W9-CMB-158

Mathematics for Christian Living Series

Mathematics for Christian Living Series

Beginning Arithmetic

Grade 1

Teacher's Manual

Rod and Staff Publishers, Inc.
P.O. Box 3, Hwy. 172
Crockett, Kentucky 41413
Telephone: (606) 522-4348

Acknowledgments

We are indebted to God for the vision of the need for a *Mathematics for Christian Living Series* and for His enabling grace. Charitable contributions from many churches have helped to cover the expenses for research and development.

This revision was styled by Amy Herr. Brother Vernon Hoover edited the course. The work was evaluated by a panel of reviewers and tested by teachers in the classroom. The artwork was drawn by Linda Shirk. Much effort was devoted to the production of the book. We are grateful for all who helped to make this book possible.

—*The Publishers*

Rod and Staff Publishers, Inc.
Crockett, Kentucky 41413

Printed in U.S.A.

ISBN 978-07399-0719-1

Catalog no. 131913

1 2 3 4 5 — 20 19 18 17 16 15 14 13 12 11

Table of Contents

Materials for This Course

Books and Worksheets

- Teacher's Manual
- Pupil's Workbook, Part 1
- Pupil's Workbook, Part 2
- Speed Drills
- Practice Sheets

Teaching Aids

- Flash cards
- Student's flash cards
- Fact Houses posters
- Classroom number line 0–100
- Student's number line 0–20
- Flannel board
- Large coins
- Clock
- Thermometer
- Cup, pint, and quart measures

Overview of Materials in This Course

Teacher's Manual

In the Teacher's Manual, each lesson is outlined under three main headings: *Preparation, Class Time,* and *Follow-up.*

Preparation lists the things to do before school in the morning. Gather the materials that are listed. Put the chalkboard samples on the board. The notation with each one tells at what point you will use it in class time.

Class Time outlines your teaching session with numbered points. These points generally begin with review drills and move on to new concepts and preparation for the workbook assignment. Bold print is to be spoken by the teacher or recited with the class. The last point is always the assignment of the lesson.

Follow-up gives further practice which may be done in various parts of the day. Do the drill activities after the children have finished their workbook pages or in another part of the day. Many of them are little activities that can put odd minutes to constructive use, perhaps even lunchtime.

As the children become accustomed to school and math, you may have them do the practice sheets independently. The papers for each day could be put in a designated place for each child to take and complete according to his ability. Encourage the goal of finishing all the papers each day. A vigorous arithmetic program is valuable for several reasons. Thoroughly learned basics will be a lifelong benefit. And the habit of industrious diligence will be a character blessing as well as academic advantage.

Many lessons in the Teacher's Manual include brief selections from the Bible placed there for your personal inspiration. As you find it suitable, you may share these bits with the children as you teach them arithmetic. You may find them a source of ideas for the devotional period.

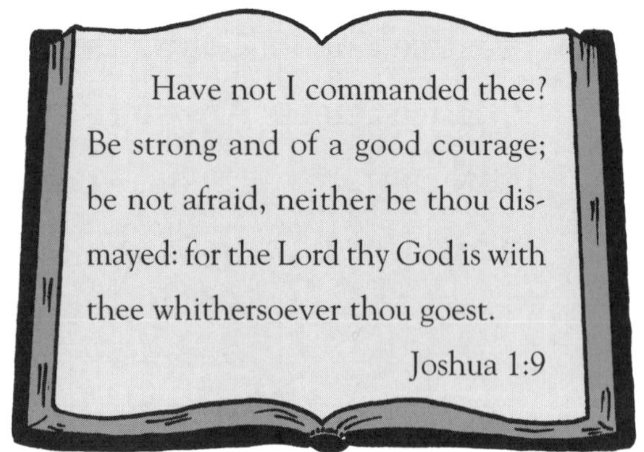

Workbooks

Two workbooks contain the pupil lessons for the entire course. Each lesson uses two facing pages. The workbook is not intended to be used in the class session. If you follow the steps in *Class Time,* the children should be able to do the workbook lesson with very minimal direction from the teacher. Workbook exercises repeat and reinforce what they have been doing in class.

Speed Drills

A separate tablet contains printed drills for every other lesson from Lesson 28 to the end of the course. Doing the speed drill is the next to last point in *Class Time* on those days. Distribute the drills, and have the children write their names on the line; then have them wait for the signal to start before they turn the paper over.

Time their work for one minute, then say, "If you are not finished, circle the problem you are doing now, then finish." Have each child immediately bring his completed drill to you. Check it and have him practice any facts he had wrong, using the boxes on the other side of the sheet. As an aid to speedy checking, the facts are arranged to produce patterns in the answers.

Practice Sheets

This practice is provided in the form of reproducible worksheets to allow the teacher to tailor the amount of work to the needs and ability of the class. Each lesson lists recommended practice sheets for that day in the *Follow-up* section of the Teacher's Manual.

Most important are the ones in the middle of the list coded with a black circle. The first ones, marked with an open square, are more fundamental, and should be done first if the students are doing them all. The last ones, marked with an open diamond, are extra activities for challenge or interest. These should be kept for last. Since the slower students might rarely have the pleasure of doing these, try to provide occasional opportunity for them to do the extras too.

□	Strengthener
●	Basic
◊	Extra

The Practice Sheets are categorized by skill. The list for each day in the Teacher's Manual names the skill and the number of that worksheet within that skill category. On the practice sheet itself, the lesson number is given in the oval at the top of the page.

Use with Lesson 25.

These numbers correspond to the recommended listing in the Teacher's Manual, but practice sheets are intended to be flexible. Use them according to your best purposes.

Some frequently used practice sheets are called Forms, they are distinguished by capital letters.

See page 365 for more detailed description of the practice sheet categories.

Flash Cards

The set of flash cards prepared for this course has nine categories. Addition and subtraction facts extend through sums and minuends of ten. Other categories supply the cards needed for drills in *Class Time* or *Follow-up* of the daily lesson plans.

Each category of the grade 1 flash card set is listed here with a description of its use. All but the basic addition and subtraction facts are shown.

Addition Families—All addition facts up to sums of 10.

Subtraction Families—All subtraction facts up to minuends of 10.

Number Flash Cards—The child says the number he sees.

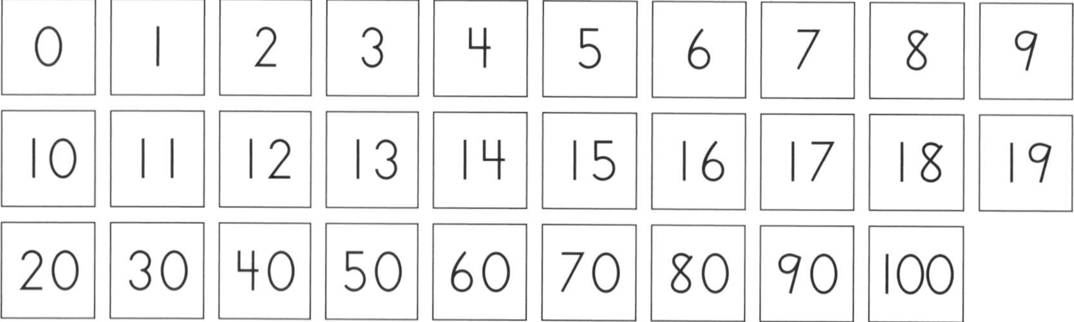

Number Pattern Cards—The child says the number of dots without counting.

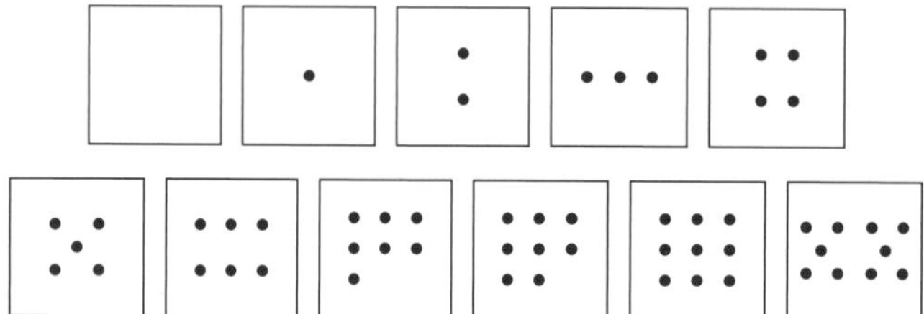

After Flash Cards—The child says the number that comes after the number he sees on the card.

Before Flash Cards—The child says the number that comes before the number he sees on the card.

_1	_2	_3	_4	_5	_6	_7	_8	_9	_10

Between Flash Cards—The child says the number that comes between the two numbers on the card.

0_2 | 1_3 | 2_4 | 3_5

4_6 | 5_7 | 6_8 | 7_9 | 8_10

Number Order Cards—The child sees the three numbers on the card and says them in the correct order.

6 8 7 | 3 4 2 | 3 5 4 | 5 6 4 | 6 5 7 | 6 8 7

9 7 8 | 8 10 9 | 11 12 10 | 11 13 12 | 12 14 13 | 14 13 15

More and Less Cards

More—The child says the number that is the greater of the two.

Less—The child says the number that is the less of the two.

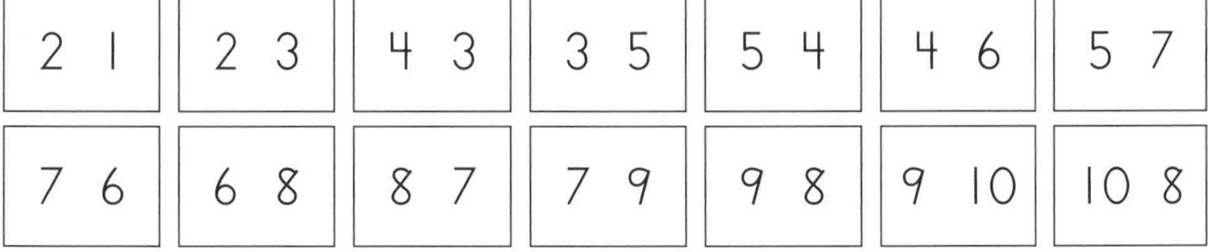

Teaching First Grade Arithmetic

Scheduling Arithmetic Class

Arithmetic is one of the basic subjects in first grade. It is best taught in the morning, when the children are most alert. Phonics, reading, and recess will also need to be scheduled during these morning hours. Circle back in the afternoon and complete any unfinished work under *Follow-up* activities.

Arithmetic activities may be scheduled in various ways. Find an order that is workable in your classroom and stick to it. This is a suggested order.

1. Conduct *Class Time* period.
2. Assign the workbook lesson.
3. Work on Practice Sheets.
4. Do *Follow-up* drills.
5. As children finish their seatwork, conduct individual flash card drill.

Hand Signals

This course is strong on counting practice and oral recitation of number facts. Use hand signals to guide the children in efficient, orderly drills. Teach some standard hand signals on the first day.

A downward sweep of your hand means "Begin together" or "Answer together."

A cupped hand at your ear means "Speak up."

A wide-spread hand means "Stop."

Hear, see, and do. Hand motions are helpful in grasping abstract concepts. Teach the children to use a consistent hand motion for the number relationships *Before, After,* and *Between*. These motions, along with the number line, will help to establish a sense of direction with the meaning of "more" or "less" in numerical value. The diagrams below show what the children see as the teacher motions; their motions will be a mirror image of yours.

0 1 2 3 4 5 6 7 8 9 10 11

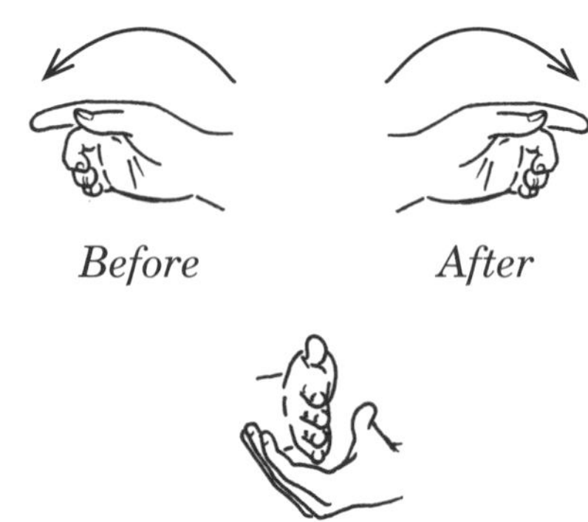

Between

First graders learn a strong left-to-right movement in reading. Place value calls for a reversal of that direction. Teach the following motion to rivet the right-to-left sequence of ones, tens, hundreds. It is valuable to have this established when they begin working multi-digit problems.

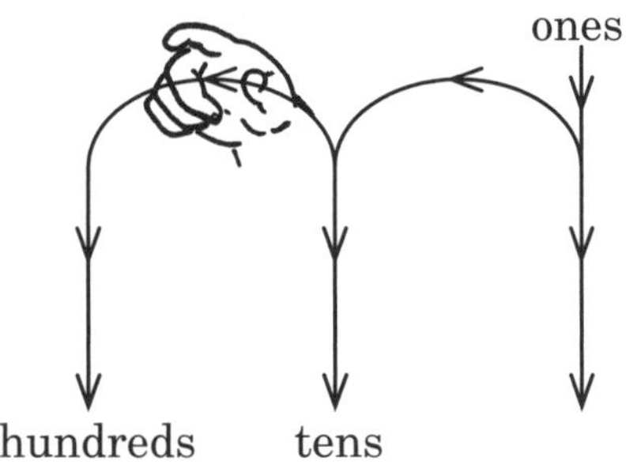

Seeing Number Groups

Children should learn to relate to quantity without saying 1-2-3 . . . When you place felt blocks on the flannel board, arrange them according to the number patterns found on the flash cards and in the workbook. The child should see each pattern as a group and know its number without counting. The addition fact 3 + 2 is seen as *a group of 3* plus *a group of 2,* **not** as 1-2-3 plus 1-2.

Memorizing Facts

Do not teach children to count for the answers to facts. The thought pattern for 7 + 3 should be 7, 3; 10, and not 7; 8-9-10. Do not teach finger counting to arrive at answers to facts.

Facts are thoroughly learned when answers come without any figuring. New facts are displayed with answers for the first while so the children can refer to them for reminders rather than counting. Lesson exercises, practice sheets, flash cards, and speed drills might seem like excessive repetition, but that is the way to thoroughly master the facts. Drill, drill, drill! Please lay a strong foundation for successful math studies to follow.

Checking the Lessons

You will need to check workbook lessons yourself, or have a helper do it.

The job can be made more efficient by laying out a series of books, overlapping them to show the same page in every book.

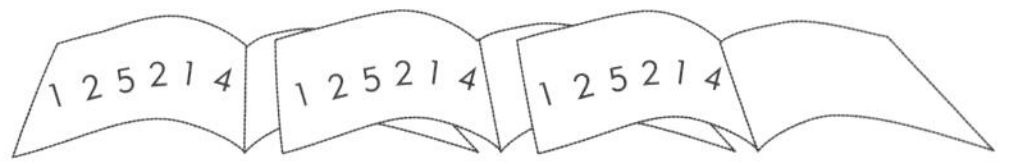

Compare the numbers across one row with the same row in the next book, and the next, and the next . . . This may even be done without the answer key, counting on a disruption of the pattern to show up mistakes.

Gain a head start on the job by teaching the children to hand in their books opened to the pages to be checked.

Grading Arithmetic

Arithmetic grades should be based on the workbook lesson, since that is the core of the work. The number of answers will vary from one lesson to another, but grade with a standard value for all the lessons alike.

The total value of each workbook lesson in first grade has been established as 36 points. Therefore if you use an E-Z Grader, always set the scale at 36 to determine arithmetic scores. Some lessons (especially in the beginning) have fewer than 36 answers. Using a grading base of 36 will grade the child less severely. Later in the book, most lessons have more than 36 points, many of which are review drills. Using a grading base of 36 will grade a child more severely, but this is realistic because he should have thorough mastery of review material.

Calendar Acquaintance

Calendar acquaintance is specifically taught in Lesson 114 and following. Your children will be at an advantage if the calendar is already familiar. Take frequent opportunity to refer to the calendar and use the current date. "Today is Tuesday, October 18."

Prepare a doughnut-shaped piece of paper that allows one day on the calendar to show through the middle. Secure it to the calendar page with plastic putty. At the end of each day, let one of the children move it to the next day's date.

Fractions

This course approaches fractions by introducing the denominator first. The child sees how many parts are in a whole, and writes that number below a line. Later one or more of the parts is shaded to indicate a number to be written above the line.

Unit fractions have a numerator of 1. A variety of unit fractions focuses attention on the meaning of the denominator.

Other fractions are introduced in the context of thirds only, or fourths only, so that the student can concentrate on the varying numerators.

Finally, a more challenging mixture is used, which includes varying numerators and varying denominators.

Number Patterns

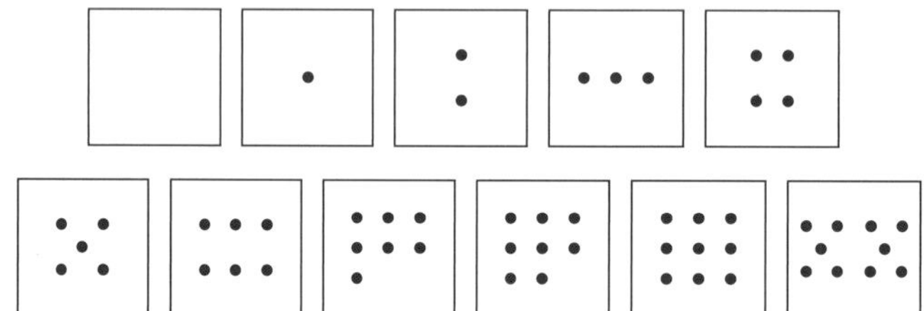

Correct Formation of Numerals

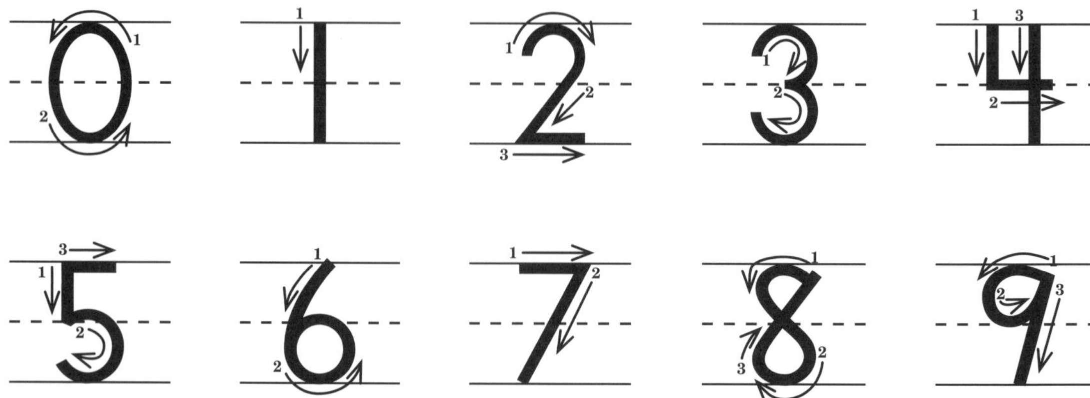

Teaching Aids

The items described here are mentioned in the daily lesson plans. Some of them may be purchased from school supply sources. Others will need to be made. Some patterns are provided at the back of this manual.

Number Lines

A number line is a long, runner-type chart showing large, clear, easy-to-read numbers. It is a valuable aid to the success of using this course. Many of the lessons call for the use of a number line from 0 to 100.

Mount the number line high on the wall before school begins. If you do not have space to put it in one continuous line, divide the line at number 50. Mount 0–50 above and 51–100 beneath.

Colored markers will be placed at intervals along the number line as you teach skip counting. (See page 600 for patterns.)

A smaller number line with numbers 0–20 is the right size for a child's desktop. On this line he can touch the numbers of *More, Less, Before, After,* and *Between,* or the correct number sequence. This smaller number line can be kept neat and clean by covering it with clear, self-adhesive covering, one inch longer and wider than the number line. A pattern for the student's desk number line is provided on page 598.

The student's desk number line may be removed about midterm.

Flannel Board

Visible objects help children to grasp the abstract idea of the quantity of a number. A variety of concrete objects are available in the classroom: fingers, pencils, erasers, books, or other items that you supply.

The flannel board is an intermediate step from concrete objects to abstract numbers. Children can see the number represented by blocks in learning numerals and later in understanding addition and subtraction.

A flannel board with a neutral background (such as beige or gray) is recommended. Prepare at least ten 1-inch red felt squares for individual counters. Draw a large X with a permanent marker on the back of each square. Make at least two red felt rectangles, one inch wide and ten inches long. Each rectangle represents one group of 10. Draw lines on these rectangles with permanent marker to show the ten 1-inch squares. Always show the plain red side of the 1-inch blocks until you are teaching subtraction.

one ☐ ☒

ten ☐☐☐☐☐☐☐☐☐☐

You will also need a divider for your flannel board to separate it into upper and lower parts. A narrow felt strip of a different color or a piece of yarn will do.

Money

Use real coins to teach money recognition and for counting money in class. Large replicas of coins are also useful.

Clock

Use a large easy-to-read clock for practice in class. It may be a cardboard clock or an old electric clock. The best representation would be one that advances the hour hand one number as the minute hand is moved one complete rotation. As you teach time, use the terms *hour hand* and *minute hand* rather than *little hand* and *big hand.*

Thermometer

A chartlike thermometer can be made for practice in counting by 2's.

Copy the scale pattern found on page 599, and paste it on a large sheet of heavy cardboard, overlapping the two 50's on the scale.

Cut a slit in the board below the 0 mark and another one above the 100 mark. Thread 20 inches of smooth white ribbon through the slits to show on the front beside the scale of numbers. The lower part of the ribbon may be colored with a red marker, or glued or sewed to the back of a red ribbon. Slide the ribbon through the slots to adjust the "mercury" level.

Place-value Chart

Crayons are used to illustrate place value in this course. An individual crayon identifies ones' place. A pack of ten crayons represents tens' place, and a case of ten packs is for hundreds' place. Prepare a chart for drilling numbers that switch digits, such as 107 and 170. See page 601 for patterns.

Liquid Measures

When you teach *cup, pint,* and *quart* near the end of the course, prepare a display of standard-measure containers. Keep them in a prominent place in the classroom.

Put a drop or two of food coloring in a pint jar and a quart jar. Fill them with water, and cap them with lids. Paste labels on the jars that say *1 pint* and *1 quart.* Also label an 8-ounce measuring cup as *1 cup.*

Flash Cards

Flash cards may be the most valuable of your teaching aids. Use them often. Use them in varied ways. Make the most of this simple, versatile helper.

A set of large flash cards is used to drill the class. Each child should have a set of small flash cards for individual study. Patterns are provided in the pattern section of this manual.

Detailed explanation of flash card activities is given on page 362.

New Skills Listed by Lessons

Lesson Number	Class Time	Workbook
1	Count to 10 The number 0	The number 0
2	The number 1 The teens	The number 1
3	Count to 19 The number 2 After Numbers	The number 2
4	Count to 29 The number 3	The number 3 Write numbers to count objects
5	Count to 39 The number 4	The number 4 After Numbers
6	Count to 49 The number 5 More Numbers	The number 5
7	Count to 59 The number 6 Between Numbers	The number 6 More Numbers
8	Count to 69 The number 7	The number 7
9	Count to 79 The number 8 Less Numbers	The number 8 Between Numbers
10	Count to 89 The number 9	The number 9 Less Numbers
11	Count to 100 Addition Family 1	Addition Family 1
12	The number 10	The number 10
13	Addition Family 2	Addition Family 2
14		
15	Before Numbers Fact recitation by memory	Mixed addition facts
16	Addition Family 3	Addition Family 3 Before Numbers
17	Flash card drill	
18	Number Order	
19		Number Order
20	Addition Family 4	Addition Family 4
21	The number 11	

22		The number 11
23		
24	The number 12	The number 12
25		
26	Addition Family 5 The number 13	The number 13
27	Reciting facts without *equals*	Addition Family 5
28	Drill fact twins The number 14 Speed Drill	The number 14
29		
30		
31		
32	The number 15	The number 15
33	The number 16	The number 16
34	The number 17	The number 17
35	Written flash card drill The number 18	The number 18
36	Addition Family 6 The number 19	The number 19
37	Missing Numbers Writing teens	Addition Family 6
38		
39	Counting pennies	Counting pennies
40	Writing 20's	
41		
42		
43	The 30's	
44		
45	Addition Family 7	
46	1- and 2-digit numbers	Addition Family 7
47	Story problems, step one	
48		Story problems, step one
49	Story problems, step two Column addition (+ 1)	
50		Column addition
51		Story problems, step two
52	Complete story problems	

53		
54		Complete story problems
55	Oral story problems Subtraction Family 1	
56		Subtraction Family 1
57	Subtraction Family 2 Count by 10's	
58	Horizontal addition Counting pennies (word)	Subtraction Family 2 Count by 10's
59	Counting dimes	Counting pennies (word)
60	Subtraction Family 3 Compare dime and penny	Counting dimes
61		Subtraction Family 3
62		
63	Clock face	
64	Telling time After Numbers by 10's	Telling time
65	Subtraction Family 4	
66		Subtraction Family 4
67	Count by 5's	
68	Counting dimes (word)	Count by 5's
69	Counting nickels	
70	Compare penny and nickel	Counting nickels
71		
72	Subtraction Family 5	
73		Subtraction Family 5
74	Counting beyond 100 Counting nickels (word)	
75	The word *minus* Place value	Counting dimes (word)
76		Place value
77		
78	Parts of a whole	
79	Distinguish 101 from 110	
80	The term *larger* Fraction denominators	Parts of a whole Missing Numbers (over 100)
81	Subtraction Family 6 Ordinal numbers	

82	The term *denominator*	Subtraction Family 6 After Numbers by 10's
83	Half hour	
84	Equality of halves Subtraction story problem	Half hour
85	Equality of thirds	Subtraction story problem
86	Equality of fourths	
87	Equality of fractional parts	
88	Horizontal subtraction Identify the ones' place	
89	Identify the tens' place	
90	Identify the hundreds' place	After Numbers by 5's Counting nickels (word)
91	Subtraction Family 7	
92	Larger and Smaller	Subtraction Family 7
93	Count by 2's	
94		Count by 2's
95		
96	Number words *one* to *five*	Number words *one* to *five*
97	Mixed addition and subtraction	
98	After Numbers by 2's Number word *six*	After Numbers by 2's Number word *six* Mixed addition and subtraction
99	Thermometer Fraction $\frac{1}{2}$	Number word *six*
100	Fraction $\frac{1}{3}$	Thermometer
101	Addition Family 8 Fraction $\frac{1}{4}$	
102	Mixed counting (10's and 1's)	Addition Family 8 Identify the ones' digit
103	Addition Family 8 twins Number word *seven*	Identify the tens' digit Number word *seven*
104	Identify the hundreds' digit	Fraction $\frac{1}{2}$
105	Column addition (+ 2)	Addition Family 8 twins Fraction $\frac{1}{3}$
106	Number word *eight*	Fraction $\frac{1}{4}$ Number word *eight*
107	Number word *nine* Count dimes with pennies	Fractions $\frac{1}{2}$, $\frac{1}{3}$ Number word *nine*
108	Addition Family 8 reflected	Count dimes with pennies Fractions $\frac{1}{3}$, $\frac{1}{4}$

109	Addition Family 7 reflected	Addition Family 8 reflected Column addition (+ 2) Fractions $\frac{1}{2}$, $\frac{1}{3}$, $\frac{1}{4}$ Identify the hundreds' digit
110	Number word *ten* Measuring inches	Number word *ten*
111	Addition Family 9	Measuring inches
112	Addition Family 9 twins	Addition Family 9
113	Counting beyond 200 Addition Family 9 reflected	Addition Family 9 twins
114		Addition Family 9 reflected
115		
116	2-digit addition	
117	Zero + zero Mixed story problems	2-digit addition
118		
119		Zero + zero
120	Counting backward 12 inches = 1 foot	
121	Addition Family 10	
122	Mixed counting (5's and 1's) Count nickels with pennies	Addition Family 10
123	Addition Family 10 twins	
124	Addition Family 10 reflected	1 nickel plus pennies
125		Addition Family 10 reflected 2 nickels plus pennies
126	Dozen	
127		Dozen 3 nickels plus pennies
128	Calendar week	
129	12:00 midnight	
130		
131	12:00 noon Subtraction Family 8	
132		Subtraction Family 8
133	Count by 25's	
134		Count by 25's
135	Counting quarters	
136	Fraction $\frac{2}{3}$	Counting quarters
137		Fractions $\frac{1}{3}$, $\frac{2}{3}$

138		
139	Number triplets	
140	Fractions $\frac{2}{4}$ and $\frac{3}{4}$	Fractions $\frac{1}{4}$, $\frac{2}{4}$, $\frac{3}{4}$
141	Subtraction Family 9 Column addition (+3)	
142		Subtraction Family 9 Column addition (+3)
143		
144	Square	
145	Circle	
146		
147	2-digit subtraction Triangle	
148		2-digit subtraction
149		
150		
151	Subtraction Family 10	
152		Subtraction Family 10
153	Rectangle	
154		Fractions with numerator 2
155		Fraction mixture
156	2-digit addition with 3-digit answers	2-digit addition with 3-digit answers
157	Count by 10's to 200	
158	Cup and pint	Count by 10's to 200
159		Cup and pint
160	2 cups = 1 pint	
161		2 cups = 1 pint
162	Quart	
163		
164	2 pints = 1 quart	Quart
165		
166		2 pints = 1 quart
167		
168		
169	2-step computation	
170		

Mathematics for Christian Living Series

Beginning Arithmetic

Grade 1

Teacher's Manual

DAILY LESSON PLANS

Objectives

New

TEACHING

Count to 10

The number 0

WORKBOOK

The number 0

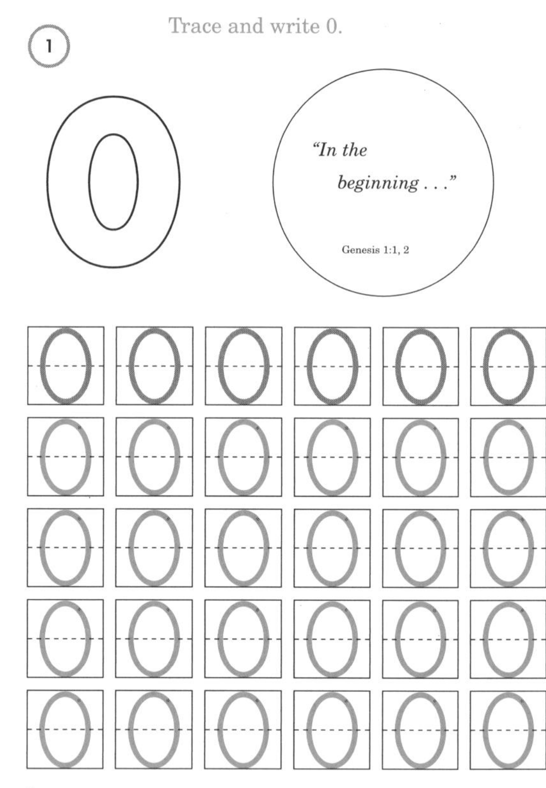

Preparation

Materials

Flannel board with three red felt blocks

Bookmark for each child, made from poster board or construction paper

Chalkboard

Make a large 0 for each child to trace. Space the 0's far apart so that each child can make three more 0's by himself.

Draw the samples below on the chalkboard for use with *Class Time* number 8.

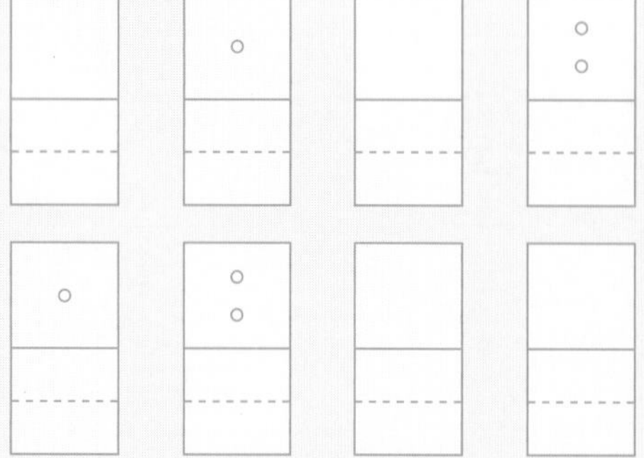

Class Time

1. *Count to 10.*
   In arithmetic class we learn about numbers. We use numbers to count. Count 1–10 several times with the children.
2. *Count objects.*
   We use numbers to count many things. Let us count the children in our class. Deliberately point to each child as you count together. Count the windows in the room. Count the doors.
3. *Introduce 0.*
   Call the children to the class center, where you have three red blocks on the flannel board. **We could count how many red blocks are here.** Remove one of the blocks. Pause and then remove another. Remove the last one. **How many red blocks are on the flannel board now? *Zero* is the number that means "not any."**

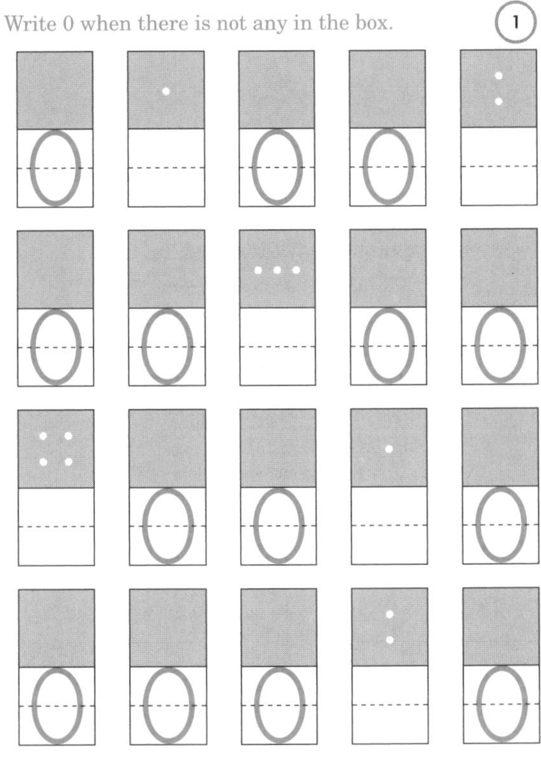

4. *See 0.*
This is how to write zero. Draw a large 0 on the chalkboard. Trace repeatedly and say, **Around—0. Around—0. . . .**

5. *Form 0 in the air.*
Stand away from the large 0 you drew, and form 0 in the air. Make the oval backwards so that it is the correct form for the children facing you. Have the children make the motion with you, saying, **Around—0. Around—0. . . .**

6. *Understanding 0.*
When God made the earth, it was empty. There was nothing in it. The earth is big and round, but it had no flowers, no animals, no trees, until God made those things. We can count the things that were on the earth the first day by saying "Zero."
   a. Have the children form a large 0 in the air as they say the answer to each of these questions.
   When God first made the earth, how many flowers were in it?
   Zero flowers.
   How many trees were there?
   Zero trees.
   How many bears? How many fish? How many birds? . . . kittens?
   b. Continue with questions about your present setting that are answered with zero. **How many trucks are in this room? How many doors are open? How many times did we wash the floor today?**

7. *Write 0.*
Have the children trace and write 0 on the chalkboard.

8. *Chalkboard samples.*
   a. Point to the first box. **How many dots are in this box?** Have them answer together while you write 0.
   b. Point to the second box. **How many dots are in this box?** When the answer is 1 or 2, do not write anything.

9. *Assign Lesson 1.*
Show each child how to place a bookmark under the first row in his book. Teach him to work row by row from left to right. **On the second page, write 0 for every box that has no dots in it. *Zero* means "not any." Do not write anything for the boxes that have dots.**

Follow-up

Drill

Have individuals **count 1–10.**

Practice Sheet

☐ Writing Practice #1

Objectives

New

TEACHING

The number 1
**Number Patterns 0, 1*

WORKBOOK

The number 1

Review

Count to 10
The number 0

*Italicized items are for *Follow-up* drill.

Preparation

Materials

Flannel board and 1 red felt block
**Number Pattern flash cards 0 and 1*

Chalkboard

Large 1 for each child to trace

Samples for *Class Time* number 7

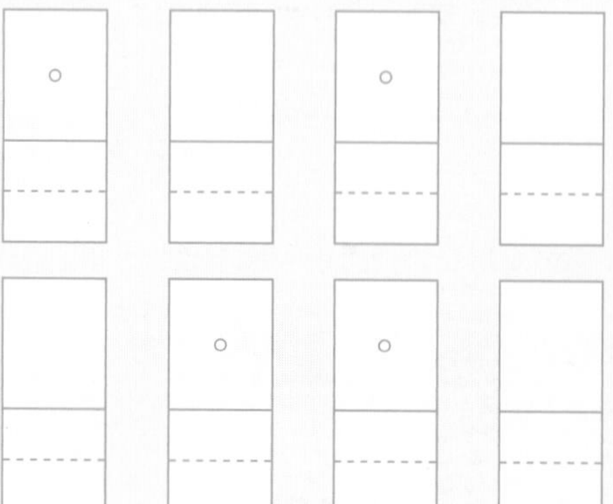

Class Time

1. *Count to 10.*
   Have the children stand near the number line. Place your pointer on 0. **We will count to 10.** Say **1** as you bounce the pointer to the 1. Say **2** as the pointer lands on 2. Continue to 10, and then place the pointer on 0 again. **Count to 10 with me.** Always begin these counting exercises with the pointer on 0, but do not say *zero* in the counting sequence.
2. *Review 0.*
   When God made the earth, how many giraffes were there? Zero. Draw a large 0 on the board. ***Zero* means "not any."**
3. *Introduce 1.*
   Then God made many wonderful things. He made everything in six days. God made 1 sun.
   a. **This is how we write the number 1.** Draw a large 1 on the board.
   b. Trace repeatedly and say, **Straight down—1. Straight down . . .**

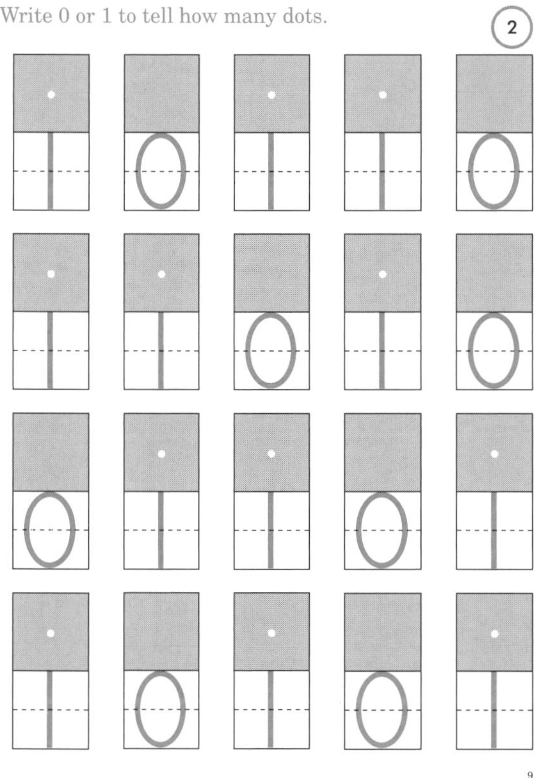

4. *Form 1 in the air.*
   a. **Straight down—1. Straight . . .**
   b. Have the children form 1 in the air and repeat the number and item for each sentence you say. **God made 1 earth.** (1 earth) **God made 1 sun.** (1 sun) **God made 1 moon. God made 1 man. God made 1 woman.**
5. *Write 1.*
   Have the children trace and write 1 on the chalkboard.
6. *Meaning of 0 and 1.*
   Place 1 red block on the flannel board.
   a. Have the children form the numeral in the air and say **1** together.
   b. Remove the block and have them respond with **0,** forming the numeral in the air and saying it.
   c. Repeat several times.
7. *Chalkboard samples.*
   Point to the first box. **How many dots are in this box?** Have them answer together as you write 0 or 1 in the bottom part of each box.
8. *Assign Lesson 2.*
   This time, write a number for every box on the second page.

Follow-up

Drill

1. Have individuals **count 1–10.**
2. Flash Number Pattern cards 0, 1. The children say the number of dots they see on the card. Number Patterns should become so familiar that the arrangement represents a number without the need to count.
3. Have the children form the numeral in the air as they answer each question. Use questions about your setting that are answered with 0 or 1.
   How many noses do you have? 1 nose
   How many cracks are in the window?
   How many mouths do you have?
   How many tongues do you have?
   How many books are in my hands?

Practice Sheets

☐ Writing Practice #2

◊ Scrambled Numbers #1

Objectives

New

TEACHING

- The teens
- Count to 19
- The number 2
- After Numbers

WORKBOOK

- The number 2

Review

- Numbers 0, 1
- Number Patterns 0–2

Preparation

Materials

(Italicized items are for *Follow-up* drill.)

Two red felt blocks

Number Pattern flash cards 0–2

Number flash cards 1–10

Chalkboard

Large 2 for each child to trace

(*Class Time* #6)

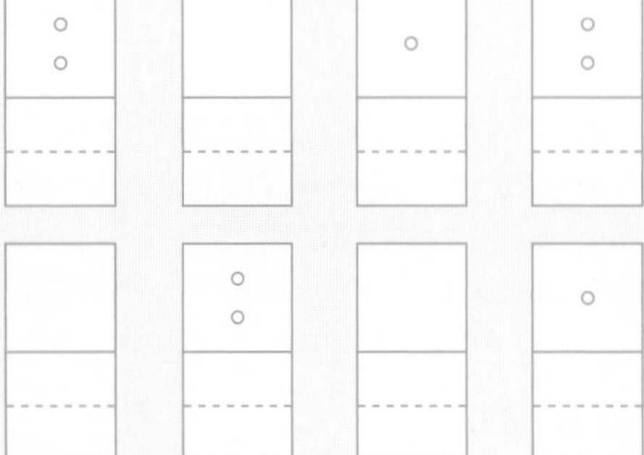

Class Time

1. *Counting.*
   Call the children to the number line. Place your pointer on 0 to begin. **Count 1–10** twice.
2. *See and say 10–19.*
   Point to the numbers 10–19. **These numbers have two digits. You see a 1 with another digit for each number. We call these numbers the teens.*** You count 10–19 as you point to each number. Everyone **count 10–19** twice.
3. *Introduce 2.*
   Draw a large 2 on the board. **Around** (curved top) **and back** (downward slant) **on a railroad track** (straight horizontal line)**—2, 2, 2.** Trace again and again. **Around and back . . .**
4. *Form 2 in the air.*
   a. **Around and back on a railroad track—2, 2, 2. . . .**

* The teens technically begin at 13. *Teens* is used here to identify the two-digit numbers that begin with 1.

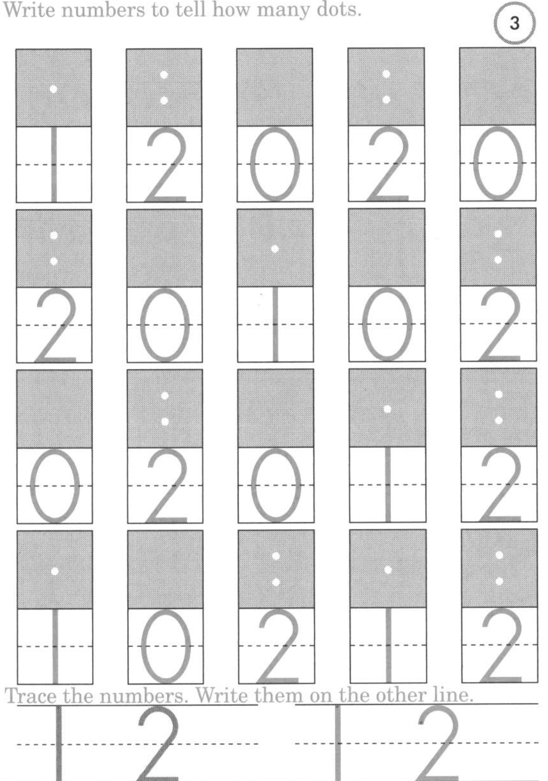

b. Have the children form 2 in the air.
c. **God told Noah to build an ark because He was going to send a flood. Noah took all kinds of animals into the ark. He took two of each kind.**
d. Have the children form 2 and say the number and animal for each answer. **How many elephants went into the ark?** (2 elephants) **How many bears went into the ark?** (2 bears) **. . . horses? . . . squirrels?**

5. *Write 2.*
Have the children trace and write 2 on the board.

6. *Meaning of 0–2.*
a. Place 2 felt blocks on the flannel board in the Number Pattern arrangement. (See page 12.) Drill the meaning of 0, 1, and 2 by changing the number of blocks and having the children say the number each time.
b. Let the children write answers in the chalkboard samples.

7. *After Numbers.*
Write these number pairs on the board horizontally. After writing each row, point to the numbers and say them.
1 2
1 2
1 2
1 __ **What number comes after 1?** Fill in the 2.
Use a consistent hand motion to help the children comprehend the abstract concept of number relationships. Because counting numbers proceed from left to right, as you face the children your motion should move from right to left, so that their motion is correct as it mirrors yours. Have the children say **after** every time they make the motion. (See page 10.)

8. *Assign Lesson 3.*

Follow-up

Drill

1. Flash Number Pattern cards 0–2.
2. Form 0–2 in the air.
3. Have individuals **count 1–19.**
4. Set Number flash cards 1–10 on the chalk tray in random order. Call on individual children to find 1 and 2. **Stand near me. Hold your card below your chin, and say your number.** 1, 2.

Practice Sheets

- ☐ Writing Practice #3
- ☐ Count and Write #1
- ◊ Scrambled Numbers #1
- ◊ Draw and Count #1

Objectives

New

TEACHING

Count to 29
The number 3

WORKBOOK

The number 3
Write numbers to count objects

Review

Numbers 0–2
Number Patterns 0–3
After Numbers

Preparation

Materials

(Italicized items are for *Follow-up* drill.)

Three red felt blocks

After flash cards 1 and 2

Number Pattern flash cards 0–3

Chalkboard

Large 3 for each child to trace

(*Class Time* #7)

1 ___ 2 ___
2 ___ 1 ___
1 ___ 2 ___

Draw the grid without any numbers. Fill in the numbers during *Class Time* #8.

1	2	3					
1	2	3					
1	2	3					
1	2	3					
1	2	3					
1	2	3					
1	2	3					

Class Time

1. *Counting.*
   Count 1–19 twice. Point to 10–19. **These numbers are the teens; they all have a 1 with another digit. Count 1–19** again.
2. *Introduce the 20's.*
   Point to the numbers 20–29. **These two-digit numbers are the twenties; they all have a 2 with another digit.** You count 20–29. **This is the twenties.** Everyone **count 1–29** twice.
3. *Introduce 3.*
   Draw a large 3 on the board. **Around a tree** (upper curve), **around a tree** (lower curve)**—3, 3, 3. Around a tree, . . .**
4. *Form 3 in the air.*
   a. **Around a tree, . . .**
   b. **One day Abraham sat in the door of his tent. He saw 3 men, and he ran to them to invite them to rest under his tree. He told his wife Sarah to take 3 measures of flour and make cakes. He got a calf and told his servant to get meat ready. He got**

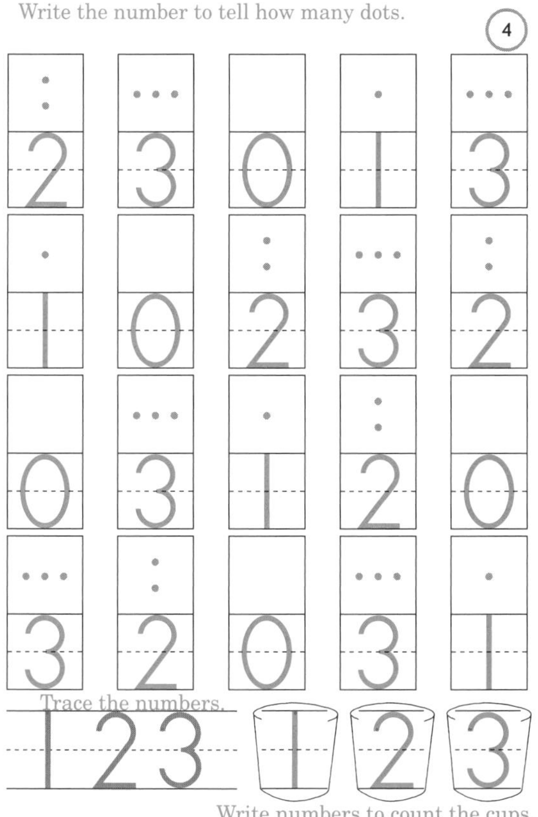

3 bowls of milk and 3 servings of butter. Abraham was kind to his 3 visitors.

c. Have the children form 3 in the air and say the items together. **3 men, 3 measures of flour, 3 cakes, 3 servings of butter, 3 bowls of milk, 3 servings of meat.**

5. *Write 3.*
   Have the children trace and write 3 on the chalkboard.
6. *Meaning of 0–3.*
   Show three blocks on the flannel board in the Number Pattern arrangement. Drill the meaning of 0–3 by changing the number.
7. *After Numbers.*
   a. Drill the hand motion for *After.*
   b. Point to the chalkboard samples. **What comes after 1?** Write their answers.
8. *Chalkboard grid.*
   Fill in the grid as the children count **1, 2, 3; 1, 2, 3; . . .** (The remainder of each row stays empty.)
9. *Assign Lesson 4.*

Follow-up

Drill

1. Flash After cards 1 and 2. The children will say the number that comes after the number they see.
2. Flash Number Pattern cards 0–3.
3. Form numbers 0–3 in the air.

Practice Sheets

- □ Writing Practice #4
- □ Form A: 1–3
- □ Count and Write #2
- ● Count and Write #3
- ◊ Scrambled Numbers #2
- ◊ Dot-to-Dot #1
- ◊ Draw and Count #2

Objectives

New

TEACHING

Count to 39
The number 4
**More Numbers*

WORKBOOK

The number 4
After Numbers

Review

Numbers 0–3
After Numbers

*Italicized items are for *Follow-up* drill.

Preparation

Materials

Four red felt blocks

Number flash cards 0–3

After flash cards 1–3

**Number Pattern flash cards 0–4*

Chalkboard

Large 4 for each child to trace

(*Class Time* #7)

2 ___ 3 ___

1 ___ 2 ___

3 ___ 1 ___

(*Class Time* #8)

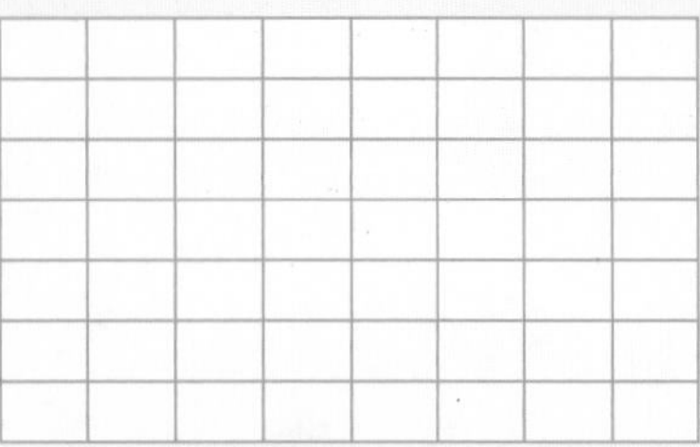

Class Time

1. *Counting.*
   Call the children to the number line. To avoid a running recitation without attention, train the children to keep their eyes on the pointer. **Follow the tip of my pointing stick with your eyes. We will travel down, down the valley and up, up the mountain.** After a few sweeps leading their eyes, bring the pointer to 0 on the number line.
   a. **Count 1–29.** Move the pointer to each number as the class says it.
   b. Review the teens and the twenties.
2. *Introduce the 30's.*
   Point to 30–39. **These numbers are the thirties; they all have a 3 with another digit. It is like a train with 30 for the engine. Count 1–39** twice.
3. *Review 0–3.*
   a. Have the children sit. **Answer together.** Flash Number cards 0–3 for them to say the number they see.
   b. Form 0–3 in the air.

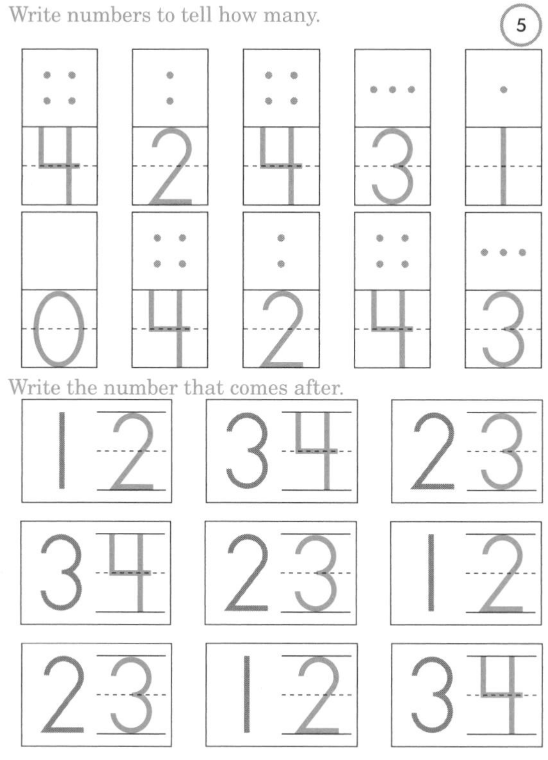
Write numbers to tell how many.

5

4 2 4 3 1

0 4 2 4 3

Write the number that comes after.

1 2	3 4	2 3
3 4	2 3	1 2
2 3	1 2	3 4

15

4. *Introduce 4.*
   a. Put four blocks on the flannel board in Number Pattern arrangement. **How many blocks are here?**
   b. **In the Old Testament, God's Law said that if a man stole a sheep, he had to give back four sheep.**
   c. Draw a large 4 on the board. **Down and over, then down some more—4, 4, 4. Down and over, . . .**
5. *Form 4 in the air.*
   Down and over, then down some more—4, 4, 4. . . .
6. *Write 4.*
   Have the children trace and write 4 on the board.
7. *After Numbers.*
   a. **What comes after 2?** Do the samples.
   b. Flash After cards 1–3.
8. *Chalkboard grid.*
   Call on individuals to write in each row of the grid **1, 2, 3, 4; 1, 2, 3, 4; . . .**
9. *Assign Lesson 5.*

Follow-up

Drill

(Chalkboard preparation)

(*Drill* #1)

1. Call one child to the front of the class. Give him 2 crayons. Call another child and give him 3 crayons.
   a. **How many crayons does [first child] have?** Write 2 on the board. **How many does [second child] have?** Write 3. **Who has more?** Circle the 3.
   b. Point to the first box of the samples. **Which number is more?**
   c. If the children have trouble grasping the concept, use crayons to demonstrate each pair of numbers.
2. Flash Number Pattern cards 0–4.
3. **How many clocks are in this room? How many doors? chairs? flower pots?** Ask questions that fit your setting. No answer should be more than 4.

Practice Sheets

- ☐ Writing Practice #5
- ☐ Count and Write #4
- ● Form A: 1–4
- ● Count and Write #5
- ◊ Scrambled Numbers #2
- ◊ Dot-to-Dot #2
- ◊ Draw and Count #3

Objectives

New

TEACHING

Count to 49
The number 5
More Numbers
**Between Numbers*

WORKBOOK

The number 5

Review

After Numbers
Numbers 0–4

*Italicized items are for *Follow-up* drill.

Preparation

Materials

Five felt blocks

More flash cards 1–5

**Number Pattern flash cards 0–5*

Chalkboard

Large 5 for each child to trace

(*Class Time* #3)

2 ___

1 ___

3 ___

2 ___

(*Class Time* #7)

Class Time

1. *Counting.*
   Call the children to the number line.
   a. **Girls, count 1–39.**
   b. **Boys, count 1–39.**
   c. Review the teens, the twenties, and the thirties.
   d. **Everyone count 1–39.**
2. *Introduce the 40's.*
   Point to 40–49. **These numbers are the forties; they all have a 4 with another digit. It is like a number train. What number is the engine?** (40) **Count 1–49.**
3. *After Numbers.*
   Have the children do the samples.
4. *Review 0–4 and introduce 5.*
   a. Have the children sit. Begin with an empty flannel board, and have the children say the number as you add blocks one by one until there are 5.
   b. **One day when Jesus was teaching many people, it became time to eat and the people were hungry. A boy gave his lunch to Jesus that day. He**

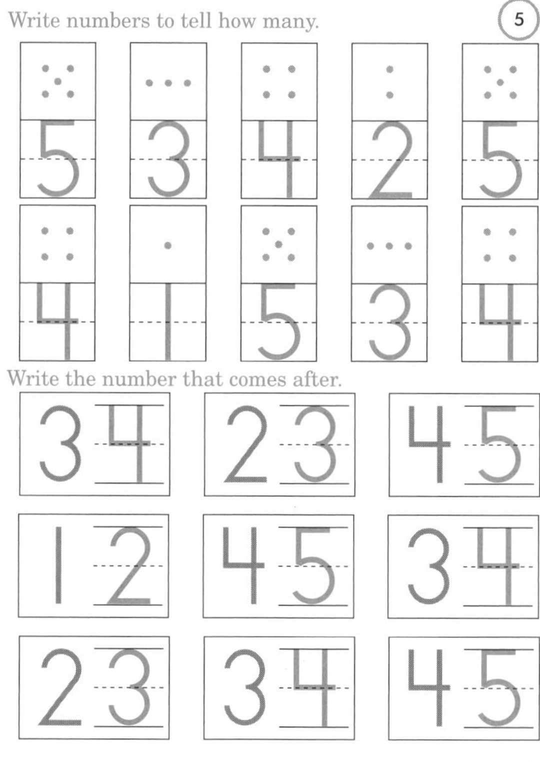

gave 5 loaves and some fish. Jesus made those 5 loaves and the fish into enough food for all the people!

c. Draw a large 5 on the board. **Down the trunk** (downward stroke) **and around the tree** (rounded part); **add a branch** (straight horizontal line)**—it's 5 you see. Down the trunk . . .**

5. *Form 5 in the air.*
   a. **Down the trunk . . .**
   b. Form 0–5 in the air.

6. *Write 5.*
   Have the children trace and write 5 on the board.

7. *More Numbers.*
   a. Point to the single dot, cover the set of five dots, and say **1.** Point to the set of five dots, cover the one, and say **5. Which is more?** Circle the set of five dots.
   b. Point to the first set of numbers in the boxes. **Which is more?** Have a child circle the number that is more in each box.
   c. Flash More cards 1–5. Have the children look at the two numbers and say the one that is more.

8. *Assign Lesson 6.*

Follow-up

Drill

(*Drill* #1)

1 ___ 3   3 ___ 5   2 ___ 4

1. a. **What number comes between 1 and 3?** Fill in the answer, then count **1, 2, 3.**
   b. Associate this hand motion with *Between:* Spread your thumb and forefinger in a wide span. Hold your other hand vertically, and move it back and forth in the gap between thumb and forefinger. (See *Hand Signals* on page 10.)
2. Flash Number Pattern cards 0–5.
3. Remove the blocks from the flannel board. Ask a child to put 2 blocks there. Remove them. Ask another child to put 5 there. . . .

Practice Sheets

- □ Form A: 1–5
- □ Count and Write #6
- ● Writing Practice #6
- ● Count and Write #7
- ◊ Dot-to-Dot #3
- ◊ Scrambled Numbers #3
- ◊ Draw and Count #4

Objectives

New

TEACHING

Count to 59
The number 6
Between Numbers
**Addition concept*

WORKBOOK

The number 6
More Numbers

Review

Number Patterns 0–6
More Numbers

*Italicized items are for *Follow-up* drill.

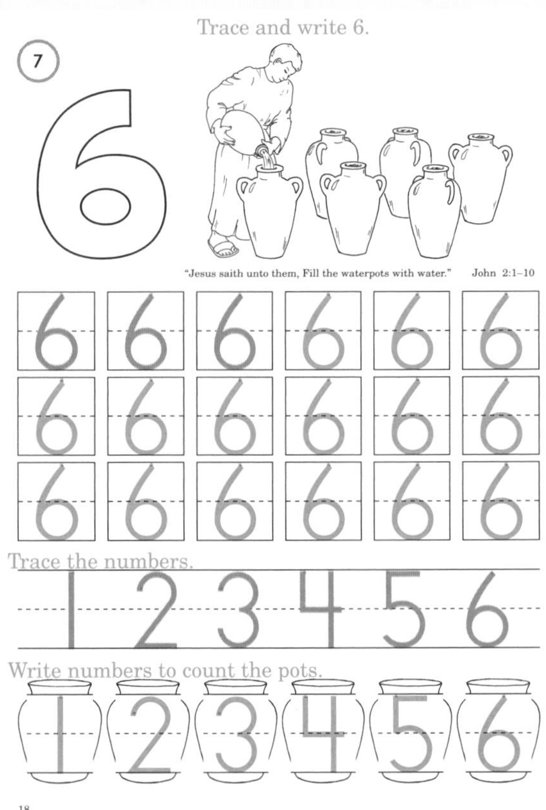

Preparation

Materials

Six felt blocks

Number Pattern flash cards 0–6

More flash cards 1–6

**Between flash cards 1–6*

**Number flash cards 1–6*

**After flash cards 1–5*

Chalkboard

Large 6 for each child to trace

(*Class Time* #7)

2 ___ 4   1 ___ 3   3 ___ 5   4 ___ 6

(*Class Time* #8)

Class Time

1. *Counting.*
   Call the children to the number line.
   a. **Let's review the number trains. Everyone say the teens. Say the twenties . . . thirties . . . forties.**
   b. **Now everyone count 1–49.**
2. *Introduce the 50's.*
   Point to 50–59. **This number train is the fifties. Each number has a 5 with another digit. What number is the engine?** (50) **Count 1–59.**
3. *Introduce 6.*
   a. Have the children sit. Put 6 red blocks on the flannel board in the Number Pattern arrangement. Have each child come and point to them one by one as he counts **1, 2, 3, 4, 5, 6.**
   b. **One day Jesus was at a wedding. The people did not have enough wine, and Jesus did something special to help them. Jesus saw 6 big waterpots. He told the servants to pour water into the pots. When**

Write numbers to tell how many. (7)

6	4	2	5	6
5	6	3	4	2
6	3	5	6	4

Circle the number that is more.

• more: (4) 2	2 (6)	5 (6)
(6) 5	0 (1)	4 (5)
(3) 1	1 (5)	2 (5)
(6) 3	(6) 4	

19

they dipped out of the pots, the water had changed into wine.

c. Draw a large 6 on the board. **Curving down into a loop—number 6 can roll a hoop.**

4. *Form 6 in the air.*
   a. Form 6. **Curving down into a loop—number 6 . . .**
   b. Form 0–6 in the air.
5. *Write 6.*
   Have the children trace and write 6 on the board.
6. *Number Patterns.*
   Flash Number Pattern cards 0–6.
7. *Between Numbers.*
   Review the hand motion associated with *Between.* Do the chalkboard samples.
8. *More Numbers.*
   a. Flash More cards 1–6.
   b. Do the chalkboard samples.
9. *Assign Lesson 7.*

Follow-up

Drill

1. Drill Between flash cards 1–6. Have the children say the number that should be on the blank between the two numbers.
2. Give Number flash cards 1–6 to the children.
   a. **Who has the number we start with when we count? Come stand beside me.**
   b. **Who has the number that comes after 1?** Continue.
   c. **Hold your card below your chin, and count 1, 2, . . .**
3. Drill After flash cards 1–5.
4. Introduce the addition concept.
   a. Call two children to the front of the class. Give each of them two books.
   b. **How many books does [first child] have?** Write 2 on the board.
   c. **How many books does [second child] have?** Write another 2 below the first one.
   d. **How many books do they have together?**
   e. **We *add* numbers when we put them together.** Write the plus sign and equal line, identifying each one as you make it: **This is a plus sign. This is the equal line. We write the number below the line to show how much these numbers are together.**
   f. Point to each number and symbol as you say the addition fact. **Two plus two equals four.**

Practice Sheets

- ☐ Writing Practice #7
- ☐ Form A: 1–6
- ☐ Count and Write #8
- ● Count and Write #9
- ● After Numbers #1
- ◊ Scrambled Numbers #3
- ◊ Dot-to-Dot #4
- ◊ Draw and Count #5

Objectives

New

TEACHING

Count to 69
The number 7
**Less Numbers*

WORKBOOK

The number 7

Review

More Numbers
Between Numbers

*Italicized items are for *Follow-up* drill.

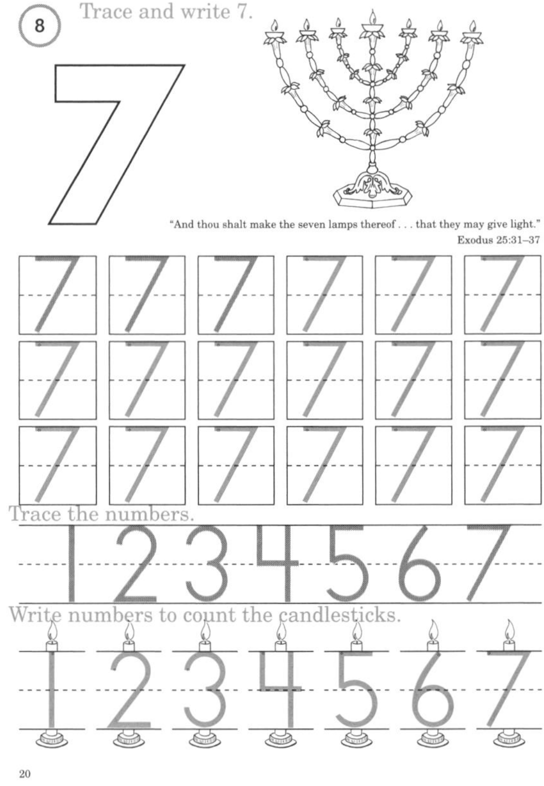

Preparation

Materials

Seven felt blocks

More flash cards 1–7

Between flash cards 1–7

**Number Pattern flash cards 0–7*

**More flash cards 1–7*

Chalkboard

Large 7 for each child to trace

(*Class Time* #6)

4 6	3 5	5 4	5 6

(*Class Time* #7)

3 ___ 5 4 ___ 6 1 ___ 3 2 ___ 4

Class Time

1. *Counting.*
   Call the children to the number line.
   a. **Let's review the number trains.**
   b. **Count 1–59.**
2. *Introduce the 60's.*
   Point to 60–69. **This number train is the sixties. They all have a 6 with another digit. Count 1–69.**
3. *Introduce 7.*
   a. Have the children sit. Begin with an empty flannel board, and have the children say the numbers as you place the blocks one at a time up to 7.
   b. Draw a large 7 on the board. **Across the sky** (horizontal line) **and down from heaven** (downward slant)—**this is how to make a 7. Across the sky . . .**
   c. **The sun, moon, and stars make light for us. The light shines down from heaven. But the sun could not shine into the tabernacle in**

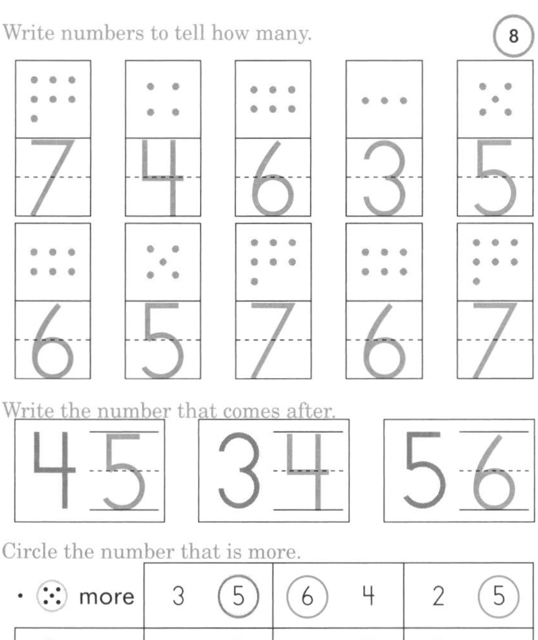
Write numbers to tell how many.
8

Write the number that comes after.

Circle the number that is more.

21

the Old Testament. The tabernacle was covered with thick curtains, and it did not have windows. God told Moses to make a candlestick for light in the tabernacle. The candlestick had 7 lights.**

4. *Form 7 in the air.*
   a. Form 7. **Across the sky and down from heaven . . .**
   b. Form 0–7 in the air.
5. *Write 7.*
   Have the children trace and write 7 on the board.
6. *More Numbers.*
   a. Flash More cards 1–7.
   b. Do the chalkboard samples.
7. *Between Numbers.*
   a. Flash Between cards 1–7.
   b. Do the chalkboard samples.
8. *Assign Lesson 8.*

Follow-up

Drill

(*Drill* #1)

1. Place 1 block on the flannel board.
   a. Call on one of the children to make it show more than 1. Let another child make it more yet.
   b. **Who can make the flannel board show *less* than what is there now?**
   c. Call one of the children to the front of the class, and give him 4 rulers. Call another one and give him 2 rulers. Ask for the number each one has, and write it on the board.
   d. **Who has less?** Circle the number when the answer is given. **2 is less than 4.**
   e. Do the samples in the boxes.
2. Flash Number Pattern cards 0–7.
3. Flash More cards 1–7.
4. Demonstrate addition.
   a. Call two children to the front of the class. Give one of them one crayon, and the other one four crayons.
   b. **How many crayons does [first child] have?** Write 1 on the board.
   c. **How many crayons does [second child] have?** Write 4 below the 1.
   d. Name the plus sign and the equal line as you make them. **How many crayons do they have together?** Write 5, and then point to each part as you say the whole fact: **One plus four equals five. This is an addition fact.**

Practice Sheets

- ☐ Writing Practice #8
- ☐ Form A: 1–7
- ☐ Count and Write #10
- ● After Numbers #2
- ● Count and Write #11
- ◊ Scrambled Numbers #4
- ◊ Dot-to-Dot #5
- ◊ Draw and Count #6

Objectives

New

TEACHING

Count to 79
The number 8
Less Numbers

WORKBOOK

The number 8
Between Numbers

Review

Numbers 0–7
Between Numbers

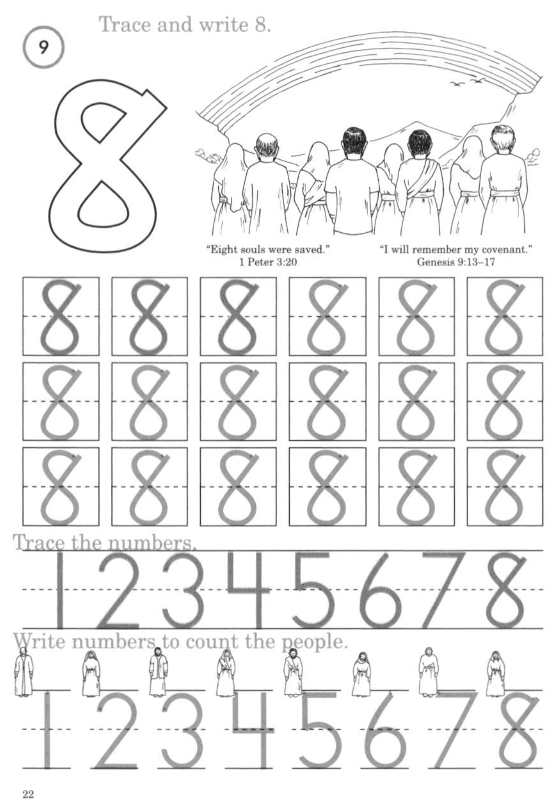

Preparation

Materials

(Italicized items are for *Follow-up* drill.)

Eight felt blocks

Number flash cards 0–7

Number Pattern flash cards 0–8

Chalkboard

Large 8 for each child to trace

(*Class Time* #7)

4 __ 6 2 __ 4 5 __ 7 3 __ 5 6 __ 8

(*Class Time* #8)

Class Time

1. *Counting.*
   Call the children to the number line. **Follow my pointing stick down, down the valley and up, up the mountain.** Lead their eyes up to 0 on the number line.
   a. **Count 1–69.**
   b. **Review the number trains. Say the engine numbers louder and slower. Say the rest of the train softer and faster.**
2. *Introduce the 70's.*
   Point to 70–79. **This is the seventies; they all have a 7 with another digit. Count 1–79.**
3. *Review 0–7.*
   Flash Number cards 0–7.
   a. **Answer together.**
   b. **If I call your name, say the number.**
4. *Introduce 8.*
   a. Have the children sit. Put 8 red blocks on the flannel board. **This is 8 blocks. 8 people went into the ark that**

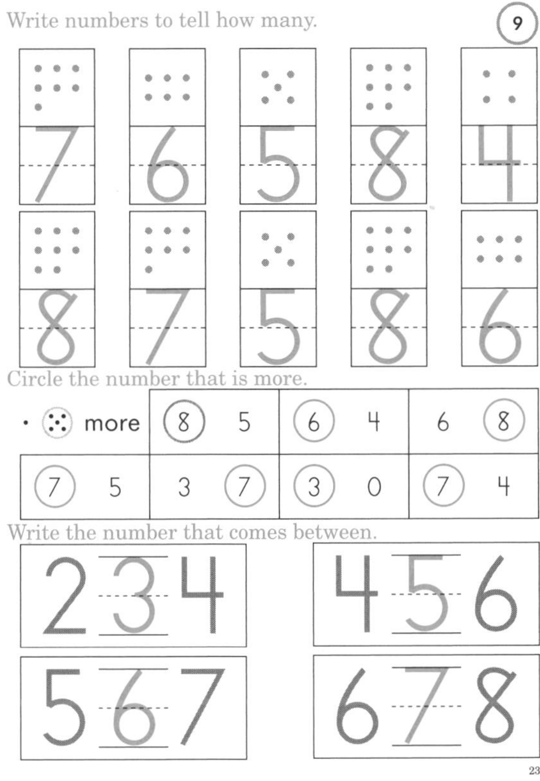
Write numbers to tell how many.

9

7 6 5 8 4

8 7 5 8 6

Circle the number that is more.

more	(8) 5	(6) 4	6 (8)
(7) 5	3 (7)	(3) 0	(7) 4

Write the number that comes between.

2 3 4 4 5 6

5 6 7 6 7 8

23

Noah built. 8 people were saved from the Flood. When the Flood was over, 8 people saw the first rainbow.

b. Draw a large 8 on the board. **Make an S, but do not wait—climb back up to make an 8. Make an S, . . .**

5. *Form 8 in the air.*
   Make an S, but do not wait . . .
6. *Write 8.*
   Have the children trace and write 8 on the board.
7. *Between Numbers.*
   Do the chalkboard samples.
8. *Less Numbers.*
   a. Call one of the children to the front of the class, and give him 2 crayons. Call another one, and give him 5 crayons. Ask for the number each one has, and write it on the board.
   b. **Who has less?** Circle the number when the answer is given. **2 is less than 5.**
   c. Point to the single dot and then point to the set of five dots. **Which is less?** Circle the single dot.
   d. Do the samples in the boxes.
9. *Assign Lesson 9.*

Follow-up

Drill

1. Flash Number Pattern cards 0–8.
2. Form numbers 0–8 in the air.
3. Have individuals count the felt blocks on the flannel board.
4. Demonstrate addition.
   a. Call two children to the front of the class. Give two chalkboard erasers to the first child, and one eraser to the other child.
   b. **How many erasers does [first child] have?** Write 2 on the board.
   c. **How many erasers does [second child] have?** Write 1 below the 2.
   d. Complete the fact and have the children say it together with you.

Practice Sheets

- ☐ Writing Practice #9
- ☐ Form A: 1–8
- ☐ Count and Write #12
- ● After Numbers #3
- ● Count and Write #13
- ◊ Scrambled Numbers #4
- ◊ Dot-to-Dot #6
- ◊ Draw and Count #7

Objectives

New

TEACHING

Count to 89
The number 9
**Number dictation*

WORKBOOK

The number 9
Less Numbers

Review

Numbers 0–8
Between Numbers
Less Numbers

*Italicized items are for *Follow-up* drill.

Preparation

Materials

Nine felt blocks
Less flash cards 2–9
**Form B for each child*
**Number Pattern flash cards 2–9*
**Number flash cards 1–9*

Chalkboard

Large 9 for each child to trace
(Draw an empty grid for *Class Time* #7.)

1	2	3	4	5	6	7	8
9							
1	2	3	4	5	6	7	8
9							
1	2	3	4	5	6	7	8
9							
1	2	3	4	5	6	7	8

(Class Time #8)

3 __ 5   4 __ 6   6 __ 8   2 __ 4

(*Class Time* #9)

Class Time

1. *Counting.*
   Call the children to the number line.
   a. **Count 1–79.**
   b. **Say each number train.**
2. *Introduce the 80's.*
   Point to 80–89. **This number train is the eighties. They all have an 8 with another digit. Count 1–89.**
3. *Review 0–8.*
   Form 0–8 in the air.
4. *Introduce 9.*
   a. Have the children sit. Put 9 red blocks on the flannel board. Have each child come and point to the blocks while counting, **1, 2, 3, 4, 5, 6, 7, 8, 9.**
   b. **Jesus told about a woman who had ten silver coins. One day when she counted her money, she counted 1, 2, 3, 4, . . . 9. Only 9 coins. She hunted until she found the lost one.**
   c. Draw a large 9 on the board. **A loop on top** (counterclockwise loop) **and then**

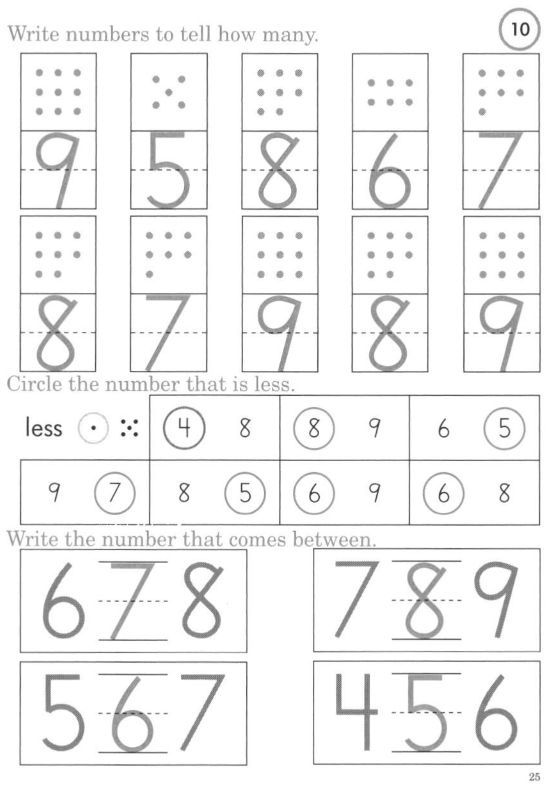

Write numbers to tell how many. (10)

9 5 8 6 7

8 7 9 8 9

Circle the number that is less.

less (·) ⁙	(4) 8	(8) 9	6 (5)
9 (7)	8 (5)	(6) 9	(6) 8

Write the number that comes between.

6 7 8   7 8 9

5 6 7   4 5 6

25

a line (downward slant)**—this is how to make a 9. A loop on top and then a line . . .**

5. *Form 9 in the air.*
   A loop on top and then a line . . .
6. *Write 9.*
   Have the children trace and write 9 on the chalkboard.
7. *Chalkboard grid.*
   Fill one row and one block of the grid as the children count to 9. Start a new row to repeat the practice.
8. *Between Numbers.*
   a. Review the motions for After and Between.
   b. Do the chalkboard samples.
9. *Less Numbers.*
   a. **Say a number that is less than 4.**
   b. Do the chalkboard samples.
   c. Flash Less cards. The same cards are used as for More Numbers, but now the children say the number that is less.
10. *Assign Lesson 10.*

Note: Be prepared with an object (such as a stuffed toy) for demonstration of Addition Family 1 in Lesson 11.

Follow-up

Drill

1. Give a copy of Form B to each child. **See the apple picture. In the first box beside the apple, write the number 6. Go across to the next box in the Apple Row. Write the number 4 in that box.**
   Go across to the last box in that row. Write the number seven.
   Now find the egg in a nest. Always start at this side of the paper and go across. Write 3 in the first box of the Egg Row.

Apple Row:	**6**	**4**	**7**
Egg Row:	**3**	**8**	**5**
Igloo Row:	**9**	**7**	**6**
Octopus Row:	**2**	**8**	**9**
Umbrella Row:	**7**	**6**	**8**

2. Flash Number Pattern cards 2–9.
3. Set Number flash cards 1–9 on the chalk tray in random order. Have the children arrange them in order.

Practice Sheets

- ● Form B (*Follow-up* drill #1)
- ☐ Writing Practice #10
- ☐ Count and Write #14
- ● Form A: 1–9
- ● After Numbers #4
- ◊ Dot-to-Dot #7
- ◊ Scrambled Numbers #5

Objectives

New

TEACHING

Count to 100
Addition Family 1

WORKBOOK

Addition Family 1

Review

Numbers 0–9

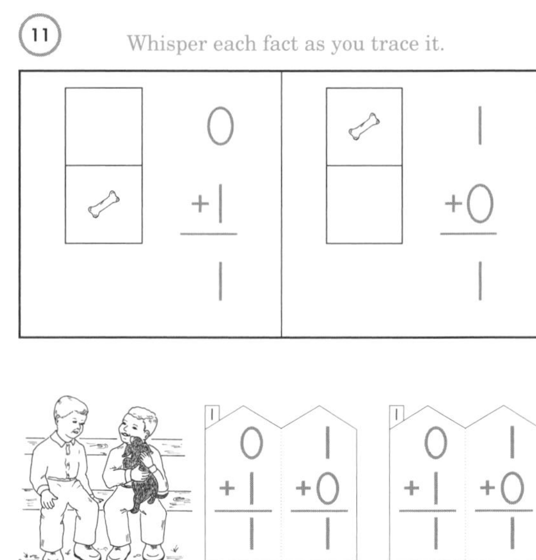
11 Whisper each fact as you trace it.

0 +1 1	1 +0 1

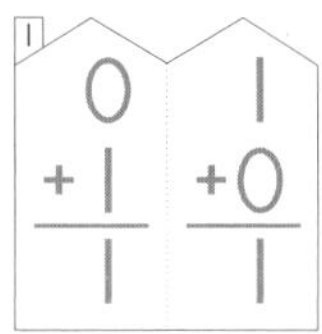

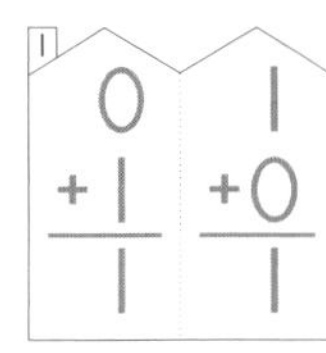

1 | 0 +1 1 | 1 +0 1

1 | 0 +1 1 | 1 +0 1

1 | 0 +1 1 | 1 +0 1

26

Preparation

Make Addition Family 1 flash cards for each child.

Materials

(Italicized items are for *Follow-up* drill.)

1 stuffed toy

1 red felt block

A strip of felt or yarn or thread to divide the flannel board into upper and lower parts

Number Pattern flash cards 3–9

Number flash cards 1–9

Addition Family 1 flash cards

Less flash cards 2–9

1 reclosable plastic sandwich bag for each child

Chalkboard

(*Class Time* #5)

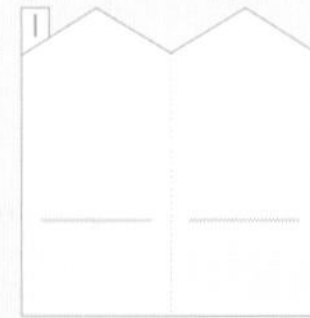

Note: When you fill the houses, always write the complete fact vertically before you write any numbers for the next fact. Addition families always begin with 0.

Class Time

1. *Counting.*
   Have the children stand beside their desks. Call one child at a time to the number line. Have each child count his steps aloud as he comes.
   a. **Let's review the number trains.**
   b. **Count 1–89.**
2. *Introduce the 90's and 100.*
   Point to 90–99. **This number train is the nineties. They all have a 9 with another digit. Count to 99. What comes next? 100!**
3. *Review 0–9.*
   a. Form 0–9 in the air.
   b. Flash Number Pattern cards 3–9.
   c. Flash Number cards 5–9 quickly.
   d. Give the Number flash cards 1–9 to the children. (If your class is small, give two consecutive numbers to each child.) **Who has the number that we begin counting with? Who has the number that comes after 1?** Continue.

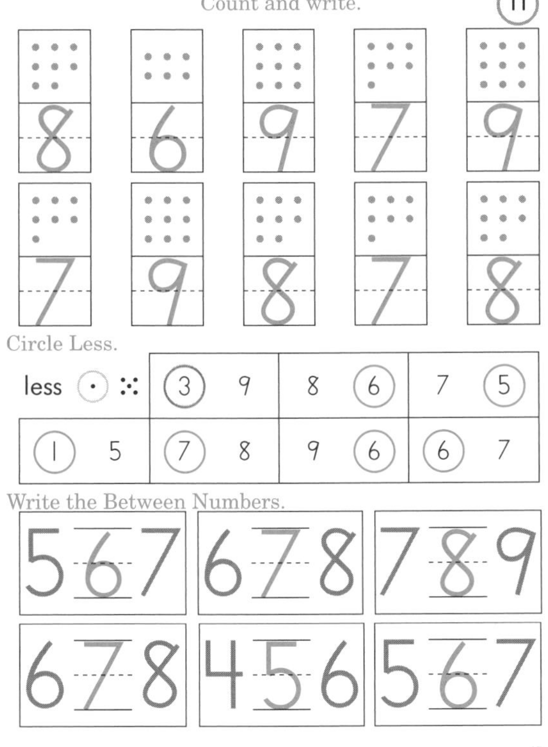

4. *Introduce Addition Family 1.*
   a. Call two children to the front of the class. Give the second one a stuffed toy.*
   b. **How many toys does [first child] have?** Write 0 on the board.
   c. **How many toys does [second child] have?** Write 1 under the 0.
   d. Write + beside the 1. **How many toys do they have together?** Draw an equal line under the problem, and write 1 below it.
   e. Trace the problem as you say, **0 plus 1 equals 1.** Repeat three times.
   f. Have the child with the toy hand it to the other one. **How many toys does [first child] have?** Write 1.
   g. **How many toys does [second child] have?** Write 0 under the 1.
   h. Write + beside the 0. **How many toys do they have together?** Draw an equal line under the problem, and write 1 below it.
   i. Trace the problem as you say, **1 plus 0 equals 1.** Repeat three times.

5. *Addition Family 1 on the flannel board.* Divide the flannel board into upper and lower parts with a strip of felt, yarn, or thread.
   a. Place 0 blocks above the dividing line and 1 block below. Point to the two parts as you say, **0 plus 1 equals 1.**
   b. Write the fact in the first section of the house on the chalkboard. Trace the fact three times as everyone says, **0 plus 1 equals 1.**
   c. Move the felt block from below to above the dividing line. Point to the two parts as you say, **1 plus 0 equals 1.**
   d. Write the fact in the other part of the house. Trace it three times as everyone says, **1 plus 0 equals 1.**

6. *Assign Lesson 11.*

* Or substitute any object, such as a book.

Follow-up

Drill

1. Show the children your Addition 1 flash cards. Say each fact three times.
2. Flash Less cards 2–9.
3. Form numbers 0–9 in the air as you say them.
4. Have the children say which number you are making as you quietly form numbers 0–9 in the air.
5. Give each child his Addition Family 1 flash cards and a reclosable plastic sandwich bag to store them in. Encourage the children to practice with their little cards individually whenever they have spare time.

Practice Sheets

- Count and Write #14
- Count and Write #15
- After Numbers #5
- ◊ Random Counting #1
- ◊ Draw and Count #8

Objectives

New

TEACHING

The number 10

WORKBOOK

The number 10

Review

Addition Family 1
Numbers 0–9
Counting (100)

Preparation

Tack Addition Family 1 flash cards above the flannel board with answers showing. Use another set when needed for the daily drill with flash cards.

Materials

Ten felt blocks

Number Pattern flash cards 4–10

Less flash cards 2–10

Form B for each child

Chalkboard

(*Class Time* #2)

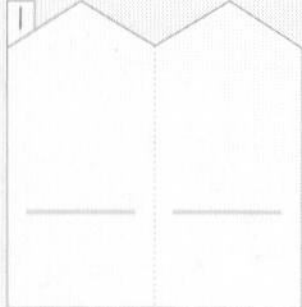

Class Time

1. *Review Addition Family 1.*
   Call the children to the flannel board.
   a. Place 1 felt block below the divider. **0 plus 1 equals 1.** Point to the parts and say the fact.
   b. Move the block above the divider. **1 plus 0 equals 1.** Point to the parts and say the fact.
   c. Ask a child to move the block as everyone repeats, **0 plus 1 equals 1. 1 plus 0 equals 1.**
2. *Drill Addition Family 1.*
   a. Point to the flash cards above the flannel board. **Let's say this pair of facts three times: 0 + 1 = 1; 1 + 0 = 1 . . .**
   b. **Say Family 1 as I fill in the houses.**
3. *Review 0–9.*
   Form 0–9 in the air.
4. *Counting.*
   Call the children to the number line.
   a. **Let's say the number trains.**
   b. **How many numbers are in the teens?** (10) **How many numbers**

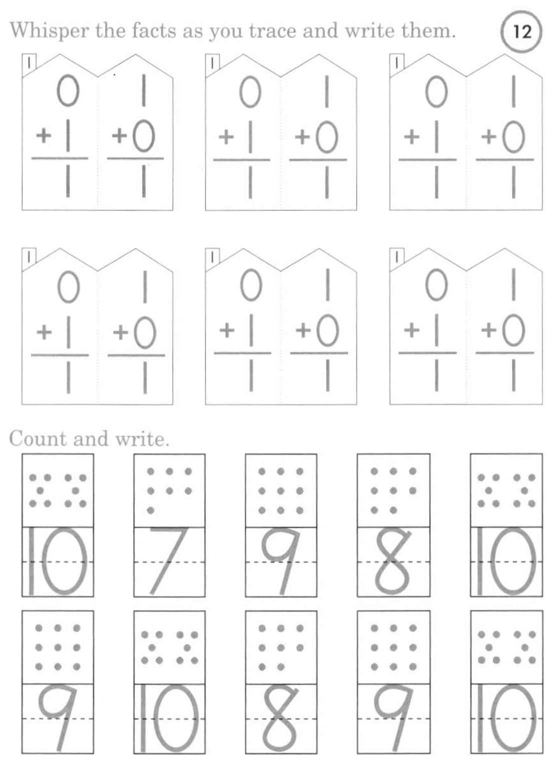
Whisper the facts as you trace and write them. (12)

0 + 1 = 1 1 + 0 = 1 (six times)

Count and write.

10 7 9 8 10

9 10 8 9 10

29

are in the twenties? (10) **How many numbers are in the thirties? . . . forties? . . . fifties? . . .**

c. **Count 1–100.**

5. *Introduce 10.*
   a. Come back to the flannel board. Remove the dividing line, and let a child add 9 more blocks as everyone counts, **1, 2, 3, 4, 5, 6, 7, 8, 9, 10.**
   b. **God gave you 10 fingers. God gave you 10 toes. He gave the 10 Commandments to the children of Israel. Jesus told about 10 young women who were waiting in the night. They had 10 lamps. Do you know what happened to some of their lamps while they waited and slept?**
6. *How to write 10.*
   10 is a very special number. It is a group number. It is different from the numbers we learned before because we write two digits to write 10.
   a. Write a large 10 on the board as you say, **One group and nothing more.**
   b. **Say 10 as I trace it. 10, . . .**
   c. Emphasize careful formation of 10. On the board, show the children that it should not look like any of these:
      10   1 0   10   10   01
7. *Assign Lesson 12.*

Note: Be prepared with two small balls or other objects for demonstration of Addition Family 2 in Lesson 13.

Follow-up

Drill

(*Drill #2*)

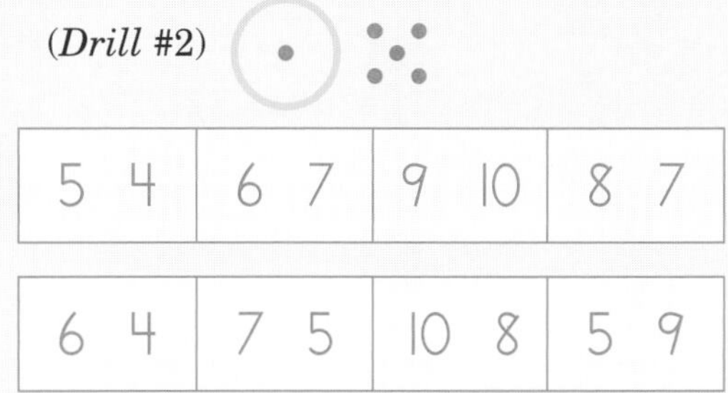

1. Flash Number Pattern cards 4–10.
2. Do the chalkboard samples. **Circle the number that is less.**
3. Flash Less cards 2–10.
4. Give a copy of Form B to each child. **Always start in the first box beside the picture and go across the row. Write the number I say. Apple Row . . .**

(apple)	10	8	9
(nest)	7	10	6
(hat)	5	9	4
(spider)	8	7	10
(umbrella)	9	10	8

Practice Sheets

- ● Form B (*Follow-up* drill #4)
- ☐ Writing Practice #11
- ☐ Between Numbers #1
- ● Form A: 1–10
- ◊ Dot-to-Dot #8
- ◊ Draw and Count #9

Objectives

New

TEACHING

Addition Family 2
Flash card drill

WORKBOOK

Addition Family 2

Review

Addition Family 1
Counting (100)
More, After, and Between
Numbers 0–10

Preparation

Make Addition Family 2 flash cards for each child.

Materials

Two felt blocks

Two small balls

Addition Families 1 and 2 flash cards

Number Pattern flash cards 4–10

Chalkboard

(*Class Time* #1)

(*Class Time* #3)

(*Class Time* #7)

Class Time

1. *Review Addition Family 1.*
   a. Call the children to the flannel board. **Say Addition Family 1 as I move the block. 0 + 1 = 1 . . .**
   b. Point to the flash cards. **Say each fact three times.**
   c. Ask a child to fill the 1 Houses as everyone says the facts.
2. *Counting.*
   Stand near the number line. **Jesus told about a shepherd who had 100 sheep. One day the shepherd counted his sheep, and they were not all there. Count with me to see how many he counted.** Use the pointer and stop at 99. **The shepherd went to look for his lost sheep, and he was very glad when he found it.**
3. *More.*
   Do the chalkboard samples.
4. *After and Between.*
   a. Review the After motion. **What comes after 7? . . . 5? . . . 8? . . . 6?**

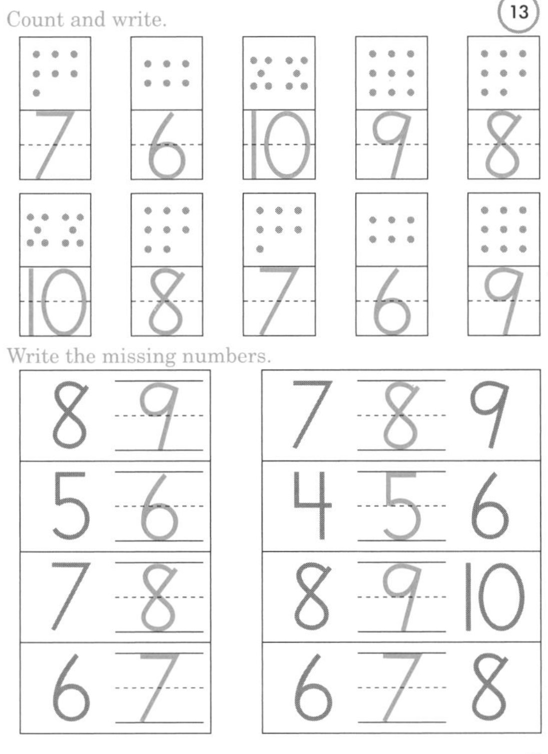

b. Review the Between motion. **What comes between 4 and 6? . . . 7 and 9? . . . 8 and 10? . . . 5 and 7?**

5. *Review 0–10.*
Form 0–10 in the air.

6. *Introduce Addition Family 2.*
   a. Call two children to the front of the class. Give the second child 2 balls.*
   (1) **How many balls does [first child] have?** Write 0 on the board.
   (2) **How many balls does [second child] have?** Write 2 under the 0.
   (3) Write + beside the 2. **How many balls do they have together?** Draw an equal line under the problem, and write 2 below it.
   (4) Trace the problem as you say, **0 plus 2 equals 2.** Repeat three times.
   b. Have the child with two balls hand one to the other child.
   (1) Repeat the questions in part *a,* and write the second fact in Family 2.
   (2) Say the fact as you trace it three times.
   c. Have the first child hand over the second ball.
   (1) Repeat the questions and do the last fact.
   (2) Say the fact as you trace it three times.

7. *Addition Family 2 on the flannel board.*
   a. Place 2 blocks in the lower part of the divided flannel board. Write the fact in the house as everyone says, **0 plus 2 equals 2.**
   b. Place 1 block in the upper part and one in the lower. Fill the second section of the house.
   c. Put both blocks in the lower part, and write the third fact.
   d. **Say each fact as I trace it.**

8. *Assign Lesson 13.*
Seeing, hearing, saying, writing—use all four channels to fix the facts in memory. Have the children whisper the facts as they fill in the houses in the lesson and on the practice sheet. They must be done vertically, with each fact completed before the next is begun.

Follow-up

Drill

1. Show flash cards for Addition Families 1 and 2.
Say the whole fact together.
2. Flash Number Pattern cards 4–10.
3. Give each child his Addition Family 2 flash cards. Encourage individual practice. The cards may also be taken home for additional drill.

Practice Sheets

- ☐ Fact Houses #1
- ☐ Form A: 1–10
- ☐ Count and Write #15
- ● Between Numbers #2
- ● After Numbers #6

* Or substitute any convenient object.

Objectives

New

TEACHING

Before Numbers

Review

Addition Families 1 and 2
Counting (100)
Numbers 1–10
Number Patterns

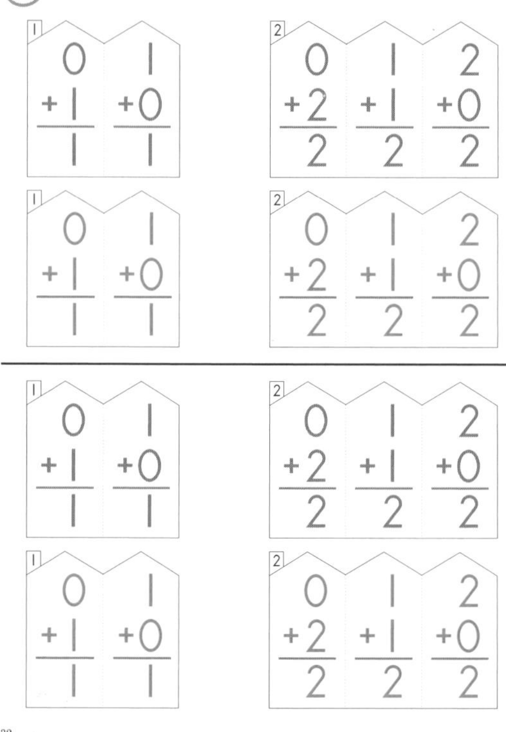

Preparation

Tack Addition Family 2 flash cards above the flannel board with answers showing. Use another set when needed for the daily drill with flash cards.

Materials

Number flash cards 1–10

Number Pattern flash cards 4–10

Form B for each child

Between flash cards 1–10

Chalkboard

(*Class Time* #1)

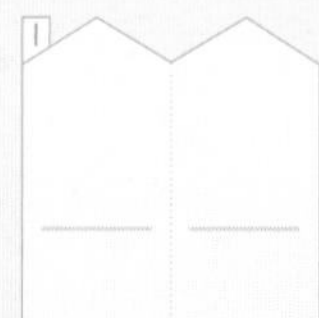

(*Class Time* #2)

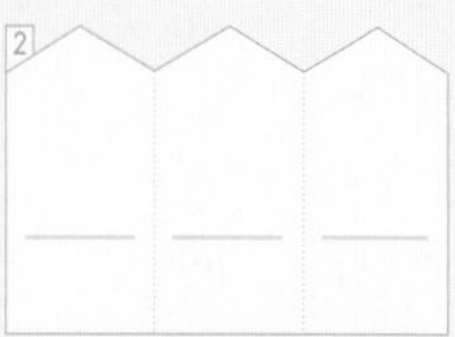

Class Time

1. *Review Addition Family 1.*
   a. Call the children to the flannel board. **Say Addition Family 1 as I move the block.**
   b. Ask a child to fill the 1 Houses as everyone says the facts.
2. *Review Addition Family 2.*
   a. **Say Addition Family 2 as I move the blocks.**
   b. Ask a child to fill the 2 Houses as everyone says the facts.
   c. Point to the Family 2 flash cards at the flannel board. **We will say each fact three times. 0 + 2 = 2; 0 + 2 = 2 . . .**
3. *Counting.*
   Stand near the number line.
   a. **The girls will say the engine number for each train. The boys will say the rest of the train.**
   b. **Count 1–100.**
4. *Review 1–10.*
   a. Form 2–10 in the air.
   b. Give your Number flash cards 1–10 to

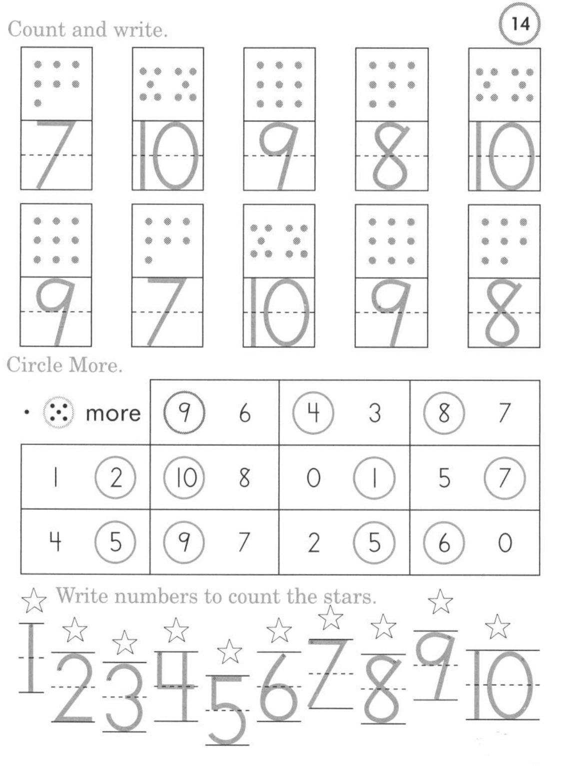

the children. Have a child slowly call **1, 2, 3, . . .** The others will come and stand in line as their numbers are called.

5. *Number Patterns.*
   Flash Number Pattern cards.
6. *Number dictation.*
   Use Form B. **Write the number I say. Remember to start in the box beside the picture, and go across.**

(apple)	**9**	**8**	**10**
(nest)	**7**	**9**	**8**
(igloo)	**10**	**6**	**10**
(spider)	**9**	**7**	**5**
(umbrella)	**8**	**10**	**9**

7. *Assign Lesson 14.*

Follow-up

Drill

(*Drill* #3)

(*Drill* #2)

__ 6	__ 7	__ 4
__ 3	__ 5	__ 2
__ 10	__ 9	__ 8

1. Flash Between cards 1–10.
2. a. As the children **count 1–10,** write 1–10 above the Before samples on the chalkboard.
   b. Review the hand motions for After and Between. Say **before, before, before,** as you motion from left to right in exactly the opposite form from what you use with After.
   c. Point to __ 6. **What comes before 6?** Refer the children to the numbers 1–10 that you have written above.
3. On the board, draw the daisy shown above. Have the children "dash around the daisy," reading the number of each petal. Do they really know their numbers? (Keep the daisy for later lessons.)

Practice Sheets

- ● Form B (*Class Time* #6)
- □ Form A: 1–10
- □ Between Numbers #1
- ● Count and Write #16
- ◊ Random Counting #2

Objectives

New

TEACHING

Before Numbers
Fact recitation by memory
Chalkboard dictation

WORKBOOK

Mixed addition facts

Review

Addition Families 1 and 2
Counting (100)
Less Numbers (choice of 3)

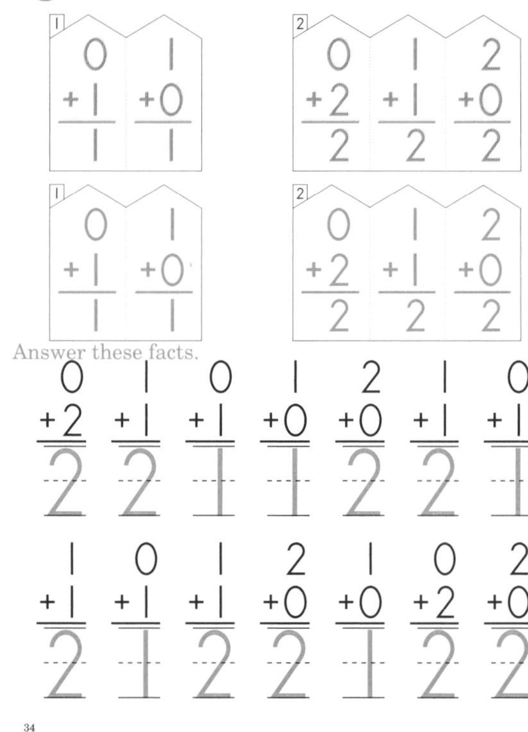

Preparation

Materials

Number Pattern flash cards 1–10

Addition Families 1 and 2 flash cards

Chalkboard

(*Class Time* #1)

(*Class Time* #4)

(*Class Time* #5)

__ 4	__ 5	__ 3
__ 6	__ 7	__ 8
__ 9	__ 10	__ 2

Class Time

1. *Review Addition Families 1 and 2.*
   Have the children stand near the flannel board. **I will move the blocks.**
   a. **Say Family 1 together. 0 + 1 = 1; 1 + 0 = 1.**
   b. **Say Family 2 together. 0 + 2 = 2; 1 + 1 . . .**
   c. **Say Families 1 and 2 as I fill the houses.**
2. *Recite fact families.*
   Stand where the children will not see any facts while looking at you. To help prevent confusion about which fact to say and to help the class stay together, use your fingers as a visual aid.
   a. **Say Addition Family 1.**
   Hold up a fist for zero.
   ***Zero* plus 1 equals 1.**
   Hold up 1 finger.
   ***One* plus 0 equals 1.**
   b. **Say Addition Family 2.**
   Hold up a fist for zero.
   ***Zero* plus 2 equals 2.**
   Hold up 1 finger.

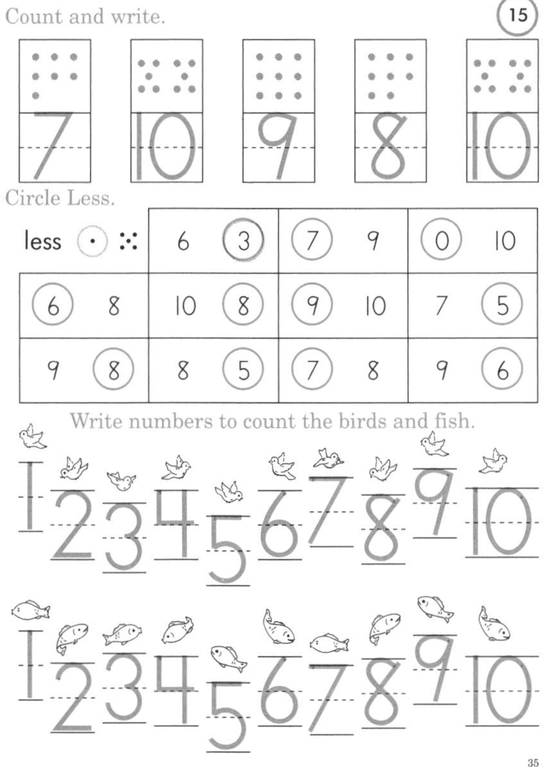

One plus 1 equals 2.
Hold up 2 fingers.
Two plus 0 equals 2.

3. *Counting.*
   Stand near the number line. **The boys will say the engine numbers. The girls will say the rest of the train. Count 1–100.**
4. *Less*
   Point to the first box in the chalkboard samples. **7 is less than 8, but 5 is less than 7. Find the number that is least of all.**
5. *Before Numbers.*
   a. As the children **count 1–10,** write 1–10 above the Before samples. Practice the Before motion.
   b. Point to __ 4. **What comes before 4?** Fill in their answers.
6. *Assign Lesson 15.*

Note: Bring three flowers or other objects for demonstration of Addition Family 3 in Lesson 16.

Follow-up

Drill

1. Flash Number Pattern cards 1–10.
2. Drill Addition Families 1 and 2 flash cards. **Say the number that is the answer for each fact.**
3. Chalkboard drill: Have the children stand at the board with chalk and eraser.
   a. **Write the number I say: 6. Now write the number that comes after 6.** Each child should have written 6, 7. **Erase.**
   b. **Write 3 and the number that comes after 3. Erase.**
   c. Continue in the same manner with **8, 4, 9, 7, 5, 2.**

Practice Sheets

- ☐ More Numbers #1
- ☐ Count and Write #16
- ● Number Facts #1
- ● Between Numbers #1
- ◊ Random Counting #3

Objectives

New

TEACHING

Addition Family 3
After (2 blanks)

WORKBOOK

Addition Family 3
Before Numbers

Review

Addition Families 1 and 2
Counting (100)

Preparation

Make Addition Family 3 flash cards for each child.

Materials

Three flowers or other objects

Three felt blocks

Number Pattern flash cards 4–10

Chalkboard

(*Class Time* #1)

(*Class Time* #3)

__ 6	__ 9	__ 2	__ 10
__ 5	__ 8	__ 4	__ 7

(*Class Time* #5)

Class Time

1. *Review Addition Families 1 and 2.*
   Call the children to the flannel board. **I will move the blocks.**
   a. **Say Family 1. 0 + 1 . . .**
   b. **Say Family 2. 0 + 2 . . .**
   c. Point to the Family 2 flash cards. **Say each fact three times.**
   d. Ask a child to fill the 2 Houses as everyone says the facts.
2. *Counting.*
   Follow my pointing stick down, down into the valley and up, up the mountain . . . Lead their eyes on up to 0. **Count 1–100.** Are they looking at the numbers?
3. *Before.*
   Write 1–10 above the samples. **What comes before 6?** Do the samples.
4. *Introduce Addition Family 3.*
   a. Call two children to the front of the class. Give the first one 0 flowers, and give the second one 3.
   (1) Write the first fact on the board as you draw response from the class. **How**

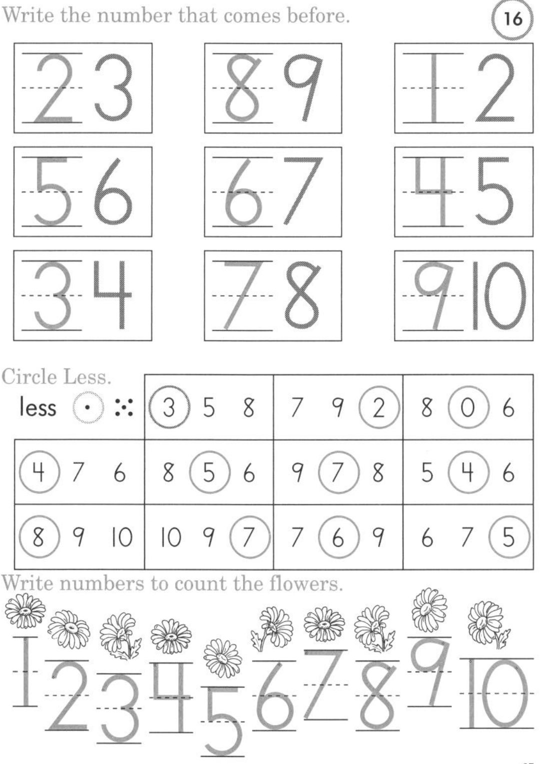
Write the number that comes before. (16)

2 3	8 9	1 2
5 6	6 7	4 5
3 4	7 8	9 10

Circle Less.

less (·) ∴	(3) 5 8	7 9 (2)	8 (0) 6
(4) 7 6	8 (5) 6	9 (7) 8	5 (4) 6
(8) 9 10	10 9 (7)	7 (6) 9	6 7 (5)

Write numbers to count the flowers.

1 2 3 4 5 6 7 8 9 10

37

many flowers does [first child] have? How many flowers does [second child] have? How many flowers do they have together?

(2) Trace and say the fact three times.

b. Have the second child give 1 flower to the first child. Repeat the questions, and write the second fact. Trace and say the fact three times.

c. Have them transfer the other flowers, and do those facts in the same manner.

5. *Addition Family 3 on the flannel board.*

a. Place 3 blocks in the lower part. Write 0 + 3 = 3 in the first section of the 3 Houses.

b. Move 1 block to the upper part of the flannel board. Write 1 + 2 = 3 in the second part of the houses.

c. Continue with 2 + 1 and 3 + 0.

d. **Say each fact as I trace it. 0 + 3 = 3; 1 + 2 = 3; 2 + 1 = 3; 3 + 0 = 3.**

6. *Assign Lesson 16.*

Follow-up

Drill

(*Drill* #2)

6 __ __ 5 __ __ 7 __ __

3 __ __ 8 __ __ 4 __ __

1. Give each child his Addition Family 3 flash cards.
2. Have the children do the After samples.
3. Flash Number Pattern cards 4–10.

Practice Sheets

- ☐ Fact Houses #2
- ☐ Less Numbers #1
- ☐ Between Numbers #2
- ● Number Facts #1
- ◊ Random Counting #4

Objectives

New

TEACHING

Flash card drill

Number Order

Review

Addition Families 1–3

Counting (100)

Numbers 1–10

Before Numbers

After (2 blanks)

Less

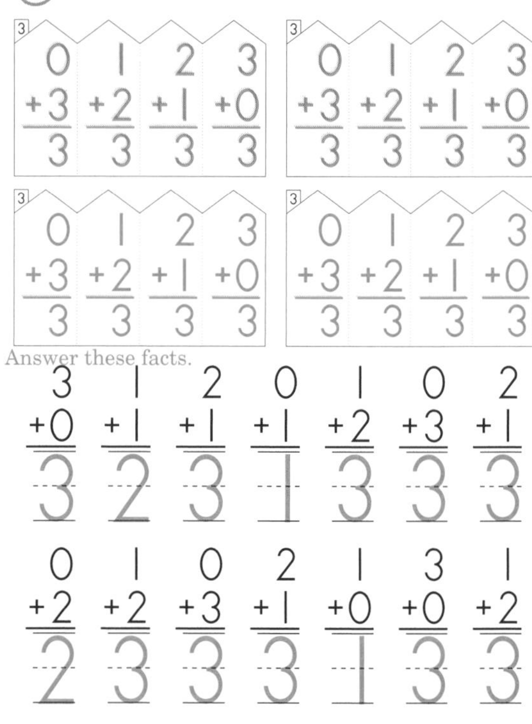
(17) Whisper the facts as you trace and write them.

0 +3 3	1 +2 3	2 +1 3	3 +0 3	0 +3 3	1 +2 3	2 +1 3	3 +0 3
0 +3 3	1 +2 3	2 +1 3	3 +0 3	0 +3 3	1 +2 3	2 +1 3	3 +0 3

Answer these facts.

3 +0 3	1 +1 2	2 +1 3	0 +1 1	1 +2 3	0 +3 3	2 +1 3
0 +2 2	1 +2 3	0 +3 3	2 +1 3	1 +0 1	3 +0 3	1 +2 3

38

Preparation

Tack a set of Addition Family 3 flash cards with answers showing above the flannel board. Use another set for the daily drill with flash cards.

Materials

Addition Families 1–3 flash cards

Number flash cards 1–10

Before flash cards 2–10

Chalkboard

(*Class Time* #1)

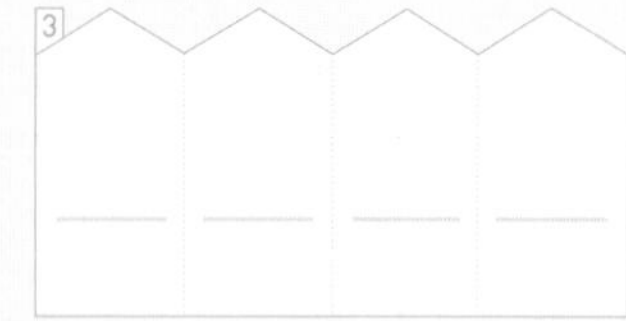

(*Class Time* #4)

7 __ __

5 __ __

8 __ __

3 __ __

6 __ __

(*Class Time* #5)

6 8 7	9 10 5	4 5 6
6 5 7	4 3 2	7 9 8

Class Time

1. *Review Addition Families 1–3.*
   a. Call the children to the flannel board. Ask a child to move the blocks as you say Family 1. Ask a child to move the blocks as you say Family 2.
   b. Flash Addition Families 1–3 cards, and have the children say the answers only.
   c. **Say Family 3 as I fill the houses.**
2. *Counting.*
   Stand near the number line.
   a. **Say the number trains. Say the engine numbers louder and slower.**
   b. **Count 1–100.**
3. *Review 1–10.*
   Pass out Number flash cards 1–10. **Come when I call your number. See if you can stand in order. 5, 2, 9, 4, 10, 6, 1, 8, 7, 3.** Are they lined up correctly with the cards below their chins?
   (For a class of less than 10 children, you could give each child two or three cards, making sure each child's numbers are consecutive. Or you could give one or two

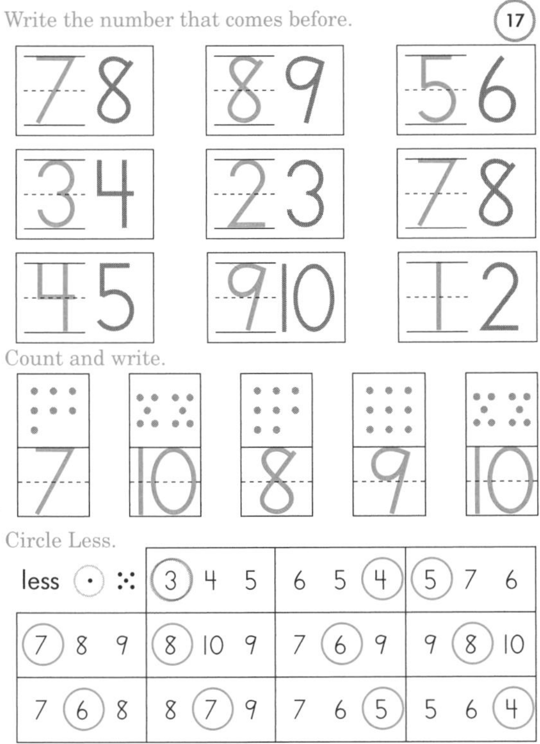
Write the number that comes before. (17)

7 8	8 9	5 6
3 4	2 3	7 8
4 5	9 10	1 2

Count and write.

7 10 8 9 10

Circle Less.

less (•) ⁙	(3) 4 5	6 5 (4)	(5) 7 6
(7) 8 9	(8) 10 9	7 (6) 9	9 (8) 10
7 (6) 8	8 (7) 9	7 6 (5)	5 6 (4)

39

children one card at a time for them to place on the table or chalk tray in correct sequence.)

4. *Before and After.*
   a. Flash Before cards. The children will say the number for the blank.
   b. Do the chalkboard samples for After Numbers.
5. *Less.*
   Do the chalkboard samples.
6. *Assign Lesson 17.*

Follow-up

Drill

(*Drill* #1)

5 4 6 _ _ _	7 8 6 _ _ _
3 5 4 _ _ _	8 10 9 _ _ _

1. Call attention to the numbers in the boxes.
   a. Ask a child to circle the number that is least in the first box.
   b. **Since 4 is least, 4 comes first.** Write 4 on the first blank in the box.
   c. **Which number comes after 4?** Write 5 on the next blank. **after 5?** Write 6. **Count 4, 5, 6. We put them in the right order!** Continue in the same manner for the other boxes.
2. Chalkboard drill: **Write the number I say, then the number that comes after it. 3, 8, 5, 1, 9, 6, 4, 7, 2.**
3. Is your daisy still on the chalkboard from Lesson 14? Let the children say the numbers on the petals as fast as they can, around one way and then reversing the direction.

Practice Sheets

- ☐ Fact Houses #2
- ☐ Before Numbers #1
- ● Number Facts #2
- ● Form A: 1–10
- ◊ Random Counting #5

Objectives

New

TEACHING

Number Order

Review

Addition Families 1–3
Counting (100)
Numbers 1–10
After

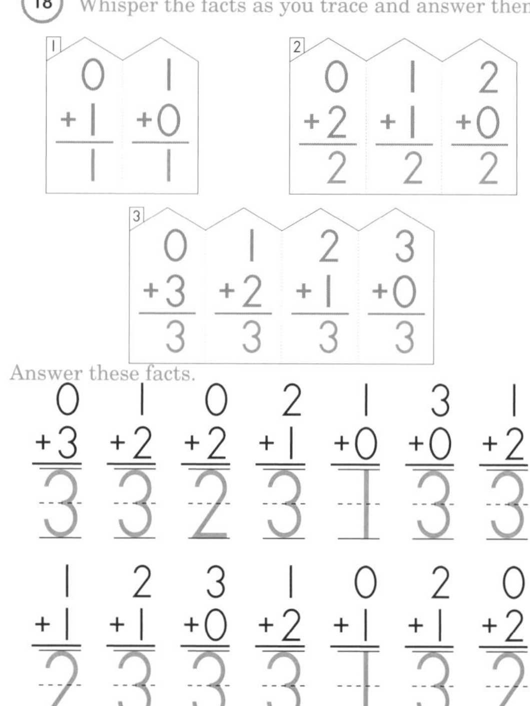

Preparation

Materials

Addition Families 1–3 flash cards

Number flash cards 1–10

After flash cards 1–9

Before flash cards 2–10

Between flash cards 1–10

Number Pattern flash cards

Chalkboard

(*Class Time* #1)

(*Class Time* #3)

7	5	6	8	6	7
_	_	_	_	_	_
2	1	3	10	8	9
_	_	_	_	_	_

Class Time

1. *Review Addition Families 1–3.*
   a. Call the children to the flannel board. **I will move the blocks. Say Addition Family 1 . . . Family 2 . . . Family 3.**
   b. Set Addition Families 1–3 flash cards on the chalk tray in family order. Point to the first card. **Let's say them together.**
   0 + 1 = 1; 1 + 0 = 1; 0 + 2 = 2 . . .
   c. **We will say each family as [Fred] fills the houses for us.**
2. *Counting.*
   The daily drill of rote counting is a cornerstone in arithmetic. Keep the drill lively. Count with a clear, punchy, expressive voice. Beware of a sing-song, drone-along chant. **Count 1–100.**
3. *Number Order.*
   a. Point to the chalkboard samples. Ask a child to circle the least number in the first box.
   b. **Tell me what to write on the blanks.**

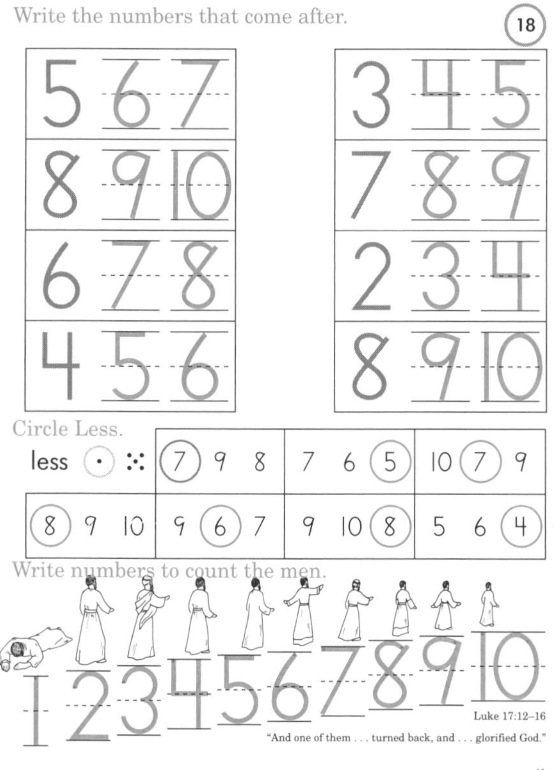

And as he entered into a certain village, there met him ten men that were lepers, which stood afar off: and they lifted up their voices, and said, Jesus, Master, have mercy on us. And when he saw them, he said unto them, Go shew yourselves unto the priests. And it came to pass, that, as they went, they were cleansed. And one of them, when he saw that he was healed, turned back, and with a loud voice glorified God, and fell down on his face at his feet, giving him thanks: and he was a Samaritan (Luke 17:12–16).

Check the work by counting **5, 6, 7.**

c. Continue.

4. *Review 1–10.*
   a. Pass out Number flash cards 1–10. **Come when I call your number. Stand in place so that your numbers are in the right order. 6, 3, 8, 10, 2, 4, 7, 5, 9, 1.**
   b. **Say your numbers.**
   c. **One day ten men with leprosy met Jesus. He told them to go to the priest, and they were healed when they went. One of them turned around to thank and worship Jesus.**
5. *After.*
   Flash After cards.
6. *Assign Lesson 18.*

Follow-up

Drill

(*Drill* #2)

1. Practice hand motions for Before, After, and Between.
   a. Flash Before cards.
   b. Flash Between cards.
2. Draw a new daisy, or change the numbers on the petals to a different order. Observe the time it takes the children to dash around the daisy. If it takes more than ten seconds for a child to read all the numbers, he needs more practice. (Keep the daisy for Lessons 19 and 20.)
3. Flash Number Pattern cards.

Practice Sheets

- ☐ Fact Houses #3
- ☐ Before Numbers #1
- ● Number Facts #2

Objectives

New

TEACHING

The number 11

WORKBOOK

Number Order

Review

Addition Families 1–3
Counting (100)
Numbers 0–10
Number Order

(19) Answer these facts.

3	1	1	2	0	0	1
+0	+2	+1	+1	+2	+1	+2
3	3	2	3	2	1	3

0	0	1	2	0	1	0
+3	+2	+1	+1	+1	+1	+3
3	2	2	3	1	2	3

0	3	1	2	1	1	2
+2	+0	+2	+1	+1	+2	+0
2	3	3	3	2	3	2

1	0	2	2	2
+2	+3	+1	+0	+1
3	3	3	2	3

42

Preparation

Materials

Addition Families 1–3 flash cards

Number Order flash cards 1–10

Number flash cards 1–10

Chalkboard

(*Class Time* #4—Daisy from Lesson 18)
Change the order of the numbers again.

(*Class Time* #5)

3 4 2	6 8 7
_ _ _	_ _ _
9 10 8	5 7 6
_ _ _	_ _ _

Class Time

1. *Review addition families.*
   a. Call the children to the flannel board. **I will move the blocks. Say Addition Family 1 . . . Family 2 . . . Family 3.**
   b. Flash Addition Families 1–3 cards. Aim to have each child answer a fact in three seconds.
2. *Recite addition families.*
   Let's say our addition families by memory. Hold up your fist or fingers to indicate the first addend for each fact.
   a. **Family 1:**
      Hold up a fist. ***Zero* + 1 = 1**
      Hold up 1 finger. ***One* + 0 = 1**
   b. **Family 2:**
      Hold up a fist. ***Zero* + 2 = 2**
      Hold up 1 finger. ***One* + 1 = 2**
      Hold up 2 fingers. ***Two* + 0 = 2**
   c. **Family 3:**
      Hold up a fist. ***Zero* + 3 = 3**
      Hold up 1 finger. ***One* + 2 = 3**
      Hold up 2 fingers. ***Two* + 1 = 3**
      Hold up 3 fingers. ***Three* + 0 = 3**

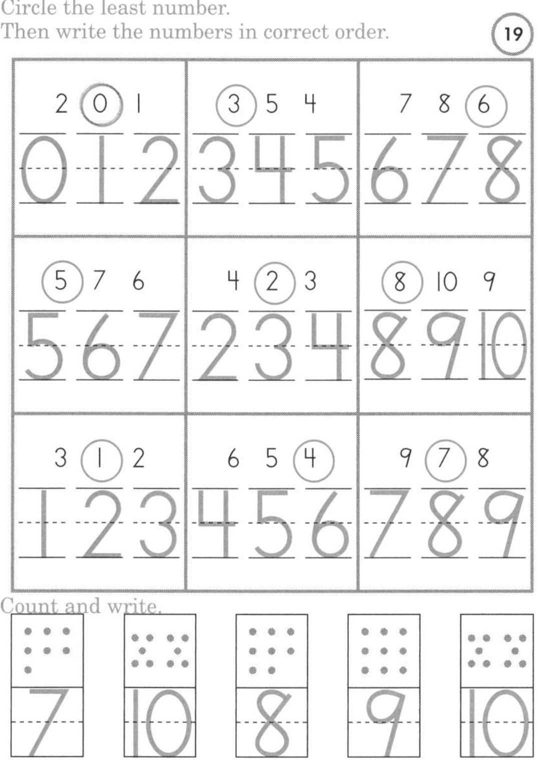

3. *Counting.*
   I will say the engine number for each number train. You say all the other numbers. Count 1–100.
4. *Review 0–10.*
   Dash around the daisy.
5. *Number Order*
   a. Flash Number Order cards.
   b. Stand near the samples. Have the children circle the number that is least and then write the numbers in correct order.
6. *Assign Lesson 19.*

Note: If children get into the habit of counting on their fingers for math facts, give them objects to count, such as buttons or other items. Counting objects helps to rivet addition concepts.

Follow-up

Drill

(*Drill* #1)

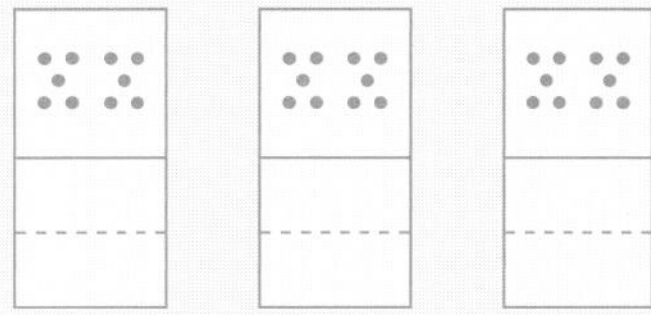

1. Stand near the samples.
   a. Point to the first box. **How many dots are in this box?** (10) **Let's put them together in one group.** Draw a circle around the 10 dots.
   b. Draw 1 dot outside the circle. **A group of 10 and 1 more. How many is that in all? 10, ___** Write 11 in the box.
   c. Do the same thing in the other boxes.
2. Pass out Number flash cards 1–10.
   a. **Come when I call your number. 7. Who has the number that comes *after* 7? Who has the number that comes *before* 7?**
   b. Have those children return to their seats. Ask the same questions about other numbers.

Practice Sheets

- ☐ Fact Houses #3
- ☐ More Numbers #1
- ● Before Numbers #1
- ● Number Facts #2

Objectives

New

TEACHING

Addition Family 4

The number 11

WORKBOOK

Addition Family 4

Review

Addition facts

Counting (100)

Numbers 0–10

Number Order

20 Whisper, trace, and answer these facts.

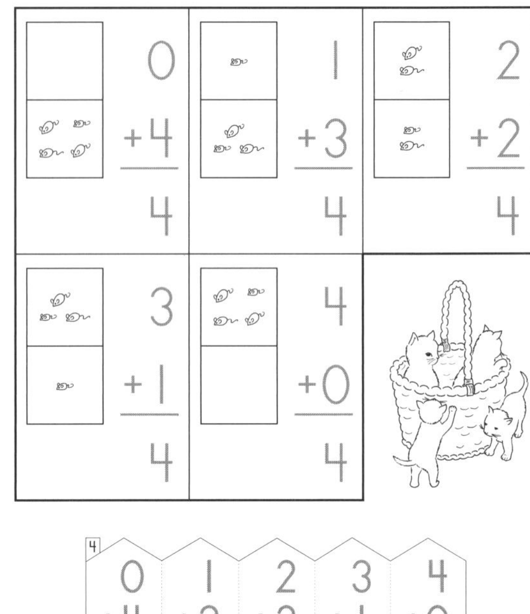

44

Preparation

Make Addition Family 4 flash cards for each child.

Materials

Addition Families 1–3 flash cards

Number Order flash cards 1–10

Number Pattern flash cards 1–10

Four felt blocks

Four rulers

Chalkboard

(*Class Time* #1)

1	2	0	2	0	1	3
+1	+0	+3	+1	+1	+2	+0

1	0	1	3	2	1	2
+2	+2	+0	+0	+1	+1	+0

(*Class Time* #3—Daisy from Lesson 18)

(*Class Time* #7)

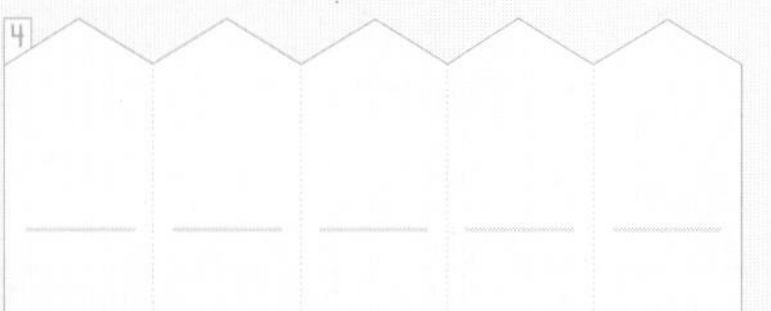

Class Time

1. *Drill Addition facts.*
   a. Flash Addition Families 1–3 flash cards.
   b. Stand near the facts on the board. **Say the answers together.** Have each child answer one row. **Answer together.** Zigzag from row to row.
2. *Counting.* **You say the engine number for each train; I will say the other numbers. Count 1–100.**
3. *Review 0–10.* Dash around the daisy.
4. *Number Order.* Flash Number Order cards.
5. *Number Patterns.* Flash Number Pattern cards.
6. *Introduce Family 4.*
   a. Call two children to the front of the

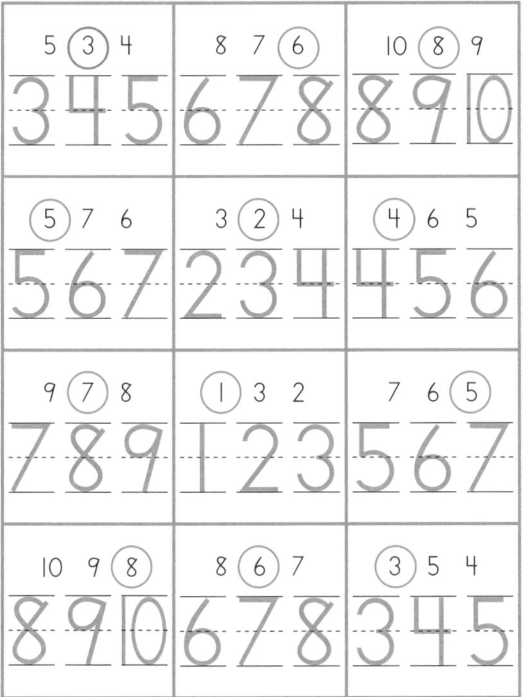

class. Give the first one 0 rulers, and give the second one 4.

(1) Write the first fact on the board as you draw response from the class. **How many rulers does [first child] have? How many rulers does [second child] have? How many rulers do they have together?**

(2) Trace and say the fact three times.

b. Have the second child give 1 ruler to the first child. Repeat the questions and write the second fact. Trace and say the fact three times.

c. Have them transfer the other rulers, and do those facts in the same manner.

7. *Addition Family 4 on the flannel board.*

a. Place 4 blocks in the lower part of the divided flannel board. Write 0 + 4 = 4 in the first section of the Fact Houses.

b. Move 1 block to the upper part of the flannel board. Write 1 + 3 = 4 in the second part of the houses.

c. Continue through the rest of the facts in Family 4.

d. **Say each fact as I trace it.**

0 + 4 = 4
1 + 3 = 4
2 + 2 = 4
3 + 1 = 4
4 + 0 = 4

8. *Assign Lesson 20.*

Follow-up

Drill

(*Drill* #2)

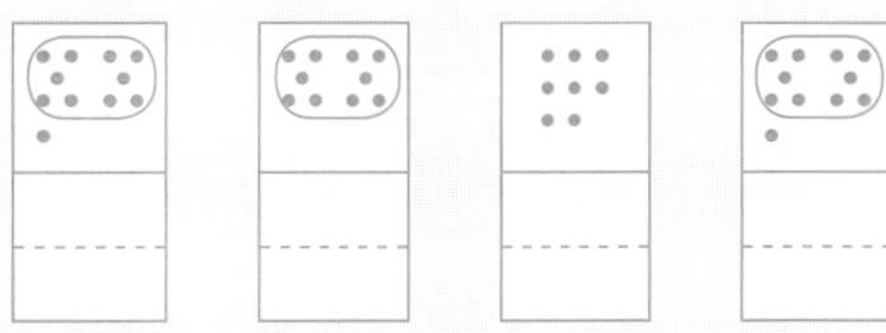

1. Give each child his Addition Family 4 flash cards.

2. Stand near the samples.

a. **How many dots are in the circle?** Point to the dot outside. Help the children think **10, 11.** Write 11 in the box as you say, **1 group and 1 more.**

b. Point to the next box. **How many dots are in the circle? 1 group and zero more.** Write 10.

c. Do the remaining samples.

Practice Sheets

- ☐ Fact Houses #4
- ● Number Facts #2
- ◊ Random Counting #6

Objectives

New

TEACHING

The number 11
After Numbers dictation
Fact Twins

Review

Addition facts
Counting (100)
Between
Number Order

Preparation

Tack Addition Family 4 flash cards above the flannel board with answers showing. Use another set for the daily drill with flash cards.

Materials

Addition Families 1–3 flash cards

Between flash cards 1–10

Number Order cards 1–10

Form B for each child

Addition Families 1–4 flash cards

Chalkboard

(*Class Time* #1)

(*Class Time* #2)

(*Class Time* #4)

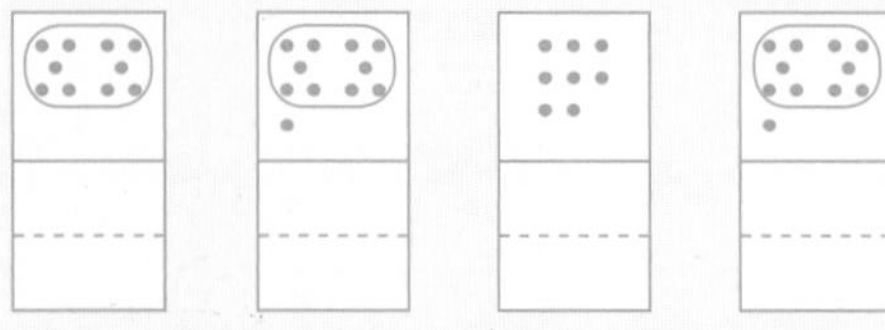

21 Whisper the facts as you trace and write them.

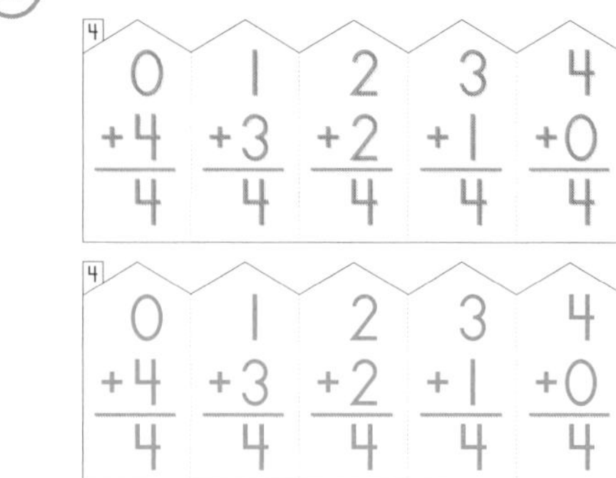

Answer these facts.

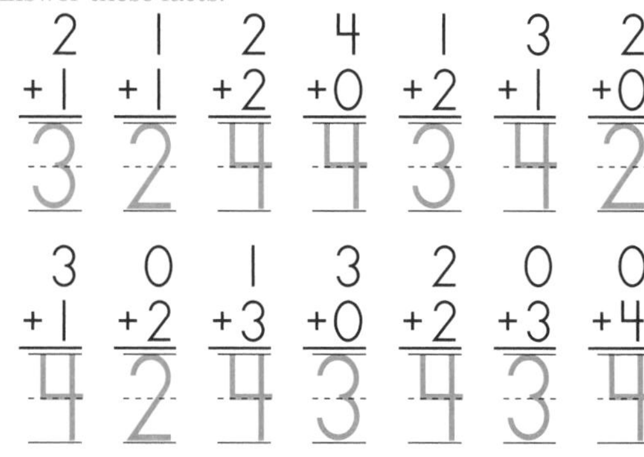

46

Class Time

1. *Review Addition Families 1–3.*
   a. Set Addition Families 1–3 flash cards on the chalk tray in family order. Point to the first card. **Let's say the facts together. 0 + 1 = 1; 1 + 0 = 1 . . .**
   b. **Say Families 1–3 by memory.** Hold up your fingers to indicate the first addend of each fact. (See Lesson 19, *Class Time* #2.)
   c. Ask a child to fill the 3 Houses as everyone says the facts.
2. *Practice Family 4.*
   a. **Say Family 4 as I move the blocks.**
   b. **Say Family 4 as I fill the houses.**
3. *Counting.*
   Call the children one by one to the number line. Have each child count his steps aloud as he comes. Then **count 1–100 together.**
4. *The number 11.*
   Have the children do the counting samples on the board.

Circle the least number.
Then write the numbers in correct order. (21)

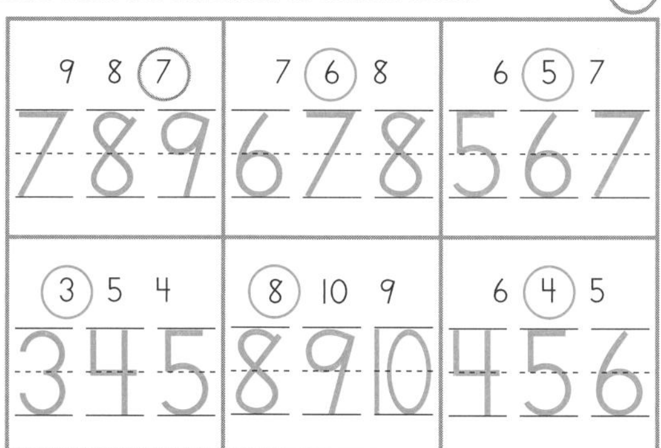

Count and write.

47

5. *Between.*
   a. Review motions Before, After, and Between.
   b. Flash Between cards.
6. *Number Order.*
   Flash Number Order cards.
7. *Assign Lesson 21.*

Follow-up

Drill

1. Teach After Numbers as an oral exercise.
   a. **Write the number 4. Look at the number you wrote, and think what comes after it. Erase your number, and write the one that comes after.** Repeat this exercise a few times with different numbers.
   b. **Now listen to the number I say, and think what comes after it. Do not write the number I say. Write what comes after 6. Erase. Write the number that comes after 2.**

2. Use Form B for After Numbers. **Write the number that comes after the number I say. What comes after 2? What comes after 4?** Repeat the question for each number. (Answers in parentheses.)

   2 (3) **4** (5) **6** (7)

   8 (9) **7** (8) **5** (6)

   3 (4) **9** (10) **1** (2)

   7 (8) **4** (5) **9** (10)

   6 (7) **8** (9) **5** (6)

3. Set these addition flash cards on the chalk tray.

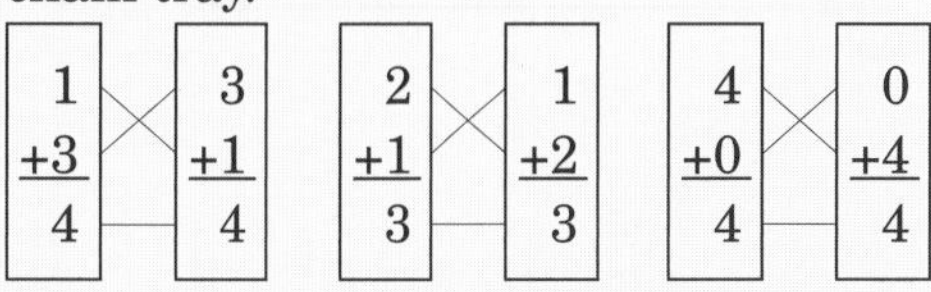

These facts have the same numbers. We call them twins. Draw the connecting lines with chalk.

Practice Sheets

- ● Form B (*Follow-up* drill #2)
- □ Fact Houses #4
- ● Number Facts #3

Objectives

New

WORKBOOK

The number 11

Review

Addition facts
Counting (100)
The number 11
Numbers 7–11

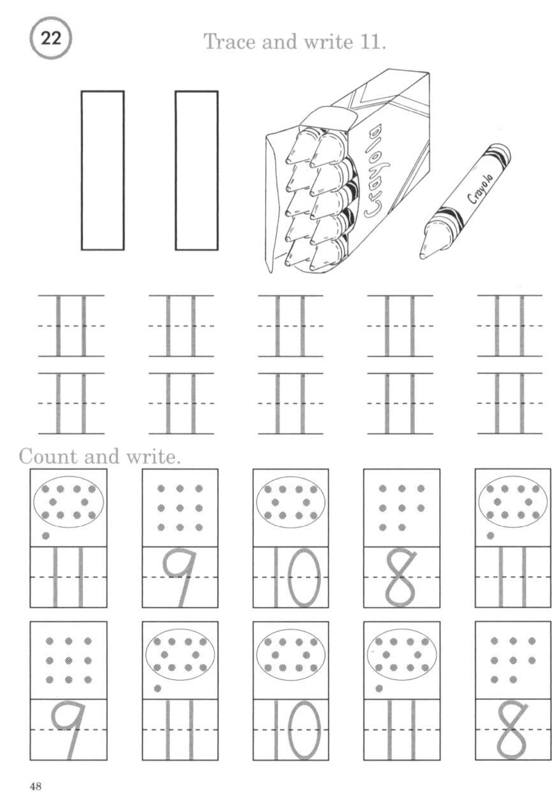

Preparation

Materials

One felt bar with 10 blocks on it, and one individual block

Addition Families 1–4 flash cards

Chalkboard

(*Class Time* #1)

Class Time

1. *Review Addition Families 1–4.*
   a. Call the children to the flannel board. **I will move the blocks. Say Addition Family 2 . . . Family 3 . . . Family 4.**
   b. Point to the flash cards above the flannel board. **Say each fact three times. 0 + 4 = 4 . . .**
   c. **Let's say our Addition Families 1–3 by memory.** Hold up your fingers to indicate the first addend of each fact.
   d. **We will say Family 4 as [Susan] fills the houses.**
2. *Counting.*
   Place a bar of 10 and one individual block on the flannel board. Point to each square of the 10 and to the one block as the class counts. **1, 2, 3, 4, 5, 6, 7, 8, 9, 10, 11.** Point to the number line and continue: **12, 13, 14, 15, . . . 100.**
3. *The number 11 on flannel board.*
   a. Return to the flannel board. Circle the bar with your finger. **Here is a group**

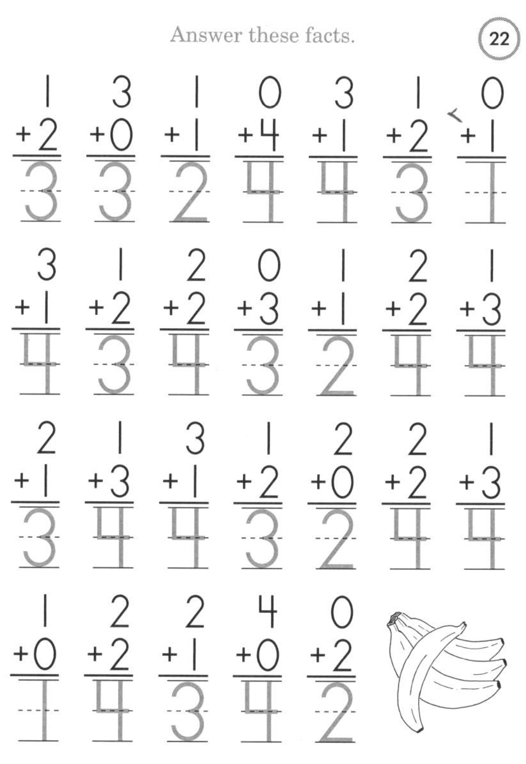

of 10 blocks. Point to the 1. **11; 10, 11; 10, 11, . . .**

b. Draw a large 11 on the board. **One group of 10—and 1 more.** Trace your number, and pronounce the syllables distinctly: **e-lev-en. One group of 10, and 1 more; e-lev-en.**

4. *Review numbers 7–11.*
   Form 7–11 in the air.
5. *Assign Lesson 22.*

Follow-up

Drill

(*Drill* #1)

__9 __6 __3 __5 __7

__8 __4 __10 __2 __11

1. Do the Before samples.
2. Chalkboard drill: **Write the number I say: 8, 11, 9, 10, 11, 9, 8, 11, 10.**
3. Flash Addition Families 1–4 cards.

Practice Sheets

- ☐ Form A: 1–11
- ● Number Facts #3
- ● Count and Write #17
- ◊ Dot-to-Dot #9

Objectives

Review

Addition facts
Counting (100)
Before and Between
Less

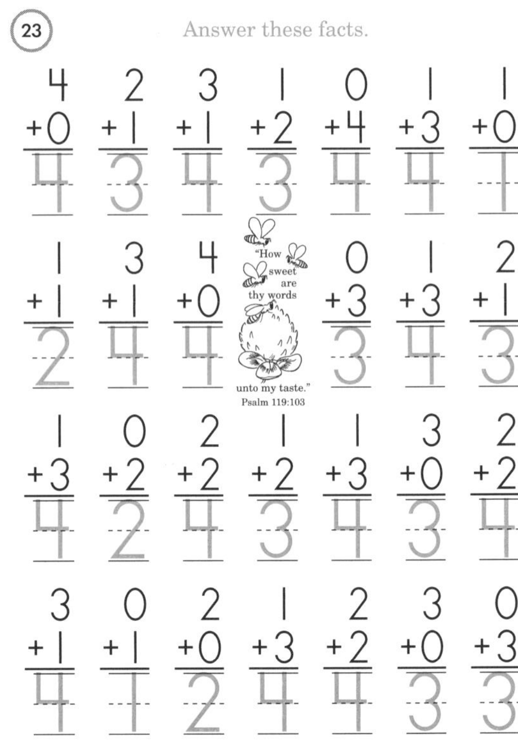
(23) Answer these facts.

4 +0 = 4	2 +1 = 3	3 +1 = 4	1 +2 = 3	0 +4 = 4	1 +3 = 4	1 +0 = 1
1 +1 = 2	3 +1 = 4	4 +0 = 4	"How sweet are thy words unto my taste." Psalm 119:103	0 +3 = 3	1 +3 = 4	2 +1 = 3
1 +3 = 4	0 +2 = 2	2 +2 = 4	1 +2 = 3	1 +3 = 4	3 +0 = 3	2 +2 = 4
3 +1 = 4	0 +1 = 1	2 +0 = 2	1 +3 = 4	2 +2 = 4	3 +0 = 3	0 +3 = 3

50

Preparation

Materials

Addition Families 1–4 flash cards
Number flash cards 1–11
Addition Families 1–4 flash cards

Chalkboard

(*Class Time* #1)

(*Class Time* #3)

___ 4 5 ___ 7
___ 6 6 ___ 8
___ 10 7 ___ 9
___ 8 4 ___ 6
___ 5 9 ___ 11

(*Class Time* #4)

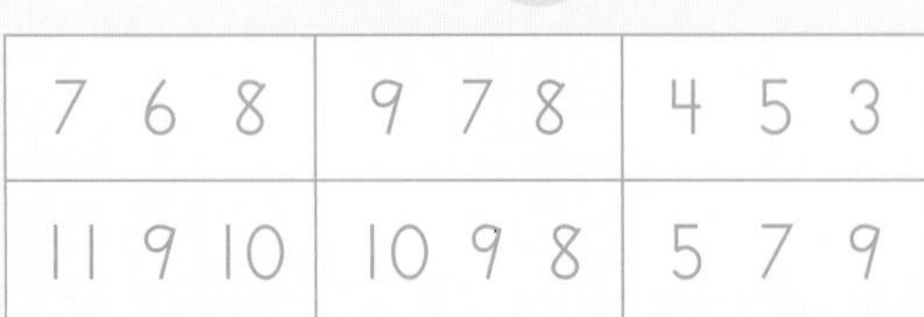

7 6 8	9 7 8	4 5 3
11 9 10	10 9 8	5 7 9

Class Time

1. *Review Addition Families 3 and 4.*
   a. Call the children to the flannel board. **I will move the blocks. Say Addition Family 3 . . . Family 4.**
   b. Give Addition Family 4 flash cards to the children. **When I call your fact, come and set it on the chalk tray in family order.**
   c. **Say Family 3 as I fill the houses.**
   d. **Say Family 4 as I fill the houses.**
2. *Forming numbers and counting.*
   Form 1–11 in the air; then point to the number line and continue counting to 100.
3. *Before and Between.*
   a. Give Number flash cards 1–10 to the children. Hold up card 11. **Who has the number that comes before 11? Who has the number that comes before 10?** Continue back to 1.
   b. Do the chalkboard samples for Before and Between Numbers.

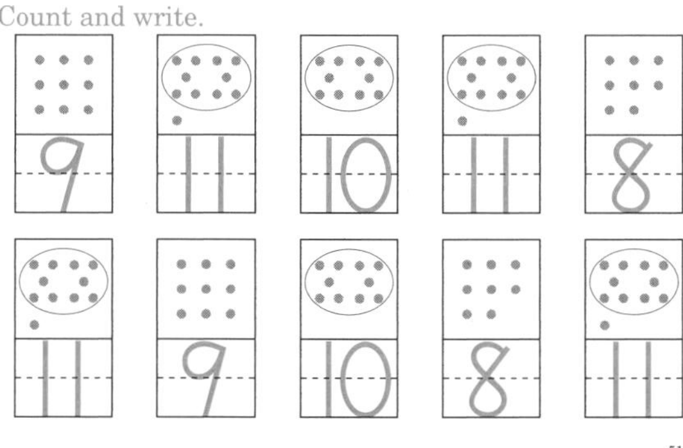

4. *Less.*
   Do the chalkboard samples.
5. *Assign Lesson 23.*

Note: Understanding a calendar page will be taught later in the term. The children should have a preliminary awareness that each day has a name and number. An excellent way to teach that awareness is to daily have the class repeat a statement such as, "Today is Monday, October 7." This tiny routine can be done at a regular time such as beginning of classes, lunchtime, recess dismissal, or pencil-sharpening time.

Follow-up

Drill

(*Drill* #3)

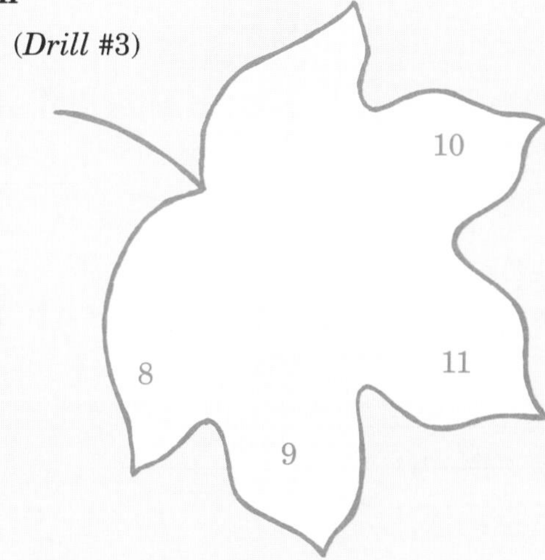

1. Drill addition flash cards with each child individually.
2. Form 11 in the air again and again. **11, 11, 11, . . . Would 11 steps take you outside? to the chalkboard? to the drinking fountain?** Have the children find out.
3. Draw an autumn leaf on the board. Call the children one by one to read the numbers. (Keep the leaf for Lessons 24 and 25.)

Practice Sheets

- ☐ Fact Houses #5
- ☐ Less Numbers #2
- ☐ Count and Write #17
- • Number Facts #4
- • Number Order #1

Objectives

New

TEACHING

The number 12

WORKBOOK

The number 12

Review

Addition facts
More (choice of 3)
Counting (100)
Numbers 10 and 11

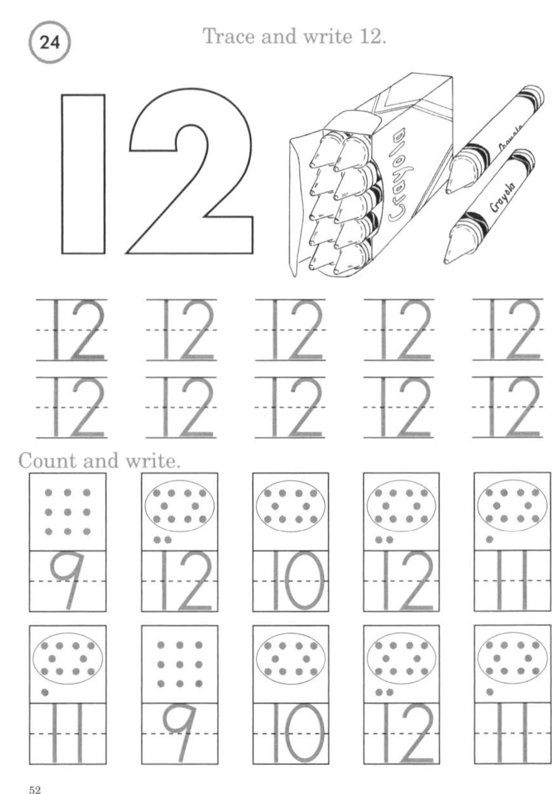

Preparation

Materials

More flash cards

Number Order flash cards 1–10

Addition Families 1–4 flash cards

Chalkboard

(*Class Time* #2)

5 4 6	7 8 6	9 8 10
9 8 7	3 5 4	7 5 6

(*Class Time* #6)

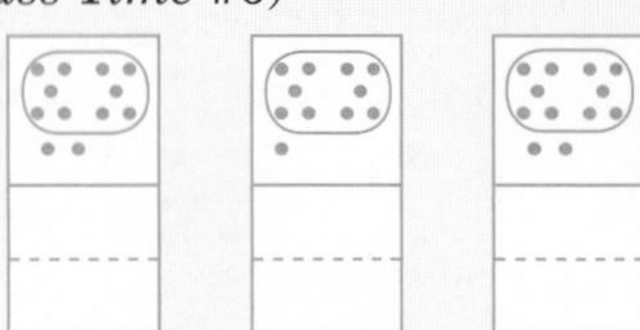

Class Time

1. *Review Addition Families 1–4.*
   a. Call the children to the flannel board. Ask a child to move the blocks as everyone says Addition Family 2 . . . Family 3 . . . Family 4.
   b. **Watch my fingers as we say Addition Family 1 . . . Family 2 . . . Family 3 . . . Family 4.**
2. *More.*
   a. Flash More cards.
   b. Do the chalkboard samples.
3. *Number Order.*
   Flash Number Order cards.
4. *Counting.*
   a. **Say the numbers in each number train.**
   b. **Count 1–100.**
5. *Introduce 12.*
   a. Put one bar of 10 on the flannel board. Add 2 blocks. Circle the bar of 10 with your finger. **10, 11, 12; 10, 11, 12 . . .**

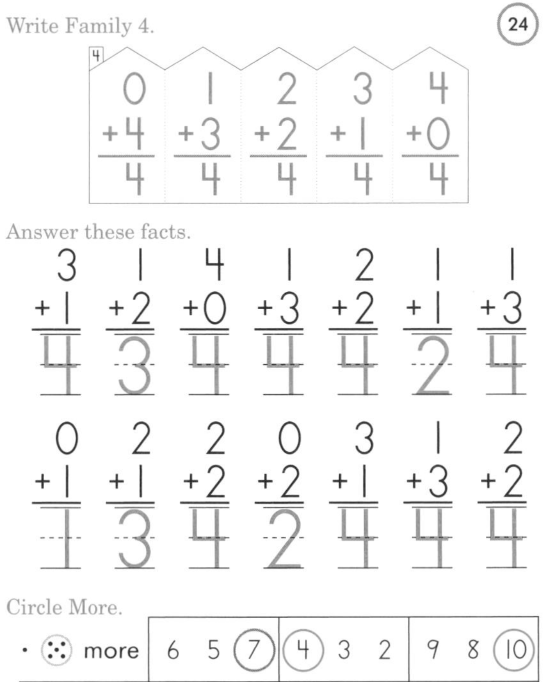

b. Draw a large 12 on the board. **One group of 10 and 2 more; 12, 12, 12.**

c. Form 12 in the air. **12, 12, . . .**

6. *Practice 10–12.*

   a. Return to the flannel board. Remove the 2 blocks. Replace them as you say, **10, 11, 12; 10, 11, 12 . . .**

   b. Write 10 11 12 on the board. Trace and say, **10, 11, 12; 10, 11, 12 . . .**

   c. **One day Jesus used a little boy's lunch to feed a great crowd of people. When everyone had enough to eat, the disciples gathered up the extra food. They gathered it into baskets, and they got 12 baskets full of bread and fish.**

   d. Do the chalkboard counting samples.

7. *Assign Lesson 24.*

Follow-up

Drill

1. Drill individuals with addition flash cards.
2. Chalkboard drill: **Write the number that comes after the number I say. What comes after 6? What comes after 9?** (Repeat the question with each number.) **5, 10, 8, 7, 4, 9, 3, 11, 8.**
3. Add 12 to the maple leaf on the board, and drill the numbers.

Practice Sheets

- ☐ Form A: 1–12
- ☐ Between Numbers #3
- ● Number Facts #5
- ● Count and Write #18
- ◊ Dot-to-Dot #10

Objectives

New

TEACHING

Addition Family 5

Review

Addition facts
Numbers 10–12
Before
Counting (100)

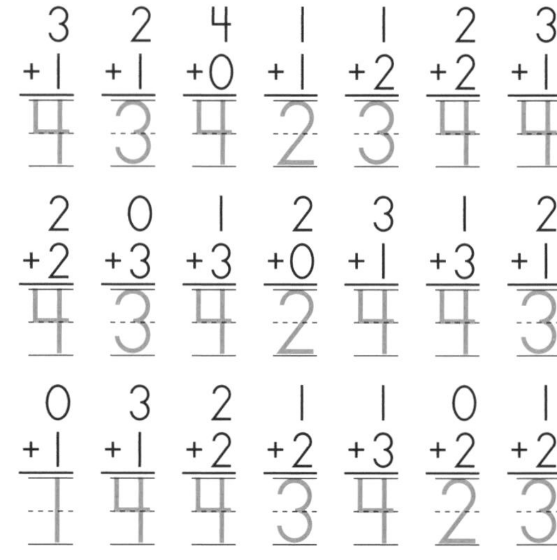

Preparation

Materials

Addition Families 1–4 flash cards

Before flash cards 2–10

Chalkboard

(*Class Time* #1)

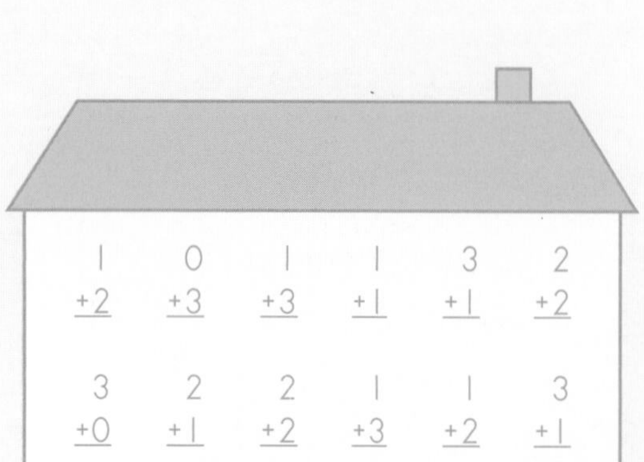

Class Time

1. *Drill addition facts.*
   a. Introduce Double Drill. Hold Addition Families 1–4 flash cards. Have the children stand before you in two straight rows. The child at the head of each row will try to answer your flash card first. Whoever answers first may go to the back of his row. If they both answer correctly at the same time, flash more cards until one of them may go to the back. Drill until each child has gone to the back five times.
   b. **Say Family 4 as I fill the houses.**
   c. Call the children to the large house. **Answer as quickly as you can!** (Keep the house for *Follow-up* drill.)
2. *Review 10–12.*
   a. Draw a large 11 and 12 on the board. **11, 12; 11, 12; 11, 12 . . .**
   b. Form 10, 11, 12 in the air.
3. *Before.*
   Flash Before cards.

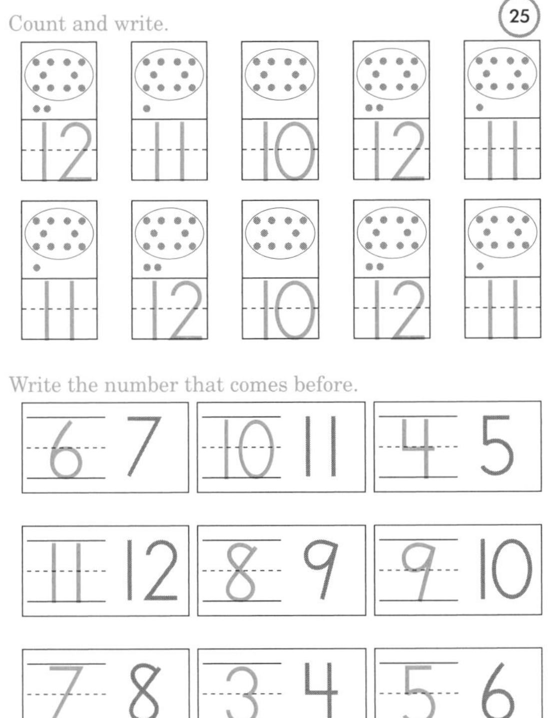

4. *Counting.*
   a. **Say the numbers in each number train.**
   b. **Count 1–100.**
5. *Assign Lesson 25.*

Follow-up

Drill

(*Drill #3*)

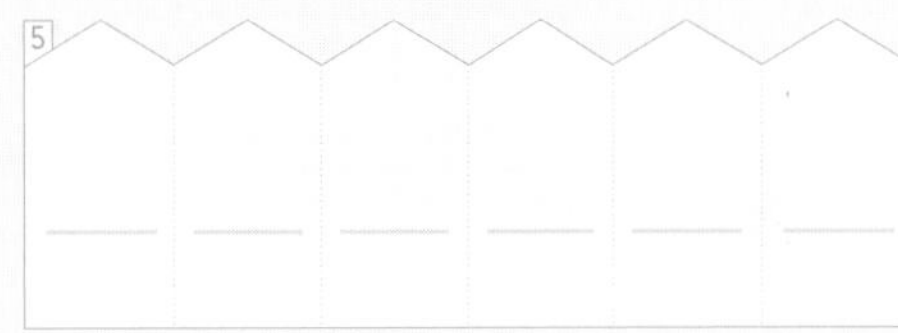

1. Drill each child at the large house on the board.
2. Call the children to the maple leaf. Give your pointing stick to one child. **Point to the number I say. 12, 10, 11, 12, 9, 10, 12, 11.** Hand the pointing stick to the next person.
3. Introduce Addition Family 5. **Can you help me fill these houses with plus problems that equal 5?** Be open to their help. Do not coax facts from them. When the houses are full, say, **We will look at Addition Family 5 tomorrow.**

Practice Sheets

- ☐ Number Order #2
- ☐ More Numbers #2
- ☐ Count and Write #18
- ● Number Facts #4
- ● After Numbers #7

Objectives

New

TEACHING

Addition Family 5
The number 13

WORKBOOK

The number 13

Review

Addition facts
Numbers 10–12

Preparation

Materials

5 erasers

Addition Families 1–4 flash cards

Before flash cards 2–10

Chalkboard

(*Class Time* #3)

Class Time

1. *Review Addition Families 1–4.*
   a. **Say Family 4 as I move the blocks.**
   b. **Watch my fingers as we say Addition Family 1 . . . Family 2 . . . Family 3 . . . Family 4.**
2. *Introduce Addition Family 5.*
   a. Call two children to the front of the class. Give the second one 5 erasers. **How many erasers does [first child] have? How many does [second child] have? How many erasers is that altogether?** Write the addition fact on the chalkboard as the children give response.
   b. Have the second child hand one of the erasers to the first child. Repeat the questions, and write the second fact in Family 5.
   c. Continue through the rest of the facts.
3. *Addition Family 5 on the flannel board.*
   a. Place 5 blocks in the lower part of the flannel board. **If Andy has 0 blocks on the table and 5 blocks on the**

Write Family 4.

26

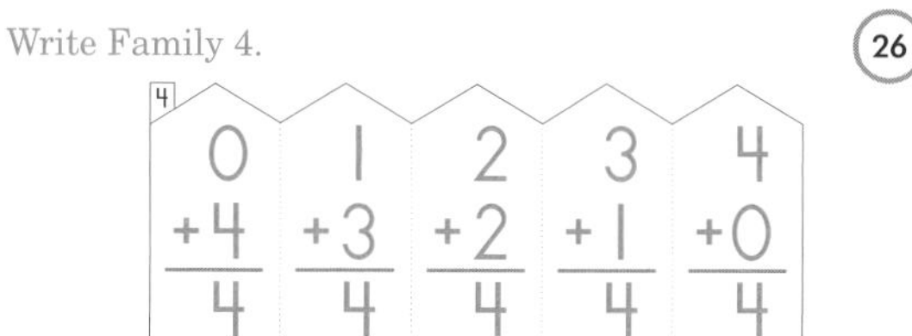

Answer these facts.

1 + 2 = 3	3 + 1 = 4	1 + 1 = 2	2 + 2 = 4	1 + 3 = 4	0 + 4 = 4	2 + 1 = 3
1 + 3 = 4	4 + 0 = 4	2 + 1 = 3	3 + 1 = 4	1 + 1 = 2	2 + 2 = 4	1 + 3 = 4
0 + 1 = 1	3 + 1 = 4	1 + 2 = 3	2 + 2 = 4	2 + 0 = 2	1 + 3 = 4	3 + 1 = 4

57

floor, he has 5 blocks. Zero blocks plus 5 blocks equals 5 blocks. 0 plus 5 equals 5. Write 0 + 5 = 5 in the first of the Fact Houses.

b. Move one block to the upper part of the flannel board. **When Andy has 1 block on the table and 4 blocks on the floor, he has 5 blocks. One block plus 4 blocks equals 5 blocks. 1 plus 4 . . .** Write 1 + 4 = 5.

c. Continue moving blocks and writing facts until you have all of Family 5.

4. *Recite Family 5.*
   Say the facts as I trace them. 0 + 5 = 5; 1 + 4 = 5; 2 + 3 = 5 . . .

5. *Introduce 13.*
   a. Place a bar of 10 and three blocks on the flannel board. Circle the bar with your finger. **This is 10.** Point to the blocks and count, **11, 12, 13; 10, 11, 12, 13 . . .**
   b. Draw a large 13 on the board. **One group of 10 and 3 more; 13, 13, 13.**
   c. Form 13 in the air. **13, 13, 13 . . .**

6. *Practice 10–13.*
   a. Return to the flannel board. Remove the three blocks, and replace them as you count, **10, 11, 12, 13; 10, 11, 12, 13 . . .**
   b. Write 11, 12, 13 on the board. Trace and say, **11, 12, 13 . . .**

7. *Assign Lesson 26.*

Follow-up

Drill

1. Form 1–13 in the air; then look up at the number line and **count to 100.**
2. Double Drill with Addition Families 1–4 flash cards. This drill should give the most practice to those who need it most. However, if a slow learner is still at the head after three or four tries, allow him to give the next answer.
3. Flash Before cards 2–10.

Practice Sheets

- ☐ Fact Houses #5
- ☐ Form A: 1–13
- ☐ Before Numbers #2
- ● Number Facts #5
- ● Count and Write #19

Objectives

New

TEACHING

Reciting facts without *equals*

WORKBOOK

Addition Family 5

Review

Addition facts
Before
Counting (100)
Numbers 8–13

27 Whisper, trace, and answer these facts.

0 +5 = 5	1 +4 = 5	2 +3 = 5
3 +2 = 5	4 +1 = 5	5 +0 = 5

5

0 +5 = 5	1 +4 = 5	2 +3 = 5	3 +2 = 5	4 +1 = 5	5 +0 = 5

58

Preparation

Make Addition Family 5 flash cards for each child.

Materials

Addition Families 1–4 flash cards
Number Pattern flash cards 5–10
Number flash cards 8–13
Addition Families 1–4 flash cards

Chalkboard

(*Class Time* #2)

___ 11	___ 7
___ 13	___ 12
___ 9	___ 10
___ 6	___ 8

(*Class Time* #3)

Class Time

1. *Review Addition Families 1–4.*
   a. Give the Addition Families 1–4 flash cards to the children. **When I call your fact, come and set it on the chalk tray in family order. 0 + 1 = 1 . . .**
   b. Point to the first card. **Let's say our families together.**
2. *Before.*
   Do the chalkboard samples.
3. *Practice Addition Family 5.*
   a. Call the children to the flannel board. **Say Family 5 as I move the blocks. 0 + 5 = 5 . . .**
   b. **Say Family 5 as I fill the houses.**
4. *Introduce more-brisk recitation.*
   Reciting facts is becoming habitual. Keep the recitation crisp and concise. Eliminate *equals* from your oral drill; 0 + 5 (pause) 5; 1 + 4 (pause) 5 . . .

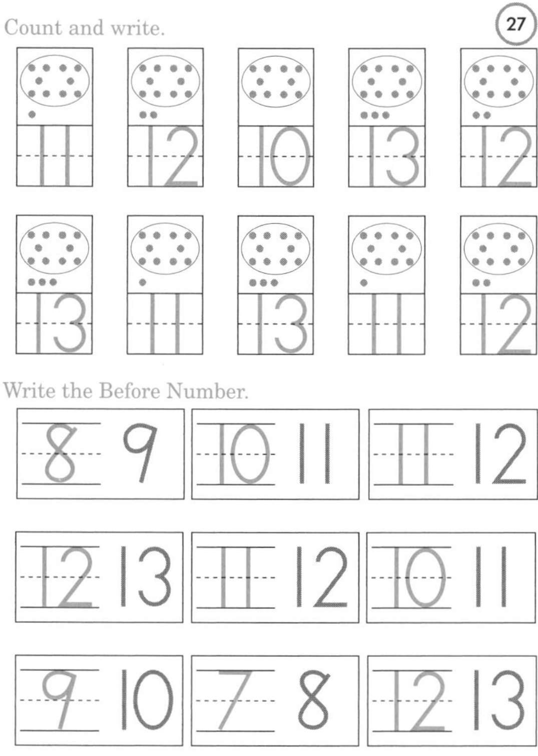

Point to the first house. **Listen. 0 + 5, 5; 0 + 5, 5. Say each fact two times. (Do not say *equals*.)**

0 + 5, 5; 0 + 5, 5

1 + 4, 5; 1 + 4, 5 . . .

5. *Counting.*
   a. Call the children to the number line. **I will say the engine number in each train; you say the other numbers.**
   b. **Count 1–100.**
6. *Number Patterns.*
   Flash Number Pattern cards.
7. *Review 12 and 13.*
   a. Draw a large 12 and 13 on the board. **12, 13; 12, 13 . . .**
   b. Flash Number cards.
8. *Assign Lesson 27.*

Follow-up

Drill

1. Double Drill: Addition Families 1–4 flash cards.
2. Chalkboard drill: **Write the number I say: 13, 11, 12, 11, 13, 10, 12, 13**
3. Give each child his Family 5 flash cards.

Practice Sheets

- □ Count and Write #19
- ● Number Facts #4
- ● Less Numbers #3
- ◊ Dot-to-Dot #11

Objectives

New

TEACHING

Drill fact twins
The number 14
Speed Drill

WORKBOOK

The number 14

Review

Addition Family 5
After

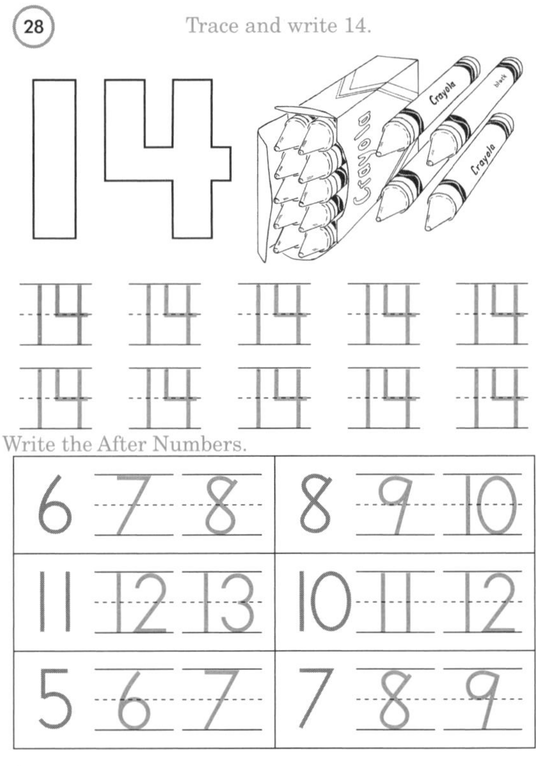
(28) Trace and write 14.

14

14 14 14 14 14
14 14 14 14 14

Write the After Numbers.

6 7 8	8 9 10
11 12 13	10 11 12
5 6 7	7 8 9

60

Preparation

Tack Addition Family 5 flash cards above the flannel board with answers showing. Use another set for daily drill with flash cards.

Materials

Number flash cards 8–14

Addition Families 1, 2, and 5 flash cards

Chalkboard

(*Class Time* #1)

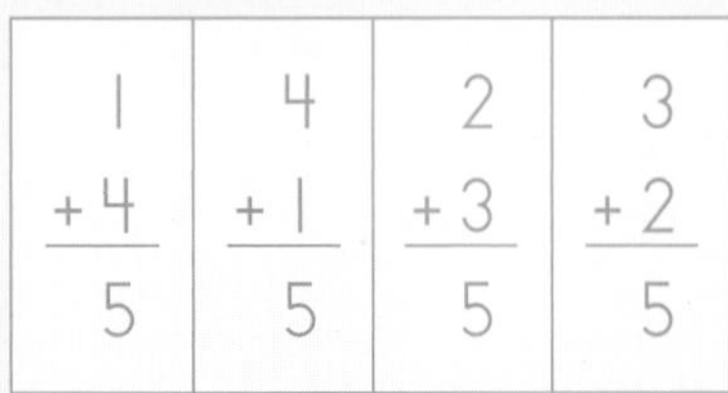

1	4	2	3
+4	+1	+3	+2
5	5	5	5

(*Class Time* #3)

5 ___ ___
9 ___ ___
8 ___ ___
6 ___ ___

Class Time

1. *Drill selected facts.*
   a. Call the children to the number facts on the board. Circle 1 + 4 = 5. **Say this three times with me. 1 + 4, 5; 1 + 4, 5 . . . Close your eyes. Say it three more times.**
   b. Circle 4 + 1 = 5. **Say it three times together. 4 + 1, 5; 4 + 1, 5 . . . Close your eyes. Say it three more times.**
   c. Circle and drill 2 + 3 = 5 and 3 + 2 = 5 in the same manner.
2. *Drill Addition Family 5.*
   Say Family 5 as I move the blocks.
3. *After.*
   Do the chalkboard samples.
4. *Introduce 14.*
   a. Place the ten-bar and 4 blocks on the flannel board. Circle the 10 with your finger. **This is 10.** Point to the blocks and continue counting. **11, 12, 13, 14; 10, 11, 12, 13, 14 . . .**

Write Family 5.

28

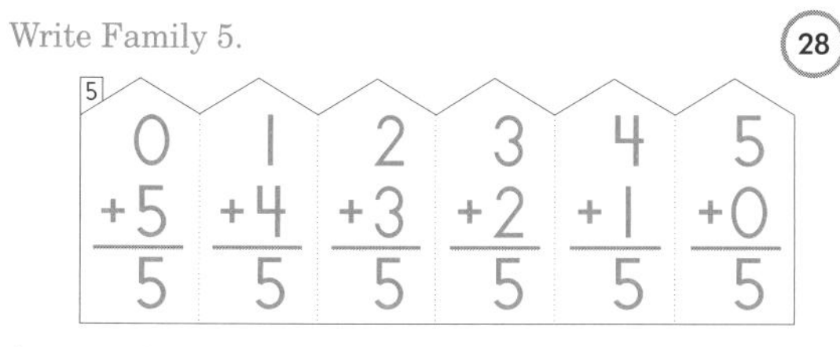

0	1	2	3	4	5
+5	+4	+3	+2	+1	+0
5	5	5	5	5	5

Answer these facts.

3	4	1	3	0	2	2
+2	+1	+1	+2	+1	+0	+3
5	5	2	5	1	2	5

1	0	1	3	1	5	1
+4	+2	+0	+2	+4	+0	+1
5	2	1	5	5	5	2

2	0	1	2	1	4	0
+3	+5	+4	+3	+1	+1	+1
5	5	5	5	2	5	1

61

Speed Drill Answers

4	3	4	2	4	1
3	4	3	4	2	4
1	3	4	3	4	2

Speed Drill #1

b. Draw a large 14 on the board. **One group of 10 and 4 more; 14, 14, 14 . . .**

c. Form 14 in the air. **14, 14, . . .**

d. Return to the flannel board. Remove the 4 blocks, and replace them as you count, **10, 11, 12, 13, 14, . . .**

5. *Do Speed Drill #1.*
Distribute the Speed Drill pages. **Write your name on the line, and then wait. When I say "go," you will turn your paper over and write the answers.** When everyone is finished writing his name, say, **Ready, set, go!** After one minute: **If you are not finished, circle the problem you are working on, and then finish.**

Have each child bring his drill to you immediately as he completes it. Check it, and tell him the number right. He will return to his seat and write that number in the pack on the camel's back.

If he had any fact wrong, he should practice writing it correctly in the boxes below his name.

6. *Assign Lesson 28.*

Follow-up

Drill

1. Flash Number cards 8–14.
2. **You say the engine number for each train. I will say the other numbers. Count 1–100.**
3. Flash Addition Families 1, 2, and 5 cards.

Practice Sheets

- ☐ Fact Houses #6
- ☐ Form A: 1–14
- ☐ Number Order #3
- ● Number Facts #5
- ● Count and Write #20
- ◊ Dot-to-Dot #12

Objectives

Review

Addition facts
Counting (100)
Less
Numbers 5–14

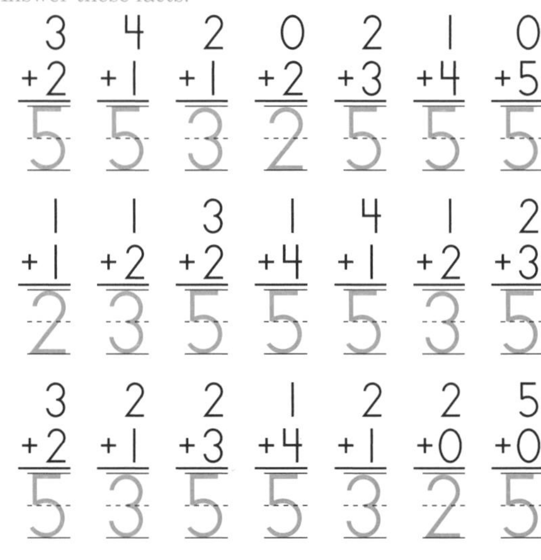

29

Write Family 5.

0	1	2	3	4	5
+5	+4	+3	+2	+1	+0
5	5	5	5	5	5

Answer these facts.

3	4	2	0	2	1	0
+2	+1	+1	+2	+3	+4	+5
5	5	3	2	5	5	5
1	1	3	1	4	1	2
+1	+2	+2	+4	+1	+2	+3
2	3	5	5	5	3	5
3	2	2	1	2	2	5
+2	+1	+3	+4	+1	+0	+0
5	3	5	5	3	2	5

62

Preparation

Materials

Addition Families 1–3 and 5 flash cards

Less flash cards 1–10

Number flash cards 5–14

Form B for each child

Chalkboard

(*Class Time* #1)

(*Class Time* #4)

Class Time

1. *Review Addition Family 5.*
   a. Ask a child to move the flannel blocks as everyone says Addition Family 5.
   b. Point to the flash cards above the flannel board. **We will say each fact three times with our eyes open, then three times with our eyes closed. 0 + 5, 5; 0 + 5, 5 . . .**
   c. **Say Family 5 as I fill the houses.**
2. *Drill addition facts.*
   Double Drill with Addition Families 1–3 and 5 flash cards.
3. *Counting.*
   Stand near the number line. **Say all the numbers in each train. Count 1–100.**
4. *Less.*
   a. Flash Less cards.
   b. Do the chalkboard samples.

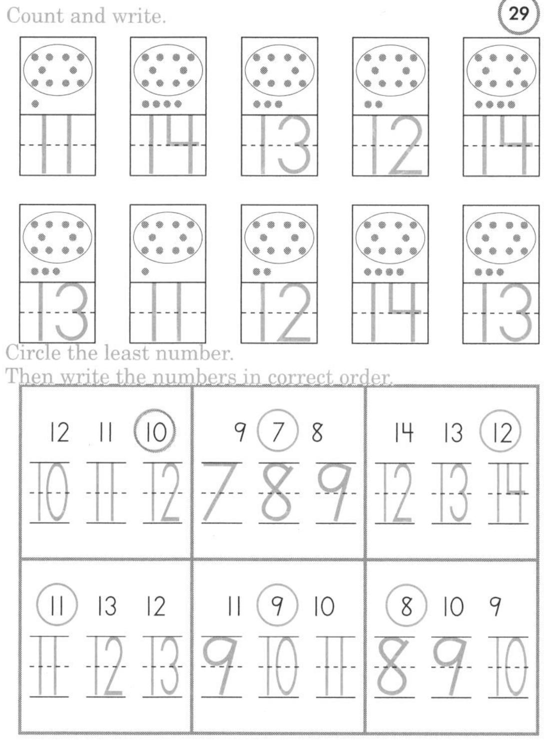
Count and write. 29

11 14 13 12 14

13 11 12 14 13

Circle the least number.
Then write the numbers in correct order.

12 11 (10)	9 (7) 8	14 13 (12)
10 11 12	7 8 9	12 13 14
(11) 13 12	11 (9) 10	(8) 10 9
11 12 13	9 10 11	8 9 10

63

5. *Review 5–14.*
   a. Place a ten-bar and 4 blocks on the flannel board. Have each child remove the 4 blocks and then replace them while counting, **10, 11, 12, 13, 14.**
   b. Pass out Number flash cards 5–14. Ask a child to slowly **count 5–14** for the children to come and stand in order.
6. *Assign Lesson 29.*

Follow-up

Drill

1. Use Form B. **Write the number I say.**

	14	**11**	**12**
	13	**14**	**10**
	12	**11**	**14**
	11	**13**	**12**
	10	**14**	**13**

2. Have two children at a time come to the board. Place them with wide space for each one. **Write 1–14.** Watch their number formation. If any digit is made incorrectly, have the child practice a whole row of that number.

Practice Sheets

- ● Form B (*Follow-up* drill #1)
- ☐ Fact Houses #6
- ☐ Between Numbers #4
- ● After Numbers #8

Objectives

Review

Addition facts
Drill fact twins
Numbers 11–14
Counting (100)
More

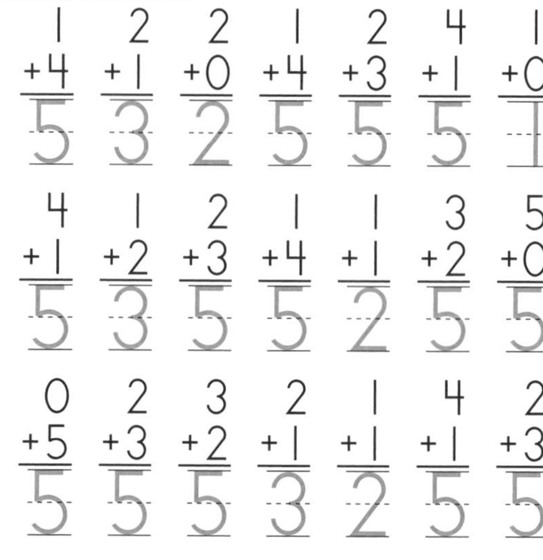
30 Write Family 5.

5

0	1	2	3	4	5
+5	+4	+3	+2	+1	+0
5	5	5	5	5	5

Answer these facts.

1	2	2	1	2	4	1
+4	+1	+0	+4	+3	+1	+0
5	3	2	5	5	5	1

4	1	2	1	1	3	5
+1	+2	+3	+4	+1	+2	+0
5	3	5	5	2	5	5

0	2	3	2	1	4	2
+5	+3	+2	+1	+1	+1	+3
5	5	5	3	2	5	5

64

Preparation

Materials

More flash cards 1–10

Number flash cards 5–14

Addition Families 1–3 and 5 flash cards

Chalkboard

(*Class Time* #2)

(Prepare one set like this for each child to trace in *Class Time* #3.)

2	3
+3	+2
5	5

(*Class Time* #4)

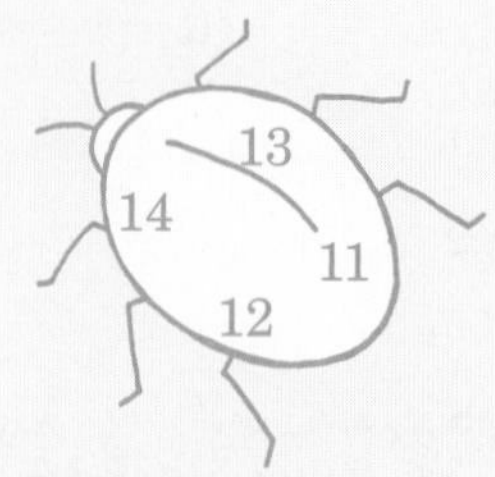

Class Time

1. *Review Addition Families 1–4.*
   Watch my fingers as we say Addition Family 1 . . . 2 . . . 3 . . . 4.
2. *Practice Addition Family 5.*
   a. **Say Family 5 as I move the blocks.**
   b. Ask a child to fill the 5 Houses as everyone says the facts.
3. *Drill selected facts.*
   Have each child stand near his set of facts on the board.
   a. **Trace and say "2 + 3 = 5" three times.**
   b. **Trace and say "3 + 2 = 5" three times.**
   c. **Whisper and trace your facts until I say "stop."**
4. *Review 11–14.*
   Stand near the ladybug. Give the pointing

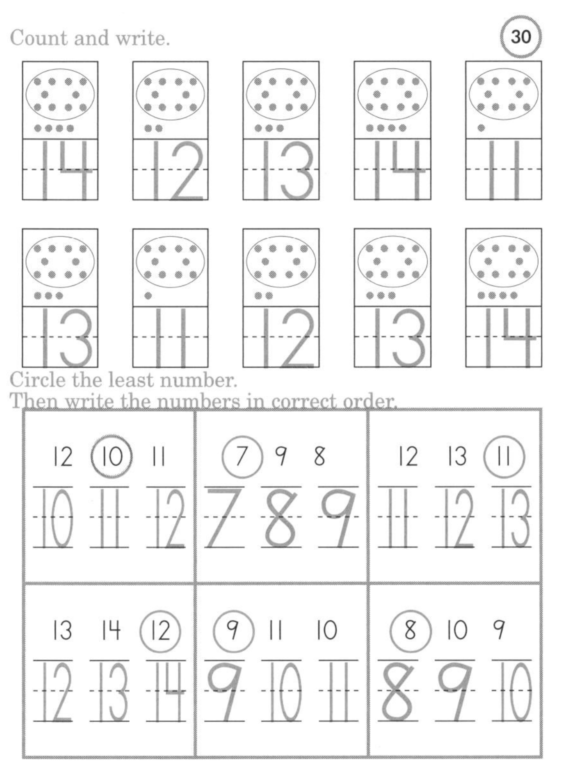

Speed Drill Answers

5 3 5 3 5 2
3 5 3 5 2 3
5 3 5 2 3 5

Speed Drill #2

stick to one child. **Point to the number I say. 13, 11, 14, 12.** Hand the stick to the next child. (Keep the ladybug on the board for Lessons 31 and 32.)

5. *Counting.*
   Count 1–100.
6. *More.*
   Flash More cards.
7. *Do Speed Drill #2.*
8. *Assign Lesson 30.*

Follow-up

Drill

1. Give the Number flash cards 5–14 to the children.
   a. **Come when I call your number. 10. Who has the number that comes after 10? Who has the number that comes before 10?**
   b. Have those children return to their seats. Ask the same questions using other numbers. **13, 6, 9, 11, 8, 12, 7.**
2. Drill flash cards for Addition Families 1–3 and 5.

Practice Sheets

- ☐ Fact Houses #6
- ☐ Count and Write #20
- ☐ More Numbers #3
- ● Before Numbers #3
- ● Form A: 1–14

Objectives

Review

Addition facts
Counting (100)
Number Order
More

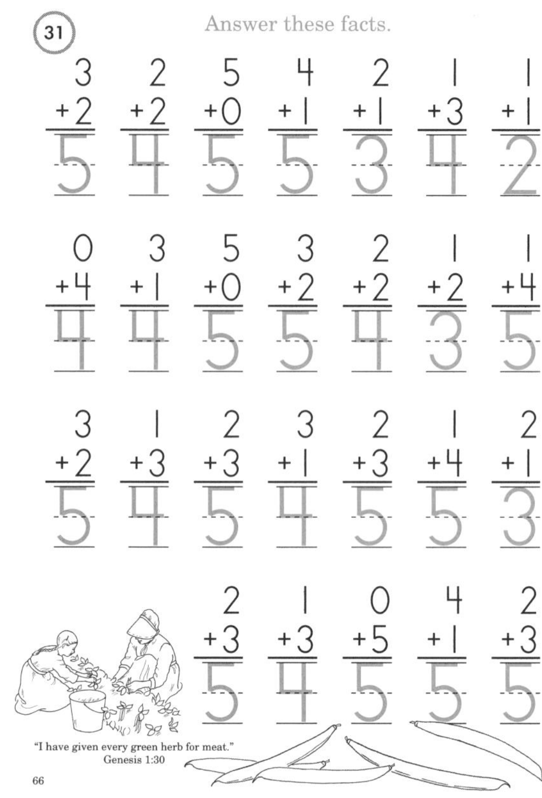

Preparation

Materials

Addition Families 1–5 flash cards

Number Order flash cards 1–14

More flash cards 1–10

Addition Families 1–5 flash cards

Chalkboard

(*Class Time* #2)

2	2	3
+2	+3	+2
4	5	5

(Ladybug from Lesson 30
for *Class Time* #4)

Class Time

1. *Review Addition Families 4 and 5.*
   Call the children to the flannel board. **I will move the blocks. Say Family 4 . . . Family 5.**
2. *Drill selected facts.*
   a. Stand near the box of facts on the board. Point to 2 + 2 = 4. **Say it three times. 2 + 2, 4 . . . Now close your eyes, and say it three more times. 2 + 2, 4 . . .**
   b. Drill the other facts in the same manner.
3. *Drill addition facts.*
   Double Drill with Addition Families 1–5.

Circle More. 31

· (dice 5) more	8 (12) 10	(14) 13 11
12 10 (13)	7 (9) 8	11 12 (13)
9 (11) 8	(8) 6 7	11 (12) 9
9 (11) 10	12 10 (14)	0 (10) 5

Circle the least number.
Then write the numbers in correct order.

7 (5) 6	11 (10) 12	10 9 (8)
5 6 7	10 11 12	8 9 10
13 (12) 14	8 9 (7)	11 12 (10)
12 13 14	7 8 9	10 11 12

67

4. *Review numbers and count.*
   a. Form 1–14 in the air, then look up at the number line and **count on to 100.**
   b. Drill the ladybug numbers.
5. *Number Order.*
   Flash Number Order cards 1–14.
6. *More.*
   Flash More cards 1–10.
7. *Assign Lesson 31.*

Follow-up

Drill

1. Drill individuals with Addition Families 1–5 flash cards. If any child has trouble answering a fact, write that fact on the board. Have him whisper and trace the fact again and again.
2. **How far will 14 steps take you?** Have each child count aloud as he steps.
3. Call the children one by one to the flannel board. **Move the blocks, and say Family 5 for me.**

Practice Sheets

- □ Fact Houses #7
- ● Number Facts #6
- ◊ Random Counting #7

Objectives

New

TEACHING

The number 15

WORKBOOK

The number 15

Review

Addition facts

Counting

More

Preparation

Materials

Addition Families 4 and 5 flash cards

Chalkboard

(*Class Time* #1)

(*Class Time* #4)

14	13	10	12
9	11	12	11
10	11	13	12

Class Time

1. *Review Addition Families 4 and 5.*
   a. **Say Family 4 as I fill in the houses.**
   b. **Say Family 5 as I fill in the houses.**
2. *Recite addition families.*
   Watch my fingers as we say Addition Family 1 . . . Family 2 . . . Family 3 . . . Family 4 . . . Family 5.
3. *Counting.*
   Stand near the number line.
   a. Review the number trains with their engines.
   b. **Joseph had some wicked brothers who were mean to him. They took away his coat and put him into a pit. When they saw some men and camels traveling to Egypt with things to sell, Joseph's brothers took him out of the pit and sold him to the men. Joseph had to go many, many miles with the men who bought him. It was more than 100 miles. Count 1–100.**

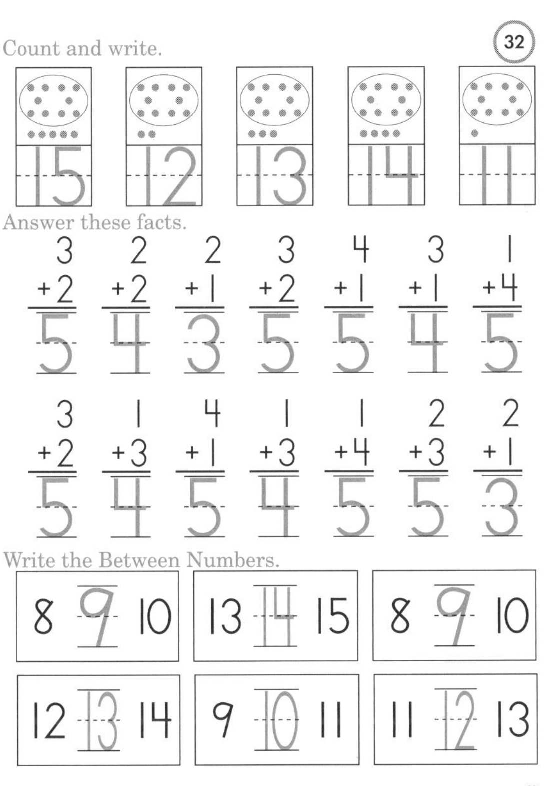
Count and write. (32)

15 12 13 14 11

Answer these facts.

3+2=5, 2+2=4, 2+1=3, 3+2=5, 4+1=5, 3+1=4, 1+4=5

3+2=5, 1+3=4, 4+1=5, 1+3=4, 1+4=5, 2+3=5, 2+1=3

Write the Between Numbers.

8 9 10 | 13 14 15 | 8 9 10

12 13 14 | 9 10 11 | 11 12 13

69

Speed Drill Answers

4	5	3	5	4	5
3	4	5	3	5	4
2	3	4	5	3	5

Speed Drill #3

4. *More.*
   Do the chalkboard samples.
5. *Introduce 15.*
   a. Place a ten-bar and 5 blocks on the flannel board. Circle the bar with your finger. **This is 10.** Point to the blocks. **11, 12, 13, 14, 15.**
   b. Draw a large 15 on the board. Trace it and say, **One group of 10 and 5 more; 15, 15, 15, . . .**
   c. Form 15 in the air. **15, 15, 15, . . .**
   d. Return to the flannel board. Remove the individual blocks, and replace them as you count, **10, 11, 12, . . .**
6. *Do Speed Drill #3.*
7. *Assign Lesson 32.*

Follow-up

Drill

1. Drill individuals with Addition Families 4 and 5 flash cards.
2. Add 15 to the ladybug. Drill the numbers.
3. Chalkboard drill: **Write the number that comes after the number I say. What comes after 13?** Continue with **11, 9, 14, 10, 8, 12, 6, 14, 7.**

Practice Sheets

- ☐ Form A: 1–15
- ☐ Number Order #4
- ● Number Facts #7
- ● Count and Write #21
- ◊ Dot-to-Dot #13

Objectives

New

TEACHING

The number 16

WORKBOOK

The number 16

Review

Addition facts
Numbers 7–15
More

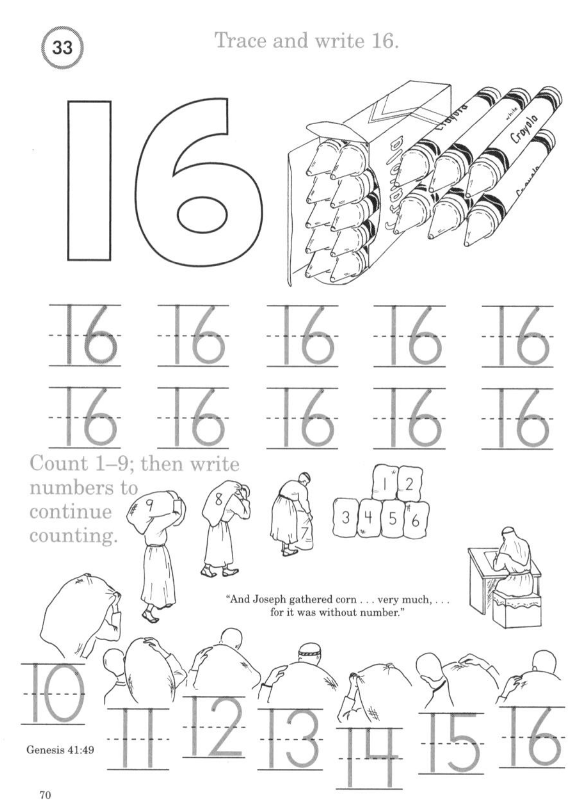

Preparation

Materials

Addition Families 4 and 5 flash cards
Number flash cards 7–15
A felt ten-bar and 6 blocks
Form B for each child

Chalkboard

(*Class Time* #2)

2 +1	2 +2	2 +3	3 +2	2 +2	2 +3
2 +2	3 +2	2 +2	2 +3	1 +2	3 +2

(*Class Time* #4)

14 12 13	11 10 12
12 13 11	11 15 10
13 12 11	15 13 14

Class Time

1. *Review Addition Families 4 and 5.*
   a. Give Families 4 and 5 flash cards to the children. **Who has the first fact in Family 4? Come set it on the chalk tray.** Continue with Families 4 and 5.
   b. Stand near the cards. **Let's say Families 4 and 5 together.**
2. *Drill addition facts.*
   a. Point to the box of facts on the board. **Say the answers together.**
   b. Have each child say one row.
   c. Zigzag from row to row.
3. *Numbers 7–15.*
   Drill Number flash cards 7–15.
4. *More.*
   a. **God was with Joseph when he went to Egypt as a slave. Joseph was faithful to God, and God blessed him. He became a ruler. He helped the people to store up food for a**

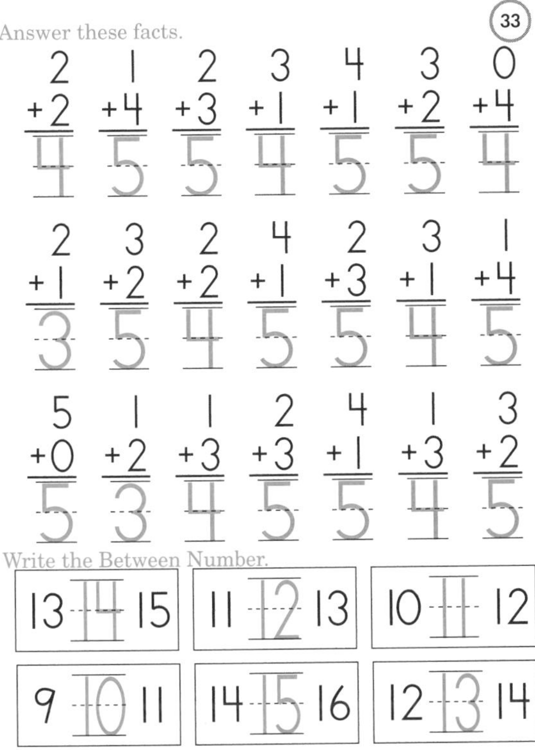
33

Answer these facts.

2	1	2	3	4	3	0
+2	+4	+3	+1	+1	+2	+4
4	5	5	4	5	5	4

2	3	2	4	2	3	1
+1	+2	+2	+1	+3	+1	+4
3	5	4	5	5	4	5

5	1	1	2	4	1	3
+0	+2	+3	+3	+1	+3	+2
5	3	4	5	5	4	5

Write the Between Number.

13 14 15	11 12 13	10 11 12
9 10 11	14 15 16	12 13 14

71

time when there would be a famine. They stored more and more food until there was so much they could not count it.

b. Do the chalkboard samples.

5. *Introduce 16.*
   a. Place 1 ten-bar and 6 blocks on the flannel board. Circle the 10 with your finger. **This is 10.** Point to the blocks and count, **11, 12, 13, 14, 15, 16.**
   b. Draw a large 16 on the board. **One group of 10 and 6 more; 16, 16, . . .**
   c. Form 16 in the air. **16, 16, . . .**
   d. Return to the flannel board. Remove the 6 blocks, and replace them. **10, 11, 12, 13, 14, 15, 16.**
6. *Assign Lesson 33.*

Follow-up

Drill

1. **Count 1–100. Say the engine number of each train louder and slower. Say the rest of the numbers in the train softer and faster.**
2. Use Form B. **Write the number that comes after the number I say. What comes after 10? What comes after 12?** Repeat the question for each number. (Answers in parentheses.)

10 (11)	**12** (13)	**9** (10)
14 (15)	**5** (6)	**7** (8)
13 (14)	**11** (12)	**9** (10)
14 (15)	**8** (9)	**13** (14)
12 (13)	**6** (7)	**10** (11)

Practice Sheets

- ● Form B (*Follow-up* drill #2)
- ☐ Form A: 1–16
- ☐ Fact Houses #7
- ● Before Numbers #4
- ● Count and Write #22
- ◊ Dot-to-Dot #14

Objectives

New

TEACHING

The number 17

WORKBOOK

The number 17

Review

Addition facts

Before

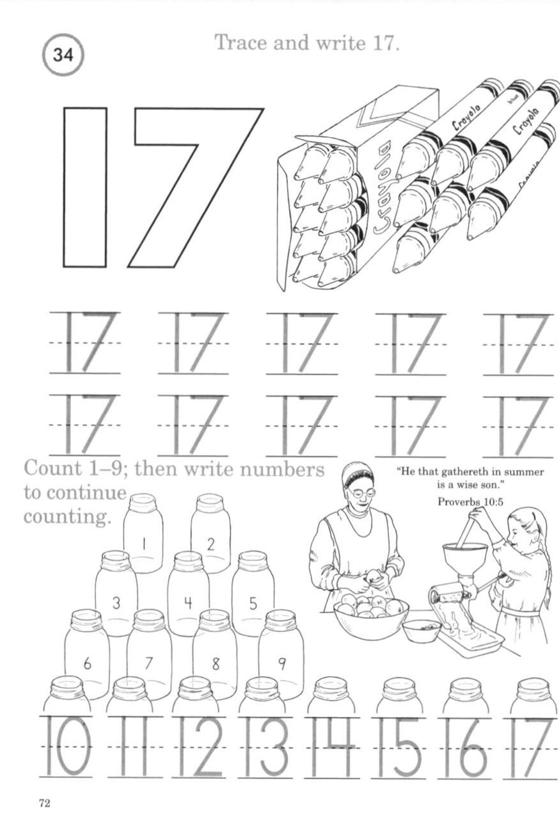

Preparation

Materials

Addition Families 1–5 flash cards

A felt ten-bar and 7 blocks

Addition Families 1–5 flash cards

Chalkboard

(*Class Time* #2)

2	2	3
+ 2	+ 3	+ 2
4	5	5

(*Class Time* #3)

___ 8	___ 13	___ 10
___ 16	___ 11	___ 14
___ 12	___ 5	___ 7
___ 9	___ 15	___ 6

Class Time

1. *Review Addition Families 3–5.*
   Call the children to the flannel board. **I will move the blocks. Say Family 3 . . . Family 4 . . . Family 5.**
2. *Drill selected facts.*
   a. Stand near the facts on the board. Circle 2 + 2 = 4. **We will say this five times. 2 + 2, 4 . . .** (Say it loudly the first time; then lower your voice with each recital.) Drill 2 + 3 and 3 + 2 in the same manner.
   b. Double Drill with Addition Families 1–5 flash cards.
3. *Before.*
   Do the chalkboard samples.
4. *Introduce 17.*
   a. Place a ten-bar and 7 blocks on the flannel board. Circle the 10 with your finger. **This is 10.** Point to the blocks. **11, 12, 13, 14, 15, 16, 17.**

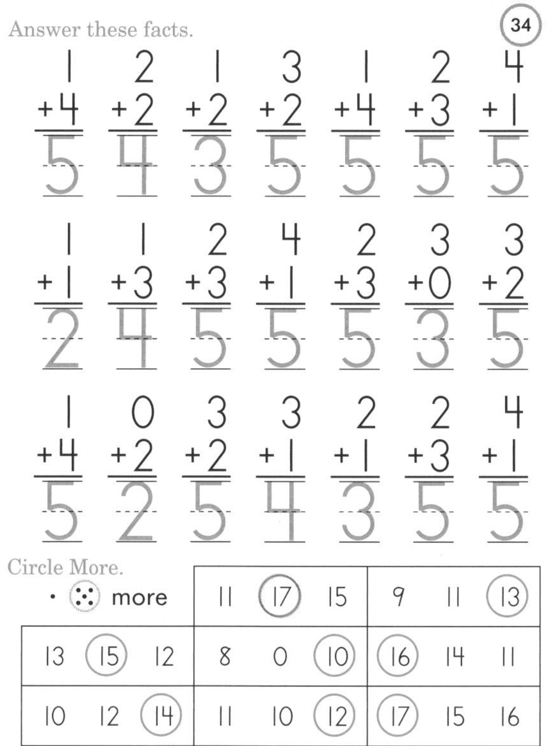

Speed Drill Answers

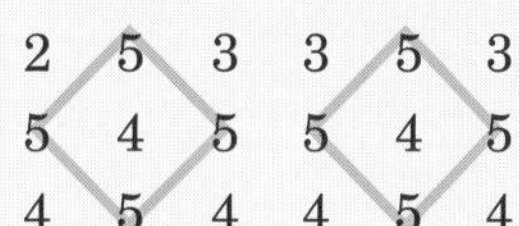

b. Draw a large 17 on the board. **One group of 10 and 7 more; 17, 17, . . .**

c. Form 17 in the air. **17, 17, . . .**

d. Remove the 7 individual blocks from the flannel board, and replace them. **10, 11, 12, 13, . . .**

5. *Do Speed Drill #4.*
6. *Assign Lesson 34.*
What is the girl helping her mother to do? They are preparing applesauce for the winter. "He that gathereth in summer is a wise son" (Proverbs 10:5).

Follow-up

Drill

(*Drill* #1)

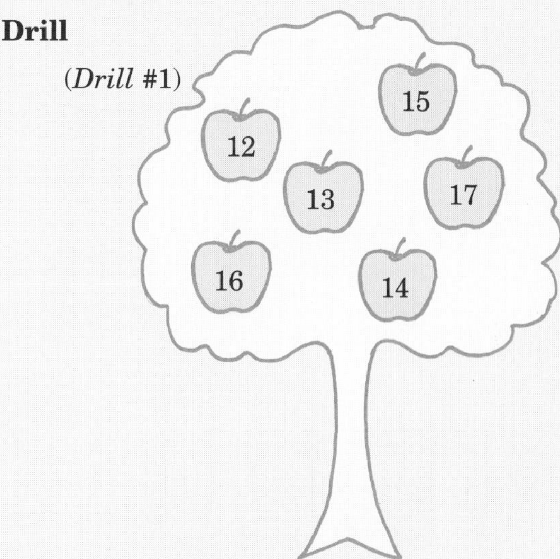

1. Draw the apple tree above on the board. Drill the numbers on the tree. (Keep the tree for Lessons 35 and 36.)
2. Drill each child with Addition Families 1–5 flash cards.
3. **Count 1–100.** Have individuals say the different number trains.

Practice Sheets

- ☐ Form A: 1–17
- ☐ Number Order #5
- ☐ After Numbers #9
- ● Number Facts #6
- ● Count and Write #23
- ◊ Dot-to-Dot #15

Objectives

New

TEACHING
- Written flash card drill
- The number 18
- *Addition Family 6*

WORKBOOK
- The number 18

Review
- Addition facts
- Less
- Counting (100)

Preparation

Materials

Addition Families 1–5 flash cards

Form C for each child

A flannel ten-bar and 8 blocks

Chalkboard

(*Class Time* #3)

16	15	13	11	10	12
14	16	17	12	14	17
15	11	13	17	15	16

Class Time

1. *Drill addition facts.*
   a. Double Drill with Addition Families 1–5 flash cards.
   b. Distribute Form C, and continue using the same flash cards. **Now you will write the answers instead of saying them. Start in the first box beside the apron picture. In Box 1, write the answer for this fact.** (Flash a card.) **Go across to Box 2, and write this answer.** (Flash a card.) **Box 3** (Flash a card.) Stop, and check if each child is writing only the answer. **Box 4—Box 5.**

   Boat Row: Box 1 . . .
   Colt Row, Dime Row, Eagle Row . . .
2. *Review addition families.*
   Ask a child to recite Family 3. Ask another child to recite Family 4; and another, Family 5.

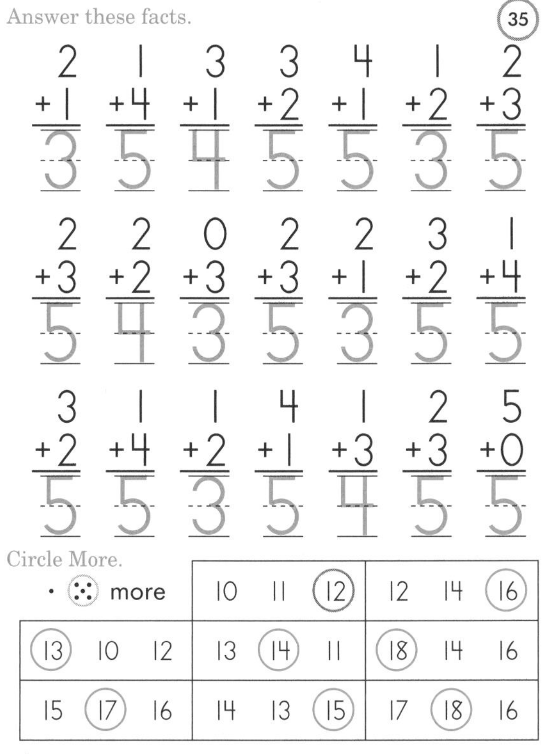
Answer these facts. (35)

2	1	3	3	4	1	2
+1	+4	+1	+2	+1	+2	+3
3	5	4	5	5	3	5

2	2	0	2	2	3	1
+3	+2	+3	+3	+1	+2	+4
5	4	3	5	3	5	5

3	1	1	4	1	2	5
+2	+4	+2	+1	+3	+3	+0
5	5	3	5	4	5	5

Circle More.

• ⁙ more	10 11 (12)	12 14 (16)
(13) 10 12	13 (14) 11	(18) 14 16
15 (17) 16	14 13 (15)	17 (18) 16

75

3. *Less.*
   Do the chalkboard samples.
4. *Introduce 18.*
   a. Place a ten-bar on the flannel board and 8 blocks. Circle the 10 with your finger. **This is 10.** Point to the blocks. **11, 12, 13, 14, 15, 16, 17, 18.**
   b. Draw a large 18 on the board. **One group of 10 and 8 more; 18, 18, . . .**
   c. Form 18 in the air. **18, 18, . . .**
   d. Remove the individual flannel blocks, and replace them. **10, 11, 12, 13, . . .**
5. *Counting.*
   Review the number trains. **Count 1–100.**
6. *Assign Lesson 35.*

Follow-up

Drill

(*Drill* #2)

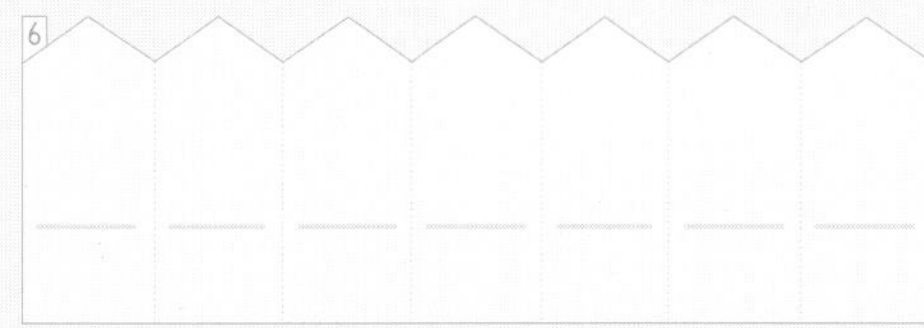

1. Add apple 18 to the apple tree from Lesson 34. Give the pointing stick to a child. **Point to the number I say. 15, 17, 12, 16, 14, 18, 13.**
2. Introduce Addition Family 6. **Let's fill the houses with plus problems that equal 6.** Welcome their suggestions. Find the twins. **We will look at Family 6 again tomorrow.**

Practice Sheets

- ● Form C (*Class Time* #1)
- ☐ Form A: 1–18
- ☐ Between Numbers #5
- ● Fact Houses #7
- ● Number Facts #7
- ◊ Dot-to-Dot #16

Objectives

New

TEACHING

Addition Family 6
The number 19

WORKBOOK

The number 19

Review

Addition facts
Counting (100)

Simon Peter saith unto them, I go a fishing. . . . That night they caught nothing. But when the morning was now come, Jesus stood on the shore. . . . Then Jesus saith unto them, . . . Cast the net on the right side of the ship, and ye shall find. They cast therefore, and now they were not able to draw it for the multitude of fishes. . . . Simon Peter went up, and drew the net to land full of great fishes, an hundred and fifty and three: and for all there were so many, yet was not the net broken (John 21:3–11).

Preparation

Materials

Six pencils

A flannel ten-bar and 9 blocks

Number flash cards 8–18

Chalkboard

(*Class Time* #3)

Class Time

1. *Review Addition Families 1–5.*
   Watch my fingers as we say Addition Family 1 . . . Family 2 . . . Family 3 . . . Family 4 . . . Family 5.
2. *Introduce Addition Family 6.*
   a. Call two children to the front of the class. Give the second one 6 pencils. **How many pencils does [first child] have?** Write 0 on the board. **How many pencils does [second child] have?** Write 6 below the 0. Put a plus sign before the 6. **How many pencils do they have together?**
   b. Have the second child hand 1 pencil to the first child. Repeat the questions as you write the second fact.
   c. Continue until you have worked through all the facts in Family 6.
3. *Addition Family 6 on the flannel board.*
   a. Begin with 0 blocks above the divider and 6 blocks below. **If Susan has 0 pennies in her hand and 6 pennies in her purse, she has 6 pennies**

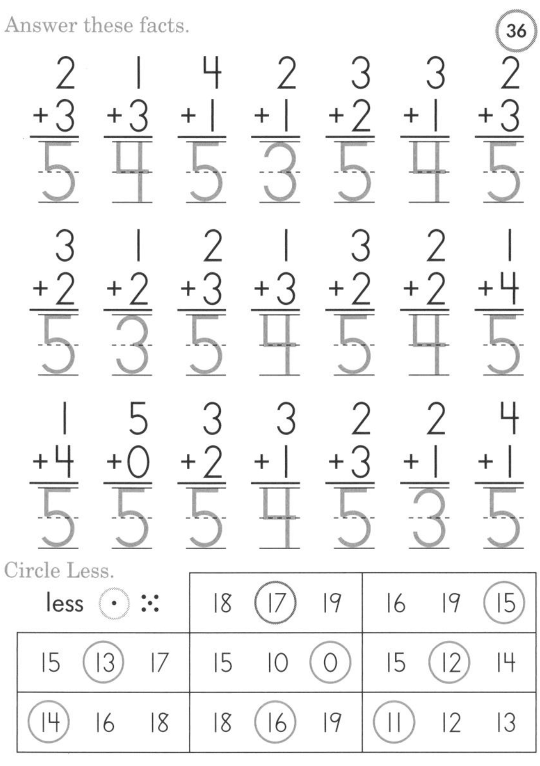

Speed Drill Answers

4	5	5	4	5	4
5	5	4	5	4	5
5	4	5	4	5	4

in all. **Zero pennies + 6 pennies = 6 pennies. 0 + 6 = 6.** Ask a child to write the fact in the first house on the board.

b. Move 1 of the 6 blocks above the divider. **When Susan has 1 penny in her hand and 5 pennies in her purse, she has 6 pennies in all. One penny + 5 pennies = 6 pennies. 1 + 5 = 6.** Ask a child to write the fact in the second house.

c. Continue to move the blocks until the houses are full.

d. Point to 0 + 6 = 6 in the first house. **Say Family 6 together.**

4. *Introduce 19.*

   a. Place 1 ten-bar and 9 blocks on the flannel board. Circle the 10 with your finger. **This is 10.** Point to the individual blocks. **11, 12, 13, 14, 15, 16, 17, 18, 19.**

   b. Draw a large 19 on the board. **One group of 10 and 9 more; 19, 19, . . .**

5. *Counting.*

   a. Write 1–19 on the board while the children **count 1–19.**

   b. **One morning Jesus helped His disciples to catch many great fish in their net. They counted them, and there were more than 100 fish. Count 1–100.**

6. *Do Speed Drill #5.*
7. *Assign Lesson 36.*

Follow-up

Drill

1. Add apple 19 to the apple tree. Drill the numbers.
2. Flash Number flash cards 8–18.
3. Chalkboard drill: **Write the number that comes before. What comes before 12?** Repeat the question for each number. **16, 10, 17, 13, 19, 11, 18, 15, 9, 14.**

Practice Sheets

- □ Fact Houses #7
- □ Before Numbers #5
- ● Number Facts #6
- ● Form A: 1–19
- ◊ Dot-to-Dot #17

Objectives

New

TEACHING

Missing Numbers
Writing teens
Penny

WORKBOOK

Addition Family 6

Review

Addition facts
Number Order

Preparation

Make Addition Family 6 flash cards for each child.

Materials

Number Order flash cards 1–15

Addition Families 1–4 and 6 flash cards

One penny for each child

Chalkboard

(*Class Time* #2)

6

(*Class Time* #3)

1 ___ ___ 4 ___ ___ ___ 8 ___ ___

11 ___ ___ ___ 15 ___ ___ ___ 19

Class Time

1. *Review Addition Families 4 and 5.*
   Watch my fingers as we say Addition Family 4 . . . Family 5.
2. *Practice Addition Family 6.*
   a. Place 0 blocks in the upper part of the flannel board and 6 blocks in the lower. **If Alice has 0 yellow leaves and 6 red leaves, she has 6 leaves in all. Zero leaves + 6 leaves = 6 leaves. 0 + 6 = 6.** Write the fact in the first house.
   b. **If Alice has 1 yellow leaf and 5 red leaves, she has 6 leaves in all. One leaf + 5 leaves = 6 leaves. 1 + 5 = 6.** Continue to move a block from the lower to the upper part and to write the facts until the houses are full.
   c. Point to the houses. **Say each fact three times. 0 + 6 = 6 . . .**
3. *Missing Numbers.*
   Do the chalkboard samples.

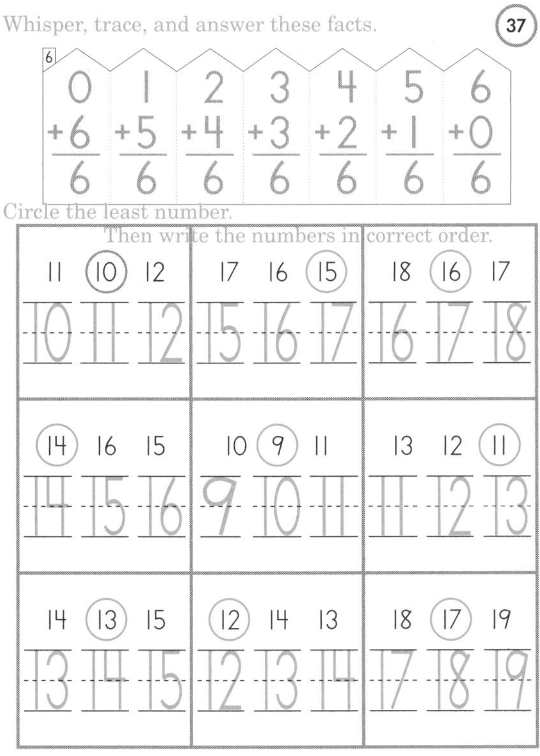

4. *The teens.*
   a. **Slowly count 10–19 while I write.** 10 11 12 13 14 15 16 17 18 19. **What do you see that looks alike in all these numbers?**
   b. **The numbers in the teens all have a 1. That digit means 1 group of 10.** Trace the 1's with colored chalk.
5. *Number Order.*
   Flash Number Order cards.
6. *Assign Lesson 37.*

Follow-up

Drill

1. Drill individuals with Addition Families 1–4 and 6 flash cards. (Avoiding Family 5 helps to concentrate on the new Family 6.)
2. Give each child his Family 6 flash cards.
3. Call the children to the teaching corner. Give each child one penny. **This is a penny. Find a man. The man's name is Abraham Lincoln. Feel the edge of the penny. The edge of a penny is smooth.**

Practice Sheets

- ☐ Writing Practice #12
- ● Fact Houses #8
- ● Number Facts #7
- ◊ Dot-to-Dot #18

Objectives

New

TEACHING

Value of penny

Review

Addition facts

The teens

Counting (100)

Before

(38) Write Family 6.

6

0	1	2	3	4	5	6
+6	+5	+4	+3	+2	+1	+0
6	6	6	6	6	6	6

Answer these facts.

1	2	4	0	1	4	3
+5	+1	+2	+6	+1	+2	+3
6	3	6	6	2	6	6

3	1	2	2	2	5	1
+3	+2	+4	+0	+4	+1	+5
6	3	6	2	6	6	6

2	5	3	2	6	4	1
+4	+1	+3	+1	+0	+2	+1
6	6	6	3	6	6	2

80

Preparation

Tack Addition Family 6 flash cards above the flannel board, answers showing.

Materials

Colored chalk

Number flash cards 11–19

Chalkboard

(*Class Time* #1)

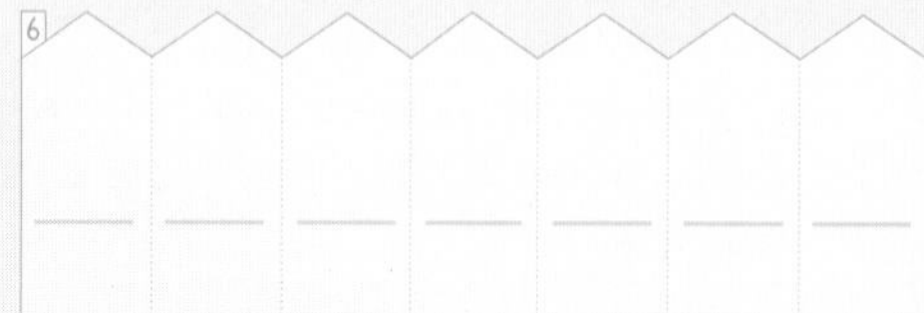

(*Class Time* #4)

___ 12	___ 18
___ 15	___ 9
___ 13	___ 16
___ 19	___ 11
___ 14	___ 17

Class Time

1. *Review Addition Family 6.*
   a. Call the children to the flannel board. **Say Family 6 as I move the blocks.**
   b. Ask a child to fill the houses as everyone says Family 6.
   c. Give the pointing stick to a child. **As [Jason] points to the houses, we will say each fact three times with our eyes open, and then three times with our eyes closed.**
2. *Review the teens.*
   Write 0 1 2 3 4 5 6 7 8 9 with colored chalk. **What shall I do with this group of numbers to make them be the teens?** Put a 1 in front of each number.

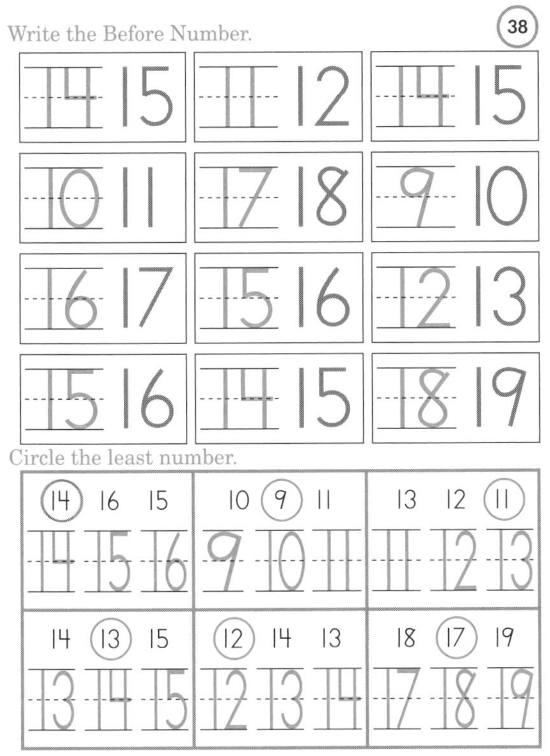
Write the Before Number. (38)

14 15	11 12	14 15
10 11	17 18	9 10
16 17	15 16	12 13
15 16	14 15	18 19

Circle the least number.

(14) 16 15	10 (9) 11	13 12 (11)
14 15 16	9 10 11	11 12 13
14 (13) 15	(12) 14 13	18 (17) 19
13 14 15	12 13 14	17 18 19

Then write the numbers in correct order. 81

Speed Drill Answers

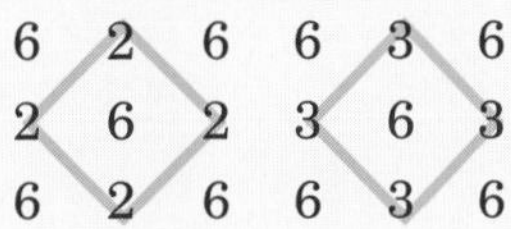

3. *Counting.*
   Count 1–100.
4. *Before.*
   Do the chalkboard samples.
5. *Do Speed Drill #6.*
6. *Assign Lesson 38.*

Follow-up

Drill

1. Flash Number cards 11–19.
2. Place a ten-bar and 9 blocks on the flannel board. Have each child circle the 10 with his finger and count: **10, 11, 12, 13, 14, 15, 16, 17, 18, 19.**
3. Call the children to the teaching corner. Give each one a penny. **Find Abraham Lincoln. Find a building. How does the edge of a penny feel?**
   a. **A penny is worth 1¢. Penny, 1¢; penny, 1¢; . . .**
   b. Write 1¢ on the board. **1¢, 1¢, . . .**
   c. Circle 1¢. **Penny, 1¢; penny, 1¢; . . .**

Practice Sheets

- ☐ Fact Houses #8
- ☐ Form A: 1–19
- ● Number Facts #8
- ◊ Dot-to-Dot #19

Objectives

New

TEACHING

- Counting pennies
- *Meaning of 20*

WORKBOOK

- Counting pennies

Review

- Addition facts
- The teens
- More

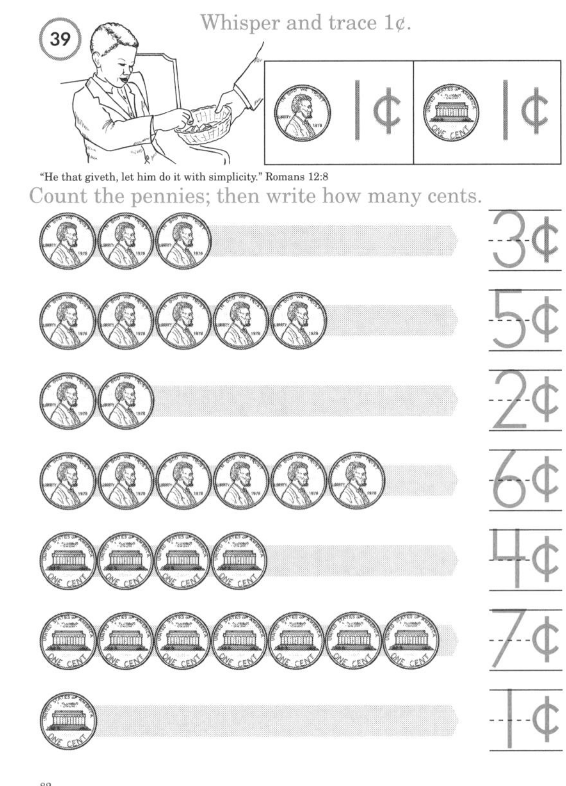

Preparation

Materials

Addition Families 1–4 and 6 flash cards

Large penny

A handful of real pennies

Addition Families 1–4 and 6 flash cards

2 felt ten-bars

Chalkboard

(*Class Time* #1)

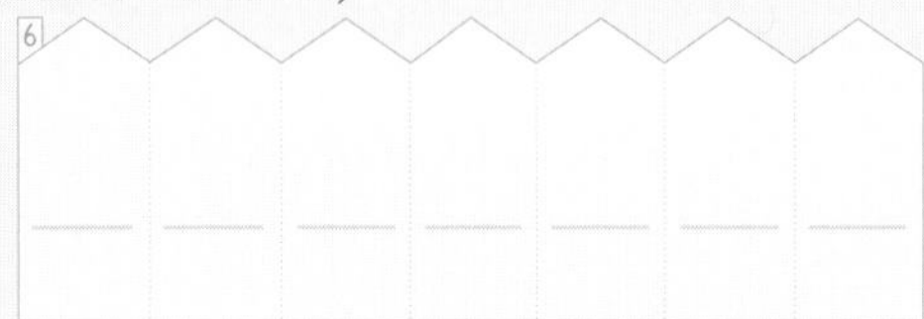

(*Class Time* #5)

(*Class Time* #6)

12 16 14	18 17 19
15 17 16	18 17 16
13 11 12	18 15 16

Class Time

1. *Review Addition Family 6.*
   a. Call the children to the flannel board. **Say Family 6 as I move the blocks.**
   b. Ask a child to fill the houses as everyone says Family 6.
2. *Flash card drill.*
   Double Drill with Addition 1–4 and 6 flash cards.
3. *Review teens.*
   With colored chalk write 1 1 1 1 1 1 1 1 1 1 (ten 1's). **What shall we do to make these numbers into the teens?** Have the children use white chalk to add 0, 1, 2, 3, 4, . . .
4. *Practice with penny.*
   a. Hold the large penny. **Can we give a penny to God?** (Accept answers.) **Yes, when we drop a penny into the offering basket at church, we are giving a penny to God.**
   b. **How much is a penny worth?**
   c. **Whose picture is on the penny?** (Abraham Lincoln)

Write Family 6.

39

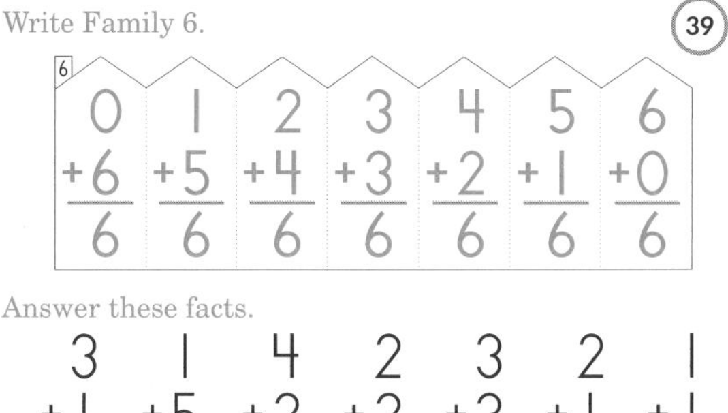

Answer these facts.

3 +1 4	1 +5 6	4 +2 6	2 +2 4	3 +3 6	2 +1 3	1 +1 2
1 +5 6	2 +4 6	2 +2 4	1 +3 4	5 +1 6	1 +2 3	4 +2 6
5 +1 6	4 +2 6	1 +3 4	3 +3 6	6 +0 6	3 +1 4	2 +4 6

83

5. *Counting pennies.*
   a. Point to the circles on the board. Trace 1¢ inside each circle as the children say, **Penny, 1¢; penny, 1¢; . . .**
   b. **Let's count the pennies in the first row. 1¢, 2¢, 3¢, 4¢.** Write 4¢ on the blank at the end of the row. Do the second row in the same way.
   c. Place a number of pennies on the table, and have individuals count them, sliding each one out and putting it in a row as it is counted.
6. *More.*
   Do the chalkboard samples.
7. *Assign Lesson 39.*

Follow-up

Drill

1. Drill individuals with Addition Families 1–4 and 6 flash cards.
2. Place a ten-bar on the flannel board.
   a. Add 1 block and say, **One 10 and 1 more.** Call on a child to write that number on the board, and have the class say the number.
   b. Add the second block and say, **One 10 and 2 more.** Have a child write that number and the class say it. Continue to 19.
   c. Add the tenth block. **What do we have when there is 1 ten and 10 more? This will be another group of 10.**
   d. Replace the 10 individual blocks with a second ten-bar. **Now we have 2 tens.** Write 20 on the chalkboard. **2 tens and nothing more; 20, 20, 20 . . .**

Practice Sheets

- ☐ Fact Houses #8
- ☐ Missing Numbers #1
- ● Number Facts #8

Objectives

New

TEACHING

Writing 20's

Review

Addition facts

Counting (100)

Penny

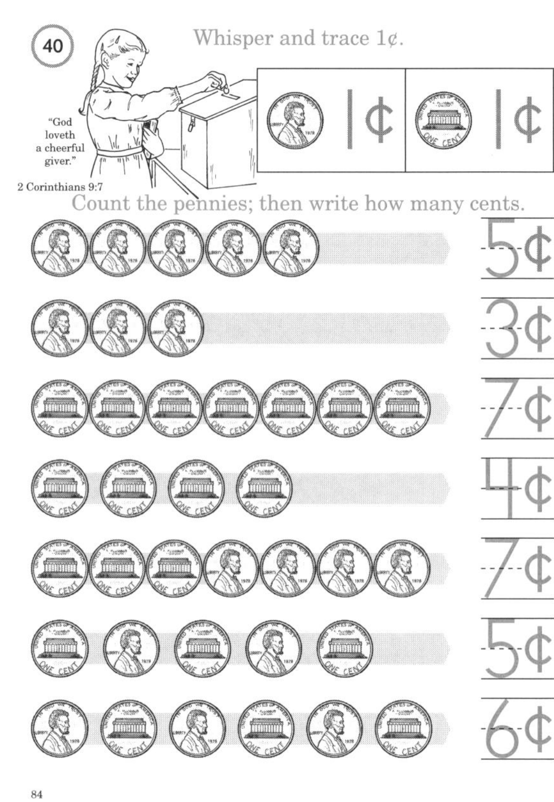

40

Whisper and trace 1¢.

"God loveth a cheerful giver."
2 Corinthians 9:7

|¢ |¢

Count the pennies; then write how many cents.

5¢

3¢

7¢

4¢

7¢

5¢

6¢

84

Preparation

Materials

Large penny

Addition Families 1–6 flash cards

Form B for each child

Chalkboard

(*Class Time* #1)

2	3	2	4
+ 3	+ 2	+ 4	+ 2
5	5	6	6

(*Class Time* #5)

Class Time

1. *Drill selected facts.*
Call the children to the facts on the board. Circle 2 + 3 = 5. **We will say it five times.** Say it loudly the first time; then lower your voice with each recital. Drill each fact in this way.

2. *Review Addition Family 6.*
Ask a child to move the blocks on the flannel board as everyone says Addition Family 6.

3. *Writing 20's.*
Write 0 1 2 3 4 5 6 7 8 9 with colored chalk. **What shall I do to show that these numbers are in the twenties?** Put a 2 in front of each number, with white chalk.

4. *Counting.*
Count 1–100. When we come to the twenties we will form the numbers in the air as we count.

Write Family 6.

40

0	1	2	3	4	5	6
+6	+5	+4	+3	+2	+1	+0
6	6	6	6	6	6	6

Answer these facts.

3	1	4	2	3	1	2
+2	+5	+2	+2	+3	+4	+1
5	6	6	4	6	5	3

2	2	4	1	5	3	4
+3	+4	+1	+3	+1	+2	+2
5	6	5	4	6	5	6

1	4	2	3	6	3	2
+2	+1	+3	+3	+0	+1	+4
3	5	5	6	6	4	6

85

5. *Review penny.*
   a. Hold the large penny. **How much is a penny worth? Penny, 1¢; penny, 1¢; . . .**
   b. **What can we do with a penny?** We can put a penny in the offering. **How does God get the pennies we drop into the offering box? Brother [deacon] uses some offering money to buy Gospel papers. We give the papers to other people. They read the papers and think about God. God is pleased when we give our pennies to Him.**
   c. Have each child write 1¢ in a circle on the board and say, **Penny, 1¢.**
   d. Count the money samples together. **1¢, 2¢, 3¢, . . .**
6. *Do Speed Drill #7.*
7. *Assign Lesson 40.*

Speed Drill Answers

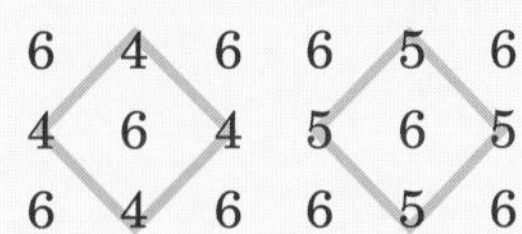

Follow-up

Drill

(*Drill* #3)

15	25	17	21
23	13	29	24
16	26	29	19

1. Use Form B. **Write the number I say.**

	15	**22**	**27**
	21	**17**	**19**
	26	**24**	**18**
	20	**19**	**28**
	23	**25**	**16**

2. Drill Addition Families 1–6 flash cards.
3. Do the chalkboard samples for More Numbers.

Practice Sheets

- ● Form B (*Follow-up* drill #1)
- ☐ Fact Houses #9
- ☐ Writing Practice #13
- ● Number Facts #8

Objectives

Review

Addition facts
The 20's
Counting (100)
More (20's)
Penny

Preparation

Materials

Addition Families 2–6 flash cards
Form C for each child
One penny for each child
Addition Families 1–6 flash cards
A handful of real pennies

Chalkboard

(*Class Time* #1)

(*Class Time* #4)

21	24	25	22
28	26	27	25

Class Time

1. *Review Addition Families 5 and 6.*
   a. Call the children to the flannel board. Quietly arrange the blocks to show 0 + 5 = 5. **Who can write this fact in a house?** Continue to rearrange the blocks until the children have the 5 and 6 Houses full.
   b. Point to the houses. **Say Family 5 . . . Family 6.**
2. *Written flash card drill.*
   Use Addition Families 2–6 flash cards and Form C. **Write the answer to the fact I show. Always start in the box beside the picture and go across. Apron Row: Box 1** (Flash a card.) **Box 2** (Flash a card.) **Box 3** (Flash a card.) **Check if each child is writing only the answer. Box 4—Box 5.**
3. *Counting.*
   a. Review the number trains.
   b. With colored chalk, write a row of ten 2's on the board: 2 2 2 2 2

Answer these facts. (41)

4 + 1 = 5	1 + 5 = 6	4 + 2 = 6	2 + 2 = 4	3 + 3 = 6	2 + 3 = 5	4 + 1 = 5
1 + 5 = 6	2 + 4 = 6	3 + 2 = 5	1 + 3 = 4	5 + 1 = 6	3 + 2 = 5	4 + 2 = 6
1 + 4 = 5	4 + 2 = 6	2 + 3 = 5	3 + 3 = 6	6 + 0 = 6	3 + 1 = 4	2 + 4 = 6

Circle More.

more	23 (25)	(21) 20	(29) 28
(28) 26	(22) 21	22 (24)	(28) 27
(29) 27	(26) 25	(23) 21	(25) 24

87

2 2 2 2 2. **What shall we do to make these numbers be the twenties?** Have the children use white chalk to insert 0, 1, 2, 3, 4, 5, . . .

c. **Count 1–100.**

4. *More.*
Do the chalkboard samples.

5. *Review penny.*
   a. Give each child a penny. **I am thinking of something that is kept on a shelf. It could be shaped like a pig. It has a hole in the top. If you shake it, you will hear *jingle, jingle, jingle!* What is it?** A penny bank. **We can save pennies in a penny bank.**
   b. **When I point to you, hold up your coin and say, "Penny, 1¢."**

6. *Assign Lesson 41.*

Follow-up

Drill

(*Drill* #1)

11	24	12	29	
22	13	16	20	18
23	27	17	28	
26	15	25	19	21

1. **See how quickly you can say all the numbers in the honeycomb.** Keep the honeycomb on the board for Lesson 42.
2. Double Drill with Addition Families 1–6 flash cards.
3. Let individuals count various amounts of real pennies.

Practice Sheets

- Form C (*Class Time* #2)
- ☐ Fact Houses #9
- ☐ Money #1
- ☐ More Numbers #4
- Number Facts #9
- Missing Numbers #2

Objectives

Review

Addition facts

Penny

Number Order

42 Write Family 6.

6						
0	1	2	3	4	5	6
+6	+5	+4	+3	+2	+1	+0
6	6	6	6	6	6	6

Answer these facts.

3	1	3	1	4	2	2
+2	+5	+3	+4	+2	+2	+1
5	6	6	5	6	4	3

2	2	5	3	4	1	4
+3	+4	+1	+2	+1	+3	+2
5	6	6	5	5	4	6

1	4	6	3	2	3	2
+2	+1	+0	+1	+3	+3	+4
3	5	6	4	5	6	6

88

Preparation

Materials

Addition Family 6 flash cards

Large penny

Assortment of real coins

Number Order flash cards 1–15

Addition Families 5 and 6 flash cards

Chalkboard

(Prepare one set like this for each child to trace in *Class Time* #2.)

2	2
+3	+4
5	6

(*Class Time* #3)

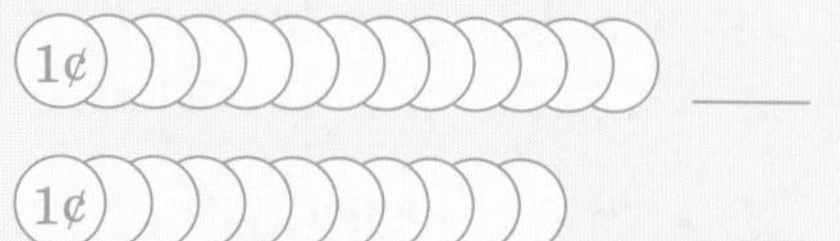

Class Time

1. *Review Addition Family 6.*
   Give the Family 6 flash cards to the children. **When I call your fact, come and stand in line in family order.**

   3 + 3 = 6
   6 + 0 = 6
   1 + 5 = 6
   4 + 2 = 6
   2 + 4 = 6
   5 + 1 = 6
   0 + 6 = 6

   Are they standing in order? Have each child say his fact.

2. *Drill selected facts.*
   a. Have each child stand near his set of facts on the board. **Trace and say "2 + 3 = 5" three times with me.**
   b. **Trace and say "2 + 4 = 6" three times with me.**
   c. **Whisper and trace the facts until I say "stop."**

3. *Review penny.*
   a. Hold the large penny. **What are two**

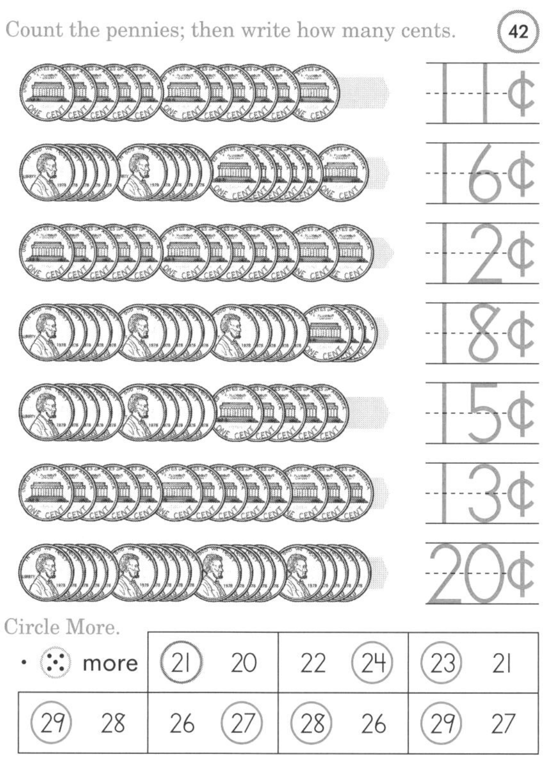

Speed Drill Answers

5 4 6 6 5 3
6 5 4 6 6 5
3 6 5 4 6 6

Speed Drill #8

things we can do with pennies? We put pennies in the offering. We save pennies in a penny bank.

b. **How much is a penny worth? What color is a penny? How does the edge of a penny feel?**

c. **We count pennies by 1's.**
1, 2, 3, 4, 5, 6, . . .
1¢, 2¢, 3¢, 4¢, . . . Do the chalkboard samples.

d. **If you saved 7 pennies in your bank, how many cents did you save?** Continue with
4 pennies **11 pennies**
2 pennies **9 pennies**

e. Place an assortment of coins on the table. Have individuals sort out the pennies and count them, putting them in a row.

4. *Number Order.*
Flash Number Order cards.

5. *Do Speed Drill #8.*

6. *Assign Lesson 42.*

Follow-up

Drill

1. Drill individuals with Addition Families 5 and 6 flash cards.
2. Drill number recognition with the honeycomb from Lesson 41. If individuals cannot say the numbers in thirty seconds, keep the honeycomb and drill again on following days.
3. Chalkboard drill: **Write the number I say: 24, 27, 21, 29, 25, 22, 20, 26, 28, 23. How many letters have we learned in phonics class?**

Practice Sheets

- ☐ Form F: 1–29
- ☐ Less Numbers #4
- ● Number Facts #9
- ● Money #2
- ◊ Dot-to-Dot #20

Objectives

New

TEACHING

The 30's

Review

Counting (100)
Addition facts
Penny
Before and After (including 20's)

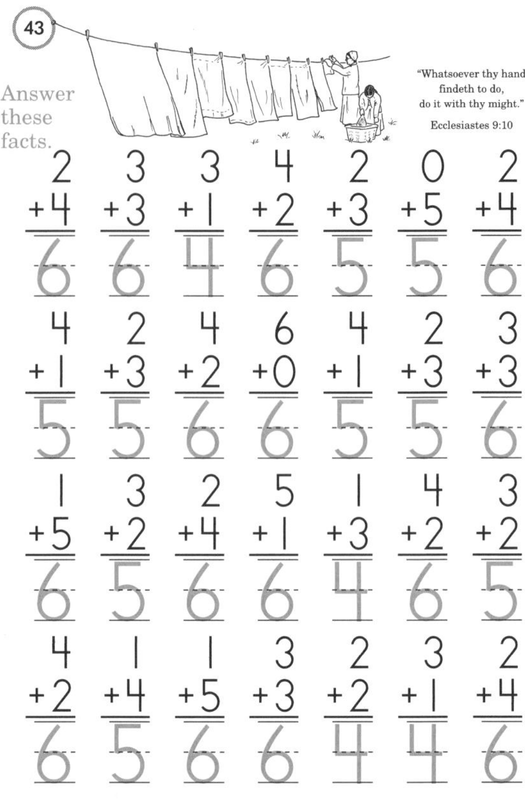

43

Answer these facts.

"Whatsoever thy hand findeth to do, do it with thy might."
Ecclesiastes 9:10

2	3	3	4	2	0	2
+4	+3	+1	+2	+3	+5	+4
6	6	4	6	5	5	6
4	2	4	6	4	2	3
+1	+3	+2	+0	+1	+3	+3
5	5	6	6	5	5	6
1	3	2	5	1	4	3
+5	+2	+4	+1	+3	+2	+2
6	5	6	6	4	6	5
4	1	1	3	2	3	2
+2	+4	+5	+3	+2	+1	+4
6	5	6	6	4	4	6

Preparation

Tape a 2" × 3" card to the end of your pointing stick.

Materials

Large penny

Addition Families 4–6 flash cards

Chalkboard

(*Class Time* #3)

2	2	3	4	1	3	4
+2	+3	+3	+2	+4	+2	+2
1	4	4	3	2	5	2
+5	+2	+1	+2	+4	+1	+3

(*Class Time* #5)

___ 27 ___

___ 21 ___

___ 18 ___

___ 24 ___

___ 15 ___

Class Time

1. *Counting.*
   a. Call the children to the number line. **Say the leading number of each train loud and slow. Say the rest of the train softer and faster. Count 1–100.**
   b. Point to the thirties. Cover the 3's with the card on the end of your pointing stick. **Count with me. 0, 1, 2, 3, 4, . . .** Count again, looking at the whole numbers. **30, 31, 32, 33, 34, . . .**
   c. **The thirties all have the digit 3. The twenties all have the digit 2. The teens all have the digit 1.**
   d. **Each group also has these same numbers in the same order: 0, 1, 2, 3, 4, 5, 6, 7, 8, 9.**
2. *Review Addition Families 5 and 6.*
   Stand near the flannel board. **I will move the blocks. Say Family 5 . . . Family 6.**

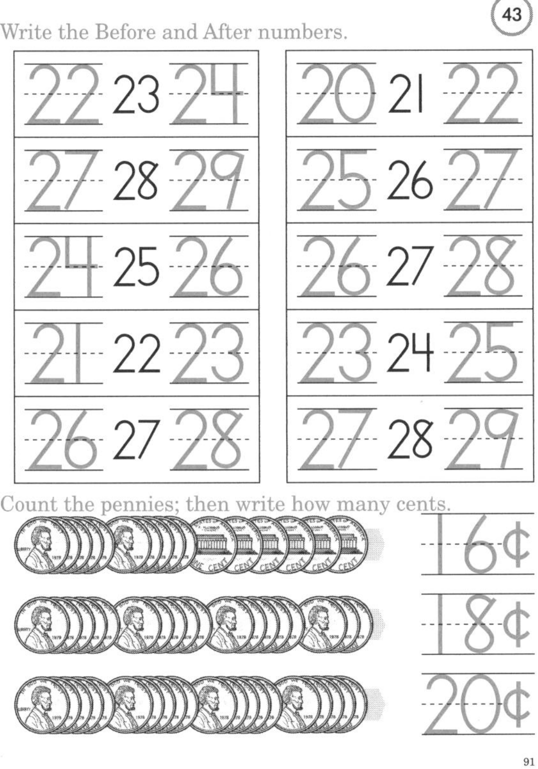
43

Write the Before and After numbers.

22 23 24	20 21 22
27 28 29	25 26 27
24 25 26	26 27 28
21 22 23	23 24 25
26 27 28	27 28 29

Count the pennies; then write how many cents.

16¢

18¢

20¢

91

3. *Drill mixed addition facts.*
   a. Stand by the house on the chalkboard. **Say the answers together.**
   b. Have each child say one row.
   c. Zigzag from row to row.
4. *Review penny.*
   Show the large penny or some real pennies. **We count pennies by 1's. If you saved 6 pennies in your bank, how many cents would you have?** Continue with
   3 pennies **13 pennies**
   5 pennies **17 pennies**
   9 pennies **10 pennies**
5. *Before and After.*
   a. Review the motions.
   b. Do the chalkboard samples.
6. *Assign Lesson 43.*

Follow-up

Drill

(*Drill* #1)

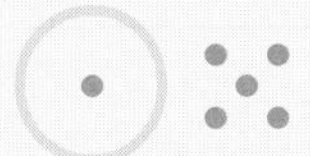

14	21	27	18
21	24	24	14
15	25	26	29

1. Do the chalkboard samples for Less Numbers.
2. Circle Drill with Addition Families 4–6 flash cards. Select a block in the room that can be circled by the children. It may be your desk, a table, or the teaching corner.
   a. **You will quietly walk around and around. As you pass me, say the answer for my flash card.**
   b. **Use your fingers to keep count of how many answers you say. As soon as you have given ten answers, you may sit down.**
   c. **If your answer is wrong, you may not count it.**

Practice Sheets

- ☐ Fact Houses #10
- ☐ Writing Practice #14
- ☐ Money #1
- ● Number Facts #9

Objectives

New

TEACHING

Addition Family 7

Review

Addition facts

Missing Numbers (20's, 30's)

Less (20's)

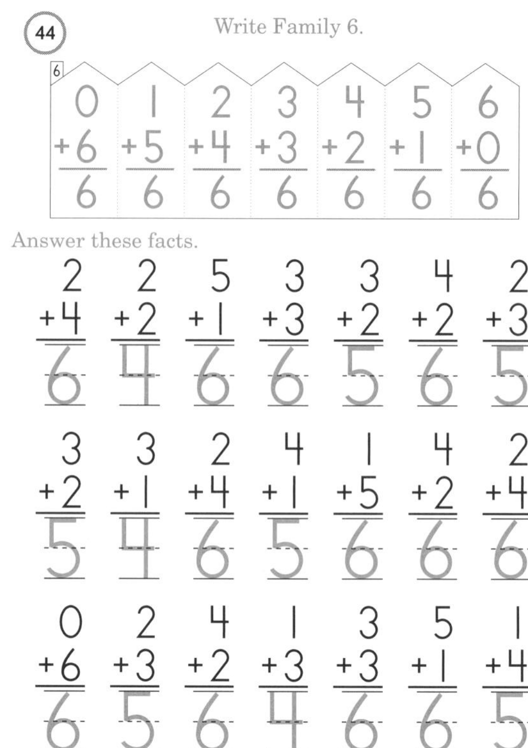

(44) Write Family 6.

0	1	2	3	4	5	6
+6	+5	+4	+3	+2	+1	+0
6	6	6	6	6	6	6

Answer these facts.

2	2	5	3	3	4	2
+4	+2	+1	+3	+2	+2	+3
6	4	6	6	5	6	5
3	3	2	4	1	4	2
+2	+1	+4	+1	+5	+2	+4
5	4	6	5	6	6	6
0	2	4	1	3	5	1
+6	+3	+2	+3	+3	+1	+4
6	5	6	4	6	6	5

92

Preparation

Materials

Form C for each child

Addition Families 2–6 flash cards

Addition Families 2–6 flash cards

Chalkboard

(*Class Time* #2)

2	3	2	4
+ 3	+ 2	+ 4	+ 2
5	5	6	6

(*Class Time* #4)

20 ___ 22 ___ ___ ___ ___ 27 ___ ___

30 ___ ___ ___ ___ ___ 36 ___ ___ ___

(*Class Time* #5)

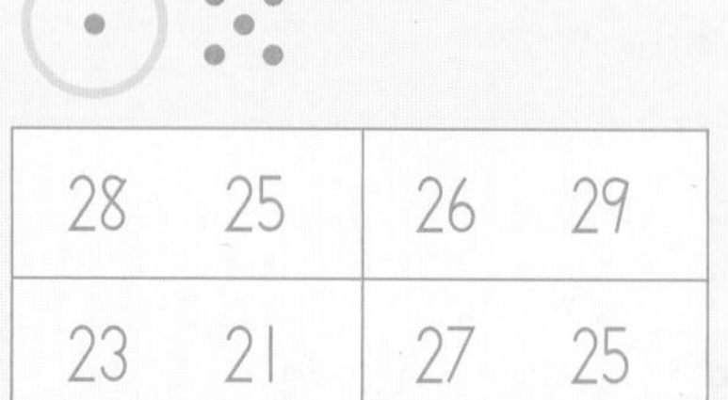

28	25	26	29
23	21	27	25

Class Time

1. *Review Addition Families 4–6.*
   Watch my fingers as we say Addition Family 4 . . . Family 5 . . . Family 6.
2. *Drill selected facts.*
   Stand near the facts on the board. Circle 2 + 3 = 5. **We will say this five times.** Say it loudly the first time; then lower your voice with each recital. Drill all the facts.
3. *Drill addition facts.*
   Use Form C. Flash Addition Families 2–6 cards. **Write the answer to the fact I show. Apron Row: Box 1—Box 2—Box 3 . . .** Check to see that the children are using the left-to-right direction across the row.
4. *Missing Numbers.*
   Fill in the chalkboard samples.

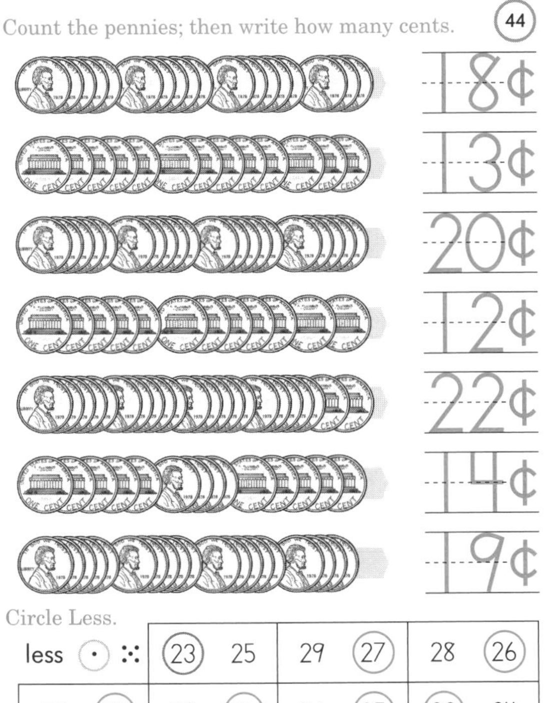

5. *Less.*
   Do the chalkboard samples.
6. *Do Speed Drill #9.*
7. *Assign Lesson 44.*

Speed Drill Answers

4	5	6	6	5	6
5	6	6	5	6	5
6	6	5	6	5	4

Follow-up

Drill

(*Drill* #2)

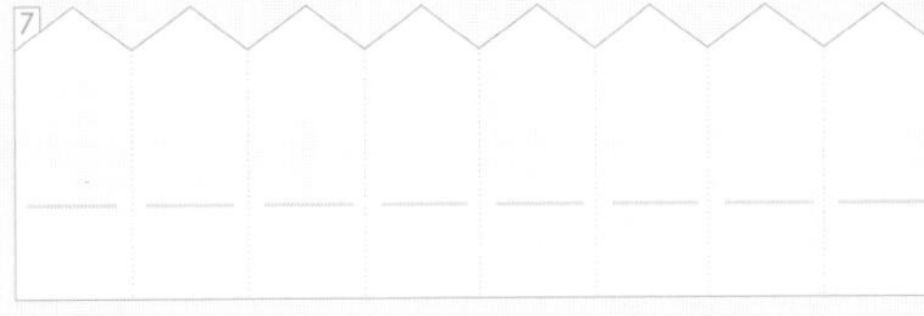

1. Circle Drill with Addition 2–6 flash cards. Review the procedure from Lesson 43. **As soon as you have ten correct answers, you may sit down.** Keep the drill quiet and orderly.
2. Introduce Family 7. **Help me fill these houses with plus problems that equal 7.** The children should volunteer all the facts. Write them in order in the houses. Pick out the twins. **We will work with Family 7 tomorrow.**
3. Write 0 1 2 3 4 5 6 7 8 9 on the board. **What shall we do to make these numbers into the thirties?** Put a 3 in front of each number.

Practice Sheets

- ● Form C (*Class Time* #3)
- ☐ Fact Houses #10
- ☐ Missing Numbers #3
- ● Number Facts #10

Objectives

New

TEACHING

Addition Family 7

Review

Addition facts

Before and After (20's, 30's)

(45) Write Family 6.

6

0	1	2	3	4	5	6
+6	+5	+4	+3	+2	+1	+0
6	6	6	6	6	6	6

Answer these facts.

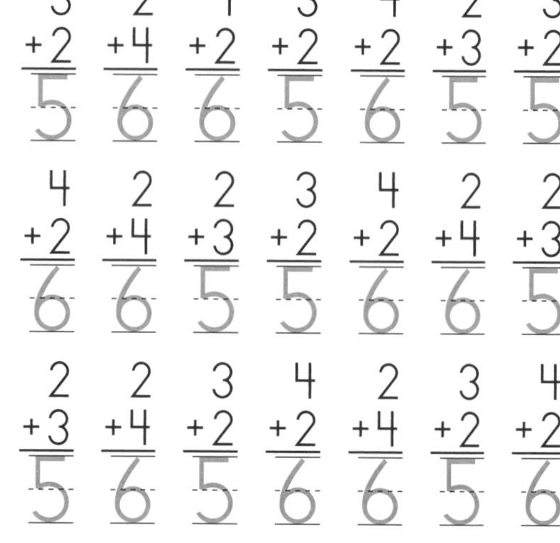

3	2	4	3	4	2	3
+2	+4	+2	+2	+2	+3	+2
5	6	6	5	6	5	5
4	2	2	3	4	2	2
+2	+4	+3	+2	+2	+4	+3
6	6	5	5	6	6	5
2	2	3	4	2	3	4
+3	+4	+2	+2	+4	+2	+2
5	6	5	6	6	5	6

94

Preparation

Materials

Addition Families 4–6 flash cards

Form B for each child

Addition Families 4–6 flash cards

Chalkboard

(*Class Time* #2)

(*Class Time* #4)

___ 36 ___	___ 23 ___
___ 32 ___	___ 27 ___
___ 38 ___	___ 21 ___
___ 34 ___	___ 25 ___

Class Time

1. *Review Addition Families 4–6.*
   a. Give the Addition Families 4–6 flash cards to the children. **If you have the first fact in Family 4, come and set it on the chalk tray.** Continue through Families 4, 5, and 6.
   b. Stand near the flash cards. **Let's say them together.**
2. *Teach Addition Family 7.*
   Call the children to the flannel board. **I will move the blocks. [Barbara] may write the facts when we are ready to put them in the houses.**
   a. If 0 ducks are in the pond and 7 ducks are in the grass, there are 7 ducks in all. 0 ducks + 7 ducks = 7 ducks. Have everyone say the fact, and then wait for it to be written. 0 + 7 = 7.
   b. **If 1 duck is in the pond and 6 ducks are in the grass, there are 7 ducks in all. One duck + 6 ducks = 7 ducks.**
   c. Continue to move a block from the lower part to the upper part until the 7 Houses are full.

Write the Before and After numbers.

45

34	35	36	32	33	34
30	31	32	37	38	39
35	36	37	31	32	33
32	33	34	36	37	38
33	34	35	35	36	37

Circle Less.

less ⊙ ∵	(20) 23	23 (21)	(25) 26
(27) 29	25 (24)	(22) 24	(22) 23
(27) 28	28 (26)	(28) 29	21 (20)

95

3. *Number dictation.*
   Use Form B. **Write the number I say.**

	25	**33**	**31**
	37	**29**	**36**
	35	**20**	**25**
	38	**24**	**23**
	34	**30**	**32**

4. *Before and After.*
   a. Practice the motions *Before, After,* and *Between.*
   b. Do the chalkboard samples.
5. *Assign Lesson 45.*

Follow-up

Drill

1. Drill individuals with Addition Families 4–6 flash cards.
2. **Count 1–100.**
   a. Ask a child to stand, begin at 1, and count until you motion for him to stop.
   b. The second child will begin where the first one stopped. (Be sure each child gets a turn on the way to 100.)
3. Review the penny.
   How much is a penny worth?
   We count pennies by ___.
   The edge of a penny is ___.
   Name two things we can do with pennies.

Practice Sheets

- ● Form B (*Class Time* #3)
- ☐ Fact Houses #10
- ☐ More Numbers #5
- ● Number Facts #10
- ● Form F: 1–39

Objectives

New

TEACHING

1- and 2-digit numbers

Story problems, step one

WORKBOOK

Addition Family 7

Review

Addition facts

Writing 30's

Preparation

Make Addition Family 7 flash cards for each child.

Materials

Addition Families 4–6 flash cards

Chalkboard

(*Class Time* #3)

Class Time

1. *Review Addition Family 6.*
   Pass out Family 6 addition flash cards to the children. **When I say the fact you have, come and stand in line in family order. 5 + 1 = 6, 3 + 3 = 6, 0 + 6 = 6, 2 + 4 = 6, 6 + 0 = 6, 1 + 5 = 6, 4 + 2 = 6.** Have each child say his fact.
2. *Drill addition facts.*
   Double Drill with Addition Families 4–6 flash cards.
3. *Review Addition Family 7.*
   a. Call the children to the flannel board. **If Delbert has 0 rabbits in one pen and 7 rabbits in another pen, he has 7 rabbits in all. Zero rabbits plus 7 rabbits equals 7 rabbits. Everyone say the story fact with me. Zero rabbits plus 7 rabbits . . .**
   b. Move 1 block. **If Delbert has 1 rabbit in one pen and 6 rabbits in another pen, he has 7 rabbits in all. Say this story fact together. One rabbit plus 6 rabbits equals 7 rabbits.**

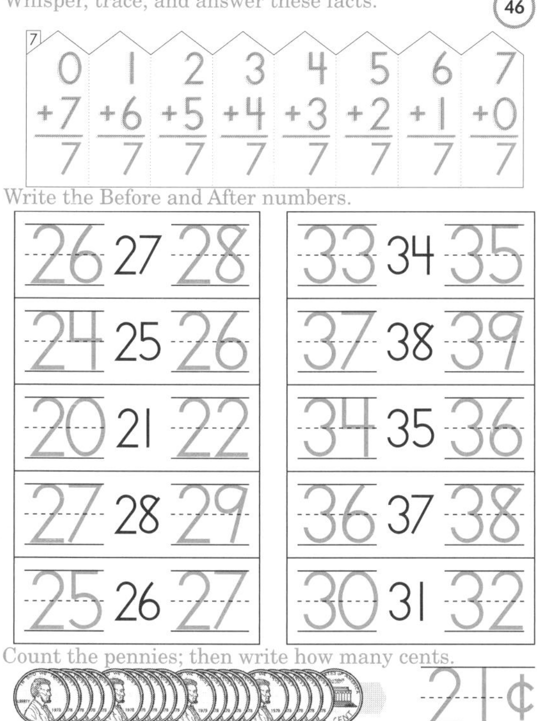

c. Work through the entire family; then ask a child to fill the 7 Houses as everyone says the facts again.

4. *Writing 30's.*
   Write 3 3 3 3 3 3 3 3 3 3 (ten 3's) on the board. **What shall we do to make the thirties?**

5. *Teach 1- and 2-digit numbers..*
   a. **All the thirties are 2-digit numbers. They each have a 3 and another number. They each have 2 *digits*.**
   b. **Think of a number that we write with only 1 digit?** Write a few on the board, using the children's samples.

6. *Do Speed Drill #10.*

7. *Assign Lesson 46.*

Speed Drill Answers

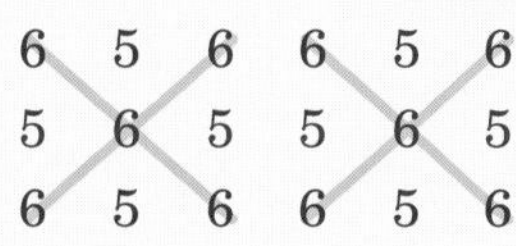

Follow-up

Drill

1. Review the penny. **If you saved 8 pennies, how many cents did you save?** Continue with

10 pennies	**30 pennies**
21 pennies	**14 pennies**
24 pennies	**12 pennies**

2. Give each child his Family 7 flash cards.

3. Introduce the first step in solving story problems. Print on the board *Tim has 3 cats.* Teach the word *has* if the children do not know it. They should be able to sound the other words phonetically.

   Tim has 3 cats.

   a. **Read this sentence three times with me.**
   b. Draw a short blank and another one about twice as long.

   ___ ______

   How many cats does Tim have? Write 3 on the short blank.
   c. **Tim has 3 ____?** Write *cats* on the longer blank.
   d. Repeat the practice with these sentences.

      Tim has 5 nuts.
      Tim has 4 pups.
      Tim has 1 hat.

Practice Sheets

- ☐ Fact Houses #11
- ☐ Number Trains #1
- ● Number Facts #10
- ● Less Numbers #5

Objectives

New

TEACHING

Story problems, step one

Review

Addition facts

1- and 2-digit numbers

More (20's, 30's)

Preparation

Tack Addition Family 7 flash cards above the flannel board, answers showing.

Materials

Addition Families 1–4 and 7 flash cards

Chalkboard

(*Class Time* #1)

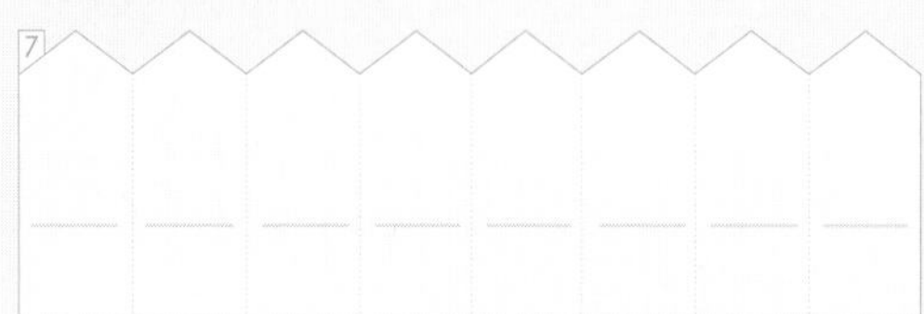

(*Class Time* #2)

18 30 7 21 5 1 22 4 36

(*Class Time* #3)

___ ______

(*Class Time* #4)

24 34	27 25
36 33	29 39
35 24	38 39

(47) Write Family 7.

7

0 + 7 = 7, 1 + 6 = 7, 2 + 5 = 7, 3 + 4 = 7, 4 + 3 = 7, 5 + 2 = 7, 6 + 1 = 7, 7 + 0 = 7

Answer these facts.

3 + 4 = 7, 3 + 1 = 4, 2 + 5 = 7, 6 + 1 = 7, 2 + 1 = 3, 7 + 0 = 7, 4 + 3 = 7

5 + 2 = 7, 4 + 3 = 7, 1 + 6 = 7, 1 + 3 = 4, 4 + 3 = 7, 2 + 2 = 4, 6 + 1 = 7

0 + 7 = 7, 3 + 4 = 7, 0 + 3 = 3, 1 + 2 = 3, 3 + 4 = 7, 2 + 5 = 7, 1 + 6 = 7

98

Class Time

1. *Drill Addition Family 7.*
   a. Call the children to the flannel board. **I will move the blocks. [Carl] will write the facts in the houses. Everyone will help to say Family 7.**
   b. Point to the first flash card above the flannel board. **Say this three times with your eyes open, and then three times with your eyes closed.** Drill all the facts.
2. *Review 1- and 2-digit numbers.*
   a. Ask someone to find a 1-digit number in the row on the board. Have him say, "__ is a 1-digit number," and erase it from the row.
   b. Have someone find a 2-digit number, identify it, and erase it.
   c. Continue until all the samples are gone.
   d. Point to the number line. **What is the first 2-digit number? What is the last 2-digit number?**

(47)

Circle More.

• ⁙ more	23 (32)	28 (35)	(33) 23
24 (32)	(39) 29	20 (30)	(34) 24
(33) 22	29 (30)	(36) 27	(31) 29
(37) 28	(38) 29	22 (32)	(30) 28

Write the After Numbers.

27 28 29	37 38 39
25 26 27	26 27 28
32 33 34	34 35 36
20 21 22	22 23 24
35 36 37	36 37 38

99

3. *Teach step one in solving story problems.*
   a. Write on the board *Sam has 2 cups.* **Read this two times with me.**
   b. Point to the blanks on the board. **How many cups does Sam have?** Write 2 on the first blank.
   c. **Sam has 2 ___?** Write *cups* on the second blank.
   d. Erase *2 cups.* Drill these sentences.
      Sam has 4 pups.
      Sam has 6 nuts.
4. *More.*
   Do the chalkboard samples.
5. *Assign Lesson 47.*

Follow-up

Drill

1. Circle Drill with Addition Families 1–4 and 7 flash cards.
2. **We will count all the 2-digit numbers. Count from 10 to 99.**

Practice Sheets

- ☐ Fact Houses #11
- ☐ Writing Practice #15
- ● Money #3
- ◊ Dot-to-Dot #21

Objectives

New

TEACHING

Column addition (+ 1)

WORKBOOK

Story problems, step one

Review

Addition facts
1- and 2-digit numbers
Counting (100)

Read each sentence. Then write the number that tells how many and the word that tells what.

48

Tim has 3 dips.	3 dips
Tim has 2 cats.	2 cats
Tim has 3 pups.	3 pups
Tim has 5 pets.	5 pets
Tim has 6 nuts.	6 nuts
Tim has 4 caps.	4 caps
Tim has 7 cups.	7 cups

100

Preparation

Materials

Addition Families 1–5 and 7 flash cards

Chalkboard

(*Class Time* #1)

____ ________ Tim has 4 cats.

Sam has 2 pens.

Ned has 6 buds.

Ben has 3 pets.

(*Class Time* #2)

7

Class Time

1. *Review the first step in story problems.*
   a. Point to the first sentence on the board. **Read together.** Ask a child to fill in the blanks.
   b. Erase *4 cats* from the blanks. Point to the second sentence. **Read together.** Ask a child to fill in the blanks.
   c. Do all the sentences.
2. *Review Addition Family 7.*
   a. Stand near the flannel board. Ask a child to move the blocks as everyone says Family 7.
   b. **Say Family 7 as I fill the houses.**
3. *Review 1-digit and 2-digit numbers.*
   a. **Tell me all the 1-digit numbers.** Write them on the board.
   b. **Tell me some 2-digit numbers.** Write them on the board.

Write Family 7. (48)

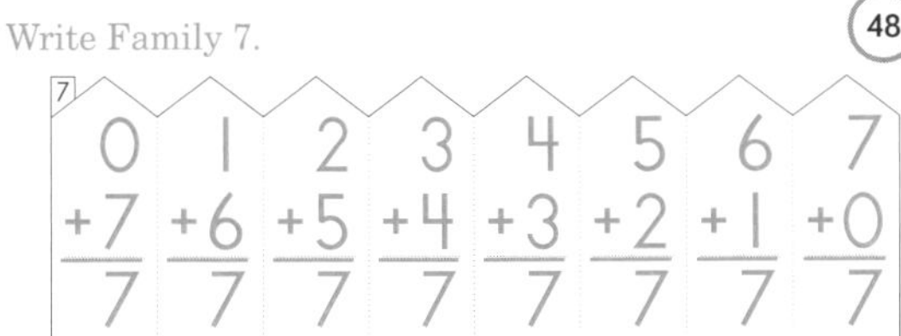

Answer these facts.

3	3	2	6	2	2	2
+4	+2	+5	+1	+1	+3	+2
7	5	7	7	3	5	4

5	2	0	3	1	4	1
+2	+3	+3	+2	+6	+3	+6
7	5	3	5	7	7	7

1	3	4	1	3	2	1
+3	+4	+3	+4	+4	+5	+2
4	7	7	5	7	7	3

101

4. *Counting.*
   a. **Say the numbers in each number train.**
   b. **When we count 1, 2, 3, 4, we are counting by 1's. We say each number, like walking along and stepping on every floor tile as we go.**
   c. **Let's count by 1's to 100.**
5. *Do Speed Drill #11.*
6. *Assign Lesson 48.*

Speed Drill Answers

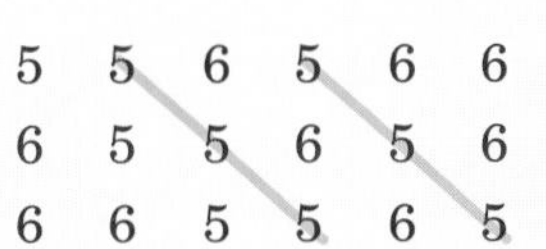

5	5	6	5	6	6
6	5	5	6	5	6
6	6	5	5	6	5

Speed Drill #11

Follow-up

Drill

(*Drill* #3)

2	2	3	1
3	4	3	4
+ 1	+ 1	+ 1	+ 1

1. Drill individuals with Addition Families 1–5 and 7 flash cards.
2. Chalkboard drill: **Write the 2-digit number I say: 31, 25, 28, 34, 42, 30, 46, 43, 45.**
3. Introduce column addition. Point to the first problem on the chalkboard. **2 + 3 = ___.** Write a small 5 beside the 3. **5 + 1 = ___.** Write 6 below. Do all the problems.

   2
   3 5
   + 1
   6

Note: It is difficult for a child to hold a partial sum in his mind. Teach the children to write the partial sum beside the second addend. Then add the third addend.

Practice Sheets

- □ Fact Houses #11
- ● Number Facts #11
- ● Missing Numbers #4
- ◊ Extra: Money #2—Color pennies; then cut and paste them back-to-back.

Objectives

New

TEACHING

Story problems, step two
Column addition (+ 1)
Subtraction concept

Review

Addition facts
Counting (100)
Before and After (including 40's)

Read each sentence. Then write the number that tells how many and the word that tells what.

49

Ben saw 5 bugs.	5 bugs
Ben did 3 jobs.	3 jobs
Ben has 1 hat.	1 hat
Ted has 4 tops in a box.	4 tops
Jim got 7 nuts in a can.	7 nuts
Tim met 3 lads in a van.	3 lads
Sam has 2 bats at home.	2 bats

102

Preparation

Materials

Addition Families 1–5 and 7 flash cards

Chalkboard

(*Class Time* #2)

___ _______   ___ _______

___ _______

(*Class Time* #4)

__ 42 __   31 __ __
__ 37 __   24 __ __
__ 26 __   43 __ __
__ 45 __   30 __ __

(*Class Time* #5)

2	3	4	3
4	2	1	3
+ 1	+ 1	+ 1	+ 1

Class Time

1. *Review Addition Family 7.*
   a. Arrange the flannel board blocks for 0 + 7. **If 0 birds are on the feeder and 7 birds are on the ground, there are 7 birds in all. Say the story fact with me. Zero birds + 7 birds = 7 birds.**
   b. Continue through all the facts of Family 7.
   c. **Watch my fingers as we say Family 7 by memory.**
2. *Teach step 2 in story problems.*
   a. Stand near the first blanks on the board. Print *Ben has 4 cats.* Ask a child to fill the blanks.
   b. Print two sentences.

      Ben has 2 nuts.
      Tim has 3 nuts.

      This story has 2 numbers. Write the two bits of information on the two sets of blanks.

Write Family 7. (49)

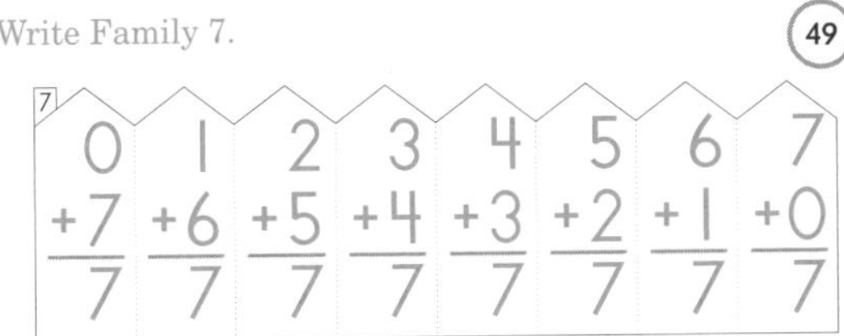

Write the After Numbers.

34	35	36	43	44	45
47	48	49	36	37	38
32	33	34	41	42	43
45	46	47	30	31	32

Circle More.

• ∵ more	35 (38)	(49) 48	32 (43)
(48) 38	(38) 37	(41) 31	(45) 44

103

3. *Counting.*
   If we count 1, 2, 3, 4, we are counting by ____. Let's count from number to number. Count to 100.
4. *Before and After.*
   Do the chalkboard samples.
5. *Teach column addition.*
   a. Go to the first sample on the chalkboard. **2 + 4 = ___.** Write a small 6 beside the 4. **6 + 1 = ___.** Write 7 below.
   b. Have the children say the numbers for you as you work through the rest of the samples.
6. *Assign Lesson 49.*

Follow-up

Drill

(*Drill #2*)

32 48 26
41
45 33 30
37
34 49 28
46
42 38 31
39
36 43 35
40
47 29 44

1. Circle Drill with Addition Families 1–5 and 7 flash cards. Allow three seconds for an answer. Is the circle of children moving quietly and orderly?
2. Call the children to the number steps on the chalkboard. **Climb the steps as fast as you can!**
3. Introduce the subtraction concept.
   a. Call a child to the front of the class. Give him 4 pencils. **How many pencils does [Jean] have?** Write 4 on the board.
   b. Take two of the pencils from the child and lay them on a desk or table where they can be seen. **How many pencils did I take away?** Write 2 below the 4.
   c. Write the subtraction sign and equal line. **This is a "take away" sign, and the equal line. We *subtract* when we "take away" with numbers.**
   d. **How many pencils does [Jean] have left?** Write 2 below the line. Point to each number and symbol as you say, **4 take away 2 equals 2.**

Practice Sheets

- ☐ More Numbers #6
- ☐ Writing Practice #16
- ● Number Facts #11
- ● Form F: 1–49

Objectives

New

WORKBOOK

Column addition

Review

Addition facts

Story problems, step two

Numbers 11–30

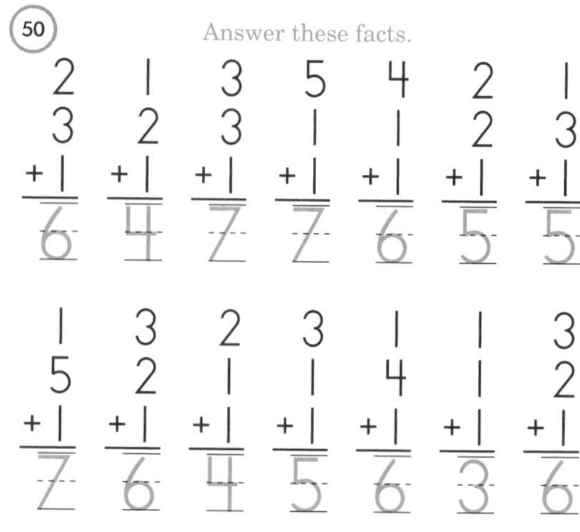

Read each sentence. Then write the number that tells how many and the word that tells what.

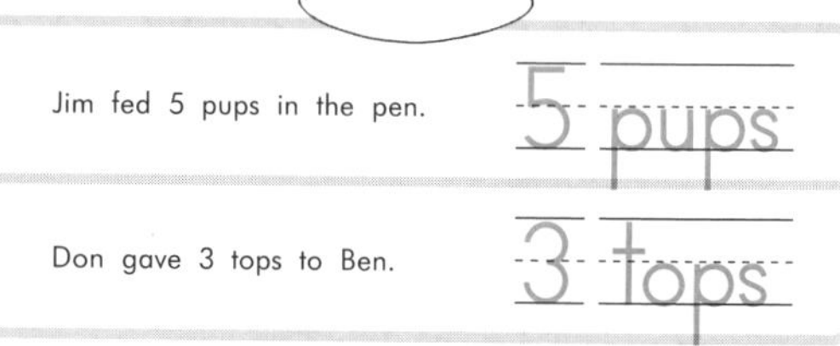

104

Preparation

Materials

Number flash cards 11–30

Addition Families 1–7 flash cards

Chalkboard

(*Class Time* #2)

4	2	5	2
+2	+4	+2	+5
6	6	7	7

(*Class Time* #3)

2	1	3	2	3	1	5
3	5	3	4	2	4	1
+1	+1	+1	+1	+1	+1	+1

(*Class Time* #4)

___ ________

___ ________

Class Time

1. *Review Addition Families 6 and 7.*
   a. **Girls, say Family 6 as I move the blocks.**
   b. **Boys, say Family 7 as I move the blocks.**
2. *Drill selected facts.*
   Stand near the facts on the board. Circle 4 + 2 = 6. **We will say this five times.** Say it loudly the first time; then lower your voice with each recital. Drill all four facts.
3. *Column addition.*
   Have the children do the samples on the board as outlined in Lesson 48 *Follow-up*.

Write Family 7. (50)

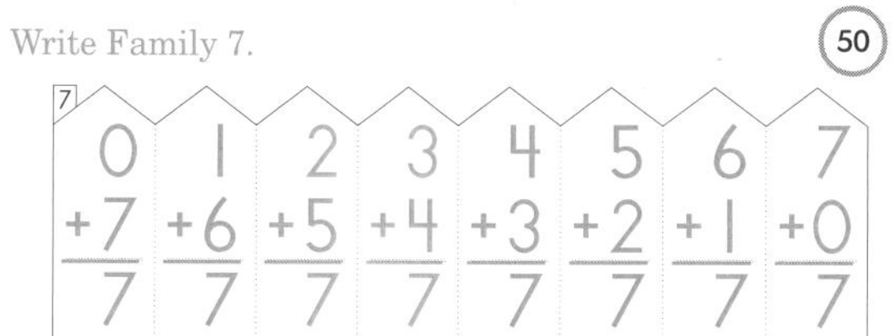

Write the Before and After numbers.

32	33	34	47	48	49
36	37	38	41	42	43
30	31	32	45	46	47
34	35	36	43	44	45

Circle More.

• more	(41) 31	(45) 44	37 (47)
36 (46)	(38) 37	41 (43)	(49) 39

105

4. *Practice two steps of story problems.*
   a. Write *Tim has 2 cups.*
      Ben has 2 cups.
      Read with me. Tell me what to write in the blanks.
   b. Erase and write:
      Ben has 3 pups.
      Tim has 4 pups.
      Read with me. Tell me what to write in the blanks.
5. *Number recognition.*
   Flash Number cards 11–30.
6. *Do Speed Drill #12.*
7. *Assign Lesson 50.*

Speed Drill Answers

5	6	7	6	7	7
6	7	6	7	7	5
7	6	7	7	5	7

Follow-up

Drill

(*Drill #1*)

34 43	36 31
45 42	47 36

1. Do the Less samples.
2. Review the penny. **If you saved 3¢ in your penny bank, how many pennies did you save?** Continue with

6¢	**9¢**	**7¢**
8¢	**12¢**	**16¢**
10¢	**4¢**	**11¢**

3. Drill each child with Addition Families 1–7 flash cards.
4. Demonstrate the subtraction concept.
   a. Call a child to the front of the class and give him 3 chalkboard erasers. **How many erasers does [Heidi] have?** Write 3 on the board.
   b. Take one of the erasers from the child and put it back on the chalk tray. **How many erasers did I take away?** Write - 1 and the equal line.
   c. **How many erasers does [Heidi] have left?** Write 2, and then point to each number and symbol as you say, **3 take away 1 equals 2. This is a subtraction fact.**

Practice Sheets

- ☐ Fact Houses #12
- ● Number Facts #12
- ● Less Numbers #6
- ◊ Dot-to-Dot #22

Objectives

New

TEACHING

Story problem answers

WORKBOOK

Story problems, step two

Review

Addition facts

(51) Read each sentence. Then write the numbers that tell how many and the words that tell what.

Tim has 5 nuts.	5	nuts
Ben has 2 nuts.	2	nuts
Tim has 3 caps.	3	caps
Ben has 3 caps.	3	caps
Tim has 1 top.	1	top
Ben has 2 tops.	2	tops
Tim has 2 cats.	2	cats
Ben has 3 cats.	3	cats
Tim has 1 hen.	1	hen
Ben has 1 hen.	1	hen

106

Preparation

Materials

Addition Families 4–7 flash cards

Form C for each child

Chalkboard

(Prepare a set of these facts for each child to trace in *Class Time* #2.)

$$\begin{array}{r} 2 \\ +4 \\ \hline 6 \end{array} \qquad \begin{array}{r} 3 \\ +4 \\ \hline 7 \end{array}$$

(*Class Time* #4)

Tim has 4 bats. ___ ______

Ben has 3 bats. ___ ______

Sam has 2 cups. ___ ______

Ted has 2 cups. ___ ______

Class Time

1. *Review Addition Families 6 and 7.*
   a. Ask a child to move the blocks as everyone repeats Family 7.
   b. **Watch my fingers as we say Addition Family 6 . . . Family 7.**
2. *Drill selected facts.*
   a. Have each child stand near his set of facts on the board. **We will trace and say each fact three times together.**
   b. **Now trace and whisper them until I say "stop."**
3. *Drill addition facts.*
   Distribute Form C, and use Addition Families 4–7 flash cards. **Write the answer to the fact I show. Apron Row: Box 1—Box 2—Box 3 . . .**

Write Family 7 (51)

7							
0	1	2	3	4	5	6	7
+7	+6	+5	+4	+3	+2	+1	+0
7	7	7	7	7	7	7	7

Answer these facts.

1	2	6	3	4	4	2
+3	+4	+1	+2	+3	+2	+5
4	6	7	5	7	6	7

3	2	5	1	1	3	1
+3	+3	+2	+6	+3	+4	+5
6	5	7	7	4	7	6

2	1	3	1	3	2	1
3	2	3	5	2	2	3
+1	+1	+1	+1	+1	+1	+1
6	4	7	7	6	5	5

107

4. *Story problems.*
   Do the two samples on the chalkboard. Leave the last set of information on the blanks for *Follow-up* drill.
5. *Assign Lesson 51.*

Tip: If a child is stumbling over any fact, write that fact on a large piece of paper. Tape the paper to the wall. Give the child a crayon, and have him trace and say the fact again and again. He may practice before school in the morning, work on it during the day, or take the paper home to practice.

Follow-up

Drill

(*Drill* #2)

2 cups
2 cups

1. Call the children to the number line.
   a. **2, 6, 4, 1, 7, and 3 are what kind of numbers?** (1-digit)
   16, 27, 34, and 49 are what kind of numbers? (2-digit)
   b. **All the teens have what digit in them?** (1)
   All the twenties have what digit? (2)
   All the thirties have what digit? (3)
   All the forties . . . All the fifties . . .
   c. **Count 1–100.**
2. Turn to the story problem blanks on the board. **2 cups + 2 cups = how many cups *in all?*** Add the plus sign and a new set of blanks below. Write *4 cups.* **Read with me. 2 cups + 2 cups = 4 cups.**
3. Chalkboard drill: **Write the 2-digit number I say. 41, 35, 38, 44, 52, 40, 56, 53, 55.**

Practice Sheets

- ● Form C (*Class Time* #3)
- ☐ Fact Houses #12
- ☐ Writing Practice #17
- ● Number Facts #12

Objectives

New

TEACHING

Complete story problems

Review

Addition facts

Missing Numbers (30's–50's)

52 Read each sentence. Then write the numbers that tell how many and the words that tell what.

Tim has 5 buns.	5	buns
Ben has 2 buns.	2	buns
Tim got 3 logs.	3	logs
Ben got 2 logs.	2	logs
Rob did 2 jobs.	2	jobs
Ben did 2 jobs.	2	jobs
Jim fed 3 pups.	3	pups
Dan fed 2 pups.	2	pups
Sam has 6 sips in a cup.	6	sips
Tom has 1 sip in his cup.	1	sip

108

Preparation

Materials

Addition Families 1–7 flash cards

Chalkboard

(*Class Time* #3)

Ben has 2 cups.

Bill has 4 cups.

___ ______

___ ______

Tim has 4 pups.

Ted has 3 pups.

How many pups is that in all?

___ ______

___ ______

___ ______

(*Class Time* #4)

___ 36 ___ ___ 39

42 ___ ___ ___ 46

___ 51 ___ ___ ___

Class Time

1. *Review Addition Families 6 and 7.*
   a. Pass out your 7 Family flash cards to the children. **When I say the fact you have, come and stand in line in family order.**
      3 + 4 = 7
      1 + 6 = 7
      5 + 2 = 7
      0 + 7 = 7
      2 + 5 = 7
      6 + 1 = 7
      4 + 3 = 7
      7 + 0 = 7
      Have each child say his fact.
   b. **Watch my fingers as we say Addition Family 6 . . . Family 7.**
2. *Drill addition facts.*
   Circle Drill with Addition Families 1–7 flash cards.

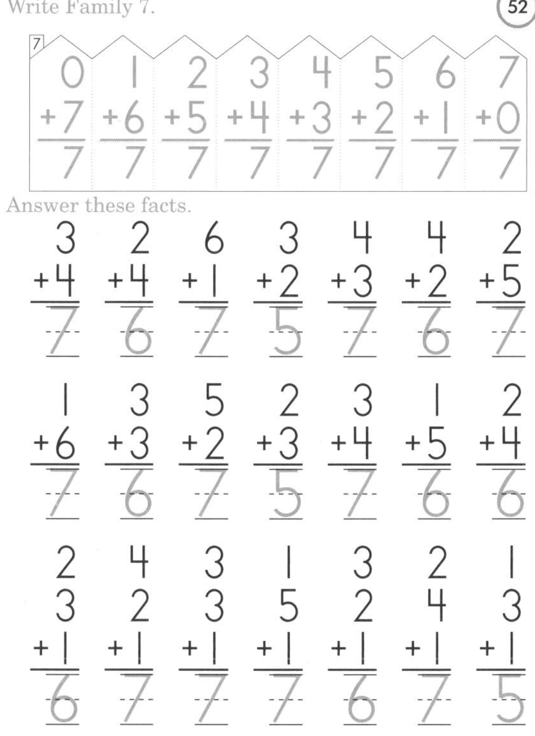

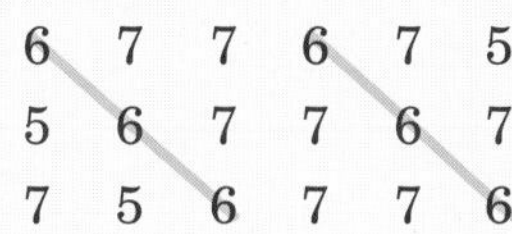

3. *Story problems.*
   a. Point to the first story problem on the board. **Read this with me.** Ask a child to fill in the blanks.
   b. Point to the second problem. **The words in the box are *how many.* Say the words with me. Read the problem with me.**
   c. Point to the key. **Our key words are *in all. In all* means that we put Tim's pups and Ted's pups together. Let's read the problem again.**
   d. Fill in the blanks, including the plus sign. **4 pups + 3 pups = 7 pups.**
4. *Missing Numbers.*
   Do the chalkboard samples.
5. *Do Speed Drill #13.*
6. *Assign Lesson 52.*

Follow-up

Drill

1. Chalkboard drill: **Write the number that comes after the number I say. What comes after 24?** Continue with **21, 28, 32, 36, 30, 45, 41, 47.**
2. Review the terms *1-digit* and *2-digit.*
3. Have individuals **count 1–100.**
4. Demonstrate the subtraction concept.
   a. Call a child to the front of the class and give him 6 crayons. **How many crayons does [Gary] have?** Write 6 on the board.
   b. Take three of the crayons and lay them on a table or desk where they can be seen. **How many crayons did I take away?** Write - 3 and the equal line.
   c. **How many crayons does [Gary] have left?** Complete the fact and have the children say it together with you.

Practice Sheets

- ☐ Missing Numbers #5
- ☐ Writing Practice #18
- ● Number Facts #12
- ● More Numbers #7

Objectives

Review

Numbers 15–50
Counting (99)
Before and After (including 50's)
Addition facts
Story problems

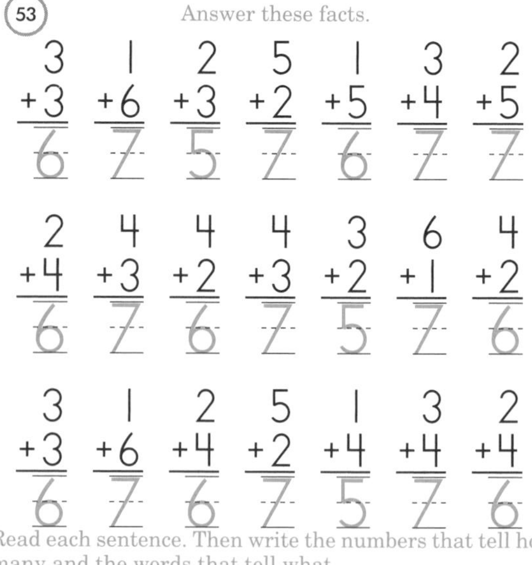

Preparation

Materials

Number flash cards 15–50

Chalkboard

(*Class Time* #3)

___ 27 ___	___ 24 ___
___ 53 ___	___ 48 ___
___ 45 ___	___ 51 ___
___ 42 ___	___ 36 ___

(*Class Time* #4)

(*Class Time* #5)

Ben has 2 pets.

Tim has 4 pets.

How many pets is that in all?

___ _______

___ _______

___ _______

Class Time

1. *Number recognition.*
   Flash Number cards 15–50.
2. *Counting.*
   Call the children to the number line. **We will say all the 2-digit numbers. Count from 10 to 99.**
3. *Before and After.*
   Do the chalkboard samples.
4. *Review Addition Families 6 and 7.*
   a. Stand near the flannel board. **I will move the blocks. Say Family 6. . . Family 7.**
   b. Ask a child to fill the houses as everyone says Family 7.
5. *Story problems.*
   Read the story problem with me. Fill in the blanks. **When we put Ben's pets and Tim's pets together, we have 6 pets *in all*.**
6. *Assign Lesson 53.*

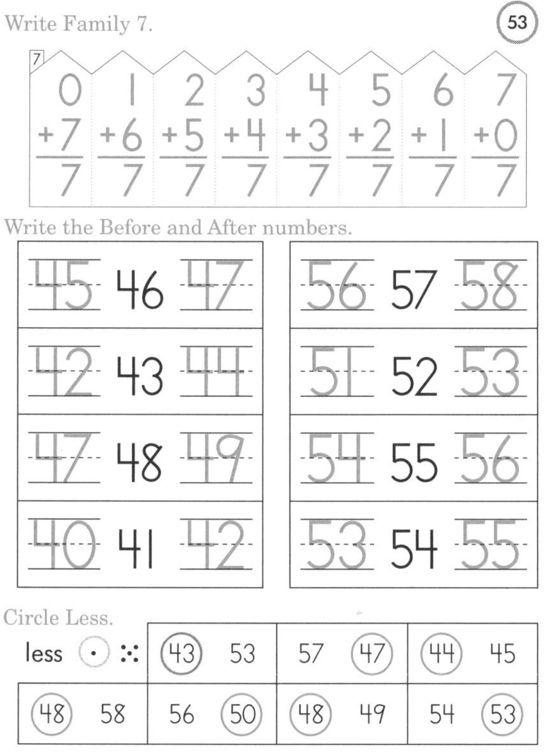

Write Family 7. (53)

7							
0	1	2	3	4	5	6	7
+7	+6	+5	+4	+3	+2	+1	+0
7	7	7	7	7	7	7	7

Write the Before and After numbers.

45 46 47	56 57 58
42 43 44	51 52 53
47 48 49	54 55 56
40 41 42	53 54 55

Circle Less.

less ⊙ ∷	(43) 53	57 (47)	(44) 45
(48) 58	56 (50)	(48) 49	54 (53)

111

Follow-up

Drill

(*Drill* #1)

2 + 3	5 + 1	4 + 3	0 + 7	3 + 3	5 + 2
1 + 5	4 + 1	4 + 2	1 + 6	3 + 2	2 + 4
4 + 3	0 + 6	1 + 4	2 + 5	6 + 1	3 + 4
4 + 2	3 + 2	2 + 5	3 + 3	5 + 2	1 + 2
2 + 3	2 + 4	1 + 6	4 + 3	6 + 1	4 + 2

1. Use the addition grid on the chalkboard. Drill the facts from left to right, right to left, top to bottom, and bottom to top. (Keep the grid to use in Lessons 54, 55, and 56.)
2. Review the penny.
3. Demonstrate the subtraction concept.
   a. Call a child to the front of the class and give him 5 pens. **How many pens does [Mary] have?** Write 5 on the board.
   b. Take two of the pens and lay them on a table or desk where they can be seen. **How many pens did I take away?** Write - 2 and the equal line.
   c. **How many pens does [Mary] have left?** Complete the fact and have the children say it together with you.

Practice Sheets

- ☐ Fact Houses #12
- ☐ Less Numbers #7
- ● Number Facts #13

Objectives

New

TEACHING

Subtraction Family 1
Counting backward

WORKBOOK

Complete story problems

Review

Addition facts
Column addition
Counting (100)

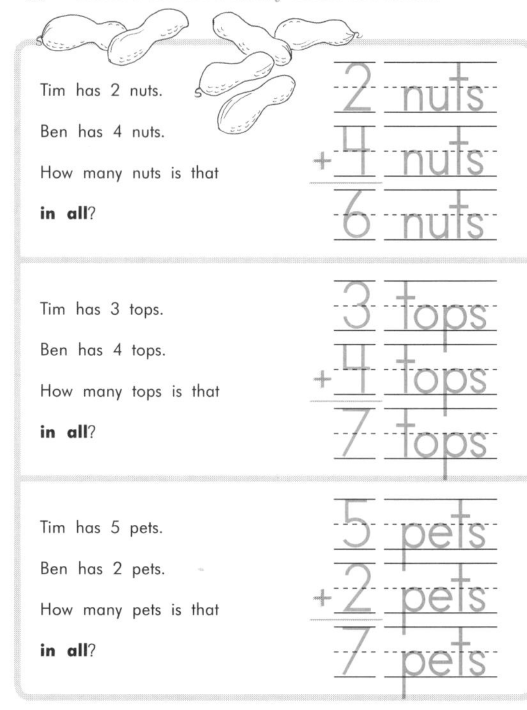

54 Read each sentence. Then write the numbers that tell how many and the words that tell what. Then write how many there are in all.

Tim has 2 nuts.
Ben has 4 nuts.
How many nuts is that **in all**?

2 nuts
+4 nuts
6 nuts

Tim has 3 tops.
Ben has 4 tops.
How many tops is that **in all**?

3 tops
+4 tops
7 tops

Tim has 5 pets.
Ben has 2 pets.
How many pets is that **in all**?

5 pets
+2 pets
7 pets

112

Preparation

Chalkboard

(*Class Time* #1)

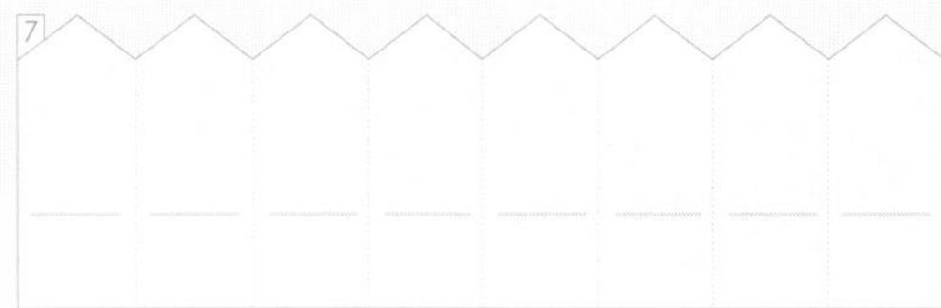

(Addition grid from Lesson 53 for *Class Time* #2)

(*Class Time* #3)

2	4	3	1
2	2	2	5
+ 1	+ 1	+ 1	+ 1

(*Class Time* #5)

___ ______
___ ______
___ ______

Class Time

1. *Review Addition Family 7.*
   a. Point to the flash cards near the flannel board. **Say each fact five times.** Say it loudly the first time; then lower your voice with each recital.
   b. **Say Family 7 as I fill the houses.**
2. *Drill addition facts.*
   Stand near the addition grid. **Answer together.**
3. *Column addition.*
   Do the chalkboard samples.
4. *Counting.*
   I will count to 100. But I will stop many times. When I stop, you say the next number.
5. *Story problems.*
   a. Write on the chalkboard:
   Dan has 3 hats.
   Jim has 1 hat.
   How many hats is that ***in all?***

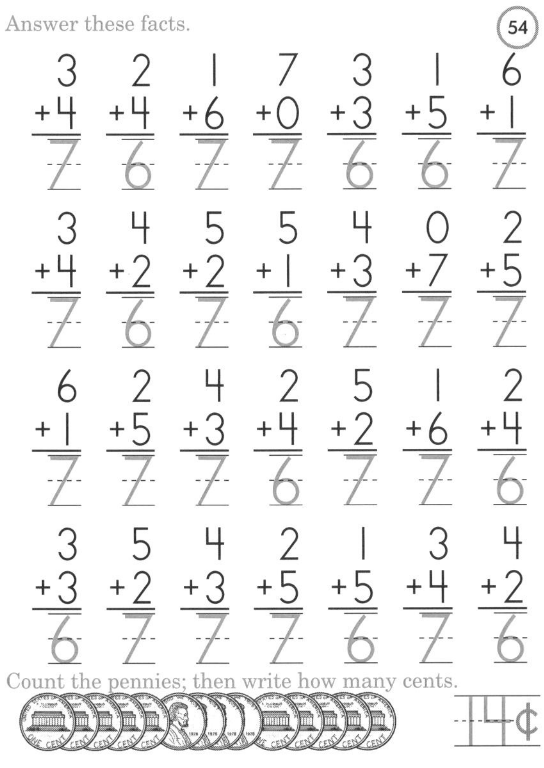
Answer these facts. 54

3 + 4 = 7 | 2 + 4 = 6 | 1 + 6 = 7 | 7 + 0 = 7 | 3 + 3 = 6 | 1 + 5 = 6 | 6 + 1 = 7

3 + 4 = 7 | 4 + 2 = 6 | 5 + 2 = 7 | 5 + 1 = 6 | 4 + 3 = 7 | 0 + 7 = 7 | 2 + 5 = 7

6 + 1 = 7 | 2 + 5 = 7 | 4 + 3 = 7 | 2 + 4 = 6 | 5 + 2 = 7 | 1 + 6 = 7 | 2 + 4 = 6

3 + 3 = 6 | 5 + 2 = 7 | 4 + 3 = 7 | 2 + 5 = 7 | 1 + 5 = 6 | 3 + 4 = 7 | 4 + 2 = 6

Count the pennies; then write how many cents. 14¢

113

Speed Drill Answers

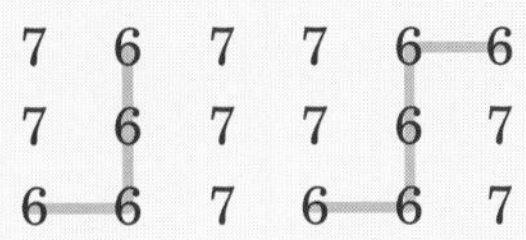
7 6 7 7 6 6
7 6 7 7 6 7
6 6 7 6 6 7

What shall I write on the blanks?

b. Erase and write:
Tim has 4 cups.
Sam has 2 cups.
How many cups is that ***in all?***

6. *Do Speed Drill #14.*
7. *Assign Lesson 54.*

Follow-up

Drill

1. Introduce Subtraction Family 1.
   a. Call a child to the front of the class. Give him one book. **How many books does [Donald] have?** Write 1 on the chalkboard.
   b. Make a motion with your hand as though to take back the book, but leave it in the child's hand. **How many books did I take away from [Donald]?** Write 0 below the 1 on the board.
   c. Put a minus sign beside the 0. **How many books does [Donald] have now?** Draw an equal line under the problem, and write 1 below it.
   d. Let the child take his seat. Trace the problem three times as the class repeats **1 take away 0 equals 1.**
   e. Call another child to the front of the class to hold the book. **How many books does [Emma] have?** Write 1 on the chalkboard.
   f. Take the book from the child. **How many books did I take away?** Write 1 below the other 1. Put a minus sign beside it.
   g. **How many books does [Emma] have now?** Draw an equal line under the problem, and write 0 below it.
   h. Trace the fact three times as the class repeats **1 take away 1 equals 0.**
2. **Can you count backward?** Let individuals count down from 10 to 0.

Practice Sheets

- ☐ Writing Practice #19
- ● Number Facts #13
- ● Fact Houses #13

Objectives

New

TEACHING

Oral story problems
Subtraction Family 1

Review

Addition facts
More (including 60's)

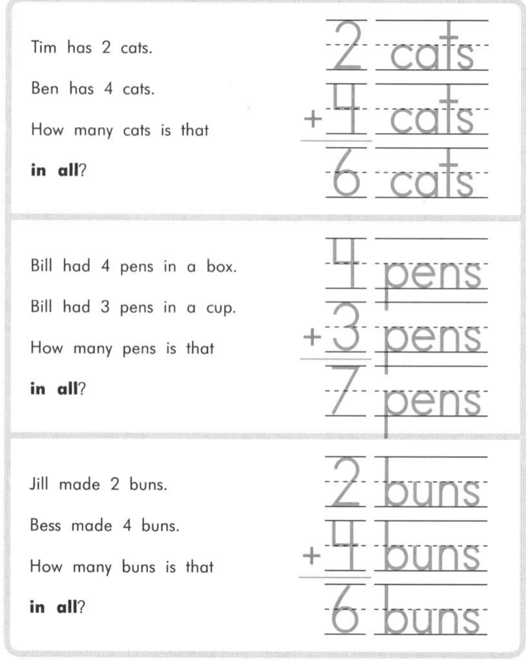

55 Read each sentence.
Then write the numbers that tell how many and the words that tell what.
Then write how many there are in all.

Tim has 2 cats.	2	cats
Ben has 4 cats.	+ 4	cats
How many cats is that **in all**?	6	cats
Bill had 4 pens in a box.	4	pens
Bill had 3 pens in a cup.	+ 3	pens
How many pens is that **in all**?	7	pens
Jill made 2 buns.	2	buns
Bess made 4 buns.	+ 4	buns
How many buns is that **in all**?	6	buns

114

Preparation

Materials

Addition Families 4–7 flash cards

Form C for each child

Chalkboard

(Addition grid from Lesson 53 for *Class Time* #2 and *Follow-up* drill)

(*Class Time* #3)

__ ______
__ ______
__ ______

(*Class Time* #4)

(*Class Time* #5)

47	57	65	56
63	68	52	62
51	50	67	69
60	50	58	63

Class Time

1. *Review Addition Family 7.*
   Ask a child to move the blocks as everyone says Family 7.
2. *Drill addition facts.*
   a. Stand near the addition grid.
      Answer together.
      Boys, say the answers.
      Girls, say the answers.
   b. Distribute Form C, and use flash cards for Addition Families 4–7.
3. *Story problem.*
   Close your eyes to listen. Jim has 5 pets. Tom has 1 pet. How many pets is that *in all?* Open your eyes. What shall I write on the blanks?
4. *Teach Subtraction Family 1.*
   a. Place 1 block on the flannel board. **One block. If I take away 0 blocks, how many will be left?**

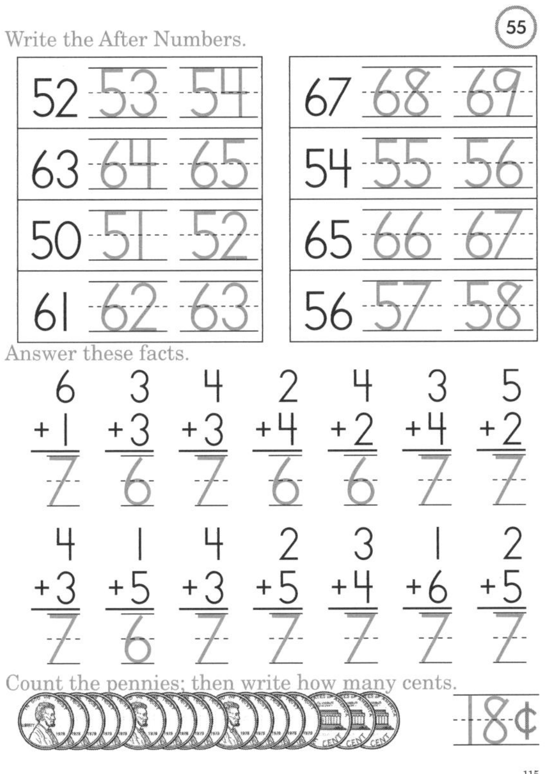

b. Write 1 - 0 = 1 in the first house. Trace the fact as the children repeat it three times.

c. Turn back to the flannel board. **One block.** Move the block to a corner of the board as you say, **If I take away 1, how many are left?**

d. Write 1 - 1 = 0 in the second house. Trace and repeat three times.

5. *More.*
   Do the chalkboard samples.

6. *Assign Lesson 55.*

Follow-up

Drill

(*Drill* #1)

1. Have the children write 1¢ in each circle and count the pennies.
2. Drill individuals at the addition grid. Keep the grid for Lesson 56.
3. **Count 1–100.**

Practice Sheets

- ● Form C (*Class Time* #2)
- □ Fact Houses #13
- □ More Numbers #8
- ● Number Facts #13
- ● Missing Numbers #6
- ◊ Extra: Draw and color a picture for one of the story problems.

Objectives

New

TEACHING

Subtraction Family 2

WORKBOOK

Subtraction Family 1

Review

Oral story problems
Numbers 18–60
Counting (99)

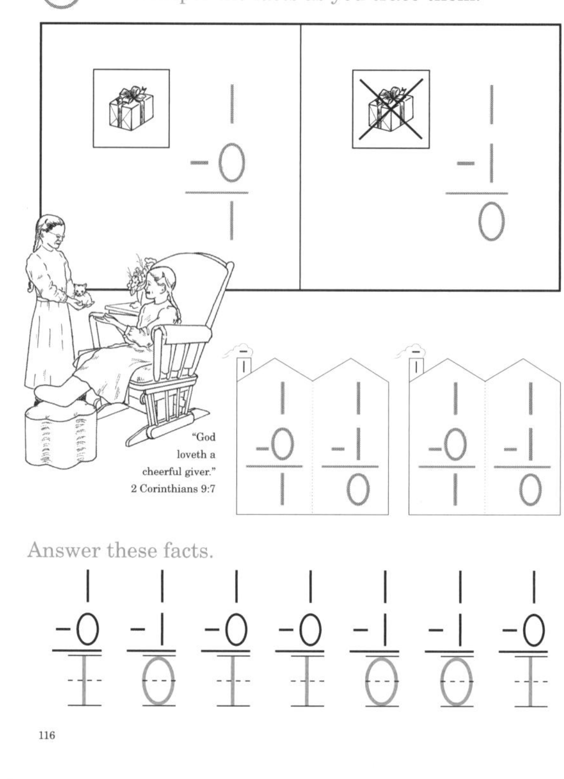

Preparation

Make Subtraction Family 1 flash cards for each child.

Materials

Number flash cards 18–60

Chalkboard

(*Class Time* #1)

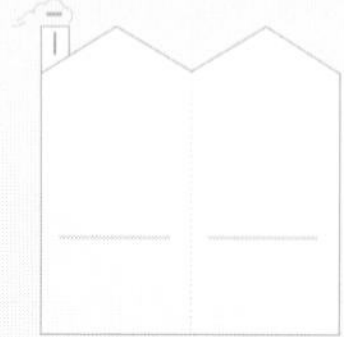

(*Class Time* #2)

Class Time

1. *Review Subtraction Family 1.*
   Call the children to the flannel board.
   a. Place 1 block on the flannel board. **One block. If I take away 0 blocks, how many will be left?**
   b. Write 1 - 0 = 1 in the first house. **1 take away 0 equals 1.** Repeat three times.
   c. Turn back to the flannel board. **1 block.** Move the block to a corner. **When I take away 1 block, how many are left?**
   d. Write 1 - 1 = 0 in the second house. **1 take away 1 equals 0 . . .**

Write the Before and After numbers. (56)

52	53	54	66	67	68
55	56	57	60	61	62
53	54	55	65	66	67
54	55	56	61	62	63

Circle More.

• ⁙ more	54 (62)	59 (67)	(64) 58
(63) 58	53 (61)	(64) 57	(67) 66

Do the story problem.

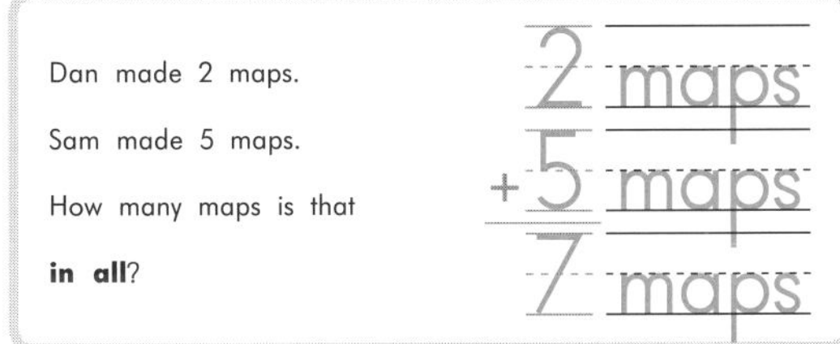

117

2. *Story problem.*
   Close your eyes. Tim has 2 tops. Ben has 3 tops. How many tops is that *in all?* Open your eyes. What shall I write on the blanks?
3. *Number recognition.*
   Flash Number cards 18–60.
4. *Counting.*
   Say all the 2-digit numbers.
5. *Do Speed Drill #15.*
6. *Assign Lesson 56.*

Speed Drill Answers

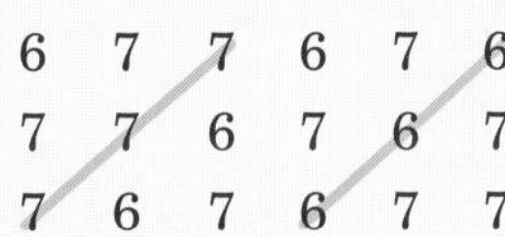

Follow-up

Drill

(*Drill* #3)

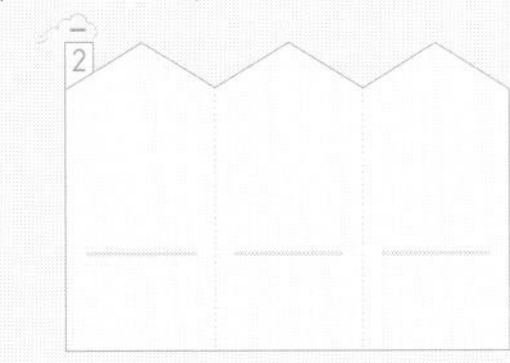

1. Give each child his Subtraction Family 1 flash cards.
2. Drill individuals at the addition grid from Lesson 53. Can each child answer all the facts in one minute?
3. Introduce Subtraction Family 2. Call the children to the flannel board with 2 felt blocks on it.
   a. **2 blocks. If I take 0 blocks away, there are 2 left.** Write 2 - 0 = 2 in the first house.
   b. **2 blocks.** Move 1 block. **Take away 1. 1 block left.** Write 2 - 1 = 1 in the second house.
   c. Put the 2 blocks together again. **2 blocks.** Move them both. **Take away 2. 0 blocks left.** Write 2 - 2 = 0 in the third house.
   d. Point to the houses. **We will say each fact three times.**

Practice Sheets

- ☐ Number Trains #2
- ☐ Writing Practice #20
- ● Form F: 1–69
- ● Less Numbers #8
- ◊ Dot-to-Dot #23

Objectives

New

TEACHING

Subtraction Family 2
Count by 10's
Horizontal addition

Review

Counting (100)
Subtraction Family 1
Column addition

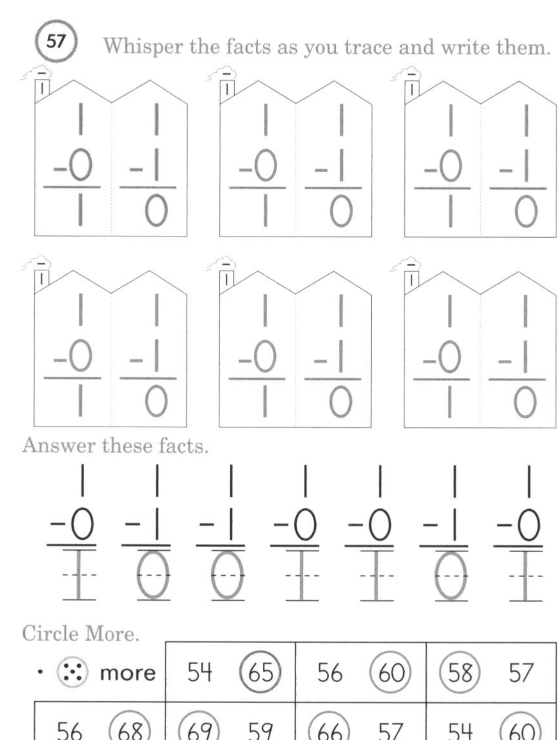

Preparation

Tack Subtraction Family 1 flash cards above the flannel board, with answers showing.

Mount purple triangles above the 10's in the number line. (See pattern on page 600.)

Materials

Number flash cards 10–100

Chalkboard

(*Class Time* #3) (*Class Time* #4)

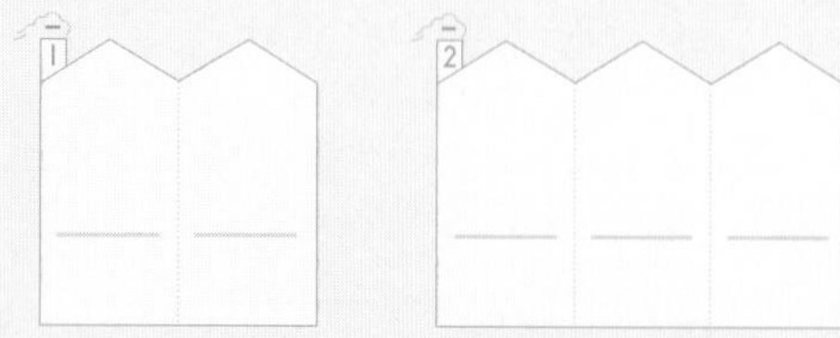

(*Class Time* #5)

2	4	1	1	3
3	2	5	3	3
+ 1	+ 1	+ 1	+ 1	+ 1

Class Time

1. *Counting.*
   a. Call the children to the number line. **Count by 1's to 100.**
   b. **When we count by 1's, we say every number.**
2. *Count by 10's.*
   a. **We can count faster if we do not say every number.** Point to the purple triangles. **10, 20, 30, . . . 100.**
   b. **Count two times with me. 10, 20, . . .**
   c. **How many fingers are in our class?** Have the children (ten or less) stand in a row and hold up both hands with their fingers spread. Point to each finger and thumb, counting by ones. Emphasize the tens number as you say the last number for each child.
   d. Count them again, counting by tens.
3. *Review Subtraction Family 1.*
   a. Call the children to the flannel board. **Say Subtraction Family 1 as I move the blocks.**
   b. **Say Family 1 as I fill the houses.**

Write the Before Numbers. (57)

61 62	58 59	67 68
56 57	62 63	55 56
65 66	54 55	63 64
50 51	66 67	57 58

Answer these facts.

1	3	2	4	1	2	2
5	3	2	2	4	3	4
+ 1	+ 1	+ 1	+ 1	+ 1	+ 1	+ 1
7	7	5	7	6	6	7

Do the story problem.

Beth has 5 buds in a cup.

Beth has 1 bud in a jug.

How many buds is that **in all**?

5 buds
+ 1 bud
6 buds

119

c. Point to the flash cards above the flannel board. **Say each fact three times.**

4. *Teach Subtraction Family 2.*
   a. **2 blocks. If I take 0 blocks away, there are 2 left.** Write 2 - 0 = 2 in the first house.
   b. **2 blocks. Take away 1.** (Move 1 block.) **1 block left.** Write 2 - 1 = 1 in the second house.
   c. Place the 2 blocks together again. **2 blocks. Take 2 away.** (Move them both.) **0 blocks left.** Write 2 - 2 = 0 in the third house.
   d. Point to the houses. **Say Family 2 with me.**
5. *Column addition.*
   Do the chalkboard samples.
6. *Assign Lesson 57.*

Follow-up

Drill

1. Pass out Number flash cards 10–100. **Who has the 10? Who has the number that comes next?** Have each child come, hold his card below his chin, and say his number. After 20, count by 10's.
2. Introduce horizontal addition.
   a. Write this vertical fact on the chalkboard. **Read this fact with me. 2 plus 5 equals 7. We start at the top and read down. We can also make a number fact go across, like the sentences we read.** Write the horizontal form 2 + 5 = 7. **This is a number sentence.** Point to each part as you read **2 plus 5 equals 7. In a number sentence, the equal line is two short lines instead of one long line.**

   $$\begin{array}{r} 2 \\ +5 \\ \hline 7 \end{array}$$

   b. Write these number sentences. Have the children write the answers and read the sentences.

   2 + 4 =　　5 + 2 =　　3 + 4 =
   2 + 3 =　　4 + 2 =　　4 + 1 =

Practice Sheets

- ☐ Writing Practice #21
- ☐ Missing Numbers #7
- ● Number Facts #14
- ● Before and After #1

Objectives

New

TEACHING

Horizontal addition
Counting pennies (word)
Dime

WORKBOOK

Subtraction Family 2
Count by 10's

Review

Subtraction Family 1

Preparation

Make Subtraction Family 2 flash cards for each child.

Materials

One dime for each child

Chalkboard

(*Class Time #2*)

(*Class Time #3*)

3 + 2 = ___ 4 + 2 = ___
2 + 5 = ___ 3 + 4 = ___
6 + 1 = ___ 4 + 1 = ___

(*Class Time #4*)

3 pennies = ___
2 pennies = ___
8 pennies = ___
6 pennies = ___
1 penny = ___
4 pennies = ___

Class Time

1. *Review Subtraction Family 1.*
   Call the children to the flannel board. **Say Subtraction Family 1 as I move the blocks.**
2. *Practice Subtraction Family 2.*
   a. Place 2 blocks on the flannel board. **2 blocks. If I take away 0 blocks, there are 2 left.** Write 2 - 0 = 2 in the first house.
   b. **2 blocks. Take away 1; 1 block left.** Write 2 - 1 = 1.
   c. **2 blocks. Take away 2; 0 blocks left.** Write 2 - 2 = 0.
   d. Point to the houses. **Say Family 2 with me.**
3. *Horizontal addition.*
   Do the chalkboard samples.
4. *Counting pennies.*
   Do the chalkboard samples.

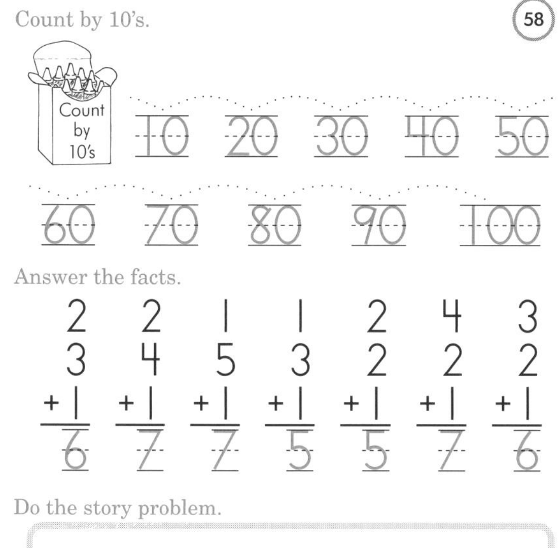

5. *Count by 10's.*
   a. Point to a few consecutive numbers on the number line. **1 number, 1 number, 1 number, . . . When we count by 1's we count *1 number* at a time.**
   b. Point to each purple triangle. **10 numbers, 10 numbers, 10 numbers. When we count by 10's, we count *10 numbers* at a time.**
   c. Count by 10's.
6. *Do Speed Drill #16.*
7. *Assign Lesson 58.*

Speed Drill Answers

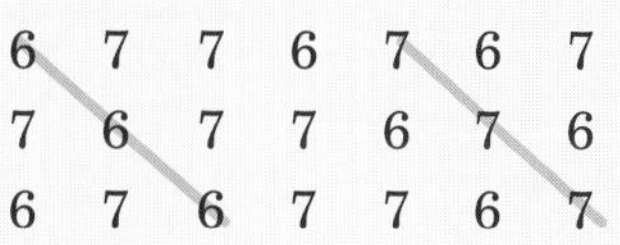

Speed Drill #16

Follow-up

Drill

(*Drill* #2)

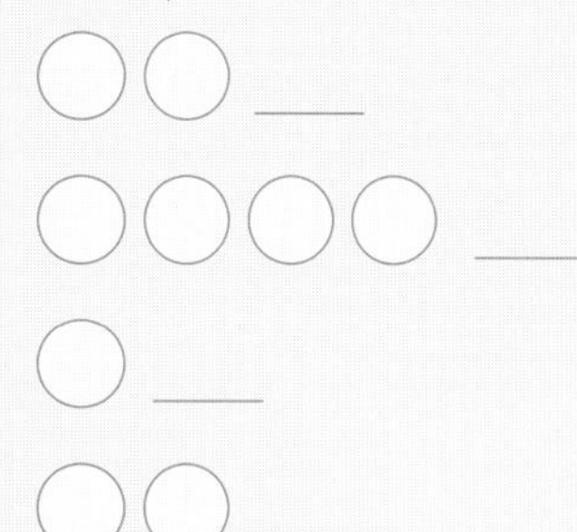

1. Give each child his Subtraction Family 2 flash cards.
2. Introduce the dime. Call the class to the teaching corner, and give each child one dime.
   a. **Look at the picture of the man. This man's name is Franklin D. Roosevelt.**
   b. **What pictures do you see on the back of the dime?** (A torch and sprigs of laurel and oak)
   c. **1 dime is worth 10¢. Say, "Dime, 10¢" as I fill each circle.**
   d. **When we count money, we count by 10's for the dimes. Count with me. 10¢, 20¢, . . .**

Practice Sheets

- ☐ Fact Houses #14
- ☐ Skip Counting #1
- ● Number Facts #14
- ● More Numbers #9

Objectives

New

TEACHING

Counting dimes
Subtraction Family 3

WORKBOOK

Counting pennies (word)

Review

Addition facts
Counting (100)
Count by 10's
Subtraction Family 2

59 Whisper the facts as you trace and write them.

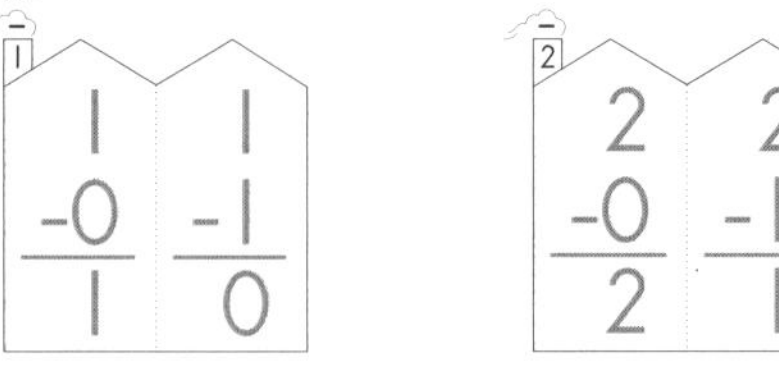

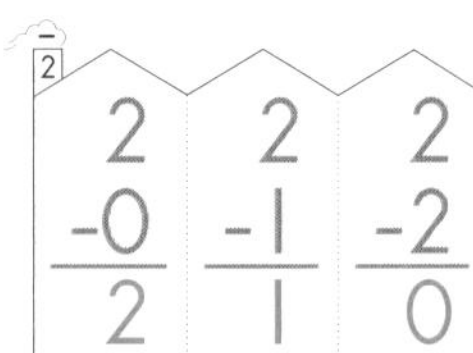

Answer these facts.

2	2	2	1	2	1	2
-0	-2	-1	-1	-1	-0	-0
2	0	1	0	1	1	2

1	1	2	1	2	2	2
-0	-1	-0	-1	-1	-2	-1
1	0	2	0	1	0	1

122

Preparation

Tack Subtraction Family 2 flash cards above the flannel board with answers showing.

Materials

Addition Families 4–7 flash cards

Large dime

Chalkboard

(*Class Time* #2)

3 pennies = ____	6 pennies = ____
5 pennies = ____	2 pennies = ____
8 pennies = ____	9 pennies = ____

(*Class Time* #3)

10¢ ○ ____

10¢ ○ ○ ○ ____

10¢ ○ ○ ○ ○ ____

10¢ ○ ○ ____

(*Class Time* #4)

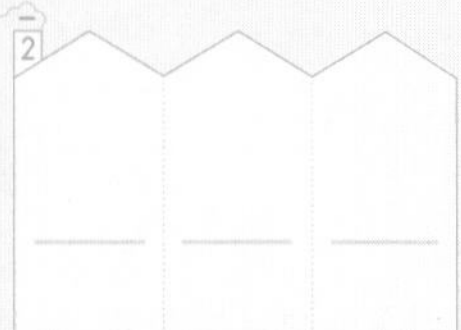

Class Time

1. *Drill addition facts.*
   Circle Drill with Addition Families 4–7 flash cards.
2. *Count by 1's and pennies.*
   a. **Count 1–100 by 1's.**
   b. Do the chalkboard penny samples.
3. *Count by 10's and dimes.*
   a. Point to the purple triangles above the number line. **10 numbers, 10 numbers, . . . When we count by 10's, we jump 10 numbers at a time. We will count 10–100 twice.**
   b. Hold the large dime. **Which coin is this? How much is a dime worth? What color is a dime?**
   c. Do the chalkboard dime samples.

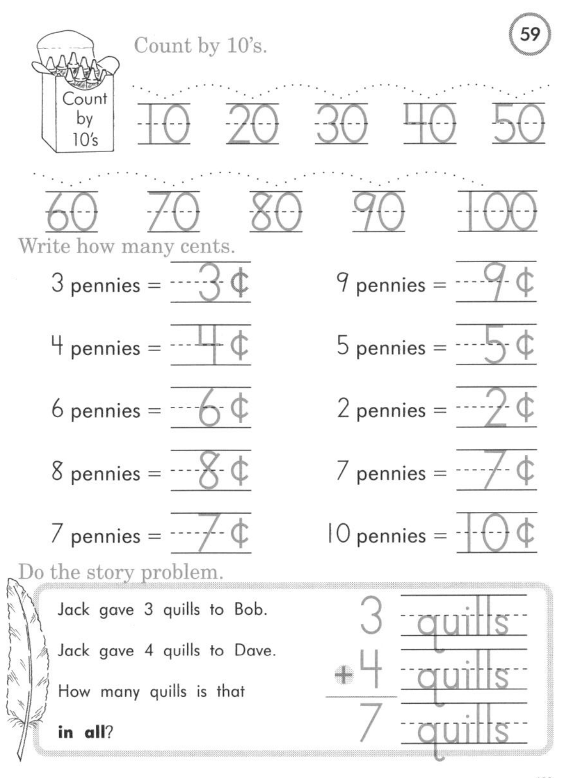

4. *Review Subtraction Family 2.*
   a. **I will move the felt blocks. [Fred] will fill the houses. Everyone will help to say Family 2.**
   b. Point to the flash cards above the flannel board. **Say each fact three times with your eyes open, and then three more times with your eyes closed.**
5. *Assign Lesson 59.*

Follow-up

Drill

(*Drill* #1)

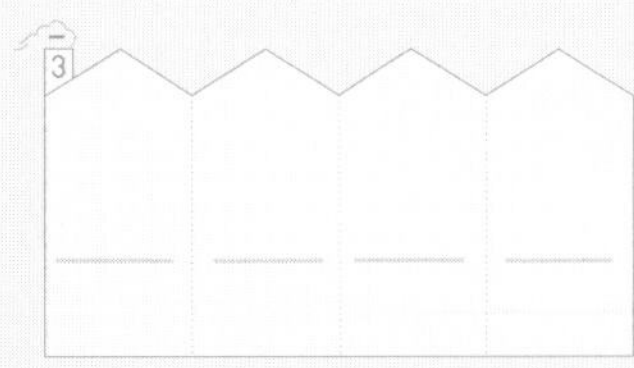

1. Introduce Subtraction Family 3 with the flannel board. Use the divider so the felt blocks can be arranged in clear number groups on both parts of the board.
   a. Place 3 blocks on the lower part of the flannel board. **3 blocks. If I take away 0 blocks, 3 blocks are left.** Write 3 - 0 = 3.
   b. **3 blocks.** Move 1 block above the divider. **Take away 1; 2 blocks left.** Write 3 - 1 = 2.
   c. Begin with 3 blocks in the lower part again. **3 blocks. Take away 2.** (Move 2 blocks above.) **1 block left.** Write 3 - 2 = 1.
   d. **3 blocks. Take away 3; 0 blocks left.** Write 3 - 3 = 0.
   e. Point to the houses. **Say Family 3 together.**
2. **What do you have that God gave you 10 of?** (Fingers and toes.) **Hold up your fingers. We will count them by 10's.** Use the total number in the following blanks.
   _____ **busy fingers to help Mother.**
   _____ **busy fingers to do our lessons.**
   _____ **busy fingers to quietly fold when we pray to God.**

Practice Sheets

- ☐ Fact Houses #14
- ☐ Skip Counting #1
- ☐ Less Numbers #9
- ● Number Facts #14
- ● Before and After #2
- ◊ Dot-to-Dot #24

Objectives

New

TEACHING

Subtraction Family 3
Compare dime and penny

WORKBOOK

Counting dimes

Review

Subtraction Families 1, 2
Count by 10's

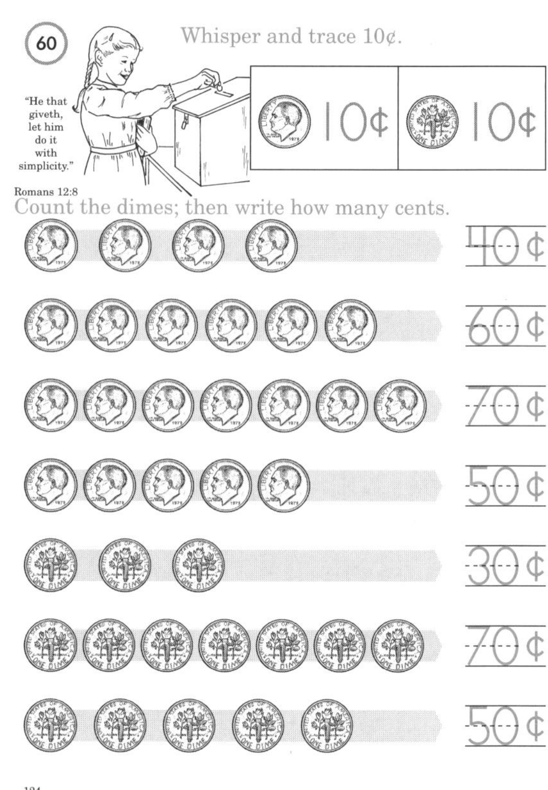

60

"He that giveth, let him do it with simplicity."
Romans 12:8

Whisper and trace 10¢.

10¢ 10¢

Count the dimes; then write how many cents.

40¢
60¢
70¢
50¢
30¢
70¢
50¢

124

Preparation

Materials

One dime and one penny for each child

Form D for each child

Chalkboard

(*Class Time* #2)

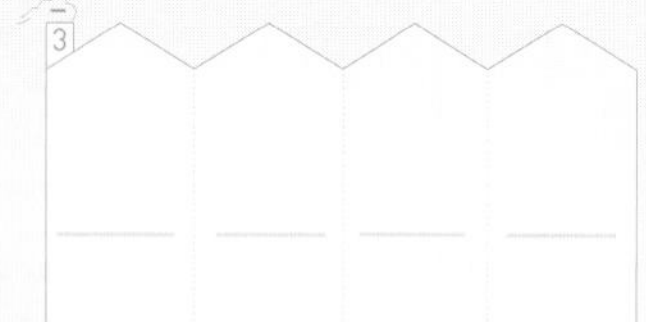

(*Class Time* #4)

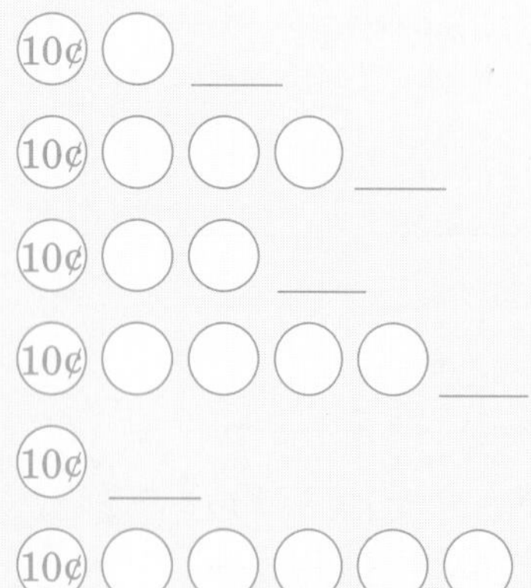

Class Time

1. *Review Subtraction Families 1 and 2.* Call the children to the flannel board. **I will move the blocks. Say Subtraction Family 1 . . . Family 2.**
2. *Teach Subtraction Family 3.*
   a. Place 3 felt blocks on the lower part of the flannel board. **3 blocks. If I take away 0 blocks, 3 blocks are left.** Write 3 - 0 = 3 in the first house.
   b. **3 blocks.** Move 1 block to the upper part as you say, **Take away 1. 2 blocks left.** Write 3 - 1 = 2.
   c. Return the moved block to the lower part of the flannel board. **3 blocks.** Move 2 blocks to the upper part. **Take away 2. 1 block left.** Write 3 - 2 = 1.
   d. Begin with all the blocks in the lower part again. **3 blocks. Take away 3. 0 blocks left.** Write 3 - 3 = 0.
   e. Point to the houses. **Say Family 3 together.**

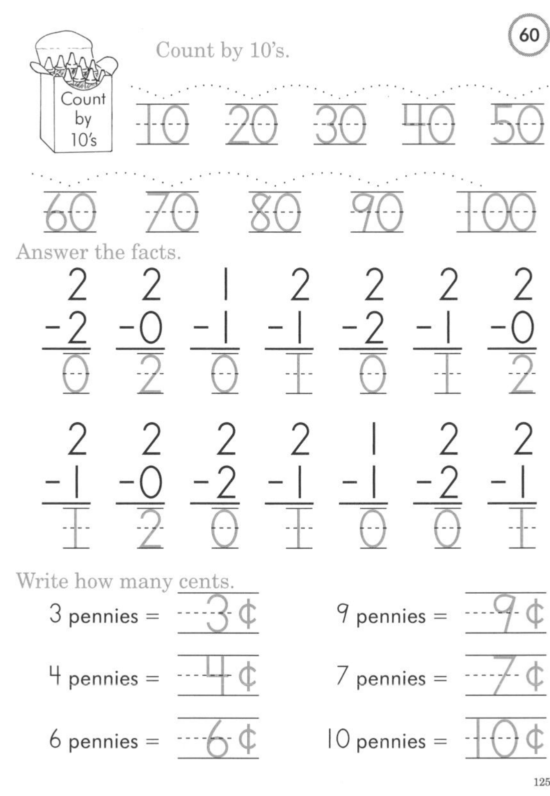

3. *Count by 10's.*
   Stand near the number line.
   a. **Boys, count by 10's to 100.**
   b. **Girls, count by 10's to 100.**
4. *Compare dime and penny.*
   Give each child a dime and a penny.
   a. **Place your dime on top of your penny. Which coin is larger? A penny is larger than a dime! Which coin is worth more? A little dime is worth more than a big penny!**
   b. Have each child stand in turn. He should first hold up his penny and say, **Penny, 1¢;** and then hold up his dime and say, **Dime, 10¢.**
   c. Do the chalkboard dime samples.
5. *Do Speed Drill #17.*
6. *Assign Lesson 60.*

Speed Drill Answers

5	7	6	7	7	6	5
7	6	7	5	7	7	6
6	7	5	5	5	7	7

Speed Drill #17

Follow-up

Drill

1. Distribute Form D for story problems. Print *hens* on the chalkboard for reference so the children do not need to concentrate on phonics.

Note: This exercise is valuable for developing skill in computing story problem, but it can be time-consuming for the teacher. See page 364 for hints on saving teacher time.

   Listen to the story. Write the numbers and the words that the story tells about. Put a plus in the gray spot when you hear the words *in all.*
   a. **Arrow Box: Ben has 4 hens.** (Pause for this information to be written.) **Sam has 3 hens.** (Pause.) **How many hens is that *in all?***
   b. **Button Box: Dorcas has 3 hens. Tim has 2 hens. How many hens is that *in all?***
   c. **Camel Box: Joe saw 4 hens in the yard. He saw 2 hens in the garden. How many hens is that *in all?***
   d. **Daffodil Box: 5 hens pecked seeds on the ground. 2 hens pecked bugs. How many . . .**
   e. **Elephant Box: Ben has 3 hens with baby chicks. He has 3 more hens sitting on eggs. How many . . .**
   f. **Feather Box: Sam has 3 white hens. He has 4 red hens. How many . . .**
2. Have individuals move the felt blocks and say Subtraction Family 3.

Practice Sheets

- Form D (*Follow-up* drill #1)
- ☐ Skip Counting #1
- Number Facts #15

Objectives

New

WORKBOOK

Subtraction Family 3

Review

Subtraction facts

Dime

Before and After (70's, 80's)

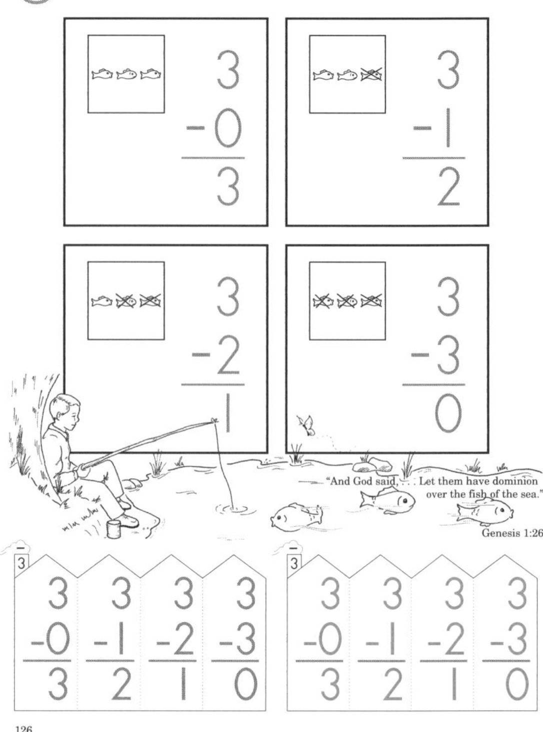

Preparation

Make Subtraction Family 3 flash cards for each child.

Materials

Large dime

Subtraction Families 1–3 flash cards

Chalkboard

(*Class Time* #1)

(*Class Time* #3)

__ 74 __	__ 86 __
__ 78 __	__ 83 __
__ 75 __	__ 88 __
__ 71 __	__ 85 __

Class Time

1. *Review Subtraction Families 1–3.*
   a. **Say Family 2 as I fill the houses. 2 - 0 = 2, 2 - 1 = 1, . . .**
   b. **Say Family 3 as I fill the houses. 3 - 0 = 3, 3 - 1 = 2, . . .**
   c. Ask a child to move the felt blocks as you say Family 3 together.
2. *Review dime.*
   a. Display the large dime. **How much is a dime worth? Whose picture is on a dime?** (Franklin D. Roosevelt)
   b. **What can we do with a dime on Sunday morning?** We can take it along to church and drop it into the offering basket. **God sees each little dime that drops into the basket. It is a gift to God.**
   c. Have each child stand and say, **Dime, 10¢.**

3. *Before and After, in 70's and 80's.* Do the chalkboard samples.
4. *Numbers in 70's and 80's.* Chalkboard drill: **Write the number I say: 82, 73, 69, 85, 70, 77, 84, 81, 75, 88, 76**
5. *Assign Lesson 61.*

Follow-up

Drill

1. Give each child his Subtraction Family 3 flash cards.
2. Drill individuals with Subtraction Families 1–3 flash cards.
3. Review the meaning of 1-digit and 2-digit numbers. **8 is a 1-digit number. 83 is a 2-digit number. What do you think 100 is?**

Practice Sheets

- ☐ Fact Houses #15
- ☐ Missing Numbers #8
- ● Skip Counting #1
- ● More Numbers #10
- ◊ Dot-to-Dot #25

Objectives

New

TEACHING
Clock face

Review

Subtraction facts
Counting dimes
More and Less (70's, 80's)

Preparation

Tack Subtraction Family 3 flash cards with answers above the flannel board.

Materials

Subtraction Families 1–3 flash cards

One dime for each child

Model clock—An ideal clock to use for displaying time is an old clock that you can set by pushing the minute hand. If you always spin the minute hand the whole way around to move the hand from one number to the next, it will help the children understand how the hands relate.

Chalkboard

(*Class Time* #2)

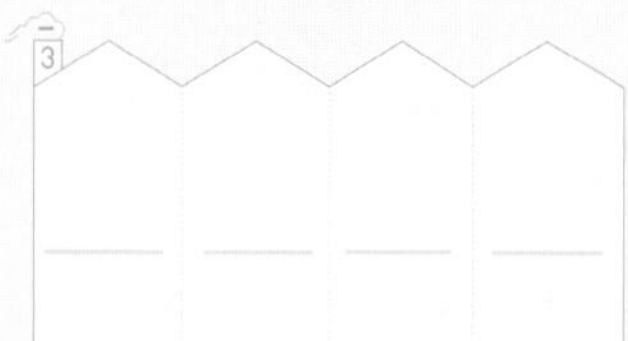

(*Class Time* #5)

82	73	75	85
84	88	78	87

81	80	73	75
84	74	79	89

(62) Whisper the facts as you trace and write them.

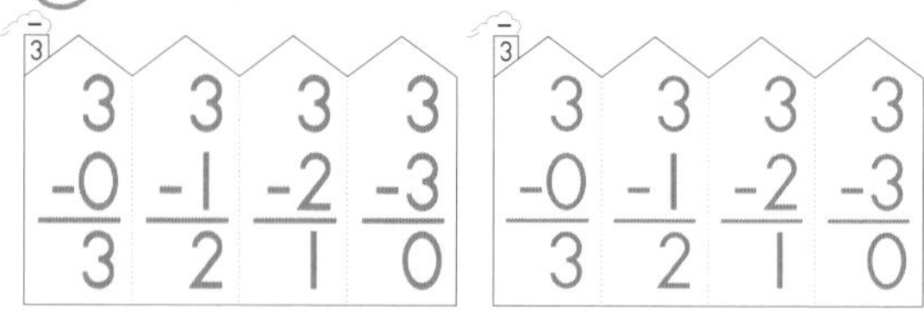

3 − 0 = 3 3 − 1 = 2 3 − 2 = 1 3 − 3 = 0 | 3 − 0 = 3 3 − 1 = 2 3 − 2 = 1 3 − 3 = 0

Answer the facts.

3 − 1 = 2 3 − 2 = 1 3 − 1 = 2 2 − 1 = 1 3 − 3 = 0 2 − 1 = 1 3 − 2 = 1

3 − 0 = 3 1 − 1 = 0 2 − 0 = 2 3 − 2 = 1 2 − 0 = 2 3 − 2 = 1 2 − 2 = 0

128

Class Time

1. *Drill subtraction facts.*
   Double Drill with Subtraction Families 1–3 flash cards.
2. *Practice Subtraction Family 3.*
   a. Place 3 felt blocks on the lower part of the flannel board, and move them according to the story facts as you say them.
      (1) **Three red beets grow in the garden. If Mother takes away 0 red beets, 3 beets are left. Three beets take away 0 beets equals 3 beets.**
      (2) **Three beets grow in the garden. If Mother pulls 1 beet, 2 beets are left. Say the story fact with me. Three beets take away 1 beet equals 2 beets.**
      (3) **Three beets grow in the garden. If Mother pulls 2 beets, 1 beet is left. Three beets take away 2 beets equals 1 beet.**
      (4) **Three beets grow in the garden. If Mother pulls 3 beets, 0 beets are left. Three beets take away 3 beets equals 0 beets.**

b. Ask a child to fill the houses as everyone says Family 3.
c. Point to the flash cards above the flannel board. **Say each fact three times.**

3. *Review dime.*
   a. Give each child a dime. **Feel the edge of the dime.**
   b. Have each child stand and say, **Dime, 10¢.**
4. *Counting dimes.*
   a. **If you saved a dime in your penny bank, how many cents did you save? If you saved 2 dimes, how many cents did you save? Hold up 2 fingers to stand for 2 dimes. 10¢, 20¢.**
   b. Continue with

3 dimes	**2 dimes**
4 dimes	**5 dimes**

5. *More and Less.*
   Do the chalkboard samples.
6. *Do Speed Drill #18.*
7. *Assign Lesson 62.*

Speed Drill Answers

6	7	5	6	7	6	5
7	6	7	5	6	7	6
7	7	6	7	5	6	7

Follow-up

Drill

(*Drill* #2)

1. Introduce the clock.
   Call the children to the teaching corner. Hold the model clock. **Say the numbers around the clock with me.**
2. Use white chalk to put numbers in the circle on the board.
   a. Write 12. **12 is the greatest number on the clock. 12 stands at the top.**
   b. Write 6. **6 curls up at the bottom of the clock.**
   c. Write 3. **3 is on the right.**
   d. Write 9. **9 is on the left.**
   e. Fill in the missing numbers.
3. Use green chalk to draw the hour hand pointing to 1. **The small hand on a clock is the hour hand. It moves very slowly and takes all day to go around the clock one time. The hour hand shows us what hour the time is.** Show the children the position of the hour hand on the classroom clock. If this is done near the end of the day, refer to the clock frequently tomorrow to point out the position of the hour hand.

Practice Sheets

- ☐ Fact Houses #15
- ☐ Money #4
- ● Number Facts #15
- ● Less Numbers #10

Objectives

New

TEACHING

Clock face

Telling time

Review

Count by 10's

Subtraction facts

Before and After (70's, 80's)

(63) Whisper the facts as you trace and write them.

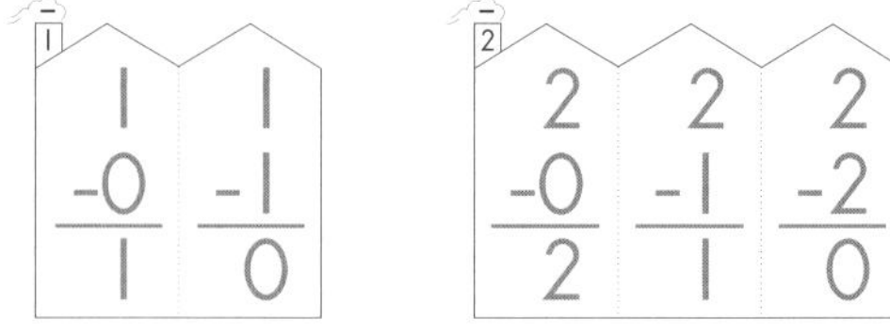

3	3	3	3
-0	-1	-2	-3
3	2	1	0

3	3	3	3
-0	-1	-2	-3
3	2	1	0

Answer these facts.

2	3	3	2	3	2	3
-0	-2	-1	-1	-3	-1	-0
2	1	2	1	0	1	3

3	2	2	3	3	3	2
-2	-1	-0	-2	-1	-2	-2
1	1	2	1	2	1	0

130

Preparation

Materials

Model clock

Subtraction Families 1–3 flash cards

Chalkboard

(*Class Time* #2)

(*Class Time* #4)

___ 77 ___	___ 88 ___
___ 82 ___	___ 74 ___
___ 86 ___	___ 78 ___
___ 71 ___	___ 85 ___

Class Time

1. *Count by 10's.*
   Call the children to the number line. **Let's count by 10's to 100 twice.**
2. *Teach the clock.*
   a. Use white chalk, and let the children tell you which numbers to fill in the circle on the board. **Which number stands at the top?** 12
   curls at the bottom? 6
   is on the right? 3
   is on the left? 9
   Fill in the missing numbers.
   b. Use green chalk to draw the hour hand pointing to 1. **What is the name of this hand? The hour hand is short and very slow. The hour hand tells us what hour the time is.**
   c. Use yellow chalk to draw the minute hand pointing to 12. **This is the minute hand. The minute hand is larger. The minute hand moves faster. The minute hand goes the whole way around the clock while**

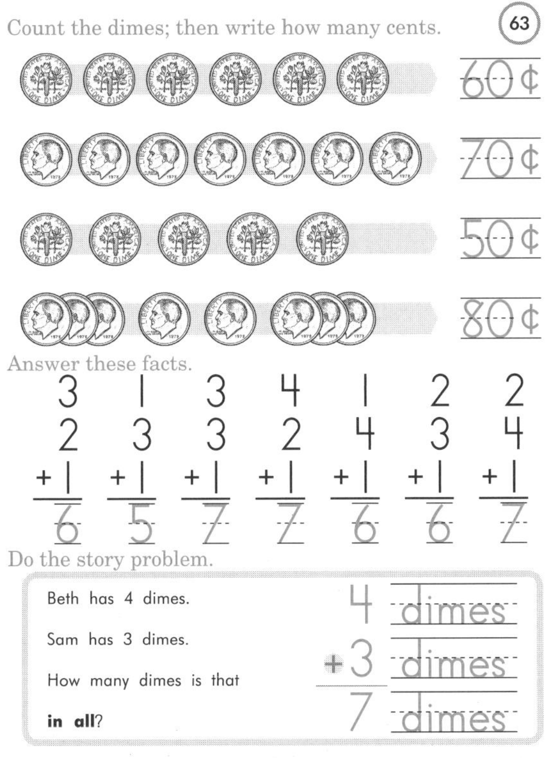

the hour hand moves just one number.

d. **This clock says one o'clock. The minute hand points straight up when it is one o'clock. This is how to write one o'clock.** Write 1:00. **The hour is 1, and the zeros show that it is zero minutes after the hour.**

3. *Review Subtraction Families 1–3.*
   a. **I will move the felt blocks. Say Subtraction Family 1 . . . 2 . . . 3.**
   b. Point to the first flash card above the flannel board. **Look at the fact. Then close your eyes and say it three times.** Treat each fact in the same way.
4. *Before and After, in 70's and 80's.* Do the chalkboard samples.
5. *Assign Lesson 63.*

Follow-up

Drill

1. Hold the model clock. **Read the time together.** Set the hands at 3:00, 6:00, 8:00, 4:00, 9:00, 2:00, 7:00, 11:00.
2. Drill individuals with Subtraction Families 1–3 flash cards.

Practice Sheets

- □ Fact Houses #16
- ● Number Facts #16
- ● Money #5
- ◊ Dot-to-Dot #26

Objectives

New

TEACHING

- Telling time
- After Numbers by 10's
- *Subtraction Family 4*

WORKBOOK

- Telling time

Review

- Subtraction facts
- Count by 10's

64 Read the times together.
Tell what each child is doing.

Write the time.

132

Preparation

Make a 2-inch square card with :00 on it. Tape it above the 12 on your classroom clock.

Materials

Model clock

Subtraction Families 1–3 flash cards

Subtraction Families 1–3 flash cards

Chalkboard

(*Class Time* #1)

___ :00	___ :00
___ :00	___ :00
___ :00	___ :00
___ :00	___ :00

(*Class Time* #3)

10 ___	30 ___
50 ___	60 ___
80 ___	20 ___
40 ___	70 ___

Class Time

1. *Clock practice.*
   a. Call the children to the teaching corner. **I am thinking of something that is in your house. It might be in the kitchen, living room, or bedroom. It tells us something with its hands. What is it?**
   b. Hold the model clock. Point to the hour hand. **Tell me something about this hand.** (It is the hour hand. It is small and very slow. It tells us what hour the time is.)
   c. Point to the minute hand. **Tell me something about this hand.** (It is the minute hand. It is large and moves faster.)
   d. Set the hands at 1:00. **[Janet], stand and read the time. Fill in the first blank on the chalkboard.** Move the hands until the children have completed all the samples.
2. *Review Subtraction Families 1–3.*
   a. Give your Subtraction Families 1–3 flash cards to the children. **Who has**

Answer these facts. (64)

3 − 1 = 2 3 − 2 = 1 1 − 1 = 0 2 − 1 = 1 3 − 2 = 1 2 − 1 = 1 3 − 2 = 1

1 − 0 = 1 3 − 2 = 1 2 − 0 = 2 2 − 1 = 1 2 − 2 = 0 2 − 1 = 1 3 − 2 = 1

3 − 1 = 2 2 − 0 = 2 3 − 1 = 2 2 − 1 = 1 3 − 3 = 0 2 − 1 = 1 3 − 2 = 1

3 − 0 = 3 3 − 2 = 1 2 − 2 = 0 2 − 1 = 1 3 − 2 = 1 2 − 0 = 2 3 − 2 = 1

133

the first fact in Family 1? Come set it on the chalk tray.**

b. Continue with Families 2 and 3.

c. Stand near the cards. **Let's say our subtraction families together.**

3. *Count by 10's.*
   a. **Count by 10's to 100. 10, 20, . . .**
   b. **What number comes after when we count by 10's?** Do the chalkboard samples.

4. *Do Speed Drill #19.*

5. *Assign Lesson 64.*

Speed Drill Answers

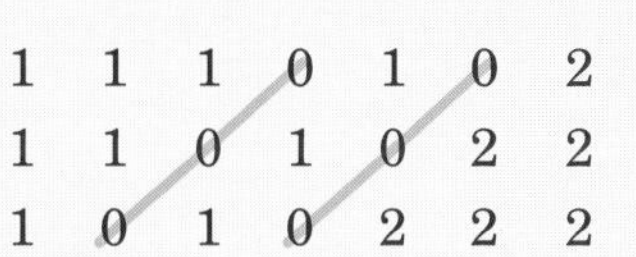

1	1	1	0	1	0	2
1	1	0	1	0	2	2
1	0	1	0	2	2	2

Follow-up

Drill

(*Drill* #2)

84	73	86	89
75	85	79	80
82	81	89	86

(*Drill* #3)

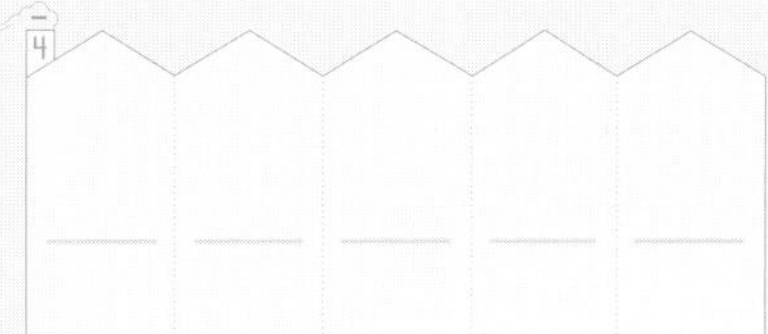

1. Drill individuals with Subtraction Families 1–3 flash cards.
2. Do the Less Number samples.
3. Introduce Subtraction Family 4. Place 4 blocks on the flannel board.
   a. **4 blocks. If I take away 0 blocks, 4 blocks are left.** Write the fact.
   b. **4 blocks. Take away 1; 3 blocks left . . .**

Practice Sheets

- ☐ Fact Houses #16
- ☐ Money #4
- ☐ More Numbers #11
- ● Number Facts #16
- ● Missing Numbers #9

Objectives

New

TEACHING

Subtraction Family 4

Review

Subtraction facts
Telling time
Count by 10's
More (80's, 90's)

(65) Answer these facts.

2 − 0 = 2	3 − 2 = 1	3 − 3 = 0	2 − 1 = 1	3 − 2 = 1	2 − 1 = 1	3 − 2 = 1
3 − 2 = 1	3 − 1 = 2	3 − 2 = 1		2 − 0 = 2	3 − 2 = 1	2 − 0 = 2
3 − 1 = 2	1 − 0 = 1	3 − 2 = 1	2 − 1 = 1	1 − 1 = 0	2 − 1 = 1	3 − 2 = 1
3 − 2 = 1	2 − 2 = 0	3 − 0 = 3	2 − 1 = 1	2 − 2 = 0	2 − 1 = 1	3 − 1 = 2

134

Preparation

Materials

Subtraction Families 1–3 flash cards
Model clock
Form D for each child

Chalkboard

(*Class Time* #2)

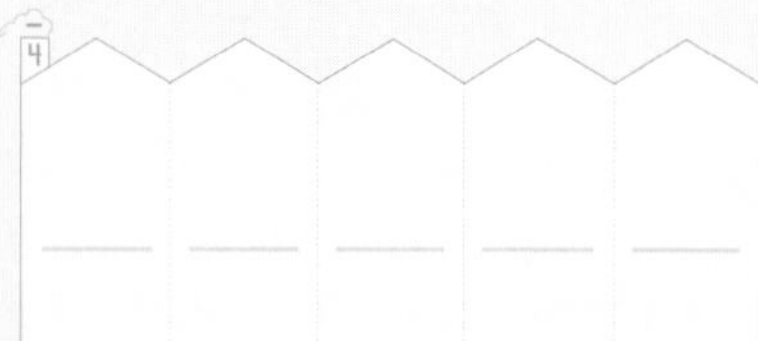

(*Class Time* #5)

85	95	92	91
96	94	83	93
97	99	85	87
90	89	82	85

Class Time

1. *Drill subtraction facts.*
   Circle Drill with Subtraction Families 1–3 flash cards.
2. *Teach Subtraction Family 4.*
   a. Place 4 felt blocks on the lower part of the flannel board. **4 blocks. If I take away 0 blocks, 4 blocks are left.** Write the fact in the first house.
   b. **4 blocks. Take away 1 block.** (Move 1 block to the upper part.) **3 blocks left. 4 - 1 = 3.** Write the fact.
   c. Continue until all the houses are filled.
3. *Clock practice.*
   a. Hold the model clock. Set the hands at 5:00. **The zeros mean that it is exactly 5 o'clock.**
   It is not one minute before 5.
   It is not one minute after 5.
   It is exactly 5:00.

65

Write the time.

1:00 3:00 10:00 6:00

12:00 7:00 4:00 5:00

Count by 10's.

Count by 10's

10 20 30 40 50

60 70 80 90 100

Count the dimes; then write how many cents.

50¢

70¢

135

b. Set the hands at 9:00. **[Kenneth], stand and read the time. Write it on the board.** Continue around the class.

4. *Count by 10's.*
   When we count by 10's, how many numbers do we jump at a time?
   a. **Boys, count by 10's.**
   b. **Girls, count by 10's.**
5. *More Numbers, in 80's and 90's.*
   Do the chalkboard samples.
6. *Assign Lesson 65.*

Follow-up

Drill

1. Distribute Form D for story problems. Print these label words on the chalkboard. *goats* *sheep*

Note: See page 364 for tips on saving teacher time.

Listen to the whole story. Write the numbers and words that the story tells about. Put a plus in the gray spot when you hear the words *in all*.
   a. **Arrow Box: Dan has 3 sheep. Ross has 2 sheep. How many sheep is that *in all?***
   b. **Button Box: Tom has 5 goats. Jim has 2 goats. How many goats is that *in all?***
   c. **Camel Box: Tim had 4 goats. He got 3 more goats. How many goats is that *in all?***
   d. **Daffodil Box: John had 6 sheep. He got 1 more sheep. How many sheep is that *in all?***
   e. **Elephant Box: Fred has 2 sheep. Dan has 3 sheep. How many sheep is that *in all?***
   f. **Feather Box: Sam had 3 goats. He got 4 more goats. How many goats is that *in all?***
2. Have individuals move the felt blocks and say Subtraction Family 4.

Practice Sheets

- ● Form D (*Follow-up* drill #1)
- ☐ Fact Houses #16
- ☐ Number Trains #3
- ● Less Numbers #11
- ◊ Dot-to-Dot #27

Objectives

New

TEACHING

Count by 5's

WORKBOOK

Subtraction Family 4

Review

Subtraction facts
Count by 10's
After, by 10's
Telling time

Preparation

Make Subtraction Family 4 flash cards for each child.

Mount pink triangles above the 5's in the number line. See pattern on page 600.

Materials

Model clock

Subtraction Families 1–3 flash cards

Chalkboard

(*Class Time* #2)

(*Class Time* #3)

40 ___ 60 ___
80 ___ 10 ___
20 ___ 50 ___
70 ___ 30 ___

Class Time

1. *Review Subtraction Families 1–3.*
   I will move the blocks. Say Subtraction Family 1 . . . 2 . . . 3.
2. *Practice Subtraction Family 4.*
   a. Place 4 blocks on the lower part of the flannel board.
      (1) **Amos had 4 cookies. He ate 0 cookies. Amos had 4 cookies left. Four cookies take away 0 cookies equals 4 cookies.**
      (2) **Bob had 4 cookies. He ate 1 cookie. Bob had 3 cookies left. Four cookies take away 1 cookie equals 3 cookies. Say the story fact with me.**
      (3) Return the moved block to the bottom part of the flannel board. **Carl had 4 cookies. He ate 2 cookies. Carl had 2 cookies left.**
      (4) **Dean had 4 cookies. He ate 3 cookies. . . .**
      (5) **Ezra had 4 cookies. . . .**
   b. **Say Family 4 as I fill the houses.**

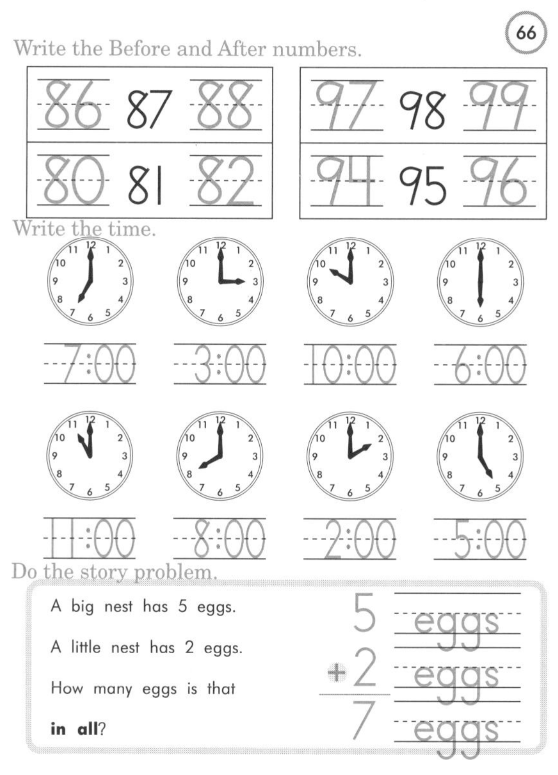
66

Write the Before and After numbers.

86	87	88	97	98	99
80	81	82	94	95	96

Write the time.

7:00 3:00 10:00 6:00

11:00 8:00 2:00 5:00

Do the story problem.

A big nest has 5 eggs.
A little nest has 2 eggs.
How many eggs is that **in all**?

5 eggs
+2 eggs
7 eggs

137

Speed Drill Answers

2	1	0	2	1	3	0
1	2	1	0	2	1	3
3	1	2	1	0	2	1

Speed Drill #20

3. *Count by 10's.*
   a. **Count by 10's to 100.**
   b. **What comes after when we count by 10's?** Do the chalkboard samples.
4. *Clock practice.*
   Hold the model clock. Set the hands at 5:00. **[Lisa], stand and read the time. Write it on the chalkboard.** Continue around the class.
5. *Do Speed Drill #20.*
6. *Assign Lesson 66.*

Follow-up

Drill

1. Give each child his Subtraction Family 4 flash cards.
2. Drill individuals with Subtraction Families 1–3 flash cards.
3. Introduce counting by 5's.
   a. Call the children to the number line.
   We can count by 1's.
   We can count by 10's.
   We can count by 5's too.
   b. Point to the triangles. **5, 10, 15, 20, . . . We are jumping 5 numbers at a time.**
   c. **Count by 5's to 100** twice.

Practice Sheets

☐ Fact Houses #17

☐ Money #3

● Number Facts #17

● Before and After #3

◊ Extra: Money #5—Color the dimes; then cut and paste them back-to-back.

Objectives

New

TEACHING

Count by 5's

Review

Subtraction facts
Telling time
Counting pennies (word)
Dime

67 Whisper each fact as you trace and write it.

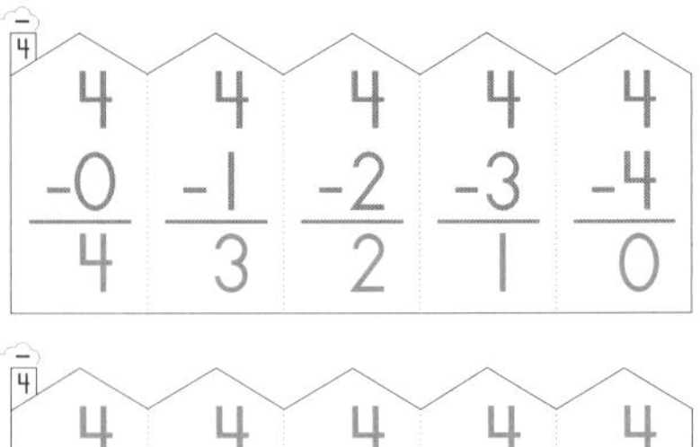

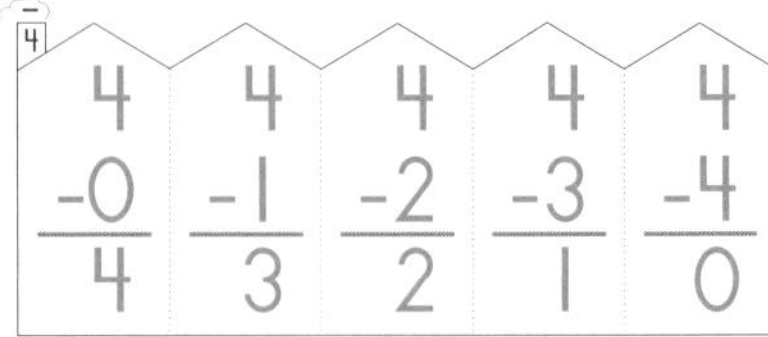

Answer these facts.

4	3	4	3	4	4	3
-3	-2	-2	-2	-1	-3	-1
1	1	2	1	3	1	2

4	4	4	2	4	4	4
-4	-2	-1	-1	-3	-2	-3
0	2	3	1	1	2	1

138

Preparation

Tack Subtraction Family 4 flash cards above the flannel board with answers showing.

Materials

Model clock

Large dime

Subtraction Family 4 flash cards

Chalkboard

(*Class Time* #2)

(*Class Time* #4)

12 pennies = ____ 14 pennies = ____
17 pennies = ____ 19 pennies = ____
10 pennies = ____ 16 pennies = ____
13 pennies = ____ 11 pennies = ____

Class Time

1. *Count by 5's.*
   a. Call the children to the number line. **When we count by 5's, we jump 5 numbers at a time.** Point to the pink and purple triangles. **Every time we come to a triangle, we have 5 more numbers.**
   b. **Count by 5's to 100** twice.
   c. Have the children stand single file and raise both hands with their fingers spread wide. **I will count by 5's to count your fingers.** Pass down one side of the students, counting fingers on their right hands and up the other side, counting the left.
2. *Review Subtraction Family 4.*
   a. Ask a child to move the felt blocks as everyone says Subtraction Family 4.
   b. Point to the flash cards above the flannel board. **Say each fact three times with your eyes open, then three times with your eyes closed.**
   c. **Say Subtraction Family 4 as I fill the houses.**

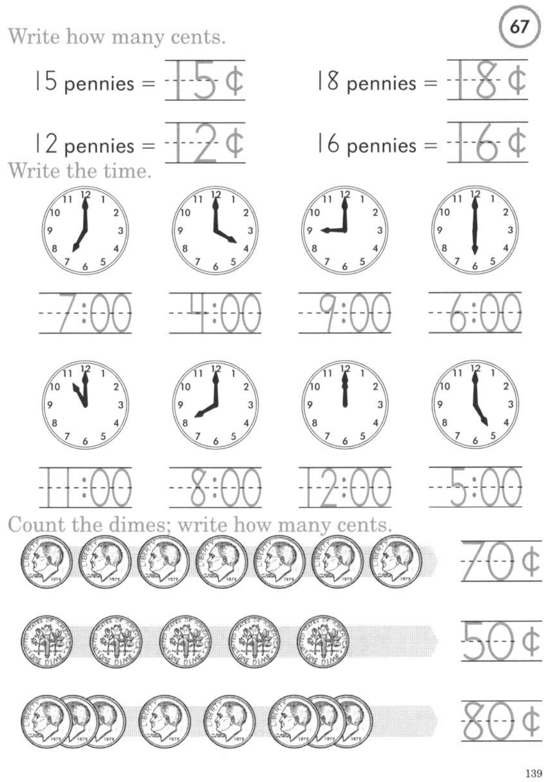

3. *Telling time.*
   Hold the model clock. **Read the time together.** Set the hands at 12:00, 5:00, 9:00, 2:00, 6:00, 11:00, 3:00, 7:00.
4. *Review money.*
   a. **We count pennies by ___.** (1's) Do the chalkboard samples.
   b. Hold the large dime. **How much is a dime worth? We count dimes by ___.** (10's) **What does the edge feel like? Name two things we can do with a dime.**
5. *Assign Lesson 67.*

Follow-up

Drill

(*Drill* #2)

58	61	49	73	85	76
48	36	50	41	52	48
65	67	76	75	55	65

1. Drill individuals with Subtraction Family 4 flash cards.
2. Ask a child to read the three numbers in the first box on the chalkboard. **Which number is less than all the others?** Let someone circle 49. Continue with the rest of the samples.
3. Chalkboard drill: **Write the number I say: 83, 96, 81, 85, 94, 97, 80, 99, 87, 84, 95, 81.**

Practice Sheets

- ☐ Fact Houses #17
- ● Number Facts #17
- ● Money #6
- ◊ Dot-to-Dot #28

Objectives

New

TEACHING

Counting dimes (word)
Nickel

WORKBOOK

Count by 5's

Review

Subtraction facts

(68) Answer these facts.

4 − 3 = 1	4 − 2 = 2	4 − 1 = 3	4 − 3 = 1	4 − 4 = 0	4 − 2 = 2	4 − 0 = 4
4 − 1 = 3	2 − 2 = 0	2 − 0 = 2	4 − 3 = 1	2 − 1 = 1	4 − 2 = 2	4 − 3 = 1
2 − 0 = 2	4 − 1 = 3	4 − 3 = 1	4 − 2 = 2	4 − 1 = 3	2 − 1 = 1	1 − 1 = 0
4 − 3 = 1	4 − 1 = 3	4 − 2 = 2	4 − 3 = 1	4 − 2 = 2	4 − 1 = 3	4 − 2 = 2

140

Preparation

Materials

Subtraction Families 1, 2, and 4 flash cards

One nickel for each child

Model clock

Chalkboard

(*Class Time* #2)

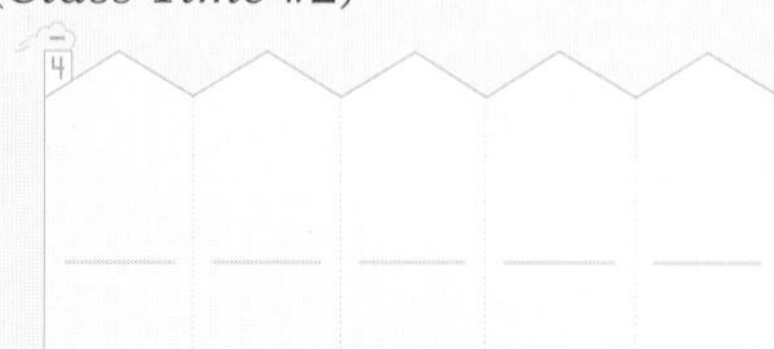

(*Class Time* #4)

3 dimes = _____

1 dime = _____

5 dimes = _____

4 dimes = _____

Class Time

1. *Count by 5's.*
   Call the children to the number line. Point to the triangles. **5 numbers, 5 numbers, 5 numbers. When we count by 5's, we jump 5 numbers at a time. Count by 5's to 100** twice.
2. *Practice Subtraction Family 4.*
   a. Place 4 felt blocks on the lower part of the flannel board.
   (1) **Four screws held a handle on the door. Zero screws fell out. Four screws were left. Four screws take away 0 screws equals 4 screws. Say the story fact with me.**
   (2) **Four screws held a handle on the door. One screw fell out.** (Move 1 block to the upper part.) **Three screws were left. Four screws take away 1 screw equals 3 screws.**
   (3) **Four screws held a handle on the door. Two screws fell out. . . .** Continue to the end of the story.
   b. **Say Subtraction Family 4 as I fill the houses.**

3. *Drill subtraction facts.*
   Circle Drill with Subtraction Families 1, 2, and 4 flash cards.
4. *Counting dimes.*
   a. Hold up 10 fingers. Touch one finger for each number as you say, **10, 20, 30, 40, 50, 60, 70, 80, 90, 100.**
   b. **Hold up your 10 fingers, and count with me. 10, 20, 30, . . .**
   c. Point to the dime samples. **3 dimes. Hold up 3 fingers, and count. 10¢, 20¢, 30¢.** Write 30¢.
   d. Have each child hold up the right number of fingers and count by 10's to discover the answers.
5. *Do Speed Drill #21.*
6. *Assign Lesson 68.*

Speed Drill Answers

4	0	2	1	3	2	1
0	2	1	3	2	1	0
2	1	3	2	1	0	2

Follow-up

Drill

(*Drill* #1)

1. Call the children to the teaching corner. Give each child one nickel.
   a. **A nickel is thick! A nickel is about the same color as a ___.** (dime) **Look at the man. His name is Thomas Jefferson.**
   b. **A nickel is worth 5¢. Say, "Nickel, 5¢" as I fill the circles.**
   c. Count the nickels by 5's.
2. Hold the model clock. Ask a child to set the hands at 7:00. Ask another child to set the hands at 12:00. . . .

Practice Sheets

- ☐ Fact Houses #18
- ☐ Skip Counting #2
- ● Number Facts #17
- ● Money #7
- ◊ Dot-to-Dot #29

Objectives

New

TEACHING

Counting nickels

Review

Subtraction facts

Counting dimes (word)

Count by 5's

Before and After (including 90's)

69 Write Family 4.

4	4	4	4	4
-0	-1	-2	-3	-4
4	3	2	1	0

Answer these facts.

4	4	3	4	4	4	1
-3	-2	-2	-3	-1	-3	-0
1	2	1	1	3	1	1

3	4	3	4	4	3	4
-2	-1	-2	-2	-3	-1	-2
1	3	1	2	1	2	2

4	3	4	4	4	2	4
-1	-1	-3	-2	-3	-1	-3
3	2	1	2	1	1	1

142

Preparation

Materials

Subtraction Families 3 and 4 flash cards

Large nickel

Model clock

Subtraction Families 3 and 4 flash cards

Chalkboard

(*Class Time* #2)

6 dimes = ____

4 dimes = ____

7 dimes = ____

3 dimes = ____

(*Class Time* #3)

5¢ ____

5¢ ____

5¢ ____

(*Class Time* #4)

___ 77 ___ ___ 95 ___

___ 63 ___ ___ 81 ___

___ 88 ___ ___ 94 ___

Class Time

1. *Review Subtraction Families 3 and 4.*
   a. Pass out Subtraction Families 3 and 4 flash cards to the children. **Who has the first fact in Family 3? Come set it on the chalk tray.** Continue.
   b. Stand near the chalk tray. **Say the Subtraction Families 3 and 4 with me.**
   c. **I will move the felt blocks. Say Subtraction Family 3 . . . Family 4.**
2. *Counting dimes.*
   a. **Show the steps on your fingers as we count by 10's to 100.**
   b. Point to the chalkboard samples. **6 dimes.** Show 6 fingers. **10¢, 20¢, 30¢, 40¢, 50¢, 60¢.**
   c. Have individuals count aloud and then write the answers to the rest of the samples.
3. *Counting nickels.*
   a. Point to the triangles on the number line. **When we count by 5's, we are jumping 5 numbers at a time. 5, 10, 15, . . . 100.**

b. Hold the large nickel. **Which coin is this? How much is a nickel worth? What is the man's name?** (Thomas Jefferson) **We count nickels by ___** (5's)

c. Do the chalkboard samples.

4. *Before and After.*
   Do the chalkboard samples.

5. *Assign Lesson 69.*

Follow-up

Drill

1. Hold the model clock.
   a. **Name the small hand. Name the large hand.**
   b. Set the clock at 1:00. **In 1 hour, it will be 2:00.** Slowly, slowly move the minute hand around the clock. **In one hour, the minute hand moves the whole way around the clock. In one hour, the hour hand creeps to the next number.**
   c. To help the children comprehend the meaning and length of 1 hour, do one of these:
      - Set a timer for 1 hour.
      - Burn a candle for 1 hour.
      - Lower a window shade for 1 hour.
2. Drill Subtraction Families 3 and 4 flash cards.

Practice Sheets

- ☐ Fact Houses #18
- ☐ Skip Counting #2
- ● Number Facts #18
- ● Clocks #1
- ● Money #8

Objectives

New

TEACHING

Compare penny and nickel

WORKBOOK

Counting nickels

Review

Subtraction facts

Count by 5's

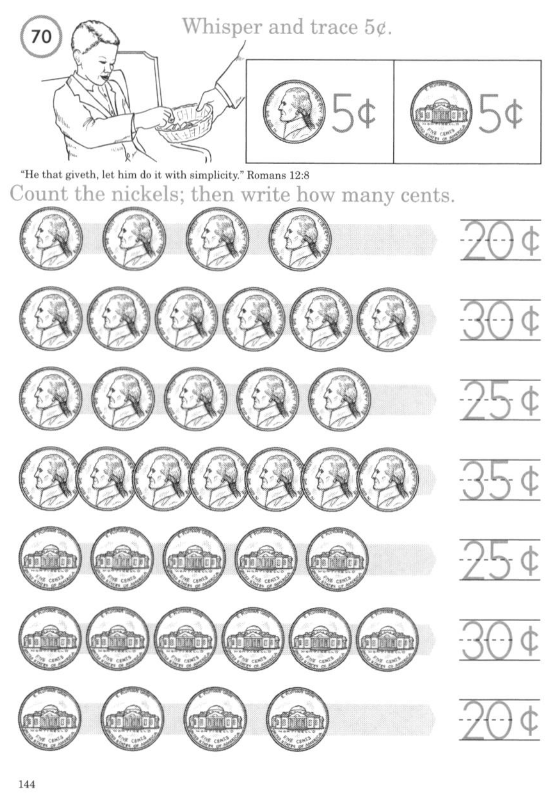

(70) Whisper and trace 5¢.

5¢ 5¢

"He that giveth, let him do it with simplicity." Romans 12:8

Count the nickels; then write how many cents.

20¢

30¢

25¢

35¢

25¢

30¢

20¢

144

Preparation

Materials

Subtraction Families 1–4 flash cards

A nickel and a penny for each child

Chalkboard

(*Class Time* #2)

(*Class Time* #3)

Class Time

1. *Drill subtraction facts.*
   Circle Drill with Subtraction Families 1–4 flash cards.
2. *Practice Subtraction Family 4.*
   a. Ask a child to move the felt blocks as everyone says Subtraction Family 4.
   b. **Say Family 4 as I fill the houses.**
3. *Count by 5's and nickels.*
   a. **Girls, count by 5's to 100.**
   Boys, count by 5's to 100.
   b. Do the chalkboard samples.
4. *Compare penny and nickel.*
   a. Give each child one penny and one nickel. Have them compare the coins: buildings, men, and so on.
   b. Have each child stand in turn. Each one should first hold up his nickel and say, **Nickel, 5¢** and then hold up his penny and say, **Penny, 1¢.**
5. *Do Speed Drill #22.*
6. *Assign Lesson 70.*

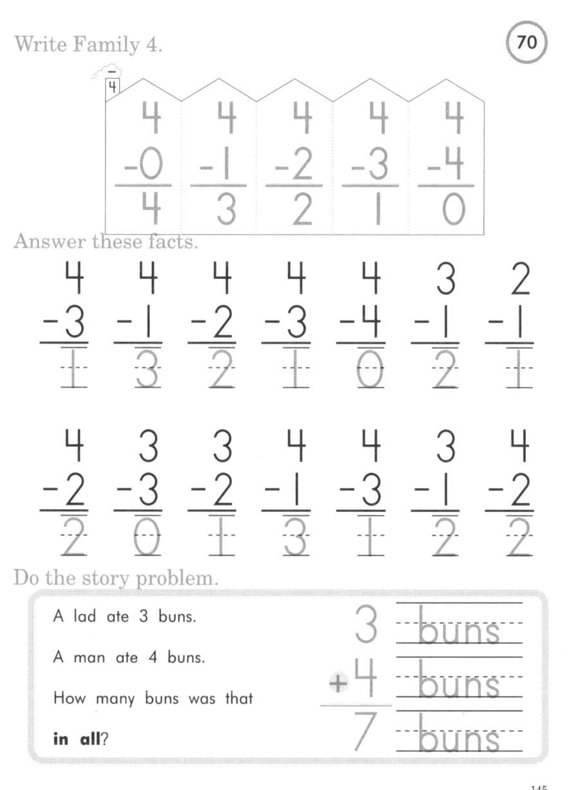
Write Family 4. (70)

4	4	4	4	4
-0	-1	-2	-3	-4
4	3	2	1	0

Answer these facts.

4	4	4	4	4	3	2
-3	-1	-2	-3	-4	-1	-1
1	3	2	1	0	2	1

4	3	3	4	4	3	4
-2	-3	-2	-1	-3	-1	-2
2	0	1	3	1	2	2

Do the story problem.

A lad ate 3 buns.
A man ate 4 buns.
How many buns was that **in all**?

3 buns
+4 buns
7 buns

145

Speed Drill Answers

3	1	2	2	2	1	0
2	3	1	2	1	0	2
3	2	3	1	0	2	0

Speed Drill #22

Follow-up

Drill

(*Drill* #1)

3 -2	3 -1	4 -2	2 -1	3 -2	3 -3
4 -1	4 -0	4 -3	3 -2	2 -1	3 -2
2 -2	4 -3	4 -4	4 -2	3 -1	1 -0
4 -3	3 -2	4 -2	4 -1	4 -2	2 -0

1. Call the children to the grid on the board. **Answer as quickly as you can!** Keep the grid for Lessons 71 and 72.

2. Have the children stand in a semicircle. **I am thinking of something God gave you. He put 5 of them in a row. 1 is large, 3 are middle-sized, and 1 is small. You cannot see them now, but you can wiggle them now.** (toes) **We will count your toes by 5's.** Point to each foot as you count. (Say the total number in the following blanks.)

   ____ **little toes to tiptoe when the baby is asleep.**
   ____ **little toes to cover with sand in the sandbox.**
   ____ **little toes to curl under our feet when we kneel beside the bed and pray to God.**

Practice Sheets

- ☐ Fact Houses #18
- ☐ Clocks #1
- ☐ Skip Counting #2
- ● Number Facts #18
- ● Number Facts #19

Objectives

New

TEACHING

Subtraction Family 5

Review

Counting (100)
Count by 5's
Nickel and penny
Telling time
Column addition
Subtraction facts

Preparation

Materials

Large nickel and penny

Model clock

Subtraction Families 1–4 flash cards

Chalkboard

(*Class Time* #4)

3	4	2	5	3	2
3	2	3	1	2	4
+ 1	+ 1	+ 1	+ 1	+ 1	+ 1

Class Time

1. *Counting.*
   a. Call the children to the number line. **Name a 1-digit number. Name a 2-digit number. Name a 3-digit number.**
   b. **Count by 1's to 100.**
   c. **Count by 5's to 100.**

2. *Review nickel and penny.*
   a. Hold the large nickel. **Nickel, 5¢; nickel, 5¢; . . .**
   b. Hold the large penny. **Penny, 1¢; penny, 1¢; . . .**
   c. **Father gave a penny to Lee and a nickel to Lee's older brother Keith. Father said, "You may put these coins in the offering today."**

   Lee looked at the penny. "Father, if I give 1¢ and Keith gives 5¢, will God give him a bigger blessing?"

   Father said, "No, Lee. God does not count blessings as we count

Write Family 4. (71)

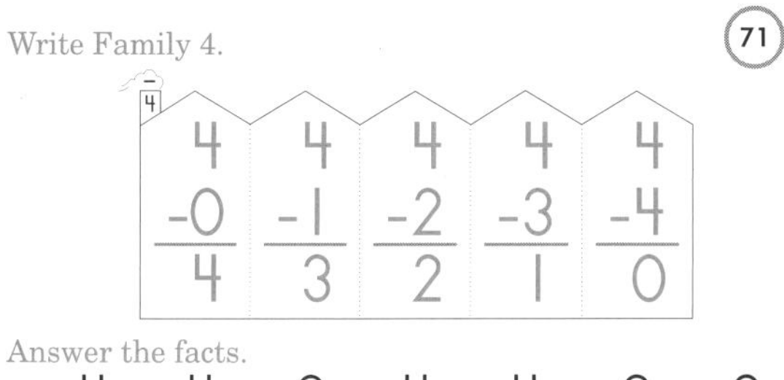

Answer the facts.

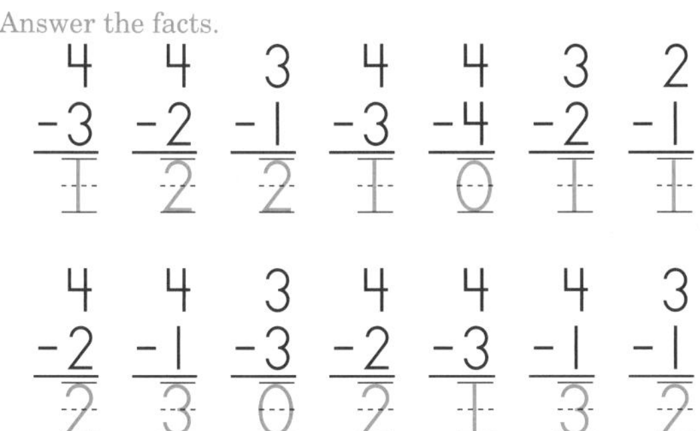

Write the time.

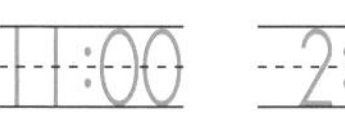
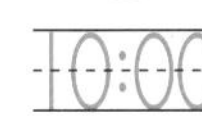

147

coins. God wants you to cheerfully give your little penny so that He can give you a big blessing."

"I will," said Lee, smiling as he tucked his penny into his pocket.

3. *Telling time.*
   a. Set the hands of the model clock at 11:00. **Mother said, "In one hour we will eat lunch." What time will we eat?**
   b. **Read the time together.** Set the hands at 3:00, 6:00, 8:00, 12:00, 4:00, 9:00, 2:00, 7:00.
4. *Column addition.*
   Do the chalkboard samples.
5. *Drill subtraction facts.*
   Use Subtraction Families 1–4 flash cards. **Answer together.**
6. *Assign Lesson 71.*

Follow-up

Drill

(*Drill* #2)

5

(*Drill* #3)

3 dimes = _____

8 dimes = _____

5 dimes = _____

7 dimes = _____

1. Drill the subtraction facts in the grid from Lesson 70.
2. Introduce Subtraction Family 5. **Help me fill these houses with Subtraction Family 5.** Write the facts in order. **We will work with Family 5 tomorrow.**
3. **Count on your fingers to find the answer for 3 dimes . . .**

Practice Sheets

- ☐ Fact Houses #18
- ☐ Skip Counting #2
- ● Number Facts #18
- ● Number Facts #19
- ◊ Dot-to-Dot #30

Objectives

New

TEACHING

Subtraction Family 5

Review

Story problems
Subtraction facts
Counting (100)
Count by 5's
More (including 90's)

Preparation

Materials

Subtraction Families 1–4 flash cards

Form B for each child

Chalkboard

(*Class Time* #1)

___ ________

___ ________

___ ________

(*Class Time* #4)

(*Class Time* #6)

76	63	68	85	94	86
80	70	90	89	98	92
81	89	83	96	92	94

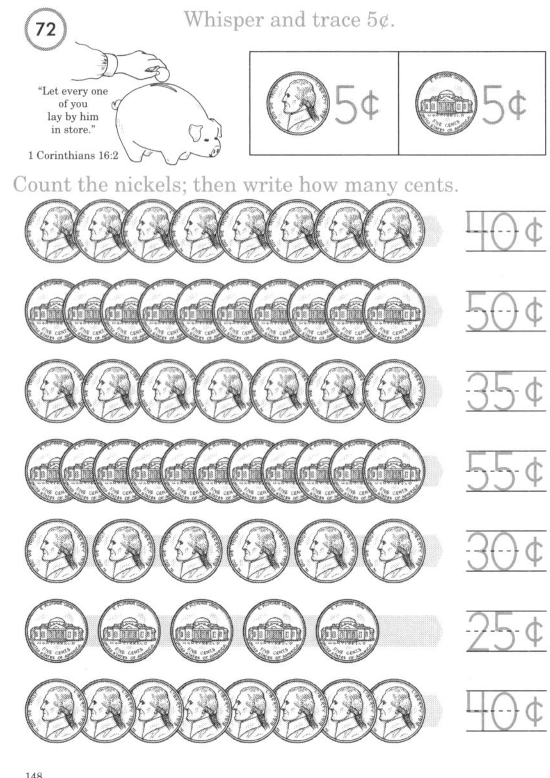

72

Whisper and trace 5¢.

"Let every one of you lay by him in store."
1 Corinthians 16:2

5¢ 5¢

Count the nickels; then write how many cents.

40¢

50¢

35¢

55¢

30¢

25¢

40¢

148

Class Time

1. *Story problems.*
   a. Call attention to the blanks on the board. **Close your eyes and listen.**
   Jim has 2 pups.
   Tom has 5 pups.
   How many pups is that *in all?*
   Open your eyes. Ask a child to fill the blanks. Erase.
   b. **Lee has 3 pups.**
   Jay has 2 pups.
   How many pups is that *in all?*
   Ask a child to fill the blanks.
2. *Practice Subtraction Families 1–4.*
   a. **Say Subtraction Family 4 as I move the blocks.**
   b. **Say the subtraction families by memory.** Use your fingers as a visual aid to keep the class together and to show which fact to say next.
   Family 1
   Hold up a fist for zero.
   1 take away *zero* = 1
   Hold up 1 finger.
   1 take away *one* = 0

Write Family 4. (72)

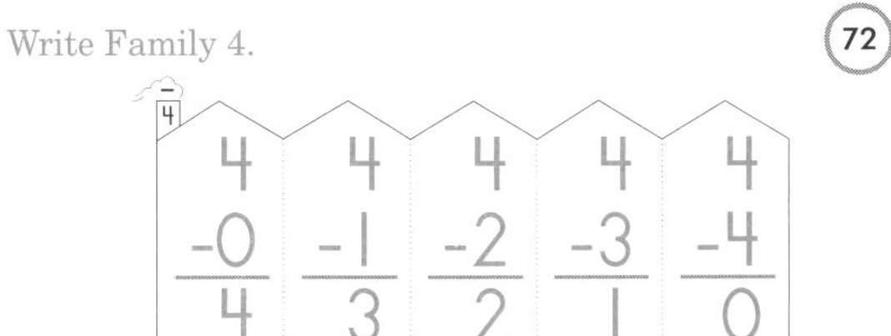

4	4	4	4	4
-0	-1	-2	-3	-4
4	3	2	1	0

Answer the facts.

4	3	4	3	4	3	4
-1	-1	-3	-3	-2	-2	-2
3	2	1	0	2	1	2

4	4	2	4	4	4	3
-2	-3	-1	-4	-3	-1	-1
2	1	1	0	1	3	2

4	3	4	3	4	3	4
-2	-2	-1	-1	-3	-3	-2
2	1	3	2	1	0	2

149

Family 2

Hold up a fist for zero.

2 take away *zero* = 2

Hold up 1 finger.

2 take away *one* = 1

Hold up 2 fingers.

2 take away *two* = 0

Continue with Families 3 and 4.

3. *Drill subtraction facts.*
Double Drill with Subtraction Families 1–4 flash cards.
4. *Teach Subtraction Family 5.*
   a. **Say Subtraction Family 5 as I move the felt blocks.**
   b. Ask a child to fill the houses as you say Family 5 together.
5. *Counting.*
   a. Stand near the number line. **Let's go over the number trains again. Say the engine number in each train louder and slower.**
   b. **Count by 5's to 100.**
6. *More Numbers.*
Do the chalkboard samples.

Speed Drill Answers

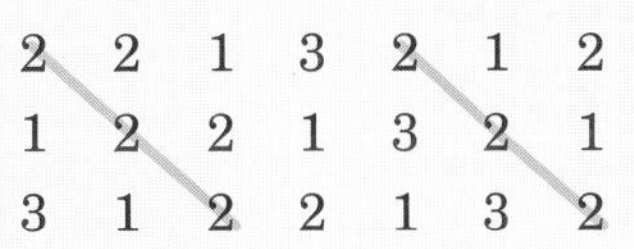

2	2	1	3	2	1	2
1	2	2	1	3	2	1
3	1	2	2	1	3	2

Speed Drill #23

7. *Do Speed Drill #23.*
8. *Assign Lesson 72.*

Follow-up

Drill

1. Use Form B. Hold up the model clock. **Write the time I show.**

	4:00	**6:00**	**11:00**
	1:00	**5:00**	**8:00**
	12:00	**3:00**	**7:00**
	9:00	**12:00**	**2:00**
	10:00	**4:00**	**6:00**

2. Drill individuals at the subtraction grid from Lesson 70.

Practice Sheets

- ● Form B (*Follow-up* drill #1)
- ☐ Money #9
- ☐ Clocks #1
- ● Number Facts #18
- ● Before and After #4

Objectives

New

WORKBOOK

Subtraction Family 5

Review

Subtraction facts
Telling time
Count by 10's
Counting dimes (word)

Preparation

Make Subtraction Family 5 flash cards for each child.

Materials

Subtraction Families 1–4 flash cards
Model clock

Chalkboard

(*Class Time* #2)

(*Class Time* #4)

3 dimes = _____
6 dimes = _____
10 dimes = _____
7 dimes = _____
5 dimes = _____
9 dimes = _____

Class Time

1. *Drill subtraction facts.*
   Circle Drill with Families 1–4 flash cards.
2. *Practice Subtraction Family 5.*
   a. Place 5 felt blocks on the lower part of the flannel board, and move them as you say the story problems.
   (1) **David had 5 stones in his bag. He threw 0 stones on the ground. David had 5 stones left. Five stones take away 0 stones equals 5 stones.**
   (2) **David had 5 stones in his bag. He slung 1 stone at the giant. David had 4 stones left. Five stones take away 1 stone equals 4 stones.**
   (3) **Jerry had 5 stones. He dropped 2 stones down a hole. Jerry had 3 stones left. Five stones take away 2 stones . . .**
   (4) **Sam had 5 stones. He gave 3 stones to his friend. Sam had 2 stones left. Five stones take away 3 stones . . .**
   (5) **Paul had 5 stones. He skipped 4 stones on the pond. Paul had**

And he took his staff in his hand, and chose him five smooth stones out of the brook, and put them in a shepherd's bag which he had, . . . and his sling was in his hand: and he drew near to the Philistine. And the Philistine came on and drew near unto David; and the man that bare the shield went before him. . . . And the Philistine cursed David by his gods. . . . Then said David to the Philistine, Thou comest to me with a sword, and with a spear, and with a shield: but I come to thee in the name of the LORD of hosts, the God of the armies of Israel. . . . This day will the LORD deliver thee into mine hand. . . . And all this assembly shall know that the LORD saveth not with sword and spear: for the battle is the LORD's (1 Samuel 17:40–47).

1 stone left. Five stones take away 4 stones . . .

(6) **Greg had 5 stones. He laid 5 stones around the flower bed. Greg had 0 stones left. Five stones take away 5 stones equals 0 stones.**

b. Ask a child to fill the houses as you say Family 5 together.

3. *Telling time.*
   a. Set the model clock at 6:00. **Father said, "In one hour, we will leave for prayer meeting." What time will we leave?**
   b. Set the hands at 9:00. **Mother said, "In one hour, the mailman will come." What time will the mailman come?**
4. *Counting dimes.*
   a. **Count by 10's to 100.**
   b. Point to the chalkboard samples. **Use your fingers to count the right number of dimes.** Have individuals count aloud and then write the answers.
5. *Assign Lesson 73.*

Follow-up

Drill

1. Give each child his Subtraction Family 5 flash cards.
2. Have individuals count by 5's to 100.
3. **If you saved 3 nickels, how many cents would you save? Hold up 3 fingers and count by 5's. 5¢, 10¢, 15¢.** Tell how many cents you would have if you saved

5 nickels	**1 nickel**
2 nickels	**6 nickels**
4 nickels	**8 nickels**

Practice Sheets

- ☐ Fact Houses #19
- ● Number Facts #20
- ● Money #10
- ◊ Dot-to-Dot #31

Objectives

New

TEACHING

Counting beyond 100
Counting nickels (word)
Place value

Review

Penny, nickel, dime
Subtraction facts

74

Write Family 5

5

5	5	5	5	5	5
-0	-1	-2	-3	-4	-5
5	4	3	2	1	0

Answer these facts.

5	5	5	5	5	5	5
-2	-5	-1	-4	-3	-2	-3
3	0	4	1	2	3	2

5	5	5	5	5	5	5
-1	-4	-3	-5	-3	-4	-2
4	1	2	0	2	1	3

5	5	5	5	5	5	5
-1	-4	-3	-2	-3	-4	-0
4	1	2	3	2	1	5

152

Preparation

Tack Subtraction Family 5 flash cards above the flannel board with answers showing.

Materials

Large penny, nickel, and dime

Subtraction Family 5 flash cards

Chalkboard

(*Class Time* #3)

6 nickels = _____

8 nickels = _____

4 nickels = _____

2 nickels = _____

7 nickels = _____

5 nickels = _____

(*Class Time* #4)

Class Time

1. *Counting beyond 100.*
   a. **Count by 1's to 99.**
   b. Pick up a piece of chalk. **Let's count on to 119.** Write numbers 100–119 on the board as you count.
2. *Review coins.*
   a. Display the large coins for the class to respond in unison.
   Penny, penny, penny; 1¢, 1¢, 1¢.
   Nickel, nickel, nickel; 5¢, 5¢, 5¢.
   Dime, dime, dime; 10¢, 10¢, 10¢.
   b. Have the children respond as you flash alternate sides of the coins. **Penny, 1¢; nickel, 5¢; dime, 10¢; . . .**
3. *Counting nickels.*
   Point to the chalkboard samples. **Count by 5's on your fingers.** Have individuals count aloud and then write the answers.
4. *Practice Subtraction Family 5.*
   a. **Say Subtraction Family 5 as I move the blocks.**
   b. Ask a child to fill the houses as you say Family 5 together.

Write the Before and After numbers. (74)

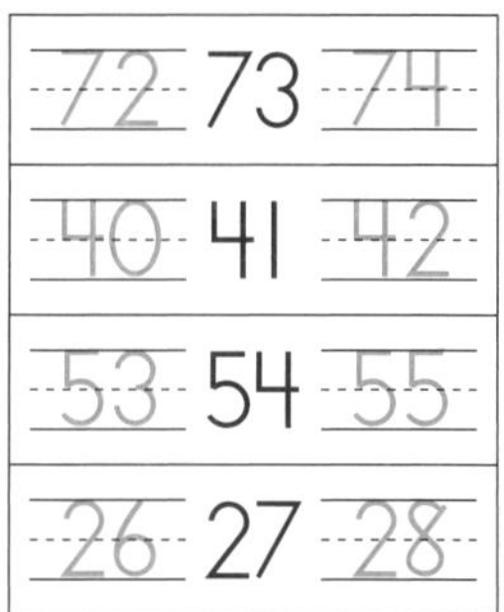

72	73	74
40	41	42
53	54	55
26	27	28

68	69	70
21	22	23
37	38	39
74	75	76

Circle More.

• ⁙ more	(88) 73 77	(31) 23 24
69 (75) 71	49 48 (51)	63 57 (64)

Do the story problem.

Sam got 1 fish.
Father got 6 fish.
How many fish is that **in all**?

$$\begin{array}{r} 1 \\ +6 \\ \hline 7 \end{array}$$ fish

153

c. Point to the flash cards above the flannel board. **Say each fact three times.**

5. *Do Speed Drill #24.*
6. *Assign Lesson 74.*

Follow-up

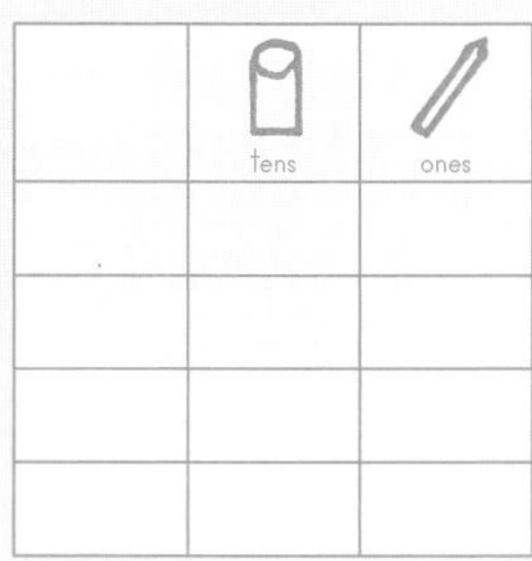

Speed Drill Answers

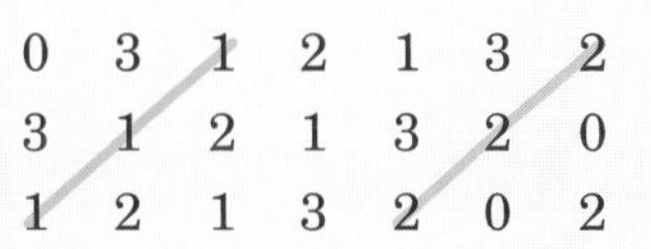

0	3	1	2	1	3	2
3	1	2	1	3	2	0
1	2	1	3	2	0	2

Speed Drill #24

Drill

1. Drill individuals with Subtraction Family 5 flash cards.
2. Introduce place value.
   a. **There is something special about the parts of a 2-digit number.** Write 12, 24, 51, and 45 in the place-value grid.
   b. **The number on the left always means so many groups of 10. If we are counting crayons, this means 1 group of 10 crayons.** (Circle the 1 in 12.) **This means 2 groups of 10 crayons.** (Circle the 2 in 24.)
   If we are counting birds, this means 5 groups of 10 birds. (Circle the 5 in 51.)
   If we are counting flowers, this means 4 groups of 10 flowers. (Circle the 4 in 45.)
   c. **The number on the right tells about more single things.** (Point to the ones numbers as you mention them.) **This is two more crayons besides the group of 10. This is just 1 more bird . . .**
   d. Erase the numbers from the grid. **A 1-digit number always means just so many things. Write 6, 9, 1, and 4 in the ones' place.**
   e. **Ones' place, tens' place.** Make the motion associated with this statement. (See page 10.) **Ones' place, tens' place; ones' place, tens' . . .**

Practice Sheets

- ☐ Fact Houses #19
- ☐ Money #9
- ● Number Facts #20
- ● Writing Practice #22

Objectives

New

TEACHING

The word *minus*
Place value

WORKBOOK

Counting dimes (word)

Review

Subtraction facts
Count by 5's

Preparation

Materials

Subtraction Families 1–3 and 5 flash cards

Addition Families 1–7 flash cards

One nickel and one dime for each child

Chalkboard

(Prepare a set of these facts for each child to trace in *Class Time* #2.)

5	5
-2	-3
3	2

(*Class Time* #4)

	hundreds	tens	ones
18			
53			
5			
47			
2			

75

Write Family 5.

5

5	5	5	5	5	5
-0	-1	-2	-3	-4	-5
5	4	3	2	1	0

Answer these facts.

5	5	5	5	3	5	5	5	5
-3	-2	-4	-2	-2	-1	-3	-4	-3
2	3	1	3	1	4	2	1	2

3	5	3	5	5	5	2	5	3
-0	-2	-1	-1	-4	-3	-1	-4	-2
3	3	2	4	1	2	1	1	1

5	5	3	5	5	5	3	5	3
-5	-3	-1	-2	-3	-2	-2	-1	-1
0	2	2	3	2	3	1	4	2

154

Class Time

1. *Introduce the term* minus.
   a. Point to the first flash card above the flannel board. **5 *take away* 0, 5. Here is another way to say that fact: 5 *minus* 0, 5. *Minus* is a word that means "less."**
   b. **Say each fact three times. 5 minus 0, 5; 5 minus 0, 5; . . .**
   c. Move the felt blocks for Subtraction Family 5 as the class says the facts using *minus*.
2. *Drill selected facts.*
   Have each child stand near his set of facts on the board. **Trace and whisper the facts until I say "stop."**
3. *Drill Subtraction Families 1–3 and 5.*
   Circle Drill with Subtraction Families 1–3 and 5 flash cards.
4. *Teach place value.*
   a. Call the children to the grid on the board. **A 2-digit number has a number in the ones' place and the tens' place.** Make the place-value

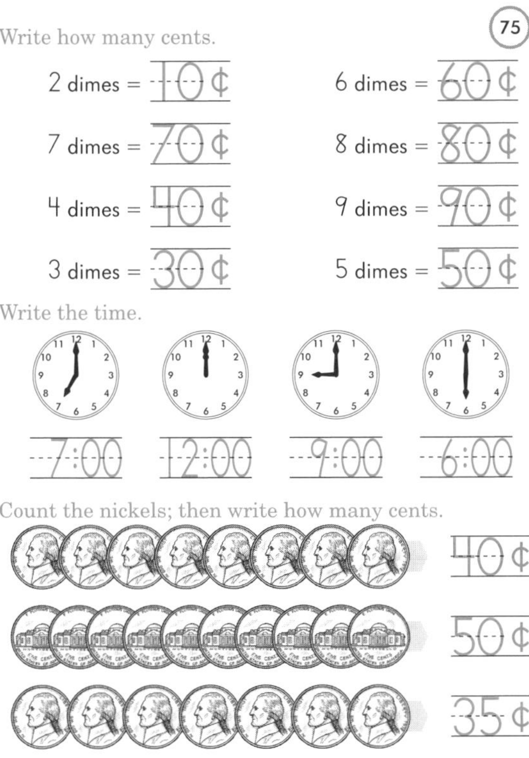

motion as you repeat the place names several times. **Ones' place, tens' place; ones' place, tens' . . .**

b. Have the children write the numbers in the grid. Erase the numbers.

c. **Some numbers have 3 digits. Ones' place, tens' place, hundreds' place.** Motion and drill the place names: **Ones, tens, hundreds; ones, tens, hundreds . . .**

d. Write these 3-digit numbers in the grid: 110, 105, 113, 119, 107.

5. *Count by 5's.*
   a. **We count nickels by ___.** (5's)
   b. **Count by 5's to 100.**

6. *Assign Lesson 75.*

Follow-up

Drill

1. Drill Addition Families 1–7 flash cards.
2. Call the children to the teaching corner, and give each child one nickel and one dime.
   a. Compare the coins, especially noting the smooth edge of the nickel.
   b. Have each child stand in turn. He should first hold up his nickel and say, **Nickel, 5¢** and then hold up his dime and say, **Dime, 10¢.**
3. **Count 1–129.** When you reach 100, write 100–129 on the board as you count.

Practice Sheets

- ☐ Fact Houses #19
- ☐ Money #11
- ● Number Facts #19
- ● Number Facts #20
- ◊ Dot-to-Dot #32

Objectives

New

WORKBOOK

Place value

Review

Subtraction facts

Penny, nickel, dime

Counting (139)

(76) Write the numbers in the correct places.

	100	10	ones
79		7	9
105	1	0	5
132	1	3	2
48		4	8
126	1	2	6

	100	10	ones
139	1	3	9
115	1	1	5
107	1	0	7
92		9	2
124	1	2	4

Answer these facts.

1	3	2	2	1	1	4	2	1
5	2	3	4	3	2	2	1	4
+1	+1	+1	+1	+1	+1	+1	+1	+1
7	6	6	7	5	4	7	4	6

1	1	3	1	3	2	4	2	5
2	4	2	5	3	2	1	4	1
+1	+1	+1	+1	+1	+1	+1	+1	+1
4	6	6	7	7	5	6	7	7

156

Preparation

Materials

Large penny, nickel, and dime

Subtraction Family 5 flash cards

Model clock

Chalkboard

(*Class Time* #1)

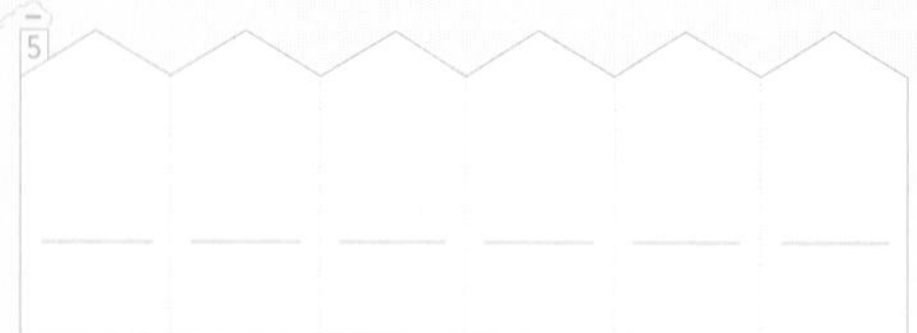

(*Class Time* #3)

	hundreds	tens	ones
73			
124			
6			
130			
89			

Class Time

1. *Drill Subtraction Families 4 and 5.*
   a. Point to the flash cards above the flannel board. **We will say each fact five times. 5 minus 0, 5; 5 minus 0, 5; . . .** Say it loudly the first time, and lower your voice with each recital.
   b. **I will move the felt blocks. Say Family 4 . . . Family 5.**
   c. Ask a child to fill the houses as you say Subtraction Family 5 together.
2. *Review coins.*
   a. Show the large coins, sometimes the front, and sometimes the back. **Name each coin as I flash it.**
   b. **Tell me how much each coin is worth as I flash it.**
3. *Review place value.*
   a. Drill the place names with the motion. **Ones, tens, hundreds; ones, tens, . . .**
   b. **All our numbers have a digit in the ones' place. The tens' place or hundreds' place could be empty,**

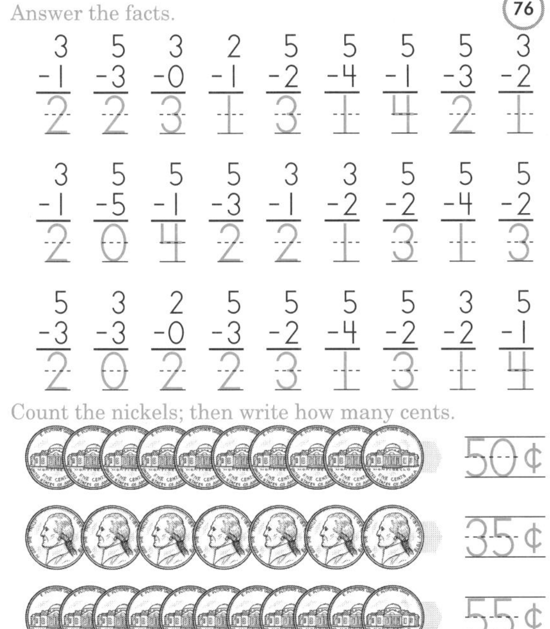

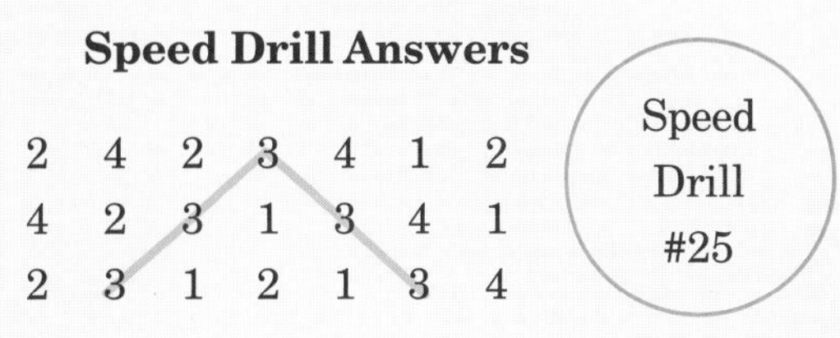

but there must be a digit in the ones' place.**

c. Have the children write the numbers in the grid.

4. *Counting.*
Count 1–139. When you reach 100, write 100–139 on the board as you go.

5. *Do Speed Drill #25.*

6. *Assign Lesson 76.*

Note: Bring an apple and a sharp knife for the fraction demonstration in the *Follow-up* drill in Lesson 77.

Follow-up

Drill

(*Drill* #3)

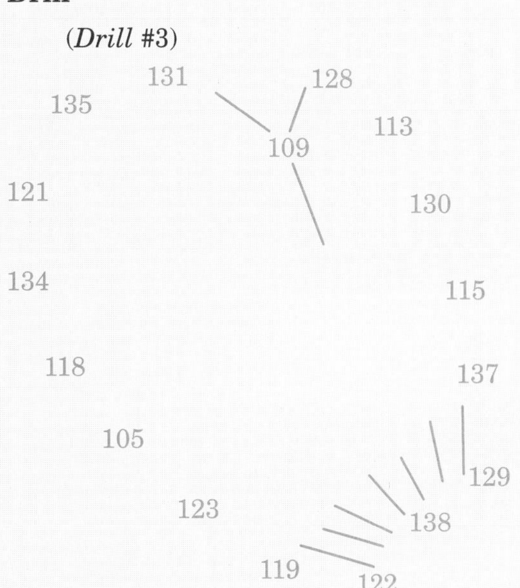

1. Drill Subtraction Family 5 flash cards.
2. Chalkboard drill: **Write the time I show.** Set these times on the model clock:

3:00	8:00	2:00	6:00
1:00	7:00	11:00	4:00
9:00	12:00	5:00	10:00

3. Have individuals read the numbers around the mitten outline.

Practice Sheets

☐ Fact Houses #20

● Money #12

● Writing Practice #23

◊ Dot-to-Dot #33

Objectives

New

TEACHING

Parts of a whole

Review

Subtraction facts
Telling time
Counting (139)
Missing Numbers (over 100)
Place value

(77) Write the numbers in the correct places.

	100	10	ones		100	10	ones
43		4	3	120	1	2	0
109	1	0	9	136	1	3	6
112	1	1	2	104	1	0	4
80		8	0	70		7	0
135	1	3	5	122	1	2	2

Write how many cents.

5 dimes = 50¢ 7 dimes = 70¢
2 dimes = 20¢ 3 dimes = 30¢
9 dimes = 90¢ 8 dimes = 80¢
4 dimes = 40¢ 6 dimes = 60¢
10 dimes = 100¢ 9 dimes = 90¢

158

Preparation

Materials

Subtraction Families 3–5 flash cards
Model clock
Form D for each child
One apple and a knife

Chalkboard

(*Class Time* #5)

100	____	____	103	____
____	107	____	____	110
____	114	____	____	____

(*Class Time* #6)

	hundreds	tens	ones
120			
8			
65			
104			
52			

Class Time

1. *Review Subtraction Families 3–5.*
   a. Pass out the flash cards to the children. **If you have the first fact in Family 3, come set it on the chalk tray. . . .**
   b. Stand near the flash cards. **Let's say them together.**
2. *Drill selected facts.*
   Hold the flash cards for 5 - 3 = 2 and 4 - 3 = 1. **We will say each fact three times with our eyes open, and then three times with our eyes closed.**
3. *Telling time.*
   a. Hold the model clock. **Name the hands. Which hand moves around the clock one time in 1 hour? Which hand moves to the next number in 1 hour?**
   b. Set the hands at 4:00. **Farmer John said, "In 1 hour I will feed the animals." What time will he feed the animals?**

4. *Counting.*
   Count 100–139.
5. *Missing Numbers.*
   Do the chalkboard samples.
6. *Place value.*
   Put the numbers in the grid.
7. *Assign Lesson 77.*

Follow-up

Drill

1. Distribute Form D for story-problem dictation. Print these labels on the chalkboard. *songs* *gifts*

   a. **Arrow Box: Esther packed 2 gifts. Robert packed 5 gifts. How many gifts was that *in all?***
   b. **Button Box: Mother tied 3 gifts with white ribbon. She tied 3 gifts with yellow ribbon. How many gifts was that *in all?***
   c. **Camel Box: When the family visited Brother Herman, they sang 4 songs about Jesus. They sang 3 songs about heaven. How many songs was that *in all?***
   d. **Daffodil Box: Father and Mother and the children took 1 gift to a large family. They took 6 gifts to old people. How many gifts was that *in all?***
   e. **Elephant Box: At Mrs. Wheeler's house, the family sang 2 songs in the living room. They sang 4 songs in her bedroom. How many songs was that *in all?***
   f. **Feather Box: Esther knew how to sing 3 songs by memory. She looked in the book to sing 4 songs. How many songs was that *in all?***
2. Introduce the fraction concept. Let the children surround your desk.
   a. **This is one whole apple.** Cut it in half.
   b. **How many pieces did I make?** Hold a piece in each hand. **I have 2 parts of one apple. This is one-half, and this is one-half.**
   c. Cut each piece in half again. **Now how many pieces do I have? This piece is one-fourth of the apple. This piece is one-fourth; this is one-fourth. . . .**

Note: See page 364 for hints on saving teacher time.

Practice Sheets

- ● Form D (*Follow-up* drill #1)
- ☐ Form E: 1–20
- ☐ Money #13
- ● Number Facts #21
- ● Fact Houses #20

Objectives

New

TEACHING

Parts of a whole

Distinguish 101 from 110

Review

Counting (149)

Before and After (over 100)

Subtraction facts

Place value

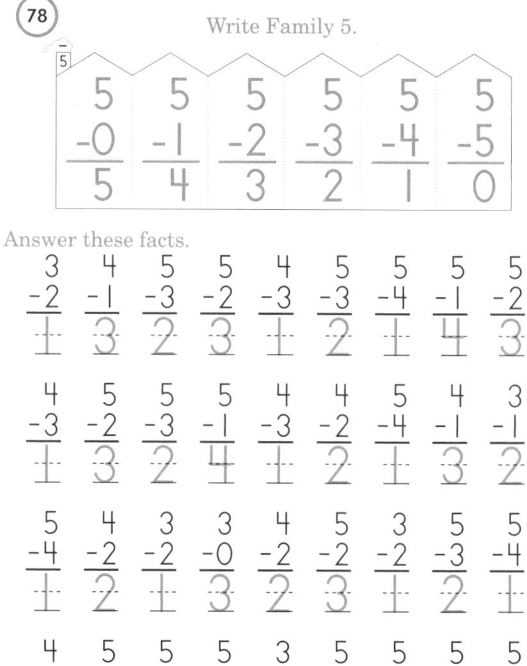

Preparation

Materials

Subtraction Families 3–5 flash cards

Three scrap-paper squares (Color a simple border around the edge of each.)

Addition Families 1–7 flash cards

Chalkboard

(*Class Time* #2)

_____ 104 _____		_____ 116 _____
_____ 101 _____		_____ 111 _____
_____ 108 _____		_____ 119 _____
_____ 105 _____		_____ 113 _____

(*Class Time* #3)

Class Time

1. *Counting.*
   Count 1–149.
2. *Before and After.*
   Do the chalkboard samples.
3. *Review Subtraction Families 4 and 5.*
   a. Ask a child to move the felt blocks as everyone says Family 5.
   b. **I will fill the houses. Say Subtraction Family 4 . . . Family 5.**
4. *Drill subtraction facts.*
   Circle Drill with Subtraction Families 3–5 flash cards.
5. *Teach the fraction concept.*
   a. Hold one square of scrap paper. **If I cut this in half, how many pieces will I have?** Cut it. Write $\frac{1}{2}$ on the chalkboard. **This says one-half. There is a 2 on the bottom because it takes 2 parts to make a whole thing.**
   b. Cut another piece of paper into three equal parts. **How many pieces did I make this time? Each piece is one-third.** Write $\frac{1}{3}$ on the chalkboard.

Write the numbers in the correct places. 78

	100	10	1			100	10	1
103	1	0	3		108	1	0	8
127	1	2	7		113	1	1	3
134	1	3	4		125	1	2	5
110	1	1	0		119	1	1	9
121	1	2	1		130	1	3	0

Count by 5's.

Count by 5's 5 10 15 20

25 30 35 40 45 50

55 60 65 70 75 80

85 90 95 100

161

This says one-third. There is a 3 on the bottom because it takes 3 parts to make the whole thing. Hold the 3 pieces so the children can see the colored frame forming the square.

c. Cut the last square into four equal parts. **How many pieces do we have in this square?** Write $\frac{1}{4}$ on the chalkboard. **This says one-fourth. There is a 4 on the bottom because it takes 4 parts to make the whole thing.**

6. *Place value.*
   Review with the motion: **Ones, tens, hundreds; ones, tens, . . .**
7. *Do Speed Drill #26.*
8. *Assign Lesson 78.*

Speed Drill Answers

1	4	3	2	1	2	3
4	3	2	1	2	3	2
3	2	1	2	3	2	5

Follow-up

Drill

(*Drill* #1) 101 110

(*Drill* #2)

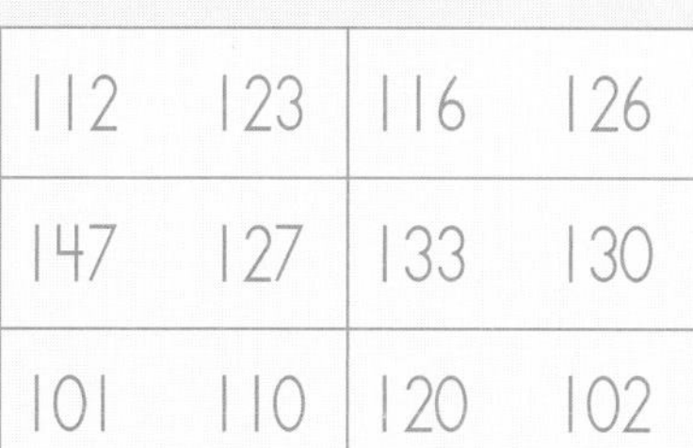

112	123	116	126
147	127	133	130
101	110	120	102

1. The numbers 101 and 110 can be confusing. Use one of these methods to drill the large numbers on the board.
   a. Motion and say, **Ones, tens, hundreds.** Point to the digits and say, **Ones, tens, hundreds. This is 1 hundred. Is the other 1 in the tens' place or the ones' place?**
   b. Add details to turn the numbers into pictures, and teach these rhymes.

   **These two boys
   are having fun;
   One hundred one,
   one hundred one.**

   **The boys will catch
   the ball again;
   One hundred ten,
   one hundred ten.**
2. Do the chalkboard samples for More Numbers.
3. Drill Addition Families 1–7 flash cards.

Practice Sheets

- ☐ Fact Houses #20
- ☐ Form E: 21–40
- ☐ Place Value #1
- ● Number Facts #21
- ◊ Extra: Money #10—Color the nickels; then cut and paste them back-to-back.

Objectives

New

TEACHING

Distinguish 101 from 110
Fraction denominators

Review

Subtraction facts
Counting (159)
Place value
Less (including 140's)
Count by 5's
Missing numbers (by 5's)

(79) Write Family 5.

5 -0 5	5 -1 4	5 -2 3	5 -3 2	5 -4 1	5 -5 0

Answer these facts.

5 -4 1	4 -1 3	5 -3 2	5 -2 3	4 -3 1	5 -3 2	5 -4 1	5 -1 4	5 -2 3
4 -2 2	5 -2 3	4 -2 2	5 -1 4	5 -4 1	5 -2 3	4 -3 1	5 -3 2	5 -4 1
4 -3 1	4 -2 2	5 -4 1	4 -1 3	4 -2 2	5 -2 3	4 -3 1	5 -3 2	5 -2 3
5 -4 1	5 -3 2	5 -1 4	4 -1 3	4 -3 1	5 -3 2	4 -3 1	5 -4 1	5 -3 2

162

Preparation

Materials

Subtraction Families 4 and 5 flash cards

Chalkboard

(*Class Time* #4)

(*Class Time* #5)

117	106	141	142
112	102	138	131
125	130	140	120

(*Class Time* #6)

50 ___ ___ 65 ___ ___ 80
10 ___ 20 ___ ___ 35 ___
70 ___ ___ ___ 90 ___ ___

Class Time

1. *Review Subtraction Families 4 and 5.*
   a. Point to Family 5 flash cards above the flannel board. **Boys, say each fact twice.**
   b. **Girls, say each fact twice.**
   c. **Watch my fingers as we say Subtraction Family 4 . . . Family 5.**
2. *Counting.*
   Count 50–159.
3. *Place value.*
   Review the motion. **Ones, tens, hundreds; ones, . . .**

79

Write the numbers in the correct places.

	100	10	1			100	10	1
71		7	1	114	1	1	4
102	1	0	2	99		9	9
46		4	6	133	1	3	3
118	1	1	8	128	1	2	8
72		7	2	98		9	8

Do the story problem.

Jane has 5 plums.

Hope has 2 plums.

How many plums is that **in all**?

$$\begin{array}{r} 5 \text{ plums} \\ +2 \text{ plums} \\ \hline 7 \text{ plums} \end{array}$$

163

4. *Teach the distinction of 101 and 110.*
   Repeat the *Follow-up* drill in Lesson 78.
5. *Less.*
   Do the chalkboard samples.
6. *Count by 5's.*
   a. **Count by 5's to 100.**
   b. Fill in the Missing Numbers, counting by 5's.
7. *Drill subtraction facts.*
   Circle Drill with Subtraction Families 4 and 5 flash cards.
8. *Assign Lesson 79.*

Follow-up

Drill

(*Drill* #1)

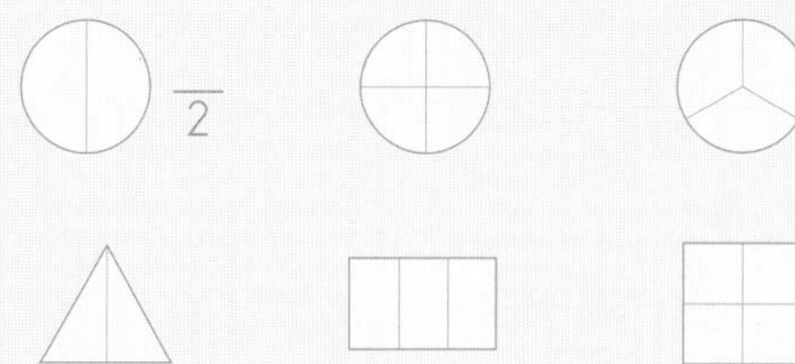

1. Introduce fraction denominators.
   a. Point to the first circle in the chalkboard samples. **How many parts are in this shape?** Draw a short horizontal line for a fraction bar, and write a 2 below it.
   b. Point to the second circle. **How many parts are in this shape? Write the number of parts with a small number. Write it under a line.**
   c. Continue with the rest of the samples.
2. Chalkboard drill: **Write the number I say: 104, 102, 108, 101, 105, 107, 115, 118, 114, 119, 110.**

Practice Sheets

- ☐ Fact Houses #20
- ☐ Form E: 41–60
- ● Number Facts #22
- ● Number Facts #21
- ● Money #13

Objectives

New

TEACHING

- The term *larger*
- Fraction denominators
- *Ordinal numbers*
- *Subtraction Family 6*

WORKBOOK

- Parts of a whole
- Missing Numbers (over 100)

Review

- Subtraction facts
- Counting (169)
- Place value
- Distinguish 101 from 110

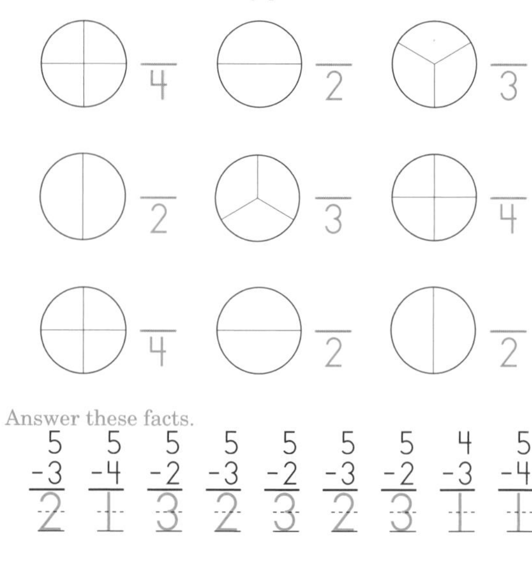

80 Trace the line. Then write a number under it to tell how many parts.

Answer these facts.

5	5	5	5	5	5	5	4	5
-3	-4	-2	-3	-2	-3	-2	-3	-4
2	1	3	2	3	2	3	1	1

4	4	5	3	5	4	5	3	5
-2	-3	-3	-2	-4	-2	-2	-2	-3
2	1	2	1	1	2	3	1	2

164

Preparation

Materials

Subtraction Families 1–5 flash cards

Subtraction Families 1–5 flash cards

Chalkboard

(*Class Time* #1)

(*Class Time* #4)

(*Class Time* #5)

146	116	107	101
120	110	133	103
117	127	131	113

(*Class Time* #6)

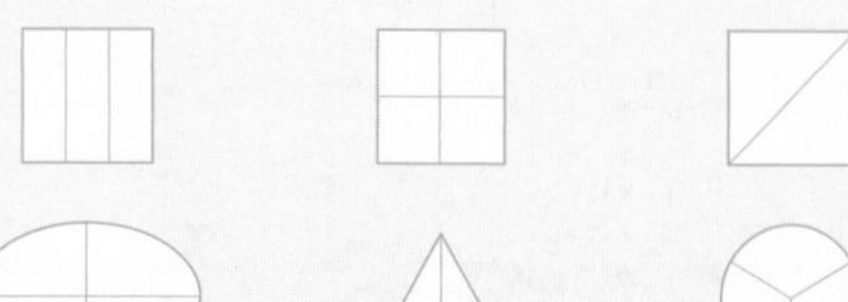

Class Time

1. *Review Subtraction Families 1–5.*
   a. Distribute the flash cards to the children. **Do you have the first fact in Family 1? Come set it on the chalk tray.** Call for the rest of the families in order.
   b. **Stand near the facts. Let's say our subtraction families together.**
   c. Ask a child to fill the houses as everyone says Family 5.
2. *Counting.*
   Count 50–169.
3. *Review place value.*
   Practice the place-value motion, saying the place names.
4. *Review distinction of 101 and 110.*
   (See *Follow-up* drill #1 in Lesson 78.)
5. *Larger numbers.*
   a. **If Peter has 13 marbles and Nevin has 26 marbles, who has more? Who has a larger pile? A *larger* number means more things.**

80

Write the Missing Numbers.

100	101	102	103	104	105
106	107	108	109	110	111
112	113	114	115	116	117
118	119	120	121	122	123
124	125	126	127	128	129
130	131	132	133	134	135

Write the time.

12:00 6:00 7:00 4:00

165

b. Point to the first box in the chalkboard samples. **Find the larger number in this box.** Circle the larger number in each sample.

6. *Teach fraction denominators.*
   a. Point to the first square. **How many parts are in this shape?** Draw a short line, and write 3 below it. **A fraction shows how many parts something has. The number below the line tells how many parts in the whole thing.**
   b. Point to the second square. **How many parts are in this shape?** Draw the line, and have one of the children write the number below it.
   c. Let the children finish the samples.
7. *Do Speed Drill #27.*
   Watch the signs!
8. *Assign Lesson 80.*

Speed Drill Answers

5	7	6	7	6	5	5
4	5	7	6	7	6	5
5	4	5	7	6	7	6

Speed Drill #27

Follow-up

Drill

(*Drill* #3)

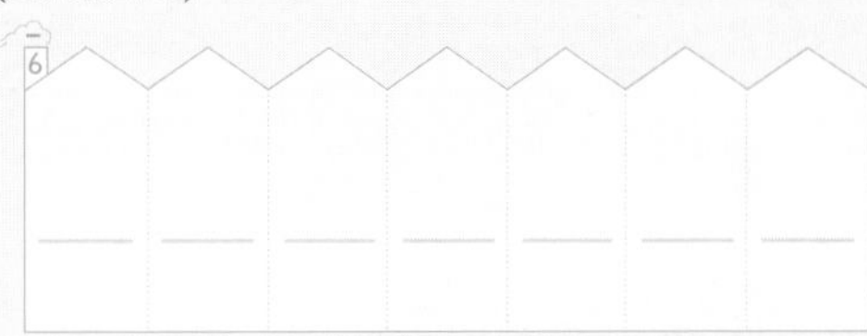

1. Drill individuals with Subtraction Families 1–5 flash cards.
2. Introduce ordinal numbers.
   a. **Count 1–10 as I write the numbers on the board.**
   b. Point to the numbers. **First, second, third, fourth, fifth, sixth, seventh, eighth, ninth, tenth.**
   c. **Count together. First, second, . . .**
3. Introduce Subtraction Family 6. **Help me fill these houses with Subtraction Family 6.** Write the facts in order. **We will work with Subtraction Family 6 tomorrow.**

Practice Sheets

- ☐ Form E: 61–80
- ☐ Place Value #2
- ● Number Facts #23
- ● Writing Practice #24

Objectives

New

TEACHING

Subtraction Family 6
Ordinal numbers

Review

Subtraction facts
Count by 10's
Larger
Parts of a whole

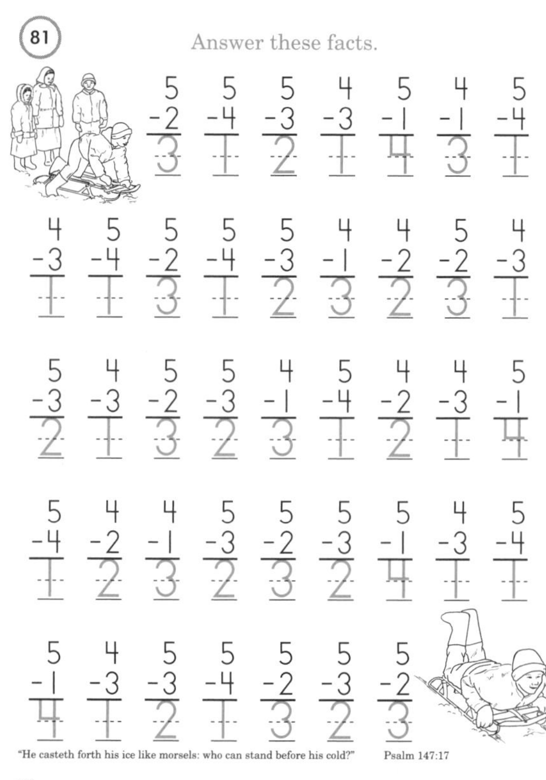
81 Answer these facts.

5 − 2 = 3 5 − 4 = 1 5 − 3 = 2 4 − 3 = 1 5 − 1 = 4 4 − 1 = 3 5 − 4 = 1

4 − 3 = 1 5 − 4 = 1 5 − 2 = 3 5 − 4 = 1 5 − 3 = 2 4 − 1 = 3 4 − 2 = 2 5 − 2 = 3 4 − 3 = 1

5 − 3 = 2 4 − 3 = 1 5 − 2 = 3 5 − 3 = 2 4 − 1 = 3 5 − 4 = 1 4 − 2 = 2 4 − 3 = 1 5 − 1 = 4

5 − 4 = 1 4 − 2 = 2 4 − 1 = 3 5 − 3 = 2 5 − 2 = 3 5 − 3 = 2 5 − 1 = 4 4 − 3 = 1 5 − 4 = 1

5 − 1 = 4 4 − 3 = 1 5 − 3 = 2 5 − 4 = 1 5 − 2 = 3 5 − 3 = 2 5 − 2 = 3

"He casteth forth his ice like morsels: who can stand before his cold?" Psalm 147:17

166

Preparation

Materials

Subtraction Families 1–5 flash cards

Form B for each child

Subtraction Families 4 and 5 flash cards

Chalkboard

(*Class Time* #2)

(*Class Time* #5)

116	106	125	152
150	140	113	131
134	143	101	110

(*Class Time* #6)

Class Time

1. *Drill subtraction facts.*
   a. Circle Drill with Subtraction Families 1–5 flash cards.
   b. **Say Family 5 as I move the felt blocks.**
2. *Teach Subtraction Family 6.*
   a. Place 6 blocks on the flannel board. **6 blocks. Take away 0 blocks. 6 blocks left. . . .**
   b. Ask a child to fill the houses as you say Family 6 together.
3. *Count by 10's.*
   Count by 10's to 100.
4. *Ordinal numbers.*
   a. Hold up your ten fingers. **I will count each finger with a number that says which one it is. First, second, third, . . .**
   b. **Count your fingers in the same way. First, second, . . .**

81

Write how many cents.

4 dimes = 40 ¢	5 dimes = 50 ¢
6 dimes = 60 ¢	9 dimes = 90 ¢
3 dimes = 30 ¢	2 dimes = 20 ¢
8 dimes = 80 ¢	7 dimes = 70 ¢
10 dimes = 100 ¢	6 dimes = 60 ¢

Trace the line. Then write a number below it to tell how many parts.

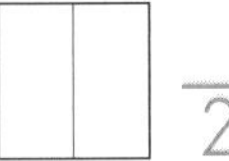
2

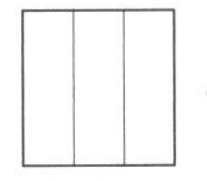
4

3

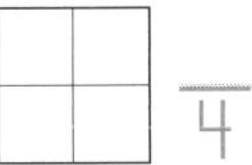
4

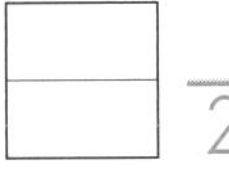
3

2

167

c. **When Grandmother asks, "What grade are you in?" what do you say?** Accept answers. ***First grade* and *grade 1* mean the same thing.**

5. *Larger Numbers.*
A number that says *more* is a *larger* number. Do the chalkboard samples.

6. *Practice fraction denominators.*
Have the children draw a short line and then write a number below it for each figure on the chalkboard. **A part of something is a fraction of the thing.**

7. *Assign Lesson 81.*
The children in the picture are wearing winter coats. Cold weather with its ice and snow is made by God.

Follow-up

Drill

1. Distribute Form B. **Write the number I say.**

	124	**108**	**152**
	105	**112**	**129**
	136	**103**	**140**
	155	**119**	**106**
	147	**131**	**120**

2. Drill individuals with Subtraction Families 4 and 5 flash cards.

Practice Sheets

- ● Form B (*Follow-up* drill #1)
- ☐ Form E: 81–100
- ☐ Skip Counting #3
- ● Number Facts #22
- ● Number Facts #23

Objectives

New

TEACHING

The term *denominator*
Half hour

WORKBOOK

Subtraction Family 6
After Numbers by 10's

Review

Subtraction facts
Ordinal numbers
Counting (179)
Less (including 150's)
Parts of a whole

Preparation

Make Subtraction Family 6 flash cards for each child.

Materials

Subtraction Families 1–5 flash cards
Model clock

Chalkboard

(*Class Time* #2)

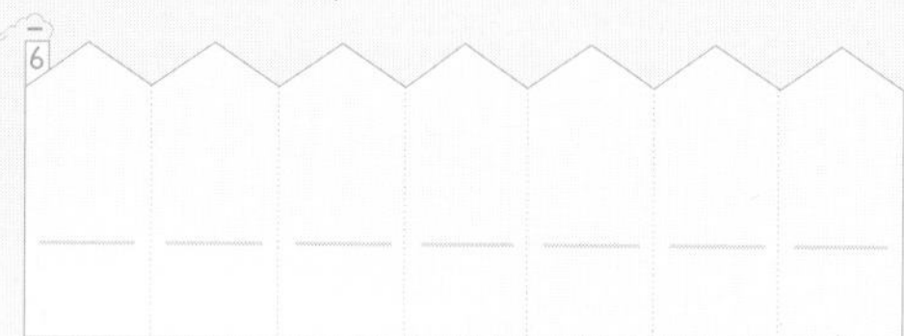

(*Class Time* #5)

111	114	152	125
106	116	128	131
135	134	159	156

(*Class Time* #6)

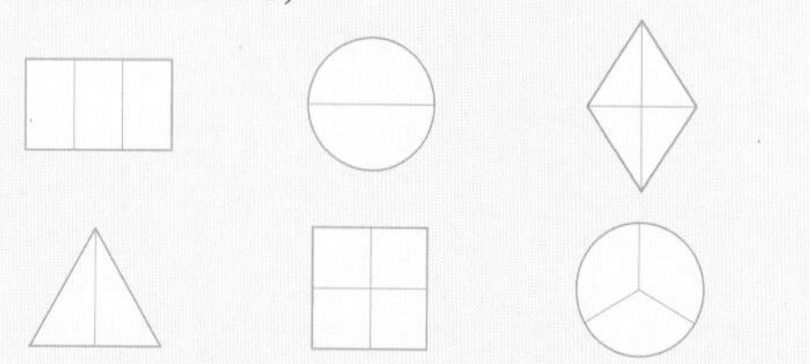

Class Time

1. *Drill subtraction facts.*
   Double Drill with Subtraction Families 1–5 flash cards.
2. *Practice Subtraction Family 6.*
   a. Use the flannel board to show story facts for Subtraction Family 6.
   (1) **There were 6 pieces of pie. We ate 0 pieces. Six pieces were left. 6 pieces take away 0 pieces equals 6 pieces.**
   (2) **There were 6 pieces of pie. We ate 1 piece. Five pieces were left. 6 pieces take away 1 piece equals 5 pieces.**
   (3) **There were 6 pieces of pie. We ate 2 pieces. . . .**
   b. **Say Family 6 as I fill the houses.**
   c. Point to the houses. **Say these facts with the word *minus*.**
3. *Ordinal Numbers.*
   a. **I will call some children to stand in a line. First will be [Sue]. Second will be [Joel]. Third . . .**

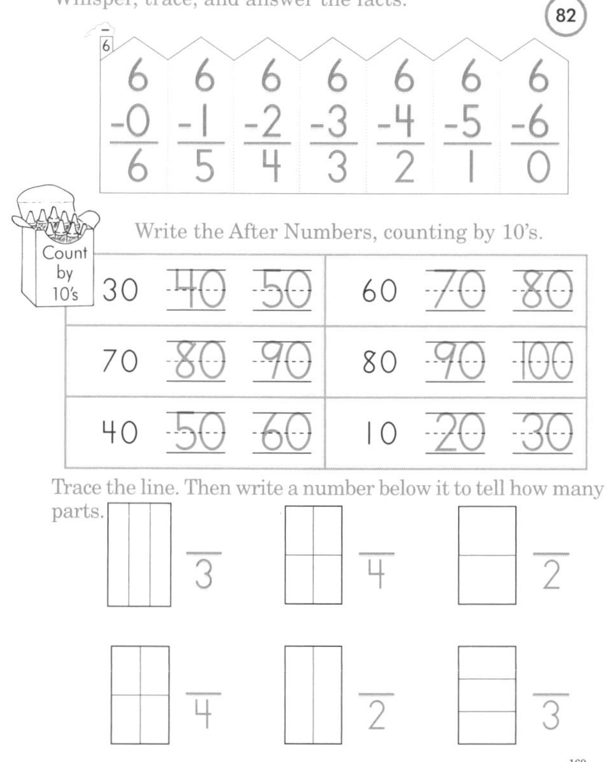

b. Point to each child in the line as you count. **First, second, third, . . .**

c. **Who is first? Who is fourth? . . . third?**

4. *Counting.*
   Count 100–179.
5. *Less Numbers.*
   Do the chalkboard samples.
6. *Introduce the term* denominator.
   Have the children write a short line and number beside each shape on the chalkboard. **The fraction number we are writing is a *denominator*. The denominator tells how many pieces something is *divided* into. The denominator is the *down* number. We write it down below the line.**
7. *Do Speed Drill #28.*
8. *Assign Lesson 82.*

Speed Drill Answers

7	6	5	7	7	6	5
6	5	7	7	6	5	7
5	7	7	6	5	7	7

Speed Drill #28

Follow-up

Drill

1. Give each child his Subtraction Family 6 flash cards.
2. Introduce the half hour.
   a. Set the model clock at 2:00. **It is 2:00. Soon it is past 2:00. The minute hand crawls past the 1, past the 2, . . .** Move it slowly to the six. **Now it is halfway around the clock.**
   b. If you do not have a clock on which the hands move together, set the hour hand halfway between the 2 and 3. **What did the hour hand do while the minute hand went halfway around? It is halfway to the next hour. This is half-past 2; half-past 2 . . .**
   c. Move the hands of the model clock through these hours and half hours. Pause at each time, and say it together.

9:00 . . .	**half past 9**
10:00 . . .	**half past 10**
11:00 . . .	**half past 11**
3:00 . . .	**half past 3**
6:00 . . .	**half past 6**

Practice Sheets

- ☐ Fact Houses #21
- ☐ Place Value #1
- ● Writing Practice #25
- ● Form E: 101–120

Objectives

New

TEACHING

Half hour
Subtraction story problem

Review

Subtraction facts
Denominators

(83)

Write Family 6.

6	6	6	6	6	6	6
-0	-1	-2	-3	-4	-5	-6
6	5	4	3	2	1	0

Answer these facts.

6	6	6	6	6	6	6	6	6
-0	-2	-1	-4	-2	-5	-3	-5	-4
6	4	5	2	4	1	3	1	2

6	6	6	6	6	6	6	6	6
-6	-2	-5	-3	-4	-5	-4	-2	-3
0	4	1	3	2	1	2	4	3

6	6	6	6	6	6	6	6	6
-1	-4	-2	-5	-3	-5	-4	-3	-2
5	2	4	1	3	1	2	3	4

6	6	6	6	6	6	6	6	6
-3	-2	-4	-5	-4	-3	-5	-1	-2
3	4	2	1	2	3	1	5	4

170

Preparation

Tack Subtraction Family 6 flash cards above the flannel board with answers showing.

Materials

Model clock

Chalkboard

(*Class Time* #1)

(*Class Time* #2)

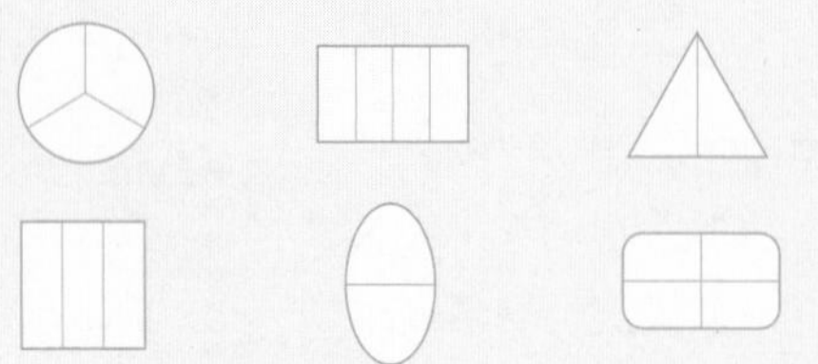

Class Time

1. *Practice Family 6 subtraction facts.*
   a. **Say Family 6 as I move the blocks.**
   b. Ask a child to fill the houses as you say Family 6 together.
   c. Point to the flash cards above the flannel board. **Say each fact three times with your eyes open, and then three times with your eyes closed.**
2. *Review fraction denominators.*
   A fraction of something is a part of the thing. We write the denominator below the line to show how many parts each shape has. Do the chalkboard samples.
3. *Teach the half hour as 30 minutes.*
   a. Set the model clock at these times, and have the children say them.

7:00 . . .	**half past 7**
10:00 . . .	**half past 10**
1:00 . . .	**half past 1**

Write the numbers in the correct places. (83)

	100	10	
103	1	0	3
5			5
129	1	2	9
84		8	4

	100	10	
139	1	3	9
145	1	4	5
107	1	0	7
2			2

Circle Less.

less	108 123	146 139	105 117
134 124	145 138	103 130	137 140

Count the nickels; then write how many cents.

35¢

55¢

30¢

171

b. Set the hands at 4:00. **We use the tiny black lines between the numbers to count minutes. 1, 2, 3, 4, 5. There are 5 minutes between each number. We can count minutes by 5's. Ready? 5, 10, 15, 20, 25, 30. Thirty minutes past 4:00, or 4:30.**

c. Write 4:30 on the board. **The first number tells the hour. The numbers after the colon tell how many minutes it is past the hour. This says 4:30.** Point to the clock. **This says 4:30.**

d. Set the clock at these times. Say and write each one. **2:30, 8:30, 10:30, 1:30, 5:30.**

4. *Assign Lesson 83.*

Follow-up

Drill

(*Drill* #2)

123 ___ ___ ___ 127 ___

146 ___ ___ 149 ___ ___

160 ___ ___ ___ ___ 165

(*Drill* #3)

___ ______

___ ______

___ ______

1. **Count 50–179.**
2. Do the Missing Number chalkboard samples.
3. Introduce a subtraction story problem. **Close your eyes and listen.**
   a. **4 pups play. Then 3 of them run away. How many pups are *left*?**
   b. **Shall we add or subtract?** Put a minus sign in place for the problem. **What shall I write on the blanks?**

Practice Sheets

- ☐ Fact Houses #21
- ☐ Skip Counting #3
- ● Number Facts #24
- ● Fractions #1
- ● Form E: 121–140

Objectives

New

TEACHING

Equality of halves
Subtraction story problem

WORKBOOK

Half hour

Review

Subtraction Family 6

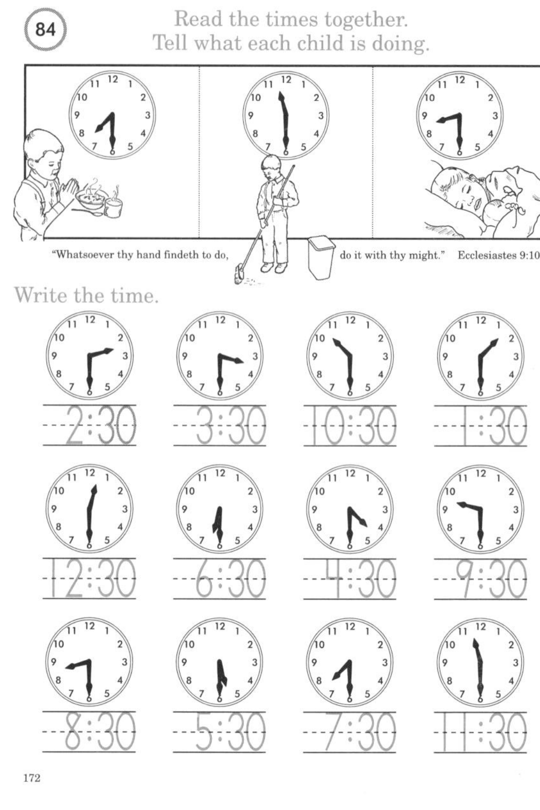
84 Read the times together.
Tell what each child is doing.

"Whatsoever thy hand findeth to do, do it with thy might." Ecclesiastes 9:10

Write the time.

2:30	3:30	10:30	1:30
12:30	6:30	4:30	9:30
8:30	5:30	7:30	11:30

172

Preparation

Make a 2-inch square card with :30 on it. Tape it below the 6 on your classroom clock.

Materials

Model clock

Chalkboard

(*Class Time* #2)

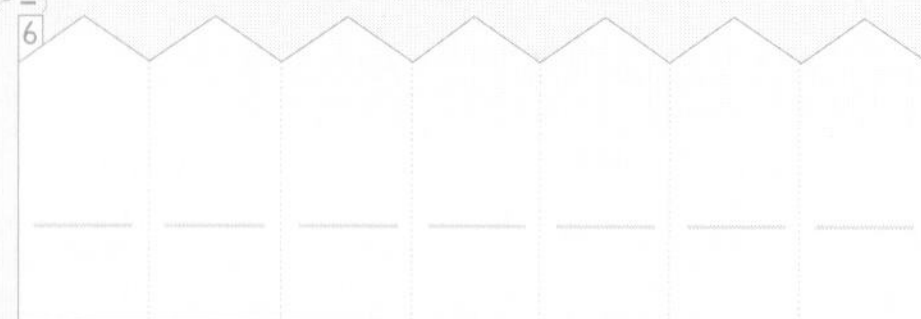

(Draw dividing lines in *Class Time* #3.)

(*Class Time* #4)

5 cats play. Then 2 of them run away. How many cats are left?

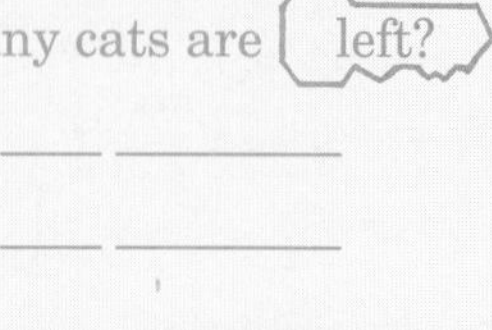

Class Time

1. *Practice half-hour time.*
   a. Set the model clock at 9:30. Say the following rhyme, and write 9:30 on the board before you have someone tell the time.
   Time to eat, time to play,
   Time to work, time to pray,
   Time to sleep, time to say . . . (9:30)
   Repeat the rhyme for 1:30 and 3:30.
   b. Set the hands at 7:30. Call on one of the children to stand, say the time, and write it on the board. Use other half-hour times to give everyone a turn.
2. *Practice Subtraction Family 6.*
   a. **Say Subtraction Family 6 as I move the blocks.**
   b. Ask a child to fill the houses as you say Family 6 together.
3. *Introduce halves as equal parts.*
   a. Draw a line through the middle of the square on the chalkboard. **How many parts does this shape have? Each piece is half of the whole thing.**

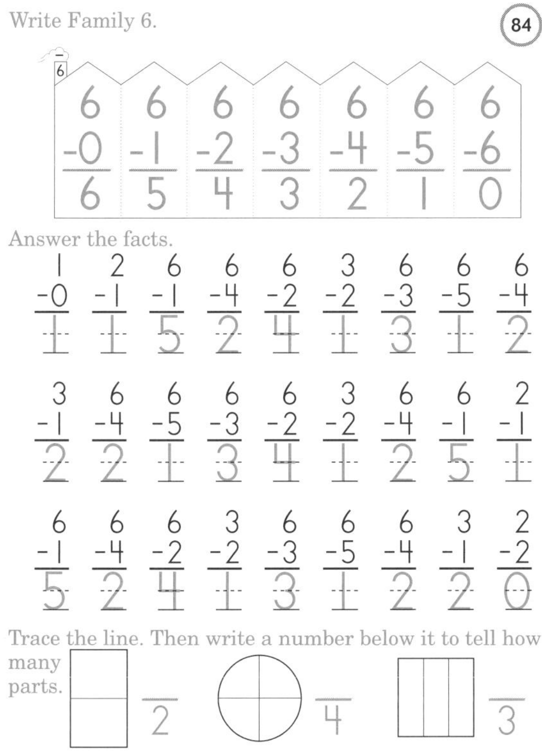

Write Family 6. (84)

6	6	6	6	6	6	6
-0	-1	-2	-3	-4	-5	-6
6	5	4	3	2	1	0

Answer the facts.

1	2	6	6	6	3	6	6	6
-0	-1	-1	-4	-2	-2	-3	-5	-4
1	1	5	2	4	1	3	1	2

3	6	6	6	6	3	6	6	2
-1	-4	-5	-3	-2	-2	-4	-1	-1
2	2	1	3	4	1	2	5	1

6	6	6	3	6	6	6	3	2
-1	-4	-2	-2	-3	-5	-4	-1	-2
5	2	4	1	3	1	2	2	0

Trace the line. Then write a number below it to tell how many parts.

2 4 3

173

Speed Drill Answers

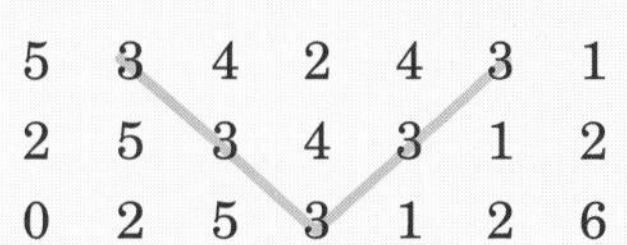

5	3	4	2	4	3	1
2	5	3	4	3	1	2
0	2	5	3	1	2	6

Write the fraction bar with a 2 below it.

b. Draw a line through one end of the rectangle. **This also has 2 parts. Are the parts the same size?** Point to one of the parts. **This is not half of the shape.** Point to the other part. **This is not half of the shape.** Erase the rectangle.

c. Divide the other shapes into 2 parts. Write the denominator if the parts are equal. Erase the shape if they are not equal.

4. *Introduce subtraction story problems.*
   a. **Read the story problem with me. The key word is *left*. *Left* sounds almost like *less*. When some cats run away, we have less.** Put a minus sign in place for the problem.
   b. **How many cats played?**
   How many cats ran away?
   Fill in the blanks.
5. *Do Speed Drill #29.*
6. *Assign Lesson 84.*

Follow-up

Drill

(*Drill* #1)

_____ 40 _____	_____ 59 _____
_____ 29 _____	_____ 39 _____
_____ 69 _____	_____ 20 _____
_____ 80 _____	_____ 50 _____

(*Drill* #2)

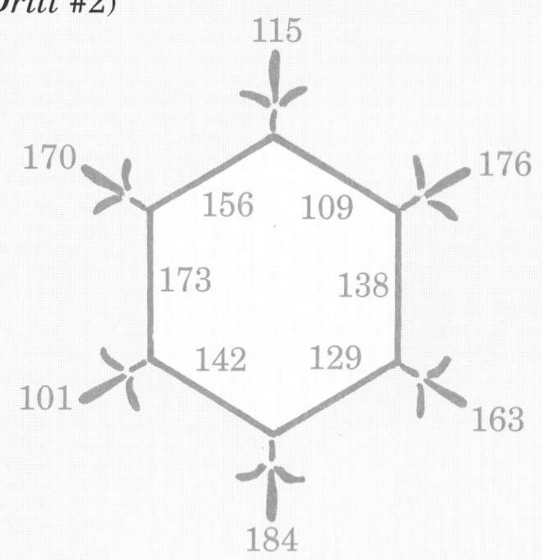

1. Do the Before and After samples, counting by ones. Each sample bridges a tens' number.
2. Call the children to the snowflake on the board. **Can you say these numbers correctly before the snowflake melts?** Drill the group. Drill individuals.

Practice Sheets

- ☐ Fact Houses #21
- ☐ Skip Counting #3
- ● Number Facts #24
- ● Form E: 141–160

Objectives

New

TEACHING

Equality of thirds

WORKBOOK

Subtraction story problem

Review

Subtraction facts

Counting (189)

Half hour

Preparation

Materials

Model clock

Subtraction Families 1–4 and 6 flash cards

Chalkboard

(*Class Time* #1)

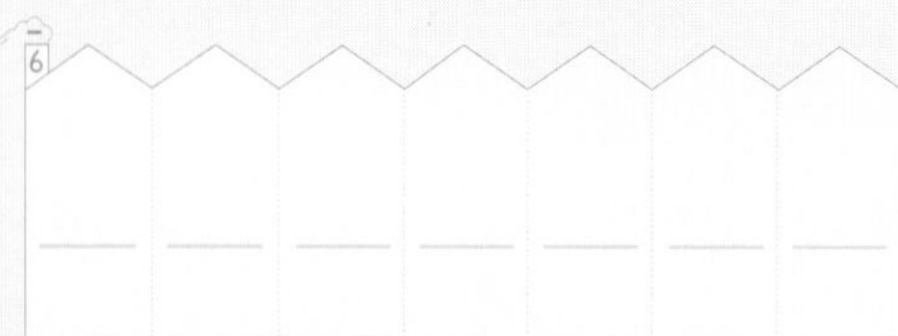

(*Class Time* #3)

6 hens peck. Then 4 of them run away. How many hens are left?

(*Class Time* #6)

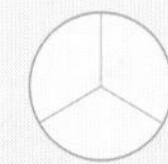

Class Time

1. *Review subtraction families.*
   a. **Watch my fingers as we say Subtraction Family 3 . . . Family 4.**
   b. **Say Family 6 as I fill the houses.**
2. *Drill selected facts.*
   Point to the flash card 6 - 2 = 4 above the flannel board. **Say this fact five times.** Say it loudly the first time, then more quietly with each recital. Drill 6 - 4 = 2 in the same way.
3. *Subtraction story problem.*
   Read the story problem with me. Ask a child to make the correct sign, and then to fill in the blanks.
4. *Counting.*
   Count 100–189.
5. *Practice half hour.*
   Ask a child to stand at the board and to write the times that the class will say. For

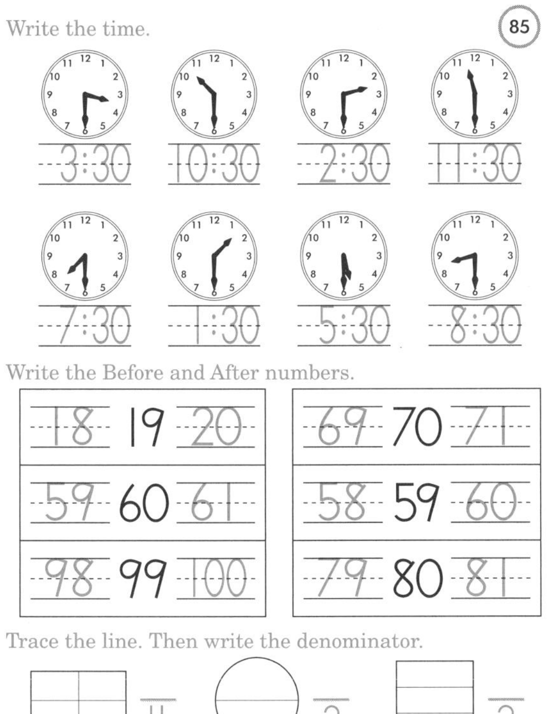
Write the time. 85

3:30 10:30 2:30 11:30

7:30 1:30 5:30 8:30

Write the Before and After numbers.

18 19 20	69 70 71
59 60 61	58 59 60
98 99 100	79 80 81

Trace the line. Then write the denominator.

4 2 3

175

each half-hour time, have the children say it both ways.

3:30—**Half past 3, or 3:30**
6:30—**Half past 6, or 6:30**
9:30—**Half past 9, or 9:30**
12:30—**Half past 12, or 12:30**

6. *Introduce thirds as equal parts.*
   a. Point to the square on the chalkboard. **How many parts are in this shape? Are the parts equal size?** Write the fraction bar and a small 3 below it.
   b. Point to the rectangle. **How many parts does this shape have? If this were a candy bar, and you wanted to divide it among 3 children, would this be a fair way to cut it?** Erase the rectangle. **Do not write a denominator when the pieces are not the same size.**
   c. Continue with the other samples.
7. *Assign Lesson 85.*

Follow-up

Drill

(*Drill* #2)

	hundreds	tens	ones
124			
85			
109			
3			
176			

1. Drill individuals with Subtraction Families 1–4 and 6 flash cards.
2. Practice the place-value motion: **Ones, tens, hundreds; ones, tens, . . .** Have the children place the numbers on the grid.

Practice Sheets

- ☐ Fact Houses #21
- ☐ Skip Counting #3
- ● Number Facts #25
- ● Number Facts #22
- ● Form E: 161–180

Objectives

New

TEACHING

Equality of fourths

Review

Subtraction facts
Counting (199)
Larger (including 180's)

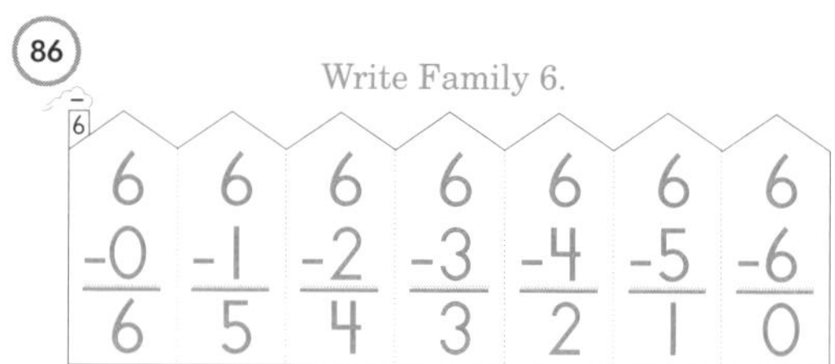

Answer these facts.

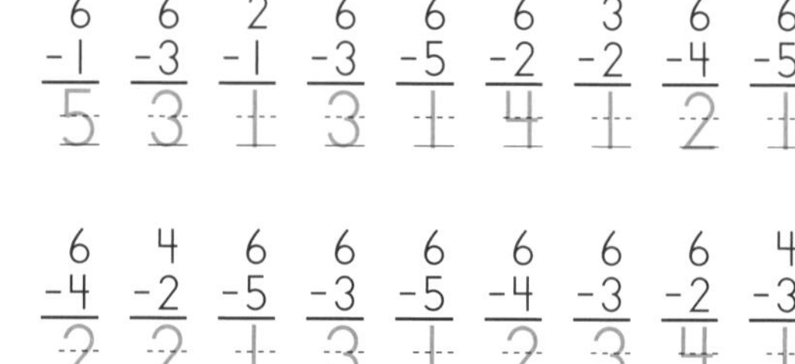

Do the story problem.

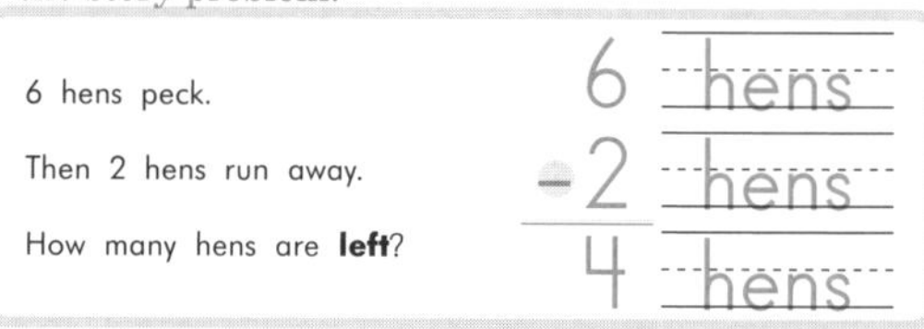

6

Preparation

Materials

Subtraction Families 1–6 flash cards

Form C for each child

Subtraction Families 1–6 flash cards

Chalkboard

(*Class Time* #3)

(*Class Time* #5)

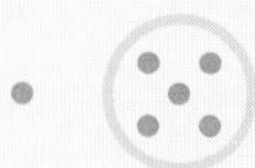

174	147	170	180
136	139	145	154
184	185	188	189

Class Time

1. *Review Subtraction Family 6.*
   a. Ask a child to move the felt blocks as everyone says Subtraction Family 6.
   b. Point to the flash cards above the flannel board. **Say each fact five times.** Say it slowly the first time, then faster with each recital.
2. *Drill subtraction facts.*
   Distribute Form C. Use Subtraction Families 1–6 flash cards. **Write the answer to the fact I show.**
   Apron Row: Box 1—Box 2 . . .
3. *Introduce fourths as equal parts.*
   a. Point to the circle on the chalkboard. **How many parts are in this shape? Are the parts equal size?** Write the fraction bar and a small 4 below it.

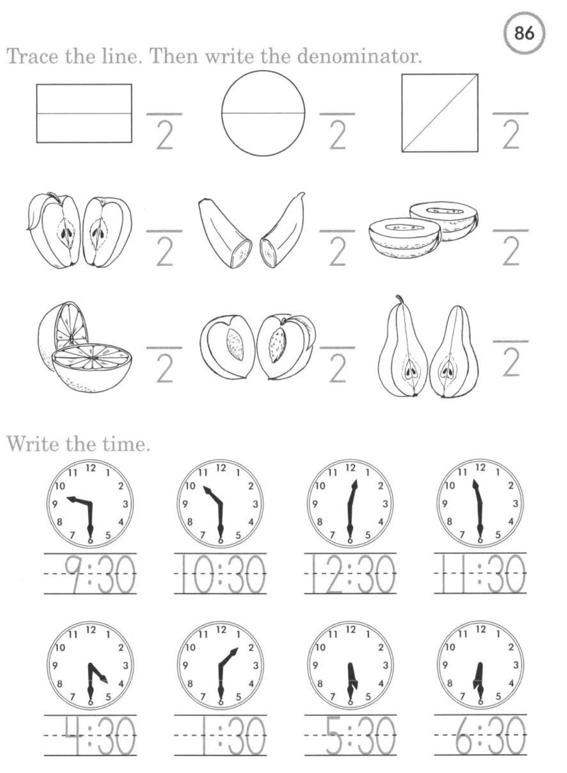

Speed Drill Answers

3	1	4	2	3	2	4
1	4	2	3	2	4	5
4	2	3	2	4	5	1

Speed Drill #30

b. Point to the triangle. **How many pieces are in this shape? Are all the pieces equal size?** Erase the triangle. **Do not write a denominator when the pieces are not the same size.**

c. Let the children finish the other shapes.

4. *Counting.*
   Count 100–199.
5. *Larger numbers.*
   Find the larger number in each box. Do the chalkboard samples.
6. *Do Speed Drill #30.*
7. *Assign Lesson 86.*

Follow-up

Drill

(*Drill* #1)

40	____	50	____	____	____
10	____	____	25	____	____
65	____	____	____	85	____

1. **Count by 5's to 100.** Count by 5's to fill in the Missing Numbers on the chalkboard.
2. Have individuals count their fingers using ordinal numbers. **First, second, third, . . .**
3. Drill Subtraction Families 1–6 flash cards.

Practice Sheets

- ● Form C (*Class Time* #2)
- ☐ Writing Practice #26
- ● Number Facts #25
- ● Form E: 181–200

Objectives

New

TEACHING

Equality of fractional parts

Review

Subtraction facts

Count by 10's

Telling time

Ordinal numbers

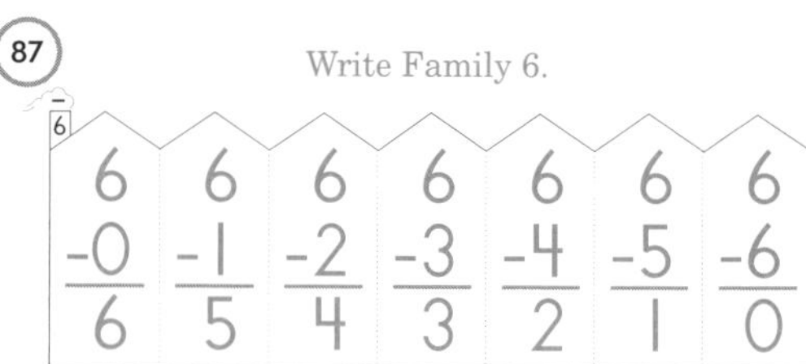

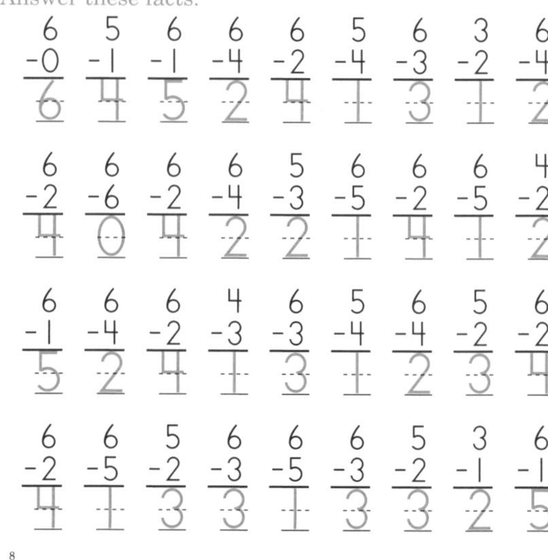

Preparation

Materials

Model clock

Large penny, nickel, and dime

Addition Families 1–7 flash cards

Chalkboard

(*Class Time* #1)

(Write a set of these facts for each child to trace in *Class Time* #2.)

5	6
-2	-2
3	4

(*Class Time* #3)

Class Time

1. *Review Subtraction Families 5 and 6.*
   I will fill the houses. Say Subtraction Family 5 . . . Family 6.
2. *Drill selected facts.*
   a. **Whisper and trace the facts until I say "stop."**
   b. **Stop. Turn toward me. We will say each fact three times. 5 - 2, 3; 5 - 2, 3; . . .**
3. *Practice fractional parts.*
   Write the correct denominator beside each equally divided shape. **Do not write a denominator when the pieces are not the same size.**

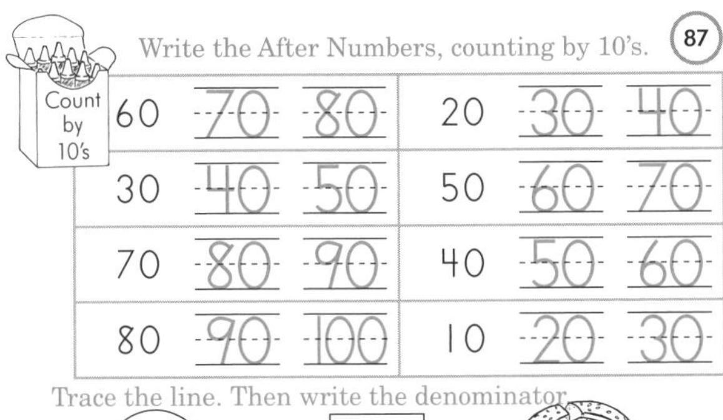
Write the After Numbers, counting by 10's. 87

Count by 10's

60	70	80	20	30	40
30	40	50	50	60	70
70	80	90	40	50	60
80	90	100	10	20	30

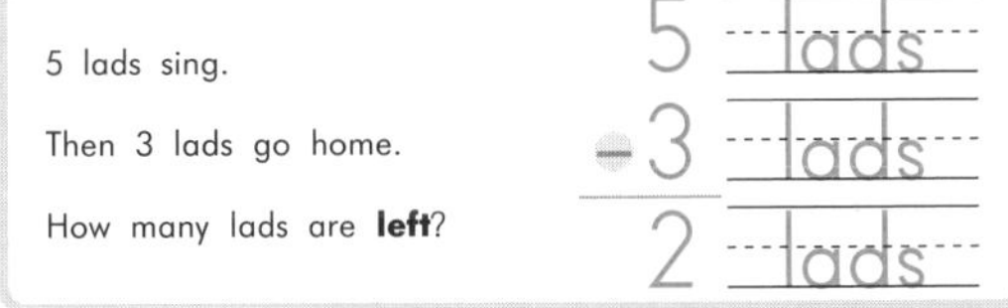

Do the story problem.

5 lads sing.
Then 3 lads go home.
How many lads are **left**?

5 lads
− 3 lads
2 lads

9

4. *Count by 10's.*
   Count by 10's to 100.
5. *Telling time.*
   Set the model clock for the children to read the time together. **8:30, 10:30, 12:30, 2:30, 6:30, . . .**
6. *Ordinal numbers.*
   What number do you think of when I say these words?

fourth	**second**	**third**
eighth	**fifth**	**ninth**
tenth	**seventh**	**sixth**

7. *Assign Lesson 87.*

Follow-up

Drill

(*Drill* #1)

1¢ ○○○○○○ ____

5¢ ○○○○○ ____

10¢ ○○○○○○ ____

10¢ ○○○○ ____

5¢ ○○○ ____

5¢ ○○○○○○ ____

1. Set the large penny, nickel, and dime in the chalk tray.
   a. **Name each coin, and say how much it is worth. Penny, 1¢ . . .**
   b. Have the children count aloud as they do the money samples.
2. Circle Drill with Addition Families 1–7 flash cards.
3. Have individuals move the felt blocks and say Subtraction Family 6.

Practice Sheets

- ☐ Fact Houses #22
- ☐ Form F: 1–100
- ● Number Facts #26
- ● Number Facts #25

Objectives

New

TEACHING

Horizontal subtraction
Identify the ones' place

Review

Subtraction facts
Count by 5's
Counting (199)
Before and After (190's)

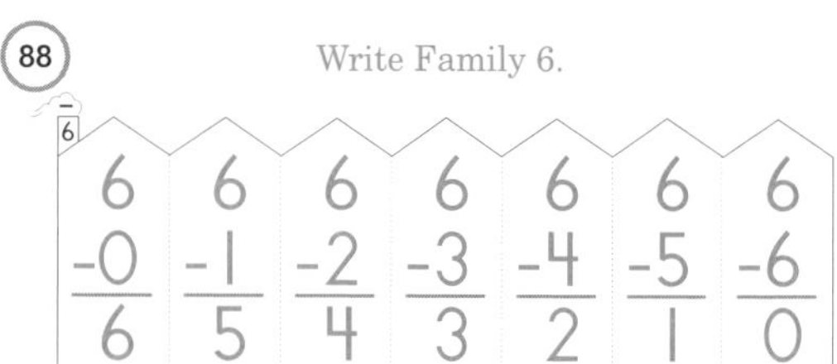

Answer these facts.

4 - 1 = 3	5 - 2 = 3	6 - 1 = 5	5 - 3 = 2	6 - 2 = 4	4 - 3 = 1	6 - 3 = 3	6 - 5 = 1	6 - 4 = 2
5 - 0 = 5	4 - 2 = 2	6 - 2 = 4	6 - 4 = 2	4 - 2 = 2	5 - 4 = 1	4 - 2 = 2	6 - 5 = 1	6 - 3 = 3
6 - 1 = 5	5 - 3 = 2	4 - 3 = 1	5 - 1 = 4	6 - 2 = 4	6 - 3 = 3	6 - 4 = 2	6 - 5 = 1	6 - 3 = 3
6 - 4 = 2	6 - 2 = 4	6 - 5 = 1	5 - 2 = 3	5 - 4 = 1	6 - 4 = 2	6 - 3 = 3	6 - 2 = 4	6 - 6 = 0

10

Preparation

Materials

Subtraction Families 3–6 flash cards

Subtraction Families 4–6 flash cards

Model clock

Chalkboard

(*Class Time* #2)

4 - 3 = ___	6 - 2 = ___	6 - 3 = ___
6 - 5 = ___	6 - 1 = ___	5 - 4 = ___
5 - 3 = ___	5 - 2 = ___	6 - 4 = ___

(*Class Time* #3)

162
179
193
120
158

(*Class Time* #5)

___ 40 ___	___ 195 ___
___ 59 ___	___ 132 ___
___ 80 ___	___ 117 ___
___ 29 ___	___ 191 ___
___ 99 ___	___ 144 ___

Class Time

1. *Review subtraction families.*
   a. Give your Subtraction Families 3–6 flash cards to the children. **If you have the first fact in Family 3, come set it on the chalk tray.** Call for Families 4, 5, and 6.
   b. Stand near the chalk tray. **Say the facts with me.**
2. *Introduce horizontal subtraction.*
   Point to the horizontal samples. **Subtraction facts can be written in number sentences the same as addition facts.** Do the samples.
3. *Place value.*
   a. Motion and say, **Ones, tens, hundreds.**
   b. Point to the numbers inside the box. **Read these numbers with me. Which numbers are in the ones' place?**
   c. Have the children circle the digit in the ones' place in each number.

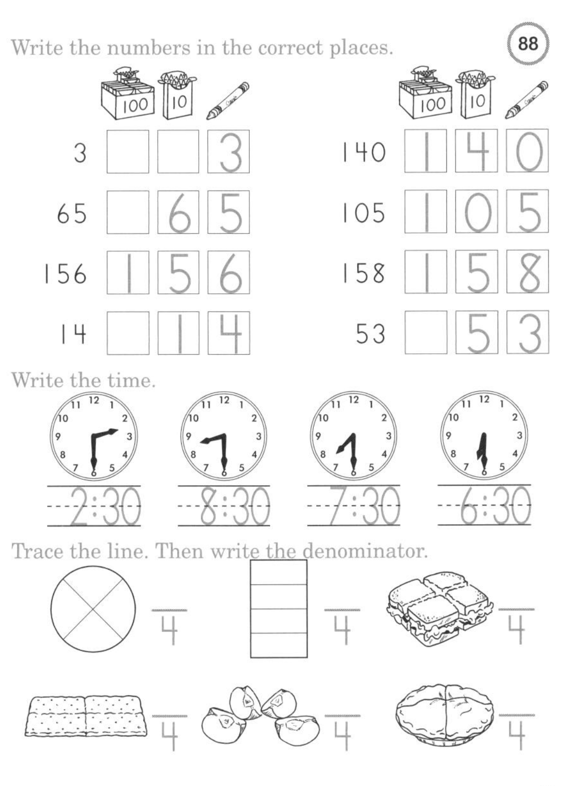
Write the numbers in the correct places. 88

	100	10	1		100	10	1
3			3	140	1	4	0
65		6	5	105	1	0	5
156	1	5	6	158	1	5	8
14		1	4	53		5	3

Write the time.

2:30 8:30 7:30 6:30

Trace the line. Then write the denominator.

4 4 4

4 4 4

11

Speed Drill Answers

4	3	4	2	3	5	1
2	4	3	4	2	3	5
5	2	4	3	4	2	3

Speed Drill #31

4. *Counting.*
   a. **Count by 5's to 100.**
   b. **Count by 1's from 100 to 199.**
5. *Before and After numbers.*
   Do the chalkboard samples.
6. *Do Speed Drill #31.*
7. *Assign Lesson 88.*

Follow-up

Drill

1. Drill individuals with Subtraction Families 4–6 flash cards.
2. Review clock skills.
   a. **Name the hands.**
   b. Set the hands at 12:00. **In 1 hour it will be ___.** Refer to the length of an hour as illustrated in Lesson 69.
   c. **How long is a minute?** To help the children grasp the meaning and length of a minute, do one of the following.
      - Have the children stand and raise both their hands for 1 minute.
      - Have them close their eyes for one minute.
      - Turn off the lights for 1 minute.

Practice Sheets

- ☐ Fact Houses #22
- ☐ Form F: 101–200
- ● Number Facts #27
- ● Money #14

Objectives

New

TEACHING

Identify tens' place
The term smaller

Review

Subtraction facts
Count by 10's, 5's
Money

(89) Answer these facts.

6 - 5 = 1	6 - 4 = 2	6 - 3 = 3	6 - 4 = 2	6 - 1 = 5	5 - 3 = 2	5 - 1 = 4	4 - 3 = 1	6 - 3 = 3
5 - 2 = 3	6 - 4 = 2	6 - 3 = 3	6 - 4 = 2	6 - 5 = 1	6 - 1 = 5	6 - 2 = 4	6 - 4 = 2	5 - 4 = 1
4 - 1 = 3	4 - 2 = 2	6 - 1 = 5	5 - 3 = 2	6 - 2 = 4	4 - 3 = 1	6 - 3 = 3	6 - 5 = 1	6 - 4 = 2
6 - 3 = 3	6 - 4 = 2	5 - 0 = 5	6 - 5 = 1	6 - 2 = 4	5 - 4 = 1	5 - 2 = 3	6 - 4 = 2	4 - 2 = 2

Do the story problem.

6 men work.
Then 3 men drive away.
How many men are **left**?

6 men
- 3 men
3 men

12

Preparation

Materials

Addition Families 1–7 flash cards

Chalkboard

(*Class Time* #3)

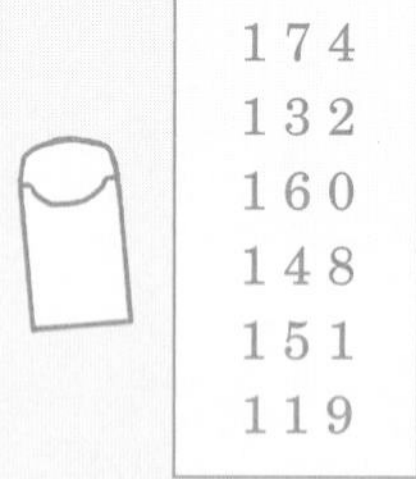

174
132
160
148
151
119

(*Class Time* #5)

15 pennies = _____
10 pennies = _____
27 pennies = _____
3 nickels = _____
6 nickels = _____
8 nickels = _____
9 dimes = _____
5 dimes = _____
7 dimes = _____

Class Time

1. *Review Subtraction Families 3–5.*
Watch my fingers as we say Subtraction Family 3 . . . Family 4 . . . 5.

2. *Practice Subtraction Family 6.*
   a. Place 6 felt blocks on the lower part of the flannel board. **Six trees grow at the side of a field. The farmer cuts down 0 trees. Six trees are left. 6 trees - 0 trees = 6 trees. Say the story fact with me. 6 trees - 0 . . .**
   b. **Six trees grow beside a field. The farmer cuts down 1 tree.** (Move 1 block to the upper part of the board.) **Five trees are left. Say the story fact together. 6 trees - 1 tree = 5 trees.**
   c. Return the moved block to the lower part of the flannel board. **Six trees grow beside a field. The farmer cuts down 2 trees.** (Move 2.) **4 trees are left. . . .**
   d. Continue through the complete subtraction family.

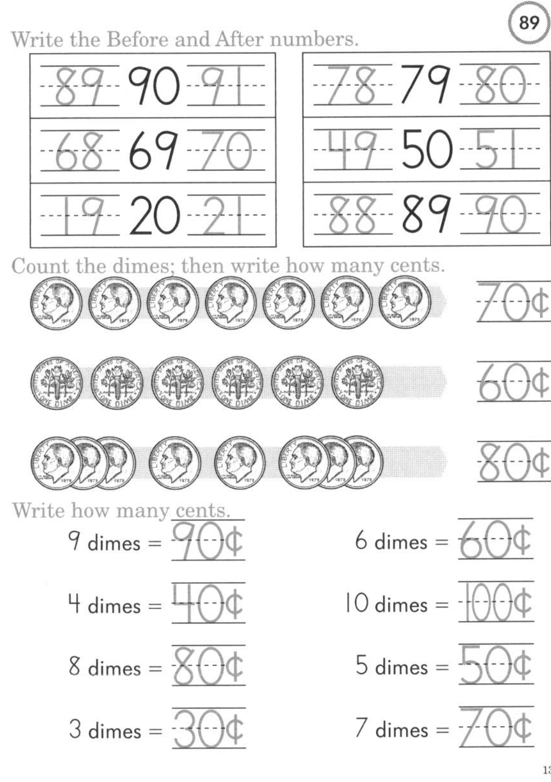

89

Write the Before and After numbers.

89	90	91	78	79	80
68	69	70	49	50	51
19	20	21	88	89	90

Count the dimes; then write how many cents.

70¢

60¢

80¢

Write how many cents.

9 dimes = 90¢ 6 dimes = 60¢

4 dimes = 40¢ 10 dimes = 100¢

8 dimes = 80¢ 5 dimes = 50¢

3 dimes = 30¢ 7 dimes = 70¢

13

3. *Place value.*
   a. Point to the numbers inside the box. **Read these with me. Which numbers are in the tens' place?**
   b. Have the children circle the digit in the tens' place of each number.
4. *Count by 10's and 5's.*
   a. **Girls, count to 100 by 10's.**
   b. **Boys, count to 100 by 5's.**
5. *Money.*
   a. Review the coin names and values.
   b. Do the chalkboard samples. **Use your fingers to help you figure the answers for nickels and dimes.**
6. *Assign Lesson 89.*

Follow-up

Drill

(*Drill* #2)

172	127	135	139
106	160	116	112
148	128	192	129
160	180	104	140

1. Double Drill with Addition Families 1–7 flash cards.
2. **If Betty has a pile of 20 pennies and Sara has a pile of 35 pennies, who has more pennies? Who has less pennies?**

   Who has the larger pile? Who has the smaller pile? A *larger* number means more things. A *smaller* number means less things.

   Point to the first pair of numbers in the samples. **Which number is smaller?** Have the children circle the smaller numbers.

Practice Sheets

- ☐ Fact Houses #23
- ● Number Facts #27
- ● Before and After #5
- ● Clocks #2

Objectives

New

TEACHING

Identify the hundreds' place
Subtraction Family 7

WORKBOOK

After Numbers by 5's
Counting nickels (word)

Review

Subtraction facts
Count by 10's
Money

90

Write Family 6.

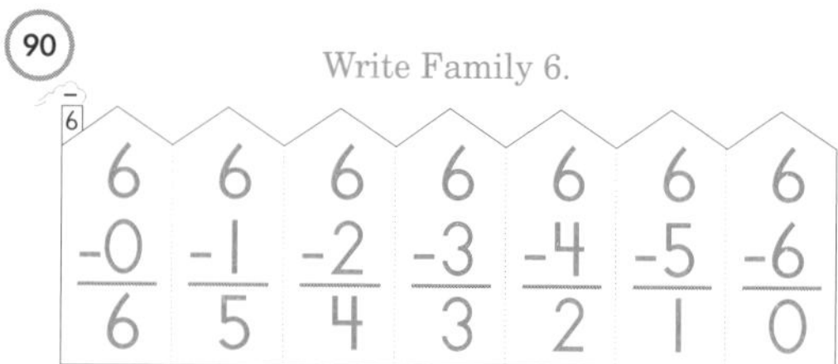

Answer these facts.

5	6	6	5	5	6	5	5	6
-0	-2	-1	-3	-1	-5	-2	-4	-4
5	4	5	2	4	1	3	1	2
5	5	6	6	5	6	6	5	6
-3	-2	-4	-2	-2	-3	-5	-5	-3
2	3	2	4	3	3	1	0	3
6	5	6	6	5	6	6	5	6
-1	-1	-2	-5	-4	-5	-4	-3	-2
5	4	4	1	1	1	2	2	4
6	6	5	6	6	6	6	6	6
-4	-2	-4	-3	-5	-4	-3	-2	-6
2	4	1	3	1	2	3	4	0

14

Preparation

Materials

Subtraction Families 1–6 flash cards

Chalkboard

(*Class Time* #1)

(*Class Time* #3)

(*Class Time* #5)

8 nickels = ____
12 nickels = ____
5 nickels = ____
3 dimes = ____
7 dimes = ____
10 dimes = ____

Class Time

1. *Review Subtraction Families 5 and 6.*
   a. Point to the first flash card above the flannel board. **Say each fact three times with your eyes open and then three times with your eyes closed.**
   b. Ask a child to fill the 5 Houses as you say Family 5 together.
   c. Ask a child to fill the 6 Houses as you say Family 6 together.
2. *Drill subtraction facts.*
   Circle Drill with Subtraction Families 1–6 flash cards.
3. *Place value.*
   a. Motion and repeat, **Ones, tens, hundreds; ones . . .**
   b. Point to the numbers inside the box. **Read these with me. Which numbers are in the hundreds' place?** Have the children circle the hundreds' digit in each number.
4. *Count by 10's.*
   Count by 10's to 100.

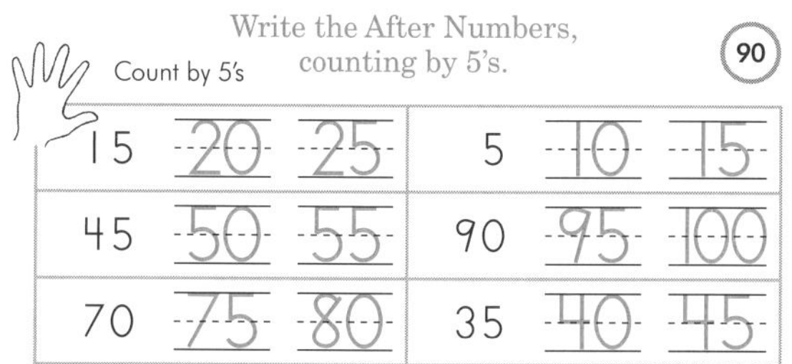

Write the After Numbers, counting by 5's. (90)

Count by 5's

15	20	25	5	10	15
45	50	55	90	95	100
70	75	80	35	40	45

Count the nickels; then write how many cents.

30¢

25¢

40¢

Write how many cents.

9 nickels = 45¢ 4 nickels = 20¢

10 nickels = 50¢ 8 nickels = 40¢

7 nickels = 35¢ 6 nickels = 30¢

15

5. *Money.*
   Do the chalkboard samples.
6. *Do Speed Drill #32.*
7. *Assign Lesson 90.*

Follow-up

Drill

(*Drill* #1)

4	2	5	1	3	2	2
2	3	1	4	3	2	4
+1	+1	+1	+1	+1	+1	+1

Speed Drill Answers

4	3	2	5	4	2	3
3	2	5	4	2	3	4
2	5	4	2	3	4	1

(*Drill* #2)

6 -2	4 -3	6 -3	5 -3	6 -2	4 -1
5 -4	4 -2	6 -4	5 -3	6 -4	6 -5
5 -2	6 -1	6 -4	6 -3	5 -2	4 -3
6 -2	6 -1	5 -3	6 -2	5 -2	6 -4

(*Drill* #3)

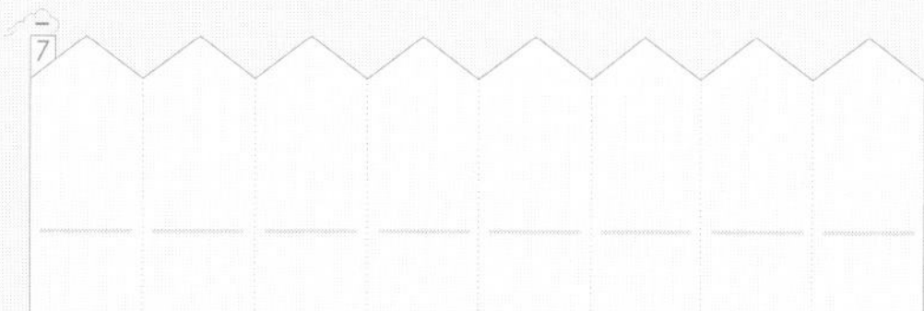

1. Do the column addition samples.
2. Drill with the subtraction grid on the chalkboard. Follow the rows up and down, right and left. Keep the grid on the board for Lesson 91.
3. Introduce Subtraction Family 7. **Help me fill these houses with Subtraction Family 7.** Write the facts in order. **We will work with Subtraction Family 7 tomorrow.**

Practice Sheets

- ☐ Fact Houses #23
- ● Number Facts #28
- ● More Numbers #12
- ● Fractions #1
- ◊ Clocks #3

Objectives

New

TEACHING

Subtraction Family 7

Review

Subtraction facts
Ordinal numbers
Counting (199)
Before and After (190's)
Parts of a whole

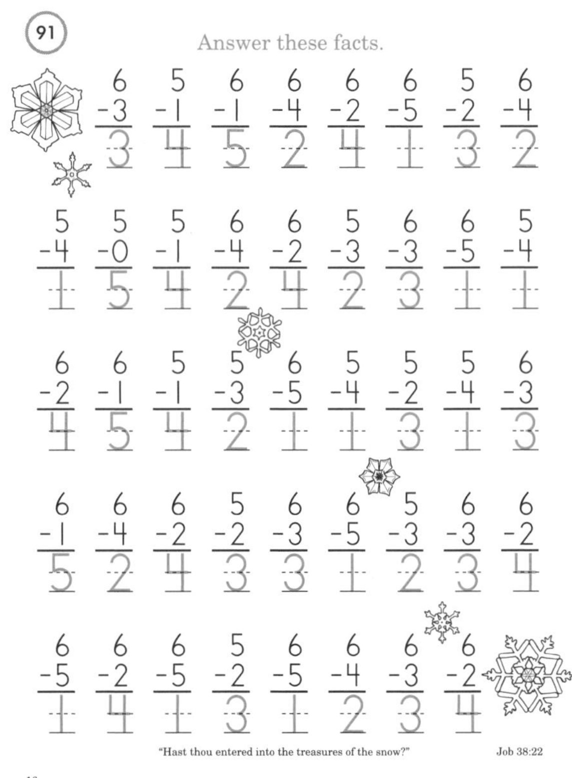

Preparation

Materials

Subtraction Families 1–6 flash cards

Form C for each child

Chalkboard

(Subtraction grid from Lesson 90 for *Class Time* #1 and *Follow-up* drill #1)

(*Class Time* #2)

(*Class Time* #5)

____ 163 ____

____ 175 ____

____ 141 ____

____ 138 ____

____ 194 ____

Class Time

1. *Drill subtraction facts.*
   a. Call the children to the subtraction grid on the board. **Answer together. Girls, answer the first column. Boys, answer the second column. Girls, . . .**
   b. Use Form C for the children to write answers to flash card drill. Flash Subtraction Families 1–6.
2. *Teach Subtraction Family 7.*
   a. **Say Subtraction Family 7 as I move the felt blocks. 7 blocks; take away 0 blocks; 7 blocks left.**
   b. **Say Family 7 as I fill the houses.**
3. *Ordinal numbers.*
   Place the 7 felt blocks in a row, and count their order together. **First, second, third, fourth, fifth, sixth, seventh.**

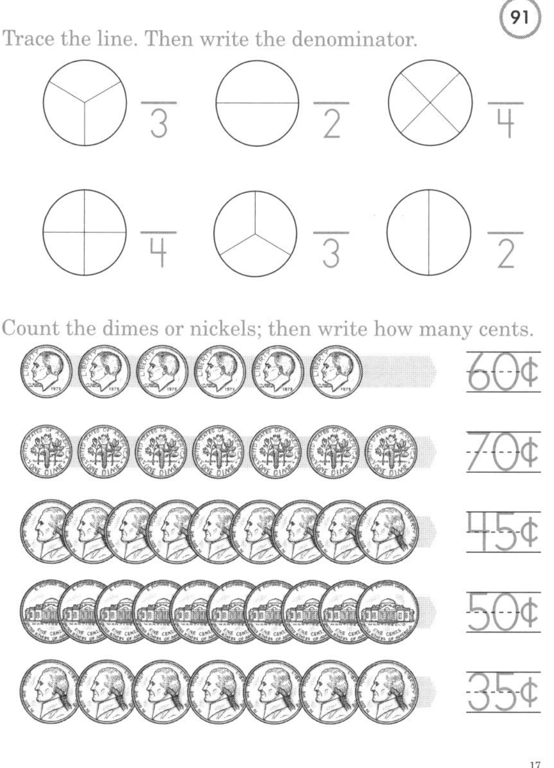

4. *Counting.*
   a. **Count 100–199.**
   b. **How far would you count if you tried to count snowflakes?**
5. *Before and After Numbers.*
   Do the chalkboard samples.
6. *Review fractional parts.*
   a. **If you cut an apple in half, how many pieces would you have?**
   b. **If you cut a cookie into thirds, how many pieces would you have?**
   c. **If you cut a candy bar into fourths, how many pieces would you have?**
7. *Assign Lesson 91.*
   God made amazing treasures when He made the snow. There are too many flakes to count, and the tiny designs are all different.

Follow-up

Drill

1. Drill individuals at the subtraction grid on the board. Can each child answer all the facts in one minute?
2. Chalkboard drill: **Write 143. Change it to 123. (You need to erase 1 digit.) Change it to 128, 120, 150, 110, 117, 137, 131, 101, 161, 169, 199, 194.**

Practice Sheets

- ● Form C (*Class Time* #1)
- ☐ Fact Houses #23
- ☐ Less Numbers #12
- ● Number Facts #28
- ● Clocks #4

Objectives

New

TEACHING

Larger and Smaller
Count by 2's

WORKBOOK

Subtraction Family 7

Review

Money
Subtraction facts

Whisper the facts as you trace them.

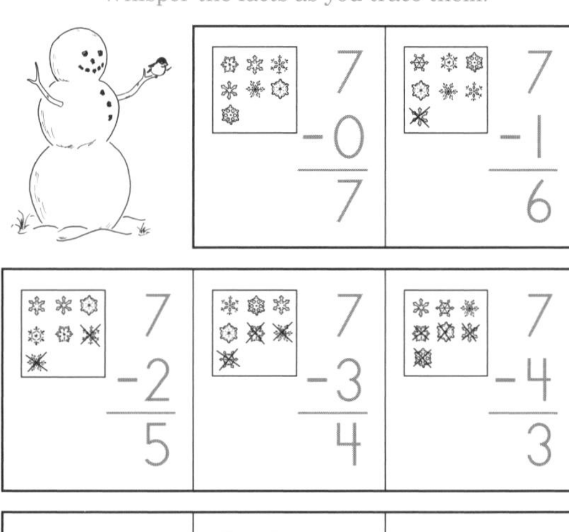

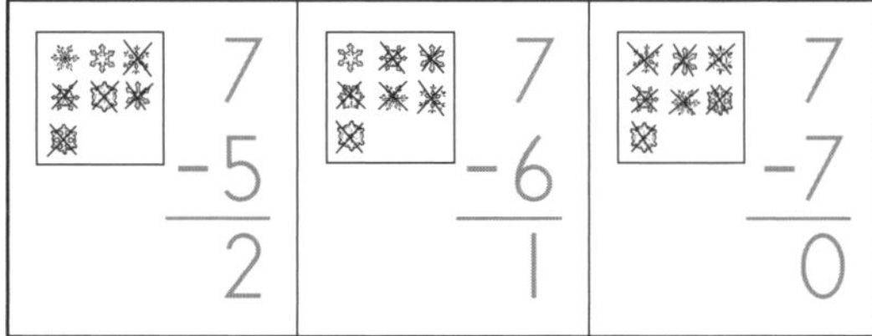

7
-5
2
7
-6
1
7
-7
0

18

Preparation

Make Subtraction Family 7 flash cards for each child.

Materials

Large penny, nickel, and dime

Chalkboard

(*Class Time* #2)

(*Class Time* #3)

113	131	152	125
137	146	140	104
166	161	118	181

Class Time

1. *Review money.*
   a. Hold the large penny, and ask for its name and value.
   Whose picture do you see? (Abraham Lincoln)
   If you saved 13 pennies, you would have ____. Continue with
   24 pennies **16 pennies**
   29 pennies **30 pennies**
   b. Hold the large nickel, and ask for its name and value.
   Whose picture do you see? (Thomas Jefferson)
   If you saved 8 nickels, you would have ____. Continue with
   7 nickels **10 nickels**
   3 nickels **5 nickels**
   c. Hold the large dime, and ask for its name and value.
   Whose picture do you see? (Franklin D. Roosevelt)

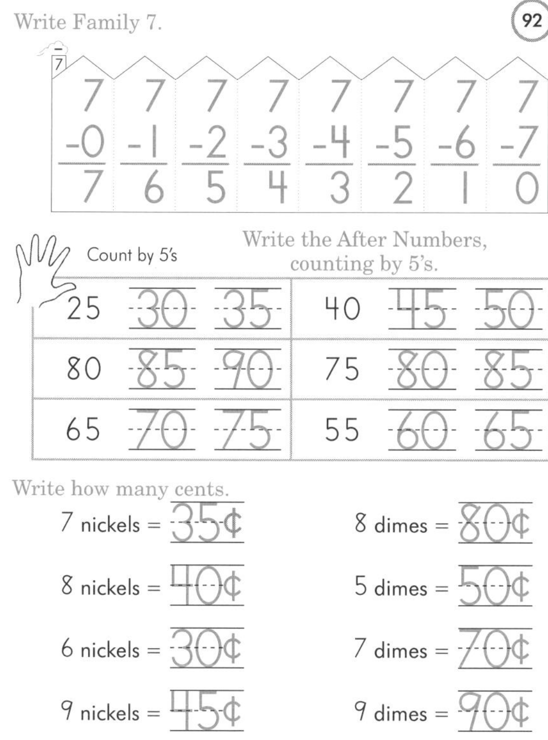

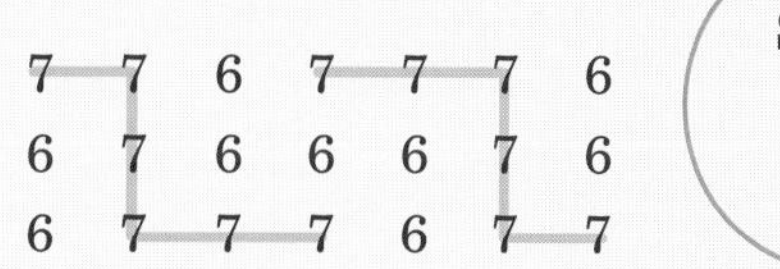

Speed Drill #33

If you saved 6 dimes, you would have ____. Continue with

4 dimes **10 dimes**
7 dimes **8 dimes**

2. *Review Subtraction Families 6 and 7.*
   a. Ask a child to fill the 6 Houses as you say Family 6 together.
   b. **I will move the felt blocks. [Peter] will fill the houses. Everyone help to say the facts. 7 take away 0 equals 7. . . .**
   c. Point to the 7 Houses. **Say the facts with me. 7 minus 0, 7 . . .**
3. *Meaning of* larger *and* smaller.
   a. **A larger number has (more, less).**
   b. **A smaller number has ____.**
   c. Have individuals circle the smaller numbers in the chalkboard samples.
4. *Do Speed Drill #33.*
5. *Assign Lesson 92.*

Follow-up

Drill

1. Give each child his Subtraction Family 7 flash cards.
2. Introduce counting by 2's.
   Call the children to the number line.
   a. **Listen while I count to 20.** 1, **2,** 3, **4,** 5, **6,** 7, **8,** 9, **10,** . . . **20.** (Whisper the odd numbers, and say the even numbers loudly.)
   b. **Count with me in the same way.** 1, **2,** 3, **4,** . . . **20.**
   c. **Count to 20 again. I will write the loud numbers on the board.** Write 2 4 6 8 . . .
   d. **Now say the numbers on the board. 2, 4, 6, 8, . . .**
   e. **This is counting by 2's. Each number takes us 2 steps down the number line. This is a good way to count mittens and shoes and socks, because they usually come in twos.**

Practice Sheets

- ☐ Fact Houses #24
- ☐ Before and After #6
- ● Number Facts #26
- ● Money #14
- ● Fractions #1

Objectives

New

TEACHING

Count by 2's

Review

Subtraction facts

Place value

Preparation

Tack Subtraction Family 7 flash cards above the flannel board with answers showing.

Materials

Addition Families 1–7 flash cards

Chalkboard

(*Class Time* #1)

(*Class Time* #2)

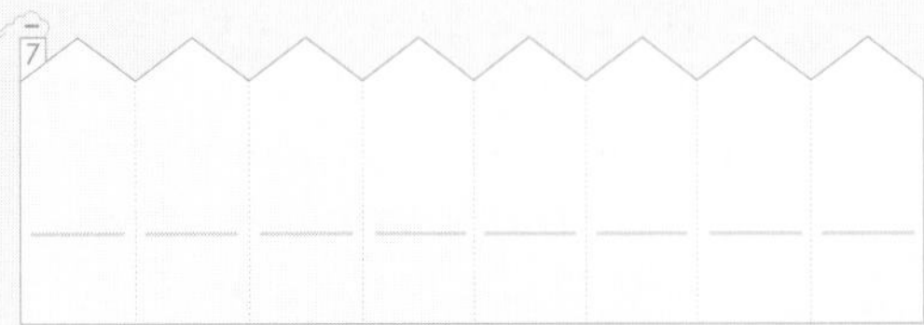

(Write a set of these facts for each child to trace in *Class Time* #3)

7	7
-3	-4
4	3

93

Write Family 7.

7	7	7	7	7	7	7	7
-0	-1	-2	-3	-4	-5	-6	-7
7	6	5	4	3	2	1	0

Answer these facts.

7	7	7	7	7	7	7	7	7
-4	-2	-5	-3	-6	-4	-1	-0	-4
3	5	2	4	1	3	6	7	3

7	7	7	7	7	7	7	7	7
-5	-0	-5	-2	-5	-3	-1	-4	-7
2	7	2	5	2	4	6	3	0

7	7	7	7	7	7	7	7	7
-3	-5	-4	-2	-5	-3	-6	-4	-1
4	2	3	5	2	4	1	3	6

7	7	7	7	7	7	7	7	7
-4	-3	-4	-5	-6	-4	-2	-3	-5
3	4	3	2	1	3	5	4	2

20

Class Time

1. *Teach counting by 2's.*
   a. Call the children to the number line. **We will count to 40. Whisper the first number. Say the next number loudly.** 1, **2,** 3, **4,** 5, **6,** 7, **8,** 9, **10,** 11, **12,** 13, **14,** . . . **40.** Write the loud numbers on the board as you go.
   b. Draw a large circle around 2, 4, 6, 8, 10 in the line of numbers you just wrote. Point to them and say, **2, 4, 6, 8, 10.** Circle 12–20. Point to the ones' digit in each of these as you say, **2, 4, 6, 8, 10.** Circle 22–30, and repeat the ones' digits again. Circle 32–40. **All the numbers have 2, 4, 6, 8, or 0 when we count by 2's.**
   c. Write 2, 4, 6, 8, 0 in the bottom of the large 2 on the chalkboard, and keep it for Lesson 94.
   d. **Now we will count by 2's as we say the numbers on the board. 2, 4, 6, 8, 10, 12, . . . 40.**
2. *Practice Subtraction Family 7.*
   a. Place 7 felt blocks on the lower part of

Write the numbers in the correct places. (93)

	100	10	1
164	1	6	4
5			5
148	1	4	8
19		1	9
173	1	7	3

	100	10	1
23		2	3
118	1	1	8
102	1	0	2
2			2
100	1	0	0

Circle More.

• more	(138) 125	105 (117)	169 (179)
(148) 142	149 (150)	(175) 157	135 (143)

Answer these facts.

2	2	3	1	3	4	2	2	1
2	4	2	5	3	2	3	4	4
+ 1	+ 1	+ 1	+ 1	+ 1	+ 1	+ 1	+ 1	+ 1
5	7	6	7	7	7	6	7	6

21

the flannel board. Move them as you say these story problems. Have the children say each story fact with you.
(1) **Fred saw 7 snowflakes land on his mitten. 0 snowflakes melted. 7 snowflakes were left. 7 snowflakes - 0 snowflakes = 7 snowflakes.**
(2) **Fred saw 7 snowflakes on his mitten. 1 snowflake melted. 6 snowflakes were left. . . .**
(3) **Fred saw 7 snowflakes on his mitten. 2 snowflakes melted. . . .**

b. Ask a child to fill the houses as everyone says Family 7.

3. *Drill selected facts.*
Have each child stand near his set of facts on the board. **Whisper and trace the facts until I say "stop."**

4. *Place value.*
Motion and say, **Ones, tens, hundreds; ones, tens, . . .**

5. *Assign Lesson 93.*

Follow-up

Drill

(*Drill* #2)

124	142	157	175
116	112	181	118
134	131	130	120

1. Circle Drill with Addition Families 1–7 flash cards.
2. **A number that has less is smaller. Find the smaller number in each sample.**
3. Have individuals count 100–150.

Practice Sheets

- □ Fact Houses #24
- □ Clocks #2
- ● Number Facts #29
- ● More Numbers #13
- ◊ Dot-to-Dot #34

Objectives

New

WORKBOOK

Count by 2's

Review

Subtraction facts
Fractional parts
Count by 5's
Missing Numbers (by 5's)
Larger and Smaller (160's)

94

Write Family 7.

7	7	7	7	7	7	7	7
-0	-1	-2	-3	-4	-5	-6	-7
7	6	5	4	3	2	1	0

Answer these facts.

3	7	7	7	4	7	7	7	7
-2	-2	-5	-3	-3	-4	-1	-6	-7
1	5	2	4	1	3	6	1	0

7	7	7	4	7	7	4	7	7
-5	-4	-1	-1	-5	-6	-2	-2	-6
2	3	6	3	2	1	2	5	1

7	7	7	7	7	4	3	7	7
-3	-4	-3	-2	-3	-0	-1	-4	-1
4	3	4	5	4	4	2	3	6

7	2	7	7	7	7	7
-4	-1	-5	-4	-2	-5	-3
3	1	2	3	5	2	4

"He sendeth out his word, and melteth them." Psalm 147:18

22

Preparation

Materials

Form D for each child

Chalkboard

(*Class Time* #1)

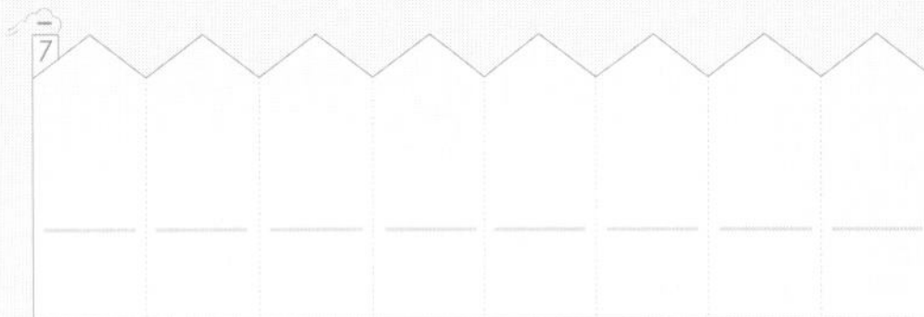

(*Class Time* #3)

(*Class Time* #4)

40	____	____	____	60	____
____	10	____	____	____	30
75	____	____	____	95	____

(*Class Time* #5)

113	131	152	125
137	146	140	104
166	161	118	181

Class Time

1. *Practice Subtraction Family 7.*
   a. **Say Family 7 as I move the felt blocks.**
   b. Point to the flash cards above the flannel board. **Say each fact three times with your eyes open and then three times with your eyes closed.**
   c. Ask a child to fill the 7 Houses as everyone says the facts.
2. *Review fractional parts.*
   a. **If you cut an orange in half, how many pieces do you have?**
   b. **If you cut a pie into thirds, how many pieces do you have?**
   c. **If you cut a sandwich into fourths, how many pieces do you have?**
3. *Count by 2's.*
   a. Point to the large 2. **The numbers for counting by 2's are 2, 4, 6, 8, 0; 2, 4, 6, 8, 0.**
   b. Point to the number line. Look for the numbers with **2, 4, 6, 8, and 0 as we**

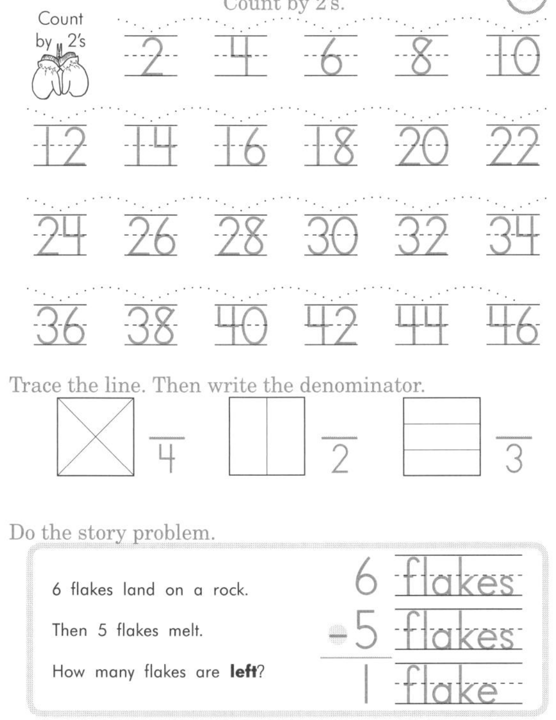

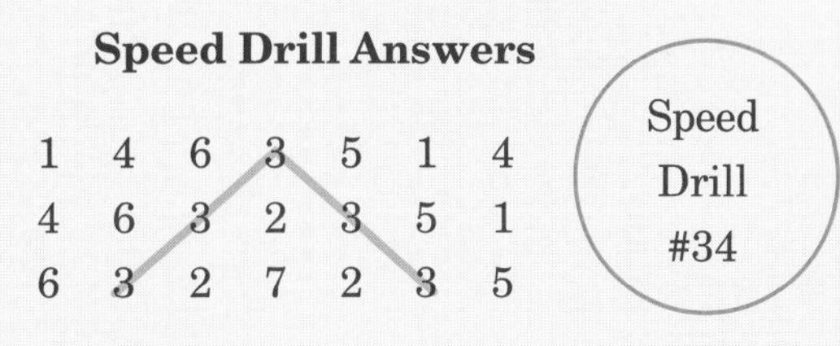

hop down the number line to 50. 2, 4, 6, 8, 10, 12, 14, . . .

c. When we count by 2's, we hop 2 numbers at a time.

4. *Count by 5's.*
   a. **Count by 5's to 100.**
   b. Do the Missing Number samples, counting by 5's.
5. *Larger and Smaller.*
   a. **A number with more is ___.**
   A number with less is ___.
   b. Let individuals circle their choice in each box and say, **This number is ___.** (larger or smaller)
6. *Do Speed Drill #34.*
7. *Assign Lesson 94.*
   God makes the cold snow, and God makes it melt again. "He sendeth out his word, and melteth them: he causeth his wind to blow, and the waters flow" (Psalm 147:18).

Follow-up

Drill

1. Distribute Form D for story problems. Print *boys* on the chalkboard for a label. **These are subtraction problems. Put a *minus* in the gray spot when you hear the word *left*.**
   a. **Arrow Box: 7 boys play. Then 1 of them runs away. How many boys are *left?***
   b. **Button Box: 7 boys play. Then 5 of them run away. How many boys are *left?***
   c. **Camel Box: 7 boys study. Then 4 of them go home. How many boys are *left?***
   d. **Daffodil Box: 7 boys stand and sing. Then 2 of them sit down. How many boys are *left?***
   e. **Elephant Box: 7 boys move chairs. Then 3 of them go out. How many boys are *left?***
   f. **Feather Box: 7 boys pass out papers. Then 6 of them go to play. How many boys are *left?***
2. Hold up your fist or fingers to lead the class in saying Subtraction Family 7.

Practice Sheets

- ● Form D (*Follow-up* drill #1)
- ☐ Fact Houses #24
- ☐ Less Numbers #13
- ☐ Money #14
- ● Number Facts #29

Objectives

New

TEACHING

Number words one *to* five

Review

Count by 2's, 5's

Subtraction facts

Telling time

(95)

Write Family 7.

7	7	7	7	7	7	7	7
-0	-1	-2	-3	-4	-5	-6	-7
7	6	5	4	3	2	1	0

Answer these facts.

7	7	5	7	7	5	7	4	5
-4	-2	-3	-3	-6	-4	-1	-3	-4
3	5	2	4	1	1	6	1	1

7	5	7	7	5	5	7	7	5
-5	-1	-2	-5	-2	-3	-4	-3	-2
2	4	5	2	3	2	3	4	3

7	7	4	7	4	7	7	7	7
-3	-4	-1	-4	-3	-3	-6	-2	-1
4	3	3	3	1	4	1	5	6

7	7	7	3	7	7	7	7	7
-4	-1	-5	-1	-2	-5	-3	-6	-4
3	6	2	2	5	2	4	1	3

24

Preparation

Prepare flash cards for the number words from one to ten. Cut ten cards 8" × 4", and write one number word on each card.

Materials

Subtraction Family 7 flash cards

Model clock

Number word cards one *to* five

Subtraction Families 6 and 7 flash cards

Chalkboard

(*Class Time* #2)

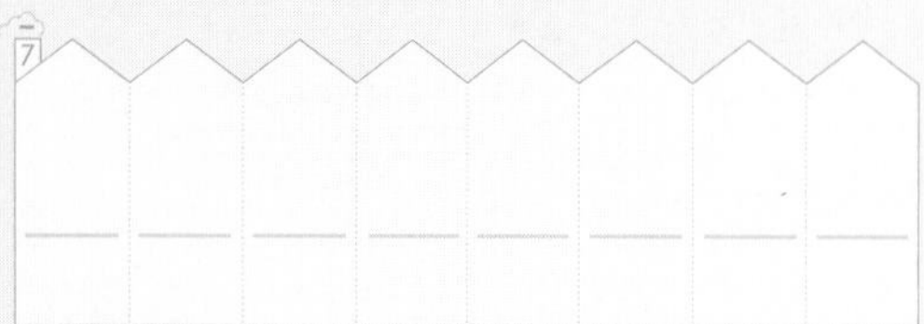

Class Time

1. *Count by 2's.*
   Stand near the number line. **The numbers for counting by 2's are 2, 4, 6, 8, 0. Ready to count by 2's to 100? 2, 4, 6, 8, 10, 12, . . .**
2. *Review Subtraction Family 7.*
   a. Ask a child to move the felt blocks as you say Family 7 together.
   b. **Say Family 7 as I fill the houses.**
3. *Drill subtraction facts.*
   Circle Drill with Subtraction Family 7 flash cards.

4. *Telling time.*
   Answer together to tell what time the clock shows. Set the hands at 7:30, 11:30, 2:30, 5:30, 9:30, 12:30.
5. *Count by 5's.*
   Boys, count by 5's to 100.
   Girls, count by 5's to 100.
6. *Assign Lesson 95.*

Follow-up

Drill

(*Drill* #2)

one ____	four ____	five ____
two ____	five ____	one ____
three ____	two ____	three ____
five ____	three ____	four ____

1. Introduce number words *one* to *five*.
   a. Print *one, two, three, four,* and *five* on the chalkboard. See if the children can sound out the words. Give help for the words that are not phonetic.
   b. Post the words with the numerals for a few days where the children can see them.
2. Practice number words.
   a. Flash number word cards *one* to *five*.
   b. Point to the chalkboard samples. **Can you write the correct number in the blank for each word?**
3. Drill individuals with Subtraction Families 6 and 7 flash cards.

Practice Sheets

- ☐ Fact Houses #24
- ☐ Before and After #7
- ● Number Facts #30
- ● Number Facts #26
- ◊ Dot-to-Dot #35

Objectives

New

TEACHING

Number words *one* to *five*

WORKBOOK

Number words *one* to *five*

Review

Count by 2's
Subtraction facts
Smaller (150's)

Preparation

Materials

Subtraction Families 4–7 flash cards

Number word cards *one* to *five*

Number word cards one *to* five

Chalkboard

(*Class Time* #4)

five	____	one	____
three	____	four	____
four	____	two	____
two	____	five	____

(*Class Time* #5)

117	115	101	110
125	135	149	129
143	134	133	113
120	130	156	146

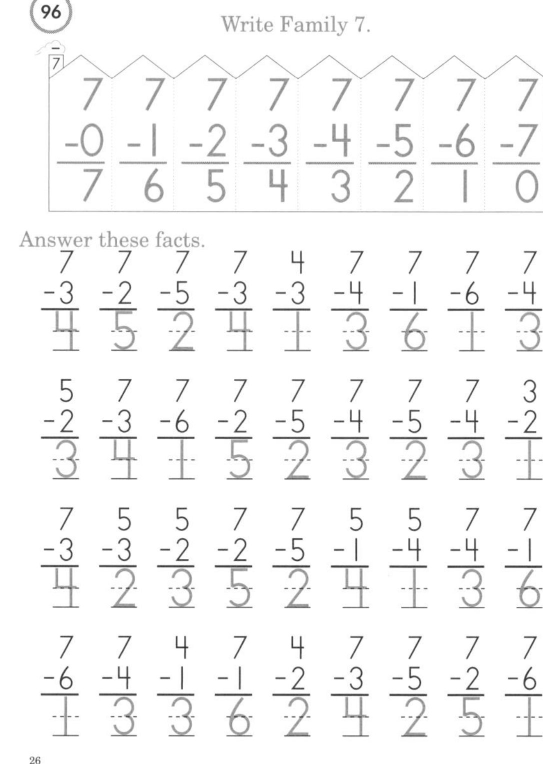

96

Write Family 7.

7	7	7	7	7	7	7	7
-0	-1	-2	-3	-4	-5	-6	-7
7	6	5	4	3	2	1	0

Answer these facts.

7	7	7	7	4	7	7	7	7
-3	-2	-5	-3	-3	-4	-1	-6	-4
4	5	2	4	1	3	6	1	3
5	7	7	7	7	7	7	7	3
-2	-3	-6	-2	-5	-4	-5	-4	-2
3	4	1	5	2	3	2	3	1
7	5	5	7	7	5	5	7	7
-3	-3	-2	-2	-5	-1	-4	-4	-1
4	2	3	5	2	4	1	3	6
7	7	4	7	4	7	7	7	7
-6	-4	-1	-1	-2	-3	-5	-2	-6
1	3	3	6	2	4	2	5	1

26

Class Time

1. *Count by 2's.*
   a. Call the children to the number line. **What is the number pattern for counting by 2's?**
   b. **When we count by 2's, we hop 2 numbers at a time. 2, 4, 6, . . . 100.**
2. *Subtraction Family 7 stories.*
   Place 7 felt blocks on the lower part of the flannel board. Move them, and have the children help to say the story facts.
   (1) **7 bunnies sat in a nest. 0 bunnies hopped out. 7 bunnies were left. 7 bunnies – 0 bunnies = 7 bunnies.**
   (2) **7 bunnies sat in a nest. 1 bunny hopped out. . . .** Continue to the end of the family.
3. *Review Subtraction Families 4–7.*
   a. Give the flash cards for Families 4–7 to the children. **If you have the first fact in Family 4, come and set it on the chalk tray.** Call for Families 5, 6, and 7.

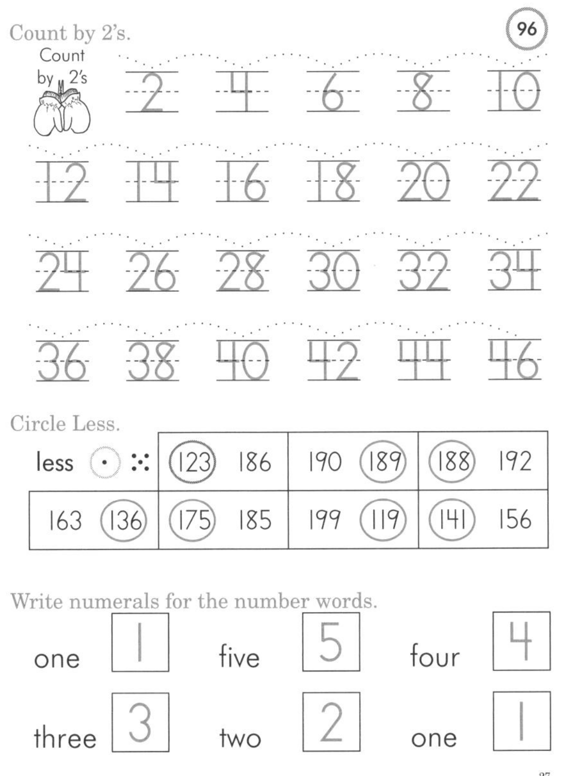

Count by 2's. (96)

Count by 2's

2 4 6 8 10

12 14 16 18 20 22

24 26 28 30 32 34

36 38 40 42 44 46

Circle Less.

less	(123) 186	190 (189)	(188) 192
163 (136)	(175) 185	199 (119)	(141) 156

Write numerals for the number words.

one 1 five 5 four 4

three 3 two 2 one 1

27

Speed Drill Answers

3	4	5	4	5	4	2
2	3	4	5	4	2	3
5	2	3	4	2	3	5

Speed Drill #35

b. Stand near the flash cards. **Say each family with me.**

4. *Teach number words* one *to* five.
   a. Print *one, two, three, four,* and *five* on the chalkboard and give any help needed for the children to recognize them. (See Lesson 95 *Follow-up.*)
   b. Flash number word cards.
   c. Do the chalkboard samples.
5. *Smaller numbers.*
   Smaller numbers means less things. Circle the number that is smaller in each sample.
6. *Do Speed Drill #35.*
7. *Assign Lesson 96.*

Follow-up

Drill

1. Give subtraction facts orally. Have the children stand before you in two rows as they do for Double Drill. **Whoever says the correct answer first may go to the back of his line.**

7 - 6 =	**3 - 2** =	**7 - 4** =
5 - 2 =	**7 - 1** =	**4 - 3** =
7 - 4 =	**7 - 5** =	**7 - 3** =
5 - 2 =	**7 - 2** =	**5 - 4** =
4 - 2 =	**7 - 3** =	**7 - 2** =

2. Drill individuals with number word cards *one* to *five*.
3. Get a box of paper clips. Have the children surround a table or your desk. Dump approximately 40 paper clips out of the box. **We will count the clips by 2's. 2, 4, 6, . . .** Slide 2 clips away from the pile for each number you say.

Practice Sheets

- ☐ Fact Houses #25
- ● Number Facts #30
- ● More Numbers #14
- ● Clocks #4

Objectives
New
TEACHING
Mixed addition and subtraction
After Numbers by 2's
Review
Subtraction facts
Count by 2's
Number words

Preparation

Materials

Subtraction Families 6 and 7 flash cards

Number word cards *one* to *five*

Addition and Subtraction Families 1–6 flash cards

Chalkboard

(*Class Time* #1)

(Write a set of these facts for each child to trace in *Class Time* #2.)

6	7
-2	-2
4	5

(*Class Time* #4. Use green chalk for plus signs and red chalk for minus signs.)

6	7	2	7	3	3
+1	-2	+3	-5	+4	+3

7	2	5	7	6	6
-4	+4	+2	-3	-4	-5

Class Time

1. *Review Subtraction Families 6 and 7.*
   a. Ask a child to fill the 6 Houses as you say Family 6 together.
   b. Ask a child to fill the 7 Houses as you say Family 7 together.
2. *Drill selected facts.*
   a. Have each child stand near his set of facts on the board. **Trace and say the facts three times with me.**
   b. **Trace and whisper the facts until I say "stop."**
3. *Drill subtraction facts.*
   Circle Drill with Subtraction Families 6 and 7 flash cards.
4. *Mixed addition and subtraction.*
   We can add row after row of plus problems. We can subtract row after row of minus problems. But can we

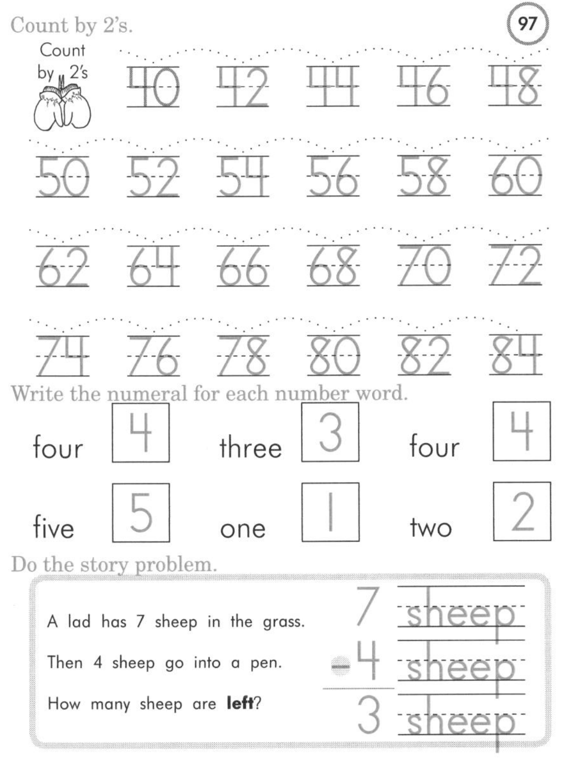
Count by 2's. 97

Count by 2's

40 42 44 46 48

50 52 54 56 58 60

62 64 66 68 70 72

74 76 78 80 82 84

Write the numeral for each number word.

four 4 three 3 four 4

five 5 one 1 two 2

Do the story problem.

A lad has 7 sheep in the grass.
Then 4 sheep go into a pen.
How many sheep are **left**?

7 sheep
−4 sheep
3 sheep

29

add and subtract in the same row? Watch the signs! Have the children answer the facts.

5. *Count by 2's.*
   Stand near the number line. **What is the number pattern for counting by 2's? Count 2, 4, 6, . . . 100.**
6. *Number words.*
   Flash number word cards *one* to *five*.
7. *Assign Lesson 97.*
   A shepherd cares for his sheep. Jesus is the loving Shepherd, who cares for us.

Follow-up

Drill

(*Drill* #1)

2 ___ ___	18 ___ ___	72 ___ ___
10 ___ ___	30 ___ ___	96 ___ ___
22 ___ ___	44 ___ ___	86 ___ ___

1. Point to the samples on the board. **Write the numbers that come after when you count by 2's.**
2. Drill individuals with Addition and Subtraction Families 1–6 flash cards.
3. Chalkboard drill: **Write the number you think of when I say:**

fourth	**seventh**	**fifth**
ninth	**first**	**eighth**
third	**sixth**	**second**

Practice Sheets

- ☐ Fact Houses #25
- ☐ Less Numbers #14
- ● Number Facts #30
- ● Fractions #1
- ◊ Dot-to-Dot #36

Objectives

New

TEACHING

After Numbers by 2's
Number word *six*
Thermometer
Fraction $\frac{1}{2}$

WORKBOOK

After Numbers by 2's
Number word *six*
Mixed addition and subtraction

Review

Subtraction facts
Count by 2's
Money
Number words

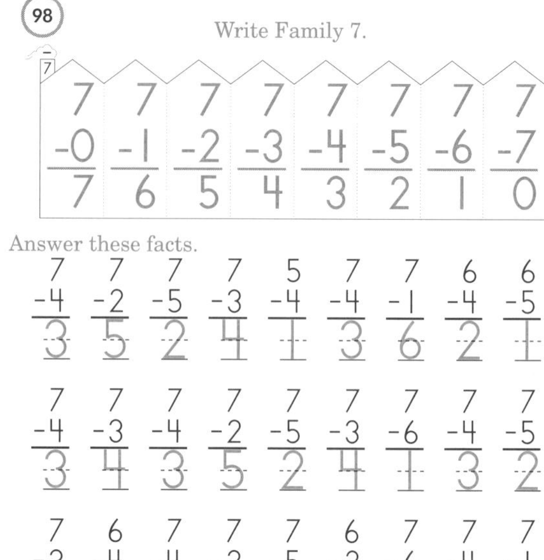

98

Write Family 7.

7	7	7	7	7	7	7	7
-0	-1	-2	-3	-4	-5	-6	-7
7	6	5	4	3	2	1	0

Answer these facts.

7	7	7	7	5	7	7	6	6
-4	-2	-5	-3	-4	-4	-1	-4	-5
3	5	2	4	1	3	6	2	1

7	7	7	7	7	7	7	7	7
-4	-3	-4	-2	-5	-3	-6	-4	-5
3	4	3	5	2	4	1	3	2

7	6	7	7	7	6	7	7	7
-3	-4	-4	-2	-5	-2	-6	-4	-1
4	2	3	5	2	4	1	3	6

7	6	6	7	7	7	5	7	5
-5	-3	-1	-5	-3	-6	-2	-1	-3
2	3	5	2	4	1	3	6	2

30

Preparation

Materials

Subtraction Families 5–7 flash cards
Large penny, nickel, and dime
Number word cards *one* to *five*
Large thermometer
Subtraction Families 1–7 flash cards

Chalkboard

(*Class Time* #1)

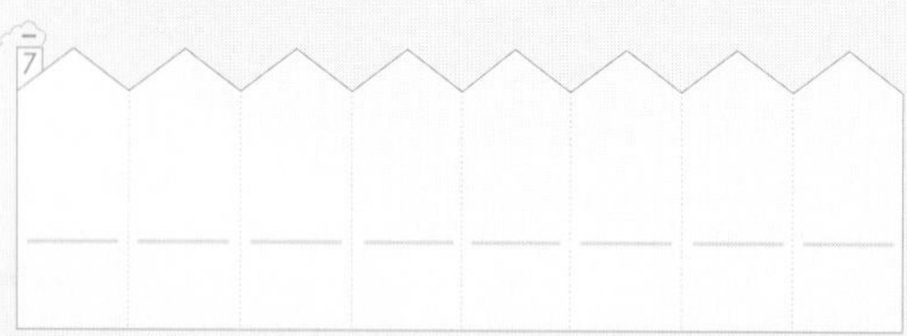

(*Class Time* #3. Use green chalk for plus signs and red chalk for minus signs.)

5	2	6	7	3	3
-3	+4	-3	-5	+4	+3

1	5	6	5	7	6
+6	+2	-4	-2	-3	+1

(*Class Time* #4)

4 ___ ___ 16 ___ ___
10 ___ ___ 24 ___ ___
32 ___ ___ 20 ___ ___

Class Time

1. *Review Subtraction Family 7.*
   a. Do story facts with the flannel board.
      (1) **7 seeds were on the windowsill. A chickadee looked at them but flew away without taking any. 7 seeds were left. 7 seeds - 0 seeds = 7 seeds.**
      (2) **7 seeds were on the windowsill. A chickadee took 1 seed. 6 seeds were left. 7 seeds - 1 seed = 6 seeds.**
      (3) **7 seeds were on the windowsill. A chickadee took 2 seeds. . . .**
   b. Ask a child to fill the houses as you say Family 7 together.
2. *Drill subtraction facts.*
   Double Drill with Subtraction Families 5–7 flash cards.
3. *Mixed computation.*
   Do the chalkboard samples. **Watch the signs!**

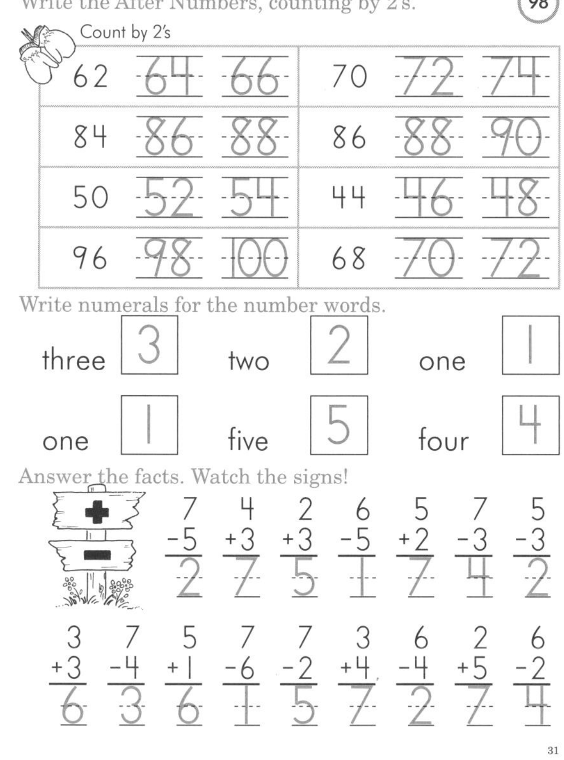
Write the After Numbers, counting by 2's. (98)

Count by 2's

62	64	66	70	72	74
84	86	88	86	88	90
50	52	54	44	46	48
96	98	100	68	70	72

Write numerals for the number words.

three 3 two 2 one 1

one 1 five 5 four 4

Answer the facts. Watch the signs!

7 − 5 = 2	4 + 3 = 7	2 + 3 = 5	6 − 5 = 1	5 + 2 = 7	7 − 3 = 4	5 − 3 = 2		
3 + 3 = 6	7 − 4 = 3	5 + 1 = 6	7 − 6 = 1	7 − 2 = 5	3 + 4 = 7	6 − 4 = 2	2 + 5 = 7	6 − 2 = 4

31

Speed Drill Answers

6	7	7	6	5	7	6
7	6	7	7	6	5	7
5	7	6	7	7	6	5

4. *After Numbers by 2's.*
   a. **What are the numbers for counting by 2's?**
   b. **Count by 2's to 100.**
   c. Do the chalkboard samples.
5. *Review coins.*
   Flash the large coins. **Name each coin, and tell me how much it is worth.**
6. *Number words.*
   a. Flash number words *one* to *five*.
   b. Ask if someone knows how to write the word for 6 on the board. Let a child do so, or write it yourself.
7. *Do Speed Drill #36.*
8. *Assign Lesson 98.*
   Watch the signs! Look for the sign picture at the bottom of the second page. Work carefully when you do this part.

Follow-up

Drill

(*Drill* #3)

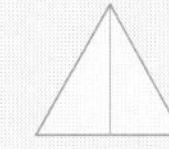 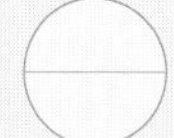 

1. Introduce the thermometer as an exercise in counting by 2's.
   a. Hold the large thermometer. (See pattern, pages 598 and 599.) **This is a ther-mom-e-ter.** Practice saying the word together.
   b. **A thermometer tells us how hot or cold something is. The numbers and little black marks help us to read the temperature.**
   c. **When we read a thermometer, we count by 2's.** Start at 0 and follow the black marks up to 100, counting together.
2. Drill individuals with Subtraction Families 1–7 flash cards.
3. Point to the triangle. **How many parts are in this shape?** Write a fraction bar with a 2 below it. **The denominator tells how many parts. It is the *down* number.** Shade in one half of the triangle. **How many parts did I shade?** Write a 1 above the fraction bar. Do the same for each of the shapes.

Practice Sheets

- ☐ Fact Houses #25
- ☐ Skip Counting #4
- ● Number Facts #31
- ● Before and After #8

Objectives

New

TEACHING

Thermometer
Fraction $\frac{1}{2}$
Fraction $\frac{1}{3}$

WORKBOOK

Number word *six*

Review

Subtraction facts

(99) Answer these facts.

7	7	7	7	7	7	7	7	7
-2	-5	-3	-6	-4	-1	-5	-6	-4
5	2	4	1	3	6	2	1	3

7	6	7	7	5	6	7	7	6
-4	-4	-4	-6	-4	-2	-1	-6	-5
3	2	3	1	1	4	6	1	1

7	6	6	7	7	6	7	6	5
-5	-3	-1	-5	-3	-4	-2	-2	-3
2	3	5	2	4	2	5	4	2

7	7	7	7	7	7	7	7	7
-3	-2	-5	-2	-5	-1	-3	-4	-1
4	5	2	5	2	6	4	3	6

Do the story problem.

7 buns are in a dish.
Then we eat 3 buns.
How many buns are **left**?

7	buns
-3	buns
4	buns

32

Preparation

Materials

Subtraction Families 5–7 flash cards

Form C for each child

Large thermometer

Addition and Subtraction Families 4–7 flash cards

Chalkboard

(Write a set of these facts for each child to trace in *Class Time* #2.)

6	7
-4	-4
2	3

(*Class Time* #5)

Class Time

1. *Review Subtraction Families 5–7.*
   a. **Watch my fingers as we say Subtraction Family 5 . . . 6.**
   b. Point to the flash cards above the flannel board. **Boys, say each fact once. Girls, say each fact once.**
2. *Drill selected facts.*
   Have each child stand near his facts on the board. **Whisper and trace the facts until I say "stop."**
3. *Drill subtraction facts.*
   Distribute Form C for the children to write the answers. Flash cards for Subtraction Families 5–7.
4. *Teach the thermometer to exercise counting by 2's.*
   a. Hold the large thermometer. **We count by 2's along the marks of a thermometer. Begin at 0 and count by 2's to 100.** Point to each little mark as you count.

Write the After Numbers, counting by 2's. (99)

Count by 2's

56	58	60	76	78	80
74	76	78	42	44	46
88	90	92	66	68	70
90	92	94	82	84	86

Write numerals for the number words.

six 6 five 5 four 4

three 3 two 2 one 1

Answer the facts. Watch the signs!

6 − 4 = 2	7 − 2 = 5	3 + 4 = 7	7 − 6 = 1	2 + 5 = 7	7 − 3 = 4	3 + 3 = 6		
5 − 3 = 2	7 − 4 = 3	5 + 1 = 6	6 − 5 = 1	3 + 4 = 7	2 + 3 = 5	7 − 5 = 2	5 + 2 = 7	6 − 2 = 4

33

b. **A thermometer tells us how hot or cold something is.** Point to the mercury. **This is the mercury. When God sends cold north winds, the mercury drops down, down, down. When God sends warm sunshine, the mercury rises up, up, up.**

c. Set the mercury at 50°. **Let's count from 0 to the top of the mercury. 2, 4, 6, . . . 50. The temperature is 50 degrees. We write 50 degrees like this:** Write 50° on the chalkboard.

d. Change the mercury to 30°, 80°, and 10°. For each setting, count from 0 to the top of the mercury; then write the temperature on the board.

5. *Teach the fraction $\frac{1}{2}$.*

a. Point to the square. **How many parts are shaded?** Write 1 above the fraction bar. **What is the denominator?** Write 2 below the fraction bar.

b. Point to the $\frac{1}{2}$ that you have just written. **This is a fraction. It says one-half.** Point to the terms as you say, **1 part out of 2 equal parts.**

c. Do one more sample, and then have the children write the fraction for the rest of the samples.

6. *Assign Lesson 99.*

Follow-up

Drill

(*Drill* #3)

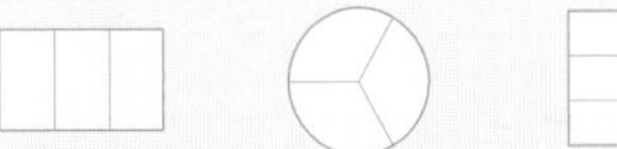

1. Mix Addition and Subtraction Families 4–7 flash cards and drill individuals.

2. **If you saved 8 nickels, how many cents would you have?** Continue with

13 pennies	**10 dimes**
3 dimes	**21 pennies**
7 nickels	**4 nickels**
41 pennies	**4 dimes**

3. Point to the rectangle. **How many parts are in this shape?** Write a fraction bar with a 3 below it. Shade in one-third of the rectangle. **How many parts did I shade?** Write a 1 above the fraction bar. Do the same for each of the shapes. Choose the middle piece for one of the items.

Practice Sheets

- ● Form C (*Class Time* #3)
- ☐ Fact Houses #26
- ☐ More Numbers #15
- ☐ Skip Counting #4
- ● Number Facts #31

Objectives

New

TEACHING

- Fraction $\frac{1}{3}$
- *Fraction* $\frac{1}{4}$
- *Addition Family 8*

WORKBOOK

- Thermometer

Review

- Subtraction facts
- Mixed addition and subtraction
- The term *digit*

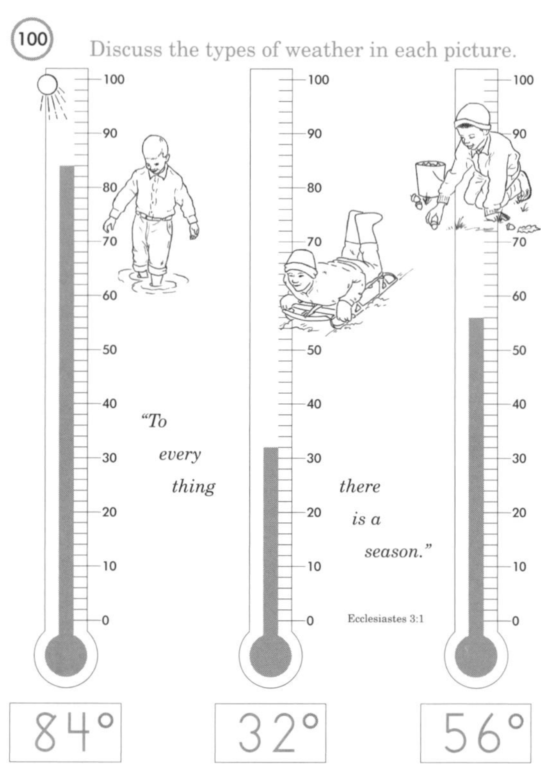

Preparation

Materials

Addition and Subtraction Families 6 and 7 flash cards

Large thermometer

Number word cards one *to* six

Chalkboard

(*Class Time* #1)

(*Class Time* #2)

6	6	7	7	7	7
-2	-4	-2	-5	-3	-4
4	2	5	2	4	3

(*Class Time* #5)

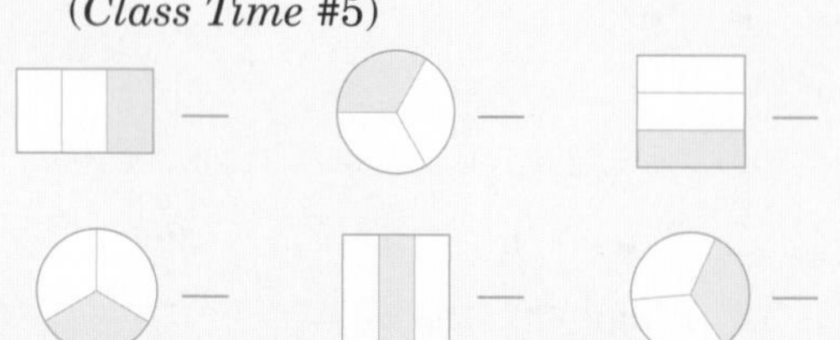

Class Time

1. *Review Subtraction Families 6 and 7.*
   a. Do story facts with the flannel board.
      (1) **7 candles were burning. Walter blew out 0 candles. 7 candles were left burning. 7 candles - 0 candles = 7 candles.**
      (2) **7 candles were burning. Walter blew out 1 candle. . . .**
   b. Ask a child to fill the 6 Houses as everyone says the facts.
   c. Ask a child to fill the 7 Houses as everyone says the facts.
2. *Drill selected facts.*
   a. Point to the first fact in the apartment houses. **Say this five times with me.** Say it quietly the first time. Raise your voice with each recital.
   b. Drill each of the facts in this way.
3. *Drill mixed addition and subtraction.* Circle Drill with Addition and Subtraction Families 6 and 7 flash cards.
4. *Count by 2's on thermometer.*
   a. Hold the large thermometer. **What**

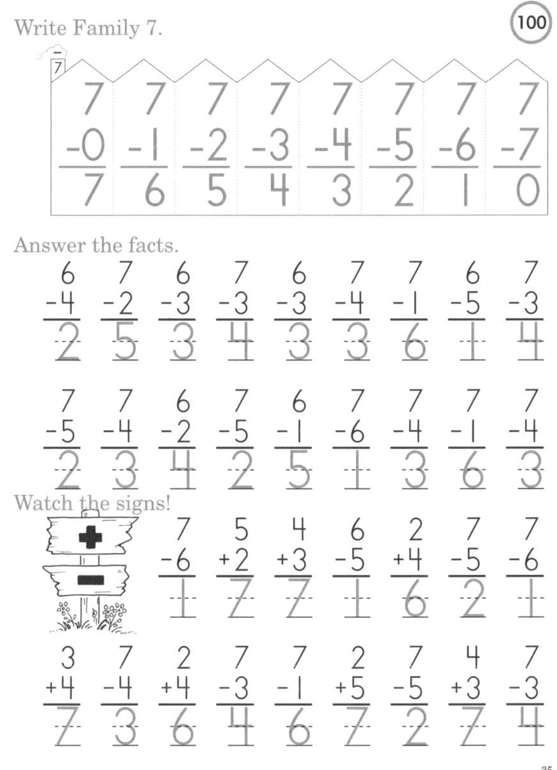

Write Family 7. (100)

7 − 0 = 7, 7 − 1 = 6, 7 − 2 = 5, 7 − 3 = 4, 7 − 4 = 3, 7 − 5 = 2, 7 − 6 = 1, 7 − 7 = 0

Answer the facts.

6 − 4 = 2, 7 − 2 = 5, 6 − 3 = 3, 7 − 3 = 4, 6 − 3 = 3, 7 − 4 = 3, 7 − 1 = 6, 6 − 5 = 1, 7 − 3 = 4

7 − 5 = 2, 7 − 4 = 3, 6 − 2 = 4, 7 − 5 = 2, 6 − 1 = 5, 7 − 6 = 1, 7 − 4 = 3, 7 − 1 = 6, 7 − 4 = 3

Watch the signs!

7 − 6 = 1, 5 + 2 = 7, 4 + 3 = 7, 6 − 5 = 1, 2 + 4 = 6, 7 − 5 = 2, 7 − 6 = 1

3 + 4 = 7, 7 − 4 = 3, 2 + 4 = 6, 7 − 3 = 4, 7 − 1 = 6, 2 + 5 = 7, 7 − 5 = 2, 4 + 3 = 7, 7 − 3 = 4

35

Speed Drill Answers

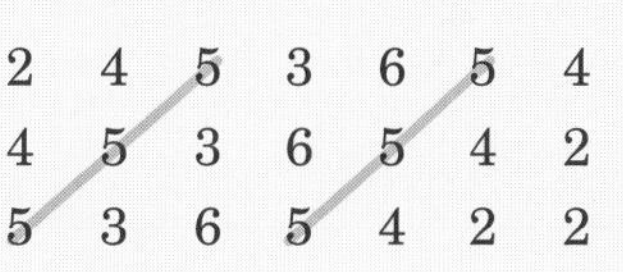

2	4	5	3	6	5	4
4	5	3	6	5	4	2
5	3	6	5	4	2	2

does the mercury do when the cold wind blows? . . . when the warm sun shines?

b. Set the mercury at 52°. **Count together from the bottom. 2, 4, 6, 8, . . . 52°.** Ask a child to write 52° on the chalkboard.

c. Continue with 74°, 12°, 28°.

5. *Teach the fraction* $\frac{1}{3}$.

   a. Point to the rectangle. **How many parts are shaded?** Write 1 above the fraction bar. **What is the denominator?** Write 3 below the fraction bar.

   b. Point to the $\frac{1}{3}$ you have just written. **This fraction says one-third.** Point to the terms as you say, **1 part out of 3 equal parts.**

   c. Do one more sample, and then have the children write the fraction for the rest of the samples.

6. *Review the term* digit.
   Name some 1-digit numbers. . . . 2-digit numbers. . . . 3-digit numbers.

7. *Do Speed Drill #37.*

8. *Assign Lesson 100.*

Follow-up

Drill

(*Drill #2*)

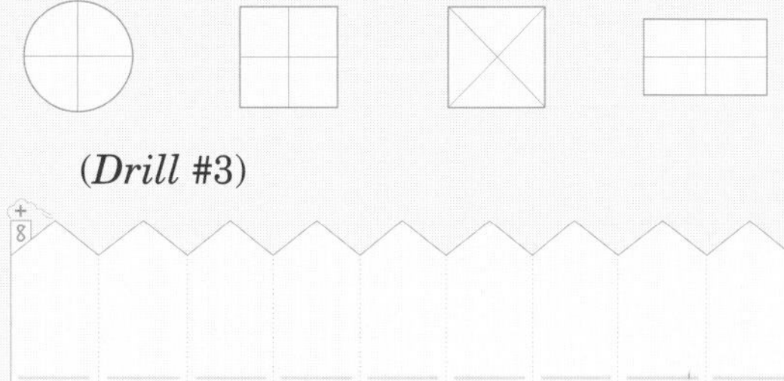

(*Drill #3*)

1. Flash number word cards *one* to *six*.

2. Point to the circle. **How many parts are in this shape?** Write a fraction bar with a 4 below it. Shade in one-fourth of the circle. **How many parts did I shade?** Write a 1 above the fraction bar. Do the same for each of the shapes. Vary the corner you choose to shade.

3. Introduce Addition Family 8. **Help me fill these houses with Addition Family 8.** Write the facts in order. Pick out the twins: 6 + 2, 2 + 6; 3 + 5, 5 + 3 . . . **We will work with Family 8 tomorrow.**

Practice Sheets

- ☐ Fact Houses #26
- ☐ Skip Counting #4
- ● Number Facts #32
- ● Number Facts #33
- ● Less Numbers #15

Objectives

New

TEACHING

Addition Family 8
Fraction $\frac{1}{4}$
Mixed counting (10's and 1's)

Review

Thermometer
Subtraction facts
Place value

Preparation

Materials

Large thermometer
Subtraction Families 4–7 flash cards

Chalkboard

(*Class Time* #2)

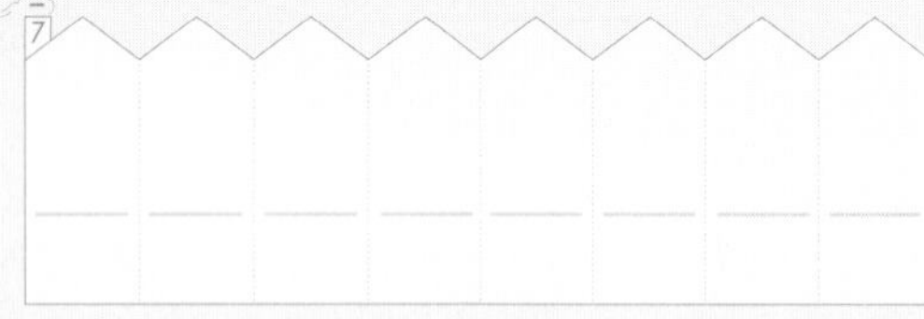

(*Class Time* #4)

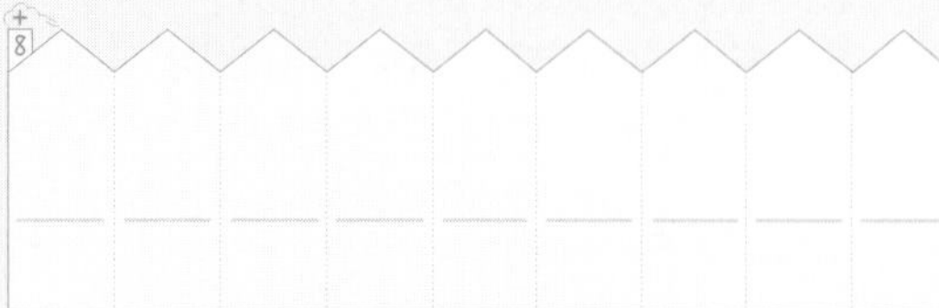

(*Class Time* #5)

(*Class Time* #6)

(101) Answer these facts.

7 − 4 = 3	6 − 5 = 1	6 − 3 = 3	7 − 3 = 4	6 − 1 = 5	7 − 4 = 3	7 − 1 = 6	7 − 5 = 2	7 − 7 = 0
7 − 5 = 2	6 − 4 = 2	7 − 2 = 5	7 − 5 = 2	6 − 4 = 2	7 − 6 = 1	6 − 5 = 1	6 − 4 = 2	6 − 0 = 6
7 − 3 = 4	6 − 3 = 3	7 − 4 = 3	7 − 2 = 5	6 − 2 = 4	7 − 3 = 4	6 − 3 = 3	7 − 4 = 3	7 − 1 = 6
7 − 4 = 3	7 − 3 = 4	7 − 5 = 2	6 − 4 = 2	7 − 2 = 5	7 − 5 = 2	7 − 3 = 4	7 − 6 = 1	7 − 4 = 3

Do the story problem.

7 cubs play.
Then 2 of them run away.
How many cubs are **left**?

7 cubs
− 2 cubs
5 cubs

36

Class Time

1. *Count by 2's on the thermometer.*
   a. Set the mercury at 58°. **What is the temperature? 2, 4, 6, . . . 58°. It feels like spring when the thermometer says 58°.** Ask a child to write 58° on the board.
   b. Set the mercury at 18°. **What is this temperature? 2, 4, 6, . . . 18°. It feels like winter when the thermometer says 18°.** Ask a child to write 18° on the board.
2. *Review Subtraction Family 7.*
   Say Family 7 as I fill the houses.
3. *Drill subtraction facts.*
   Circle Drill with Subtraction Families 4–7 flash cards.
4. *Teach Addition Family 8.*
   a. Call two children to the front of the class. Give the second one 8 crayons. **How many crayons does [first child] have?** Write 0 on the chalkboard. Ask the second child, **How many crayons do you have?** Write 8 below the 0.

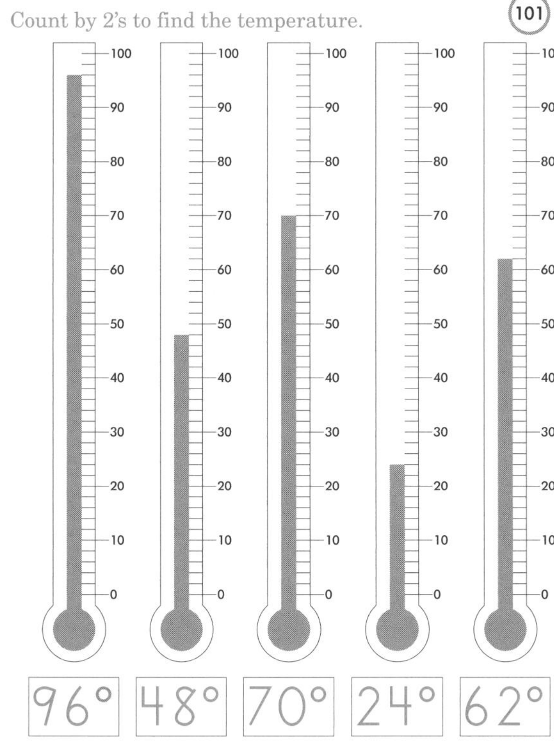

How many crayons do they have in all? Place the plus sign and equal line, and write the answer.

b. Have the second child give 1 crayon to the first. Repeat the questions as you work out the second fact.
c. Move through the rest of Addition Family 8.
d. Show Addition Family 8 with flannel board blocks, and let a child fill in the 8 Houses.

5. *Teach the fraction $\frac{1}{4}$.*
   a. Point to the circle. **How many parts are shaded?** Write 1 above the fraction bar. **What is the denominator?** Write 4 below the fraction bar.
   b. Point to $\frac{1}{4}$. **This fraction says one-fourth.** Point to the terms as you say, **1 part out of 4 equal parts.**
   c. Do one more sample, and then have the children write the fractions for the rest of the samples.
6. *Place value.*
   a. Drill **ones, tens, hundreds** with the motion.
   b. Turn to the chalkboard samples. Point to each digit in 15 as you say, **Ones, tens.** Point to each digit in 162 and say, **Ones, tens, hundreds.** Point to the 9 and say, **Ones.** Continue across the row.
   c. Go back to each number and ask the class which digit is in the ones' place. Circle that digit.
7. *Assign Lesson 101.*

Follow-up

Drill

(*Drill* #2)

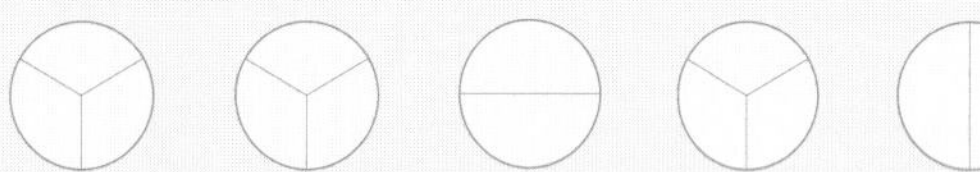

1. Oral drill: Have the children stand before you in two rows. **Whoever says the correct answer first may go to the back of his line.**

6 - 5 =	**7 - 3** =	**7 - 2** =	**7 - 4** =
7 - 5 =	**6 - 2** =	**5 - 3** =	**7 - 5** =
6 - 4 =	**7 - 6** =	**6 - 3** =	**6 - 4** =

2. Shade one part in each of the circles on the chalkboard. Have the children write the fraction for each shaded part.
3. Call the children to the number line. **Carefully follow my pointing stick. We will count by 10's for a bit, and then change to counting by 1's.**
   10, 20, 21, 22, 23
   10, 20, 30, 40, 41, 42, 43, 44, 45
   10, 20, 30, 31, 32, 33, 34

Practice Sheets

- ☐ Fact Houses #26
- ☐ Before and After #9
- ● Number Facts #32
- ● Clocks #2

Objectives

New

TEACHING

Mixed counting (10's and 1's)

WORKBOOK

Addition Family 8
Identify the ones' digit

Review

Place value
Telling time
Fractions $\frac{1}{2}$, $\frac{1}{3}$
Count by 5's

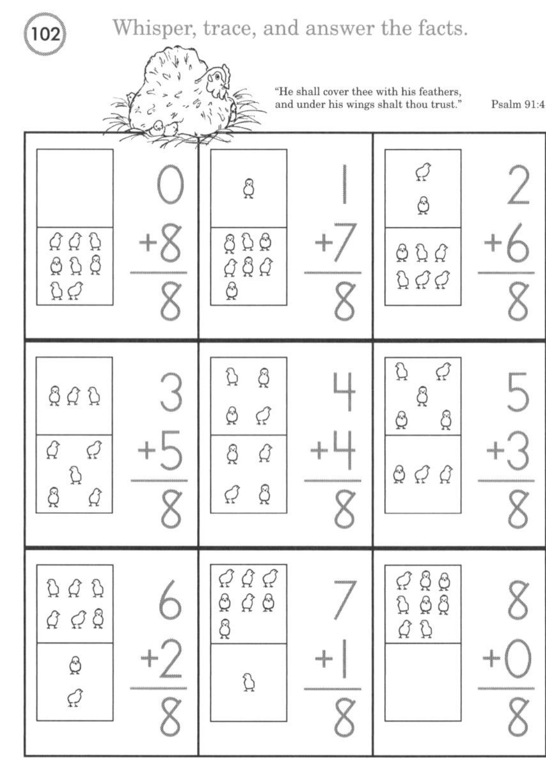

Preparation

Make Addition Family 8 flash cards for each child.

Materials

Model clock

Chalkboard

(*Class Time* #2)

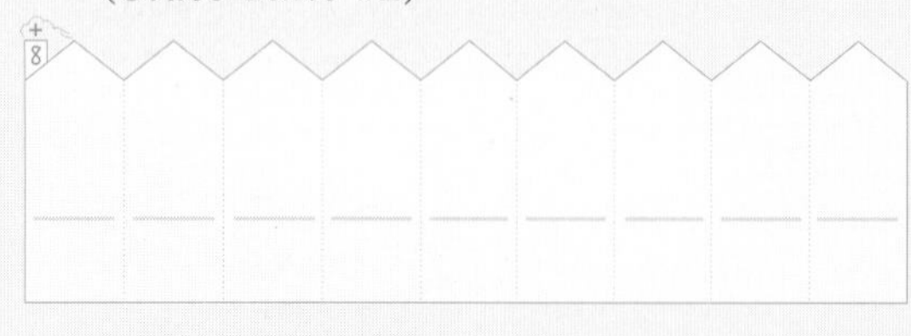

(*Class Time* #3)

(*Class Time* #5)

Class Time

1. *Mixed counting.*
   Follow my pointing stick as we count by 10's and by 1's.
   10, 11, 12, 13, 14, 15, 16, 17, 18
   10, 20, 30, 40, 50, 51, 52
   10, 20, 30, 31, 32, 33, 34
2. *Practice Addition Family 8.*
   a. Place 0 blocks on the upper and 8 blocks on the lower part of the divided flannel board. **0 + 8 = 8.** Continue with the rest of the facts.
   b. **Say Family 8 as I fill the houses.**
   c. Point to the first house. **Say these with me: 0 + 8, 8; 1 + 7, 8 . . .**
3. *Place value.*
   a. Practice the motion and say, **Ones, tens, hundreds.**
   b. Have the children circle the numbers that are in the ones' place.

Write Family 8. (102)

0	1	2	3	4	5	6	7	8
+8	+7	+6	+5	+4	+3	+2	+1	+0
8	8	8	8	8	8	8	8	8

Circle the numeral in the ones' place.

ones

19 148 5 62 112 47

Write the After Numbers, counting by 5's.

Count by 5's

15	20	25	35	40	45
90	95	100	20	25	30
55	60	65	45	50	55

Count the nickels; then write how many cents.

35¢

55¢

39

Speed Drill Answers

6	4	7	3	2	5	3
5	6	4	7	3	2	5
3	5	6	4	7	3	2

Speed Drill #38

4. *Telling time.*
   Answer together. Set the hands on the model clock to 6:30, 10:30, 1:30, 3:30, 5:30, 9:30, 11:30.
5. *Fractions* $\frac{1}{2}$ *and* $\frac{1}{3}$.
   a. Point to the first square. **How many parts are shaded?** Write the numerator. **What is the denominator?** Write the denominator. **What part of the whole shape is shaded?** Trace the fraction. **One-half, one-half.**
   b. Do the same for the rest of the squares.
6. *Count by 5's.*
   Count by 5's to 100.
7. *Do Speed Drill #38.*
8. *Assign Lesson 102.*

Follow-up

Drill

(*Drill* #2)

143 52 7 69 183 110

(*Drill* #3)

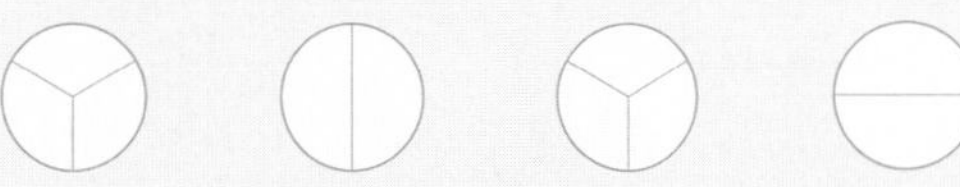

1. Give each child his Family 8 flash cards.
2. Stand near the row of numbers on the board. Point to individual digits as you say, **Ones, tens, hundreds.** Ask the class which digit is in the tens' place of each number; then circle it. (7 has no tens; circle nothing for that one.)
3. Shade one part in each of the circles on the chalkboard. Write the appropriate fraction for each one.

Practice Sheets

- ☐ Fact Houses #27
- ☐ Skip Counting #4
- ● Number Facts #34
- ● More Numbers #16

Objectives

New

TEACHING

- Addition Family 8 twins
- Number word *seven*
- *Identify the hundreds' digit*

WORKBOOK

- Identify the tens' digit
- Number word *seven*

Review

- Before and After (170's)
- Thermometer
- Fractions $\frac{1}{3}$, $\frac{1}{4}$

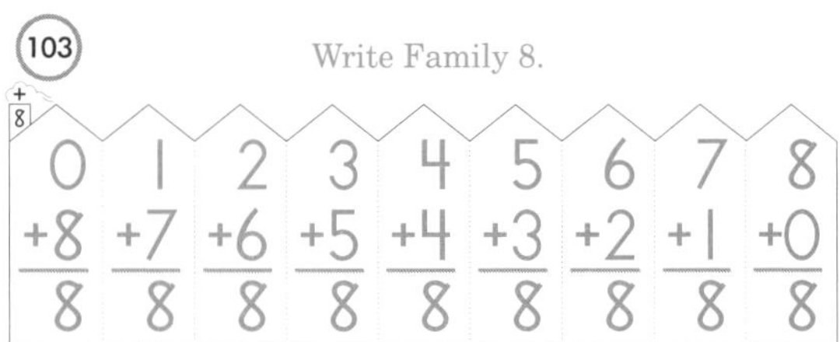
(103) Write Family 8.

0	1	2	3	4	5	6	7	8
+8	+7	+6	+5	+4	+3	+2	+1	+0
8	8	8	8	8	8	8	8	8

Answer these facts.

3 +5 = 8	6 +2 = 8	2 +3 = 5	0 +8 = 8	1 +3 = 4	2 +6 = 8	4 +4 = 8	1 +4 = 5	1 +7 = 8
5 +3 = 8	4 +1 = 5	2 +2 = 4	4 +4 = 8	2 +3 = 5	1 +7 = 8	3 +5 = 8	5 +3 = 8	1 +7 = 8
2 +3 = 5	2 +6 = 8	5 +3 = 8	8 +0 = 8	3 +2 = 5	6 +2 = 8	3 +1 = 4	4 +4 = 8	3 +5 = 8
7 +1 = 8	2 +6 = 8	1 +4 = 5	3 +2 = 5	7 +1 = 8	3 +5 = 8	2 +2 = 4	5 +3 = 8	6 +2 = 8

40

Preparation

Tack Addition Family 8 flash cards above the flannel board with answers showing.

Materials

Large thermometer

Number word cards one *to* seven

Chalkboard

(*Class Time* #1)

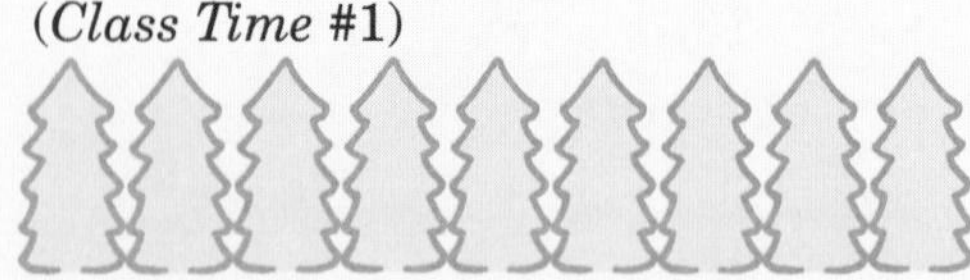

(*Class Time* #2)

____ 131 ____	____ 153 ____
____ 148 ____	____ 128 ____
____ 165 ____	____ 136 ____
____ 172 ____	____ 112 ____

(*Class Time* #5)

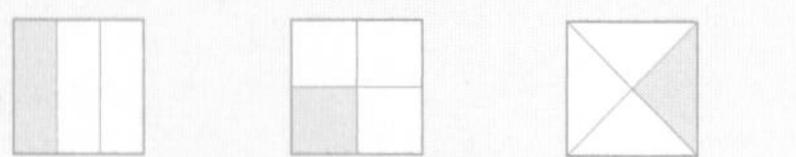

(*Class Time* #6)

6 55 108 147 182 74

Class Time

1. *Practice Addition Family 8.*
   a. Ask a child to move the felt blocks as you say Addition Family 8 together.
   b. **Today I will write the facts on trees as you say Family 8.** As the children say the facts in order, write them in every other tree. From the 4 + 4 tree at the end of the row, come back across the row, filling in the gaps. **Do you see the twin facts standing next to each other?**

   0
   +8
   8

   c. Point to the flash cards above the flannel board. **Say each fact three times with your eyes open and three times with your eyes closed.**
2. *Before and After.*
   Do the chalkboard samples.
3. *Count by 2's with the thermometer.*
   a. **Warm sunshine makes the mercury go ____.** Set the mercury at 88°.
   b. **Count to find out how warm it is: 2, 4, 6, . . . 88°.**

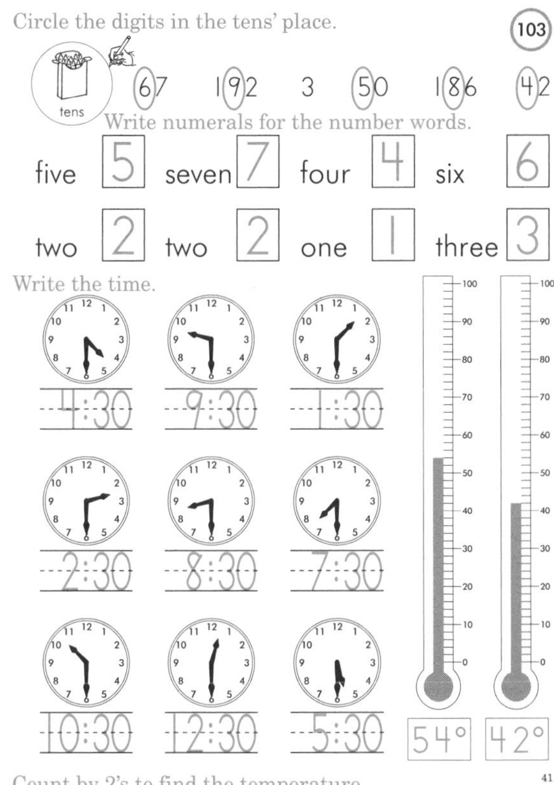

4. *Introduce the word* seven.
   a. Print the word *seven* on the chalkboard, and ask the children what it says. Point out phonetic hints if any of the children need help.
   b. Print *six* under *seven,* and let the class tell you what it is. Print *five,* and continue on down to *one.*
5. *Fractions* $\frac{1}{3}$ *and* $\frac{1}{4}$.
   a. Point to the first square. **How many parts are shaded?** Write the numerator. **What is the denominator?** Write the denominator. **What part of the whole shape is shaded?** Trace the fraction. **One-third, one-third.**
   b. Do the same for the rest of the squares.
6. *Place value.*
   a. Drill place value with the motion.
   b. Point to the row of numbers on the board. **Look for numbers that are in the tens' place.** Have the children circle the numbers.
7. *Assign Lesson 103.*

Follow-up

Drill

(*Drill* #1)

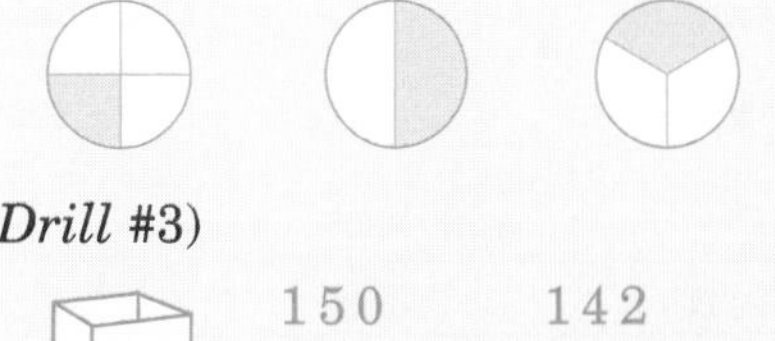

(*Drill* #3)

150	142	29
100	137	182

1. a. Ask someone to tell which circle shows $\frac{1}{2}$. Let another child write $\frac{1}{2}$ under it.
   b. Ask someone to tell which circle shows $\frac{1}{3}$. Let another child write $\frac{1}{3}$ under it.
   c. Let someone label $\frac{1}{4}$.
2. Pass out the number word cards *one* to *seven.* **If you have the word that means *first,* come stand beside me.** Continue with ***second, third, fourth, fifth, sixth,*** and ***seventh.***
3. Point to the row of numbers on the chalkboard. **This is a case of 100 crayons. Tell me which numbers are in the hundreds' place.** Circle each digit in the hundreds' place.

Practice Sheets

- ☐ Fact Houses #27
- ☐ Less Numbers #16
- ● Number Facts #35
- ◊ Dot-to-Dot #37

Objectives

New

TEACHING

Identify the hundreds' digit

WORKBOOK

Fraction $\frac{1}{2}$

Review

Addition Family 8 twins

Number words

Count by 10's

(104) Write Family 8.

0	1	2	3	4	5	6	7	8
+8	+7	+6	+5	+4	+3	+2	+1	+0
8	8	8	8	8	8	8	8	8

Answer these facts.

1	3	2	3	4	2	4	1	2
+7	+5	+3	+5	+2	+6	+4	+5	+4
8	8	5	8	6	8	8	6	6
6	2	1	3	4	1	3	5	2
+2	+4	+7	+5	+1	+7	+2	+3	+6
8	6	8	8	5	8	5	8	8
4	4	5	4	3	6	8	4	3
+4	+2	+3	+2	+3	+2	+0	+4	+5
8	6	8	6	6	8	8	8	8
3	1	3	2	7	1	5	2	6
+1	+5	+5	+6	+1	+4	+3	+4	+2
4	6	8	8	8	5	8	6	8

42

Preparation

Materials

Number word cards *one* to *seven*

Addition Families 1–6 and 8 flash cards

Chalkboard

(*Class Time* #1)

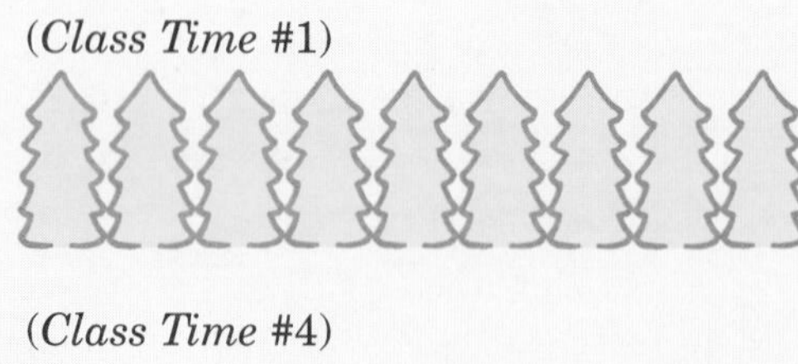

(*Class Time* #4)

58	129	143
127	165	8

(*Class Time* #5)

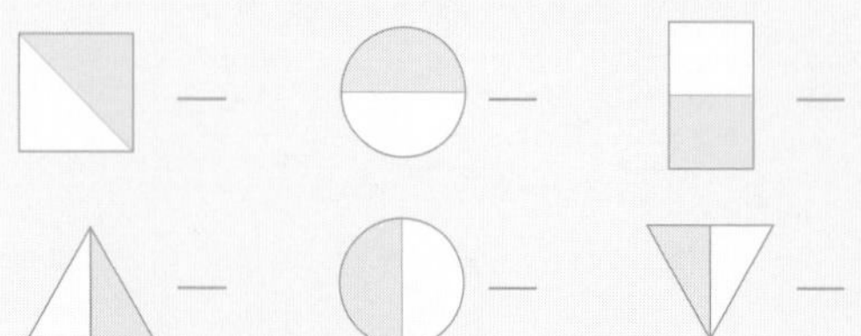

Class Time

1. *Review Addition Family 8.*
   a. **Say Family 8 as I write the facts on the trees.** Write the facts on every other tree so that when you are finished the twin facts are beside each other.
   b. **Say the addition facts in the trees as I point to them: 0 + 8, 8; 8 + 0, 8, . . .**
2. *Number words.*
   Flash number word cards *one* to *seven*.
3. *Count by 10's.*
   Count by 10's to 100.
4. *Place value.*
   a. Practice the place-value motion.
   b. **Look for the digit in the hundreds' place.** Have the children circle each one.

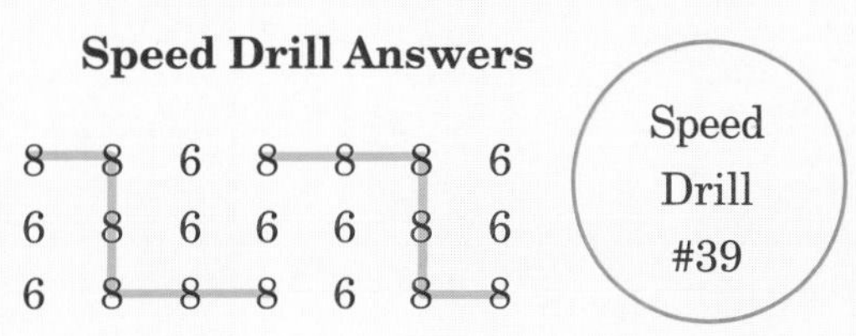

5. *Fraction ½.*
   Let the children write the fraction for the shaded part beside each shape.
6. *Do Speed Drill #39.*
7. *Assign Lesson 104.*
   Zacchaeus was a rich man. When Jesus came to his house, Zacchaeus said, "The half of my goods I give to the poor" (Luke 19:8). **He divided his riches into two parts. He kept one part, and he gave the other part to poor people.**

Follow-up

Drill

(*Drill* #2)

163	136	131	113
127	172	143	142
105	150	138	148
158	159	128	130

1. Chalkboard drill: **Write 135. Change it to 185. (Erase 1 digit.) Change it to 105, 101, 161, 168, 198, 128, 125, 155, 150, 140.**
2. **Numbers that are *smaller* are *Less* Numbers. Circle the number that is smaller.** Do the chalkboard samples.
3. Drill Addition Families 1–6 and 8 flash cards.

Practice Sheets

- ☐ Fact Houses #27
- ☐ Before and After #10
- ☐ Clocks #4
- ● Number Facts #34
- ● Number Facts #35

Objectives

New

TEACHING

Column addition (+ 2)

WORKBOOK

Addition Family 8 twins
Fraction $\frac{1}{3}$

Review

Addition facts
Mixed counting (10's and 1's)
Thermometer
Number words

(105) Whisper and trace the fact twins.

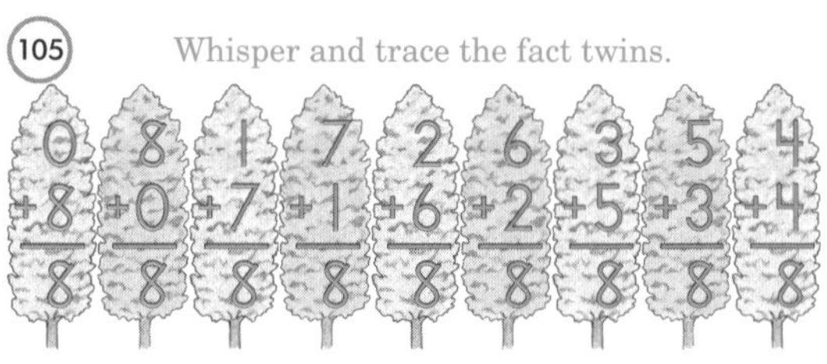

Answer these facts.

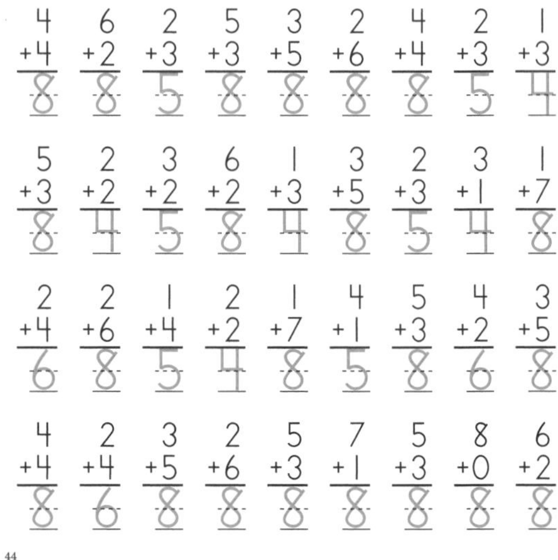

4 +4 = 8	6 +2 = 8	2 +3 = 5	5 +3 = 8	3 +5 = 8	2 +6 = 8	4 +4 = 8	2 +3 = 5	1 +3 = 4
5 +3 = 8	2 +2 = 4	3 +2 = 5	6 +2 = 8	1 +3 = 4	3 +5 = 8	2 +3 = 5	3 +1 = 4	1 +7 = 8
2 +4 = 6	2 +6 = 8	1 +4 = 5	2 +2 = 4	1 +7 = 8	4 +1 = 5	5 +3 = 8	4 +2 = 6	3 +5 = 8
4 +4 = 8	2 +4 = 6	3 +5 = 8	2 +6 = 8	5 +3 = 8	7 +1 = 8	5 +3 = 8	8 +0 = 8	6 +2 = 8

44

Preparation

Materials

Addition Families 4–6 and 8 flash cards
Form C for each child
Large thermometer
Number word cards *one* to *seven*
Subtraction Families 1–7 flash cards

Chalkboard

(*Class Time* #1)

(*Class Time* #3)

4	3	1	3	5	2	2
2	2	6	3	1	4	3
+2	+2	+1	+2	+2	+2	+1

(*Class Time* #7)

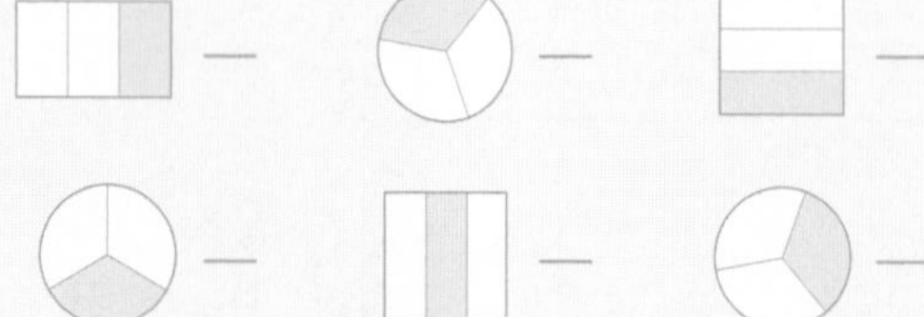

Class Time

1. *Review Addition Family 8.*
   a. Point to the first flash card above the flannel board. **Look at the fact. Close your eyes, and say it three times.** Practice each of the facts.
   b. **Can you say Family 8 with the twins together as I fill the trees?** Hold up your fist for 0 + 8. Do not show any number for the twin fact 8 + 0. Hold up one finger for 1 + 7, but nothing for 7 + 1. Continue until you get to four fingers for 4 + 4. **This fact has twin numbers. It does not have a twin addition fact.**
2. *Drill addition facts.*
   Use Form C for the children to write their answers. Flash cards from Addition Families 4–6 and 8. **Apron Row: Box 1—Box 2—Box 3 . . .**
3. *Column addition.*
   Do the chalkboard samples. Some of the problems have 2 as the last addend.

4. *Mixed counting.*
   Call the children to the number line. **We will count by 10's and then change to counting by 1's. Watch the pointer carefully!**
   10, 20, 21, 22, 23, 24
   10, 20, 30, 40, 50, 60, 61
   10, 20, 30, 40, 41, 42, 43, 44, 45
5. *Count by 2's with the thermometer.*
   a. Set the mercury at 16°. **What is the temperature? 2, 4, 6, . . . 16°. Bundle up in your coat, scarf, and mittens when the thermometer says 16°.**
   b. Set the mercury at 62°. **What is the temperature? 2, 4, 6, . . . 62°. You may only need your sweater when the thermometer says 62°.**
6. *Number words.*
   Flash number word cards *one* to *seven*.
7. *Fraction $\frac{1}{3}$.*
   Let the children write the fraction for the shaded part beside each shape.
8. *Assign Lesson 105.*

Follow-up

Drill

(*Drill* #1)

152 ___ ___ ___ ___ 157 ___

___ 133 ___ ___ ___ ___ ___

___ 165 ___ ___ ___ ___ ___

1. Do the Missing Numbers samples.
2. Circle Drill: Subtraction Families 1–7 flash cards.
3. Ask individuals to set the clock at 7:30, 9:30, 1:30, 3:30, 5:30, 10:30, 2:30.

Practice Sheets

- ● Form C (*Class Time* #2)
- ☐ Fact Houses #27
- ☐ More Numbers #17
- ● Number Facts #33
- ● Number Facts #35
- ◊ Dot-to-Dot #38

Objectives

New

TEACHING

Number word *eight*
Count dimes with pennies

WORKBOOK

Fraction $\frac{1}{4}$
Number word *eight*

Review

Subtraction Family 7
Addition facts
Counting (199)

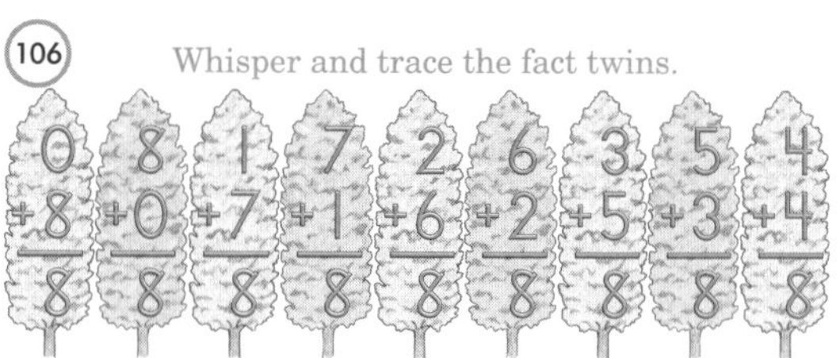

Answer these facts.

3 + 5 = 8	6 + 2 = 8	3 + 4 = 7	2 + 4 = 6	2 + 5 = 7	2 + 6 = 8	2 + 5 = 7	3 + 2 = 5	4 + 2 = 6
5 + 3 = 8	4 + 4 = 8	1 + 7 = 8	3 + 4 = 7	3 + 5 = 8	5 + 3 = 8	1 + 7 = 8	3 + 3 = 6	2 + 3 = 5
2 + 3 = 5	2 + 6 = 8	5 + 3 = 8	2 + 6 = 8	4 + 3 = 7	6 + 2 = 8	5 + 2 = 7	4 + 4 = 8	4 + 2 = 6
5 + 3 = 8	3 + 2 = 5	3 + 5 = 8	2 + 6 = 8	7 + 1 = 8	5 + 2 = 7	3 + 5 = 8	4 + 3 = 7	6 + 2 = 8

46

Preparation

Materials

Addition Families 6–8 flash cards

Number word cards *one* to *eight*

Addition Families 7 and 8 flash cards

Chalkboard

(*Class Time* #1)

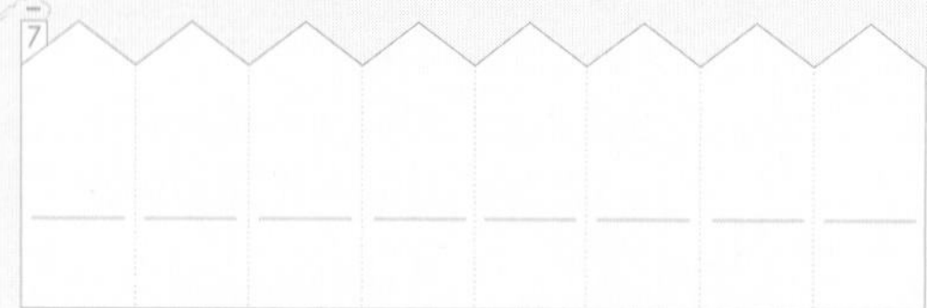

(*Class Time* #2)

(*Class Time* #5)

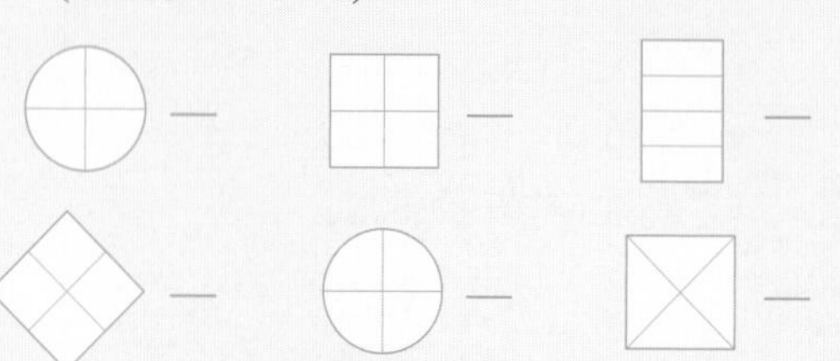

Class Time

1. *Review Subtraction Family 7.*
   Ask a child to fill the 7 Houses as you say Subtraction Family 7 together.
2. *Review Addition Family 8.*
   a. Show Addition Family 8 on the flannel board for these story facts.
   (1) **Susan has 0 yellow chicks and 8 brown chicks. She has 8 chicks in all. 0 chicks + 8 chicks = 8 chicks.**
   (2) Move one felt block to the upper part of the flannel board. **Susan has 1 yellow chick and 7 brown chicks. She has 8 chicks in all. 1 chick + 7 chicks = 8 chicks.**
   (3) Move the second block. **Susan has 2 yellow chicks and 6 brown chicks. She has 8 chicks in all. 2 chicks + 6 chicks . . .**
   b. **Say the addition facts for Family 8 in twin sets as I fill in the trees. Watch my fingers when we begin each set.** Hold up a fist for 0 + 8. (Do not show a number for the twin fact, 8 + 0.) Hold up one finger for 1 + 7, and so on.

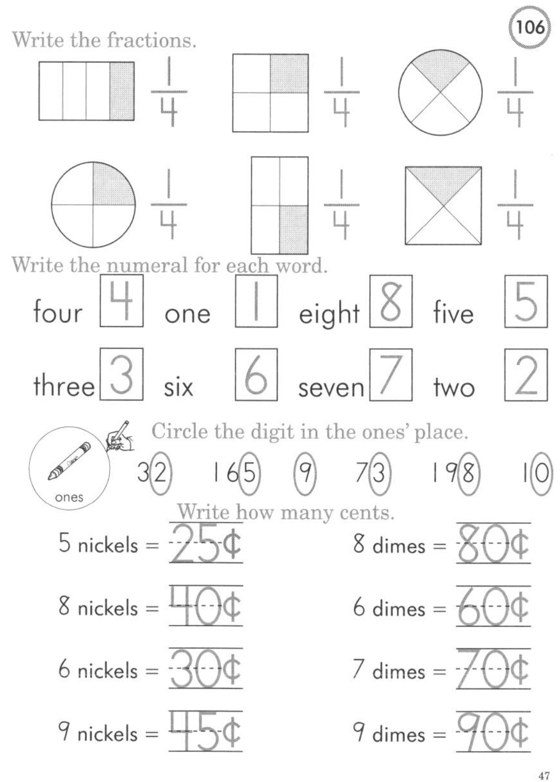

Speed Drill Answers

8	2	5	6	3	8	4
2	5	6	3	8	4	7
5	6	3	8	4	7	2

3. *Drill addition facts.*
   Circle Drill with Addition Families 6–8 flash cards.
4. *Counting.*
   Have the children stand in a circle with you. **We will count around the circle by 1's from 100 to 199. Listen closely and count clearly. I will begin. 100, . . .**
5. *Fraction $\frac{1}{4}$.*
   Let individuals shade one part of each shape and write the fraction.
6. *Number words.*
   a. Print number words *one* through *seven* on the chalkboard in mixed order and have the children say them.
   b. Print *eight.* Discuss the phonetic exceptions. If you need a mnemonic device, trace the *g* in the middle of the word in the form of a figure 8.
   c. Flash number word cards *one* to *eight*.
7. *Do Speed Drill #40.*
8. *Assign Lesson 106.*

Follow-up

Drill

(10¢) (10¢) (10¢) (1¢) (1¢) (1¢) ____

(10¢) (10¢) (1¢) (1¢) (1¢) (1¢) ____

(10¢) (1¢) (1¢) (1¢) ____

1. Introduce counting money mixtures.
   a. Call the children to the number line. **Count by 10's and by 1's.**
   10, 20, 30, 40, 50, 51, 52, 53, 54
   10, 11, 12, 13, 14, 15, 16, 17
   10, 20, 30, 40, 41, 42, 43, 44, 45
   b. Point to the money samples. **Count the dimes and pennies with me. 10¢, 20¢, 30¢, 31¢, 32¢, 33¢.** Write 33¢. Do the rest of the samples.
2. Drill individuals with Addition Families 7 and 8 flash cards.

Practice Sheets

- ☐ Fact Houses #28
- ☐ Number Trains #4
- ● Number Facts #36
- ● Less Numbers #17

Objectives

New

TEACHING

Number word *nine*
Count dimes with pennies

WORKBOOK

Fractions $\frac{1}{2}$, $\frac{1}{3}$
Number word *nine*

Review

Addition facts
Mixed facts
Telling time
Count by 2's
After, by 2's
Place value

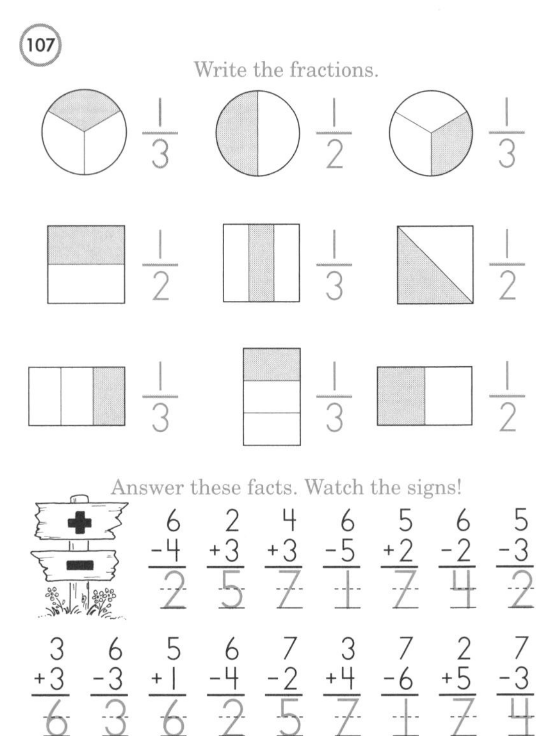
107

Write the fractions.

$\frac{1}{3}$ $\frac{1}{2}$ $\frac{1}{3}$

$\frac{1}{2}$ $\frac{1}{3}$ $\frac{1}{2}$

$\frac{1}{3}$ $\frac{1}{3}$ $\frac{1}{2}$

Answer these facts. Watch the signs!

6 − 4 = 2, 2 + 3 = 5, 4 + 3 = 7, 6 − 5 = 1, 5 + 2 = 7, 6 − 2 = 4, 5 − 3 = 2

3 + 3 = 6, 6 − 3 = 3, 5 + 1 = 6, 6 − 4 = 2, 7 − 2 = 5, 3 + 4 = 7, 7 − 6 = 1, 2 + 5 = 7, 7 − 3 = 4

48

Preparation

Materials

Mixed flash cards: Addition Families 5–8 and Subtraction Families 5–7

Model clock

Number word cards *one* to *eight*

Chalkboard

(Write a set of these for each child to trace in *Class Time* #2.)

3	3
+4	+5
7	8

(*Class Time* #5)

44 __ __   26 __ __

32 __ __   74 __ __

50 __ __

(*Class Time* #8)

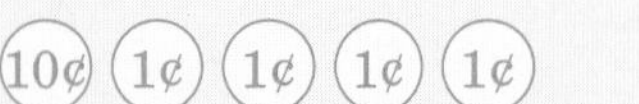
10¢ 1¢ 1¢ 1¢ 1¢ ____

10¢ 10¢ 1¢ ____

10¢ 10¢ 1¢ 1¢ ____

10¢ 10¢ 10¢ 1¢ 1¢ ____

Class Time

1. *Review Addition Family 8.*
   a. Move the felt blocks on the flannel board to illustrate Addition Family 8. Have the children say each story fact.
   (1) **John has 0 crayons, and Paula has 8 crayons. They have 8 crayons in all. 0 crayons + 8 crayons = 8 crayons.**
   (2) **John has 1 crayon, and Paula has 7 crayons. They have 8 crayons in all. 1 crayon + 7 crayons = 8 crayons.**
   (3) **John has 2 crayons, and Paula has 6 . . .**
   b. Point to the flash cards above the flannel board. **Say each fact three times with your eyes open, and then three times with your eyes closed.**
2. *Drill selected facts.*
   Have each child stand near his set of facts on the board. **Whisper and trace the facts until I say "stop."**

107

Write the numeral for each word.

six 6 eight 8 three 3 nine 9

four 4 five 5 seven 7 two 2

Circle the digits in the tens' place.

tens

45 6 178 92 184 57

Count the dimes or pennies; then write how many cents.

60¢

6¢

70¢

7¢

90¢

49

3. *Drill mixed number facts.*
   Circle Drill with Addition Families 5–8 and Subtraction Families 5–7 flash cards.
4. *Telling time.*
   Answer together to say the time. Set the model clock at 12:30, 2:00, 8:30, 10:00, 5:30, 7:00.
5. *Count by 2's.*
   a. **Count by 2's to 100.**
   b. **Count by 2's to fill in the After Number blanks.**
6. *Number words.*
   a. Flash number word cards *one* to *eight*.
   b. Introduce *nine*.
7. *Place value.*
   Practice the motion, saying, **Ones, tens, hundreds.**
8. *Counting dimes with pennies.*
   Do the chalkboard samples. Have the children count aloud as they work.
9. *Assign Lesson 107.*

Follow-up

Drill

(*Drill* #1)

7 −6	1 +7	6 −3	7 −5	6 −4	4 +4
5 +2	5 −2	4 +3	2 +6	7 −2	5 −2
6 −4	3 +5	7 −2	7 −3	2 +5	6 +2
0 +6	4 −2	2 +4	5 −4	5 +3	7 −4
7 −6	2 +3	4 +2	7 −4	3 −2	4 +4
6 +1	6 −2	7 −3	4 −3	3 +5	7 −4

1. Drill the children at the number-fact grid on the chalkboard. Save the grid for use with Lessons 108 and 109.
2. **If you saved 7 dimes, you would have ___¢.** Continue with

8 nickels	**25 pennies**
14 pennies	**4 nickels**
3 dimes	**8 dimes**
5 nickels	**11 pennies**

Practice Sheets

- ☐ Fact Houses #28
- ☐ Before and After #11
- ● Number Facts #37
- ● Number Facts #36
- ● Clocks #5

Objectives

New

TEACHING

Addition Family 8 reflected

WORKBOOK

Count dimes with pennies

Fractions $\frac{1}{3}$, $\frac{1}{4}$

Review

Thermometer

Mixed counting (10's and 1's)

Addition facts

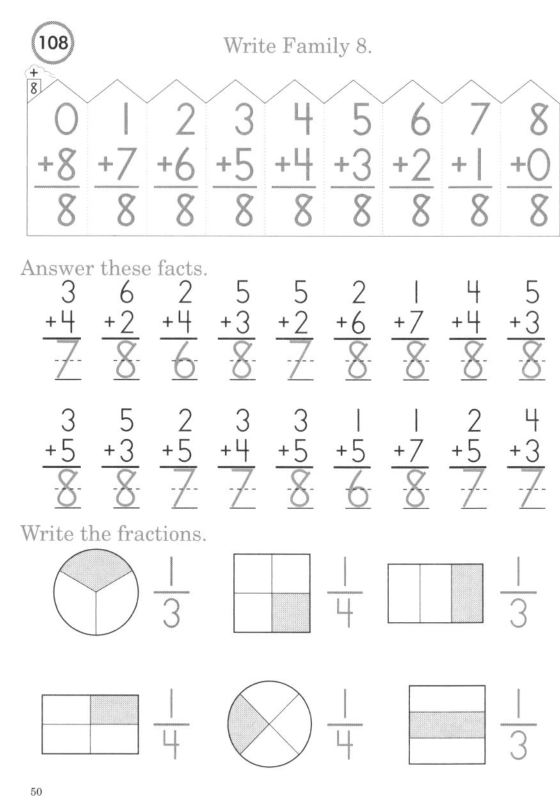

Preparation

Materials

Large thermometer

Addition Families 6–8 flash cards

Number word cards one *to* nine

Chalkboard

(Class Time #2)

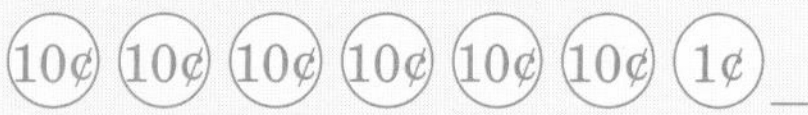

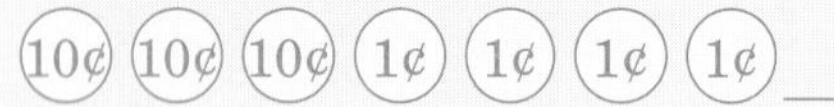

(Class Time #3)

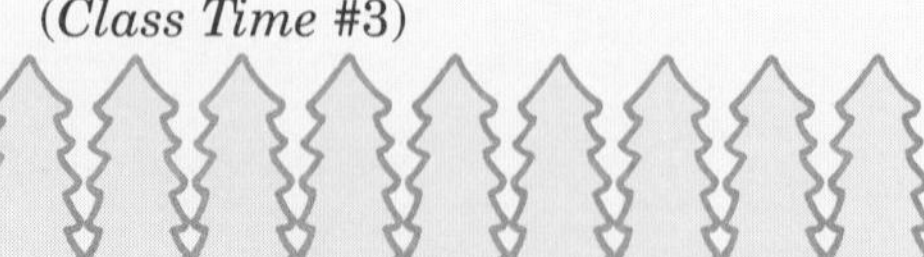

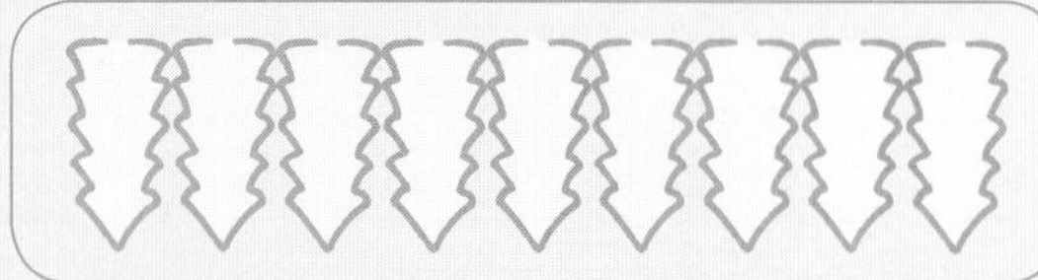

(Class Time #4)

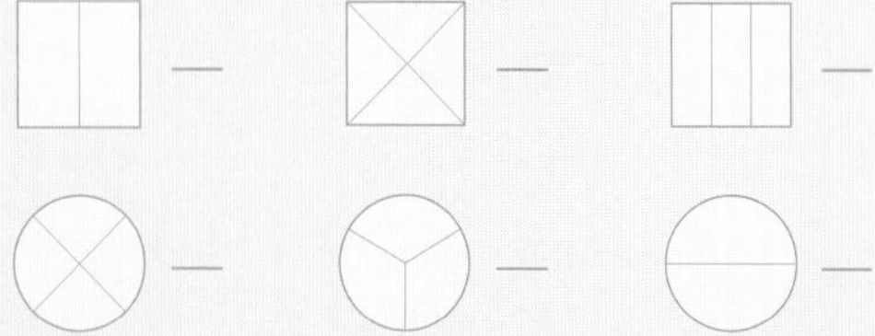

Class Time

1. *Count by 2's with the thermometer.*
   a. Have the children stand near enough to see the marks on the thermometer. Set the mercury at 84°. **What is the temperature? 2, 4, 6, . . . 84°. A cold drink of lemonade tastes good when the thermometer says 84°.**
   b. Set the mercury at 12°. **What is the temperature? 2, 4, 6, . . . 12°. Is that warmer or colder than 84°? A cup of hot chocolate tastes good when the thermometer says 12°.**
2. *Counting dimes with pennies.*
   a. Point to the number line. **Count by 10's and 1's.**
   10, 20, 30, 40, 50, 60, 70, 71, 72
   10, 11, 12, 13, 14, 15
   10, 20, 30, 31, 32, 33
   b. Do the money samples. Have the children count aloud as they work.
3. *Introduce Subtraction Family 8.*
   a. **Say Addition Family 8 in twin sets**

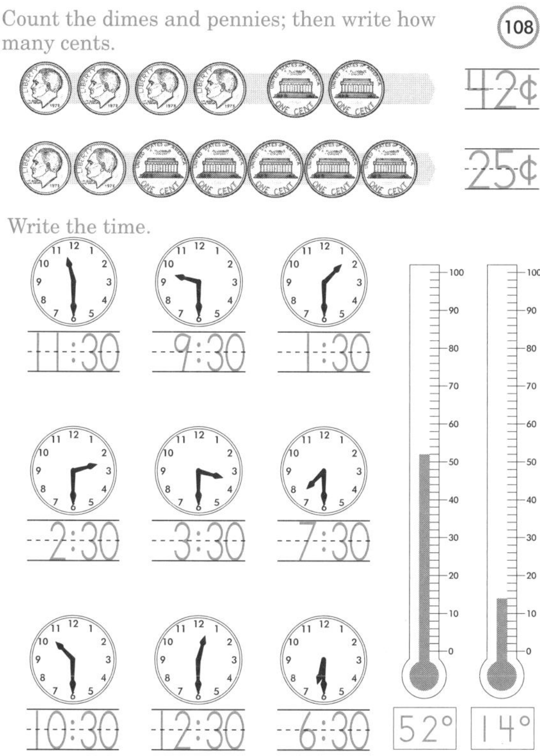
Count the dimes and pennies; then write how many cents. (108)

42¢

25¢

Write the time.

11:30 9:30 1:30

2:30 3:30 7:30

10:30 12:30 6:30

52° 14°

Count by 2's to find the temperature.

51

as I fill the trees. Hold up a fist for 0 + 8, one finger for 1 + 7, . . . (Do not show any number for the second twin in each pair.)

b. **Do you know what facts are in Subtraction Family 8?** Write Subtraction Family 8 facts in the upside-down trees. Put the subtrahend − 8 in the reflection for the addition fact that has + 8. The subtrahend − 7 goes below the fact that has + 7, and so forth. **Subtraction is like a reflection of addition. It uses the same numbers in different order.**

4. *Fractions.*
Let individuals shade one part of each shape and write the appropriate fraction.
5. *Drill addition facts.*
Double Drill with Addition Families 6–8 flash cards.
6. *Do Speed Drill #41.*
7. *Assign Lesson 108.*

Speed Drill Answers

2	8	5	4	1	7	6
8	2	8	5	4	1	7
3	8	2	8	5	4	1

Follow-up

Drill

(*Drill* #1)

4	5	2	3	2
2	1	3	1	2
+ 2	+ 2	+ 2	+ 2	+ 2
3	4	6	5	2
3	1	1	2	4
+ 2	+ 2	+ 1	+ 1	+ 1

1. Do the column addition samples.
2. Review number words.
   a. Flash number word cards *one* to *nine*.
   b. Give the cards to the children. **When I call your word, come stand in order. 3, 8, 1, 6, 4, 9, 5, 2, 7.**
3. Drill each child at the number-fact grid from Lesson 107. Save the grid for Lesson 109.

Practice Sheets

- ☐ Fact Houses #28
- ☐ More Numbers #18
- ☐ Missing Numbers #10
- ● Number Facts #38
- ● Number Facts #36

Objectives

New

TEACHING

- Addition Family 7 reflected
- *Measuring inches*

WORKBOOK

- Addition Family 8 reflected
- Column addition (+ 2)
- Fractions $\frac{1}{2}$, $\frac{1}{3}$, $\frac{1}{4}$
- Identify the hundreds' digit

Review

- Subtraction facts
- Addition facts
- Mixed counting (10's and 1's)

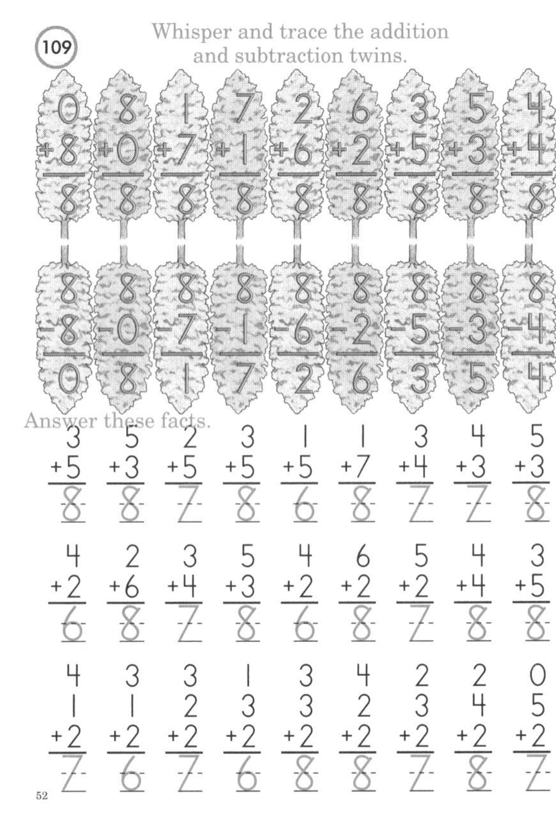

109 Whisper and trace the addition and subtraction twins.

0	8	1	7	2	6	3	5	4
+8	+0	+7	+1	+6	+2	+5	+3	+4
8	8	8	8	8	8	8	8	8

8	8	8	8	8	8	8	8	8
−8	−0	−7	−1	−6	−2	−5	−3	−4
0	8	1	7	2	6	3	5	4

Answer these facts.

3	5	2	3	1	1	3	4	5
+5	+3	+5	+5	+5	+7	+4	+3	+3
8	8	7	8	6	8	7	7	8

4	2	3	5	4	6	5	4	3
+2	+6	+4	+3	+2	+2	+2	+4	+5
6	8	7	8	6	8	7	8	8

4	3	3	1	3	4	2	2	0
1	1	2	3	3	2	3	4	5
+2	+2	+2	+2	+2	+2	+2	+2	+2
7	6	7	6	8	8	7	8	7

52

Preparation

Materials

- Form C for each child
- Addition Families 5–8 flash cards
- *12-inch ruler (preferably with inches only—no metric numbers)*

Chalkboard

(*Class Time* #1)

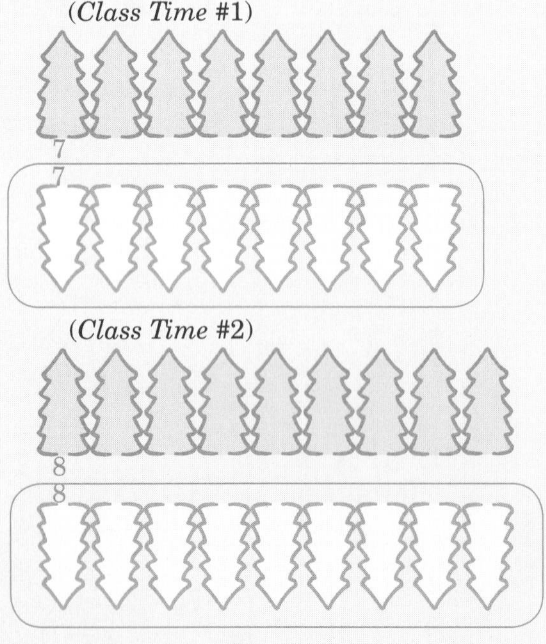

(*Class Time* #2)

(*Class Time* #4)

2	2	1	4	6	3	1
4	3	5	1	0	3	3
+2	+2	+2	+2	+2	+2	+2

Class Time

1. *Review Addition and Subtraction Family 7.*
   a. **Can you say the addition facts for 7 in sets of twins as I write them in the trees?** Hold up a fist for 0 + 7, one finger for 1 + 6, and so on.
   b. **Now say each addition fact again with its reflecting subtraction fact as I write it. Under the fact that says "plus 7," the subtraction fact will say "minus 7."**
2. *Review Addition and Subtraction Family 8.*
   a. Ask a child to move the felt blocks as you say Addition Family 8 together.
   b. **Say Family 8 in sets of twins as I write in the trees.**

(*Class Time* #6)

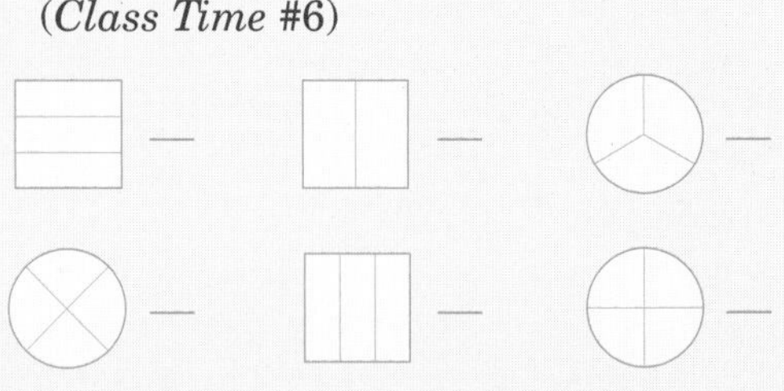

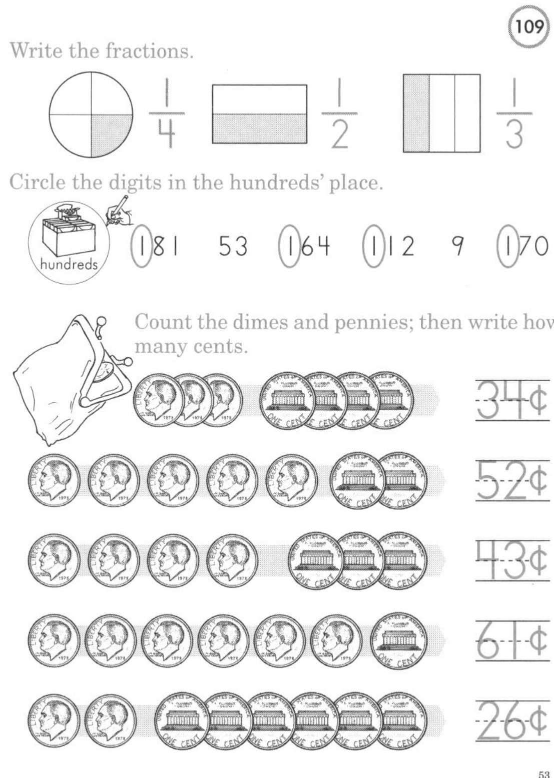

c. Let a child write the subtraction facts in the reflection as the class recites them. The number that is beside the plus sign in each addition fact should also go beside the minus sign in the reflection.

3. *Drill addition facts.*
Use Form C for the children to write their answers. Flash cards from Addition Families 4–6 and 8. **Apron Row: Box 1—Box 2 . . .**

4. *Column addition.*
Do the chalkboard samples.

5. *Mixed counting.*
Stand near the number line. **Count by 10's and by 1's.**
10, 20, 30, 31, 32
10, 11, 12, 13
10, 20, 30, 40, 50, 51, 52

6. *Fractions.*
Let individuals shade one part of each shape and write the fraction.

7. *Assign Lesson 109.*

Follow-up

Drill

(*Drill* #2)
(Draw these lines 4", 2", and 6" long.)

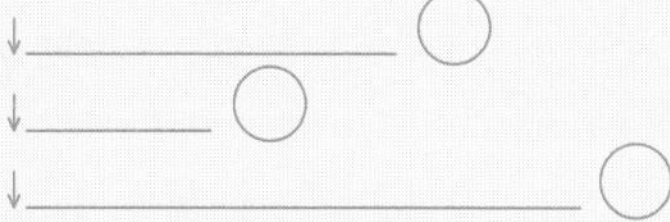

1. Drill individuals at the number-fact grid from Lesson 107.

2. Introduce measuring inches.
   a. Call the children to the teaching corner, and show them a 12-inch ruler. **This is a ruler. We use a ruler to measure inches. This is like a little number line. Can you find the place for zero? Count the inches. 1 inch, 2 inches, . . .**
   b. Point to the first line in the samples. **Let's measure this line. The arrow means "start here." I must put the "zero" of my ruler at the tip of the line. Where does the line stop?** (4 inches) **This line is 4 inches long. We can write 4 inches like this:** Write 4" in the circle.
   c. Measure the other lines, and write the measurements in the circles.

Practice Sheets

- Form C (*Class Time* #3)
- ☐ Fact Houses #29
- ☐ Number Trains #5
- Number Facts #39
- Less Numbers #18

Objectives

New

TEACHING

Number word *ten*
Measuring inches
Addition Family 9

WORKBOOK

Number word *ten*

Review

Addition facts
Count by 2's
Telling time
Fractions

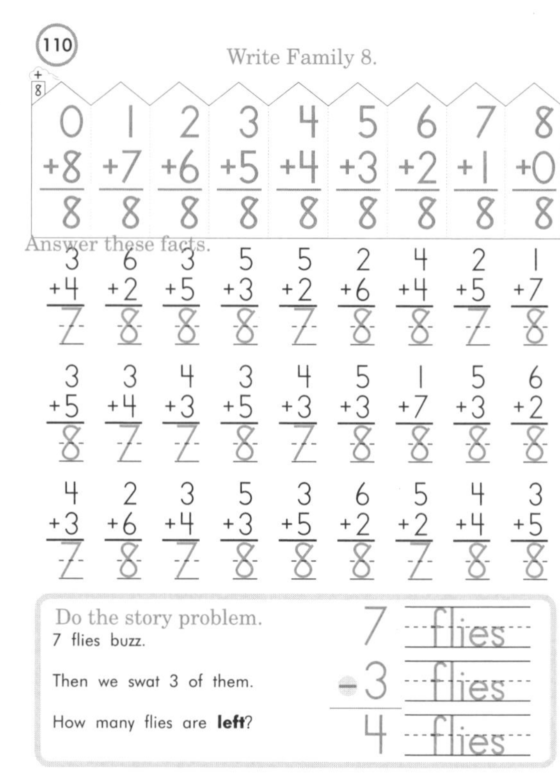

110 Write Family 8.

0	1	2	3	4	5	6	7	8
+8	+7	+6	+5	+4	+3	+2	+1	+0
8	8	8	8	8	8	8	8	8

Answer these facts.

3	6	3	5	5	2	4	2	1
+4	+2	+5	+3	+2	+6	+4	+5	+7
7	8	8	8	7	8	8	7	8
3	3	4	3	4	5	1	5	6
+5	+4	+3	+5	+3	+3	+7	+3	+2
8	7	7	8	7	8	8	8	8
4	2	3	5	3	6	5	4	3
+3	+6	+4	+3	+5	+2	+2	+4	+5
7	8	7	8	8	8	7	8	8

Do the story problem.
7 flies buzz.
Then we swat 3 of them.
How many flies are **left**?

7 flies
−3 flies
4 flies

54

Preparation

Materials

Addition Families 7 and 8 flash cards
Model clock
Number word cards *one* to *nine*
12-inch ruler
Number word cards one *to* ten
Addition Families 6–8 flash cards
Subtraction Families 6 and 7 flash cards

Chalkboard

(*Class Time* #4)

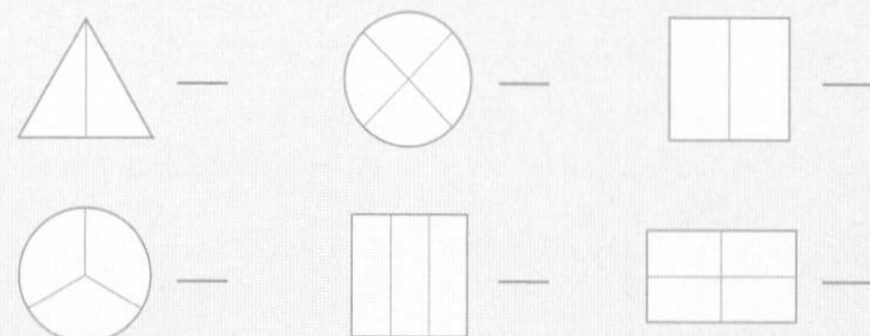

(Draw these lines 5", 3", and 7" long for *Class Time* #6.)

Class Time

1. *Review Addition Families 7 and 8.*
   a. Give the Addition Families 7 and 8 flash cards to the children. **Who has the first fact in Family 7? Come set it on the chalk tray. . . .**
   b. Stand near the cards. **Say Family 7 . . . Family 8.**
2. *Count by 2's.*
   a. Call the children to the number line. **What is the number pattern for counting by 2's?**
   b. **Count by 2's to 100.**
3. *Telling time.*
   a. **Answer together to tell the time.** Set the model clock at 1:00, 5:30, 7:00, 9:30, 11:00, 12:30, 3:00, 6:30.
   b. Set the hands at 3:30. **Father said, "Joseph, in 1 hour you may bring the cows in from the pasture." What time will Joseph fetch the cows?**
   c. Set the hands at 10:30. **Mother said, "Mary, in 1 hour you may set the**

Write the After Numbers, counting by 2's. (110)

Count by 2's

72	74	76	54	56	58
26	28	30	38	40	42
60	62	64	96	98	100

Write the numeral for each word.

one 1 seven 7 three 3 eight 8

two 2 ten 10 four 4 nine 9

Count the dimes and pennies; then write how many cents.

33¢

52¢

51¢

55

Speed Drill Answers

8	7	8	8	7	8	7
7	8	8	7	8	7	7
8	8	7	8	7	7	8

table for dinner." What time will Mary set the table?

4. *Fractions.*
   Let individuals shade one part of each shape and write the fraction.
5. *Number words.*
   a. Flash number word cards *one* to *nine*.
   b. Introduce *ten*.
6. *Measuring inches.*
   a. Hold the ruler. **A ruler measures inches. Count with me. 1 inch, 2 inches, . . .**
   b. **The arrow means "start here." Where is the "zero" on the ruler?** Hold the ruler for measuring the first line. Ask a child to read and write the inches. **We can use two little straight marks to mean "inches."**
   c. Measure the rest of the lines.
7. *Do Speed Drill #42.*
8. *Assign Lesson 110.*

Follow-up

(*Drill* #3)

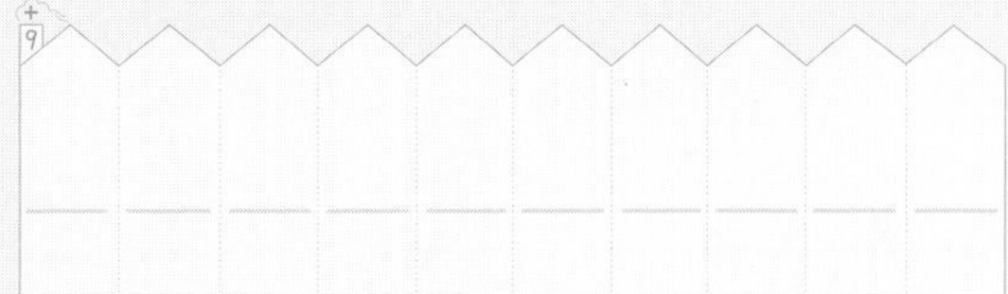

Drill

1. Drill individuals with number word cards *one* to *ten*.
2. Mix the flash cards for Addition Families 6–8 and Subtraction Families 6 and 7. Drill the facts.
3. Introduce Addition Family 9. **Can you think of plus problems that equal 9?** Write the facts in order. Pick out the twins: 2 + 7 and 7 + 2, 3 + 6 and 6 + 3, . . . **We will work with Addition Family 9 tomorrow.**

Practice Sheets

- ☐ Fact Houses #29
- ☐ Before and After #12
- ☐ Missing Numbers #10
- ● Number Facts #37
- ● Number Facts #39
- ● Fractions #2

Objectives

New

TEACHING

Addition Family 9

WORKBOOK

Measuring inches

Review

Addition facts

Number words

Larger (170's)

(111) Answer these facts.

5	3	6	5	4	3	4	2	3
+3	+5	+2	+2	+4	+5	+3	+6	+4
8	8	8	7	8	8	7	8	7

2	3	5	4	3	3	4	6	1
+6	+4	+2	+3	+5	+4	+4	+2	+7
8	7	7	7	8	7	8	8	8

3	2	5	2	3	3	1	5	4
+5	+5	+3	+6	+5	+4	+7	+3	+3
8	7	8	8	8	7	8	8	7

Write the fractions.

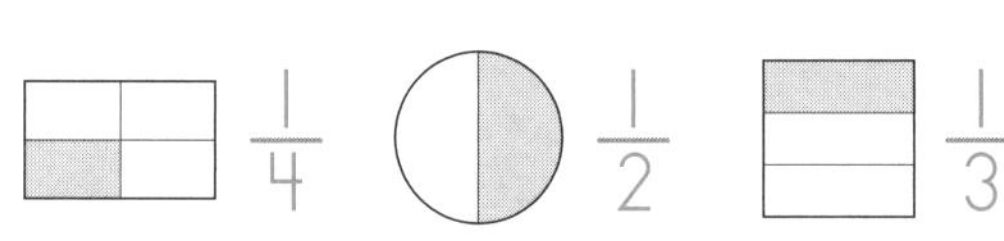

$\frac{1}{2}$ $\frac{1}{4}$ $\frac{1}{3}$

$\frac{1}{4}$ $\frac{1}{2}$ $\frac{1}{3}$

56

Preparation

Materials

Addition Families 7 and 8 flash cards

12-inch ruler

Number word cards *one* to *ten*

Subtraction Families 1–7 flash cards

Large thermometer

Chalkboard

(*Class Time* #2)

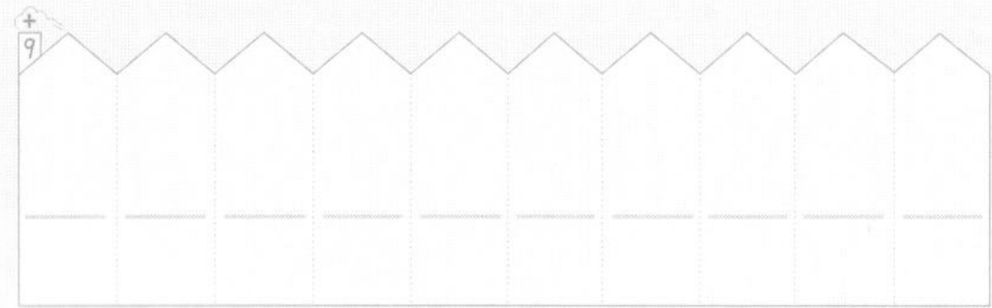

(Draw these lines 3", 1", and 5" long for *Class Time* #3.)

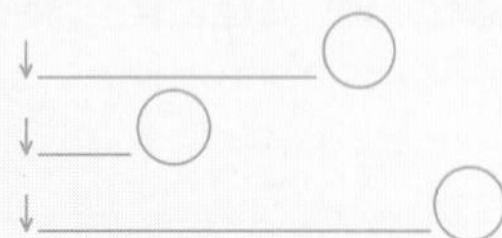

(*Class Time* #5)

155	150	146	164
106	160	114	141
174	173	169	159

Class Time

1. *Review Addition Families 7 and 8.*
   a. Circle Drill with Addition Families 7 and 8 flash cards.
   b. **Watch my fingers. Boys, say Family 7. Girls, say Family 8.**
2. *Introduce Addition Family 9.*
   a. Place 9 felt blocks below the divider on the flannel board. **0 + 9 = 9.** Move 1 of the blocks above the divider, and proceed through Addition Family 9.
   b. **Say Family 9 as I fill the houses.**
3. *Measuring inches.*
   a. Hold the ruler. **Count with me. 1 inch, 2 inches, 3 inches, . . .**
   b. Ask individuals to hold the ruler, measure the lines, and write the inches. **Put the "zero" of your ruler at the beginning of the line. Write the number and the mark that means "inches."**

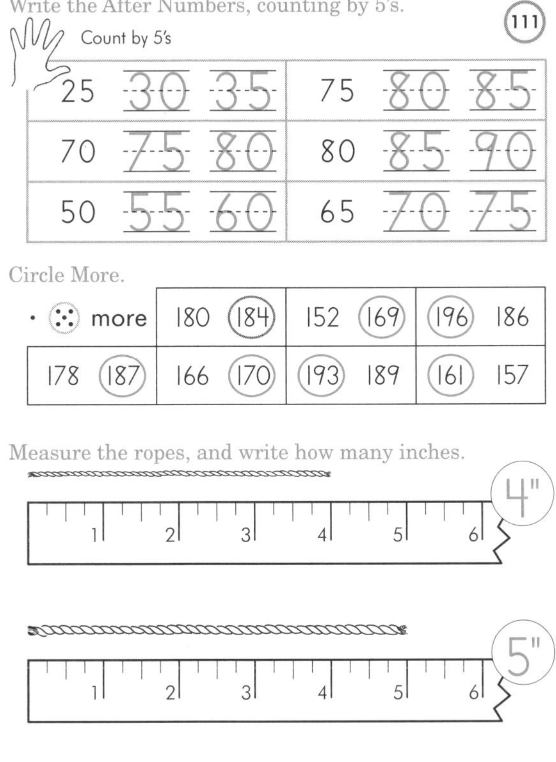

4. *Number words.*
   Flash number word cards.
5. *Larger numbers.*
   A number that says *more* is a *larger* number. Circle the larger number.
6. *Assign Lesson 111.*

Follow-up

Drill

1. Drill individuals with Subtraction Families 1–7 flash cards.
2. Practice counting by 2's on the thermometer.
   a. Set the mercury at 22°. **2, 4, 6, . . . 22°. Would you wear a winter coat?**
   b. Set the mercury at 96°. **2, 4, 6, . . . 96°. Would you go barefoot?**
   c. **If this mercury were real, it would show the temperature of our classroom.** Set the mercury at 72°. **2, 4, 6, . . . 72°. Our room is 72°.**
3. Have individuals count by 5's to 100.

Practice Sheets

- ☐ Fact Houses #29
- ● Number Facts #39
- ● More Numbers #19
- ● Clocks #5

Objectives

New

TEACHING

Addition Family 9 twins

WORKBOOK

Addition Family 9

Review

Column addition
Fractions
Place value
Money

Preparation

Make Addition Family 9 flash cards for each child.

Materials

Large penny, nickel, and dime

One 12-inch ruler for each child

Chalkboard

(*Class Time* #1)

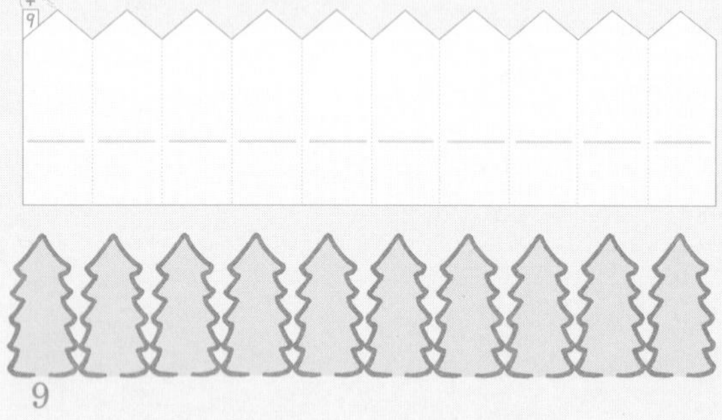

(*Class Time* #2)

3	4	3	2	5
4	2	5	3	1
+1	+2	+1	+2	+2

2	2	4	3	1
3	4	3	2	3
+2	+2	+1	+2	+2

(Class Time #3)

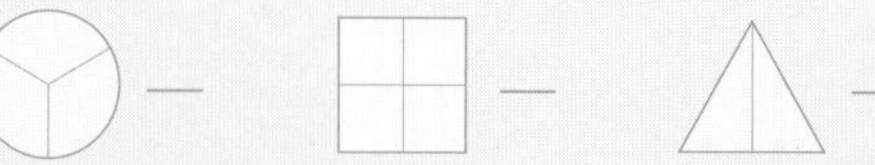

Class Time

1. *Practice Addition Family 9.*
   a. Illustrate Addition Family 9 with felt blocks on the flannel board as you say these story facts.
      (1) **Zero fish are in the boat, and 9 fish are in the net. There are 9 fish in all. 0 fish + 9 fish = 9 fish.**
      (2) **One fish is in the boat, and 8 fish are in the net. There are 9 fish in all. 1 fish + 8 fish = 9 fish.**
   b. Ask a child to fill the 9 Houses as you say Family 9 together.
   c. **Say Family 9 again in the same order as I write in the trees.** (Write in every other tree the first time across.)
   d. **Now say Family 9 in twin order. Point to each fact as you say it.**
2. *Column addition.*
   Do the chalkboard samples.
3. *Fractions.*
   Do the chalkboard samples.

Speed Drill Answers

2 1 3 4 3 1 2
1 3 4 5 4 3 1
3 4 5 2 5 4 3

Speed Drill #43

And Simon answering said unto him, Master, we have toiled all the night, and have taken nothing: nevertheless at thy word I will let down the net. And . . . they inclosed a great multitude of fishes: and their net brake. And they beckoned unto their partners, which were in the other ship. . . . And they came, and filled both the ships, so that they began to sink. . . . And Jesus said unto Simon, Fear not; from henceforth thou shalt catch men. And . . . they forsook all, and followed him.
Luke 5:5–11

4. *Place value.*
   Review the motion: **Ones, tens, hundreds; ones, . . .**
5. *Money.*
   a. Flash the coins as the children say, **Penny, 1¢; nickel, 5¢; dime, 10¢; . . .**
   b. **We count pennies by ___, nickels by ___, and dimes by ___.**
   c. **Tell how many dimes would make**
   30¢ 10¢ 90¢ 60¢ 100¢
   80¢ 50¢ 40¢ 20¢ 70¢
   If the children do not readily see the connection, tell them that dimes are tens, and the digit in tens' place tells how many tens. Or have them touch their fingers as they skip count to the right amount, and then see how many fingers were needed.
6. *Do Speed Drill #43.*
7. *Assign Lesson 112.*

Follow-up

Drill

1. Give each child his Addition Family 9 flash cards.
2. Chalkboard drill: **Listen as I count. When I stop, write the number that comes next.**
   5, 10, 15, ___ 75, 80, 85, ___
   50, 55, 60, ___ 60, 65, 70, ___
   25, 30, 35, ___ 40, 45, 50, ___
3. Give each child a 12-inch ruler. **Count the inches. 1 inch, 2 inches, . . . You may keep the ruler in your desk.**

Practice Sheets

- ☐ Fact Houses #30
- ☐ Less Numbers #19
- ☐ Number Trains #6
- ● Number Facts #38
- ● Fractions #3

Objectives

New

TEACHING

Counting beyond 200
Addition Family 9 reflected

WORKBOOK

Addition Family 9 twins

Review

Subtraction facts
Count by 5's
Before and After, by 10's
Money
Fraction concept

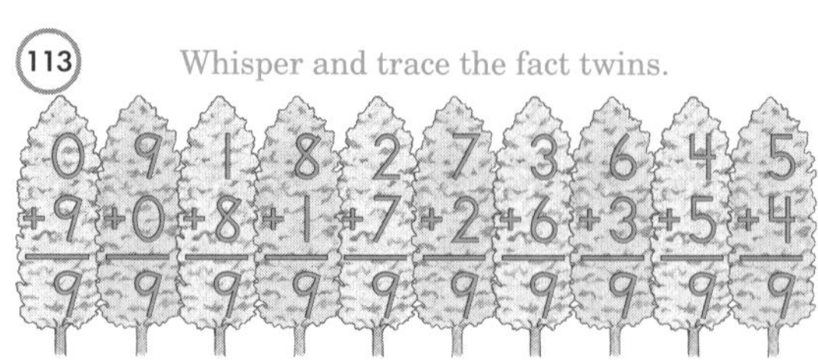

Answer these facts.

2 +3 5	3 +6 9	7 +2 9	3 +3 6	4 +5 9	1 +8 9	4 +2 6	5 +4 9	0 +9 9
6 +3 9	4 +5 9	3 +2 5	6 +3 9	4 +2 6	3 +6 9	2 +7 9	5 +1 6	6 +3 9
2 +7 9	1 +5 6	5 +4 9	7 +2 9	2 +4 6	3 +6 9	4 +1 5	4 +5 9	8 +1 9
9 +0 9	5 +4 9	3 +6 9	2 +3 5	5 +4 9	1 +8 9	2 +4 6	6 +3 9	4 +5 9

60

Preparation

Tack Addition Family 9 flash cards above the flannel board with answers showing.

Materials

Subtraction Families 1–7 flash cards

Form D for each child

Chalkboard

(*Class Time* #2)

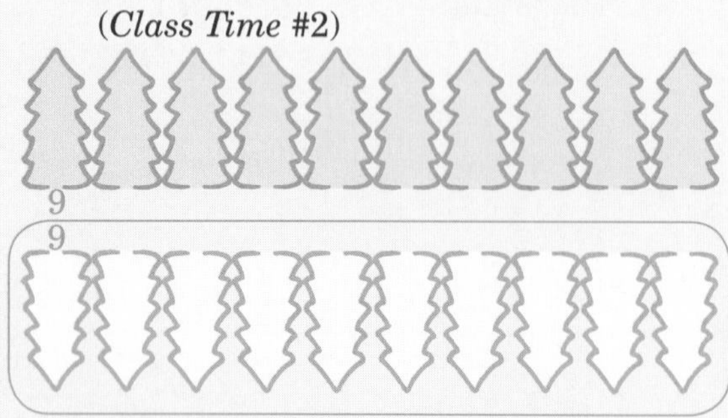

(*Class Time* #5)

___ 20 ___	___ 60 ___
___ 40 ___	___ 30 ___
___ 90 ___	___ 80 ___
___ 70 ___	___ 50 ___

Class Time

1. *Practice Addition Family 9.*
   a. Ask a child to move the felt blocks as you say Family 9 together.
   b. Point to the flash cards above the flannel board. **Say each fact three times with your eyes open, and then three times with your eyes closed.**
2. *Introduce Subtraction Family 9.*
   a. **Say Addition Family 9 as I fill the trees.**
   b. **Can you say Subtraction Family 9 as I fill the reflection?** Use the lower addend in each fact addition for the subtrahend in the reflection.
3. *Drill subtraction facts.*
   Double Drill with Subtraction Families 1–7 flash cards.
4. *Counting.*
   a. **Count by 1's from 100 to 199.**
   b. **Do you know what comes after 199?** Write 200–219 on the board as the children count.
   c. **Count by 5's to 100.**

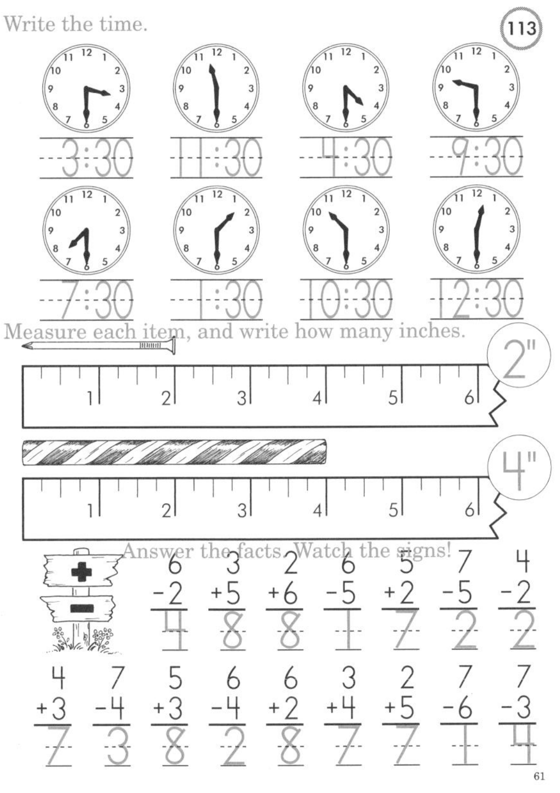
Write the time. 113

3:30 11:30 4:30 9:30

7:30 1:30 10:30 12:30

Measure each item, and write how many inches.

2"

4"

Answer the facts. Watch the signs!

6 − 2 = 4, 3 + 5 = 8, 2 + 6 = 8, 6 − 5 = 1, 5 + 2 = 7, 7 − 5 = 2, 4 − 2 = 2

4 + 3 = 7, 7 − 4 = 3, 5 + 3 = 8, 6 − 4 = 2, 6 + 2 = 8, 3 + 4 = 7, 2 + 5 = 7, 7 − 6 = 1, 7 − 3 = 4

61

5. *Before and After Numbers by 10's.*
   Do the chalkboard samples.
6. *Money.*
   a. **We count pennies by ___, nickels by ___, and dimes by ___.**
   b. **Tell how many nickels would make**
      5¢ 25¢ 50¢ 40¢ 20¢
      10¢ 40¢ 30¢ 15¢ 35¢
7. *Review fraction concept.*
   a. **How many parts does an apple have that is cut in half?**
   b. **How many parts does a sandwich have that is cut into fourths?**
   c. **How many parts does a rope have that is cut into thirds? What if the parts are not equal?** (Then the parts are not thirds.)
8. *Assign Lesson 113.*

Follow-up

Drill

(*Drill #2*)

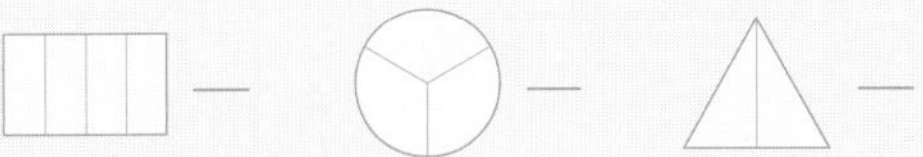

1. Distribute Form D for story problem dictation. Print these labels on the chalkboard. *books* *jobs*
   a. **Arrow Box: Sister Mary had 7 jobs for the children to do. The boys did 3 of them. How many jobs were *left* for the girls?**
   b. **Button Box: 6 books needed tape on the covers. George helped Sister Mary to tape 2 of them. How many books were *left* that still needed tape?**
   c. **Camel Box: 7 books were on the table. Then Nora put 4 of them in a box. How many books were *left* on the table?**
   d. **Daffodil Box: 7 jobs were written on the chalkboard. Then 5 of them were erased. How many jobs were *left* on the board?**
   e. **Elephant Box: Joan had 7 books to pass out. She put 2 of them in her own desk. How many books were *left* to pass out to others?**
   f. **Feather Box: 7 jobs had to be done. Before the children went home, they did 6 of them. How many jobs were *left* for Sister Mary to do?**
2. Have the children shade one part and write the fraction for the samples on the board.

Practice Sheets

- ● Form D (*Follow-up* drill #1)
- ☐ Fact Houses #30
- ☐ Form F: 101–200
- ☐ Measures #1
- ● Number Facts #40
- ● Number Facts #37

Objectives

New

TEACHING

Calendar date

WORKBOOK

Addition Family 9 reflected

Review

Count by 5's, 10's
Addition facts
Column addition
Larger and Smaller (190's)

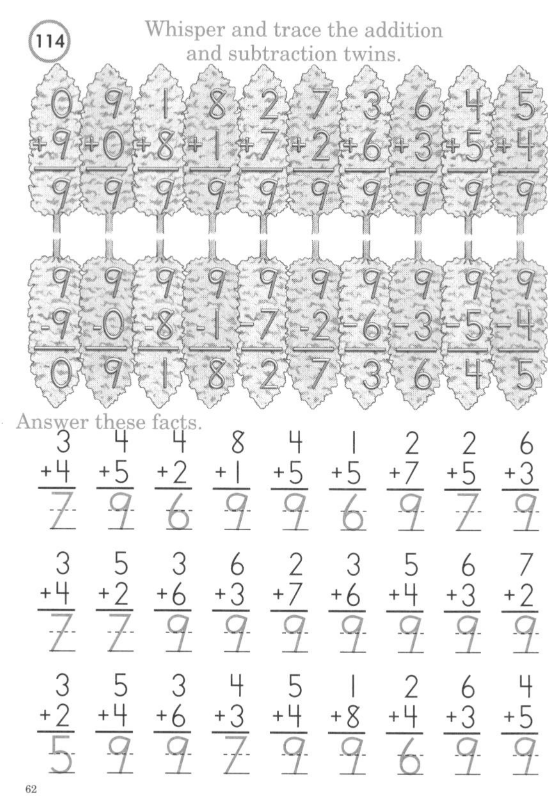

Answer these facts.

3 +4 7	4 +5 9	4 +2 6	8 +1 9	4 +5 9	1 +5 6	2 +7 9	2 +5 7	6 +3 9
3 +4 7	5 +2 7	3 +6 9	6 +3 9	2 +7 9	3 +6 9	5 +4 9	6 +3 9	7 +2 9
3 +2 5	5 +4 9	3 +6 9	4 +3 7	5 +4 9	1 +8 9	2 +4 6	6 +3 9	4 +5 9

62

Preparation

Materials

Addition Families 5–7 and 9 flash cards
Addition Families 5–7 and 9 flash cards
Subtraction Families 5–7 flash cards
Model clock

Chalkboard

(*Class Time #3*)

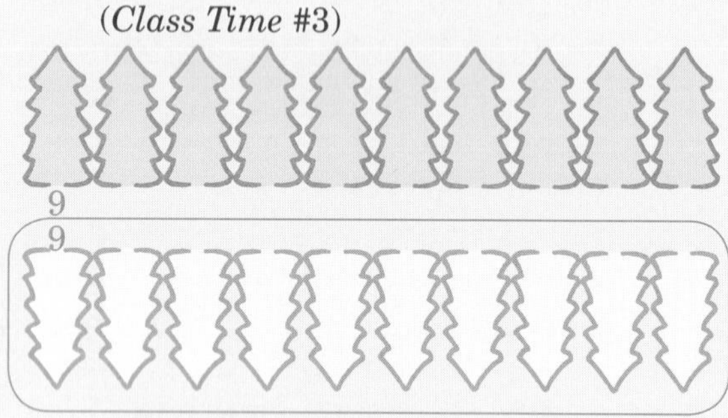

(*Class Time #6*)

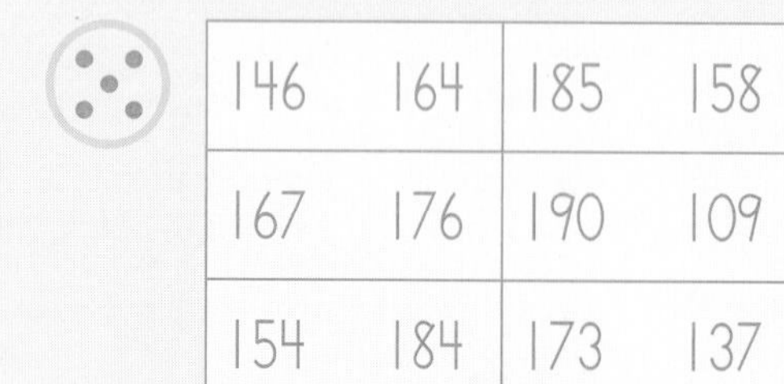

146	164	185	158
167	176	190	109
154	184	173	137

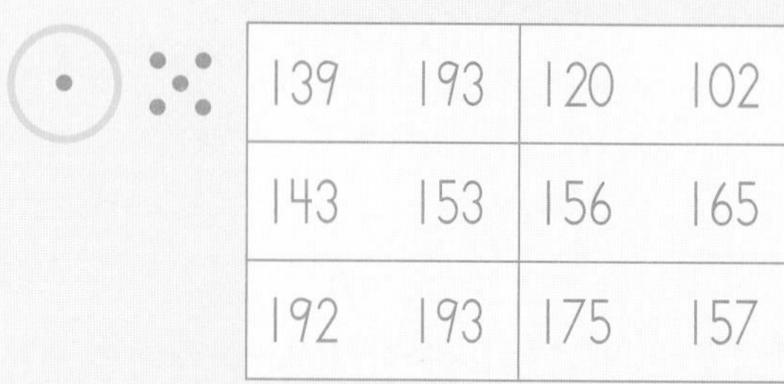

139	193	120	102
143	153	156	165
192	193	175	157

Class Time

1. *Count by 5's and 10's.*
   a. **Count by 5's to 100.**
   b. **Count by 10's to 100.**
2. *Review Addition Families 6 and 7.*
   Watch my fingers as we say Addition Family 6 . . . Family 7.
3. *Practice Addition and Subtraction Family 9.*
   a. Use the flannel board for story facts. Have the children say the fact together at the end of each story.
   (1) **Linda and Diane gather the eggs for Mother. Linda found 0 eggs, and Diane found 9 eggs. They found 9 eggs in all. 0 eggs + 9 eggs = 9 eggs.**
   (2) **Linda found 1 egg, and Diane found 8 eggs. They found 9 eggs in all. 1 egg + 8 eggs = 9 eggs.**
   (3) **Linda found 2 eggs, and Diane found 7 eggs. They found . . .**
   b. **Can you say Family 9 in twin order as I fill the trees?**

Speed Drill Answers

7	6	9	9	7	9	9
9	7	6	9	9	7	9
9	9	7	6	9	9	7

Speed Drill #44

c. **Say each addition fact and then the subtraction fact that goes with it.** Write the subtraction facts in the reflection as you say them.

4. *Drill addition facts.*
   Double Drill with Addition Families 5–7 and 9 flash cards.
5. *Column addition.*
   Chalkboard drill: **Write these three numbers in a column—2, 3, 1. Draw a line below 1. Write + beside the bottom number. Add the numbers.** Continue with the following problems.

3	3	5	4	2	2	1	3
5	4	2	2	6	3	5	3
+1	+2	+1	+2	+1	+2	+1	+2

6. *Larger and Smaller numbers.*
   Do the chalkboard samples.
7. *Do Speed Drill #44.*
8. *Assign Lesson 114.*

Follow-up

Drill

1. Call the children to the calendar in your room.
   a. Point to number 1. **Count with me. 1, 2, 3, . . .**
   b. Point to number 1. **Count with me again. First, second, . . .**
   c. **Today is number [18]. Today is the [18th].** (Use the number of the present day.)
   d. **Yesterday was the ___.**
   Tomorrow will be the ___.
2. Mix the flash cards for Addition Families 5–7 and 9, and Subtraction Families 5–7. Drill the facts.
3. Hold the model clock. Ask individuals to set the clock at 6:30, 9:30, 1:30, 4:30, 8:30, 11:30, 2:30.

Practice Sheets

- □ Fact Houses #30
- ● Number Facts #40
- ● Writing Practice #27
- ● Clocks #5

Objectives

New

TEACHING

2-digit addition

Review

Addition facts
Count by 2's
Number words
Count dimes with pennies
Fractions

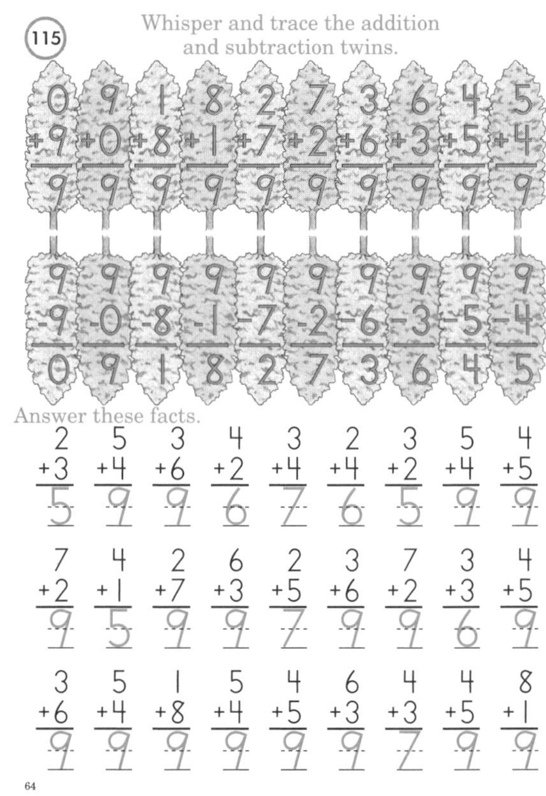

Preparation

Materials

Addition Families 6, 7, and 9 flash cards

Form C for each child

Number word cards

Subtraction Families 1–7 flash cards

Chalkboard

(*Class Time* #5)

(*Class Time* #6)

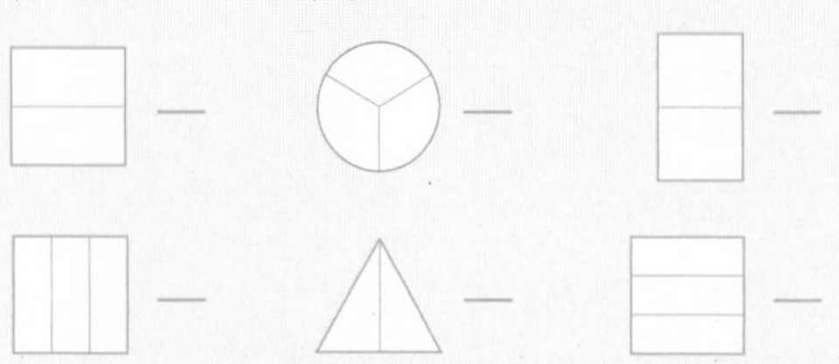

Class Time

1. *Review Addition Family 9.*
   Point to the flash cards above the flannel board. **Say each fact five times.** Say it quietly the first time. Raise your voice with each recital.
2. *Drill addition facts.*
   Use Form C for the children to write answers to flash card drill of Addition Families 6, 7, and 9.
3. *Count by 2's.*
   a. **What is the number pattern for counting by 2's?**
   b. **Count by 2's to 100.**

4. *Number words.*
   Flash number word cards.
5. *Counting dimes with pennies.*
   Do the chalkboard samples.
6. *Fractions.*
   Do the chalkboard samples.
7. *Numbers in the hundreds.*
   Chalkboard drill: **Write 157. Change it to 167, 107, 197, 190, 140, 148, 158, 138, 131, 101.**
8. *Assign Lesson 115.*

Follow-up

Drill

(*Drill* #1)

(Use white chalk to write the digits in the ones' place and green chalk for digits in the tens' place.)

↓	↓	↓	↓	↓	↓
42	16	45	20	34	52
+ 13	+ 51	+ 22	+ 36	+ 23	+ 45

1. Introduce 2-digit addition.
   a. Review place value with the motion. Point to the arrow above the ones' place in the first problem. **The arrow means "start here."** Trace the arrow. **Ones' place first, ones' place first.**
   b. **2 + 3 = ___.** Write 5 in the ones' place of the answer. **4 + 1 = ___.** Write 5. **The answer is 55.**
   c. Trace the arrow above the next problem. **Ones' place first, ones' place first.** Call on one of the children to do the problem. Continue.
2. **Count 100–219.**
3. Drill individuals with Subtraction Families 1–7 flash cards.

Practice Sheets

- ● Form C (*Class Time* #2)
- ☐ Number Words #1
- ☐ Missing Numbers #10
- ● Number Facts #38
- ● Number Facts #40

Objectives

New

TEACHING

2-digit addition

Review

Addition facts
Subtraction facts
Telling time

Preparation

Materials

Model clock

Addition Families 6–9 flash cards

Chalkboard

(*Class Time* #1)

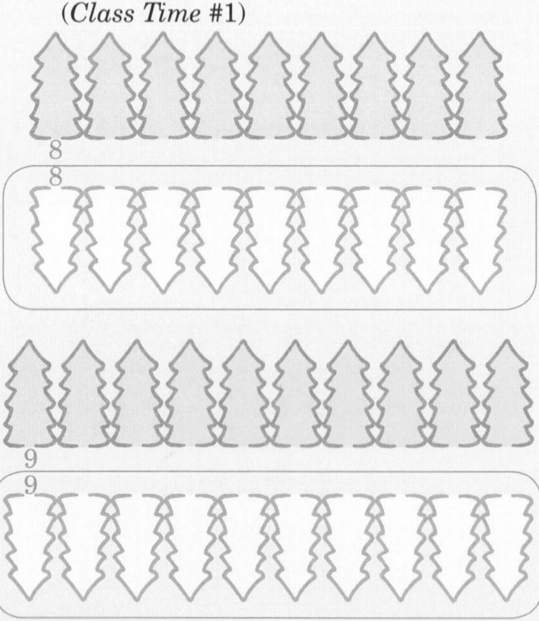

(*Class Time* #2. Use white chalk to write the digits in the ones' place and green chalk for digits in the tens' place.)

12	35	44	60	32	26
+ 63	+ 52	+ 42	+ 23	+ 41	+ 52

116 Whisper and trace the addition and subtraction twins.

0	9	1	8	2	7	3	6	4	5
+9	+0	+8	+1	+7	+2	+6	+3	+5	+4
9	9	9	9	9	9	9	9	9	9

9	9	9	9	9	9	9	9	9	9
-9	-0	-8	-1	-7	-2	-6	-3	-5	-4
0	9	1	8	2	7	3	6	4	5

Answer these facts.

5	2	4	3	4	3	3	5	3
+3	+7	+5	+5	+5	+5	+4	+4	+6
8	9	9	8	9	8	7	9	9

7	6	5	6	2	6	5	6	4
+2	+2	+2	+3	+7	+2	+4	+3	+2
9	8	7	9	9	8	9	9	6

1	5	1	6	3	1	3	5	4
+7	+4	+7	+3	+3	+8	+6	+3	+5
8	9	8	9	6	9	9	8	9

66

Class Time

1. *Review Addition and Subtraction Families 8 and 9.*
   a. **Say Family 8 as I move the felt blocks.**
   b. Ask a child to fill the 8 Trees as you say the facts together in twin order.
   c. **Say each addition fact and the subtraction fact that goes with it as I fill the reflection.** (The addend beside the plus sign should go beside the minus sign in the reflection.)
   d. **Say Family 9 as I move the felt blocks.**
   e. Ask a child to fill the 9 Trees as you say the facts together.
   f. **Say each addition fact and the subtraction fact that goes with it as I fill the reflection.**

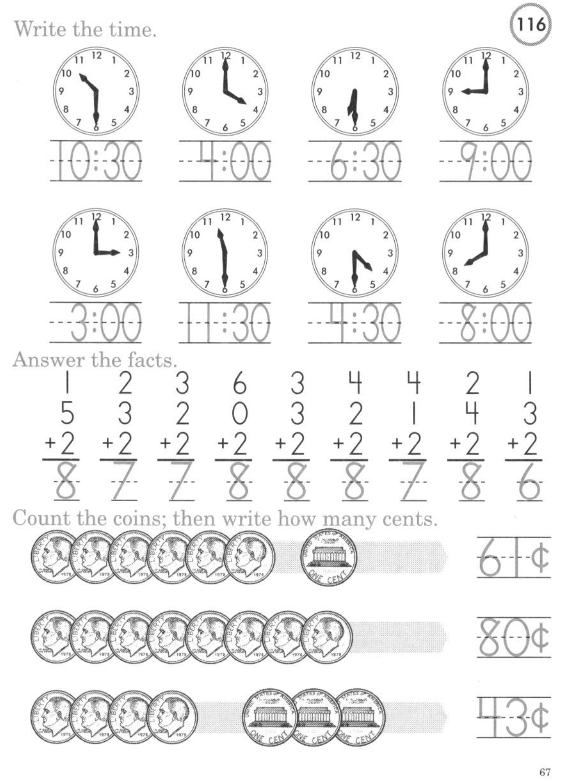

116

Write the time.

10:30 4:00 6:30 9:00

3:00 11:30 4:30 8:00

Answer the facts.

1	2	3	6	3	4	4	2	1
5	3	2	0	3	2	1	4	3
+2	+2	+2	+2	+2	+2	+2	+2	+2
8	7	7	8	8	8	7	8	6

Count the coins; then write how many cents.

61¢

80¢

43¢

67

2. *Two-digit addition.*
   a. Review place value with the motion.
   b. Trace the arrows above the two-digit samples. **Ones' place first, ones' place first.**
   c. Have individuals come and say, **Ones' place first, ones' place first,** and then answer the problem.
3. *Telling time.*
   Have the children answer together as you set the model clock. 5:00, 7:30, 9:00, 12:30, 2:00, 10:30, 12:00, 6:00, 8:30.
4. *Do Speed Drill #45.*
5. *Assign Lesson 116.*

Speed Drill Answers

9	7	4	5	6	9	3
7	4	5	6	9	3	6
4	5	6	9	3	6	9

Follow-up

Drill

(*Drill* #2)

___	60	___	70	___	___
___	60	___	___	90	___
___	10	___	___	25	___
___	30	___	50	___	___

1. Circle Drill with Addition Families 6–9 flash cards.
2. Call the children to the number line.
   a. **Girls, count by 5's to 100.**
   b. **Boys, count by 10's to 100.**
   c. Point to the first row of Missing Numbers on the chalkboard. **Can you tell which skip counting to use to fill in the Missing Numbers?**
   d. Do the rest of the rows.
3. Chalkboard drill with column addition. **Write these three numbers in a column: 3, 4, 2. Draw a plus sign and equal line. Add the numbers, and write the answer.**

2	4	1	3	4	5	3	0
4	3	6	5	0	1	4	6
+2	+2	+2	+1	+2	+2	+1	+2

Practice Sheets

- ☐ Fact Houses #31
- ☐ Measures #3
- ● Number Facts #41
- ● Measures #2
- ● Fractions #2

Objectives

New

TEACHING

Zero + zero
Mixed story problems

WORKBOOK

2-digit addition

Review

Addition facts
Fractions
Count by 2's

117 Whisper and trace the addition and subtraction twins.

0	9	1	8	2	7	3	6	4	5
+9	+0	+8	+1	+7	+2	+6	+3	+5	+4
9	9	9	9	9	9	9	9	9	9

9	9	9	9	9	9	9	9	9	9
-9	-0	-8	-1	-7	-2	-6	-3	-5	-4
0	9	1	8	2	7	3	6	4	5

Answer these facts.

2	5	2	5	3	1	5	3	4
+7	+4	+4	+3	+4	+8	+4	+5	+5
9	9	6	8	7	9	9	8	9

7	6	4	4	2	3	7	2	4
+2	+2	+5	+4	+5	+6	+2	+6	+5
9	8	9	8	7	9	9	8	9

3	1	6	3	4	5	4	8	5
+5	+7	+3	+6	+3	+4	+5	+1	+3
8	8	9	9	7	9	9	9	8

68

Preparation

Materials

Number word cards

Chalkboard

(*Class Time* #2)

3	5	4	5
+5	+3	+5	+4
8	8	9	9

(*Class Time* #3)

25	33	40	73	65	32
+74	+46	+20	+25	+14	+25

(Class Time #4)

Class Time

1. *Review Addition Family 9.*
   Point to the flash cards above the flannel board.
   a. **Boys, say each fact once.**
   b. **Girls, say each fact once.**
   c. **Say the facts together.**
2. *Drill selected facts.*
   a. Stand near the box on the board. Circle the first fact in the box. **Say this three times with your eyes open, and then three times with your eyes closed.**
   b. Circle and drill the other facts.
3. *Two-digit addition.*
   a. **Ones' place first, ones' place first.**
   b. Ask individuals to answer the problems. Give help if there is any confusion about zero plus zero.
4. *Fractions.*
   Do the chalkboard samples.

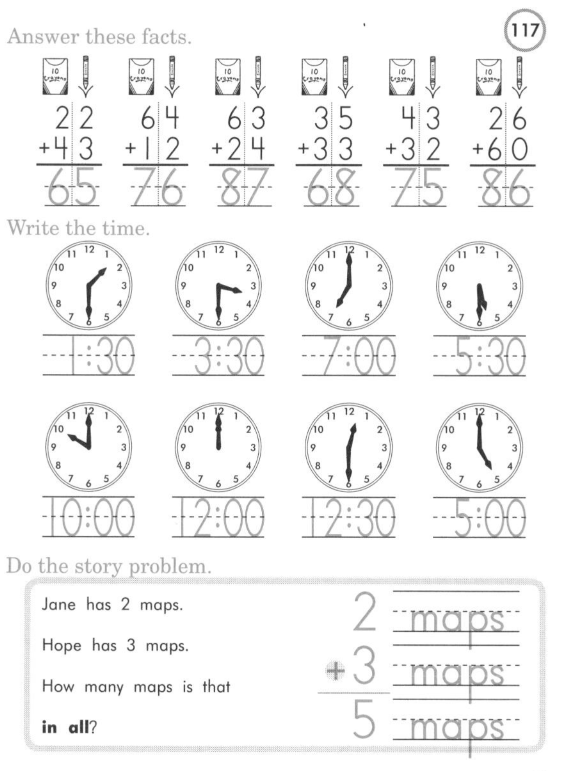

5. *Count by 2's.*
   Have the children stand in a circle with you. **We will count by 2's. I will begin, and we will take turns around the circle. 2, . . .**
6. *Oral story problems.*
   a. **Close your eyes and listen. 7 birds sing. Then 2 of them fly away. How many birds are *left?* Open your eyes. Who can give the whole problem?** (7 birds - 2 birds = 5 birds)
   b. **Close your eyes. Jay has 5 balls. Roy has 4 balls. How many balls is that *in all?* Open your eyes. Who can give the whole problem?** (5 balls + 4 balls = 9 balls)
7. *Assign Lesson 117.*

Follow-up

Drill

1. Double Drill with oral facts. Have the children stand before you in two rows. **Listen for a fact. Whoever says the correct answer first may go to the back of his row.**

5 - 3	**3 + 5**	**6 - 3**	**7 + 1**	**7 - 5**
7 - 3	**7 + 2**	**7 - 2**	**5 + 4**	**5 - 2**
5 - 4	**4 + 4**	**4 - 3**	**2 + 7**	**7 - 4**
6 - 2	**6 + 3**	**7 - 6**	**2 + 6**	**6 - 4**

2. Flash number word cards.
3. Have individuals move the felt blocks and say Addition Family 9 for you.

Practice Sheets

- ☐ Fact Houses #31
- ☐ Missing Numbers #11
- ☐ Money #15
- ● Number Facts #42
- ● Number Facts #41

Objectives

Review

Addition and subtraction
Money
Fractions
Count by 10's
Counting (200)

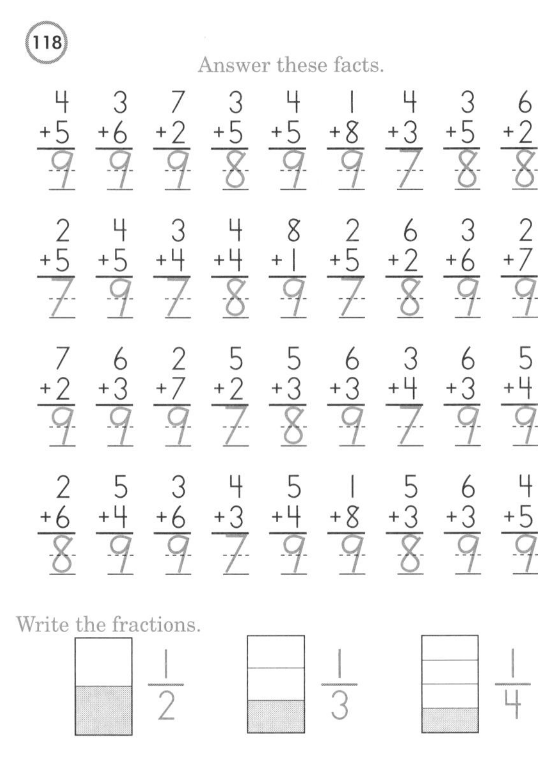

118

Answer these facts.

4 +5 = 9	3 +6 = 9	7 +2 = 9	3 +5 = 8	4 +5 = 9	1 +8 = 9	4 +3 = 7	3 +5 = 8	6 +2 = 8
2 +5 = 7	4 +5 = 9	3 +4 = 7	4 +4 = 8	8 +1 = 9	2 +5 = 7	6 +2 = 8	3 +6 = 9	2 +7 = 9
7 +2 = 9	6 +3 = 9	2 +7 = 9	5 +2 = 7	5 +3 = 8	6 +3 = 9	3 +4 = 7	6 +3 = 9	5 +4 = 9
2 +6 = 8	5 +4 = 9	3 +6 = 9	4 +3 = 7	5 +4 = 9	1 +8 = 9	5 +3 = 8	6 +3 = 9	4 +5 = 9

Write the fractions.

$\frac{1}{2}$ $\frac{1}{3}$ $\frac{1}{4}$

70

Preparation

Materials

Addition Families 7–9 flash cards
Form C for each child
Large penny, nickel, and dime
Subtraction Families 5–7 flash cards

Chalkboard

(*Class Time* #1)

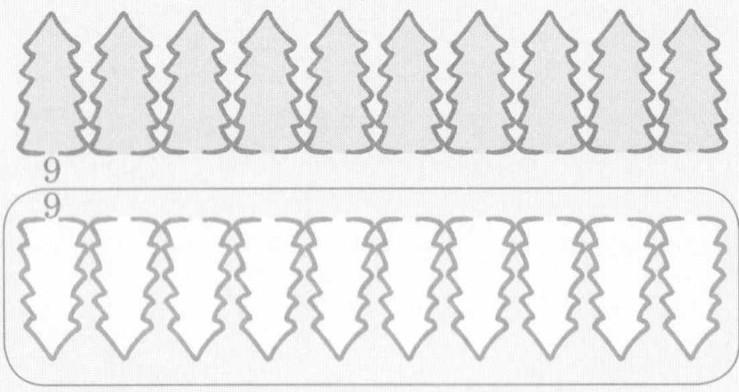

(*Class Time* #3)

7 nickels = _____ 2 dimes = _____
3 dimes = _____ 6 nickels = _____
4 nickels = _____ 5 dimes = _____
8 nickels = _____ 3 nickels = _____

(*Class Time* #4)

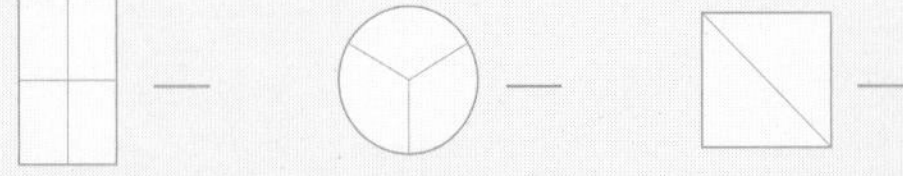

Class Time

1. *Review Addition Family 8 and Addition and Subtraction Family 9.*
   a. **I will move the blocks. Say Addition Family 8 . . . Family 9.**
   b. Ask a child to fill the trees as you say the addition facts together in twin order. Guide recitation by showing the beginning number for each set of twins with your fingers.
   c. Ask a child to fill the reflection as you say the subtraction facts together in twin order. (The subtrahend of each subtraction fact should be the second addend from the fact above it.)
   d. **Now say the addition facts with the reflecting subtraction fact after each one.** Point to the facts as you say them.

118

Answer these facts.

32	34	65	45	40	52
+33	+42	+22	+23	+35	+14
65	76	87	68	75	66

Circle More.

• ⁘ more	210 (219)	(217) 211	203 (213)
(201) 200	208 (218)	(216) 206	207 (209)

Write the time.

7:30 1:00 10:30 11:00

6:30 12:00 2:30 2:00

71

Speed Drill Answers

8 9 9 8 9 8 8
9 8 9 9 8 9 8
9 9 8 9 9 8 9

Speed Drill #46

2. *Drill addition facts.*
   a. Circle Drill with Addition Families 7–9 flash cards.
   b. Distribute Form C for the children to write answers to the flash cards.
3. *Money.*
   a. Flash the large coins, including the reverse sides. **Penny, 1¢; nickel, 5¢; dime, 10¢ . . .**
   b. Do the chalkboard samples. **Use your fingers to help you figure the answers.**
4. *Fractions.*
   Do the chalkboard samples.
5. *Counting.*
   Count by 10's to 100, and then continue to 200 by 1's.
6. *Do Speed Drill #46.*
7. *Assign Lesson 118.*

Follow-up

Drill

1. Chalkboard drill: **Write the number I say: 200, 210, 216, 204, 208, 211, 218, 203, 212, 201, 217.**
2. Drill Subtraction Families 5–7 flash cards.
3. Call the children to the teaching corner. Give each child a songbook. **See how quietly and quickly you can find the number I say. As soon as you have found it, turn your book toward me. 57, 89, 63, 12, 46, 92, 3, 35, 70, 24, *___**

*Announce a favorite number. **Stand; we will sing this song together.**

Practice Sheets

- ● Form C (*Class Time* #2)
- ☐ Fact Houses #31
- ☐ Number Words #1
- ● Number Facts #41
- ● Money #15

Objectives

New

TEACHING

12 inches = 1 foot

WORKBOOK

Zero + zero

Review

Addition facts

2-digit addition

Count by 2's

Before and After (200's)

Preparation

Materials

Addition Families 7–9 flash cards

Large thermometer

Footprint poster

12-inch ruler

Addition Families 7–9 flash cards

Chalkboard

(Write a set of these facts for each child to trace in *Class Time* #2.)

5	5
+3	+4
8	9

(*Class Time* #3)

14	62	40	73	52	50
+53	+27	+30	+16	+35	+40

(*Class Time* #5)

____ 173 ____   ____ 212 ____

____ 164 ____   ____ 205 ____

____ 181 ____   ____ 216 ____

____ 198 ____   ____ 209 ____

Class Time

1. *Review Addition Families 7–9.*
   a. Give the flash cards for Addition Families 7–9 to the children. **If you have part of Family 7, come set it on the chalk tray.** Continue.
   b. Stand near the cards. **Say them together.**
2. *Drill selected facts.*
   a. Have each child stand at his set of facts on the board. **Trace and whisper the facts until I say "stop."**
   b. **Stop. Turn toward me. Say each fact three times. 5 + 3, 8; 5 + 3 . . .**
3. *Two-digit addition.*
   a. Review place value with the motion.
   b. **Ones' place first; ones' place first.** Do the chalkboard samples.

119

Answer these facts.

53	58	23	34	47	10
+26	+30	+74	+45	+41	+80
79	88	97	79	88	90

Circle Less.

less	213 219	210 209	207 208
203 201	214 204	216 209	208 218
217 207	214 206	205 212	215 213

Write how many cents.

7 nickels = 35¢ 9 dimes = 90¢

9 nickels = 45¢ 6 dimes = 60¢

5 nickels = 25¢ 7 dimes = 70¢

8 nickels = 40¢ 8 dimes = 80¢

73

4. *Count by 2's with the thermometer.*
   a. Set the mercury at 48°. **What is the temperature? 2, 4, 6, . . . 48°. A snowman will melt if the mercury rises to 48°.**
   b. Set the mercury at 18°. **What is the temperature? 2, 4, 6, . . . 18°. A water puddle will freeze if the mercury sinks to 18°.**
5. *Before and After numbers.*
   Do the chalkboard samples.
6. *Assign Lesson 119.*

Follow-up

Drill

1. Hold the footprint poster.*
   a. Count **1 inch, 2 inches, . . .**
   b. **12 inches make 1 foot; 12 inches make 1 foot.**
   c. **Do you think your footprint is 12 inches long? Do you think your father's footprint is 12 inches long?**
   d. Hold a 12-inch ruler beside the footprint. **This is a 12-inch ruler; this is a 12-inch footprint. This is a 1-foot ruler; this is a 1-foot footprint.**
2. Circle Drill with Addition Families 7–9 flash cards.
3. **Count by 1's from 150 to 220.**

* See pattern on page 602.

Practice Sheets

- ☐ Fact Houses #32
- ☐ Before and After #13
- ☐ Measures #4
- ● Number Facts #43
- ● Number Facts #44

Objectives

New

TEACHING

Counting backward
12 inches = 1 foot
Addition Family 10

Review

Addition facts
Mixed counting (10's and 1's)
Fractions

Preparation

Materials

Footprint poster
Form D for each child

Chalkboard

(*Class Time #5*)

(*Class Time #6*)

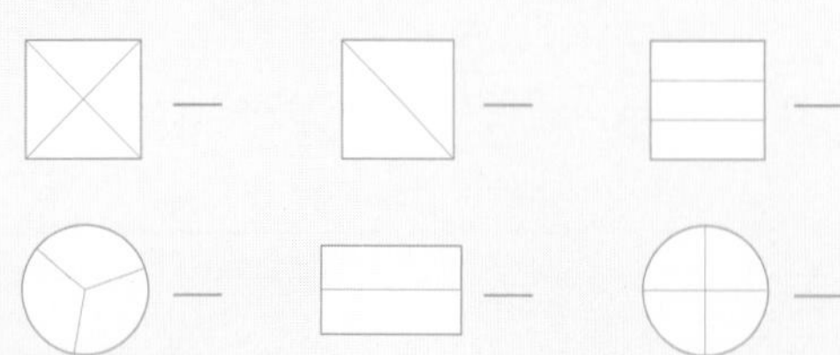

Class Time

1. *Practice Addition Family 9.*
   a. Ask a child to move the felt blocks as you say Addition Family 9.
   b. Point to the first flash card above the flannel board. **Look at the fact. Close your eyes, and say it three times . . .**
2. *Review Addition Families 6, 7, and 8.*
   Watch my fingers. Say Addition Family 6 . . . Family 7 . . . Family 8.
3. *Mixed counting.*
   Stand near the number line. **Follow the pointer and count.**
   10, 20, 30, 31, 32, 33, 34
   10, 20, 30, 40, 50, 51, 52, 53, 54, 55
   10, 20, 30, 40, 50, 60, 70, 71, 72
4. *Counting backward.*
   Chalkboard drill: **I will count backward. When I stop, you write the number I should say next.**

10, 9, 8, ___	**56, 55, 54, ___**
19, 18, 17, ___	**45, 44, 43, ___**
23, 22, 21, ___	**77, 76, 75, ___**
69, 68, 67, ___	**84, 83, 82, ___**

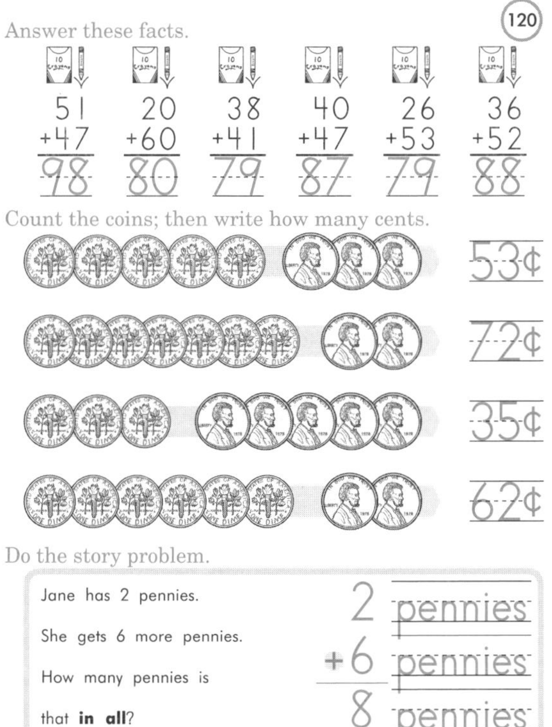
120

Answer these facts.

51	20	38	40	26	36
+47	+60	+41	+47	+53	+52
98	80	79	87	79	88

Count the coins; then write how many cents.

53¢

72¢

35¢

62¢

Do the story problem.

Jane has 2 pennies.
She gets 6 more pennies.
How many pennies is that **in all**?

2 pennies
+6 pennies
8 pennies

75

5. *12 inches = 1 foot.*
   a. Hold the footprint poster. **12 inches = 1 foot; 12 inches . . .**
   b. Point to the pictures on the board. **If these pictures were real things, which ones would be 12 inches tall?** Circle the flower, cat, family Bible, and cereal box.
6. *Fractions.*
   Do the chalkboard samples.
7. *Do Speed Drill #47.*
8. *Assign Lesson 120.*

Follow-up

Drill

(*Drill* #2)

Speed Drill Answers

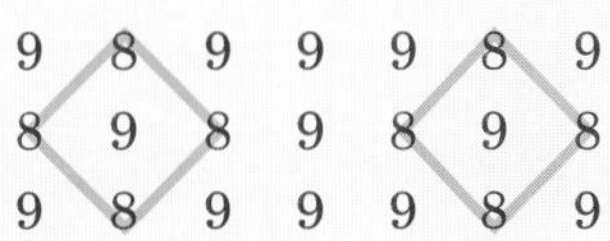

1. Distribute Form D for story problem dictation. Print these labels on the chalkboard. *hens* *eggs*
   Some stories will tell us to add. Some stories will tell us to subtract. Put the correct sign in the gray spot.
   a. **Arrow Box: Glen found 4 eggs in one nest. He found 5 eggs in another nest. How many eggs is that *in all?***
   b. **Button Box: Mother had 7 eggs. She fried 5 of them for breakfast. How many eggs were *left?***
   c. **Camel Box: 6 hens scratch and peck. Then 4 of them run away. How many hens are *left?***
   d. **Daffodil Box: 3 hens are brown, and 5 hens are white. How many hens is that *in all?***
   e. **Elephant Box: Glen had 7 eggs in a basket. He dropped the basket, and 3 eggs broke. How many eggs were *left?***
   f. **Feather Box: 6 hens are scratching in the garden. 3 hens are scratching in the yard. How many hens is that *in all?***
2. Introduce Addition Family 10. **Help me fill the houses with Addition Family 10.**

Practice Sheets

- ● Form D (*Follow-up* drill #1)
- ☐ Fact Houses #32
- ☐ Missing Numbers #11
- ☐ Clocks #6
- ● Number Facts #42
- ● Number Facts #43

Objectives

New

TEACHING

Addition Family 10

Mixed counting (5's and 1's)

Review

Mixed facts

Telling time

12 inches = 1 foot

Count by 10's, by 5's

Money

(121) Answer these facts.

4	6	4	6	4	3	2	3	6
+5	+2	+5	+3	+4	+6	+7	+5	+2
9	8	9	9	8	9	9	8	8

7	5	6	8	2	5	1	6	5
+2	+3	+3	+1	+7	+3	+7	+3	+4
9	8	9	9	9	8	8	9	9

3	3	7	3	4	1	2	6	4
+5	+6	+2	+5	+5	+8	+6	+3	+5
8	9	9	8	9	9	8	9	9

4	2	5	8	3	4	6	5	3
+5	+7	+3	+1	+6	+4	+2	+4	+5
9	9	8	9	9	8	8	9	8

5	6	2	4	5	6	1
+3	+3	+7	+5	+4	+3	+7
8	9	9	9	9	9	8

"There he maketh the hungry to dwell, that they may . . . sow the fields, and plant vineyards, which may yield fruits of increase."
Psalm 107:36, 37

76

Preparation

Materials

Mixed flash cards: Addition Families 5–9 and Subtraction Families 5–7

Model clock

Number word cards

Chalkboard

(*Class Time* #2)

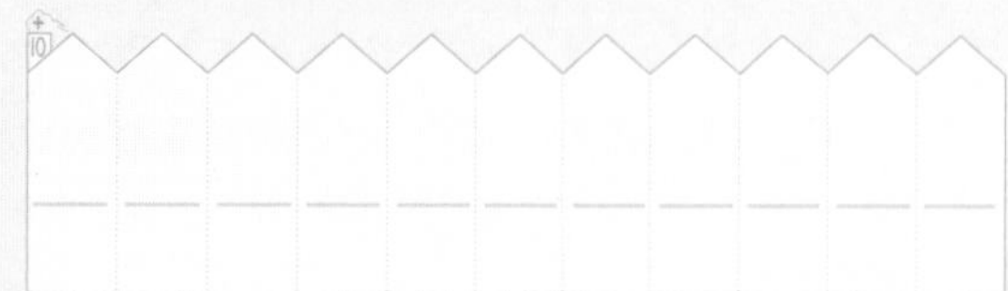

(*Class Time* #6)

6 dimes = ____	12¢ = ____ pennies
12 pennies = ____	21¢ = ____ pennies
3 nickels = ____	20¢ = ____ dimes
15 pennies = ____	40¢ = ____ dimes
10 nickels = ____	25¢ = ____ nickels
8 dimes = ____	15¢ = ____ nickels

Class Time

1. *Drill addition and subtraction facts.*
   Circle Drill with flash cards for Addition Families 5–9 and Subtraction Families 5–7.

2. *Introduce Addition Family 10.*
   a. Call the children to the flannel board. **Say Family 10 as I move the blocks.**
   b. **Say Family 10 as I fill the houses.** Write the answers as two-digit numbers, placing 1 below the plus sign, except for the fact that has 10 for the lower addend.
   c. **10 is a 2-digit number. We may not squeeze 1 and 0 into the ones' place. Write 1 below the plus, and write 0 in the ones' place.**

3. *Telling time.*
   a. Set the clock at 2:30. **Mother said, "Mary awoke 1 hour ago." What time did Mary wake up?**

b. Set the clock at 8:30. **Father said, "Uncle John left 1 hour ago." What time did Uncle John leave?**

4. *12 inches = 1 foot.*
   Drill the statement **12 inches make 1 foot; 12 inches make . . .**
5. *Skip counting.*
   a. **Boys, count by 10's to 100.**
   b. **Girls, count by 5's to 100.**
6. *Money.*
   Do the chalkboard samples. For the second column, have the children do skip counting on their fingers until they reach the right amount, then see how many fingers they used.
7. *Assign Lesson 121.*
   What do you think the boy in the picture is planting? God makes our crops grow, but we need to plant the seeds.

Follow-up

Drill

1. Give the number word cards to the children. **When I say your number, come stand in line so that the numbers are in order. Two, six, ten, five, nine, four, seven, one, eight, three.**
2. Call the children to the number line for mixed counting. **We will count by 5's and by 1's. Follow the pointer.**
   5, 6, 7, 8, 9
   5, 10, 11, 12, 13, 14
   5, 10, 15, 20, 21
   5, 10, 15, 16, 17, 18, 19

Practice Sheets

- ☐ Fact Houses #32
- ☐ Number Words #1
- ☐ Money #15
- ● Number Facts #43
- ● More Numbers #20
- ● Fractions #3

Objectives

New

TEACHING

Mixed counting (5's and 1's)
Count nickels with pennies

WORKBOOK

Addition Family 10

Review

2-digit addition
12 inches = 1 foot
Fraction concept

Preparation

Make Addition Family 10 flash cards for each child.

Materials

Footprint poster
Large thermometer

Chalkboard

(*Class Time* #1)

(*Class Time* #2)

74	36	53	32	27	49	26
+ 12	+ 43	+ 46	+ 25	+ 61	+ 50	+ 72

(*Class Time* #3)

(5¢) (1¢) ____

(5¢) (1¢) (1¢) (1¢) ____

(5¢) (1¢) (1¢) (1¢) (1¢) (1¢) ____

(5¢) (1¢) (1¢) (1¢) (1¢) ____

(5¢) (1¢) (1¢) ____

(5¢) (1¢) (1¢) (1¢) (1¢) (1¢) (1¢) (1¢) ____

(122) Whisper, trace, and answer the facts.

0 + 10 = 10	1 + 9 = 10	
2 + 8 = 10	3 + 7 = 10	4 + 6 = 10
5 + 5 = 10	6 + 4 = 10	7 + 3 = 10
8 + 2 = 10	9 + 1 = 10	10 + 0 = 10

"God . . . giveth the increase."
1 Corinthians 3:7

78

Class Time

1. *Practice Addition Family 10.*
   a. **Say Addition Family 10 as I move the felt blocks.**
   b. Ask a child to fill the 10 Houses as everyone says Family 10. Is he writing the answers as 2-digit numbers? (1 below the plus sign)
2. *Two-digit addition.*
   Do the chalkboard samples. **Ones' place first!**
3. *Counting nickels and pennies.*
   a. Stand near the number line. **Count by 5's and by 1's.**
   5, 6, 7, 8
   5, 10, 11, 12, 13, 14
   5, 10, 15, 20, 21, 22, 23, 24, 25
   5, 10, 15, 16, 17, 18
   b. Point to the nickel and penny samples. **Count with me. 5¢, 6¢.** Write 6¢. Continue with the rest of the samples.

Write Family 10. (122)

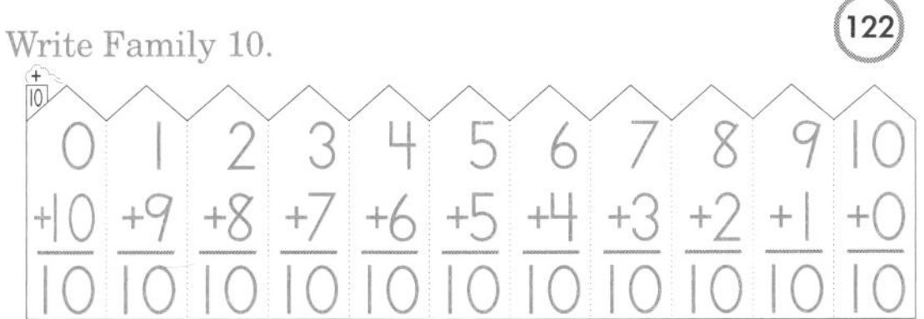

0	1	2	3	4	5	6	7	8	9	10
+10	+9	+8	+7	+6	+5	+4	+3	+2	+1	+0
10	10	10	10	10	10	10	10	10	10	10

Write the After Numbers, counting by 2's.

Count by 2's

46	48	50	20	22	24
82	84	86	74	76	78
94	96	98	36	38	40
18	20	22	52	54	56

Do the story problem.

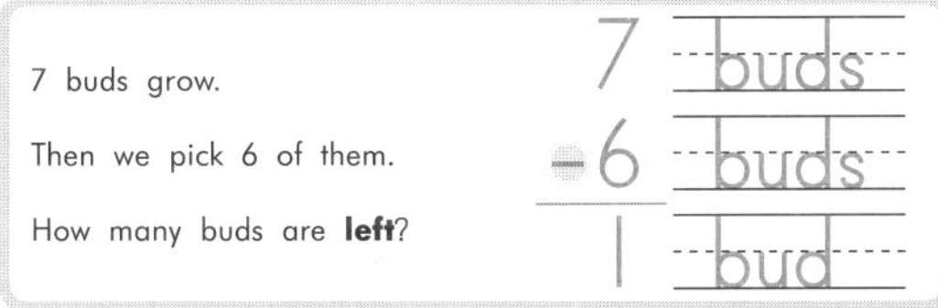

7 buds grow.

Then we pick 6 of them.

How many buds are **left**?

7 buds
−6 buds
1 bud

79

Speed Drill Answers

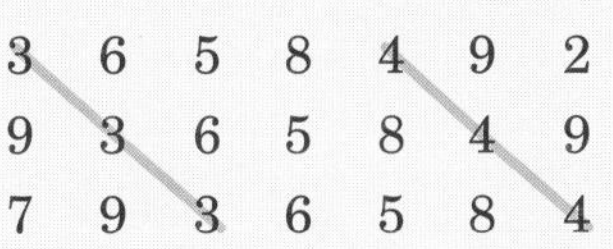

3	6	5	8	4	9	2
9	3	6	5	8	4	9
7	9	3	6	5	8	4

4. *12 inches = 1 foot.*
   Hold the footprint poster. **12 inches make 1 foot; 12 inches make . . .**
5. *Fraction concept.*
   a. **If a whole orange is cut into 2 equal pieces, each piece is ____.** ($\frac{1}{2}$)
   b. **If a log is cut into 3 equal pieces, each piece is ___.**
   c. **If a garden is divided into 4 equal sections, each part is ___.**
6. *Do Speed Drill #48.*
7. *Assign Lesson 122.*
   What makes seeds grow? We can put them in the earth. We can water them. But we cannot make them grow. "God . . . giveth the increase" (1 Corinthians 3:7).

Follow-up

Drill

(*Drill* #3)

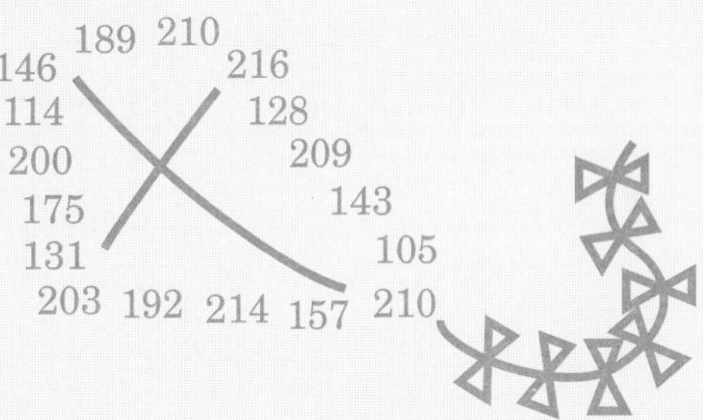

1. Give each child his Addition Family 10 flash cards.
2. Count up the thermometer by 2's.
3. Call the children to the number kite on the chalkboard. **When God sends warm spring breezes, you can fly a kite. Read the numbers around this kite.** If the children say *and* after the hundreds, coach them to say just numbers: one hundred forty-six, ***not*** one hundred *and* forty-six.

Practice Sheets

- ☐ Fact Houses #33
- ☐ Less Numbers #20
- ☐ Measures #1
- ● Number Facts #44
- ● Measures #5

Objectives

New

TEACHING

Addition Family 10 twins

Review

Addition facts
Mixed counting (5's and 1's)
Count nickels with pennies
Place value
12 inches = 1 foot

123 Whisper and trace the fact twins.

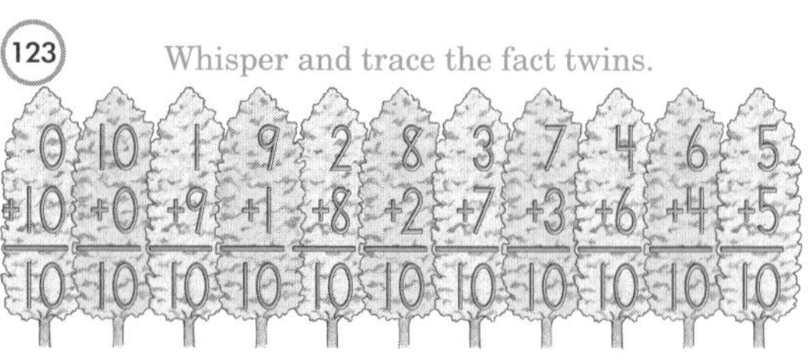

Answer these facts.

2 +4 6	3 +7 10	6 +4 10	3 +4 7	8 +2 10	1 +6 7	7 +3 10	2 +8 10	3 +7 10
1 +9 10	2 +5 7	4 +6 10	7 +3 10	3 +3 6	2 +4 6	1 +9 10	4 +6 10	9 +1 10
2 +8 10	5 +5 10	4 +3 7	2 +8 10	5 +2 7	2 +4 6	6 +4 10	9 +1 10	3 +7 10
6 +4 10	4 +3 7	8 +2 10	3 +7 10	5 +5 10	8 +2 10	5 +2 7	4 +6 10	3 +4 7

80

Preparation

Tack Addition Family 10 flash cards above the flannel board with answers showing.

Materials

Footprint poster

Subtraction Families 5–7 flash cards

Chalkboard

(*Class Time* #1)

(*Class Time* #2)

5¢ 1¢ 1¢ ____

5¢ 1¢ 1¢ 1¢ 1¢ ____

5¢ 1¢ 1¢ 1¢ ____

5¢ 1¢ 1¢ 1¢ 1¢ 1¢ ____

(*Class Time* #3)

143	22	218	190	3
165	206	7	133	204
185	227	79	210	30

Class Time

1. *Review Addition Family 10.*
   a. Start with 10 felt blocks on the lower part of the flannel board for these story facts. Have the children say the story facts together.
   (1) **Jane planted 0 seeds, and Paul planted 10 seeds. They planted 10 seeds in all.** Story fact: **0 seeds** + **10 seeds** = **10 seeds.**
   (2) **Jane planted 1 seed, and Paul planted 9 seeds. They planted 10 seeds in all.** Story fact: **1 seed** + **9 seeds** = **10 seeds.**
   (3) **Jane planted 2 seeds, . . .**
   b. **Say Family 10 together as I fill the trees.** Write in every other tree the first time across. **Now let's say Family 10 in twin order.**

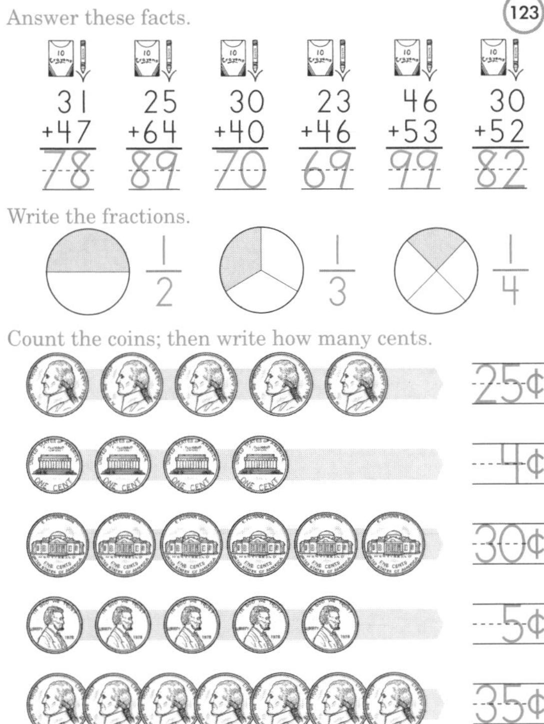

2. *Counting nickels and pennies.*
   a. Point to the number line. **Count by 5's and by 1's.**
      5, 10, 11, 12, 13, 14
      5, 6, 7, 8, 9
      5, 10, 15, 16, 17, 18
      5, 10, 15, 20, 21, 22, 23, 24
   b. Do the chalkboard samples. Have the children count aloud and then write the answers.
3. *Place value.*
   a. Review place value with the motion.
   b. Point to the numbers on the board. **Circle the numbers in the tens' place.**
4. *12 inches = 1 foot.*
   a. Hold the footprint poster. **12 inches make 1 foot; . . .**
   b. **1 foot is 12 inches; . . .**
5. *Assign Lesson 123.*

Follow-up

Drill

(*Drill #2*)

___ 25 ___	___ 15 ___
___ 40 ___	___ 30 ___
___ 75 ___	___ 65 ___
___ 90 ___	___ 50 ___

1. Drill individuals with Subtraction Families 5–7 flash cards.
2. **Count by 5's to 100.** Fill in the Before and After samples by 5's.
3. Review ordinal numbers.
   a. **Stand beside your seat. Hold up your fingers and count with me: first, second, third, . . .**
   b. **If this means you, sit down:**
      The second person in the first row. (Use directions that fit your setting.)
      The third person in the second row. Continue until all the children are seated.

Practice Sheets

- ☐ Fact Houses #33
- ☐ Missing Numbers #11
- ☐ Clocks #7
- ● Number Facts #45
- ● Number Facts #42

Objectives

New

TEACHING

Addition Family 10 reflected

WORKBOOK

1 nickel plus pennies

Review

Addition facts

2-digit addition

Place value

Mixed counting (5's and 1's)

Count by 2's

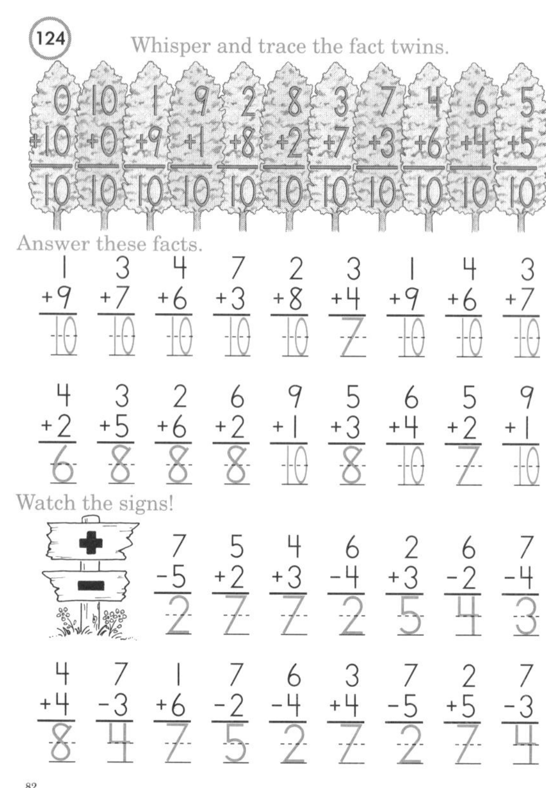

(124) Whisper and trace the fact twins.

0	10	1	9	2	8	3	7	4	6	5
+10	+0	+9	+1	+8	+2	+7	+3	+6	+4	+5
10	10	10	10	10	10	10	10	10	10	10

Answer these facts.

1	3	4	7	2	3	1	4	3
+9	+7	+6	+3	+8	+4	+9	+6	+7
10	10	10	10	10	7	10	10	10

4	3	2	6	9	5	6	5	9
+2	+5	+6	+2	+1	+3	+4	+2	+1
6	8	8	8	10	8	10	7	10

Watch the signs!

7	5	4	6	2	6	7
-5	+2	+3	-4	+3	-2	-4
2	7	7	2	5	4	3

4	7	1	7	6	3	7	2	7
+4	-3	+6	-2	-4	+4	-5	+5	-3
8	4	7	5	2	7	2	7	4

82

Preparation

Materials

Form E for each child

Addition Families 6–8 and 10 flash cards

12-inch ruler

Chalkboard

(*Class Time* #2)

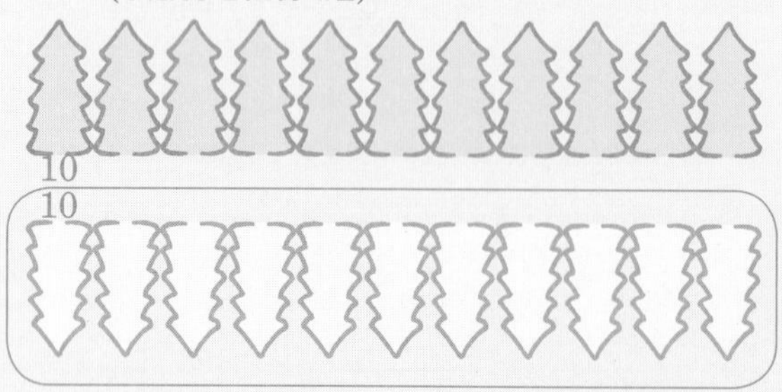

(*Class Time* #4)

56	12	40	28	35	63	52
+42	+56	+35	+61	+34	+21	+16

Class Time

1. *Review Addition Family 8.*
   Watch my fingers as we say Family 8. 0 + 8, 8; 1 + 7, 8; . . .
2. *Practice Addition Family 10.*
   a. Point to the flash cards above the flannel board. **Say each fact three times with your eyes open, and then three times with your eyes closed.**
   b. **Say Family 10 as I fill the trees.**
3. *Introduce Subtraction Family 10.*
   a. **Say the addition facts again, and say the reflecting subtraction fact after each one.** Write the subtraction facts in the reflection as you say them.
   b. **Now say a pair of addition twins and then the reflecting pair of subtraction twins.**
4. *2-digit addition.*
   Do the chalkboard samples. **Ones' place first!**
5. *Place value.*
   a. Review place value with the motion.
   b. Give each child a copy of Form E for

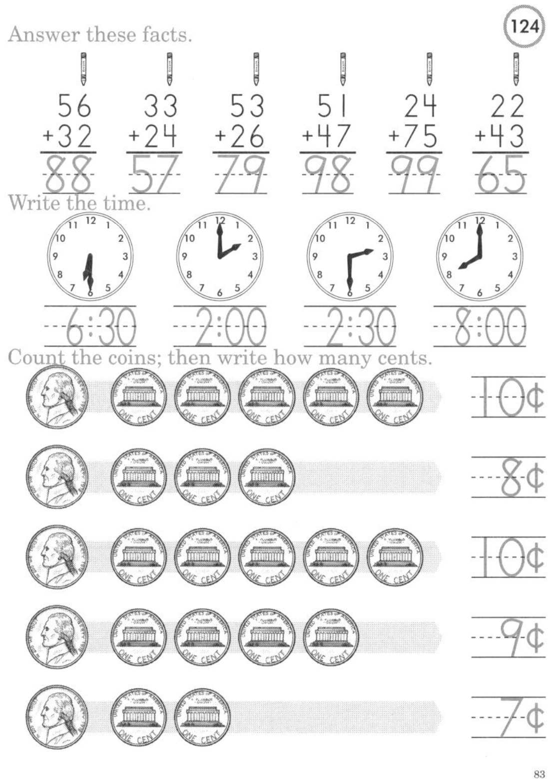

number dictation. **Begin in the first column. Write the numbers I say in the correct places.** Say all the numbers in column 1; then say column 2.

78	**218**
125	**133**
3	**91**
49	**205**
6	**9**
167	**147**
101	**200**
22	**184**
214	**62**
150	**209**

6. *Mixed counting.*
   Call the children to the number line. **Count by 5's and by 1's.**
   5, 6, 7, 8, 9
   5, 10, 11, 12, 13, 14
   5, 10, 15, 20, 21, 22, 23, 24
   5, 10, 15, 16, 17, 18
7. *Count by 2's.*
   Count by 2's to 100. 2, 4, 6, . . .
8. *Do Speed Drill #49.*
9. *Assign Lesson 124.*

Speed Drill Answers

Speed Drill #49

10	10	7	10	7	10	10
10	7	6	10	6	7	10
7	6	10	10	10	6	7

Follow-up

Drill

1. Circle Drill with Addition Families 6–8 and 10 flash cards.
2. **I will say two addition steps. Raise your hand as soon as you think of the answer.** Speak slowly.
   3 + 3 + 2 = (8)
   4 + 5 + 1 = (10)
   2 + 7 + 1 = (10)
   1 + 6 + 2 = (9)
   5 + 3 + 2 = (10)
   4 + 3 + 2 = (9)
   2 + 6 + 1 = (9)
   4 + 4 + 2 = (10)
3. Hold a 12-inch ruler. Ask one child at a time to bring his pencil, lay it on the ruler, and say, **My pencil is about ___ inches long.**

Practice Sheets

- Form E (*Class Time* #5)
- ☐ Fact Houses #33
- ☐ Clocks #6
- ☐ Measures #2
- Number Facts #45
- Number Trains #7

Objectives

New

TEACHING

Dozen

WORKBOOK

Addition Family 10 reflected
2 nickels plus pennies

Review

Addition facts
Count by 5's
Mixed counting (5's and 1's)
Place value
Number words
12 inches = 1 foot

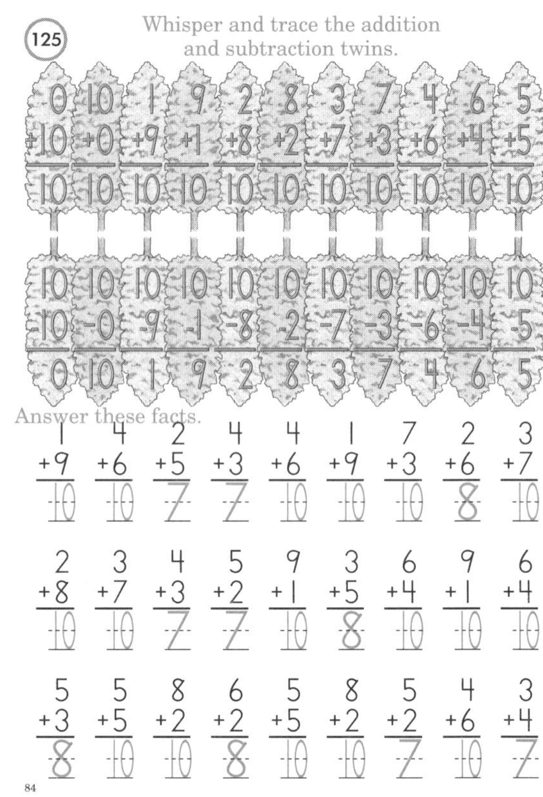

Preparation

Materials

Addition Families 7, 8, and 10 flash cards

Number word cards

Footprint poster

Subtraction Families 5–7 flash cards

Box of one dozen new pencils

Chalkboard

(*Class Time* #1)

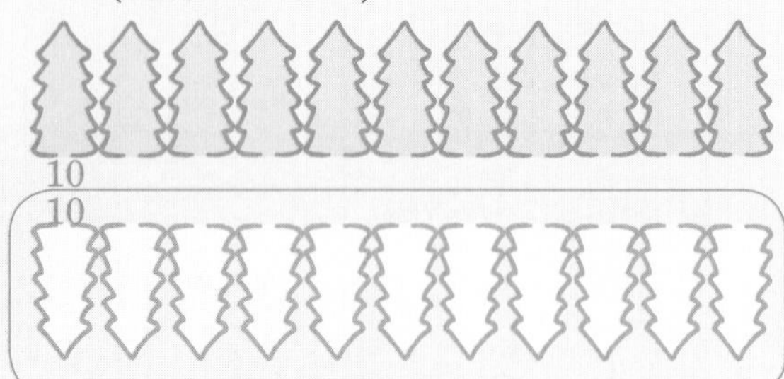

(*Class Time* #3)

5¢ 5¢ 1¢ ____

5¢ 5¢ 1¢ 1¢ 1¢ ____

5¢ 5¢ 1¢ 1¢ 1¢ 1¢ 1¢ ____

Class Time

1. *Practice Addition and Subtraction Family 10.*
   a. Use the flannel board to illustrate Addition Family 10. Have the children say each story fact with you.
      (1) **George blew 0 big bubbles and 10 little bubbles. He blew 10 bubbles in all. 0 bubbles + 10 bubbles = 10 bubbles.**
      (2) **George blew 1 big bubble and 9 little bubbles. He blew 10 bubbles in all. 1 bubble + 9 bubbles = 10 bubbles.**
      (3) **George blew 2 big bubbles . . .**
   b. Ask a child to fill the trees as everyone says the addition facts in twin order.
   c. Let another child fill the reflection as everyone says the subtraction facts.
   d. **Now say the addition twins and subtraction twins in sets of four.**

$$\begin{array}{r}0\\+10\\\hline10\end{array}\quad\begin{array}{r}10\\+0\\\hline10\end{array}\quad\begin{array}{r}10\\-10\\\hline0\end{array}\quad\begin{array}{r}10\\-0\\\hline10\end{array}$$

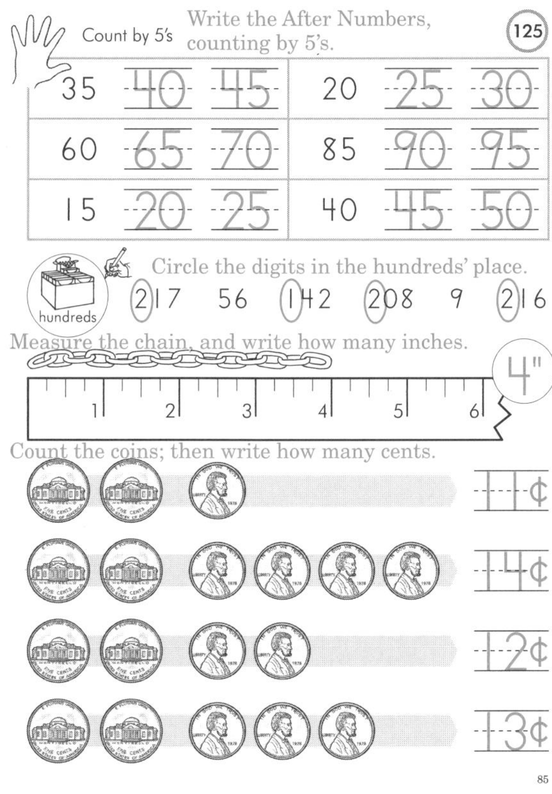

2. *Drill addition facts.*
   Flash Addition Families 7, 8, and 10 cards for one minute. **Answer together.**
3. *Counting nickels and pennies.*
   a. **Count by 5's to 100.**
   b. **Count by 5's and by 1's.**
   5, 6, 7, 8, 9
   5, 10, 15, 16, 17, 18
   5, 10, 11, 12, 13, 14, 15
   c. Do the chalkboard samples. Ask individuals to count aloud and then write the answers.
4. *Place value.*
   Review place value with the motion.
5. *Number words.*
   Flash number word cards.
6. *12 inches = 1 foot.*
   a. Hold the footprint poster. **12 inches make 1 foot; . . .**
   b. **1 foot is 12 inches; . . .**
7. *Assign Lesson 125.*

Note: You will need an empty egg carton for Lesson 126. You may wish to ask a child to bring it to school.

Follow-up

Drill

1. Drill individuals with Subtraction Families 5–7 flash cards.
2. Call the children to the teaching corner. Empty the box of pencils.
   a. **Count with me. 1, 2, 3, . . . 12 pencils.**
   b. **12 pencils make 1 dozen pencils. 12 things make 1 dozen; 12 things make 1 dozen.**
3. Chalkboard drill: **I will count by 2's. When I stop, everyone write the number that should come next.**

2, 4, 6, ___	**80, 82, 84, ___**
42, 44, 46, ___	**14, 16, 18, ___**
56, 58, 60, ___	**36, 38, 40, ___**

Practice Sheets

- ☐ Fact Houses #33
- ☐ Measures #3
- ● Number Facts #44
- ● Number Facts #45
- ● Writing Practice #28

Objectives

New

TEACHING

Dozen

Review

Addition and subtraction

Count nickels with pennies

Preparation

Materials

Egg carton

Addition Families 7–10 flash cards

Pennies, nickels, and dimes

Chalkboard

(*Class Time* #1)

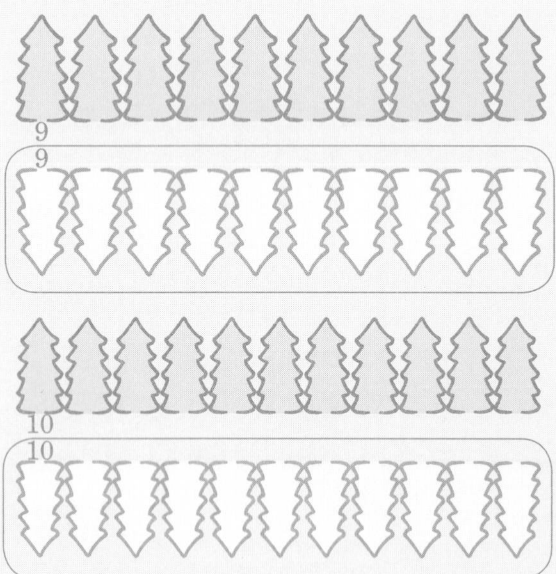

(*Class Time* #3)

5¢ 1¢ 1¢ ____

5¢ 5¢ 1¢ 1¢ ____

5¢ 1¢ 1¢ 1¢ 1¢ ____

5¢ 1¢ 1¢ 1¢ 1¢ 1¢ ____

5¢ 5¢ 1¢ 1¢ 1¢ 1¢ 1¢ ____

Class Time

1. *Review Addition and Subtraction Families 9 and 10.*
   a. **Say Addition Family 9 as I move the felt blocks.**
   b. Ask a child to fill the 9 Trees as you say the facts together in twin order.
   c. **Say each addition fact and its reflecting subtraction fact as I fill the reflection.**
   d. **Say Addition Family 10 as I move the felt blocks.**
   e. Ask a child to fill the 10 Trees as you say the facts together in twin order.
   f. **Say the addition and subtraction facts as I fill the reflection.**
2. *Teach dozen.*
   a. Print 1 dozen on the chalkboard. **1 dozen, 1 dozen, . . .**
   b. Hold the egg carton. **How many eggs could we put into this box? 1, 2, 3, 4, . . . 12 eggs.**

126

Answer these facts.

43	56	51	42	20	53
+35	+23	+36	+55	+60	+46
78	79	87	97	80	99

Count the coins; then write how many cents.

15¢

11¢

14¢

10¢

Do the story problem.

6 eggs are in a nest.
Then 2 of them hatch.
How many eggs are **left**?

6 eggs
−2 eggs
4 eggs

87

Speed Drill Answers

2	10	5	9	4	3	8
10	5	9	4	3	8	10
5	9	4	3	8	10	10

Speed Drill #50

c. **12 eggs make 1 dozen. 12 pencils make 1 dozen. 12 things make 1 dozen; 12 things make 1 dozen.**

3. *Counting nickels and pennies.*
Do the chalkboard samples. Have individuals count aloud and then write the answers.
4. *Do Speed Drill #50.*
5. *Assign Lesson 126.*

Note: Write *1 dozen* on a 3" × 6" card. Tape the card to the egg carton, and put the carton in a prominent place. Use it when you drill **12 things make 1 dozen.**

Follow-up

Drill

1. Double Drill with Addition Families 7–10 flash cards.
2. Lay a mixture of pennies, nickels, and dimes on your desktop. Call individuals to your desk.
   a. **Find a nickel** (pause until they find one); **a dime; a penny.**
   b. **Find a 10¢ coin; a 5¢ coin; a 1¢ coin.**
3. **Count by 2's to 100.**

Practice Sheets

- ☐ Fact Houses #34
- ☐ Number Words #2
- ☐ Form E: 221–240
- ● Number Facts #46
- ● Missing Numbers #12
- ● Fractions #2

Objectives

New

WORKBOOK

Dozen

3 nickels plus pennies

Review

Addition facts

Count by 10's, by 5's

Preparation

Materials

Addition Families 9 and 10 flash cards

Footprint poster

Chalkboard

(Write a set of these facts for each child to trace in *Class Time* #2)

3	3
+6	+7
9	10

(*Class Time* #3)

5¢ 5¢ 5¢ 1¢ 1¢ ____

5¢ 5¢ 5¢ 1¢ ____

5¢ 5¢ 5¢ 1¢ 1¢ 1¢ 1¢ ____

5¢ 5¢ 5¢ 1¢ 1¢ 1¢ ____

(*Class Time* #4)

Class Time

1. *Review Addition Families 9 and 10.*
   a. Give your Addition Families 9 and 10 flash cards to the children. **If you have the first fact in Family 9, come set it on the chalk tray. Who has the next fact?** Continue.
   b. Stand near the flash cards. **Say Addition Family 9 . . . Family 10.**
2. *Drill selected facts.*
   Have each child stand near his set of facts on the board. **Trace and whisper the facts until I say "stop."**
3. *Skip counting and money.*
   a. **Boys, if you were counting dimes, how would you count?** (by 10's) **Count to 100.**
   b. **Girls, if you were counting nickels, how would you count?** (by 5's) **Count to 100.**
   c. Do the chalkboard samples. Have individuals count aloud and then write the answers.

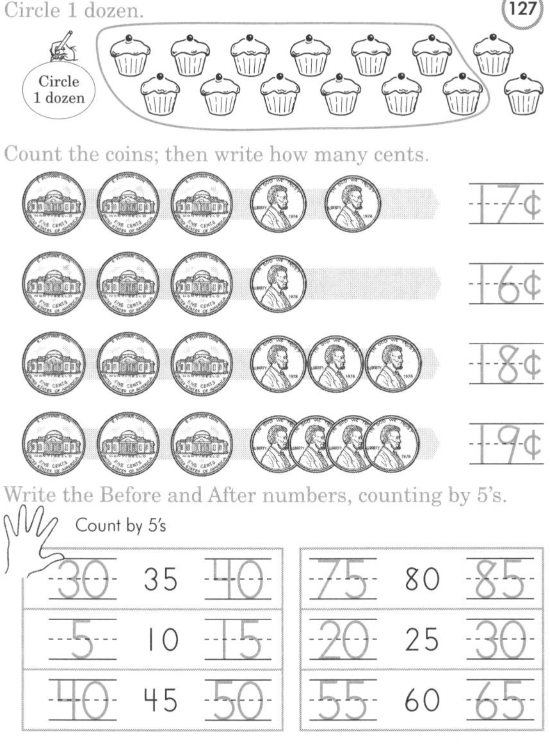

4. *Dozen.*
   a. Write *1 dozen* on the chalkboard. **1 dozen, 1 dozen. 12 things make 1 dozen; 12 things . . .**
   b. Ask a child to circle 1 dozen oranges on the chalkboard (one large circle, not 12 small circles).
   c. **Let's count the oranges inside the circle.**
5. *Assign Lesson 127.*

Follow-up

Drill

(*Drill* #1)

2 + 7 =	8 + 2 =	7 + 2 =	8 + 2 =	4 + 2 =
5 + 2 =	6 + 2 =	8 + 2 =	2 + 3 =	9 + 1 =
1 + 9 =	2 + 7 =	2 + 4 =	7 + 1 =	2 + 6 =
2 + 8 =	1 + 8 =	7 + 1 =	2 + 5 =	1 + 6 =
7 + 2 =	6 + 2 =	2 + 8 =	8 + 1 =	7 + 1 =

1. Call the children to the grid on the chalkboard. Drill the facts up and down, right and left. Keep the grid on the board for Lesson 128.
2. Review 12 inches = 1 foot.
   a. Hold the footprint poster. **12 inches make 1 foot; 12 inches make . . .**
   b. **Take your 12-inch ruler out of your desk. Count 1 inch, 2 inches, . . .**
   c. **Put your left elbow on your desktop and hold your left hand straight up. Hold your ruler beside your left arm. Is it about 12 inches from your elbow to your fingertips?**

Practice Sheets

- ☐ Fact Houses #34
- ☐ Before and After #14
- ● Number Facts #47
- ● Number Facts #46
- ● Measures #5

Objectives

New

TEACHING

Calendar week

Review

Mixed story problems
Subtraction Family 10
Addition facts
Fractions

128 Whisper and trace the addition and subtraction twins.

0	10	1	9	2	8	3	7	4	6	5
+10	+0	+9	+1	+8	+2	+7	+3	+6	+4	+5
10	10	10	10	10	10	10	10	10	10	10

10	10	10	10	10	10	10	10	10	10	10
-10	-0	-9	-1	-8	-2	-7	-3	-6	-4	-5
0	10	1	9	2	8	3	7	4	6	5

Answer these facts.

7	3	4	7	2	1	7	4	3
+3	+6	+6	+3	+6	+9	+2	+6	+7
10	9	10	10	8	10	9	10	10

2	3	6	1	9	3	4	2	9
+7	+5	+4	+8	+1	+7	+5	+8	+1
9	8	10	9	10	10	9	10	10

6	8	8	6	5	8	4	4	4
+4	+1	+2	+3	+5	+2	+4	+6	+5
10	9	10	9	10	10	8	10	9

90

Preparation

Materials

Addition Families 8–10 flash cards

Form C for each child

Chalkboard

(*Class Time* #1)

(*Class Time* #2)

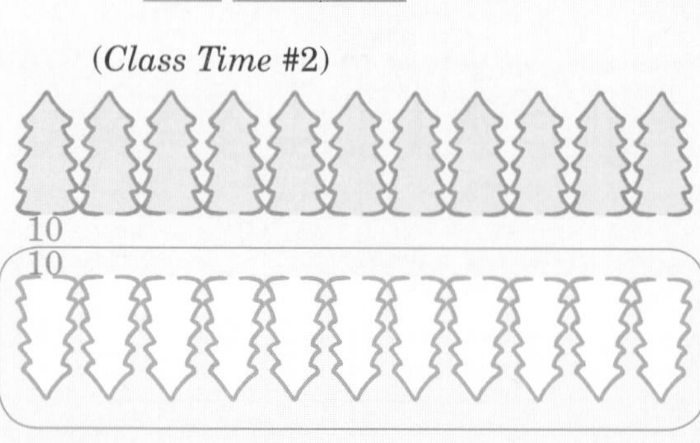

(*Class Time* #4)

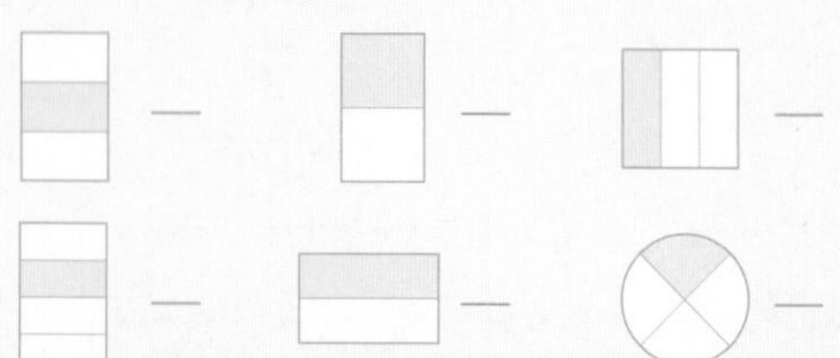

Class Time

1. *Story problems.*
   a. **Close your eyes and listen. 7 boys sled. Then 5 boys go into the house. How many boys are *left*?** Ask a child to put the right sign in the circle and fill the blanks. Erase.
   b. **Listen again. Beth has 4 pens. Ruth has 5 pens. How many pens do *both* girls have?** Ask a child to do the problem.
2. *Review Addition and Subtraction Family 10.*
   a. Point to the flash cards above the flannel board. **Boys, say each fact once. . . . Girls, say each fact once.**
   b. **Can you say Family 10 in twin order as I fill the trees?**
   c. Call on individuals to say one addition fact and then to say and write the reflecting subtraction fact below it.
3. *Drill addition facts.*
   a. Flash Addition Families 8–10 cards for one minute. **Answer together.**

Speed Drill Answers

9	4	10	2	5	8	10
9	9	4	10	2	5	8
10	9	9	4	10	2	5

Speed Drill #51

b. Distribute Form C for written answer. Continue flashing Addition Families 8–10 flash cards. **Apron Row: Box 1—Box 2 . . .**

4. *Fractions.*
   Do the chalkboard samples.

5. *Introduce the calendar week.*
   a. Call the children to the calendar. Point to number 1. **Count first, second, third, . . .**
   b. **Yesterday was the ___.** (Point to the number.)
   Tomorrow will be the ___. (Point to the number.)
   c. **Each row of numbers is 1 week. The Lord's Day is the first day of the week. Can you name the days with me? Sunday, Monday, . . .**
   d. **How many days are in 1 week? 1, 2, 3, . . . 7. 1 week is 7 days.**

6. *Do Speed Drill #51.*

7. *Assign Lesson 128.*

Follow-up

Drill

(*Drill* #2)

214 ___ hundreds 119 ___ tens
165 ___ hundreds 63 ___ tens
171 ___ hundreds 188 ___ tens
23 ___ ones
56 ___ ones
145 ___ ones

1. Chalkboard drill: **Write the number 124. Change it to 127. (Erase 1 digit.) Change it to 227, 217, 210, 110, 140, 143, 103, 203.**
2. Review place value. **How many hundreds are in 214?** Have the children do the chalkboard samples.
3. Drill individuals at the addition grid from Lesson 127.

Practice Sheets

- ● Form C (*Class Time* #3)
- ☐ Fact Houses #34
- ☐ Clocks #7
- ● Number Facts #46
- ● Money #16

Objectives
New
TEACHING
12:00 midnight
Review
Addition facts
Count by 10's, 5's, 2's
Missing Numbers, by 10's, by 5's
More (230's)

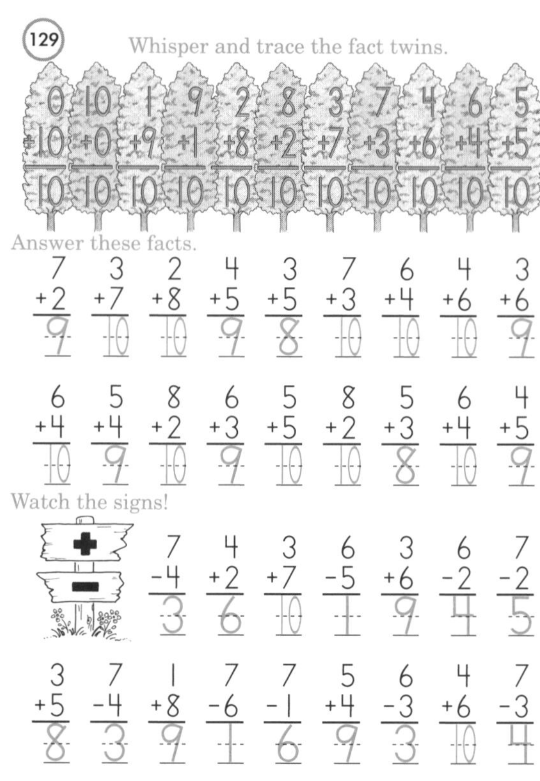
129 Whisper and trace the fact twins.

0 + 10 = 10, 10 + 0 = 10, 1 + 9 = 10, 9 + 1 = 10, 2 + 8 = 10, 8 + 2 = 10, 3 + 7 = 10, 7 + 3 = 10, 4 + 6 = 10, 6 + 4 = 10, 5 + 5 = 10

Answer these facts.

7 + 2 = 9, 3 + 7 = 10, 2 + 8 = 10, 4 + 5 = 9, 3 + 5 = 8, 7 + 3 = 10, 6 + 4 = 10, 4 + 6 = 10, 3 + 6 = 9

6 + 4 = 10, 5 + 4 = 9, 8 + 2 = 10, 6 + 3 = 9, 5 + 5 = 10, 8 + 2 = 10, 5 + 3 = 8, 6 + 4 = 10, 4 + 5 = 9

Watch the signs!

7 − 4 = 3, 4 + 2 = 6, 3 + 7 = 10, 6 − 5 = 1, 3 + 6 = 9, 6 − 2 = 4, 7 − 2 = 5

3 + 5 = 8, 7 − 4 = 3, 1 + 8 = 9, 7 − 6 = 1, 7 − 1 = 6, 5 + 4 = 9, 6 − 3 = 3, 4 + 6 = 10, 7 − 3 = 4

92

Preparation

Materials

Addition Families 8–10 flash cards

Model clock

Chalkboard

(*Class Time* #2)

4 + 5 = 9	5 + 4 = 9	4 + 6 = 10	6 + 4 = 10

(*Class Time* #3)

___ 50 ___ ___ 80 ___ ___

___ 10 ___ ___ ___ 30 ___

60 ___ ___ 75 ___ ___ ___

___ ___ 30 ___ ___ 60 ___

(*Class Time* #4)

231	213	205	209
230	220	217	215
229	239	203	230

Class Time

1. *Practice Addition Family 10.*
   a. Use the flannel board to illustrate Addition Family 10, and have the children say the story facts.
   (1) **Mother served 0 cupcakes with cherries and 10 cupcakes with nuts. She served 10 cupcakes in all.** Story fact: **0 cupcakes + 10 cupcakes = 10 cupcakes.**
   (2) **Mother served 1 cupcake with a cherry and 9 cupcakes with nuts. She served 10 cupcakes in all.** Story fact: **1 cupcake + 9 cupcake = 10 cupcakes.**
   (3) **Mother served 2 cupcakes with cherries and 8 cupcakes with nuts. . . .**
   b. Point to the flash cards above the flannel board. **Say each fact three times with your eyes open, and then three times with your eyes closed.**

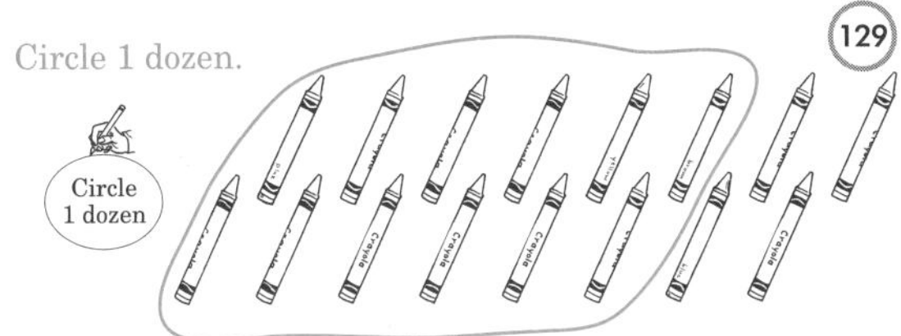

Circle More.

• ⁙ more	211 (219)	(207) 201	204 (214)
(235) 234	226 (227)	(217) 209	212 (221)
205 (215)	208 (228)	(220) 206	237 (239)

Write the After Numbers, counting by 2's.

Count by 2's

56	58	60	14	16	18
78	80	82	30	32	34
20	22	24	84	86	88
52	54	56	16	18	20

93

2. *Drill selected facts.*
   Stand near the facts on the board. Circle the first fact. **Say it five times with me.** Say it quietly the first time, and then raise your voice with each recital. Drill the other facts.
3. *Skip counting for Missing Numbers.*
   a. **Count to 100 by 10's.**
   b. **Count to 100 by 5's.**
   c. Point to the first row with Missing Numbers on the chalkboard. **Think! Should I count by 5's or 10's?** Have the children fill in the blanks in each row.
   d. **Count by 2's to 100.**
4. *More.*
   Do the chalkboard samples.
5. *Assign Lesson 129.*

Follow-up

Drill

(*Drill #2*)

43	30	56	54	27	34	28
+ 25	+ 53	+ 23	+ 15	+ 52	+ 42	+ 40

1. Circle Drill with Addition Families 8–10 flash cards.
2. Do the 2-digit addition samples.
3. Introduce the meaning of midnight. **Yesterday was [Thursday]. Today is [Friday]. When did Thursday stop and Friday start?**
   a. Hold the model clock, and move the hands as you tell this story.
   It is 8:00. Mother says, "Put your toys away. Get ready for your bedtime story."
   It is 9:00. The story is finished. You prayed your bedtime prayer. Now you are snuggled under your cozy blanket.
   It is 10:00. You are asleep.
   It is 11:00. Stars twinkle as you sleep on and on. It is still Thursday.
   The minute hand creeps around to 12. It is 12:00 midnight. Thursday is gone.
   The minute hand creeps away from 12. It is Friday morning.
   b. **When did Thursday stop and Friday start?** (at midnight)

Practice Sheets

- ☐ Fact Houses #35
- ☐ More Numbers #21
- ☐ Story Problems #1
- ● Number Facts #48
- ● Number Facts #47

Objectives

New

TEACHING

Subtraction Family 8

Review

Addition facts
Dozen
Place value
Mixed counting (5's and 1's)
Count nickels with pennies
Counting (239)

Preparation

Materials

Addition Families 8–10 flash cards
Egg carton
Subtraction Families 4–7 flash cards
Model clock

Chalkboard

(*Class Time* #1)

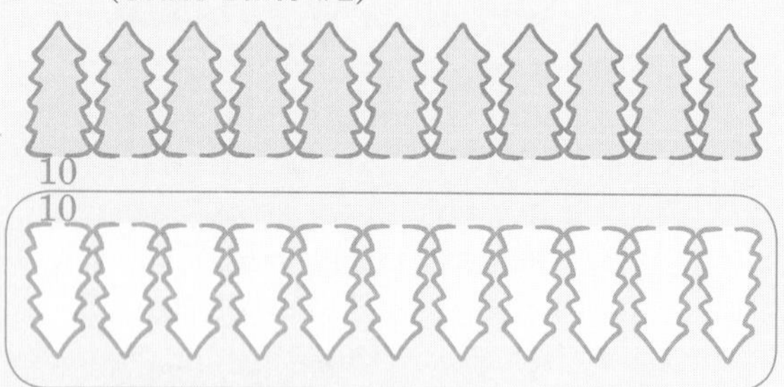

(*Class Time* #4)

156	___ hundreds	54	___ ones
219	___ hundreds	247	___ hundreds
143	___ tens	63	___ ones
70	___ tens	103	___ tens
15	___ ones	112	___ tens

(*Class Time* #5)

Class Time

1. *Review Addition Families 8–10.*
   a. **Watch my fingers. Say Addition Family 8 . . . Family 9.**
   b. Challenge the class to say Family 10 facts in the order that will fill one tree and its reflection, then the next tree and its reflection, and so on with the twins beside each other. Write the facts in the trees and reflection as the class says them. When you are ready to begin each new set of four facts, show the number of the first addend with your fingers.
2. *Drill addition facts.*
   Double Drill with Addition Families 8–10 facts.
3. *Dozen.*
   Show the egg carton and drill the statement **12 things make 1 dozen.**

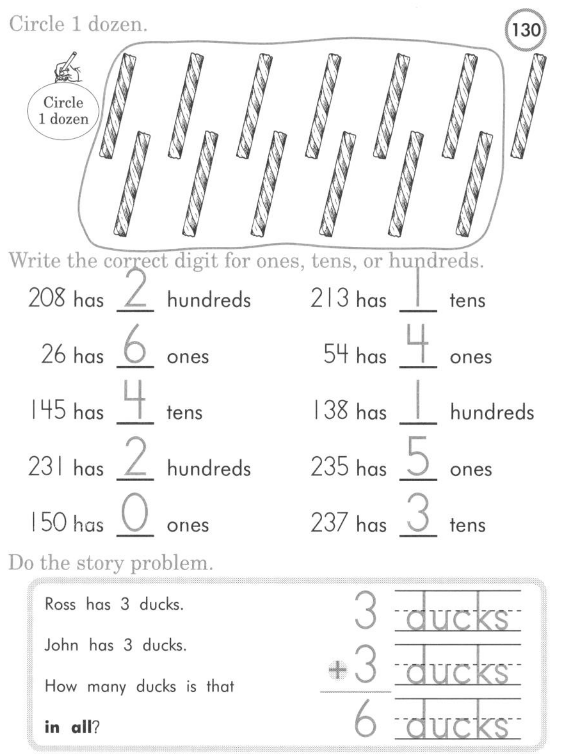
Circle 1 dozen. (130)

Circle 1 dozen

Write the correct digit for ones, tens, or hundreds.

208 has 2 hundreds 213 has 1 tens

26 has 6 ones 54 has 4 ones

145 has 4 tens 138 has 1 hundreds

231 has 2 hundreds 235 has 5 ones

150 has 0 ones 237 has 3 tens

Do the story problem.

Ross has 3 ducks.
John has 3 ducks.
How many ducks is that **in all**?

3 ducks
+3 ducks
6 ducks

95

4. *Place value.*
   a. Drill place value.
   b. Point to the chalkboard samples. **How many hundreds are in 156?** Have the children fill in the blanks.
5. *Counting nickels and pennies.*
   a. Stand near the number line. **Follow the pointer and count.**
   5, 10, 11, 12, 13, 14, 15
   5, 10, 15, 20, 21, 22, 23, 24, 25
   5, 10, 15, 20, 25, 30, 31, 32, 33
   b. Do the money samples. Have the children count aloud and then write the answers.
6. *Counting beyond 200.*
   Count by 1's from 200–239.
7. *Do Speed Drill #52.*
8. *Assign Lesson 130.*

Speed Drill Answers

10	9	10	10	10	9	10
9	10	10	10	9	10	9
10	10	10	9	10	9	10

Speed Drill #52

Follow-up

Drill

(*Drill #2*)

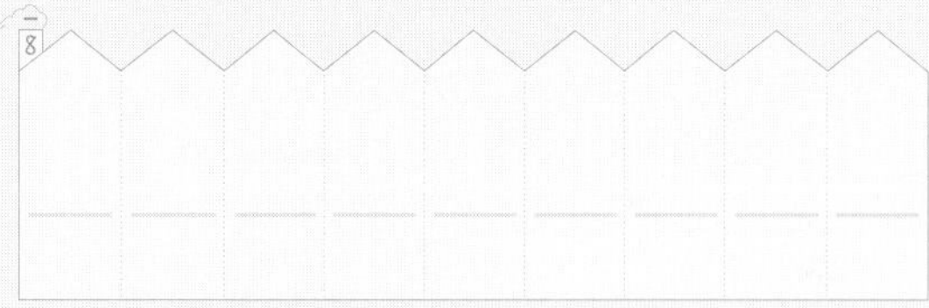

1. Drill Subtraction Families 4–7 flash cards.
2. Introduce Subtraction Family 8. **Can you help me fill these houses with Subtraction Family 8?** Write the facts in order. **We will work with Family 8 tomorrow.**
3. Hold the model clock.
   a. **What does the clock say at midnight?**
   b. **What happens at midnight?** (One day ends and the next one begins.)
   c. **Read the time together.** Set the clock at 12:00, 2:30, 4:00, 6:30, 8:00, 10:30, 12:30, 5:30.

Practice Sheets

- ☐ Fact Houses #35
- ☐ Missing Numbers #12
- ☐ Number Words #2
- ● Number Facts #48
- ● Fractions #3

Objectives

New

TEACHING

12:00 noon
Subtraction Family 8

Review

Addition facts
Place value
Before and After (240's)

131 Answer these facts.

7 +3 = 10	6 +3 = 9	4 +5 = 9	3 +7 = 10	2 +7 = 9	6 +4 = 10	5 +5 = 10	4 +6 = 10	4 +5 = 9
5 +4 = 9	4 +5 = 9	6 +4 = 10	7 +2 = 9	6 +4 = 10	1 +9 = 10	3 +7 = 10	6 +3 = 9	2 +8 = 10
5 +5 = 10	2 +7 = 9	9 +1 = 10	8 +1 = 9	5 +4 = 9	8 +2 = 10	4 +5 = 9	4 +6 = 10	3 +7 = 10
1 +8 = 9	7 +3 = 10	2 +8 = 10	7 +3 = 10	3 +6 = 9	4 +6 = 10	3 +6 = 9	7 +2 = 9	6 +4 = 10
		8 +2 = 10	5 +4 = 9	5 +5 = 10	2 +7 = 9	5 +4 = 9	4 +6 = 10	4 +5 = 9

"Whatsoever thy hand findeth to do, do it with thy might." Ecclesiastes 9:10

96

Preparation

Materials

Addition Families 9 and 10 flash cards
Model clock
Addition Families 8–10 flash cards
Footprint poster

Chalkboard

(*Class Time* #1)

+ 10

(*Class Time* #2)

162	___ tens	137	___ ones
23	___ tens	245	___ hundreds
50	___ ones	199	___ hundreds

(*Class Time* #3)

___ 217 ___	___ 206 ___
___ 185 ___	___ 241 ___
___ 223 ___	___ 199 ___
___ 242 ___	___ 234 ___

(*Class Time* #5)

− 8

Class Time

1. *Practice Addition Families 9 and 10.*
   a. **Say Family 10 as I fill the houses.**
   b. Circle Drill with Addition Families 9 and 10 flash cards.
2. *Place value.*
   a. Review the motion and statement.
   b. Fill in the chalkboard samples.
3. *Before and After Numbers.*
   Have the children fill in the chalkboard samples.
4. *Teach 12:00 noon.*
   a. Set the clock hands at 12:00. **Where are you when the clock says 12:00 midnight?**
   b. **The clock says 12:00 again when we are at school. It is not 12:00 midnight. It is 12:00 noon.**

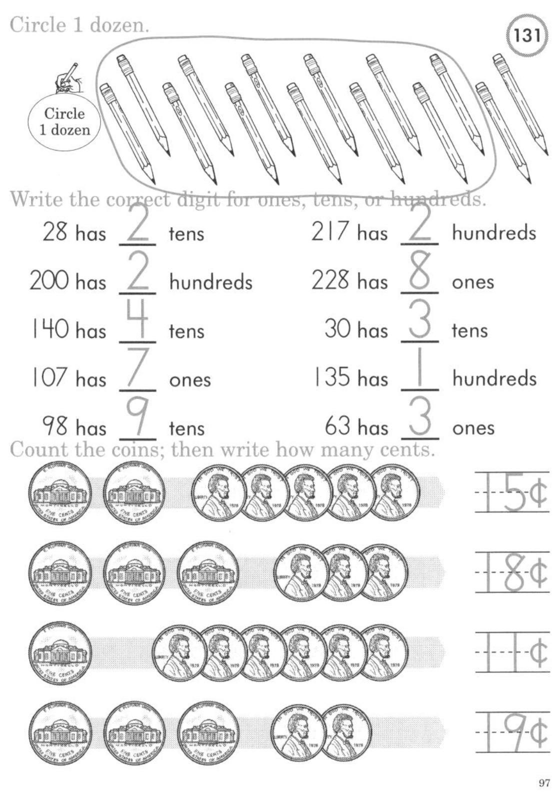

131

Circle 1 dozen.

Circle 1 dozen

Write the correct digit for ones, tens, or hundreds.

28 has	2	tens	217 has	2	hundreds
200 has	2	hundreds	228 has	8	ones
140 has	4	tens	30 has	3	tens
107 has	7	ones	135 has	1	hundreds
98 has	9	tens	63 has	3	ones

Count the coins; then write how many cents.

15¢

18¢

11¢

19¢

97

5. *Practice Subtraction Family 8.*
   a. **Say Family 8 as I move the blocks. 8 blocks; take away 0 . . .**
   b. **Say Family 8 as I fill the houses.**
6. *Assign Lesson 131.*

Note: Subtraction on the flannel board previously called for all the blocks to be moved back to the starting point for each minuend. Subtraction is not new, so you can drop that increasing manipulation. As you begin each subtraction fact, move your hands to the minuend area and show the minuend number with your fingers. Then pick off the next block, and move it to the subtrahend area as you say the subtrahend.

Follow-up

Drill

1. Drill individuals with Addition Families 8–10 flash cards.
2. **If you had 12 pencils, you would have ___ pencils.** (1 dozen)
   If I had 12 eggs, I would have ___ eggs. (1 dozen)
3. Hold the footprint poster.
   a. **12 inches make 1 foot; 12 inches make 1 foot.**
   b. **Which of these might be 12 inches tall: a pup, a cow, a chicken, a donkey?**
   c. Have the children find things in the room that measure 12 inches.

Practice Sheets

- ☐ Fact Houses #35
- ☐ Form E: 241–260
- ● Number Facts #48
- ● Less Number #21
- ● Clocks #6

Objectives

New

TEACHING

Count by 25's
Number triplets

WORKBOOK

Subtraction Family 8

Review

Story problems
Money
Counting (150)
Number words

132 Whisper, trace, and answer the facts.

Cross out the right amount.

$8 - 0 = 8$	$8 - 1 = 7$	$8 - 2 = 6$
$8 - 3 = 5$	$8 - 4 = 4$	$8 - 5 = 3$
$8 - 6 = 2$	$8 - 7 = 1$	$8 - 8 = 0$

98

Preparation

Make Subtraction Family 8 flash cards for each child.

Tape green rings on the number line to circle 25, 50, 75, 100. (See pattern on page 600.)

Materials

One penny, nickel, and dime for each child

Number word cards

Chalkboard

(*Class Time* #1)

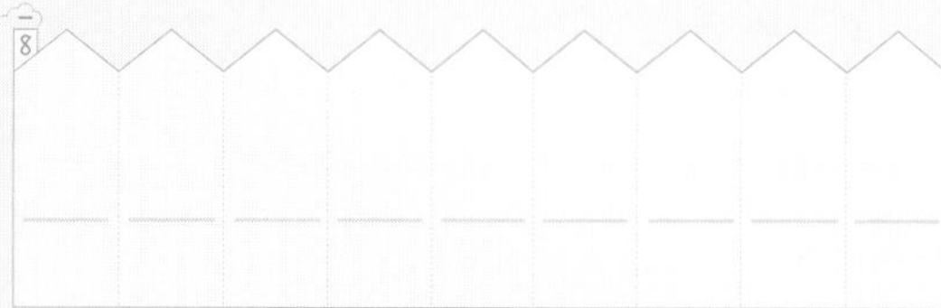

(*Class Time* #2)

Six hens sit.
Then three hens run away.
How many are left?

Mark has six books.
Fred has four books.
How many books do both boys have?

Class Time

1. *Review Subtraction Family 8.*
   a. Use the flannel board to illustrate Subtraction Family 8. Have the children say each story fact with you.
   (1) **James had 8 screws in his hand. He put 0 screws in a jar. He had 8 screws left in his hand.** Story fact: **8 screws minus 0 screws equals 8 screws.**
   (2) **James had 8 screws in his hand. He put 1 screw in a jar. He had 7 screws left in his hand.** Story fact: **8 screws minus 1 . . .**
   (3) **James had 8 screws in his hand. He put 2 screws in a jar. . . .**
   b. Ask a child to fill the 8 Houses as you say the facts together.
2. *Story problems.*
   a. Point to the first story problem. **Read this with me.** Ask a child to make the correct sign in the circle and fill in the blanks.

Write Family 8. (132)

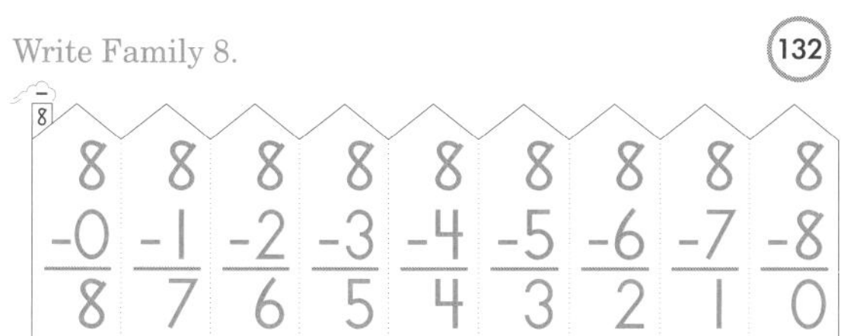

Circle Less.

less ⊙ ∴	(213) 223	219 (209)	209 (208)
(203) 205	(214) 234	239 (209)	228 (218)
(217) 227	(214) 224	232 (212)	231 (213)

Write the correct digit for ones, tens, or hundreds.

149 has 1 hundreds — 23 has 2 tens
198 has 8 ones — 234 has 4 ones
65 has 6 tens — 150 has 1 hundreds
208 has 2 hundreds — 206 has 2 hundreds
201 has 0 tens — 54 has 5 tens

99

b. Point to the second story problem. **Read this with me.** Ask a child to fill in the sign and blanks.

3. *Money.*
   a. Give each child one penny, nickel, and dime. **Can you name the man on the penny? . . . the nickel? . . . the dime?**
   b. **Which coin is worth the most? . . . the least?**
   c. **Which coin is the same as 5 pennies? . . . 10 pennies? . . . 2 nickels?**

4. *Counting.*
   Count by 1's from 50 to 150.

5. *Number words.*
   Give the number word cards to the children. **If your card answers my problem, come stand beside me.**

2 + 7	**4 + 2**	**7 − 4**	**3 + 2**	**7−3**
6 − 4	**5 − 4**	**3 + 7**	**5 + 2**	**3+5**

6. *Do Speed Drill #53.*

7. *Assign Lesson 132.*

Speed Drill Answers

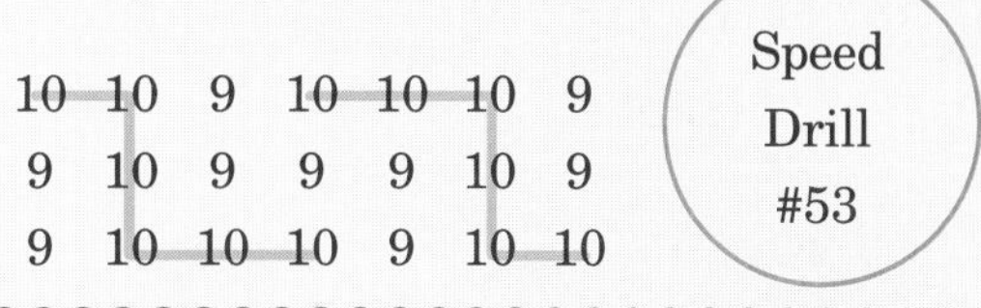

Follow-up

Drill

(*Drill*#3)

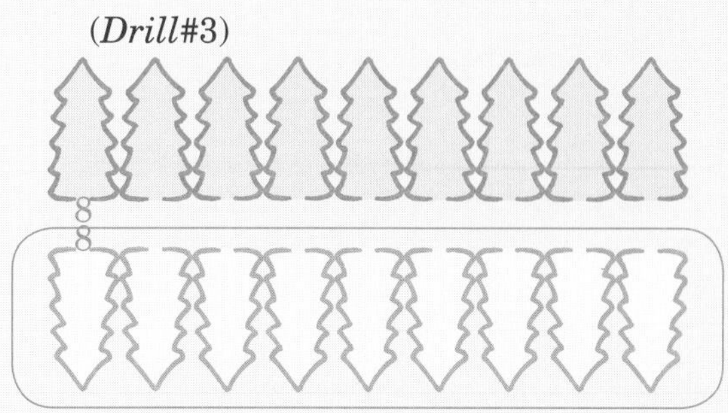

1. Give each child his Subtraction Family 8 flash cards.
2. Call the children to the number line.
   a. **Count to 100 by 2's, by 5's, and by 10's.**
   b. **We can count by 25's. Listen! 25, 50, 75, 100; 25, 50, 75, 100. Such big jumps get to 100 quickly. Count with me: 25, 50, 75, 100; . . .**
3. Use number triplets to make four facts.
   a. Write 0 + 8 = 8 in the first tree. Point to the three numbers. **With these three numbers we can make four number facts.** Write the twin addition fact in the next tree. **Two of the facts are addition. Two of them are subtraction.** Write the subtraction facts in the reflection.
   b. Write 1 + 7 = 8 in the third tree. **Who can write the other three facts with these numbers?**
   c. When you write 4 + 4 in the last tree, point out that switching the numbers gives the same fact again, so we have only one addition and one subtraction for these three numbers.

Practice Sheets

- ☐ Fact Houses #36
- ☐ Money #16
- ☐ Measures #6
- ● Number Facts #48
- ● Form F: 51–150

Objectives

New

TEACHING

Count by 25's

Review

Subtraction Family 8

Fractions

Money

12 inches = 1 foot

133

Write Family 8.

8	8	8	8	8	8	8	8	8
-0	-1	-2	-3	-4	-5	-6	-7	-8
8	7	6	5	4	3	2	1	0

Answer these facts.

8	8	8	8	8	8	8	8	8
-6	-5	-2	-4	-7	-1	-3	-0	-8
2	3	6	4	1	7	5	8	0

8	8	8	8	8	8	8	8	8
-3	-5	-6	-5	-2	-4	-7	-1	-3
5	3	2	3	6	4	1	7	5

8	8	8	8	8	8	8	8	8
-5	-6	-5	-2	-4	-7	-1	-3	-0
3	2	3	6	4	1	7	5	8

8	8	8	8	8	8	8	8	8
-8	-3	-5	-6	-5	-2	-4	-7	-1
0	5	3	2	3	6	4	1	7

100

Preparation

Tack Subtraction Family 8 flash cards above the flannel board with answers showing.

Materials

Large nickel and dime

Footprint poster

Form D for each child

Chalkboard

(*Class Time #2*)

(*Class Time #3*)

Class Time

1. *Count by 25's.*
   Call the children to the number line. **We will count with big jumps that go 25 numbers at a time. 25, 50, 75, 100.** Count four times.
2. *Practice Subtraction Family 8.*
   a. Stand near the flannel board. **8 blocks; take away 0 blocks; 8 blocks left.** Continue through Family 8.
   b. Point to the flash cards above the flannel board. **Say each fact three times with your eyes open, and then three times with your eyes closed.**
   c. Ask a child to fill the 8 Houses as you say the facts together.
3. *Fractions.*
   Do the chalkboard samples.

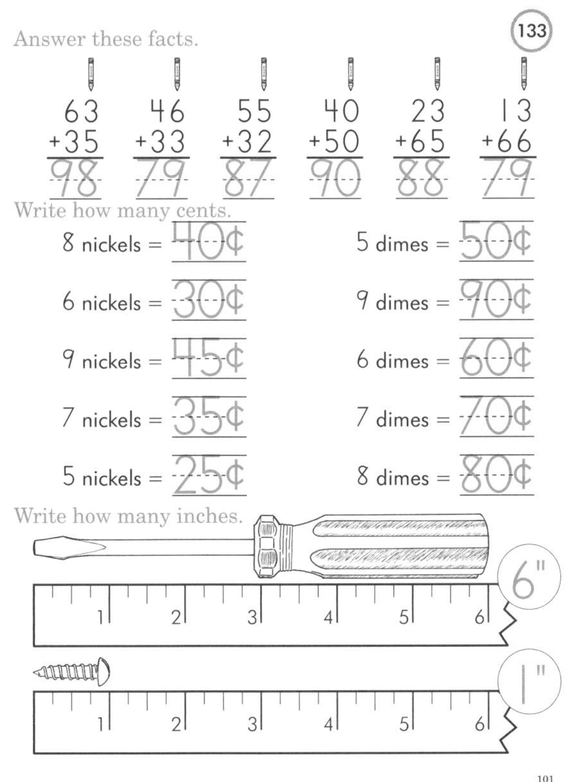

4. *Nickel and dime.*
   a. Hold up the large nickel. **Nickel, 5¢; nickel, 5¢; . . .**

      4 nickels = **10 nickels =**
      2 nickels = **6 nickels =**
      8 nickels = **3 nickels =**

   b. Hold up the large dime. **Dime, 10¢; dime, 10¢; . . .**

      5 dimes = **9 dimes =**
      7 dimes = **6 dimes =**
      3 dimes = **8 dimes =**

5. *12 inches = 1 foot.*
   a. **Jay caught a catfish that is 12 inches long, or _____.** (1 foot long)
   b. **Joy's tulips grew 12 inches tall, or _____.** (1 foot tall)

6. *Assign Lesson 133.*

Follow-up

Drill

1. Distribute Form D for story problem dictation. Print these labels on the chalkboard.

   seeds *buds*

   Sometimes we will add. Sometimes we will subtract. Put the correct sign in the gray spot.

   a. **Arrow Box: Mother planted 7 seeds beside the door. She planted 3 seeds at the mailbox. How many seeds is that *in all?***
   b. **Button Box: Freda planted 7 seeds. A chipmunk dug up 4 seeds and ate them. How many seeds were *left?***
   c. **Camel Box: Fred gave 4 buds to Mother. Roy gave her 5 buds. How many buds did *both* boys give?**
   d. **Daffodil Box: Freda picked 2 buds that will make yellow flowers. She picked 7 buds of pink flowers. How many buds is that *in all?***
   e. **Elephant Box: A flower pot has 6 seeds. The next flower pot has 4 seeds. How many seeds do *both* pots have?**
   f. **Feather Box: Mother put 6 buds in a vase. The next day 4 of the buds wilted. How many buds were *left?***

2. Chalkboard drill: **Write 216. Change it to 116, 146, 149, 249, 209, 239, 139, 131, 181, 111, 211, 201.**

Practice Sheets

- ● Form D (*Follow-up* drill #1)
- ☐ Fact Houses #37
- ☐ Missing Numbers #12
- ☐ Clocks #7
- ● Number Facts #49
- ● Number Facts #47

Objectives

New

TEACHING

Quarter

WORKBOOK

Count by 25's

Review

Addition and Subtraction Family 8

Count by 2's

Missing Numbers, by 2's

Fractions

134

Write Family 8.

8	8	8	8	8	8	8	8	8
-0	-1	-2	-3	-4	-5	-6	-7	-8
8	7	6	5	4	3	2	1	0

Answer these facts.

8	4	8	8	8	8	4	8	8
-4	-3	-1	-3	-5	-3	-2	-5	-2
4	1	7	5	3	5	2	3	6
8	8	5	6	5	8	8	8	5
-5	-6	-2	-0	-1	-7	-1	-3	-4
3	2	3	6	4	1	7	5	1
8	8	8	5	5	8	8	8	3
-1	-3	-7	-2	-3	-5	-2	-4	-2
7	5	1	3	2	3	6	4	1
8	8	8	8	4	8	8	8	8
-6	-3	-5	-6	-1	-2	-4	-7	-1
2	5	3	2	3	6	4	1	7

102

Preparation

Materials

Subtraction Family 8 flash cards

One quarter for each child

Chalkboard

(*Class Time* #1)

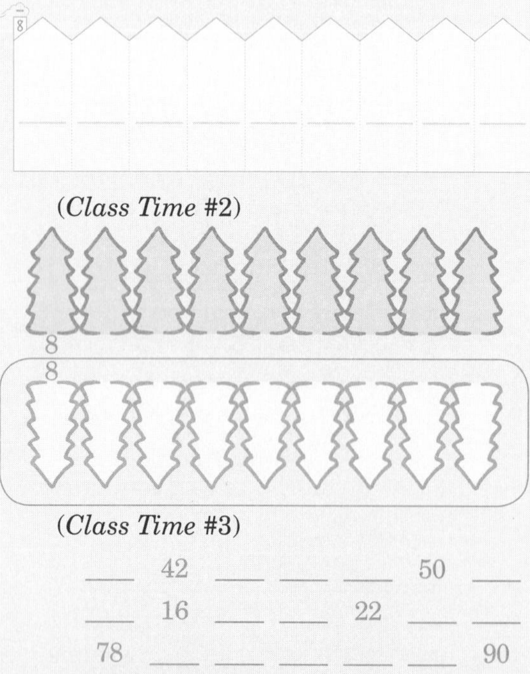

Class Time

1. *Practice Subtraction Family 8.*
   a. Point to the flash cards near the flannel board. **Girls, say each fact once. Boys, say each fact once.**
   b. **Say Subtraction Family 8 as I move the blocks.**
   c. Ask a child to fill the 8 Houses as you say Family 8 together.
2. *Drill Addition and Subtraction Family 8.*
   a. Let individuals fill in twin groups of addition and subtraction facts.
   b. Recite Family 8 facts in groups of four—addition twins and the reflecting subtraction twins. Point to the facts in order as you go.
3. *Count by 2's.*
   a. Stand near the number line. **The number pattern for counting by 2's is ___. Let's count by 2's to 100.**
   b. Count by 2's to do the Missing Number chalkboard samples.

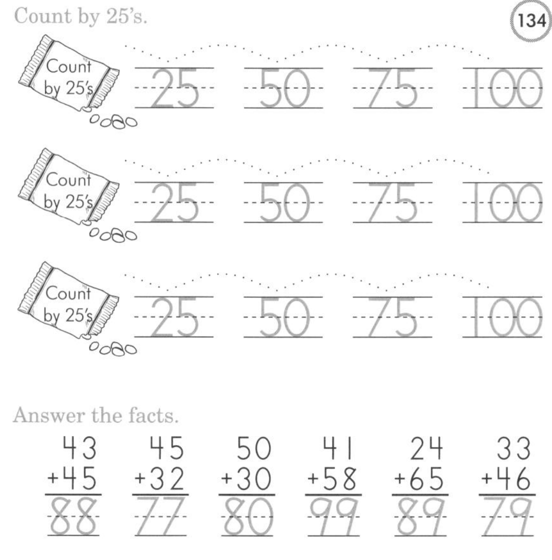

Write the fractions.

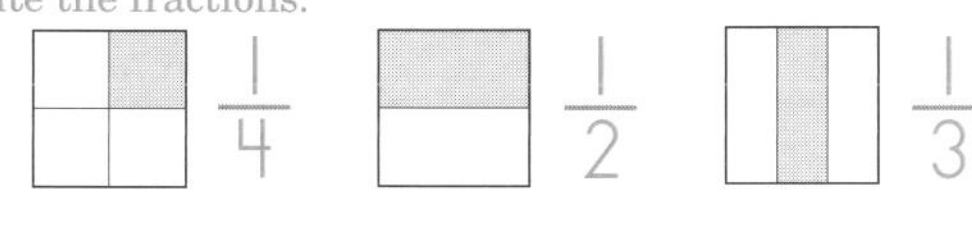

103

4. *Count by 25's.*
   a. **Count by 25's. 25, 50, 75, 100.** Count three times.
   b. **When we count to 100, there is a number that we say whether we count by 2's, by 5's, by 10's, or by 25's. What number is it?** (50)
5. *Fractions.*
   Let a child shade one part of the circle and write the fraction to show what is shaded. Do the same for the other shapes.
6. *Do Speed Drill #54.*
7. *Assign Lesson 134.*

Speed Drill Answers

6	3	5	4	5	3	2
1	6	3	5	3	2	4
0	1	6	3	2	4	7

Speed Drill #54

Follow-up

Drill

(*Drill* #2)

1. Drill individuals with Subtraction Family 8 flash cards.
2. Introduce the quarter. Call the class to the teaching corner, and give each child one quarter.
   a. **What a large coin! This is a quarter. The man's name is George Washington. Can you name the bird on the back of the coin?** (eagle—if your coins are dated before 1999)
   b. **One quarter is worth 25¢.** Write 25¢ in each circle as everyone says, **Quarter, 25¢; quarter, 25¢; quarter, 25¢; . . .**
   c. Count the quarters, and fill in the blanks.

Practice Sheets

- ☐ Fact Houses #36
- ☐ Measures #2
- ● Number Facts #49
- ● Writing Practice #29
- ● Money #16

Objectives

New

TEACHING

Counting quarters

Fraction $\frac{2}{3}$

Review

Addition and Subtraction Family 8

Dozen

Telling time

Count by 25's

Preparation

Materials

Model clock

Large quarter

Subtraction Families 4–6 and 8 flash cards

Large thermometer

Chalkboard

(*Class Time* #1)

(*Class Time* #2)

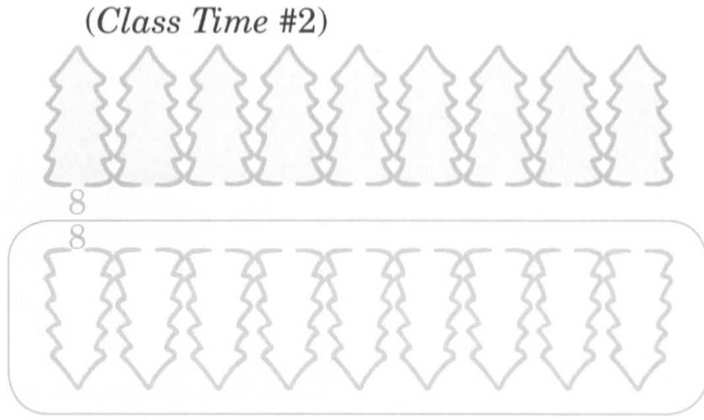

(*Class Time* #5)

135

Write Family 8.

8	8	8	8	8	8	8	8	8
-0	-1	-2	-3	-4	-5	-6	-7	-8
8	7	6	5	4	3	2	1	0

Answer these facts.

6	6	8	6	8	8	8	4	8
-4	-3	-2	-2	-7	-5	-3	-2	-6
2	3	6	4	1	3	5	2	2

8	8	8	5	8	8	8	8	8
-1	-5	-6	-2	-2	-4	-7	-5	-3
7	3	2	3	6	4	1	3	5

8	5	8	6	8	6	6	6	8
-5	-3	-5	-0	-4	-5	-3	-1	-6
3	2	3	6	4	1	3	5	2

8	8	8	8	8	8	8	5	4
-3	-1	-5	-6	-5	-2	-4	-4	-1
5	7	3	2	3	6	4	1	3

104

Class Time

1. *Practice Subtraction Family 8.*
   a. Point to the flash cards near the flannel board. **We will say each fact three times.**
   b. Use the flannel board for story facts.
      (1) **Betty had 8 little candies. She ate 0 candies. She had 8 candies left.**
      (2) **Betty had 8 little candies. She ate 1 candy. . . .**
   c. Ask a child to fill the houses as you say Family 8 together.
2. *Drill Addition and Subtraction Family 8.* Write the facts in groups of four as you say them together.
3. *Review dozen.*
   a. **Paul husked 12 ears of corn, or ___ ears of corn.** (1 dozen)
   b. **Mother put 12 cookies on the tray, or ___ cookies on the tray.** (1 dozen)
   c. **12 things make 1 dozen. 12 things make 1 dozen.**

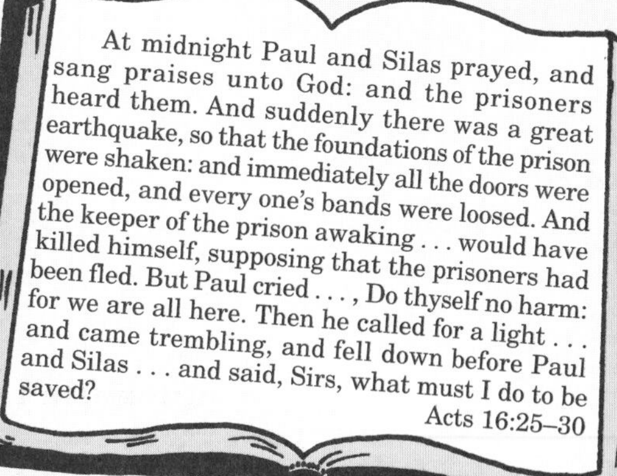

At midnight Paul and Silas prayed, and sang praises unto God: and the prisoners heard them. And suddenly there was a great earthquake, so that the foundations of the prison were shaken: and immediately all the doors were opened, and every one's bands were loosed. And the keeper of the prison awaking . . . would have killed himself, supposing that the prisoners had been fled. But Paul cried . . . , Do thyself no harm: for we are all here. Then he called for a light . . . and came trembling, and fell down before Paul and Silas . . . and said, Sirs, what must I do to be saved?

Acts 16:25–30

4. *Telling time.*
   a. **Name the hands of a clock.**
   b. **When the minute hand and the hour hand both point to 12 in the daytime, it is ___.** (12:00 noon)
   c. **When the minute hand and the hour hand both point to 12 in the nighttime, it is ___.** (12:00 midnight) **One time at midnight, two men in prison prayed and sang praises.**
   d. **Answer together.** Set the model clock at 6:30, 8:00, 11:00, 12:30, 3:30, 5:00.
5. *Counting quarters.*
   a. Stand near the number line. **Take great big jumps of 25 numbers at a time. 25, 50, 75, 100.** Count three times.
   b. **Quarter, 25¢; quarter, 25¢. We count quarters by 25's.** Write 25¢ in each circle on the chalkboard as everyone says, **Quarter, 25¢.**
   c. Answer the chalkboard samples.
6. *Assign Lesson 135.*

Follow-up

Drill

(*Drill #2*)

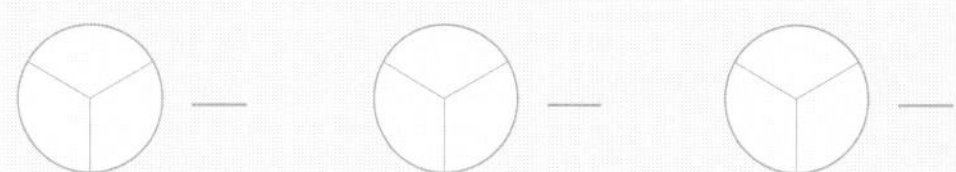

1. Circle Drill: Subtraction Families 4–6 and 8.
2. Introduce the fraction $\frac{2}{3}$.
   a. Shade one part of the first circle on the board, and call on someone to write the fraction.
   b. Shade a second part of the same circle. **Now how many parts are shaded? Erase the numerator 1, and write 2 in its place.**
   c. **This fraction says two-thirds. 2 of the 3 equal parts are shaded.**
   d. Shade two-thirds of the other circles, choosing thirds in various positions. Let individuals write the fractions.
3. Hold the large thermometer. Set the mercury at 68°. **What is the temperature? 2, 4, 6, . . . 68°. Pussy willows will pop out of their shells when springtime days are 68°.**

Practice Sheets

- ☐ Fact Houses #37
- ☐ Number Trains #8
- ☐ Number Words #2
- ● Number Facts #50
- ● Measures #7

Objectives

New

TEACHING

Fraction $\frac{2}{3}$

WORKBOOK

Counting quarters

Review

Subtraction facts

Count by 25's

136

Write Family 8.

8	8	8	8	8	8	8	8	8
-0	-1	-2	-3	-4	-5	-6	-7	-8
8	7	6	5	4	3	2	1	0

Answer these facts.

4	8	8	8	5	8	8	6	8
-2	-5	-2	-4	-4	-5	-3	-4	-3
2	3	6	4	1	3	5	2	5

8	4	5	5	8	8	8	8	6
-1	-1	-3	-2	-2	-4	-7	-5	-1
7	3	2	3	6	4	1	3	5

6	8	8	6	6	6	6	8	8
-3	-6	-5	-0	-2	-5	-3	-3	-6
3	2	3	6	4	1	3	5	2

8	8	8	8	8	8	8	8	4
-6	-1	-5	-6	-5	-2	-4	-7	-1
2	7	3	2	3	6	4	1	3

106

Preparation

Materials

Subtraction Families 4–6 and 8 flash cards

Form C for each child

Large quarter

One slice of bread and a knife

Addition Families 8–10 flash cards

Chalkboard

(Write a set of these facts for each child to trace in *Class Time* #1.)

8	8
- 3	- 5
5	3

(*Class Time* #3)

Class Time

1. *Practice Subtraction Family 8.*
   a. Have each child stand near his set of facts on the board. **Trace and whisper the facts until I say "stop."**
   b. **Stop. Turn toward me. Watch my fingers as we say Family 8.** Show each subtrahend with your fingers. **8 - 0, 8; 8 - 1, 7 . . .**
   c. **Can you say the addition and subtraction facts in twin order?**
2. *Drill subtraction facts.*
   a. Double Drill with Subtraction Families 4–6 and 8 flash cards.
   b. Use Form C for written flash card drill. Continue with Subtraction Families 4–6 and 8. **Write the answer to the fact I show. Apron Row: Box 1—Box 2 . . .**
3. *Counting quarters.*
   a. Call the children to the number line. **Count by 25's to 100** three times.
   b. Hold the large quarter. **Quarter, 25¢; quarter, 25¢; . . .** Write 25¢ in each

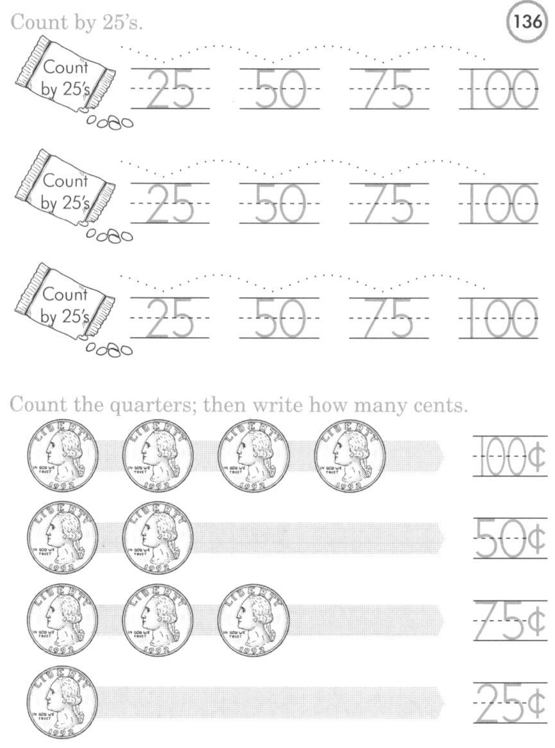
Count by 25's. 136

Count by 25's 25 50 75 100

Count by 25's 25 50 75 100

Count by 25's 25 50 75 100

Count the quarters; then write how many cents.

100¢

50¢

75¢

25¢

107

chalkboard circle as everyone says, **Quarter, 25¢; . . .**

c. Have individuals do the samples aloud and write the answers.

4. *Teach two-thirds.*
   a. **Hold up a slice of bread. If I cut this bread into 2 pieces, how much will each piece be? If I cut it into 3 pieces, what will each piece be? If I cut it into 4 pieces, what will each piece be?**
   b. Cut the bread into 3 equal parts. Hold up each part one at a time and say, **This is $\frac{1}{3}$.**
   c. Hold up 2 of the pieces. **This is $\frac{2}{3}$.** Write the fraction on the chalkboard.
   d. Point to the denominator. **The bread is cut into 3 parts.** Point to the numerator. **I have 2 of the parts. 2 of 3 equal parts is $\frac{2}{3}$.**
5. *Do Speed Drill #55.*
6. *Assign Lesson 136.*

Speed Drill Answers

2	4	6	3	4	5	3
6	2	4	6	3	4	5
5	6	2	4	6	3	4

Speed Drill #55

Follow-up

Drill

(*Drill* #2)

___	24	___	28	___	___
50	___	___	___	90	___
143	___	145	___	___	___
___	20	___	___	35	___

1. Drill individuals with Addition Families 8–10 flash cards.
2. Point to the first row of chalkboard samples. **Should we count by 1's, 2's, 5's, or 10's?** Fill in the Missing Numbers.
3. Call the children to the calendar.
   a. **Name the days of the week.**
   b. Point to each column as you explain. **All the numbers in the first column are Sundays. All the numbers in the second column are Mondays.** Continue to Saturday.
   c. **What day of the week is [March] 12?** Continue with

      March 5 March 15 March 21
      March 1 March 17 March 30

Practice Sheets

- ● Form C (*Class Time* #2)
- ☐ Fact Houses #38
- ☐ Money #17
- ● Number Facts #50
- ● Story Problems #2

Objectives

New

WORKBOOK

Fractions $\frac{1}{3}$, $\frac{2}{3}$

Review

Subtraction facts
Story problems
Money
Count by 25's

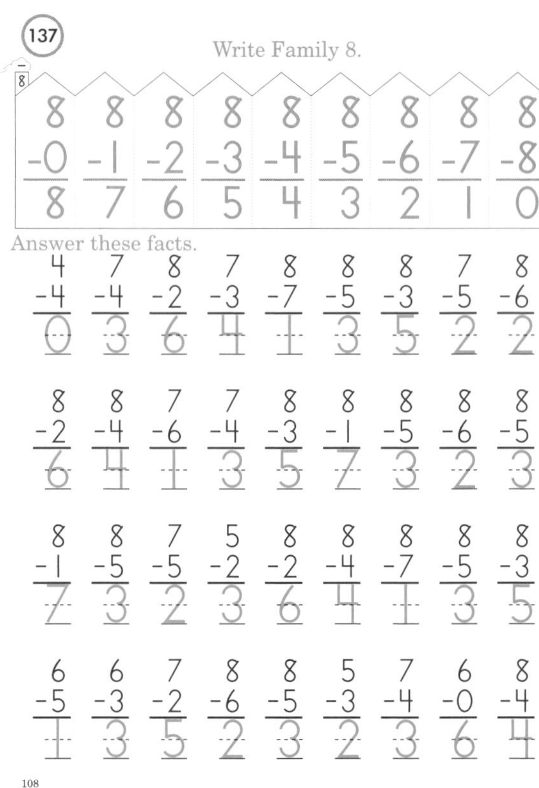

Preparation

Materials

Large coins

Subtraction Families 6–8 flash cards

One quarter for each child

Chalkboard

(*Class Time* #1)

(*Class Time* #3)

Class Time

1. *Review Subtraction Families 7 and 8.*
   a. **Say Subtraction Family 7 as I move the felt blocks.**
   b. Ask a child to fill the 7 Houses as you say the facts together.
   c. **Say Subtraction Family 8 as I move the blocks.**
   d. Ask a child to fill the 8 Houses as you say the facts together.
2. *Oral story problems.*
   a. **Close your eyes and listen. Jason has 7 sheep. David has 3 sheep. How many sheep is that *altogether*? Open your eyes. Who can give us the whole problem?**
   b. **Close your eyes. 8 pups play. Then 6 of them go to sleep. How many pups are *still* playing? Who can give us the whole problem?**

Count by 25's. 137

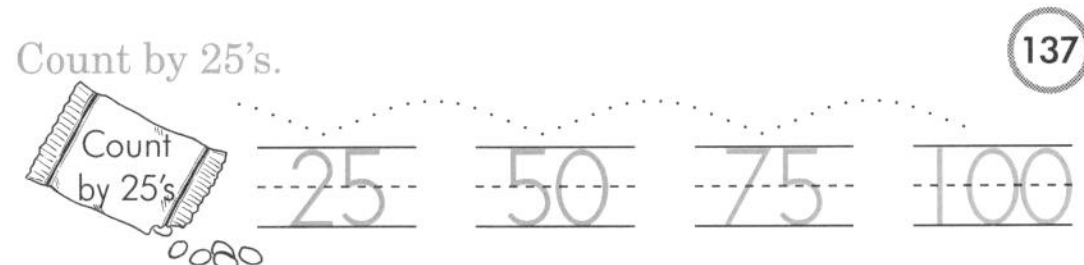

Count the quarters; then write how many cents.

Answer the facts.

32	36	30	52	26	43
+35	+52	+47	+46	+73	+42
67	88	77	98	99	85

Write the fractions.

$\frac{2}{3}$ $\frac{1}{3}$ $\frac{2}{3}$

109

3. *Fractions $\frac{1}{3}$ and $\frac{2}{3}$.*
   a. Point to the first rectangle. **How many parts does this shape have? How many parts are shaded?** Write the fraction.
   b. Point to the second rectangle. **How many parts does this shape have? How many parts are shaded?** Write the fraction.
   c. Let the children write fractions for the other shapes.
4. *Review money.*
   Flash the large coins. **Nickel, 5¢; quarter, 25¢; penny, 1¢; dime, 10¢.**
5. *Count by 25's.*
   Point to the number line. **Count by 25's.** Count three times.
6. *Assign Lesson 137.*
   Remember to add the ones' place first when you are adding 2-digit numbers.

Follow-up

Drill

1. Circle Drill with Subtraction Families 6–8 flash cards.
2. Have individuals count by 25's.
3. Call the children to the teaching corner. Give each an eagle-back quarter.
   a. **This coin is a ___. It is worth ___. Can you name the bird on the back?** (eagle) **Can you name the man on the front?** (George Washington)
   b. **See the tiny words below the man's chin?** IN GOD WE TRUST (These words are behind the man's neck on the states-series quarters.)
   c. **We trust in God. We do not trust in George Washington. God is alive. God is our Father. He is the greatest one.**
   d. **Every quarter, dime, nickel, and penny says IN GOD WE TRUST.**

Practice Sheets

- ☐ Fact Houses #38
- ☐ Form F: 61–160
- ● Number Facts #50
- ● Before and After #15
- ● Money #18

Objectives

Review

Subtraction facts
Number words
Fractions $\frac{1}{3}$, $\frac{2}{3}$
Count by 2's, 5's, 10's, 25's
Larger (200's)

138

Write Family 8.

8	8	8	8	8	8	8	8	8
-0	-1	-2	-3	-4	-5	-6	-7	-8
8	7	6	5	4	3	2	1	0

Answer these facts.

7	8	8	8	7	8	8	7	8
-5	-5	-2	-4	-6	-5	-3	-5	-6
2	3	6	4	1	3	5	2	2

7	7	8	6	8	6	6	8	8
-3	-4	-4	-2	-5	-6	-3	-7	-6
4	3	4	4	3	0	3	1	2

8	7	8	8	8	8	6	6	8
-1	-1	-6	-5	-2	-6	-1	-4	-3
7	6	2	3	6	2	5	2	5

7	8	7	8	7	8	8	8	8
-2	-1	-3	-4	-4	-2	-4	-7	-5
5	7	4	4	3	6	4	1	3

110

Preparation

Materials

Number word cards

Subtraction Families 6–8 flash cards

Chalkboard

(*Class Time* #2)

7	7	8	8
-3	-4	-3	-5
4	3	5	3

(*Class Time* #4)

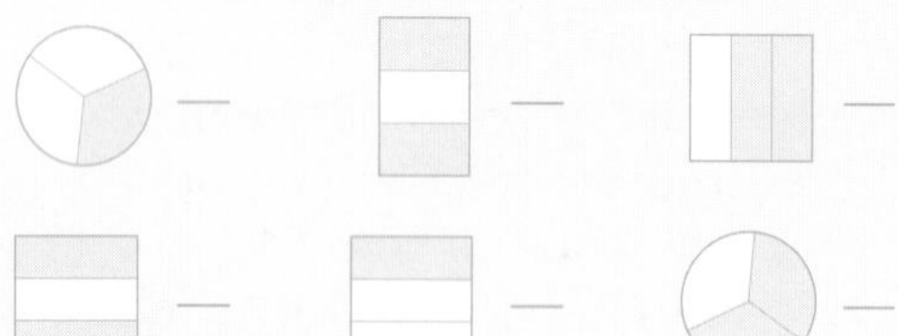

(*Class Time* #6)

143	137	173	168	108	186
201	211	210	125	135	152
174	147	107	156	165	185

Class Time

1. *Review Subtraction Families 7 and 8.*
   a. **Watch my fingers as we say Subtraction Family 7.**
   b. Point to the flash cards near the flannel board. **Girls, say each fact once. Boys, say each fact once. Say the facts together.**
2. *Drill selected facts.*
   Stand near the box on the board. Circle 7 - 3 = 4. **Say this five times.** Say it slowly the first time, and then a little faster with each recital. Circle and drill each fact.
3. *Number words.*
   Flash number word cards.

Count by 25's. 138

25 50 75 100

Write how many cents.

50¢

100¢

25¢

75¢

Write the correct digit for ones, tens, or hundreds'.

226 has 6 ones	163 has 1 hundreds
48 has 4 tens	207 has 0 tens
235 has 2 hundreds	53 has 3 ones
201 has 0 tens	167 has 6 tens

111

4. *Fractions $\frac{1}{3}$ and $\frac{2}{3}$.*
   Do the chalkboard samples.
5. *Skip counting.*
   a. **Count by 2's to 100.**
   b. **Count by 5's to 100.**
   c. **Count by 10's to 100.**
   d. **Count by 25's to 100.**
6. *Larger numbers.*
   Point to the chalkboard samples. **Find the largest number in each box.**
7. *Do Speed Drill #56.*
8. *Assign Lesson 138.*

Speed Drill Answers

6	3	7	4	5	8	2
3	7	4	5	8	2	9
7	4	5	8	2	9	6

Follow-up

Drill

(*Drill* #3)

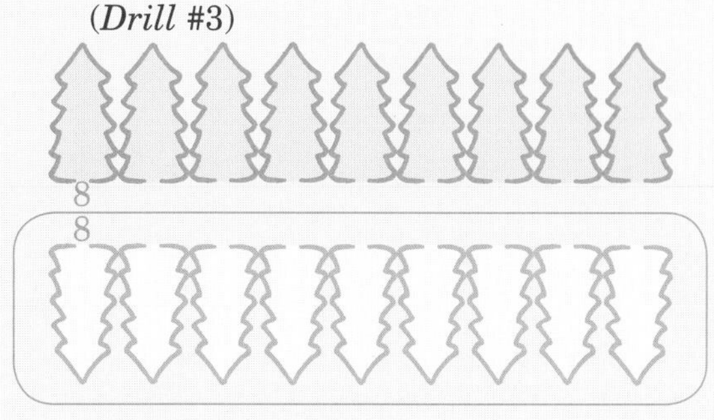

1. Chalkboard drill:
   Write 143. Circle the digit in the tens' place.
   Write 206. Circle the digit in the ones' place. Continue with
   221 . . . the hundreds' place
   135 . . . the tens' place
   187 . . . the hundreds' place
   210 . . . the ones' place
2. Drill individuals with Subtraction Families 6–8 flash cards.
3. Drill Addition and Subtraction Family 8.
   a. Write 0 + 8 in the first tree. Ask a child to finish the four facts that are made with the same numbers.
   b. Let individuals do the other groups of four.
   c. Recite the facts together in groups of four.

Practice Sheets

- ☐ Fact Houses #38
- ☐ Missing Numbers #13
- ☐ Money #17
- ● Number Facts #51
- ● Number Facts #52
- ● Measures #8

Objectives

New

TEACHING

Number triplets
Fractions $\frac{2}{4}$, $\frac{3}{4}$

Review

Mixed addition and subtraction
Fractions
Count by 25's
Counting money
Dozen

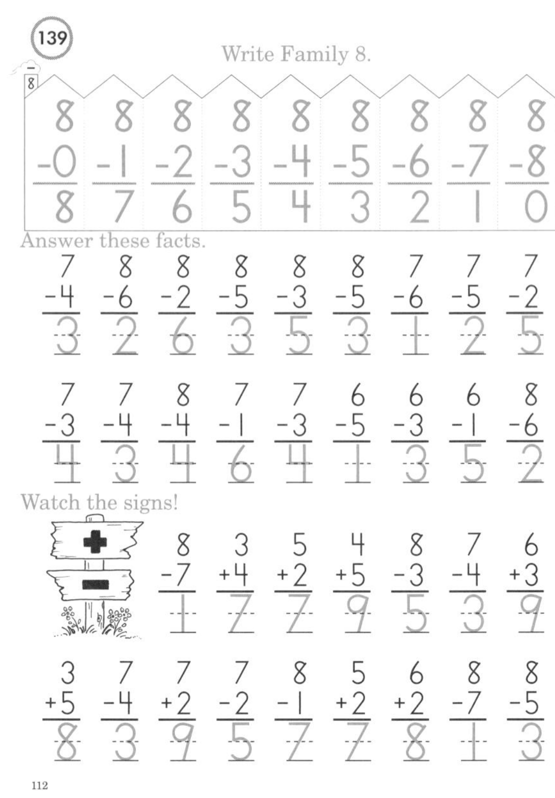

Preparation

Materials

Mixed flash cards: Addition Families 8–10 and Subtraction Families 6–8

Large quarter

Pennies, nickels, dimes, and quarters

Chalkboard

(*Class Time* #1)

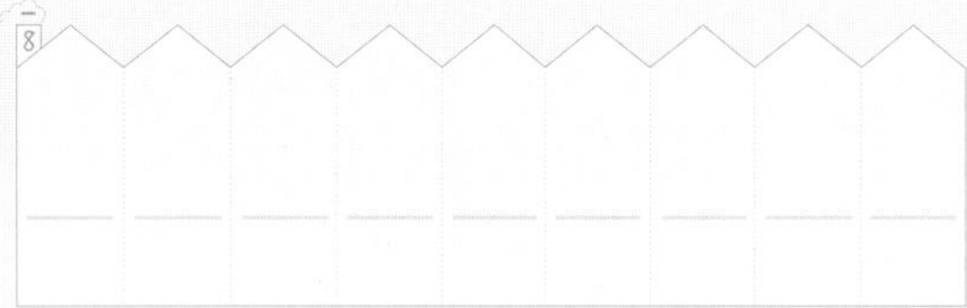

(*Class Time* #3)

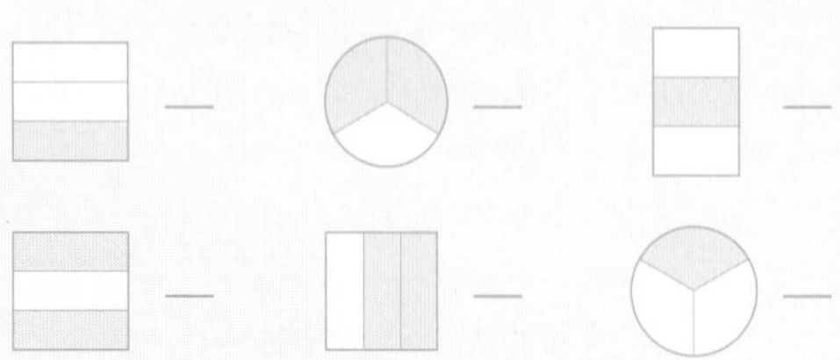

(*Class Time* #4)

25¢ 25¢ 25¢ ____

25¢ ____

25¢ 25¢ 25¢ 25¢ ____

25¢ 25¢ ____

6 nickels = ____
6 dimes = ____
12 pennies = ____
7 nickels = ____
4 dimes = ____
8 nickels = ____

Class Time

1. *Review Subtraction Family 8.*
   a. Use the flannel board for story facts.
      (1) **Faith saw 8 daffodil buds. She picked 0 buds. Eight buds were left.**
      (2) **Faith saw 8 daffodil buds. She picked 1 bud. Seven buds . . .**
   b. Ask a child to fill the 8 Houses as you say the facts together.
2. *Mixed fact drill.*
   a. Ask a child to recite four facts for the numbers 8, 0, 8. Ask someone else for the facts for 8, 1, 7. Call on others for the rest of the triplets in Family 8.
   b. Circle Drill with mixed flash cards for Addition Families 8–10 and Subtraction Families 6–8.

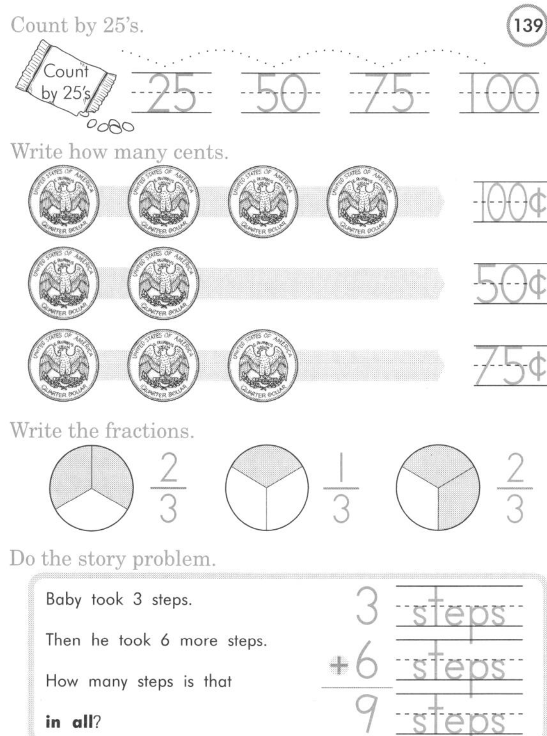

3. *Fractions.*
   Do the chalkboard samples.
4. *Counting money.*
   a. Stand near the number line. **Count by 25's** three times.
   b. Hold the large quarter and drill its name and value. Do the quarter samples that are on the chalkboard.
   c. Have the children use their fingers and count aloud for the samples with money words.
5. *Dozen.*
   a. **Mary picked 12 daffodils, or Mary picked ___ daffodils.** (1 dozen)
   b. **Jason helped Mother plant 12 cabbage plants, or Jason helped Mother plant ___ cabbage plants.** (1 dozen)
6. *Assign Lesson 139.*

Follow-up

Drill

(*Drill* #3)

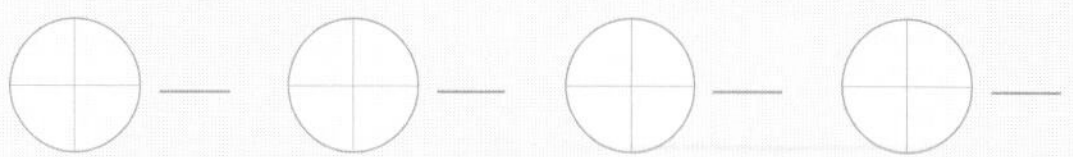

1. Lay a mixture of pennies, nickels, dimes, and quarters on your desk. Call individuals to identify them.
   a. **Find a 10¢ coin . . . 25¢ coin . . . 1¢ coin . . . 5¢ coin.**
   b. **Now find a quarter . . . nickel . . . dime . . . penny.**
2. Have individuals move the felt blocks and say Subtraction Family 8.
3. Introduce multiple fourths.
   a. Point to the first circle on the chalkboard. **How many parts does this shape have?** Write the denominator. Shade in one of the fourths. **How many parts are shaded?** Write the numerator.
   b. Shade another quarter of the same circle. **Now how many parts are shaded?** Erase the numerator 1, and write 2 in its place. **This fraction says two-fourths. 2 of the 4 equal parts are shaded.**
   c. Shade a third quarter, and change the numerator again. Let someone tell what that fraction says.
   d. Shade 1, 2, or 3 parts of the other circles, and let individuals write the fractions.

Practice Sheets

- ☐ Fact Houses #39
- ☐ Skip Counting #5
- ● Number Facts #51
- ● More Numbers #22
- ◊ Extra: Money #18—Color quarters; then cut and paste them back-to-back.

Objectives

New

TEACHING

Fractions $\frac{2}{4}$, $\frac{3}{4}$

Subtraction Family 9

WORKBOOK

Fractions $\frac{1}{4}$, $\frac{2}{4}$, $\frac{3}{4}$

Review

Addition and subtraction

2-digit addition

Telling time

140

Write Family 8.

8	8	8	8	8	8	8	8	8
-0	-1	-2	-3	-4	-5	-6	-7	-8
8	7	6	5	4	3	2	1	0

Answer these facts.

8	7	8	7	8	8	8	7	8
-6	-2	-2	-3	-7	-5	-3	-5	-6
2	5	6	4	1	3	5	2	2

8	7	8	8	7	7	8	7	8
-4	-5	-5	-4	-1	-6	-2	-4	-6
4	2	3	4	6	1	6	3	2

7	7	7	7	8	7	7	8	8
-2	-3	-4	-5	-7	-3	-4	-5	-3
5	4	3	2	1	4	3	3	5

8	8	8	8	8	8	8	7	7
-1	-3	-4	-6	-5	-2	-4	-6	-4
7	5	4	2	3	6	4	1	3

114

Preparation

Materials

Subtraction Families 7 and 8 flash cards

Model clock

Form B for each child

Crackers designed to break into fourths

Large penny, nickel, dime, and quarter

Chalkboard

(*Class Time* #2)

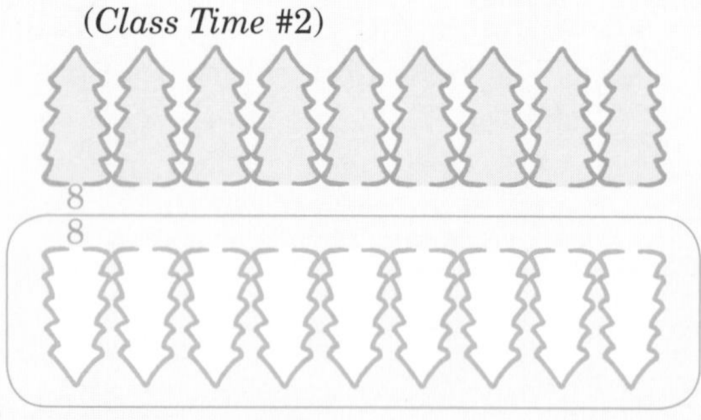

(*Class Time* #3)

75	50	36	34	65	28	35
+ 22	+ 40	+ 43	+ 54	+ 13	+ 60	+ 60

(*Class Time* #5)

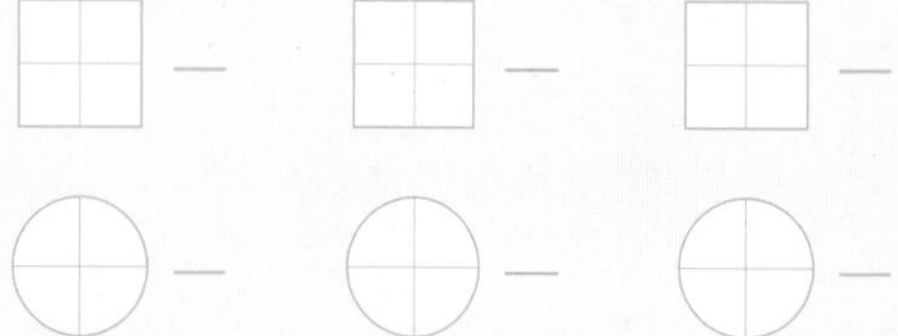

Class Time

1. *Review Subtraction Families 7 and 8.*
   a. Distribute the flash cards for Subtraction Families 7 and 8. **If you have the first fact in Family 7, come set it on the chalk tray . . .**
   b. Stand near the flash cards. **Say these facts with me.**
2. *Drill Addition and Subtraction Family 8.* Let individuals fill in the trees and reflection in sets of four as you say the facts together.
3. *Two-digit addition.* Do the chalkboard samples. **Ones' place first!**
4. *Telling time.* Distribute Form B, and show these times on the model clock for the children to write.

(apple)	8:30	12:30	3:30
(nest)	7:30	11:30	1:30
(igloo)	4:00	6:30	9:30

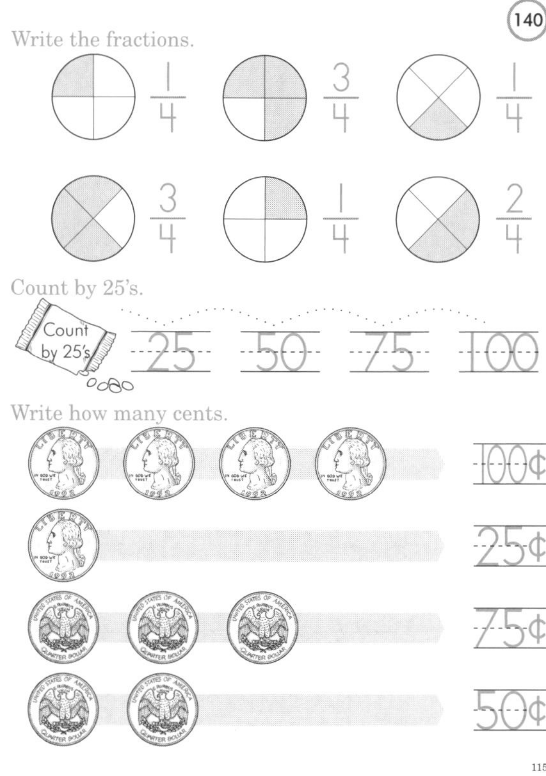
140

Write the fractions.

1/4 3/4 1/4

3/4 1/4 2/4

Count by 25's.

25 50 75 100

Write how many cents.

100¢

25¢

75¢

50¢

115

	2:30	11:30	5:30
	8:00	10:30	4:30

5. *Teach multiple fourths.*
   a. Show the class an unbroken cracker scored to break into fourths. **If I break this cracker into fourths, how many pieces will I have?**
   b. Break it, and hold up 1 piece. **This is one-fourth.** Write the fraction on the board. Hold up 2 pieces. **This is two-fourths.** Write the fraction. Show 3 pieces, and write that fraction. **This is three-fourths.**
   c. Put the 4 pieces down, and invite a child to take $\frac{3}{4}$ of the cracker and share it with some of the others. If you wish, divide more crackers so all can have a taste.
   d. Ask individuals to shade 1, 2, or 3 parts of the shapes on the board and write the appropriate fractions.
6. *Do Speed Drill #57.*
7. *Assign Lesson 140.*

Speed Drill Answers

7	5	2	4	3	5	7
5	2	4	6	4	3	5
2	4	6	6	6	4	3

Speed Drill #57

Follow-up

Drill

(*Drill* #3)

9

1. Flash the large coins, sometimes showing the front and sometimes the back. **Quarter, 25¢; nickel, 5¢; dime, 10¢; penny, 1¢ . . .**
2. Point to the number line. **Count with me. Watch for changes in the counting.**
   10, 20, 30, 31, 32, 33, 34
   5, 10, 15, 20, 21, 22, 23, 24
   10, 20, 30, 40, 50, 60, 61, 62
   5, 10, 15, 20, 25, 30, 35, 40, 41, 42, 43
3. Introduce Subtraction Family 9. **Can you think of problems for Subtraction Family 9?** Write the facts in order. **Tomorrow we will work with Family 9 again.**

Practice Sheets

- Form B (*Class Time* #4)
- ☐ Fact Houses #39
- ☐ Measures #4
- Number Facts #51
- Money #19

Objectives

New

TEACHING

- Subtraction Family 9
- Column addition (+ 3)

Review

- Subtraction facts
- Count by 10's, 5's, 25's
- Counting (169)
- Fractions $\frac{1}{3}$, $\frac{2}{3}$

141

Answer these facts.

7	8	8	7	8	8	7	8	8
-4	-2	-4	-6	-5	-3	-5	-6	-7
3	6	4	1	3	5	2	2	1

7	8	7	7	8	7	8	8	8
-5	-6	-3	-1	-7	-4	-3	-5	-6
2	2	4	6	1	3	5	3	2

"Consider her ways, and be wise."

8	8	8	7	7	7	8
-5	-2	-4	-2	-5	-6	-6
3	6	4	5	2	1	2

Proverbs 6:6

7	8	7	7	8	7	8	8	8
-2	-4	-5	-4	-2	-3	-7	-5	-3
5	4	2	3	6	4	1	3	5

8	8	7	8	8	8	8	8	7
-1	-3	-3	-6	-4	-2	-5	-7	-4
7	5	4	2	4	6	3	1	3

116

Preparation

Materials

Form D for each child

Chalkboard

(*Class Time* #2)

9

(*Class Time* #3)

6	2	5	3	2	7	3
1	4	1	2	5	0	3
+3	+3	+3	+3	+3	+3	+3

(*Class Time* #6)

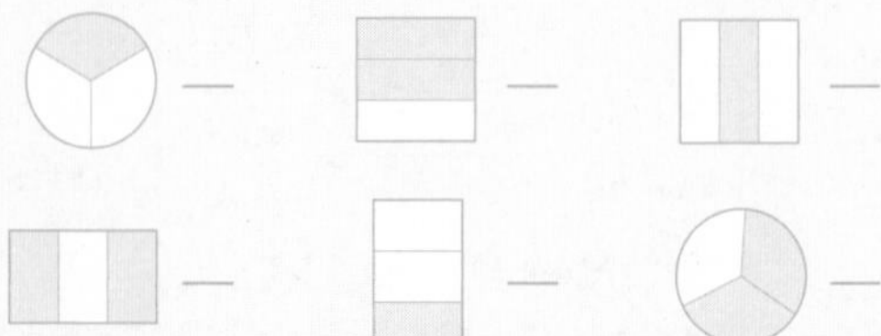

Class Time

1. *Review Subtraction Families 7 and 8.*
   I will move the felt blocks. Say Subtraction Family 7 . . . Family 8.
2. *Teach Subtraction Family 9.*
   a. **Let's try Subtraction Family 9. 9 blocks; take away 0 blocks; 9 blocks left . . .**
   b. Ask a child to fill the houses as you say Family 9 together.
3. *Column addition with 3 for last addend.*
   Do the chalkboard samples.
4. *Skip counting.*
   Have responsive counting. **I will say the first number, you say the next number, then I will say one, and then you say one.**
   a. **Count by 10's.**
   b. **Count by 5's.**
   c. **Count by 25's.**

141

Write the fractions.

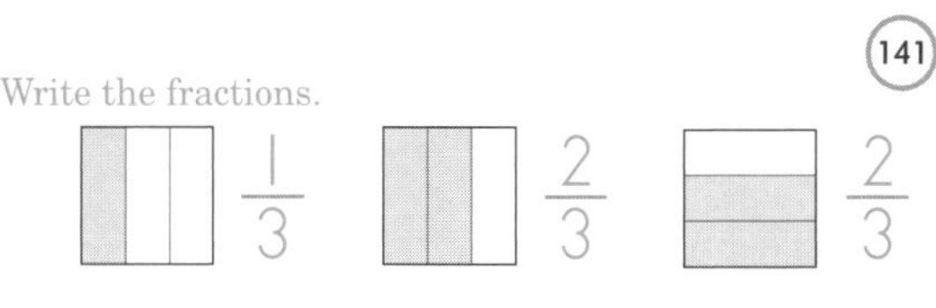

Circle More.

• ∴ more	221 219	229 227	245 205
231 234	215 217	243 242	237 238

Write Before and After numbers, counting by 5's.

Count by 5's

40	45	50	20	25	30
55	60	65	70	75	80
10	15	20	5	10	15
80	85	90	45	50	55

117

5. *Counting.*
   Let's say the number trains, starting at 70 and counting to 169. I will say the seventies. You will say the eighties, and so on.
6. *Fractions.*
   Do the chalkboard samples.
7. *Assign Lesson 141.*
   What can we learn from ants? They are little creatures that work together and work hard. If we follow their example, we will not be lazy.

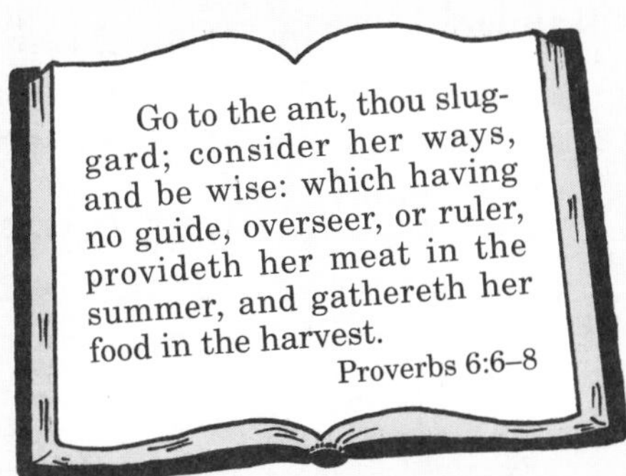

Follow-up

Drill

(*Drill* #2)

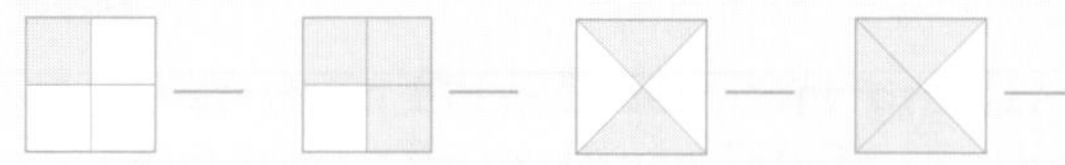

1. Distribute Form D for story problem dictation. Print these labels on the chalkboard. *birds nests*
   Decide if you should add or subtract. Put the correct sign in the shaded spot.
   a. **Arrow Box: Sara saw 4 red birds. Ruth saw 6 brown birds. How many birds was that *altogether?***
   b. **Button Box: Ruth saw 5 nests in the trees. Sara saw 4 nests in the hedge. How many nests did *both* girls see?**
   c. **Camel Box: 8 birds sang. Then 6 of them flew away. How many birds were *left?***
   d. **Daffodil Box: 8 nests were in the trees. Then a storm blew down 3 of them. How many nests were *still* in the trees?**
   e. **Elephant Box: Sara saw 7 yellow birds. Ruth saw 3 green birds. How many birds did *both* girls see?**
   f. **Feather Box: 8 birds were eating on the feeder. Then 7 of them flew away. How many birds were *still* on the feeder?**
2. Do the fraction samples on the chalkboard.

Practice Sheets

- ● Form D (*Follow-up* drill #1)
- ☐ Fact Houses #39
- ☐ Form F: 71–170
- ☐ Skip Counting #5
- ● Number Facts #51
- ● Clocks #8

Objectives

New

WORKBOOK

Subtraction Family 9
Column addition (+ 3)

Review

Mixed addition and subtraction
Smaller (150's)
Fractions $\frac{1}{4}$, $\frac{2}{4}$, $\frac{3}{4}$

Preparation

Make Subtraction Family 9 flash cards for each child.

Materials

Mixed flash cards: Addition and Subtraction Families 7 and 8

Form C for each child

Chalkboard

(*Class Time* #2)

(*Class Time* #3)

110	111	101	120	150	130
159	139	129	146	126	136
152	142	132	117	118	119

(*Class Time* #4)

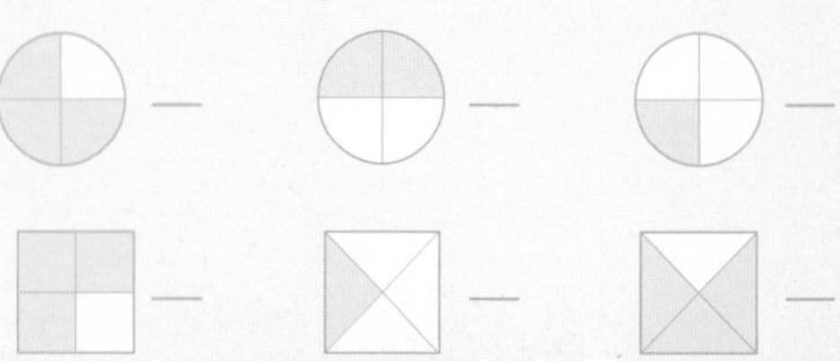

Class Time

1. *Mixed fact drill.*
   a. Double Drill with mixed flash cards for Addition and Subtraction Families 7 and 8.
   b. Distribute Form C, and continue with mixed facts. **Watch the signs! Apron Row: Box 1—Box 2 . . .**
2. *Practice Subtraction Family 9.*
   a. Use the flannel board for story facts.
   (1) **9 ants crawled on the picnic table. Nobody brushed them off. 9 ants still crawled on the picnic table. 9 ants - 0 ants = 9 ants.**
   (2) **9 ants crawled on the picnic table. Jean brushed 1 off. 8 ants still crawled on the picnic table. 9 ants - 1 ant = 8 ants.**
   (3) **9 ants crawled on the picnic table. Jean brushed 2 ants off. . . .**
   b. **Say Subtraction Family 9 as I fill the houses.**

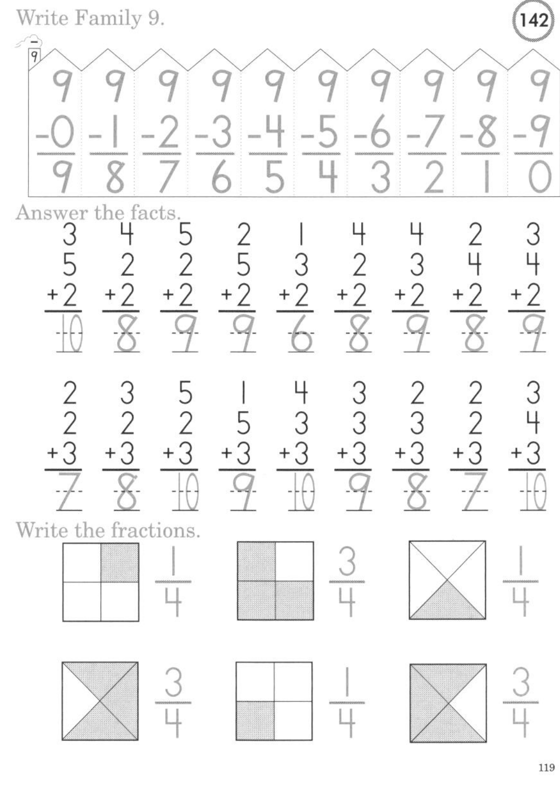
Write Family 9. (142)

9	9	9	9	9	9	9	9	9	9
-0	-1	-2	-3	-4	-5	-6	-7	-8	-9
9	8	7	6	5	4	3	2	1	0

Answer the facts.

3	4	5	2	1	4	4	2	3
5	2	2	5	3	2	3	4	4
+2	+2	+2	+2	+2	+2	+2	+2	+2
10	8	9	9	6	8	9	8	9

2	3	5	1	4	3	2	2	3
2	2	2	5	3	3	3	2	4
+3	+3	+3	+3	+3	+3	+3	+3	+3
7	8	10	9	10	9	8	7	10

Write the fractions.

$\frac{1}{4}$ $\frac{3}{4}$ $\frac{1}{4}$

$\frac{3}{4}$ $\frac{1}{4}$ $\frac{3}{4}$

119

Speed Drill Answers

3	9	2	4	8	6	7
10	3	9	2	4	8	6
5	10	3	9	2	4	8

Speed Drill #58

3. *Smaller numbers.*
   Point to the chalkboard samples. **Can you find the smallest number in each box?**
4. *Fractions.*
   Do the chalkboard samples.
5. *Do Speed Drill #58.*
6. *Assign Lesson 142.*

Follow-up

Drill

(*Drill* #2)

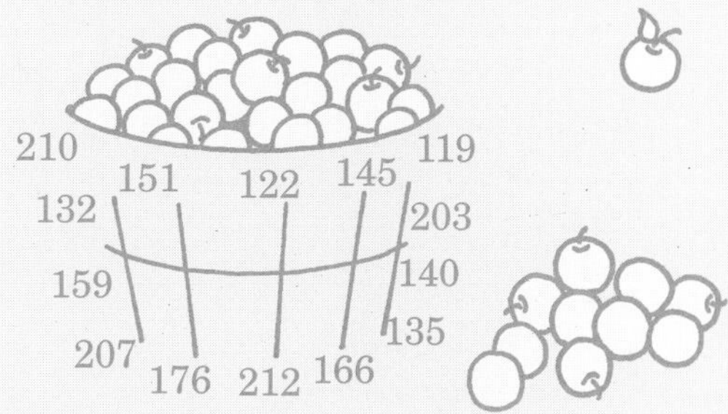

1. Give each child his Subtraction Family 9 flash cards.
2. Call the children to the basket of apples on the board.
   a. Review place value with the motion.
   b. Point to the apple with the leaf.
      1 apple.
      Point to the apples on the ground.
      1 pile of 10 apples.
      Point to the apples in the basket.
      1 basket of 100 apples.
   c. **1 apple, 10 apples, 100 apples. Which amount is the greatest? A number in the hundreds' place is greater than a number in the tens' place. A number in the hundreds' place is much greater than a number in the ones' place.**
   d. **Let's read the numbers.**
3. Stand in a circle. **We will count around the circle by 5's. I will say the first number. 5, . . .**

Practice Sheets

- Form C (*Class Time* #1)
- ☐ Fact Houses #40
- ☐ Measures #6
- Number Facts #52
- Less Numbers #22

Objectives

Review

Addition and Subtraction Family 9
Count by 25's
Mixed counting (5's and 1's)
Fractions $\frac{1}{3}$, $\frac{2}{3}$
Money
Place value

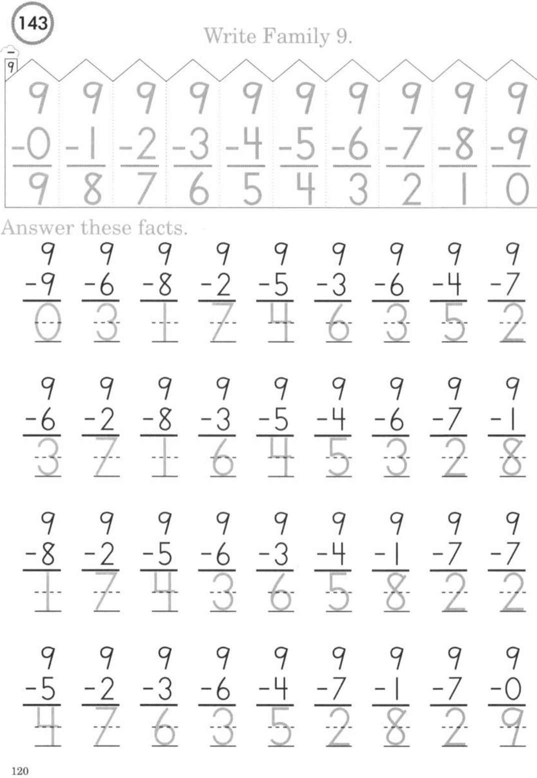

Preparation

Tack Subtraction Family 9 flash cards above the flannel board with answers showing.

Materials

Large coins

Addition Families 8–10 flash cards

Chalkboard

(*Class Time* #1)

(*Class Time* #2)

(*Class Time* #4)

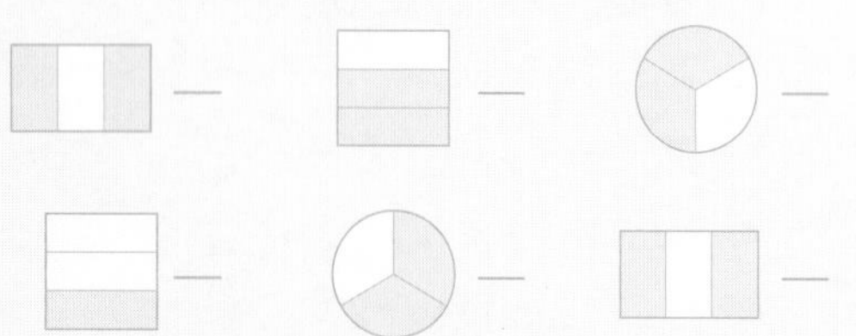

Class Time

1. *Practice Subtraction Family 9.*
   a. Call the children to the flannel board. **Say Subtraction Family 9 as I move the felt blocks.**
   b. Point to the flash cards above the flannel board. **Say each fact once. 9 minus 0, 9 . . .**
   c. Ask a child to fill the houses as you say Family 9 together.
2. *Drill Addition and Subtraction Family 9.*
   a. Write 0 + 9 in the first tree. Ask a child to write the other three facts that are made with the same numbers.
   b. Let individuals fill in other groups of four facts.
   c. Point to the facts as you say them together in groups of four—addition twins followed by reflecting subtraction twins.
3. *Skip counting and mixed counting.*
   a. **Count by 25's** three times.
   b. **Count by 5's and 1's.**
   5, 10, 15, 20, 25, 30, 35, 36, 37, 38

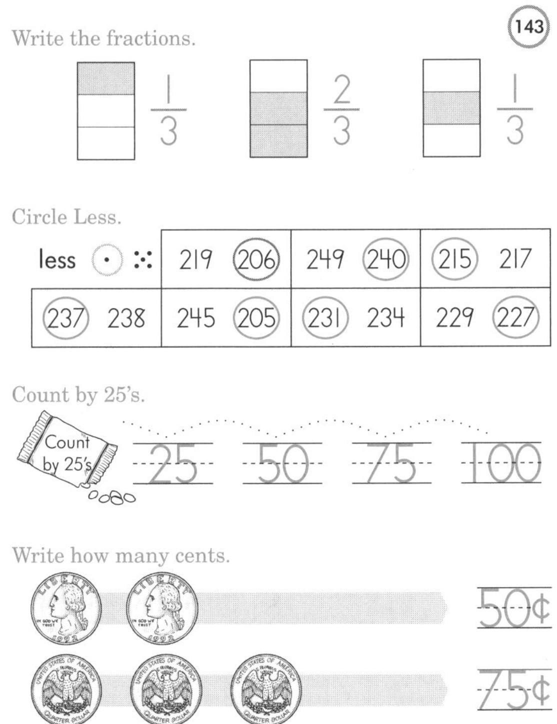
Write the fractions. 143

1/3 2/3 1/3

Circle Less.

less ⊙ ∴	219 (206)	249 (240)	(215) 217
(237) 238	245 (205)	(231) 234	229 (227)

Count by 25's.

25 50 75 100

Write how many cents.

50¢

75¢

121

5, 10, 11, 12, 13, 14, 15
5, 10, 15, 20, 21, 22, 23, 24
5, 10, 15, 20, 25, 30, 35, 40, 45, 46, 47

4. *Fractions.*
   Do the chalkboard samples.
5. *Money.*
   Set the large coins on the chalk tray. To answer each of your questions, have a child choose one of the coins, hold it up, and say its name and value.
   a. **Which coin is worth 5¢?**
      Which coin is worth 25¢?
      Which coin is worth 1¢? . . . 10¢?
   b. **Which coin is worth the same as 25 pennies? . . . 5 pennies? . . . 10 pennies?**
   c. **Which coin is worth the same as 2 nickels? . . . 5 nickels?**
6. *Place value.*
   Review place value with the motion. **Which place has the greatest numbers?** (the hundreds' place)
7. *Assign Lesson 143.*

Follow-up

Drill

1. Drill Addition Families 8–10 flash cards.
2. Chalkboard drill: **I will count a few numbers. When I stop, write the number that I should say next.**
   165, 166, 167, ___
   101, 102, 103, ___
   20, 30, 40, ___
   70, 80, 90, ___
   22, 24, 26, ___
   16, 18, 20, ___
   89, 88, 87, ___
   33, 32, 31, ___
3. Call individuals to the flannel board. **Move the felt blocks and say Subtraction Family 9 for me.**

Practice Sheets

- ☐ Fact Houses #41
- ☐ Money #19
- ☐ Measures #3
- ● Number Facts #53
- ● Story Problems #3

Objectives

New

TEACHING

Square

Review

Addition and Subtraction Family 9

Number triplets

12 inches = 1 foot

Fractions $\frac{1}{4}$, $\frac{2}{4}$, $\frac{3}{4}$

Count by 2's

After (by 2's)

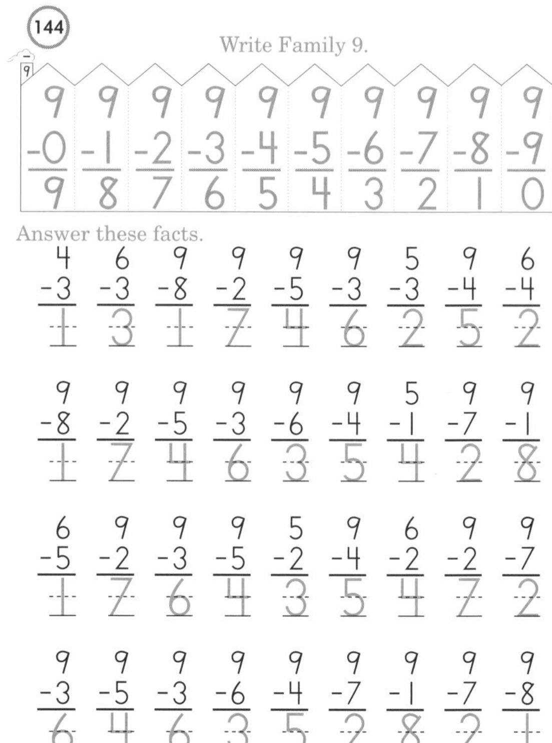

Preparation

Materials

12-inch ruler

Subtraction Families 5, 6, and 9 flash cards

Penny, nickel, dime, and quarter

Chalkboard

(Draw a square with 12-inch sides for *Class Time* #4.)

(*Class Time* #5)

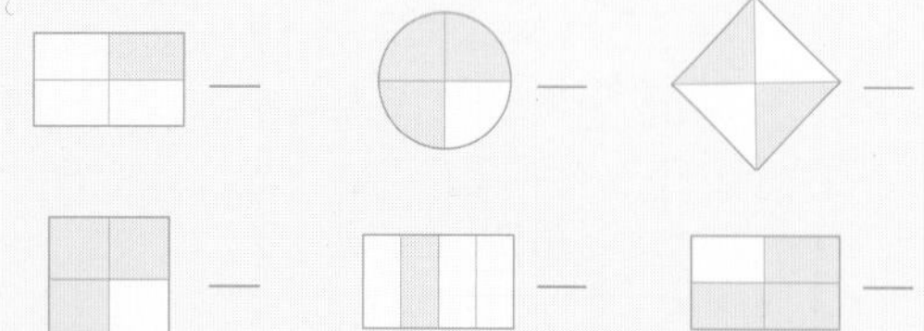

(*Class Time* #6)

8 ___ ___	64 ___ ___
52 ___ ___	46 ___ ___
80 ___ ___	92 ___ ___
30 ___ ___	28 ___ ___

Class Time

1. *Review Subtraction Family 9.*
   a. Use the flannel board for story facts.
      (1) **9 robins hopped on the lawn. 0 robins flew away. 9 robins were still hopping on the lawn. 9 robins – 0 robins = 9 robins.**
      (2) **9 robins hopped on the lawn. 1 robin flew away. . . .**
   b. Point to the flash cards above the flannel board. **Say each fact three times with your eyes open, and then three times with your eyes closed.**
2. *Drill Addition and Subtraction Family 9.* **Who can say four facts with the numbers 9, 3, 6?** Practice with other triplets of Family 9 as well.
3. *Review 12 inches = 1 foot.* Hold a 12-inch ruler. **12 inches make 1 foot. 12 inches make . . .**
4. *Teach* square.
   a. Measure each side of the square on the chalkboard. **12 inches, 12 inches, . . .**

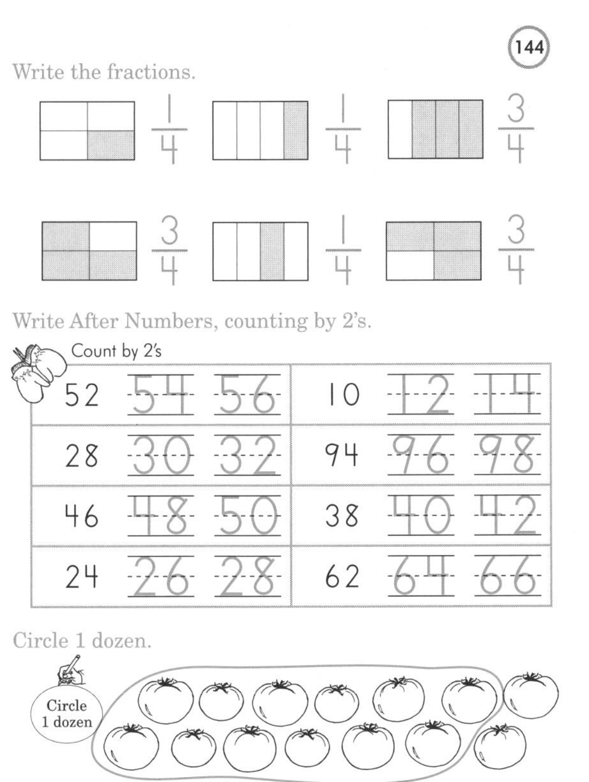

144

Write the fractions.

1/4 1/4 3/4

3/4 1/4 3/4

Write After Numbers, counting by 2's.

Count by 2's

52	54	56	10	12	14
28	30	32	94	96	98
46	48	50	38	40	42
24	26	28	62	64	66

Circle 1 dozen.

123

Speed Drill Answers

2	6	8	2	5	7	4
6	8	2	5	7	4	3
8	2	5	7	4	3	1

Speed Drill #59

Each side of this block measures the same.

b. **This block is square.** Write the word inside the block with a large square S. Drill the term. **Square, square, square.**

Square

5. *Fractions.*
   Do the chalkboard samples.
6. *Count by 2's.*
   a. Call the children to the number line. **Count by 2's to 100.**
   b. Count by 2's to do the After Number samples on the chalkboard.
7. *Do Speed Drill #59.*
8. *Assign Lesson 144.*

Note: Basic shapes have been employed in fraction figures. If you have been using the names of these shapes, the children probably know them. A series of lessons now includes specific teaching on recognition of shapes for those who need it, and can be used to teach the words.

Follow-up

Drill

1. Circle Drill with Subtraction Families 5, 6, and 9 flash cards.
2. Stand near the calendar. **What day of the week is April 21?**
   April 9? **April 12?**
   April 25? **April 3?**
   April 6? **April 15?**
3. Show the large coins. Have individuals name them and tell how much each is worth.

Practice Sheets

- ☐ Fact Houses #40
- ☐ Skip Counting #5
- ☐ Clocks #9
- ● Number Facts #52
- ● Number Facts #53

Objectives

New

TEACHING
- Circle

Review
- Subtraction facts
- Square
- Telling time
- Place value

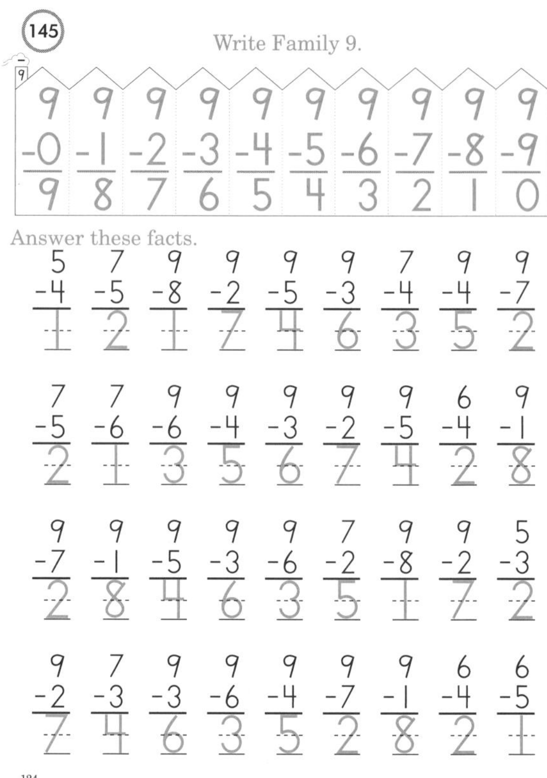

Preparation

Materials

Subtraction Families 5–7 and 9 flash cards

Model clock

Addition Families 7–10 flash cards

Chalkboard

(*Class Time* #1)

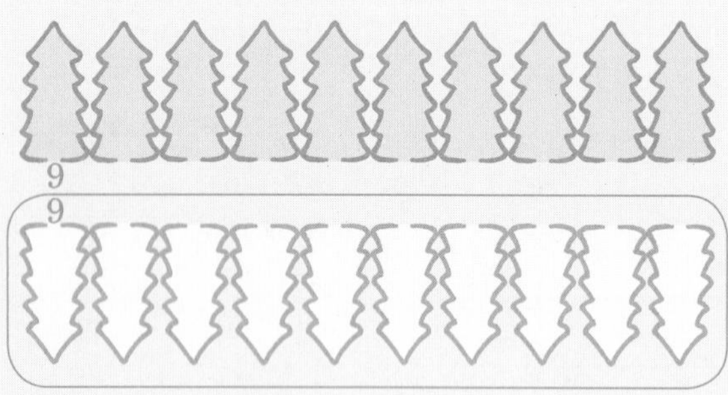

(*Class Time* #3)

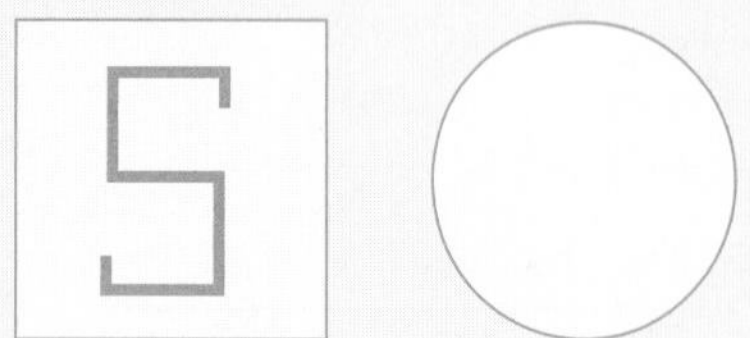

(*Class Time* #5)

Class Time

1. *Review Subtraction Family 9.*
   a. Point to the flash cards above the flannel board. **Say each fact five times.**
   b. **Watch my fingers as you say Family 9 together.** (Show the subtrahend number for each fact.)
   c. **Say Addition and Subtraction Family 9 as I fill the trees.**
2. *Drill subtraction facts.*
   Double Drill with Subtraction Families 5–7 and 9 flash cards.
3. *Shapes.*
   a. Review the square. **This is a ___.**
   A square has 1, 2, 3, 4 corners.
   A square has 1, 2, 3, 4 sides. The four sides are the same size.
   b. Introduce the circle. **This is a circle.** Follow the ring with your finger, around and around. **A circle does not have any corners. A circle does not show any place to start and stop.**

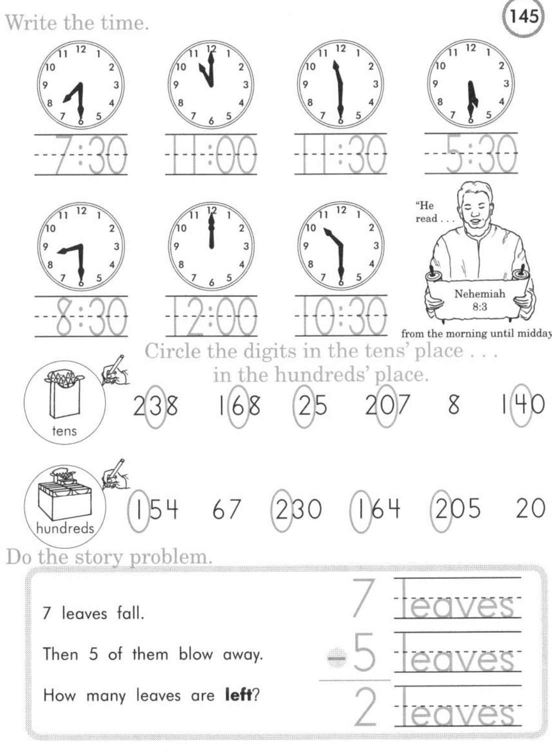
145

Write the time.

7:30 11:00 11:30 5:30

8:30 12:00 10:30

Circle the digits in the tens' place . . .
in the hundreds' place.

tens: 238 168 25 207 8 140

hundreds: 154 67 230 164 205 20

Do the story problem.

7 leaves fall.
Then 5 of them blow away.
How many leaves are **left**?

7 leaves
− 5 leaves
2 leaves

125

c. Write the word inside the figure, using a large round C that circles part of the word. **Circle, circle, circle.**

4. *Telling time.*
   a. Hold the model clock. **Name the clock hands.**
   b. Set the clock at 12:30. **Say the time together.** 4:30, 6:30, 8:00, 11:30, 1:00, 3:30, 6:00, 12:00.
   c. **God's silver moonbeams light the earth at 12:00 ___.** (midnight)
   d. **God's golden sunbeams light the earth at 12:00 ___.** (noon) **One day the people of Israel were so eager to hear the Word of God that Ezra the priest read the Law to them from morning until noon.**
5. *Place value.*
   a. Review **Ones, tens, hundreds** with the motion.
   b. Point to the smallest apple. **Which number is in the ones' place?**
   c. Point to the middle-sized apple. **Which number is in the tens' place?**
   d. Point to the largest apple. **Which number is in the hundreds' place?**
   e. Circle the three 2's. **2 ones, 2 tens, 2 hundreds. Which 2 means the greatest amount?** (2 hundreds)
6. *Assign Lesson 145.*

Follow-up

Drill

(*Drill* #1)

___ 46 ___ ___ 98 ___
___ 24 ___ ___ 60 ___
___ 32 ___ ___ 74 ___

1. **Count by 2's to fill in the Before and After Numbers on the board.**
2. Drill individuals with Addition Families 7–10 flash cards.
3. **If you saved 8 dimes in your bank, you would have ___. Continue with**

6 nickels	(30¢)	**24 pennies**	(24¢)
1 quarter	(25¢)	**3 dimes**	(30¢)
8 nickels	(40¢)	**7 nickels**	(35¢)
9 dimes	(90¢)	**2 quarters**	(50¢)
3 nickels	(15¢)	**9 nickels**	(45¢)

Practice Sheets

- ☐ Fact Houses #41
- ☐ Missing Numbers #13
- ☐ Measures #4
- ● Number Facts #54
- ● Form F: 81–180
- ● Fractions #4

Objectives

New

TEACHING

2-digit subtraction

Review

Number triplets
Subtraction facts
Count by 2's
Mixed counting (10's and 1's)
Unit fractions
Circle and square

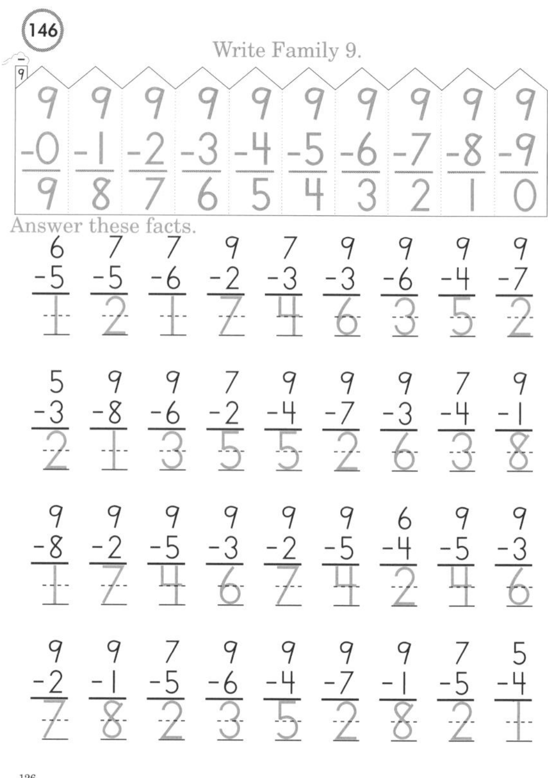

146

Write Family 9.

9	9	9	9	9	9	9	9	9	9
-0	-1	-2	-3	-4	-5	-6	-7	-8	-9
9	8	7	6	5	4	3	2	1	0

Answer these facts.

6	7	7	9	7	9	9	9	9
-5	-5	-6	-2	-3	-3	-6	-4	-7
1	2	1	7	4	6	3	5	2

5	9	9	7	9	9	9	7	9
-3	-8	-6	-2	-4	-7	-3	-4	-1
2	1	3	5	5	2	6	3	8

9	9	9	9	9	9	6	9	9
-8	-2	-5	-3	-2	-5	-4	-5	-3
1	7	4	6	7	4	2	4	6

9	9	7	9	9	9	9	7	5
-2	-1	-5	-6	-4	-7	-1	-5	-4
7	8	2	3	5	2	8	2	1

126

Preparation

Materials

Shape cards for square and circle (See patterns on page 603.)

Subtraction Families 5–7 and 9 flash cards

Large thermometer

Subtraction Families 5–7 and 9 flash cards

Chalkboard

(Write a set of these facts for each child to trace in *Class Time* #1.)

9	9
-6	-7
3	2

(*Class Time* #5)

Class Time

1. *Practice Subtraction Family 9.*
   a. Use the flannel board for story facts.
   (1) **9 bugs crawled on a bush. A hen ate 0 bugs. 9 bugs were left on the bush. 9 bugs - 0 bugs = 9 bugs.**
   (2) **9 bugs crawled on a bush. A hen ate 1 bug. . . .**
   b. Have each child stand near his set of facts on the board. **Trace and whisper the facts until I say "stop."**
   c. Say one of the triplets for Family 9. Ask for the addition and subtraction facts that can be made with those numbers.
2. *Drill subtraction facts.*
   For one minute, flash Subtraction Families 5–7 and 9 cards. **Answer together.**

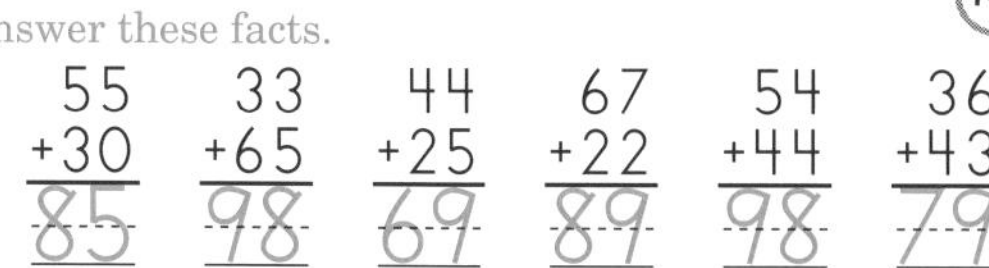

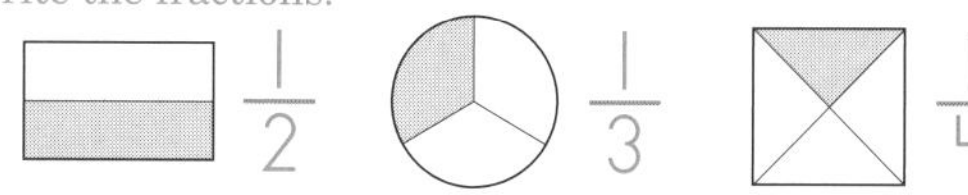

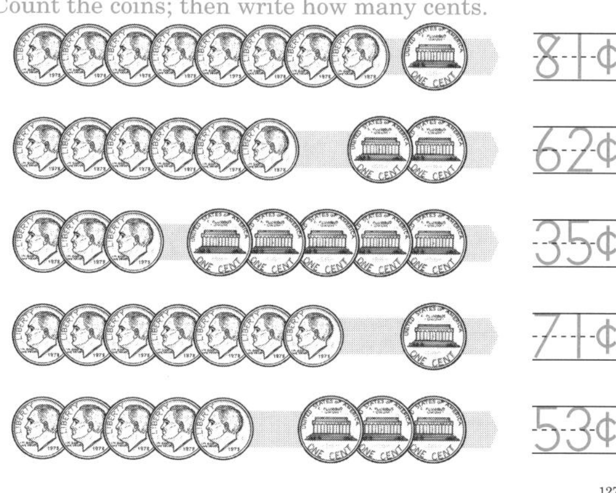

Speed Drill Answers

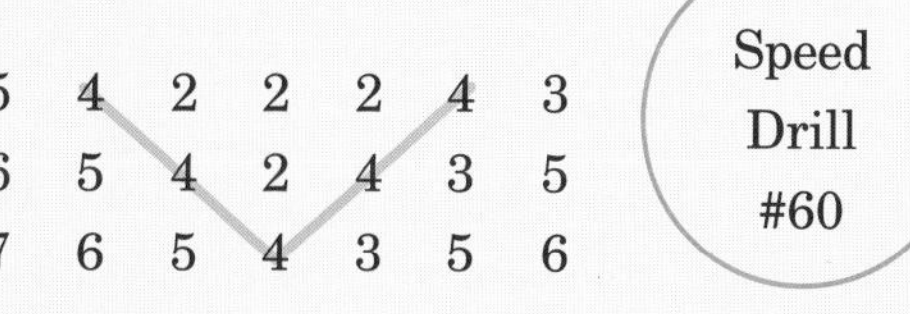

3. *Count by 2's on the thermometer.*
   Set the mercury at 92°. **What is the temperature? 2, 4, 6, . . . 92°. Ice cream melts quickly when the thermometer says 92°.**
4. *Count by 10's and 1's.*
   Watch the pointer as we count by 10's and 1's.
   10, 20, 30, 40, 41, 42, 43, 44, 45
   10, 11, 12, 13, 14, 15, 16, 17
   10, 20, 30, 40, 50, 60, 61, 62
   10, 20, 21, 22, 23, 24, 25
5. *Fractions.*
   Do the chalkboard samples.
6. *Shapes.*
   Drill the cards for circle and square.
7. *Do Speed Drill #60.*
8. *Assign Lesson 146.*

Follow-up

Drill

(*Drill* #2)

(Use white chalk to write the digits in the ones' place and green chalk for digits in the tens' place.)

↓	↓	↓	↓	↓	↓
65	39	92	50	74	49
- 52	- 26	- 61	- 20	- 32	- 37

1. Drill individuals with Subtraction Families 5–7 and 9 flash cards.
2. Introduce two-digit subtraction.
   a. Point to the first two-digit problem. **See two number facts standing together. Which fact is in the ones' place?** (5 - 2)
   b. Trace the arrow. **Ones' place first, ones' place first. 5 - 2 = ___.** (Write 3.) **6 - 5 = ___.** (Write 1.)
   c. Trace the arrow in the next problem. **Ones' place first, ones' place first.** Ask a child to answer the problem. Continue.

Practice Sheets

- ☐ Fact Houses #42
- ● Number Facts #54
- ● Before and After #16
- ● Place Value #3
- ◊ Shapes #1

Objectives

New

TEACHING

2-digit subtraction
Triangle

Review

Addition and subtraction
Number triplets
Money
Count by 25's
Fractions $\frac{1}{3}$, $\frac{2}{3}$

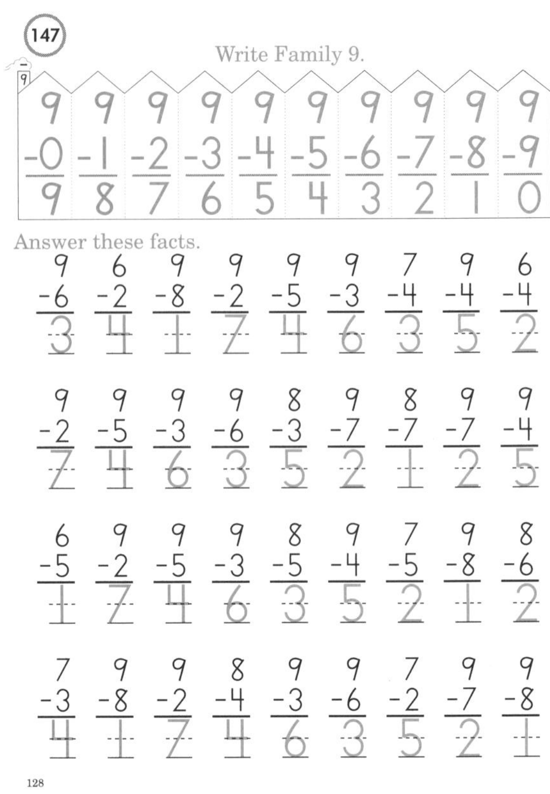

147

Write Family 9.

9	9	9	9	9	9	9	9	9	9
-0	-1	-2	-3	-4	-5	-6	-7	-8	-9
9	8	7	6	5	4	3	2	1	0

Answer these facts.

9	6	9	9	9	9	7	9	6
-6	-2	-8	-2	-5	-3	-4	-4	-4
3	4	1	7	4	6	3	5	2

9	9	9	9	8	9	8	9	9
-2	-5	-3	-6	-3	-7	-7	-7	-4
7	4	6	3	5	2	1	2	5

6	9	9	9	8	9	7	9	8
-5	-2	-5	-3	-5	-4	-5	-8	-6
1	7	4	6	3	5	2	1	2

7	9	9	8	9	9	7	9	9
-3	-8	-2	-4	-3	-6	-2	-7	-8
4	1	7	4	6	3	5	2	1

128

Preparation

Materials

Large coins
Subtraction Families 6–9 flash cards
Shape cards for square and circle

Chalkboard

(*Class Time* #1)

(*Class Time* #3)

49	76	97	65	78	94	83
- 35	- 43	- 25	- 42	- 53	- 41	- 63

(*Class Time* #6)

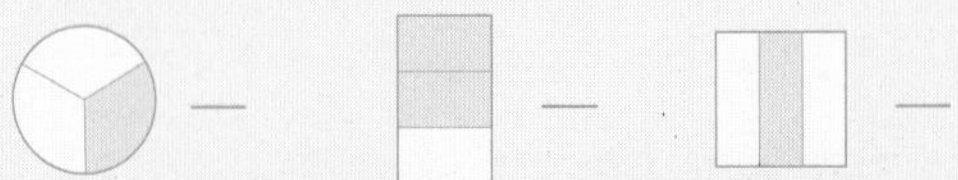

Class Time

1. *Review Subtraction Families 8 and 9.*
   a. **Say Subtraction Family 8 as I move the felt blocks.**
   b. Ask a child to fill the 8 Houses as you repeat the facts together.
   c. **Say Subtraction Family 9 as I move the blocks.**
   d. Ask a child to fill the 9 Houses as you repeat the facts together.
2. *Drill Addition and Subtraction Family 9.* Ask someone for three numbers that can be used to make fact twins in Family 9. Let another child say the four facts and then give three more numbers for the next facts.
3. *Two-digit subtraction.* Point to the samples. **Ones' place first, ones' place first.** Have the children answer the problems.

147

Answer these facts.

45	33	74	37	56	35
+33	+56	+25	+30	+42	+42
78	89	99	67	98	77

Write the Before and After numbers.

139	140	141	168	169	170
136	137	138	151	152	153
103	104	105	195	196	197
169	170	171	118	119	120

Write how many cents.

100¢

50¢

75¢

129

4. *Review money.*
   a. Hold up each coin.
   Penny, 1¢; penny, 1¢; . . .
   Nickel, 5¢; nickel, 5¢; . . .
   Dime, 10¢; dime, 10¢; . . .
   Quarter, 25¢; quarter, 25¢; . . .
   b. **We count pennies by ___, nickels by ___, dimes by ___, and quarters by ___.**
5. *Count by 25's.*
   Point to the number line. **Count by 25's** three times.
6. *Fractions.*
   Do the chalkboard samples.
7. *Assign Lesson 147.*

Follow-up

Drill

(*Drill* #2)

6 nickels = ___	1 quarter = ___
3 dimes = ___	3 nickels = ___
2 quarters = ___	10 dimes = ___
8 nickels = ___	3 quarters = ___
9 dimes = ___	5 nickels = ___

(*Drill* #3)

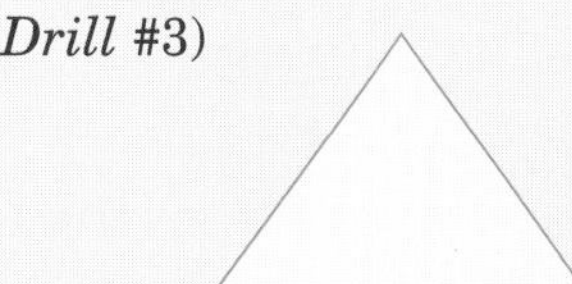

1. Circle Drill with Subtraction Families 6–9 flash cards.
2. Have the children answer the money samples. **Use your fingers to help you figure the answers.**
3. Drill the shape cards for square and circle. Introduce the triangle.
   a. Point to the shape on the board. **This is a triangle.** Label the triangle, using a large *T* with a slanting top.

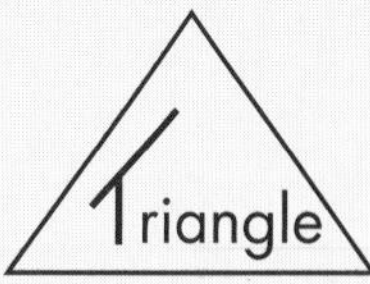

   Triangle, triangle, . . .
   b. **A triangle has 1, 2, 3 corners.**
   A triangle has 1, 2, 3 sides.
   Post geometric shape cards on the wall for convenient review.

Practice Sheets

- ☐ Fact Houses #42
- ☐ Skip Counting #6
- ● Number Facts #54
- ● Story Problems #4
- ● Fractions #4

Objectives

New

WORKBOOK

2-digit subtraction

Review

Addition and subtraction
Count by 2's
Mixed counting (5's and 1's)
Money

148

Write Family 9.

9	9	9	9	9	9	9	9	9	9
-0	-1	-2	-3	-4	-5	-6	-7	-8	-9
9	8	7	6	5	4	3	2	1	0

Answer these facts.

7	7	9	9	8	9	8	9	9
-3	-4	-8	-2	-4	-3	-5	-4	-7
4	3	1	7	4	6	3	5	2

9	9	9	9	8	9	9	9	9
-2	-5	-3	-6	-3	-7	-8	-7	-1
7	4	6	3	5	2	1	2	8

9	9	9	8	9	9	8	7	9
-8	-2	-5	-2	-6	-4	-6	-6	-7
1	7	4	6	3	5	2	1	2

9	9	8	9	9	9	7	9	8
-6	-8	-1	-5	-3	-6	-2	-7	-7
3	1	7	4	6	3	5	2	1

130

Preparation

Materials

Subtraction Families 7–9 flash cards
Form C for each child
Subtraction Families 8 and 9 flash cards
Shape cards: square, circle, and triangle

Chalkboard

(*Class Time* #4)

86	99	75	91	46	88	69
-52	-57	-54	-30	-26	-65	-46

(*Class Time* #6)

5¢ 1¢ ___
5¢ 1¢ ___
5¢ 1¢ ___
5¢ 1¢ ___
5¢ 1¢ ___
5¢ 1¢ ___

Class Time

1. *Drill Addition and Subtraction Family 9.* Ask someone for three numbers that can be used to make fact twins in Family 9. Let another child say the four facts and then give three more numbers for the next facts.
2. *Review Subtraction Families 7–9.*
   a. Distribute the Subtraction Families 7–9 flash cards among the children. **If you have the first fact in Family 7, come set it on the chalk tray . . .**
   b. Stand near the flash cards. **Let's say our fact families together.**
3. *Drill subtraction facts.* Scramble Subtraction Families 7–9 flash cards. Give each child a copy of Form C to write answers. **Apron Row: Box 1—Box 2 . . .**

Answer these facts. (148)

76	64	78	85	73	86
-42	-14	-24	-33	-32	-60
34	50	54	52	41	26

Write Before and After numbers, counting by 2's.

Count by 2's

22	24	26	90	92	94
58	60	62	52	54	56
16	18	20	30	32	34
44	46	48	76	78	80

Circle More.

• (5) more	(249) 234	(248) 247	245 (246)
223 (233)	(217) 207	221 (231)	(239) 235

131

Speed Drill Answers

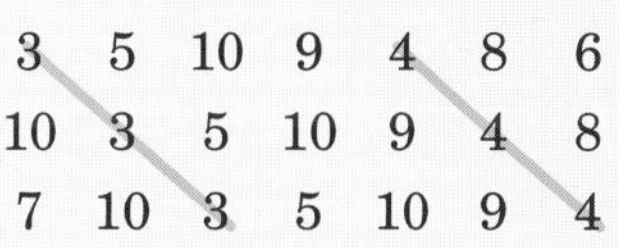

3	5	10	9	4	8	6
10	3	5	10	9	4	8
7	10	3	5	10	9	4

Speed Drill #61

4. *Two-digit subtraction.*
   Do the chalkboard samples. **Ones' place first!**
5. *Count by 2's.*
   Point to the number line. **Count along the number line by 2's.**
6. *Mixed counting and money.*
   a. **Watch the pointer as we count by 5's and change to 1's.**
      5, 10, 15, 20, 21, 22, 23, 24, 25
      5, 6, 7, 8, 9
      5, 10, 15, 16, 17, 18
      5, 10, 15, 20, 25, 26, 27, 28
   b. **Count by 5's and 1s to count the money.** Have the children count aloud and then write the answers to the chalkboard samples.
7. *Do Speed Drill #61.*
8. *Assign Lesson 148.*

Follow-up

Drill

1. Drill individuals with Subtraction Families 8 and 9 flash cards.
2. Drill the shape cards.
   a. **Name some things that have the shape of a square.** (floor or ceiling tile, side of a toy block, hot pad, quilt patch, Post-it Notes, . . .)
   b. **Name some things that have the shape of a circle.** (plate, doughnut, coin, clock face, . . .)
   c. **Name some things that have the shape of a triangle.** (house gable, coat hanger, cat's ear, music note *do*, . . .)
3. Chalkboard drill: **Write 232. Circle the numeral in the ones' place.**
   Write 241—Circle . . . the hundreds' place.
   208 . . . the ones' place
   214 . . . the ones' place
   222 . . . the tens' place
   239 . . . the hundreds' place
   193 . . . the ones' place
   185 . . . the tens' place

Practice Sheets

- ● Form C (*Class Time* #3)
- ☐ Fact Houses #42
- ☐ Money #20
- ☐ Before and After #16
- ● Number Facts #55
- ● Number Facts #56

Objectives

Review

Addition and subtraction
Place value
Counting (190)
Count nickels with pennies
Dozen
12 inches = 1 foot

Preparation

Materials

Footprint poster

Addition and Subtraction Families 6–9 flash cards

Shape cards: circle, square, and triangle

Chalkboard

(*Class Time #2*)

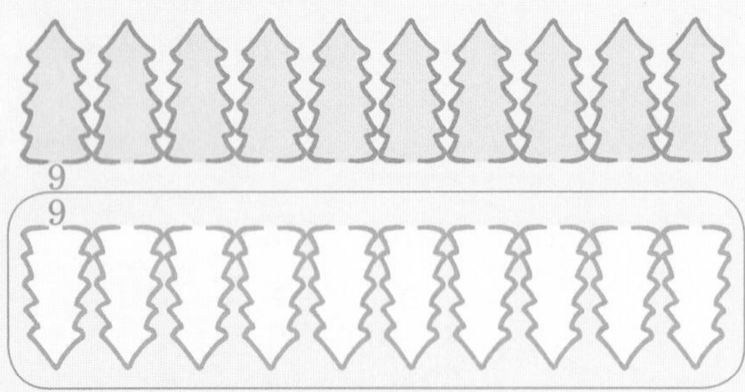

(*Class Time #5*)

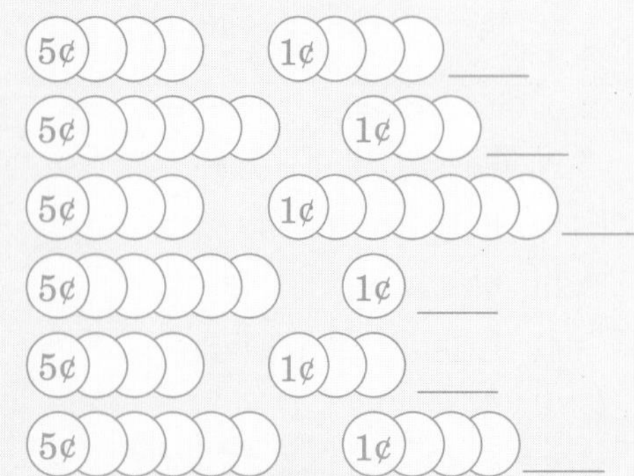

Class Time

1. *Review Subtraction Families 8 and 9.*
   a. **Watch my fingers as we say Subtraction Family 8.**
   b. Use the flannel board for story facts.
   (1) **9 eggs were in mother duck's nest. 0 eggs hatched. 9 eggs were still in the nest. 9 eggs - 0 eggs = 9 eggs.**
   (2) **9 eggs were in mother duck's nest. 1 egg hatched. 8 eggs were still in the nest. 9 eggs - 1 egg . . .**
   c. Point to the flash cards above the flannel board. **Say each fact three times. 9 - 0, 9; 9 - 0, 9 . . .**
   d. **Watch my fingers as we say Subtraction Family 9.**

2. *Drill Addition and Subtraction Family 9.*
   a. Let individuals fill in sets of four facts on the trees and reflection.
   b. Say the facts together in twin order.

149

Answer these facts.

88	68	67	85	48	78
-34	-15	-23	-70	-36	-48
54	53	44	15	12	30

Write the correct digit for ones', tens', or hundreds'.

143 has 1 hundreds		240 has 2 hundreds	
203 has 3 ones		47 has 7 ones	
28 has 2 tens		230 has 3 tens	

Count the coins; then write how many cents.

133

3. *Place value.*
   Motion and say, **Ones, tens, hundreds. Which place has the greatest number?**
4. *Counting.*
   Count by 1's from 90 to 190.
5. *Counting nickels and pennies.*
   Have individuals count the chalkboard samples aloud and then write the answers.
6. *Review dozen and foot.*
   a. **In the henhouse David found 12 brown eggs, or ___ brown eggs.**
   b. **Mary put 12 buns, or ___ buns, in the bag.**
   c. Hold the footprint poster. **12 inches make 1 foot; 12 inches make . . .**
7. *Assign Lesson 149.*

Follow-up

Drill

(*Drill* #2)

___	30	___	___	60	___
___	___	6	___	___	12
___	___	15	___	25	___
36	___	___	42	___	___

1. Double Drill with mixed flash cards: Addition and Subtraction Families 6–9.
2. Stand near the number line.
   a. **Boys, count by 10's to 100.**
   b. **Girls, count by 5's to 100.**
   c. **Everyone count by 2's to 100.**
   d. Point to the chalkboard samples with Missing Numbers. **Decide if you should count by 10's, 5's, or 2's.**
3. Drill the shape cards.

Practice Sheets

- ☐ Fact Houses #43
- ☐ Form F: 91–190
- ☐ Skip Counting #6
- ● Number Facts #55
- ● Clocks #10
- ● Fractions #5

Objectives

New

TEACHING

Subtraction Family 10

Review

Mixed facts
Money
Fractions $\frac{1}{4}$, $\frac{2}{4}$, $\frac{3}{4}$

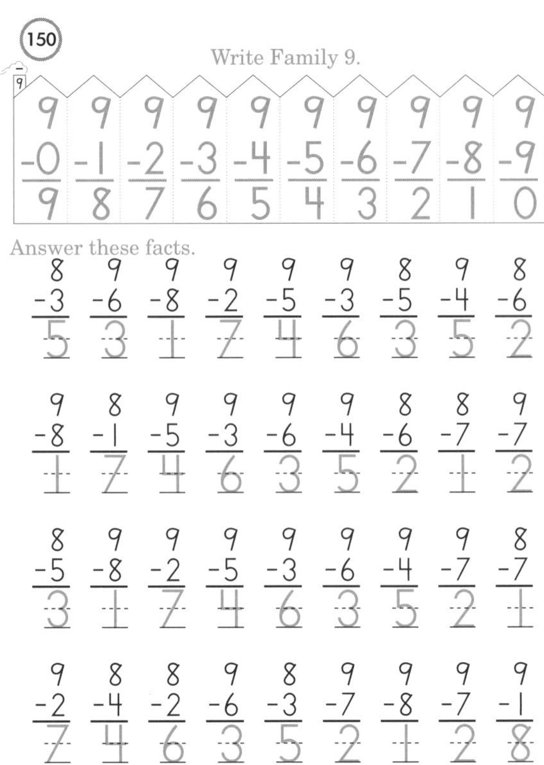

150

Write Family 9.

9	9	9	9	9	9	9	9	9	9
-0	-1	-2	-3	-4	-5	-6	-7	-8	-9
9	8	7	6	5	4	3	2	1	0

Answer these facts.

8	9	9	9	9	9	8	9	8
-3	-6	-8	-2	-5	-3	-5	-4	-6
5	3	1	7	4	6	3	5	2

9	8	9	9	9	9	8	8	9
-8	-1	-5	-3	-6	-4	-6	-7	-7
1	7	4	6	3	5	2	1	2

8	9	9	9	9	9	9	9	8
-5	-8	-2	-5	-3	-6	-4	-7	-7
3	1	7	4	6	3	5	2	1

9	8	8	9	8	9	9	9	9
-2	-4	-2	-6	-3	-7	-8	-7	-1
7	4	6	3	5	2	1	2	8

134

Preparation

Materials

Addition and Subtraction Families 7–9 flash cards

Form C for each child

Large coins

Shape cards: circle, square, triangle

Chalkboard

(*Class Time* #1)

8	8	9	9
- 3	- 5	- 3	- 6
5	3	6	3

(*Class Time* #3)

7 nickels = ____	3 nickels = ____
8 dimes = ____	5 dimes = ____
3 quarters = ____	4 nickels = ____
6 nickels = ____	4 quarters = ____
2 quarters = ____	10 dimes = ____

(*Class Time* #4)

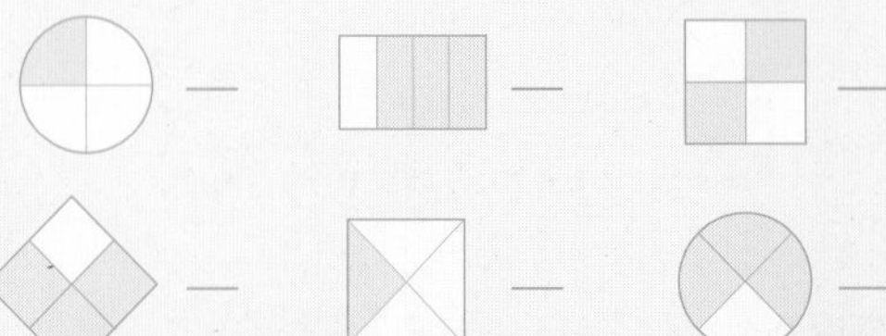

Class Time

1. *Drill selected facts.*
Circle the first fact in the box on the chalkboard. **We will say this fact five times.** Say it slowly the first time, and then faster with each recital. Drill each fact in this way.

2. *Drill mixed facts.*
   a. **Say Addition and Subtraction Family 9 in twin order.** At the beginning of each set of four facts, show the number for the first addend with your fingers.
   b. Distribute Form C. Use Addition and Subtraction Families 7–9 flash cards. **Watch the signs! Apron Row: Box 1—Box 2 . . .**

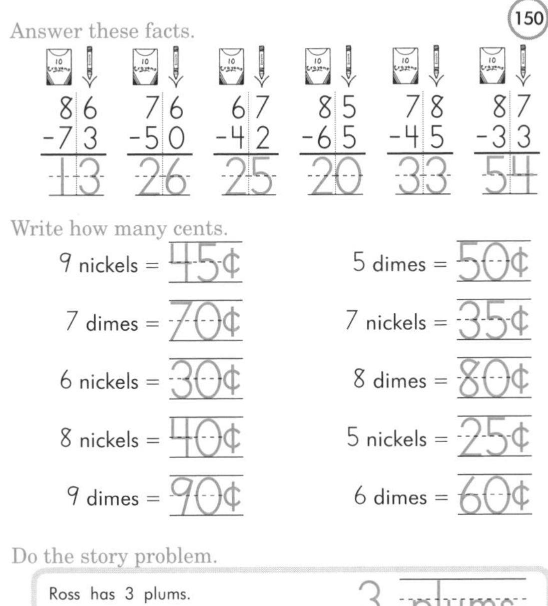

3. *Review and count money.*
   a. Set the large coins on the chalk tray. **Which coin is worth the same as 25 pennies? . . . 10 pennies? . . . 5 pennies?**
   b. **Which coin is worth the same as 2 nickels? . . . 5 nickels?**
   c. **Which coin is worth the same as 1 nickel and 5 pennies? . . . 2 dimes and 5 pennies?**
   d. Do the chalkboard samples.
4. *Fractions.*
   Do the chalkboard samples.
5. *Do Speed Drill #62.*
6. *Assign Lesson 150.*

Speed Drill Answers

3 5 2 4 7 3 6
5 2 4 7 3 6 5
2 4 7 3 6 5 4

Follow-up

Drill

(*Drill* #1)

9 − 3 =	8 − 2 =	7 − 4 =	9 − 6 =	8 − 5 =
9 − 4 =	9 − 7 =	8 − 4 =	7 − 5 =	8 − 3 =
9 − 5 =	9 − 4 =	8 − 6 =	9 − 8 =	8 − 5 =
9 − 2 =	9 − 6 =	9 − 4 =	7 − 5 =	9 − 7 =
9 − 5 =	7 − 3 =	9 − 3 =	7 − 3 =	7 − 2 =

(*Drill* #3)

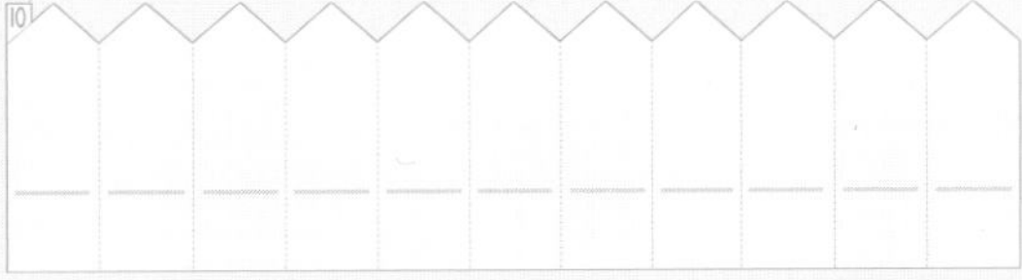

1. Call individuals to the subtraction grid on the chalkboard. Can each child answer all the facts in one minute? (Keep the grid for Lesson 151.)
2. Flash the shape cards.
3. Introduce Subtraction Family 10. **Can you help me fill these houses with Subtraction Family 10?** Write the facts in order.

Practice Sheets

- ● Form C (*Class Time* #2)
- ☐ Fact Houses #43
- ☐ Measures #7
- ● Number Facts #55
- ● Money #20
- ◊ Shapes #2

Objectives

New

TEACHING

Subtraction Family 10

Review

Subtraction Family 9
Telling time
Story problems
Smaller (240's)

151 Answer these facts.

9 − 6 = 3	8 − 7 = 1	9 − 2 = 7	9 − 5 = 4	8 − 2 = 6	8 − 5 = 3	9 − 4 = 5		
8 − 4 = 4	9 − 3 = 6	9 − 6 = 3	9 − 4 = 5	9 − 1 = 8	8 − 5 = 3	9 − 8 = 1	9 − 2 = 7	9 − 7 = 2
9 − 6 = 3	9 − 8 = 1	9 − 2 = 7	9 − 5 = 4	9 − 3 = 6	8 − 5 = 3	8 − 3 = 5	8 − 6 = 2	8 − 7 = 1
9 − 6 = 3	9 − 4 = 5	9 − 7 = 2	9 − 8 = 1	9 − 4 = 5	9 − 2 = 7	9 − 5 = 4	8 − 2 = 6	9 − 7 = 2
8 − 1 = 7	9 − 5 = 4	9 − 3 = 6	9 − 6 = 3	9 − 8 = 1	8 − 6 = 2	8 − 7 = 1	9 − 7 = 2	8 − 3 = 5

136

Preparation

Materials

Model clock
Form E for each child

Chalkboard

(*Class Time* #1)

(*Class Time* #2)

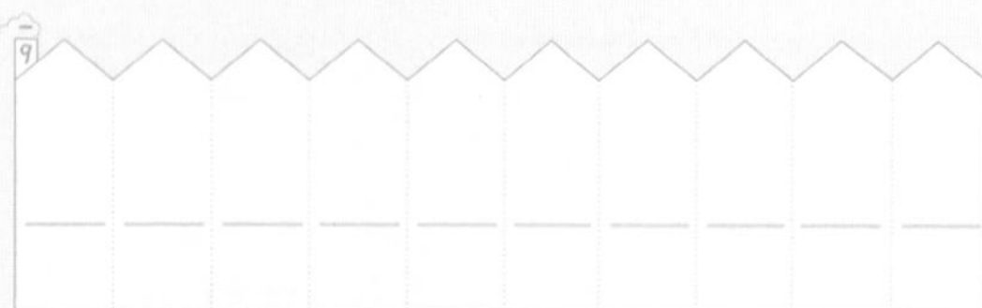

(*Class Time* #5)

202	230	220	156	186	136
214	210	240	120	110	140
231	221	241	189	139	179

Class Time

1. *Review Subtraction Family 9.*
   Station a child at the 9 Houses. **Say the facts as I move the felt blocks and [Hannah] fills the houses.**
2. *Teach Subtraction Family 10.*
   a. **Let's try Subtraction Family 10. 10 blocks; take away 0 blocks . . .**
   b. **Say Family 10 as I fill the houses.** Be careful to write the subtrahend and all 1-digit answers below the zero of the minuend. **Ten is a 2-digit number. All the numbers in the ones' place should be in a straight line.**
3. *Telling time.*
   Set the hands on the model clock at
   2:30. **In 2 hours it will be ___.**
   6:00. **In 2 hours it will be ___.**
   9:00. **Two hours ago it was ___.**
   5:30. **Two hours ago it was ___.**

4. *Oral story problems.*
   a. **Close your eyes to listen. 9 goats are in the meadow. 6 of them run inside the barn. How many goats are *still* in the meadow? Who can give the complete problem?**
   b. **Close your eyes. Jane has 6 pens. Aunt Alice gives her 2 more. How many pens does Jane have *now?* Who can give . . . ?**
5. *Smaller numbers.*
   Point to the chalkboard samples. **Find the number that is smallest.**
6. *Assign Lesson 151.*

Follow-up

Drill

1. Give each child a copy of Form E. **When I say a number, write it in the correct places for ones, tens, and hundreds.**

Column 1	Column 2
175	**9**
241	**164**
63	**203**
207	**54**
5	**211**
130	**7**
101	**138**
228	**12**
56	**239**
189	**106**

2. Drill individuals at the subtraction grid on the chalkboard. (See *Follow-up* in Lesson 150.)
3. **Count by 2's to 100.**

Practice Sheets

- ● Form E (*Follow-up* drill #1)
- ☐ Fact Houses #43
- ☐ Skip Counting #6
- ● Number Facts #55
- ● Before and After #17

Objectives

New

TEACHING

Rectangle

WORKBOOK

Subtraction Family 10

Review

Money

Before and After (by 2's, 5's, 10's)

12 inches = 1 foot

Preparation

Make Subtraction Family 10 flash cards for each child.

Materials

Footprint poster

Shape cards: circle, square, and triangle

Addition Families 8–10 flash cards

Chalkboard

(*Class Time* #1)

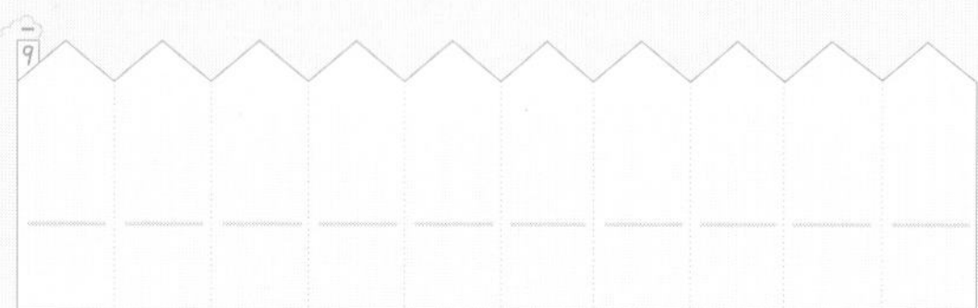

(*Class Time* #2)

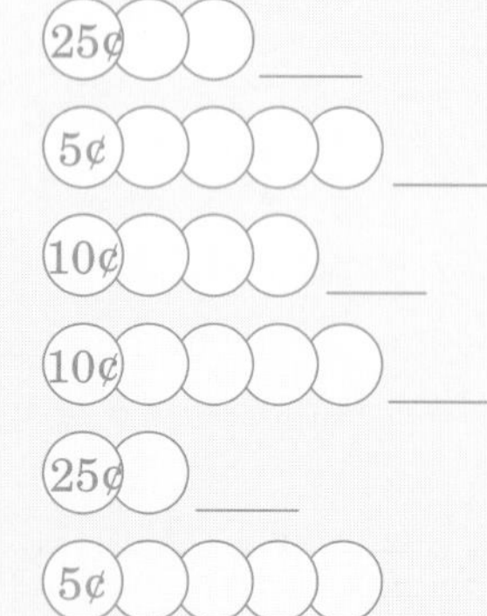

(*Class Time* #3)

___ 42 ___	___ 45 ___	___ 90 ___
___ 68 ___	___ 20 ___	___ 40 ___
___ 36 ___	___ 95 ___	___ 60 ___
___ 50 ___	___ 65 ___	___ 20 ___

Class Time

1. *Review Subtraction Family 10.*
   a. **Say Subtraction Family 10 as I move the felt blocks.**
   b. Ask a child to fill the houses as you say Family 10. Remind him to keep the one-digit numbers in line in the ones' place.
2. *Counting money.*
   a. **We count pennies by ___, nickels by ___, dimes by ___, and quarters by ___.**
   b. Have individuals count aloud and then write answers for the chalkboard samples.
3. *Before and After Numbers in skip counting.* Do the chalkboard samples. Can the children figure out that the first column is counting by 2's, the second column counting by 5's, and the third column counting by 10's?

Write Family 10.

152

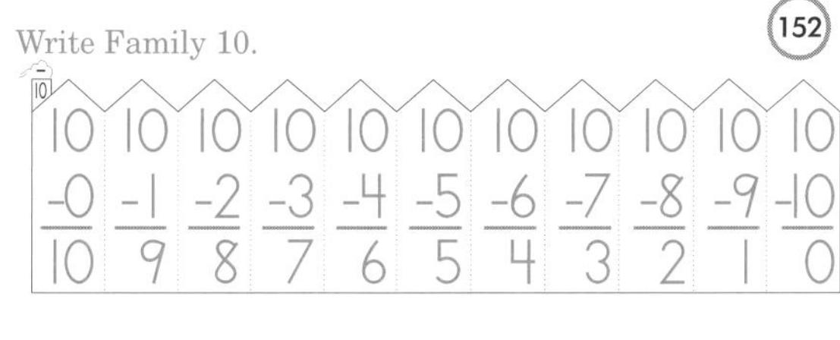

Circle Less.

less ⊙ ∴	241 (211)	249 (248)	210 (209)
243 (242)	238 (237)	(229) 230	218 (208)

Count the coins; then write how many cents.

139

4. *12 inches = 1 foot.*
   a. **12 inches make 1 foot; 12 inches make . . .**
   b. **Nevin sawed a board 12 inches long, or ___ long.**
   c. **Sharon's doll is 12 inches long, or ___ long.**
5. *Do Speed Drill #63.*
6. *Assign Lesson 152.*
   Does this shirt show a time? It is a time to sew, because a button is missing.

Speed Drill Answers

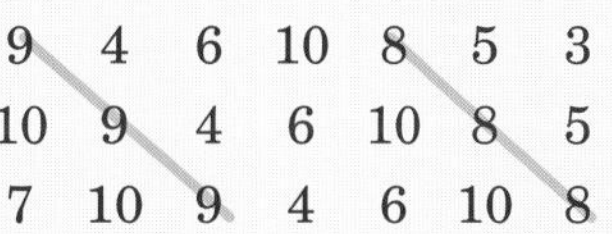

9	4	6	10	8	5	3
10	9	4	6	10	8	5
7	10	9	4	6	10	8

Follow-up

Drill

(*Drill* #2)

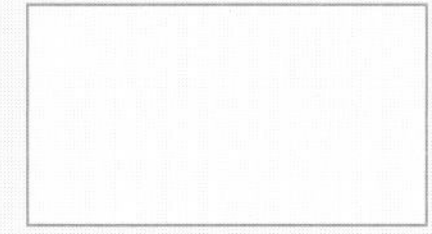

1. Give each child his Subtraction Family 10 flash cards.
2. Drill the shape cards, and then introduce the rectangle.
   a. Point to the shape on the board. **This is a rectangle.** Write the label inside the shape with a rectangular capital *R*.

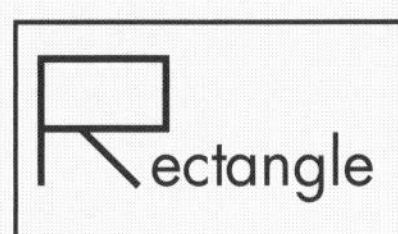

   b. Practice saying the word together. **Rec-tan-gle, rec-tan-gle, . . .**
   c. **A rectangle has 1, 2, 3, 4 corners. A rectangle has two long sides and two short sides.**

   Add a rectangle to the shapes displayed on the wall.
3. Drill Addition Families 8–10 flash cards.

Practice Sheets

- ☐ Fact Houses #44
- ☐ Missing Numbers #14
- ● Number Facts #56
- ● Story Problems #5
- ● Fractions #4

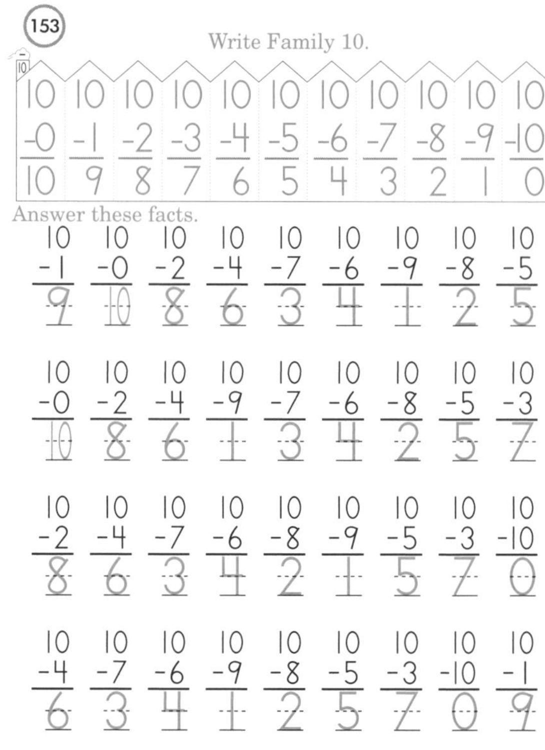
153

Write Family 10.

10	10	10	10	10	10	10	10	10	10	10
-0	-1	-2	-3	-4	-5	-6	-7	-8	-9	-10
10	9	8	7	6	5	4	3	2	1	0

Answer these facts.

10	10	10	10	10	10	10	10	10
-1	-0	-2	-4	-7	-6	-9	-8	-5
9	10	8	6	3	4	1	2	5

10	10	10	10	10	10	10	10	10
-0	-2	-4	-9	-7	-6	-8	-5	-3
10	8	6	1	3	4	2	5	7

10	10	10	10	10	10	10	10	10
-2	-4	-7	-6	-8	-9	-5	-3	-10
8	6	3	4	2	1	5	7	0

10	10	10	10	10	10	10	10	10
-4	-7	-6	-9	-8	-5	-3	-10	-1
6	3	4	1	2	5	7	0	9

140

Objectives

New

TEACHING

Rectangle

Review

Addition facts

Subtraction Family 10

Unit fractions

Preparation

Tack Subtraction Family 10 flash cards above the flannel board with answers showing.

Materials

Addition Families 8–10 flash cards

Shape cards

Form D for each child

Chalkboard

(*Class Time* #2)

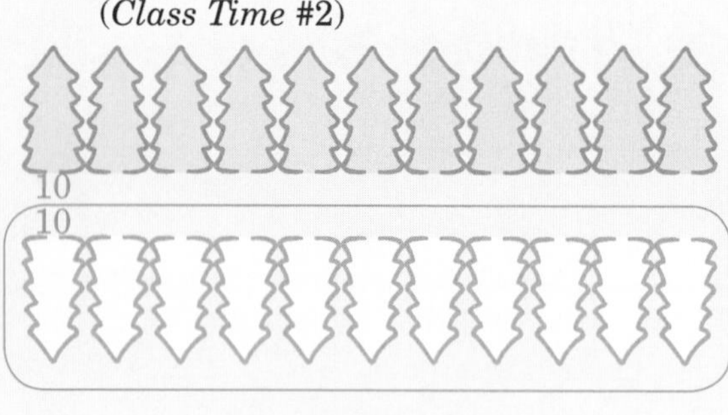

(*Class Time* #3)

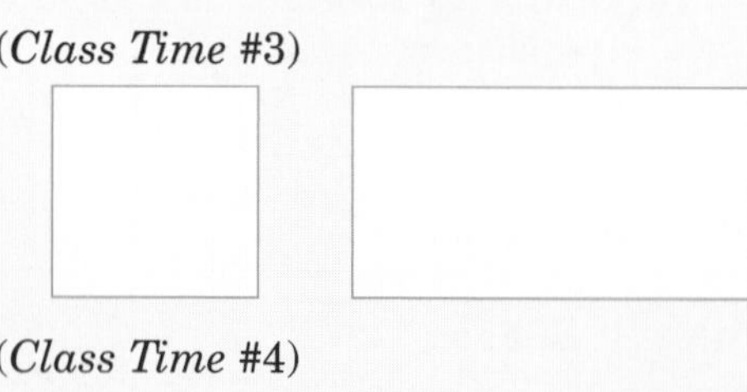

(*Class Time* #4)

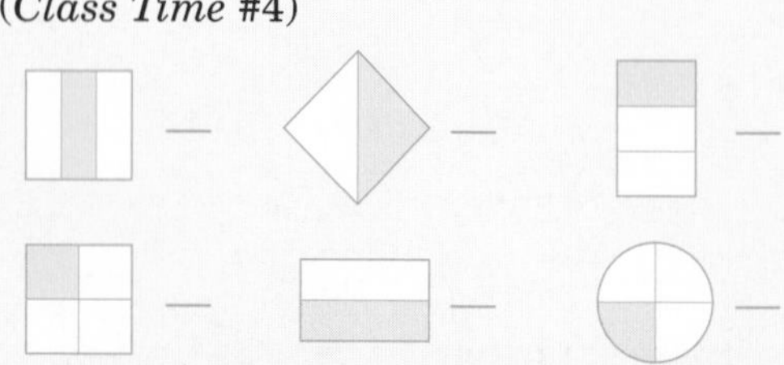

Class Time

1. *Drill addition facts.*
   Flash Addition Families 8–10 cards for one minute. **Answer together.**
2. *Practice Subtraction Family 10.*
   a. Use the flannel board for story facts.
      (1) **10 new pencils were in a box. Leroy sharpened 0 pencils. 10 pencils were left in the box. 10 pencils – 0 pencils = 10 pencils.**
      (2) **Ten pencils were in a box. Leroy sharpened 1 pencil. . . .**
   b. Point to the flash cards above the flannel board. **Say each fact three times with your eyes open, and then three times with your eyes closed.**
   c. Write 0 + 10 in the first tree. Let someone fill in the rest of the facts that use the same numbers. Does he have the ones' place in line?
   d. Let others fill in other groups of four facts. Check the ones' place for alignment.

153

Answer these facts.

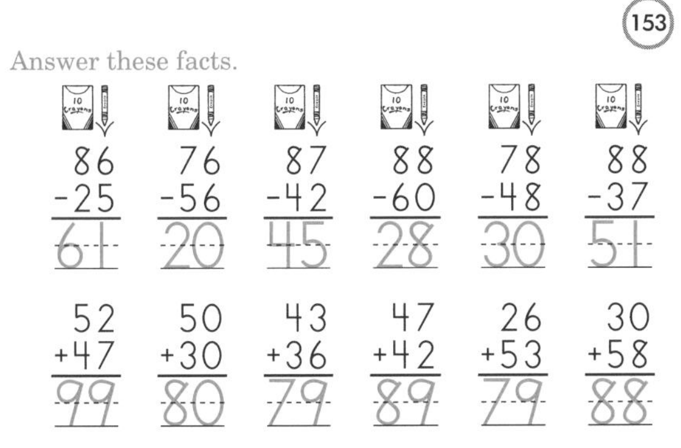

Write the fractions.

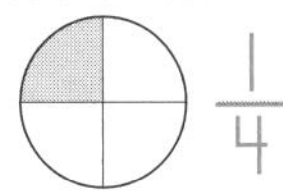

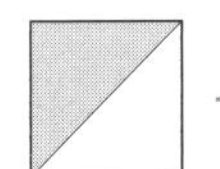

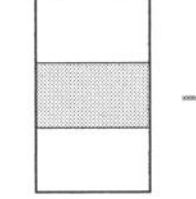

Do the story problem.

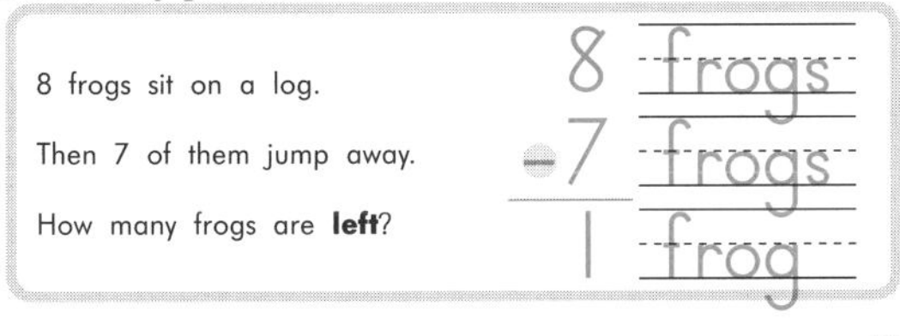

141

3. *Distinguish between square and rectangle.*
   a. Point to the shapes on the board. **Square, square, . . .** **Rectangle, rectangle, . . .**
   b. **They both have 1, 2, 3, 4 corners. They both have 1, 2, 3, 4 sides. A rectangle has two long sides and two short sides. A rectangle might be called a "wrecked square."**
   c. **Name things that are the shape of a rectangle.** (door, bed, window, desktop, book, . . .)
   d. Drill the shape cards.
4. *Fractions.*
   Do the chalkboard samples.
5. *Assign Lesson 153.*

Follow-up

Drill

1. Distribute Form D for story problem dictation. Print *goats* on the chalkboard for a label.
   Decide if you should add or subtract. Put the correct sign in the gray spot.
   a. **Arrow Box: 9 goats eat. Then 5 of them run away. How many goats are *still* eating?**
   b. **Button Box: Father has 6 goats. He buys 3 more goats. How many is that *altogether?***
   c. **Camel Box: 8 brown goats play. Then 3 of them sleep. How many goats are *still* playing?**
   d. **Daffodil Box: 9 white goats climb a hill. Then 2 of them run away. How many goats are *left?***
   e. **Elephant Box: 9 white goats are in the barn. Father sells 6 of them. How many goats are *still* in the barn?**
   f. **Feather Box: 3 brown goats eat hay. 7 brown goats eat grain. How many is that *in all?***
2. Count by 1's from 110–210.

Practice Sheets

- ● Form D (*Follow-up* drill #1)
- ☐ Fact Houses #45
- ☐ Money #21
- ☐ Measures #8
- ● Number Facts #57
- ● Form F: 101–200

Objectives

New

TEACHING

Fraction mixture

WORKBOOK

Fractions with numerator 2

Review

Subtraction Family 10
Place value
Count by 2's
Shapes
Column addition
Mixed addition and subtraction

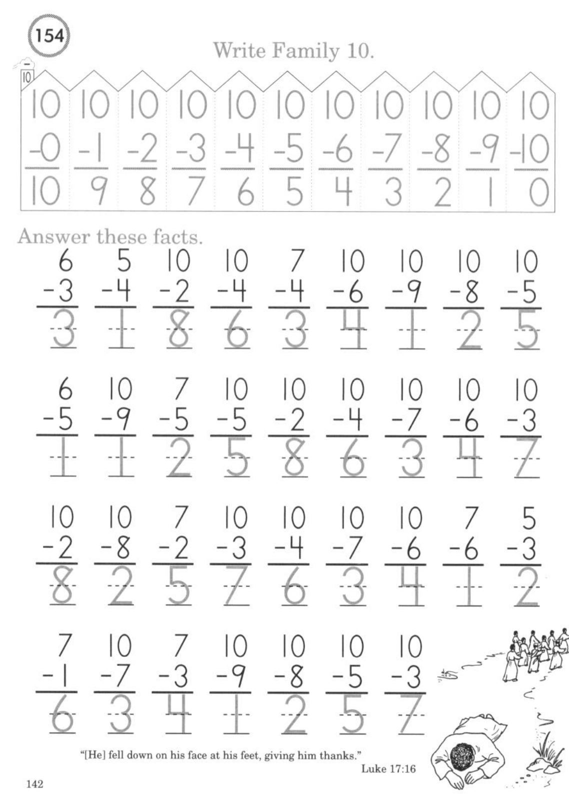

154

Write Family 10.

10	10	10	10	10	10	10	10	10	10	10
-0	-1	-2	-3	-4	-5	-6	-7	-8	-9	-10
10	9	8	7	6	5	4	3	2	1	0

Answer these facts.

6	5	10	10	7	10	10	10	10
-3	-4	-2	-4	-4	-6	-9	-8	-5
3	1	8	6	3	4	1	2	5

6	10	7	10	10	10	10	10	10
-5	-9	-5	-5	-2	-4	-7	-6	-3
1	1	2	5	8	6	3	4	7

10	10	7	10	10	10	10	7	5
-2	-8	-2	-3	-4	-7	-6	-6	-3
8	2	5	7	6	3	4	1	2

7	10	7	10	10	10	10
-1	-7	-3	-9	-8	-5	-3
6	3	4	1	2	5	7

"[He] fell down on his face at his feet, giving him thanks."
Luke 17:16

142

Preparation

Materials

Shape cards

Mixed flash cards: Addition Families 8–10 and Subtraction Families 5–7 and 10

Model clock

Chalkboard

(*Class Time* #1)

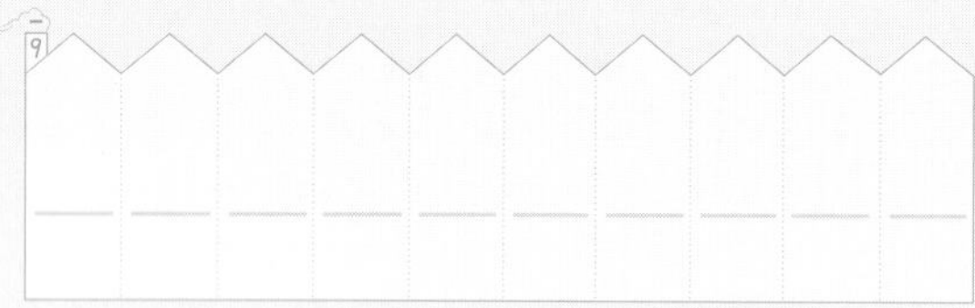

(*Class Time* #4)

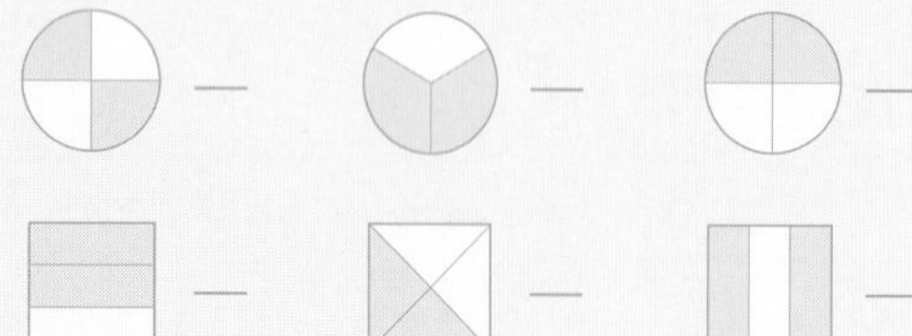

(*Class Time* #6)

3	5	2	3	4	2
4	3	3	3	4	5
+3	+2	+2	+3	+1	+3

2	6	1	5	7	7
4	1	5	2	1	0
+3	+3	+3	+3	+2	+3

Class Time

1. *Review Subtraction Family 10.*
   a. **Say Subtraction Family 10 as I move the felt blocks.**
   b. Ask a child to fill the houses as you say Family 10 together.
   c. **Ten lepers were cleansed. Nine went away without thanking Jesus. How many lepers were left to give thanks?**
2. *Place value.*
   a. Drill and motion **Ones, tens, hundreds.**
   b. **Which place has the greatest number?**
3. *Count by 2's.*
   Count by 2's to 100.
4. *Fractions.*
   Do the chalkboard samples.
5. *Shapes.*
   Drill the shape cards.

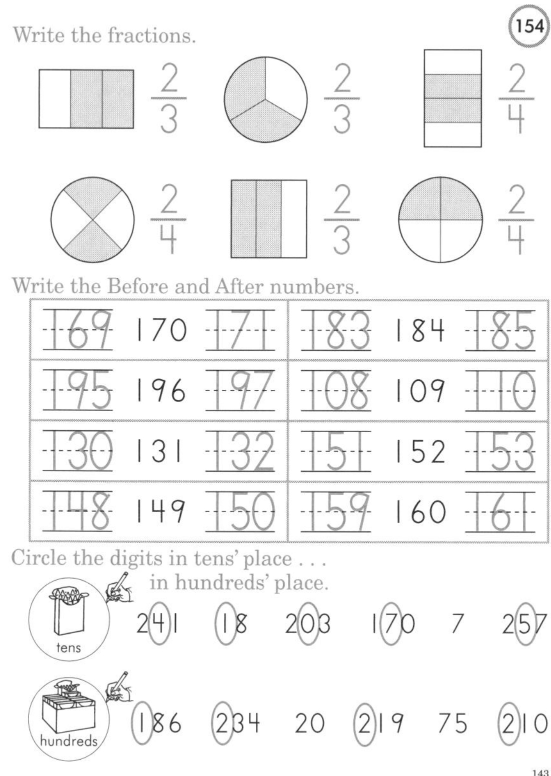

Speed Drill Answers

6	3	8	4	2	7	3
4	7	9	5	8	1	6
2	5	6	3	8	4	2

6. *Column addition.*
   Do the chalkboard samples.
7. *Drill mixed facts.*
   Circle Drill with Addition Families 8–10 and Subtraction Families 5–7 and 10.
8. *Do Speed Drill #64.*
9. *Assign Lesson 154.*

Follow-up

Drill

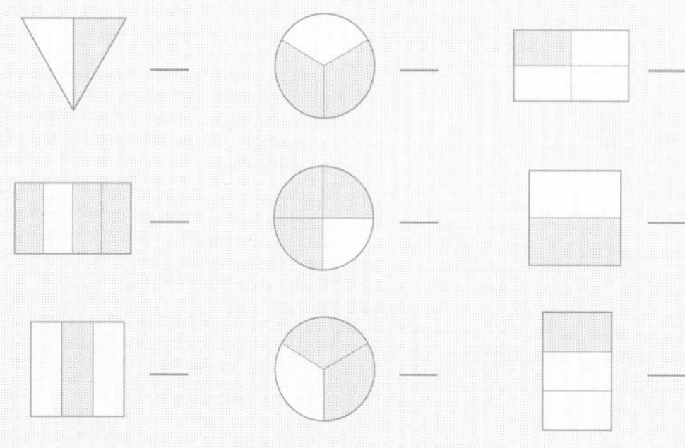

(*Drill* #2)

1. Have individuals count by 25's to 100.
2. Do the fraction samples on the chalkboard.
3. Hold the model clock. Have individuals set the hands at 5:30, 8:30, 1:00, 4:30, 6:00, 12:30, . . .

Practice Sheets

- ☐ Fact Houses #44
- ☐ Before and After #17
- ● Number Facts #56
- ● Number Facts #57
- ● Clocks #8
- ◊ Shapes #3

Objectives

New

WORKBOOK

Fraction mixture

Review

Addition and subtraction

Mixed counting

Before and After (by 2's, 5's, 10's)

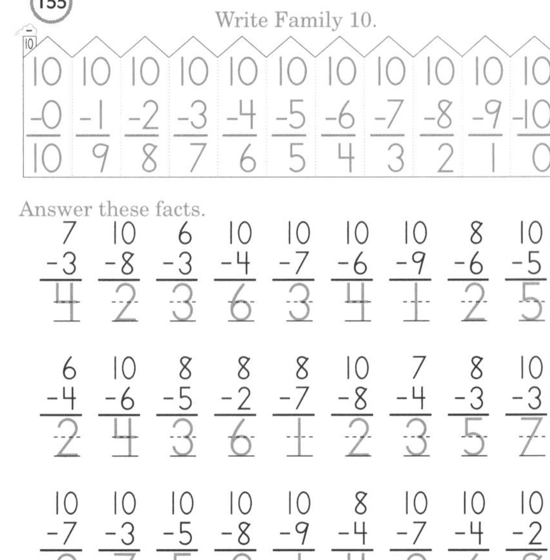

155

Write Family 10.

10	10	10	10	10	10	10	10	10	10	10
-0	-1	-2	-3	-4	-5	-6	-7	-8	-9	-10
10	9	8	7	6	5	4	3	2	1	0

Answer these facts.

7	10	6	10	10	10	10	8	10
-3	-8	-3	-4	-7	-6	-9	-6	-5
4	2	3	6	3	4	1	2	5

6	10	8	8	8	10	7	8	10
-4	-6	-5	-2	-7	-8	-4	-3	-3
2	4	3	6	1	2	3	5	7

10	10	10	10	10	8	10	10	10
-7	-3	-5	-8	-9	-4	-7	-4	-2
3	7	5	2	1	4	3	6	8

10	10	10	10	10	10	10	10	10
-4	-7	-6	-9	-8	-5	-3	-2	-1
6	3	4	1	2	5	7	8	9

144

Preparation

Materials

Subtraction Family 10 flash cards

Mixed flash cards: Addition Families 8–10 and Subtraction Families 6–8 and 10

Chalkboard

(*Class Time #2*)

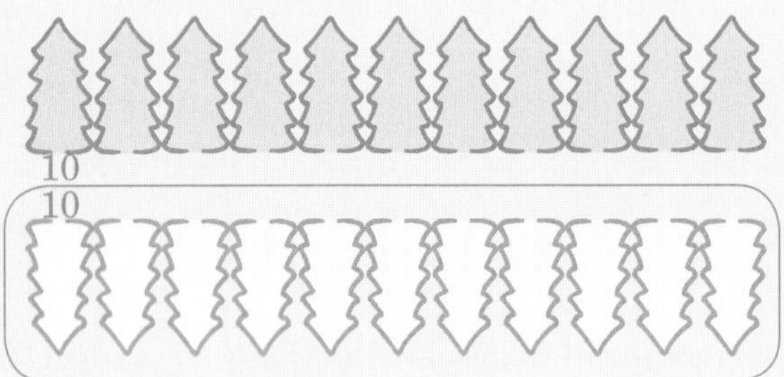

(*Class Time #4*)

___ 42 ___	___ 25 ___	___ 40 ___
___ 56 ___	___ 55 ___	___ 90 ___
___ 18 ___	___ 80 ___	___ 60 ___
___ 70 ___	___ 15 ___	___ 20 ___
___ 38 ___	___ 70 ___	___ 80 ___

(*Class Time #5*)

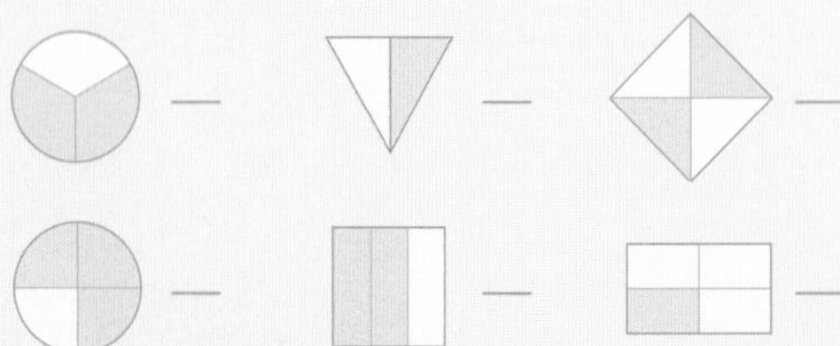

Class Time

1. *Practice Subtraction Families 8 and 10.*
   a. **Watch my fingers. Say Subtraction Family 8.**
   b. Use the flannel board to do story facts for Subtraction Family 10.
   (1) **10 sheep were eating grass in the pasture. 0 sheep went into the fold. 10 sheep were left in the pasture. 10 sheep – 0 sheep = 10 sheep.**
   (2) **10 sheep were in the pasture. 1 sheep went into the fold. . . .**
   c. Watch my fingers as we say Subtraction Family 10.
   d. Flash Subtraction Family 10 cards for one minute. **Answer together.**
2. *Drill Addition and Subtraction Family 10.*
   a. Let individuals fill the trees and reflection with sets of four facts.
   b. Divide the class into two teams. Say three numbers for a set of facts in Family 10. Have one team say an addition fact with the numbers (smaller addend first). Have the other team echo the twin addition fact. Then the first team

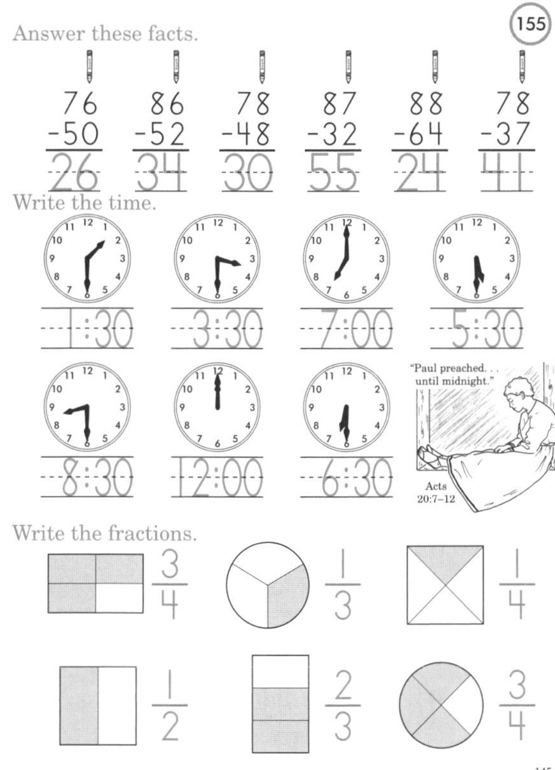
Answer these facts. 155

76	86	78	87	88	78
-50	-52	-48	-32	-64	-37
26	34	30	55	24	41

Write the time.

1:30 3:30 7:00 5:30

8:30 12:00 6:30

"Paul preached. . . until midnight." Acts 20:7–12

Write the fractions.

$\frac{3}{4}$ $\frac{1}{3}$ $\frac{1}{4}$

$\frac{1}{2}$ $\frac{2}{3}$ $\frac{3}{4}$

145

Paul preached unto them . . . and continued his speech until midnight. . . . And there sat in a window a certain young man named Eutychus, being fallen into a deep sleep: and as Paul was long preaching, he sunk down with sleep, and fell down from the third loft, and was taken up dead. And Paul went down . . . and . . . said . . . his life is in him. When he therefore was come up again, and had broken bread, . . . and talked a long while, even till break of day, so he departed, and they brought the young man alive, and were not a little comforted.

Acts 20:7–12

says a subtraction fact (larger addend as subtrahend) and the second team echoes the subtraction twin.

3. *Mixed counting.*
   a. **Follow the pointer as we count by 10's and 1's.**
      10, 20, 30, 40, 41, 42, 43, 44
      10, 11, 12, 13, 14, 15, 16, 17
      10, 20, 30, 40, 50, 60, 70, 71, 72, 73
   b. **Follow the pointer as we count by 5's and 1's.**
      5, 10, 15, 16, 17, 18
      5, 10, 15, 20, 25, 26, 27, 28, 29
      5, 10, 15, 20, 25, 30, 35, 40, 45, 46, 47
4. *Before and After, skip counting.*
   Fill in the chalkboard samples (first column by 2's, second column by 5's, third column by 10's).
5. *Fractions.*
   Do the chalkboard samples.
6. *Assign Lesson 155.*

Follow-up

Drill

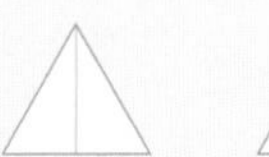  

(*Drill* #2)

1. Double Drill with mixed flash cards: Addition Families 8–10 and Subtraction Families 6–8 and 10.
2. Review the concept that halves must be equal.
   a. Point to the first triangle. **How many parts are in this triangle?** Shade one of the parts. **Is this one-half of the triangle?** Write $\frac{1}{2}$ beside the shape.
   b. Point to the second triangle. **How many parts are in this triangle?** Shade one of the parts. **Is this one-half of the triangle? No, the parts are not equal. We will not write a fraction.** Erase the triangle.
   c. Do the rest of the samples.

Practice Sheets

- ☐ Fact Houses #45
- ☐ Missing Numbers #14
- ● Number Facts #58
- ● Money #21
- ● Place Value #4

Objectives

New

TEACHING

2-digit addition with 3-digit answers

Count by 10's to 200

WORKBOOK

2-digit addition with 3-digit answers

Review

Mixed addition and subtraction

Count by 2's

Shapes

Fraction mixture

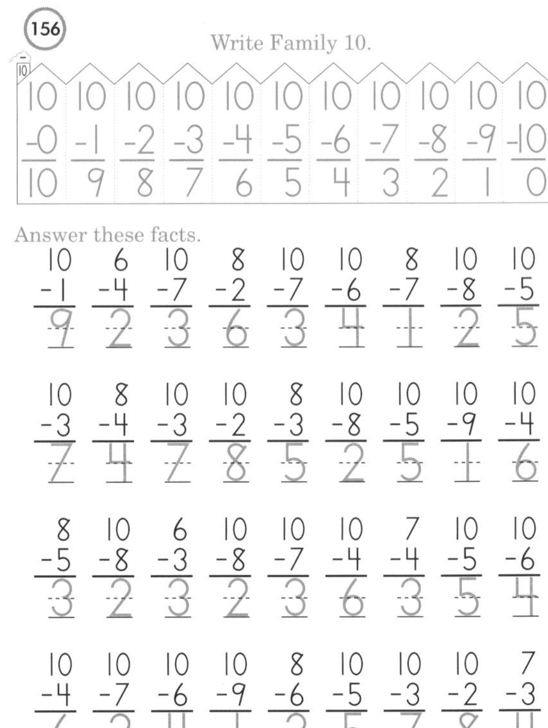

Preparation

Materials

Mixed flash cards: Addition and Subtraction Families 8–10

Shape cards

Subtraction Family 10 flash cards

Chalkboard

(*Class Time* #1)

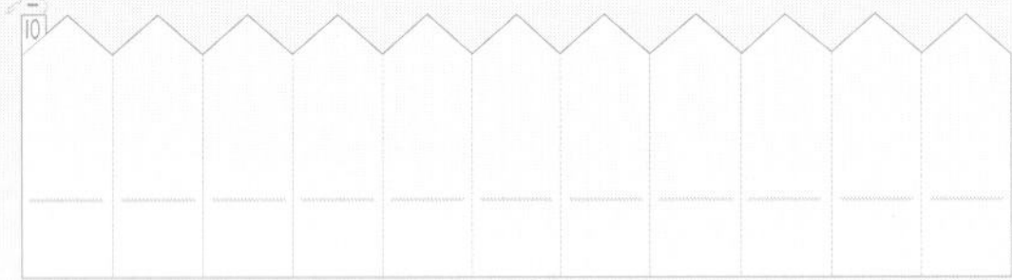

(*Class Time* #3)

76	44	50	23	34	82	60
+ 32	+ 65	+ 57	+ 85	+ 73	+ 27	+ 40

(*Class Time* #5)

(*Class Time* #6)

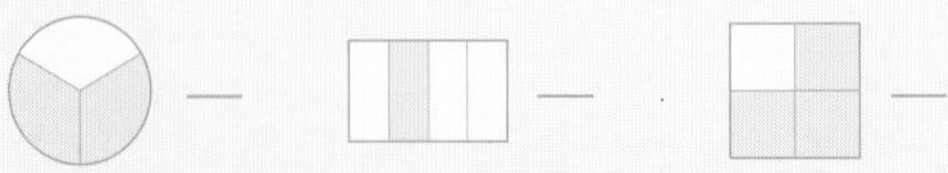

Class Time

1. *Review Subtraction Family 10.*
   a. Ask a child to move the felt blocks as you say Subtraction Family 10.
   b. **Say Family 10 as I fill the houses.**
2. *Drill mixed facts.*
   Circle Drill with Addition and Subtraction Families 8–10 flash cards.
3. *Two-digit addition with 3-digit answers.*
   Do the chalkboard samples. **Ones' place first!** These problems have 2-digit answers for adding the tens. The answers have a digit in the hundreds' place. Teach the children to put the hundreds' digit under the plus sign.
4. *Count by 2's.*
   Have the children stand in a circle with you. **We will count by 2's. Everybody say one number as we go around the circle. I will begin. 2, . . .**

156

Answer these facts.

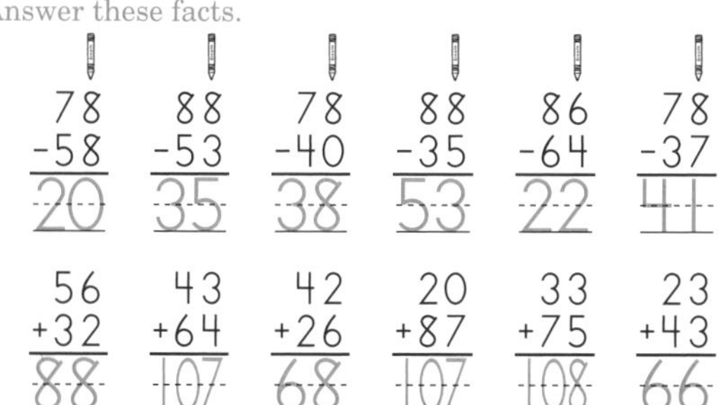

Write the fractions.

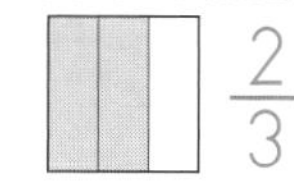

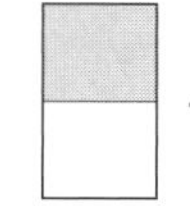

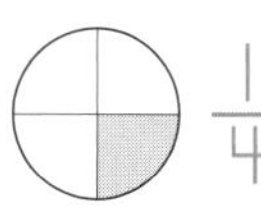

Answer the facts.

1	5	3	4	2	4	5	2	3
5	2	2	4	4	3	3	3	4
+2	+3	+3	+2	+2	+3	+2	+2	+3
8	10	8	10	8	10	10	7	10

147

Speed Drill Answers

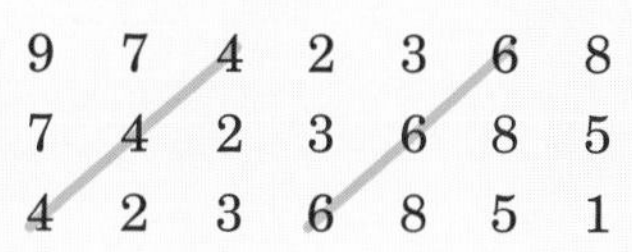

5. *Distinguish triangle and rectangle.*
   a. Drill the shape cards.
   b. Show the triangle card. **A triangle has 3 corners. A triangle has 3 sides.**
   c. Show the rectangle card. **A rectangle has 4 corners. A rectangle has 4 sides.**
   d. Point to the shapes on the board. **Name these shapes.** Write the special *T* or *R* inside each shape.
6. *Fractions.*
   Do the chalkboard samples.
7. *Do Speed Drill #65.*
8. *Assign Lesson 156.*

Follow-up

Drill

1. Drill individuals with Subtraction Family 10 flash cards.
2. **Count by 10's the whole way to 200.**
3. Have individuals recite the days of the week.

Practice Sheets

- ☐ Fact Houses #46
- ☐ Clocks #9
- ● Number Facts #59
- ● Number Facts #58
- ● Story Problems #6
- ◊ Shapes #4

Objectives

New

TEACHING

Count by 10's to 200

Cup and pint

Review

Counting (220)

Addition and subtraction

12 inches = 1 foot

Days of the week

157

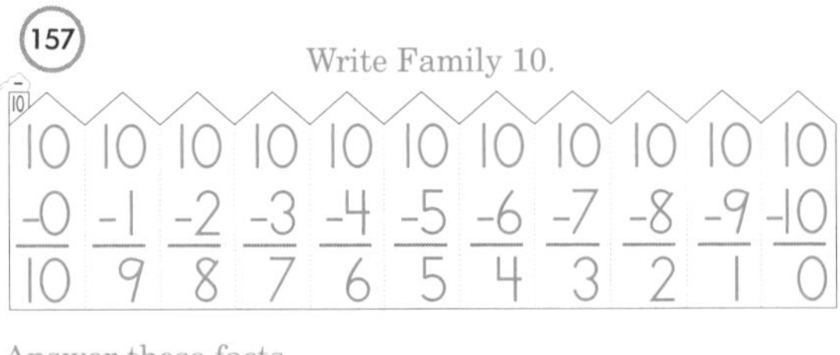

Answer these facts.

9	10	9	10	8	10	9	10	10
-8	-7	-5	-9	-6	-8	-6	-4	-5
1	3	4	1	2	2	3	6	5

7	7	9	8	10	8	10	8	10
-5	-4	-3	-5	-6	-7	-8	-3	-3
2	3	6	3	4	1	2	5	7

10	10	9	10	10	10	10	8	10
-7	-9	-7	-5	-3	-4	-7	-4	-2
3	1	2	5	7	6	3	4	8

10	10	10	10	10	9	10	10	10
-4	-7	-6	-9	-8	-4	-3	-2	-1
6	3	4	1	2	5	7	8	9

148

Preparation

Materials

Footprint poster

Subtraction Families 9 and 10 flash cards

One 8-ounce cup and one pint jar

Shape cards

Chalkboard

(*Class Time* #2)

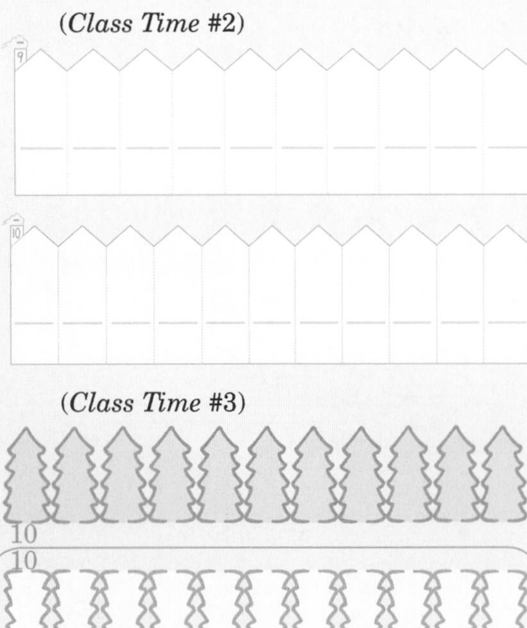

(*Class Time* #3)

Class Time

1. *Counting.*
   a. **Count by 1's from 120 to 220.**
   b. **Count by 10's to 200.**
2. *Review Subtraction Families 9 and 10.*
   a. **Say Subtraction Family 9 as I move the felt blocks.**
   b. Ask a child to fill the 9 Houses as you say the facts together.
   c. **Say Subtraction Family 10 for these story facts.**
   (1) **10 spoons were in the drawer. Marla put 0 spoons on the table. 10 spoons were still in the drawer. 10 spoons - 0 spoons = 10 spoons.**
   (2) **10 spoons were in the drawer. Marla put 1 spoon on the table. . . .**
   d. Ask a child to fill the 10 Houses as you say the facts together.
3. *Drill Addition and Subtraction Family 10 with twin teams.*
   a. Let individuals fill the trees and reflection with groups of four facts.

157

Answer these facts.

97	89	99	99	89	88
-30	-56	-59	-74	-68	-37
67	33	40	25	21	51

Write Before and After numbers.

214	215	216	257	258	259
206	207	208	241	242	243
238	239	240	218	219	220
249	250	251	253	254	255
228	229	230	232	233	234

Do the story problem.

Don has 3 red hens and 6 white hens. How many hens is that **in all**?

3 hens
+6 hens
9 hens

149

b. Say three numbers. Team 1 gives an addition fact (beginning with the smaller addend). Team 2 gives the twin addition fact. Team 1 says a subtraction fact (with the larger addend as subtrahend). Team 2 says the twin subtraction fact.

c. Divide the class into four teams. Each team says one fact for your three numbers. Follow the same order with the arrangement of facts.

4. *12 inches = 1 foot.*
   a. Hold the footprint poster. **12 inches make 1 foot; 12 inches make . . .**
   b. **God made some creatures long and some creatures short. Which of these might be 1 foot long: a fish, . . . a snail, . . . a turtle, . . . a lizard, . . . a tadpole?**

5. *Days of the week.*
   Call the children to the calendar. **When I point to a number, tell me what day of the week it is.**

6. *Assign Lesson 157.*

Follow-up

Drill

1. Drill individuals with Subtraction Families 9 and 10 flash cards.
2. Introduce the cup and the pint.
   a. Hold the cup. **This is 1 cup, 1 cup. We use a cup to measure things in the kitchen. Mother poured 1 cup of milk into the baby's bottle.**
   b. Hold the pint. **This is 1 pint, 1 pint. We use a pint to measure things too. Lee poured 1 pint of milk into the cats' dish.**
3. Drill the shape cards.

Practice Sheets

- ☐ Fact Houses #46
- ☐ Form F: 121–220
- ● Number Facts #58
- ● Money #22
- ● Fractions #5

Objectives

New

TEACHING

Cup and pint

WORKBOOK

Count by 10's to 200

Review

Subtraction facts

Money

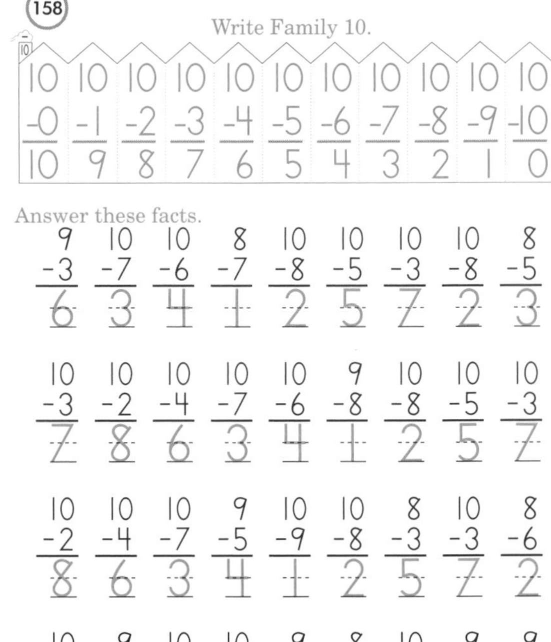
158

Write Family 10.

10	10	10	10	10	10	10	10	10	10	10
-0	-1	-2	-3	-4	-5	-6	-7	-8	-9	-10
10	9	8	7	6	5	4	3	2	1	0

Answer these facts.

9	10	10	8	10	10	10	10	8
-3	-7	-6	-7	-8	-5	-3	-8	-5
6	3	4	1	2	5	7	2	3

10	10	10	10	10	9	10	10	10
-3	-2	-4	-7	-6	-8	-8	-5	-3
7	8	6	3	4	1	2	5	7

10	10	10	9	10	10	8	10	8
-2	-4	-7	-5	-9	-8	-3	-3	-6
8	6	3	4	1	2	5	7	2

10	9	10	10	9	8	10	9	9
-1	-2	-2	-4	-6	-4	-9	-7	-4
9	7	8	6	3	4	1	2	5

150

Preparation

Materials

Subtraction Families 8–10 flash cards

Large coins

Cup and pint

Shape cards

Chalkboard

(*Class Time* #1)

(Write a set of these facts for each child to trace in *Class Time* #2.)

9	10
-4	-4
5	6

(*Class Time* #6)

cup	pint
pint	cup
pint	cup

Class Time

1. *Review Subtraction Families 9 and 10.*
   a. **Say Subtraction Family 9 as I fill the houses.**
   b. Point to Family 10 flash cards above the flannel board. **Look at the first fact; then close your eyes and say it three times.** Continue with the other facts.
2. *Drill selected facts.*
   a. Have each child stand near his set of facts on the board. **Trace and say each fact three times with me. 9 - 4 = 5 . . .**
   b. **Whisper and trace the facts until I say "stop."**
3. *Drill subtraction facts.*
   Flash Subtraction Families 8–10 flash cards for one minute. **Answer together.**
4. *Count by 10's.*
   a. **Count by 10's to 200.**
   b. **One day when Jesus wanted to feed the people, Philip said, "Two hundred pennyworth of bread**

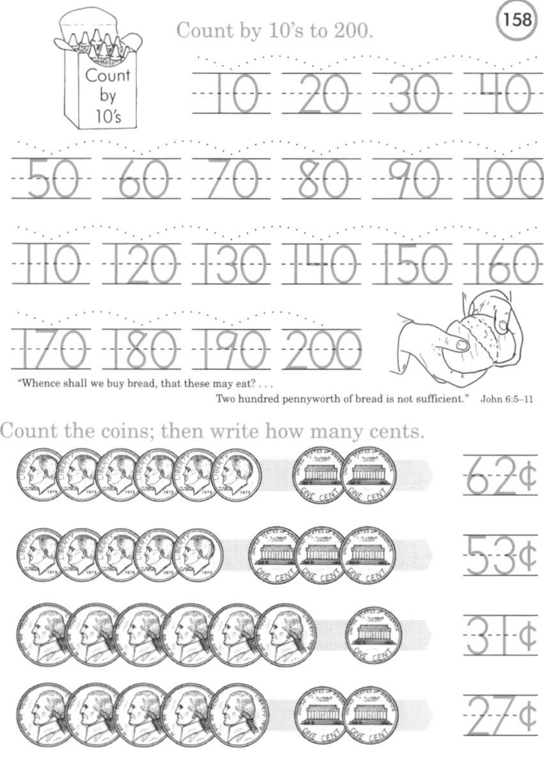
158

Count by 10's

Count by 10's to 200.

10 20 30 40
50 60 70 80 90 100
110 120 130 140 150 160
170 180 190 200

"Whence shall we buy bread, that these may eat? . . .
Two hundred pennyworth of bread is not sufficient." John 6:5–11

Count the coins; then write how many cents.

62¢
53¢
31¢
27¢

151

Speed Drill Answers

7	5	2	6	3	8	2
2	7	5	2	6	3	8
5	2	7	5	2	6	3

Speed Drill #66

When Jesus . . . saw a great company come unto him, he saith unto Philip, Whence shall we buy bread, that these may eat? And this he said to prove him: for he himself knew what he would do. Philip answered him, Two hundred pennyworth of bread is not sufficient for them, that every one of them may take a little. . . . Andrew . . . saith . . . , There is a lad here, which hath five barley loaves, and two small fishes: but what are they among so many? . . . And Jesus took the loaves; and when he had given thanks, he distributed to the disciples, and the disciples to them that were set down; and likewise of the fishes as much as they would.

John 6:5–11

would not be enough." It seemed impossible to Philip, but Jesus can do anything.

5. *Review money.*
   a. Flash the large coins. **Penny, 1¢; nickel, 5¢; dime, . . .**
   b. **Name the man on each coin.**
   c. **Which coin is worth the same amount as 2 nickels? . . . as 25 pennies? . . . as 5 nickels? . . . as 10 pennies? . . . as 2 dimes and 1 nickel?**
6. *Teach the cup and the pint.*
   a. Show the cup measure. **This is 1 cup, 1 cup, . . . You can give 1 cup of cold water to your thirsty brother.**
   b. Hold the pint. **This is 1 pint, 1 pint, . . . You might fetch 1 pint of pickles from the cellar for Mother.**
   c. **Which holds more, 1 cup or 1 pint?** Circle the larger measure in each box in the chalkboard samples.
7. *Do Speed Drill #66.*
8. *Assign Lesson 158.*

Follow-up

Drill

1. Have individuals count by 10's to 200.
2. Drill the shape cards.
3. Chalkboard drill: **Write 220. Circle the numeral in the ones' place.** Continue with
   189 . . . the tens' place
   201 . . . the ones' place
   130 . . . the hundreds' place
   217 . . . the tens' place
   243 . . . the tens' place
   208 . . . the hundreds' place

Practice Sheets

- ☐ Fact Houses #46
- ☐ Missing Numbers #15
- ● Number Facts #60
- ● Number Facts #59
- ● Place Value #5

Objectives

New

TEACHING

2 cups = 1 pint

WORKBOOK

Cup and pint

Review

Subtraction facts

Count by 10's to 200

Dozen

159

Write Family 10.

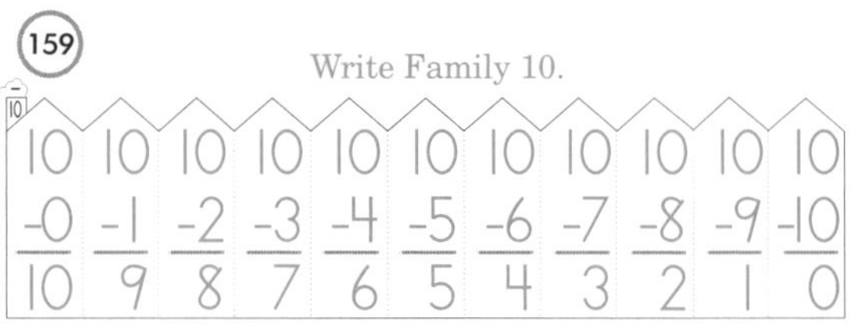

10	10	10	10	10	10	10	10	10	10	10
-0	-1	-2	-3	-4	-5	-6	-7	-8	-9	-10
10	9	8	7	6	5	4	3	2	1	0

Answer these facts.

8	10	9	10	10	10	10	10	9
-5	-7	-5	-9	-8	-3	-2	-4	-4
3	3	4	1	2	7	8	6	5
9	10	9	10	10	8	10	10	10
-2	-2	-3	-7	-6	-7	-8	-5	-3
7	8	6	3	4	1	2	5	7
8	10	9	8	10	10	10	10	9
-4	-9	-7	-3	-3	-8	-2	-4	-6
4	1	2	5	7	2	8	6	3
10	10	10	9	10	10	10	8	10
-4	-7	-6	-8	-8	-5	-3	-6	-1
6	3	4	1	2	5	7	2	9

152

Preparation

Materials

Subtraction Families 8–10 flash cards

Cup and pint

Chalkboard

(*Class Time* #1)

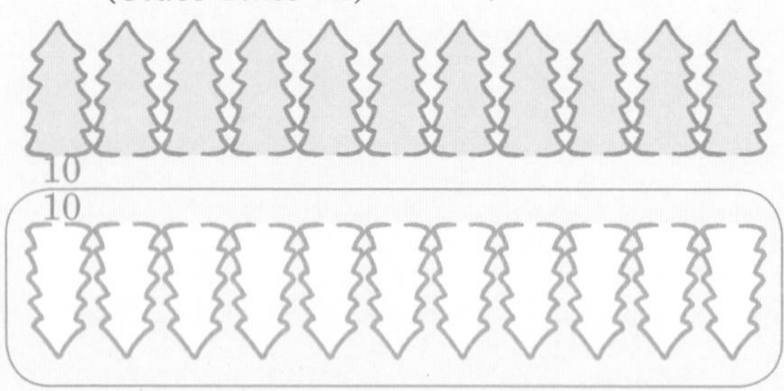

(*Class Time* #2)

9	9	10	10
-3	-6	-3	-7
6	3	7	3

(*Class Time* #6)

cup

pint

Class Time

1. *Review Subtraction Family 10.*
   a. Use the flannel board for story facts.
      (1) **10 beads were on a string. 0 beads slipped off. 10 beads were left on the string. 10 beads - 0 beads = 10 beads.**
      (2) **10 beads were on a string. 1 bead slipped off. . . .**
   b. Let individuals fill the trees and reflection with sets of four facts.
2. *Drill selected facts.*
   Point to the first fact in the box. **Say "9 - 3 = 6" as I trace it again and again.** Trace and drill each fact.
3. *Drill subtraction facts.*
   Circle Drill with Subtraction Families 8–10 flash cards.
4. *Count by 10's.*
   Count by 10's to 200.

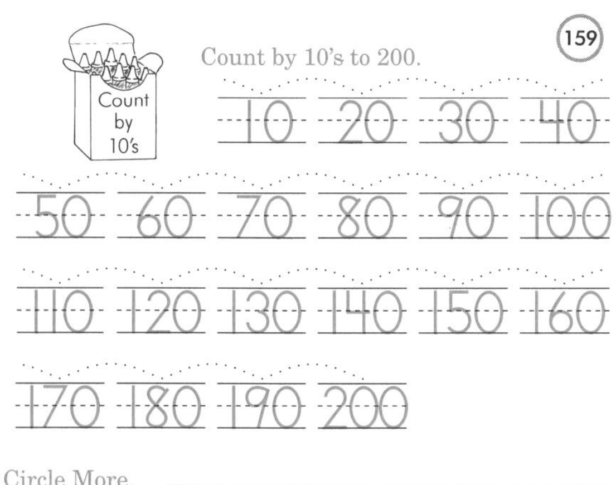

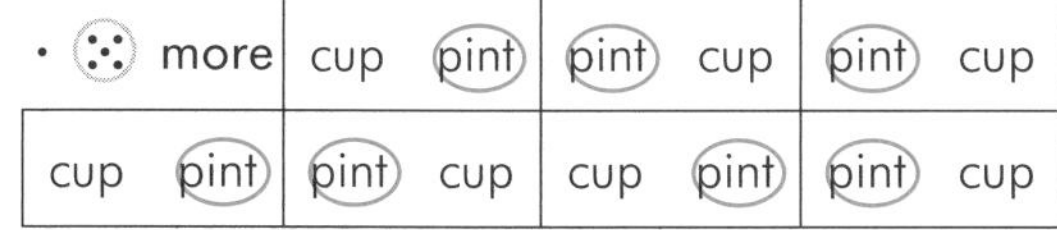

5. *Dozen.*
   a. **The baker put 12 doughnuts, or ___ doughnuts, into the box.**
   b. **The carpenter put 1 dozen nails, or ___ nails, into his pocket.**
6. *Cup and pint.*
   a. Hold the cup and pint. **1 cup, 1 pint; 1 cup, 1 pint; . . .**
   b. **Grandmother set 1 pint of pickles and 1 cup of jam on the table. She put more ___ on the table.** (pickles)
   c. **Big brother Roy ate 1 pint of noodle soup and 1 cup of vanilla pudding. He ate more ___.** (soup)
   d. Have everyone say, **1 cup, 1 pint** as individuals label the diagrams on the board.
7. *Assign Lesson 159.*

Follow-up

Drill

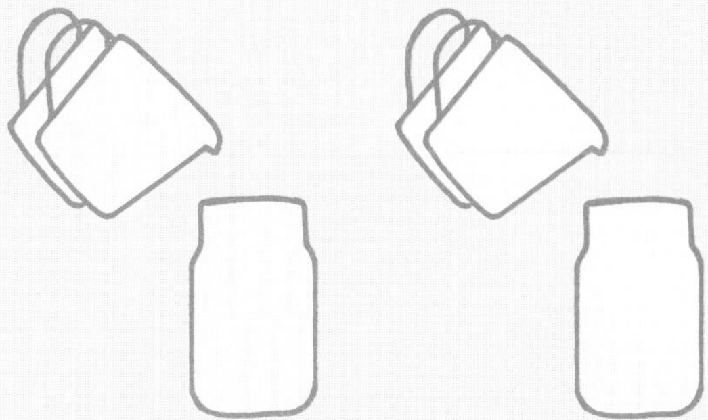

(*Drill* #2)

1. Oral drill: Have the children stand before you in two rows. **I'll call a fact. Whoever can give the correct answer first may go to the back of his line.**

9 - 2	**10 - 5**	**7 - 3**	**6 - 4**
3 + 7	**8 + 2**	**4 + 6**	**10 - 6**
4 + 2	**3 + 6**	**10 - 2**	**3 + 4**
10 - 4	**4 + 5**	**6 + 3**	**8 - 5**

2. Point to the diagrams on the board. Write the labels as shown below while you say, **2 cups fill 1 pint; 2 cups fill 1 pint.**

Practice Sheets

- ☐ Fact Houses #47
- ☐ Money #22
- ● Number Facts #60
- ● Story Problems #7
- ● Fractions #5
- ◊ Shapes #4

Objectives

New

TEACHING

2 cups = 1 pint

Review

Addition and subtraction
Count by 2's
Count by 10's to 200
Before and After (by 10's)

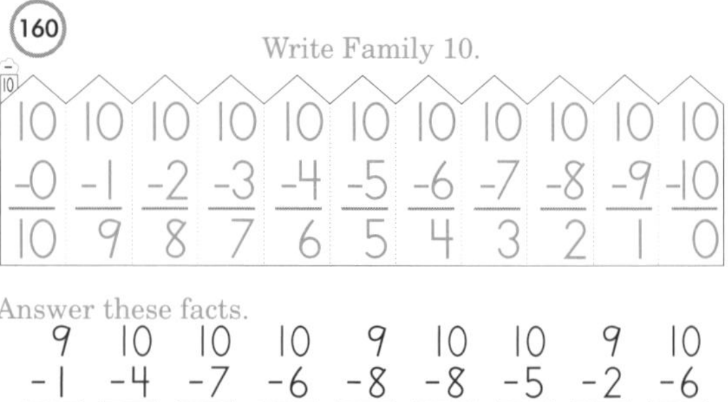

160

Write Family 10.

10	10	10	10	10	10	10	10	10	10	10
-0	-1	-2	-3	-4	-5	-6	-7	-8	-9	-10
10	9	8	7	6	5	4	3	2	1	0

Answer these facts.

9	10	10	10	9	10	10	9	10
-1	-4	-7	-6	-8	-8	-5	-2	-6
8	6	3	4	1	2	5	7	4

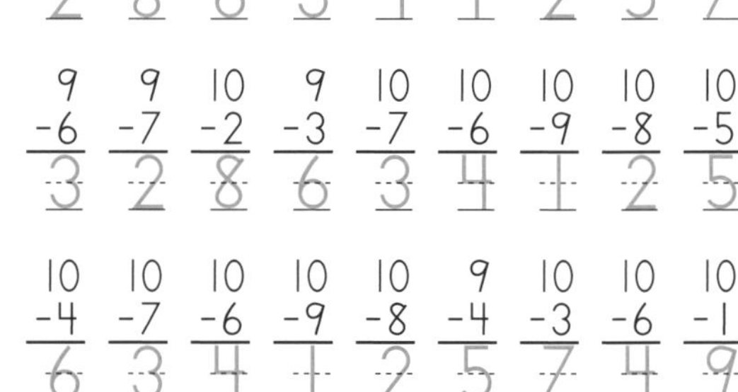

9	10	10	9	9	10	10	10	10
-7	-2	-4	-6	-5	-9	-8	-5	-3
2	8	6	3	4	1	2	5	7

9	9	10	9	10	10	10	10	10
-6	-7	-2	-3	-7	-6	-9	-8	-5
3	2	8	6	3	4	1	2	5

10	10	10	10	10	9	10	10	10
-4	-7	-6	-9	-8	-4	-3	-6	-1
6	3	4	1	2	5	7	4	9

154

Preparation

Materials

Subtraction Families 8–10 flash cards
Form C for each child
Large thermometer
Addition Families 6–10 flash cards

Chalkboard

(*Class Time* #1)

(*Class Time* #5)

___	70	___	___	160	___
___	40	___	___	130	___
___	90	___	___	180	___
___	20	___	___	150	___

(*Class Time* #6)

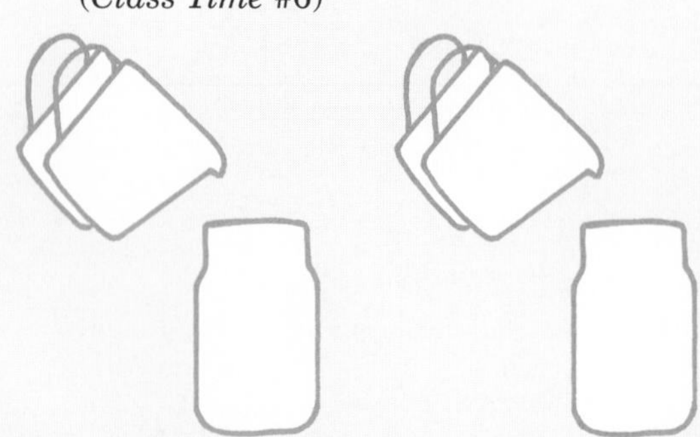

Class Time

1. *Review Subtraction Families 8–10.*
   a. **Watch my fingers. Say Subtraction Family 8 . . . Family 9.**
   b. **Say Family 10 as I fill the houses.**
2. *Drill Addition and Subtraction Family 10 facts with twin teams.*
   Say the triplets orally and have four teams recite the four different facts. Follow this pattern to keep recitation orderly:
   (1) Addition with smaller addend first
   (2) Addition twin
   (3) Subtraction with larger addend as subtrahend
   (4) Subtraction twin.
3. *Drill subtraction facts.*
   Distribute Form C, and use flash cards from Subtraction Families 8–10. **Apron Row: Box 1—Box 2 . . .**

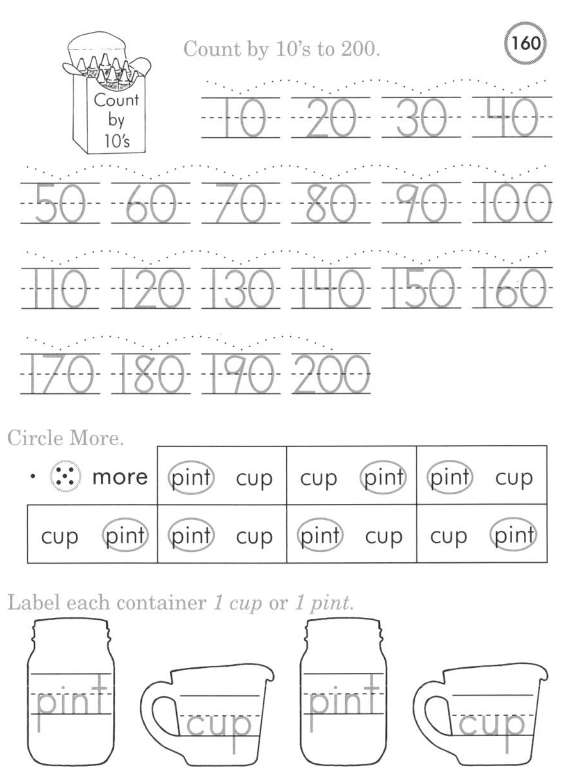

Speed Drill Answers

8	3	5	6	2	4	3
3	5	6	2	4	3	7
5	6	2	4	3	7	8

Speed Drill #67

4. *Count by 2's with the thermometer.*
   a. Set the mercury at 20°. **2, 4, 6, . . . 20°. What would you wear at recess if the temperature were 20°?**
   b. Set the mercury at 76°. **2, 4, 6, . . . 76°. What would you wear at recess if the temperature were 76°?**
5. *Before and After, counting by 10's.*
   a. **Count by 10's to 200.**
   b. Count by 10's to do the Before and After chalkboard samples.
6. *Cup and pint.*
   Point to the cups and pints on the board. **2 cups fill 1 pint; 2 cups fill 1 pint . . .** Have everyone say, **2 cups fill 1 pint** as individuals label the diagrams.
7. *Do Speed Drill #67.*
8. *Assign Lesson 160.*

Follow-up

Drill

(*Drill* #2)

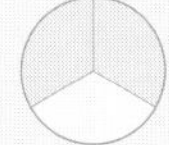 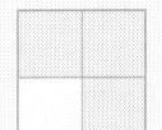 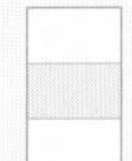 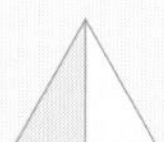

1. Drill Addition Families 6–10 flash cards.
2. Do the chalkboard fraction samples.

Practice Sheets

- ● Form C (*Class Time* #3)
- ☐ Fact Houses #47
- ☐ Clocks #10
- ☐ Missing Numbers #15
- ● Number Facts #60
- ● Before and After #18
- ◊ Shapes #5

Objectives

New

WORKBOOK

2 cups = 1 pint

Review

Subtraction facts
Money
Count by 25's
Counting (230)
Fractions

Preparation

Materials

Subtraction Families 9 and 10 flash cards

Large coins

Cup and pint

Shape cards

Chalkboard

(*Class Time* #3)

7 dimes = ____
1 quarter = ____
8 nickels = ____
6 nickels = ____
3 quarters = ____
9 dimes = ____
7 nickels = ____
2 quarters = ____

(*Class Time* #5)

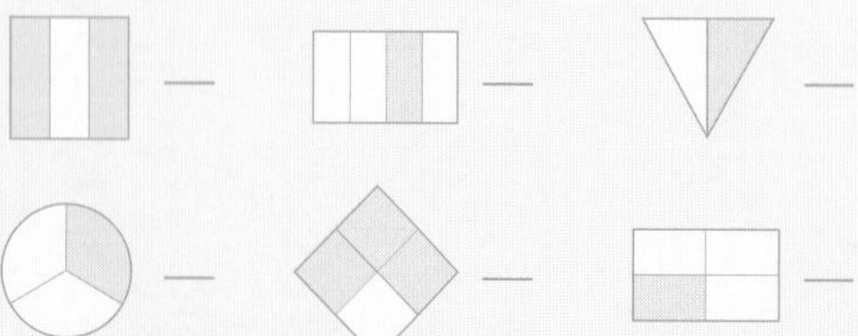

Class Time

1. *Review Subtraction Family 10.*
   a. Point to the first flash card above the flannel board. **Look at the fact. Close your eyes, and say it three times.** Practice each fact in this way.
   b. Ask a child to move the felt blocks as you say Family 10 together.
2. *Drill subtraction facts.*
   Flash Subtraction Families 9 and 10 cards for one minute. **Answer together.**
3. *Review money.*
   a. Flash the large coins for the children to say the name and value.
   b. **We count pennies by ___, nickels by ___, dimes by ___, and quarters by ___.**
   c. Have the children use their fingers and count aloud to do the chalkboard samples.

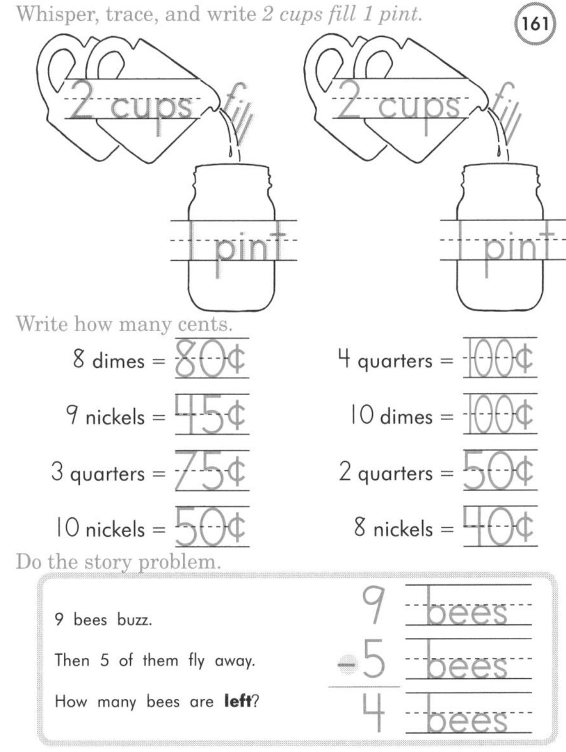
Whisper, trace, and write *2 cups fill 1 pint.* 161

2 cups fill
1 pint
2 cups fill
1 pint

Write how many cents.

8 dimes = 80¢ 4 quarters = 100¢

9 nickels = 45¢ 10 dimes = 100¢

3 quarters = 75¢ 2 quarters = 50¢

10 nickels = 50¢ 8 nickels = 40¢

Do the story problem.

9 bees buzz. 9 bees

Then 5 of them fly away. −5 bees

How many bees are **left**? 4 bees

157

4. *Counting.*
   a. **Count by 25's to 100.** Count four times.
   b. **Count by 1's from 130–230.**
5. *Fractions.*
   Do the chalkboard samples.
6. *Cup and pint.*
   a. Show the measures. **1 cup, 1 pint . . .**
   b. **2 cups fill 1 pint; 2 cups . . .**
   c. **Mother poured 2 cups of juice into the Thermos, or Mother poured ___ of juice into the Thermos.** (1 pint)
7. *Assign Lesson 161.*

Follow-up

Drill

(*Drill* #3)

1. Drill individuals with the shape cards.
2. Chalkboard drill: **Listen as I count. When I stop, write the number I should say next.**

25, 50, 75, ___	**160, 170, 180, ___**
50, 60, 70, ___	**100, 110, 120, ___**
85, 90, 95, ___	**170, 180, 190, ___**

3. Drill number triplets.
   For the first triplet of numbers, point to the 9 in the circle on the chalkboard. Write 3 on the first blank below the circle, and say, **The numbers for the first facts will be 9, 3, and . . .** (Let the class supply the 6 for you to write in the blank.)
   Change the numbers on the blanks for other facts in Family 9.

Practice Sheets

- ☐ Fact Houses #47
- ☐ Skip Counting #7
- ☐ Measures #9
- ● Number Facts #59
- ● Number Facts #60
- ● Fractions #4

Objectives

New

TEACHING

Quart

Review

Addition and subtraction

2 cups = 1 pint

Fractions

Count by 10's to 200

Column addition

162

Answer these facts.

1	7	2	9	5	2	7	6	6
+6	+1	+3	+1	+3	+4	+2	+1	+4
7	8	5	10	8	6	9	7	10
1	6	5	7	3	1	2	6	1
+7	+3	+2	+3	+3	+4	+8	+2	+8
8	9	7	10	6	5	10	8	9
3	5	4	4	5	4	4	2	2
+2	+5	+4	+2	+4	+3	+6	+7	+2
5	10	8	6	9	7	10	9	4
1	8	8	1	2	3	5	3	2
+9	+2	+1	+3	+5	+5	+1	+6	+1
10	10	9	4	7	8	6	9	3
	1	4	3	3	3	3	1	1
	+5	+5	+4	+7	+6	+1	+2	+1
	6	9	7	10	9	4	3	2

158

Preparation

Materials

Addition Families 2–10 flash cards

Cup, pint, and quart

Form D for each child

Chalkboard

(*Class Time* #5)

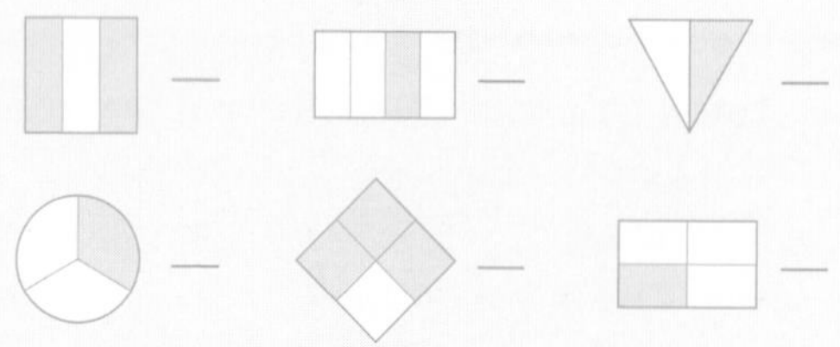

(*Class Time* #7)

2	3	5	3	5	2
3	5	2	4	1	4
+3	+2	+3	+2	+3	+1
4	3	2	2	4	3
2	4	5	6	4	5
+3	+3	+2	+2	+2	+0

Class Time

1. *Drill addition facts.*
   a. Double Drill with Addition Families 2–10 flash cards. You may eliminate the combinations with 0, to concentrate practice of the harder facts.
   b. Flash Addition Families 2–10 flash cards for one minute. **Answer together.**
2. *Recite Family 8 facts with twin teams.*
   (1) Addition with smaller addend first
   (2) Addition twin
   (3) Subtraction with larger addend as subtrahend
   (4) Subtraction twin
3. *Review the cup and pint.*
   a. Hold the cup and pint. **1 cup, 1 pint . . .**
   b. **2 cups fill 1 pint; 2 cups . . .**

Whisper, trace, and write *2 cups fill 1 pint.* (162)

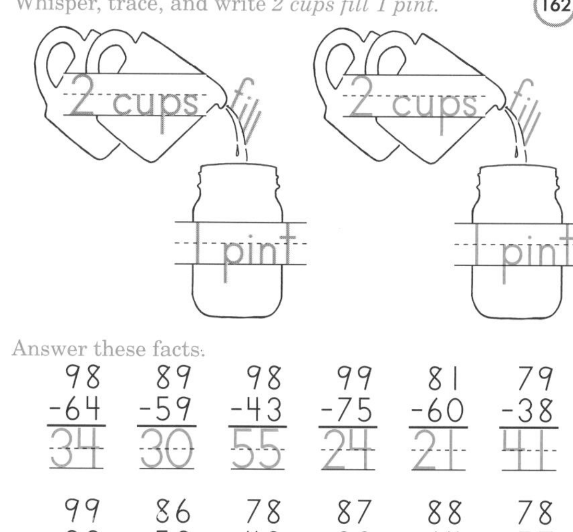

Answer these facts.

98	89	98	99	81	79
-64	-59	-43	-75	-60	-38
34	30	55	24	21	41

99	86	78	87	88	78
-32	-52	-48	-32	-64	-57
67	34	30	55	24	21

Write the fractions.

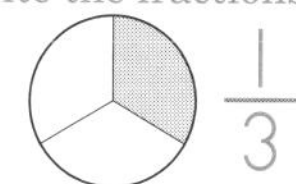 $\frac{1}{3}$ 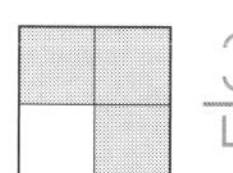 $\frac{3}{4}$ 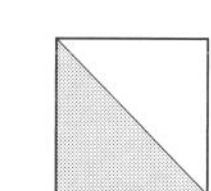 $\frac{1}{2}$

159

4. *Introduce the quart.*
   a. Hold the quart. **This is 1 quart, 1 quart, 1 quart.**
   b. **When Mother says, "Please bring 1 quart of cherries from the cellar," you look for a jar this size.**
5. *Fractions.*
   Do the chalkboard samples.
6. *Skip counting.*
   a. **Boys, count by 10's to 200.**
   b. **Girls, count by 10's to 200.**
7. *Column addition.*
   Do the chalkboard samples.
8. *Do Speed Drill #68.*
9. *Assign Lesson 162.*

Speed Drill Answers

8	4	2	7	3	6	9
5	8	4	2	7	3	6
6	5	8	4	2	7	3

Follow-up

Drill

1. Distribute Form D for story problem dictation. Print *bugs* on the chalkboard for a label. **Put the correct sign in the gray spot.**
   a. **Arrow Box: 3 black bugs and 7 brown bugs eat leaves. How many bugs is that *altogether?***
   b. **Button Box: 10 red bugs crawl up a tree. Then 6 of them fly away. How many bugs are *still* in the tree?**
   c. **Camel Box: 10 brown bugs sleep in a log. A woodpecker eats 2 of them. How many bugs are *still* in the log?**
   d. **Daffodil Box: 4 green bugs sit on a leaf. 5 brown bugs come. How many bugs is that *in all?***
   e. **Elephant Box: 10 black bugs crawl from under a rock. A bear eats 7 of them. How many bugs are *left?***
   f. **Feather Box: 6 black bugs sit on a beanstalk. 4 red bugs come. How many bugs is that *altogether?***
2. Stand near the number line with the pointer. **Can we count backwards? 100, 99, 98, 97, . . . 1.**

Practice Sheets

- ● Form D (*Follow-up* drill #1)
- ☐ Form F: 131–230
- ☐ Measures #9
- ● Number Facts #61
- ● Money #23
- ◊ Missing Numbers #16

Objectives

Review

Subtraction facts
Count by 2's, 10's
Cup, pint, quart
Money
Shapes

Preparation

Materials

Subtraction Families 2–10 flash cards

Cup, pint, and quart

Shape cards

Subtraction Families 2–10 flash cards

Chalkboard

(*Class Time* #1)

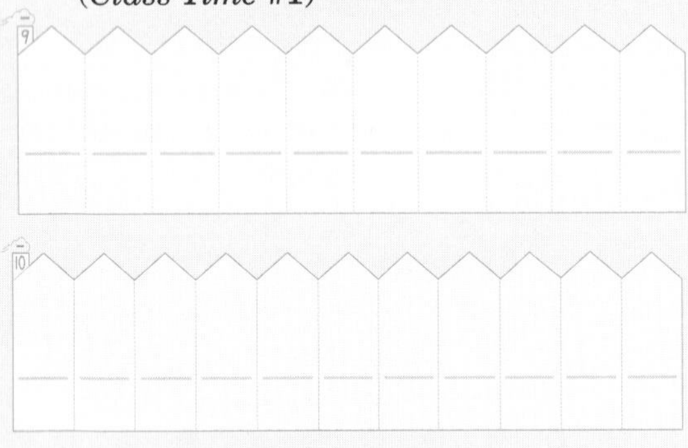

(*Class Time* #4)

pint	quart
quart	pint
pint	quart

(*Class Time* #5)

35¢ = ___ nickels 4 nickels = ___

15¢ = ___ nickels 9 nickels = ___

25¢ = ___ quarters 4 quarters = ___

75¢ = ___ quarters 2 quarters = ___

Class Time

1. *Review Subtraction Families 9 and 10.*
   a. Ask a child to fill the 9 Houses as you say Family 9 together.
   b. **Say Family 10 as I fill the 10 Houses.**
2. *Drill subtraction facts.*
   Flash Subtraction Families 2–10 cards for one minute. **Answer together.**
3. *Skip counting.*
   a. **Count by 2's to 100.**
   b. **Count by 10's to 200.**
4. *Measures.*
   a. Review the cup, pint, and quart by pointing to the containers. **Say the name of the measure I point to.**
   b. Hold up the cup and pint. **2 cups fill 1 pint; 2 cups . . .**
   c. **Which holds the most—1 cup, 1 pint, or 1 quart?**
   d. Circle the larger measure of each pair in the chalkboard samples.

163

Whisper, trace, and write *2 cups fill 1 pint.*

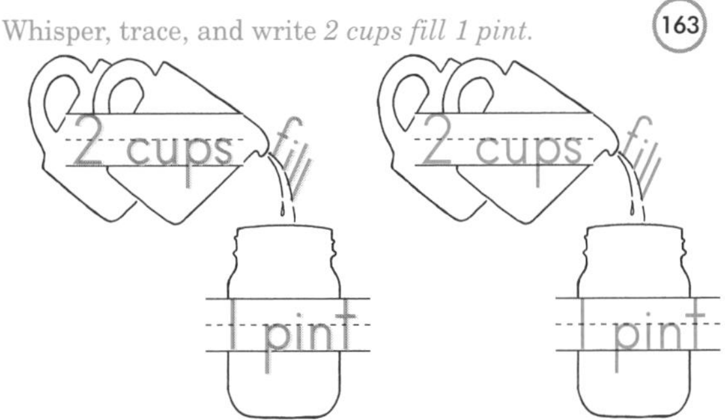

Write Before and After Numbers, counting by 2's.

Count by 2's

68	70	72	54	56	58
92	94	96	80	82	84
36	38	40	58	60	62

Circle 1 dozen.

Circle 1 dozen

161

5. *Money.*
   Do the chalkboard samples. For the first column, have the children count on their fingers until they reach the correct amount. How many fingers did they need to use?
6. *Shapes.*
   Drill the shape cards.
7. *Assign Lesson 163.*

Follow-up

Drill

(*Drill* #1)

1. Practice facts with number triplets for 8, 9, and 10.
   a. Let individuals write two numbers on the blanks below a circle and say all four facts.
   b. Draw additional blanks below the numbers for other combinations.
2. Drill individuals with Subtraction Families 2–10 flash cards.
3. Quiz fraction concepts orally.
   a. **If I cut a sandwich into 2 equal pieces, how much of the sandwich is 1 of the pieces?**
   b. **If I cut an apple into 4 equal pieces, how much of the apple is 1 of the pieces? If I eat 3 of those pieces, how much of the apple did I eat?**
   c. **If I cut a doughnut into 3 equal pieces, how much of the doughnut is 1 piece? If I give you 2 of the pieces, how much of the doughnut do you have?**

Practice Sheets

- □ Skip Counting #7
- ● Number Facts #62
- ● Fact Houses #48
- ● Place Value #3
- ◊ Shapes #5

Objectives

New

TEACHING

2 pints = 1 quart

WORKBOOK

Quart

Review

Mixed facts

Number triplets

Count by 10's to 200

Telling time

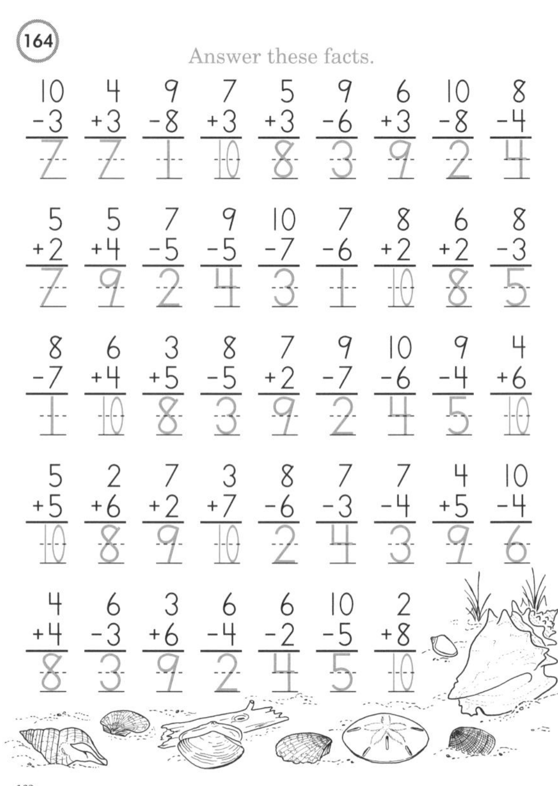
164

Answer these facts.

10 −3 = 7	4 +3 = 7	9 −8 = 1	7 +3 = 10	5 +3 = 8	9 −6 = 3	6 +3 = 9	10 −8 = 2	8 −4 = 4
5 +2 = 7	5 +4 = 9	7 −5 = 2	9 −5 = 4	10 −7 = 3	7 −6 = 1	8 +2 = 10	6 +2 = 8	8 −3 = 5
8 −7 = 1	6 +4 = 10	3 +5 = 8	8 −5 = 3	7 +2 = 9	9 −7 = 2	10 −6 = 4	9 −4 = 5	4 +6 = 10
5 +5 = 10	2 +6 = 8	7 +2 = 9	3 +7 = 10	8 −6 = 2	7 −3 = 4	7 −4 = 3	4 +5 = 9	10 −4 = 6
4 +4 = 8	6 −3 = 3	3 +6 = 9	6 −4 = 2	6 −2 = 4	10 −5 = 5	2 +8 = 10		

162

Preparation

Materials

Cup, pint, and quart

Model clock

Chalkboard

(*Class Time* #1)

2 + 8 =	8 − 5 =	5 + 4 =	10 − 7 =	5 + 5 =
9 − 7 =	7 + 3 =	10 − 5 =	9 − 5 =	9 − 6 =
10 − 3 =	3 + 6 =	9 − 2 =	4 + 6 =	10 − 2 =
6 − 2 =	10 − 6 =	5 − 3 =	4 + 5 =	6 + 4 =
9 − 3 =	9 − 4 =	8 − 6 =	2 + 7 =	10 − 8 =
8 + 2 =	8 − 5 =	3 + 7 =	10 − 4 =	6 + 3 =

(*Class Time* #2)

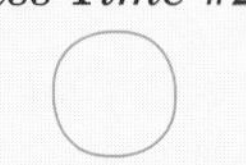

____ ____

(*Class Time* #3)

Class Time

1. *Drill mixed facts.*
   a. Divide the children into two groups to answer the facts in the grid. **Group A will say the first answer. Group B will say the next answer.**
   b. Drill the facts, moving up and down, left and right with your pointer. Keep the grid for later drill.
2. *Drill number triplets.*
   a. Write a family number in the circle on the chalkboard. Say one of the addends for an addition fact in that family, and call on someone to say the three numbers. Ask for other pairs of numbers for the blanks.
   b. Change the family number in the circle for more practice.
3. *Measures.*
   a. Point to the containers. **Name each measure as I point to it.**
   b. **2 cups fill 1 pint; 2 cups . . .**

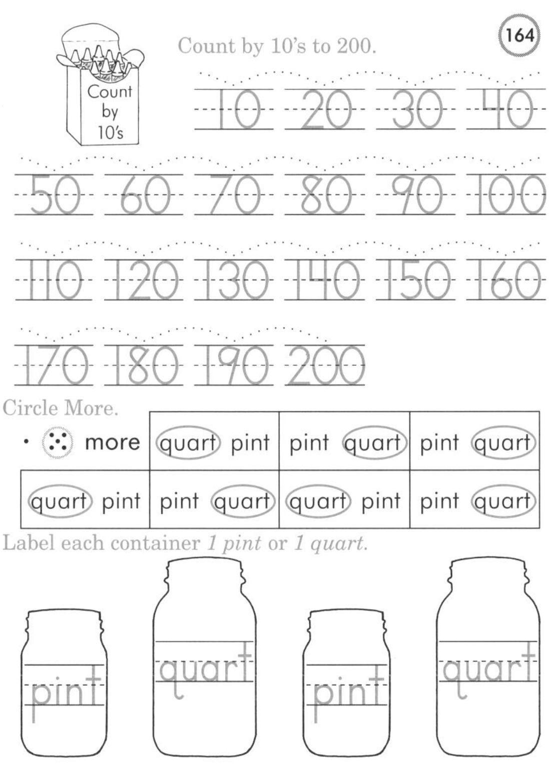

Speed Drill Answers

4	5	7	3	8	6	2
5	7	3	8	6	2	7
7	3	8	6	2	7	8

c. Move to the diagrams on the board. Label them with the equation as you repeat **2 pints fill 1 quart; 2 pints fill . . .**

4. *Count by 10's.*
   a. **Count by 10's to 100.**
   b. **Now hop back again. 100, 90, . . . 10.**
   c. **Count by 10's to 200.**
5. *Telling time.*
   a. Set the model clock at 12:00. **What time is it?**
   b. **In half an hour it will be ___.** (12:30—set the hands to that time.)
   c. **In another half an hour it will be ___.** (1:00—move the hands to that time.)
   d. **In 2 hours it will be ___.** (3:00—move the hands.)
   e. **In 2 more hours it will be ___.** (5:00)
6. *Do Speed Drill #69.*
7. *Assign Lesson 164.*

Follow-up

Drill

1. Chalkboard drill: **I will say two numbers. Think about them and write the number that is larger.**

156	**152**	**205**	**215**
124	**128**	**106**	**160**
190	**180**	**119**	**109**
212	**220**	**143**	**134**
176	**167**	**201**	**210**

2. Drill each child at the grid on the chalkboard. Can he answer all the facts in one minute?
3. **Get your 12-inch ruler. Can you find something in the room that measures 8 inches?**

Practice Sheets

- ☐ Money #23
- ☐ Measures #10
- ● Number Facts #63
- ● Missing Numbers #16
- ● Fractions #5

Objectives

Review

Mixed facts
Story problems
2 cups = 1 pint
2 pints = 1 quart
Fractions
Shapes

165 Answer these facts.

4 + 1 = 5 | 3 + 5 = 8 | 2 + 8 = 10 | 9 + 1 = 10 | 5 + 3 = 8 | 2 + 4 = 6 | 5 + 4 = 9

"Her sons . . .

5 + 3 = 8 | 4 + 3 = 7 | 6 + 3 = 9 | 7 + 3 = 10 | 3 + 3 = 6 | 7 + 3 = 10 | 4 + 6 = 10 | 6 + 2 = 8 | 5 + 4 = 9

brought the vessels

8 + 2 = 10 | 3 + 7 = 10 | 2 + 6 = 8 | 4 + 2 = 6 | 7 + 2 = 9 | 4 + 3 = 7 | 4 + 6 = 10 | 2 + 7 = 9 | 8 + 2 = 10

to her;

6 + 4 = 10 | 5 + 5 = 10 | 4 + 5 = 9 | 8 + 2 = 10 | 2 + 5 = 7 | 3 + 6 = 9 | 2 + 4 = 6 | 4 + 4 = 8 | 6 + 3 = 9

and she poured out."

2 + 4 = 6 | 4 + 5 = 9 | 3 + 4 = 7 | 3 + 7 = 10 | 3 + 6 = 9 | 1 + 9 = 10 | 2 + 7 = 9 | 7 + 2 = 9

2 Kings 4:1–7

164

Preparation

Materials

Mixed flash cards—Addition and Subtraction Families 9 and 10

Form C for each child

Cup, pint, and quart

Shape cards

Chalkboard

(*Class Time* #3)

(*Class Time* #4)

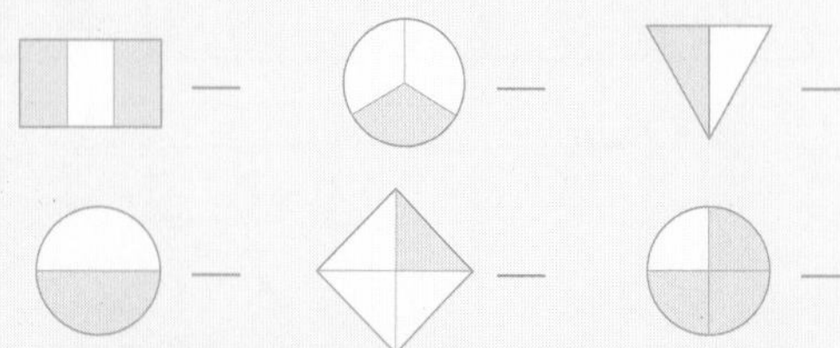

Class Time

1. *Drill mixed facts.*
   a. Circle Drill with mixed Addition and Subtraction Families 9 and 10 flash cards.
   b. Distribute Form C for written answers, and continue with Addition and Subtraction Families 9 and 10. **Watch the signs! Apron Row: Box 1—Box 2 . . .**
2. *Story problems.*
   a. **Close your eyes. Nevin has 10 gumdrops. He gives 6 of them to Wa yne. How many gumdrops does Nevin have *now?* Open your eyes. Who can give me the whole problem?**
   b. **Close your eyes. 5 girls jump rope. 4 girls swing. How many girls is that *altogether?***
3. *Measures.*
   a. **Name each measure as I point to it. 1 pint, 1 quart . . .**
   b. **2 cups fill 1 pint; 2 pints fill 1 quart . . .**

c. Have individuals label the diagrams as everyone says, **2 pints fill 1 quart; 2 pints fill 1 quart.**

d. **One quart can fill 2 pint jars, and then the quart jar is empty. One day God made a widow's jar pour out more and more oil to fill many pots, and her jar still was not empty. That was a miracle.**

4. *Fractions.*
   Do the chalkboard samples.

5. *Shapes.*
   a. Drill the shape cards.
   b. **What shape do you think of when I say, "3 corners"?**
   0 corners?
   4 corners?
   cat's ears?
   shoe box?
   music note *la*?

6. *Assign Lesson 165.*

Follow-up

Drill

(*Drill #2*)

5 7 

1. Have individuals count by 10's to 200.
2. Drill number triplets and their facts. Call on individuals to write two numbers on the blanks and say four facts with the triplet.

Practice Sheets

- ● Form C (*Class Time* #1)
- ☐ Form F: 141–240
- ☐ Skip Counting #7
- ☐ Measures #11
- ● Number Facts #64
- ● Number Facts #61

Objectives

New

WORKBOOK

2 pints = 1 quart

Review

Subtraction facts
Cup, pint, quart
Money
Place value
Calendar

(166) Answer these facts.

8	10	5	10	10	10	8	8	6
-6	-7	-3	-4	-6	-8	-3	-5	-5
2	3	2	6	4	2	5	3	1
9	9	9	10	8	10	9	7	9
-6	-4	-6	-9	-6	-8	-3	-3	-2
3	5	3	1	2	2	6	4	7
9	8	9	7	9	10	7	10	10
-7	-2	-5	-5	-4	-7	-6	-3	-6
2	6	4	2	5	3	1	7	4
10	8	8	9	7	8	6	10	10
-4	-7	-1	-5	-4	-4	-4	-5	-9
6	1	7	4	3	4	2	5	1
6	9	7	6		10	8	9	9
-2	-7	-2	-3		-3	-4	-8	-4
4	2	5	3		7	4	1	5

166

Preparation

Materials

Subtraction Families 2–10 flash cards
Cup, pint, and quart
Large coins

Chalkboard

(*Class Time* #1)

Class Time

1. *Subtraction drill.*
   a. Call the children to the subtraction flowers on the chalkboard. **I will say the problem; you say the answer.**
   b. Point to the first flower and say these problems. Give a new fact rapidly following each answer. **7 - 2; 9 - 2; 8 - 2; 6 - 2 . . .** Drill all the flowers. Save them for later drill.
   c. Flash Subtraction Families 2–10 cards for one minute. **Answer together.**

2. *Measures.*
   a. **Name each measure as I point to it. 1 cup, 1 pint, 1 quart . . .**
   b. Hold the cup and pint. **2 cups fill 1 pint; 2 cups . . .**
   c. Hold the pint and quart. **2 pints fill 1 quart; 2 pints . . .**

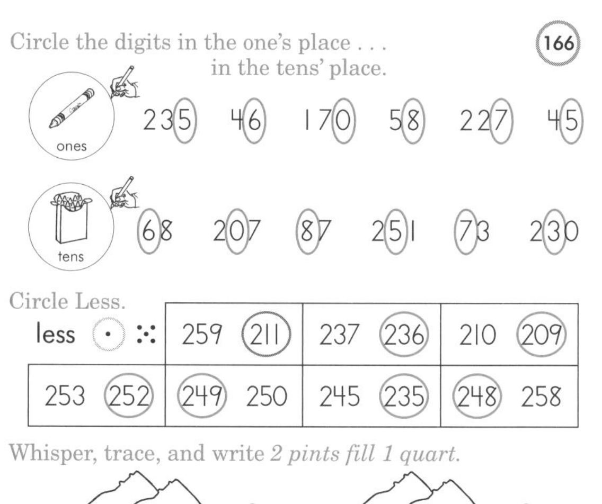
Circle the digits in the one's place . . . in the tens' place. 166

ones: 23(5) 4(6) 17(0) 5(8) 22(7) 4(5)

tens: (6)8 2(0)7 (8)7 2(5)1 (7)3 2(3)0

Circle Less.

less ⊙ ∴	259 (211)	237 (236)	210 (209)
253 (252)	(249) 250	245 (235)	(248) 258

Whisper, trace, and write *2 pints fill 1 quart.*

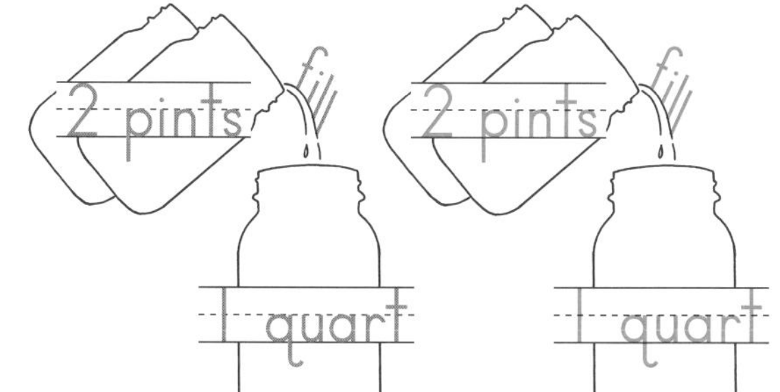

Speed Drill Answers

6	7	4	8	6	5	10
7	4	8	6	5	10	3
4	8	6	5	10	3	9

3. *Money.*
   a. Flash the large coins. **Penny, 1¢; nickel, 5¢; dime, 10¢; quarter, 25¢.**
   b. **Can you name the man on each coin?**
4. *Place value.*
   a. Review the motion **Ones, tens, hundreds; one, tens, . . .**
   b. **Which place has the greatest numbers?**
5. *Calendar.*
   Call the children to the calendar.
   a. **This is the month of ___.**
   b. **Today is the ___.**
   c. **Let's begin at the first day and count to the end of the month. First, second, third, . . .**
6. *Do Speed Drill #70.*
7. *Assign Lesson 166.*

Follow-up

Drill

(*Drill* #1)

(6) (8) (10)

1. Drill number triplets and their facts. Call on individuals to write two numbers on the blanks and say four facts with the triplet.
2. Drill individuals with the subtraction flowers on the chalkboard.
3. Oral drill: Have the children line up in two rows. **Whoever says the answer first may go to the back of his row.**

9 - 3	**10 - 5**	**8 - 3**	**10 - 3**
8 - 5	**8 - 2**	**9 - 5**	**9 - 6**
10 - 1	**10 - 9**	**10 - 6**	**10 - 7**
10 - 8	**10 - 4**	**9 - 4**	**10 - 2**

Practice Sheets

- ☐ Money #24
- ☐ Measures #10
- ● Number Facts #62
- ● Number Facts #64
- ● Story Problems #8
- ◊ Missing Numbers #17

Objectives

New

TEACHING

2-step computation

Review

Mixed facts
Skip counting
Money
Cup, pint, quart
Shapes

167

Answer these facts.

9	4	8	7	3	9	6	10	9
-2	+3	-2	+3	+5	-6	+3	-8	-5
7	7	6	10	8	3	9	2	4

4	3	7	4	6	7	7	3	10
+6	+5	-4	+5	-4	-3	-2	+7	-2
10	8	3	9	2	4	5	10	8

10	6	6	8	3	9	10	8	4
-4	+4	+2	-5	+6	-7	-6	-3	+6
6	10	8	3	9	2	4	5	10

2	9	3	5	10	5	7	8	9
+5	-3	+7	+3	-7	+4	-5	-4	-4
7	6	10	8	3	9	2	4	5

9	2	8	6	10	2	10	4
-6	+7	-6	-2	-5	+8	-2	+2
3	9	2	4	5	10	8	6

168

Preparation

Materials

Mixed flash cards—Addition and Subtraction Families 2–10

Cup, pint, and quart

Shape cards

Chalkboard

(*Class Time* #2)

25 ___ ___ 40 ___ 50 ___

___ 20 ___ ___ 50 ___ ___

___ ___ 24 26 ___ ___ ___

70 ___ 80 ___ ___ ___ ___

Class Time

1. *Drill mixed facts.*
   Flash mixed cards for Addition and Subtraction Families 2–10 for one minute. **Answer together.**
2. *Skip counting.*
   a. **Girls, count by 5's to 100.**
   b. **Boys, count by 10's to 200.**
   c. **Girls, count by 25's to 100.**
   d. **Everyone count by 2's to 100.**
   e. Point to the Missing Number exercises on the board. **Decide if you should count by 2's, by 5's, or by 10's for each row.**
3. *Money.*
   Can you tell what I am counting?
   10¢, 20¢, 30¢, . . . (dimes)
   25¢, 50¢, 75¢, . . . (quarters)
   1¢, 2¢, 3¢, . . . (pennies)
   5¢, 10¢, 15¢, . . . (nickels)

4. *Measures.*
   Show the three measuring containers.
   Name which one of these measures I am thinking of.
   It holds 2 cups. (pint)
   It holds more than 1 pint. (quart)
   It holds less than 1 pint. (cup)
   It holds 2 pints. (quart)
   It holds the least. (cup)
   It holds the most. (quart)
5. *Shapes.*
   Drill the shape cards.
6. *Assign Lesson 167.*

Follow-up

Drill

1. **I am going to say some two-step problems. Think of the answer to each step. When I say "equals," you may raise your hand to give the answer.**

6 + 3 - 1 =	**2 + 7 - 4 =**
5 + 5 - 2 =	**2 + 6 - 7 =**
6 + 4 - 3 =	**3 + 5 - 6 =**
8 + 1 - 3 =	**7 + 3 - 6 =**
2 + 8 - 4 =	**5 + 4 - 9 =**

2. Chalkboard drill: **I will say two numbers. You write the number that is smaller.**

256	**246**	**196**	**198**
230	**130**	**199**	**209**
214	**234**	**225**	**252**
202	**220**	**227**	**207**

Practice Sheets

- ☐ Skip Counting #8
- ☐ Measures #12
- ☐ Clocks #9
- ● Number Facts #63
- ● Fact Houses #49

Objectives

Review

Mixed facts
Cup, pint, quart
Column addition
12 inches = 1 foot

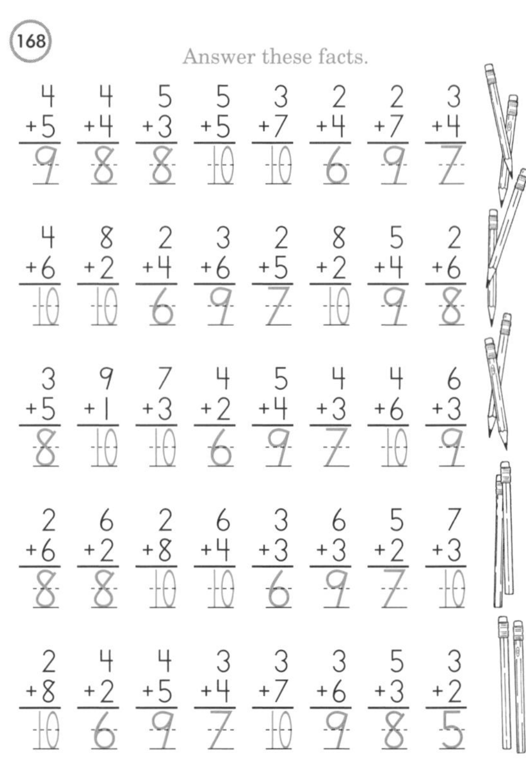

(168)

Answer these facts.

4 +5 9	4 +4 8	5 +3 8	5 +5 10	3 +7 10	2 +4 6	2 +7 9	3 +4 7
4 +6 10	8 +2 10	2 +4 6	3 +6 9	2 +5 7	8 +2 10	5 +4 9	2 +6 8
3 +5 8	9 +1 10	7 +3 10	4 +2 6	5 +4 9	4 +3 7	4 +6 10	6 +3 9
2 +6 8	6 +2 8	2 +8 10	6 +4 10	3 +3 6	6 +3 9	5 +2 7	7 +3 10
2 +8 10	4 +2 6	4 +5 9	3 +4 7	3 +7 10	3 +6 9	5 +3 8	3 +2 5

170

Preparation

Materials

Mixed flash cards—Addition and Subtraction Families 9 and 10

Form C for each child

Cup, pint, and quart

Footprint poster

Mixed flash cards—Addition and Subtraction Families 2–10

Chalkboard

(*Class Time* #2)

(*Class Time* #3)

5 3 +2	6 1 +3	4 3 +3	2 6 +2	3 3 +3	5 2 +3
5 2 +2	2 4 +3	2 7 +1	3 5 +0	4 2 +4	2 4 +1

Class Time

1. *Drill mixed facts.*
   a. Circle Drill with mixed flash cards for Addition and Subtraction Families 9 and 10.
   b. Distribute Form C for written answers, and continue with mixed facts from Families 9 and 10. **Watch the signs! Apron Row: Box 1—Box 2 . . .**
2. *Measures.*
   a. Hold up each container, and have the children name it.
   b. Drill measure equivalents: **2 cups fill 1 pint; 2 pints fill 1 quart; . . .**
   c. Have the children label the chalkboard diagrams with the equivalents as everyone says, **2 cups fill 1 pint; 2 pints fill 1 quart.**

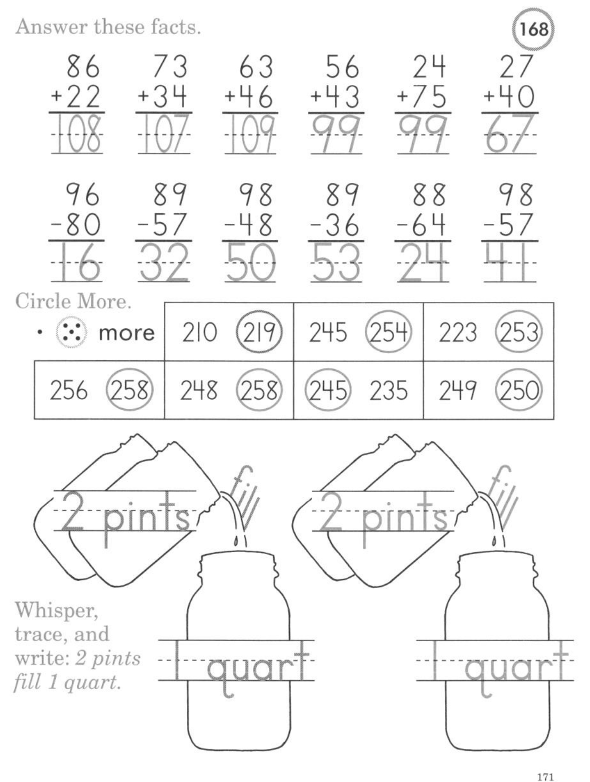

Speed Drill Answers

6 9 5 7 4 10 10
8 6 9 5 7 4 10
5 8 6 9 5 7 4

Speed Drill #71

3. *Column addition.*
   Do the chalkboard samples.
4. *12 inches = 1 foot.*
   a. Hold the footprint poster. **12 inches make 1 foot; 12 inches . . .**
   b. **God made many kinds of vegetables for us to eat. Which of these vegetables may grow to be 1 foot long: an ear of corn, a pea pod, rhubarb, celery, a green pepper?**
5. *Do Speed Drill #71.*
6. *Assign Lesson 168.*
   Remember to do the ones' place first when you add or subtract 2-digit numbers.

Follow-up

Drill

1. Drill mixed flash cards for Addition and Subtraction Families 2–10. Divide the children into two groups. **If you should add, Group A will give the answer. If you should subtract, Group B will give the answer.**
2. Chalkboard drill: **I will say a few numbers. When I stop counting, write the number that I should say next.**
   144, 143, 142, ___ 110, 120, 130, ___
   189, 188, 187, ___ 160, 170, 180, ___
   225, 224, 223, ___ 120, 130, 140, ___
   207, 206, 205, ___ 170, 180, 190, ___

Practice Sheets

- ● Form C (*Class Time* #1)
- ☐ Money #24
- ☐ Measures #12
- ● Number Facts #61
- ● Number Facts #64
- ◊ Missing Numbers #17

Objectives

New

TEACHING

2-step computation

Review

Mixed facts
Fractions
Count by 10's to 200
Counting (250)
Money
Cup, pint, quart

(169)

Answer these facts.

6	9	5	10	10	10	7	10	9
-4	-2	-3	-4	-6	-8	-2	-7	-8
2	7	2	6	4	2	5	3	1

10	8	7	10	7	8	8	9	10
-4	-4	-5	-5	-4	-7	-5	-5	-9
6	4	2	5	3	1	3	4	1

8	8	9	9	9	8	7	10	6
-6	-2	-5	-7	-4	-5	-6	-7	-2
2	6	4	2	5	3	1	3	4

10	9	7	8	9	9	10	9
-8	-3	-3	-6	-4	-6	-9	-6
2	6	4	2	5	3	1	3

9	8	10	9	7	10	9	10
-7	-3	-7	-8	-4	-6	-8	-2
2	5	3	1	3	4	1	8

Psalm 23

"Surely goodness and mercy shall follow me."

172

Preparation

Materials

Mixed flash cards—Addition and Subtraction Families 8–10

Pint and quart

Form D for each child

Chalkboard

(*Class Time* #2)

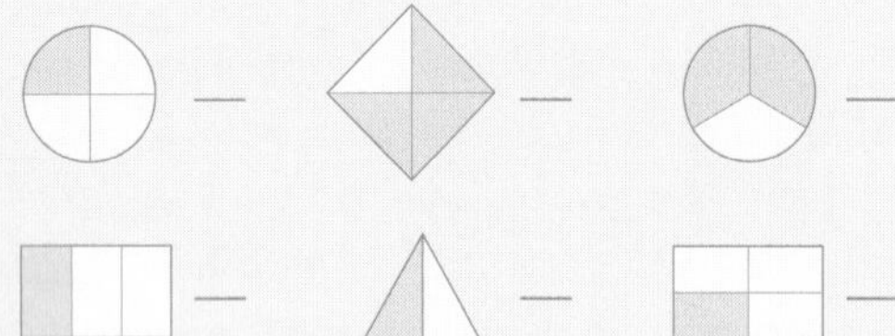

(*Class Time* #4)

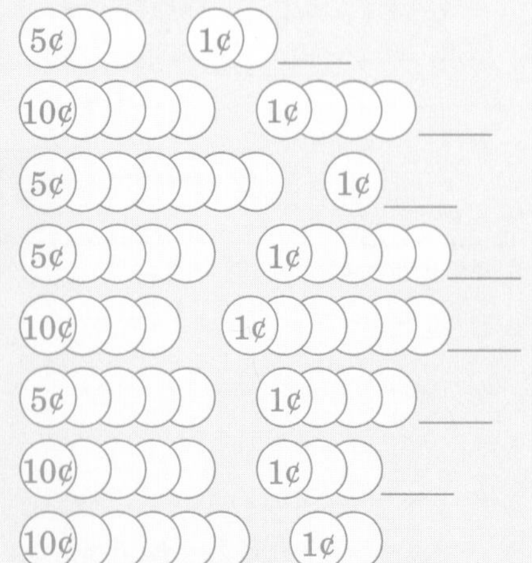

Class Time

1. *Drill mixed facts.*
   Double Drill with mixed flash cards for Addition and Subtraction Families 8–10.
2. *Fractions.*
   Do the chalkboard samples.
3. *Counting.*
   a. **Count by 10's to 200.**
   b. **Count by 1's from 150 to 250.**
4. *Money.*
   Do the chalkboard samples.

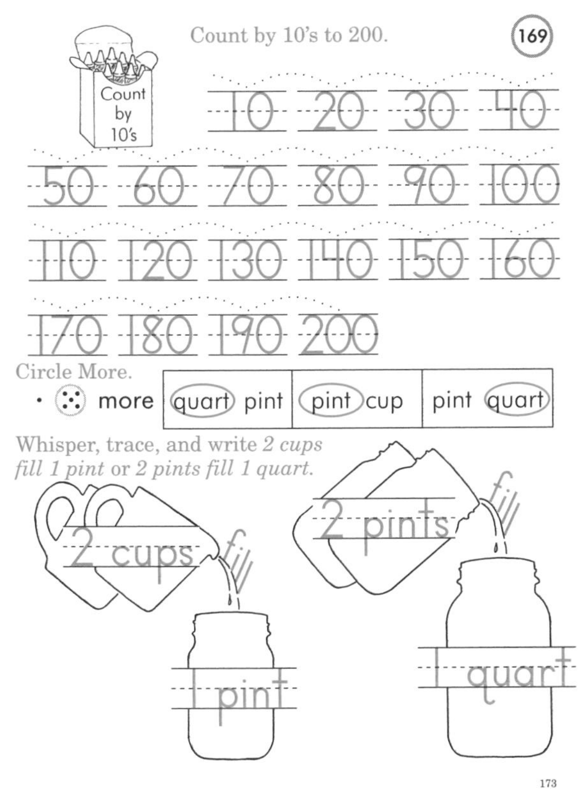

5. *Measures.*
   Hold the pint and the quart. **2 pints fill 1 quart; 2 pints fill 1 quart; . . .**
6. *Two-step problems.*
   I will say some two-step problems. When I say "equals," you may raise your hand to give the answer.

6 + 2 − 3 =	**4 + 3 − 5 =**
5 + 5 − 3 =	**5 + 4 − 2 =**
3 + 6 − 6 =	**2 + 8 − 7 =**
7 + 3 − 5 =	**7 + 2 − 4 =**

7. *Assign Lesson 169.*

Follow-up

Drill

1. Distribute Form D for story problem dictation. Print the label *cows* on the chalkboard. **Put the correct sign in the gray spot.**
   a. **Arrow Box: 10 cows are in a pen. Father loads 4 of them on a truck. How many cows are *still* in the pen?**
   b. **Button Box: 10 cows stand under a tree. 2 cows walk away. How many cows are *still* under the tree?**
   c. **Camel Box: 3 cows wade in the stream. 7 more cows come. How many cows is that *altogether?***
   d. **Daffodil Box: 4 cows eat clover. 6 cows eat corn. How many cows *are* eating?**
   e. **Elephant Box: Father has 10 cows. He sells 4 of them. How many cows does Father have *now?***
   f. **Feather Box: 10 cows are in the barn. Father chases 7 of them out. How many cows are *still* in the barn?**
2. Count backward from 100–1.

Practice Sheets

- ● Form D (*Follow-up* drill #1)
- ☐ Form F: 151–250
- ☐ Measures #13
- ☐ Skip Counting #8
- ● Number Facts #62
- ● Number Facts #64

Objectives

Review

Mixed facts
Story problems
Missing Numbers (by 2's, 5's, 10's)
Cup, pint, quart
2-step computation

(170) Answer these facts.

10	4	9	7	5	10	6	7	8
-3	+3	-8	+3	+3	-7	+3	-5	-4
7	7	1	10	8	3	9	2	4
5	2	7	4	8	7	9	3	10
+5	+6	-4	+5	-6	-3	-4	+7	-4
10	8	3	9	2	4	5	10	6
8	6	3	8	7	9	10	7	4
-7	+4	+5	-5	+2	-7	-6	-2	+6
1	10	8	3	9	2	4	5	10
5	7	4	6	9	5	10	9	8
+2	-6	+6	+2	-6	+4	-8	-5	-3
7	1	10	8	3	9	2	4	5
		3	6	6	10	2	9	3
		+6	-2	-4	-5	+8	-3	+4
		9	4	2	5	10	6	7

174

Preparation

Materials

Cup, pint, and quart
Model clock

Chalkboard

(*Class Time* #1)

9 - 6	4 + 4	10 - 7	10 - 6	8 - 4	2 + 8
8 - 3	7 + 3	5 + 3	9 - 3	5 + 4	9 - 7
5 + 5	9 - 4	4 + 5	4 + 6	8 - 6	10 - 3
3 + 6	10 - 5	9 - 2	10 - 8	7 + 2	3 + 5
6 + 4	6 + 2	8 + 2	8 - 2	3 + 7	9 - 5
8 - 5	6 + 3	10 - 4	2 + 7	2 + 6	10 - 2

(*Class Time* #3)

___ 30 ___ 50 ___ ___
___ 15 ___ ___ 30 ___
___ ___ 56 ___ 60 ___
___ 140 ___ ___ ___ 180

Class Time

1. *Drill mixed facts.*
   Call the children to the number-fact grid on the chalkboard.
   a. **Boys, answer the subtraction facts. Girls, answer the addition facts.**
   b. **Answer together. Can we say them all in one minute? 1, 2, 3, go!**
2. *Story problems.*
   a. **Close your eyes to listen. Linda has 6 white flowers and 4 blue flowers. How many is that *altogether*? Open your eyes. Who can give the whole problem?**
   b. **Close your eyes. Wayne has 10 rabbits. He sells 7 of them. How many rabbits does Wayne have *now*? Open your eyes. Who can give the whole problem?**
3. *Missing Numbers in skip counting.*
   Do the chalkboard samples. **Count by 2's, 5's, or 10's to fill in the blanks.**

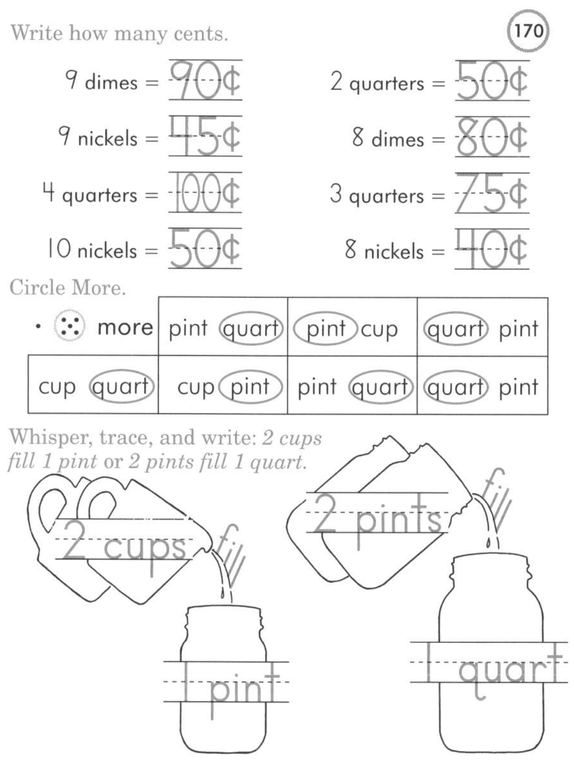

Write how many cents. (170)

9 dimes = 90¢ 2 quarters = 50¢

9 nickels = 45¢ 8 dimes = 80¢

4 quarters = 100¢ 3 quarters = 75¢

10 nickels = 50¢ 8 nickels = 40¢

Circle More.

• more	pint (quart)	(pint) cup	(quart) pint
cup (quart)	cup (pint)	pint (quart)	(quart) pint

Whisper, trace, and write: *2 cups fill 1 pint* or *2 pints fill 1 quart.*

175

Speed Drill Answers

3 8 6 10 5 9 4
8 6 10 5 9 4 10
6 10 5 9 4 10 2

4. *Measures.*
   a. **Name each measure as I point to it.**
   b. Hold the cup and pint. **2 cups fill 1 pint; 2 cups fill . . .**
   c. Hold the pint and quart. **2 pints fill 1 quart; 2 pints fill . . .**
5. *Two-step problems.*
   Listen to these two-step problems. When I say "equals," you may raise your hand to answer.

2 + 7 - 4 =	**7 + 3 - 6** =
4 + 6 - 5 =	**6 + 4 - 3** =
4 + 5 - 8 =	**2 + 8 - 4** =
5 + 3 - 4 =	**3 + 4 - 5** =
3 + 7 - 2 =	**8 + 0 - 3** =

6. *Do Speed Drill #72.*
7. *Assign Lesson 170.*

Follow-up

Drill

(*Drill* #1)

8 9 10

1. Ask individuals to write two numbers on the blanks and say four number facts for the triplet.
2. Drill individuals at the grid on the chalkboard.
3. Practice telling time.
   a. Set the hands on the model clock at 4:30. **1 hour ago it was ___.**
   Set the hands at 10:00. **1 hour ago it was ___.**
   6:00 . . . **In 1 hour it will be ___.**
   11:30 . . . **In 1 hour it will be ___.**
   b. Ask individuals to set the hands at 2:00, 5:30, 7:00, 9:30, . . .

Practice Sheets

- ☐ Measures #13
- ☐ Skip Counting #8
- ☐ Clocks #10
- ● Number Facts #63
- ● Story Problems #9
- ● Money #24

Flash Card Activities

Introduction to Flash Cards

Step 1

Hold the pack of flash cards with the side that shows the answer facing the students. Have the class recite the complete fact in unison. Page to the next card, and the next, saying each one rapidly.

Step 2

Hold the flash cards with answers showing. Go around the class and have the children take turns saying the entire fact rapidly.

Step 3

Hold the pack of flash cards, showing the side without the answer. Have the class say the entire fact in unison.

Step 4

With answers not showing, have individuals say the entire fact.

Step 5

Say the answer only, in unison or individually by turn.

Individual Study

Have students follow these steps when they receive new flash cards for individual drill:

1. Look at the answer side and say the entire fact.
2. Look at the side without the answer and say the entire fact. Check the answer on the back after each one.
3. Look at the side without the answer and say the answer only. Check the back of the card after each one.
4. Flip through the stack, saying the answers only, going rapidly from card to card.

Variations for Teacher-led Drills

1. Waterwheel

Have the class form a circle around the room or a smaller area. Flash the cards for individuals to say the answer as they file past you in turn. How steadily and how fast does the water run for your class?

2. Selective Answers

When drilling mixed addition and subtraction, tell the boys to answer all the addition cards and the girls all the subtraction.

3. Silent answers

Let the children hold up the number of fingers to tell the answer to the card you show.

4. My Number

Assign each child a number or two. Have him say the answer only when it is his number.

5. Clock Race

Set a timer for one minute, and flash the cards as rapidly as the class can answer. Count the cards that were answered correctly when the time is up. Repeat the activity daily, striving to break the record again and again.

This may be done with individual students, each keeping his own record on a chart.

Competition Drills

Use these activities with consideration for the slower student. Do not frequently create a situation that shows the slower ones as inferior if they are doing their best.

1. Double Drill

Divide the class into two teams and have them stand in two lines, single file, facing you. The children at the head of the lines compete to say the answer first. The one who gives the correct answer first goes to the back of his line, and the other competes again.

This activity gives more practice to the slower children.

2. Travel

The child in the first seat of row one stands beside the seated child behind him, and they compete to say the answer first. If the standing child gives the correct answer first, he moves on to stand beside the next child in the row. If the standing child loses, he sits in the seat of the one who said the answer first, and that child moves on to the next one.

This activity gives more practice to the faster children.

3. Gather

This is a lively competition for a small group of two or three. All try to say the answer first. If you can perceive who first said the correct answer, give the card to him. If you hear a tie, the card goes back into the pack to resurface later.

Who has gathered the most cards when your hands are empty?

Written Drill

Have the children silently write the answer for each card you flash, using Form C of the Practice Sheets set.

Late in the first grade year, children may be taught to check written flash card drill in class. Use flash cards with a hole punched in the top. Hang the cards one at a time on a nail as the children write their answers.

At the end of the drill, pull the pack of cards off the nail and turn the stack over. Now the card on the top of the pack is the first card of the drill, answer side up. Place this card on the nail, answer showing, and tell the children to compare the answer with the number they wrote in the first box. After they have checked this answer, have them point their checking pencil at the next answer on the paper and look for the answer on the next card as you place it on the nail.

As the children become practiced in checking, you can increase speed, or read the answers aloud.

Oral Story Problems

Oral story problems are valuable practice, but they can be time-consuming. If your own schedule does not allow you to do the job thoroughly, use some of these tips to save time instead of skipping the work.

Consider the alternative of having a helper give the story problems for the class. If a helper is not available, you may economize your time with the class by using some of the following suggestions.

- Dictate the first problem. Then instruct the children to fill in only the two numbers they hear during dictation. After you are finished giving the stories, they shall go back and print all the labels and finish the problems.

- Give just one label for all the story problems, and have the children wait until after dictation to fill in the labels and answers.

- Tell the children to print the two numbers and the first letter of each label while you give the stories. Afterward, have them finish the problems. (All the labels for one problem are always the same.)

Practice Sheets Guide

Each Practice Sheet category is listed here with brief directions.

Forms

Form A—*Number Writing*

The child writes his name, and then turns the page crosswise to write numbers in the rows. Vertical lines form the rows into a grid. Do not allow the children to work in columns, but require them to go across and write the numbers in sequence in every row. At first only a few spaces are used in each row.

Form B—*Number Dictation*

The children will write the number you say. Use the pictures in the left margin to identify which row you are working on.

Form C—*Flash Card Drill*

As you flash number-fact cards, the children will silently write the answer to each fact in a box. Use the pictures in the left margin to identify which row you are working on.

Form D—*Story Problem Dictation*

Write a label or labels on the chalkboard for the children to copy. Carefully give an oral story problem as the children listen. They will write the numbers and labels and the correct sign of operation.

Form E—*Place-value Grid*

Practice writing numbers according to place value. The children write twenty numbers each day.

Form F—*Number Grid*

Practice writing numbers. This sheet has 100 blocks. The children will write their names, and then turn the paper crosswise and write numbers.

Practice Sheets Priority Scale

□ Strengthener

● Basic

◊ Extra

In the daily lesson plan, the Practice Sheets marked with the black circle are the most important, and should be done by all students. The open box marks more fundamental skills; if doing all the sheets, do these first. The open diamond indicates greater challenge or special interest; save these for last.

Practice Sheets Skill Sets

After Numbers

Write the number that comes after the number given.

Before and After

Write the numbers that come before and after.

Before Numbers

Write the number that comes before.

Between Numbers

Write the number that comes between.

Clocks

Write the time each clock shows.

Count and Write

When the items show dot patterns, write the number by recognizing the pattern. When the items show pictures, count the pictures and write the number.

Dot-to-Dot

Draw straight lines from dot to dot. Occasionally an extra activity is involved, as directed in small print at the bottom of the sheet.

Draw and Count

Draw the design shown at the beginning of each row, repeating it to have as many as the number given for that row.

Fact Houses

Write the number facts in order by families. Always have the children write each fact complete with answer before beginning the fact beside it.

A variation when the facts are well known is to write them as twin pairs instead of in the order originally learned. Standard order:

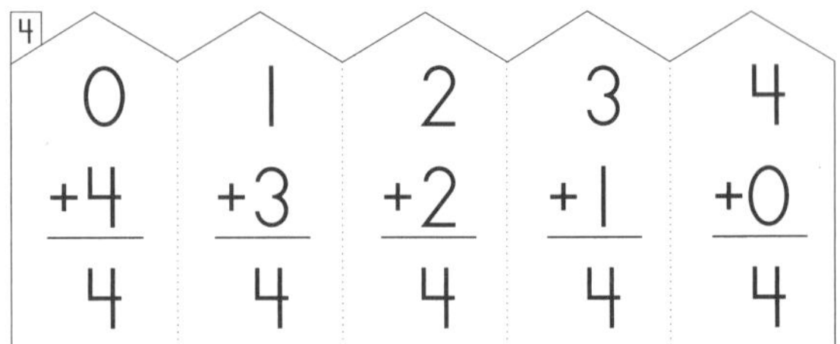

Variation:

4

0	4	1	3	2
+4	+0	+3	+1	+2
4	4	4	4	4

As a diversion, let the children say the facts as they write them in the houses, just loudly enough to hear themselves.

Fractions

On the first sheet, the children trace the fraction bar and write the number of parts in the shape (denominator). For the rest of the sheets, they write the complete fraction, the numerator telling how many of the parts are shaded.

Less Numbers

Circle the number that is less in each box.

Measures

Thermometers: Use a red crayon to color a column of mercury the right height for the temperature given.

Inches: Measure the length or height of each picture. Write the measure.

Dozen: Draw a large circle around twelve

objects in each group.

Liquid:

#9—Write *2 cups fill 1 pint.*

#10—Label each container.

#11—Circle the measure that is more.

#12—Write *2 pints fill 1 quart.*

Missing Numbers

Write the numbers that are missing.

Money

#1—Write 1¢ inside each circle. Then count the pennies and write how many cents.

#2—Color all the coins that look like the ones in the boxes at the top. Use realistic colors.

#3—Count the coins, and write how many cents in the bank.

More Numbers

Circle the number that is more in each box.

Number Facts

Write the answer to each fact.

Number Order

Circle the number that is less. Then write the numbers in correct order on the blanks below.

Number Trains

Write the numbers in the train cars that follow the number in the engine.

Number Words

Write the numeral for each word.

Place Value

Write the digits in the correct places.

Random Counting

For each small picture in the boxes at the bottom, find some like it in the large picture. Count how many there are, and write the number beside the small picture in the box.

Scrambled Numbers

#1 with Lesson 2—Color all the 1's.

#1 with Lesson 3—Color all the 2's.

The remainder will follow suit.

Shapes

Color each shape on the page according to the color guide above.

Skip Counting

Write skip-counting numbers in the blanks according to directions.

Story Problems

Read the sentences. Write the numbers and words and the correct sign. Write the answer to the problem.

Writing Practice

Trace and write the numbers.

Practice Sheets Priority Scale

- □ Strengthener
- ● Basic
- ◊ Extra

In the daily lesson plan, the Practice Sheets marked with the black circle are the most important, and should be done by all students. The open box marks more fundamental skills; if doing all the sheets, do these first. The open diamond indicates greater challenge or special interest; save these for last.

Contents

Practice Sheets Listed by Lesson

Contents

Practice Sheets Listed by Type

Practice Sheets Answer Key

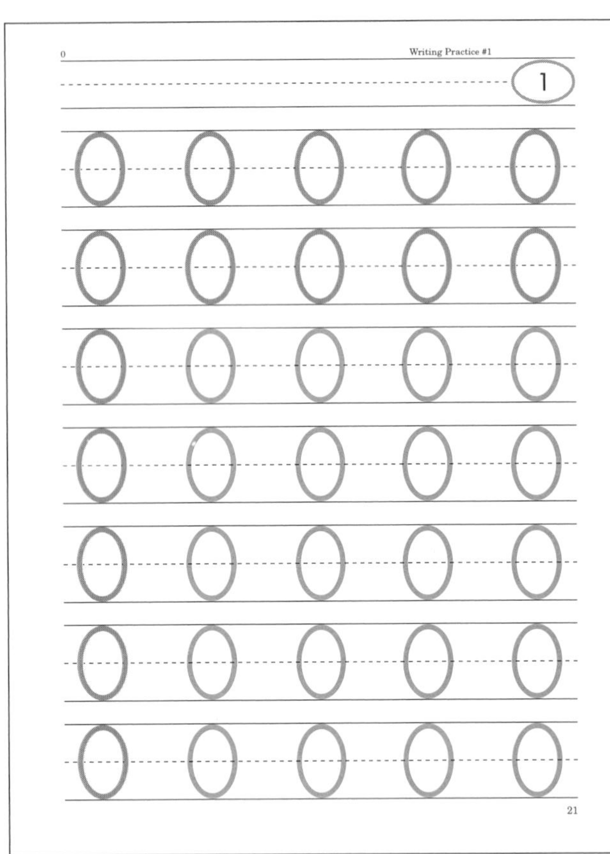

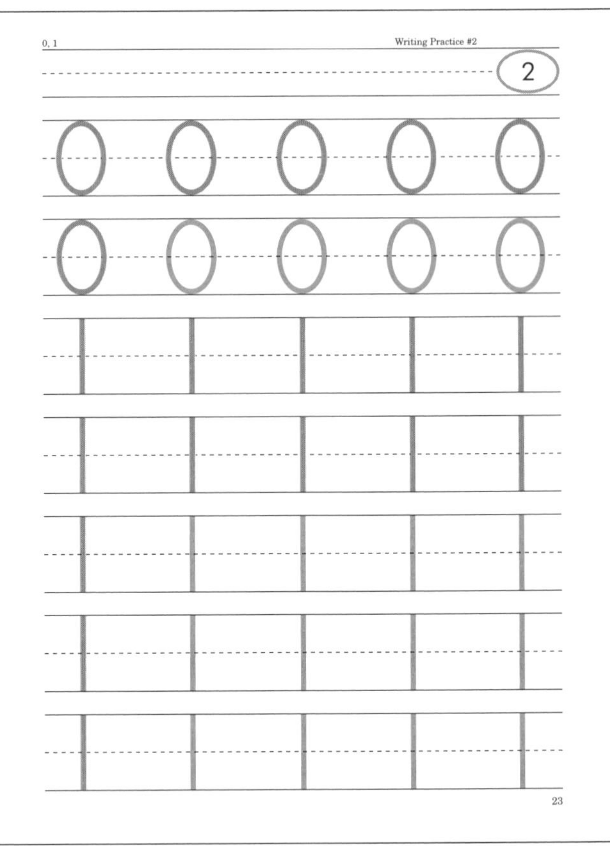

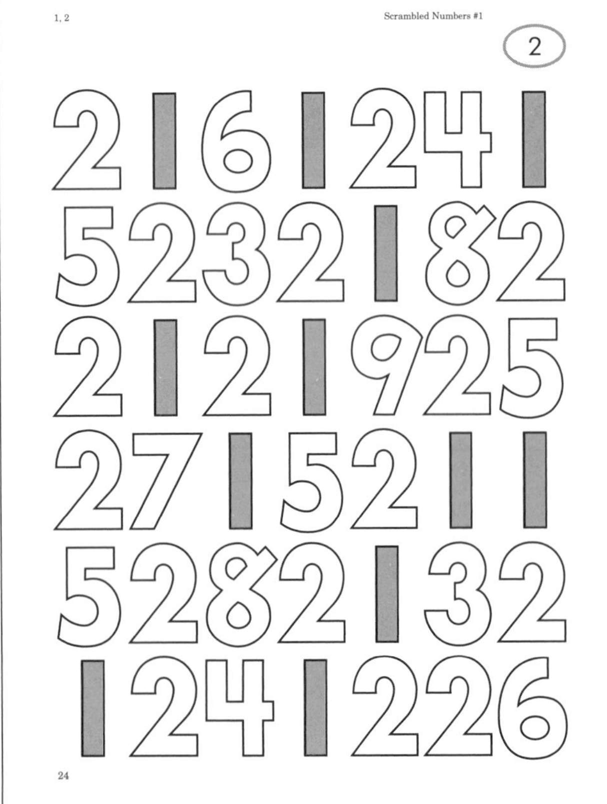

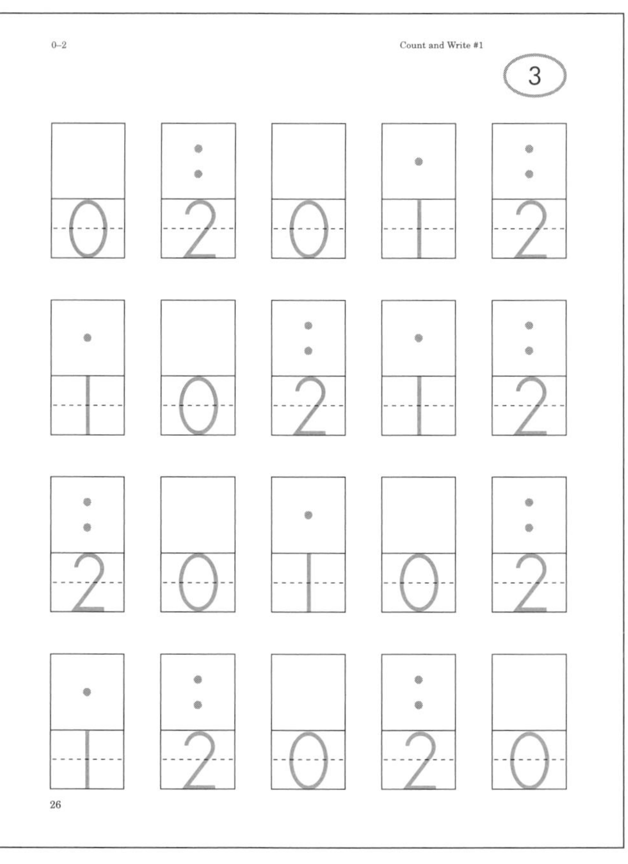
0–2
Count and Write #1
3
0 2 0 1 2
1 0 2 1 2
2 0 1 0 2
1 2 0 2 0
26

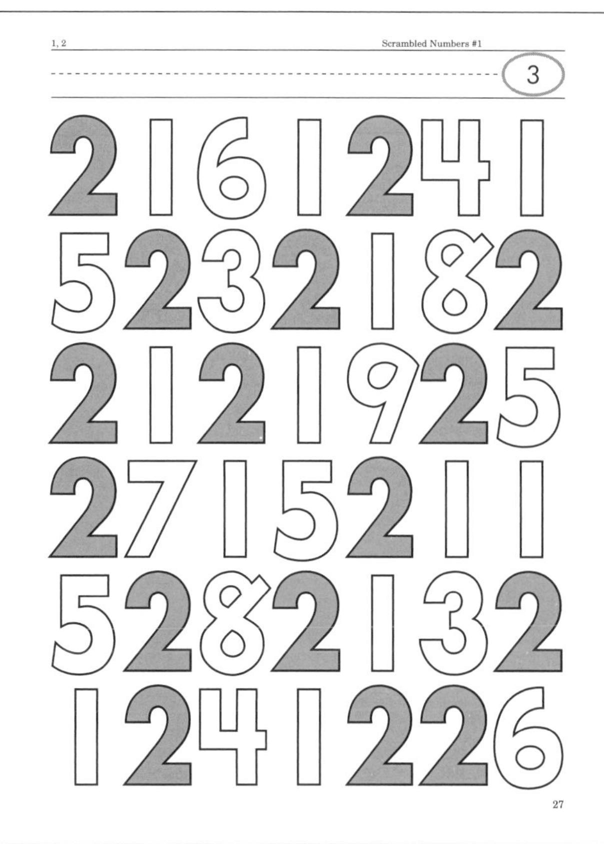
1, 2
Scrambled Numbers #1
3
2 1 6 1 2 4 1
5 2 3 2 1 8 2
2 1 2 1 9 2 5
2 7 1 5 2 1 1
5 2 8 2 1 3 2
1 2 4 1 2 2 6
27

1, 2
Draw and Count #1
3
1
2
2
1
2
1
2
2
1
28

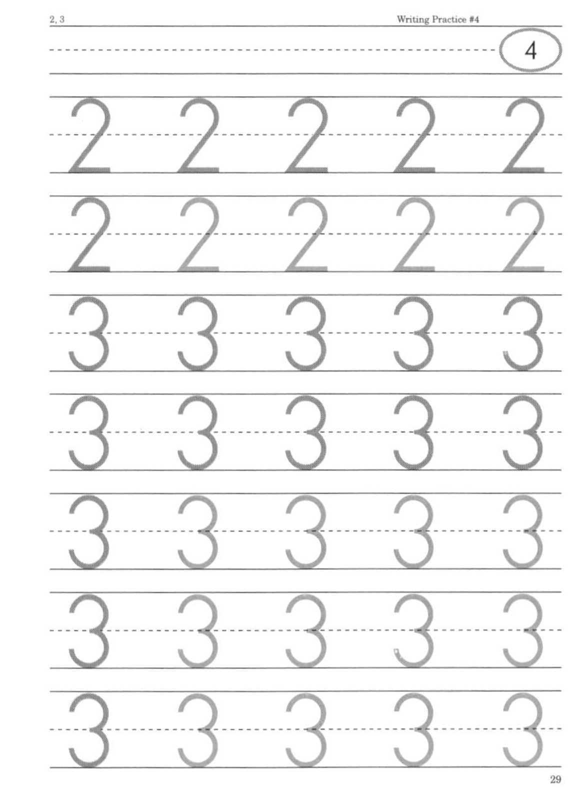
2, 3
Writing Practice #4
4
2 2 2 2 2
2 2 2 2 2
3 3 3 3 3
3 3 3 3 3
3 3 3 3 3
3 3 3 3 3
3 3 3 3 3
29

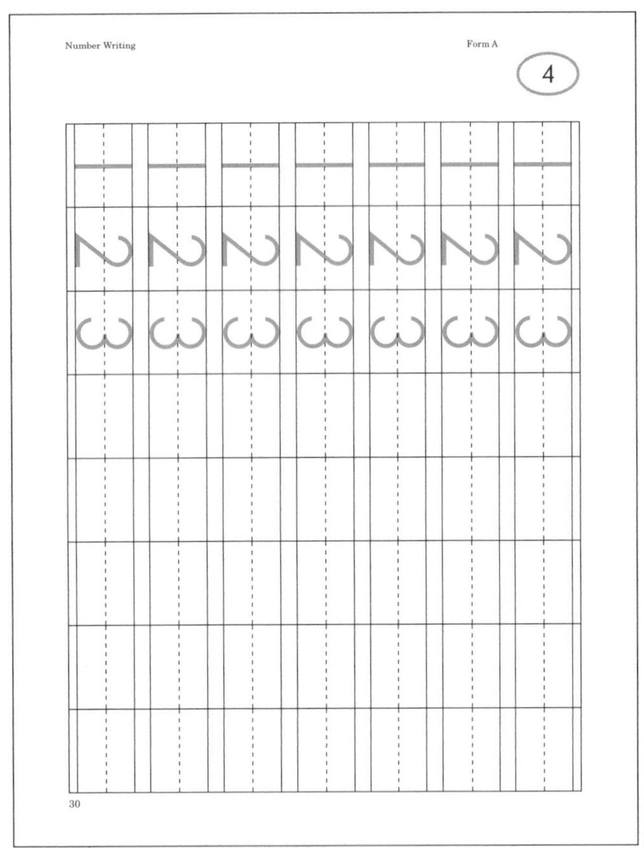
Number Writing
Form A
4
30

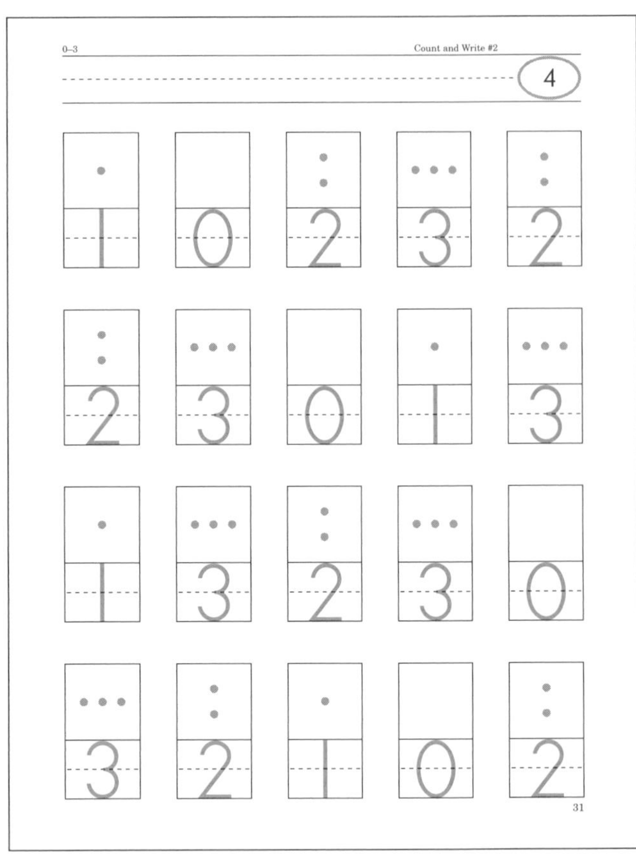
0–3
Count and Write #2
4
31

1–3
Count and Write #3
4
32

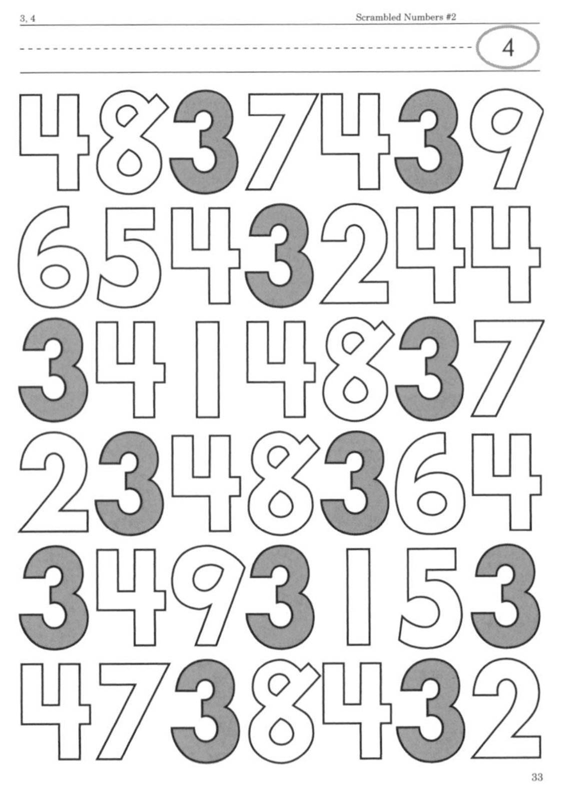
3, 4
Scrambled Numbers #2
4
33

1–3
Dot-to-Dot #1
4
1
2
3
34

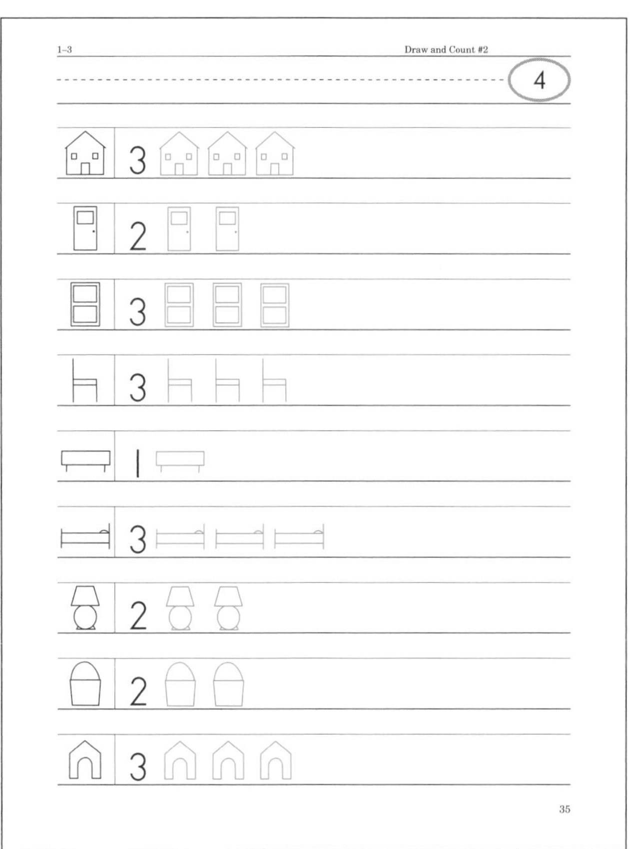
1–3
Draw and Count #2
4
3
2
3
3
1
3
2
2
3
35

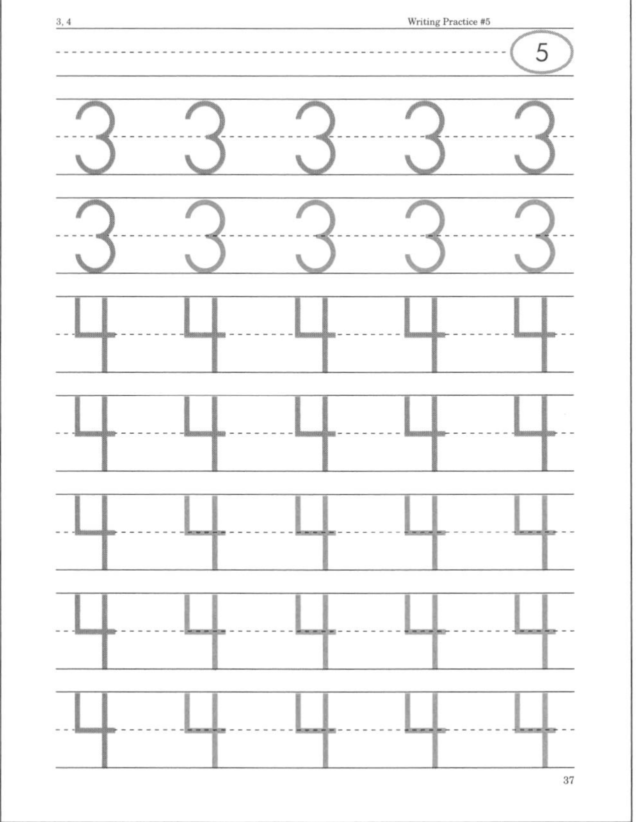
3, 4
Writing Practice #5
5
37

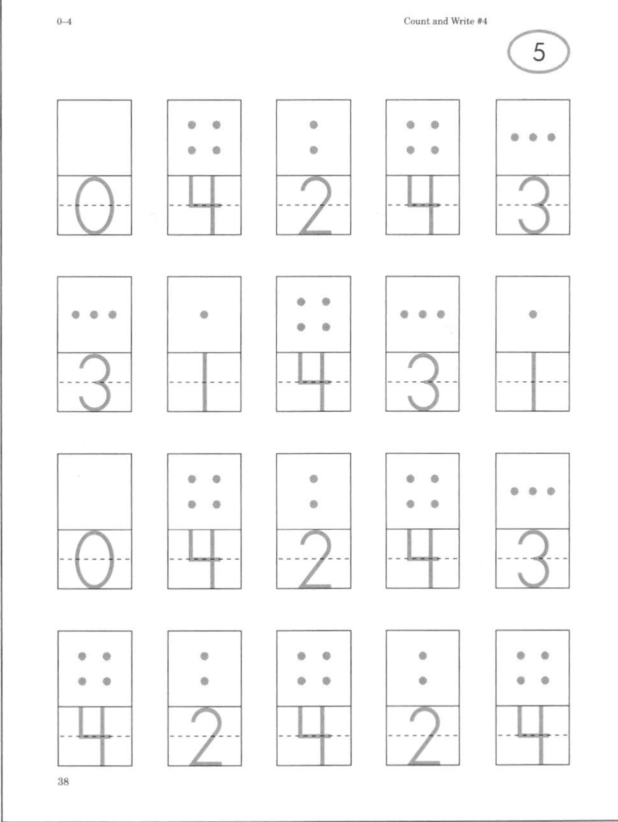
0–4
Count and Write #4
5
0
4
2
4
3
3
1
4
3
1
0
4
2
4
3
4
2
4
2
4
38

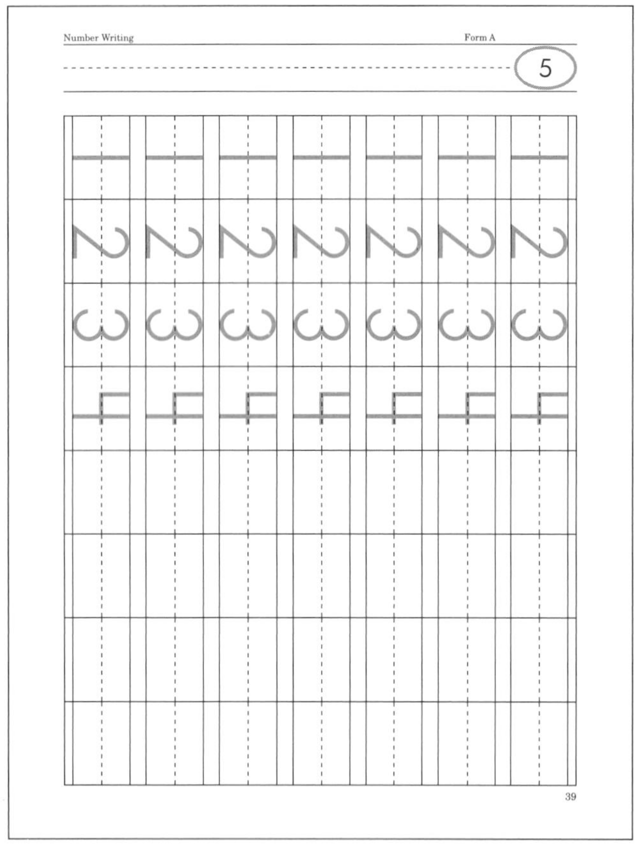
Number Writing
Form A
5
39

1–4
Count and Write #5
5
40

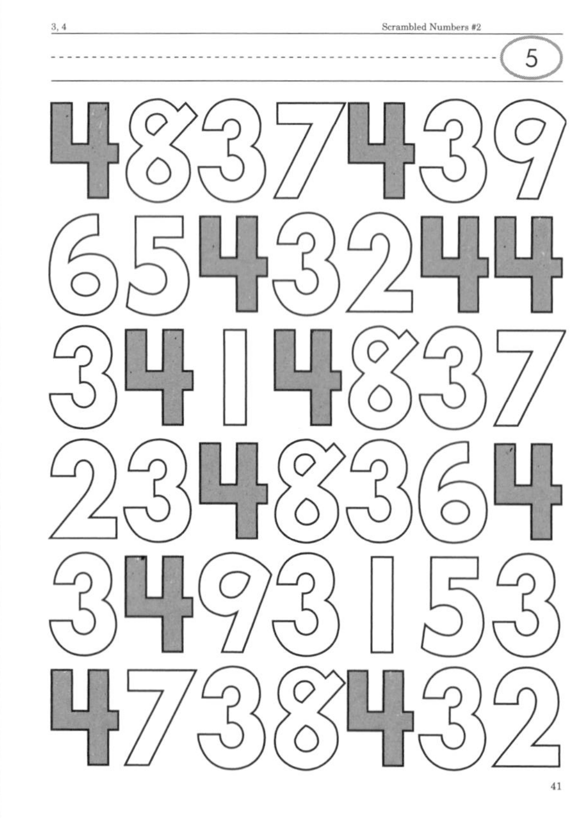
3, 4
Scrambled Numbers #2
5
4837439
6543244
3414837
2348364
3493153
4738432
41

1–4
Dot-to-Dot #2
5
42

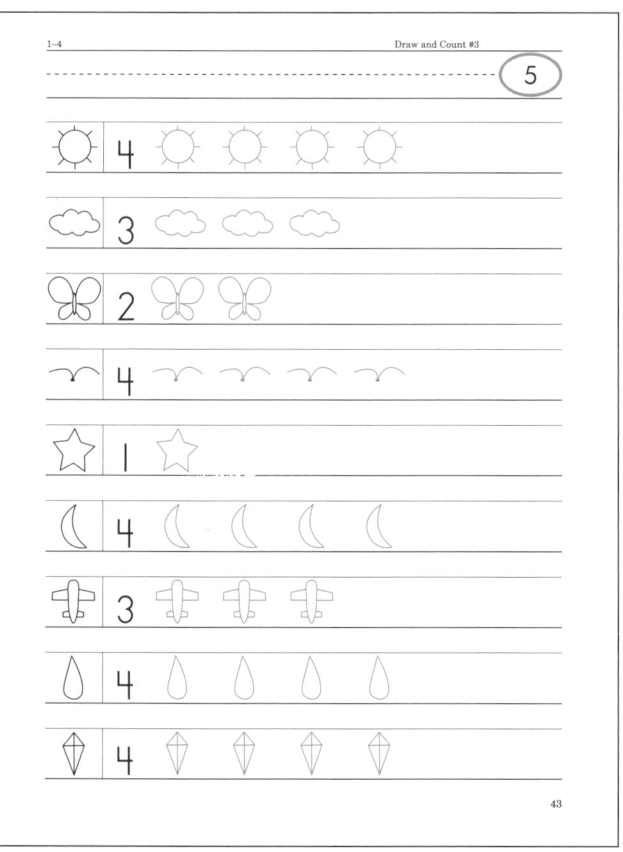
1-4
Draw and Count #3
5
4
3
2
4
1
4
3
4
4
43

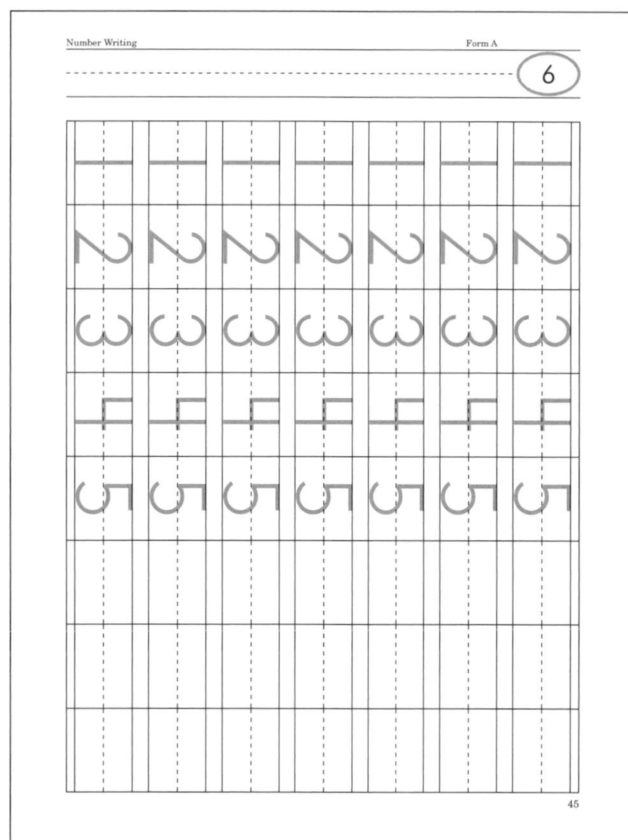
Number Writing
Form A
6
45

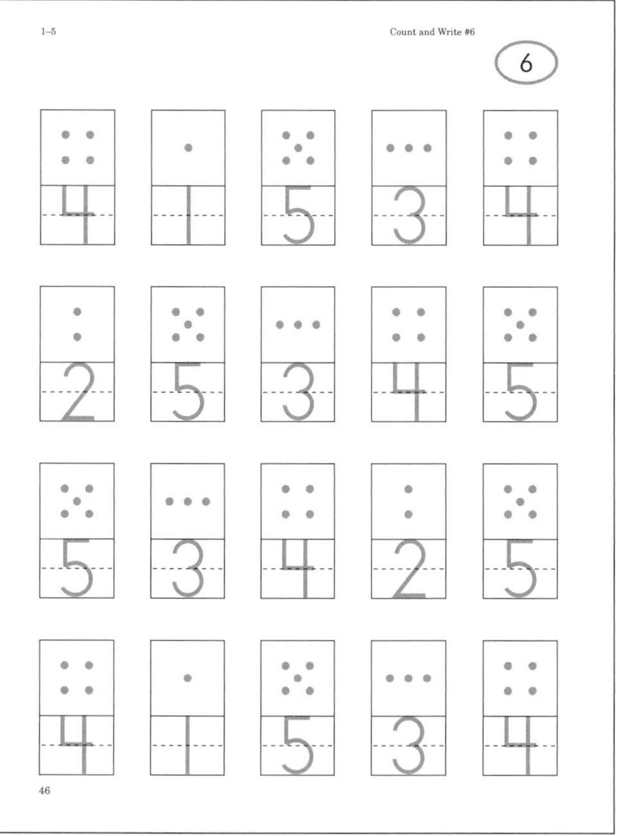
1-5
Count and Write #6
6
4 1 5 3 4
2 5 3 4 5
5 3 4 2 5
4 1 5 3 4
46

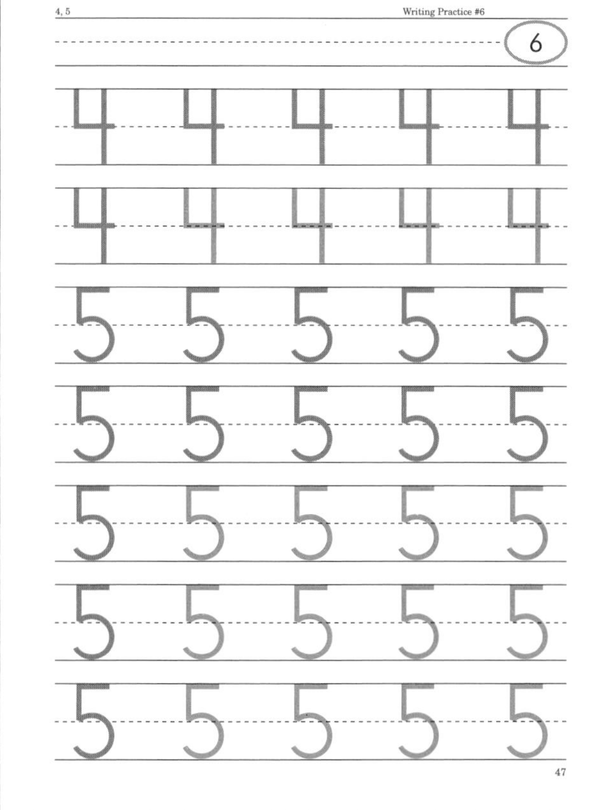
4, 5
Writing Practice #6
6
47

2–5
Count and Write #7
6
5
3
3
5
5
4
5
4
2
5
48

1–5
Dot-to-Dot #3
6
1
2
3
4
5
49

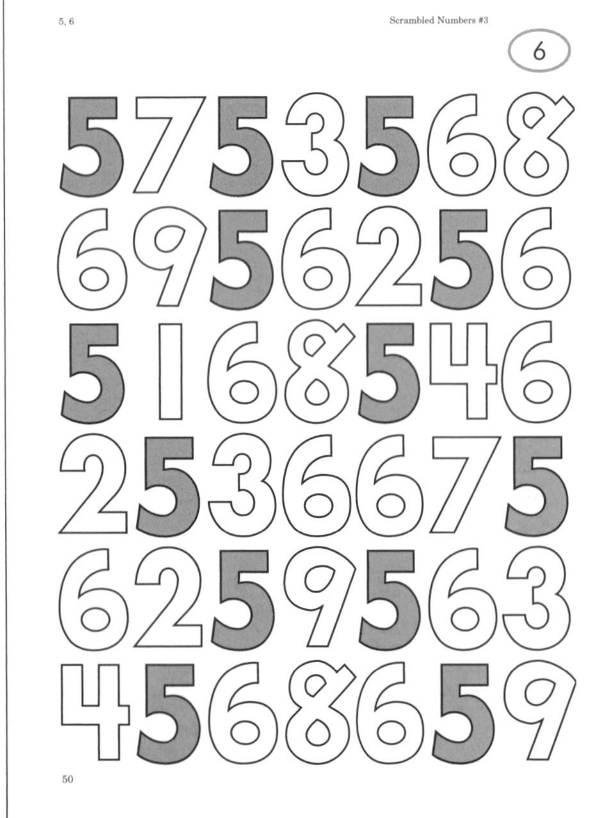
5, 6
Scrambled Numbers #3
6
5753568
6956256
5168546
2536675
6259563
4568659
50

2–5
Draw and Count #4
6
2
5
4
4
5
5
3
4
5
51

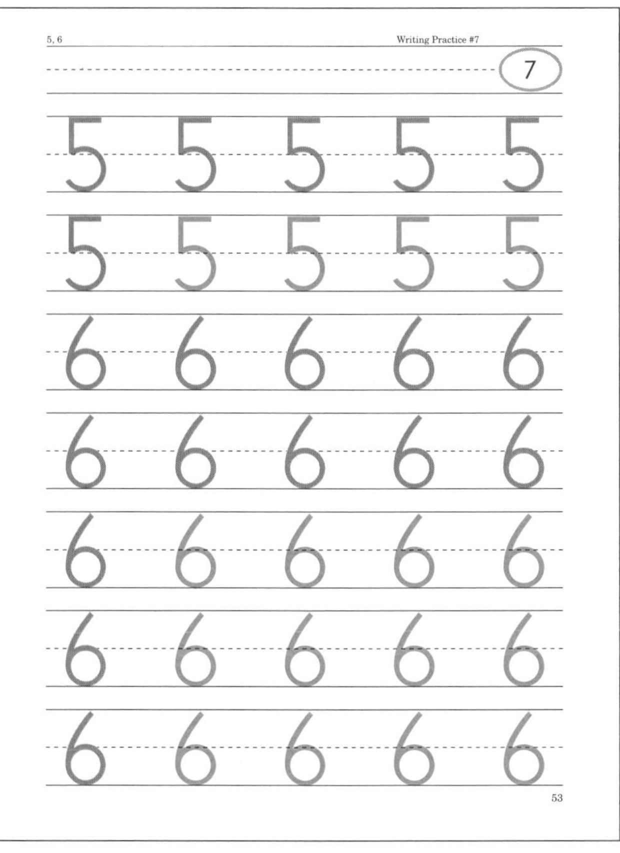
5, 6
Writing Practice #7
7
53

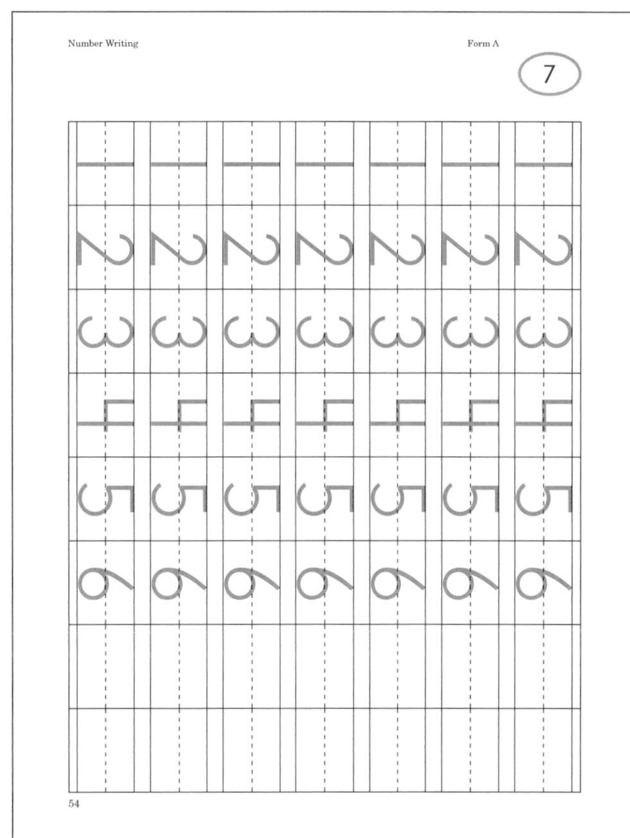
Number Writing
Form A
7
54

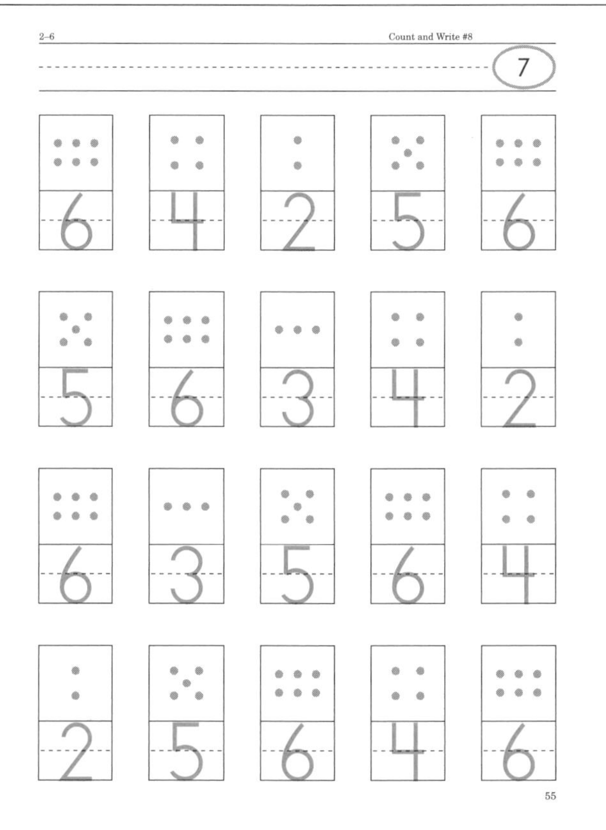
2–6
Count and Write #8
7
6 4 2 5 6
5 6 3 4 2
6 3 5 6 4
2 5 6 4 6
55

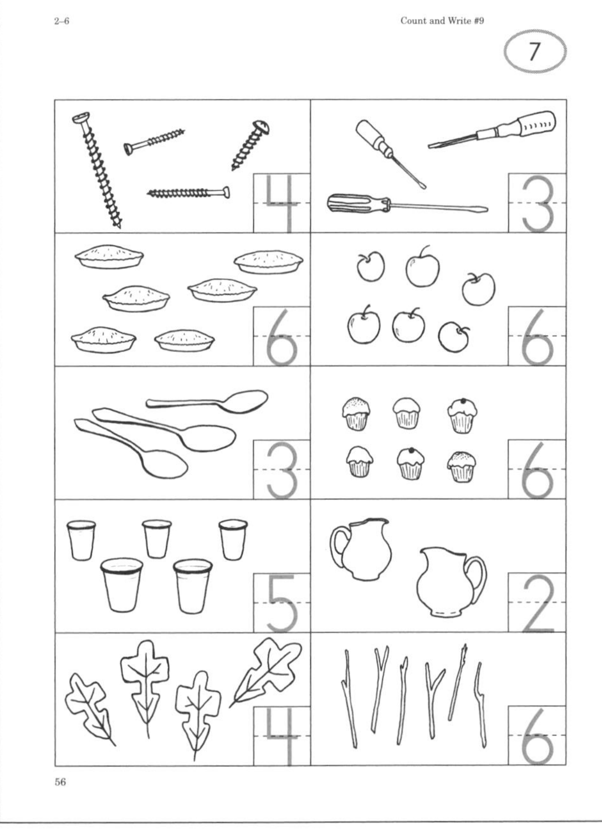
2–6
Count and Write #9
7
4 3
6 6
3 6
5 2
4 6
56

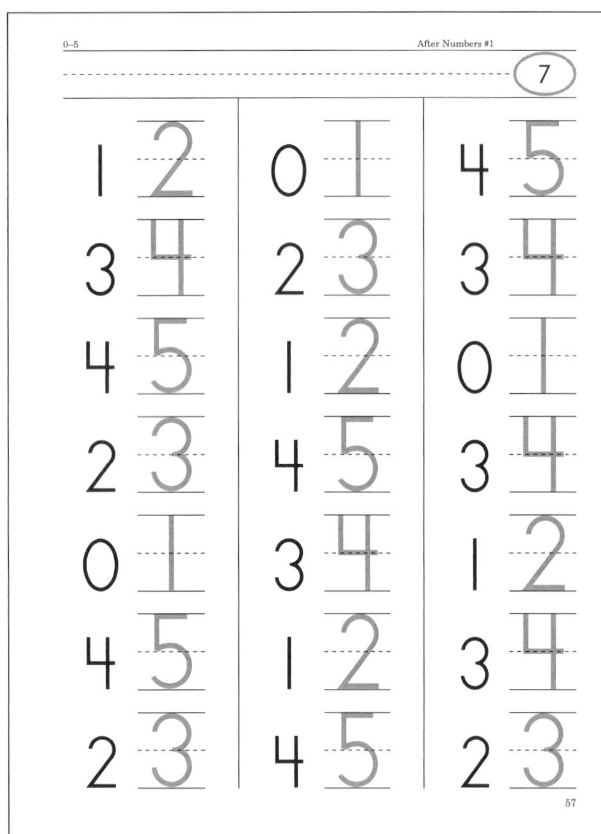
0–5
After Numbers #1
7
1 2
3 4
4 5
2 3
0 1
4 5
2 3
0 1
2 3
1 2
4 5
3 4
1 2
4 5
4 5
3 4
0 1
3 4
1 2
3 4
2 3
57

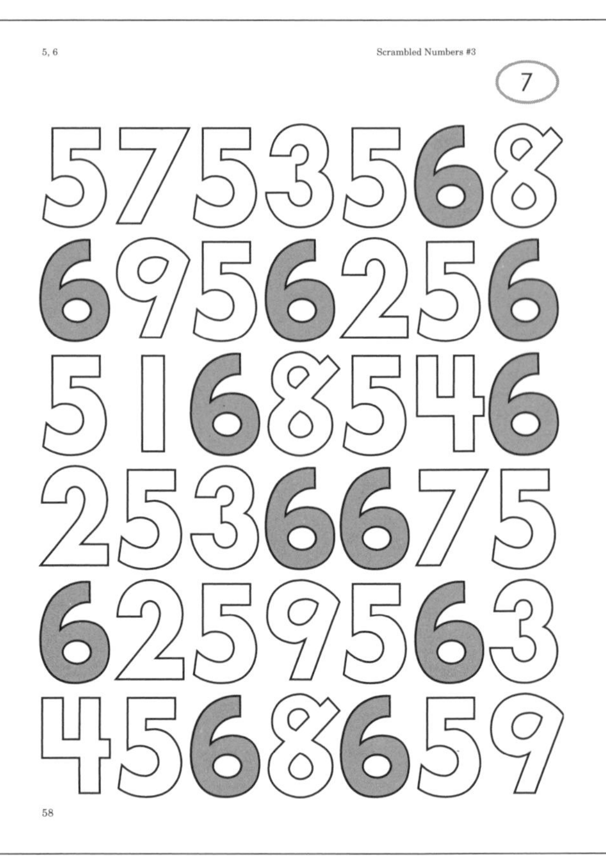
5, 6
Scrambled Numbers #3
7
5753568
6956256
5168546
2536675
6259563
4568659
58

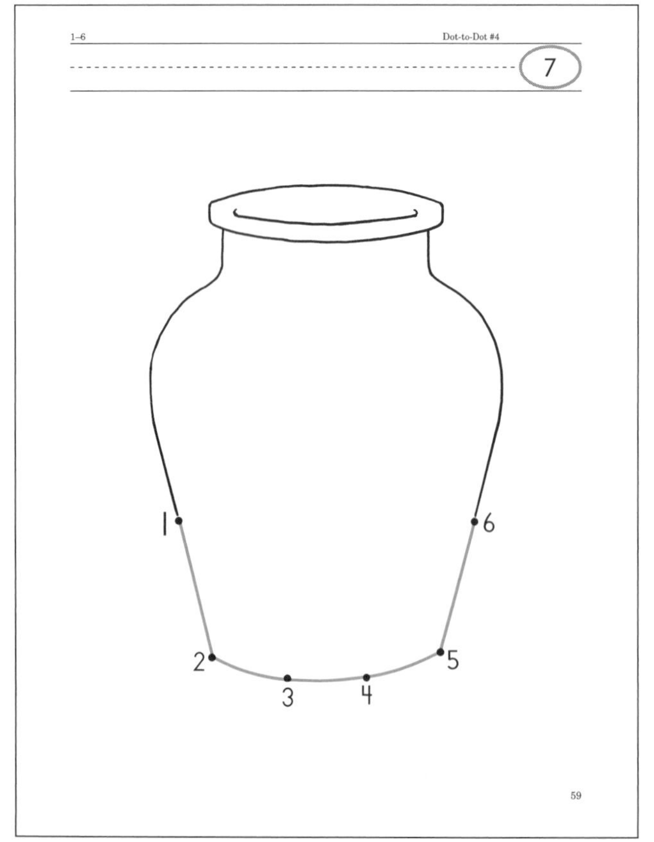
1–6
Dot-to-Dot #4
7
1
2
3
4
5
6
59

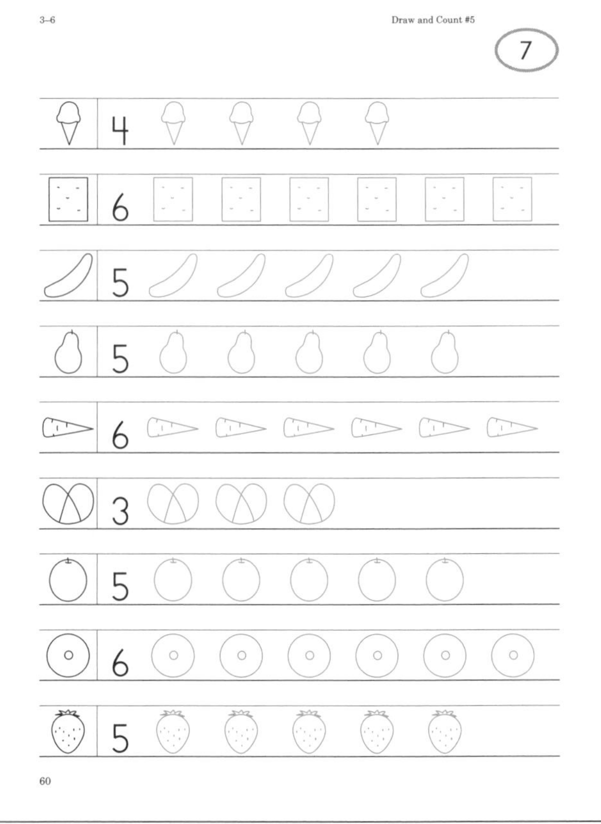
3–6
Draw and Count #5
7
4
6
5
5
6
3
5
6
5
60

6, 7 Writing Practice #8

8

6 6 6 6 6
6 6 6 6 6
7 7 7 7 7
7 7 7 7 7
7 7 7 7 7
7 7 7 7 7
7 7 7 7 7

61

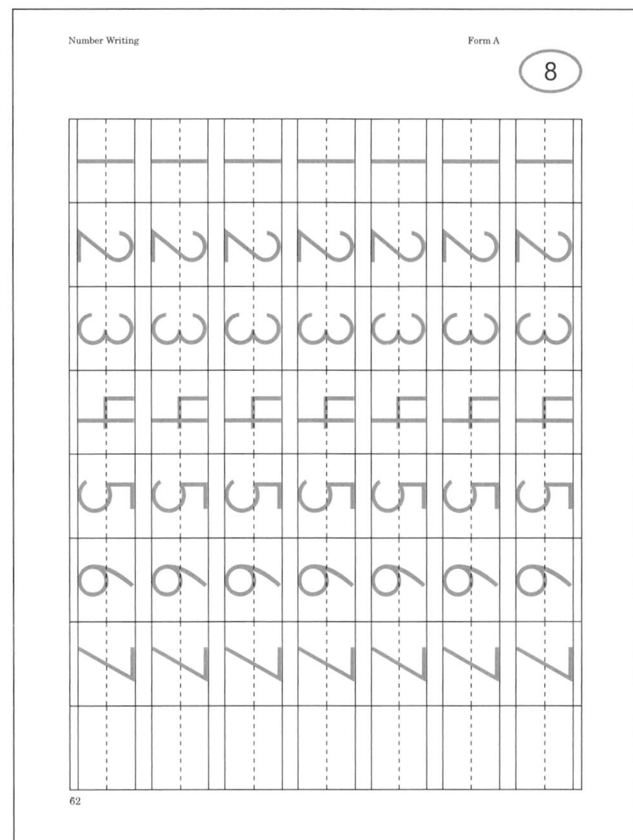
Number Writing Form A

8

1 1 1 1 1 1 1
2 2 2 2 2 2 2
3 3 3 3 3 3 3
4 4 4 4 4 4 4
5 5 5 5 5 5 5
6 6 6 6 6 6 6
7 7 7 7 7 7 7

62

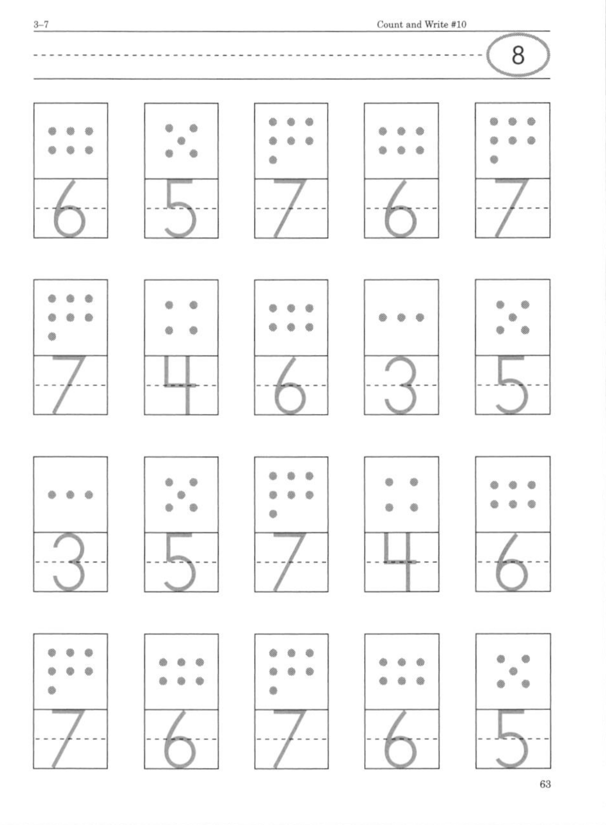
3–7 Count and Write #10

8

6 5 7 6 7
7 4 6 3 5
3 5 7 4 6
7 6 7 6 5

63

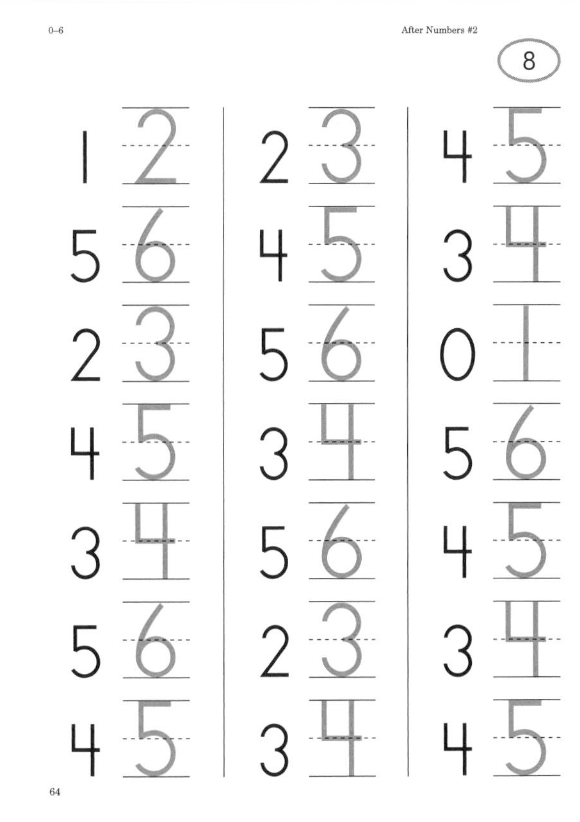
0–6 After Numbers #2

8

1 2	2 3	4 5
5 6	4 5	3 4
2 3	5 6	0 1
4 5	3 4	5 6
3 4	5 6	4 5
5 6	2 3	3 4
4 5	3 4	4 5

64

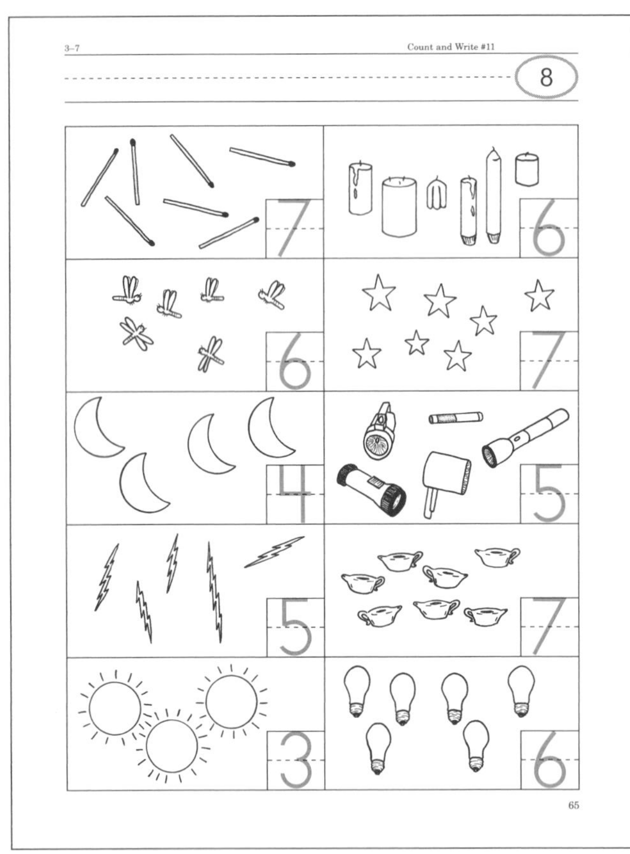
3–7
Count and Write #11
8
7
6
6
7
4
5
5
7
3
6
65

7, 8
Scrambled Numbers #4
8
3872768
71895774
87473863
58287977
37861778
89478837
66

1–7
Dot-to-Dot #5
8
1
7
2 3 4 5 6
67

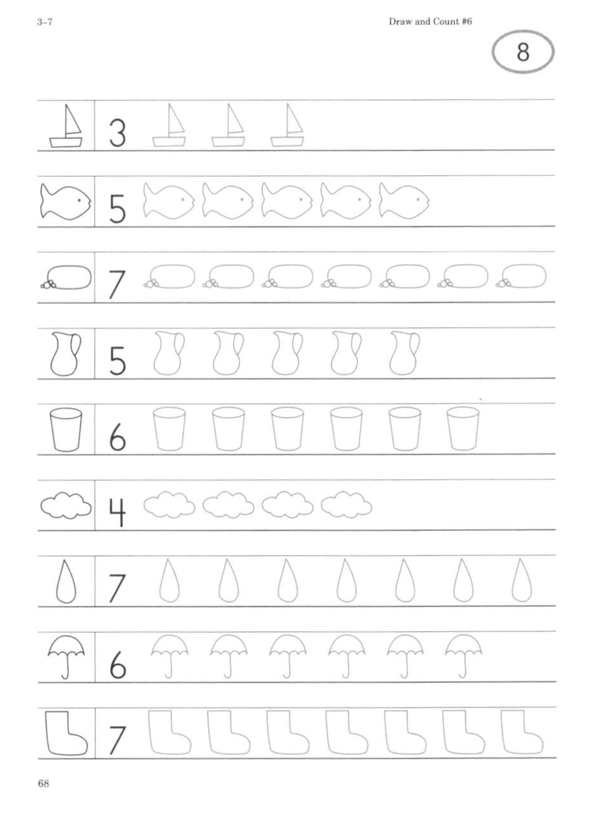
3–7
Draw and Count #6
8
3
5
7
5
6
4
7
6
7
68

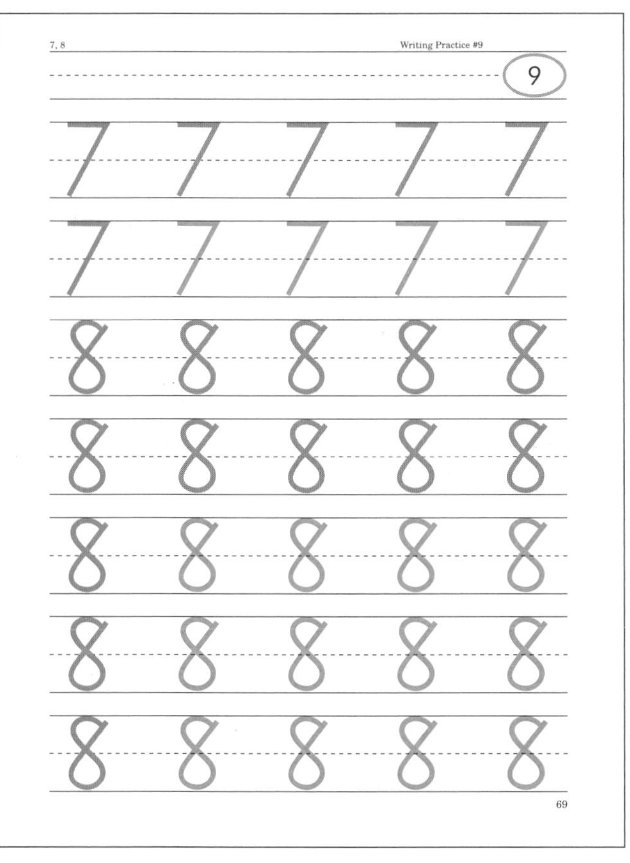
7, 8 Writing Practice #9

9

7 7 7 7 7

7 7 7 7 7

8 8 8 8 8

8 8 8 8 8

8 8 8 8 8

8 8 8 8 8

8 8 8 8 8

69

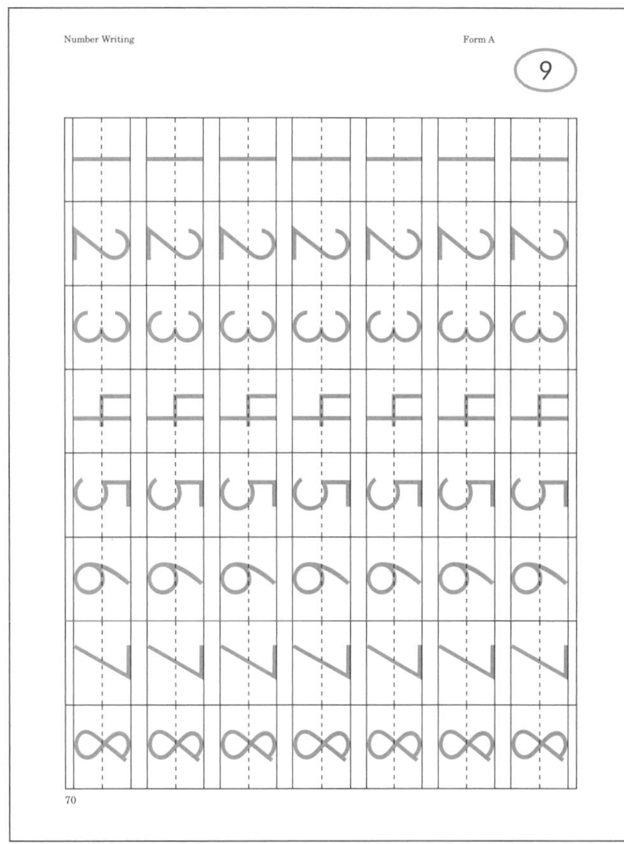
Number Writing Form A

9

1	1	1	1	1	1	1
2	2	2	2	2	2	2
3	3	3	3	3	3	3
4	4	4	4	4	4	4
5	5	5	5	5	5	5
6	6	6	6	6	6	6
7	7	7	7	7	7	7
8	8	8	8	8	8	8

70

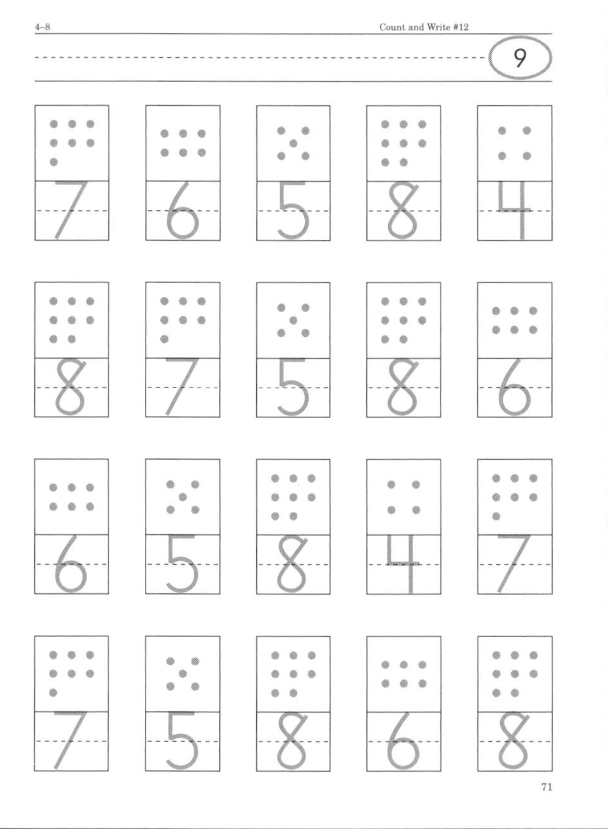
4–8 Count and Write #12

9

7 6 5 8 4

8 7 5 8 6

6 5 8 4 7

7 5 8 6 8

71

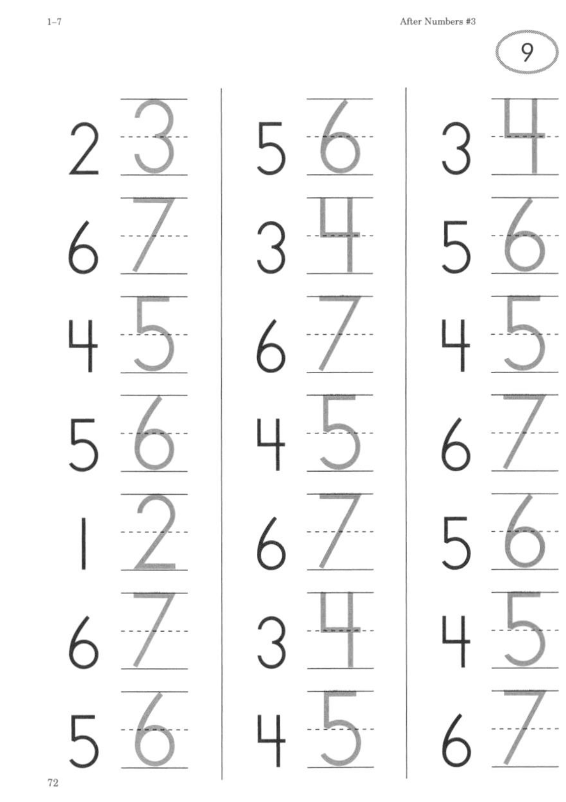
1–7 After Numbers #3

9

2 3	5 6	3 4
6 7	3 4	5 6
4 5	6 7	4 5
5 6	4 5	6 7
1 2	6 7	5 6
6 7	3 4	4 5
5 6	4 5	6 7

72

4–8
Count and Write #13
9
8
7
6
8
8
4
7
6
5
8
73

7, 8
Scrambled Numbers #4
9
3872768
7189574
8747386
5828797
3786178
8947837
74

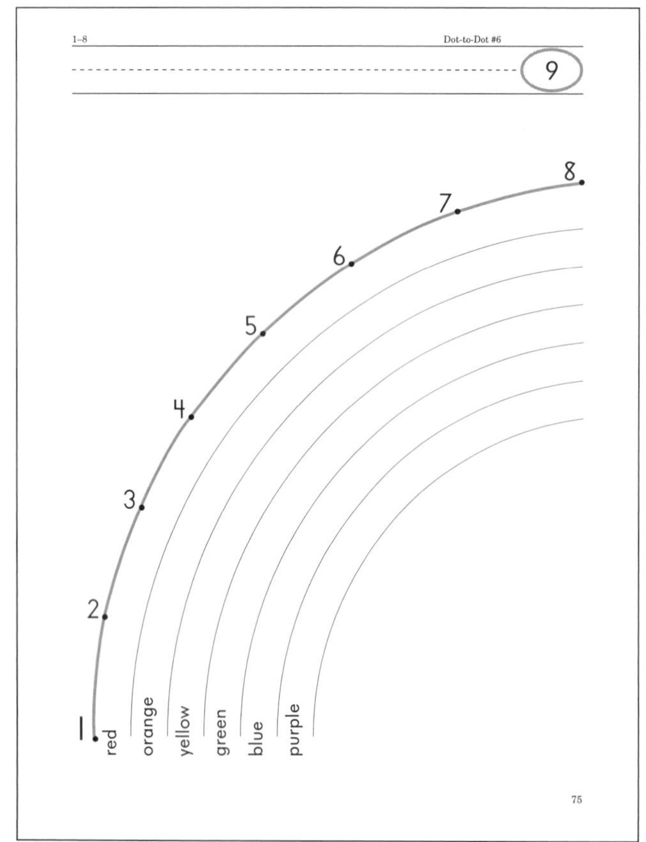
1–8
Dot-to-Dot #6
9
1
2
3
4
5
6
7
8
red
orange
yellow
green
blue
purple
75

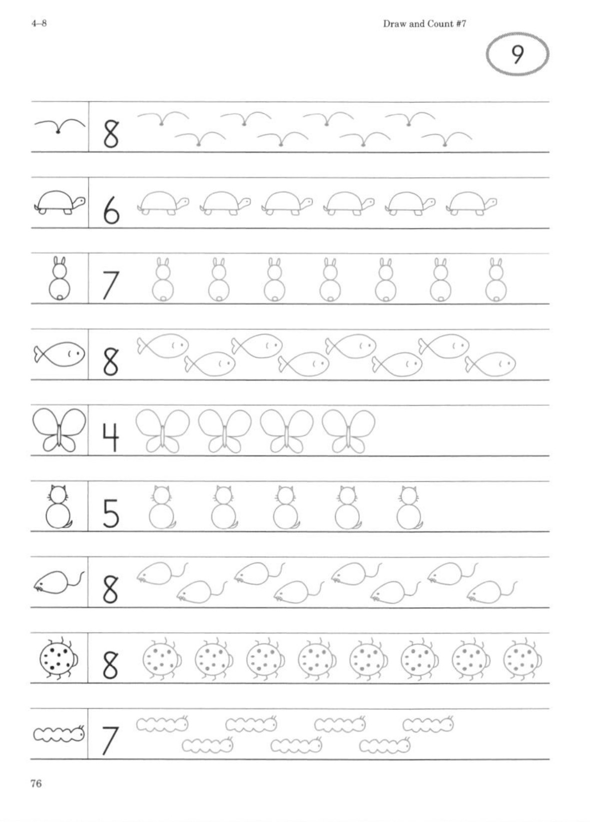
4–8
Draw and Count #7
9
8
6
7
8
4
5
8
8
7
76

Number Dictation
Form B
10
1 6 2 4 3 7
1 3 2 8 3 5
1 9 2 7 3 6
1 2 2 8 3 9
1 7 2 6 3 8
77

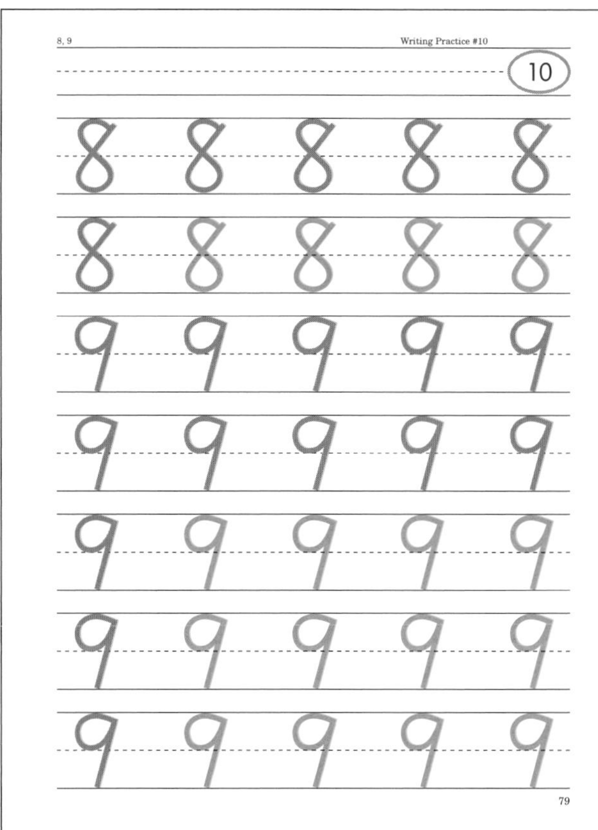
8, 9
Writing Practice #10
10
79

5–9
Count and Write #14
10
8 6 9 7 9
7 9 8 7 8
9 5 8 6 7
8 7 9 8 9
80

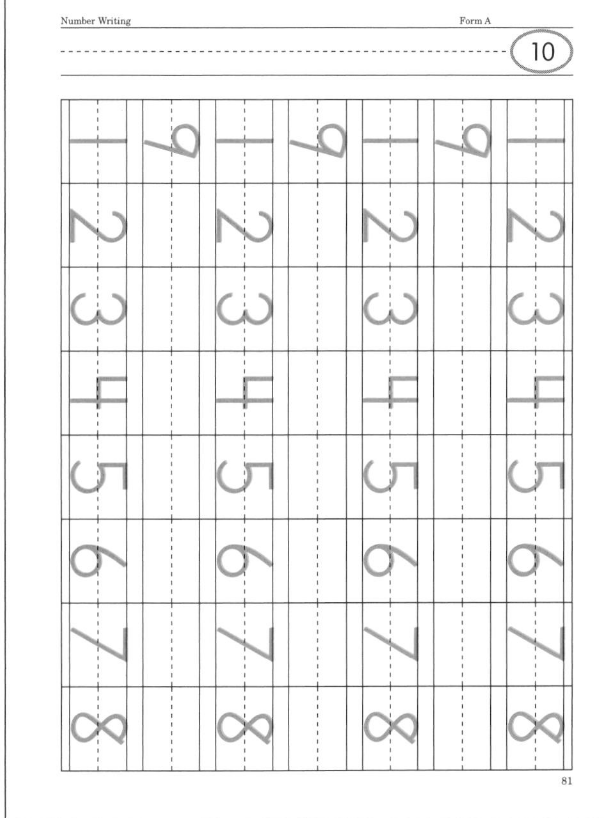
Number Writing
Form A
10
81

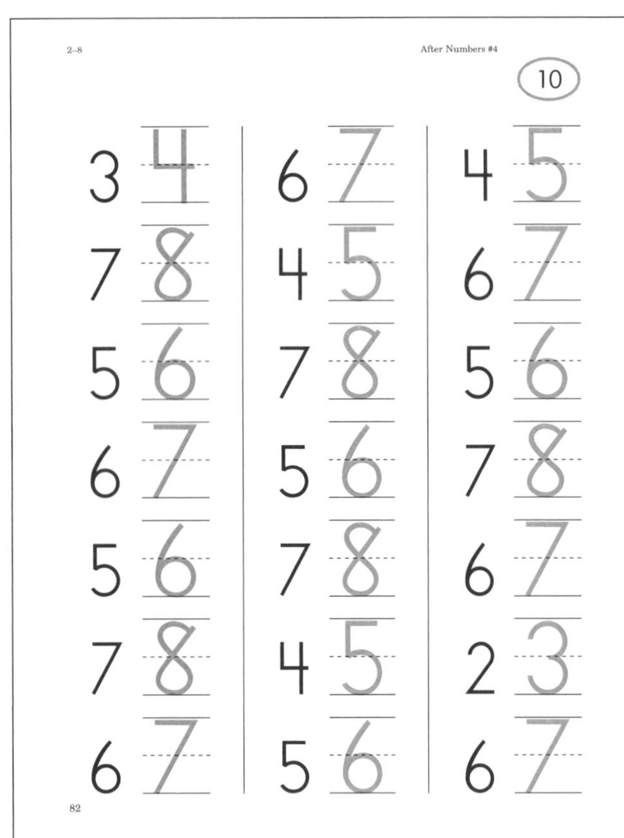
2–8
After Numbers #4
10
3 4 6 7 4 5
7 8 4 5 6 7
5 6 7 8 5 6
6 7 5 6 7 8
5 6 7 8 6 7
7 8 4 5 2 3
6 7 5 6 6 7
82

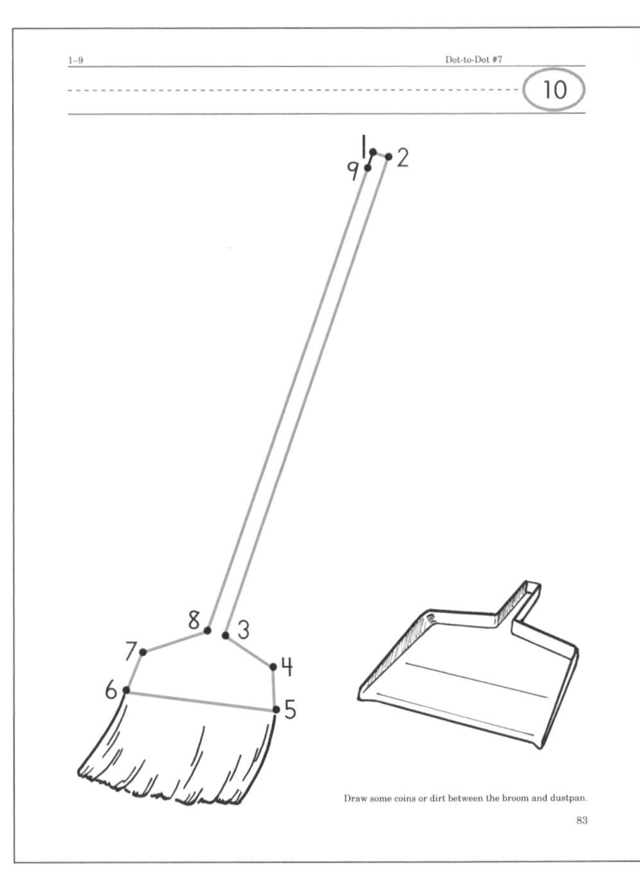
1–9
Dot-to-Dot #7
10
Draw some coins or dirt between the broom and dustpan.
83

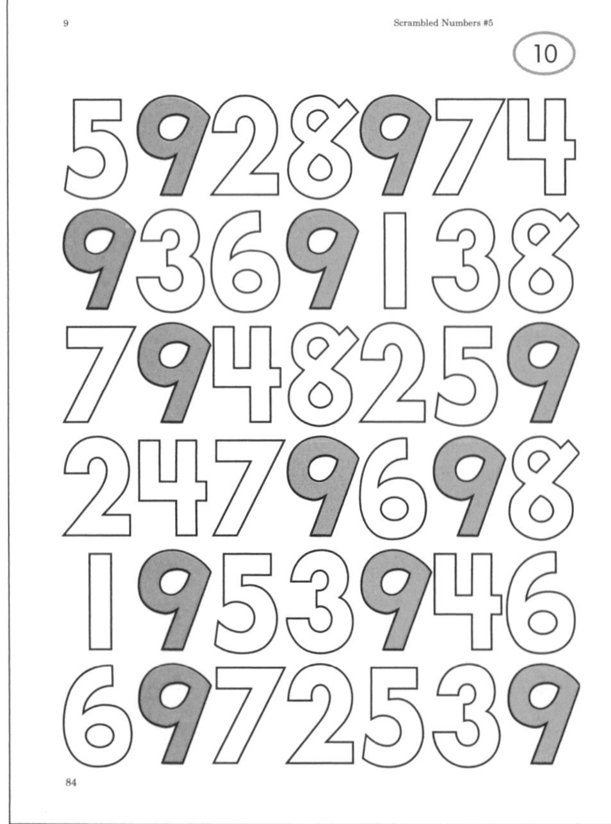
9
Scrambled Numbers #5
10
5928974
9369138
7948259
2479698
1953946
6972539
84

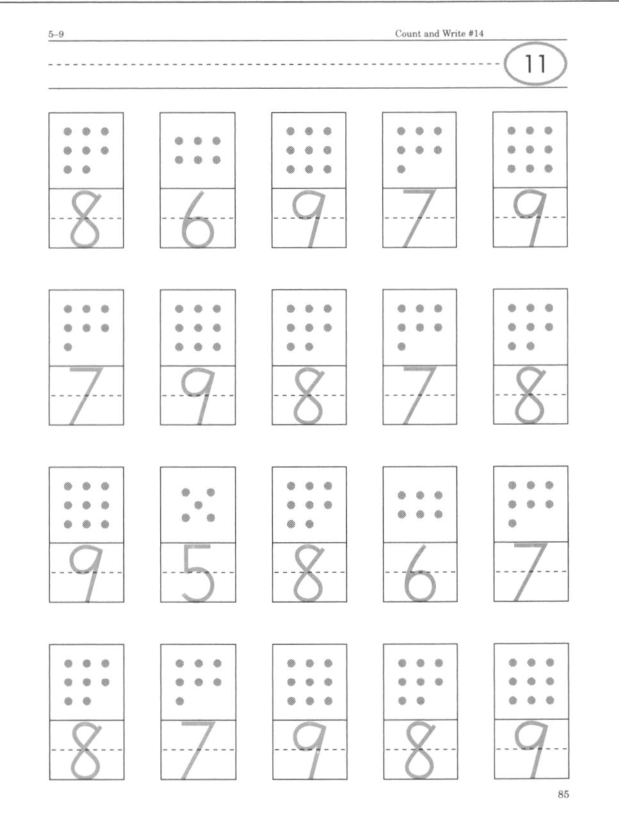
5–9
Count and Write #14
11
8 6 9 7 9
7 9 8 7 8
9 5 8 6 7
8 7 9 8 9
85

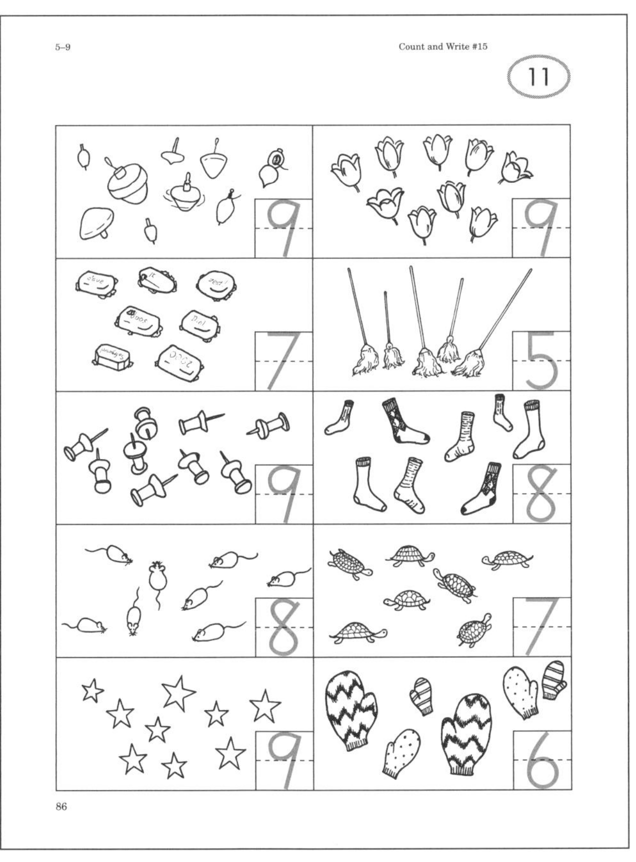
5–9
Count and Write #15
11
9
9
7
5
9
8
8
7
9
6
86

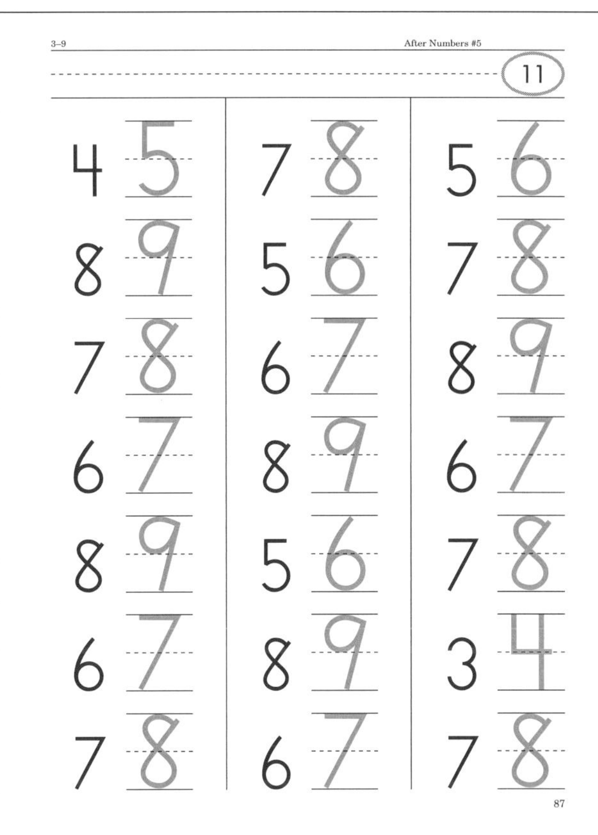
3–9
After Numbers #5
11
4 5
7 8
5 6
8 9
5 6
7 8
7 8
6 7
8 9
6 7
8 9
6 7
8 9
5 6
7 8
6 7
8 9
3 4
7 8
6 7
7 8
87

1–9
Random Counting #1
11
2
1
3
7
6
9
4
5
8
88

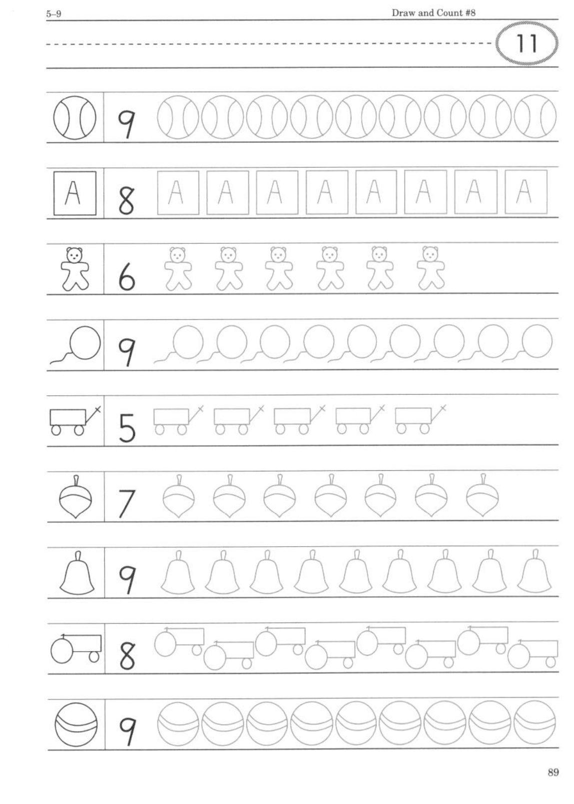
5–9
Draw and Count #8
11
9
A 8 A A A A A A A A
6
9
5
7
9
8
9
89

Number Dictation Form B

12

	1	2	3
(apple)	10	8	9
(nest)	7	10	6
(igloo)	5	9	4
(octopus)	8	7	10
(umbrella)	9	10	8

91

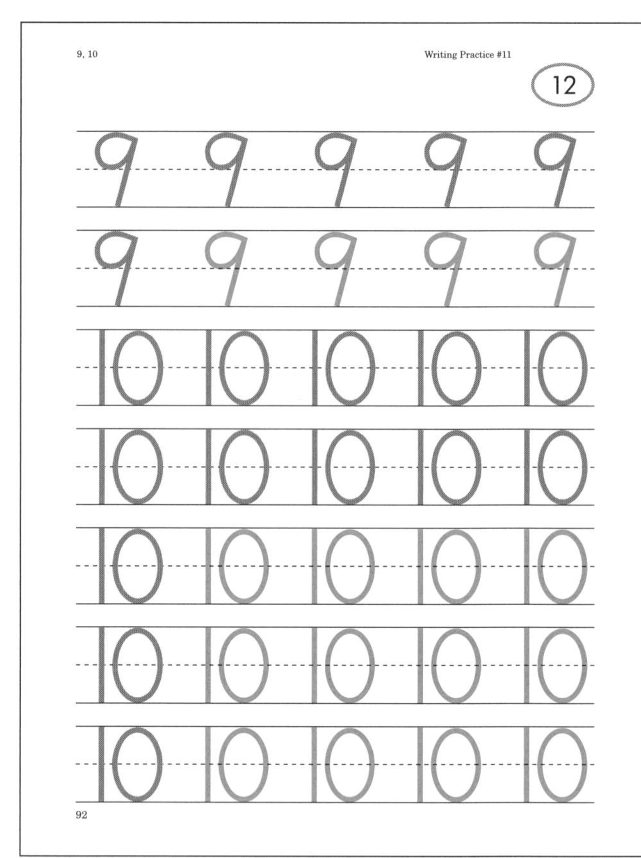
9, 10 Writing Practice #11

12

9 9 9 9 9
9 9 9 9 9
10 10 10 10 10
10 10 10 10 10
10 10 10 10 10
10 10 10 10 10
10 10 10 10 10

92

0–10 Between Numbers #1

12

2 3 4	8 9 10	7 8 9
6 7 8	5 6 7	3 4 5
0 1 2	1 2 3	6 7 8
5 6 7	8 9 10	5 6 7
8 9 10	7 8 9	4 5 6
3 4 5	5 6 7	8 9 10
7 8 9	8 9 10	4 5 6

93

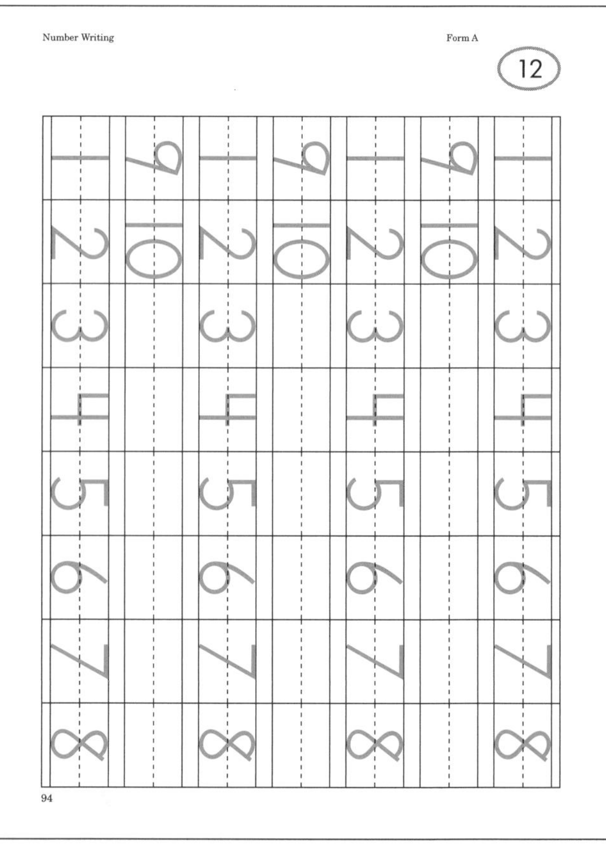
Number Writing Form A

12

94

1–10
Dot-to-Dot #8
12
95

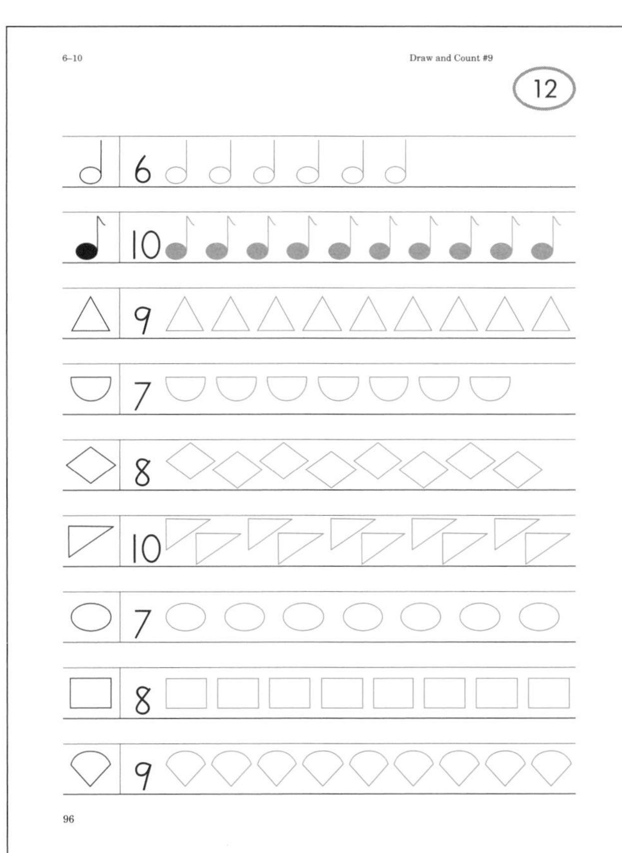
6–10
Draw and Count #9
12
6
10
9
7
8
10
7
8
9
96

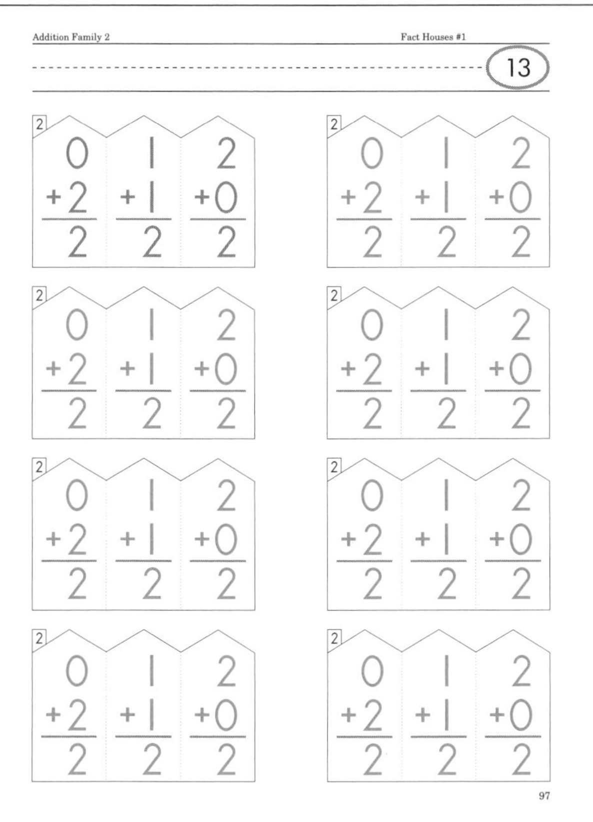
Addition Family 2
Fact Houses #1
13
97

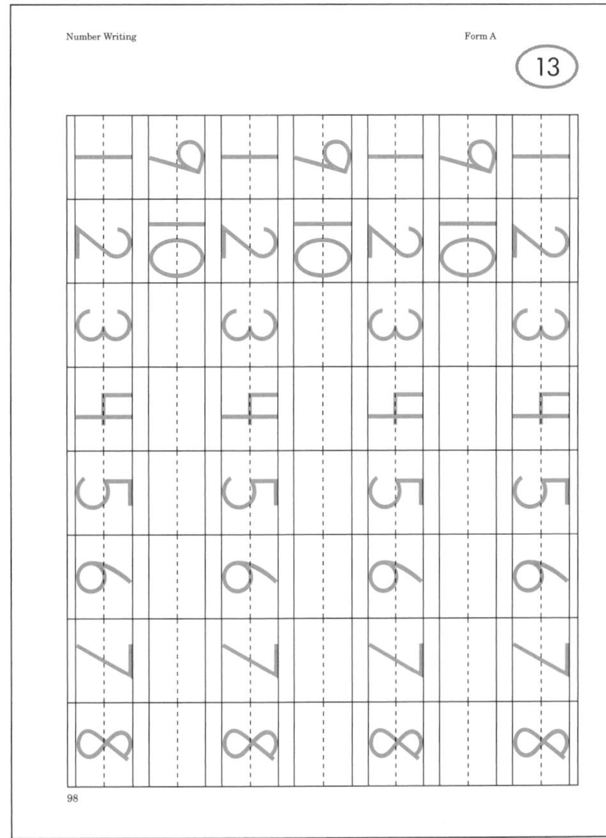
Number Writing
Form A
13
98

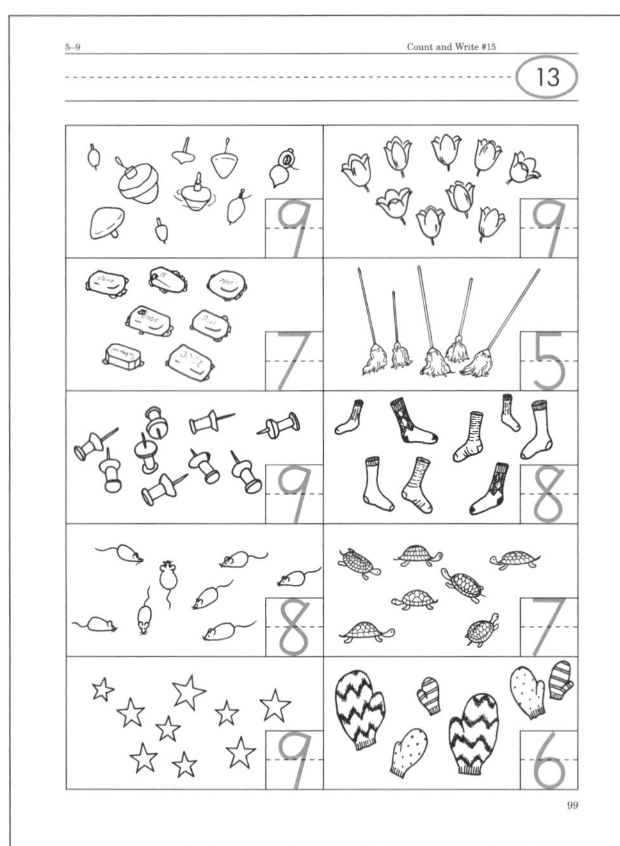
5–9 Count and Write #15

13

9	9
7	5
9	8
8	7
9	6

99

0–10 Between Numbers #2

13

7 8 9	0 1 2	1 2 3
2 3 4	8 9 10	7 8 9
6 7 8	1 2 3	8 9 10
4 5 6	8 9 10	4 5 6
2 3 4	5 6 7	7 8 9
6 7 8	3 4 5	8 9 10
5 6 7	6 7 8	3 4 5

100

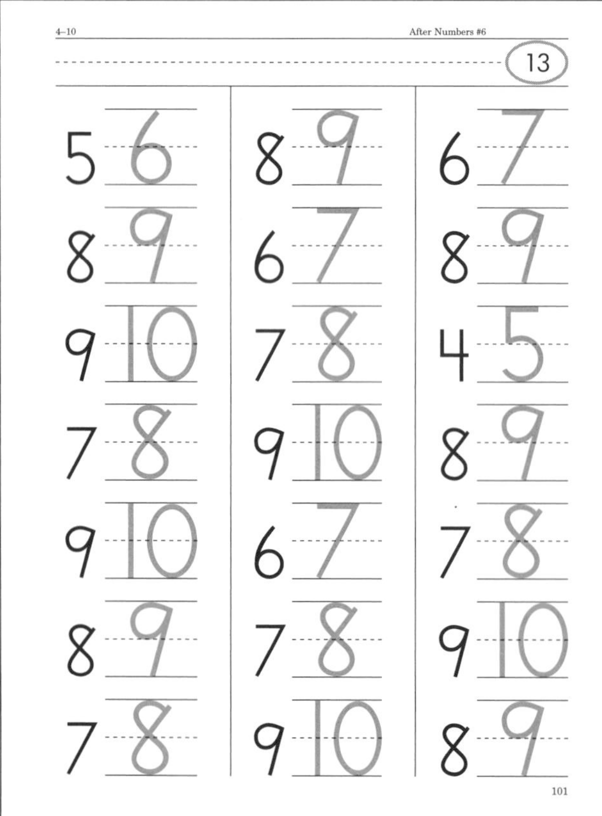
4–10 After Numbers #6

13

5 6	8 9	6 7
8 9	6 7	8 9
9 10	7 8	4 5
7 8	9 10	8 9
9 10	6 7	7 8
8 9	7 8	9 10
7 8	9 10	8 9

101

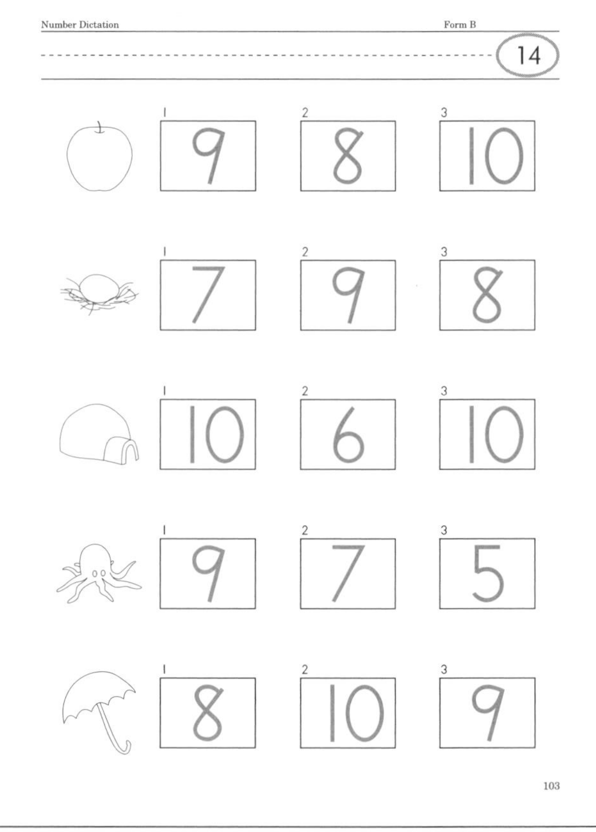
Number Dictation Form B

14

	1	2	3
	9	8	10
	7	9	8
	10	6	10
	9	7	5
	8	10	9

103

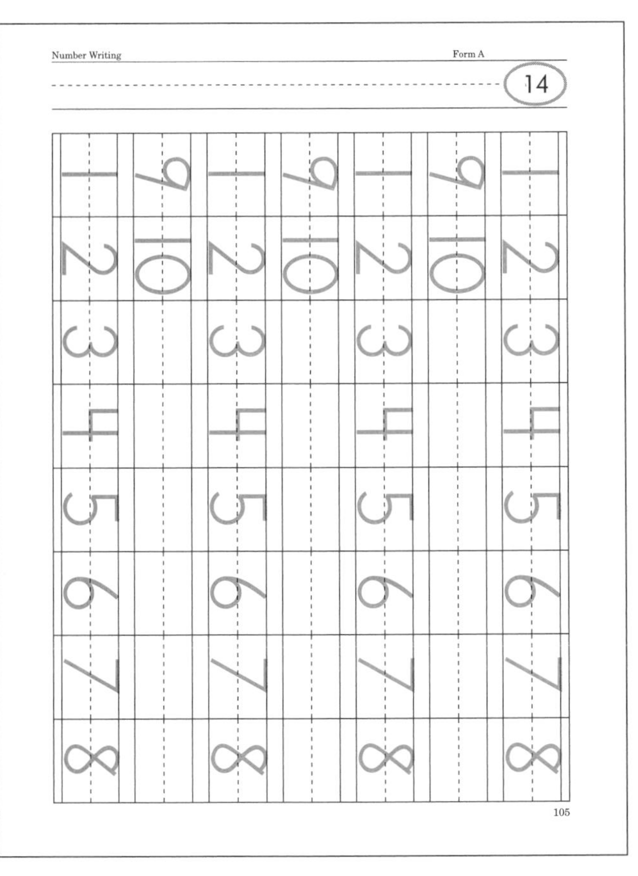
Number Writing Form A

14

1	9	1	9	1	9	1
2	10	2	10	2	10	2
3		3		3		3
4		4		4		4
5		5		5		5
6		6		6		6
7		7		7		7
8		8		8		8

105

0–10 Between Numbers #1

14

2 3 4	8 9 10	7 8 9
6 7 8	5 6 7	3 4 5
0 1 2	1 2 3	6 7 8
5 6 7	8 9 10	5 6 7
8 9 10	7 8 9	4 5 6
3 4 5	5 6 7	8 9 10
7 8 9	8 9 10	4 5 6

106

5–10 Count and Write #16

14

9	8
7	10
10	6
9	8
5	7
10	9

107

1–10 Random Counting #2

14

9	3	4
7	1	6
10	8	5

108

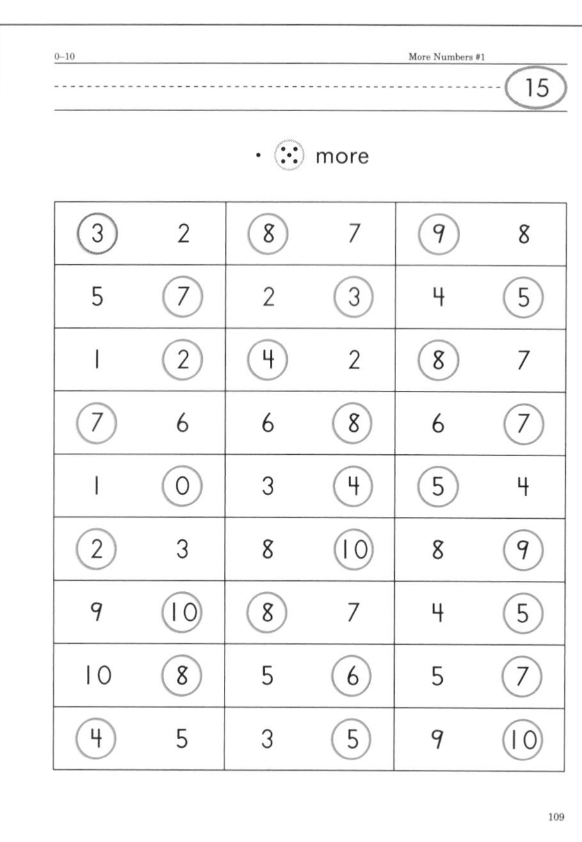

0–10 More Numbers #1

15

• ⁙ more

3	2	8	7	9	8
5	7	2	3	4	5
1	2	4	2	8	7
7	6	6	8	6	7
1	0	3	4	5	4
2	3	8	10	8	9
9	10	8	7	4	5
10	8	5	6	5	7
4	5	3	5	9	10

109

5–10 Count and Write #16

15

9	8
7	10
10	6
9	8
5	7
10	9

110

1, 2 [+] Number Facts #1

15

A	1 +0 = 1	0 +1 = 1	1 +0 = 1	2 +0 = 2	1 +0 = 1	0 +1 = 1	1 +0 = 1
B	0 +2 = 2	2 +0 = 2	1 +1 = 2	0 +1 = 1	1 +1 = 2	0 +2 = 2	2 +0 = 2
C	1 +1 = 2	0 +1 = 1	0 +2 = 2	1 +1 = 2	1 +0 = 1	2 +0 = 2	0 +2 = 2
D	0 +2 = 2	1 +0 = 1	1 +1 = 2	1 +0 = 1	1 +1 = 2	0 +1 = 1	1 +1 = 2
E	2 +0 = 2	1 +1 = 2	0 +2 = 2	1 +0 = 1	1 +1 = 2	2 +0 = 2	0 +2 = 2

111

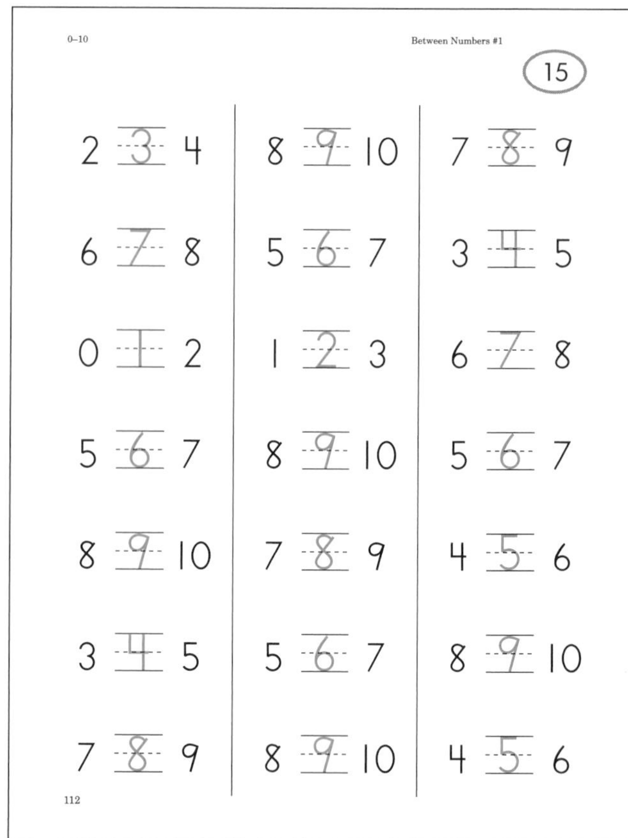

0–10 Between Numbers #1

15

2 3 4	8 9 10	7 8 9
6 7 8	5 6 7	3 4 5
0 1 2	1 2 3	6 7 8
5 6 7	8 9 10	5 6 7
8 9 10	7 8 9	4 5 6
3 4 5	5 6 7	8 9 10
7 8 9	8 9 10	4 5 6

112

5–10 Random Counting #3

15

5	6	8
7	6	5
5	8	10

113

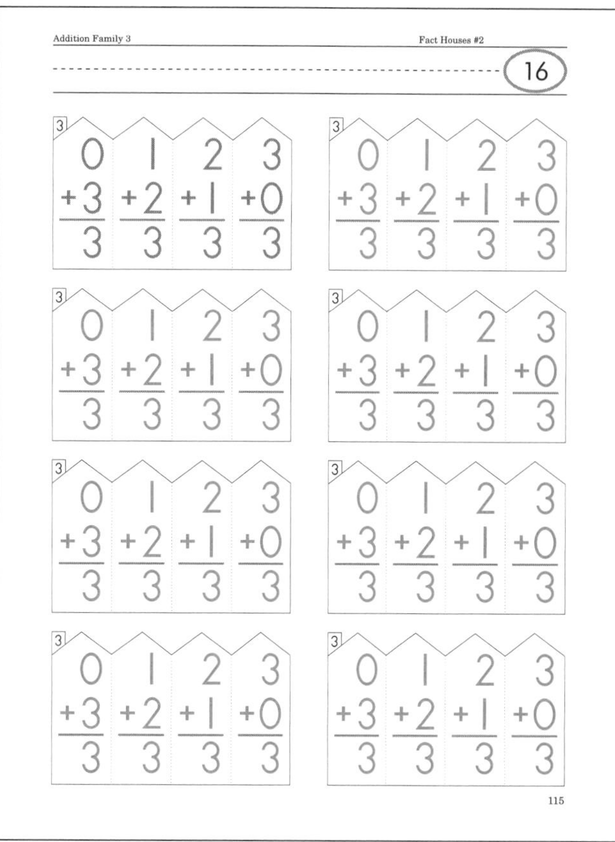

Addition Family 3 Fact Houses #2

16

3

0	1	2	3
+3	+2	+1	+0
3	3	3	3

(The same fact house is repeated eight times.)

115

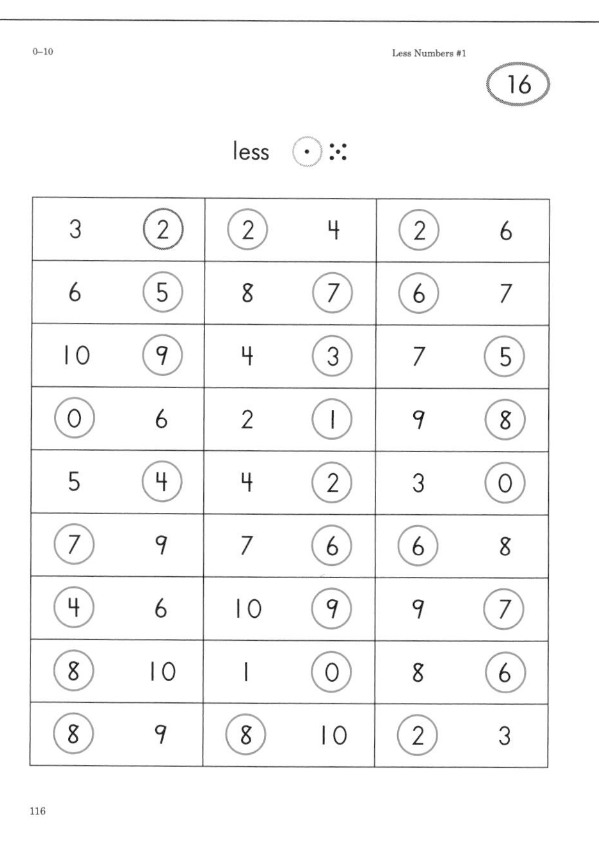

0–10 Less Numbers #1

16

less

3	2	2	4	2	6
6	5	8	7	6	7
10	9	4	3	7	5
0	6	2	1	9	8
5	4	4	2	3	0
7	9	7	6	6	8
4	6	10	9	9	7
8	10	1	0	8	6
8	9	8	10	2	3

116

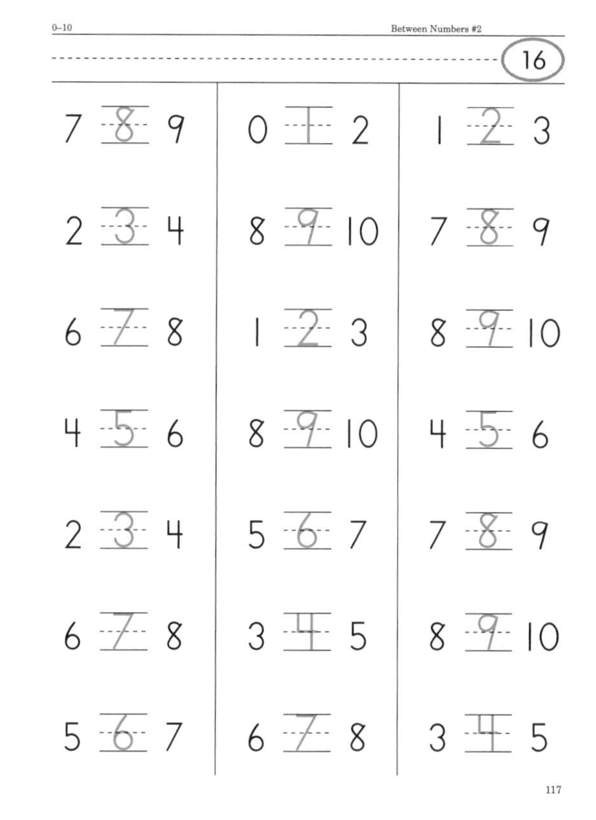

0–10 Between Numbers #2

16

7 8 9	0 1 2	1 2 3
2 3 4	8 9 10	7 8 9
6 7 8	1 2 3	8 9 10
4 5 6	8 9 10	4 5 6
2 3 4	5 6 7	7 8 9
6 7 8	3 4 5	8 9 10
5 6 7	6 7 8	3 4 5

117

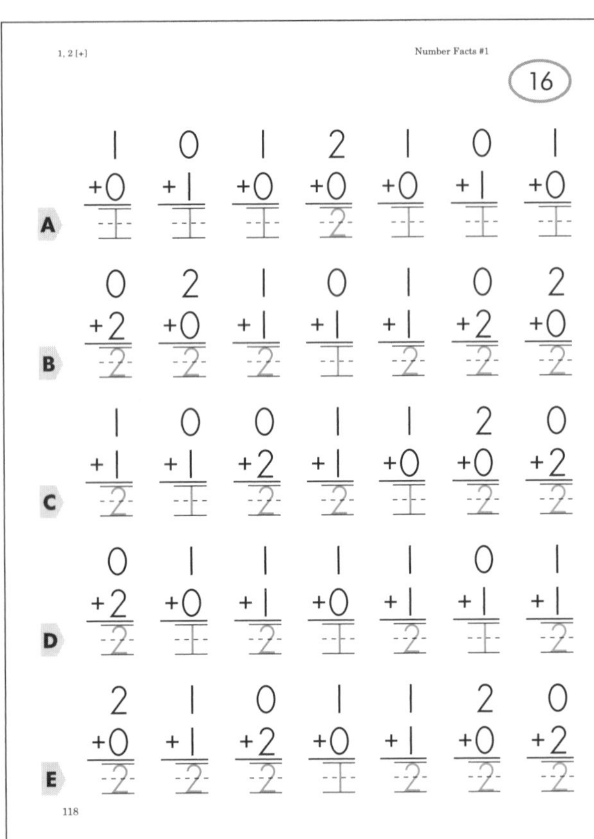

1, 2 [+] Number Facts #1

16

A	1 +0 = 1	0 +1 = 1	1 +0 = 1	2 +0 = 2	1 +0 = 1	0 +1 = 1	1 +0 = 1
B	0 +2 = 2	2 +0 = 2	1 +1 = 2	0 +1 = 1	1 +1 = 2	0 +2 = 2	2 +0 = 2
C	1 +1 = 2	0 +1 = 1	0 +2 = 2	1 +1 = 2	1 +0 = 1	2 +0 = 2	0 +2 = 2
D	0 +2 = 2	1 +0 = 1	1 +1 = 2	1 +0 = 1	1 +1 = 2	0 +1 = 1	1 +1 = 2
E	2 +0 = 2	1 +1 = 2	0 +2 = 2	1 +0 = 1	1 +1 = 2	2 +0 = 2	0 +2 = 2

118

7–10 Random Counting #4

16

10	7	7
7	10	9
10	9	8

119

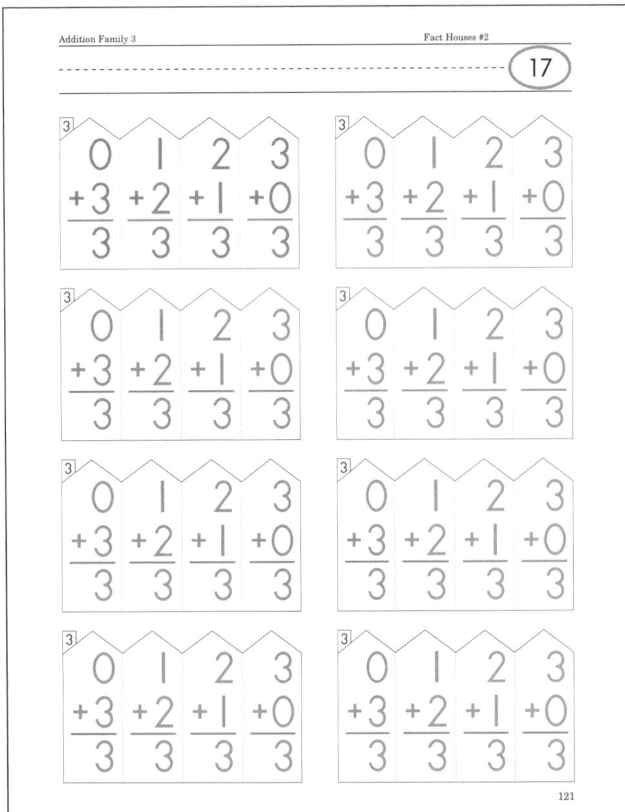

Addition Family 3 Fact Houses #2

17

3	0 +3 = 3	1 +2 = 3	2 +1 = 3	3 +0 = 3
3	0 +3 = 3	1 +2 = 3	2 +1 = 3	3 +0 = 3
3	0 +3 = 3	1 +2 = 3	2 +1 = 3	3 +0 = 3
3	0 +3 = 3	1 +2 = 3	2 +1 = 3	3 +0 = 3
3	0 +3 = 3	1 +2 = 3	2 +1 = 3	3 +0 = 3
3	0 +3 = 3	1 +2 = 3	2 +1 = 3	3 +0 = 3
3	0 +3 = 3	1 +2 = 3	2 +1 = 3	3 +0 = 3
3	0 +3 = 3	1 +2 = 3	2 +1 = 3	3 +0 = 3

121

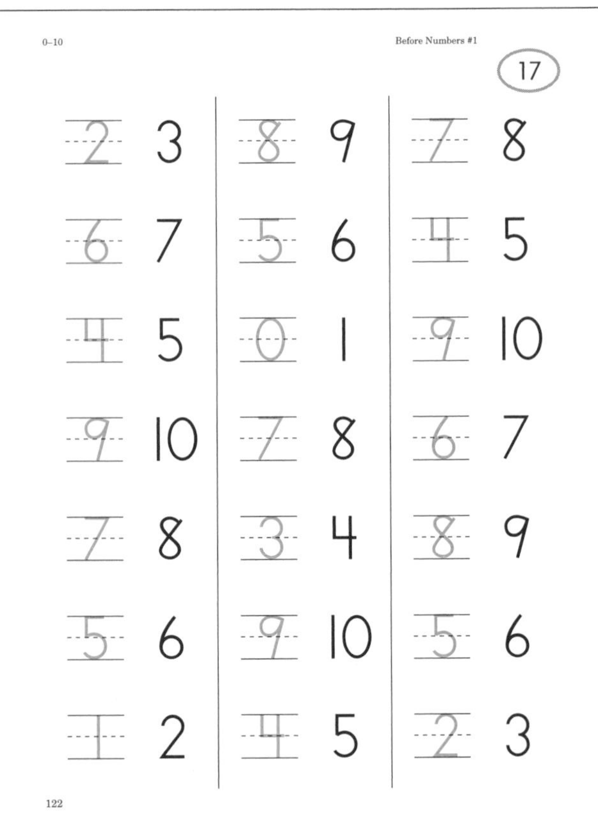

0–10 Before Numbers #1

17

2 3	8 9	7 8
6 7	5 6	4 5
4 5	0 1	9 10
9 10	7 8	6 7
7 8	3 4	8 9
5 6	9 10	5 6
1 2	4 5	2 3

122

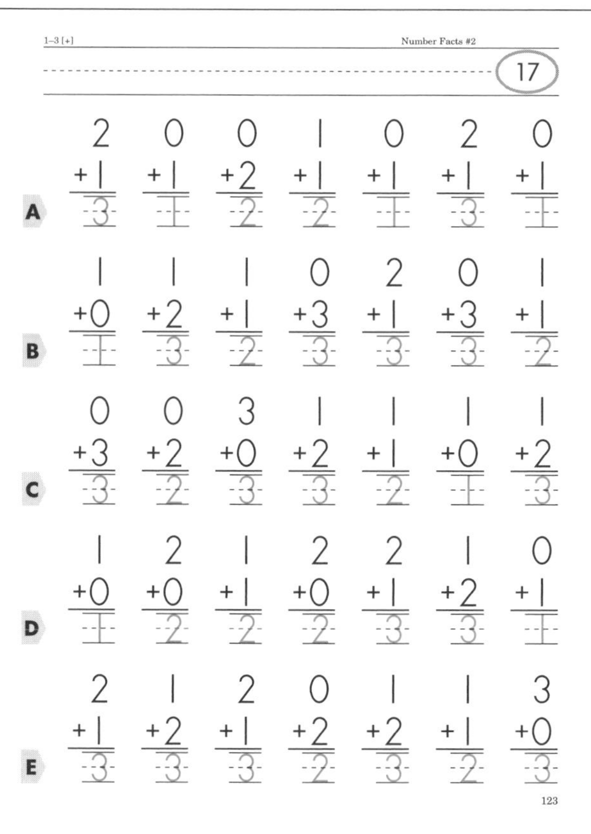

1–3 [+] Number Facts #2

17

A	2 +1 = 3	0 +1 = 1	0 +2 = 2	1 +1 = 2	0 +1 = 1	2 +1 = 3	0 +1 = 1
B	1 +0 = 1	1 +2 = 3	1 +1 = 2	0 +3 = 3	2 +1 = 3	0 +3 = 3	1 +1 = 2
C	0 +3 = 3	0 +2 = 2	3 +0 = 3	1 +2 = 3	1 +1 = 2	1 +0 = 1	1 +2 = 3
D	1 +0 = 1	2 +0 = 2	1 +1 = 2	2 +0 = 2	2 +1 = 3	1 +2 = 3	0 +1 = 1
E	2 +1 = 3	1 +2 = 3	2 +1 = 3	0 +2 = 2	1 +2 = 3	1 +1 = 2	3 +0 = 3

123

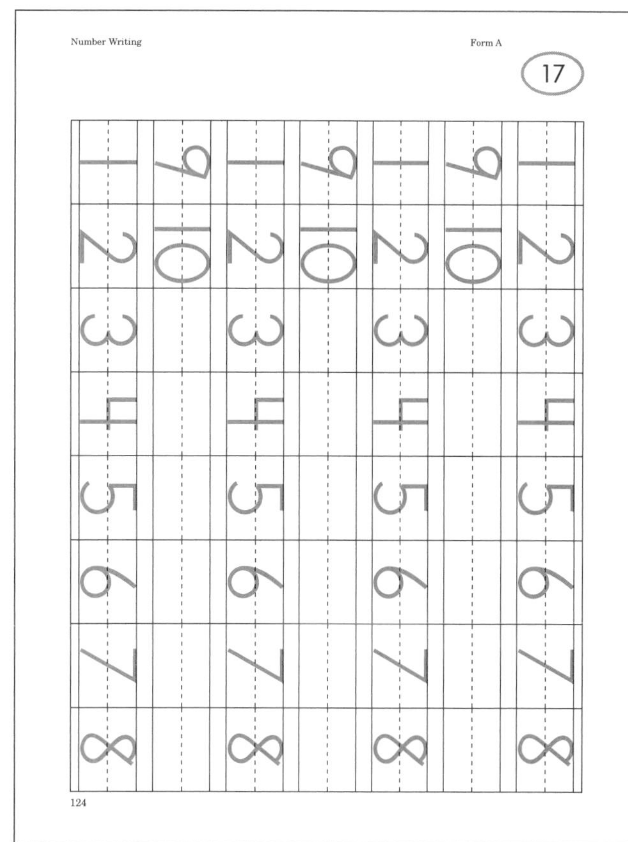

Number Writing Form A

17

1	9	1	9	1	9	1
2	10	2	10	2	10	2
3		3		3		3
4		4		4		4
5		5		5		5
6		6		6		6
7		7		7		7
8		8		8		8

124

7–10 Random Counting #5

17

10	9	7
9	10	10
8	8	8

125

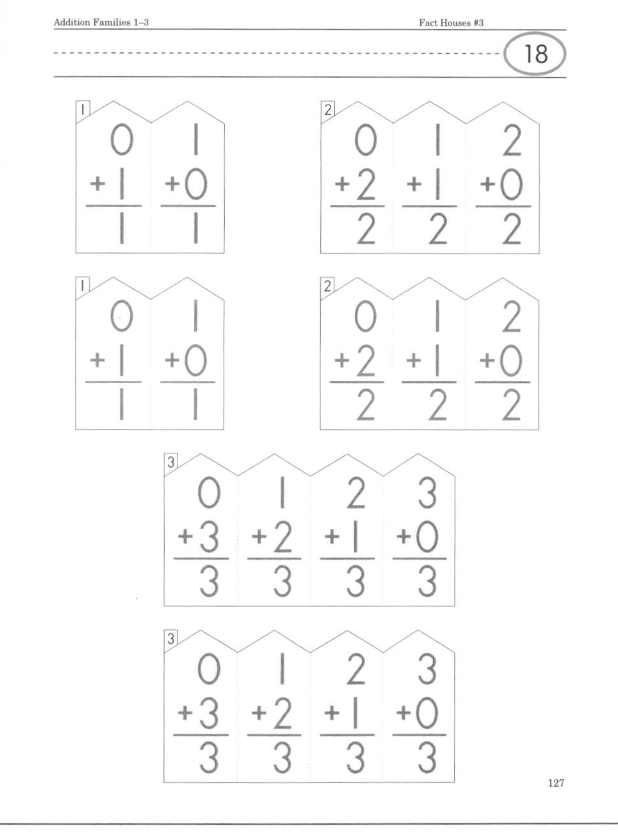

Addition Families 1–3 Fact Houses #3

18

1: 0 +1 = 1; 1 +0 = 1

2: 0 +2 = 2; 1 +1 = 2; 2 +0 = 2

1: 0 +1 = 1; 1 +0 = 1

2: 0 +2 = 2; 1 +1 = 2; 2 +0 = 2

3: 0 +3 = 3; 1 +2 = 3; 2 +1 = 3; 3 +0 = 3

3: 0 +3 = 3; 1 +2 = 3; 2 +1 = 3; 3 +0 = 3

127

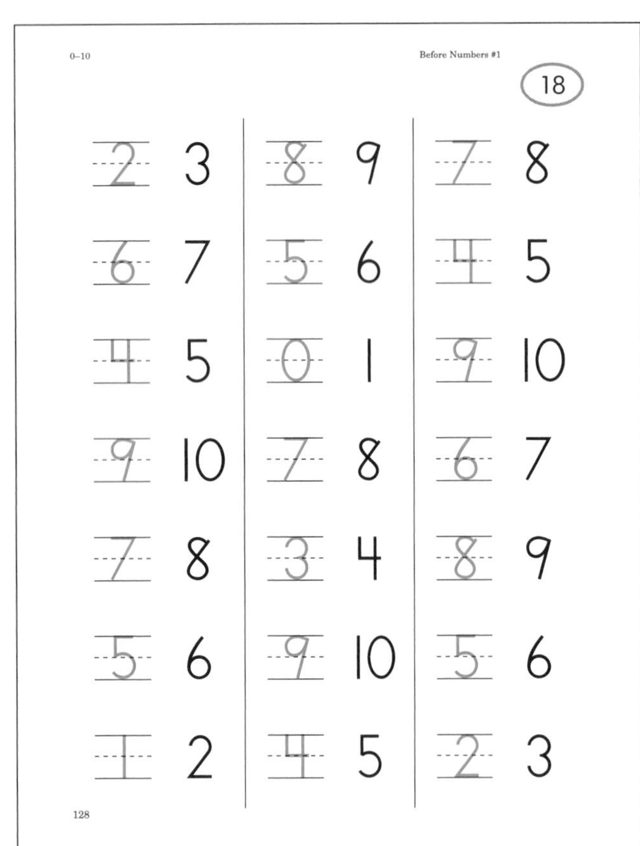
0–10 Before Numbers #1 18

2	3	8	9	7	8
6	7	5	6	4	5
4	5	0	1	9	10
9	10	7	8	6	7
7	8	3	4	8	9
5	6	9	10	5	6
1	2	4	5	2	3

128

1–3 [+] Number Facts #2 18

A	2 + 1 = 3	0 + 1 = 1	0 + 2 = 2	1 + 1 = 2	0 + 1 = 1	2 + 1 = 3	0 + 1 = 1
B	1 + 0 = 1	1 + 2 = 3	1 + 1 = 2	0 + 3 = 3	2 + 1 = 3	0 + 3 = 3	1 + 1 = 2
C	0 + 3 = 3	1 + 2 = 3	3 + 0 = 3	1 + 2 = 3	1 + 1 = 2	1 + 0 = 1	1 + 2 = 3
D	1 + 0 = 1	2 + 0 = 2	1 + 1 = 2	2 + 0 = 2	2 + 1 = 3	1 + 2 = 3	0 + 1 = 1
E	2 + 1 = 3	1 + 2 = 3	2 + 1 = 3	0 + 2 = 2	1 + 2 = 3	1 + 1 = 2	3 + 0 = 3

129

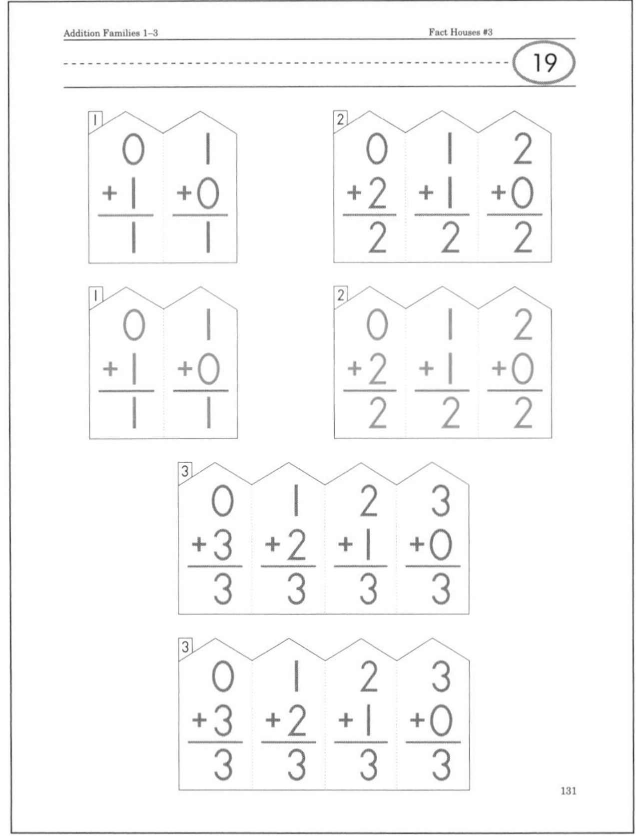
Addition Families 1–3 Fact Houses #3 19

1: 0 + 1 = 1, 1 + 0 = 1

2: 0 + 2 = 2, 1 + 1 = 2, 2 + 0 = 2

1: 0 + 1 = 1, 1 + 0 = 1

2: 0 + 2 = 2, 1 + 1 = 2, 2 + 0 = 2

3: 0 + 3 = 3, 1 + 2 = 3, 2 + 1 = 3, 3 + 0 = 3

3: 0 + 3 = 3, 1 + 2 = 3, 2 + 1 = 3, 3 + 0 = 3

131

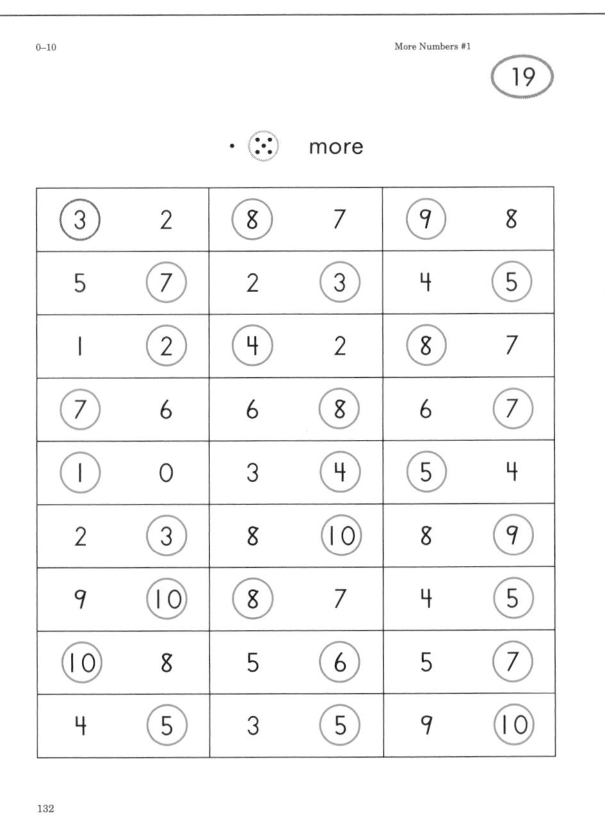
0–10 More Numbers #1 19

• ⁙ more

(3)	2	(8)	7	(9)	8
5	(7)	2	(3)	4	(5)
1	(2)	(4)	2	(8)	7
(7)	6	6	(8)	6	(7)
(1)	0	3	(4)	(5)	4
2	(3)	8	(10)	8	(9)
9	(10)	(8)	7	4	(5)
(10)	8	5	(6)	5	(7)
4	(5)	3	(5)	9	(10)

132

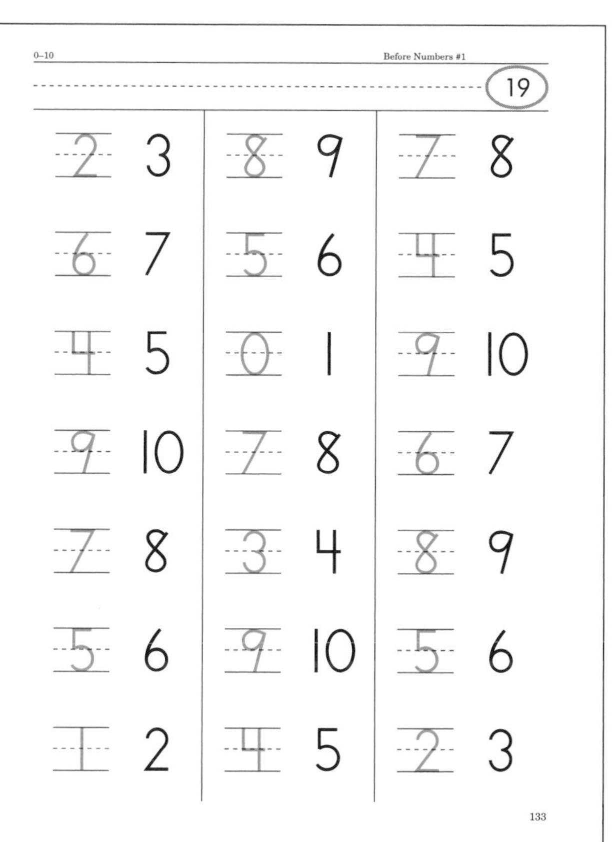

0–10 Before Numbers #1

19

2	3	8	9	7	8
6	7	5	6	4	5
4	5	0	1	9	10
9	10	7	8	6	7
7	8	3	4	8	9
5	6	9	10	5	6
1	2	4	5	2	3

133

1–3 [+] Number Facts #2

19

A	2 + 1 = 3	0 + 1 = 1	0 + 2 = 2	1 + 1 = 2	0 + 1 = 1	2 + 1 = 3	0 + 1 = 1
B	1 + 0 = 1	1 + 2 = 3	1 + 1 = 2	0 + 3 = 3	2 + 1 = 3	0 + 3 = 3	1 + 1 = 2
C	0 + 3 = 3	0 + 2 = 2	3 + 0 = 3	1 + 2 = 3	1 + 1 = 2	1 + 0 = 1	1 + 2 = 3
D	1 + 0 = 1	2 + 0 = 2	1 + 1 = 2	2 + 0 = 2	2 + 1 = 3	1 + 2 = 3	0 + 1 = 1
E	2 + 1 = 3	1 + 2 = 3	2 + 1 = 3	0 + 2 = 2	1 + 2 = 3	1 + 1 = 2	3 + 0 = 3

134

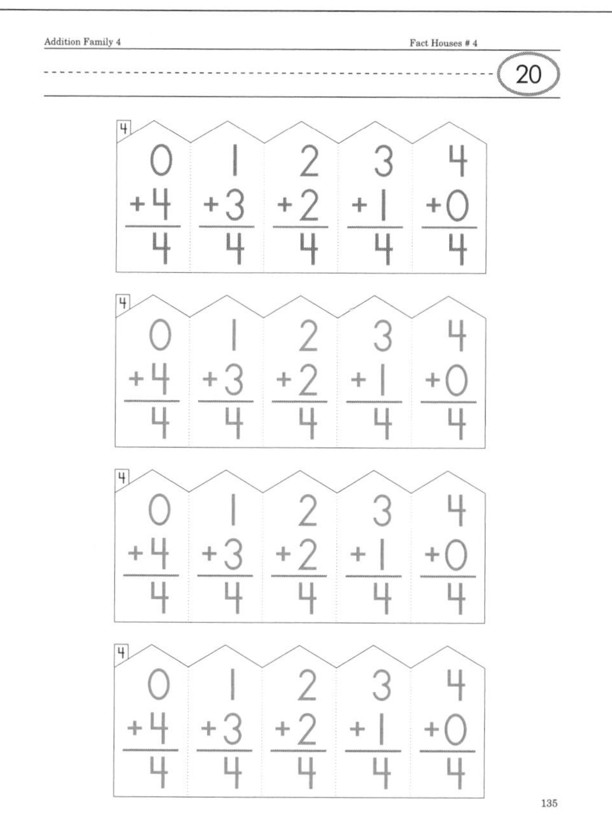

Addition Family 4 Fact Houses # 4

20

4	0 + 4 = 4	1 + 3 = 4	2 + 2 = 4	3 + 1 = 4	4 + 0 = 4
4	0 + 4 = 4	1 + 3 = 4	2 + 2 = 4	3 + 1 = 4	4 + 0 = 4
4	0 + 4 = 4	1 + 3 = 4	2 + 2 = 4	3 + 1 = 4	4 + 0 = 4
4	0 + 4 = 4	1 + 3 = 4	2 + 2 = 4	3 + 1 = 4	4 + 0 = 4

135

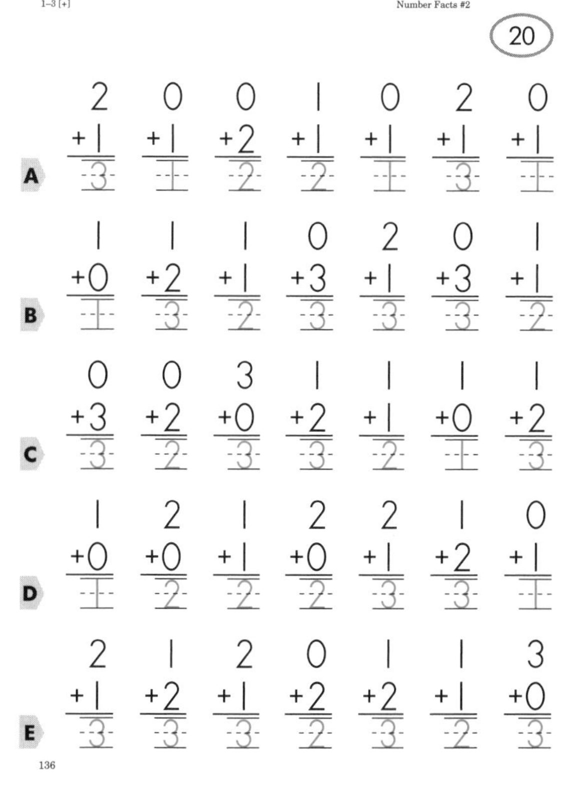

1–3 [+] Number Facts #2

20

A	2 + 1 = 3	0 + 1 = 1	0 + 2 = 2	1 + 1 = 2	0 + 1 = 1	2 + 1 = 3	0 + 1 = 1
B	1 + 0 = 1	1 + 2 = 3	1 + 1 = 2	0 + 3 = 3	2 + 1 = 3	0 + 3 = 3	1 + 1 = 2
C	0 + 3 = 3	0 + 2 = 2	3 + 0 = 3	1 + 2 = 3	1 + 1 = 2	1 + 0 = 1	1 + 2 = 3
D	1 + 0 = 1	2 + 0 = 2	1 + 1 = 2	2 + 0 = 2	2 + 1 = 3	1 + 2 = 3	0 + 1 = 1
E	2 + 1 = 3	1 + 2 = 3	2 + 1 = 3	0 + 2 = 2	1 + 2 = 3	1 + 1 = 2	3 + 0 = 3

136

7–10 Random Counting #6

20

10	8	9
8	8	9
7	10	10

137

Number Dictation Form B

21

	1	2	3
	3	5	7
	9	8	6
	4	10	2
	8	5	10
	7	9	6

139

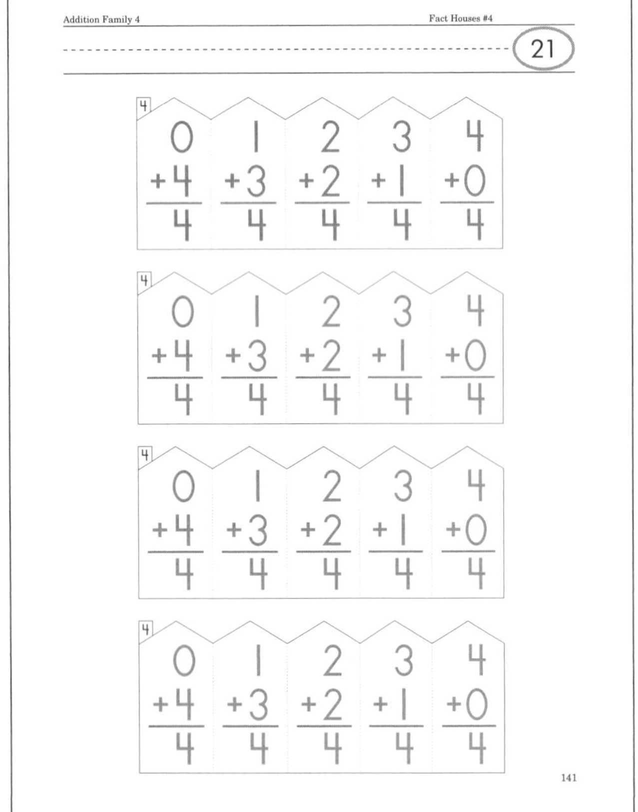

Addition Family 4 Fact Houses #4

21

4: 0 + 4 = 4, 1 + 3 = 4, 2 + 2 = 4, 3 + 1 = 4, 4 + 0 = 4

4: 0 + 4 = 4, 1 + 3 = 4, 2 + 2 = 4, 3 + 1 = 4, 4 + 0 = 4

4: 0 + 4 = 4, 1 + 3 = 4, 2 + 2 = 4, 3 + 1 = 4, 4 + 0 = 4

4: 0 + 4 = 4, 1 + 3 = 4, 2 + 2 = 4, 3 + 1 = 4, 4 + 0 = 4

141

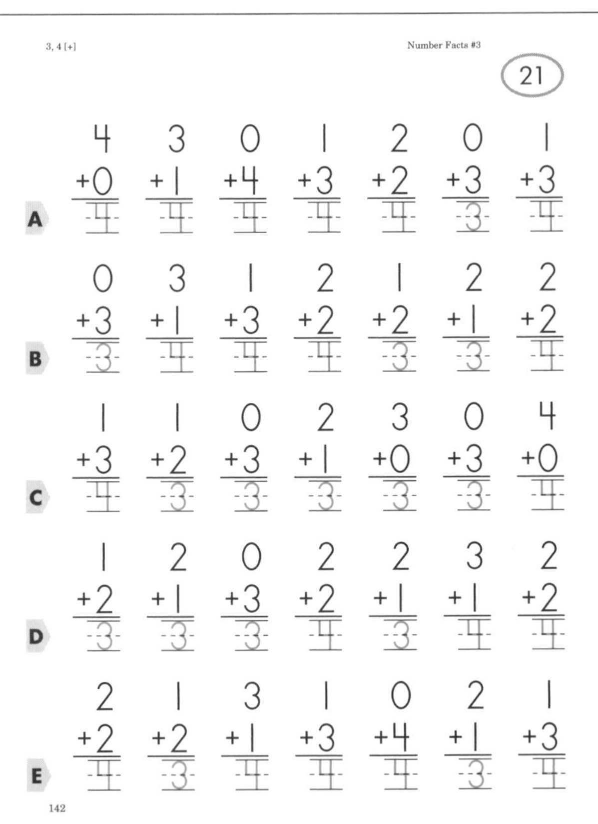

3, 4 [+] Number Facts #3

21

A	4 + 0 = 4	3 + 1 = 4	0 + 4 = 4	1 + 3 = 4	2 + 2 = 4	0 + 3 = 3	1 + 3 = 4
B	0 + 3 = 3	3 + 1 = 4	1 + 3 = 4	2 + 2 = 4	1 + 2 = 3	2 + 1 = 3	2 + 2 = 4
C	1 + 3 = 4	1 + 2 = 3	0 + 3 = 3	2 + 1 = 3	3 + 0 = 3	0 + 3 = 3	4 + 0 = 4
D	1 + 2 = 3	2 + 1 = 3	0 + 3 = 3	2 + 2 = 4	2 + 1 = 3	3 + 1 = 4	2 + 2 = 4
E	2 + 2 = 4	1 + 2 = 3	3 + 1 = 4	1 + 3 = 4	0 + 4 = 4	2 + 1 = 3	1 + 3 = 4

142

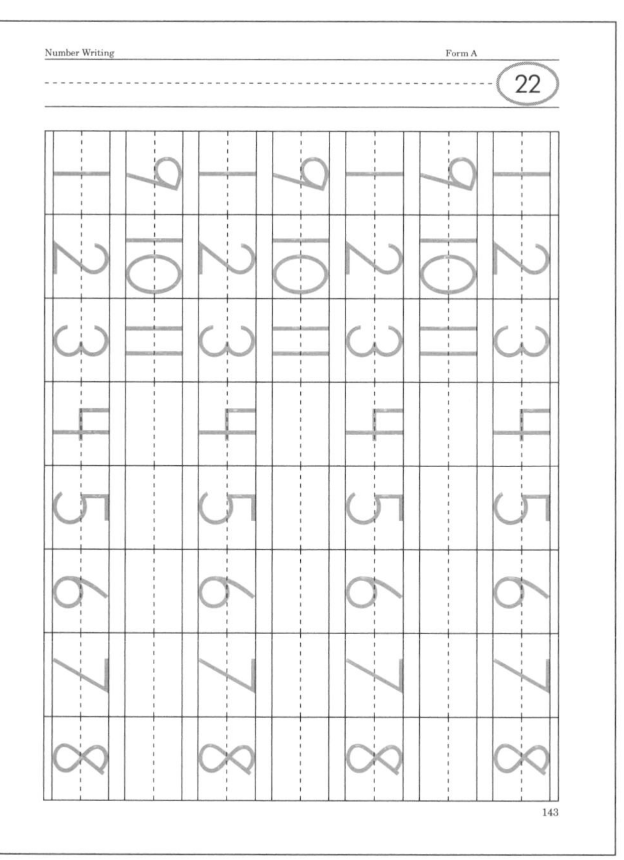
Number Writing
Form A
22
143

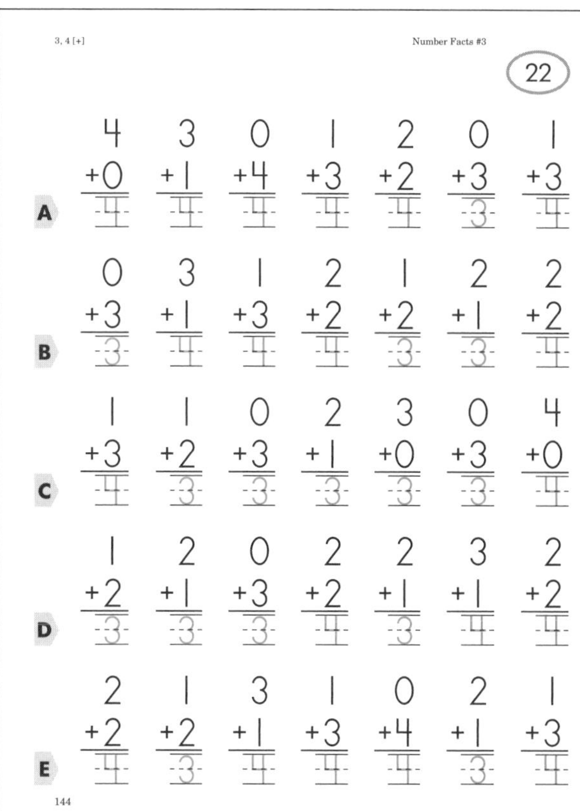
3, 4 [+]
Number Facts #3
22
A
B
C
D
E
144

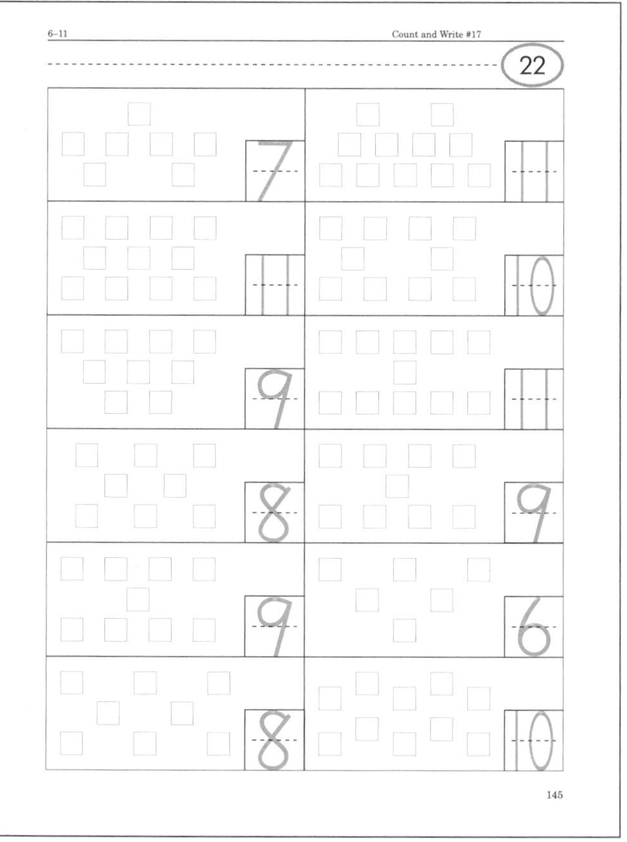
6–11
Count and Write #17
22
145

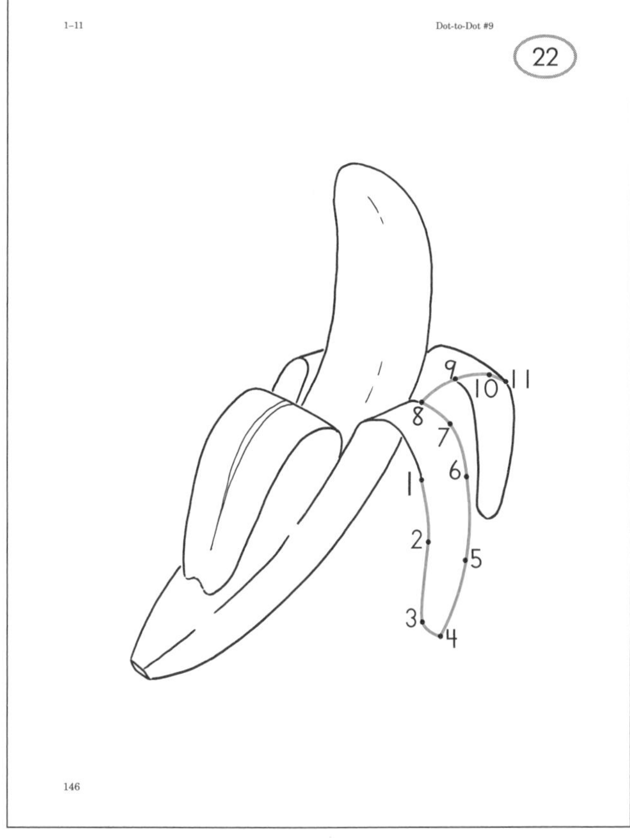
1–11
Dot-to-Dot #9
22
146

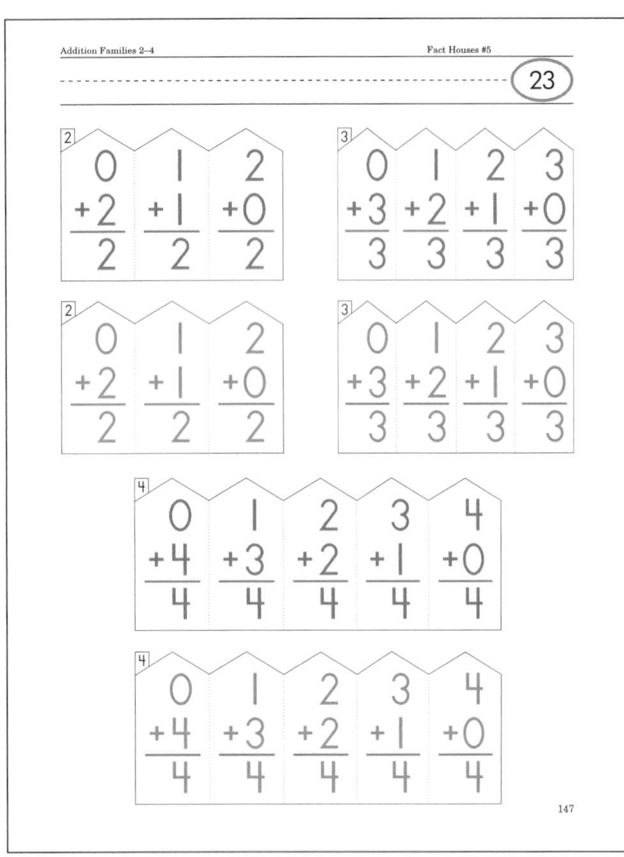

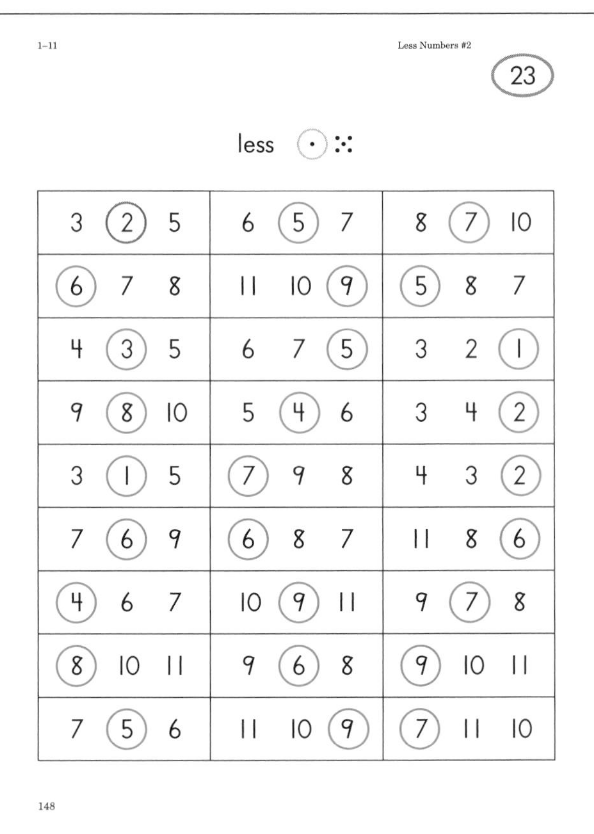

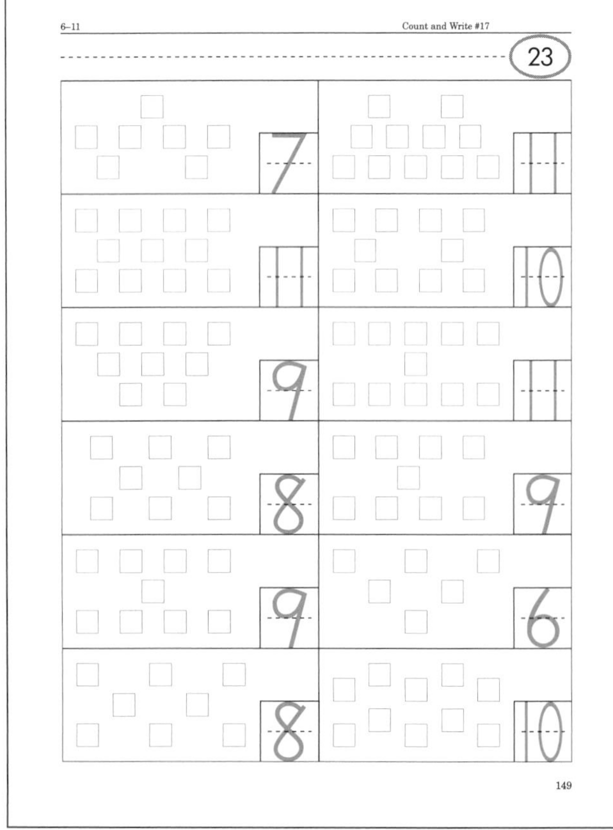

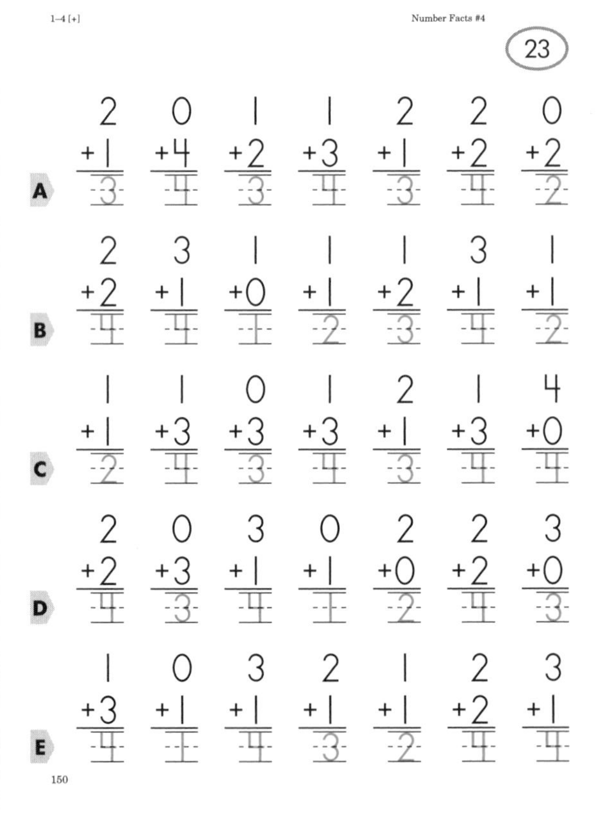

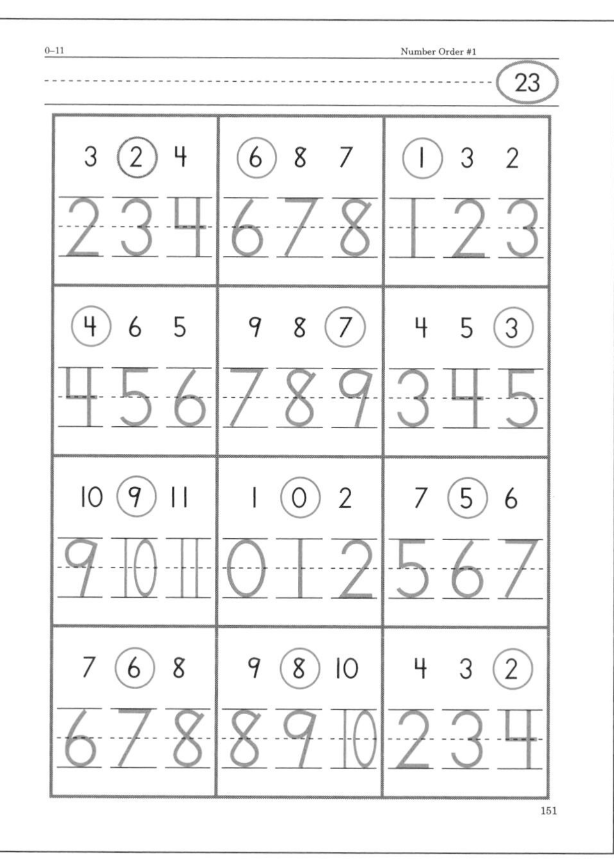

0–11 Number Order #1

23

3 (2) 4 — 2 3 4	(6) 8 7 — 6 7 8	(1) 3 2 — 1 2 3
(4) 6 5 — 4 5 6	9 8 (7) — 7 8 9	4 5 (3) — 3 4 5
10 (9) 11 — 9 10 11	1 (0) 2 — 0 1 2	7 (5) 6 — 5 6 7
7 (6) 8 — 6 7 8	9 (8) 10 — 8 9 10	4 3 (2) — 2 3 4

151

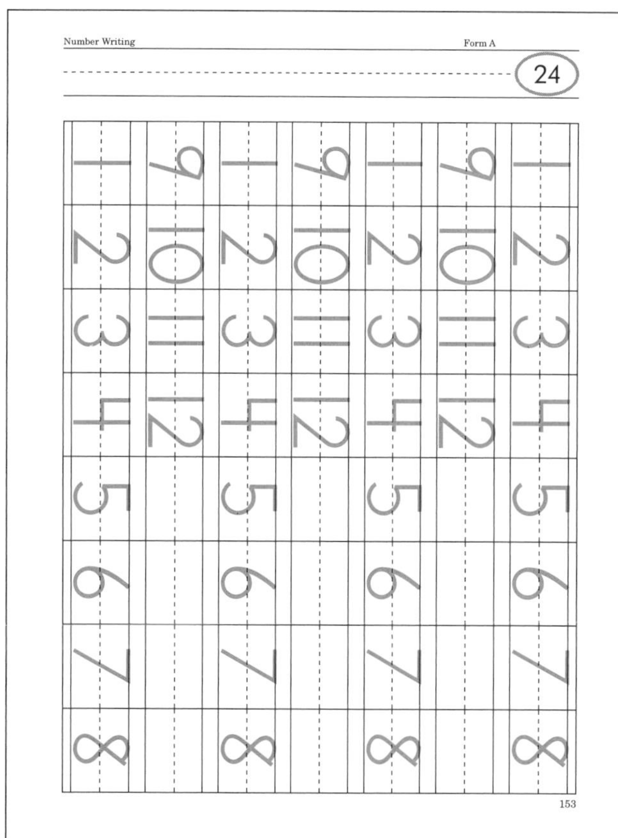

Number Writing Form A

24

153

1–11 Between Numbers #3

24

2 3 4	1 2 3	8 9 10
8 9 10	9 10 11	3 4 5
9 10 11	2 3 4	7 8 9
5 6 7	9 10 11	5 6 7
8 9 10	6 7 8	3 4 5
9 10 11	4 5 6	7 8 9
4 5 6	7 8 9	6 7 8

154

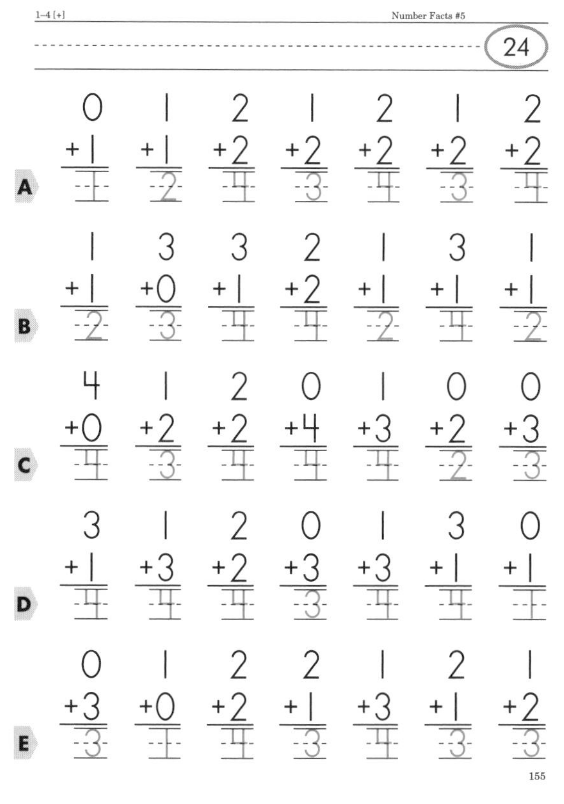

1–4 [+] Number Facts #5

24

A	0 + 1 = 1	1 + 1 = 2	2 + 2 = 4	1 + 2 = 3	2 + 2 = 4	1 + 2 = 3	2 + 2 = 4
B	1 + 1 = 2	3 + 0 = 3	3 + 1 = 4	2 + 2 = 4	1 + 1 = 2	3 + 1 = 4	1 + 1 = 2
C	4 + 0 = 4	1 + 2 = 3	2 + 2 = 4	0 + 4 = 4	1 + 3 = 4	0 + 2 = 2	0 + 3 = 3
D	3 + 1 = 4	1 + 3 = 4	2 + 2 = 4	0 + 3 = 3	1 + 3 = 4	3 + 1 = 4	0 + 1 = 1
E	0 + 3 = 3	1 + 0 = 1	2 + 2 = 4	2 + 1 = 3	1 + 3 = 4	2 + 1 = 3	1 + 2 = 3

155

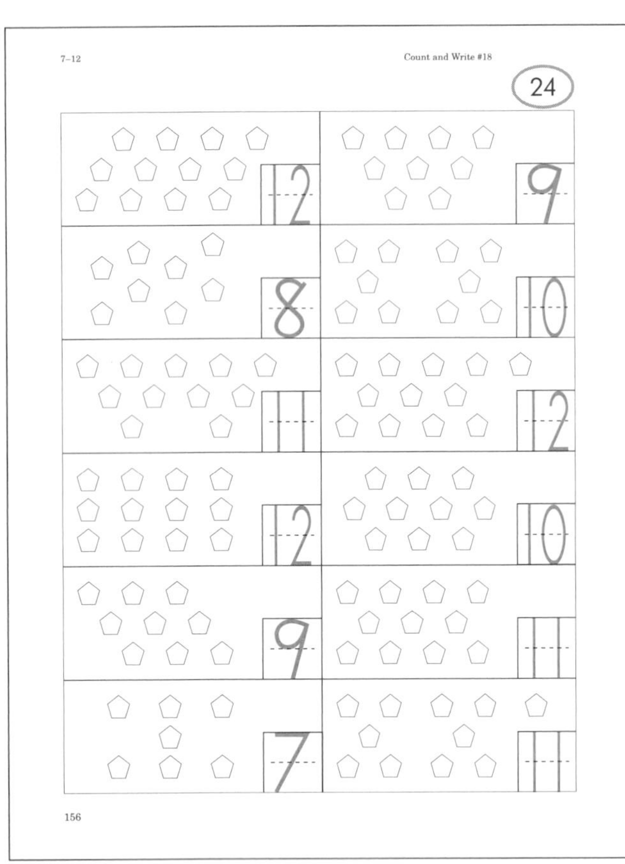

7–12 Count and Write #18

24

12	9
8	10
11	12
12	10
9	11
7	11

156

1–12 Dot-to-Dot #10

24

157

1–12 Number Order #2

25

4 (3) 5 3 4 5	10 9 (8) 8 9 10	11 (10) 12 10 11 12
(7) 9 8 7 8 9	2 (1) 3 1 2 3	8 (7) 9 7 8 9
(2) 4 3 2 3 4	10 (9) 11 9 10 11	8 (6) 7 6 7 8
(5) 7 6 5 6 7	5 6 (4) 4 5 6	5 4 (3) 3 4 5

159

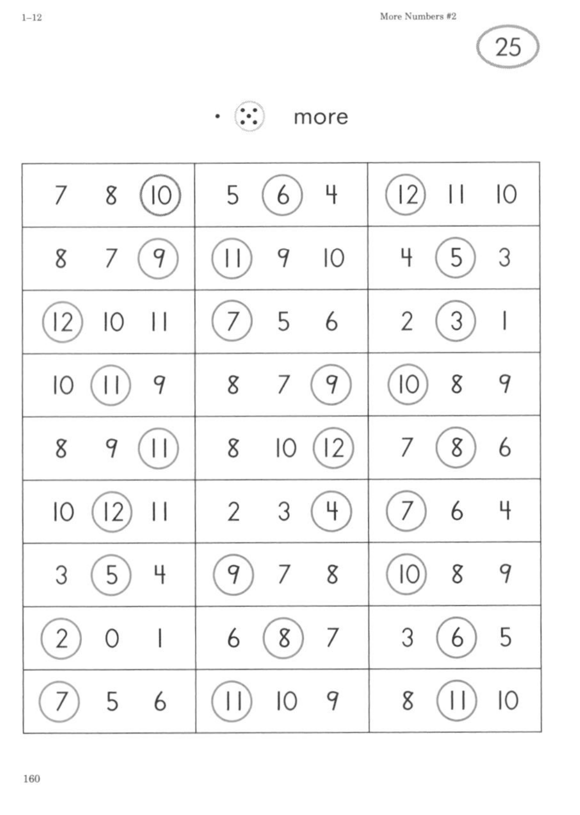

1–12 More Numbers #2

25

• more

7 8 (10)	5 (6) 4	(12) 11 10
8 7 (9)	(11) 9 10	4 (5) 3
(12) 10 11	(7) 5 6	2 (3) 1
10 (11) 9	8 7 (9)	(10) 8 9
8 9 (11)	8 10 (12)	7 (8) 6
10 (12) 11	2 3 (4)	(7) 6 4
3 (5) 4	(9) 7 8	(10) 8 9
(2) 0 1	6 (8) 7	3 (6) 5
(7) 5 6	(11) 10 9	8 (11) 10

160

7–12 Count and Write #18

25

12	9
8	10
11	12
12	10
9	11
7	11

161

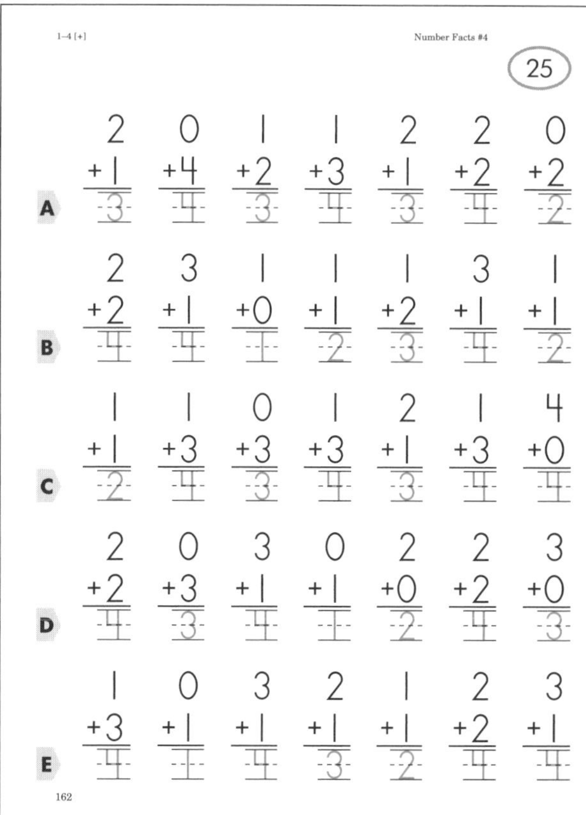

1–4 [+] Number Facts #4

25

A	2 + 1 = 3	0 + 4 = 4	1 + 2 = 3	1 + 3 = 4	2 + 1 = 3	2 + 2 = 4	0 + 2 = 2
B	2 + 2 = 4	3 + 1 = 4	1 + 0 = 1	1 + 1 = 2	1 + 2 = 3	3 + 1 = 4	1 + 1 = 2
C	1 + 1 = 2	1 + 3 = 4	0 + 3 = 3	1 + 3 = 4	2 + 1 = 3	1 + 3 = 4	4 + 0 = 4
D	2 + 2 = 4	0 + 3 = 3	3 + 1 = 4	0 + 1 = 1	2 + 0 = 2	2 + 2 = 4	3 + 0 = 3
E	1 + 3 = 4	0 + 1 = 1	3 + 1 = 4	2 + 1 = 3	1 + 1 = 2	2 + 2 = 4	3 + 1 = 4

162

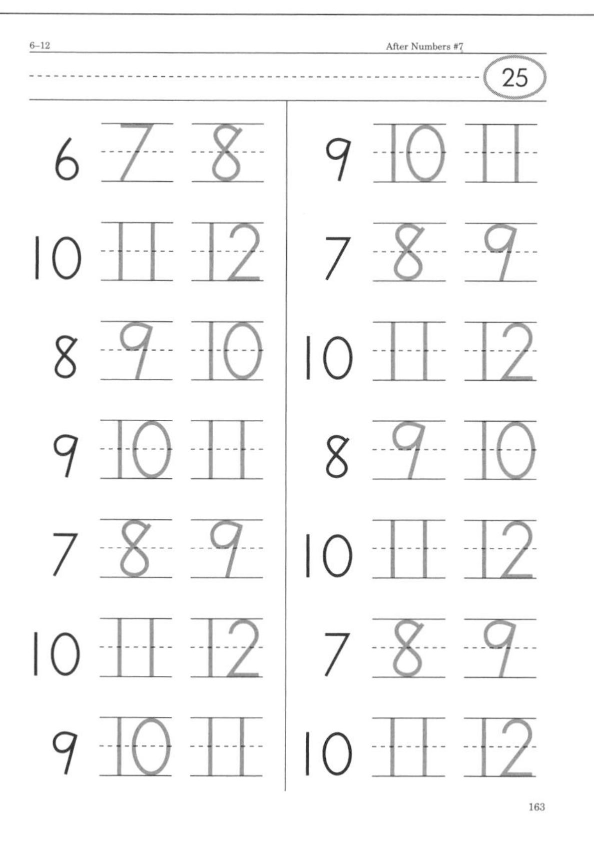

6–12 After Numbers #7

25

6	7	8	9	10	11
10	11	12	7	8	9
8	9	10	10	11	12
9	10	11	8	9	10
7	8	9	10	11	12
10	11	12	7	8	9
9	10	11	10	11	12

163

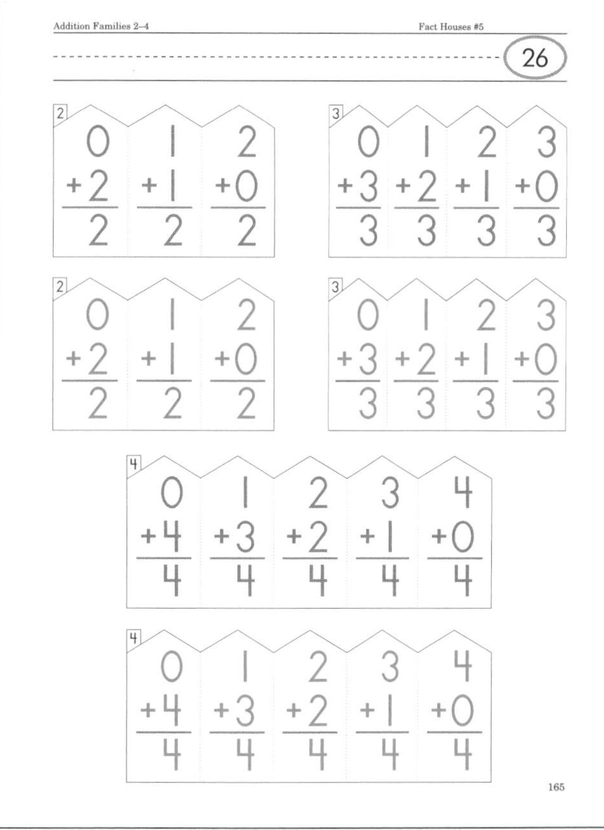

Addition Families 2–4 Fact Houses #5

26

2: 0 + 2 = 2, 1 + 1 = 2, 2 + 0 = 2

3: 0 + 3 = 3, 1 + 2 = 3, 2 + 1 = 3, 3 + 0 = 3

2: 0 + 2 = 2, 1 + 1 = 2, 2 + 0 = 2

3: 0 + 3 = 3, 1 + 2 = 3, 2 + 1 = 3, 3 + 0 = 3

4: 0 + 4 = 4, 1 + 3 = 4, 2 + 2 = 4, 3 + 1 = 4, 4 + 0 = 4

4: 0 + 4 = 4, 1 + 3 = 4, 2 + 2 = 4, 3 + 1 = 4, 4 + 0 = 4

165

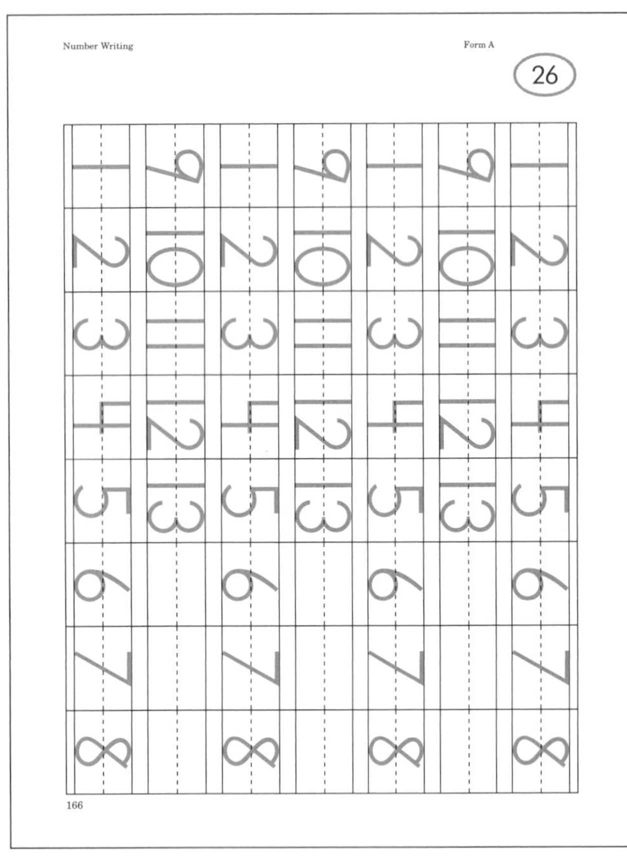

2–12

Before Numbers #2

26

4	5	2	3	9	10
10	11	6	7	7	8
9	10	11	12	11	12
8	9	9	10	7	8
7	8	8	9	10	11
6	7	10	11	6	7
11	12	5	6	4	5

167

1–4 [+]

Number Facts #5

26

A	$0+1=1$	$1+1=2$	$2+2=4$	$1+2=3$	$2+2=4$	$1+2=3$	$2+2=4$
B	$1+1=2$	$3+0=3$	$3+1=4$	$2+2=4$	$1+1=2$	$3+1=4$	$1+1=2$
C	$4+0=4$	$1+2=3$	$2+2=4$	$0+4=4$	$1+3=4$	$0+2=2$	$0+3=3$
D	$3+1=4$	$1+3=4$	$2+2=4$	$0+3=3$	$1+3=4$	$3+1=4$	$0+1=1$
E	$0+3=3$	$1+0=1$	$2+2=4$	$2+1=3$	$1+3=4$	$2+1=3$	$1+2=3$

168

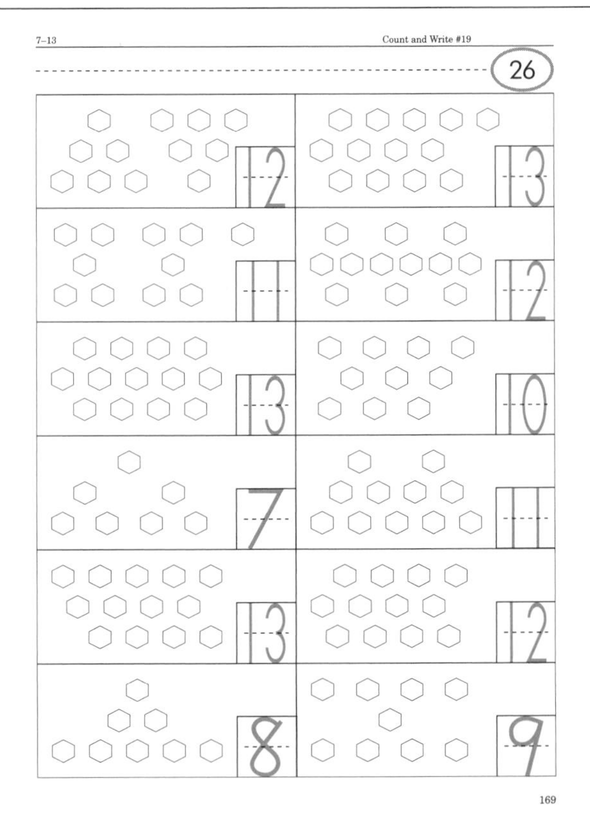

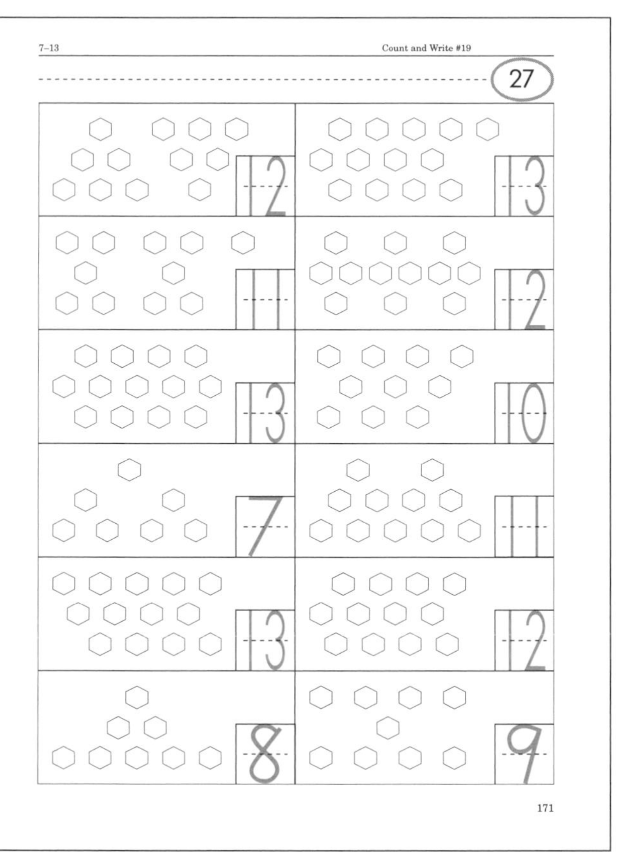

7–13 Count and Write #19

27

12	13
11	12
13	10
7	11
13	12
8	9

171

1–4 [+] Number Facts #4

27

A	2 + 1 = 3	0 + 4 = 4	1 + 2 = 3	1 + 3 = 4	2 + 1 = 3	2 + 2 = 4	0 + 2 = 2
B	2 + 2 = 4	3 + 1 = 4	1 + 0 = 1	1 + 1 = 2	1 + 2 = 3	3 + 1 = 4	1 + 1 = 2
C	1 + 1 = 2	1 + 3 = 4	0 + 3 = 3	1 + 3 = 4	2 + 1 = 3	1 + 3 = 4	4 + 0 = 4
D	2 + 2 = 4	0 + 3 = 3	3 + 1 = 4	0 + 1 = 1	2 + 0 = 2	2 + 2 = 4	3 + 0 = 3
E	1 + 3 = 4	0 + 1 = 1	3 + 1 = 4	2 + 1 = 3	1 + 1 = 2	2 + 2 = 4	3 + 1 = 4

172

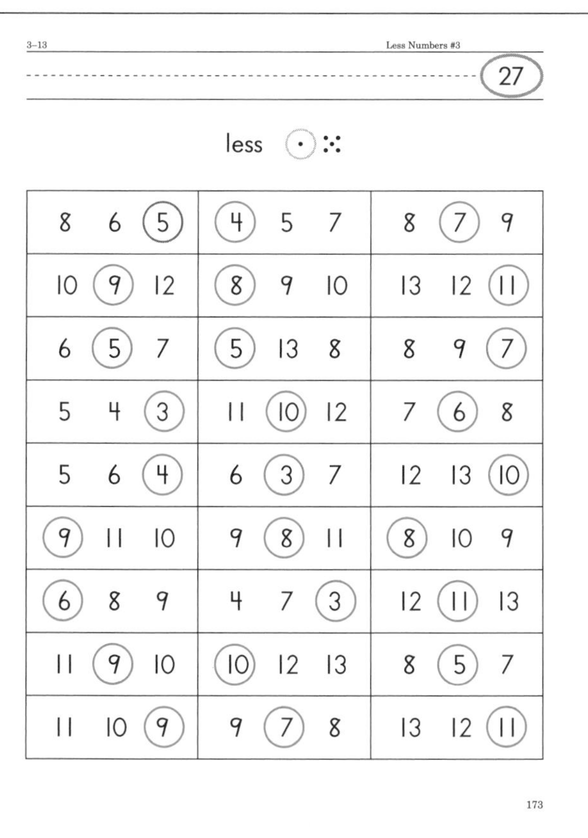

3–13 Less Numbers #3

27

less

8 6 (5)	(4) 5 7	8 (7) 9
10 (9) 12	(8) 9 10	13 12 (11)
6 (5) 7	(5) 13 8	8 9 (7)
5 4 (3)	11 (10) 12	7 (6) 8
5 6 (4)	6 (3) 7	12 13 (10)
(9) 11 10	9 (8) 11	(8) 10 9
(6) 8 9	4 7 (3)	12 (11) 13
11 (9) 10	(10) 12 13	8 (5) 7
11 10 (9)	9 (7) 8	13 12 (11)

173

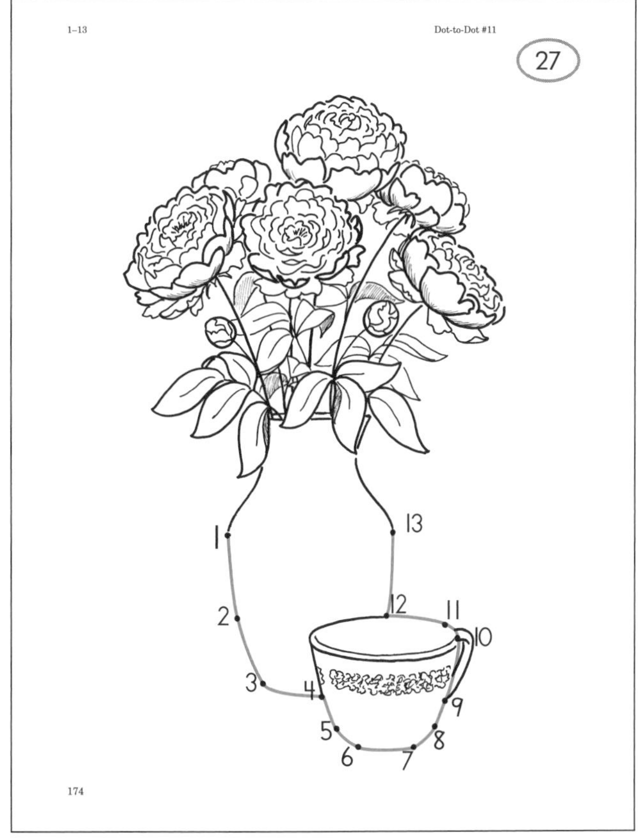

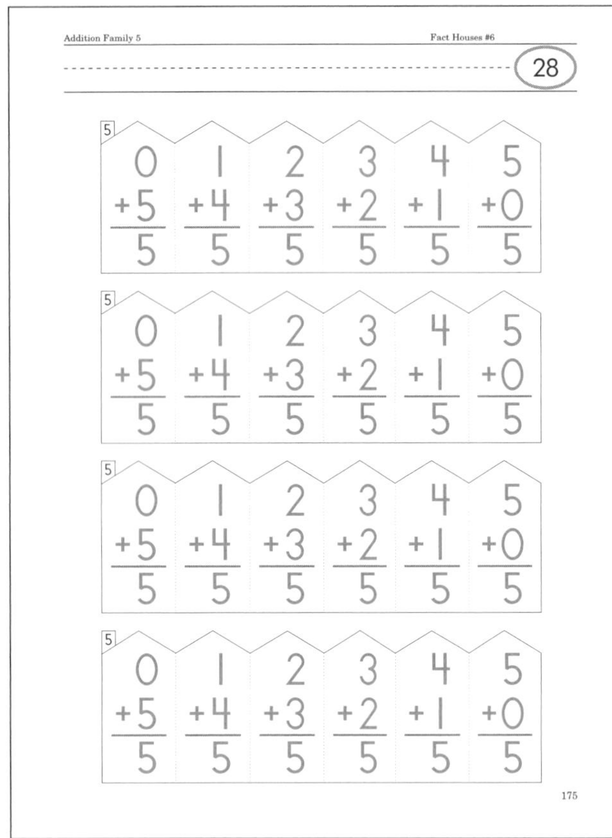

Addition Family 5 | Fact Houses #6

28

5					
0 + 5 = 5	1 + 4 = 5	2 + 3 = 5	3 + 2 = 5	4 + 1 = 5	5 + 0 = 5
0 + 5 = 5	1 + 4 = 5	2 + 3 = 5	3 + 2 = 5	4 + 1 = 5	5 + 0 = 5
0 + 5 = 5	1 + 4 = 5	2 + 3 = 5	3 + 2 = 5	4 + 1 = 5	5 + 0 = 5
0 + 5 = 5	1 + 4 = 5	2 + 3 = 5	3 + 2 = 5	4 + 1 = 5	5 + 0 = 5

175

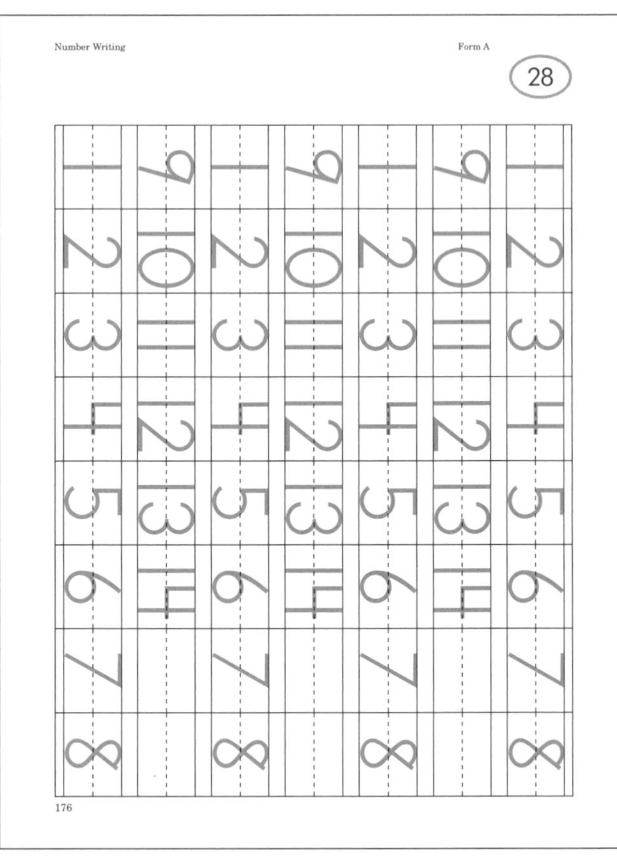

Number Writing | Form A

28

1	9	1	9	1	9	1
2	10	2	10	2	10	2
3	11	3	11	3	11	3
4	12	4	12	4	12	4
5	13	5	13	5	13	5
6	14	6	14	6	14	6
7		7		7		7
8		8		8		8

176

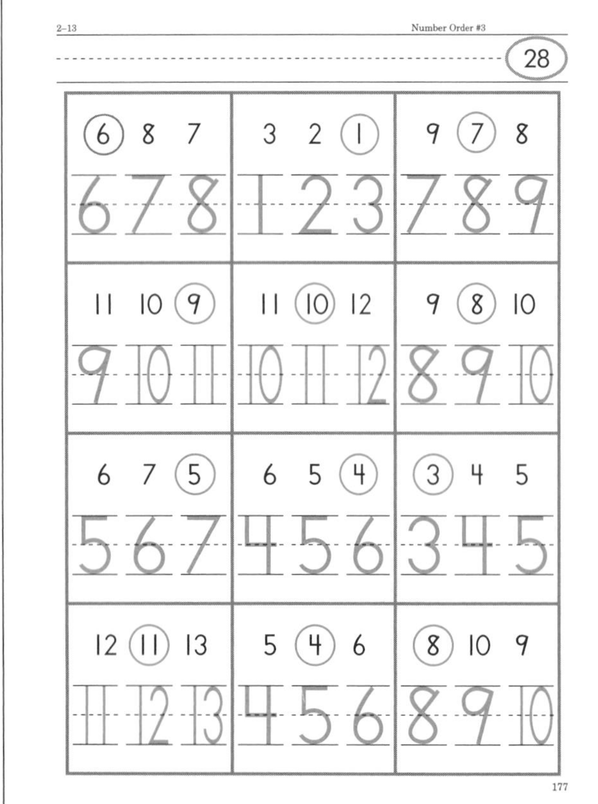

2–13 | Number Order #3

28

(6) 8 7 → 6 7 8	3 2 (1) → 1 2 3	9 (7) 8 → 7 8 9
11 10 (9) → 9 10 11	11 (10) 12 → 10 11 12	9 (8) 10 → 8 9 10
6 7 (5) → 5 6 7	6 5 (4) → 4 5 6	(3) 4 5 → 3 4 5
12 (11) 13 → 11 12 13	5 (4) 6 → 4 5 6	(8) 10 9 → 8 9 10

177

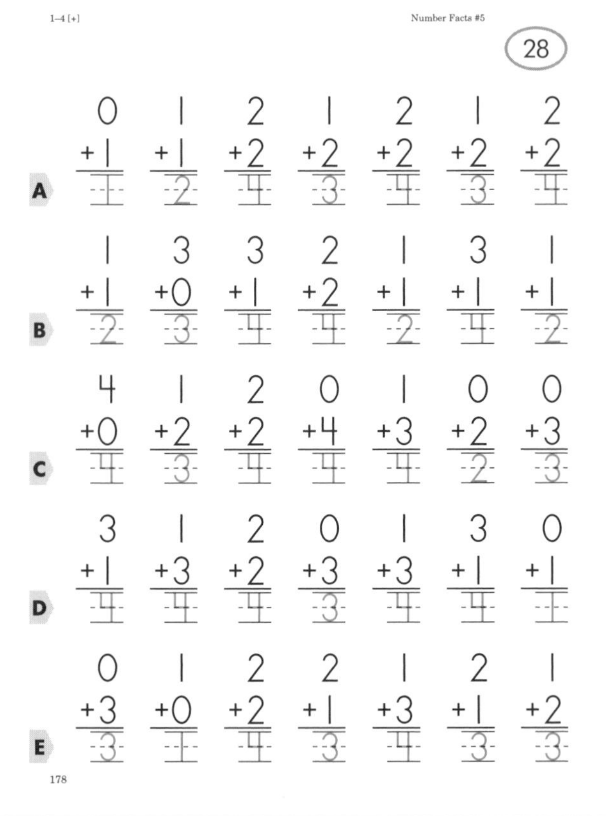

1–4 [+] | Number Facts #5

28

A	0 + 1 = 1	1 + 1 = 2	2 + 2 = 4	1 + 2 = 3	2 + 2 = 4	1 + 2 = 3	2 + 2 = 4
B	1 + 1 = 2	3 + 0 = 3	3 + 1 = 4	2 + 2 = 4	1 + 1 = 2	3 + 1 = 4	1 + 1 = 2
C	4 + 0 = 4	1 + 2 = 3	2 + 2 = 4	0 + 4 = 4	1 + 3 = 4	0 + 2 = 2	0 + 3 = 3
D	3 + 1 = 4	1 + 3 = 4	2 + 2 = 4	0 + 3 = 3	1 + 3 = 4	3 + 1 = 4	0 + 1 = 1
E	0 + 3 = 3	1 + 0 = 1	2 + 2 = 4	2 + 1 = 3	1 + 3 = 4	2 + 1 = 3	1 + 2 = 3

178

8–14
Count and Write #20
28
9
11
12
13
10
14
12
11
10
8
14
13
179

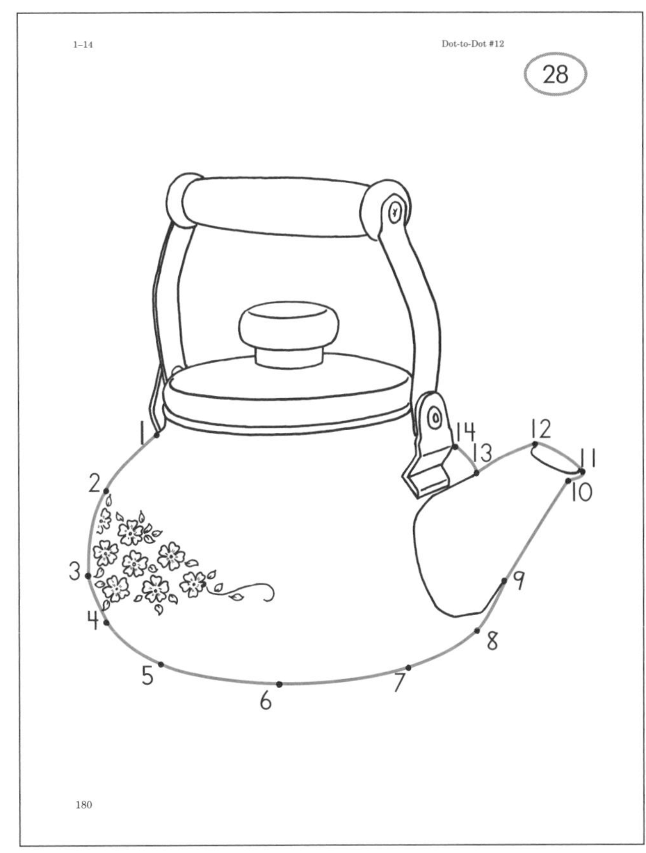
1–14
Dot-to-Dot #12
28
1
2
3
4
5
6
7
8
9
10
11
12
13
14
180

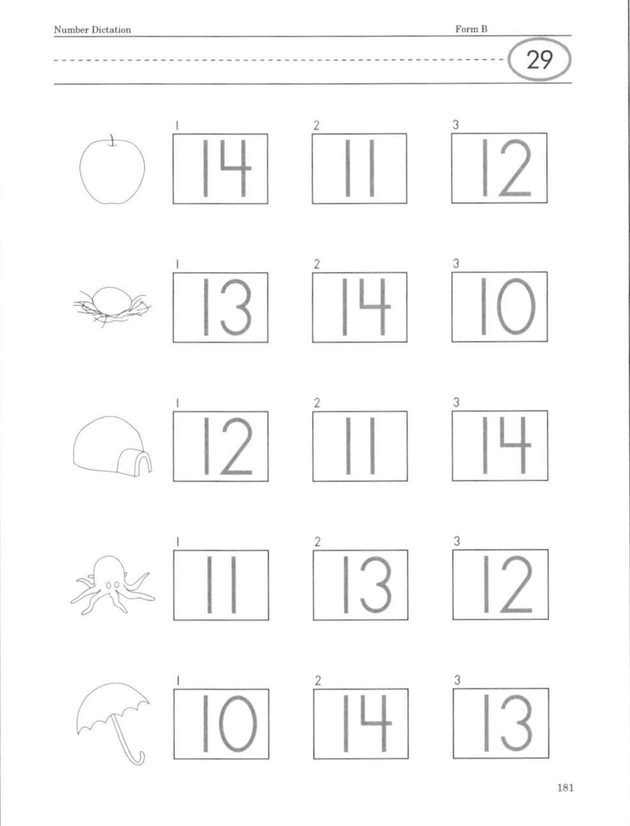
Number Dictation
Form B
29
14 11 12
13 14 10
12 11 14
11 13 12
10 14 13
181

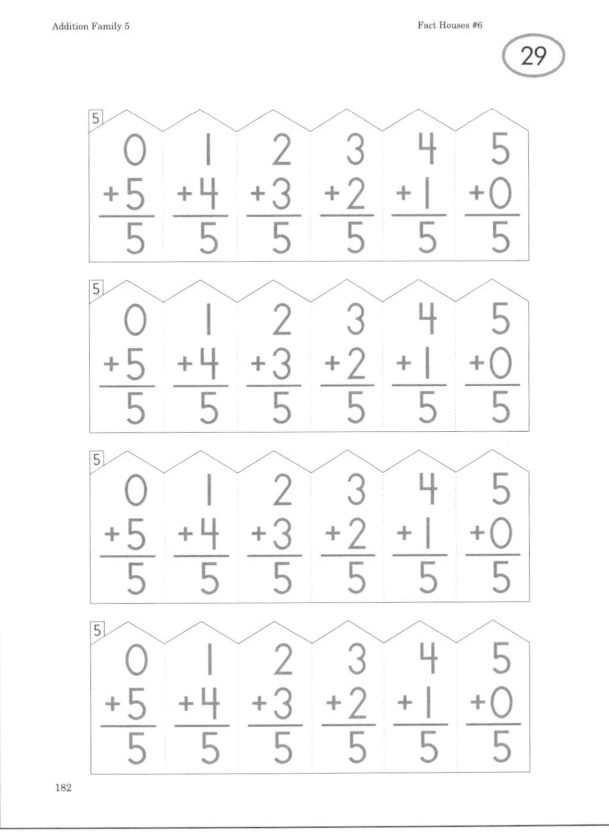
Addition Family 5
Fact Houses #6
29
0 +5 5
1 +4 5
2 +3 5
3 +2 5
4 +1 5
5 +0 5
182

3–14 Between Numbers #4

29

3 4 5	5 6 7	11 12 13
12 13 14	11 12 13	6 7 8
5 6 7	12 13 14	10 11 12
12 13 14	8 9 10	8 9 10
9 10 11	11 12 13	6 7 8
7 8 9	12 13 14	9 10 11
10 11 12	7 8 9	12 13 14

183

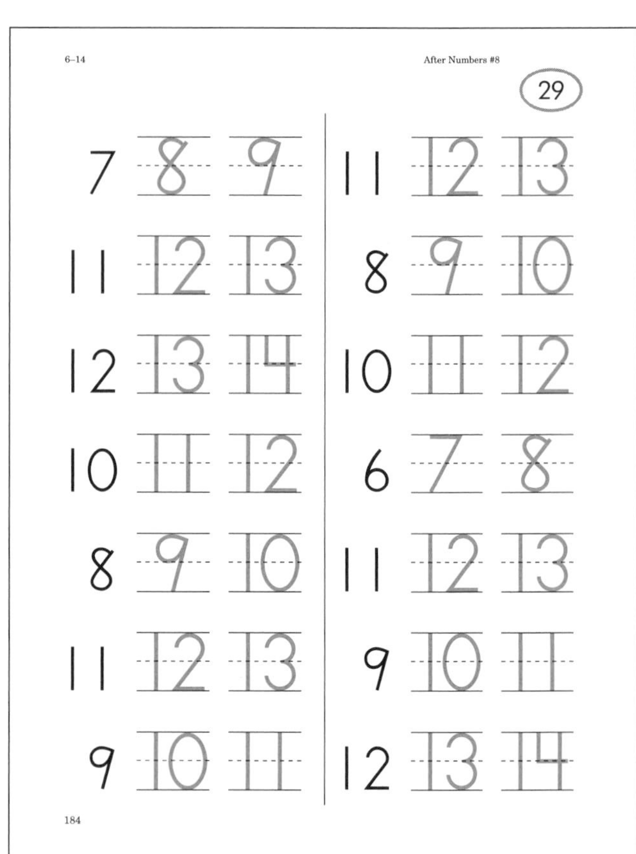

6–14 After Numbers #8

29

7 8 9	11 12 13
11 12 13	8 9 10
12 13 14	10 11 12
10 11 12	6 7 8
8 9 10	11 12 13
11 12 13	9 10 11
9 10 11	12 13 14

184

Addition Family 5 Fact Houses #6

30

0 +5 = 5	1 +4 = 5	2 +3 = 5	3 +2 = 5	4 +1 = 5	5 +0 = 5
0 +5 = 5	1 +4 = 5	2 +3 = 5	3 +2 = 5	4 +1 = 5	5 +0 = 5
0 +5 = 5	1 +4 = 5	2 +3 = 5	3 +2 = 5	4 +1 = 5	5 +0 = 5
0 +5 = 5	1 +4 = 5	2 +3 = 5	3 +2 = 5	4 +1 = 5	5 +0 = 5

185

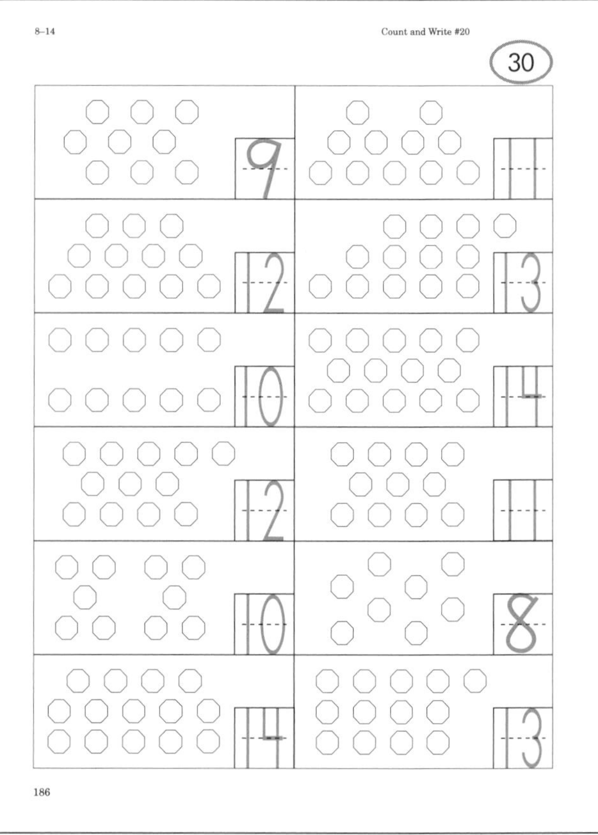

8–14 Count and Write #20

30

9	11
12	13
10	14
12	11
10	8
14	13

186

3–14 More Numbers #3

30

• ⁙ more

11 12 (14)	9 (10) 8	12 (14) 13
4 5 (6)	10 12 (13)	5 (8) 7
10 9 (11)	11 12 (14)	11 (13) 12
(9) 7 8	4 (5) 3	12 (13) 11
(12) 10 11	(13) 11 12	6 (7) 5
(14) 12 13	9 10 (11)	(14) 13 12
8 (10) 9	7 (8) 6	9 10 (12)
2 (4) 3	(14) 10 12	6 (10) 8
(9) 8 6	5 (7) 6	(11) 9 10

187

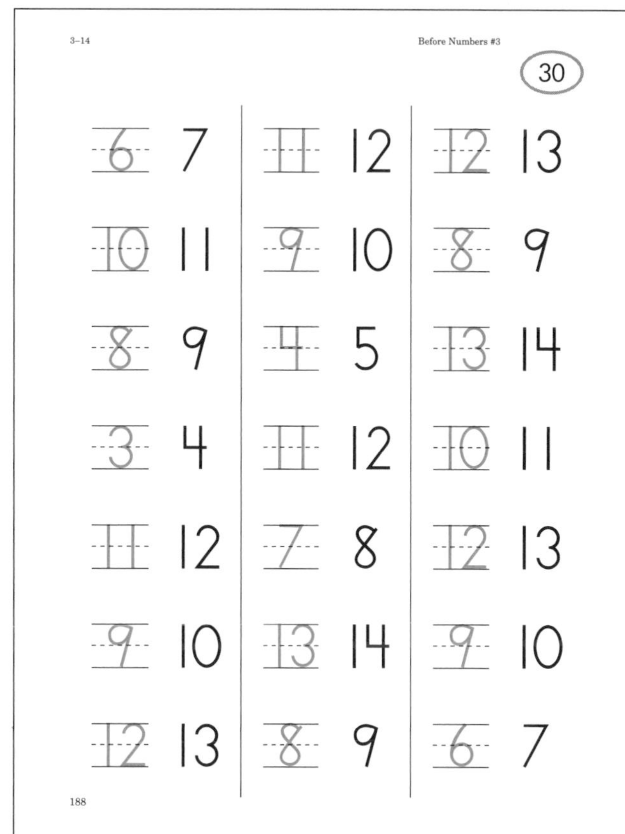

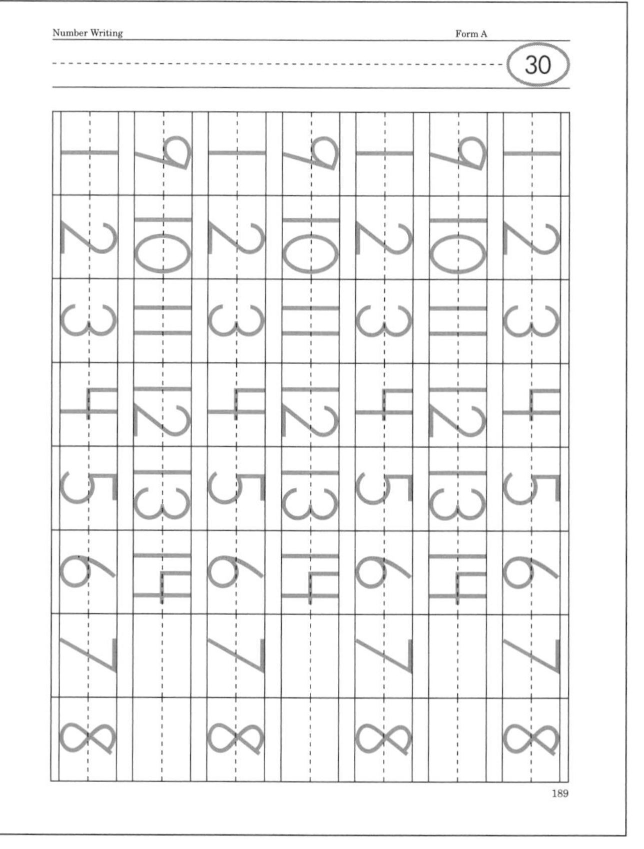

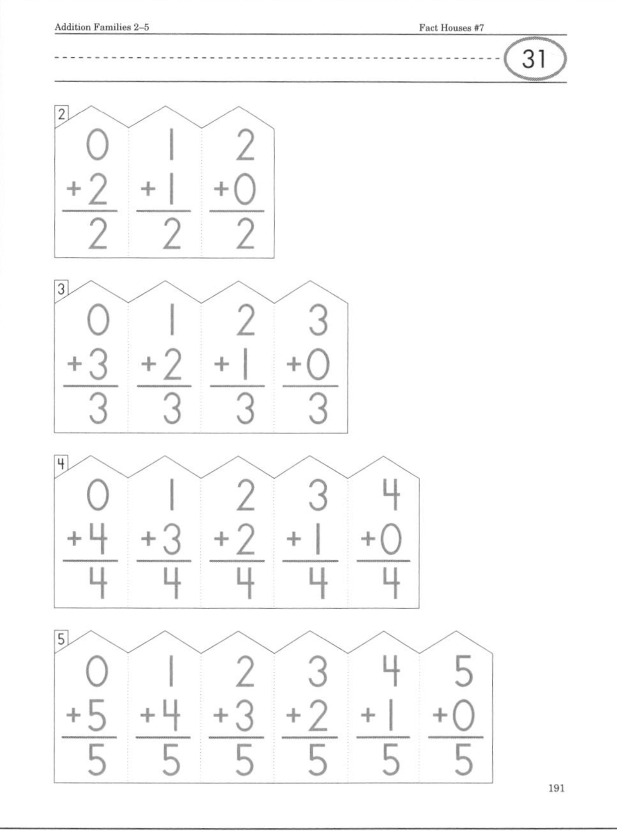

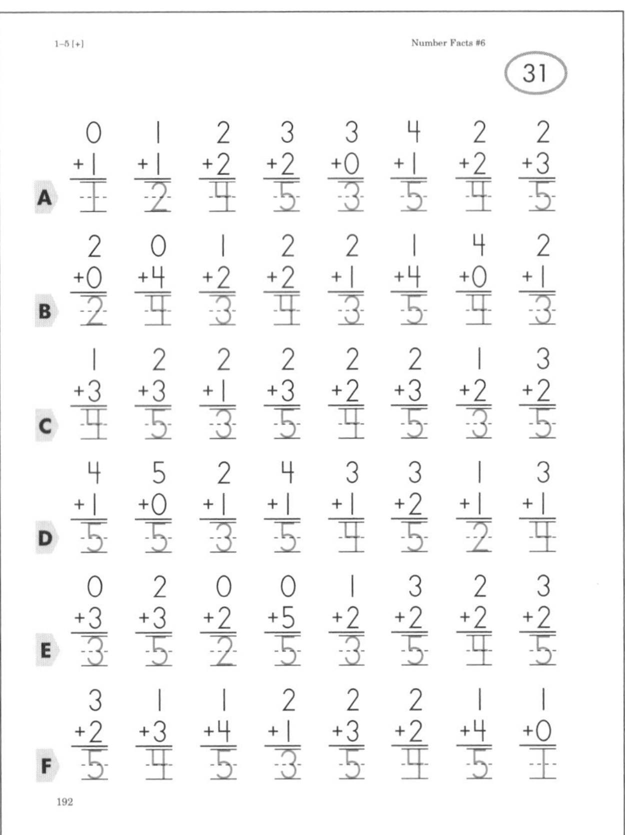

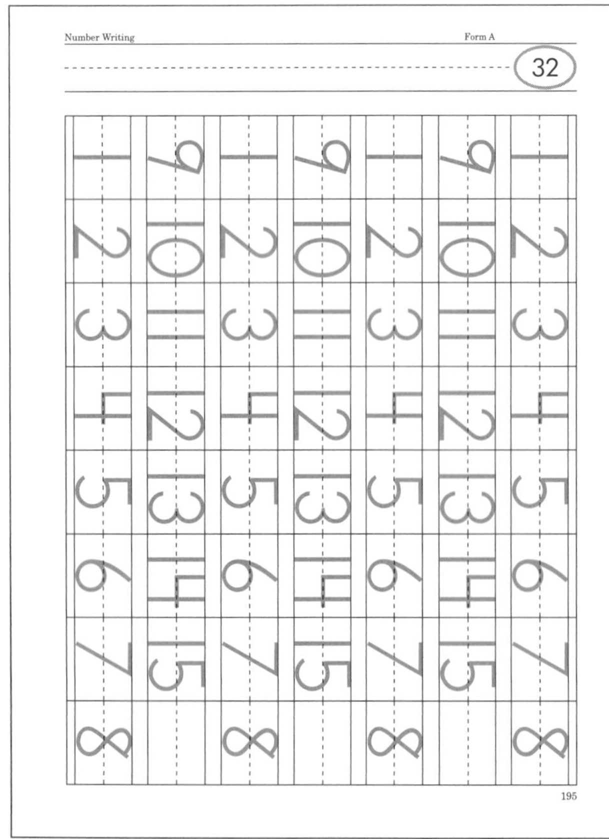

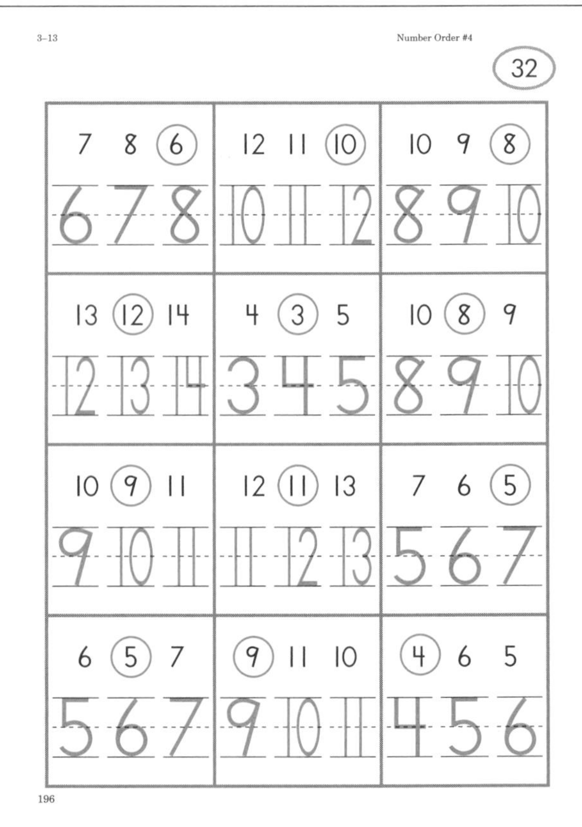

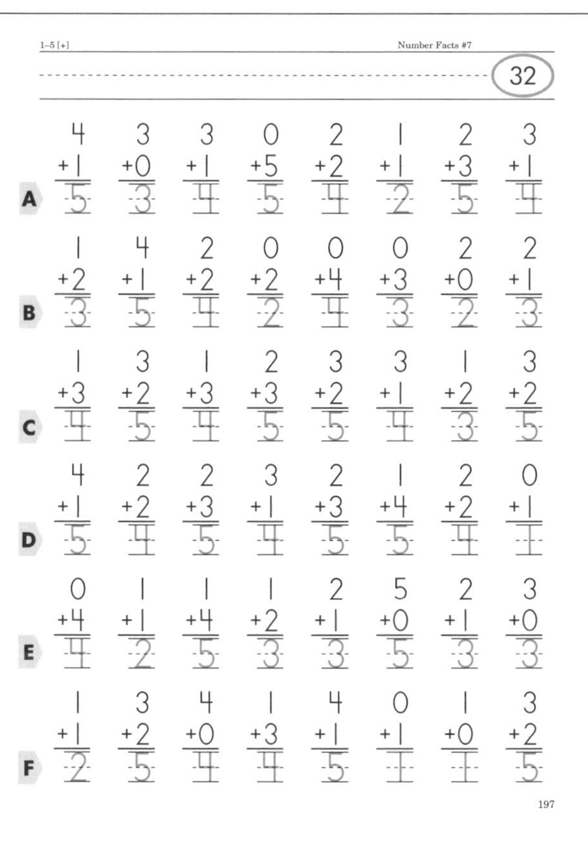

1–5 [+] Number Facts #7

32

A	4 +1 5	3 +0 3	3 +1 4	0 +5 5	2 +2 4	1 +1 2	2 +3 5	3 +1 4
B	1 +2 3	4 +1 5	2 +2 4	0 +2 2	0 +4 4	0 +3 3	2 +0 2	2 +1 3
C	1 +3 4	3 +2 5	1 +3 4	2 +3 5	3 +2 5	3 +1 4	1 +2 3	3 +2 5
D	4 +1 5	2 +2 4	2 +3 5	3 +1 4	2 +3 5	1 +4 5	2 +2 4	0 +1 1
E	0 +4 4	1 +1 2	1 +4 5	1 +2 3	2 +1 3	5 +0 5	2 +1 3	3 +0 3
F	1 +1 2	3 +2 5	4 +0 4	1 +3 4	4 +1 5	0 +1 1	1 +0 1	3 +2 5

197

9–15 Count and Write #21

32

10	13
12	14
11	15
14	9
12	13
14	15

198

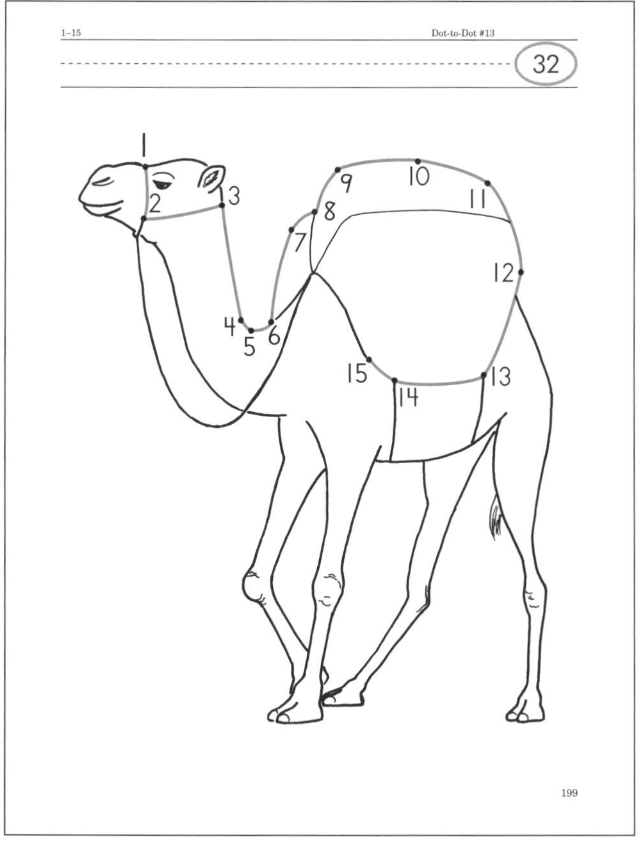

1–15 Dot-to-Dot #13

32

199

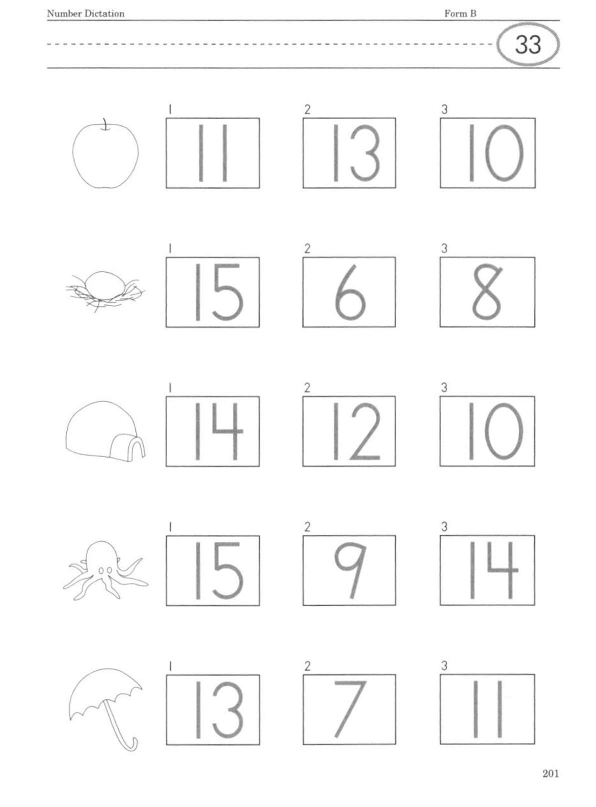

Number Dictation Form B

33

	1	2	3
	11	13	10
	15	6	8
	14	12	10
	15	9	14
	13	7	11

201

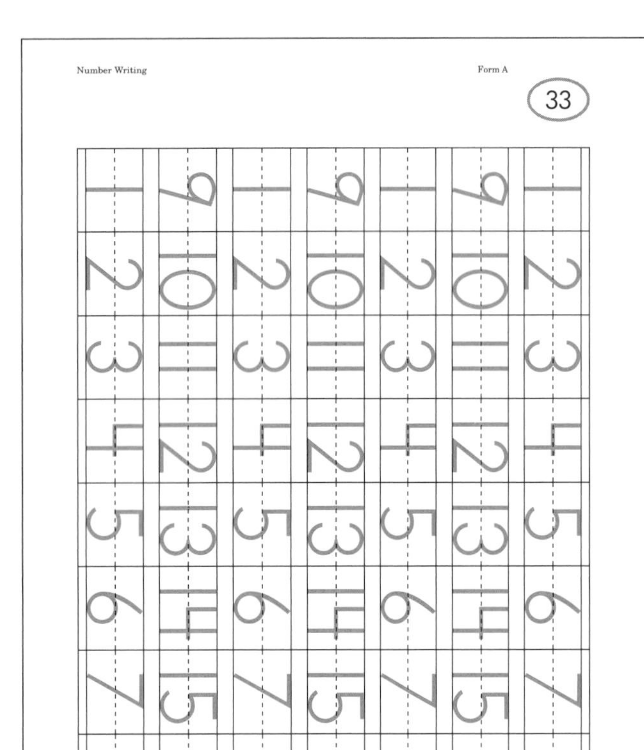
Number Writing
Form A
33
1 9 1 9 1 9 1
2 10 2 10 2 10 2
3 11 3 11 3 11 3
4 12 4 12 4 12 4
5 13 5 13 5 13 5
6 14 6 14 6 14 6
7 15 7 15 7 15 7
8 16 8 16 8 16 8
202

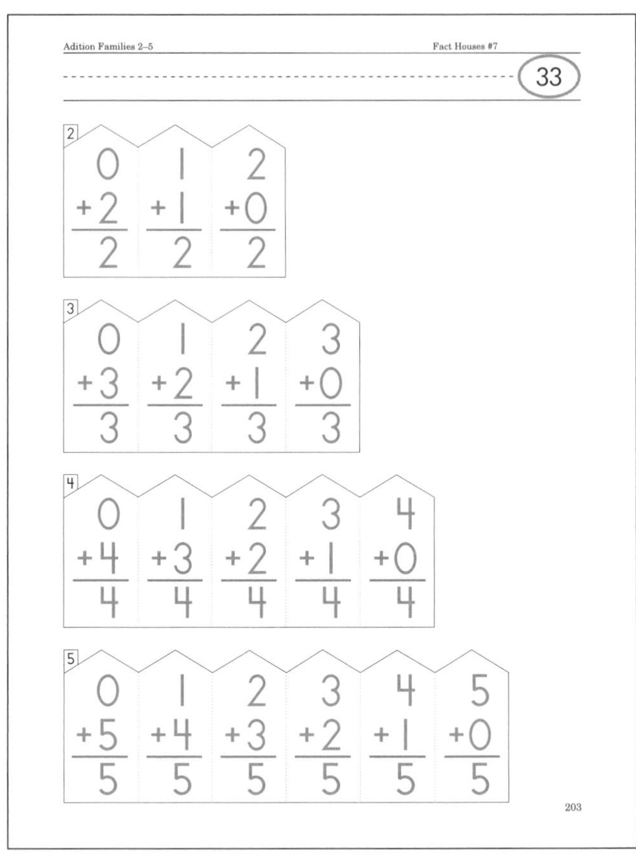
Adition Families 2–5
Fact Houses #7
33
2
0 +2 = 2; 1 +1 = 2; 2 +0 = 2
3
0 +3 = 3; 1 +2 = 3; 2 +1 = 3; 3 +0 = 3
4
0 +4 = 4; 1 +3 = 4; 2 +2 = 4; 3 +1 = 4; 4 +0 = 4
5
0 +5 = 5; 1 +4 = 5; 2 +3 = 5; 3 +2 = 5; 4 +1 = 5; 5 +0 = 5
203

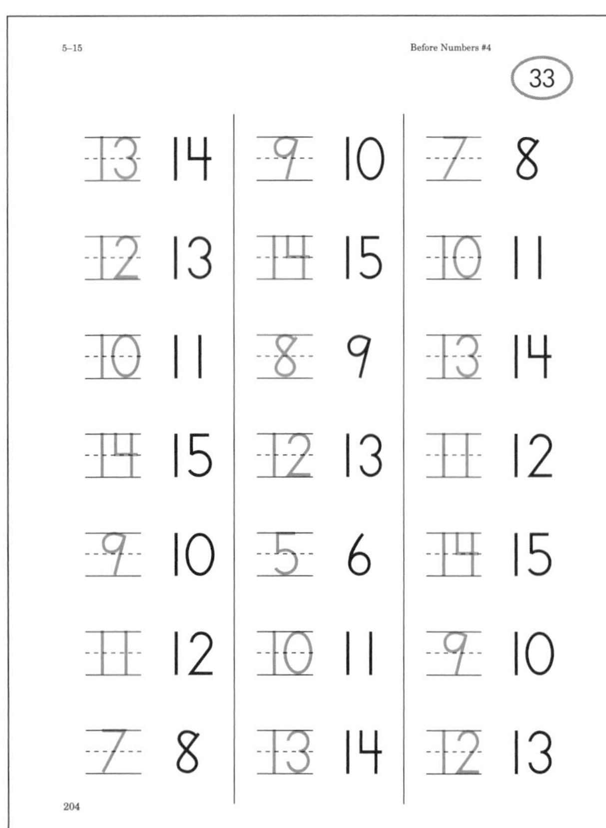
5–15
Before Numbers #4
33
13 14 | 9 10 | 7 8
12 13 | 14 15 | 10 11
10 11 | 8 9 | 13 14
14 15 | 12 13 | 11 12
9 10 | 5 6 | 14 15
11 12 | 10 11 | 9 10
7 8 | 13 14 | 12 13
204

10–16
Count and Write #22
33
14 16
15 16
15 14
13 16
11 10
12 13
205

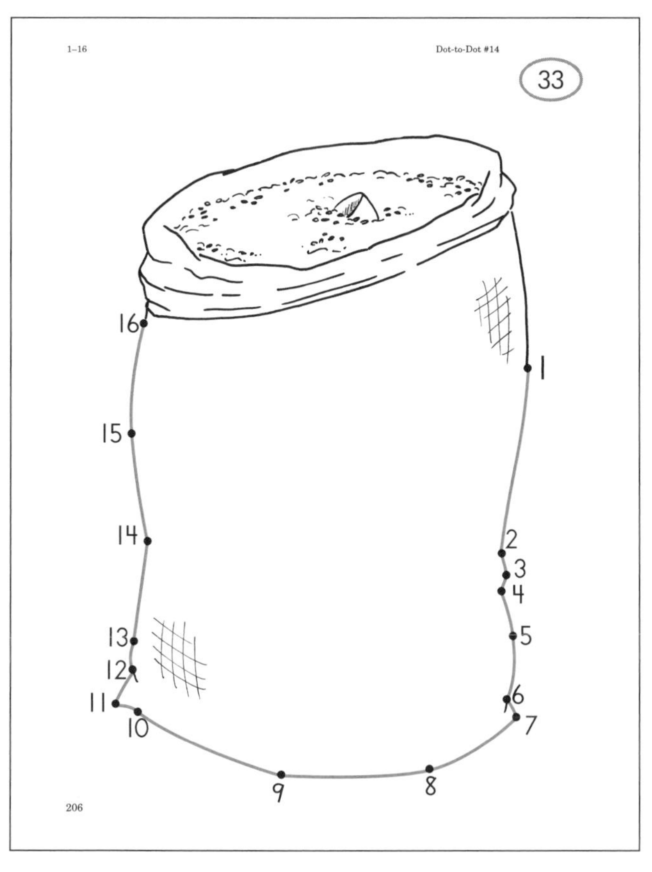
1–16
Dot-to-Dot #14
33
206

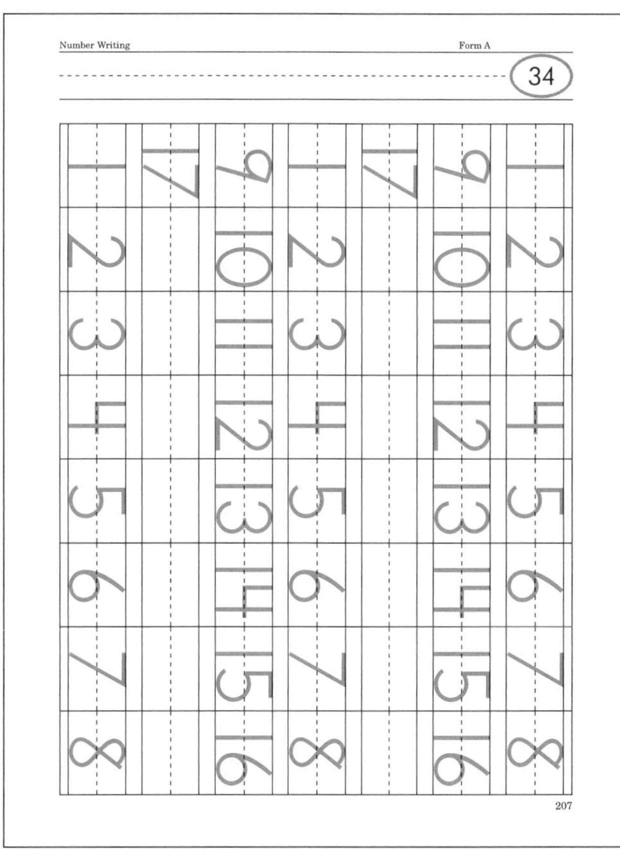
Number Writing
Form A
34
207

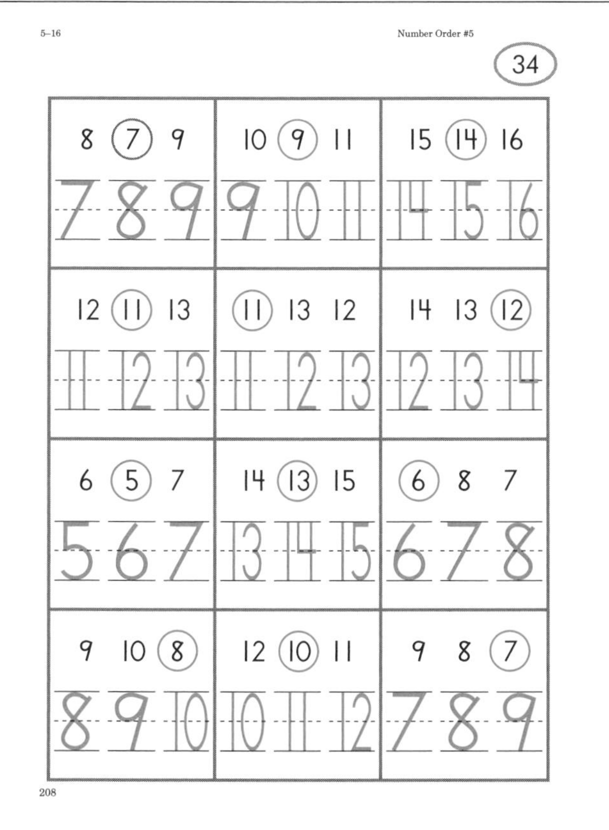
5–16
Number Order #5
34
208

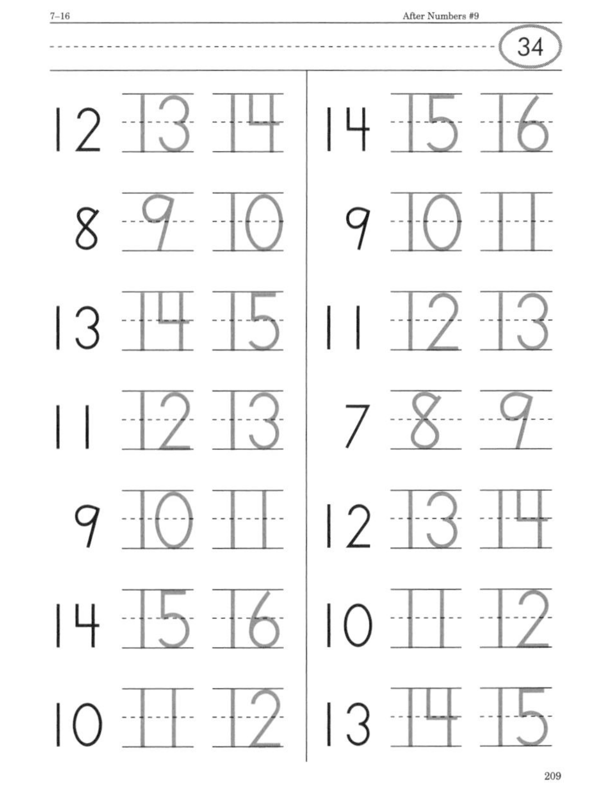
7–16
After Numbers #9
34
209

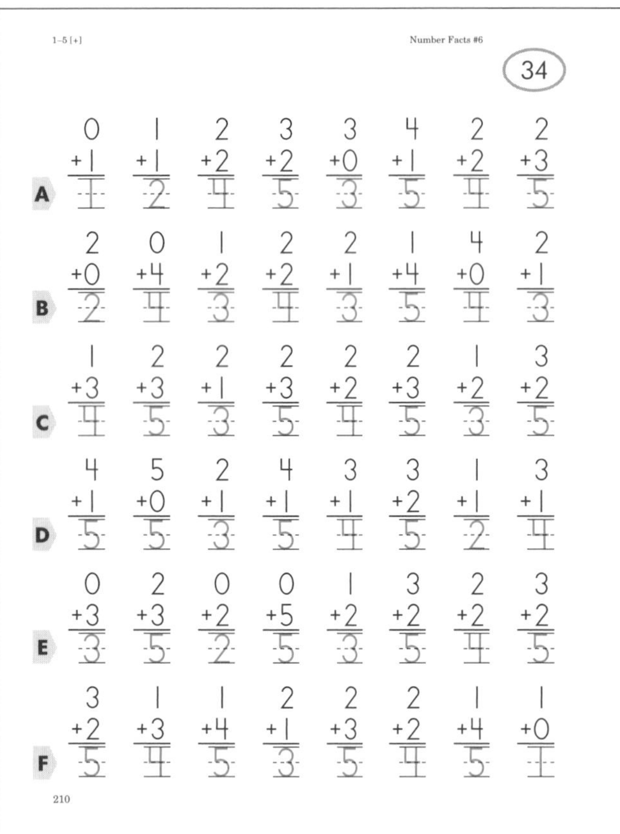
1-5 [+] Number Facts #6

34

A	0 +1 = 1	1 +1 = 2	2 +2 = 4	3 +2 = 5	3 +0 = 3	4 +1 = 5	2 +2 = 4	2 +3 = 5
B	2 +0 = 2	0 +4 = 4	1 +2 = 3	2 +2 = 4	2 +1 = 3	1 +4 = 5	4 +0 = 4	2 +1 = 3
C	1 +3 = 4	2 +3 = 5	2 +1 = 3	2 +3 = 5	2 +2 = 4	2 +3 = 5	1 +2 = 3	3 +2 = 5
D	4 +1 = 5	5 +0 = 5	2 +1 = 3	4 +1 = 5	3 +1 = 4	3 +2 = 5	1 +1 = 2	3 +1 = 4
E	0 +3 = 3	2 +3 = 5	0 +2 = 2	0 +5 = 5	1 +2 = 3	3 +2 = 5	2 +2 = 4	3 +2 = 5
F	3 +2 = 5	1 +3 = 4	1 +4 = 5	2 +1 = 3	2 +3 = 5	2 +2 = 4	1 +4 = 5	1 +0 = 1

210

11-16 Count and Write #23

34

15	11
16	12
14	16
13	13
14	15
11	12

211

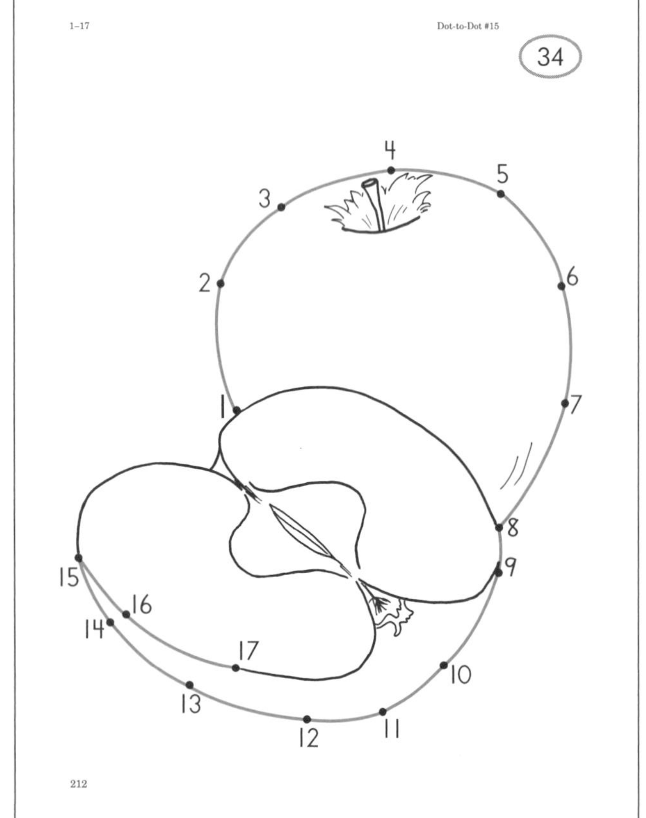
1-17 Dot-to-Dot #15

34

212

Flash Card Drill Form C

35

1 2 3 4 5

Individual answers (See page 365 for instructions.)

213

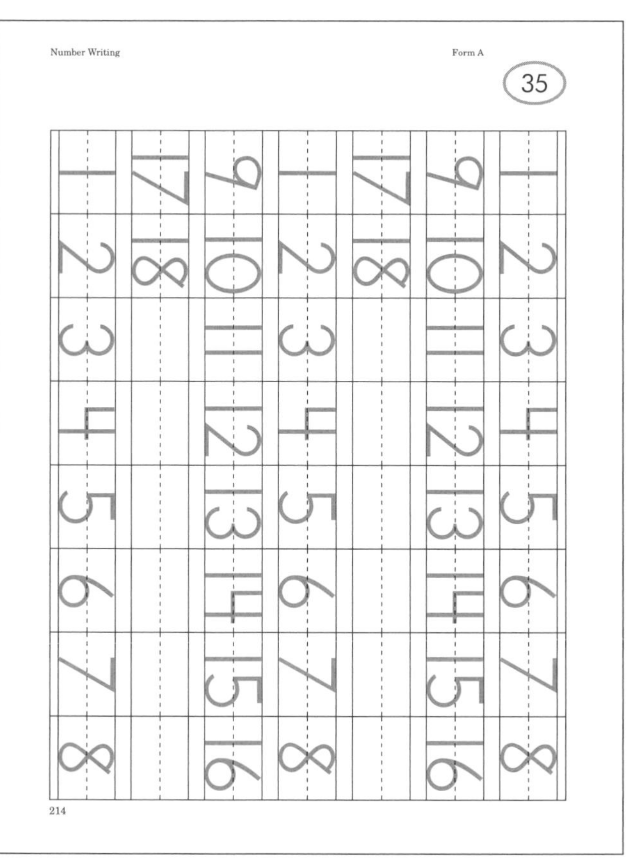

Number Writing Form A

35

1	17	9	1	17	9	1
2	18	10	2	18	10	2
3		11	3		11	3
4		12	4		12	4
5		13	5		13	5
6		14	6		14	6
7		15	7		15	7
8		16	8		16	8

214

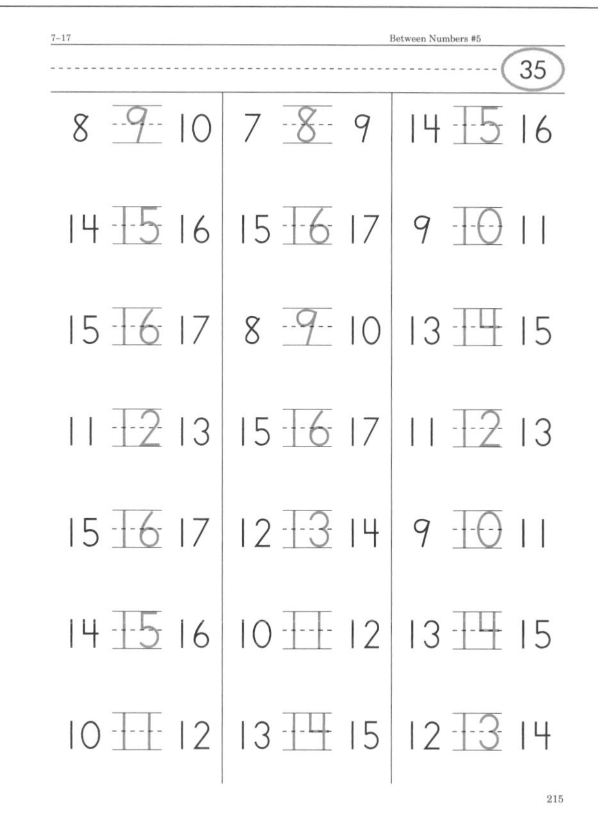

7–17 Between Numbers #5

35

8 9 10	7 8 9	14 15 16
14 15 16	15 16 17	9 10 11
15 16 17	8 9 10	13 14 15
11 12 13	15 16 17	11 12 13
15 16 17	12 13 14	9 10 11
14 15 16	10 11 12	13 14 15
10 11 12	13 14 15	12 13 14

215

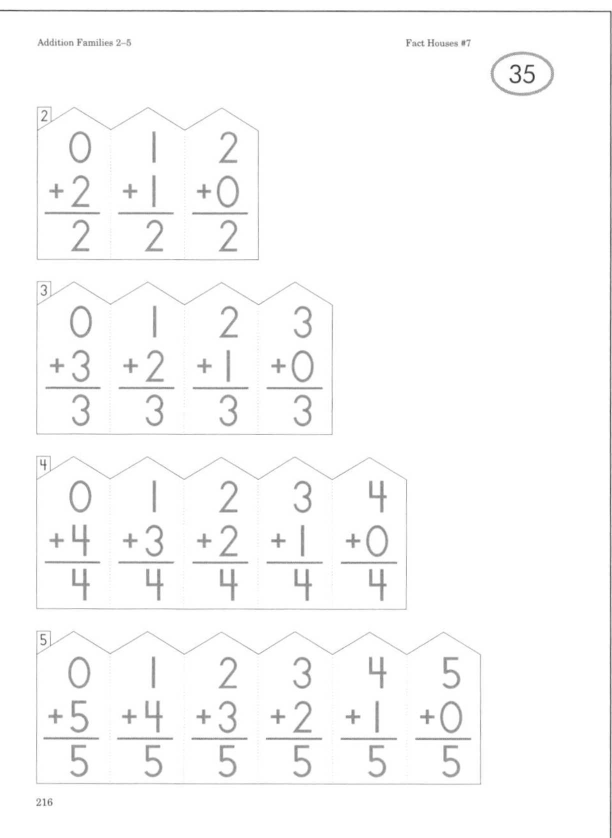

Addition Families 2–5 Fact Houses #7

35

Family						
2	0 + 2 = 2	1 + 1 = 2	2 + 0 = 2			
3	0 + 3 = 3	1 + 2 = 3	2 + 1 = 3	3 + 0 = 3		
4	0 + 4 = 4	1 + 3 = 4	2 + 2 = 4	3 + 1 = 4	4 + 0 = 4	
5	0 + 5 = 5	1 + 4 = 5	2 + 3 = 5	3 + 2 = 5	4 + 1 = 5	5 + 0 = 5

216

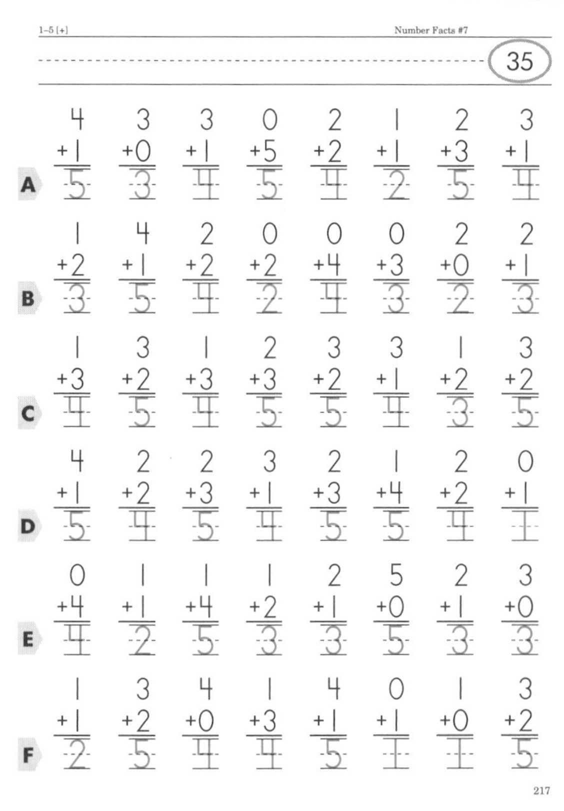

1–5 [+] Number Facts #7

35

A	4 + 1 = 5	3 + 0 = 3	3 + 1 = 4	0 + 5 = 5	2 + 2 = 4	1 + 1 = 2	2 + 3 = 5	3 + 1 = 4
B	1 + 2 = 3	4 + 1 = 5	2 + 2 = 4	0 + 2 = 2	0 + 4 = 4	0 + 3 = 3	2 + 0 = 2	2 + 1 = 3
C	1 + 3 = 4	3 + 2 = 5	1 + 3 = 4	2 + 3 = 5	3 + 2 = 5	3 + 1 = 4	1 + 2 = 3	3 + 2 = 5
D	4 + 1 = 5	2 + 2 = 4	2 + 3 = 5	3 + 1 = 4	2 + 3 = 5	1 + 4 = 5	2 + 2 = 4	0 + 1 = 1
E	0 + 4 = 4	1 + 1 = 2	1 + 4 = 5	1 + 2 = 3	2 + 1 = 3	5 + 0 = 5	2 + 1 = 3	3 + 0 = 3
F	1 + 1 = 2	3 + 2 = 5	4 + 0 = 4	1 + 3 = 4	4 + 1 = 5	0 + 1 = 1	1 + 0 = 1	3 + 2 = 5

217

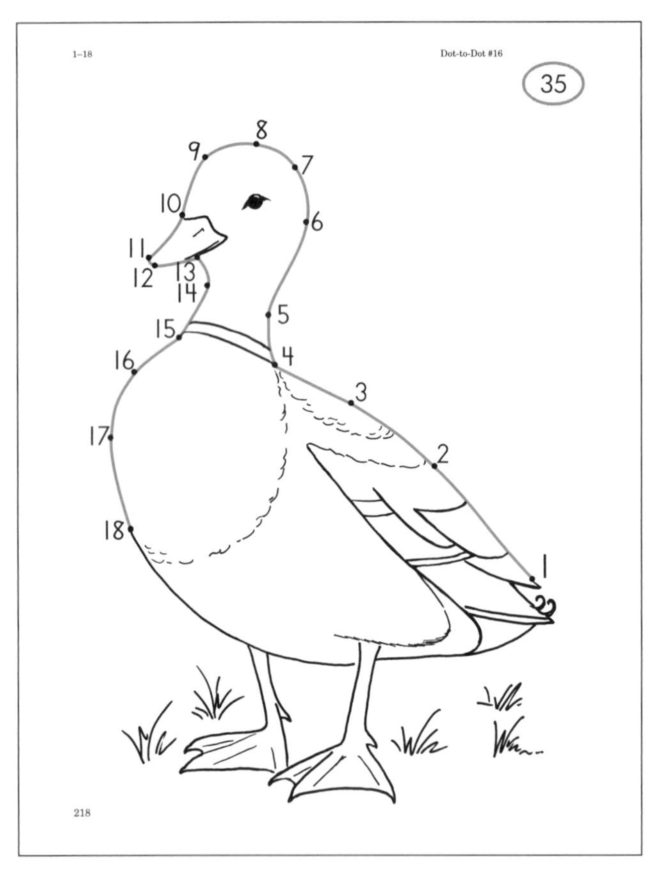

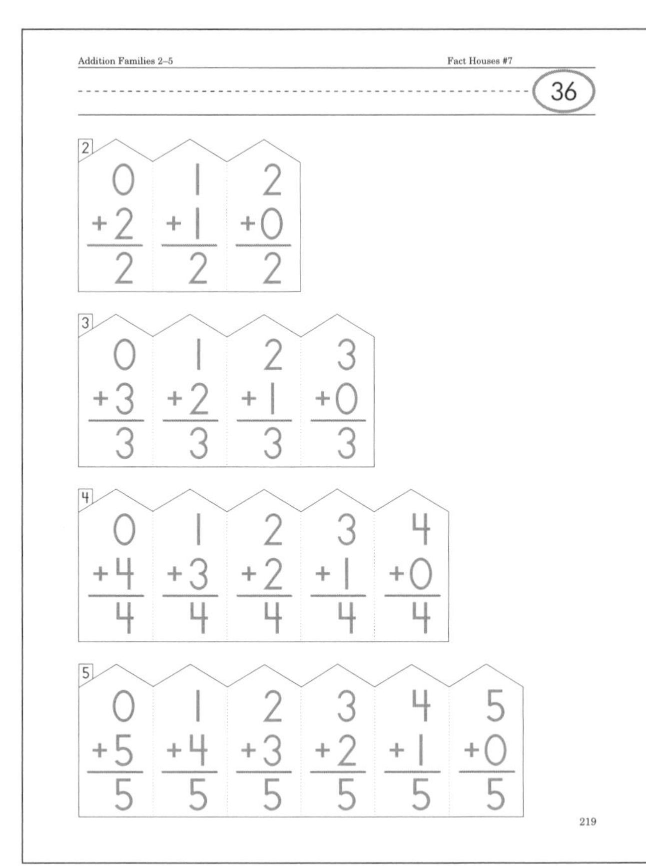
Addition Families 2–5

Fact Houses #7

36

2		
0 +2 2	1 +1 2	2 +0 2

3			
0 +3 3	1 +2 3	2 +1 3	3 +0 3

4				
0 +4 4	1 +3 4	2 +2 4	3 +1 4	4 +0 4

5					
0 +5 5	1 +4 5	2 +3 5	3 +2 5	4 +1 5	5 +0 5

219

8–18

Before Numbers #5

36

10	11	8	9	16	17
16	17	12	13	13	14
15	16	17	18	17	18
14	15	15	16	13	14
13	14	14	15	16	17
12	13	15	16	12	13
17	18	11	12	10	11

220

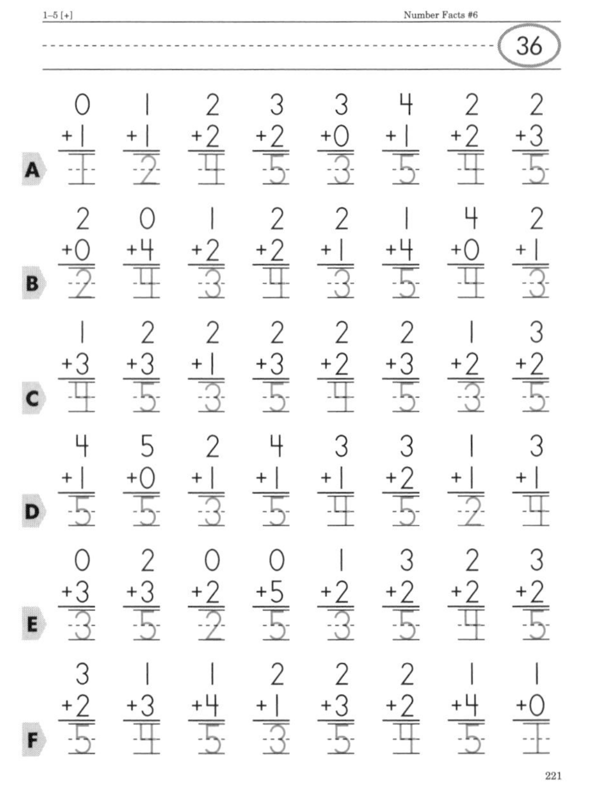
1–5 [+]

Number Facts #6

36

A	0 +1 1	1 +1 2	2 +2 4	3 +2 5	3 +0 3	4 +1 5	2 +2 4	2 +3 5
B	2 +0 2	0 +4 4	1 +2 3	2 +2 4	2 +1 3	1 +4 5	4 +0 4	2 +1 3
C	1 +3 4	2 +3 5	2 +1 3	2 +3 5	2 +2 4	2 +3 5	1 +2 3	3 +2 5
D	4 +1 5	5 +0 5	2 +1 3	4 +1 5	3 +1 4	3 +2 5	1 +1 2	3 +1 4
E	0 +3 3	2 +3 5	0 +2 2	0 +5 5	1 +2 3	3 +2 5	2 +2 4	3 +2 5
F	3 +2 5	1 +3 4	1 +4 5	2 +1 3	2 +3 5	2 +2 4	1 +4 5	1 +0 1

221

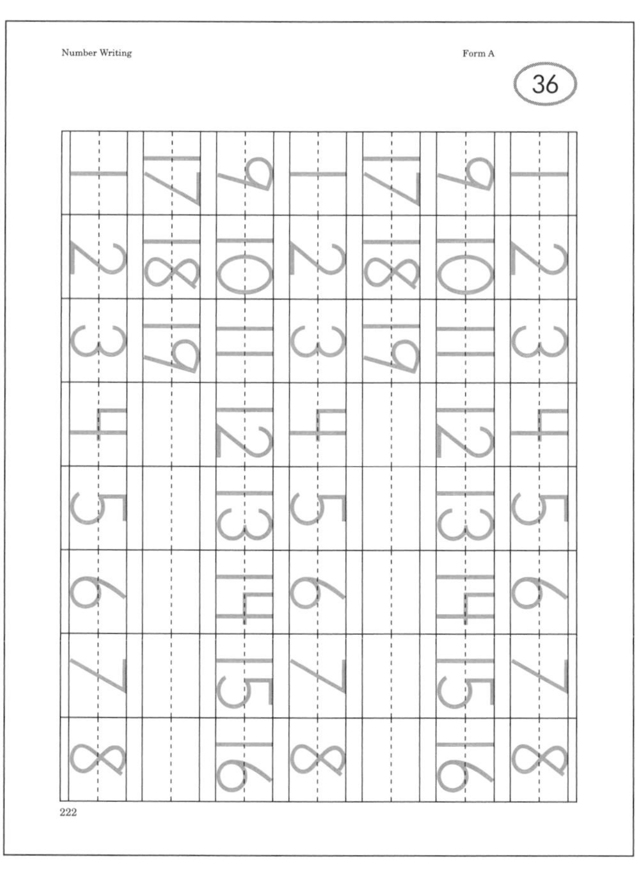
Number Writing
Form A
36
222

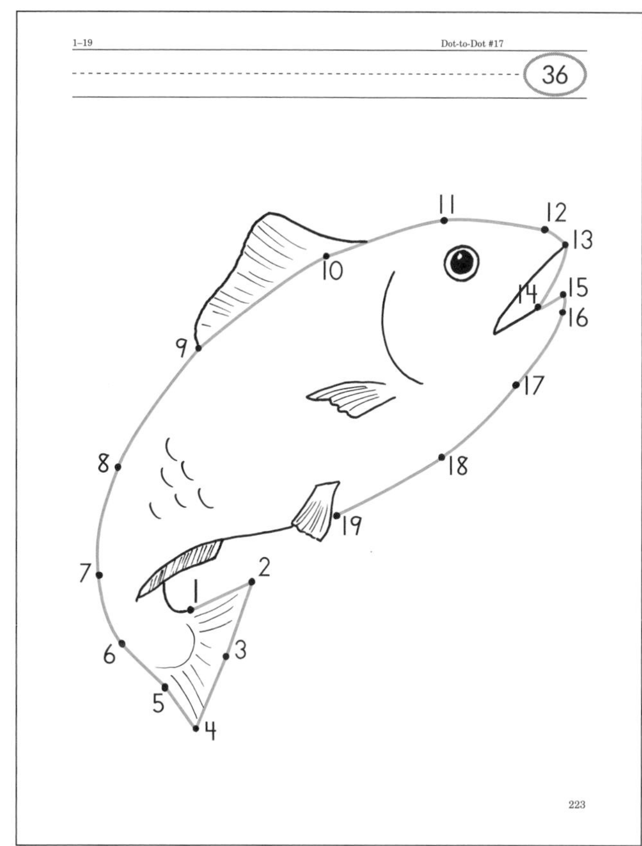
1–19
Dot-to-Dot #17
36
1
2
3
4
5
6
7
8
9
10
11
12
13
14
15
16
17
18
19
223

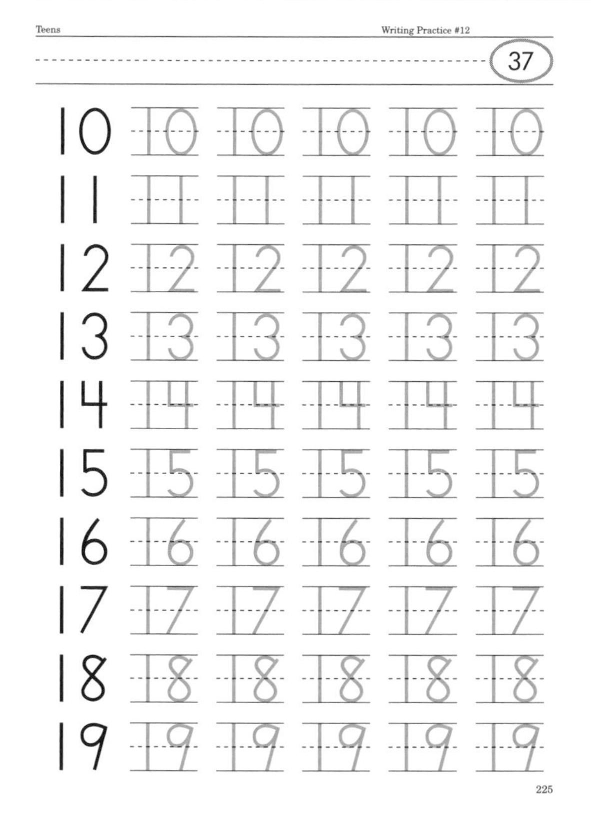
Teens
Writing Practice #12
37
10 10 10 10 10 10
11 11 11 11 11 11
12 12 12 12 12 12
13 13 13 13 13 13
14 14 14 14 14 14
15 15 15 15 15 15
16 16 16 16 16 16
17 17 17 17 17 17
18 18 18 18 18 18
19 19 19 19 19 19
225

Addition Family 6
Fact Houses #8
37
6
0 +6 6 | 1 +5 6 | 2 +4 6 | 3 +3 6 | 4 +2 6 | 5 +1 6 | 6 +0 6
6
0 +6 6 | 1 +5 6 | 2 +4 6 | 3 +3 6 | 4 +2 6 | 5 +1 6 | 6 +0 6
6
0 +6 6 | 1 +5 6 | 2 +4 6 | 3 +3 6 | 4 +2 6 | 5 +1 6 | 6 +0 6
6
0 +6 6 | 1 +5 6 | 2 +4 6 | 3 +3 6 | 4 +2 6 | 5 +1 6 | 6 +0 6
226

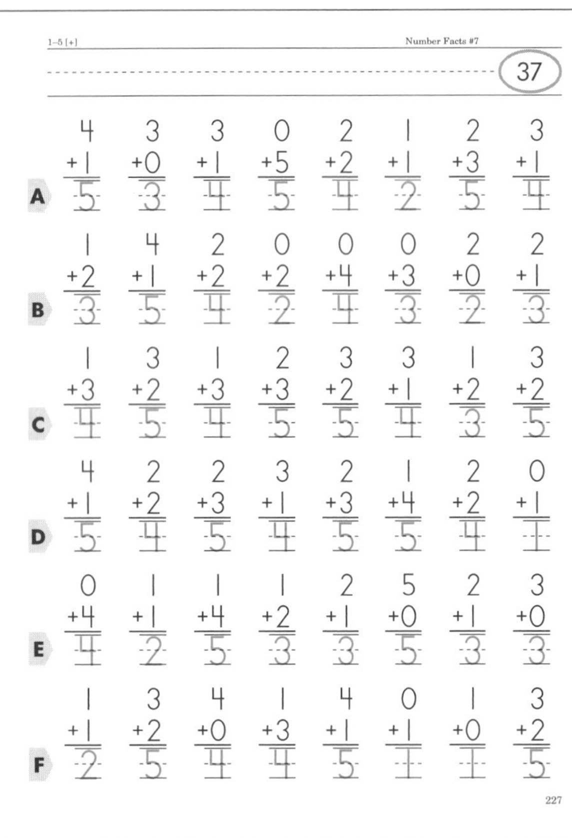

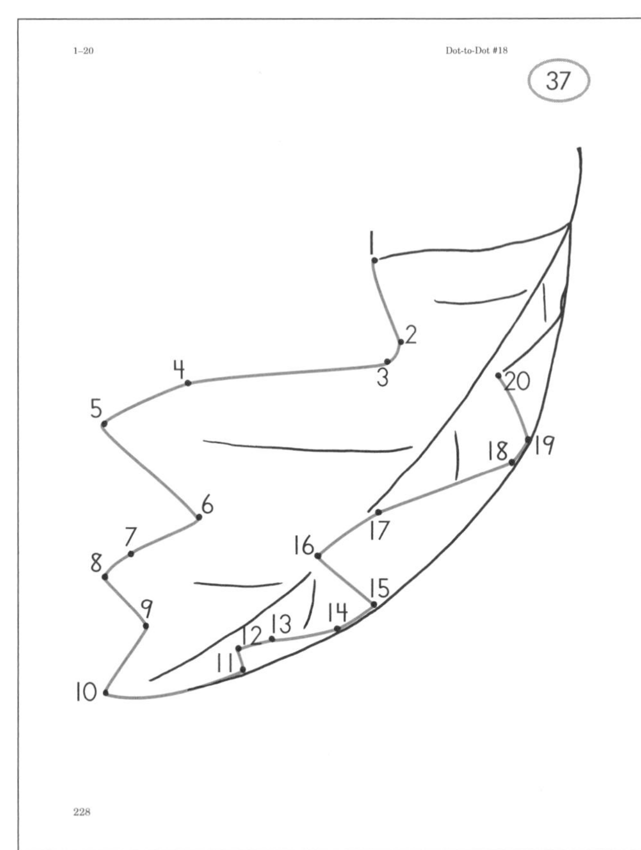

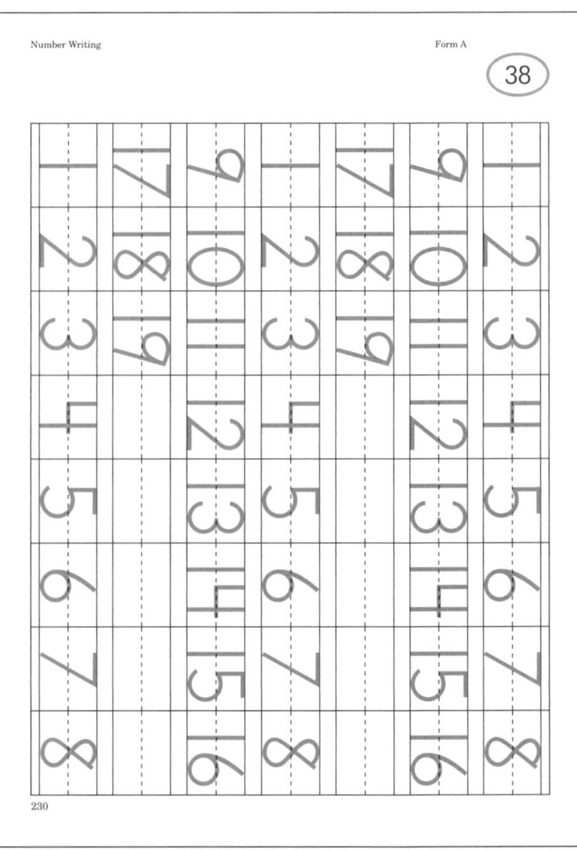

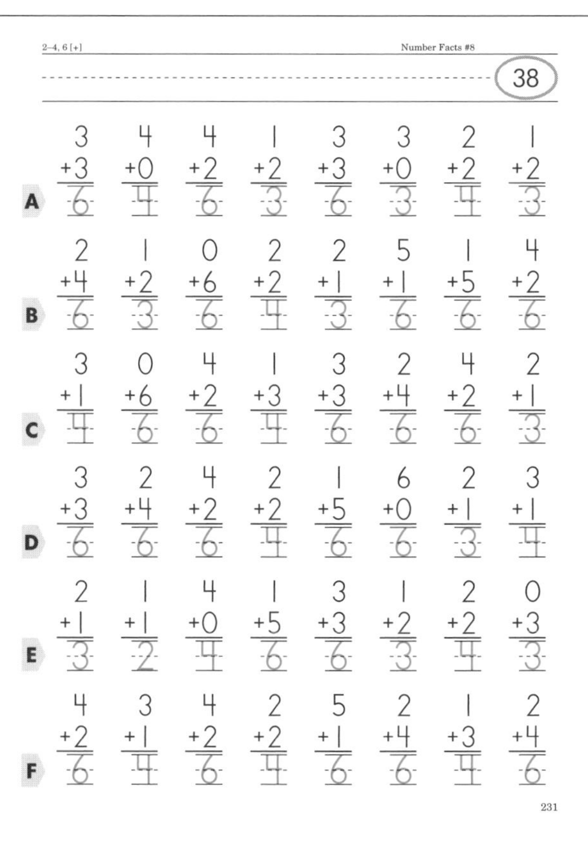
2–4, 6 [+]
Number Facts #8
38
A
B
C
D
E
F
231

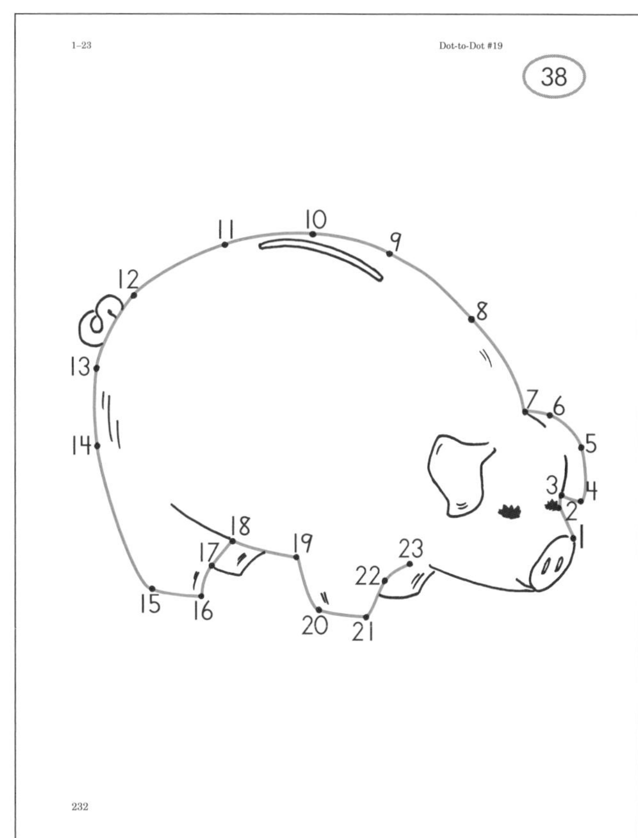
1–23
Dot-to-Dot #19
38
232

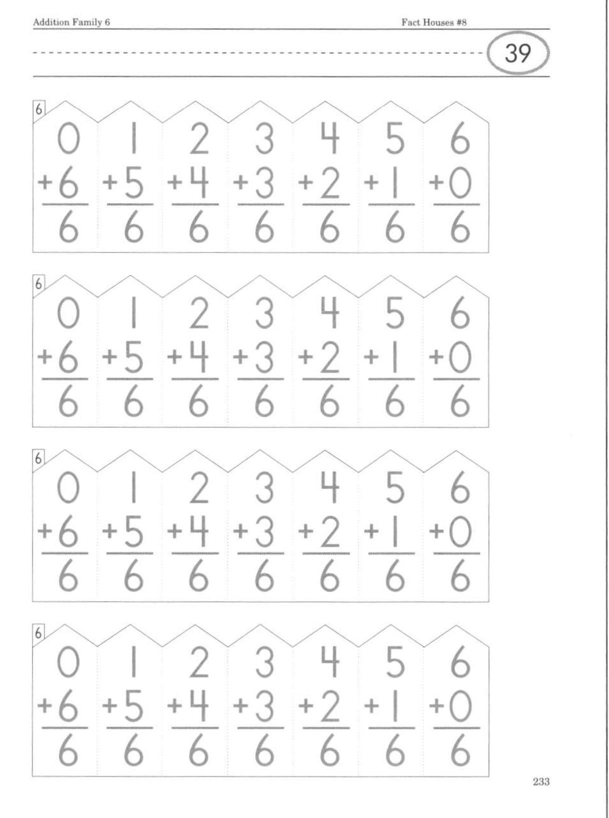
Addition Family 6
Fact Houses #8
39
233

1–20
Missing Numbers #1
39
234

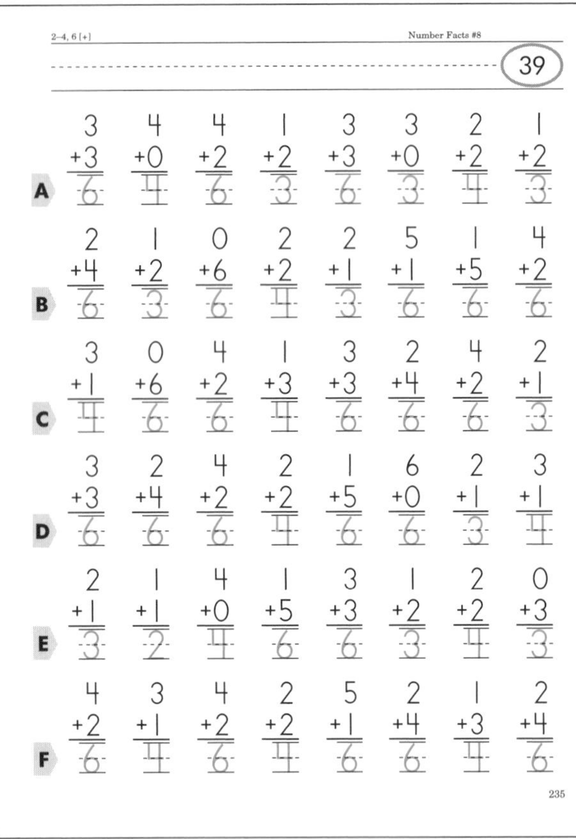

2–4, 6 [+] Number Facts #8

39

A	3 +3 = 6	4 +0 = 4	4 +2 = 6	1 +2 = 3	3 +3 = 6	3 +0 = 3	2 +2 = 4	1 +2 = 3
B	2 +4 = 6	1 +2 = 3	0 +6 = 6	2 +2 = 4	2 +1 = 3	5 +1 = 6	1 +5 = 6	4 +2 = 6
C	3 +1 = 4	0 +6 = 6	4 +2 = 6	1 +3 = 4	3 +3 = 6	2 +4 = 6	4 +2 = 6	2 +1 = 3
D	3 +3 = 6	2 +4 = 6	4 +2 = 6	2 +2 = 4	1 +5 = 6	6 +0 = 6	2 +1 = 3	3 +1 = 4
E	2 +1 = 3	1 +1 = 2	4 +0 = 4	1 +5 = 6	3 +3 = 6	1 +2 = 3	2 +2 = 4	0 +3 = 3
F	4 +2 = 6	3 +1 = 4	4 +2 = 6	2 +2 = 4	5 +1 = 6	2 +4 = 6	1 +3 = 4	2 +4 = 6

235

Number Dictation Form B

40

	1	2	3
apple	15	22	27
nest	21	17	19
igloo	26	24	18
octopus	20	19	28
umbrella	23	25	16

237

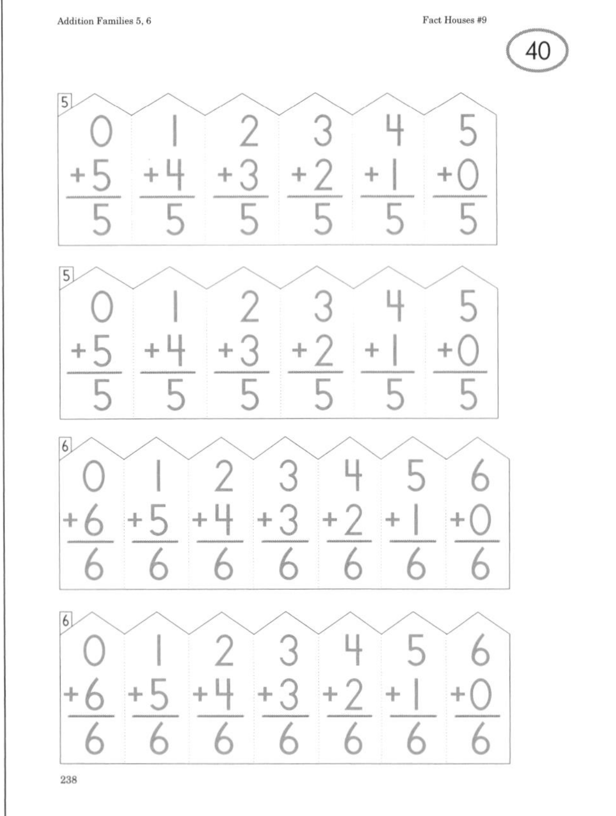

Addition Families 5, 6 Fact Houses #9

40

5						
	0 +5 = 5	1 +4 = 5	2 +3 = 5	3 +2 = 5	4 +1 = 5	5 +0 = 5

5						
	0 +5 = 5	1 +4 = 5	2 +3 = 5	3 +2 = 5	4 +1 = 5	5 +0 = 5

6							
	0 +6 = 6	1 +5 = 6	2 +4 = 6	3 +3 = 6	4 +2 = 6	5 +1 = 6	6 +0 = 6

6							
	0 +6 = 6	1 +5 = 6	2 +4 = 6	3 +3 = 6	4 +2 = 6	5 +1 = 6	6 +0 = 6

238

20's Writing Practice #13

40

20	20	20	20	20	20
21	21	21	21	21	21
22	22	22	22	22	22
23	23	23	23	23	23
24	24	24	24	24	24
25	25	25	25	25	25
26	26	26	26	26	26
27	27	27	27	27	27
28	28	28	28	28	28
29	29	29	29	29	29

239

2–4, 6 [+] Number Facts #8

40

A	3 +3 = 6	4 +0 = 4	4 +2 = 6	1 +2 = 3	3 +3 = 6	3 +0 = 3	2 +2 = 4	1 +2 = 3
B	2 +4 = 6	1 +2 = 3	0 +6 = 6	2 +2 = 4	2 +1 = 3	5 +1 = 6	1 +5 = 6	4 +2 = 6
C	3 +1 = 4	0 +6 = 6	4 +2 = 6	1 +3 = 4	3 +3 = 6	2 +4 = 6	4 +2 = 6	2 +1 = 3
D	3 +3 = 6	2 +4 = 6	4 +2 = 6	2 +2 = 4	1 +5 = 6	6 +0 = 6	2 +1 = 3	3 +1 = 4
E	2 +1 = 3	1 +1 = 2	4 +0 = 4	1 +5 = 6	3 +3 = 6	1 +2 = 3	2 +2 = 4	0 +3 = 3
F	4 +2 = 6	3 +1 = 4	4 +2 = 6	2 +2 = 4	5 +1 = 6	2 +4 = 6	1 +3 = 4	2 +4 = 6

240

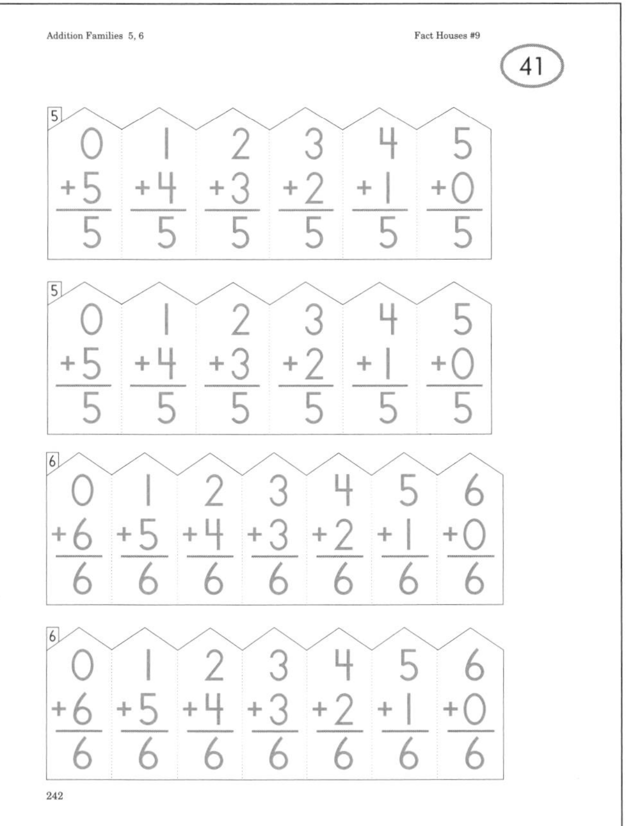

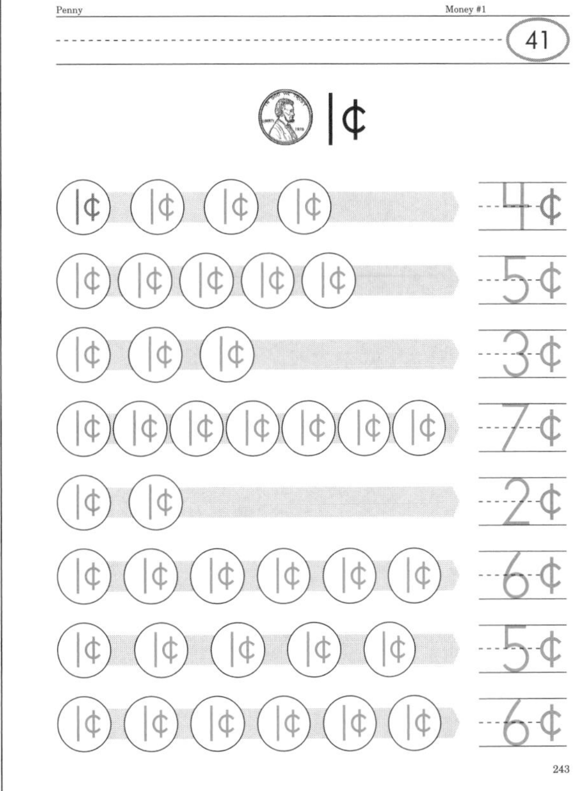

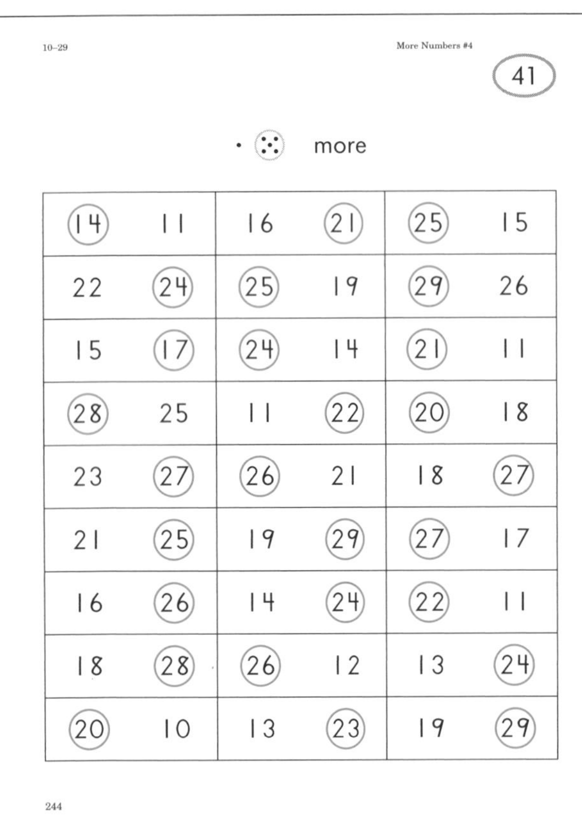

10–29 More Numbers #4 41

• ⁙ more

14	11	16	**21**	**25**	15
22	**24**	**25**	19	**29**	26
15	**17**	**24**	14	**21**	11
28	25	11	**22**	**20**	18
23	**27**	**26**	21	18	**27**
21	**25**	19	**29**	**27**	17
16	**26**	14	**24**	**22**	11
18	**28**	**26**	12	13	**24**
20	10	13	**23**	19	**29**

244

4–6 [+] Number Facts #9 41

A	1 +5 = 6	4 +1 = 5	2 +4 = 6	2 +2 = 4	3 +3 = 6	1 +4 = 5	2 +4 = 6	3 +2 = 5
B	2 +4 = 6	2 +3 = 5	3 +2 = 5	1 +4 = 5	4 +2 = 6	3 +1 = 4	4 +2 = 6	3 +3 = 6
C	3 +2 = 5	3 +3 = 6	4 +2 = 6	6 +0 = 6	5 +1 = 6	2 +2 = 4	4 +2 = 6	2 +3 = 5
D	1 +3 = 4	1 +5 = 6	2 +3 = 5	5 +1 = 6	3 +2 = 5	1 +3 = 4	4 +2 = 6	3 +3 = 6
E	1 +4 = 5	2 +3 = 5	3 +2 = 5	3 +3 = 6	4 +2 = 6	0 +6 = 6	2 +3 = 5	3 +1 = 4
F	3 +3 = 6	2 +2 = 4	3 +1 = 4	1 +4 = 5	4 +2 = 6	5 +1 = 6	4 +1 = 5	2 +4 = 6

245

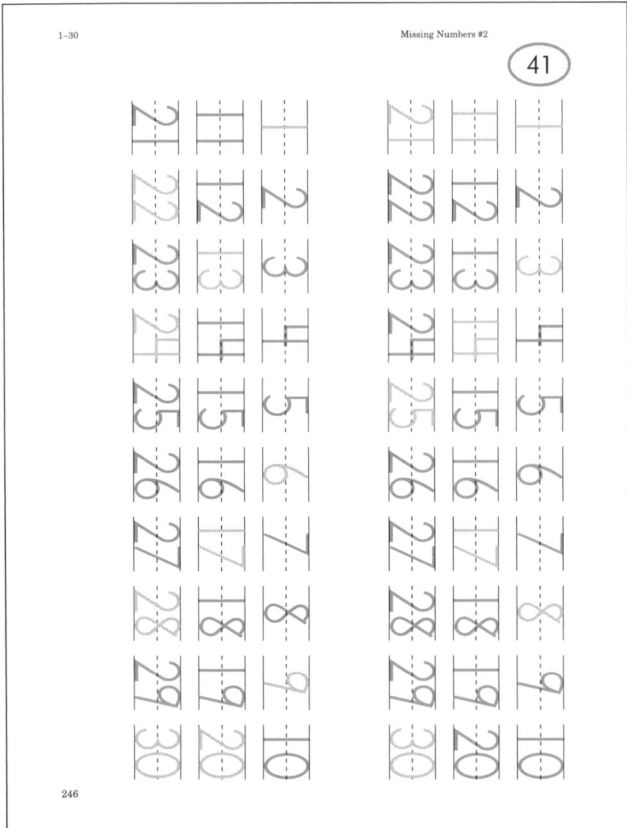

1–30 Missing Numbers #2 41

21	11	1	21	11	1
22	12	2	22	12	2
23	13	3	23	13	3
24	14	4	24	14	4
25	15	5	25	15	5
26	16	6	26	16	6
27	17	7	27	17	7
28	18	8	28	18	8
29	19	9	29	19	9
30	20	10	30	20	10

246

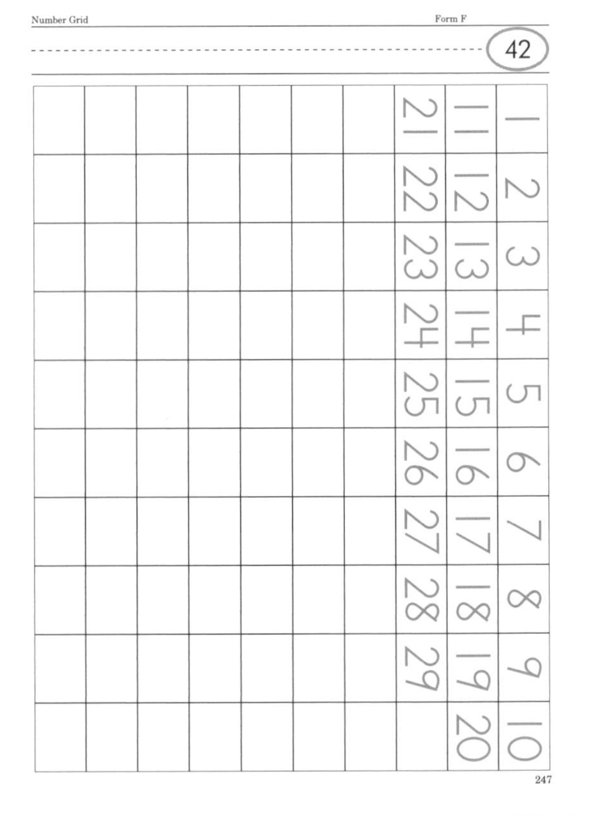

Number Grid Form F 42

							21	11	1
							22	12	2
							23	13	3
							24	14	4
							25	15	5
							26	16	6
							27	17	7
							28	18	8
							29	19	9
								20	10

247

10–29 Less Numbers #4

42

less

22	**11**	**18**	28	**19**	29
14	24	26	**12**	**13**	23
16	26	**13**	24	20	**10**
27	**17**	**18**	27	26	**21**
19	29	**21**	25	**23**	27
28	**25**	**11**	22	20	**18**
15	17	24	**14**	21	**11**
29	**26**	25	**19**	**22**	24
14	**11**	**16**	21	25	**15**

248

4–6 [+] Number Facts #9

42

A	1 + 5 = 6	4 + 1 = 5	2 + 4 = 6	2 + 2 = 4	3 + 3 = 6	1 + 4 = 5	2 + 4 = 6	3 + 2 = 5
B	2 + 4 = 6	2 + 3 = 5	3 + 2 = 5	1 + 4 = 5	4 + 2 = 6	3 + 1 = 4	4 + 2 = 6	3 + 3 = 6
C	3 + 2 = 5	3 + 3 = 6	4 + 2 = 6	6 + 0 = 6	5 + 1 = 6	2 + 2 = 4	4 + 2 = 6	2 + 3 = 5
D	1 + 3 = 4	1 + 5 = 6	2 + 3 = 5	5 + 1 = 6	3 + 2 = 5	1 + 3 = 4	4 + 2 = 6	3 + 3 = 6
E	1 + 4 = 5	2 + 3 = 5	3 + 2 = 5	3 + 3 = 6	4 + 2 = 6	0 + 6 = 6	2 + 3 = 5	3 + 1 = 4
F	3 + 3 = 6	2 + 2 = 4	3 + 1 = 4	1 + 4 = 5	4 + 2 = 6	5 + 1 = 6	4 + 1 = 5	2 + 4 = 6

249

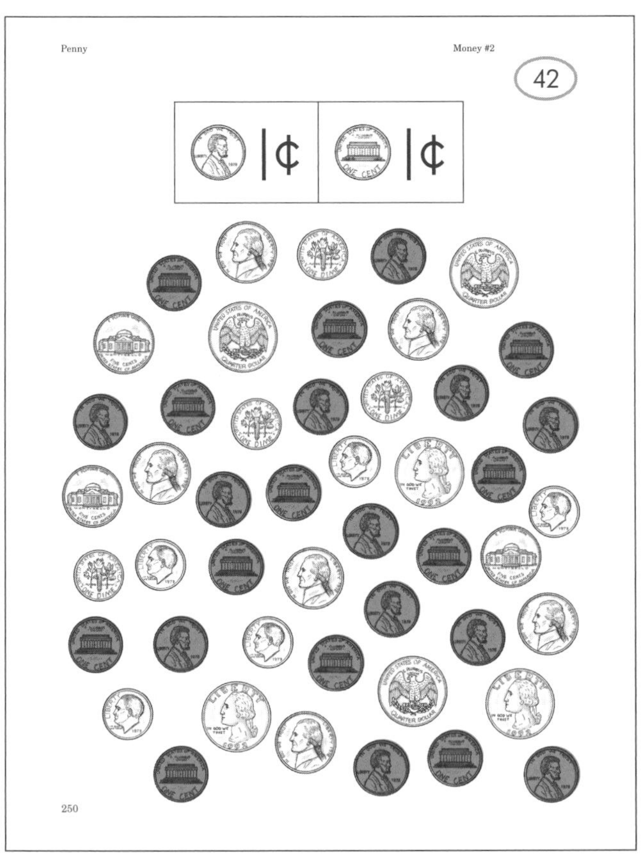

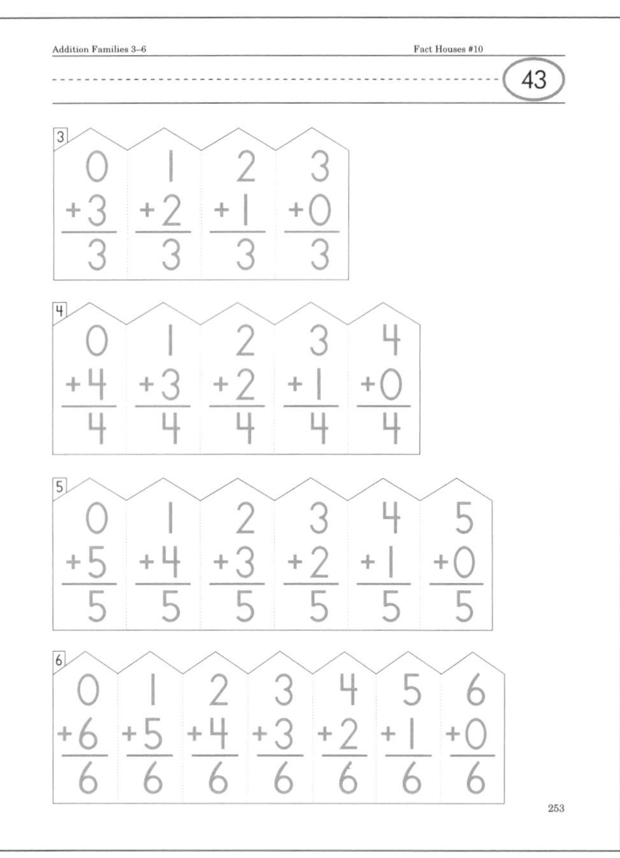

Addition Families 3–6 Fact Houses #10

43

3			
0 +3 3	1 +2 3	2 +1 3	3 +0 3

4				
0 +4 4	1 +3 4	2 +2 4	3 +1 4	4 +0 4

5					
0 +5 5	1 +4 5	2 +3 5	3 +2 5	4 +1 5	5 +0 5

6						
0 +6 6	1 +5 6	2 +4 6	3 +3 6	4 +2 6	5 +1 6	6 +0 6

253

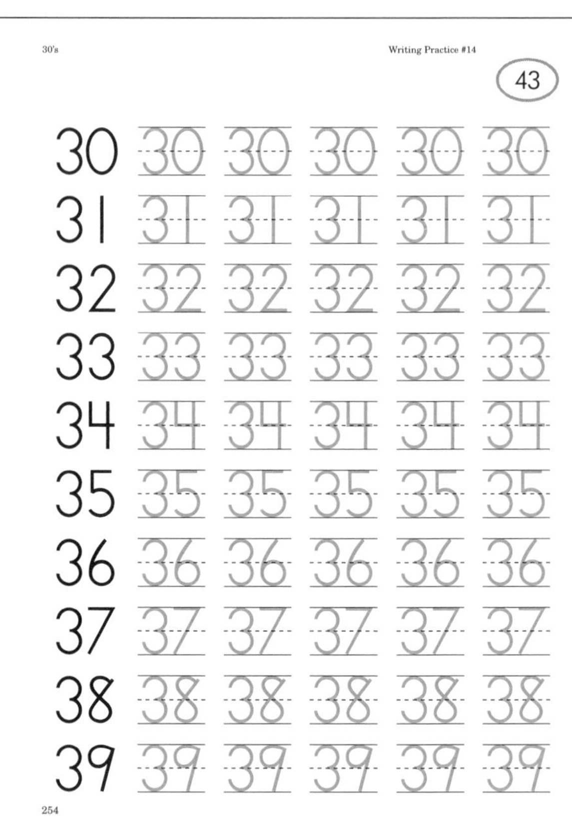

30's Writing Practice #14

43

30 30 30 30 30 30
31 31 31 31 31 31
32 32 32 32 32 32
33 33 33 33 33 33
34 34 34 34 34 34
35 35 35 35 35 35
36 36 36 36 36 36
37 37 37 37 37 37
38 38 38 38 38 38
39 39 39 39 39 39

254

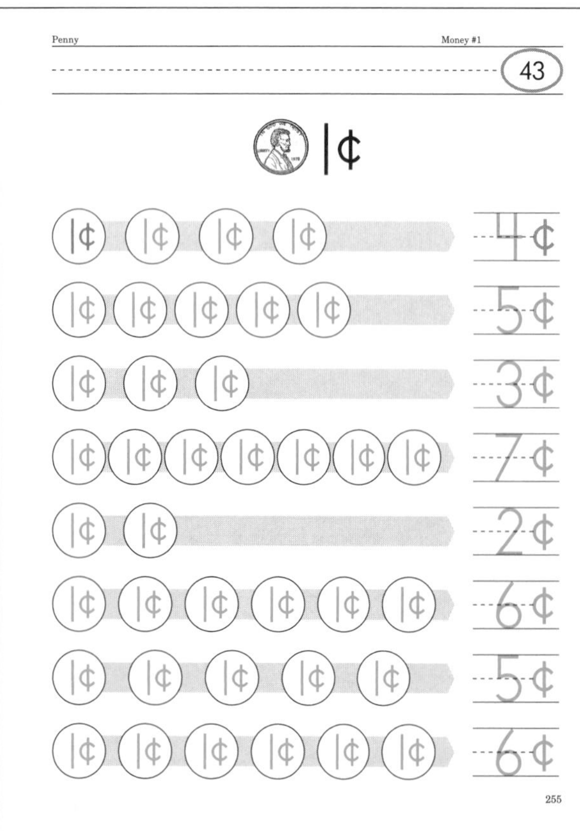

Penny Money #1

43

1¢

1¢ 1¢ 1¢ 1¢ — 4¢
1¢ 1¢ 1¢ 1¢ 1¢ — 5¢
1¢ 1¢ 1¢ — 3¢
1¢ 1¢ 1¢ 1¢ 1¢ 1¢ 1¢ — 7¢
1¢ 1¢ — 2¢
1¢ 1¢ 1¢ 1¢ 1¢ 1¢ — 6¢
1¢ 1¢ 1¢ 1¢ 1¢ — 5¢
1¢ 1¢ 1¢ 1¢ 1¢ 1¢ — 6¢

255

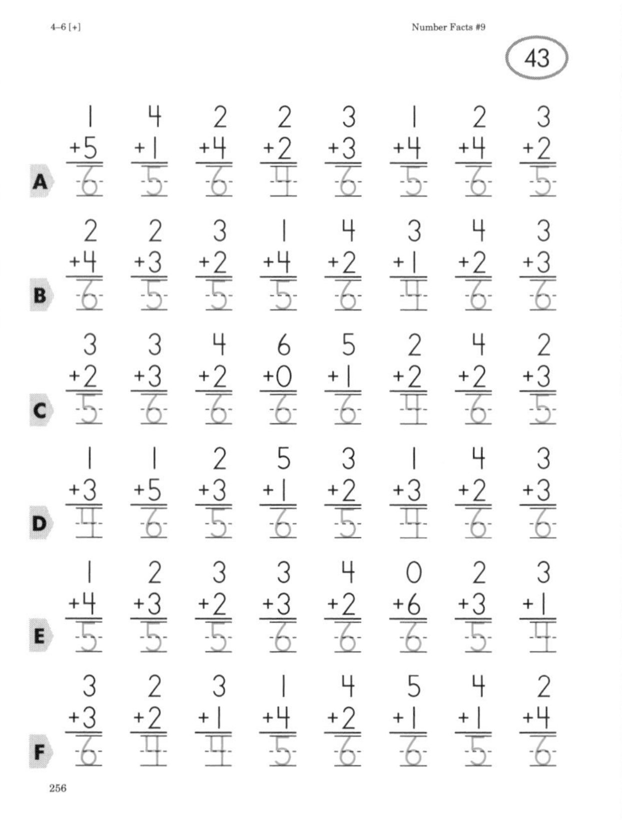

4–6 [+] Number Facts #9

43

A	1 +5 6	4 +1 5	2 +4 6	2 +2 4	3 +3 6	1 +4 5	2 +4 6	3 +2 5
B	2 +4 6	2 +3 5	3 +2 5	1 +4 5	4 +2 6	3 +1 4	4 +2 6	3 +3 6
C	3 +2 5	3 +3 6	4 +2 6	6 +0 6	5 +1 6	2 +2 4	4 +2 6	2 +3 5
D	1 +3 4	1 +5 6	2 +3 5	5 +1 6	3 +2 5	1 +3 4	4 +2 6	3 +3 6
E	1 +4 5	2 +3 5	3 +2 5	3 +3 6	4 +2 6	0 +6 6	2 +3 5	3 +1 4
F	3 +3 6	2 +2 4	3 +1 4	1 +4 5	4 +2 6	5 +1 6	4 +1 5	2 +4 6

256

Flash Card Drill — Form C

44

1	2	3	4	5
1	2	3	4	5
1	2	3	4	5
1	2	3	4	5
1	2	3	4	5

Individual answers (See page 365 for instructions.)

257

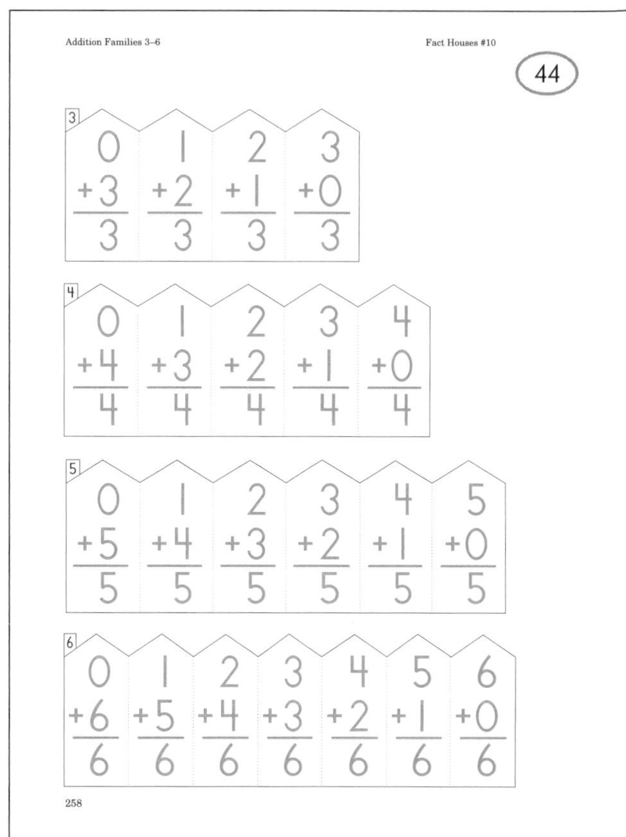
Addition Families 3–6 — Fact Houses #10

44

3: 0+3=3, 1+2=3, 2+1=3, 3+0=3

4: 0+4=4, 1+3=4, 2+2=4, 3+1=4, 4+0=4

5: 0+5=5, 1+4=5, 2+3=5, 3+2=5, 4+1=5, 5+0=5

6: 0+6=6, 1+5=6, 2+4=6, 3+3=6, 4+2=6, 5+1=6, 6+0=6

258

1–40 — Missing Numbers #3

44

31	21	11	1	31	21	11	1
32	22	12	2	32	22	12	2
33	23	13	3	33	23	13	3
34	24	14	4	34	24	14	4
35	25	15	5	35	25	15	5
36	26	16	6	36	26	16	6
37	27	17	7	37	27	17	7
38	28	18	8	38	28	18	8
39	29	19	9	39	29	19	9
40	30	20	10	40	30	20	10

259

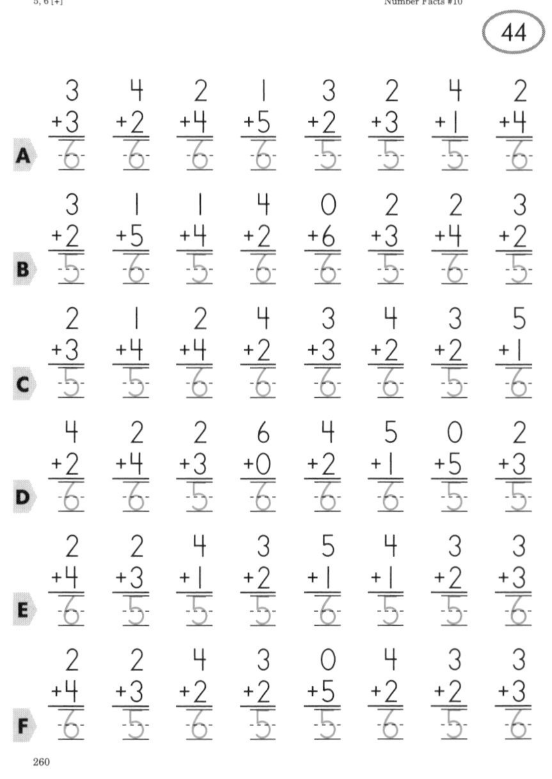
5, 6 [+] — Number Facts #10

44

A	3+3=6	4+2=6	2+4=6	1+5=6	3+2=5	2+3=5	4+1=5	2+4=6
B	3+2=5	1+5=6	1+4=5	4+2=6	0+6=6	2+3=5	2+4=6	3+2=5
C	2+3=5	1+4=5	2+4=6	4+2=6	3+3=6	4+2=6	3+2=5	5+1=6
D	4+2=6	2+4=6	2+3=5	6+0=6	4+2=6	5+1=6	0+5=5	2+3=5
E	2+4=6	2+3=5	4+1=5	3+2=5	5+1=6	4+1=5	3+2=5	3+3=6
F	2+4=6	2+3=5	4+2=6	3+2=5	0+5=5	4+2=6	3+2=5	3+3=6

260

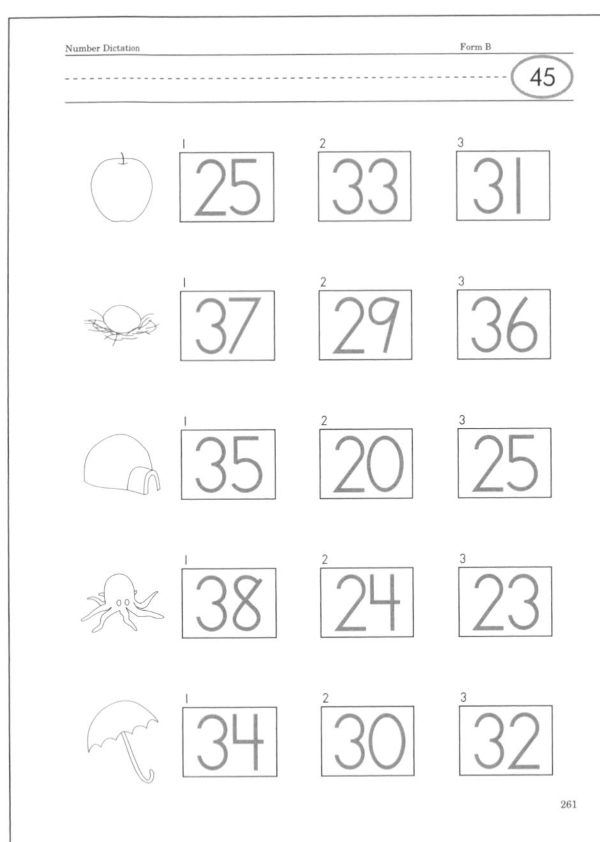
Number Dictation — Form B — 45

	1	2	3
apple	25	33	31
nest	37	29	36
igloo	35	20	25
octopus	38	24	23
umbrella	34	30	32

261

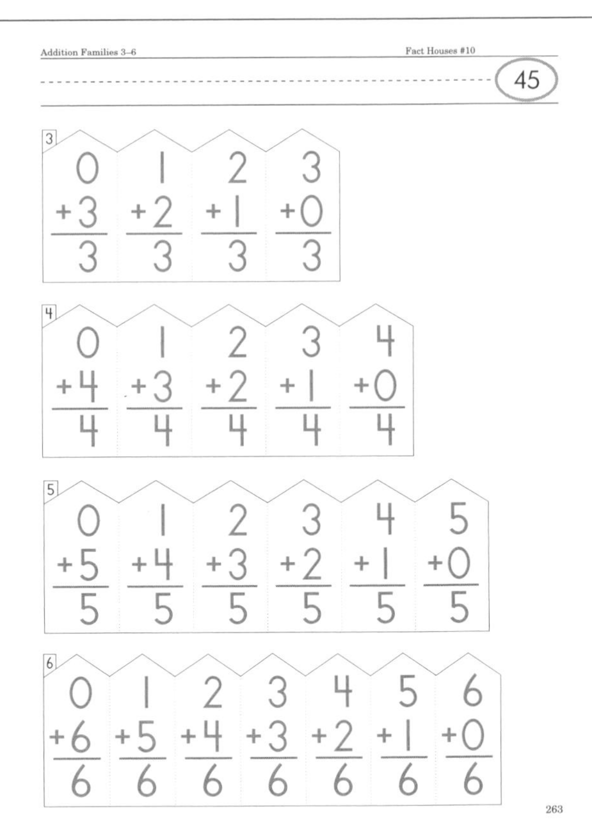
Addition Families 3–6 — Fact Houses #10 — 45

3: 0 + 3 = 3, 1 + 2 = 3, 2 + 1 = 3, 3 + 0 = 3

4: 0 + 4 = 4, 1 + 3 = 4, 2 + 2 = 4, 3 + 1 = 4, 4 + 0 = 4

5: 0 + 5 = 5, 1 + 4 = 5, 2 + 3 = 5, 3 + 2 = 5, 4 + 1 = 5, 5 + 0 = 5

6: 0 + 6 = 6, 1 + 5 = 6, 2 + 4 = 6, 3 + 3 = 6, 4 + 2 = 6, 5 + 1 = 6, 6 + 0 = 6

263

20–39 — More Numbers #5 — 45

• ⁙ more

29	**39**	23	**33**	**30**	20
36	31	33	**37**	**30**	28
31	21	27	**38**	32	**34**
35	29	27	**37**	**34**	24
21	**32**	31	**35**	28	**37**
23	**34**	**36**	22	28	**38**
32	21	24	**34**	26	**36**
37	27	29	**39**	**38**	35
25	**27**	**33**	30	**39**	36

264

5, 6 [+] — Number Facts #10 — 45

A	3 + 3 = 6	4 + 2 = 6	2 + 4 = 6	1 + 5 = 6	3 + 2 = 5	2 + 3 = 5	4 + 1 = 5	2 + 4 = 6
B	3 + 2 = 5	1 + 5 = 6	1 + 4 = 5	4 + 2 = 6	0 + 6 = 6	2 + 3 = 5	2 + 4 = 6	3 + 2 = 5
C	2 + 3 = 5	1 + 4 = 5	2 + 4 = 6	4 + 2 = 6	3 + 3 = 6	4 + 2 = 6	3 + 2 = 5	5 + 1 = 6
D	4 + 2 = 6	2 + 4 = 6	2 + 3 = 5	6 + 0 = 6	4 + 2 = 6	5 + 1 = 6	0 + 5 = 5	2 + 3 = 5
E	2 + 4 = 6	2 + 3 = 5	4 + 1 = 5	3 + 2 = 5	5 + 1 = 6	4 + 1 = 5	3 + 2 = 5	3 + 3 = 6
F	2 + 4 = 6	2 + 3 = 5	4 + 2 = 6	3 + 2 = 5	0 + 5 = 5	4 + 2 = 6	3 + 2 = 5	3 + 3 = 6

265

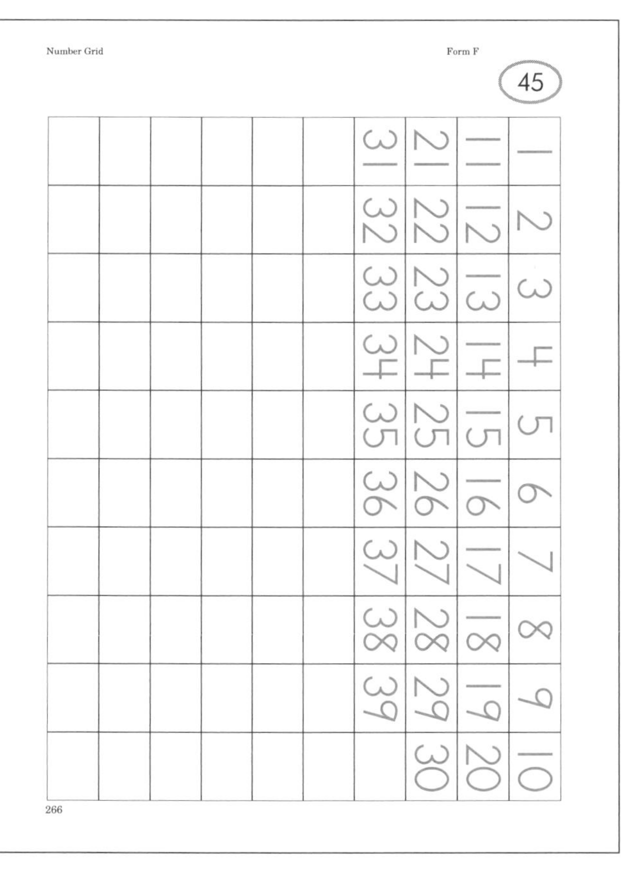

Number Grid Form F

45

1	2	3	4	5	6	7	8	9	10
11	12	13	14	15	16	17	18	19	20
21	22	23	24	25	26	27	28	29	30
31	32	33	34	35	36	37	38	39	

266

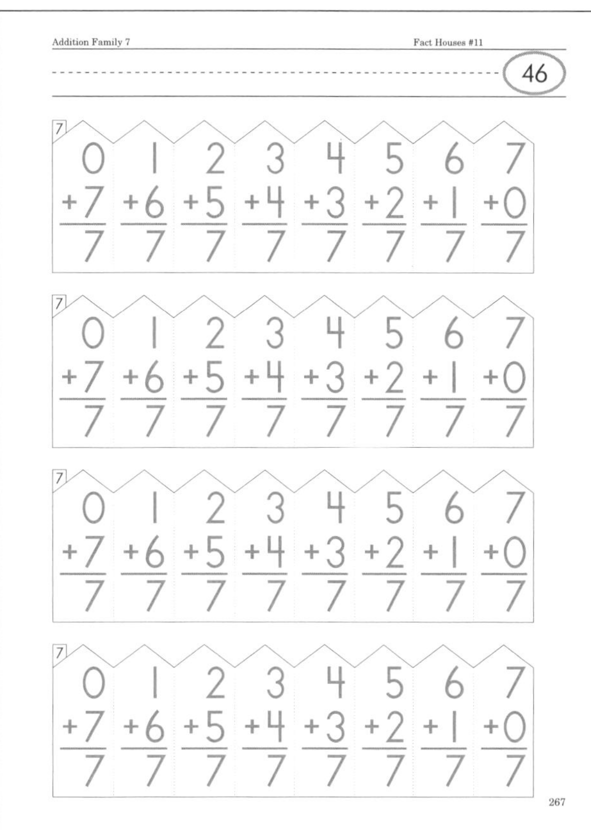

Addition Family 7 Fact Houses #11

46

0 +7 = 7	1 +6 = 7	2 +5 = 7	3 +4 = 7	4 +3 = 7	5 +2 = 7	6 +1 = 7	7 +0 = 7
0 +7 = 7	1 +6 = 7	2 +5 = 7	3 +4 = 7	4 +3 = 7	5 +2 = 7	6 +1 = 7	7 +0 = 7
0 +7 = 7	1 +6 = 7	2 +5 = 7	3 +4 = 7	4 +3 = 7	5 +2 = 7	6 +1 = 7	7 +0 = 7
0 +7 = 7	1 +6 = 7	2 +5 = 7	3 +4 = 7	4 +3 = 7	5 +2 = 7	6 +1 = 7	7 +0 = 7

267

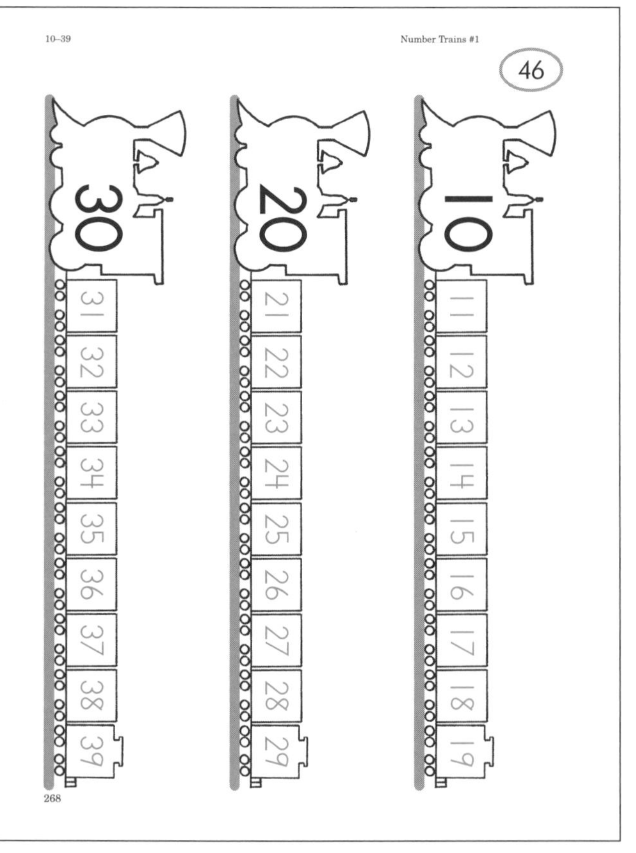

10–39 Number Trains #1

46

30	20	10
31	21	11
32	22	12
33	23	13
34	24	14
35	25	15
36	26	16
37	27	17
38	28	18
39	29	19

268

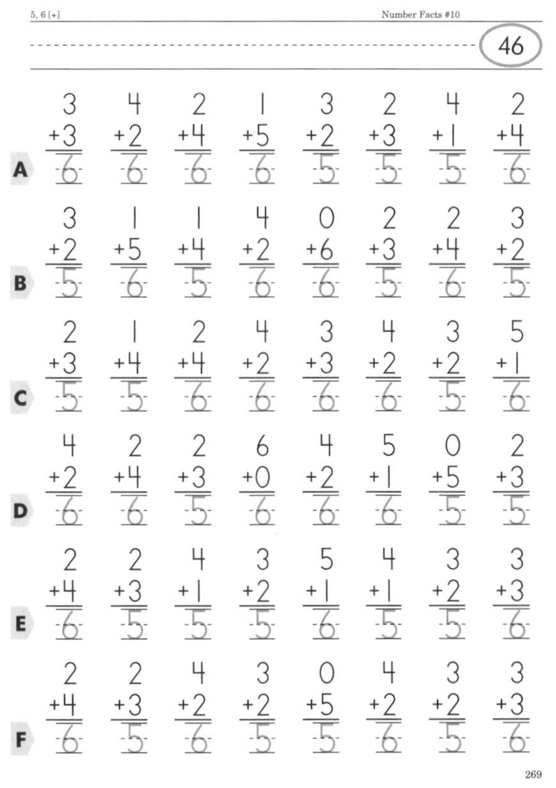

5, 6 [+] Number Facts #10

46

A	3 +3 = 6	4 +2 = 6	2 +4 = 6	1 +5 = 6	3 +2 = 5	2 +3 = 5	4 +1 = 5	2 +4 = 6
B	3 +2 = 5	1 +5 = 6	1 +4 = 5	4 +2 = 6	0 +6 = 6	2 +3 = 5	2 +4 = 6	3 +2 = 5
C	2 +3 = 5	1 +4 = 5	2 +4 = 6	4 +2 = 6	3 +3 = 6	4 +2 = 6	3 +2 = 5	5 +1 = 6
D	4 +2 = 6	2 +4 = 6	2 +3 = 5	6 +0 = 6	4 +2 = 6	5 +1 = 6	0 +5 = 5	2 +3 = 5
E	2 +4 = 6	2 +3 = 5	4 +1 = 5	3 +2 = 5	5 +1 = 6	4 +1 = 5	3 +2 = 5	3 +3 = 6
F	2 +4 = 6	2 +3 = 5	4 +2 = 6	3 +2 = 5	0 +5 = 5	4 +2 = 6	3 +2 = 5	3 +3 = 6

269

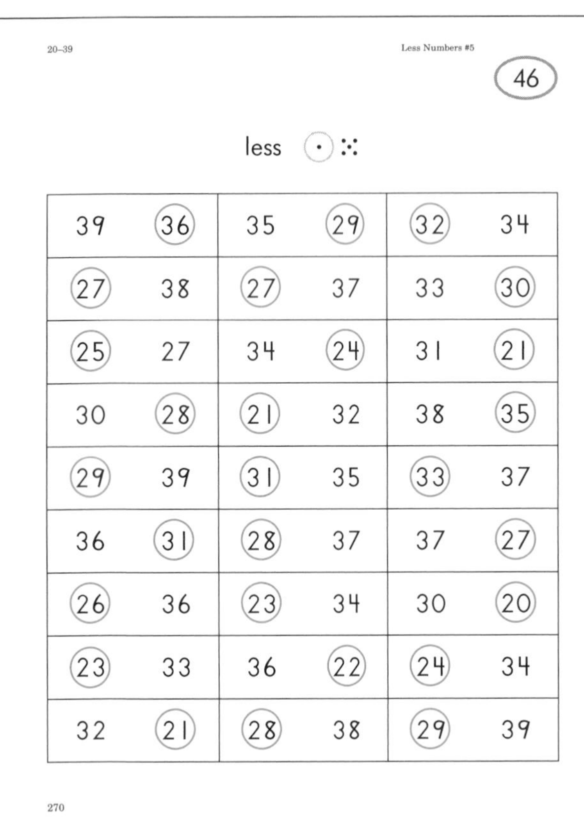
20–39
Less Numbers #5
46
less
39 36 35 29 32 34
27 38 27 37 33 30
25 27 34 24 31 21
30 28 21 32 38 35
29 39 31 35 33 37
36 31 28 37 37 27
26 36 23 34 30 20
23 33 36 22 24 34
32 21 28 38 29 39
270

Addition Family 7
Fact Houses #11
47
0 +7 7
1 +6 7
2 +5 7
3 +4 7
4 +3 7
5 +2 7
6 +1 7
7 +0 7
271

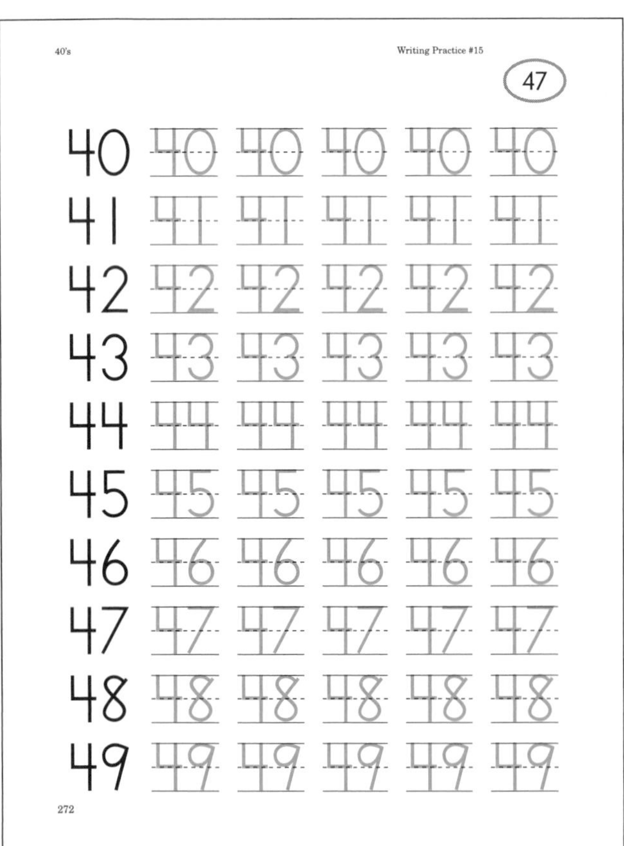
40's
Writing Practice #15
47
40
41
42
43
44
45
46
47
48
49
272

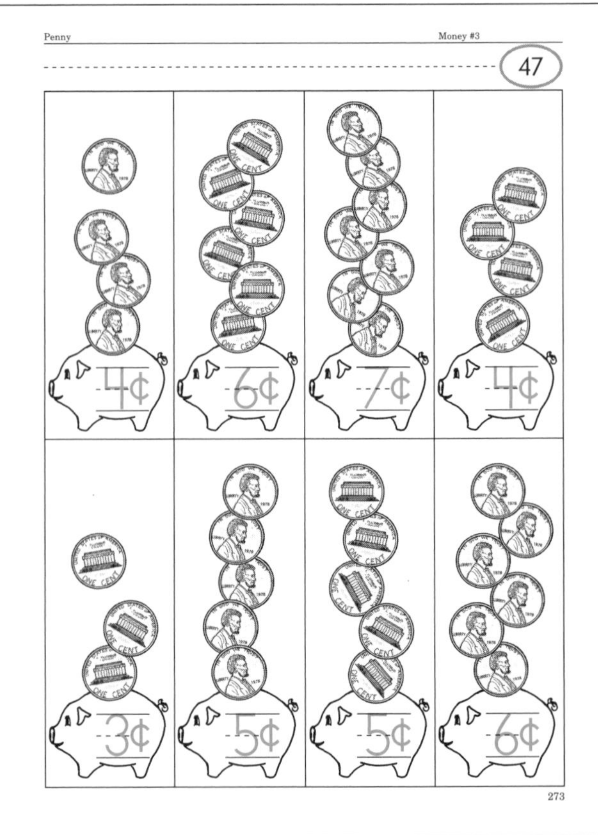
Penny
Money #3
47
4¢
6¢
7¢
4¢
3¢
5¢
5¢
6¢
273

1–36 Dot-to-Dot #21

47

274

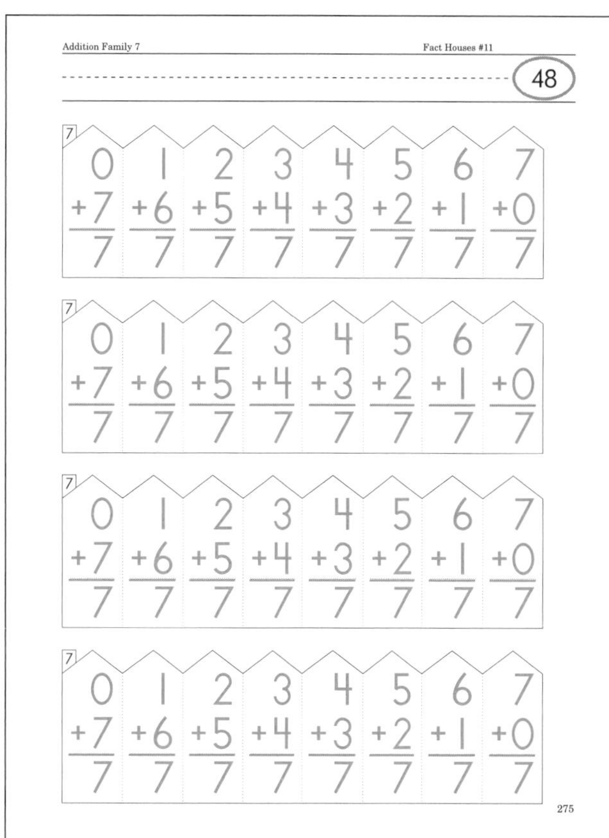
Addition Family 7 Fact Houses #11

48

7							
0	1	2	3	4	5	6	7
+7	+6	+5	+4	+3	+2	+1	+0
7	7	7	7	7	7	7	7

7							
0	1	2	3	4	5	6	7
+7	+6	+5	+4	+3	+2	+1	+0
7	7	7	7	7	7	7	7

7							
0	1	2	3	4	5	6	7
+7	+6	+5	+4	+3	+2	+1	+0
7	7	7	7	7	7	7	7

7							
0	1	2	3	4	5	6	7
+7	+6	+5	+4	+3	+2	+1	+0
7	7	7	7	7	7	7	7

275

3–5, 7 [+] Number Facts #11

48

A	2 +3 = 5	1 +6 = 7	4 +1 = 5	3 +4 = 7	2 +2 = 4	5 +2 = 7	1 +2 = 3	3 +4 = 7
B	4 +3 = 7	2 +5 = 7	3 +2 = 5	3 +4 = 7	1 +4 = 5	2 +5 = 7	1 +3 = 4	3 +4 = 7
C	5 +2 = 7	1 +6 = 7	3 +2 = 5	3 +4 = 7	1 +4 = 5	5 +2 = 7	3 +4 = 7	2 +5 = 7
D	3 +1 = 4	6 +1 = 7	2 +1 = 3	5 +2 = 7	4 +1 = 5	2 +3 = 5	1 +6 = 7	2 +2 = 4
E	2 +1 = 3	1 +2 = 3	3 +2 = 5	6 +1 = 7	3 +4 = 7	6 +1 = 7	4 +3 = 7	5 +2 = 7
F	3 +1 = 4	2 +2 = 4	1 +3 = 4	2 +5 = 7	4 +1 = 5	2 +3 = 5	4 +3 = 7	3 +2 = 5

276

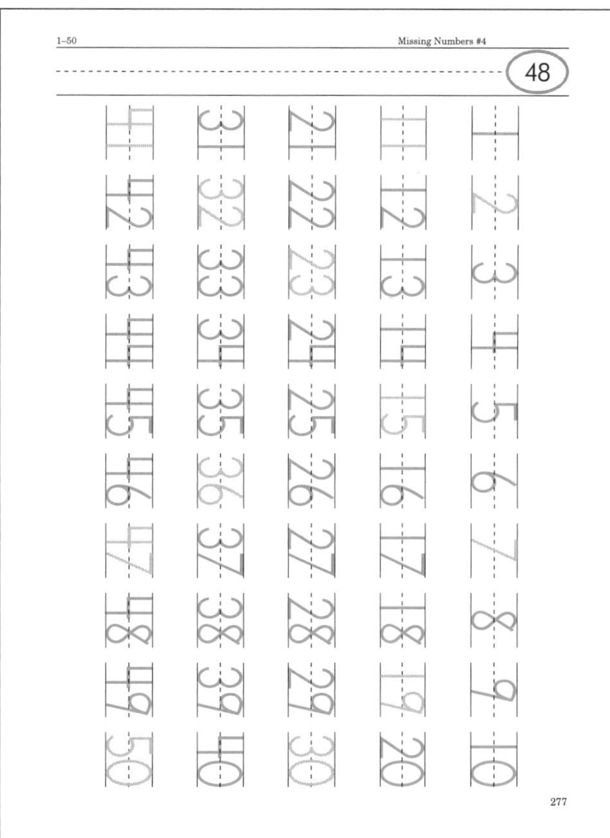
1–50 Missing Numbers #4

48

1	11	21	31	41
2	12	22	32	42
3	13	23	33	43
4	14	24	34	44
5	15	25	35	45
6	16	26	36	46
7	17	27	37	47
8	18	28	38	48
9	19	29	39	49
10	20	30	40	50

277

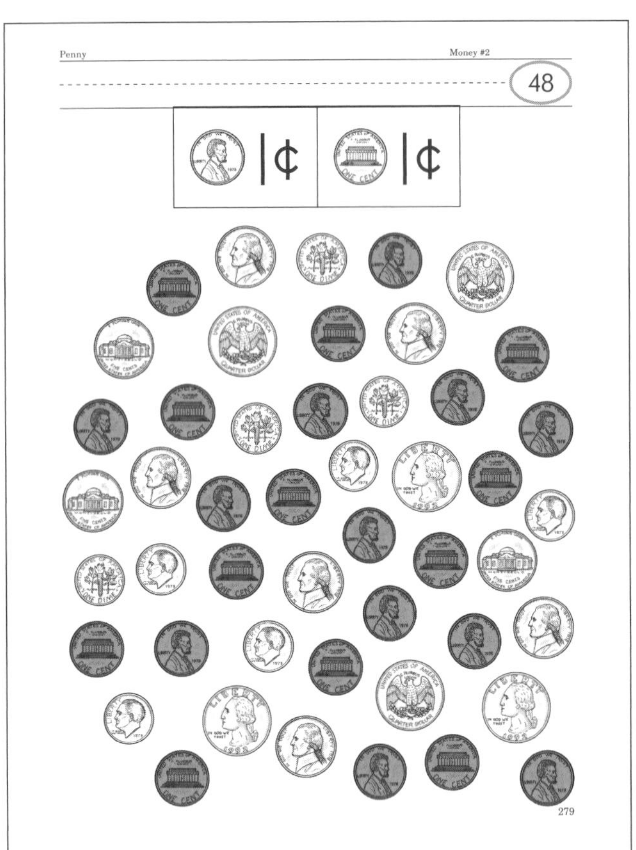

30–49 More Numbers #6

49

• ⁙ more

38	48	42	31	34	44
46	32	33	43	36	46
33	44	40	30	47	37
38	47	46	41	39	49
41	45	43	47	48	45
31	42	40	38	35	37
44	34	41	31	43	40
37	47	37	48	49	46
45	39	42	44	39	49

281

50's Writing Practice #16

49

50 50 50 50 50 50
51 51 51 51 51 51
52 52 52 52 52 52
53 53 53 53 53 53
54 54 54 54 54 54
55 55 55 55 55 55
56 56 56 56 56 56
57 57 57 57 57 57
58 58 58 58 58 58
59 59 59 59 59 59

282

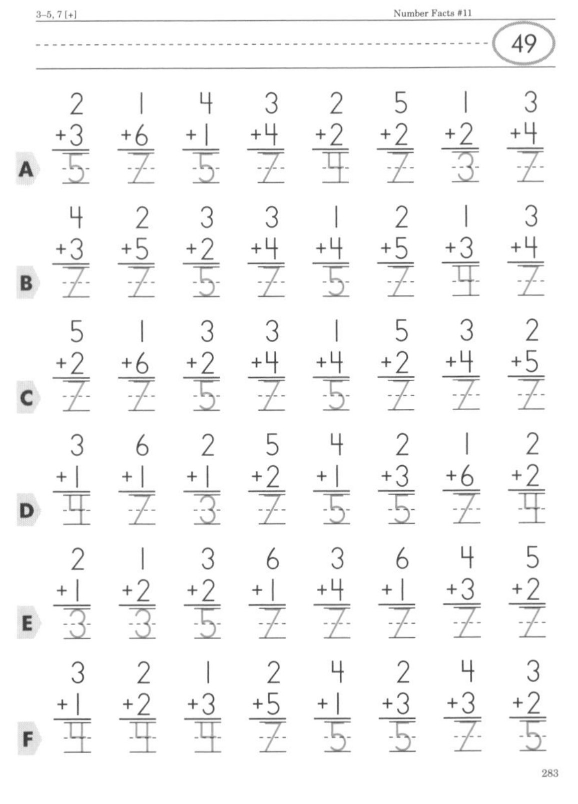

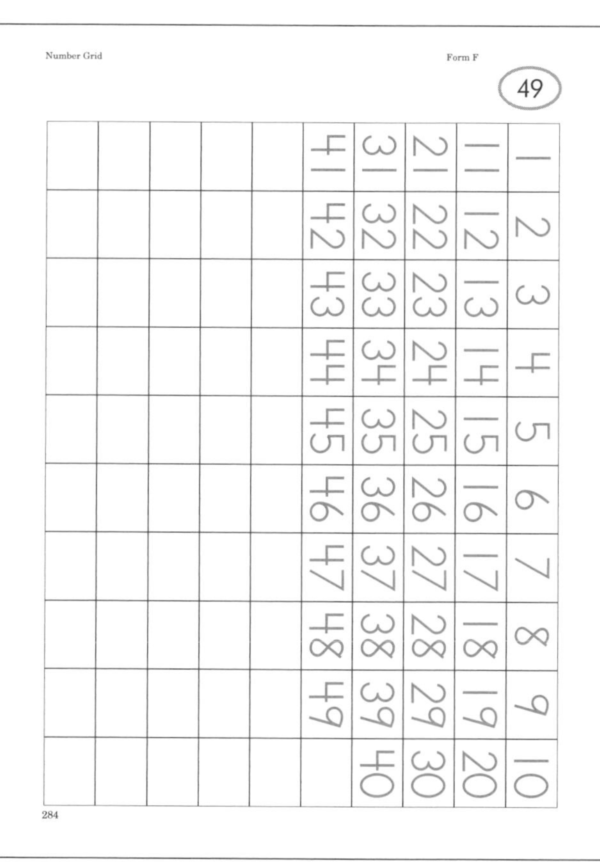
Number Grid

Form F

49

1	2	3	4	5	6	7	8	9	10
11	12	13	14	15	16	17	18	19	20
21	22	23	24	25	26	27	28	29	30
31	32	33	34	35	36	37	38	39	40
41	42	43	44	45	46	47	48	49	

284

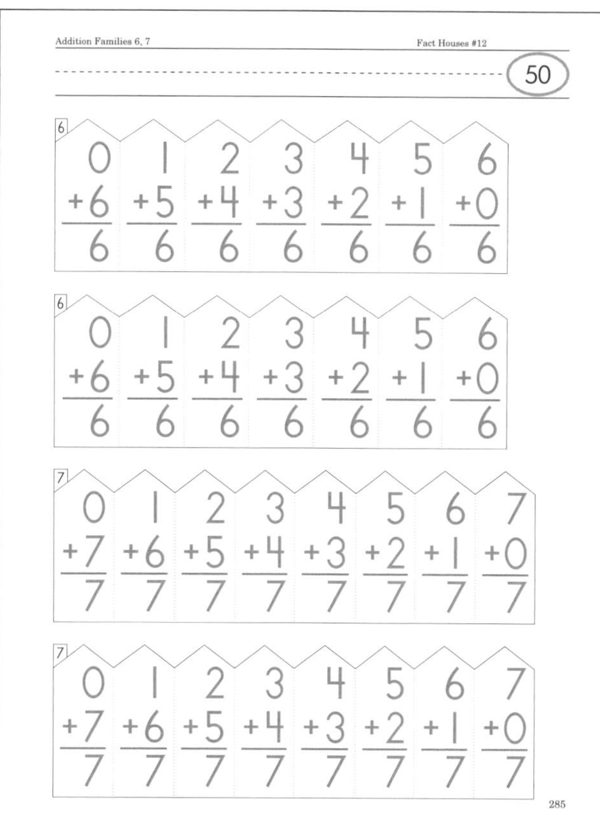
Addition Families 6, 7

Fact Houses #12

50

6: 0+6=6, 1+5=6, 2+4=6, 3+3=6, 4+2=6, 5+1=6, 6+0=6

6: 0+6=6, 1+5=6, 2+4=6, 3+3=6, 4+2=6, 5+1=6, 6+0=6

7: 0+7=7, 1+6=7, 2+5=7, 3+4=7, 4+3=7, 5+2=7, 6+1=7, 7+0=7

7: 0+7=7, 1+6=7, 2+5=7, 3+4=7, 4+3=7, 5+2=7, 6+1=7, 7+0=7

285

5–7 [+]

Number Facts #12

50

A	3+2=5	2+5=7	4+2=6	3+4=7	2+5=7	5+1=6	2+3=5	1+5=6
B	3+4=7	5+2=7	3+3=6	2+4=6	1+6=7	1+4=5	2+5=7	3+2=5
C	5+1=6	4+3=7	2+5=7	4+2=6	3+4=7	3+2=5	2+4=6	3+3=6
D	6+1=7	3+4=7	1+5=6	4+1=5	4+3=7	3+2=5	2+3=5	4+3=7
E	5+2=7	3+2=5	2+4=6	2+3=5	5+2=7	1+5=6	1+6=7	3+3=6
F	4+2=6	2+3=5	6+1=7	4+1=5	2+4=6	5+2=7	2+5=7	3+2=5

286

30–49

Less Numbers #6

50

less

(38)	48	46	(32)	(33)	44
(38)	47	(41)	45	(21)	42
44	(34)	(37)	47	45	(39)
49	(46)	43	(40)	(35)	37
48	(45)	(39)	49	47	(37)
(36)	46	(34)	44	42	(31)
(39)	49	(33)	43	40	(30)
46	(41)	(43)	47	40	(38)
41	(31)	(37)	48	(42)	44

287

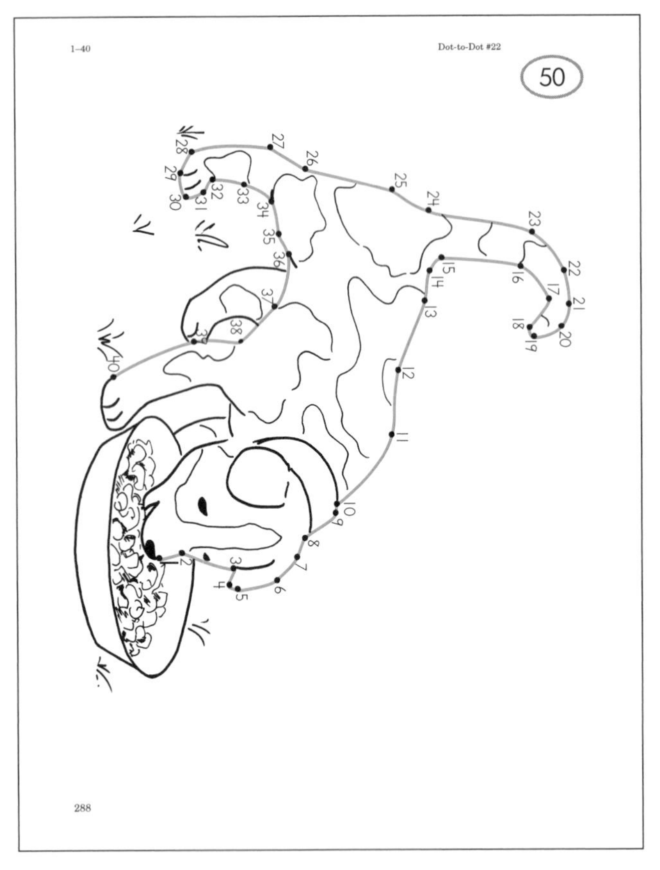
1–40 Dot-to-Dot #22

50

Flash Card Drill Form C

51

	1	2	3	4	5

Individual answers (See page 365 for instructions.)

Addition Families 6, 7 Fact Houses #12

51

6						
0	1	2	3	4	5	6
+6	+5	+4	+3	+2	+1	+0
6	6	6	6	6	6	6

6						
0	1	2	3	4	5	6
+6	+5	+4	+3	+2	+1	+0
6	6	6	6	6	6	6

7							
0	1	2	3	4	5	6	7
+7	+6	+5	+4	+3	+2	+1	+0
7	7	7	7	7	7	7	7

7							
0	1	2	3	4	5	6	7
+7	+6	+5	+4	+3	+2	+1	+0
7	7	7	7	7	7	7	7

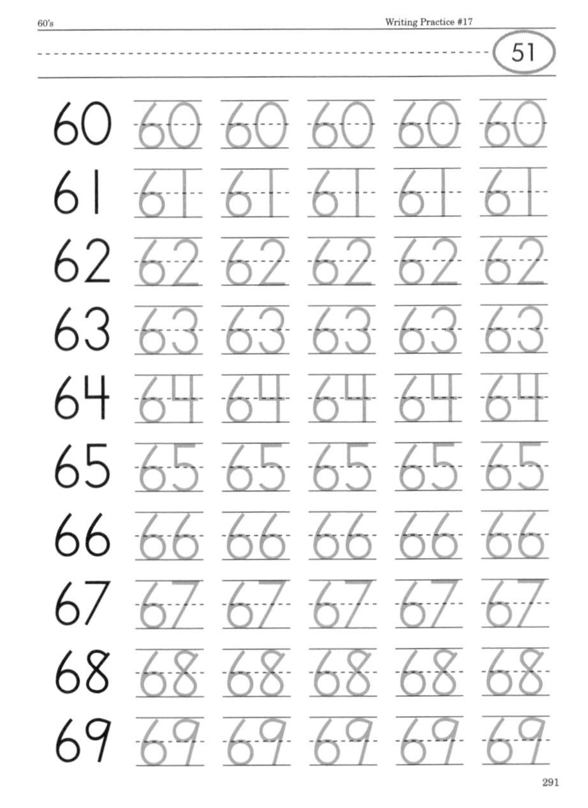
60's Writing Practice #17

51

60	60	60	60	60	60
61	61	61	61	61	61
62	62	62	62	62	62
63	63	63	63	63	63
64	64	64	64	64	64
65	65	65	65	65	65
66	66	66	66	66	66
67	67	67	67	67	67
68	68	68	68	68	68
69	69	69	69	69	69

5–7 [+] Number Facts #12

51

A	3 +2 5	2 +5 7	4 +2 6	3 +4 7	2 +5 7	5 +1 6	2 +3 5	1 +5 6
B	3 +4 7	5 +2 7	3 +3 6	2 +4 6	1 +6 7	1 +4 5	2 +5 7	3 +2 5
C	5 +1 6	4 +3 7	2 +5 7	4 +2 6	3 +4 7	3 +2 5	2 +4 6	3 +3 6
D	6 +1 7	3 +4 7	1 +5 6	4 +1 5	4 +3 7	3 +2 5	2 +3 5	4 +3 7
E	5 +2 7	3 +2 5	2 +4 6	2 +3 5	5 +2 7	1 +5 6	1 +6 7	3 +3 6
F	4 +2 6	2 +3 5	6 +1 7	4 +1 5	2 +4 6	5 +2 7	2 +5 7	3 +2 5

292

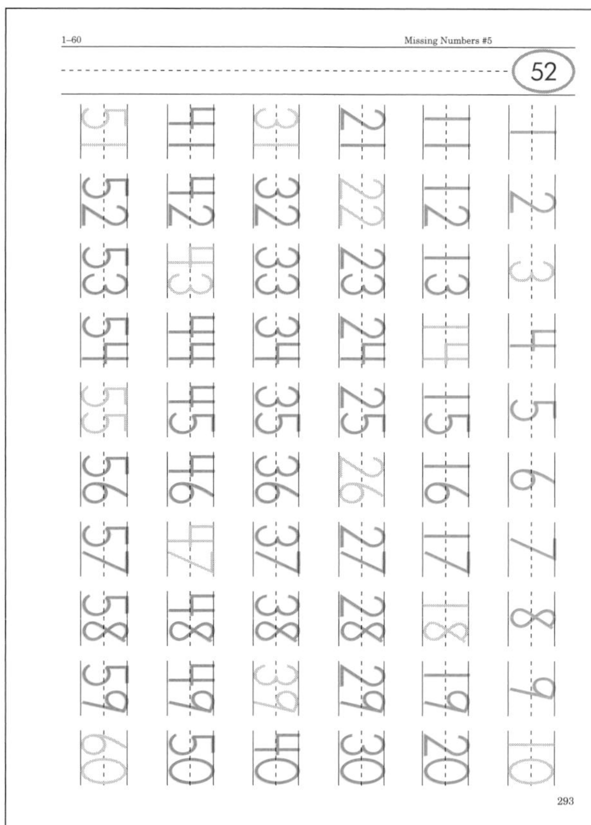

70's Writing Practice #18

52

70 70 70 70 70 70
71 71 71 71 71 71
72 72 72 72 72 72
73 73 73 73 73 73
74 74 74 74 74 74
75 75 75 75 75 75
76 76 76 76 76 76
77 77 77 77 77 77
78 78 78 78 78 78
79 79 79 79 79 79

294

5–7 [+] Number Facts #12

52

A	3 +2 5	2 +5 7	4 +2 6	3 +4 7	2 +5 7	5 +1 6	2 +3 5	1 +5 6
B	3 +4 7	5 +2 7	3 +3 6	2 +4 6	1 +6 7	1 +4 5	2 +5 7	3 +2 5
C	5 +1 6	4 +3 7	2 +5 7	4 +2 6	3 +4 7	3 +2 5	2 +4 6	3 +3 6
D	6 +1 7	3 +4 7	1 +5 6	4 +1 5	4 +3 7	3 +2 5	2 +3 5	4 +3 7
E	5 +2 7	3 +2 5	2 +4 6	2 +3 5	5 +2 7	1 +5 6	1 +6 7	3 +3 6
F	4 +2 6	2 +3 5	6 +1 7	4 +1 5	2 +4 6	5 +2 7	2 +5 7	3 +2 5

295

40–59 More Numbers #7

52

• ⁙ more

52	41	48	**58**	49	**59**
44	**54**	**56**	42	43	**53**
46	**56**	43	**54**	**50**	40
57	47	48	**57**	**56**	51
49	**59**	51	**55**	53	**57**
58	55	41	**52**	**50**	48
45	**47**	**54**	44	**51**	41
53	50	47	**57**	47	**58**
59	56	**55**	49	52	**54**

296

Addition Families 6, 7 Fact Houses #12

53

6						
0	1	2	3	4	5	6
+6	+5	+4	+3	+2	+1	+0
6	6	6	6	6	6	6

6						
0	1	2	3	4	5	6
+6	+5	+4	+3	+2	+1	+0
6	6	6	6	6	6	6

7							
0	1	2	3	4	5	6	7
+7	+6	+5	+4	+3	+2	+1	+0
7	7	7	7	7	7	7	7

7							
0	1	2	3	4	5	6	7
+7	+6	+5	+4	+3	+2	+1	+0
7	7	7	7	7	7	7	7

297

40–59 Less Numbers #7

53

less ⊙ ⁙

49	59	**44**	54	56	**42**
43	53	**46**	56	**43**	54
50	**40**	57	**47**	**48**	57
56	**51**	**49**	59	**51**	55
53	57	58	**55**	**41**	52
50	**48**	**45**	47	54	**44**
51	**41**	53	**50**	**47**	57
47	58	59	**56**	55	**49**
52	54	52	**41**	**48**	58

298

6, 7 [+] Number Facts #13

53

A	4 +3 = 7	6 +1 = 7	3 +4 = 7	4 +2 = 6	2 +5 = 7	5 +1 = 6	3 +4 = 7	2 +5 = 7
B	5 +2 = 7	3 +3 = 6	3 +4 = 7	2 +4 = 6	1 +6 = 7	2 +4 = 6	3 +3 = 6	4 +2 = 6
C	1 +6 = 7	4 +2 = 6	5 +2 = 7	4 +3 = 7	2 +5 = 7	3 +3 = 6	3 +4 = 7	2 +4 = 6
D	2 +4 = 6	4 +3 = 7	1 +5 = 6	6 +1 = 7	4 +2 = 6	2 +4 = 6	3 +3 = 6	1 +6 = 7
E	2 +5 = 7	4 +2 = 6	3 +4 = 7	4 +3 = 7	3 +3 = 6	2 +5 = 7	4 +2 = 6	2 +4 = 6
F	2 +4 = 6	6 +1 = 7	5 +2 = 7	1 +5 = 6	2 +4 = 6	2 +5 = 7	3 +4 = 7	4 +3 = 7

299

80's | Writing Practice #19 | 54

80	80	80	80	80	80
81	81	81	81	81	81
82	82	82	82	82	82
83	83	83	83	83	83
84	84	84	84	84	84
85	85	85	85	85	85
86	86	86	86	86	86
87	87	87	87	87	87
88	88	88	88	88	88
89	89	89	89	89	89

301

6, 7 [+] | Number Facts #13 | 54

A	4 + 3 = 7	6 + 1 = 7	3 + 4 = 7	4 + 2 = 6	2 + 5 = 7	5 + 1 = 6	3 + 4 = 7	2 + 5 = 7
B	5 + 2 = 7	3 + 3 = 6	3 + 4 = 7	2 + 4 = 6	1 + 6 = 7	2 + 4 = 6	3 + 3 = 6	4 + 2 = 6
C	1 + 6 = 7	4 + 2 = 6	5 + 2 = 7	4 + 3 = 7	2 + 5 = 7	3 + 3 = 6	3 + 4 = 7	2 + 4 = 6
D	2 + 4 = 6	4 + 3 = 7	1 + 5 = 6	6 + 1 = 7	4 + 2 = 6	2 + 4 = 6	3 + 3 = 6	1 + 6 = 7
E	2 + 5 = 7	4 + 2 = 6	3 + 4 = 7	4 + 3 = 7	3 + 3 = 6	2 + 5 = 7	4 + 2 = 6	2 + 4 = 6
F	2 + 4 = 6	6 + 1 = 7	5 + 2 = 7	1 + 5 = 6	2 + 4 = 6	2 + 5 = 7	3 + 4 = 7	4 + 3 = 7

302

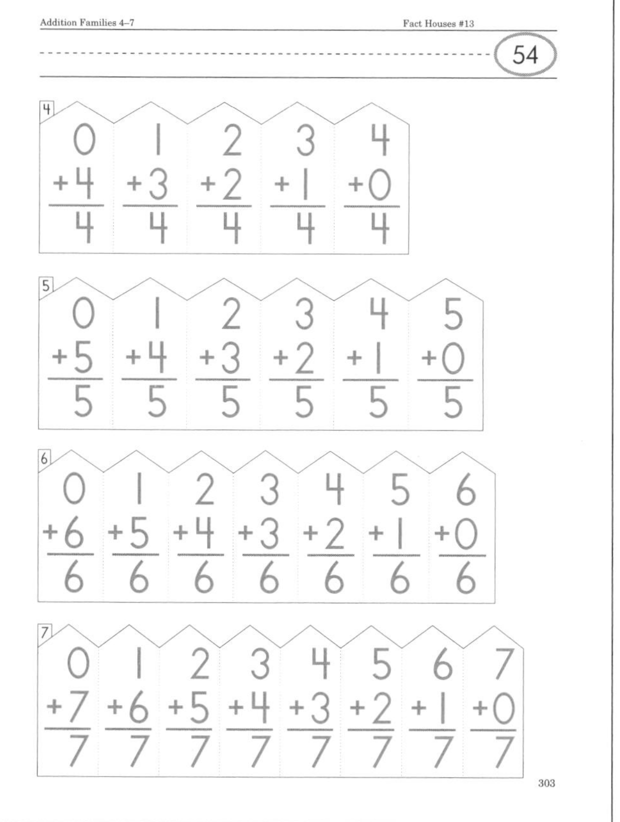

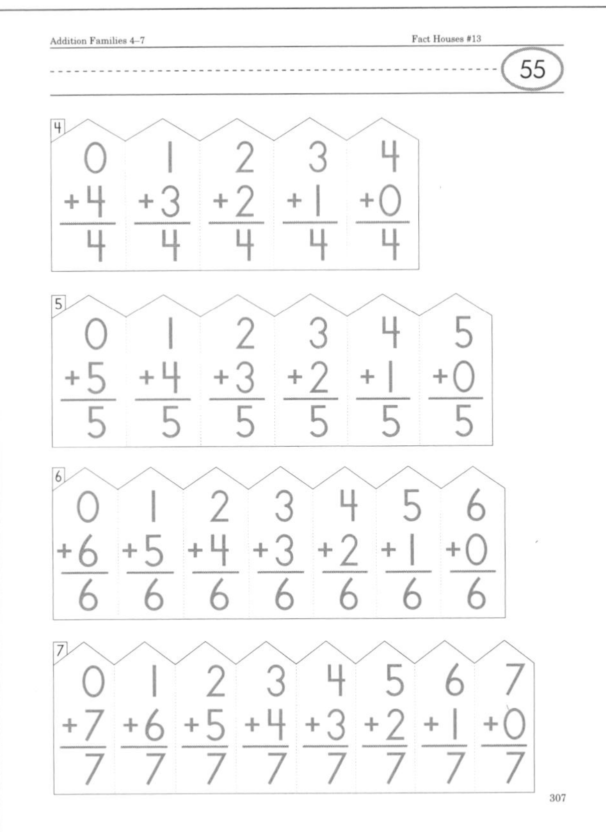

50–69 | More Numbers #8

55

• [5 dots] more

62	64	65	59	69	66
63	60	57	67	57	68
55	57	67	54	61	51
68	65	51	62	60	58
63	67	61	65	59	69
67	57	58	67	66	61
56	66	53	64	60	50
54	64	66	52	53	63
59	69	58	68	62	51

308

6, 7 [+] | Number Facts #13

55

A	4 + 3 = 7	6 + 1 = 7	3 + 4 = 7	4 + 2 = 6	2 + 5 = 7	5 + 1 = 6	3 + 4 = 7	2 + 5 = 7
B	5 + 2 = 7	3 + 3 = 6	3 + 4 = 7	2 + 4 = 6	1 + 6 = 7	2 + 4 = 6	3 + 3 = 6	4 + 2 = 6
C	1 + 6 = 7	4 + 2 = 6	5 + 2 = 7	4 + 3 = 7	2 + 5 = 7	3 + 3 = 6	3 + 4 = 7	2 + 4 = 6
D	2 + 4 = 6	4 + 3 = 7	1 + 5 = 6	6 + 1 = 7	4 + 2 = 6	2 + 4 = 6	3 + 3 = 6	1 + 6 = 7
E	2 + 5 = 7	4 + 2 = 6	3 + 4 = 7	4 + 3 = 7	3 + 3 = 6	2 + 5 = 7	4 + 2 = 6	2 + 4 = 6
F	2 + 4 = 6	6 + 1 = 7	5 + 2 = 7	1 + 5 = 6	2 + 4 = 6	2 + 5 = 7	3 + 4 = 7	4 + 3 = 7

309

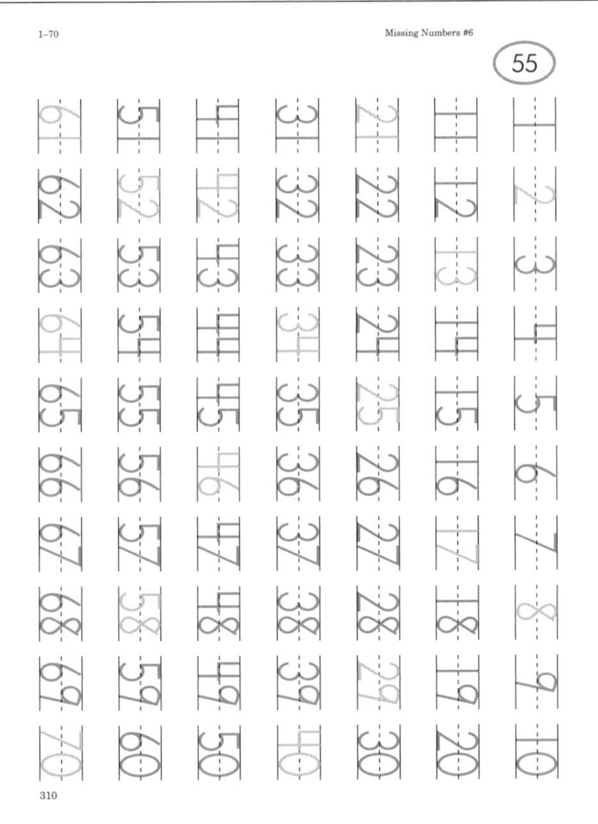

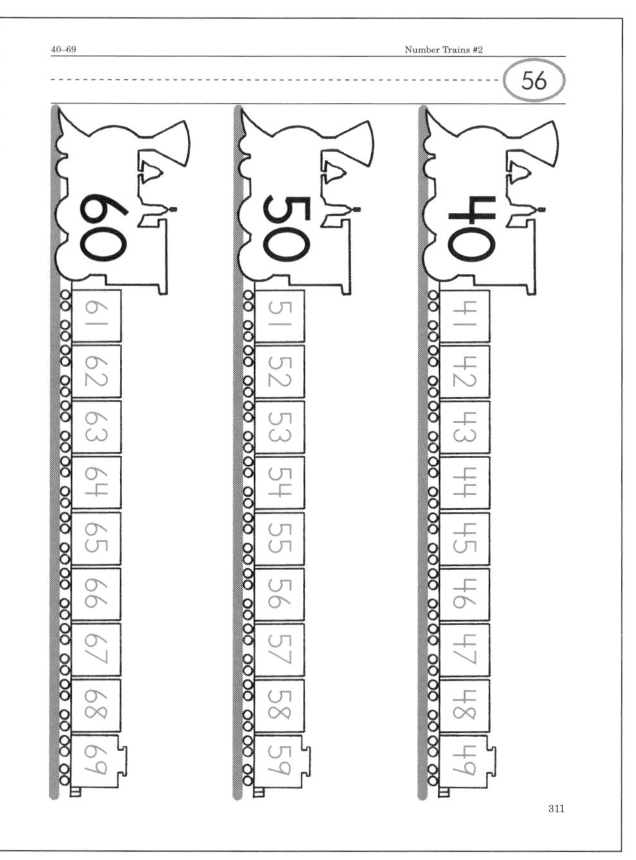
40–69 Number Trains #2

56

60	50	40
61	51	41
62	52	42
63	53	43
64	54	44
65	55	45
66	56	46
67	57	47
68	58	48
69	59	49

311

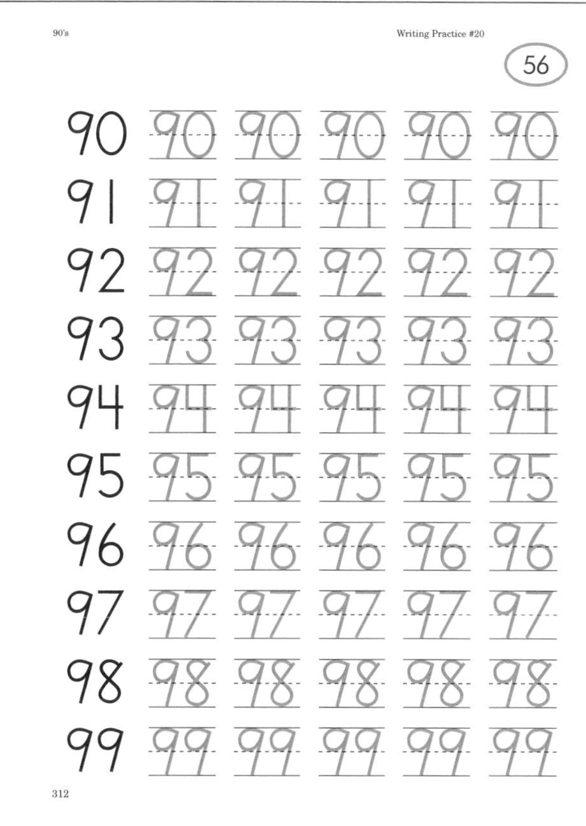
90's Writing Practice #20

56

90 90 90 90 90 90
91 91 91 91 91 91
92 92 92 92 92 92
93 93 93 93 93 93
94 94 94 94 94 94
95 95 95 95 95 95
96 96 96 96 96 96
97 97 97 97 97 97
98 98 98 98 98 98
99 99 99 99 99 99

312

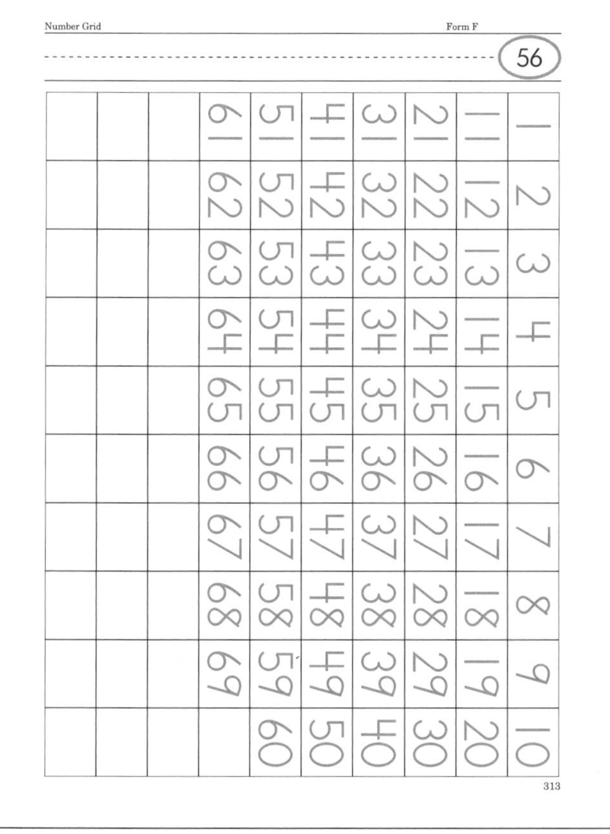
Number Grid Form F

56

1	2	3	4	5	6	7	8	9	10
11	12	13	14	15	16	17	18	19	20
21	22	23	24	25	26	27	28	29	30
31	32	33	34	35	36	37	38	39	40
41	42	43	44	45	46	47	48	49	50
51	52	53	54	55	56	57	58	59	60
61	62	63	64	65	66	67	68	69	

313

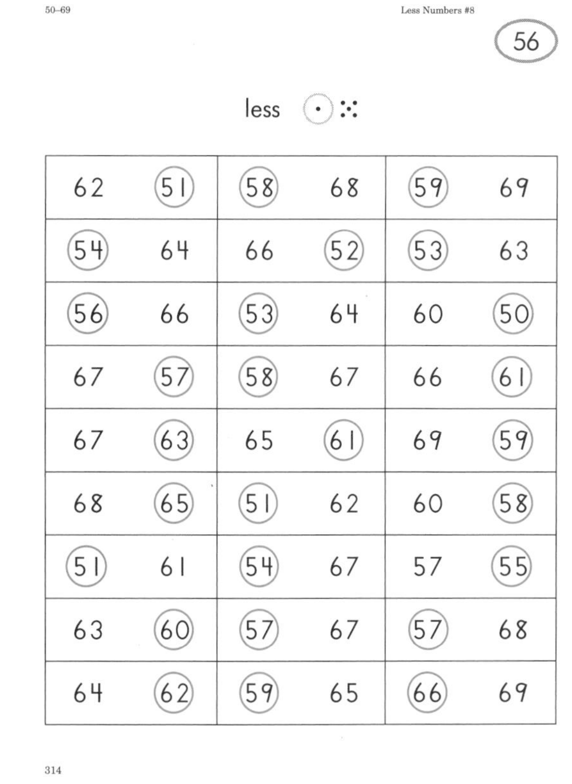
50–69 Less Numbers #8

56

less

62	(51)	(58)	68	(59)	69
(54)	64	66	(52)	(53)	63
(56)	66	(53)	64	60	(50)
67	(57)	(58)	67	66	(61)
67	(63)	65	(61)	69	(59)
68	(65)	(51)	62	60	(58)
(51)	61	(54)	67	57	(55)
63	(60)	(57)	67	(57)	68
64	(62)	(59)	65	(66)	69

314

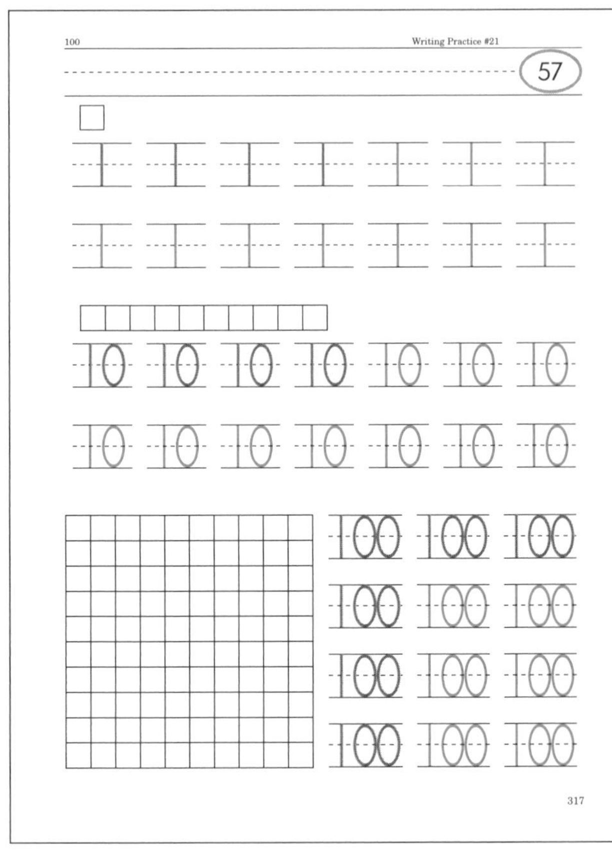

3–7 [+] Number Facts #14

57

A	4+3=7	2+2=4	3+2=5	1+4=5
B	2+3=5	4+3=7	2+2=4	5+2=7
C	2+1=3	2+4=6	4+2=6	3+3=6
D	2+3=5	1+6=7	5+1=6	3+4=7
E	5+2=7	2+3=5	2+5=7	1+3=4
F	3+3=6	4+3=7	3+1=4	2+5=7
G	3+4=7	2+4=6	4+2=6	4+3=7
H	3+2=5	3+3=6	2+5=7	4+2=6
I	2+5=7	3+4=7	3+1=4	2+2=4
J	4+2=6	2+2=4	4+3=7	5+2=7
K	1+5=6	5+2=7	2+5=7	3+3=6
L	4+3=7	2+1=3	2+4=6	6+1=7
M	3+1=4	4+1=5	2+3=5	3+4=7
N	2+5=7	3+3=6	3+4=7	3+2=5
O	3+2=5	2+5=7	4+2=6	4+3=7
P	1+2=3	3+4=7	1+6=7	5+1=6

319

41–69 Before and After #1

57

54	55	56	50	51	52
62	63	64	55	56	57
60	61	62	67	68	69
65	66	67	53	54	55
44	45	46	61	62	63
51	52	54	66	67	68
56	57	58	41	42	43
64	65	66	63	64	65
52	53	54	57	58	59

320

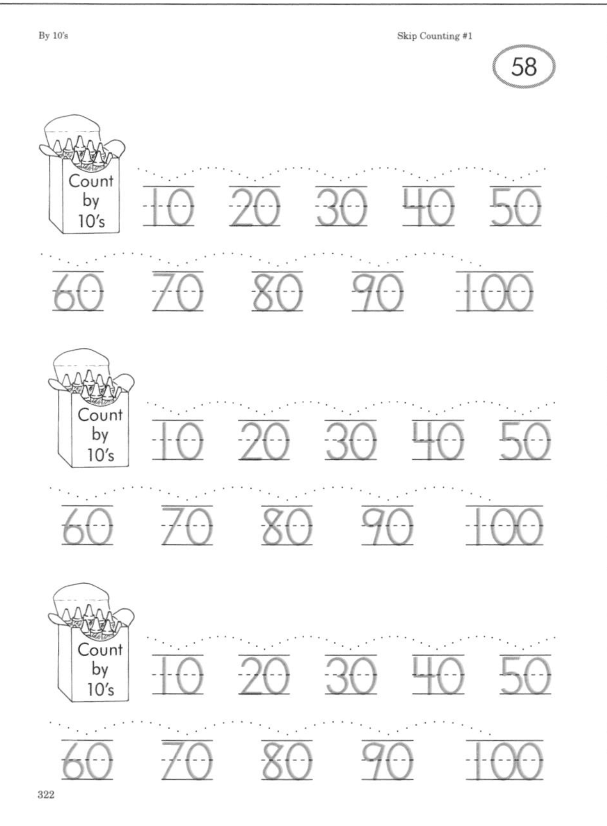

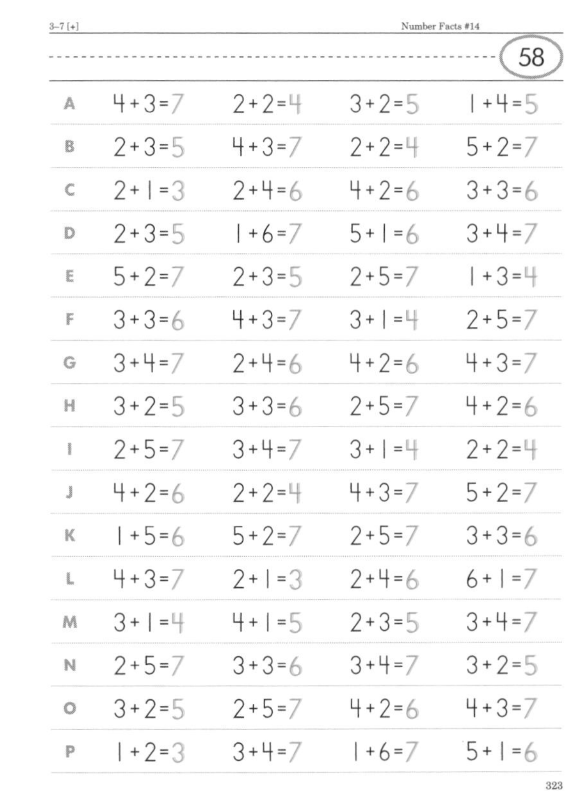
3–7 [+] Number Facts #14

58

A	4+3=7	2+2=4	3+2=5	1+4=5
B	2+3=5	4+3=7	2+2=4	5+2=7
C	2+1=3	2+4=6	4+2=6	3+3=6
D	2+3=5	1+6=7	5+1=6	3+4=7
E	5+2=7	2+3=5	2+5=7	1+3=4
F	3+3=6	4+3=7	3+1=4	2+5=7
G	3+4=7	2+4=6	4+2=6	4+3=7
H	3+2=5	3+3=6	2+5=7	4+2=6
I	2+5=7	3+4=7	3+1=4	2+2=4
J	4+2=6	2+2=4	4+3=7	5+2=7
K	1+5=6	5+2=7	2+5=7	3+3=6
L	4+3=7	2+1=3	2+4=6	6+1=7
M	3+1=4	4+1=5	2+3=5	3+4=7
N	2+5=7	3+3=6	3+4=7	3+2=5
O	3+2=5	2+5=7	4+2=6	4+3=7
P	1+2=3	3+4=7	1+6=7	5+1=6

323

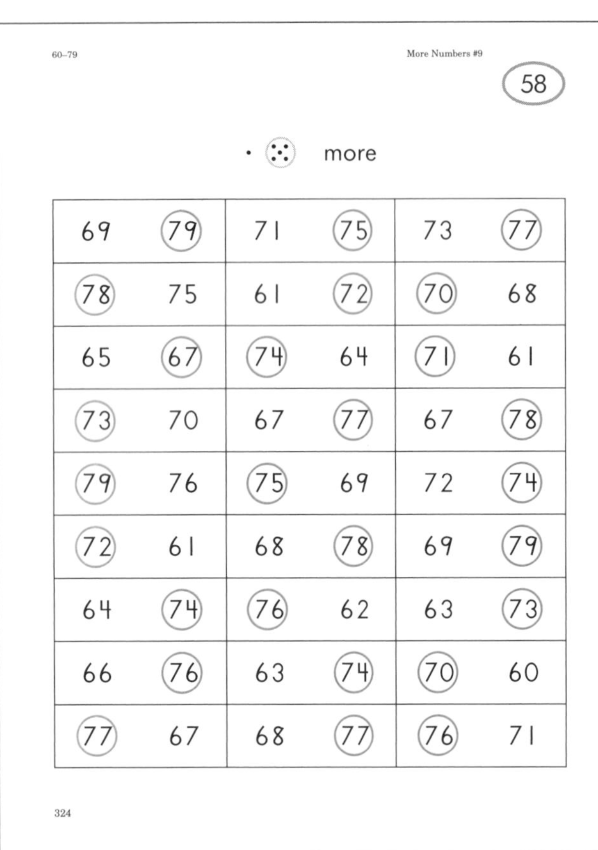

60–79 More Numbers #9

58

• more

69	79	71	75	73	77
78	75	61	72	70	68
65	67	74	64	71	61
73	70	67	77	67	78
79	76	75	69	72	74
72	61	68	78	69	79
64	74	76	62	63	73
66	76	63	74	70	60
77	67	68	77	76	71

324

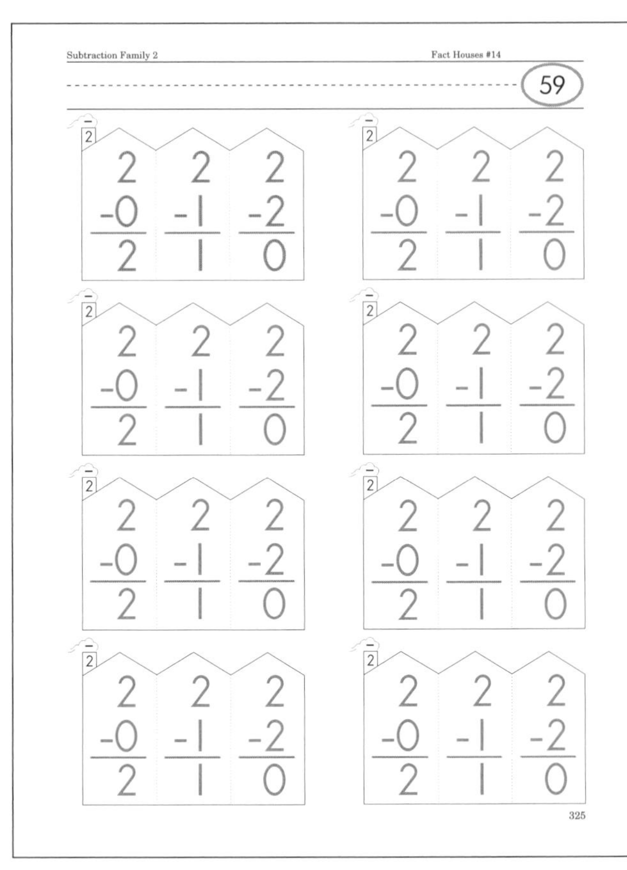

Subtraction Family 2 Fact Houses #14

59

2
2 − 0 = 2 | 2 − 1 = 1 | 2 − 2 = 0

2
2 − 0 = 2 | 2 − 1 = 1 | 2 − 2 = 0

2
2 − 0 = 2 | 2 − 1 = 1 | 2 − 2 = 0

2
2 − 0 = 2 | 2 − 1 = 1 | 2 − 2 = 0

2
2 − 0 = 2 | 2 − 1 = 1 | 2 − 2 = 0

2
2 − 0 = 2 | 2 − 1 = 1 | 2 − 2 = 0

2
2 − 0 = 2 | 2 − 1 = 1 | 2 − 2 = 0

2
2 − 0 = 2 | 2 − 1 = 1 | 2 − 2 = 0

325

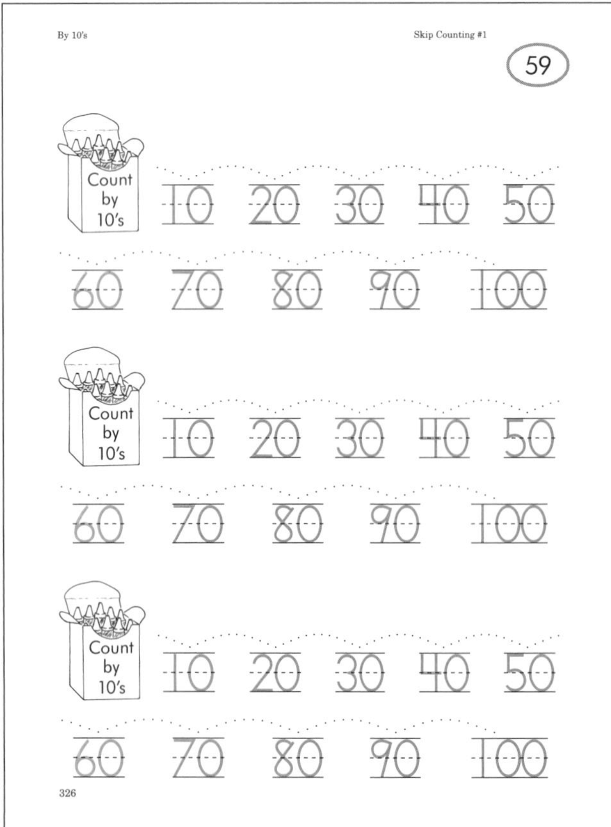

By 10's Skip Counting #1

59

Count by 10's
10 20 30 40 50
60 70 80 90 100

Count by 10's
10 20 30 40 50
60 70 80 90 100

Count by 10's
10 20 30 40 50
60 70 80 90 100

326

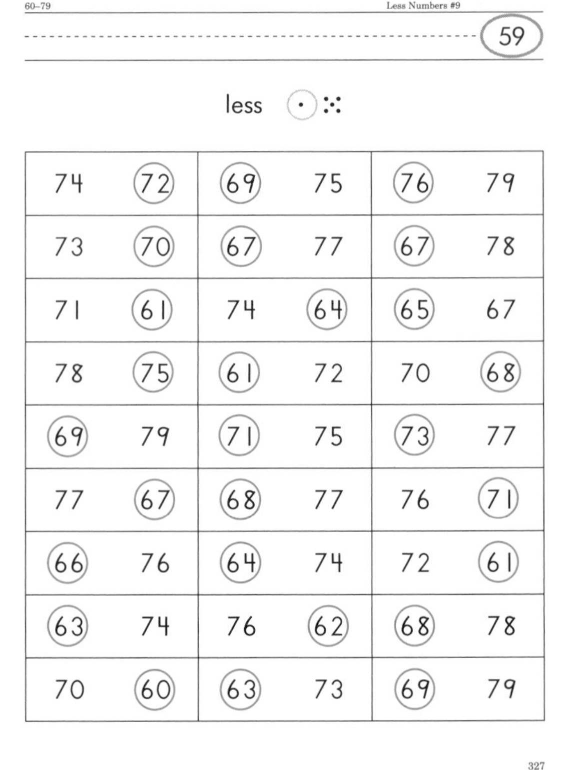

60–79 Less Numbers #9

59

less •

74	72	69	75	76	79
73	70	67	77	67	78
71	61	74	64	65	67
78	75	61	72	70	68
69	79	71	75	73	77
77	67	68	77	76	71
66	76	64	74	72	61
63	74	76	62	68	78
70	60	63	73	69	79

327

3–7 [+] Number Facts #14 (59)

A	4+3=7	2+2=4	3+2=5	1+4=5
B	2+3=5	4+3=7	2+2=4	5+2=7
C	2+1=3	2+4=6	4+2=6	3+3=6
D	2+3=5	1+6=7	5+1=6	3+4=7
E	5+2=7	2+3=5	2+5=7	1+3=4
F	3+3=6	4+3=7	3+1=4	2+5=7
G	3+4=7	2+4=6	4+2=6	4+3=7
H	3+2=5	3+3=6	2+5=7	4+2=6
I	2+5=7	3+4=7	3+1=4	2+2=4
J	4+2=6	2+2=4	4+3=7	5+2=7
K	1+5=6	5+2=7	2+5=7	3+3=6
L	4+3=7	2+1=3	2+4=6	6+1=7
M	3+1=4	4+1=5	2+3=5	3+4=7
N	2+5=7	3+3=6	3+4=7	3+2=5
O	3+2=5	2+5=7	4+2=6	4+3=7
P	1+2=3	3+4=7	1+6=7	5+1=6

328

51–79 Before and After #2 (59)

64	65	66	71	72	73
72	73	74	77	78	79
70	71	72	63	64	65
61	62	63	65	66	67
54	55	56	56	57	58
75	76	77	76	77	78
67	68	69	73	74	75
74	75	76	51	52	53
62	63	64	60	61	62

329

22–50 Dot-to-Dot #24 (59)

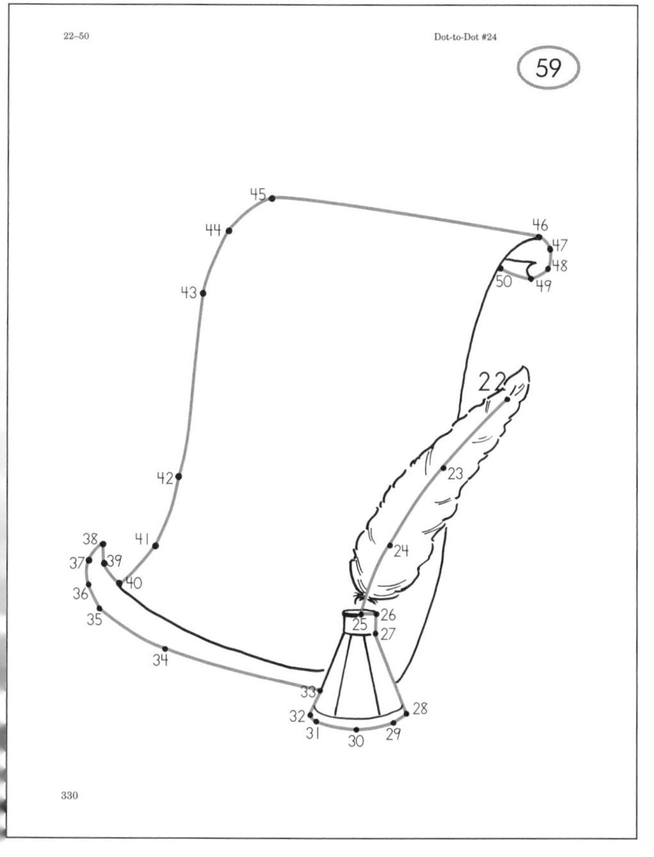

330

Story Problem Dictation Form D (60)

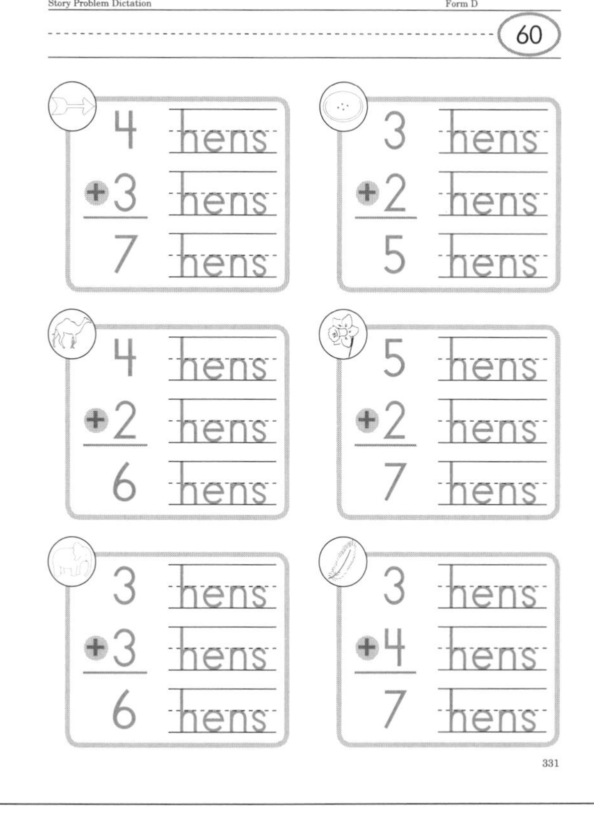

331

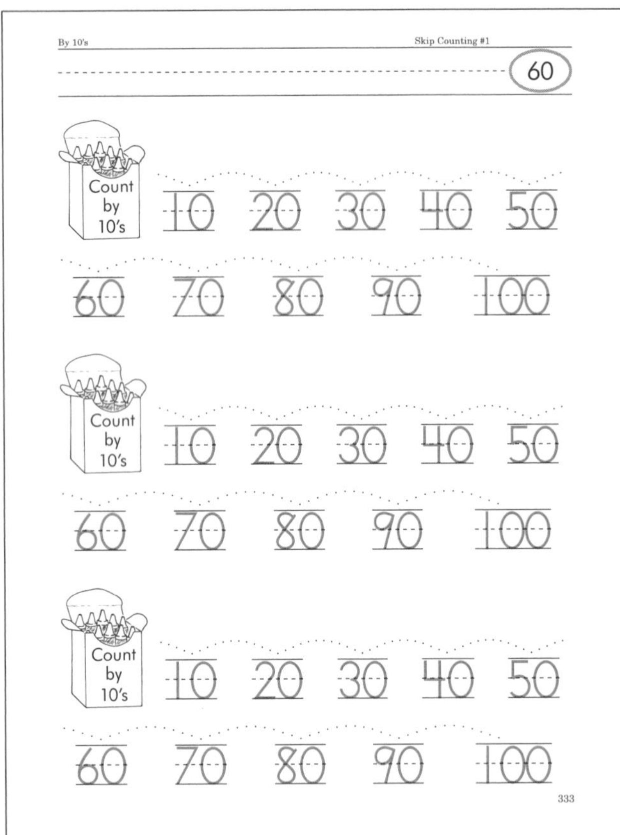

4–7 [+] Number Facts #15

60

A	5+2=7	2+5=7	4+2=6	3+3=6
B	4+1=5	4+2=6	3+4=7	4+3=7
C	2+2=4	3+2=5	5+2=7	2+5=7
D	4+1=5	4+3=7	1+5=6	1+4=5
E	2+4=6	3+3=6	4+3=7	1+3=4
F	5+2=7	4+3=7	6+1=7	4+2=6
G	4+3=7	1+6=7	3+2=5	5+2=7
H	2+4=6	4+2=6	2+2=4	4+2=6
I	3+4=7	5+2=7	3+2=5	2+3=5
J	2+4=6	1+4=5	4+3=7	2+5=7
K	3+2=5	2+2=4	3+3=6	4+2=6
L	5+2=7	4+1=5	3+2=5	3+4=7
M	4+3=7	5+2=7	1+6=7	5+2=7
N	3+2=5	1+5=6	3+3=6	2+4=6
O	1+3=4	3+2=5	2+5=7	5+2=7
P	2+3=5	5+2=7	3+4=7	6+1=7

334

Subtraction Family 3 Fact Houses #15

61

3	3	3	3		3	3	3	3
-0	-1	-2	-3		-0	-1	-2	-3
3	2	1	0		3	2	1	0

3	3	3	3		3	3	3	3
-0	-1	-2	-3		-0	-1	-2	-3
3	2	1	0		3	2	1	0

3	3	3	3		3	3	3	3
-0	-1	-2	-3		-0	-1	-2	-3
3	2	1	0		3	2	1	0

3	3	3	3		3	3	3	3
-0	-1	-2	-3		-0	-1	-2	-3
3	2	1	0		3	2	1	0

335

By 10's Skip Counting #1

61

10 20 30 40 50

60 70 80 90 100

10 20 30 40 50

60 70 80 90 100

10 20 30 40 50

60 70 80 90 100

337

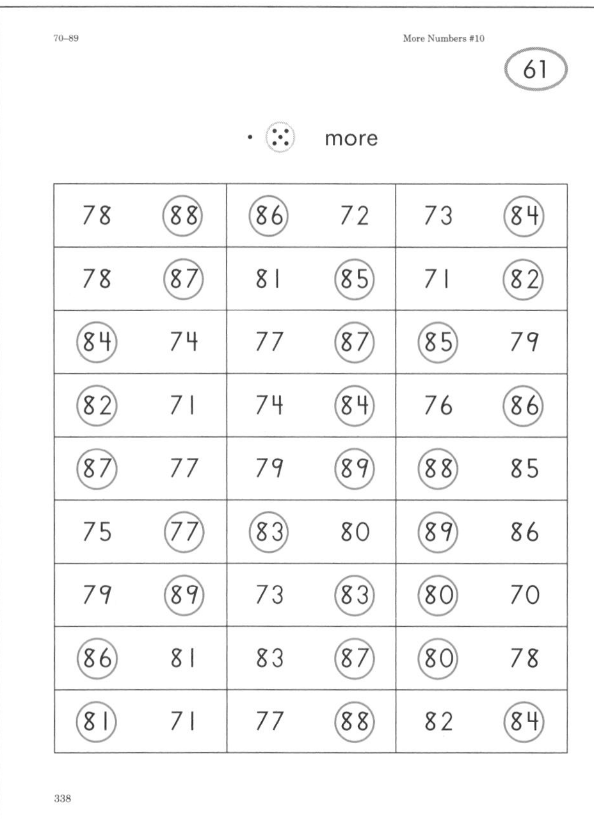
70–89 More Numbers #10

61

• ⁙ more

78	**88**	**86**	72	73	**84**
78	**87**	81	**85**	71	**82**
84	74	77	**87**	**85**	79
82	71	74	**84**	76	**86**
87	77	79	**89**	**88**	85
75	**77**	**83**	80	**89**	86
79	**89**	73	**83**	**80**	70
86	81	83	**87**	**80**	78
81	71	77	**88**	82	**84**

338

By 10's to 100 Dot-to-Dot #25

61

339

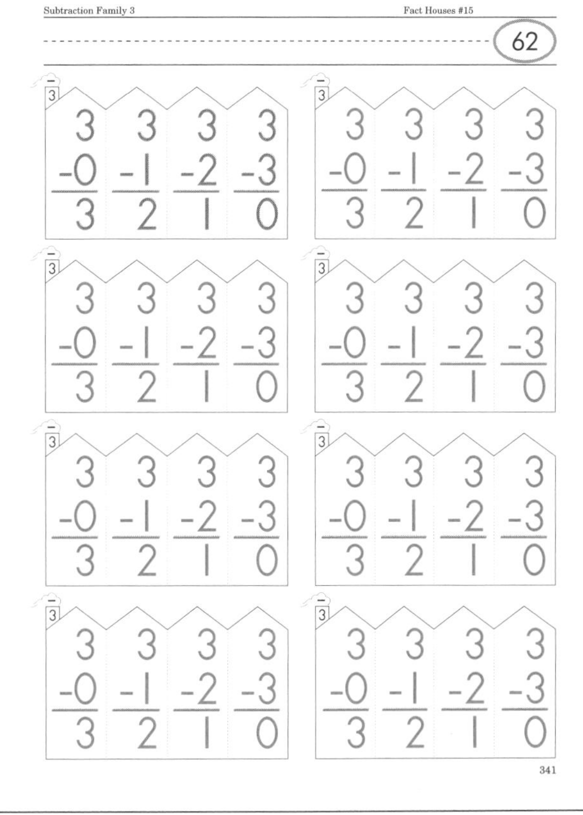
Subtraction Family 3 Fact Houses #15

62

3	3	3	3
-0	-1	-2	-3
3	2	1	0

(This fact house is printed 8 times on the sheet.)

341

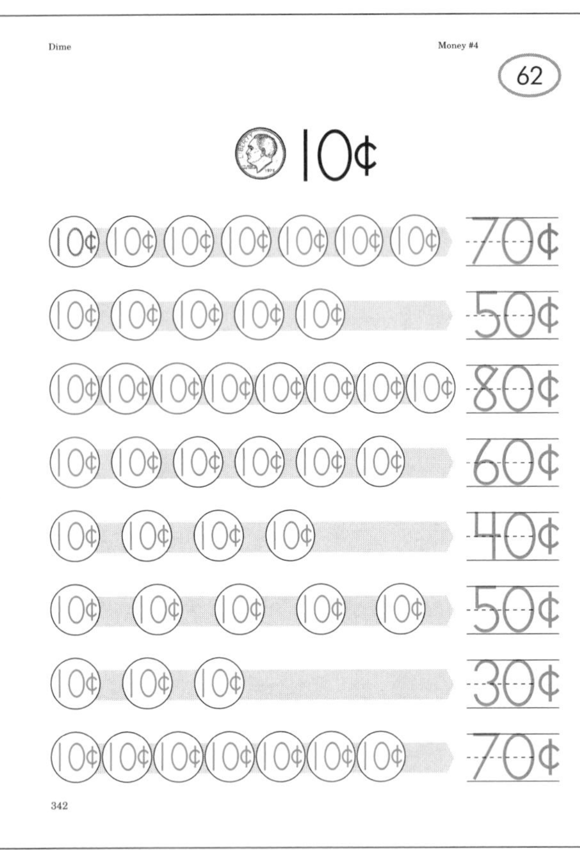

4–7 [+] Number Facts #15

62

A	5+2=7	2+5=7	4+2=6	3+3=6
B	4+1=5	4+2=6	3+4=7	4+3=7
C	2+2=4	3+2=5	5+2=7	2+5=7
D	4+1=5	4+3=7	1+5=6	1+4=5
E	2+4=6	3+3=6	4+3=7	1+3=4
F	5+2=7	4+3=7	6+1=7	4+2=6
G	4+3=7	1+6=7	3+2=5	5+2=7
H	2+4=6	4+2=6	2+2=4	4+2=6
I	3+4=7	5+2=7	3+2=5	2+3=5
J	2+4=6	1+4=5	4+3=7	2+5=7
K	3+2=5	2+2=6	3+3=6	4+2=6
L	5+2=7	4+1=5	3+2=5	3+4=7
M	4+3=7	5+2=7	1+6=7	5+2=7
N	3+2=5	1+5=6	3+3=6	2+4=6
O	1+3=4	3+2=5	2+5=7	5+2=7
P	2+3=5	5+2=7	3+4=7	6+1=7

343

70–89 Less Numbers #10

62

less

82	**71**	**78**	88	**79**	89
74	84	86	**72**	**73**	83
76	86	**73**	84	80	**70**
87	**77**	**78**	87	86	**81**
79	89	**81**	85	**83**	87
88	**85**	**71**	82	80	**78**
75	77	84	**74**	81	**71**
83	**80**	**77**	87	**77**	88
89	**86**	85	**79**	**82**	84

344

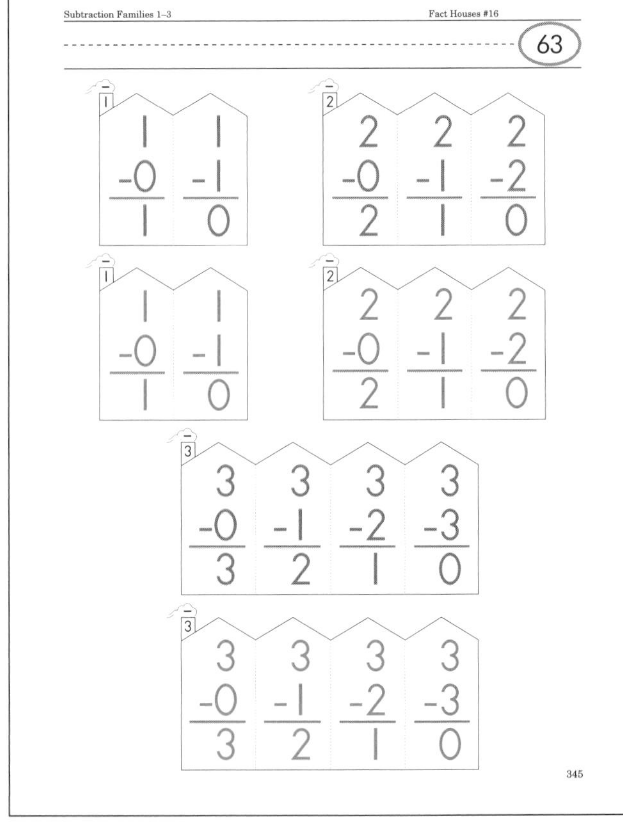

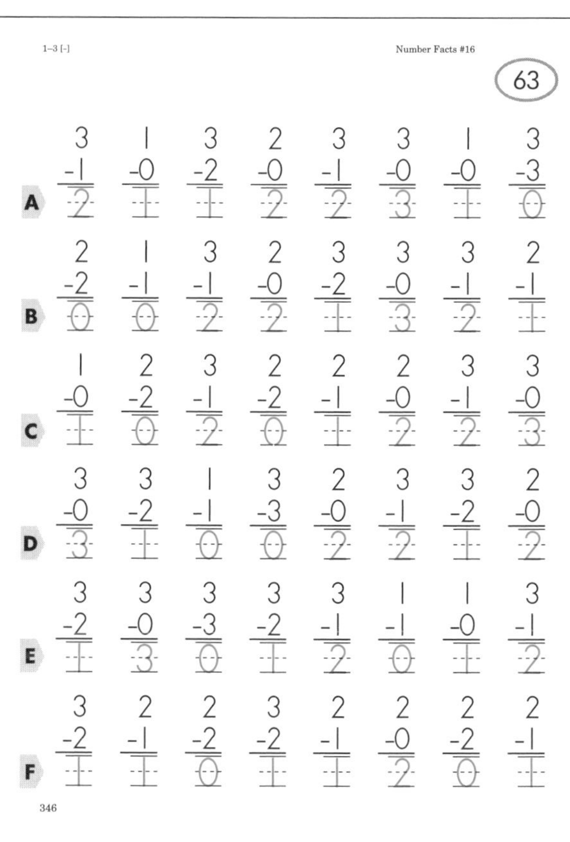

1–3 [-] Number Facts #16 63

A	3 − 1 = 2	1 − 0 = 1	3 − 2 = 1	2 − 0 = 2	3 − 1 = 2	3 − 0 = 3	1 − 0 = 1	3 − 3 = 0
B	2 − 2 = 0	1 − 1 = 0	3 − 1 = 2	2 − 0 = 2	3 − 2 = 1	3 − 0 = 3	3 − 1 = 2	2 − 1 = 1
C	1 − 0 = 1	2 − 2 = 0	3 − 1 = 2	2 − 2 = 0	2 − 1 = 1	2 − 0 = 2	3 − 1 = 2	3 − 0 = 3
D	3 − 0 = 3	3 − 2 = 1	1 − 1 = 0	3 − 3 = 0	2 − 0 = 2	3 − 1 = 2	3 − 2 = 1	2 − 0 = 2
E	3 − 2 = 1	3 − 0 = 3	3 − 3 = 0	3 − 2 = 1	3 − 1 = 2	1 − 1 = 0	1 − 0 = 1	3 − 1 = 2
F	3 − 2 = 1	2 − 1 = 1	2 − 2 = 0	3 − 2 = 1	2 − 1 = 1	2 − 0 = 2	2 − 2 = 0	2 − 1 = 1

346

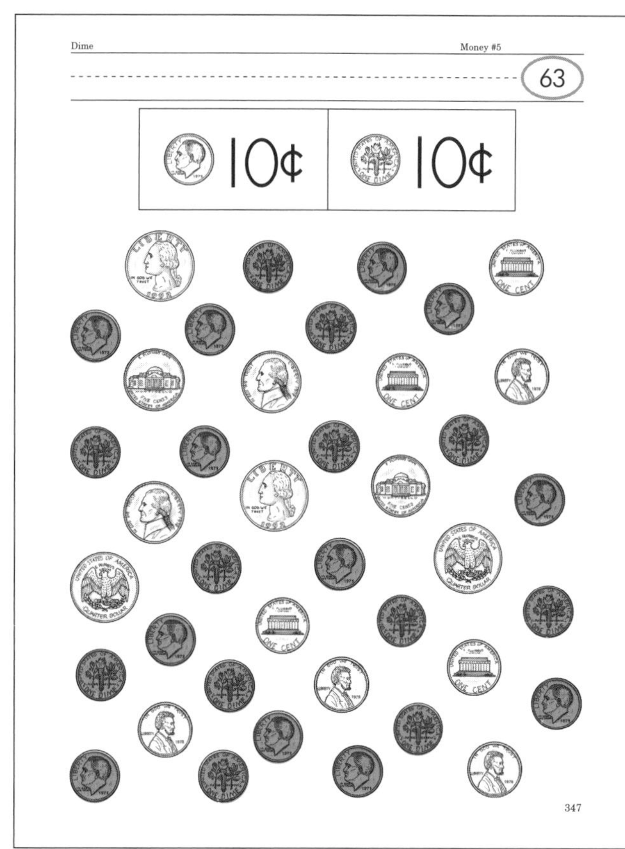

Dime Money #5 63

10¢ 10¢

347

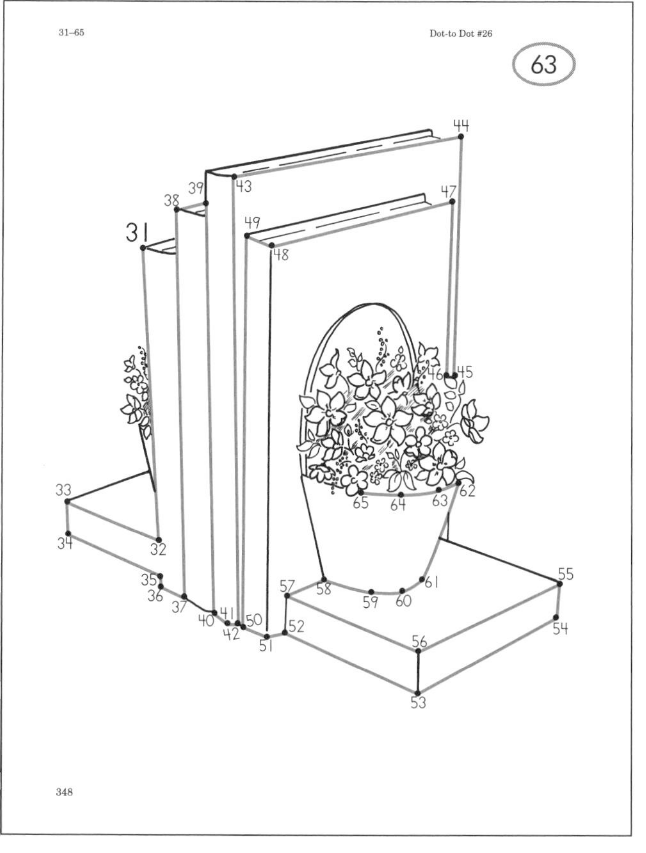

31–65 Dot-to Dot #26 63

348

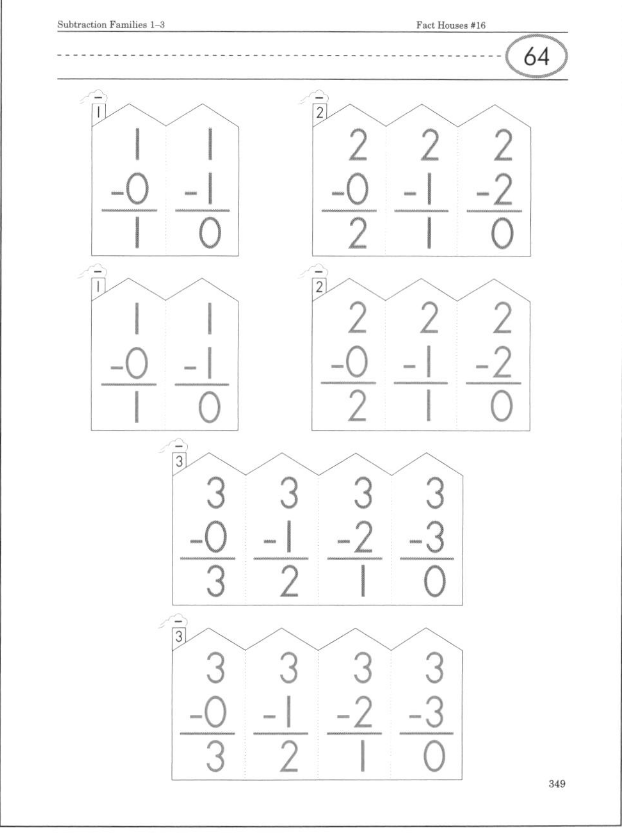

Subtraction Families 1–3 Fact Houses #16 64

1: 1 − 0 = 1, 1 − 1 = 0

2: 2 − 0 = 2, 2 − 1 = 1, 2 − 2 = 0

1: 1 − 0 = 1, 1 − 1 = 0

2: 2 − 0 = 2, 2 − 1 = 1, 2 − 2 = 0

3: 3 − 0 = 3, 3 − 1 = 2, 3 − 2 = 1, 3 − 3 = 0

3: 3 − 0 = 3, 3 − 1 = 2, 3 − 2 = 1, 3 − 3 = 0

349

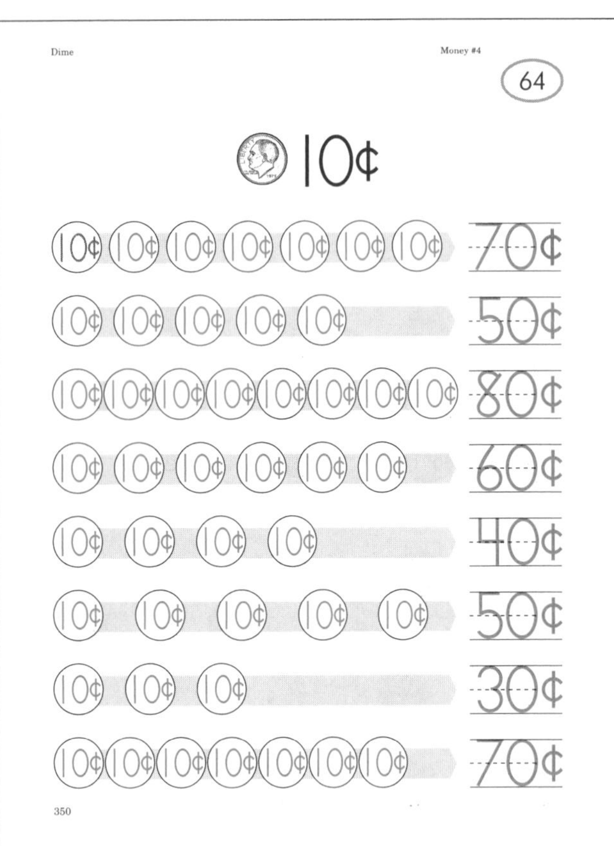
Dime

Money #4

64

10¢

70¢

50¢

80¢

60¢

40¢

50¢

30¢

70¢

350

80–99

More Numbers #11

64

more

99	96	**93**	90	85	**87**
94	84	87	**97**	**95**	89
92	**94**	87	**98**	**91**	81
90	88	93	**97**	**96**	91
88	**97**	91	**95**	81	**92**
98	95	89	**99**	**97**	87
86	**96**	84	**94**	**92**	81
88	**98**	**96**	82	83	**94**
89	**99**	83	**93**	**90**	80

351

1–3 [-]

Number Facts #16

64

A	3 − 1 = 2	1 − 0 = 1	3 − 2 = 1	2 − 0 = 2	3 − 1 = 2	3 − 0 = 3	1 − 0 = 1	3 − 3 = 0
B	2 − 2 = 0	1 − 1 = 0	3 − 1 = 2	2 − 0 = 2	3 − 2 = 1	3 − 0 = 3	3 − 1 = 2	2 − 1 = 1
C	1 − 0 = 1	2 − 2 = 0	3 − 1 = 2	2 − 2 = 0	2 − 1 = 1	2 − 0 = 2	3 − 1 = 2	3 − 0 = 3
D	3 − 0 = 3	3 − 2 = 1	1 − 1 = 0	3 − 3 = 0	2 − 0 = 2	3 − 1 = 2	3 − 2 = 1	2 − 0 = 2
E	3 − 2 = 1	3 − 0 = 3	3 − 3 = 0	3 − 2 = 1	3 − 1 = 2	1 − 1 = 0	1 − 0 = 1	3 − 1 = 2
F	3 − 2 = 1	2 − 1 = 1	2 − 2 = 0	3 − 2 = 1	2 − 1 = 1	2 − 0 = 2	2 − 2 = 0	2 − 1 = 1

352

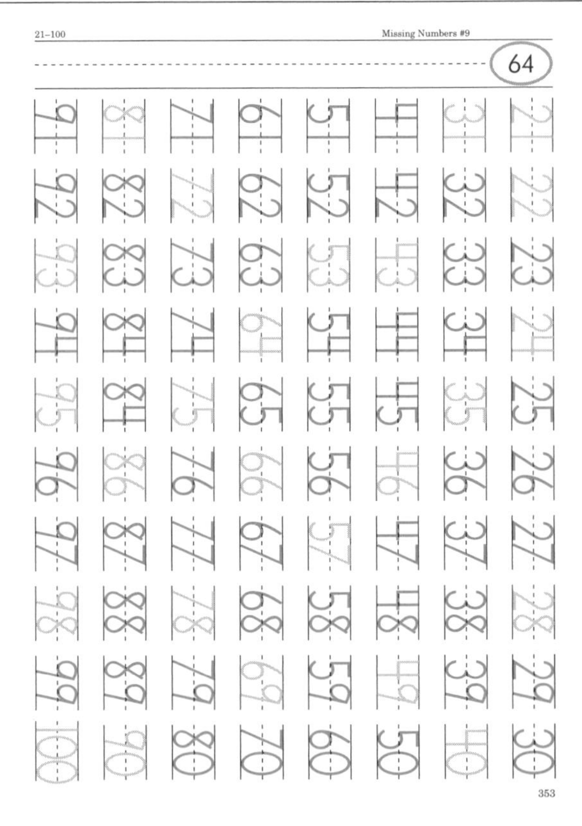
21–100

Missing Numbers #9

64

353

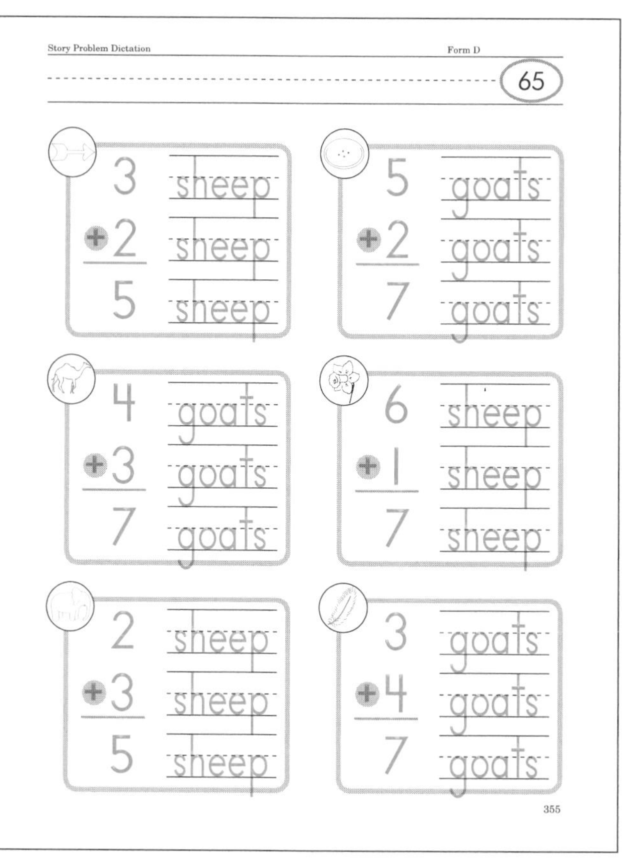
Story Problem Dictation — Form D — 65

3 sheep + 2 sheep = 5 sheep	5 goats + 2 goats = 7 goats
4 goats + 3 goats = 7 goats	6 sheep + 1 sheep = 7 sheep
2 sheep + 3 sheep = 5 sheep	3 goats + 4 goats = 7 goats

355

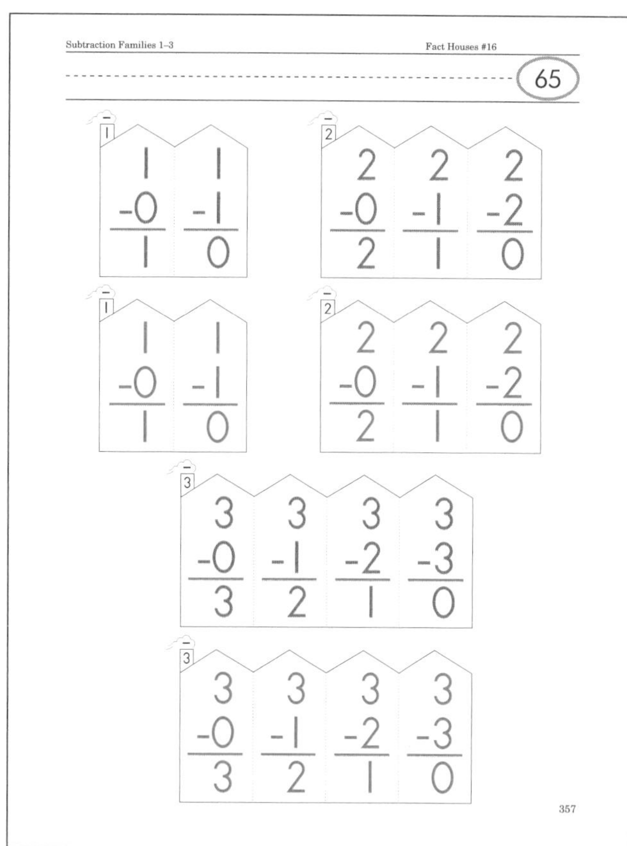
Subtraction Families 1–3 — Fact Houses #16 — 65

1	1 − 0 = 1; 1 − 1 = 0
2	2 − 0 = 2; 2 − 1 = 1; 2 − 2 = 0
1	1 − 0 = 1; 1 − 1 = 0
2	2 − 0 = 2; 2 − 1 = 1; 2 − 2 = 0
3	3 − 0 = 3; 3 − 1 = 2; 3 − 2 = 1; 3 − 3 = 0
3	3 − 0 = 3; 3 − 1 = 2; 3 − 2 = 1; 3 − 3 = 0

357

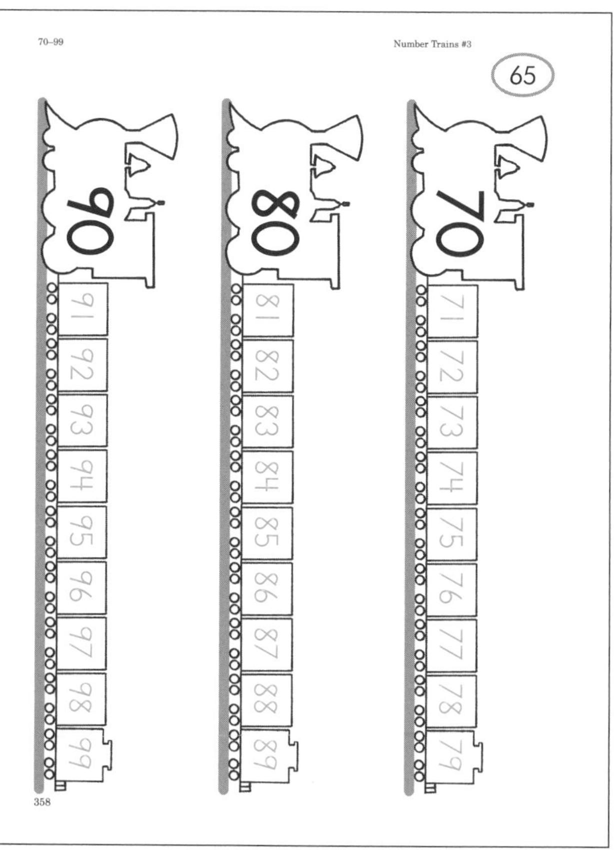
70–99 — Number Trains #3 — 65

Engine	Cars
90	91, 92, 93, 94, 95, 96, 97, 98, 99
80	81, 82, 83, 84, 85, 86, 87, 88, 89
70	71, 72, 73, 74, 75, 76, 77, 78, 79

358

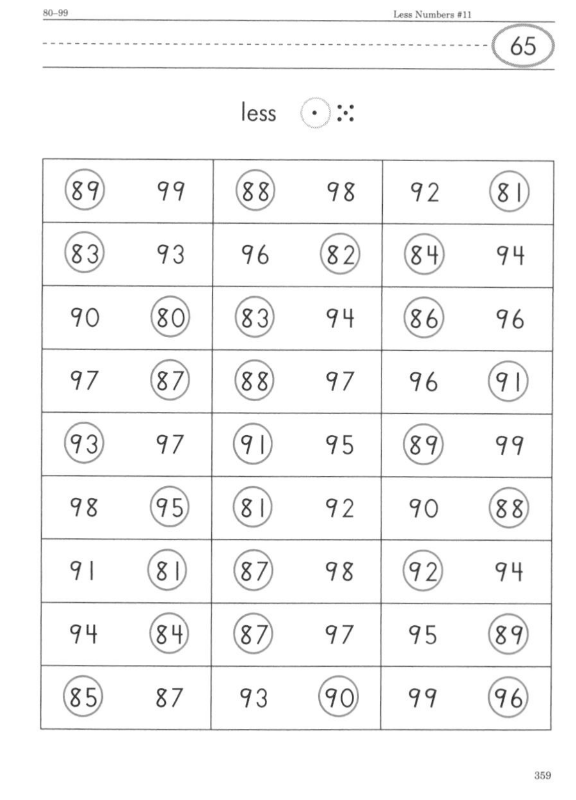
80–99 — Less Numbers #11 — 65

less

(89)	99	(88)	98	92	(81)
(83)	93	96	(82)	(84)	94
90	(80)	(83)	94	(86)	96
97	(87)	(88)	97	96	(91)
(93)	97	(91)	95	(89)	99
98	(95)	(81)	92	90	(88)
91	(81)	(87)	98	(92)	94
94	(84)	(87)	97	95	(89)
(85)	87	93	(90)	99	(96)

359

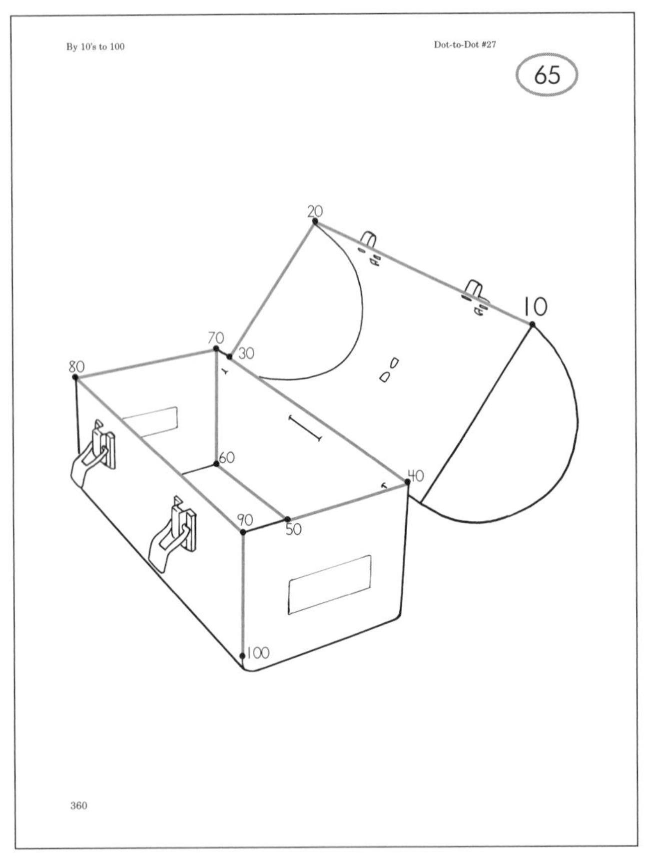
By 10's to 100
Dot-to-Dot #27
65
20
10
70
30
80
60
40
90
50
100
360

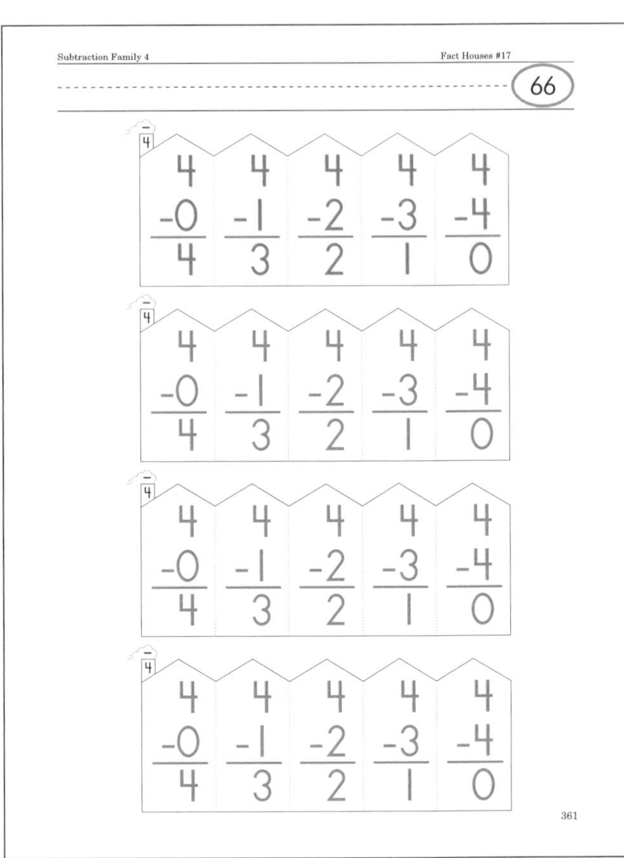
Subtraction Family 4
Fact Houses #17
66
4 - 0 = 4
4 - 1 = 3
4 - 2 = 2
4 - 3 = 1
4 - 4 = 0
361

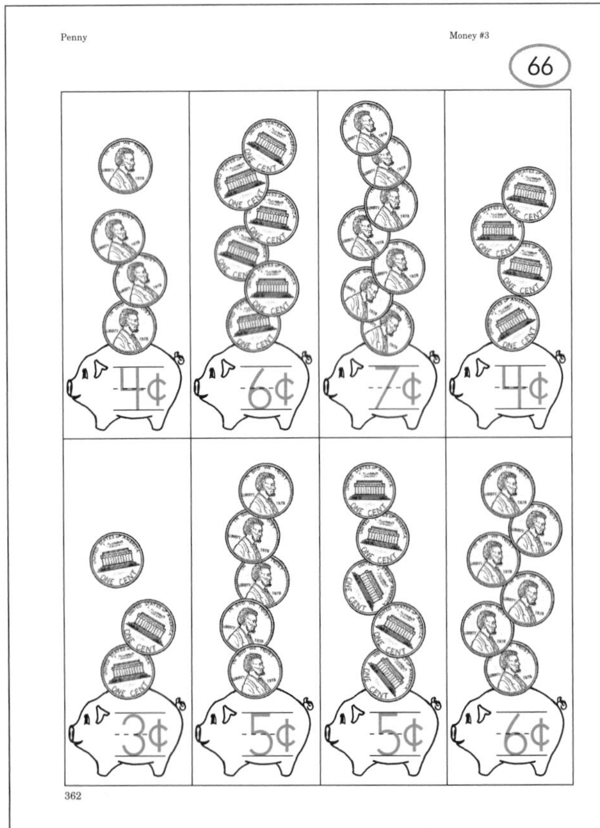
Penny
Money #3
66
4¢
6¢
7¢
4¢
3¢
5¢
5¢
6¢
362

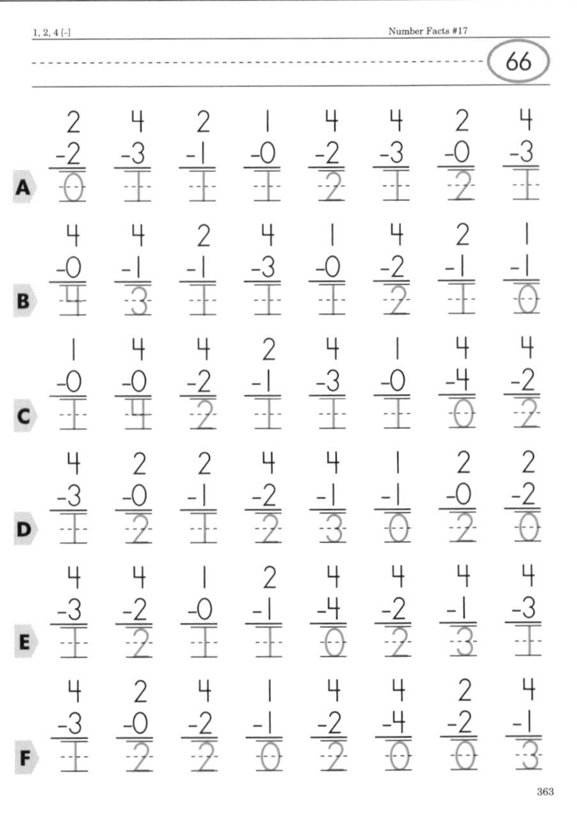
1, 2, 4 [-]
Number Facts #17
66
A 2-2=0 4-3=1 2-1=1 1-0=1 4-2=2 4-3=1 2-0=2 4-3=1
B 4-0=4 4-1=3 2-1=1 4-3=1 1-0=1 4-2=2 2-1=1 1-1=0
C 1-0=1 4-0=4 4-2=2 2-1=1 4-3=1 1-0=1 4-4=0 4-2=2
D 4-3=1 2-0=2 2-1=1 4-2=2 4-1=3 1-1=0 2-0=2 2-2=0
E 4-3=1 4-2=2 1-0=1 2-1=1 4-4=0 4-2=2 4-1=3 4-3=1
F 4-3=1 2-0=2 4-2=2 1-1=0 4-2=2 4-4=0 2-2=0 4-1=3
363

61–89 Before and After #3

66

74	75	76	70	71	72
82	83	84	81	82	83
76	77	78	86	87	88
84	85	86	73	74	75
72	73	74	63	64	65
80	81	82	61	62	63
85	86	87	75	76	77
71	72	73	87	88	89
65	66	67	83	84	85

364

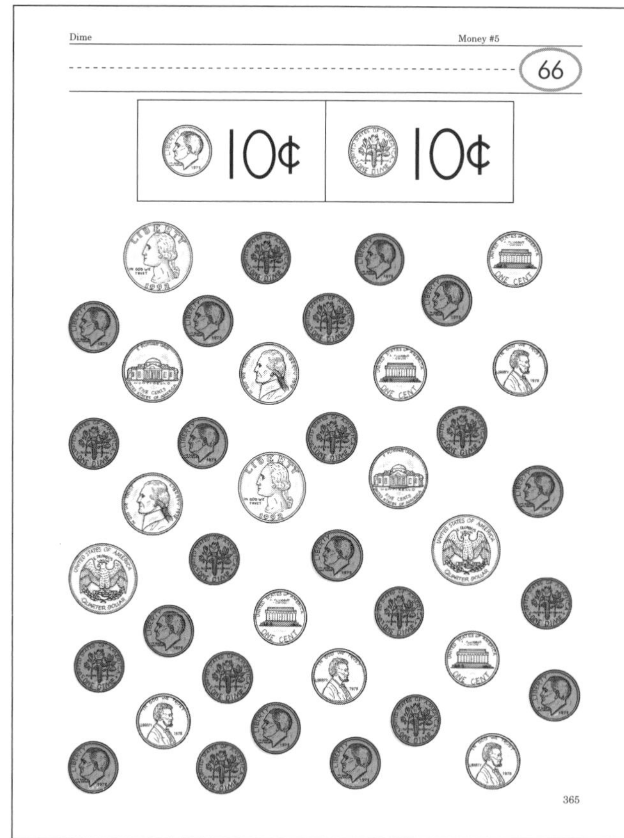
Dime Money #5

66

10¢ 10¢

365

Subtraction Family 4 Fact Houses #17

67

4 - 0 = 4	4 - 1 = 3	4 - 2 = 2	4 - 3 = 1	4 - 4 = 0
4 - 0 = 4	4 - 1 = 3	4 - 2 = 2	4 - 3 = 1	4 - 4 = 0
4 - 0 = 4	4 - 1 = 3	4 - 2 = 2	4 - 3 = 1	4 - 4 = 0
4 - 0 = 4	4 - 1 = 3	4 - 2 = 2	4 - 3 = 1	4 - 4 = 0

367

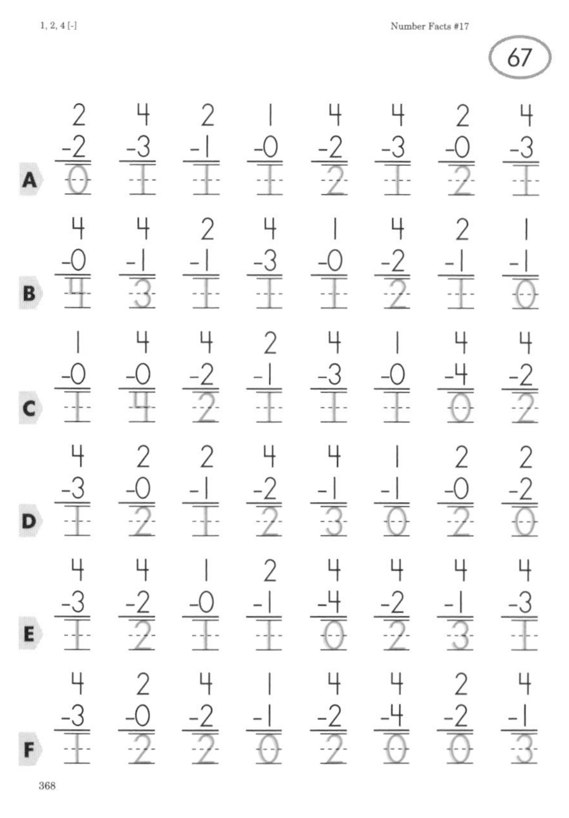
1, 2, 4 [-] Number Facts #17

67

A	2 - 2 = 0	4 - 3 = 1	2 - 1 = 1	1 - 0 = 1	4 - 2 = 2	4 - 3 = 1	2 - 0 = 2	4 - 3 = 1
B	4 - 0 = 4	4 - 1 = 3	2 - 1 = 1	4 - 3 = 1	1 - 0 = 1	4 - 2 = 2	2 - 1 = 1	1 - 1 = 0
C	1 - 0 = 1	4 - 0 = 4	4 - 2 = 2	2 - 1 = 1	4 - 3 = 1	1 - 0 = 1	4 - 4 = 0	4 - 2 = 2
D	4 - 3 = 1	2 - 0 = 2	2 - 1 = 1	4 - 2 = 2	4 - 1 = 3	1 - 1 = 0	2 - 0 = 2	2 - 2 = 0
E	4 - 3 = 1	4 - 2 = 2	1 - 0 = 1	2 - 1 = 1	4 - 4 = 0	4 - 2 = 2	4 - 1 = 3	4 - 3 = 1
F	4 - 3 = 1	2 - 0 = 2	4 - 2 = 2	1 - 1 = 0	4 - 2 = 2	4 - 4 = 0	2 - 2 = 0	4 - 1 = 3

368

Dime — Money #6 — 67

50¢	60¢	80¢	70¢
80¢	40¢	70¢	80¢

369

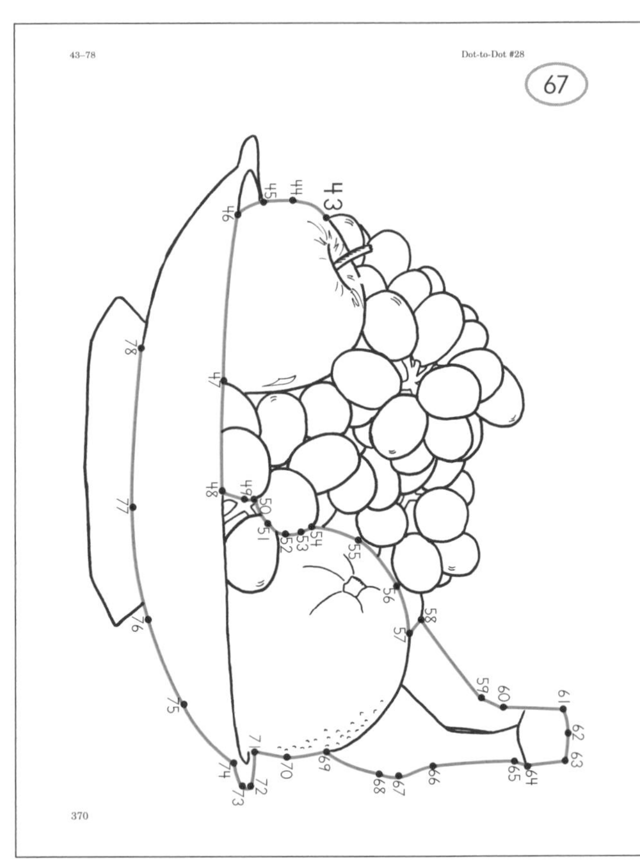
43–78 — Dot-to-Dot #28 — 67

370

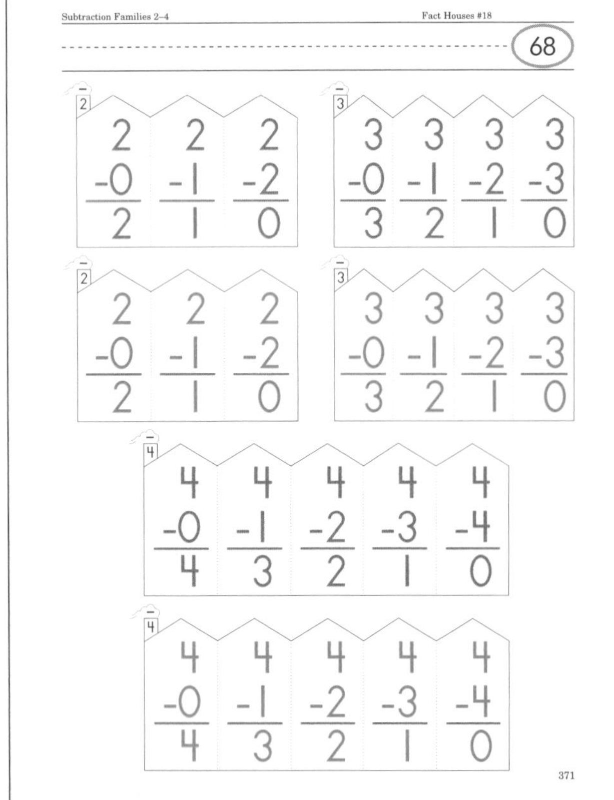
Subtraction Families 2–4 — Fact Houses #18 — 68

2 − 0 = 2, 2 − 1 = 1, 2 − 2 = 0

3 − 0 = 3, 3 − 1 = 2, 3 − 2 = 1, 3 − 3 = 0

2 − 0 = 2, 2 − 1 = 1, 2 − 2 = 0

3 − 0 = 3, 3 − 1 = 2, 3 − 2 = 1, 3 − 3 = 0

4 − 0 = 4, 4 − 1 = 3, 4 − 2 = 2, 4 − 3 = 1, 4 − 4 = 0

4 − 0 = 4, 4 − 1 = 3, 4 − 2 = 2, 4 − 3 = 1, 4 − 4 = 0

371

By 5's — Skip Counting #2 — 68

Count by 5's

5 10 15 20
25 30 35 40 45 50
55 60 65 70 75 80
85 90 95 100

Count by 5's

5 10 15 20
25 30 35 40 45 50
55 60 65 70 75 80
85 90 95 100

372

1, 2, 4 [-] — Number Facts #17

68

A	2 -2 0	4 -3 1	2 -1 1	1 -0 1	4 -2 2	4 -3 1	2 -0 2	4 -3 1
B	4 -0 4	4 -1 3	2 -1 1	4 -3 1	1 -0 1	4 -2 2	2 -1 1	1 -1 0
C	1 -0 1	4 -0 4	4 -2 2	2 -1 1	4 -3 1	1 -0 1	4 -4 0	4 -2 2
D	4 -3 1	2 -0 2	2 -1 1	4 -2 2	4 -1 3	1 -1 0	2 -0 2	2 -2 0
E	4 -3 1	4 -2 2	1 -0 1	2 -1 1	4 -4 0	4 -2 2	4 -1 3	4 -3 1
F	4 -3 1	2 -0 2	4 -2 2	1 -1 0	4 -2 2	4 -4 0	2 -2 0	4 -1 3

373

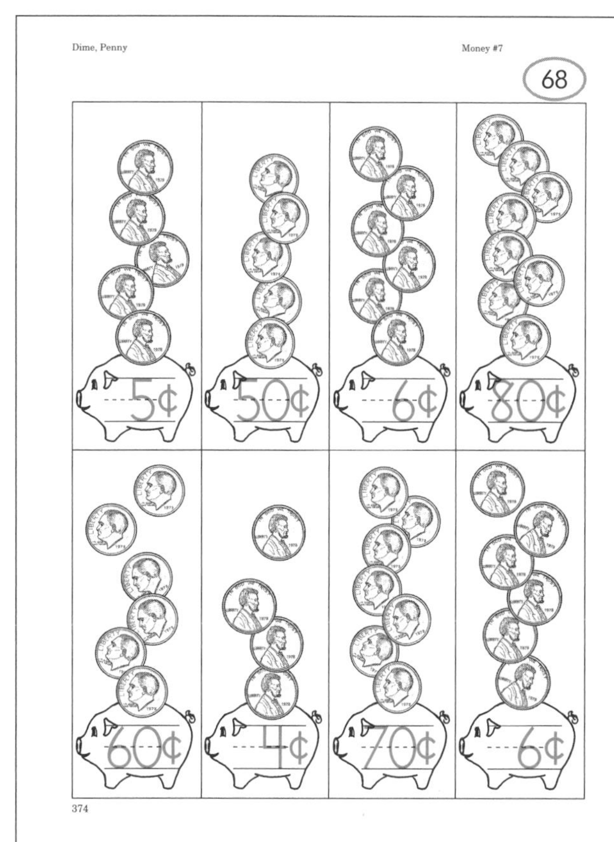

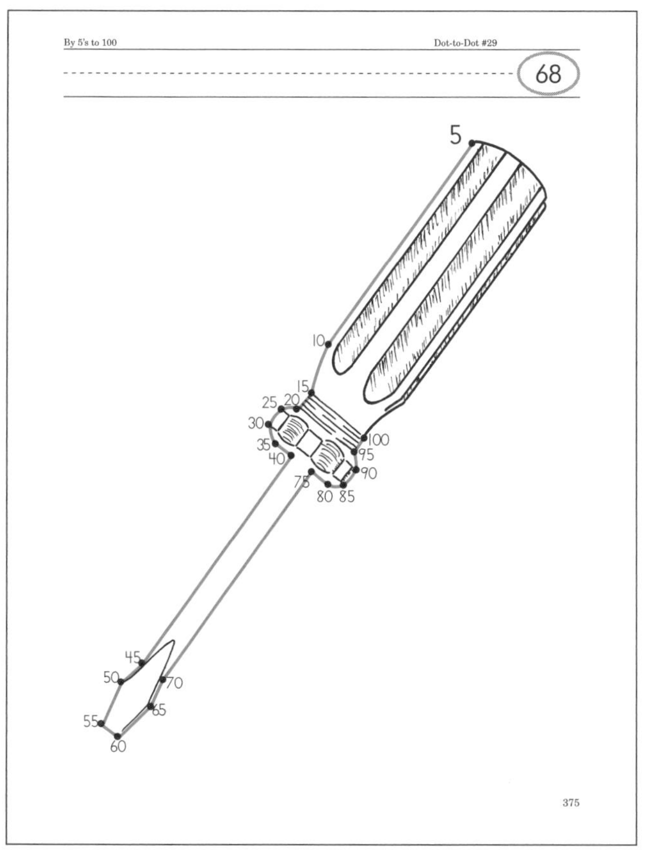

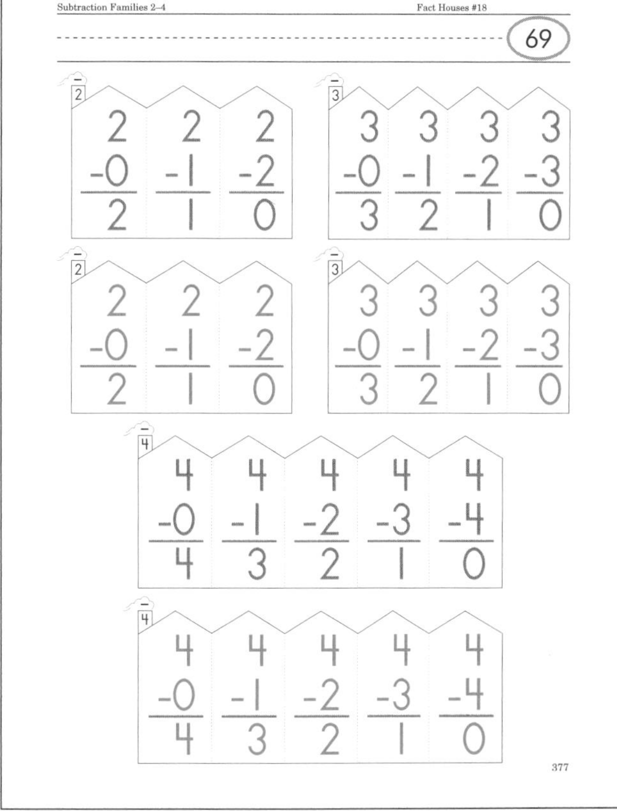

By 5's — Skip Counting #2

69

Count by 5's

5 10 15 20

25 30 35 40 45 50

55 60 65 70 75 80

85 90 95 100

Count by 5's

5 10 15 20

25 30 35 40 45 50

55 60 65 70 75 80

85 90 95 100

378

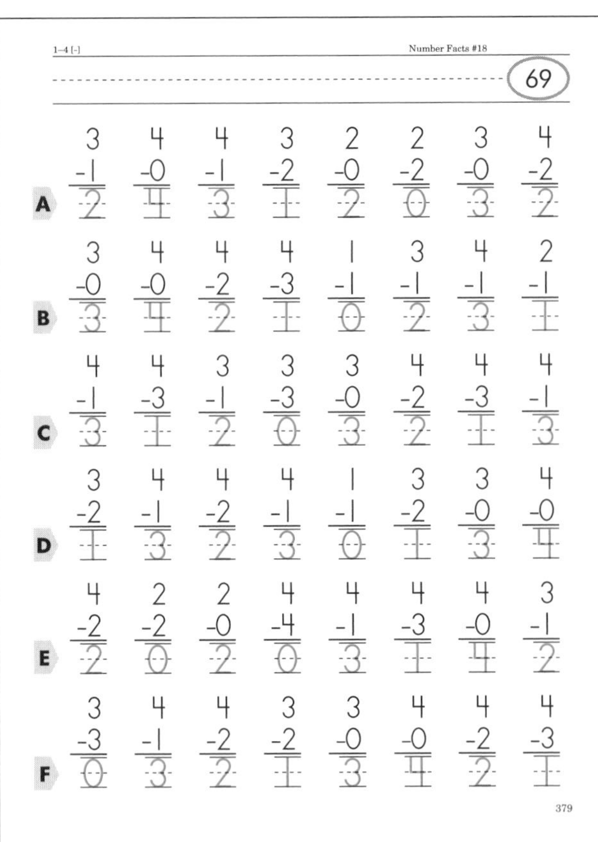

1–4 [-] — Number Facts #18

69

A	3 -1 = 2	4 -0 = 4	4 -1 = 3	3 -2 = 1	2 -0 = 2	2 -2 = 0	3 -0 = 3	4 -2 = 2
B	3 -0 = 3	4 -0 = 4	4 -2 = 2	4 -3 = 1	1 -1 = 0	3 -1 = 2	4 -1 = 3	2 -1 = 1
C	4 -1 = 3	4 -3 = 1	3 -1 = 2	3 -3 = 0	3 -0 = 3	4 -2 = 2	4 -3 = 1	4 -1 = 3
D	3 -2 = 1	4 -1 = 3	4 -2 = 2	4 -1 = 3	1 -1 = 0	3 -2 = 1	3 -0 = 3	4 -0 = 4
E	4 -2 = 2	2 -2 = 0	2 -0 = 2	4 -4 = 0	4 -1 = 3	4 -3 = 1	4 -0 = 4	3 -1 = 2
F	3 -3 = 0	4 -1 = 3	4 -2 = 2	3 -2 = 1	3 -0 = 3	4 -0 = 4	4 -2 = 2	4 -3 = 1

379

Hour — Clocks #1

69

2:00 6:00 9:00 4:00

12:00 10:00 1:00 5:00

7:00 12:00 9:00 6:00

11:00 8:00 3:00 5:00

380

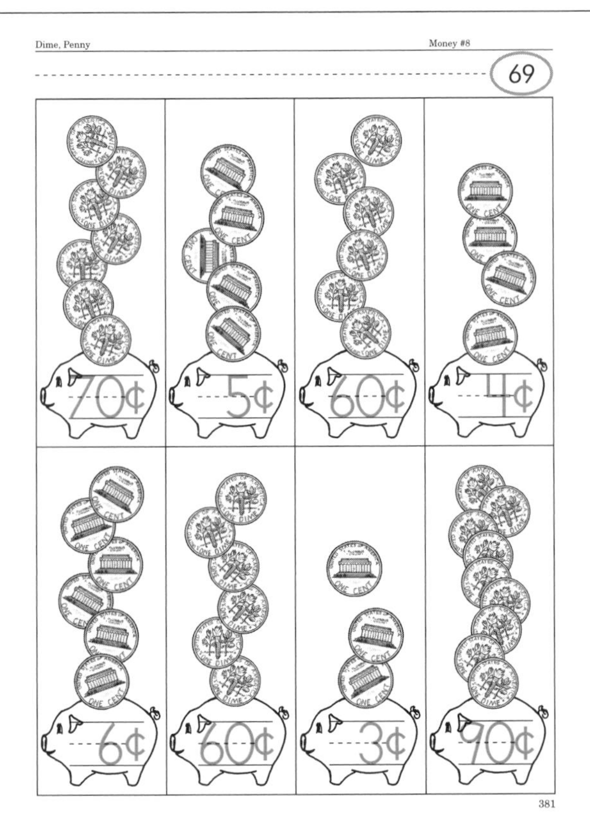

Dime, Penny — Money #8

69

70¢ 5¢ 60¢ 4¢

6¢ 60¢ 3¢ 90¢

381

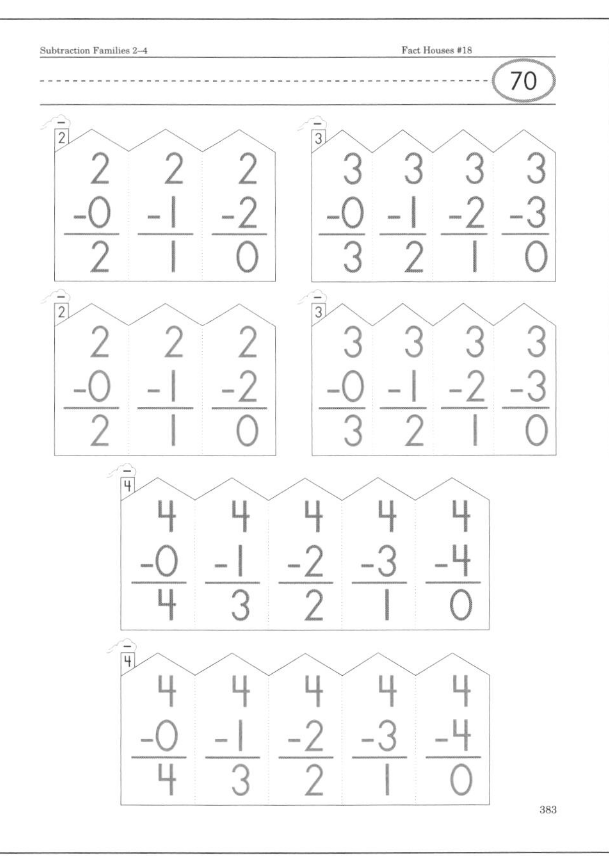

Subtraction Families 2–4 | Fact Houses #18

70

2		
2 -0 2	2 -1 1	2 -2 0

3			
3 -0 3	3 -1 2	3 -2 1	3 -3 0

2		
2 -0 2	2 -1 1	2 -2 0

3			
3 -0 3	3 -1 2	3 -2 1	3 -3 0

4				
4 -0 4	4 -1 3	4 -2 2	4 -3 1	4 -4 0

4				
4 -0 4	4 -1 3	4 -2 2	4 -3 1	4 -4 0

383

Hour | Clocks #1

70

2:00 6:00 9:00 4:00

12:00 10:00 1:00 5:00

7:00 12:00 9:00 6:00

11:00 8:00 3:00 5:00

384

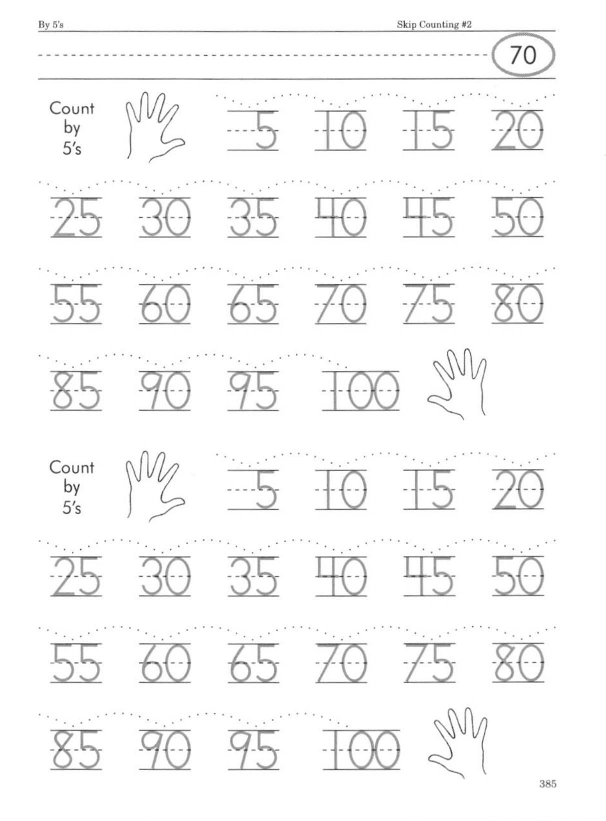

By 5's | Skip Counting #2

70

Count by 5's 5 10 15 20

25 30 35 40 45 50

55 60 65 70 75 80

85 90 95 100

Count by 5's 5 10 15 20

25 30 35 40 45 50

55 60 65 70 75 80

85 90 95 100

385

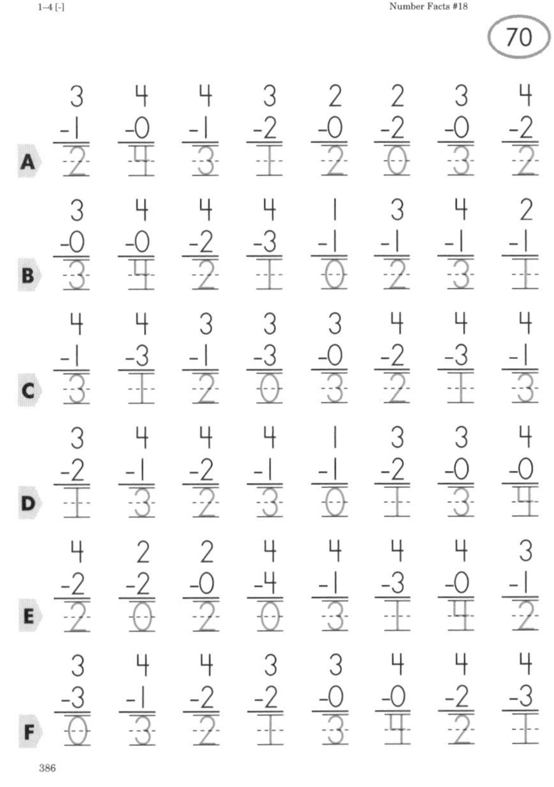

1–4 [-] | Number Facts #18

70

A	3 -1 2	4 -0 4	4 -1 3	3 -2 1	2 -0 2	2 -2 0	3 -0 3	4 -2 2
B	3 -0 3	4 -0 4	4 -2 2	4 -3 1	1 -1 0	3 -1 2	4 -1 3	2 -1 1
C	4 -1 3	4 -3 1	3 -1 2	3 -3 0	3 -0 3	4 -2 2	4 -3 1	4 -1 3
D	3 -2 1	4 -1 3	4 -2 2	4 -1 3	1 -1 0	3 -2 1	3 -0 3	4 -0 4
E	4 -2 2	2 -2 0	2 -0 2	4 -4 0	4 -1 3	4 -3 1	4 -0 4	3 -1 2
F	3 -3 0	4 -1 3	4 -2 2	3 -2 1	3 -0 3	4 -0 4	4 -2 2	4 -3 1

386

2–7 [+] Number Facts #19

70

A	1+1=2	1+6=7	6+1=7	5+2=7
B	2+4=6	5+1=6	2+4=6	3+2=5
C	3+2=5	1+3=4	3+2=5	6+1=7
D	4+3=7	4+1=5	3+3=6	2+5=7
E	2+4=6	4+3=7	1+2=3	4+3=7
F	5+2=7	6+1=7	3+3=6	2+3=5
G	2+3=5	2+4=6	5+2=7	3+3=6
H	4+2=6	3+4=7	6+1=7	5+2=7
I	2+2=4	6+1=7	4+2=6	3+4=7
J	4+3=7	2+4=6	4+3=7	5+1=6
K	5+1=6	3+2=5	3+3=6	3+2=5
L	2+5=7	4+2=6	5+1=6	2+1=3
M	3+4=7	3+1=4	4+3=7	2+4=6
N	1+5=6	5+2=7	1+5=6	5+2=7
O	4+1=5	3+3=6	3+4=7	4+1=5
P	5+1=6	5+2=7	1+4=5	3+4=7

387

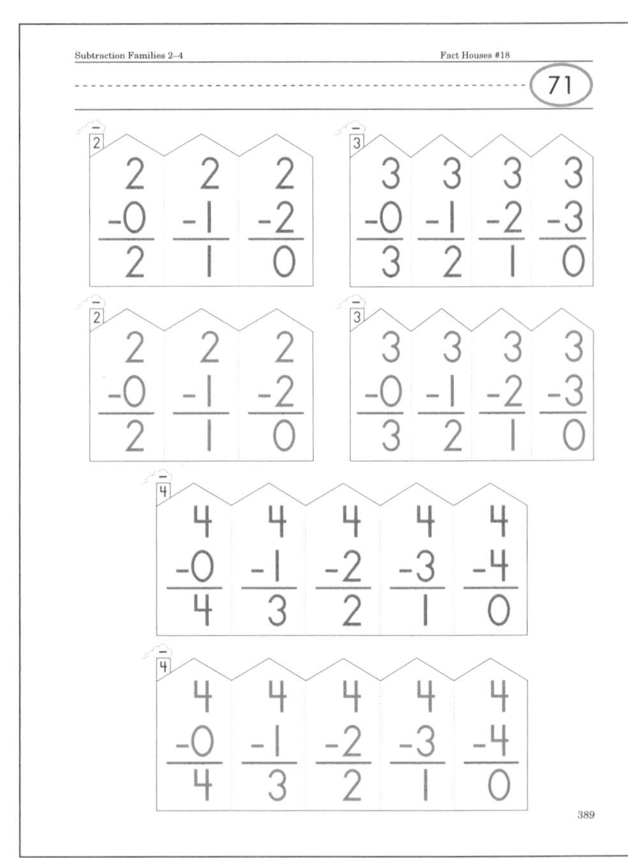
Subtraction Families 2–4 Fact Houses #18

71

2	2	2
-0	-1	-2
2	1	0

3	3	3	3
-0	-1	-2	-3
3	2	1	0

2	2	2
-0	-1	-2
2	1	0

3	3	3	3
-0	-1	-2	-3
3	2	1	0

4	4	4	4	4
-0	-1	-2	-3	-4
4	3	2	1	0

4	4	4	4	4
-0	-1	-2	-3	-4
4	3	2	1	0

389

By 5's Skip Counting #2

71

Count by 5's 5 10 15 20
25 30 35 40 45 50
55 60 65 70 75 80
85 90 95 100

Count by 5's 5 10 15 20
25 30 35 40 45 50
55 60 65 70 75 80
85 90 95 100

390

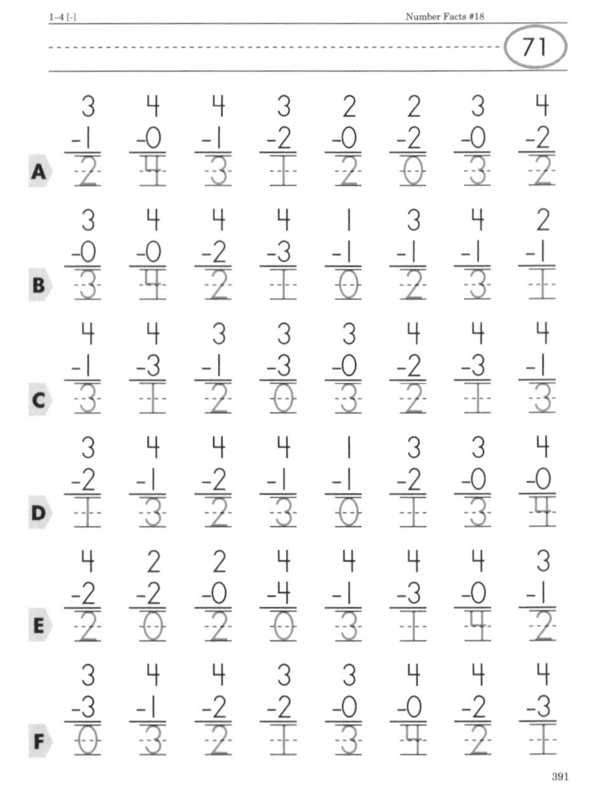
1–4 [-] Number Facts #18

71

A	3-1=2	4-0=4	4-1=3	3-2=1	2-0=2	2-2=0	3-0=3	4-2=2
B	3-0=3	4-0=4	4-2=2	4-3=1	1-1=0	3-1=2	4-1=3	2-1=1
C	4-1=3	4-3=1	3-1=2	3-3=0	3-0=3	4-2=2	4-3=1	4-1=3
D	3-2=1	4-1=3	4-2=2	4-1=3	1-1=0	3-2=1	3-0=3	4-0=4
E	4-2=2	2-2=0	2-0=2	4-4=0	4-1=3	4-3=1	4-0=4	3-1=2
F	3-3=0	4-1=3	4-2=2	3-2=1	3-0=3	4-0=4	4-2=2	4-3=1

391

2-7 [+] Number Facts #19

71

A	1+1=2	1+6=7	6+1=7	5+2=7
B	2+4=6	5+1=6	2+4=6	3+2=5
C	3+2=5	1+3=4	3+2=5	6+1=7
D	4+3=7	4+1=5	3+3=6	2+5=7
E	2+4=6	4+3=7	1+2=3	4+3=7
F	5+2=7	6+1=7	3+3=6	2+3=5
G	2+3=5	2+4=6	5+2=7	3+3=6
H	4+2=6	3+4=7	6+1=7	5+2=7
I	2+2=4	6+1=7	4+2=6	3+4=7
J	4+3=7	2+4=6	4+3=7	5+1=6
K	5+1=6	3+2=5	3+3=6	3+2=5
L	2+5=7	4+2=6	5+1=6	2+1=3
M	1+5=6	3+1=4	4+3=7	2+4=6
N	3+4=7	5+2=7	1+5=6	5+2=7
O	4+1=5	3+3=6	3+4=7	4+1=5
P	5+1=6	5+2=7	1+4=5	3+4=7

392

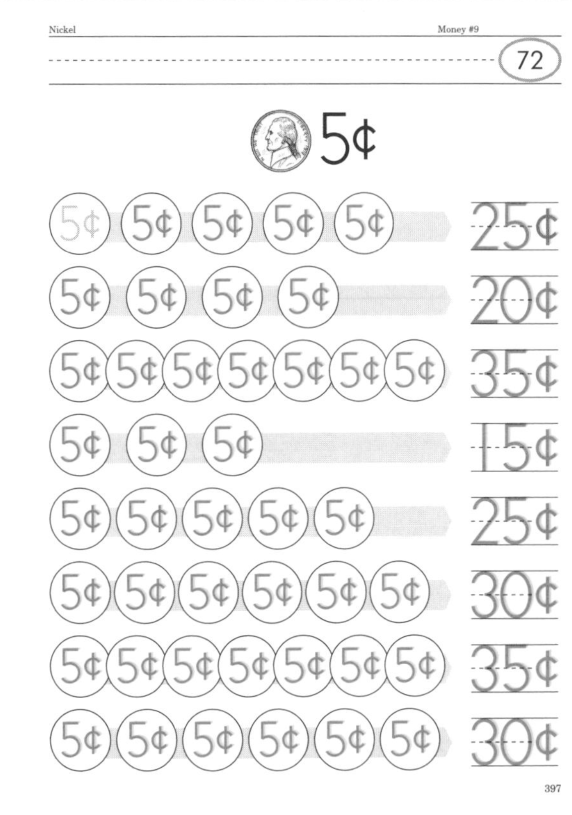

Hour Clocks #1

72

2:00	6:00	9:00	4:00
12:00	10:00	1:00	5:00
7:00	12:00	9:00	6:00
11:00	8:00	3:00	5:00

398

1–4 [-] Number Facts #18

72

A	3 -1 = 2	4 -0 = 4	4 -1 = 3	3 -2 = 1	2 -0 = 2	2 -2 = 0	3 -0 = 3	4 -2 = 2
B	3 -0 = 3	4 -0 = 4	4 -2 = 2	4 -3 = 1	1 -1 = 0	3 -1 = 2	4 -1 = 3	2 -1 = 1
C	4 -1 = 3	4 -3 = 1	3 -1 = 2	3 -3 = 0	3 -0 = 3	4 -2 = 2	4 -3 = 1	4 -1 = 3
D	3 -2 = 1	4 -1 = 3	4 -2 = 2	4 -1 = 3	1 -1 = 0	3 -2 = 1	3 -0 = 3	4 -0 = 4
E	4 -2 = 2	2 -2 = 0	2 -0 = 2	4 -4 = 0	4 -1 = 3	4 -3 = 1	4 -0 = 4	3 -1 = 2
F	3 -3 = 0	4 -1 = 3	4 -2 = 2	3 -2 = 1	3 -0 = 3	4 -0 = 4	4 -2 = 2	4 -3 = 1

399

71–99 Before and After #4

72

87	88	89	80	81	82
92	93	94	97	98	99
90	91	92	85	86	87
95	96	97	83	84	85
77	78	79	76	77	78
81	82	83	96	97	98
86	87	88	71	72	73
94	95	96	93	94	95
82	83	84	91	92	93

400

Subtraction Family 5 Fact Houses #19

73

5	5 -0 = 5	5 -1 = 4	5 -2 = 3	5 -3 = 2	5 -4 = 1	5 -5 = 0
5	5 -0 = 5	5 -1 = 4	5 -2 = 3	5 -3 = 2	5 -4 = 1	5 -5 = 0
5	5 -0 = 5	5 -1 = 4	5 -2 = 3	5 -3 = 2	5 -4 = 1	5 -5 = 0
5	5 -0 = 5	5 -1 = 4	5 -2 = 3	5 -3 = 2	5 -4 = 1	5 -5 = 0

401

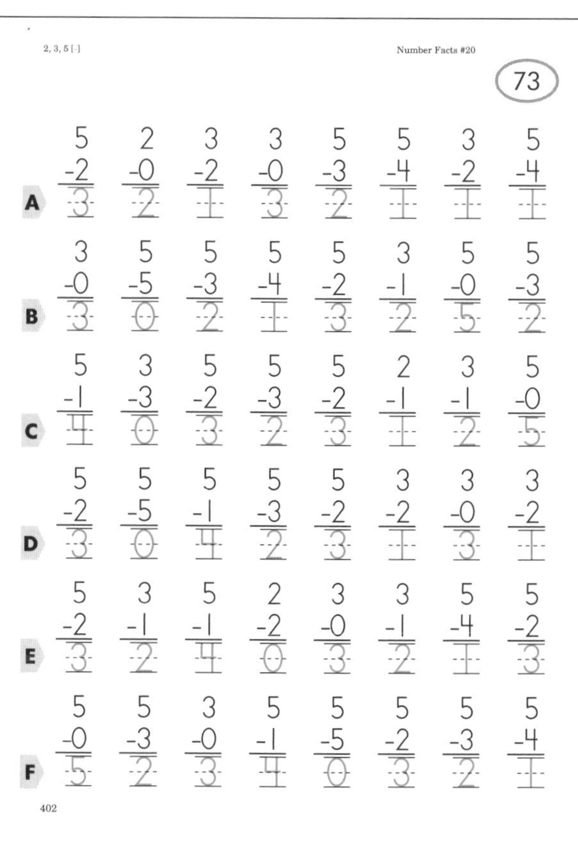

2, 3, 5 [-] Number Facts #20

73

A	5 −2 = 3	2 −0 = 2	3 −2 = 1	3 −0 = 3	5 −3 = 2	5 −4 = 1	3 −2 = 1	5 −4 = 1
B	3 −0 = 3	5 −5 = 0	5 −3 = 2	5 −4 = 1	5 −2 = 3	3 −1 = 2	5 −0 = 5	5 −3 = 2
C	5 −1 = 4	3 −3 = 0	5 −2 = 3	5 −3 = 2	5 −2 = 3	2 −1 = 1	3 −1 = 2	5 −0 = 5
D	5 −2 = 3	5 −5 = 0	5 −1 = 4	5 −3 = 2	5 −2 = 3	3 −2 = 1	3 −0 = 3	3 −2 = 1
E	5 −2 = 3	3 −1 = 2	5 −1 = 4	2 −2 = 0	3 −0 = 3	3 −1 = 2	5 −4 = 1	5 −2 = 3
F	5 −0 = 5	5 −3 = 2	3 −0 = 3	5 −1 = 4	5 −5 = 0	5 −2 = 3	5 −3 = 2	5 −4 = 1

402

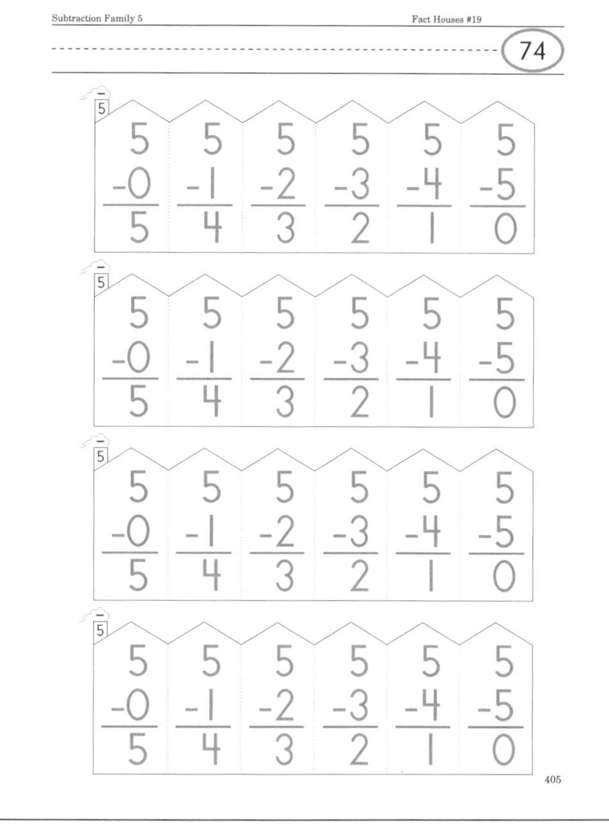

Subtraction Family 5 Fact Houses #19

74

5 −0 = 5	5 −1 = 4	5 −2 = 3	5 −3 = 2	5 −4 = 1	5 −5 = 0
5 −0 = 5	5 −1 = 4	5 −2 = 3	5 −3 = 2	5 −4 = 1	5 −5 = 0
5 −0 = 5	5 −1 = 4	5 −2 = 3	5 −3 = 2	5 −4 = 1	5 −5 = 0
5 −0 = 5	5 −1 = 4	5 −2 = 3	5 −3 = 2	5 −4 = 1	5 −5 = 0

405

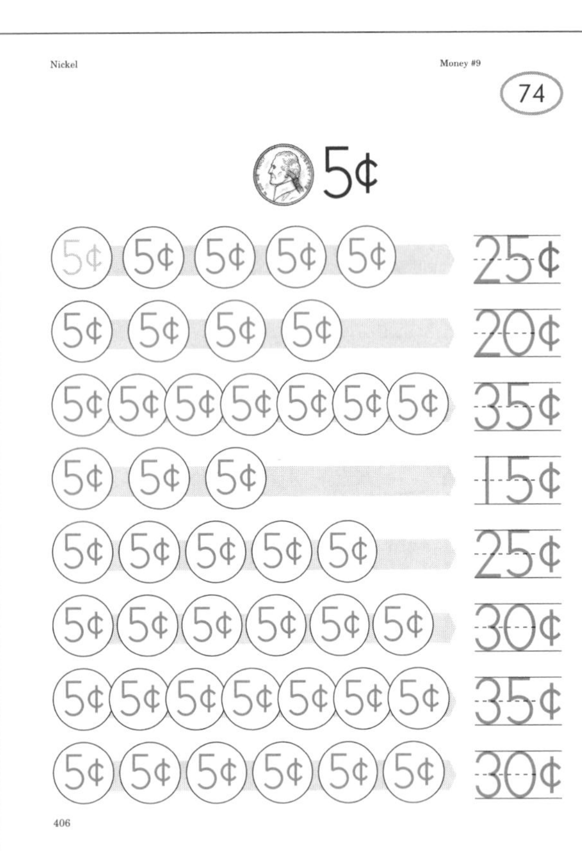

2, 3, 5 [-] Number Facts #20

74

A	5 -2 = 3	2 -0 = 2	3 -2 = 1	3 -0 = 3	5 -3 = 2	5 -4 = 1	3 -2 = 1	5 -4 = 1
B	3 -0 = 3	5 -5 = 0	5 -3 = 2	5 -4 = 1	5 -2 = 3	3 -1 = 2	5 -0 = 5	5 -3 = 2
C	5 -1 = 4	3 -3 = 0	5 -2 = 3	5 -3 = 2	5 -2 = 3	2 -1 = 1	3 -1 = 2	5 -0 = 5
D	5 -2 = 3	5 -5 = 0	5 -1 = 4	5 -3 = 2	5 -2 = 3	3 -2 = 1	3 -0 = 3	3 -2 = 1
E	5 -2 = 3	3 -1 = 2	5 -1 = 4	2 -2 = 0	3 -0 = 3	3 -1 = 2	5 -4 = 1	5 -2 = 3
F	5 -0 = 5	5 -3 = 2	3 -0 = 3	5 -1 = 4	5 -5 = 0	5 -2 = 3	5 -3 = 2	5 -4 = 1

407

101–120 Writing Practice #22

74

101	101	111	111
102	102	112	112
103	103	113	113
104	104	114	114
105	105	115	115
106	106	116	116
107	107	117	117
108	108	118	118
109	109	119	119
110	110	120	120

408

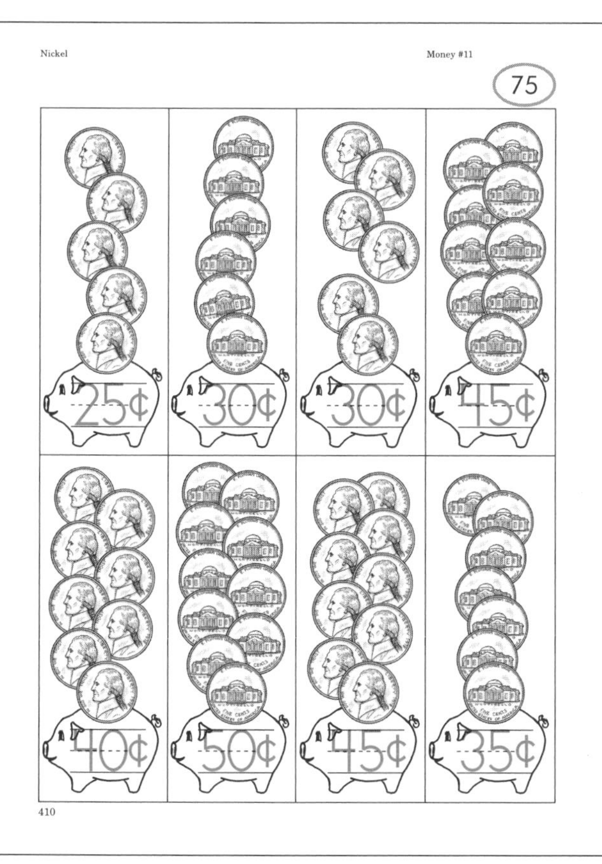

2–7 [+] Number Facts #19

75

A	1+1=2	1+6=7	6+1=7	5+2=7
B	2+4=6	5+1=6	2+4=6	3+2=5
C	3+2=5	1+3=4	3+2=5	6+1=7
D	4+3=7	4+1=5	3+3=6	2+5=7
E	2+4=6	4+3=7	1+2=3	4+3=7
F	5+2=7	6+1=7	3+3=6	2+3=5
G	2+3=5	2+4=6	5+2=7	3+3=6
H	4+2=6	3+4=7	6+1=7	5+2=7
I	2+2=4	6+1=7	4+2=6	3+4=7
J	4+3=7	2+4=6	4+3=7	5+1=6
K	5+1=6	3+2=5	3+3=6	3+2=5
L	2+5=7	4+2=6	5+1=6	2+1=3
M	3+4=7	3+1=4	4+3=7	2+4=6
N	1+5=6	5+2=7	1+5=6	5+2=7
O	4+1=5	3+3=6	3+4=7	4+1=5
P	5+1=6	5+2=7	1+4=5	3+4=7

411

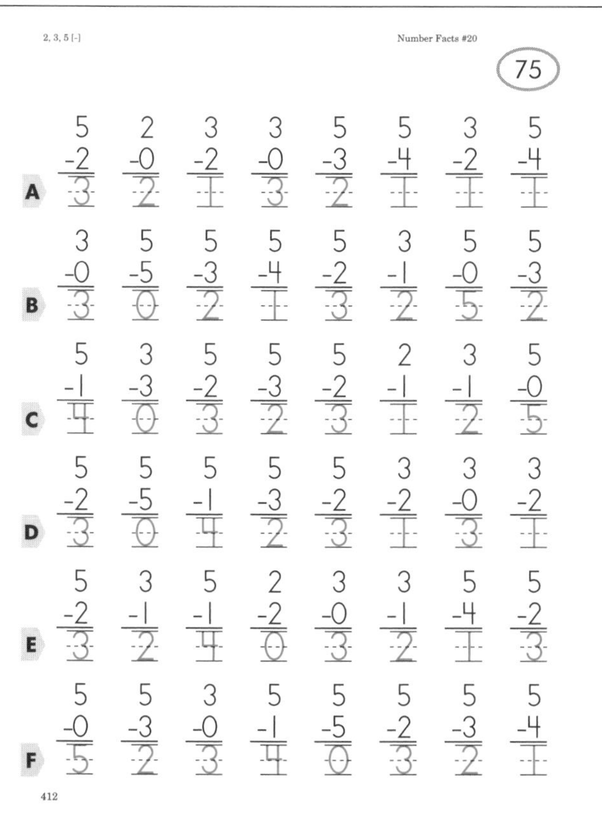
2, 3, 5 [-] Number Facts #20

75

A	5 -2 3	2 -0 2	3 -2 1	3 -0 3	5 -3 2	5 -4 1	3 -2 1	5 -4 1
B	3 -0 3	5 -5 0	5 -3 2	5 -4 1	5 -2 3	3 -1 2	5 -0 5	5 -3 2
C	5 -1 4	3 -3 0	5 -2 3	5 -3 2	5 -2 3	2 -1 1	3 -1 2	5 -0 5
D	5 -2 3	5 -5 0	5 -1 4	5 -3 2	5 -2 3	3 -2 1	3 -0 3	3 -2 1
E	5 -2 3	3 -1 2	5 -1 4	2 -2 0	3 -0 3	3 -1 2	5 -4 1	5 -2 3
F	5 -0 5	5 -3 2	3 -0 3	5 -1 4	5 -5 0	5 -2 3	5 -3 2	5 -4 1

412

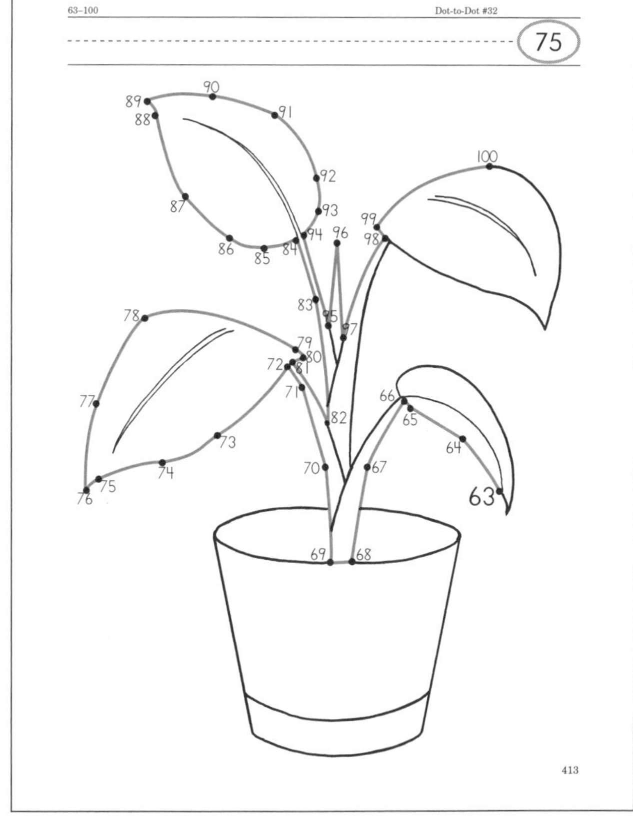

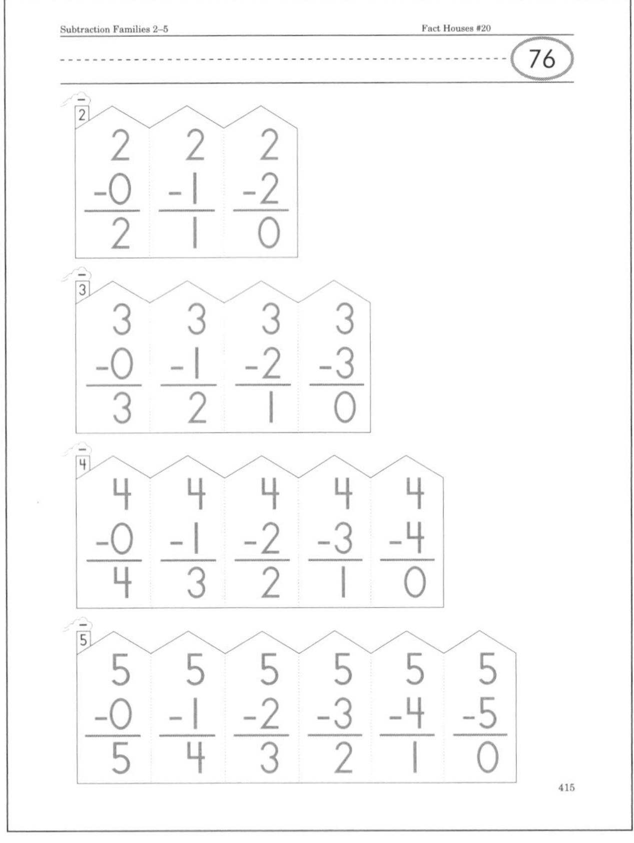
Subtraction Families 2–5
Fact Houses #20
76
415

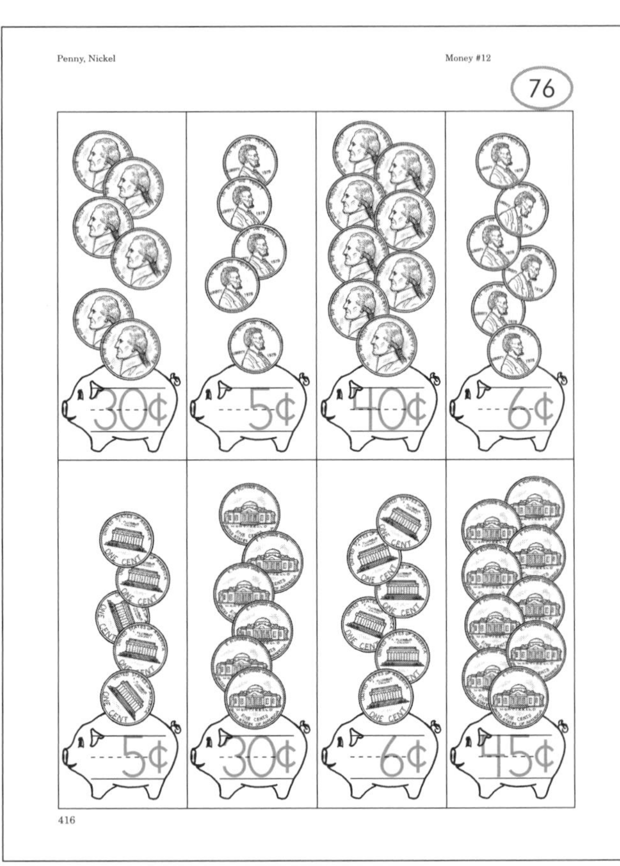
Penny, Nickel
Money #12
76
30¢
5¢
40¢
6¢
5¢
30¢
6¢
45¢
416

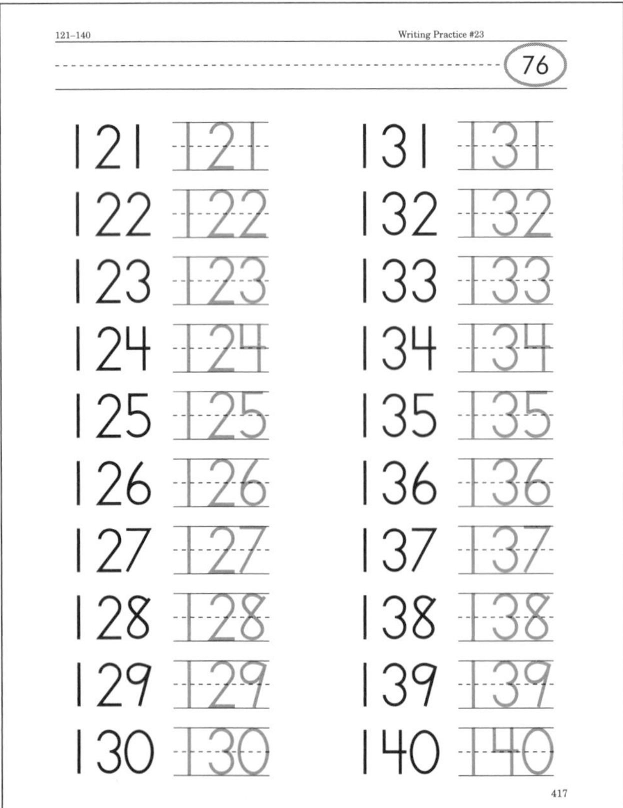
121–140
Writing Practice #23
76
417

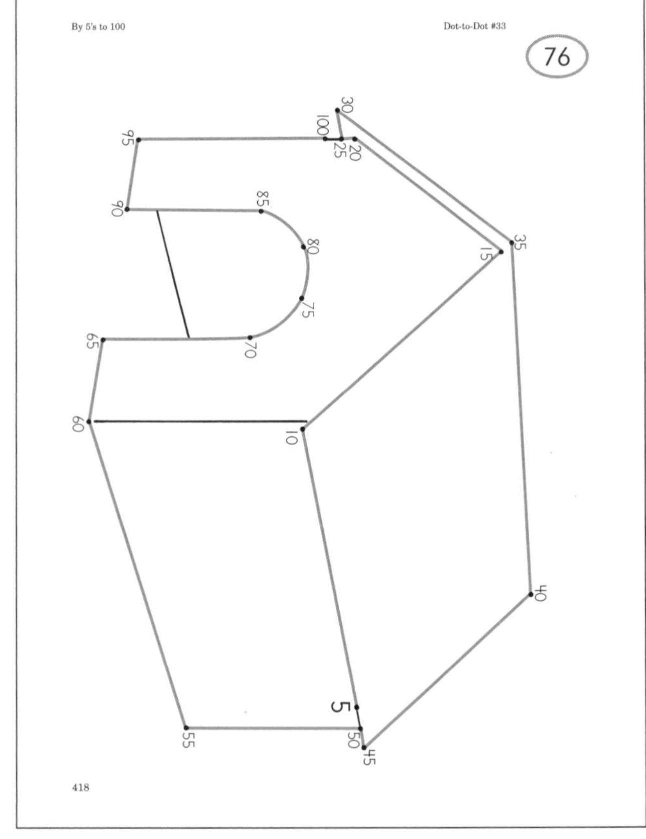
By 5's to 100
Dot-to-Dot #33
76
418

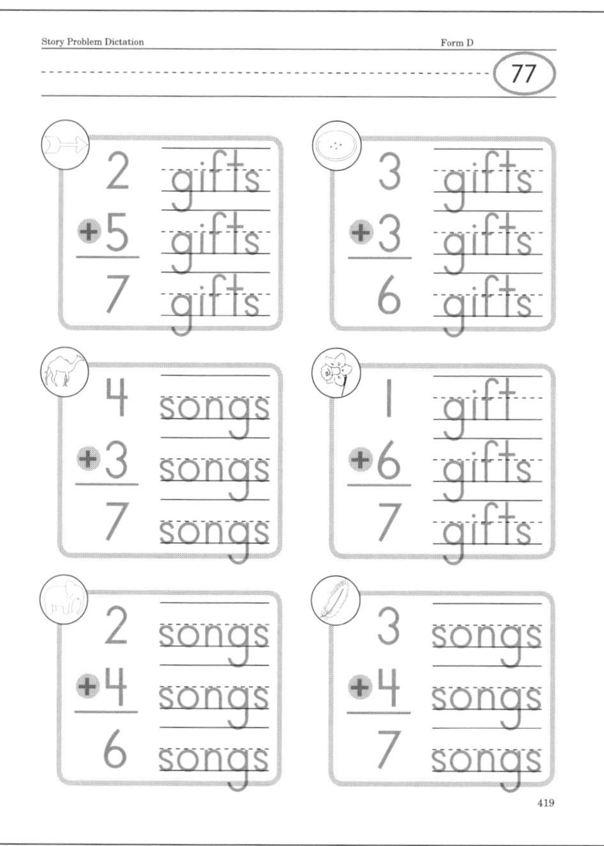
Story Problem Dictation — Form D — 77

2 gifts +5 gifts 7 gifts	3 gifts +3 gifts 6 gifts
4 songs +3 songs 7 songs	1 gift +6 gifts 7 gifts
2 songs +4 songs 6 songs	3 songs +4 songs 7 songs

419

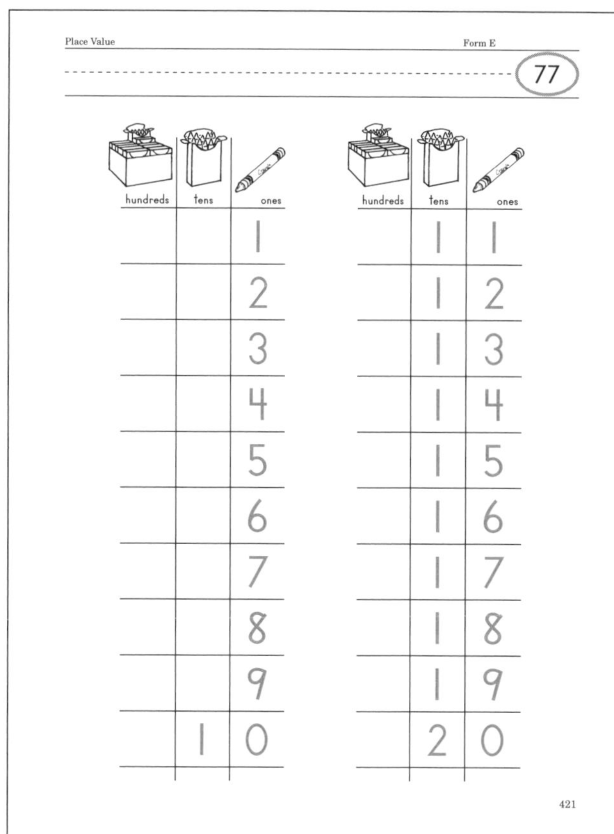
Place Value — Form E — 77

hundreds	tens	ones
		1
		2
		3
		4
		5
		6
		7
		8
		9
	1	0

hundreds	tens	ones
	1	1
	1	2
	1	3
	1	4
	1	5
	1	6
	1	7
	1	8
	1	9
	2	0

421

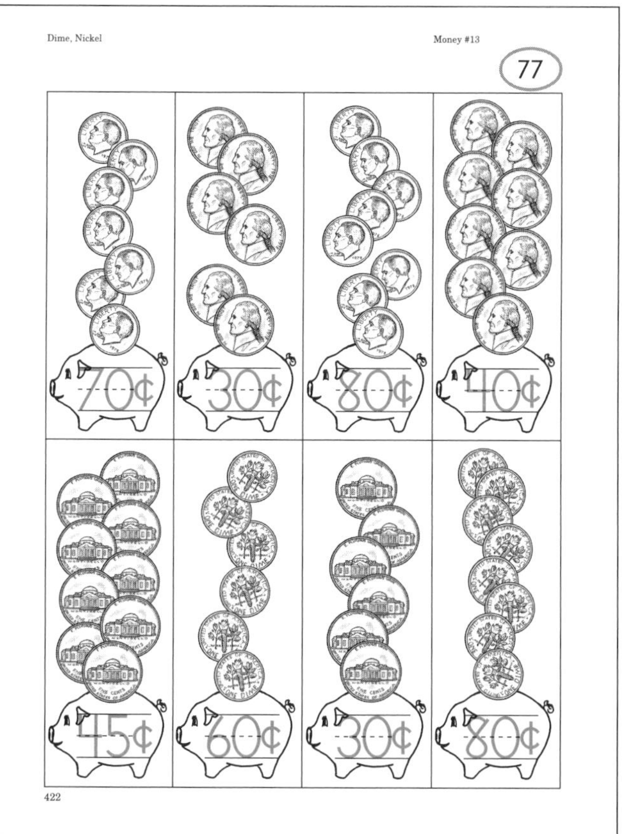
Dime, Nickel — Money #13 — 77

70¢	30¢	80¢	40¢
45¢	60¢	30¢	80¢

422

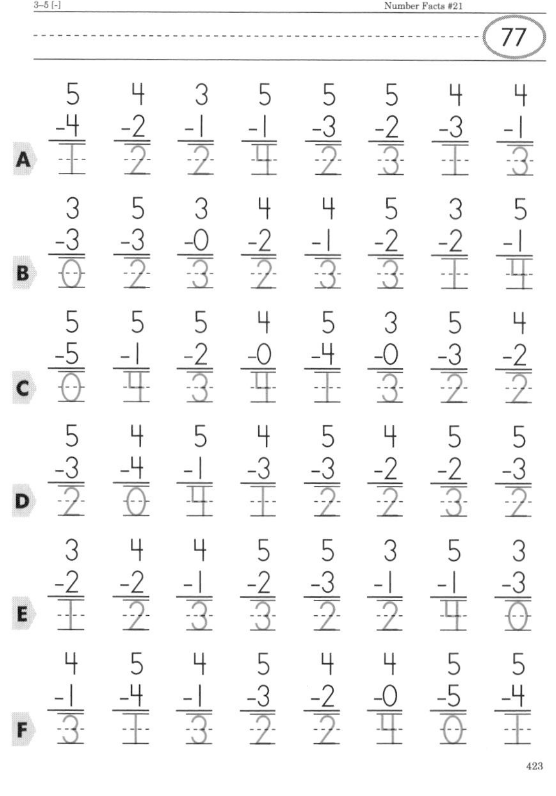
3–5 [-] — Number Facts #21 — 77

A	5 -4 = 1	4 -2 = 2	3 -1 = 2	5 -1 = 4	5 -3 = 2	5 -2 = 3	4 -3 = 1	4 -1 = 3
B	3 -3 = 0	5 -3 = 2	3 -0 = 3	4 -2 = 2	4 -1 = 3	5 -2 = 3	3 -2 = 1	5 -1 = 4
C	5 -5 = 0	5 -1 = 4	5 -2 = 3	4 -0 = 4	5 -4 = 1	3 -0 = 3	5 -3 = 2	4 -2 = 2
D	5 -3 = 2	4 -4 = 0	5 -1 = 4	4 -3 = 1	5 -3 = 2	4 -2 = 2	5 -2 = 3	5 -3 = 2
E	3 -2 = 1	4 -2 = 2	4 -1 = 3	5 -2 = 3	5 -3 = 2	3 -1 = 2	5 -1 = 4	3 -3 = 0
F	4 -1 = 3	5 -4 = 1	4 -1 = 3	5 -3 = 2	4 -2 = 2	4 -0 = 4	5 -5 = 0	5 -4 = 1

423

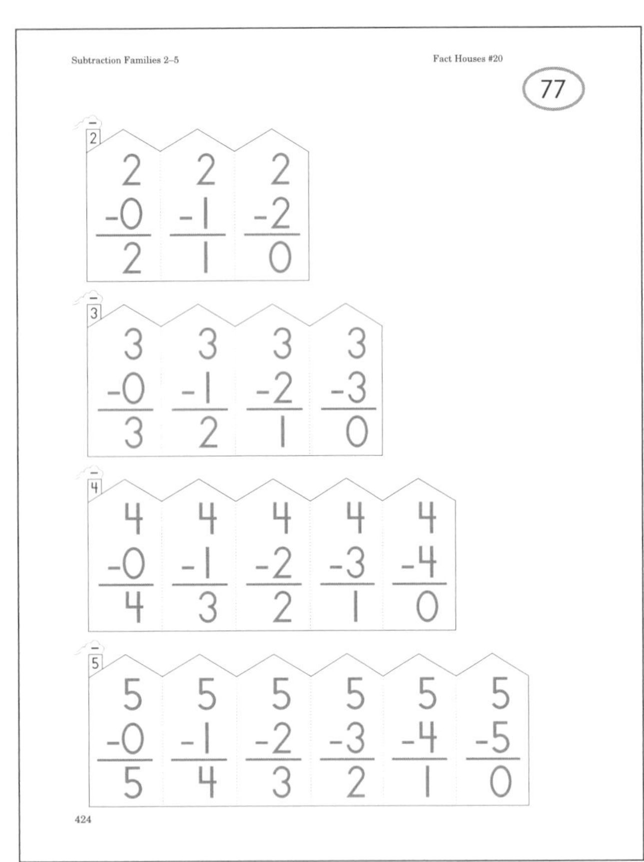
Subtraction Families 2–5 Fact Houses #20

77

2	2	2
-0	-1	-2
2	1	0

3	3	3	3
-0	-1	-2	-3
3	2	1	0

4	4	4	4	4
-0	-1	-2	-3	-4
4	3	2	1	0

5	5	5	5	5	5
-0	-1	-2	-3	-4	-5
5	4	3	2	1	0

424

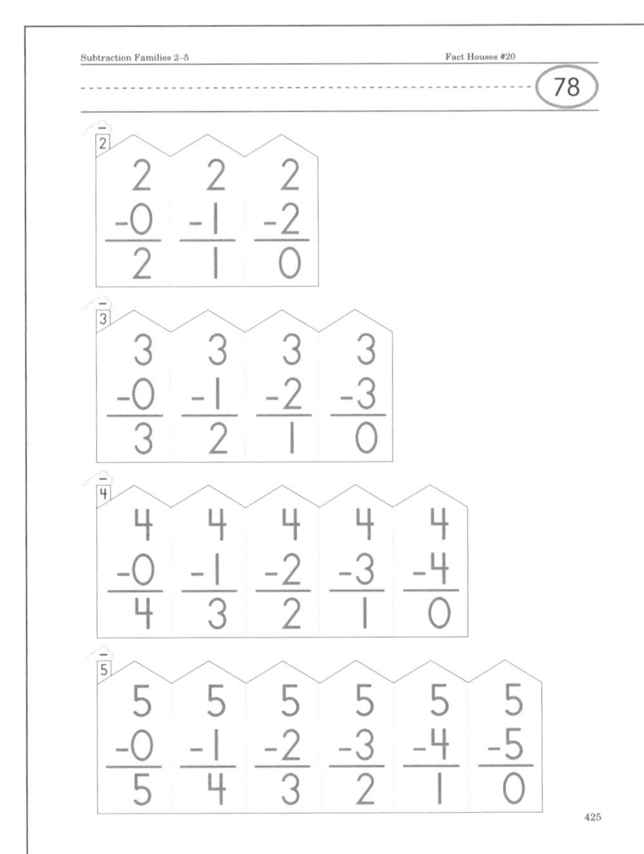
Subtraction Families 2–5 Fact Houses #20

78

2	2	2
-0	-1	-2
2	1	0

3	3	3	3
-0	-1	-2	-3
3	2	1	0

4	4	4	4	4
-0	-1	-2	-3	-4
4	3	2	1	0

5	5	5	5	5	5
-0	-1	-2	-3	-4	-5
5	4	3	2	1	0

425

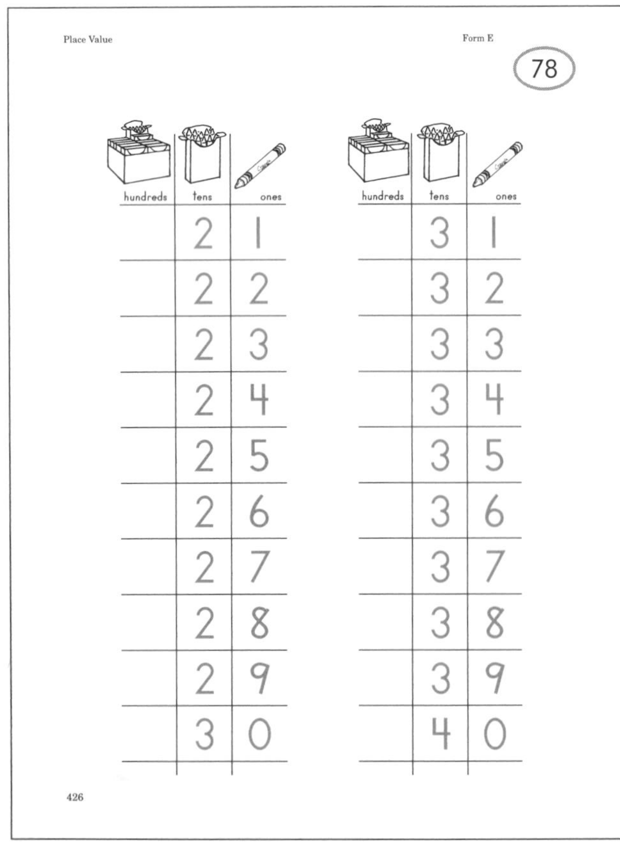
Place Value Form E

78

hundreds	tens	ones
	2	1
	2	2
	2	3
	2	4
	2	5
	2	6
	2	7
	2	8
	2	9
	3	0

hundreds	tens	ones
	3	1
	3	2
	3	3
	3	4
	3	5
	3	6
	3	7
	3	8
	3	9
	4	0

426

Place Value #1

78

	hundreds	tens	ones
127	1	2	7
100	1	0	0
132	1	3	2
84		8	4
134	1	3	4

	hundreds	tens	ones
139	1	3	9
115	1	1	5
138	1	3	8
130	1	3	0
129	1	2	9

	hundreds	tens	ones
20		2	0
105	1	0	5
132	1	3	2
84		8	4
103	1	0	3

	hundreds	tens	ones
109	1	0	9
4			4
107	1	0	7
116	1	1	6
24		2	4

427

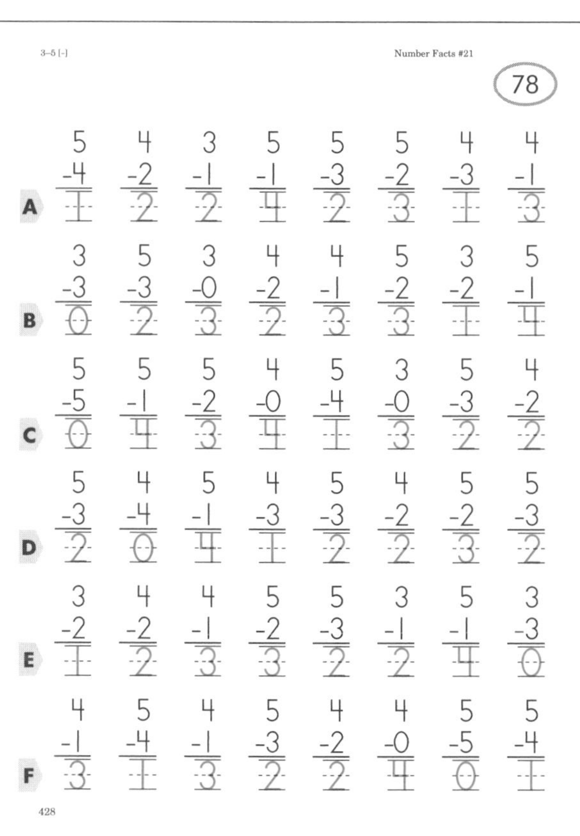

3–5 [-] Number Facts #21

78

A	5 -4 1	4 -2 2	3 -1 2	5 -1 4	5 -3 2	5 -2 3	4 -3 1	4 -1 3
B	3 -3 0	5 -3 2	3 -0 3	4 -2 2	4 -1 3	5 -2 3	3 -2 1	5 -1 4
C	5 -5 0	5 -1 4	5 -2 3	4 -0 4	5 -4 1	3 -0 3	5 -3 2	4 -2 2
D	5 -3 2	4 -4 0	5 -1 4	4 -3 1	5 -3 2	4 -2 2	5 -2 3	5 -3 2
E	3 -2 1	4 -2 2	4 -1 3	5 -2 3	5 -3 2	3 -1 2	5 -1 4	3 -3 0
F	4 -1 3	5 -4 1	4 -1 3	5 -3 2	4 -2 2	4 -0 4	5 -5 0	5 -4 1

428

Nickel Money #10

78

5¢ 5¢

429

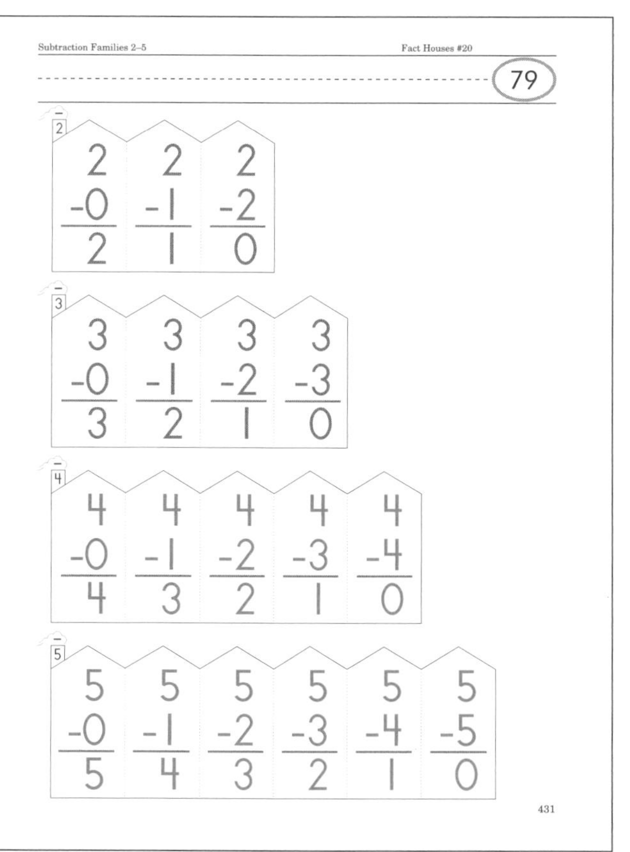

Subtraction Families 2–5 Fact Houses #20

79

2

2 -0 2	2 -1 1	2 -2 0

3

3 -0 3	3 -1 2	3 -2 1	3 -3 0

4

4 -0 4	4 -1 3	4 -2 2	4 -3 1	4 -4 0

5

5 -0 5	5 -1 4	5 -2 3	5 -3 2	5 -4 1	5 -5 0

431

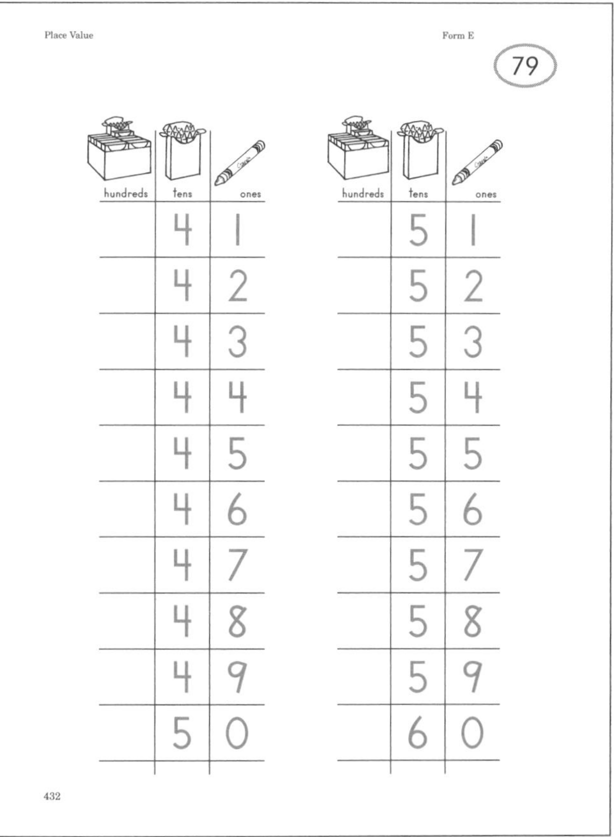

Place Value Form E

79

hundreds	tens	ones
	4	1
	4	2
	4	3
	4	4
	4	5
	4	6
	4	7
	4	8
	4	9
	5	0

hundreds	tens	ones
	5	1
	5	2
	5	3
	5	4
	5	5
	5	6
	5	7
	5	8
	5	9
	6	0

432

2–7 [+] Number Facts #22

79

A	2+5=7	4+3=7	4+1=5	5+1=6
B	1+6=7	3+2=5	5+2=7	2+5=7
C	1+4=5	3+4=7	1+2=3	4+2=6
D	2+5=7	1+5=6	1+4=5	2+5=7
E	4+3=7	2+3=5	5+2=7	4+3=7
F	1+5=6	2+1=3	3+4=7	1+3=4
G	2+4=6	4+2=6	2+2=4	4+1=5
H	3+2=5	1+6=7	2+3=5	4+2=6
I	2+5=7	3+3=6	5+1=6	1+6=7
J	4+2=6	2+5=7	1+6=7	1+1=2
K	3+3=6	1+6=7	3+4=7	3+3=6
L	3+4=7	1+3=4	2+3=5	3+4=7
M	2+5=7	1+4=5	3+4=7	1+5=6
N	2+2=4	2+4=6	3+3=6	1+6=7
O	3+2=5	6+1=7	3+2=5	2+4=6
P	2+5=7	4+2=6	3+4=7	4+3=7

3–5 [-] Number Facts #21

79

A	5 -4 = 1	4 -2 = 2	3 -1 = 2	5 -1 = 4	5 -3 = 2	5 -2 = 3	4 -3 = 1	4 -1 = 3
B	3 -3 = 0	5 -3 = 2	3 -0 = 3	4 -2 = 2	4 -1 = 3	5 -2 = 3	3 -2 = 1	5 -1 = 4
C	5 -5 = 0	5 -1 = 4	5 -2 = 3	4 -0 = 4	5 -4 = 1	3 -0 = 3	5 -3 = 2	4 -2 = 2
D	5 -3 = 2	4 -4 = 0	5 -1 = 4	4 -3 = 1	5 -3 = 2	4 -2 = 2	5 -2 = 3	5 -3 = 2
E	3 -2 = 1	4 -2 = 2	4 -1 = 3	5 -2 = 3	5 -3 = 2	3 -1 = 2	5 -1 = 4	3 -3 = 0
F	4 -1 = 3	5 -4 = 1	4 -1 = 3	5 -3 = 2	4 -2 = 2	4 -0 = 4	5 -5 = 0	5 -4 = 1

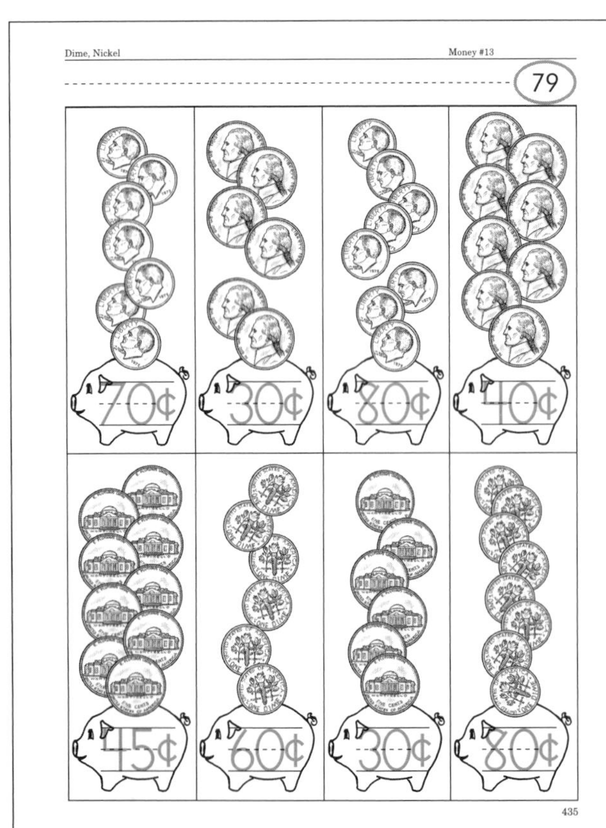
Dime, Nickel Money #13

79

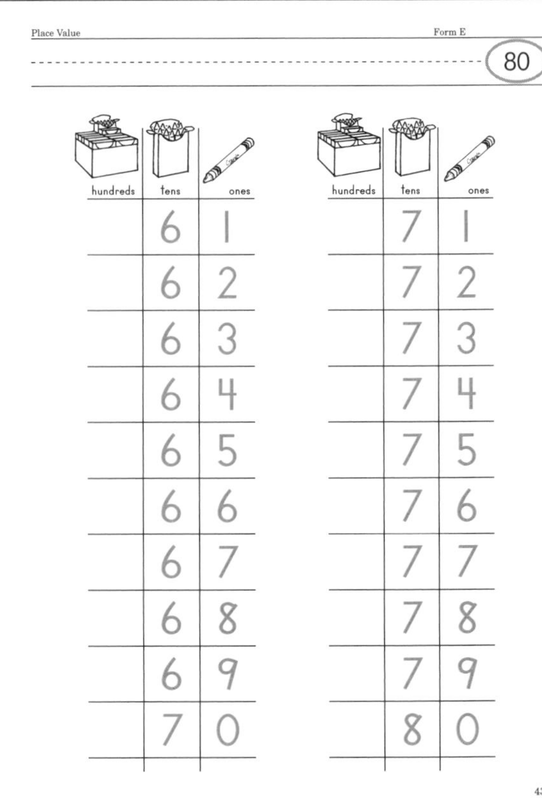
Place Value Form E

80

hundreds	tens	ones
	6	1
	6	2
	6	3
	6	4
	6	5
	6	6
	6	7
	6	8
	6	9
	7	0

hundreds	tens	ones
	7	1
	7	2
	7	3
	7	4
	7	5
	7	6
	7	7
	7	8
	7	9
	8	0

Place Value #2

80

	hundreds	tens	ones
130	1	3	0
145	1	4	5
152	1	5	2
8			8
126	1	2	6

	hundreds	tens	ones
159	1	5	9
108	1	0	8
145	1	4	5
92		9	2
124	1	2	4

	hundreds	tens	ones
79		7	9
125	1	2	5
102	1	0	2
23		2	3
126	1	2	6

	hundreds	tens	ones
7			7
126	1	2	6
157	1	5	7
36		3	6
144	1	4	4

438

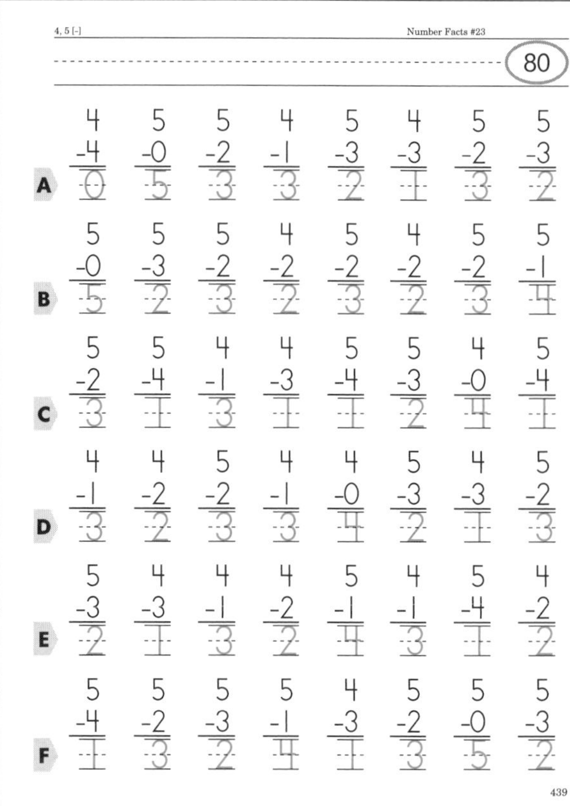

4, 5 [-] Number Facts #23

80

A	4 − 4 = 0	5 − 0 = 5	5 − 2 = 3	4 − 1 = 3	5 − 3 = 2	4 − 3 = 1	5 − 2 = 3	5 − 3 = 2
B	5 − 0 = 5	5 − 3 = 2	5 − 2 = 3	4 − 2 = 2	5 − 2 = 3	4 − 2 = 2	5 − 2 = 3	5 − 1 = 4
C	5 − 2 = 3	5 − 4 = 1	4 − 1 = 3	4 − 3 = 1	5 − 4 = 1	5 − 3 = 2	4 − 0 = 4	5 − 4 = 1
D	4 − 1 = 3	4 − 2 = 2	5 − 2 = 3	4 − 1 = 3	4 − 0 = 4	5 − 3 = 2	4 − 3 = 1	5 − 2 = 3
E	5 − 3 = 2	4 − 3 = 1	4 − 1 = 3	4 − 2 = 2	5 − 1 = 4	4 − 1 = 3	5 − 4 = 1	4 − 2 = 2
F	5 − 4 = 1	5 − 2 = 3	5 − 3 = 2	5 − 1 = 4	4 − 3 = 1	5 − 2 = 3	5 − 0 = 5	5 − 3 = 2

439

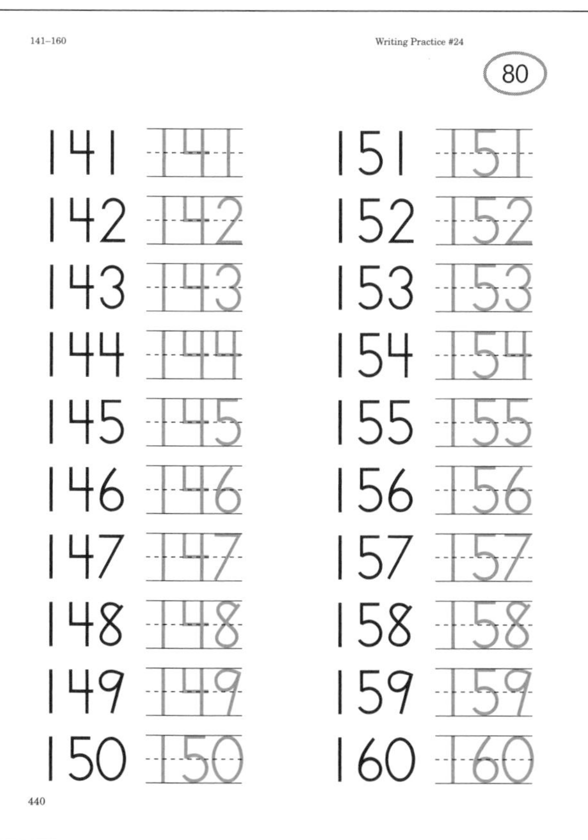

141–160 Writing Practice #24

80

141	141	151	151
142	142	152	152
143	143	153	153
144	144	154	154
145	145	155	155
146	146	156	156
147	147	157	157
148	148	158	158
149	149	159	159
150	150	160	160

440

Number Dictation Form B

81

1	2	3
124	108	152
105	112	129
136	103	140
155	119	106
147	131	120

441

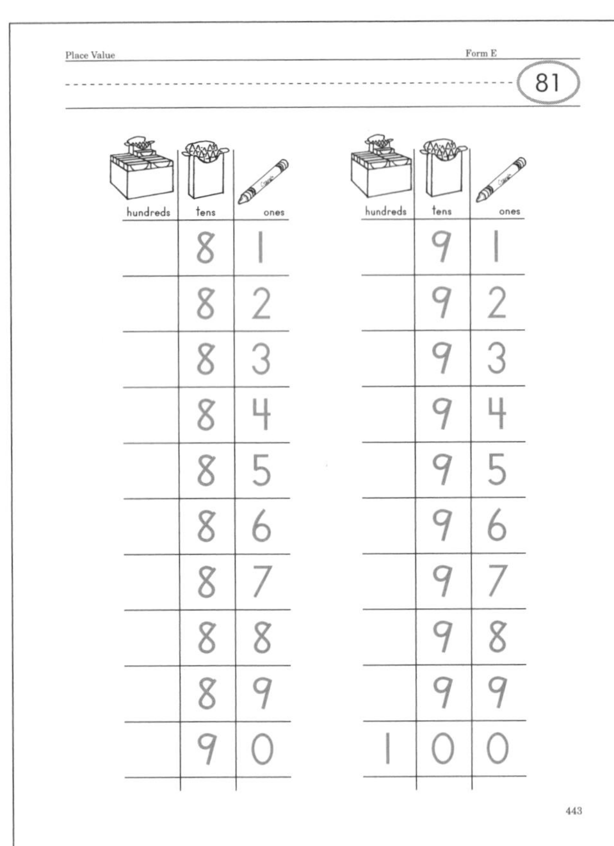

Place Value — Form E — 81

hundreds	tens	ones
	8	1
	8	2
	8	3
	8	4
	8	5
	8	6
	8	7
	8	8
	8	9
	9	0

hundreds	tens	ones
	9	1
	9	2
	9	3
	9	4
	9	5
	9	6
	9	7
	9	8
	9	9
1	0	0

443

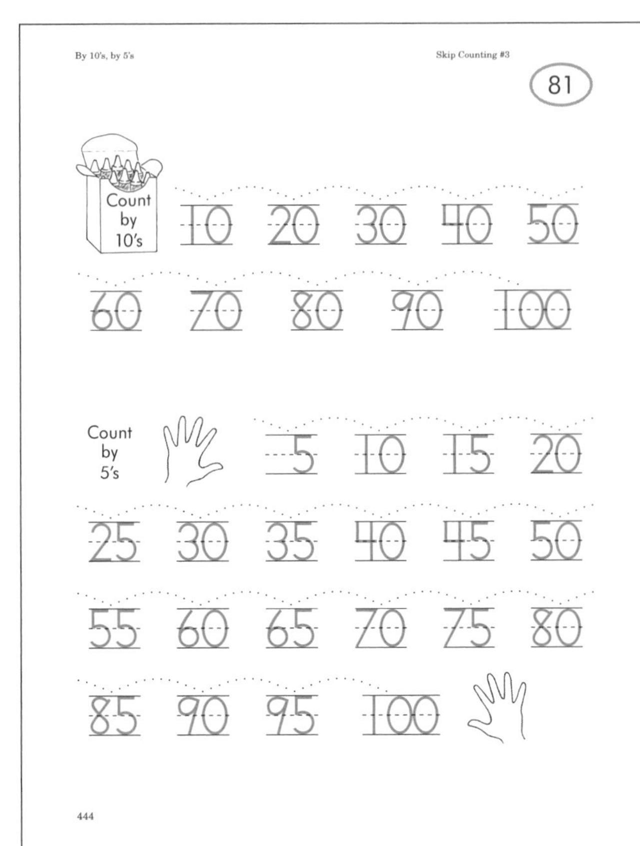

By 10's, by 5's — Skip Counting #3 — 81

Count by 10's

10 20 30 40 50

60 70 80 90 100

Count by 5's

5 10 15 20

25 30 35 40 45 50

55 60 65 70 75 80

85 90 95 100

444

2–7 [+] — Number Facts #22 — 81

A	2+5=7	4+3=7	4+1=5	5+1=6
B	1+6=7	3+2=5	5+2=7	2+5=7
C	1+4=5	3+4=7	1+2=3	4+2=6
D	2+5=7	1+5=6	1+4=5	2+5=7
E	4+3=7	2+3=5	5+2=7	4+3=7
F	1+5=6	2+1=3	3+4=7	1+3=4
G	2+4=6	4+2=6	2+2=4	4+1=5
H	3+2=5	1+6=7	2+3=5	4+2=6
I	2+5=7	3+3=6	5+1=6	1+6=7
J	4+2=6	2+5=7	1+6=7	1+1=2
K	3+3=6	1+6=7	3+4=7	3+3=6
L	3+4=7	1+3=4	2+3=5	3+4=7
M	2+5=7	1+4=5	3+4=7	1+5=6
N	2+2=4	2+4=6	3+3=6	1+6=7
O	3+2=5	6+1=7	3+2=5	2+4=6
P	2+5=7	4+2=6	3+4=7	4+3=7

445

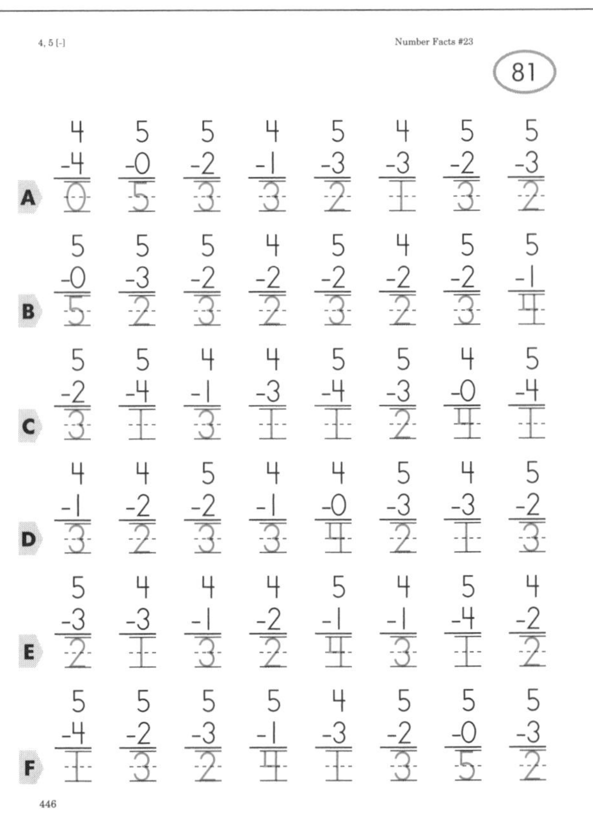

4, 5 [-] — Number Facts #23 — 81

A	4-4=0	5-0=5	5-2=3	4-1=3	5-3=2	4-3=1	5-2=3	5-3=2
B	5-0=5	5-3=2	5-2=3	4-2=2	5-2=3	4-2=2	5-2=3	5-1=4
C	5-2=3	5-4=1	4-1=3	4-3=1	5-4=1	5-3=2	4-0=4	5-4=1
D	4-1=3	4-2=2	5-2=3	4-1=3	4-0=4	5-3=2	4-3=1	5-2=3
E	5-3=2	4-3=1	4-1=3	4-2=2	5-1=4	4-1=3	5-4=1	4-2=2
F	5-4=1	5-2=3	5-3=2	5-1=4	4-3=1	5-2=3	5-0=5	5-3=2

446

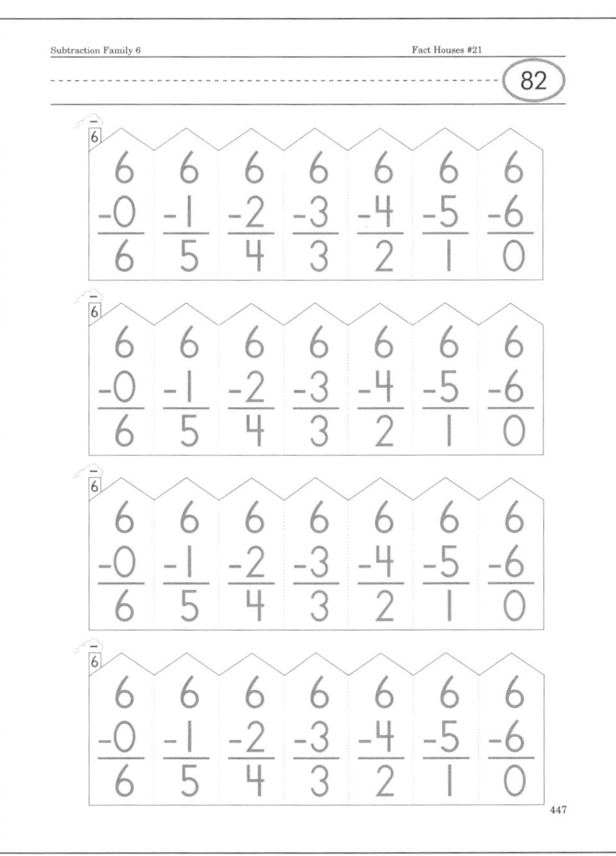
Subtraction Family 6 Fact Houses #21

82

6	6	6	6	6	6	6
-0	-1	-2	-3	-4	-5	-6
6	5	4	3	2	1	0

6	6	6	6	6	6	6
-0	-1	-2	-3	-4	-5	-6
6	5	4	3	2	1	0

6	6	6	6	6	6	6
-0	-1	-2	-3	-4	-5	-6
6	5	4	3	2	1	0

6	6	6	6	6	6	6
-0	-1	-2	-3	-4	-5	-6
6	5	4	3	2	1	0

447

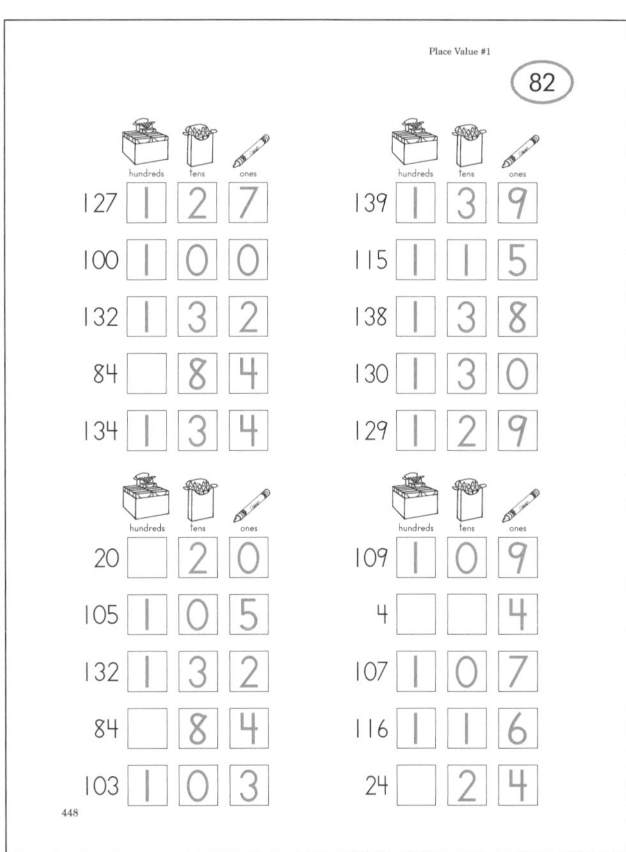
Place Value #1

82

	hundreds	tens	ones
127	1	2	7
100	1	0	0
132	1	3	2
84		8	4
134	1	3	4

	hundreds	tens	ones
139	1	3	9
115	1	1	5
138	1	3	8
130	1	3	0
129	1	2	9

	hundreds	tens	ones
20		2	0
105	1	0	5
132	1	3	2
84		8	4
103	1	0	3

	hundreds	tens	ones
109	1	0	9
4			4
107	1	0	7
116	1	1	6
24		2	4

448

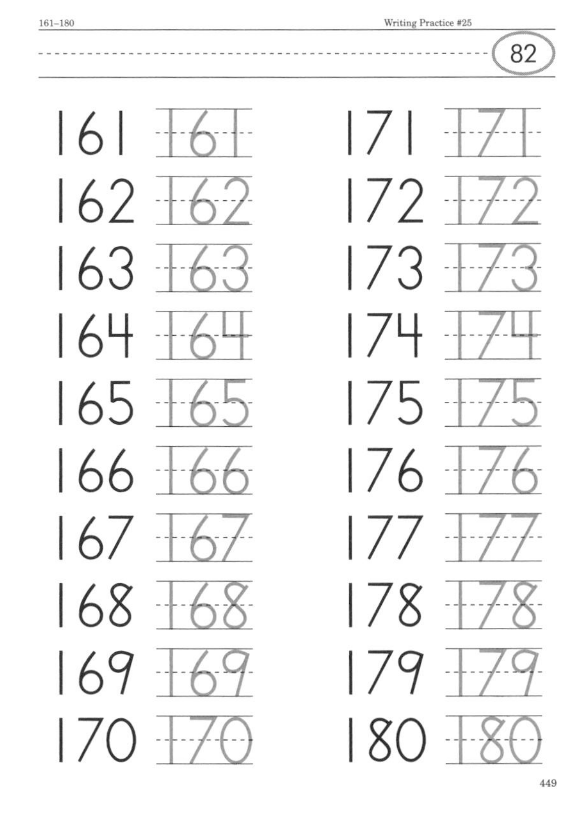
161–180 Writing Practice #25

82

161 161 171 171
162 162 172 172
163 163 173 173
164 164 174 174
165 165 175 175
166 166 176 176
167 167 177 177
168 168 178 178
169 169 179 179
170 170 180 180

449

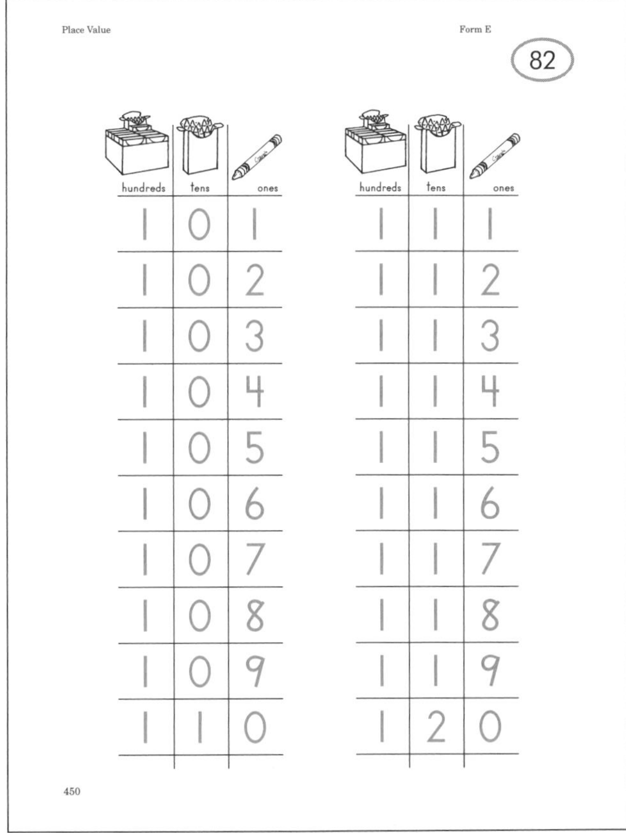
Place Value Form E

82

hundreds	tens	ones
1	0	1
1	0	2
1	0	3
1	0	4
1	0	5
1	0	6
1	0	7
1	0	8
1	0	9
1	1	0

hundreds	tens	ones
1	1	1
1	1	2
1	1	3
1	1	4
1	1	5
1	1	6
1	1	7
1	1	8
1	1	9
1	2	0

450

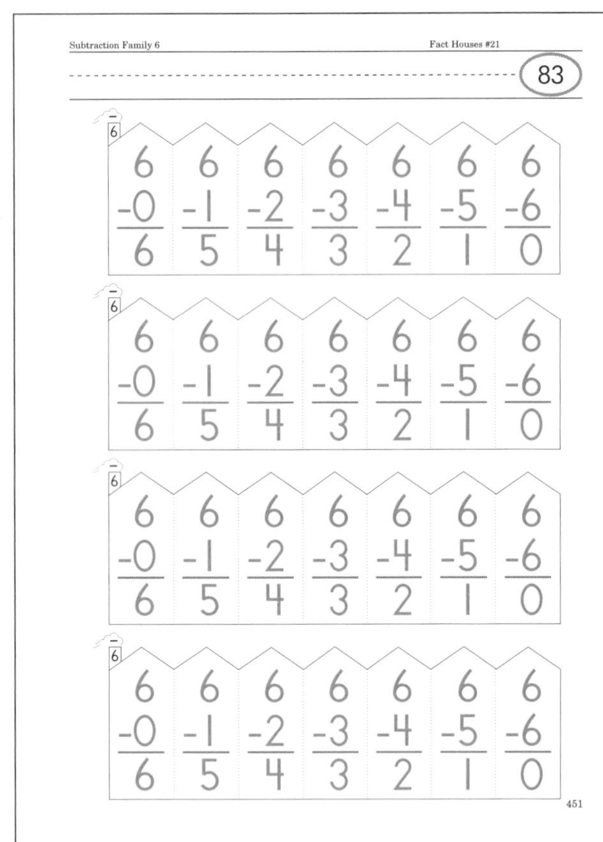

Subtraction Family 6 | Fact Houses #21

83

6	6	6	6	6	6	6
-0	-1	-2	-3	-4	-5	-6
6	5	4	3	2	1	0
6	6	6	6	6	6	6
-0	-1	-2	-3	-4	-5	-6
6	5	4	3	2	1	0
6	6	6	6	6	6	6
-0	-1	-2	-3	-4	-5	-6
6	5	4	3	2	1	0
6	6	6	6	6	6	6
-0	-1	-2	-3	-4	-5	-6
6	5	4	3	2	1	0

451

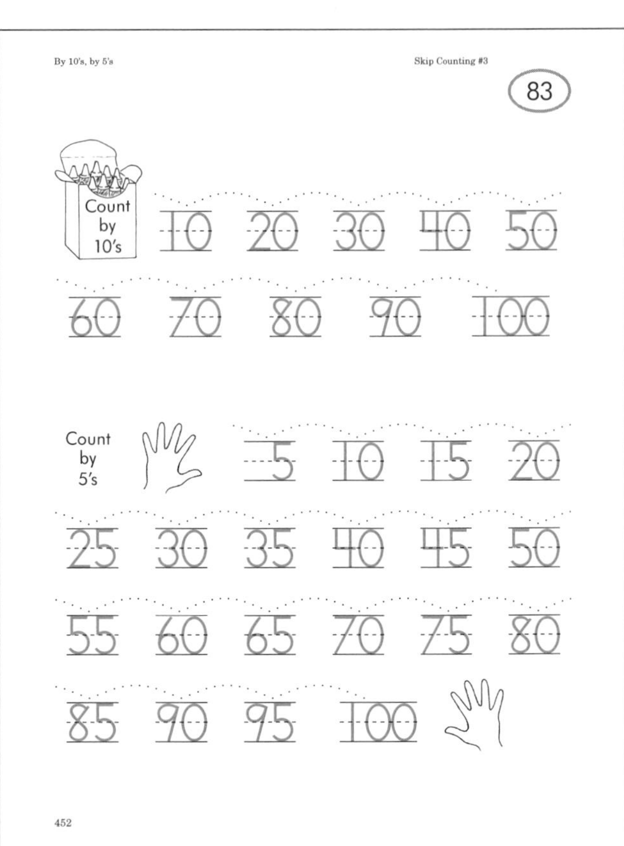

By 10's, by 5's | Skip Counting #3

83

Count by 10's

10 20 30 40 50
60 70 80 90 100

Count by 5's

5 10 15 20
25 30 35 40 45 50
55 60 65 70 75 80
85 90 95 100

452

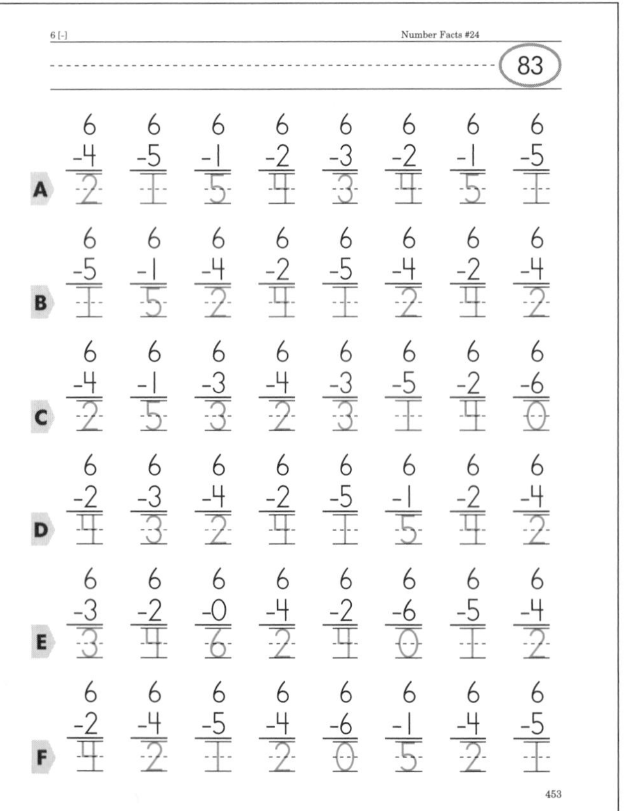

6 [-] | Number Facts #24

83

A	6 -4 = 2	6 -5 = 1	6 -1 = 5	6 -2 = 4	6 -3 = 3	6 -2 = 4	6 -1 = 5	6 -5 = 1
B	6 -5 = 1	6 -1 = 5	6 -4 = 2	6 -2 = 4	6 -5 = 1	6 -4 = 2	6 -2 = 4	6 -4 = 2
C	6 -4 = 2	6 -1 = 5	6 -3 = 3	6 -4 = 2	6 -3 = 3	6 -5 = 1	6 -2 = 4	6 -6 = 0
D	6 -2 = 4	6 -3 = 3	6 -4 = 2	6 -2 = 4	6 -5 = 1	6 -1 = 5	6 -2 = 4	6 -4 = 2
E	6 -3 = 3	6 -2 = 4	6 -0 = 6	6 -4 = 2	6 -2 = 4	6 -6 = 0	6 -5 = 1	6 -4 = 2
F	6 -2 = 4	6 -4 = 2	6 -5 = 1	6 -4 = 2	6 -6 = 0	6 -1 = 5	6 -4 = 2	6 -5 = 1

453

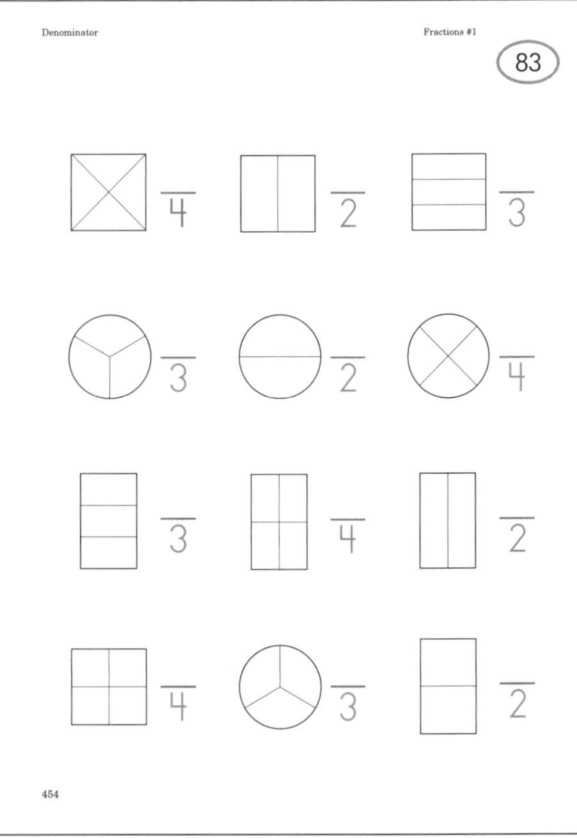

Denominator | Fractions #1

83

4 2 3
3 2 4
3 4 2
4 3 2

454

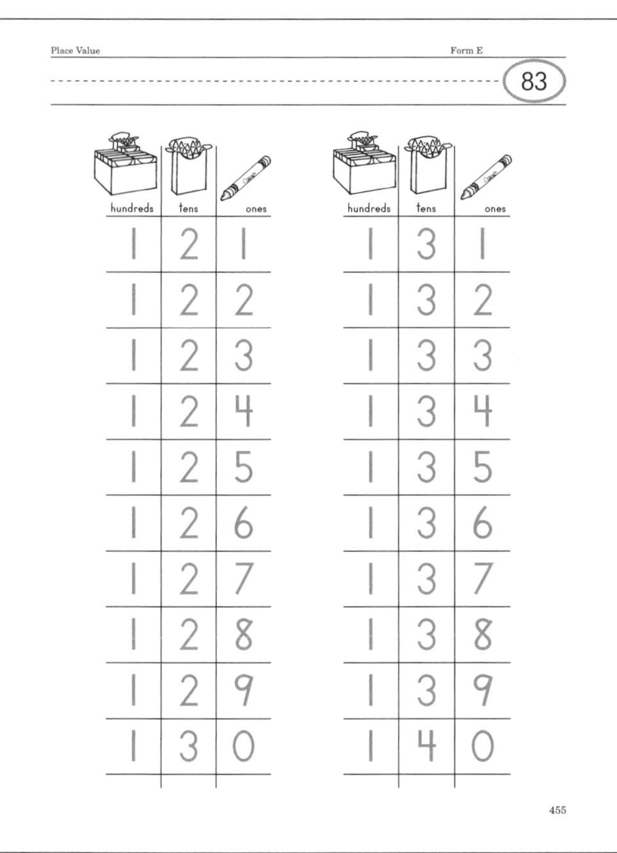

Place Value — Form E

83

hundreds	tens	ones
1	2	1
1	2	2
1	2	3
1	2	4
1	2	5
1	2	6
1	2	7
1	2	8
1	2	9
1	3	0

hundreds	tens	ones
1	3	1
1	3	2
1	3	3
1	3	4
1	3	5
1	3	6
1	3	7
1	3	8
1	3	9
1	4	0

455

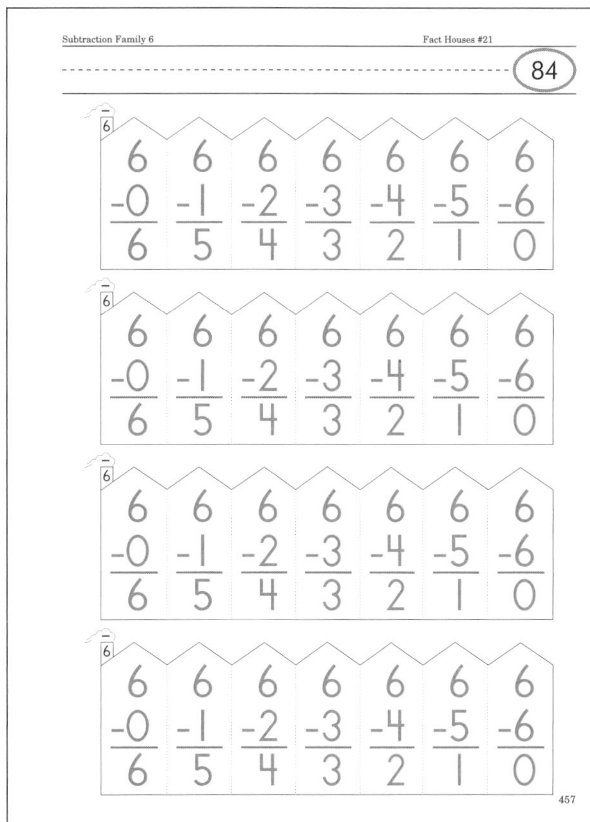

Subtraction Family 6 — Fact Houses #21

84

6	6	6	6	6	6	6
-0	-1	-2	-3	-4	-5	-6
6	5	4	3	2	1	0

6	6	6	6	6	6	6
-0	-1	-2	-3	-4	-5	-6
6	5	4	3	2	1	0

6	6	6	6	6	6	6
-0	-1	-2	-3	-4	-5	-6
6	5	4	3	2	1	0

6	6	6	6	6	6	6
-0	-1	-2	-3	-4	-5	-6
6	5	4	3	2	1	0

457

By 10's, by 5's — Skip Counting #3

84

Count by 10's

10 20 30 40 50

60 70 80 90 100

Count by 5's

5 10 15 20

25 30 35 40 45 50

55 60 65 70 75 80

85 90 95 100

458

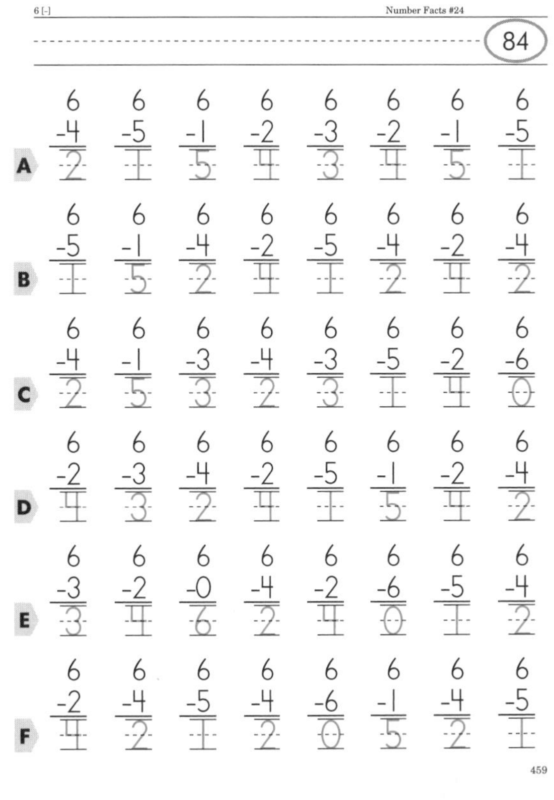

6 [-] — Number Facts #24

84

A	6 -4 = 2	6 -5 = 1	6 -1 = 5	6 -2 = 4	6 -3 = 3	6 -2 = 4	6 -1 = 5	6 -5 = 1
B	6 -5 = 1	6 -1 = 5	6 -4 = 2	6 -2 = 4	6 -5 = 1	6 -4 = 2	6 -2 = 4	6 -4 = 2
C	6 -4 = 2	6 -1 = 5	6 -3 = 3	6 -4 = 2	6 -3 = 3	6 -5 = 1	6 -2 = 4	6 -6 = 0
D	6 -2 = 4	6 -3 = 3	6 -4 = 2	6 -2 = 4	6 -5 = 1	6 -1 = 5	6 -2 = 4	6 -4 = 2
E	6 -3 = 3	6 -2 = 4	6 -0 = 6	6 -4 = 2	6 -2 = 4	6 -6 = 0	6 -5 = 1	6 -4 = 2
F	6 -2 = 4	6 -4 = 2	6 -5 = 1	6 -4 = 2	6 -6 = 0	6 -1 = 5	6 -4 = 2	6 -5 = 1

459

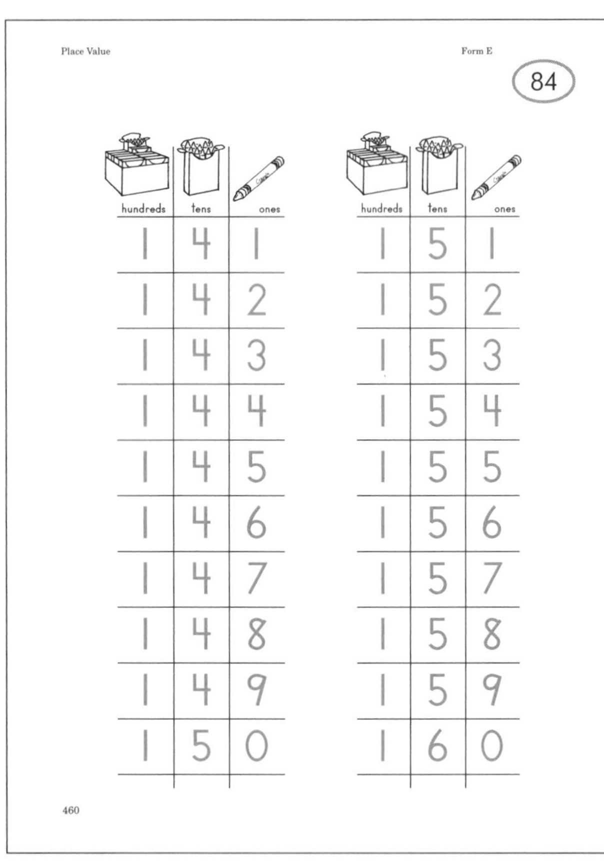

Place Value — Form E — 84

hundreds	tens	ones
1	4	1
1	4	2
1	4	3
1	4	4
1	4	5
1	4	6
1	4	7
1	4	8
1	4	9
1	5	0

hundreds	tens	ones
1	5	1
1	5	2
1	5	3
1	5	4
1	5	5
1	5	6
1	5	7
1	5	8
1	5	9
1	6	0

460

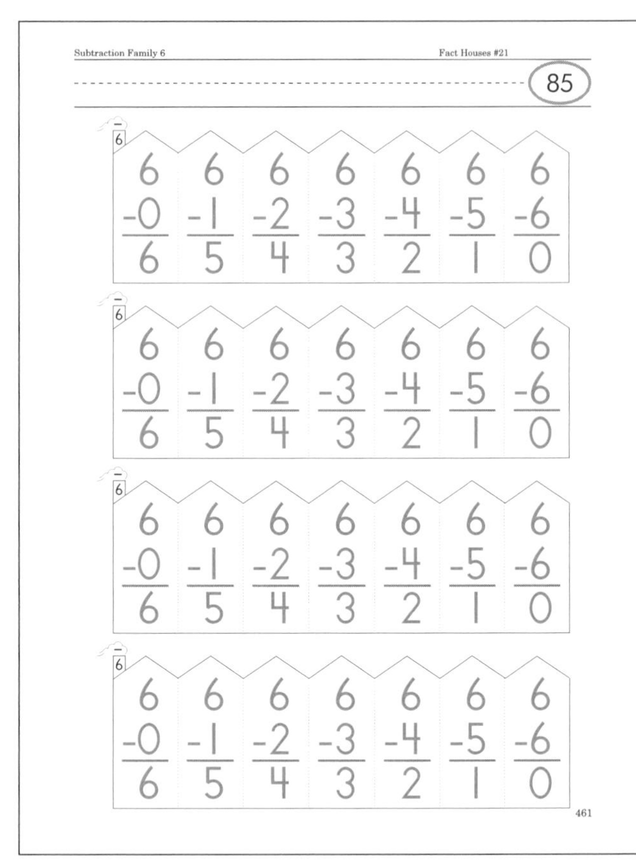

Subtraction Family 6 — Fact Houses #21 — 85

6	6	6	6	6	6	6
-0	-1	-2	-3	-4	-5	-6
6	5	4	3	2	1	0

6	6	6	6	6	6	6
-0	-1	-2	-3	-4	-5	-6
6	5	4	3	2	1	0

6	6	6	6	6	6	6
-0	-1	-2	-3	-4	-5	-6
6	5	4	3	2	1	0

6	6	6	6	6	6	6
-0	-1	-2	-3	-4	-5	-6
6	5	4	3	2	1	0

461

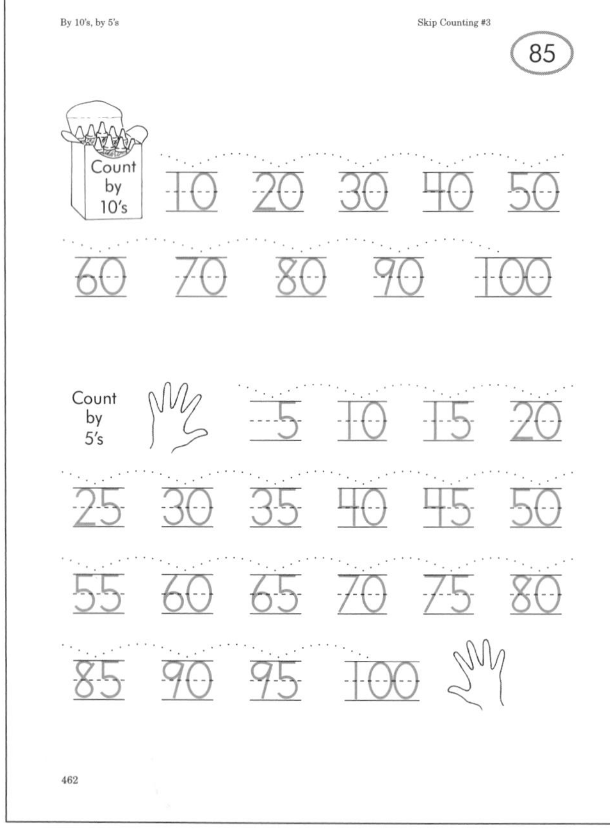

By 10's, by 5's — Skip Counting #3 — 85

Count by 10's: 10 20 30 40 50 60 70 80 90 100

Count by 5's: 5 10 15 20 25 30 35 40 45 50 55 60 65 70 75 80 85 90 95 100

462

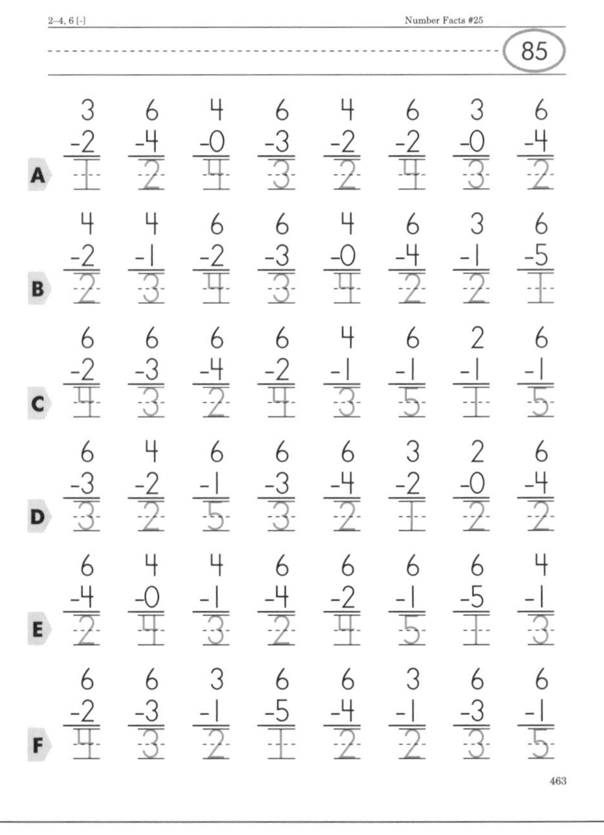

2–4, 6 [-] — Number Facts #25 — 85

A	3 − 2 = 1	6 − 4 = 2	4 − 0 = 4	6 − 3 = 3	4 − 2 = 2	6 − 2 = 4	3 − 0 = 3	6 − 4 = 2
B	4 − 2 = 2	4 − 1 = 3	6 − 2 = 4	6 − 3 = 3	4 − 0 = 4	6 − 4 = 2	3 − 1 = 2	6 − 5 = 1
C	6 − 2 = 4	6 − 3 = 3	6 − 4 = 2	6 − 2 = 4	4 − 1 = 3	6 − 1 = 5	2 − 1 = 1	6 − 1 = 5
D	6 − 3 = 3	4 − 2 = 2	6 − 1 = 5	6 − 3 = 3	6 − 4 = 2	3 − 2 = 1	2 − 0 = 2	6 − 4 = 2
E	6 − 4 = 2	4 − 0 = 4	4 − 1 = 3	6 − 4 = 2	6 − 2 = 4	6 − 1 = 5	6 − 5 = 1	4 − 1 = 3
F	6 − 2 = 4	6 − 3 = 3	3 − 1 = 2	6 − 5 = 1	6 − 4 = 2	3 − 1 = 2	6 − 3 = 3	6 − 1 = 5

463

2–7 [+] Number Facts #22

85

A	2+5=7	4+3=7	4+1=5	5+1=6
B	1+6=7	3+2=5	5+2=7	2+5=7
C	1+4=5	3+4=7	1+2=3	4+2=6
D	2+5=7	1+5=6	1+4=5	2+5=7
E	4+3=7	2+3=5	5+2=7	4+3=7
F	1+5=6	2+1=3	3+4=7	1+3=4
G	2+4=6	4+2=6	2+2=4	4+1=5
H	3+2=5	1+6=7	2+3=5	4+2=6
I	2+5=7	3+3=6	5+1=6	1+6=7
J	4+2=6	2+5=7	1+6=7	1+1=2
K	3+3=6	1+6=7	3+4=7	3+3=6
L	3+4=7	1+3=4	2+3=5	3+4=7
M	2+5=7	1+4=5	3+4=7	1+5=6
N	2+2=4	2+4=6	3+3=6	1+6=7
O	3+2=5	6+1=7	3+2=5	2+4=6
P	2+5=7	4+2=6	3+4=7	4+3=7

464

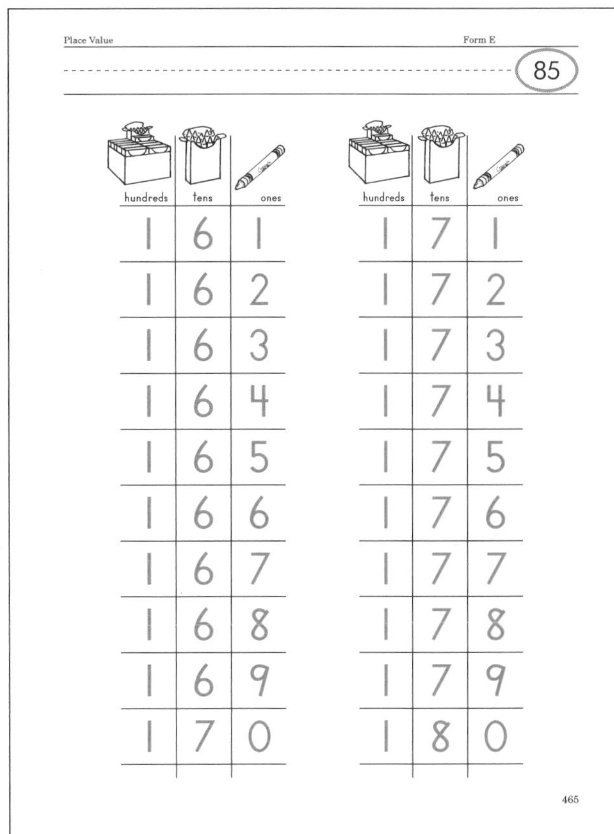

Place Value Form E

85

hundreds	tens	ones	hundreds	tens	ones
1	6	1	1	7	1
1	6	2	1	7	2
1	6	3	1	7	3
1	6	4	1	7	4
1	6	5	1	7	5
1	6	6	1	7	6
1	6	7	1	7	7
1	6	8	1	7	8
1	6	9	1	7	9
1	7	0	1	8	0

465

Flash Card Drill Form C

86

1 2 3 4 5

Individual answers (See page 365 for instructions.)

467

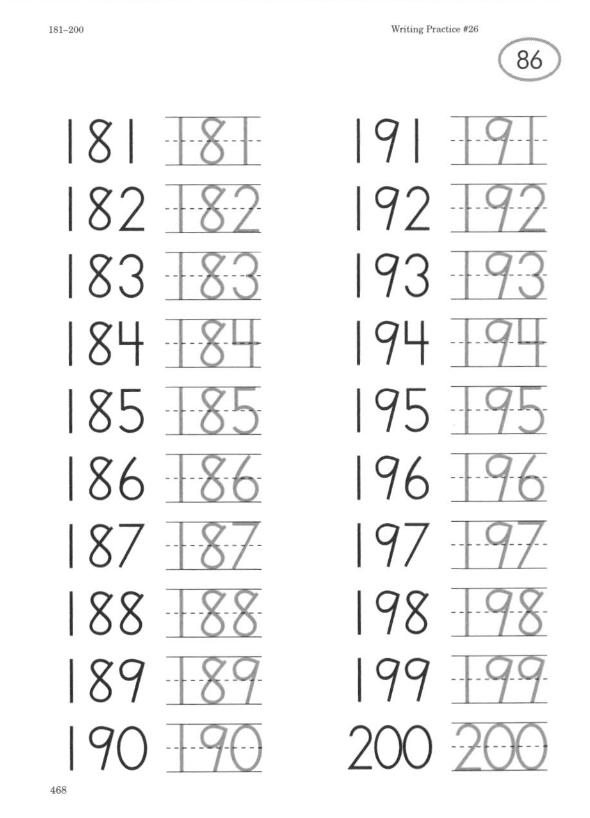

181–200 Writing Practice #26

86

181	181	191	191
182	182	192	192
183	183	193	193
184	184	194	194
185	185	195	195
186	186	196	196
187	187	197	197
188	188	198	198
189	189	199	199
190	190	200	200

468

2–4, 6 [-] Number Facts #25

86

A	3 − 2 = 1	6 − 4 = 2	4 − 0 = 4	6 − 3 = 3	4 − 2 = 2	6 − 2 = 4	3 − 0 = 3	6 − 4 = 2
B	4 − 2 = 2	4 − 1 = 3	6 − 2 = 4	6 − 3 = 3	4 − 0 = 4	6 − 4 = 2	3 − 1 = 2	6 − 5 = 1
C	6 − 2 = 4	6 − 3 = 3	6 − 4 = 2	6 − 2 = 4	4 − 1 = 3	6 − 1 = 5	2 − 1 = 1	6 − 1 = 5
D	6 − 3 = 3	4 − 2 = 2	6 − 1 = 5	6 − 3 = 3	6 − 4 = 2	3 − 2 = 1	2 − 0 = 2	6 − 4 = 2
E	6 − 4 = 2	4 − 0 = 4	4 − 1 = 3	6 − 4 = 2	6 − 2 = 4	6 − 1 = 5	6 − 5 = 1	4 − 1 = 3
F	6 − 2 = 4	6 − 3 = 3	3 − 1 = 2	6 − 5 = 1	6 − 4 = 2	3 − 1 = 2	6 − 3 = 3	6 − 1 = 5

469

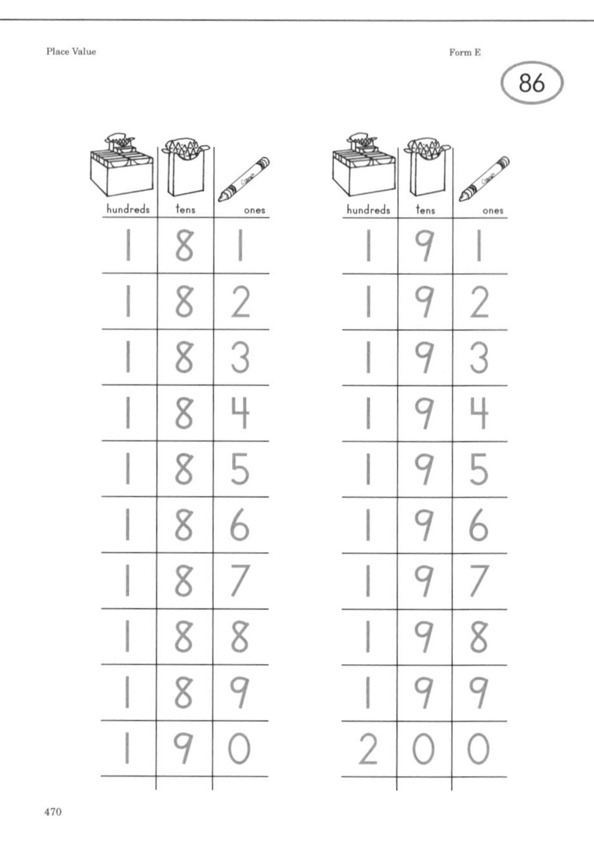
Place Value Form E

86

hundreds	tens	ones
1	8	1
1	8	2
1	8	3
1	8	4
1	8	5
1	8	6
1	8	7
1	8	8
1	8	9
1	9	0

hundreds	tens	ones
1	9	1
1	9	2
1	9	3
1	9	4
1	9	5
1	9	6
1	9	7
1	9	8
1	9	9
2	0	0

470

Subtraction Families 5, 6 Fact Houses #22

87

5: 5 − 0 = 5, 5 − 1 = 4, 5 − 2 = 3, 5 − 3 = 2, 5 − 4 = 1, 5 − 5 = 0

5: 5 − 0 = 5, 5 − 1 = 4, 5 − 2 = 3, 5 − 3 = 2, 5 − 4 = 1, 5 − 5 = 0

6: 6 − 0 = 6, 6 − 1 = 5, 6 − 2 = 4, 6 − 3 = 3, 6 − 4 = 2, 6 − 5 = 1, 6 − 6 = 0

6: 6 − 0 = 6, 6 − 1 = 5, 6 − 2 = 4, 6 − 3 = 3, 6 − 4 = 2, 6 − 5 = 1, 6 − 6 = 0

471

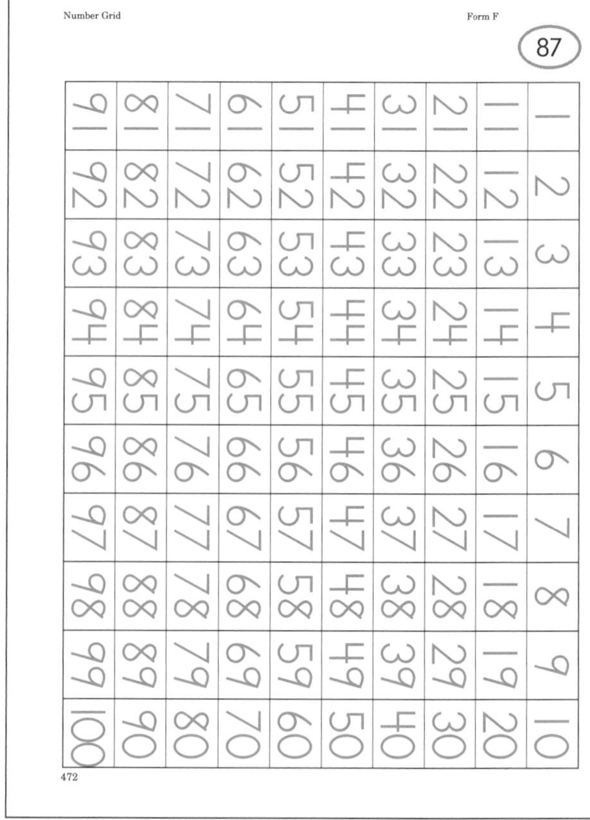
Number Grid Form F

87

1	2	3	4	5	6	7	8	9	10
11	12	13	14	15	16	17	18	19	20
21	22	23	24	25	26	27	28	29	30
31	32	33	34	35	36	37	38	39	40
41	42	43	44	45	46	47	48	49	50
51	52	53	54	55	56	57	58	59	60
61	62	63	64	65	66	67	68	69	70
71	72	73	74	75	76	77	78	79	80
81	82	83	84	85	86	87	88	89	90
91	92	93	94	95	96	97	98	99	100

472

2–7 [+] Number Facts #26

87

A	2+0=2	4+1=5	1+3=4	4+2=6
B	3+2=5	4+3=7	1+4=5	2+2=4
C	6+1=7	3+4=7	5+1=6	3+2=5
D	2+1=3	4+1=5	4+3=7	1+5=6
E	3+4=7	4+2=6	1+2=3	5+2=7
F	3+1=4	2+2=4	5+2=7	2+5=7
G	4+1=5	2+3=5	5+2=7	3+1=4
H	4+2=6	3+3=6	3+4=7	3+2=5
I	2+5=7	6+1=7	2+4=6	6+1=7
J	6+1=7	3+3=6	3+2=5	2+3=5
K	2+4=6	3+0=3	4+2=6	2+4=6
L	3+1=4	3+2=5	4+2=6	2+1=3
M	2+3=5	4+3=7	2+2=4	5+1=6
N	2+4=6	1+3=4	2+3=5	1+1=2
O	3+2=5	3+4=7	1+4=5	1+2=3
P	4+2=6	5+2=7	4+2=6	6+1=7

473

2–4, 6 [-] Number Facts #25

87

A	3 -2 = 1	6 -4 = 2	4 -0 = 4	6 -3 = 3	4 -2 = 2	6 -2 = 4	3 -0 = 3	6 -4 = 2
B	4 -2 = 2	4 -1 = 3	6 -2 = 4	6 -3 = 3	4 -0 = 4	6 -4 = 2	3 -1 = 2	6 -5 = 1
C	6 -2 = 4	6 -3 = 3	6 -4 = 2	6 -2 = 4	4 -1 = 3	6 -1 = 5	2 -1 = 1	6 -1 = 5
D	6 -3 = 3	4 -2 = 2	6 -1 = 5	6 -3 = 3	6 -4 = 2	3 -2 = 1	2 -0 = 2	6 -4 = 2
E	6 -4 = 2	4 -0 = 4	4 -1 = 3	6 -4 = 2	6 -2 = 4	6 -1 = 5	6 -5 = 1	4 -1 = 3
F	6 -2 = 4	6 -3 = 3	3 -1 = 2	6 -5 = 1	6 -4 = 2	3 -1 = 2	6 -3 = 3	6 -1 = 5

474

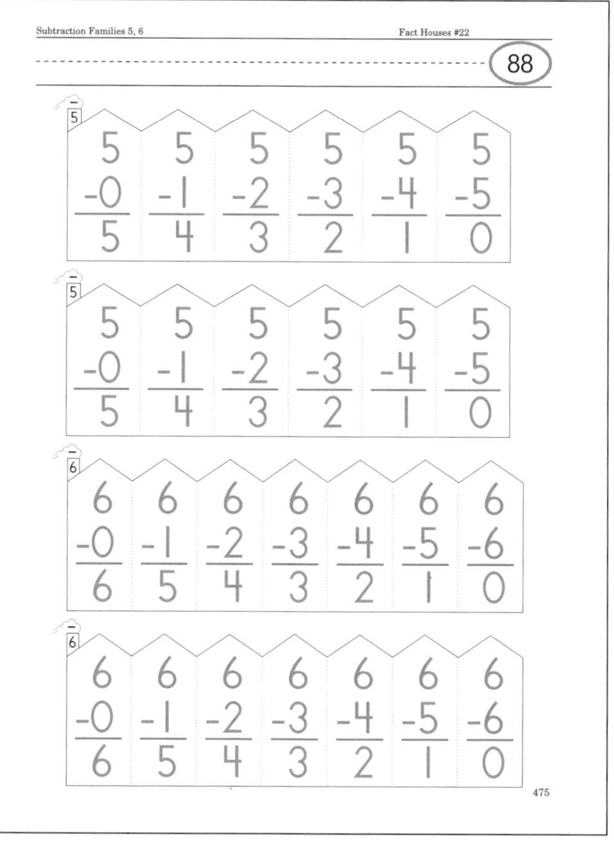
Subtraction Families 5, 6 Fact Houses #22

88

5							
	5 -0 = 5	5 -1 = 4	5 -2 = 3	5 -3 = 2	5 -4 = 1	5 -5 = 0	
5							
	5 -0 = 5	5 -1 = 4	5 -2 = 3	5 -3 = 2	5 -4 = 1	5 -5 = 0	
6							
	6 -0 = 6	6 -1 = 5	6 -2 = 4	6 -3 = 3	6 -4 = 2	6 -5 = 1	6 -6 = 0
6							
	6 -0 = 6	6 -1 = 5	6 -2 = 4	6 -3 = 3	6 -4 = 2	6 -5 = 1	6 -6 = 0

475

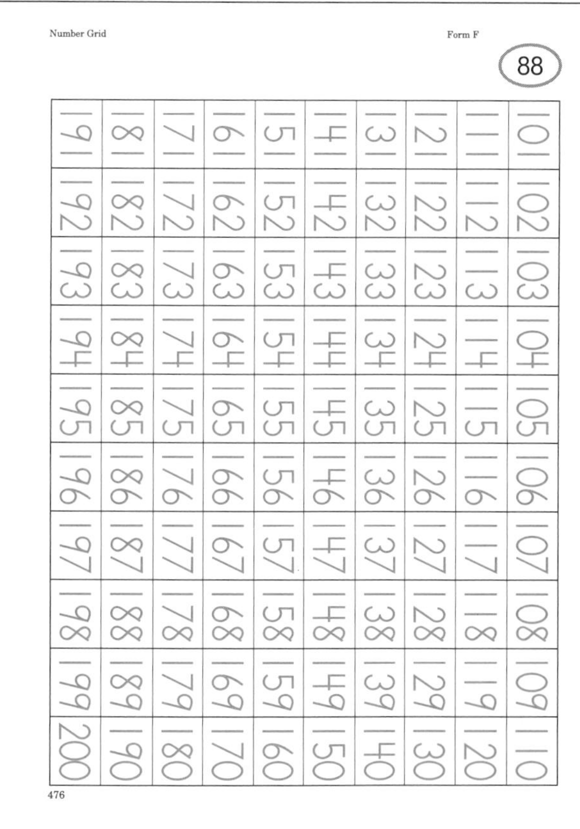
Number Grid Form F

88

101	102	103	104	105	106	107	108	109	110
111	112	113	114	115	116	117	118	119	120
121	122	123	124	125	126	127	128	129	130
131	132	133	134	135	136	137	138	139	140
141	142	143	144	145	146	147	148	149	150
151	152	153	154	155	156	157	158	159	160
161	162	163	164	165	166	167	168	169	170
171	172	173	174	175	176	177	178	179	180
181	182	183	184	185	186	187	188	189	190
191	192	193	194	195	196	197	198	199	200

476

4–6 [-] Number Facts #27

88

A	6-4=2	4-0=4	6-1=5	6-3=3
B	5-1=4	4-2=2	5-1=4	6-4=2
C	5-0=5	6-1=5	5-2=3	5-3=2
D	5-2=3	6-3=3	5-3=2	4-2=2
E	6-4=2	5-4=1	4-1=3	6-2=4
F	5-2=3	4-0=4	6-5=1	5-4=1
G	6-5=1	5-0=5	5-3=2	6-2=4
H	6-1=5	4-2=2	6-5=1	5-3=2
I	5-3=2	6-4=2	6-1=5	6-3=3
J	4-3=1	4-2=2	5-2=3	5-4=1
K	6-2=4	6-3=3	4-3=1	5-0=5
L	6-4=2	4-3=1	6-4=2	5-2=3
M	5-3=2	6-2=4	5-3=2	6-5=1
N	6-2=4	6-3=3	5-1=4	6-1=5
O	6-5=1	6-4=2	5-4=1	5-3=2
P	6-2=4	6-3=3	6-1=5	6-4=2

477

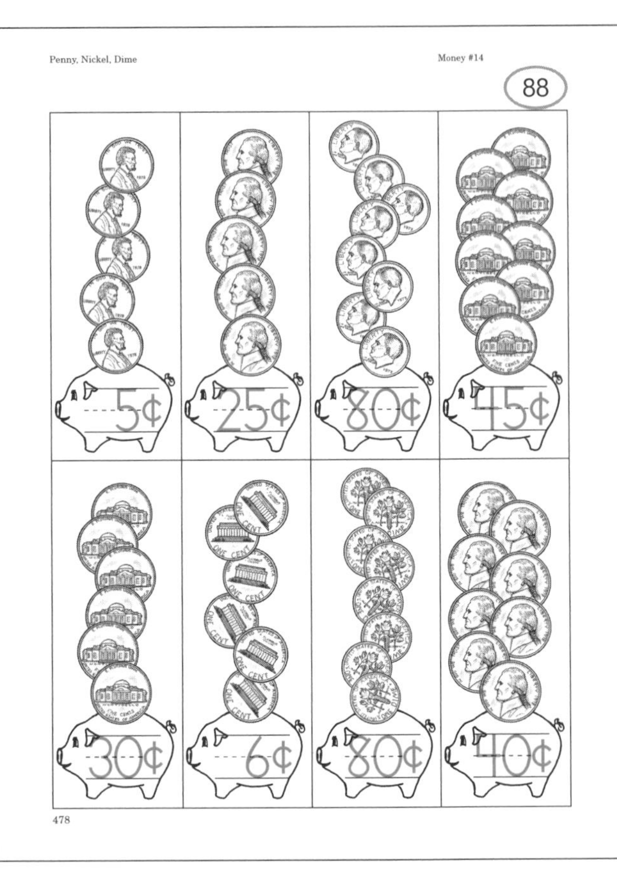

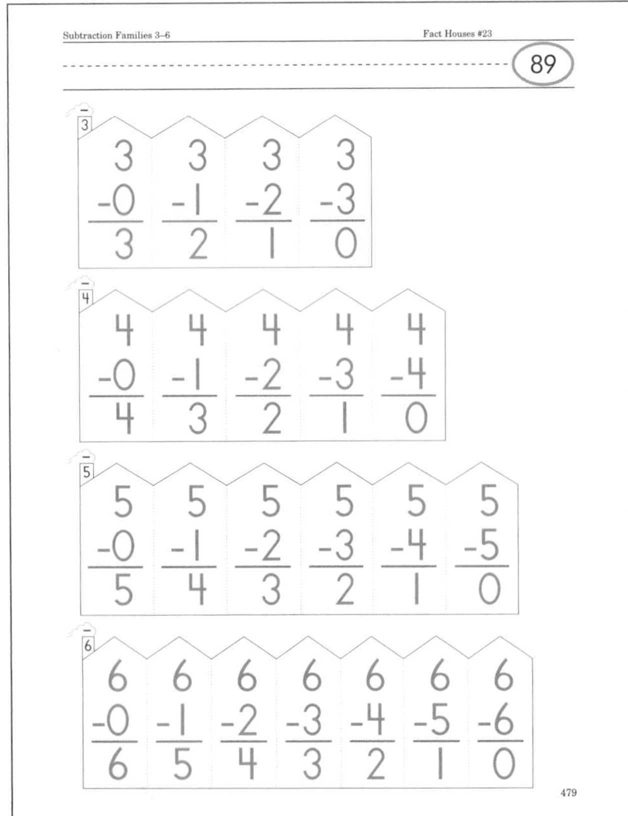
Subtraction Families 3–6 Fact Houses #23

89

3: 3 - 0 = 3, 3 - 1 = 2, 3 - 2 = 1, 3 - 3 = 0

4: 4 - 0 = 4, 4 - 1 = 3, 4 - 2 = 2, 4 - 3 = 1, 4 - 4 = 0

5: 5 - 0 = 5, 5 - 1 = 4, 5 - 2 = 3, 5 - 3 = 2, 5 - 4 = 1, 5 - 5 = 0

6: 6 - 0 = 6, 6 - 1 = 5, 6 - 2 = 4, 6 - 3 = 3, 6 - 4 = 2, 6 - 5 = 1, 6 - 6 = 0

479

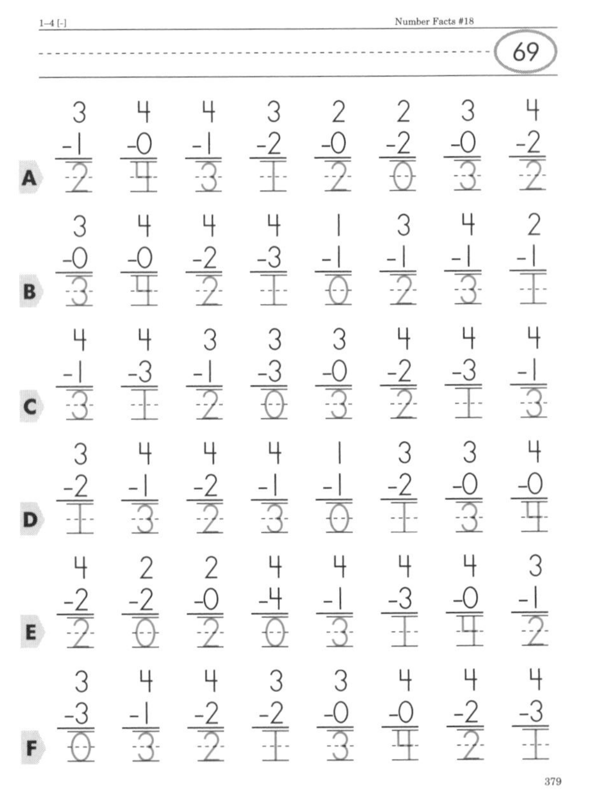
1–4 [-] Number Facts #18

69

A	3 - 1 = 2	4 - 0 = 4	4 - 1 = 3	3 - 2 = 1	2 - 0 = 2	2 - 2 = 0	3 - 0 = 3	4 - 2 = 2
B	3 - 0 = 3	4 - 0 = 4	4 - 2 = 2	4 - 3 = 1	1 - 1 = 0	3 - 1 = 2	4 - 1 = 3	2 - 1 = 1
C	4 - 1 = 3	4 - 3 = 1	3 - 1 = 2	3 - 3 = 0	3 - 0 = 3	4 - 2 = 2	4 - 3 = 1	4 - 1 = 3
D	3 - 2 = 1	4 - 1 = 3	4 - 2 = 2	4 - 1 = 3	1 - 1 = 0	3 - 2 = 1	3 - 0 = 3	4 - 0 = 4
E	4 - 2 = 2	2 - 2 = 0	2 - 0 = 2	4 - 4 = 0	4 - 1 = 3	4 - 3 = 1	4 - 0 = 4	3 - 1 = 2
F	3 - 3 = 0	4 - 1 = 3	4 - 2 = 2	3 - 2 = 1	3 - 0 = 3	4 - 0 = 4	4 - 2 = 2	4 - 3 = 1

379

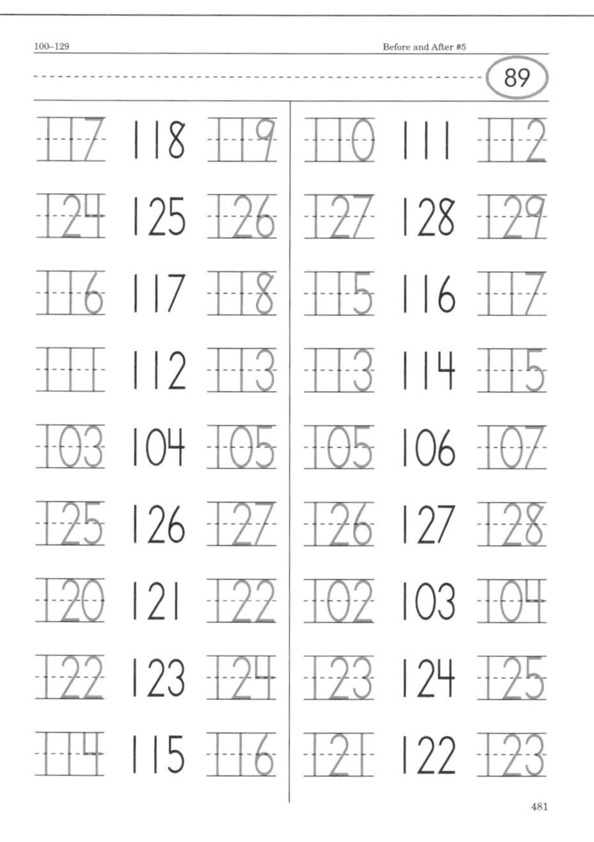

100–129 Before and After #5

89

117	118	119	110	111	112
124	125	126	127	128	129
116	117	118	115	116	117
111	112	113	113	114	115
103	104	105	105	106	107
125	126	127	126	127	128
120	121	122	102	103	104
122	123	124	123	124	125
114	115	116	121	122	123

481

Half Hour Clocks #2

89

3:30	10:30	2:30	11:30
7:30	1:30	5:30	8:30
9:30	10:30	12:30	11:30
4:30	1:30	5:30	6:30

482

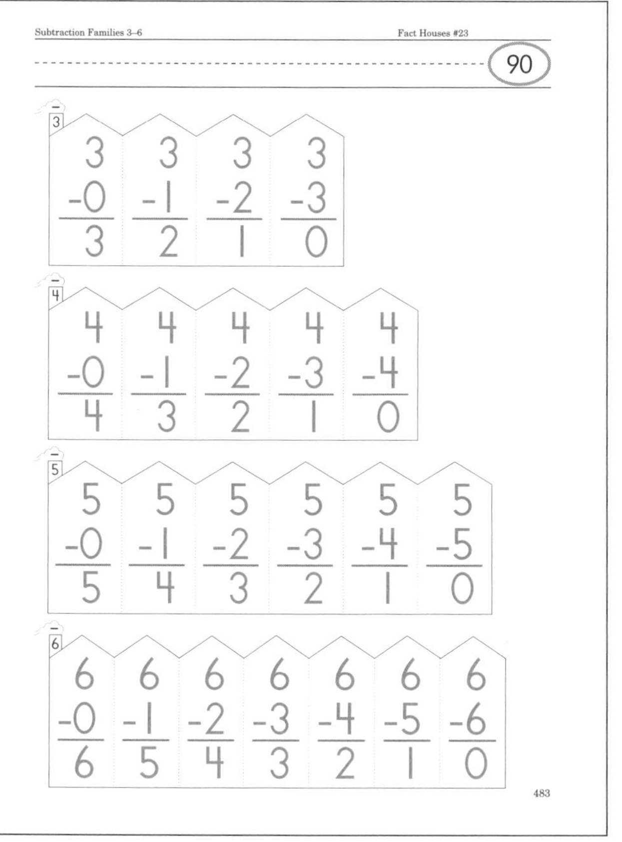

Subtraction Families 3–6 Fact Houses #23

90

− 3

3	3	3	3
-0	-1	-2	-3
3	2	1	0

− 4

4	4	4	4	4
-0	-1	-2	-3	-4
4	3	2	1	0

− 5

5	5	5	5	5	5
-0	-1	-2	-3	-4	-5
5	4	3	2	1	0

− 6

6	6	6	6	6	6	6
-0	-1	-2	-3	-4	-5	-6
6	5	4	3	2	1	0

483

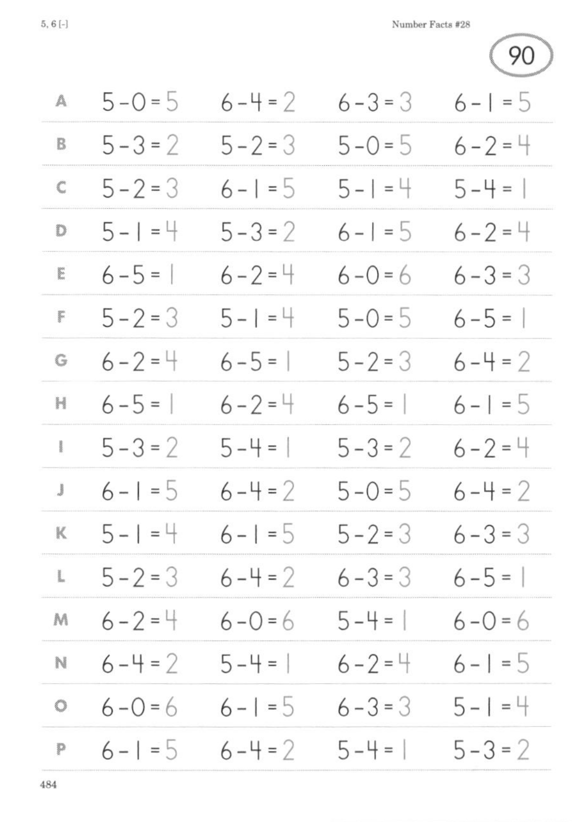

5, 6 [-] Number Facts #28

90

A	5-0=5	6-4=2	6-3=3	6-1=5
B	5-3=2	5-2=3	5-0=5	6-2=4
C	5-2=3	6-1=5	5-1=4	5-4=1
D	5-1=4	5-3=2	6-1=5	6-2=4
E	6-5=1	6-2=4	6-0=6	6-3=3
F	5-2=3	5-1=4	5-0=5	6-5=1
G	6-2=4	6-5=1	5-2=3	6-4=2
H	6-5=1	6-2=4	6-5=1	6-1=5
I	5-3=2	5-4=1	5-3=2	6-2=4
J	6-1=5	6-4=2	5-0=5	6-4=2
K	5-1=4	6-1=5	5-2=3	6-3=3
L	5-2=3	6-4=2	6-3=3	6-5=1
M	6-2=4	6-0=6	5-4=1	6-0=6
N	6-4=2	5-4=1	6-2=4	6-1=5
O	6-0=6	6-1=5	6-3=3	5-1=4
P	6-1=5	6-4=2	5-4=1	5-3=2

484

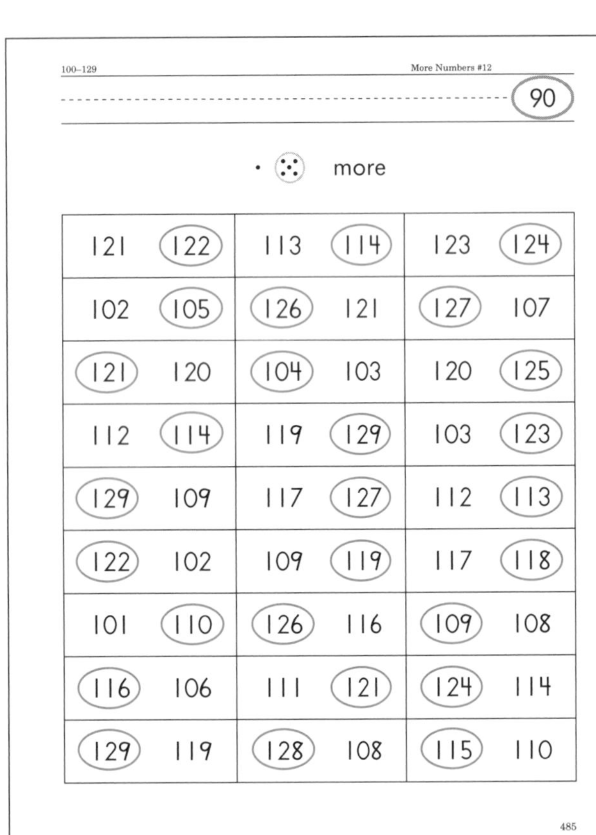
100–129 More Numbers #12

90

• ⁙ more

121	**122**	113	**114**	123	**124**
102	**105**	**126**	121	**127**	107
121	120	**104**	103	120	**125**
112	**114**	119	**129**	103	**123**
129	109	117	**127**	112	**113**
122	102	109	**119**	117	**118**
101	**110**	**126**	116	**109**	108
116	106	111	**121**	**124**	114
129	119	**128**	108	**115**	110

485

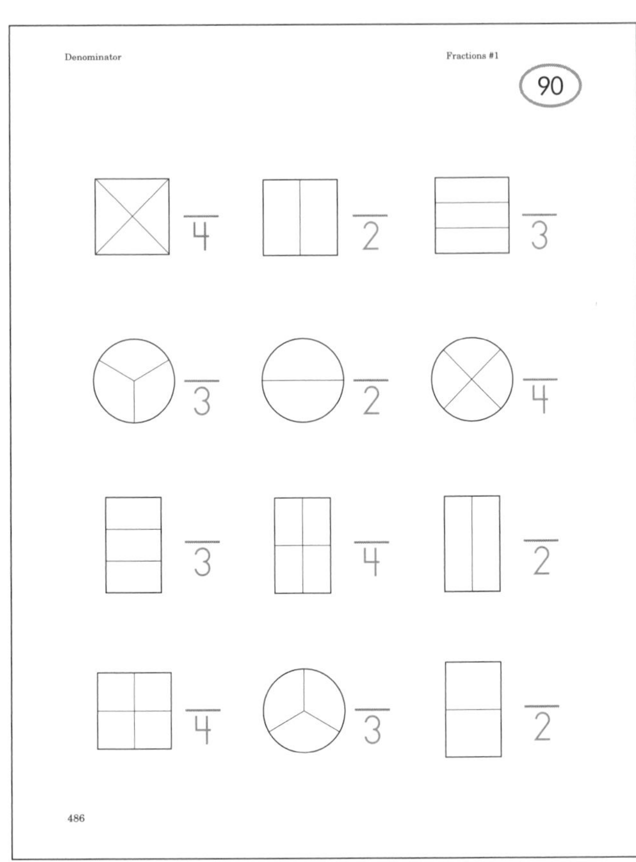
Denominator Fractions #1

90

486

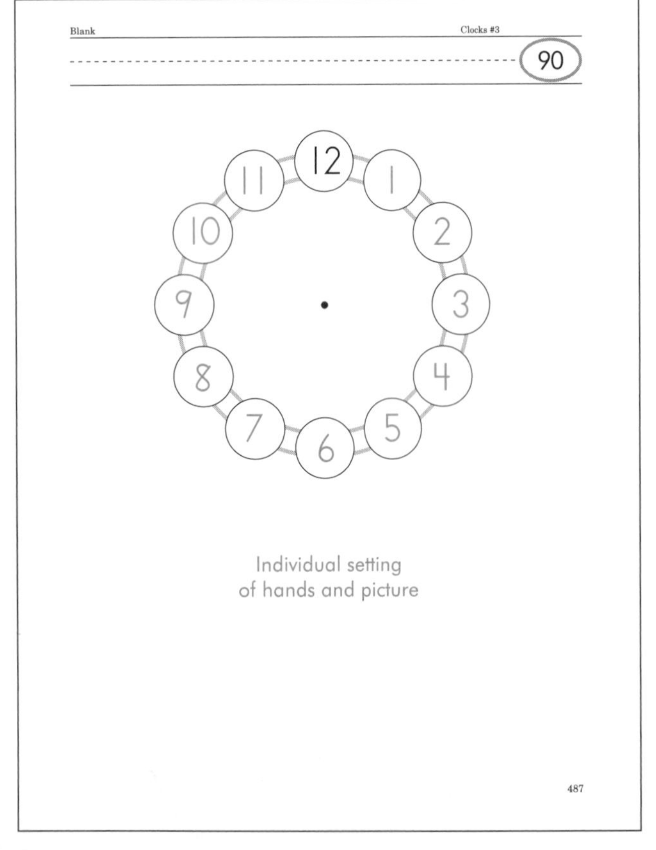
Blank Clocks #3

90

Individual setting of hands and picture

487

Flash Card Drill Form C

91

489

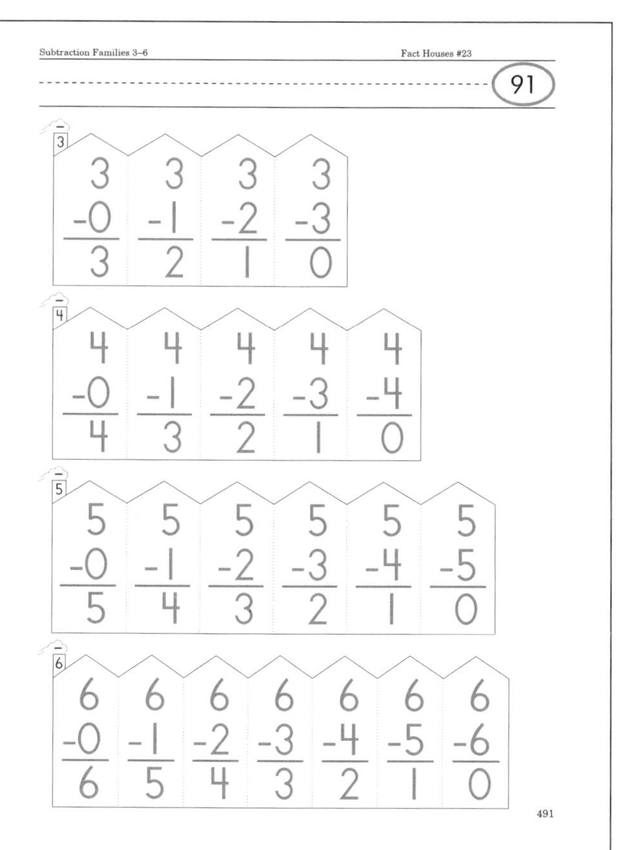

Subtraction Families 3–6 Fact Houses #23

91

3	3	3	3
-0	-1	-2	-3
3	2	1	0

4	4	4	4	4
-0	-1	-2	-3	-4
4	3	2	1	0

5	5	5	5	5	5
-0	-1	-2	-3	-4	-5
5	4	3	2	1	0

6	6	6	6	6	6	6
-0	-1	-2	-3	-4	-5	-6
6	5	4	3	2	1	0

491

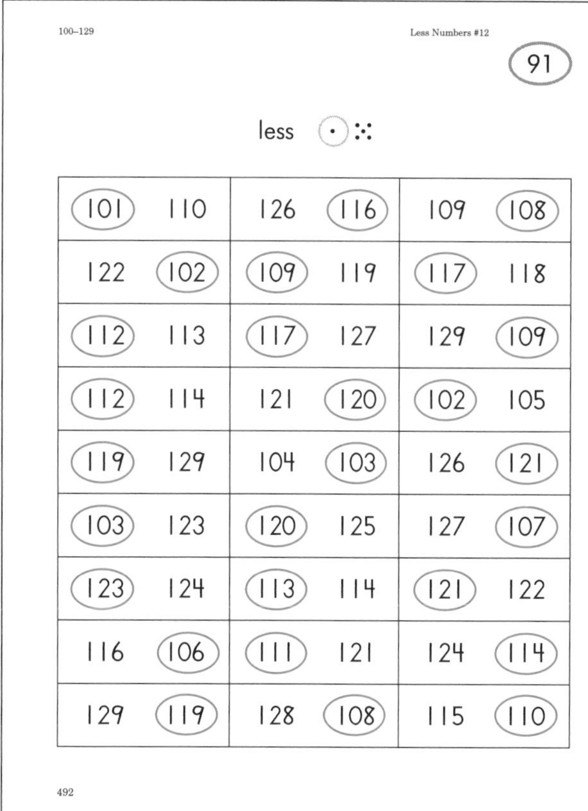

100–129 Less Numbers #12

91

less

101	110	126	**116**	109	**108**
122	**102**	**109**	119	**117**	118
112	113	**117**	127	129	**109**
112	114	121	**120**	**102**	105
119	129	104	**103**	126	**121**
103	123	**120**	125	127	**107**
123	124	**113**	114	**121**	122
116	**106**	**111**	121	124	**114**
129	**119**	128	**108**	115	**110**

492

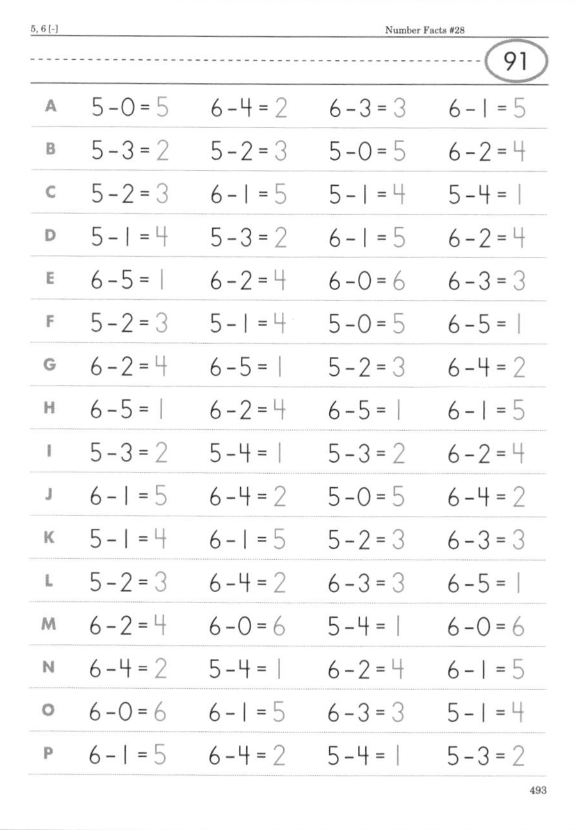

5, 6 [-] Number Facts #28

91

A	5-0=5	6-4=2	6-3=3	6-1=5
B	5-3=2	5-2=3	5-0=5	6-2=4
C	5-2=3	6-1=5	5-1=4	5-4=1
D	5-1=4	5-3=2	6-1=5	6-2=4
E	6-5=1	6-2=4	6-0=6	6-3=3
F	5-2=3	5-1=4	5-0=5	6-5=1
G	6-2=4	6-5=1	5-2=3	6-4=2
H	6-5=1	6-2=4	6-5=1	6-1=5
I	5-3=2	5-4=1	5-3=2	6-2=4
J	6-1=5	6-4=2	5-0=5	6-4=2
K	5-1=4	6-1=5	5-2=3	6-3=3
L	5-2=3	6-4=2	6-3=3	6-5=1
M	6-2=4	6-0=6	5-4=1	6-0=6
N	6-4=2	5-4=1	6-2=4	6-1=5
O	6-0=6	6-1=5	6-3=3	5-1=4
P	6-1=5	6-4=2	5-4=1	5-3=2

493

Half Hour Clocks #4

91

4:30	10:30	12:30	5:30
2:30	8:30	7:30	6:30
7:30	1:30	10:30	12:30
3:30	11:30	4:30	9:30

494

Subtraction Family 7 — Fact Houses #24 — 92

7	7	7	7	7	7	7	7
-0	-1	-2	-3	-4	-5	-6	-7
7	6	5	4	3	2	1	0
7	7	7	7	7	7	7	7
-0	-1	-2	-3	-4	-5	-6	-7
7	6	5	4	3	2	1	0
7	7	7	7	7	7	7	7
-0	-1	-2	-3	-4	-5	-6	-7
7	6	5	4	3	2	1	0
7	7	7	7	7	7	7	7
-0	-1	-2	-3	-4	-5	-6	-7
7	6	5	4	3	2	1	0

495

110–139 — Before and After #6 — 92

124	125	126	120	121	122
131	132	133	135	136	137
137	138	139	125	126	127
133	134	135	113	114	115
114	115	116	123	124	125
121	122	123	117	118	119
116	117	118	132	133	134
134	135	136	127	128	129
122	123	124	130	131	132

496

2–7 [+] — Number Facts #26 — 92

A	2+0=2	4+1=5	1+3=4	4+2=6
B	3+2=5	4+3=7	1+4=5	2+2=4
C	6+1=7	3+4=7	5+1=6	3+2=5
D	2+1=3	4+1=5	4+3=7	1+5=6
E	3+4=7	4+2=6	1+2=3	5+2=7
F	3+1=4	2+2=4	5+2=7	2+5=7
G	4+1=5	2+3=5	5+2=7	3+1=4
H	4+2=6	3+3=6	3+4=7	3+2=5
I	2+5=7	6+1=7	2+4=6	6+1=7
J	6+1=7	3+3=6	3+2=5	2+3=5
K	2+4=6	3+0=3	4+2=6	2+4=6
L	3+1=4	3+2=5	4+2=6	2+1=3
M	2+3=5	4+3=7	2+2=4	5+1=6
N	2+4=6	1+3=4	2+3=5	1+1=2
O	3+2=5	3+4=7	1+4=5	1+2=3
P	4+2=6	5+2=7	4+2=6	6+1=7

497

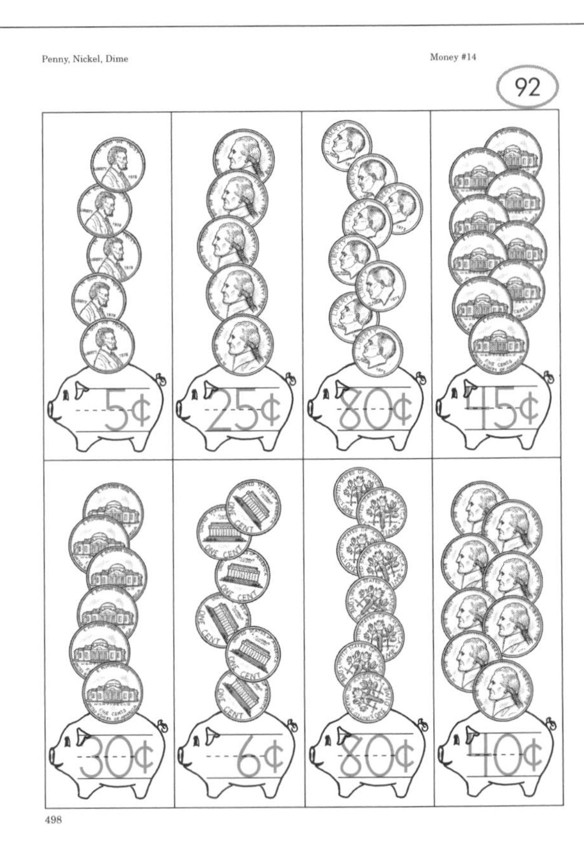

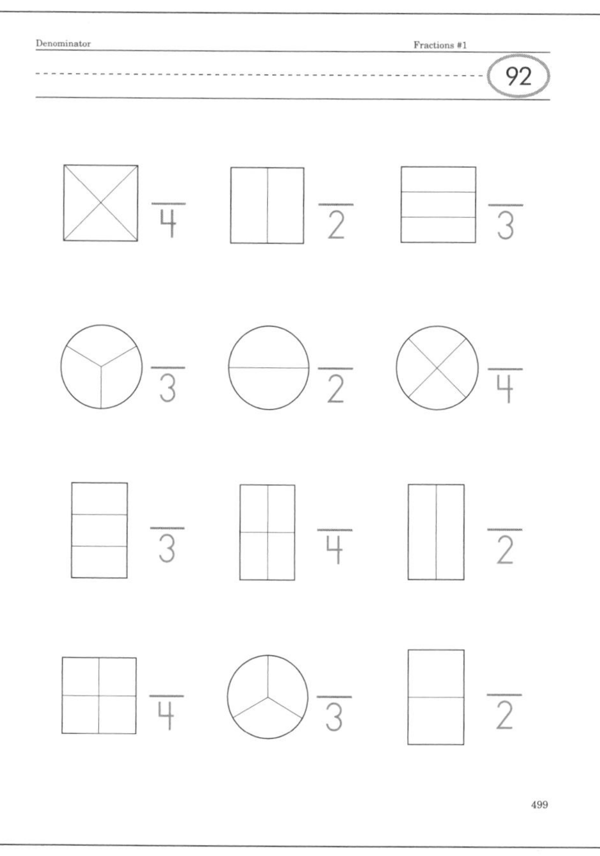
Denominator Fractions #1

92

4	2	3
3	2	4
3	4	2
4	3	2

499

Subtraction Family 7 Fact Houses #24

93

7	7	7	7	7	7	7	7
-0	-1	-2	-3	-4	-5	-6	-7
7	6	5	4	3	2	1	0

7	7	7	7	7	7	7	7
-0	-1	-2	-3	-4	-5	-6	-7
7	6	5	4	3	2	1	0

7	7	7	7	7	7	7	7
-0	-1	-2	-3	-4	-5	-6	-7
7	6	5	4	3	2	1	0

7	7	7	7	7	7	7	7
-0	-1	-2	-3	-4	-5	-6	-7
7	6	5	4	3	2	1	0

501

Half Hour Clocks #2

93

3:30	10:30	2:30	11:30
7:30	1:30	5:30	8:30
9:30	10:30	12:30	11:30
4:30	1:30	5:30	6:30

502

7 [-] Number Facts #29

93

A	7 -6 1	7 -4 3	7 -2 5	7 -3 4	7 -6 1	7 -4 3	7 -1 6	7 -5 2
B	7 -5 2	7 -1 6	7 -4 3	7 -2 5	7 -6 1	7 -3 4	7 -2 5	7 -5 2
C	7 -3 4	7 -5 2	7 -6 1	7 -4 3	7 -5 2	7 -3 4	7 -6 1	7 -2 5
D	7 -4 3	7 -3 4	7 -2 5	7 -3 4	7 -4 3	7 -2 5	7 -3 4	7 -6 1
E	7 -5 2	7 -6 1	7 -2 5	7 -5 2	7 -3 4	7 -4 3	7 -2 5	7 -6 1
F	7 -0 7	7 -1 6	7 -4 3	7 -3 4	7 -5 2	7 -6 1	7 -4 3	7 -2 5

503

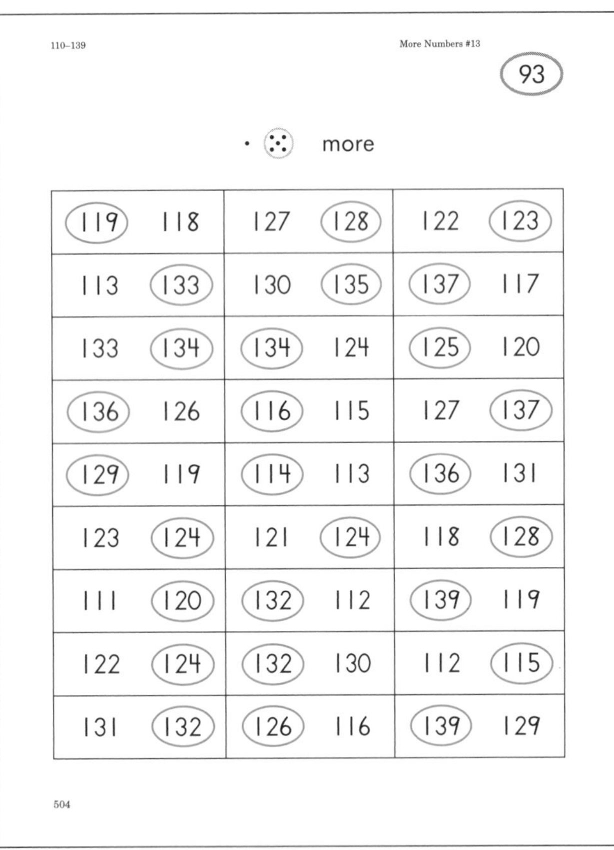

110–139 More Numbers #13

93

• ⁙ more

(119)	118	127	(128)	122	(123)
113	(133)	130	(135)	(137)	117
133	(134)	(134)	124	(125)	120
(136)	126	(116)	115	127	(137)
(129)	119	(114)	113	(136)	131
123	(124)	121	(124)	118	(128)
111	(120)	(132)	112	(139)	119
122	(124)	(132)	130	112	(115)
131	(132)	(126)	116	(139)	129

504

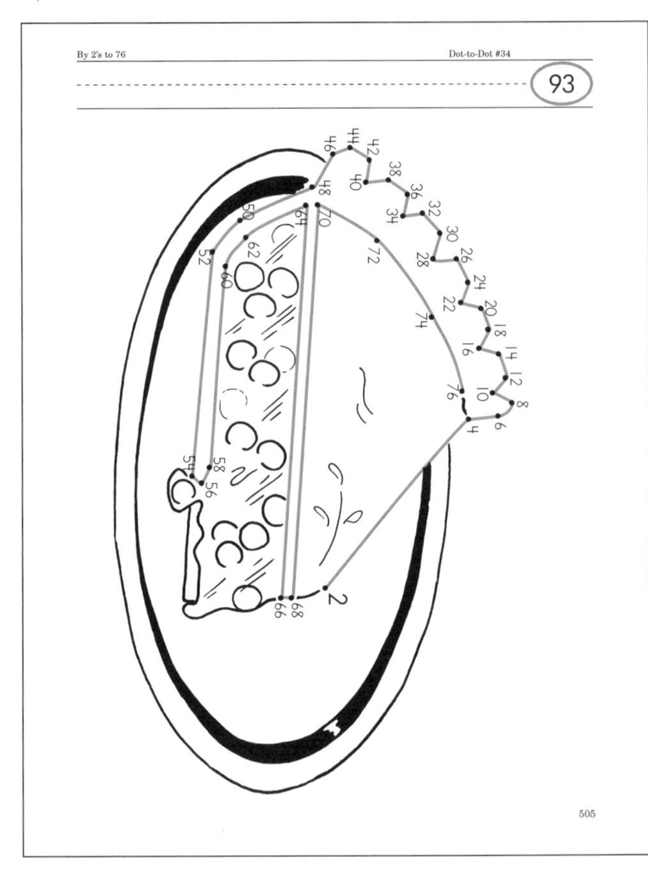

By 2's to 76 Dot-to-Dot #34

93

505

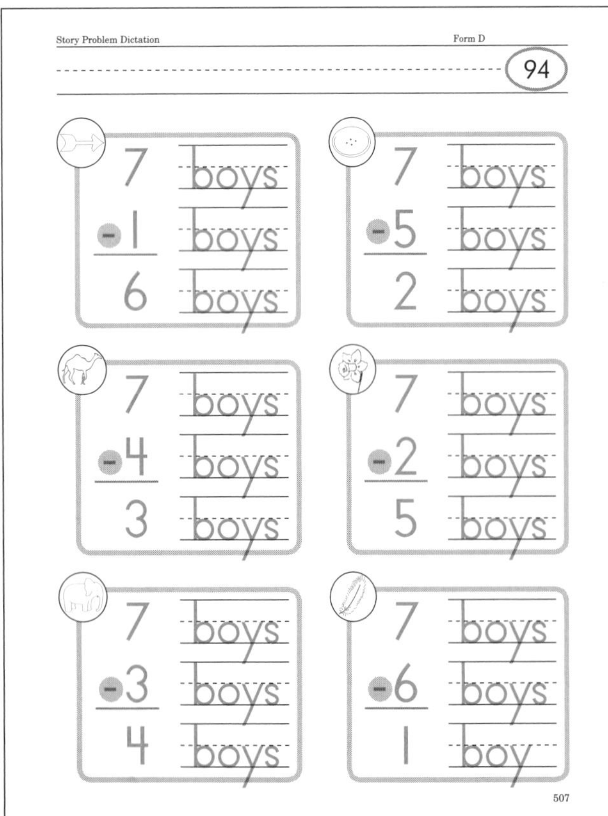

Story Problem Dictation Form D

94

7 boys − 1 boys 6 boys		7 boys − 5 boys 2 boys	
7 boys − 4 boys 3 boys		7 boys − 2 boys 5 boys	
7 boys − 3 boys 4 boys		7 boys − 6 boys 1 boy	

507

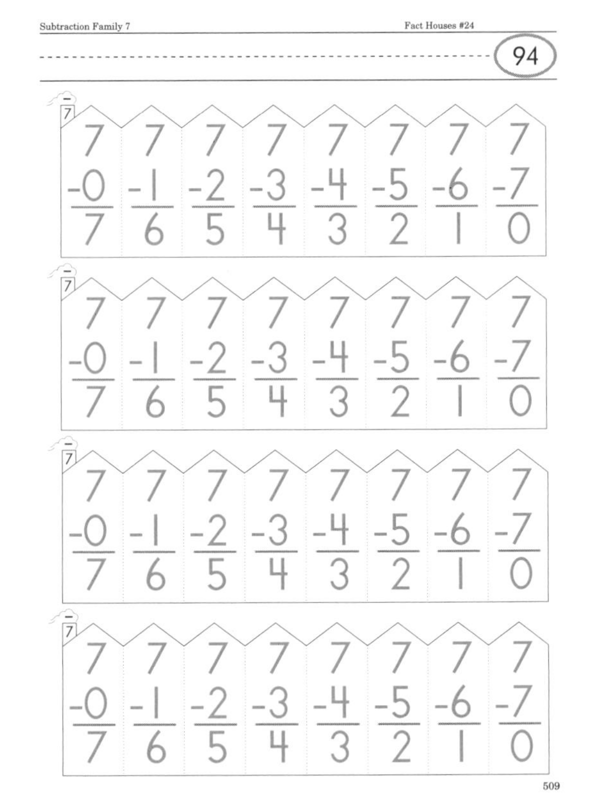

Subtraction Family 7 Fact Houses #24

94

7	7	7	7	7	7	7	7
-0	-1	-2	-3	-4	-5	-6	-7
7	6	5	4	3	2	1	0

7	7	7	7	7	7	7	7
-0	-1	-2	-3	-4	-5	-6	-7
7	6	5	4	3	2	1	0

7	7	7	7	7	7	7	7
-0	-1	-2	-3	-4	-5	-6	-7
7	6	5	4	3	2	1	0

7	7	7	7	7	7	7	7
-0	-1	-2	-3	-4	-5	-6	-7
7	6	5	4	3	2	1	0

509

100–129 Less Numbers #13

94

less

111	120	132	**112**	139	**119**
122	124	132	**130**	**112**	115
131	132	126	**116**	139	**129**
118	128	**121**	124	**123**	124
136	**131**	114	**113**	129	**119**
127	137	116	**115**	136	**126**
119	**118**	**127**	128	**122**	123
113	133	**130**	135	137	**117**
125	**120**	134	**124**	**133**	134

510

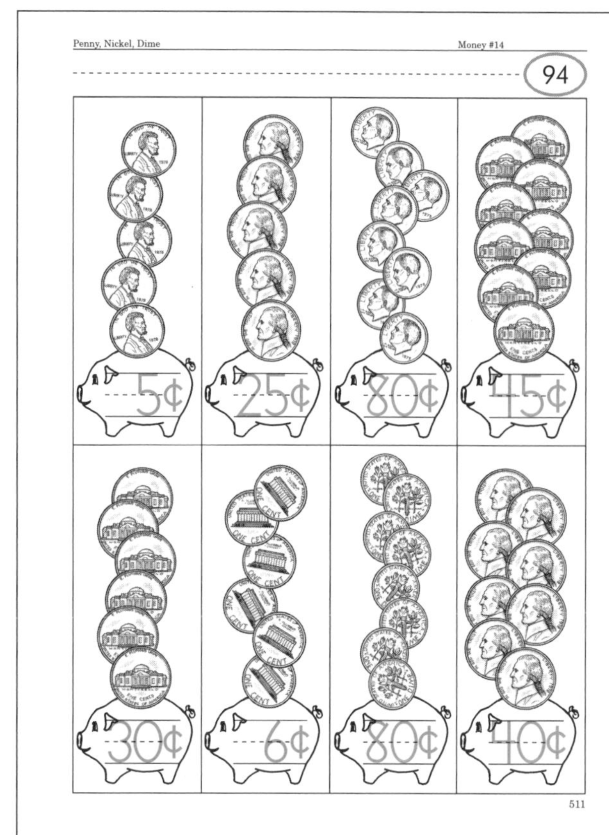

7 [-] Number Facts #29

94

A	7 − 6 = 1	7 − 4 = 3	7 − 2 = 5	7 − 3 = 4	7 − 6 = 1	7 − 4 = 3	7 − 1 = 6	7 − 5 = 2
B	7 − 5 = 2	7 − 1 = 6	7 − 4 = 3	7 − 2 = 5	7 − 6 = 1	7 − 3 = 4	7 − 2 = 5	7 − 5 = 2
C	7 − 3 = 2	7 − 5 = 2	7 − 6 = 1	7 − 4 = 3	7 − 5 = 2	7 − 2 = 5	7 − 6 = 1	7 − 2 = 5
D	7 − 4 = 3	7 − 3 = 4	7 − 2 = 5	7 − 3 = 4	7 − 4 = 3	7 − 2 = 5	7 − 3 = 4	7 − 6 = 1
E	7 − 5 = 2	7 − 6 = 1	7 − 2 = 5	7 − 5 = 2	7 − 3 = 4	7 − 4 = 3	7 − 2 = 5	7 − 6 = 1
F	7 − 0 = 7	7 − 1 = 6	7 − 4 = 3	7 − 3 = 4	7 − 5 = 2	7 − 6 = 1	7 − 4 = 3	7 − 2 = 5

512

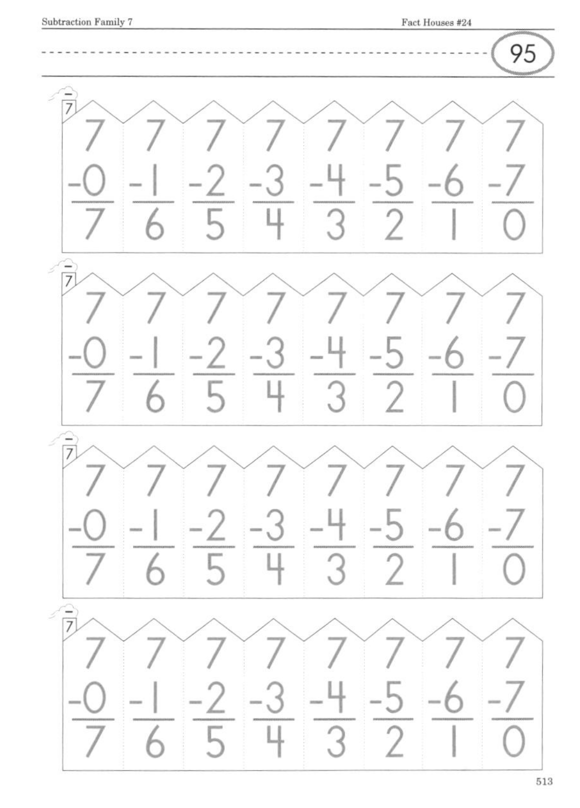

100–129 Before and After #7

95

134	135	136	133	134	135
142	143	144	147	148	149
137	138	139	126	127	128
140	141	142	143	144	145
124	125	126	146	147	148
131	132	133	121	122	123
136	137	138	145	146	147
144	145	146	130	131	132
132	133	134	141	142	143

514

4, 5, 7 [-] Number Facts #30

95

A	7 − 5 = 2	7 − 4 = 3	5 − 4 = 1	7 − 3 = 4	5 − 0 = 5	5 − 3 = 2	7 − 6 = 1	7 − 1 = 6
B	5 − 1 = 4	5 − 3 = 2	4 − 1 = 3	7 − 4 = 3	7 − 6 = 1	7 − 5 = 2	5 − 3 = 2	7 − 4 = 3
C	7 − 1 = 6	7 − 5 = 2	4 − 2 = 2	5 − 2 = 3	4 − 3 = 1	7 − 3 = 4	7 − 2 = 5	7 − 4 = 3
D	7 − 2 = 5	7 − 6 = 1	7 − 1 = 6	5 − 3 = 2	5 − 2 = 3	7 − 3 = 4	5 − 1 = 4	7 − 2 = 5
E	5 − 2 = 3	7 − 4 = 3	7 − 3 = 4	5 − 1 = 4	7 − 2 = 5	4 − 1 = 3	7 − 6 = 1	4 − 0 = 4
F	7 − 6 = 1	7 − 2 = 5	5 − 0 = 5	7 − 1 = 6	5 − 1 = 4	7 − 5 = 2	7 − 4 = 3	4 − 3 = 1

515

2–7 [+] Number Facts #26

95

A	2+0=2	4+1=5	1+3=4	4+2=6
B	3+2=5	4+3=7	1+4=5	2+2=4
C	6+1=7	3+4=7	5+1=6	3+2=5
D	2+1=3	4+1=5	4+3=7	1+5=6
E	3+4=7	4+2=6	1+2=3	5+2=7
F	3+1=4	2+2=4	5+2=7	2+5=7
G	4+1=5	2+3=5	5+2=7	3+1=4
H	4+2=6	3+3=6	3+4=7	3+2=5
I	2+5=7	6+1=7	2+4=6	6+1=7
J	6+1=7	3+3=6	3+2=5	2+3=5
K	2+4=6	3+0=3	4+2=6	2+4=6
L	2+4=6	3+2=5	4+2=6	2+1=3
M	2+3=5	4+3=7	2+2=4	5+1=6
N	2+4=6	1+3=4	2+3=5	1+1=2
O	3+2=5	3+4=7	1+4=5	1+2=3
P	4+2=6	5+2=5	4+2=6	6+1=7

516

By 2's to 40 Dot-to-Dot #35

95

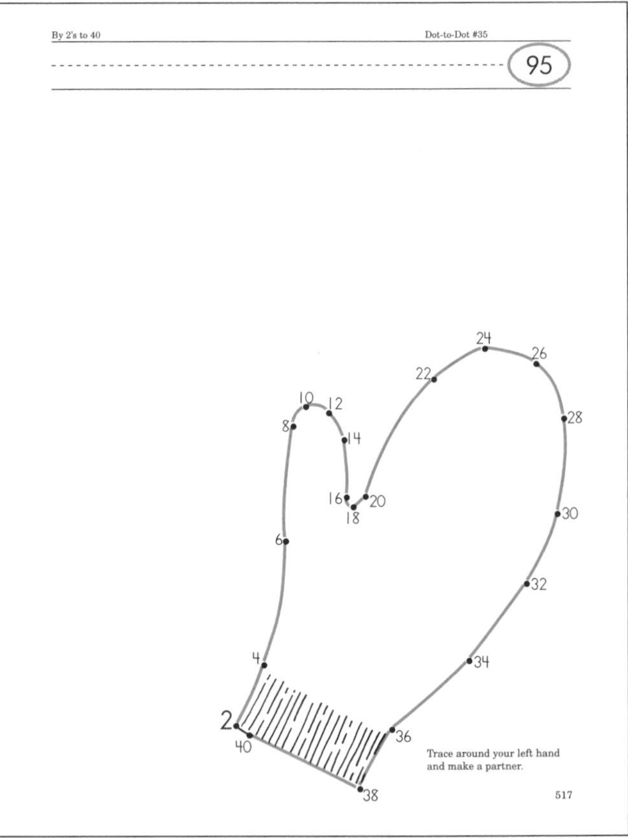

Trace around your left hand and make a partner.

517

Subtraction Families 6, 7 — Fact Houses #25 — 96

6 − 0 = 6	6 − 1 = 5	6 − 2 = 4	6 − 3 = 3	6 − 4 = 2	6 − 5 = 1	6 − 6 = 0	
6 − 0 = 6	6 − 1 = 5	6 − 2 = 4	6 − 3 = 3	6 − 4 = 2	6 − 5 = 1	6 − 6 = 0	
7 − 0 = 7	7 − 1 = 6	7 − 2 = 5	7 − 3 = 4	7 − 4 = 3	7 − 5 = 2	7 − 6 = 1	7 − 7 = 0
7 − 0 = 7	7 − 1 = 6	7 − 2 = 5	7 − 3 = 4	7 − 4 = 3	7 − 5 = 2	7 − 6 = 1	7 − 7 = 0

519

4, 5, 7 [-] — Number Facts #30 — 96

A	7 − 5 = 2	7 − 4 = 3	5 − 4 = 1	7 − 3 = 4	5 − 0 = 5	5 − 3 = 2	7 − 6 = 1	7 − 1 = 6
B	5 − 1 = 4	5 − 3 = 2	4 − 1 = 3	7 − 4 = 3	7 − 6 = 1	7 − 5 = 2	5 − 3 = 2	7 − 4 = 3
C	7 − 1 = 6	7 − 5 = 2	4 − 2 = 2	5 − 2 = 3	4 − 3 = 1	7 − 3 = 4	7 − 2 = 5	7 − 4 = 3
D	7 − 2 = 5	7 − 6 = 1	7 − 1 = 6	5 − 3 = 2	5 − 2 = 3	7 − 3 = 4	5 − 1 = 4	7 − 2 = 5
E	5 − 2 = 3	7 − 4 = 3	7 − 3 = 4	5 − 1 = 4	7 − 2 = 5	4 − 1 = 3	7 − 6 = 1	4 − 0 = 4
F	7 − 6 = 1	7 − 2 = 5	5 − 0 = 5	7 − 1 = 6	5 − 1 = 4	7 − 5 = 2	7 − 4 = 3	4 − 3 = 1

520

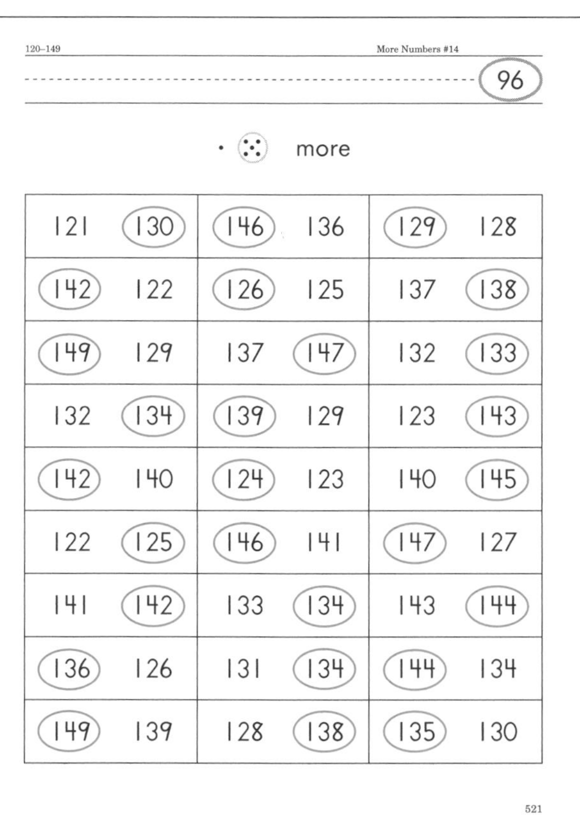

120–149 — More Numbers #14 — 96

• more

121	(130)	(146)	136	(129)	128
(142)	122	(126)	125	137	(138)
(149)	129	137	(147)	132	(133)
132	(134)	(139)	129	123	(143)
(142)	140	(124)	123	140	(145)
122	(125)	(146)	141	(147)	127
141	(142)	133	(134)	143	(144)
(136)	126	131	(134)	(144)	134
(149)	139	128	(138)	(135)	130

521

Half Hour — Clocks #4 — 96

4:30 10:30 12:30 5:30
2:30 8:30 7:30 6:30
7:30 1:30 10:30 12:30
3:30 11:30 4:30 9:30

522

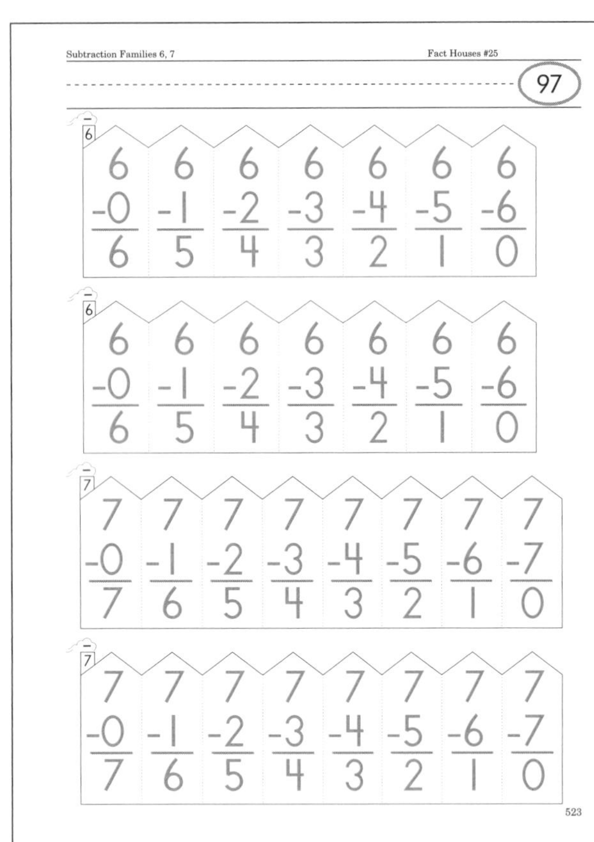

Subtraction Families 6, 7 — Fact Houses #25 — 97

6	6	6	6	6	6	6
-0	-1	-2	-3	-4	-5	-6
6	5	4	3	2	1	0

6	6	6	6	6	6	6
-0	-1	-2	-3	-4	-5	-6
6	5	4	3	2	1	0

7	7	7	7	7	7	7	7
-0	-1	-2	-3	-4	-5	-6	-7
7	6	5	4	3	2	1	0

7	7	7	7	7	7	7	7
-0	-1	-2	-3	-4	-5	-6	-7
7	6	5	4	3	2	1	0

523

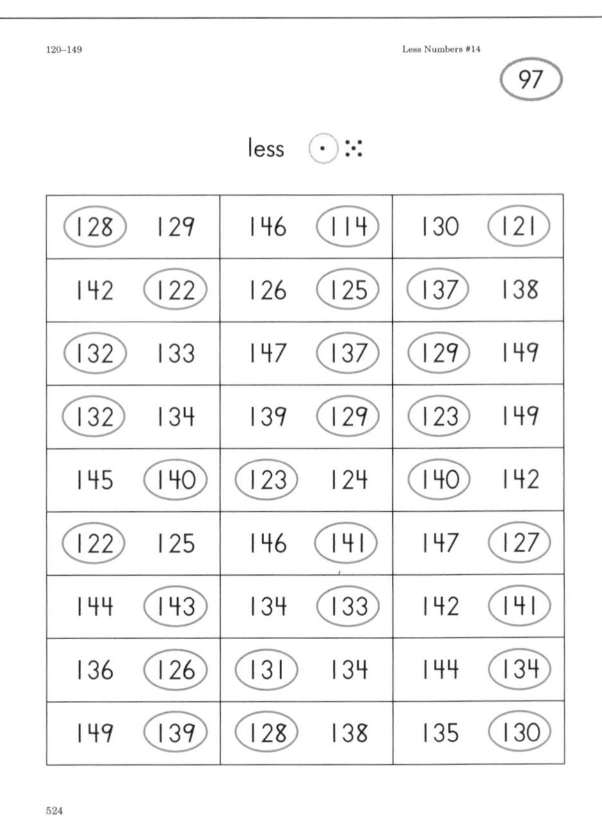

120–149 — Less Numbers #14 — 97

less

128	129	146	**114**	130	**121**
142	**122**	126	**125**	**137**	138
132	133	147	**137**	**129**	149
132	134	139	**129**	**123**	149
145	**140**	**123**	124	**140**	142
122	125	146	**141**	147	**127**
144	**143**	134	**133**	142	**141**
136	**126**	**131**	134	144	**134**
149	**139**	**128**	138	135	**130**

524

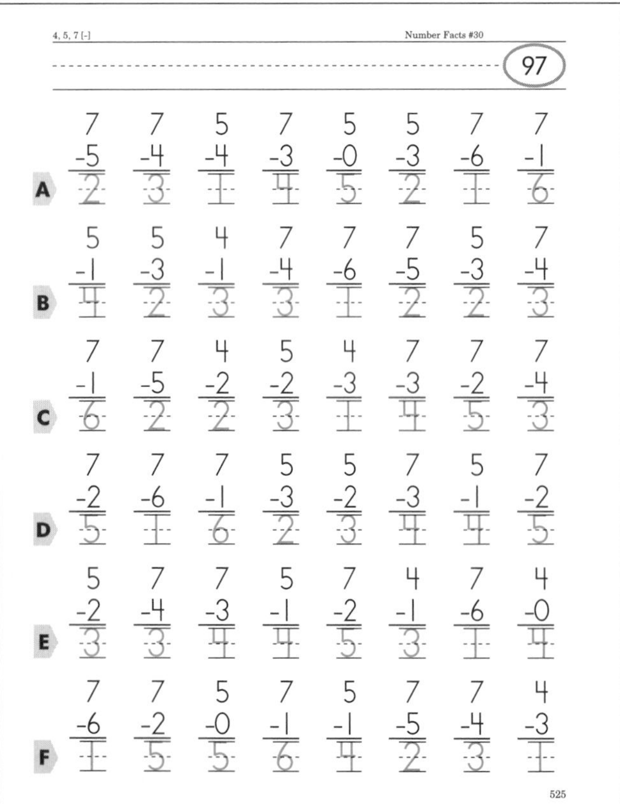

4, 5, 7 [-] — Number Facts #30 — 97

A	7 - 5 = 2	7 - 4 = 3	5 - 4 = 1	7 - 3 = 4	5 - 0 = 5	5 - 3 = 2	7 - 6 = 1	7 - 1 = 6
B	5 - 1 = 4	5 - 3 = 2	4 - 1 = 3	7 - 4 = 3	7 - 6 = 1	7 - 5 = 2	5 - 3 = 2	7 - 4 = 3
C	7 - 1 = 6	7 - 5 = 2	4 - 2 = 2	5 - 2 = 3	4 - 3 = 1	7 - 3 = 4	7 - 2 = 5	7 - 4 = 3
D	7 - 2 = 5	7 - 6 = 1	7 - 1 = 6	5 - 3 = 2	5 - 2 = 3	7 - 3 = 4	5 - 1 = 4	7 - 2 = 5
E	5 - 2 = 3	7 - 4 = 3	7 - 3 = 4	5 - 1 = 4	7 - 2 = 5	4 - 1 = 3	7 - 6 = 1	4 - 0 = 4
F	7 - 6 = 1	7 - 2 = 5	5 - 0 = 5	7 - 1 = 6	5 - 1 = 4	7 - 5 = 2	7 - 4 = 3	4 - 3 = 1

525

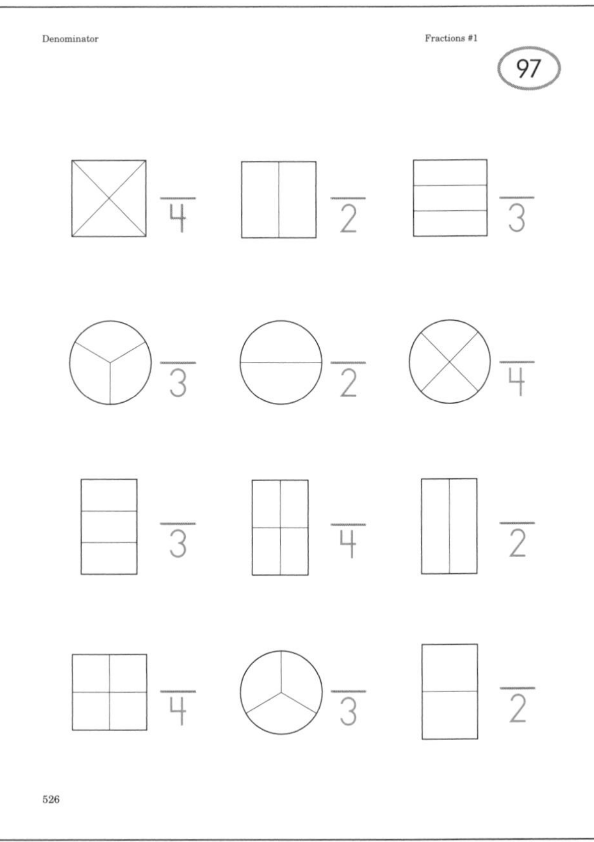

Denominator — Fractions #1 — 97

4 2 3

3 2 4

3 4 2

4 3 2

526

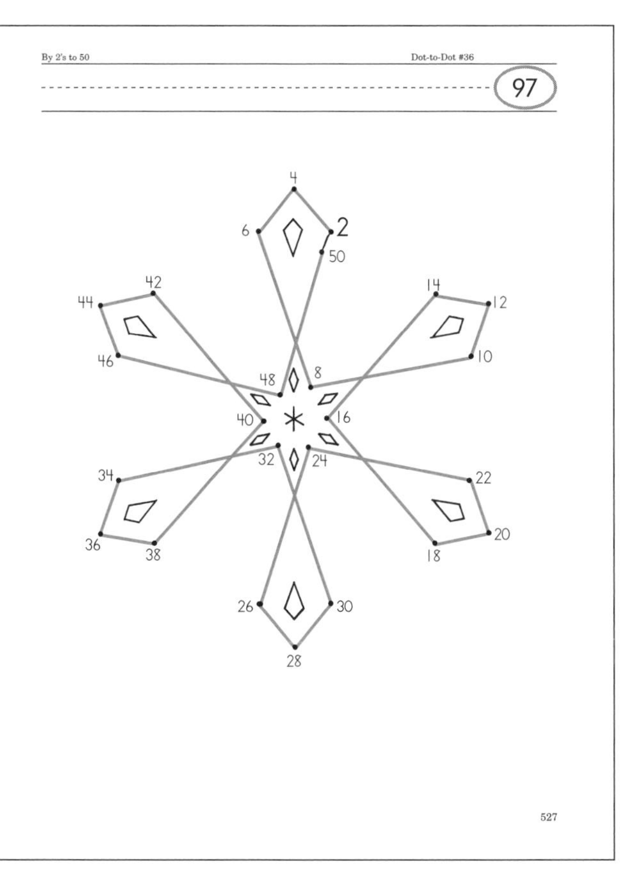

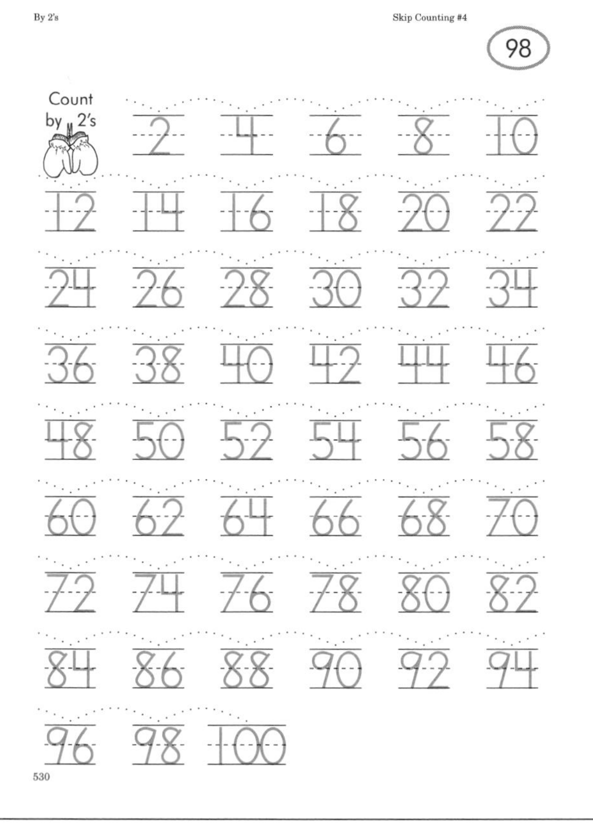

5–7 [-] Number Facts #31

98

A	7 - 1 = 6	6 - 4 = 2	6 - 1 = 5	7 - 0 = 7
B	5 - 3 = 2	7 - 3 = 4	7 - 4 = 3	6 - 2 = 4
C	7 - 2 = 5	6 - 1 = 5	5 - 4 = 1	7 - 2 = 5
D	6 - 2 = 4	6 - 3 = 3	7 - 5 = 2	7 - 4 = 3
E	7 - 4 = 3	7 - 6 = 1	6 - 2 = 4	7 - 5 = 2
F	7 - 2 = 5	7 - 4 = 3	7 - 2 = 5	6 - 4 = 2
G	7 - 3 = 4	6 - 5 = 1	6 - 3 = 3	7 - 4 = 3
H	7 - 2 = 5	5 - 3 = 2	7 - 6 = 1	5 - 4 = 1
I	6 - 5 = 1	7 - 2 = 5	7 - 1 = 6	6 - 4 = 2
J	5 - 3 = 2	7 - 1 = 6	6 - 4 = 2	7 - 2 = 5
K	7 - 1 = 6	6 - 5 = 1	7 - 5 = 2	6 - 0 = 6
L	7 - 5 = 2	5 - 1 = 4	6 - 1 = 5	7 - 5 = 2
M	6 - 3 = 3	7 - 2 = 5	7 - 1 = 6	7 - 3 = 4
N	6 - 2 = 4	6 - 0 = 6	6 - 4 = 2	6 - 1 = 5
O	6 - 4 = 2	5 - 3 = 2	7 - 3 = 4	5 - 2 = 3
P	7 - 2 = 5	6 - 4 = 2	7 - 2 = 5	7 - 6 = 1
Q	6 - 0 = 6	7 - 3 = 4	7 - 1 = 6	7 - 5 = 2

531

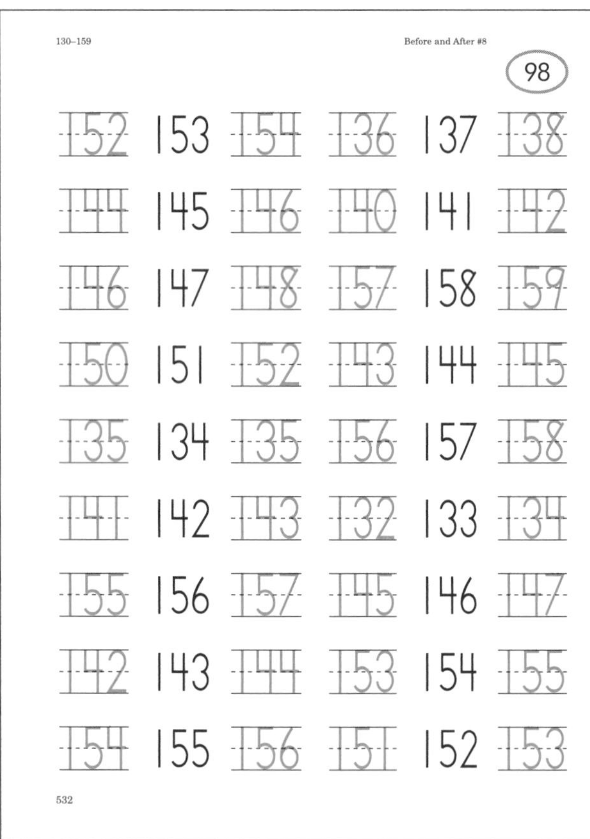

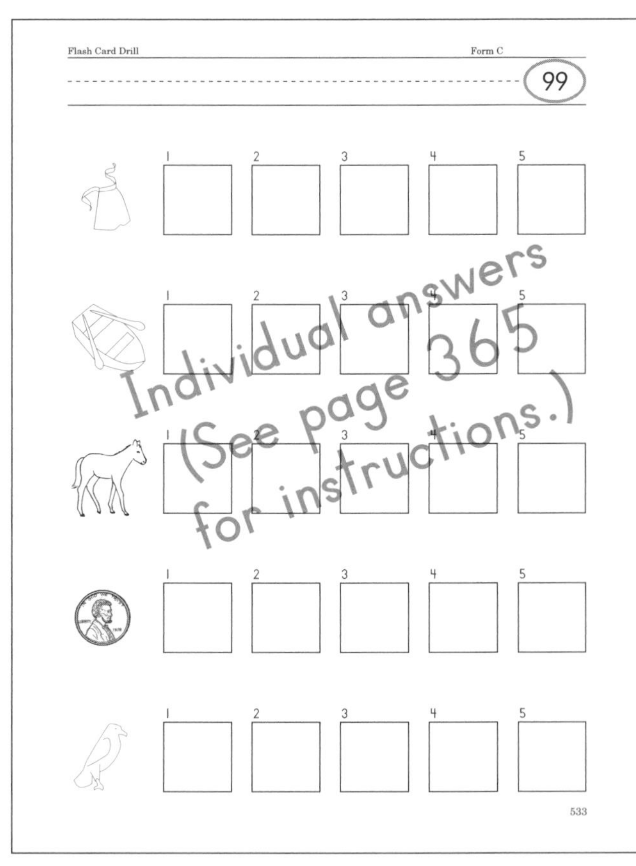
Individual answers
(See page 365
for instructions.)

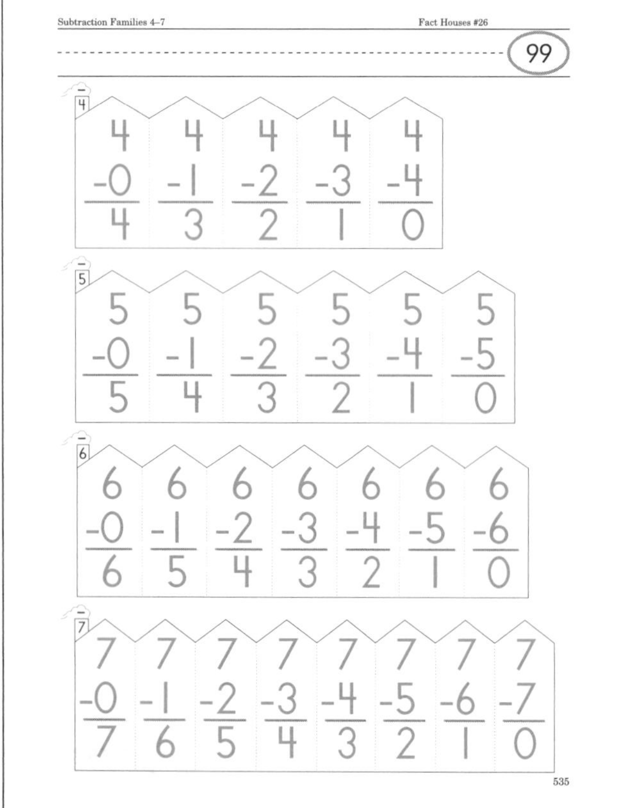

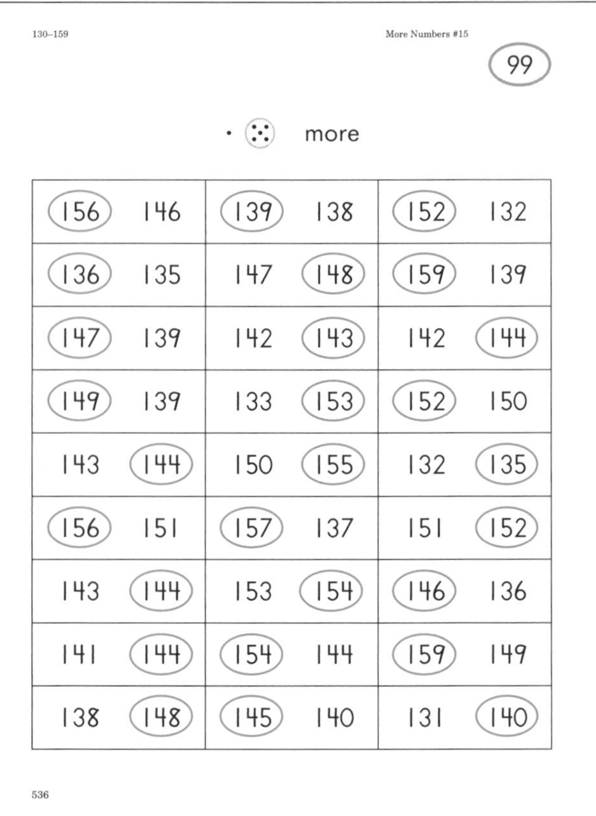

By 2's — Skip Counting #4 — 99

Count by 2's

2 4 6 8 10
12 14 16 18 20 22
24 26 28 30 32 34
36 38 40 42 44 46
48 50 52 54 56 58
60 62 64 66 68 70
72 74 76 78 80 82
84 86 88 90 92 94
96 98 100

537

5–7 [–] — Number Facts #31 — 99

A	7 - 1 = 6	6 - 4 = 2	6 - 1 = 5	7 - 0 = 7
B	5 - 3 = 2	7 - 3 = 4	7 - 4 = 3	6 - 2 = 4
C	7 - 2 = 5	6 - 1 = 5	5 - 4 = 1	7 - 2 = 5
D	6 - 2 = 4	6 - 3 = 3	7 - 5 = 2	7 - 4 = 3
E	7 - 4 = 3	7 - 6 = 1	6 - 2 = 4	7 - 5 = 2
F	7 - 2 = 5	7 - 4 = 3	7 - 2 = 5	6 - 4 = 2
G	7 - 3 = 4	6 - 5 = 1	6 - 3 = 3	7 - 4 = 3
H	7 - 2 = 5	5 - 3 = 2	7 - 6 = 1	5 - 4 = 1
I	6 - 5 = 1	7 - 2 = 5	7 - 1 = 6	6 - 4 = 2
J	5 - 3 = 2	7 - 1 = 6	6 - 4 = 2	7 - 2 = 5
K	7 - 1 = 6	6 - 5 = 1	7 - 5 = 2	6 - 0 = 6
L	7 - 5 = 2	5 - 1 = 4	6 - 1 = 5	7 - 5 = 2
M	6 - 3 = 3	7 - 2 = 5	7 - 1 = 6	7 - 3 = 4
N	6 - 2 = 4	6 - 0 = 6	6 - 4 = 2	6 - 1 = 5
O	6 - 4 = 2	5 - 3 = 2	7 - 3 = 4	5 - 2 = 3
P	7 - 2 = 5	6 - 4 = 2	7 - 2 = 5	7 - 6 = 1
Q	6 - 0 = 6	7 - 3 = 4	7 - 1 = 6	7 - 5 = 2

538

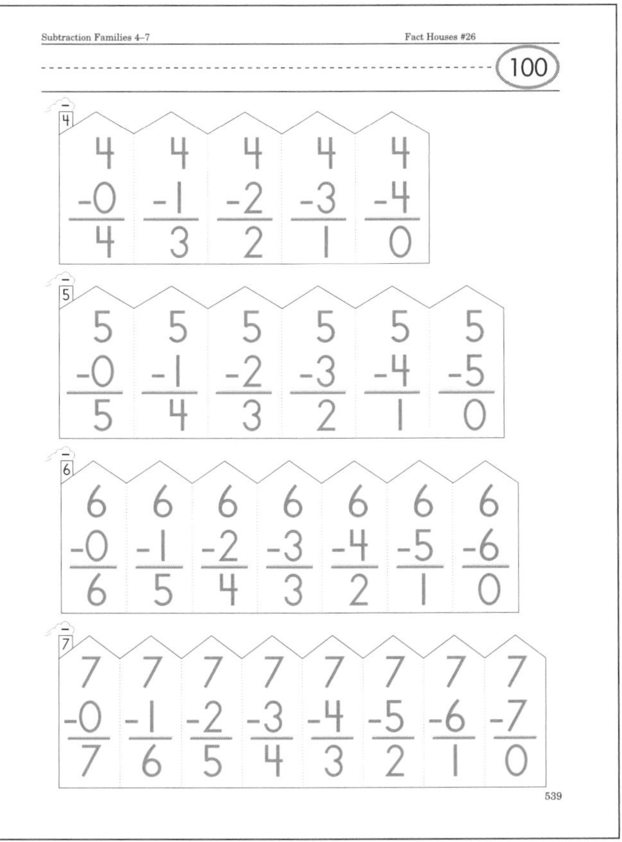

Subtraction Families 4–7 — Fact Houses #26 — 100

4: 4 - 0 = 4, 4 - 1 = 3, 4 - 2 = 2, 4 - 3 = 1, 4 - 4 = 0

5: 5 - 0 = 5, 5 - 1 = 4, 5 - 2 = 3, 5 - 3 = 2, 5 - 4 = 1, 5 - 5 = 0

6: 6 - 0 = 6, 6 - 1 = 5, 6 - 2 = 4, 6 - 3 = 3, 6 - 4 = 2, 6 - 5 = 1, 6 - 6 = 0

7: 7 - 0 = 7, 7 - 1 = 6, 7 - 2 = 5, 7 - 3 = 4, 7 - 4 = 3, 7 - 5 = 2, 7 - 6 = 1, 7 - 7 = 0

539

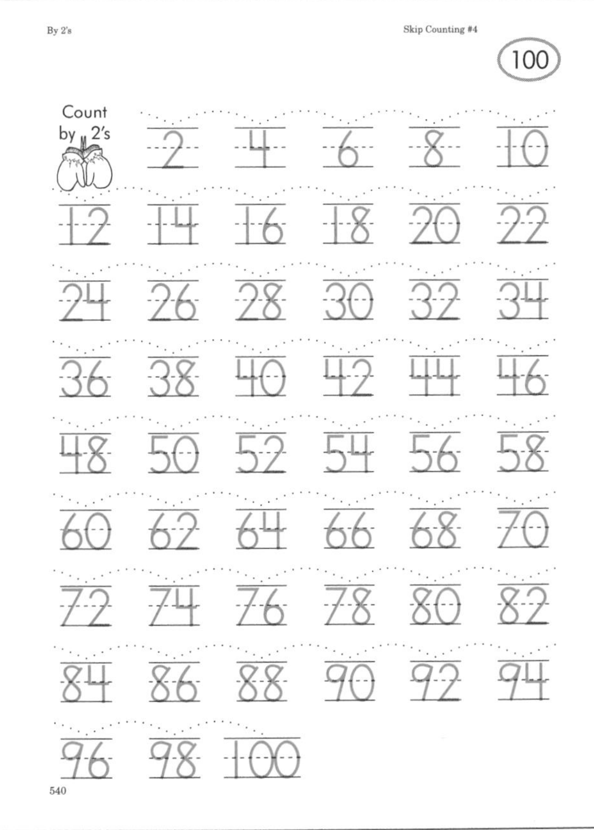

By 2's — Skip Counting #4 — 100

Count by 2's

2 4 6 8 10
12 14 16 18 20 22
24 26 28 30 32 34
36 38 40 42 44 46
48 50 52 54 56 58
60 62 64 66 68 70
72 74 76 78 80 82
84 86 88 90 92 94
96 98 100

540

6, 7 [-] Number Facts #32

100

A	6 -1 5	7 -5 2	6 -3 3	6 -5 1	6 -4 2	7 -3 4	7 -2 5	7 -4 3	7 -2 5	6 -2 4	7 -1 6	6 -3 3
B	7 -4 3	6 -5 1	7 -1 6	6 -3 3	7 -2 5	6 -0 6	7 -5 2	6 -1 5	7 -3 4	7 -4 3	7 -5 2	7 -0 7
C	7 -3 4	7 -1 6	6 -2 4	7 -4 3	6 -3 3	6 -5 1	6 -4 2	6 -3 3	6 -4 2	7 -3 4	6 -2 4	6 -1 5
D	7 -5 2	7 -2 5	6 -3 3	7 -5 2	7 -4 3	6 -1 5	6 -4 2	7 -6 1	7 -4 3	6 -5 1	7 -4 3	7 -5 2
E	7 -6 1	6 -4 2	7 -1 6	6 -2 4	7 -6 1	6 -4 2	7 -4 3	6 -5 1	7 -2 5	6 -3 3	6 -1 5	7 -4 3
F	6 -3 3	7 -2 5	6 -1 5	7 -5 2	7 -2 5	7 -1 6	7 -3 4	6 -2 4	7 -5 2	6 -4 2	6 -2 4	7 -4 3
G	7 -5 2	6 -5 1	6 -4 2	7 -2 5	6 -2 4	7 -5 2	7 -6 1	7 -3 4	7 -4 3	6 -3 3	7 -6 1	6 -5 1

541

1–7 [+ -] Number Facts #33

100

A	6 -2 4	2 +5 7	1 +6 7	6 -2 4	3 +2 5	7 -3 4	2 +3 5	6 -1 5	1 +2 3	5 +1 6	4 -2 2	2 +2 4
B	3 -1 2	3 +4 7	2 +4 6	7 -2 5	7 -4 2	5 +2 7	5 +1 6	5 -2 3	7 -3 4	2 +5 7	7 -4 3	6 -5 1
C	2 +2 4	6 -3 3	7 -5 2	7 -2 5	3 +1 4	3 +4 7	3 +2 5	2 +2 4	5 -4 1	1 +0 1	6 -1 5	3 +2 5
D	6 -5 1	2 +3 5	3 +1 4	1 +5 6	7 -5 2	4 +2 6	2 +4 6	6 -4 2	7 -2 5	7 -5 2	4 +3 7	7 -4 3
E	7 -2 5	3 +3 6	7 -6 1	7 -5 2	5 +2 7	2 +5 7	5 -3 2	2 +4 6	6 -3 3	6 +1 7	3 +2 5	6 -2 4
F	6 -3 3	6 -4 2	2 +3 5	6 -2 4	4 +3 7	6 -1 5	3 +1 4	4 +3 7	2 +2 4	6 +1 7	3 +3 6	5 -3 2
G	1 +3 4	7 -5 2	2 +1 3	4 -3 1	6 -1 5	2 +2 4	7 -6 1	7 -2 5	7 -5 2	4 +2 6	7 -2 5	2 +5 7

542

130–159 Less Numbers #15

100

less

138	148	**141**	144	**143**	144
156	**151**	**143**	144	149	**139**
147	157	136	**135**	156	**146**
139	**138**	**147**	148	**142**	143
133	153	**150**	155	157	**137**
153	154	154	**144**	145	**140**
131	140	152	**132**	159	**139**
142	144	152	**150**	**132**	135
151	**149**	**138**	148	145	**140**

543

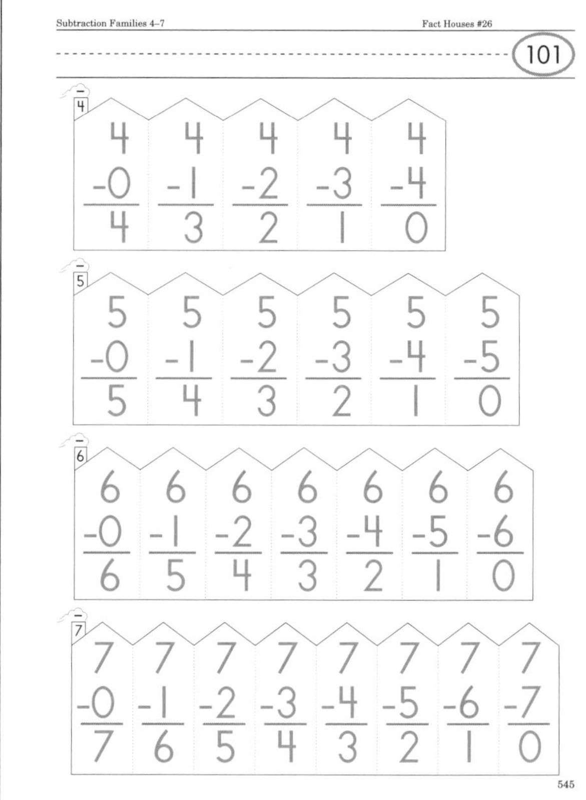

140–169 Before and After #9 (101)

151	152	153	153	154	155
162	163	164	167	168	169
155	156	157	143	144	145
160	161	162	163	164	165
144	145	146	166	167	168
154	155	156	141	142	143
156	157	158	165	166	167
164	165	166	150	151	152
152	153	154	161	162	163

546

6, 7 [-] Number Facts #32 (101)

A	6 -1 5	7 -5 2	6 -3 3	6 -5 1	6 -4 2	7 -3 4	7 -2 5	7 -4 3	7 -2 5	6 -2 4	7 -1 6	6 -3 3
B	7 -4 3	6 -5 1	7 -1 6	6 -3 3	7 -2 5	6 -0 6	7 -5 2	6 -1 5	7 -3 4	7 -4 3	7 -5 2	7 -0 7
C	7 -3 4	7 -1 6	6 -2 4	7 -4 3	6 -3 3	6 -5 1	6 -4 2	6 -3 3	6 -4 2	7 -3 4	6 -2 4	6 -1 5
D	7 -5 2	7 -2 5	6 -3 3	7 -5 2	7 -4 3	6 -1 5	6 -4 2	7 -6 1	7 -4 3	6 -5 1	7 -4 3	7 -5 2
E	7 -6 1	6 -4 2	7 -1 6	6 -2 4	7 -6 1	6 -4 2	7 -4 3	6 -5 1	7 -2 5	6 -3 3	6 -1 5	7 -4 3
F	6 -3 3	7 -2 5	6 -1 5	7 -5 2	7 -2 5	7 -1 6	7 -3 4	6 -2 4	7 -5 2	6 -4 2	6 -2 4	7 -4 3
G	7 -5 2	6 -5 1	6 -4 2	7 -2 5	6 -2 4	7 -5 2	7 -6 1	7 -3 4	7 -4 3	6 -3 3	7 -6 1	6 -5 1

547

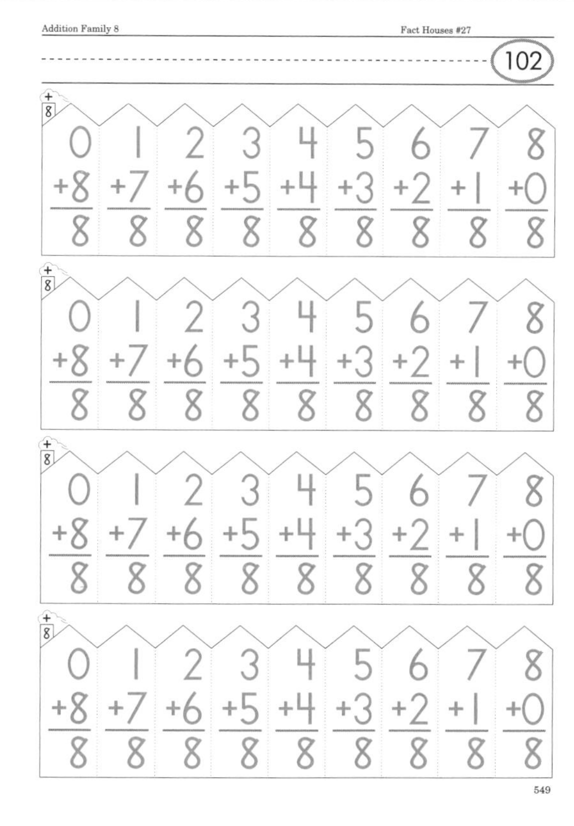

By 2's — Skip Counting #4 — 102

Count by 2's

	2	4	6	8	10
12	14	16	18	20	22
24	26	28	30	32	34
36	38	40	42	44	46
48	50	52	54	56	58
60	62	64	66	68	70
72	74	76	78	80	82
84	86	88	90	92	94
96	98	100			

550

1-7 [-] — Number Facts #34 — 102

A	3 - 2 = 1	7 - 2 = 5	7 - 4 = 3	6 - 4 = 2
B	7 - 3 = 4	6 - 3 = 3	4 - 2 = 2	5 - 4 = 1
C	5 - 3 = 2	6 - 1 = 5	5 - 2 = 3	6 - 2 = 4
D	7 - 2 = 5	5 - 3 = 2	6 - 2 = 4	7 - 1 = 6
E	6 - 4 = 2	6 - 3 = 3	7 - 2 = 5	7 - 3 = 4
F	7 - 5 = 2	3 - 2 = 1	7 - 5 = 2	6 - 2 = 4
G	7 - 0 = 7	6 - 2 = 4	7 - 6 = 1	7 - 2 = 5
H	7 - 2 = 5	6 - 0 = 6	5 - 1 = 4	2 - 1 = 1
I	6 - 5 = 1	7 - 2 = 5	7 - 1 = 6	6 - 3 = 3
J	6 - 4 = 2	5 - 2 = 3	7 - 5 = 2	4 - 3 = 1
K	7 - 4 = 3	7 - 5 = 2	7 - 3 = 4	7 - 2 = 5
L	6 - 2 = 4	6 - 4 = 2	5 - 4 = 1	6 - 4 = 2
M	6 - 1 = 5	6 - 2 = 4	7 - 2 = 5	6 - 3 = 3
N	7 - 5 = 2	7 - 6 = 1	5 - 3 = 2	5 - 1 = 4
O	1 - 0 = 1	5 - 0 = 5	7 - 4 = 3	7 - 2 = 5
P	7 - 3 = 4	6 - 1 = 5	7 - 3 = 4	6 - 4 = 2
Q	7 - 1 = 6	7 - 4 = 3	6 - 1 = 5	6 - 5 = 1

551

140–169 — More Numbers #16 — 102

more

169	159	**156**	146	161	**162**
142	**145**	**162**	160	152	**154**
169	149	**162**	142	141	**150**
166	156	**146**	145	157	**167**
159	149	**144**	143	**166**	161
153	**154**	151	**154**	148	**158**
155	150	**164**	154	163	**164**
167	147	160	**165**	143	**163**
152	**153**	157	**158**	**149**	148

552

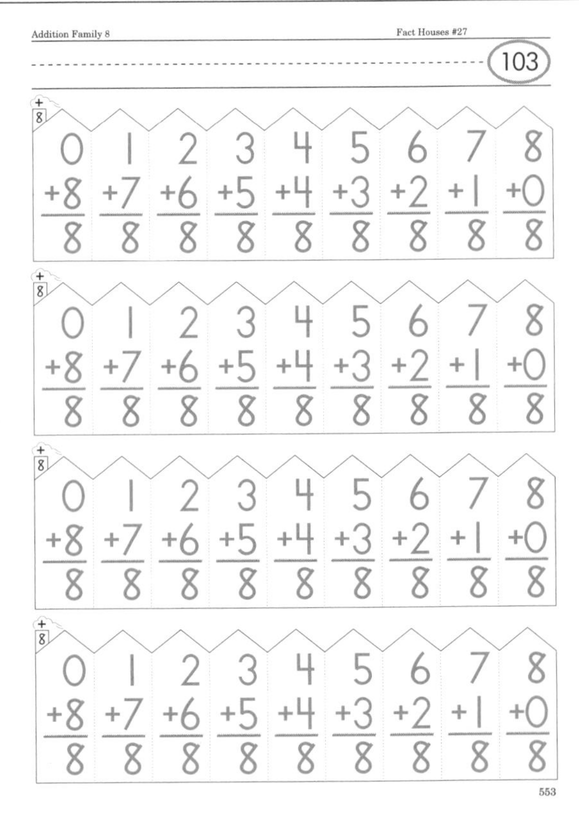
Addition Family 8 — Fact Houses #27 — 103

0	1	2	3	4	5	6	7	8
+8	+7	+6	+5	+4	+3	+2	+1	+0
8	8	8	8	8	8	8	8	8

0	1	2	3	4	5	6	7	8
+8	+7	+6	+5	+4	+3	+2	+1	+0
8	8	8	8	8	8	8	8	8

0	1	2	3	4	5	6	7	8
+8	+7	+6	+5	+4	+3	+2	+1	+0
8	8	8	8	8	8	8	8	8

0	1	2	3	4	5	6	7	8
+8	+7	+6	+5	+4	+3	+2	+1	+0
8	8	8	8	8	8	8	8	8

553

140–169 Less Numbers #16

103

less

141	150	162	142	169	149
166	156	149	148	146	145
157	158	157	167	152	153
163	143	149	159	154	152
162	160	144	143	160	165
142	145	161	162	156	146
166	161	153	154	151	154
167	147	163	164	164	154
169	159	148	158	155	150

554

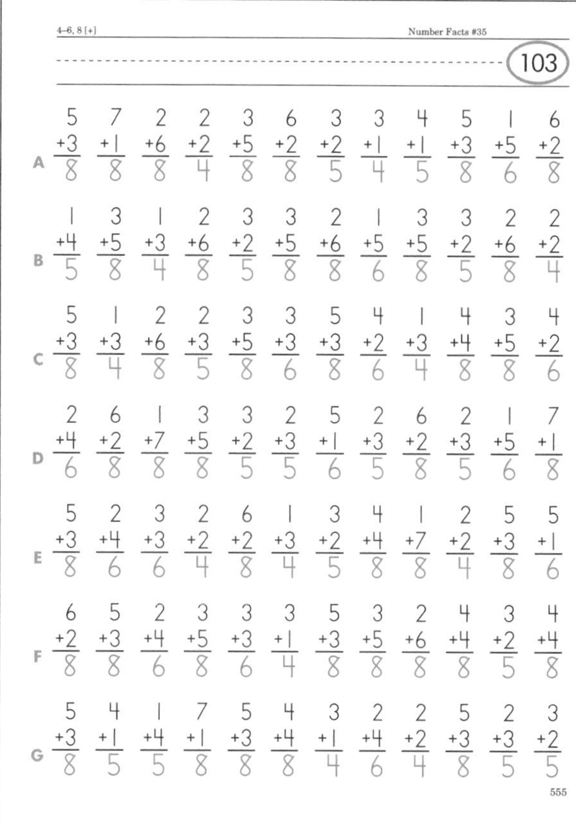

4–6, 8 [+] Number Facts #35

103

A	5+3=8	7+1=8	2+6=8	2+2=4	3+5=8	6+2=8	3+2=5	3+1=4	4+1=5	5+3=8	1+5=6	6+2=8
B	1+4=5	3+5=8	1+3=4	2+6=8	3+2=5	3+5=8	2+6=8	1+5=6	3+5=8	3+2=5	2+6=8	2+2=4
C	5+3=8	1+3=4	2+6=8	2+3=5	3+5=8	3+3=6	5+3=8	4+2=6	1+3=4	4+4=8	3+5=8	4+2=6
D	2+4=6	6+2=8	1+7=8	3+5=8	3+2=5	2+3=5	5+1=6	2+3=5	6+2=8	2+3=5	1+5=6	7+1=8
E	5+3=8	2+4=6	3+3=6	2+2=4	6+2=8	1+3=4	3+2=5	4+4=8	1+7=8	2+2=4	5+3=8	5+1=6
F	6+2=8	5+3=8	2+4=6	3+5=8	3+3=6	3+1=4	5+3=8	3+5=8	2+6=8	4+4=8	3+2=5	4+4=8
G	5+3=8	4+1=5	1+4=5	7+1=8	5+3=8	4+4=8	3+1=4	2+4=6	2+2=4	5+3=8	2+3=5	3+2=5

555

By 2's to 64 Dot-to-Dot #37

103

556

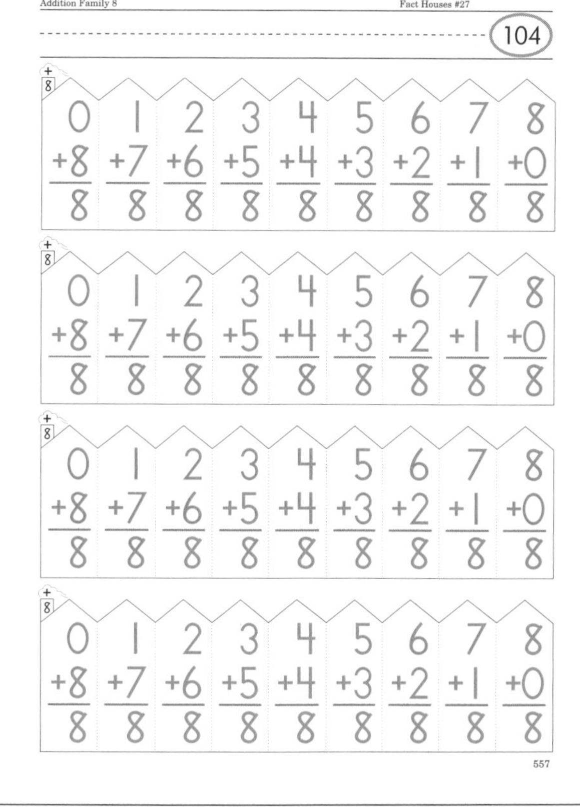

Addition Family 8 Fact Houses #27

104

+ 8								
0+8=8	1+7=8	2+6=8	3+5=8	4+4=8	5+3=8	6+2=8	7+1=8	8+0=8
0+8=8	1+7=8	2+6=8	3+5=8	4+4=8	5+3=8	6+2=8	7+1=8	8+0=8
0+8=8	1+7=8	2+6=8	3+5=8	4+4=8	5+3=8	6+2=8	7+1=8	8+0=8
0+8=8	1+7=8	2+6=8	3+5=8	4+4=8	5+3=8	6+2=8	7+1=8	8+0=8

557

150–179 Before and After #10

(104)

164	165	166	160	161	162
172	173	174	176	177	178
165	166	167	151	152	153
170	171	172	175	176	177
174	175	176	177	178	179
166	167	168	156	157	158
161	162	163	173	174	175
154	155	156	167	168	169
162	163	164	171	172	173

558

Half Hour Clocks #4

(104)

4:30	10:30	12:30	5:30
2:30	8:30	7:30	6:30
7:30	1:30	10:30	12:30
3:30	11:30	4:30	9:30

559

1–7 [-] Number Facts #34

(104)

A	3 - 2 = 1	7 - 2 = 5	7 - 4 = 3	6 - 4 = 2
B	7 - 3 = 4	6 - 3 = 3	4 - 2 = 2	5 - 4 = 1
C	5 - 3 = 2	6 - 1 = 5	5 - 2 = 3	6 - 2 = 4
D	7 - 2 = 5	5 - 3 = 2	6 - 2 = 4	7 - 1 = 6
E	6 - 4 = 2	6 - 3 = 3	7 - 2 = 5	7 - 3 = 4
F	7 - 5 = 2	3 - 2 = 1	7 - 5 = 2	6 - 2 = 4
G	7 - 0 = 7	6 - 2 = 4	7 - 6 = 1	7 - 2 = 5
H	7 - 2 = 5	6 - 0 = 6	5 - 1 = 4	2 - 1 = 1
I	6 - 5 = 1	7 - 2 = 5	7 - 1 = 6	6 - 3 = 3
J	6 - 4 = 2	5 - 2 = 3	7 - 5 = 2	4 - 3 = 1
K	7 - 4 = 3	7 - 5 = 2	7 - 3 = 4	7 - 2 = 5
L	6 - 2 = 4	6 - 4 = 2	5 - 4 = 1	6 - 4 = 2
M	6 - 1 = 5	6 - 2 = 4	7 - 2 = 5	6 - 3 = 3
N	7 - 5 = 2	7 - 6 = 1	5 - 3 = 2	5 - 1 = 4
O	1 - 0 = 1	5 - 0 = 5	7 - 4 = 3	7 - 2 = 5
P	7 - 3 = 4	6 - 1 = 5	7 - 3 = 4	6 - 4 = 2
Q	7 - 1 = 6	7 - 4 = 3	6 - 1 = 5	6 - 5 = 1

560

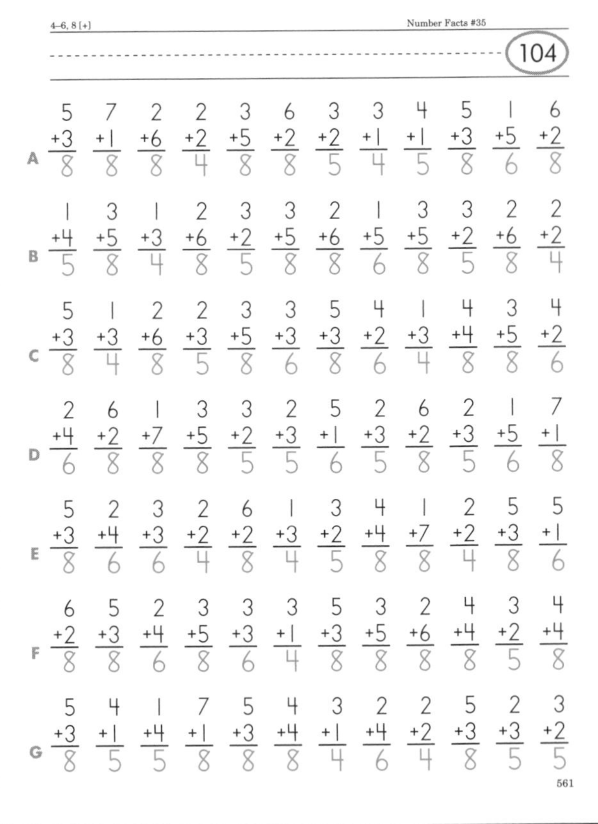
4–6, 8 [+] Number Facts #35

(104)

A	5 +3 = 8	7 +1 = 8	2 +6 = 8	2 +2 = 4	3 +5 = 8	6 +2 = 8	3 +2 = 5	3 +1 = 4	4 +1 = 5	5 +3 = 8	1 +5 = 6	6 +2 = 8
B	1 +4 = 5	3 +5 = 8	1 +3 = 4	2 +6 = 8	3 +2 = 5	3 +5 = 8	2 +6 = 8	1 +5 = 6	3 +5 = 8	3 +2 = 5	2 +6 = 8	2 +2 = 4
C	5 +3 = 8	1 +3 = 4	2 +6 = 8	2 +3 = 5	3 +5 = 8	3 +3 = 6	5 +3 = 8	4 +2 = 6	1 +3 = 4	4 +4 = 8	3 +5 = 8	4 +2 = 6
D	2 +4 = 6	6 +2 = 8	1 +7 = 8	3 +5 = 8	3 +2 = 5	2 +3 = 5	5 +1 = 6	2 +3 = 5	6 +2 = 8	2 +3 = 5	1 +5 = 6	7 +1 = 8
E	5 +3 = 8	2 +4 = 6	3 +3 = 6	2 +2 = 4	6 +2 = 8	1 +3 = 4	3 +2 = 5	4 +4 = 8	1 +7 = 8	2 +2 = 4	5 +3 = 8	5 +1 = 6
F	6 +2 = 8	5 +3 = 8	2 +4 = 6	3 +5 = 8	3 +3 = 6	3 +1 = 4	5 +3 = 8	3 +5 = 8	2 +6 = 8	4 +4 = 8	3 +2 = 5	4 +4 = 8
G	5 +3 = 8	4 +1 = 5	1 +4 = 5	7 +1 = 8	5 +3 = 8	4 +4 = 8	3 +1 = 4	2 +4 = 6	2 +2 = 4	5 +3 = 8	2 +3 = 5	3 +2 = 5

561

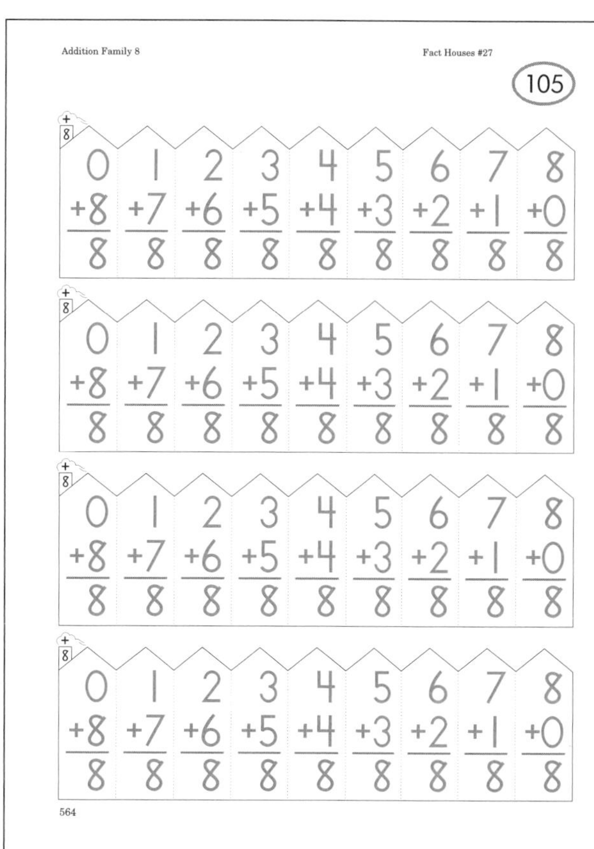

150–179 More Numbers #17

105

• more

151	**160**	**176**	166	**159**	158
179	169	158	**168**	**165**	160
172	152	**156**	155	167	**168**
166	156	161	**164**	**174**	164
179	159	167	**177**	162	**163**
171	**172**	163	**164**	173	**174**
162	**164**	**169**	159	153	**173**
152	**155**	**176**	171	**177**	157
173	170	**154**	153	170	**175**

565

1–7 [+ -] Number Facts #33

105

A	6 -2 = 4	2 +5 = 7	1 +6 = 7	6 -2 = 4	3 +2 = 5	7 -3 = 4	2 +3 = 5	6 -1 = 5	1 +2 = 3	5 +1 = 6	4 -2 = 2	2 +2 = 4
B	3 -1 = 2	3 +4 = 7	2 +4 = 6	7 -2 = 5	7 -4 = 2	5 +2 = 7	5 +1 = 6	5 -2 = 3	7 -3 = 4	2 +5 = 7	7 -4 = 3	6 -5 = 1
C	2 +2 = 4	6 -3 = 3	7 -5 = 2	7 -2 = 5	3 +1 = 4	3 +4 = 7	3 +2 = 5	2 +2 = 4	5 -4 = 1	1 +0 = 1	6 -1 = 5	3 +2 = 5
D	6 -5 = 1	2 +3 = 5	3 +1 = 4	1 +5 = 6	7 -5 = 2	4 +2 = 6	2 +4 = 6	6 -4 = 2	7 -2 = 5	7 -5 = 2	4 +3 = 7	7 -4 = 3
E	7 -2 = 5	3 +3 = 6	7 -6 = 1	7 -5 = 2	5 +2 = 7	2 +5 = 7	5 -3 = 2	2 +4 = 6	6 -3 = 3	6 +1 = 7	3 +2 = 5	6 -2 = 4
F	6 -3 = 3	6 -4 = 2	2 +3 = 5	6 -2 = 4	4 +3 = 7	6 -1 = 5	3 +1 = 4	4 +3 = 7	2 +2 = 4	6 +1 = 7	3 +3 = 6	5 -3 = 2
G	1 +3 = 4	7 -5 = 2	2 +1 = 3	4 -3 = 1	6 -1 = 5	2 +2 = 4	7 -6 = 1	7 -2 = 5	7 -5 = 2	4 +2 = 6	7 -2 = 5	2 +5 = 7

566

4–6, 8 [+] Number Facts #35

105

A	5 +3 8	7 +1 8	2 +6 8	2 +2 4	3 +5 8	6 +2 8	3 +2 5	3 +1 4	4 +1 5	5 +3 8	1 +5 6	6 +2 8
B	1 +4 5	3 +5 8	1 +3 4	2 +6 8	3 +2 5	3 +5 8	2 +6 8	1 +5 6	3 +5 8	3 +2 5	2 +6 8	2 +2 4
C	5 +3 8	1 +3 4	2 +6 8	2 +3 5	3 +5 8	3 +3 6	5 +3 8	4 +2 6	1 +3 4	4 +4 8	3 +5 8	4 +2 6
D	2 +4 6	6 +2 8	1 +7 8	3 +5 8	3 +2 5	2 +3 5	5 +1 6	2 +3 5	6 +2 8	2 +3 5	1 +5 6	7 +1 8
E	5 +3 8	2 +4 6	3 +3 6	2 +2 4	6 +2 8	1 +3 4	3 +2 5	4 +4 8	1 +7 8	2 +2 4	5 +3 8	5 +1 6
F	6 +2 8	5 +3 8	2 +4 6	3 +5 8	3 +3 6	3 +1 4	5 +3 8	3 +5 8	2 +6 8	4 +4 8	3 +2 5	4 +4 8
G	5 +3 8	4 +1 5	1 +4 5	7 +1 8	5 +3 8	4 +4 8	3 +1 4	2 +4 6	2 +2 4	5 +3 8	2 +3 5	3 +2 5

567

By 2's to 76 Dot-to-Dot #38

105

568

Addition Families 7, 8 Fact Houses #28

106

+ 7	0 +7 7	1 +6 7	2 +5 7	3 +4 7	4 +3 7	5 +2 7	6 +1 7	7 +0 7
+ 7	0 +7 7	1 +6 7	2 +5 7	3 +4 7	4 +3 7	5 +2 7	6 +1 7	7 +0 7
+ 8	0 +8 8	1 +7 8	2 +6 8	3 +5 8	4 +4 8	5 +3 8	6 +2 8	7 +1 8	8 +0 8
+ 8	0 +8 8	1 +7 8	2 +6 8	3 +5 8	4 +4 8	5 +3 8	6 +2 8	7 +1 8	8 +0 8

569

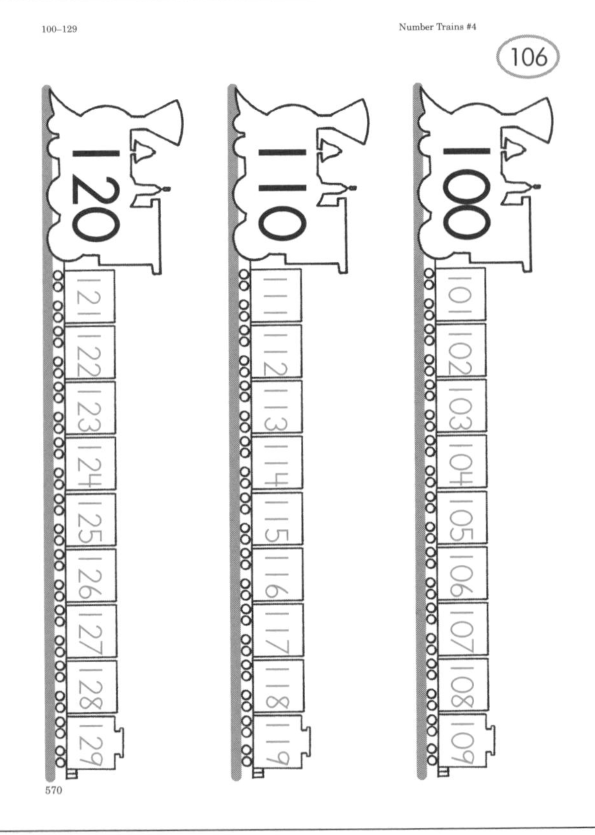

100–129 Number Trains #4

106

120: 121 122 123 124 125 126 127 128 129

110: 111 112 113 114 115 116 117 118 119

100: 101 102 103 104 105 106 107 108 109

570

5–8 [+] — Number Facts #36 — 106

A	5 + 1 = 6	7 + 1 = 8	5 + 2 = 7	2 + 6 = 8
B	2 + 3 = 5	1 + 7 = 8	2 + 6 = 8	3 + 5 = 8
C	6 + 2 = 8	2 + 3 = 5	5 + 3 = 8	3 + 2 = 5
D	3 + 5 = 8	5 + 2 = 7	2 + 3 = 5	2 + 6 = 8
E	5 + 2 = 7	2 + 6 = 8	4 + 2 = 6	3 + 2 = 5
F	2 + 6 = 8	3 + 4 = 7	4 + 3 = 7	6 + 1 = 7
G	5 + 3 = 8	3 + 3 = 6	2 + 6 = 8	5 + 3 = 8
H	4 + 1 = 5	4 + 4 = 8	2 + 4 = 6	2 + 5 = 7
I	6 + 1 = 7	4 + 3 = 7	2 + 6 = 8	2 + 4 = 6
J	5 + 3 = 8	3 + 2 = 5	3 + 4 = 7	6 + 1 = 7
K	5 + 2 = 7	4 + 3 = 7	1 + 7 = 8	2 + 3 = 5
L	6 + 2 = 8	2 + 6 = 8	6 + 2 = 8	1 + 7 = 8
M	7 + 1 = 8	3 + 4 = 7	2 + 3 = 5	4 + 3 = 7
N	5 + 3 = 8	2 + 4 = 6	4 + 3 = 7	5 + 3 = 8
O	4 + 1 = 5	2 + 6 = 8	4 + 4 = 8	5 + 1 = 6
P	3 + 3 = 6	3 + 5 = 8	4 + 3 = 7	3 + 5 = 8
Q	2 + 5 = 7	4 + 2 = 6	5 + 3 = 8	6 + 2 = 8

571

150–179 — Less Numbers #17 — 106

less

151	160	172	**152**	179	**159**
162	164	173	**170**	**152**	155
171	172	166	**156**	179	**169**
158	168	**161**	164	**163**	164
176	**171**	154	**153**	169	**159**
167	177	156	**155**	176	**166**
159	**158**	**167**	168	**162**	163
153	173	**170**	175	**173**	174
177	**157**	174	**164**	165	**160**

572

Addition Families 7, 8 — Fact Houses #28 — 107

0 + 7 = 7, 1 + 6 = 7, 2 + 5 = 7, 3 + 4 = 7, 4 + 3 = 7, 5 + 2 = 7, 6 + 1 = 7, 7 + 0 = 7

0 + 7 = 7, 1 + 6 = 7, 2 + 5 = 7, 3 + 4 = 7, 4 + 3 = 7, 5 + 2 = 7, 6 + 1 = 7, 7 + 0 = 7

0 + 8 = 8, 1 + 7 = 8, 2 + 6 = 8, 3 + 5 = 8, 4 + 4 = 8, 5 + 3 = 8, 6 + 2 = 8, 7 + 1 = 8, 8 + 0 = 8

0 + 8 = 8, 1 + 7 = 8, 2 + 6 = 8, 3 + 5 = 8, 4 + 4 = 8, 5 + 3 = 8, 6 + 2 = 8, 7 + 1 = 8, 8 + 0 = 8

573

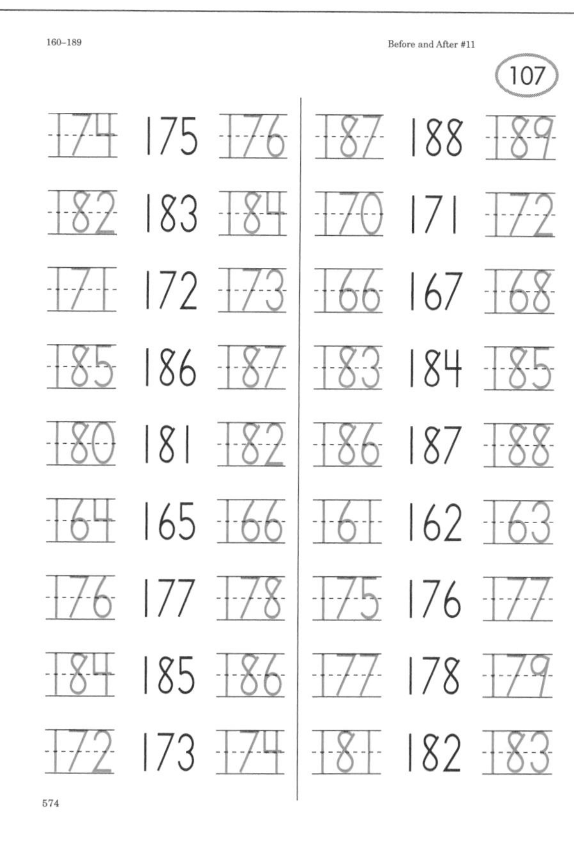

160–189 — Before and After #11 — 107

174	175	176	187	188	189
182	183	184	170	171	172
171	172	173	166	167	168
185	186	187	183	184	185
180	181	182	186	187	188
164	165	166	161	162	163
176	177	178	175	176	177
184	185	186	177	178	179
172	173	174	181	182	183

574

2–7 [-] Number Facts #37 (107)

A	7 - 2 = 5	5 - 3 = 2	6 - 4 = 2	6 - 1 = 5
B	7 - 6 = 1	7 - 3 = 4	6 - 3 = 3	7 - 5 = 2
C	5 - 1 = 4	2 - 1 = 1	6 - 0 = 6	7 - 3 = 4
D	3 - 2 = 1	7 - 4 = 3	7 - 2 = 5	5 - 4 = 1
E	6 - 3 = 3	6 - 0 = 6	7 - 3 = 4	7 - 4 = 3
F	6 - 4 = 2	3 - 2 = 1	5 - 1 = 4	6 - 4 = 2
G	7 - 1 = 6	4 - 1 = 3	6 - 4 = 2	4 - 2 = 2
H	5 - 4 = 1	6 - 2 = 4	5 - 2 = 3	7 - 1 = 6
I	6 - 2 = 4	7 - 1 = 6	7 - 5 = 2	6 - 1 = 5
J	5 - 2 = 3	7 - 2 = 5	7 - 1 = 6	2 - 0 = 2
K	7 - 5 = 2	5 - 2 = 3	7 - 6 = 1	5 - 3 = 2
L	6 - 3 = 3	6 - 2 = 4	6 - 5 = 1	7 - 4 = 3
M	7 - 1 = 6	7 - 5 = 2	4 - 1 = 3	7 - 2 = 5
N	6 - 1 = 5	7 - 1 = 6	5 - 3 = 2	7 - 3 = 4
O	6 - 3 = 3	7 - 6 = 1	6 - 0 = 6	6 - 2 = 4
P	5 - 4 = 1	5 - 2 = 3	7 - 5 = 2	7 - 6 = 1
Q	7 - 2 = 5	5 - 0 = 5	7 - 3 = 4	6 - 3 = 3

575

5–8 [+] Number Facts #36 (107)

A	5 + 1 = 6	7 + 1 = 8	5 + 2 = 7	2 + 6 = 8
B	2 + 3 = 5	1 + 7 = 8	2 + 6 = 8	3 + 5 = 8
C	6 + 2 = 8	2 + 3 = 5	5 + 3 = 8	3 + 2 = 5
D	3 + 5 = 8	5 + 2 = 7	2 + 3 = 5	2 + 6 = 8
E	5 + 2 = 7	2 + 6 = 8	4 + 2 = 6	3 + 2 = 5
F	2 + 6 = 8	3 + 4 = 7	4 + 3 = 7	6 + 1 = 7
G	5 + 3 = 8	3 + 3 = 6	2 + 6 = 8	5 + 3 = 8
H	4 + 1 = 5	4 + 4 = 8	2 + 4 = 6	2 + 5 = 7
I	6 + 1 = 7	4 + 3 = 7	2 + 6 = 8	2 + 4 = 6
J	5 + 3 = 8	3 + 2 = 5	3 + 4 = 7	6 + 1 = 7
K	5 + 2 = 7	4 + 3 = 7	1 + 7 = 8	2 + 3 = 5
L	6 + 2 = 8	2 + 6 = 8	6 + 2 = 8	1 + 7 = 8
M	7 + 1 = 8	3 + 4 = 7	2 + 3 = 5	4 + 3 = 7
N	5 + 3 = 8	2 + 4 = 6	4 + 3 = 7	5 + 3 = 8
O	4 + 1 = 5	2 + 6 = 8	4 + 4 = 8	5 + 1 = 6
P	3 + 3 = 6	3 + 5 = 8	4 + 3 = 7	3 + 5 = 8
Q	2 + 5 = 7	4 + 2 = 6	5 + 3 = 8	6 + 2 = 8

576

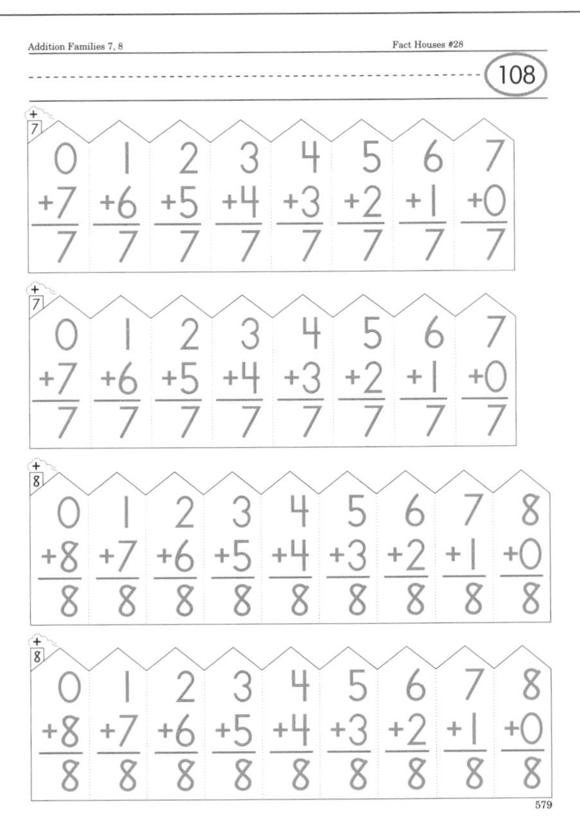

160–189 | More Numbers #18

108

• ⁙ more

183	180	**164**	163	180	**185**
162	**165**	**186**	181	**187**	167
181	**182**	173	**174**	183	**184**
176	166	171	**174**	**184**	174
189	179	168	**178**	**175**	170
161	**170**	**186**	176	**169**	168
182	162	**166**	165	177	**178**
189	169	177	**187**	172	**173**
172	**174**	**179**	169	163	**183**

580

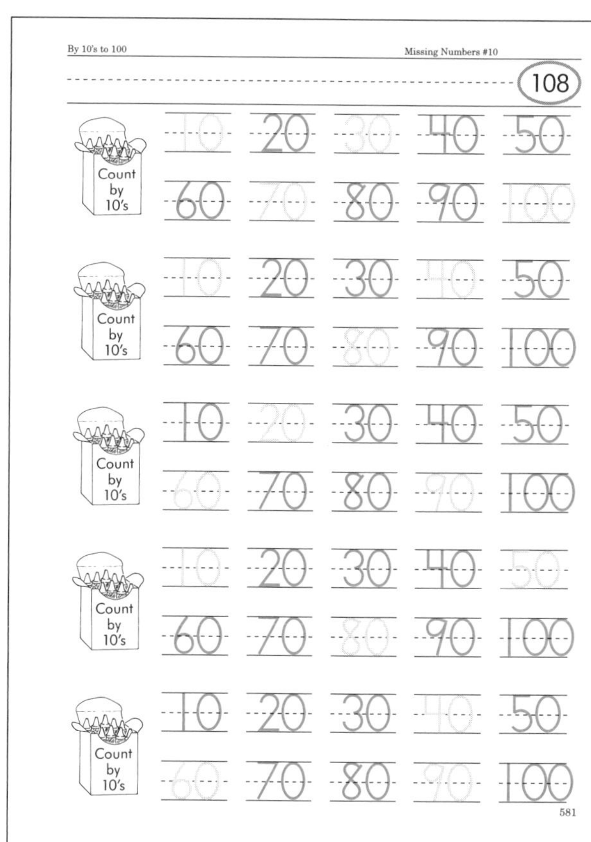

2–8 [+] 4–7 [-] | Number Facts #38

108

A	6 + 2 = 8	7 − 2 = 5	7 − 3 = 4	5 + 3 = 8	2 + 2 = 4	7 − 3 = 4	4 + 2 = 6	6 − 4 = 2	3 + 5 = 8	7 − 1 = 6	7 − 2 = 5	3 + 2 = 5
B	7 − 4 = 3	6 − 4 = 2	3 + 4 = 7	6 − 3 = 3	7 − 5 = 2	2 + 6 = 8	3 + 1 = 4	2 + 5 = 7	7 − 3 = 4	1 + 1 = 2	2 + 1 = 3	2 + 4 = 6
C	3 + 2 = 5	2 + 5 = 7	7 − 4 = 3	3 + 2 = 5	6 + 1 = 7	7 − 4 = 3	6 − 4 = 2	5 − 2 = 3	7 − 2 = 5	3 + 1 = 4	2 + 4 = 6	6 − 4 = 2
D	1 + 1 = 2	6 − 3 = 3	3 + 2 = 5	7 − 5 = 2	5 − 2 = 3	3 + 2 = 5	4 + 3 = 7	7 − 2 = 5	4 − 2 = 2	6 + 2 = 8	5 − 2 = 3	7 − 3 = 4
E	4 + 3 = 7	2 + 3 = 5	7 − 1 = 6	1 + 6 = 7	6 − 1 = 5	5 − 3 = 2	6 − 3 = 3	4 + 2 = 6	4 + 3 = 7	6 − 3 = 3	7 − 5 = 2	3 + 5 = 8
F	4 + 2 = 6	2 + 4 = 6	1 + 1 = 2	4 + 2 = 6	3 + 3 = 6	4 + 3 = 7	3 + 2 = 5	6 − 4 = 2	7 − 4 = 3	4 + 1 = 5	3 + 4 = 7	7 − 4 = 3
G	3 + 5 = 8	6 − 4 = 2	3 + 1 = 4	5 + 3 = 8	5 − 3 = 2	3 + 3 = 6	3 + 1 = 4	6 − 2 = 4	7 − 1 = 6	6 − 4 = 2	7 − 4 = 3	3 + 2 = 5

582

5–8 [+] | Number Facts #36

108

A	5 + 1 = 6	7 + 1 = 8	5 + 2 = 7	2 + 6 = 8
B	2 + 3 = 5	1 + 7 = 8	2 + 6 = 8	3 + 5 = 8
C	6 + 2 = 8	2 + 3 = 5	5 + 3 = 8	3 + 2 = 5
D	3 + 5 = 8	5 + 2 = 7	2 + 3 = 5	2 + 6 = 8
E	5 + 2 = 7	2 + 6 = 8	4 + 2 = 6	3 + 2 = 5
F	2 + 6 = 8	3 + 4 = 7	4 + 3 = 7	6 + 1 = 7
G	5 + 3 = 8	3 + 3 = 6	2 + 6 = 8	5 + 3 = 8
H	4 + 1 = 5	4 + 4 = 8	2 + 4 = 6	2 + 5 = 7
I	6 + 1 = 7	4 + 3 = 7	2 + 6 = 8	2 + 4 = 6
J	5 + 3 = 8	3 + 2 = 5	3 + 4 = 7	6 + 1 = 7
K	5 + 2 = 7	4 + 3 = 7	1 + 7 = 8	2 + 3 = 5
L	6 + 2 = 8	2 + 6 = 8	6 + 2 = 8	1 + 7 = 8
M	7 + 1 = 8	3 + 4 = 7	2 + 3 = 5	4 + 3 = 7
N	5 + 3 = 8	2 + 4 = 6	4 + 3 = 7	5 + 3 = 8
O	4 + 1 = 5	2 + 6 = 8	4 + 4 = 8	5 + 1 = 6
P	3 + 3 = 6	3 + 5 = 8	4 + 3 = 7	3 + 5 = 8
Q	2 + 5 = 7	4 + 2 = 6	5 + 3 = 8	6 + 2 = 8

583

Flash Card Drill — Form C — 109

Individual answers (See page 365 for instructions.)

585

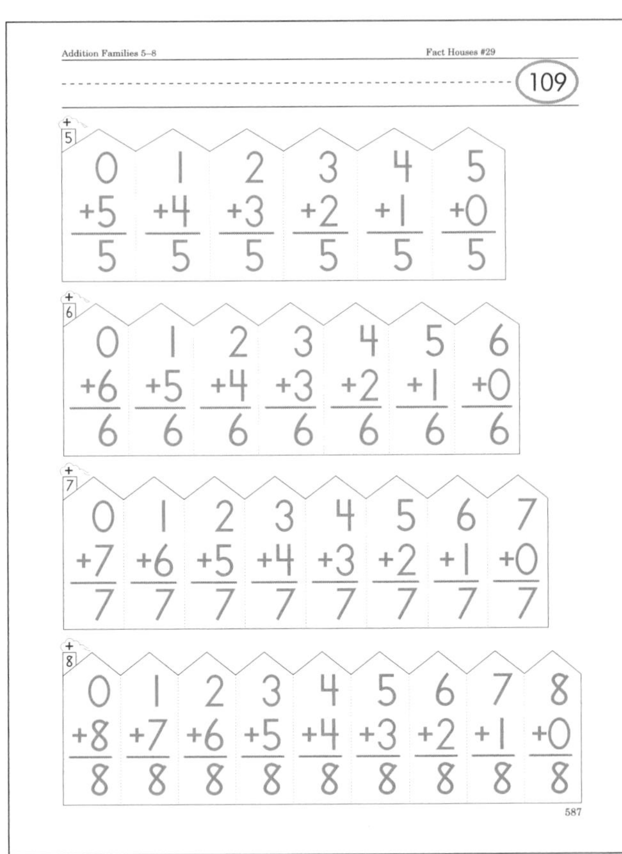
Addition Families 5–8 — Fact Houses #29 — 109

+ 5					
0 + 5 = 5	1 + 4 = 5	2 + 3 = 5	3 + 2 = 5	4 + 1 = 5	5 + 0 = 5

+ 6						
0 + 6 = 6	1 + 5 = 6	2 + 4 = 6	3 + 3 = 6	4 + 2 = 6	5 + 1 = 6	6 + 0 = 6

+ 7							
0 + 7 = 7	1 + 6 = 7	2 + 5 = 7	3 + 4 = 7	4 + 3 = 7	5 + 2 = 7	6 + 1 = 7	7 + 0 = 7

+ 8								
0 + 8 = 8	1 + 7 = 8	2 + 6 = 8	3 + 5 = 8	4 + 4 = 8	5 + 3 = 8	6 + 2 = 8	7 + 1 = 8	8 + 0 = 8

587

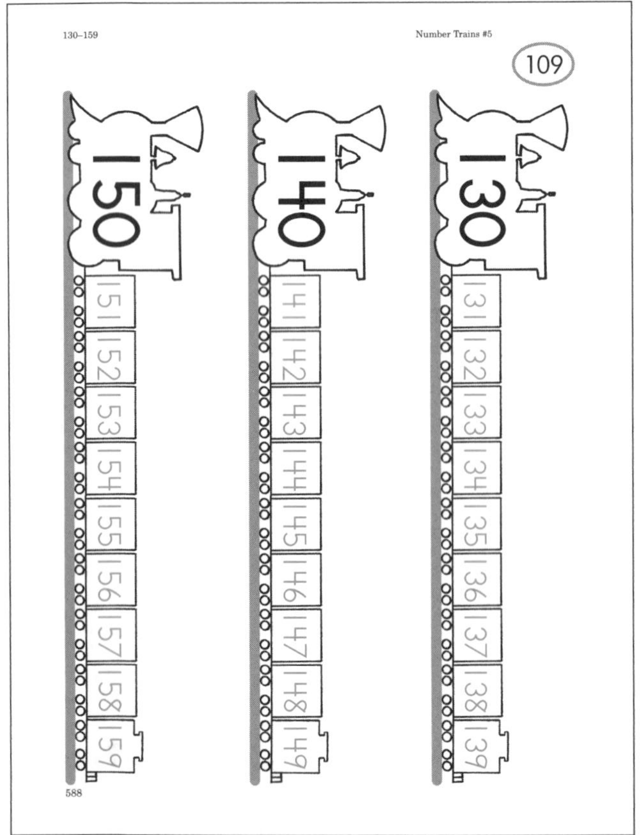
130–159 — Number Trains #5 — 109

150: 151 152 153 154 155 156 157 158 159

140: 141 142 143 144 145 146 147 148 149

130: 131 132 133 134 135 136 137 138 139

588

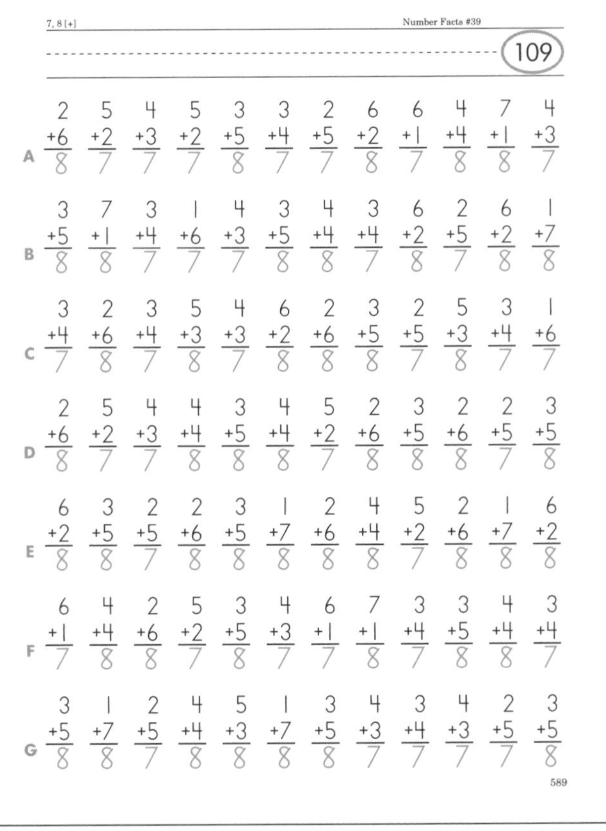
7, 8 [+] — Number Facts #39 — 109

A	2+6=8	5+2=7	4+3=7	5+2=7	3+5=8	3+4=7	2+5=7	6+2=8	6+1=7	4+4=8	7+1=8	4+3=7
B	3+5=8	7+1=8	3+4=7	1+6=7	4+3=7	3+5=8	4+4=8	3+4=7	6+2=8	2+5=7	6+2=8	1+7=8
C	3+4=7	2+6=8	3+4=7	5+3=8	4+3=7	6+2=8	2+6=8	3+5=8	2+5=7	5+3=8	3+4=7	1+6=7
D	2+6=8	5+2=7	4+3=7	4+4=8	3+5=8	4+4=8	5+2=7	2+6=8	3+5=8	2+6=8	2+5=7	3+5=8
E	6+2=8	3+5=8	2+5=7	2+6=8	3+5=8	1+7=8	2+6=8	4+4=8	5+2=7	2+6=8	1+7=8	6+2=8
F	6+1=7	4+4=8	2+6=8	5+2=7	3+5=8	4+3=7	6+1=7	7+1=8	3+4=7	3+5=8	4+4=8	3+4=7
G	3+5=8	1+7=8	2+5=7	4+4=8	5+3=8	1+7=8	3+5=8	4+3=7	3+4=7	4+3=7	2+5=7	3+5=8

589

160–189 Less Numbers #18

109

less

175	170	168	178	189	179
184	174	171	174	176	166
161	170	186	176	169	168
182	162	166	165	177	178
189	169	177	187	172	173
172	174	179	169	163	183
183	180	164	163	180	185
162	165	186	181	187	167
181	182	173	174	183	184

Addition Families 5–8 Fact Houses #29

110

+5

0	1	2	3	4	5
+5	+4	+3	+2	+1	+0
5	5	5	5	5	5

+6

0	1	2	3	4	5	6
+6	+5	+4	+3	+2	+1	+0
6	6	6	6	6	6	6

+7

0	1	2	3	4	5	6	7
+7	+6	+5	+4	+3	+2	+1	+0
7	7	7	7	7	7	7	7

+8

0	1	2	3	4	5	6	7	8
+8	+7	+6	+5	+4	+3	+2	+1	+0
8	8	8	8	8	8	8	8	8

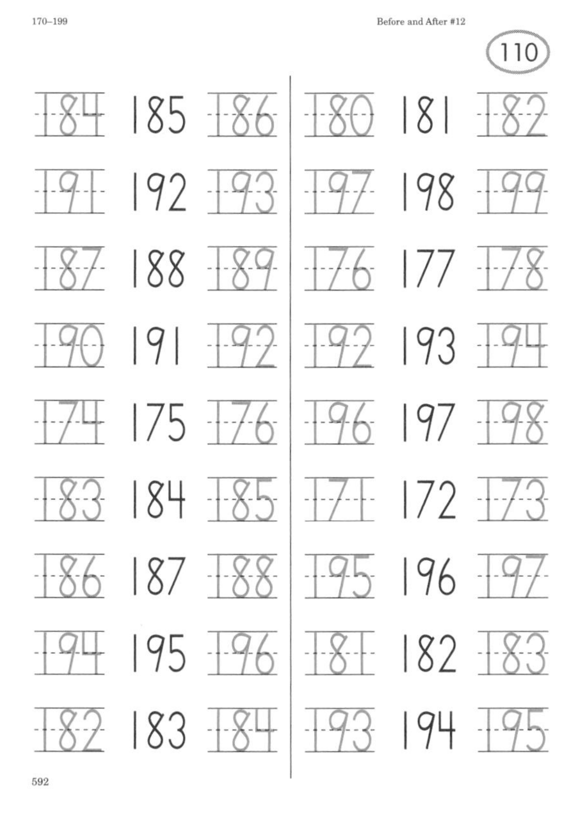

170–199 Before and After #12

110

184	185	186	180	181	182
191	192	193	197	198	199
187	188	189	176	177	178
190	191	192	192	193	194
174	175	176	196	197	198
183	184	185	171	172	173
186	187	188	195	196	197
194	195	196	181	182	183
182	183	184	193	194	195

592

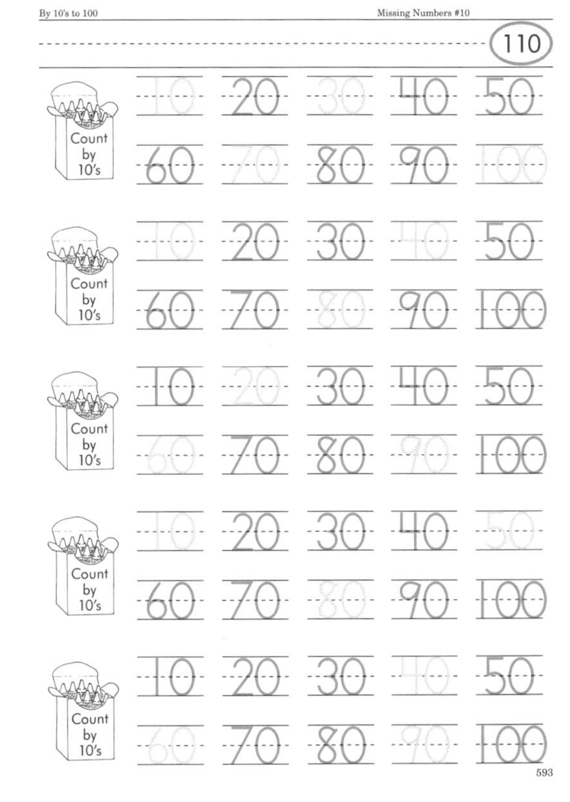

By 10's to 100 Missing Numbers #10

110

10 20 30 40 50
60 70 80 90 100

10 20 30 40 50
60 70 80 90 100

10 20 30 40 50
60 70 80 90 100

10 20 30 40 50
60 70 80 90 100

10 20 30 40 50
60 70 80 90 100

593

2–7 [–] Number Facts #37 (110)

A	7-2=5	5-3=2	6-4=2	6-1=5
B	7-6=1	7-3=4	6-3=3	7-5=2
C	5-1=4	2-1=1	6-0=6	7-3=4
D	3-2=1	7-4=3	7-2=5	5-4=1
E	6-3=3	6-0=6	7-3=4	7-4=3
F	6-4=2	3-2=1	5-1=4	6-4=2
G	7-1=6	4-1=3	6-4=2	4-2=2
H	5-4=1	6-2=4	5-2=3	7-1=6
I	6-2=4	7-1=6	7-5=2	6-1=5
J	5-2=3	7-2=5	7-1=6	2-0=2
K	7-5=2	5-2=3	7-6=1	5-3=2
L	6-3=3	6-2=4	6-5=1	7-4=3
M	7-1=6	7-5=2	4-1=3	7-2=5
N	6-1=5	7-1=6	5-3=2	7-3=4
O	6-3=3	7-6=1	6-0=6	6-2=4
P	5-4=1	5-2=3	7-5=2	7-6=1
Q	7-2=5	5-0=5	7-3=4	6-3=3

594

7, 8 [+] Number Facts #39 (110)

A	2+6=8	5+2=7	4+3=7	5+2=7	3+5=8	3+4=7	2+5=7	6+2=8	6+1=7	4+4=8	7+1=8	4+3=7
B	3+5=8	7+1=8	3+4=7	1+6=7	4+3=7	3+5=8	4+4=8	3+4=7	6+2=8	2+5=7	6+2=8	1+7=8
C	3+4=7	2+6=8	3+4=7	5+3=8	4+3=7	6+2=8	2+6=8	3+5=8	2+5=7	5+3=8	3+4=7	1+6=7
D	2+6=8	5+2=7	4+3=7	4+4=8	3+5=8	4+4=8	5+2=7	2+6=8	3+5=8	2+6=8	2+5=7	3+5=8
E	6+2=8	3+5=8	2+5=7	2+6=8	3+5=8	1+7=8	2+6=8	4+4=8	5+2=7	2+6=8	1+7=8	6+2=8
F	6+1=7	4+4=8	2+6=8	5+2=7	3+5=8	4+3=7	6+1=7	7+1=8	3+4=7	3+5=8	4+4=8	3+4=7
G	3+5=8	1+7=8	2+5=7	4+4=8	5+3=8	1+7=8	3+5=8	4+3=7	3+4=7	4+3=7	2+5=7	3+5=8

595

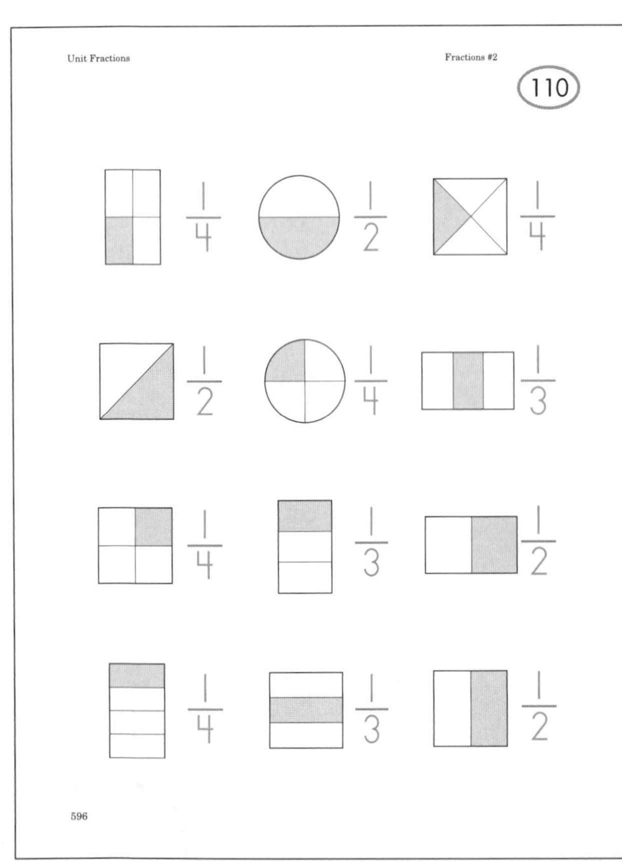

Unit Fractions Fractions #2 (110)

1/4 1/2 1/4

1/2 1/4 1/3

1/4 1/3 1/2

1/4 1/3 1/2

596

Addition Families 5–8 Fact Houses #29 (111)

+									
5	0+5=5	1+4=5	2+3=5	3+2=5	4+1=5	5+0=5			
6	0+6=6	1+5=6	2+4=6	3+3=6	4+2=6	5+1=6	6+0=6		
7	0+7=7	1+6=7	2+5=7	3+4=7	4+3=7	5+2=7	6+1=7	7+0=7	
8	0+8=8	1+7=8	2+6=8	3+5=8	4+4=8	5+3=8	6+2=8	7+1=8	8+0=8

597

7, 8 [+] Number Facts #39

111

A	2 +6 = 8	5 +2 = 7	4 +3 = 7	5 +2 = 7	3 +5 = 8	3 +4 = 7	2 +5 = 7	6 +2 = 8	6 +1 = 7	4 +4 = 8	7 +1 = 8	4 +3 = 7
B	3 +5 = 8	7 +1 = 8	3 +4 = 7	1 +6 = 7	4 +3 = 7	3 +5 = 8	4 +4 = 8	3 +4 = 7	6 +2 = 8	2 +5 = 7	6 +2 = 8	1 +7 = 8
C	3 +4 = 7	2 +6 = 8	3 +4 = 7	5 +3 = 8	4 +3 = 7	6 +2 = 8	2 +6 = 8	3 +5 = 8	2 +5 = 7	5 +3 = 8	3 +4 = 7	1 +6 = 7
D	2 +6 = 8	5 +2 = 7	4 +3 = 7	4 +4 = 8	3 +5 = 8	4 +4 = 8	5 +2 = 7	2 +6 = 8	3 +5 = 8	2 +6 = 8	2 +5 = 7	3 +5 = 8
E	6 +2 = 8	3 +5 = 8	2 +5 = 7	2 +6 = 8	3 +5 = 8	1 +7 = 8	2 +6 = 8	4 +4 = 8	5 +2 = 7	2 +6 = 8	1 +7 = 8	6 +2 = 8
F	6 +1 = 7	4 +4 = 8	2 +6 = 8	5 +2 = 7	3 +5 = 8	4 +3 = 7	6 +1 = 7	7 +1 = 8	3 +4 = 7	3 +5 = 8	4 +4 = 8	3 +4 = 7
G	3 +5 = 8	1 +7 = 8	2 +5 = 7	4 +4 = 8	5 +3 = 8	1 +7 = 8	3 +5 = 8	4 +3 = 7	3 +4 = 7	4 +3 = 7	2 +5 = 7	3 +5 = 8

598

170–199 More Numbers #19

111

• more

178	**179**	**196**	186	171	**180**
192	172	**176**	175	187	**188**
183	182	**197**	187	179	**199**
182	**184**	**189**	179	173	**193**
195	190	**174**	173	190	**193**
172	**175**	**196**	191	**197**	177
194	193	**184**	183	**192**	191
186	176	181	**184**	**194**	184
180	**185**	**188**	178	189	**197**

599

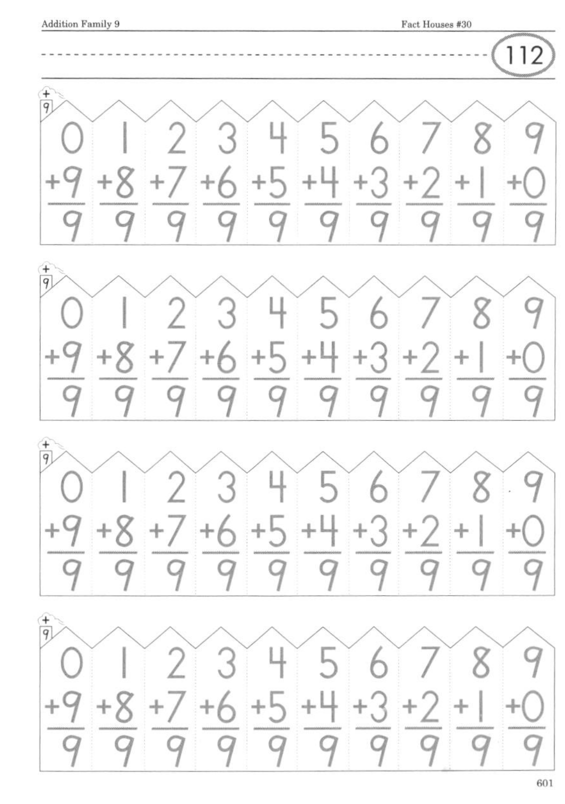

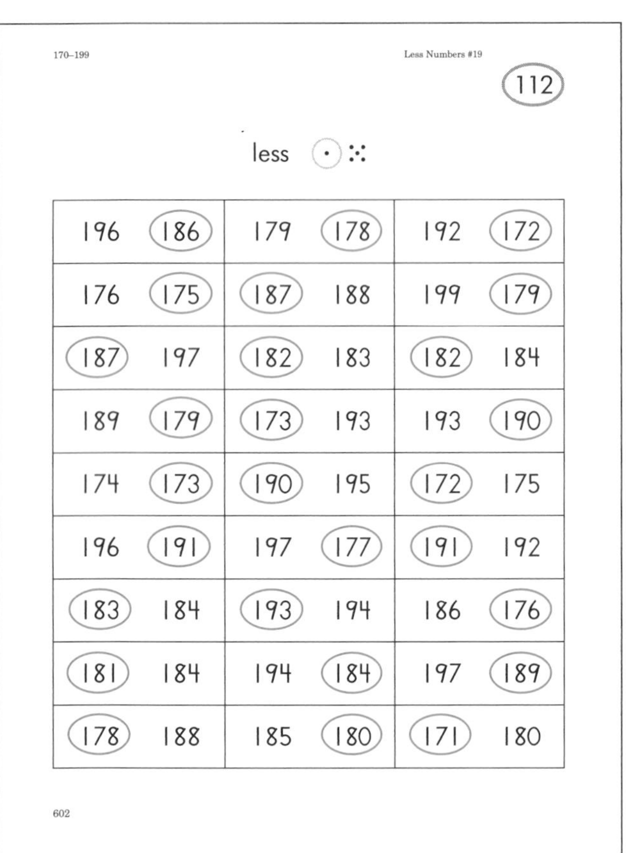
170–199 Less Numbers #19

112

less

196	186	179	178	192	172
176	175	187	188	199	179
187	197	182	183	182	184
189	179	173	193	193	190
174	173	190	195	172	175
196	191	197	177	191	192
183	184	193	194	186	176
181	184	194	184	197	189
178	188	185	180	171	180

602

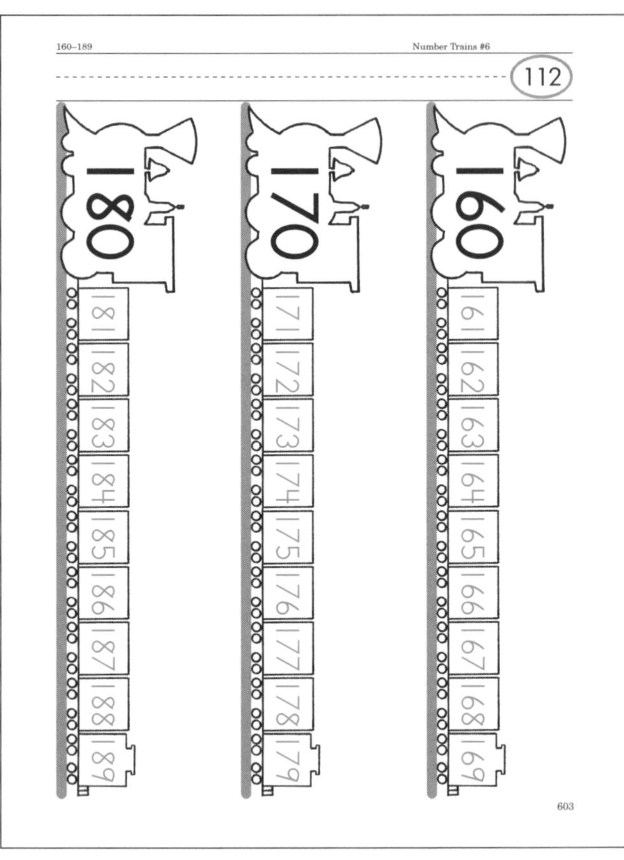

2–8 [+] 4–7 [-] Number Facts #38

112

A	6 +2 8	7 -2 5	7 -3 4	5 +3 8	2 +2 4	7 -3 4	4 +2 6	6 -4 2	3 +5 8	7 -1 6	7 -2 5	3 +2 5
B	7 -4 3	6 -4 2	3 +4 7	6 -3 3	7 -5 2	2 +6 8	3 +1 4	2 +5 7	7 -3 4	1 +1 2	2 +1 3	2 +4 6
C	3 +2 5	2 +5 7	7 -4 3	3 +2 5	6 +1 7	7 -4 3	6 -4 2	5 -2 3	7 -2 5	3 +1 4	2 +4 6	6 -4 2
D	1 +1 2	6 -3 3	3 +2 5	7 -5 2	5 -2 3	3 +2 5	4 +3 7	7 -2 5	4 -2 2	6 +2 8	5 -2 3	7 -3 4
E	4 +3 7	2 +3 5	7 -1 6	1 +6 7	6 -1 5	5 -3 2	6 -3 3	4 +2 6	4 +3 7	6 -3 3	7 -5 2	3 +5 8
F	4 +2 6	2 +4 6	1 +1 2	4 +2 6	3 +3 6	4 +3 7	3 +2 5	6 -4 2	7 -4 3	4 +1 5	3 +4 7	7 -4 3
G	3 +5 8	6 -4 2	3 +1 4	5 +3 8	5 -3 2	3 +3 6	3 +1 4	6 -2 4	7 -1 6	6 -4 2	7 -4 3	3 +2 5

604

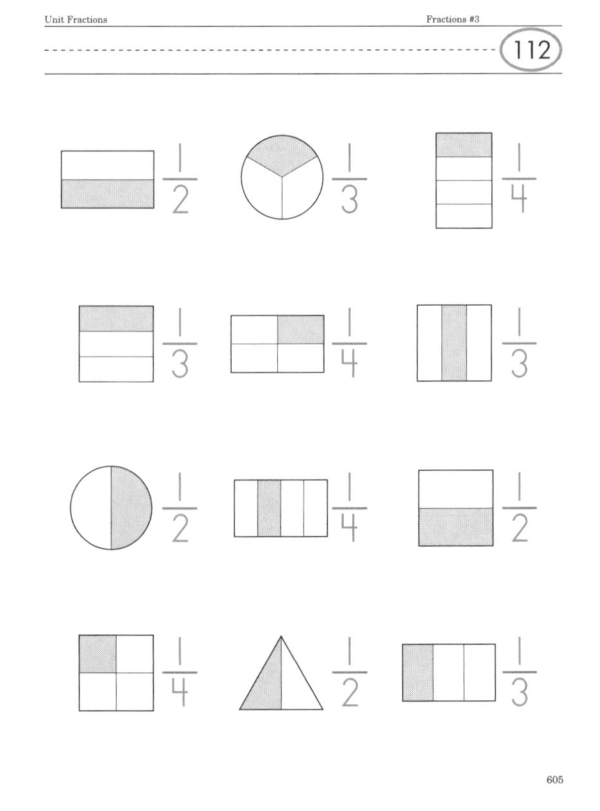

Story Problem Dictation — Form D — 113

7	jobs	
−3	jobs	
4	jobs	

6	books
−2	books
4	books

7	books
−4	books
3	books

7	jobs
−5	jobs
2	jobs

7	books
−2	books
5	books

7	jobs
−6	jobs
1	job

607

Addition Family 9 — Fact Houses #30 — 113

0	1	2	3	4	5	6	7	8	9
+9	+8	+7	+6	+5	+4	+3	+2	+1	+0
9	9	9	9	9	9	9	9	9	9

0	1	2	3	4	5	6	7	8	9
+9	+8	+7	+6	+5	+4	+3	+2	+1	+0
9	9	9	9	9	9	9	9	9	9

0	1	2	3	4	5	6	7	8	9
+9	+8	+7	+6	+5	+4	+3	+2	+1	+0
9	9	9	9	9	9	9	9	9	9

0	1	2	3	4	5	6	7	8	9
+9	+8	+7	+6	+5	+4	+3	+2	+1	+0
9	9	9	9	9	9	9	9	9	9

608

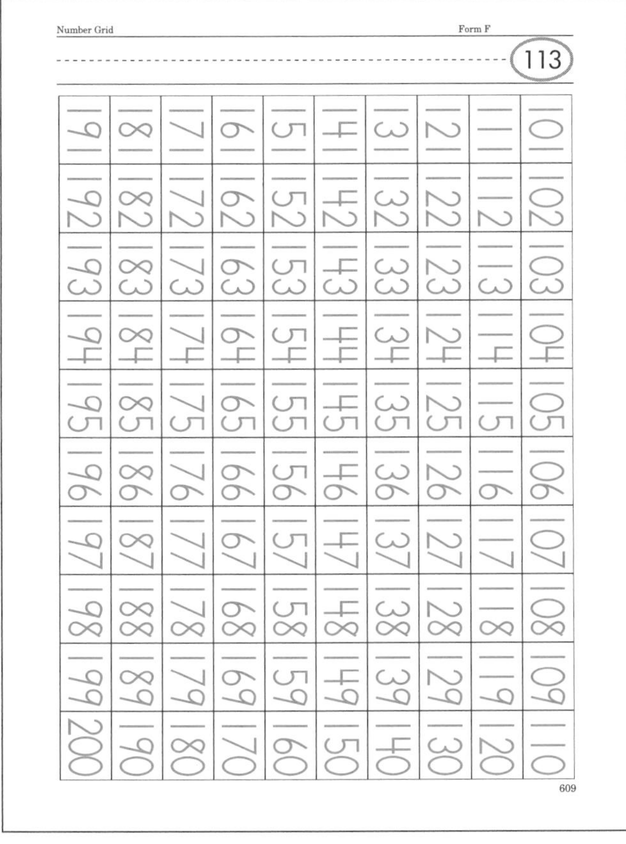

Number Grid — Form F — 113

101	102	103	104	105	106	107	108	109	110
111	112	113	114	115	116	117	118	119	120
121	122	123	124	125	126	127	128	129	130
131	132	133	134	135	136	137	138	139	140
141	142	143	144	145	146	147	148	149	150
151	152	153	154	155	156	157	158	159	160
161	162	163	164	165	166	167	168	169	170
171	172	173	174	175	176	177	178	179	180
181	182	183	184	185	186	187	188	189	190
191	192	193	194	195	196	197	198	199	200

609

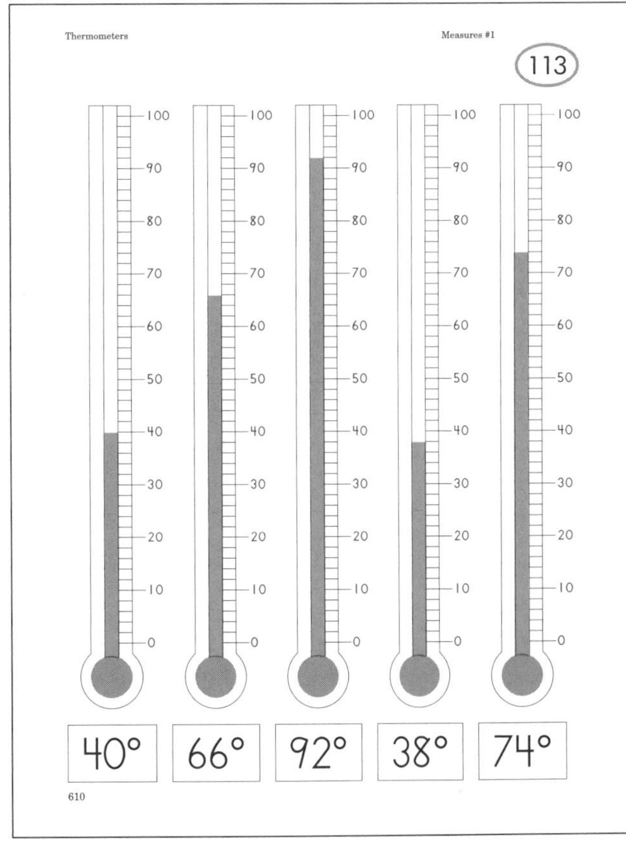

Thermometers — Measures #1 — 113

40°	66°	92°	38°	74°

610

5, 6, 9 [+] Number Facts #40

113

A	1 +8 = 9	2 +4 = 6	2 +7 = 9	2 +3 = 5	2 +4 = 6	1 +5 = 6	4 +5 = 9	7 +2 = 9	5 +1 = 6	6 +3 = 9	3 +3 = 6	3 +2 = 5
B	5 +4 = 9	3 +3 = 6	3 +6 = 9	2 +4 = 6	2 +7 = 9	8 +1 = 9	2 +3 = 5	6 +3 = 9	4 +5 = 9	2 +3 = 5	2 +7 = 9	5 +1 = 6
C	8 +1 = 9	4 +2 = 6	4 +1 = 5	7 +2 = 9	4 +5 = 9	2 +7 = 9	3 +6 = 9	5 +4 = 9	1 +4 = 5	5 +1 = 6	7 +2 = 9	3 +6 = 9
D	2 +3 = 5	2 +7 = 9	2 +4 = 6	5 +4 = 9	6 +3 = 9	3 +3 = 6	7 +2 = 9	2 +3 = 5	2 +4 = 6	4 +1 = 5	2 +7 = 9	7 +2 = 9
E	3 +3 = 6	3 +6 = 9	4 +5 = 9	6 +3 = 9	4 +5 = 9	4 +2 = 6	5 +4 = 9	7 +2 = 9	4 +5 = 9	2 +4 = 6	3 +3 = 6	2 +7 = 9
F	5 +4 = 9	3 +2 = 5	8 +1 = 9	5 +4 = 9	3 +2 = 5	3 +3 = 6	6 +3 = 9	2 +7 = 9	3 +3 = 6	4 +5 = 9	8 +1 = 9	3 +6 = 9
G	3 +2 = 5	3 +3 = 6	3 +6 = 9	2 +3 = 5	4 +2 = 6	7 +2 = 9	8 +1 = 9	2 +4 = 6	5 +4 = 9	2 +3 = 5	4 +5 = 9	6 +3 = 9

611

2–7 [-] Number Facts #37

113

A	7 - 2 = 5	5 - 3 = 2	6 - 4 = 2	6 - 1 = 5
B	7 - 6 = 1	7 - 3 = 4	6 - 3 = 3	7 - 5 = 2
C	5 - 1 = 4	2 - 1 = 1	6 - 0 = 6	7 - 3 = 4
D	3 - 2 = 1	7 - 4 = 3	7 - 2 = 5	5 - 4 = 1
E	6 - 3 = 3	6 - 0 = 6	7 - 3 = 4	7 - 4 = 3
F	6 - 4 = 2	3 - 2 = 1	5 - 1 = 4	6 - 4 = 2
G	7 - 1 = 6	4 - 1 = 3	6 - 4 = 2	4 - 2 = 2
H	5 - 4 = 1	6 - 2 = 4	5 - 2 = 3	7 - 1 = 6
I	6 - 2 = 4	7 - 1 = 6	7 - 5 = 2	6 - 1 = 5
J	5 - 2 = 3	7 - 2 = 5	7 - 1 = 6	2 - 0 = 2
K	7 - 5 = 2	5 - 2 = 3	7 - 6 = 1	5 - 3 = 2
L	6 - 3 = 3	6 - 2 = 4	6 - 5 = 1	7 - 4 = 3
M	7 - 1 = 6	7 - 5 = 2	4 - 1 = 3	7 - 2 = 5
N	6 - 1 = 5	7 - 1 = 6	5 - 3 = 2	7 - 3 = 4
O	6 - 3 = 3	7 - 6 = 1	6 - 0 = 6	6 - 2 = 4
P	5 - 4 = 1	5 - 2 = 3	7 - 5 = 2	7 - 6 = 1
Q	7 - 2 = 5	5 - 0 = 5	7 - 3 = 4	6 - 3 = 3

612

Addition Family 9 Fact Houses #30

114

+9

0 +9 = 9	1 +8 = 9	2 +7 = 9	3 +6 = 9	4 +5 = 9	5 +4 = 9	6 +3 = 9	7 +2 = 9	8 +1 = 9	9 +0 = 9

+9

0 +9 = 9	1 +8 = 9	2 +7 = 9	3 +6 = 9	4 +5 = 9	5 +4 = 9	6 +3 = 9	7 +2 = 9	8 +1 = 9	9 +0 = 9

+9

0 +9 = 9	1 +8 = 9	2 +7 = 9	3 +6 = 9	4 +5 = 9	5 +4 = 9	6 +3 = 9	7 +2 = 9	8 +1 = 9	9 +0 = 9

+9

0 +9 = 9	1 +8 = 9	2 +7 = 9	3 +6 = 9	4 +5 = 9	5 +4 = 9	6 +3 = 9	7 +2 = 9	8 +1 = 9	9 +0 = 9

613

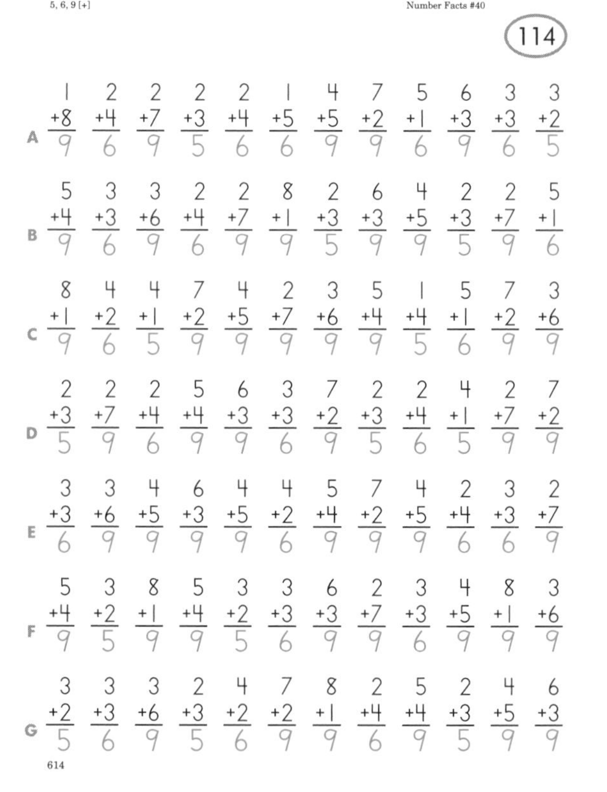

5, 6, 9 [+] Number Facts #40

114

A	1 +8 = 9	2 +4 = 6	2 +7 = 9	2 +3 = 5	2 +4 = 6	1 +5 = 6	4 +5 = 9	7 +2 = 9	5 +1 = 6	6 +3 = 9	3 +3 = 6	3 +2 = 5
B	5 +4 = 9	3 +3 = 6	3 +6 = 9	2 +4 = 6	2 +7 = 9	8 +1 = 9	2 +3 = 5	6 +3 = 9	4 +5 = 9	2 +3 = 5	2 +7 = 9	5 +1 = 6
C	8 +1 = 9	4 +2 = 6	4 +1 = 5	7 +2 = 9	4 +5 = 9	2 +7 = 9	3 +6 = 9	5 +4 = 9	1 +4 = 5	5 +1 = 6	7 +2 = 9	3 +6 = 9
D	2 +3 = 5	2 +7 = 9	2 +4 = 6	5 +4 = 9	6 +3 = 9	3 +3 = 6	7 +2 = 9	2 +3 = 5	2 +4 = 6	4 +1 = 5	2 +7 = 9	7 +2 = 9
E	3 +3 = 6	3 +6 = 9	4 +5 = 9	6 +3 = 9	4 +5 = 9	4 +2 = 6	5 +4 = 9	7 +2 = 9	4 +5 = 9	2 +4 = 6	3 +3 = 6	2 +7 = 9
F	5 +4 = 9	3 +2 = 5	8 +1 = 9	5 +4 = 9	3 +2 = 5	3 +3 = 6	6 +3 = 9	2 +7 = 9	3 +3 = 6	4 +5 = 9	8 +1 = 9	3 +6 = 9
G	3 +2 = 5	3 +3 = 6	3 +6 = 9	2 +3 = 5	4 +2 = 6	7 +2 = 9	8 +1 = 9	2 +4 = 6	5 +4 = 9	2 +3 = 5	4 +5 = 9	6 +3 = 9

614

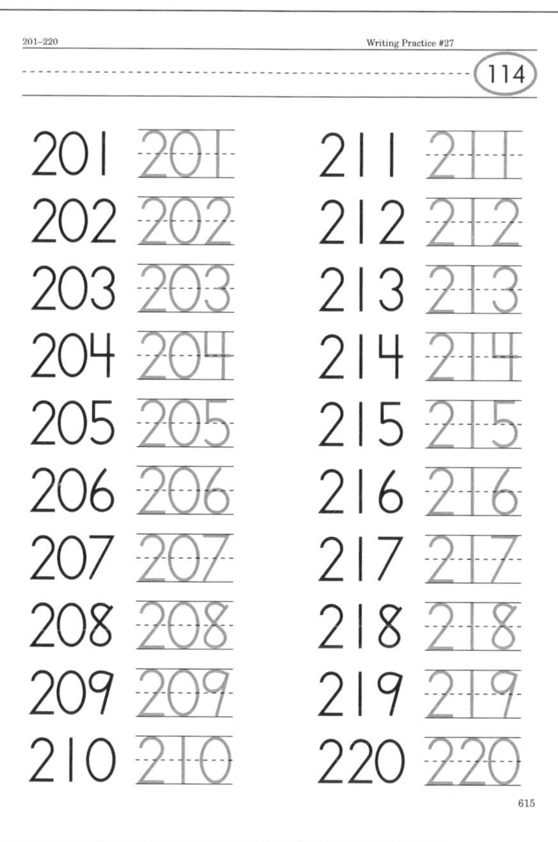
201–220
Writing Practice #27
114
201 201
202 202
203 203
204 204
205 205
206 206
207 207
208 208
209 209
210 210
211 211
212 212
213 213
214 214
215 215
216 216
217 217
218 218
219 219
220 220
615

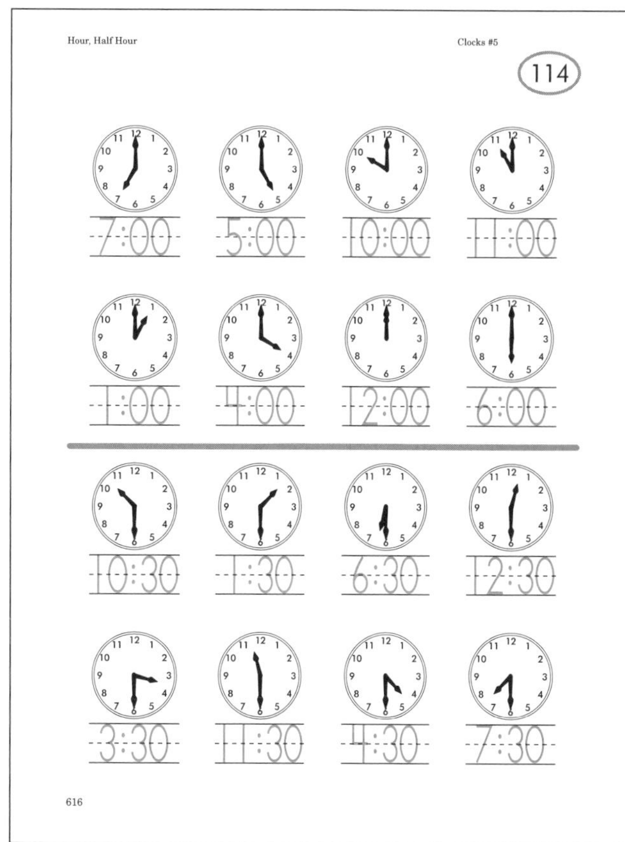
Hour, Half Hour
Clocks #5
114
7:00
5:00
10:00
11:00
1:00
4:00
12:00
6:00
10:30
1:30
6:30
12:30
3:30
11:30
4:30
7:30
616

Flash Card Drill
Form C
115
Individual answers
(See page 365
for instructions.)
617

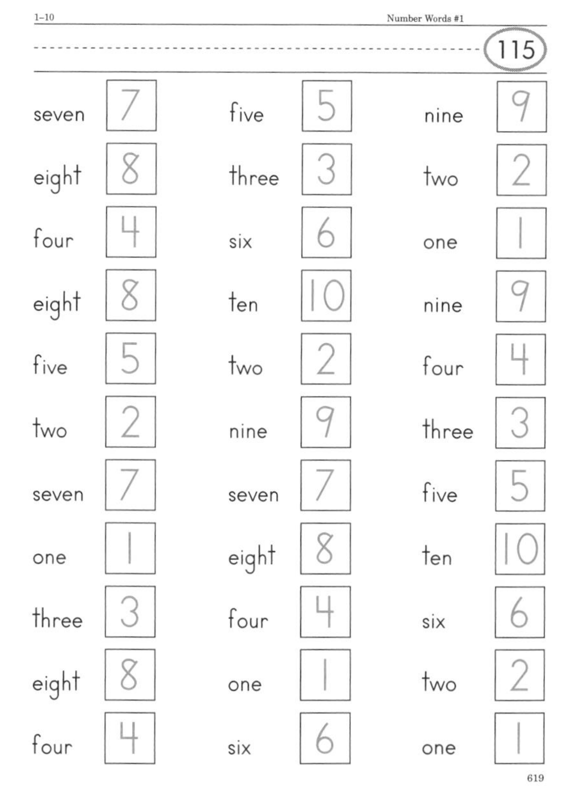
1–10
Number Words #1
115
seven 7
eight 8
four 4
eight 8
five 5
two 2
seven 7
one 1
three 3
eight 8
four 4
five 5
three 3
six 6
ten 10
two 2
nine 9
seven 7
eight 8
four 4
one 1
six 6
nine 9
two 2
one 1
nine 9
four 4
three 3
five 5
ten 10
six 6
two 2
one 1
619

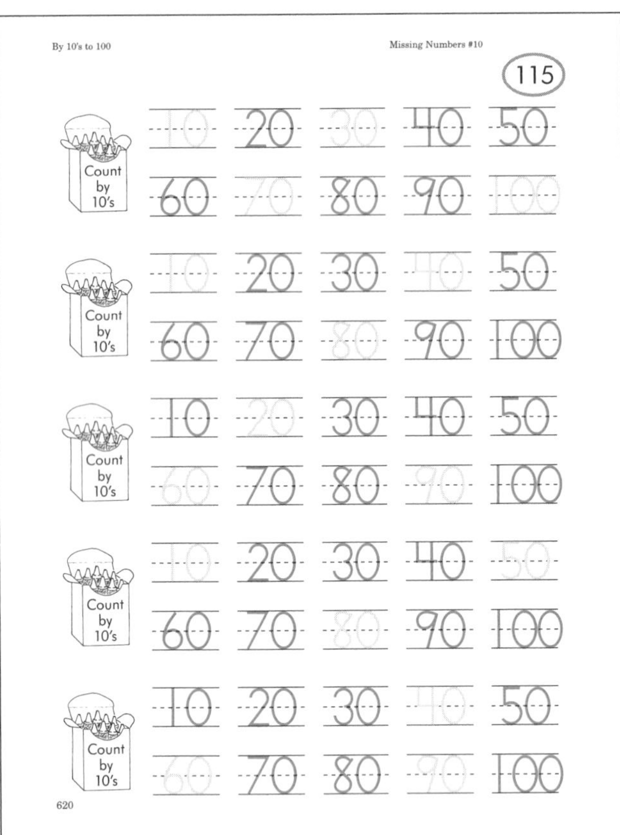

By 10's to 100 | Missing Numbers #10 | 115

620

2–8 [+] 4–7 [-] | Number Facts #38 | 115

A	6 +2 8	7 -2 5	7 -3 4	5 +3 8	2 +2 4	7 -3 4	4 +2 6	6 -4 2	3 +5 8	7 -1 6	7 -2 5	3 +2 5
B	7 -4 3	6 -4 2	3 +4 7	6 -3 3	7 -5 2	2 +6 8	3 +1 4	2 +5 7	7 -3 4	1 +1 2	2 +1 3	2 +4 6
C	3 +2 5	2 +5 7	7 -4 3	3 +2 5	6 +1 7	7 -4 3	6 -4 2	5 -2 3	7 -2 5	3 +1 4	2 +4 6	6 -4 2
D	1 +1 2	6 -3 3	3 +2 5	7 -5 2	5 -2 3	3 +2 5	4 +3 7	7 -2 5	4 -2 2	6 +2 8	5 -2 3	7 -3 4
E	4 +3 7	2 +3 5	7 -1 6	1 +6 7	6 -1 5	5 -3 2	6 -3 3	4 +2 6	4 +3 7	6 -3 3	7 -5 2	3 +5 8
F	4 +2 6	2 +4 6	1 +1 2	4 +2 6	3 +3 6	4 +3 7	3 +2 5	6 -4 2	7 -4 3	4 +1 5	3 +4 7	7 -4 3
G	3 +5 8	6 -4 2	3 +1 4	5 +3 8	5 -3 2	3 +3 6	3 +1 4	6 -2 4	7 -1 6	6 -4 2	7 -4 3	3 +2 5

621

5, 6, 9 [+] | Number Facts #40 | 115

A	1 +8 9	2 +4 6	2 +7 9	2 +3 5	2 +4 6	1 +5 6	4 +5 9	7 +2 9	5 +1 6	6 +3 9	3 +3 6	3 +2 5
B	5 +4 9	3 +3 6	3 +6 9	2 +4 6	2 +7 9	8 +1 9	2 +3 5	6 +3 9	4 +5 9	2 +3 5	2 +7 9	5 +1 6
C	8 +1 9	4 +2 6	4 +1 5	7 +2 9	4 +5 9	2 +7 9	3 +6 9	5 +4 9	1 +4 5	5 +1 6	7 +2 9	3 +6 9
D	2 +3 5	2 +7 9	2 +4 6	5 +4 9	6 +3 9	3 +3 6	7 +2 9	2 +3 5	2 +4 6	4 +1 5	2 +7 9	7 +2 9
E	3 +3 6	3 +6 9	4 +5 9	6 +3 9	4 +5 9	4 +2 6	5 +4 9	7 +2 9	4 +5 9	2 +4 6	3 +3 6	2 +7 9
F	5 +4 9	3 +2 5	8 +1 9	5 +4 9	3 +2 5	3 +3 6	6 +3 9	2 +7 9	3 +3 6	4 +5 9	8 +1 9	3 +6 9
G	3 +2 5	3 +3 6	3 +6 9	2 +3 5	4 +2 6	7 +2 9	8 +1 9	2 +4 6	5 +4 9	2 +3 5	4 +5 9	6 +3 9

622

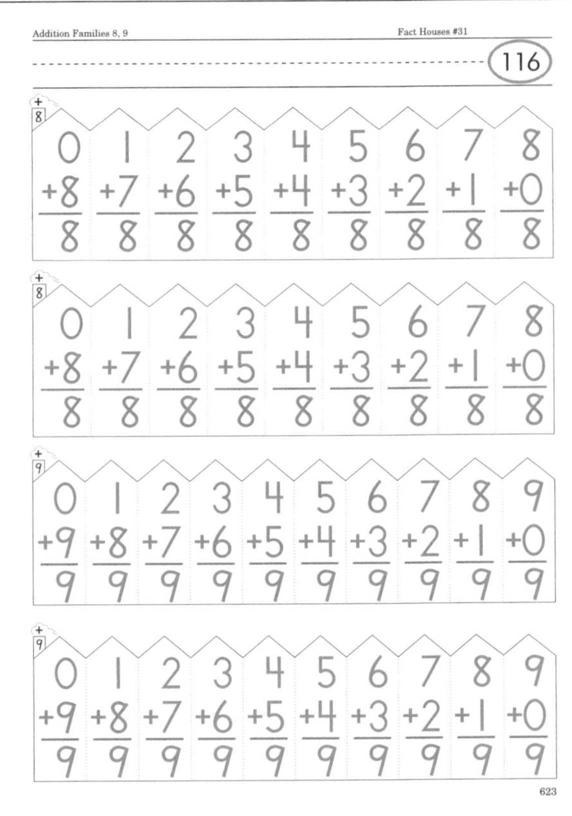

Addition Families 8, 9 | Fact Houses #31 | 116

623

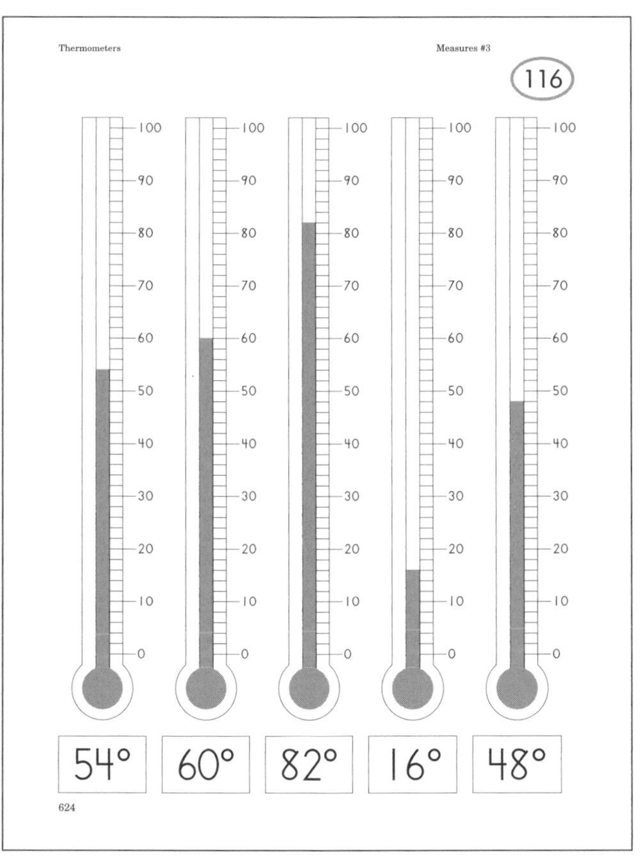

6–9 [+] Number Facts #41

116

A	3+5=8	3+6=9	7+2=9	3+5=8
B	3+3=6	2+7=9	5+3=8	2+7=9
C	3+6=9	7+1=8	2+5=7	3+3=6
D	7+2=9	4+3=7	6+2=8	6+3=9
E	2+6=8	5+4=9	6+3=9	2+7=9
F	1+6=7	2+5=7	4+5=9	3+6=9
G	5+3=8	1+7=8	7+2=9	3+5=8
H	2+7=9	6+3=9	5+3=8	5+2=7
I	4+5=9	3+6=9	5+1=6	5+3=8
J	5+4=9	4+4=8	4+5=9	2+7=9
K	3+5=8	3+4=7	6+2=8	2+4=6
L	4+3=7	5+3=8	4+5=9	3+4=7
M	4+4=8	4+3=7	6+2=8	4+4=8
N	6+3=9	2+6=8	7+2=9	5+4=9
O	2+4=6	5+4=9	8+1=9	6+3=9
P	5+4=9	4+2=6	6+2=8	5+2=7
Q	2+7=9	4+5=9	3+4=7	5+3=8

625

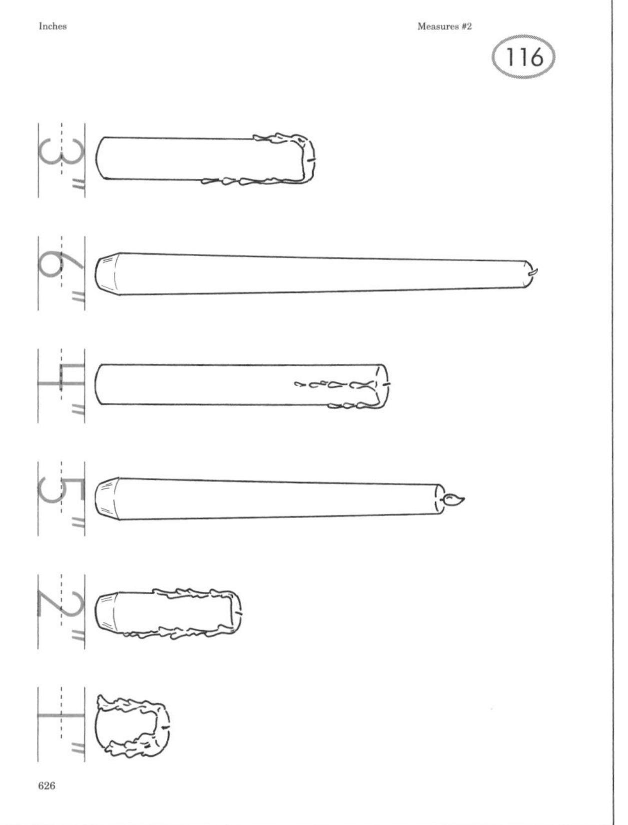

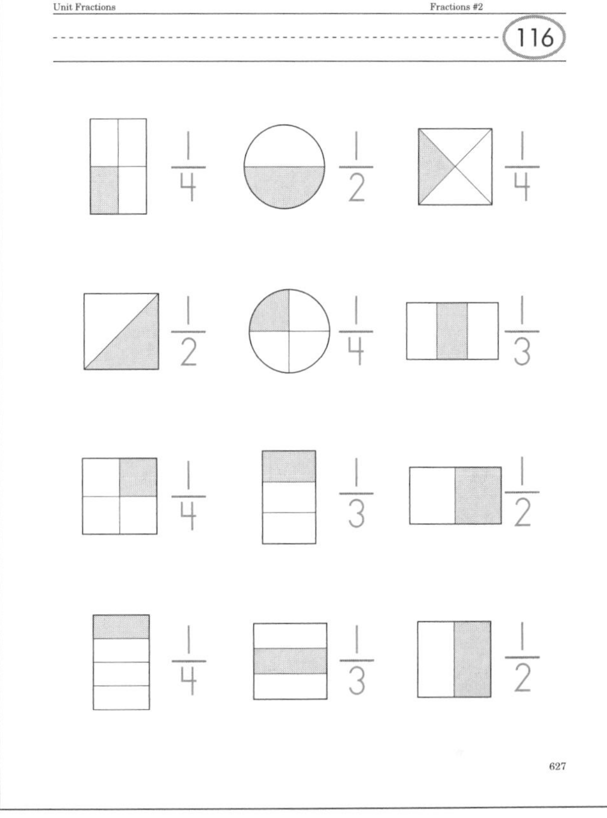

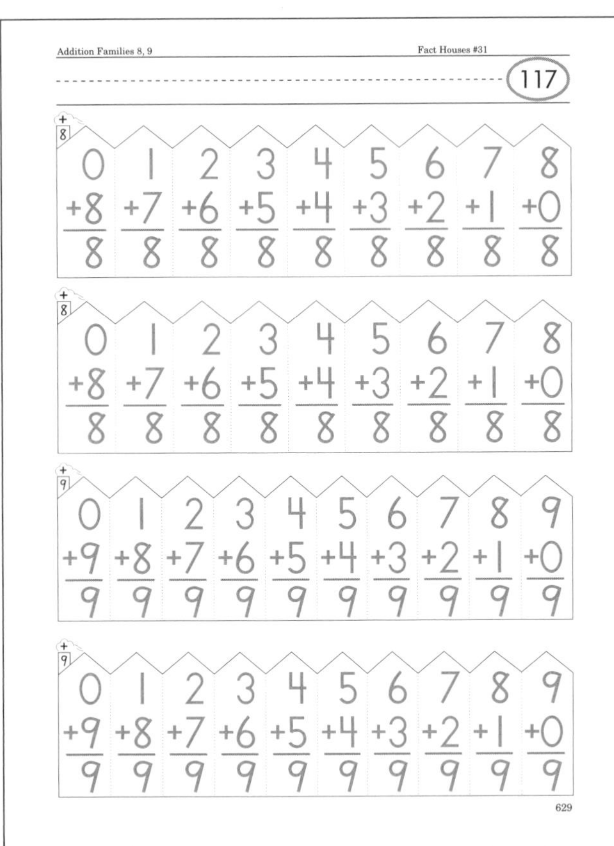

Addition Families 8, 9 — Fact Houses #31 — 117

0	1	2	3	4	5	6	7	8
+8	+7	+6	+5	+4	+3	+2	+1	+0
8	8	8	8	8	8	8	8	8

0	1	2	3	4	5	6	7	8
+8	+7	+6	+5	+4	+3	+2	+1	+0
8	8	8	8	8	8	8	8	8

0	1	2	3	4	5	6	7	8	9
+9	+8	+7	+6	+5	+4	+3	+2	+1	+0
9	9	9	9	9	9	9	9	9	9

0	1	2	3	4	5	6	7	8	9
+9	+8	+7	+6	+5	+4	+3	+2	+1	+0
9	9	9	9	9	9	9	9	9	9

629

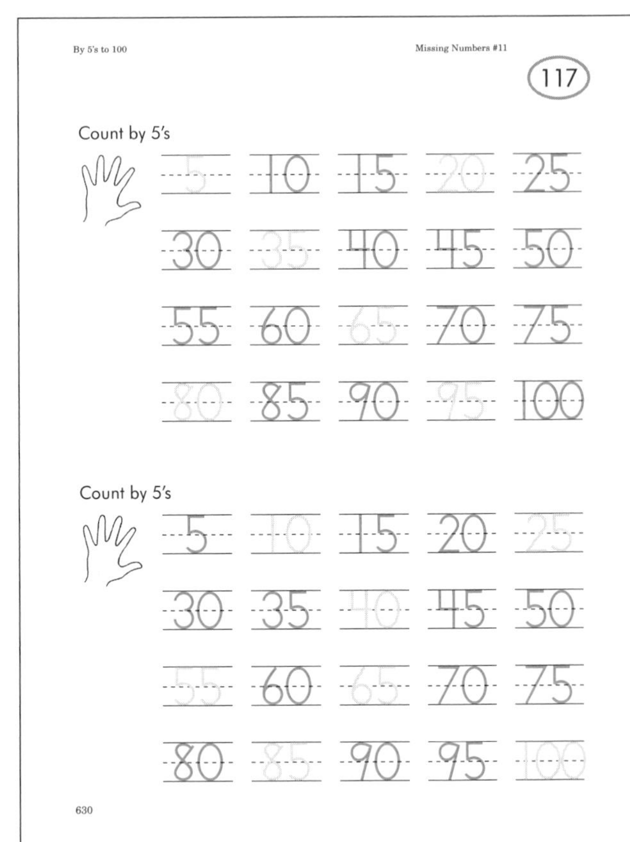

By 5's to 100 — Missing Numbers #11 — 117

Count by 5's

5 10 15 20 25
30 35 40 45 50
55 60 65 70 75
80 85 90 95 100

Count by 5's

5 10 15 20 25
30 35 40 45 50
55 60 65 70 75
80 85 90 95 100

630

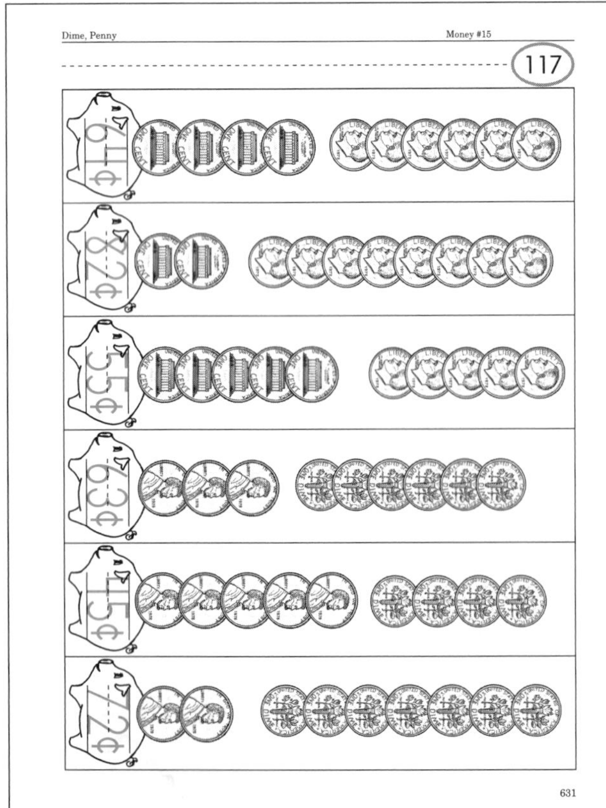

Dime, Penny — Money #15 — 117

64¢

82¢

55¢

63¢

45¢

72¢

631

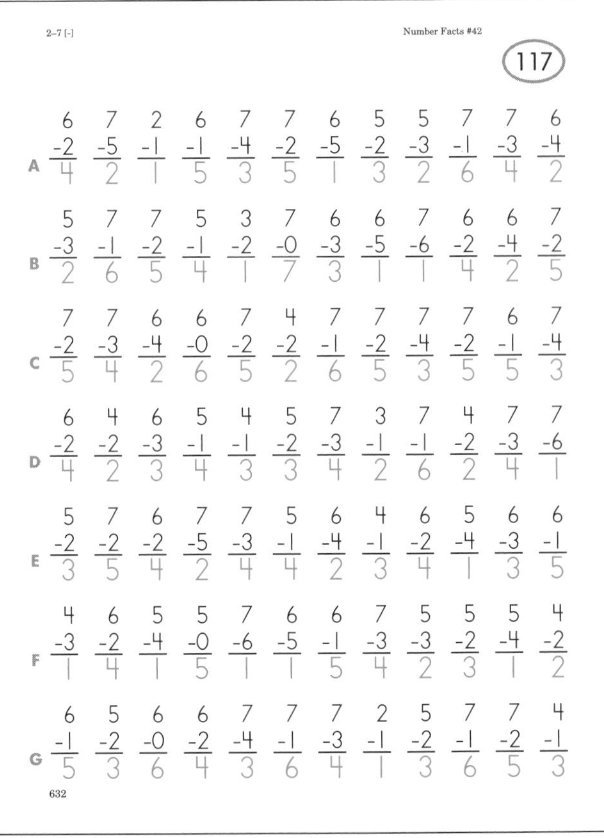

2–7 [-] — Number Facts #42 — 117

A	6 -2 4	7 -5 2	2 -1 1	6 -1 5	7 -4 3	7 -2 5	6 -5 1	5 -2 3	5 -3 2	7 -1 6	7 -3 4	6 -4 2
B	5 -3 2	7 -1 6	7 -2 5	5 -1 4	3 -2 1	7 -0 7	6 -3 3	6 -5 1	7 -6 1	6 -2 4	6 -4 2	7 -2 5
C	7 -2 5	7 -3 4	6 -4 2	6 -0 6	7 -2 5	4 -2 2	7 -1 6	7 -2 5	7 -4 3	7 -2 5	6 -1 5	7 -4 3
D	6 -2 4	4 -2 2	6 -3 3	5 -1 4	4 -1 3	5 -2 3	7 -3 4	3 -1 2	7 -1 6	4 -2 2	7 -3 4	7 -6 1
E	5 -2 3	7 -2 5	6 -2 4	7 -5 2	7 -3 4	5 -1 4	6 -4 2	4 -1 3	6 -2 4	5 -4 1	6 -3 3	6 -1 5
F	4 -3 1	6 -2 4	5 -4 1	5 -0 5	7 -6 1	6 -5 1	6 -1 5	7 -3 4	5 -3 2	5 -2 3	5 -4 1	4 -2 2
G	6 -1 5	5 -2 3	6 -0 6	6 -2 4	7 -4 3	7 -1 6	7 -3 4	2 -1 1	5 -2 3	7 -1 6	7 -2 5	4 -1 3

632

6–9 [+] Number Facts #41

117

A	3+5=8	3+6=9	7+2=9	3+5=8
B	3+3=6	2+7=9	5+3=8	2+7=9
C	3+6=9	7+1=8	2+5=7	3+3=6
D	7+2=9	4+3=7	6+2=8	6+3=9
E	2+6=8	5+4=9	6+3=9	2+7=9
F	1+6=7	2+5=7	4+5=9	3+6=9
G	5+3=8	1+7=8	7+2=9	3+5=8
H	2+7=9	6+3=9	5+3=8	5+2=7
I	4+5=9	3+6=9	5+1=6	5+3=8
J	5+4=9	4+4=8	4+5=9	2+7=9
K	3+5=8	3+4=7	6+2=8	2+4=6
L	4+3=7	5+3=8	4+5=9	3+4=7
M	4+4=8	4+3=7	6+2=8	4+4=8
N	6+3=9	2+6=8	7+2=9	5+4=9
O	2+4=6	5+4=9	8+1=9	6+3=9
P	5+4=9	4+2=6	6+2=8	5+2=7
Q	2+7=9	4+5=9	3+4=7	5+3=8

633

Flash Card Drill Form C

118

Individual answers (See page 365 for instructions.)

635

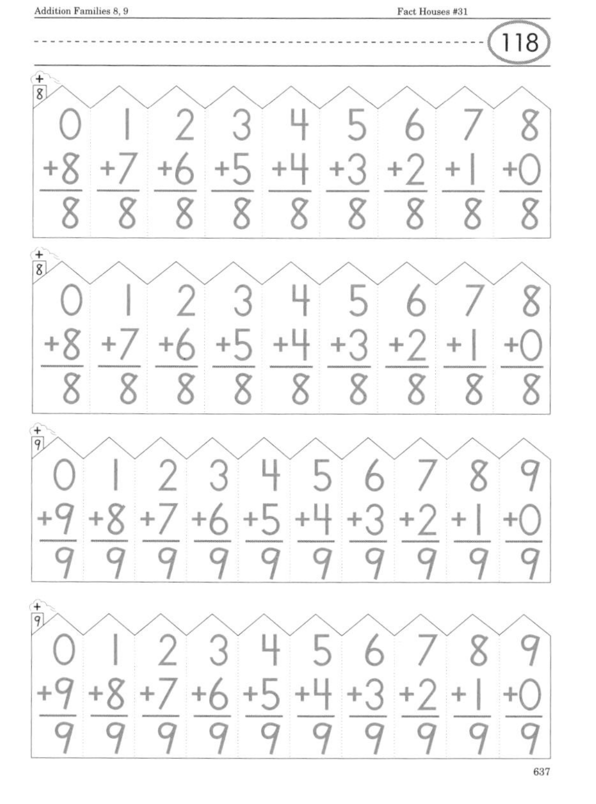
Addition Families 8, 9 Fact Houses #31

118

+ 8	0+8=8	1+7=8	2+6=8	3+5=8	4+4=8	5+3=8	6+2=8	7+1=8	8+0=8
+ 8	0+8=8	1+7=8	2+6=8	3+5=8	4+4=8	5+3=8	6+2=8	7+1=8	8+0=8
+ 9	0+9=9	1+8=9	2+7=9	3+6=9	4+5=9	5+4=9	6+3=9	7+2=9	8+1=9	9+0=9
+ 9	0+9=9	1+8=9	2+7=9	3+6=9	4+5=9	5+4=9	6+3=9	7+2=9	8+1=9	9+0=9

637

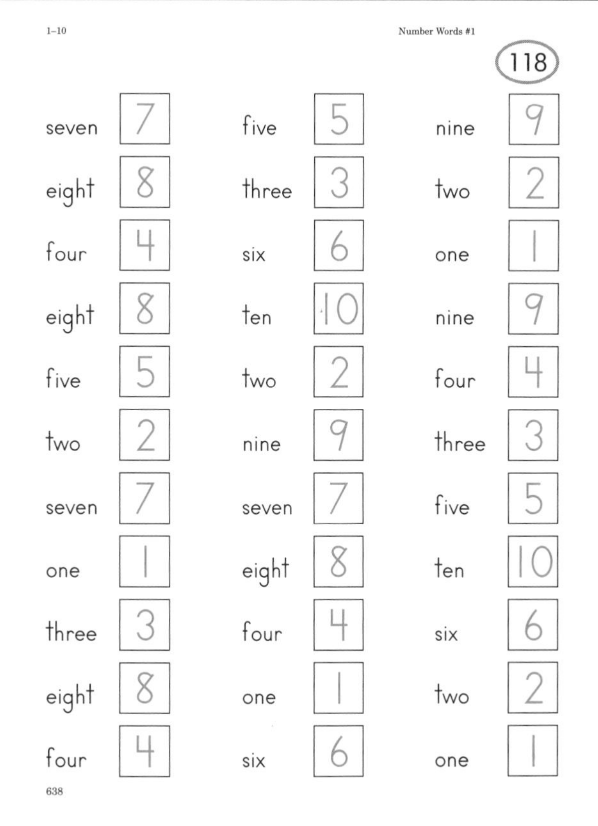
1–10 Number Words #1

118

seven	7	five	5	nine	9
eight	8	three	3	two	2
four	4	six	6	one	1
eight	8	ten	10	nine	9
five	5	two	2	four	4
two	2	nine	9	three	3
seven	7	seven	7	five	5
one	1	eight	8	ten	10
three	3	four	4	six	6
eight	8	one	1	two	2
four	4	six	6	one	1

638

6–9 [+] Number Facts #41

118

A	3+5=8	3+6=9	7+2=9	3+5=8
B	3+3=6	2+7=9	5+3=8	2+7=9
C	3+6=9	7+1=8	2+5=7	3+3=6
D	7+2=9	4+3=7	6+2=8	6+3=9
E	2+6=8	5+4=9	6+3=9	2+7=9
F	1+6=7	2+5=7	4+5=9	3+6=9
G	5+3=8	1+7=8	7+2=9	3+5=8
H	2+7=9	6+3=9	5+3=8	5+2=7
I	4+5=9	3+6=9	5+1=6	5+3=8
J	5+4=9	4+4=8	4+5=9	2+7=9
K	3+5=8	3+4=7	6+2=8	2+4=6
L	4+3=7	5+3=8	4+5=9	3+4=7
M	4+4=8	4+3=7	6+2=8	4+4=8
N	6+3=9	2+6=8	7+2=9	5+4=9
O	2+4=6	5+4=9	8+1=9	6+3=9
P	5+4=9	4+2=6	6+2=8	5+2=7
Q	2+7=9	4+5=9	3+4=7	5+3=8

639

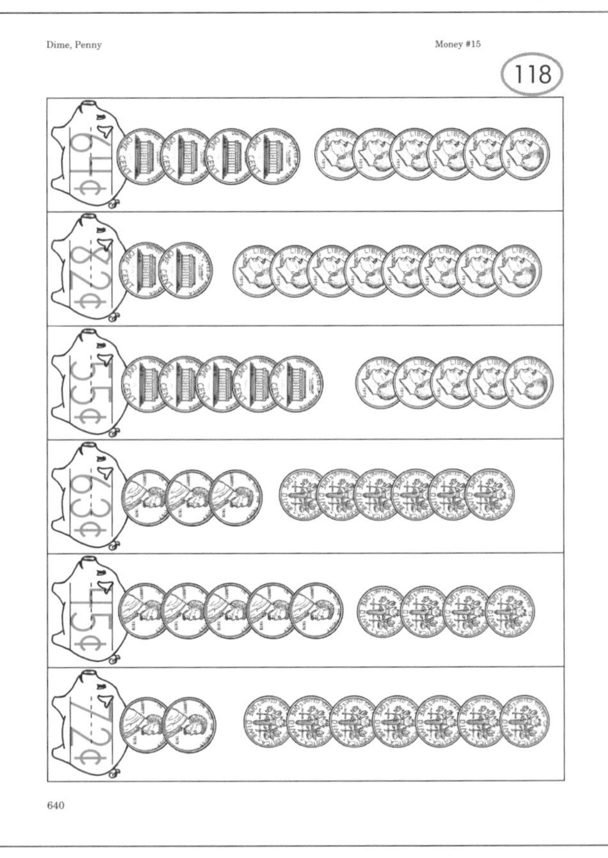

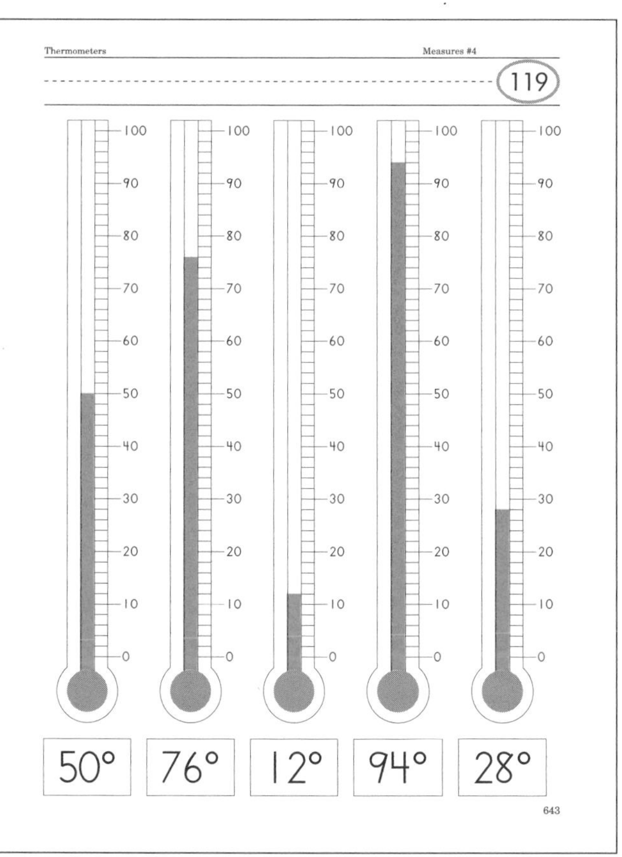
Thermometers — Measures #4 — 119

50°	76°	12°	94°	28°

643

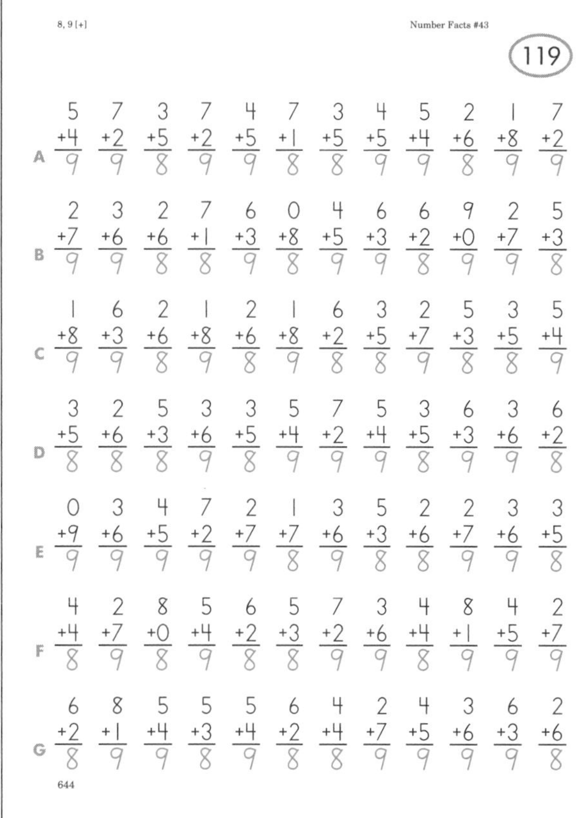
8, 9 [+] — Number Facts #43 — 119

	1	2	3	4	5	6	7	8	9	10	11	12
A	5+4=9	7+2=9	3+5=8	7+2=9	4+5=9	7+1=8	3+5=8	4+5=9	5+4=9	2+6=8	1+8=9	7+2=9
B	2+7=9	3+6=9	2+6=8	7+1=8	6+3=9	0+8=8	4+5=9	6+3=9	6+2=8	9+0=9	2+7=9	5+3=8
C	1+8=9	6+3=9	2+6=8	1+8=9	2+6=8	1+8=9	6+2=8	3+5=8	2+7=9	5+3=8	3+5=8	5+4=9
D	3+5=8	2+6=8	5+3=8	3+6=9	3+5=8	5+4=9	7+2=9	5+4=9	3+5=8	6+3=9	3+6=9	6+2=8
E	0+9=9	3+6=9	4+5=9	7+2=9	2+7=9	1+7=8	3+6=9	5+3=8	2+6=8	2+7=9	3+6=9	3+5=8
F	4+4=8	2+7=9	8+0=8	5+4=9	6+2=8	5+3=8	7+2=9	3+6=9	4+4=8	8+1=9	4+5=9	2+7=9
G	6+2=8	8+1=9	5+4=9	5+3=8	5+4=9	6+2=8	4+4=8	2+7=9	4+5=9	3+6=9	6+3=9	2+6=8

644

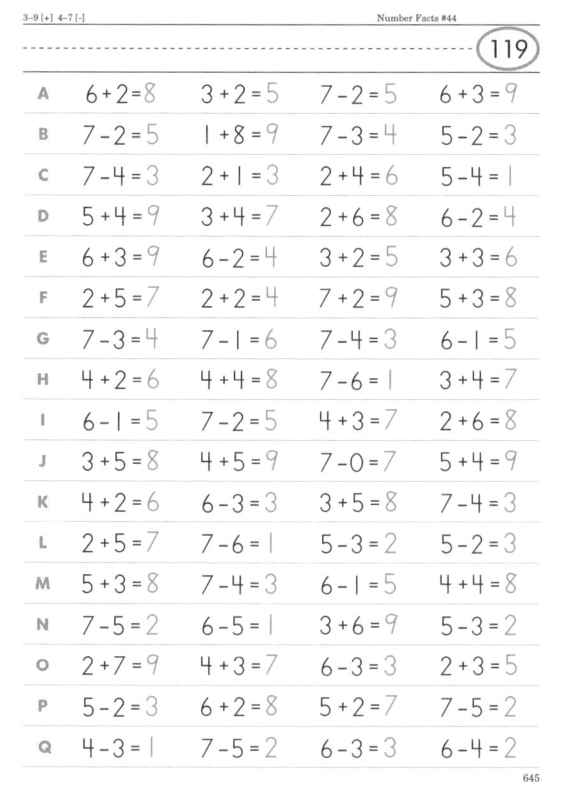
3-9 [+] 4-7 [-] — Number Facts #44 — 119

A	6+2=8	3+2=5	7-2=5	6+3=9
B	7-2=5	1+8=9	7-3=4	5-2=3
C	7-4=3	2+1=3	2+4=6	5-4=1
D	5+4=9	3+4=7	2+6=8	6-2=4
E	6+3=9	6-2=4	3+2=5	3+3=6
F	2+5=7	2+2=4	7+2=9	5+3=8
G	7-3=4	7-1=6	7-4=3	6-1=5
H	4+2=6	4+4=8	7-6=1	3+4=7
I	6-1=5	7-2=5	4+3=7	2+6=8
J	3+5=8	4+5=9	7-0=7	5+4=9
K	4+2=6	6-3=3	3+5=8	7-4=3
L	2+5=7	7-6=1	5-3=2	5-2=3
M	5+3=8	7-4=3	6-1=5	4+4=8
N	7-5=2	6-5=1	3+6=9	5-3=2
O	2+7=9	4+3=7	6-3=3	2+3=5
P	5-2=3	6+2=8	5+2=7	7-5=2
Q	4-3=1	7-5=2	6-3=3	6-4=2

645

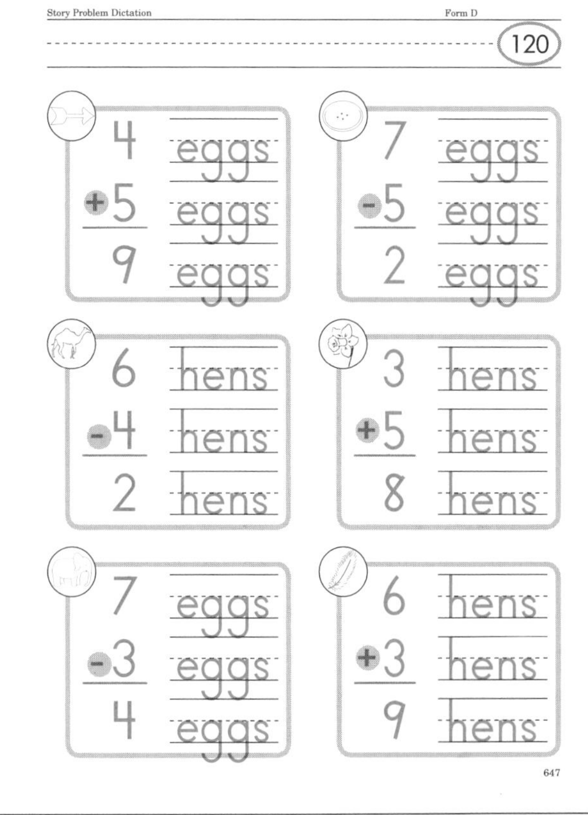
Story Problem Dictation — Form D — 120

4 eggs +5 eggs 9 eggs	7 eggs −5 eggs 2 eggs
6 hens −4 hens 2 hens	3 hens +5 hens 8 hens
7 eggs −3 eggs 4 eggs	6 hens +3 hens 9 hens

647

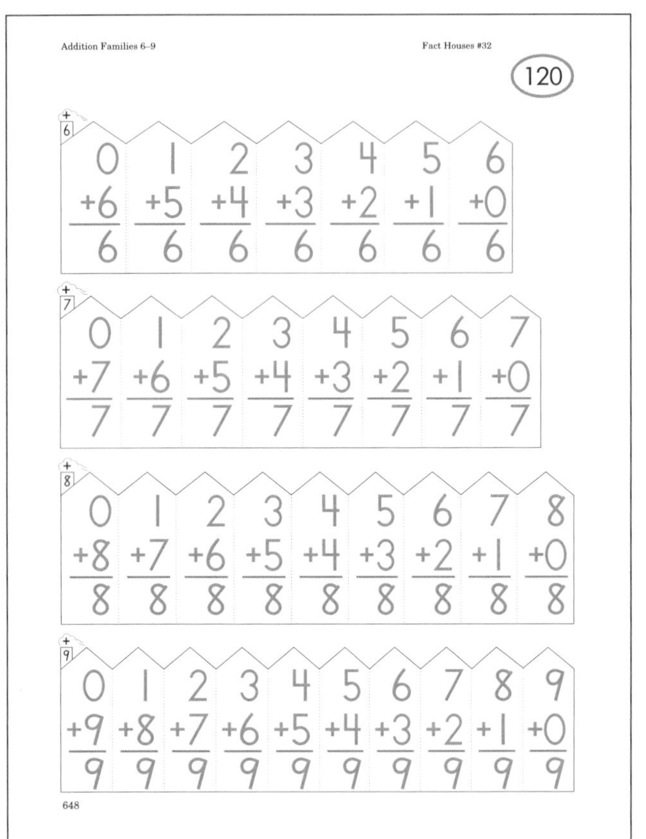

Addition Families 6–9 Fact Houses #32

120

+ 6						
0 +6 6	1 +5 6	2 +4 6	3 +3 6	4 +2 6	5 +1 6	6 +0 6

+ 7							
0 +7 7	1 +6 7	2 +5 7	3 +4 7	4 +3 7	5 +2 7	6 +1 7	7 +0 7

+ 8								
0 +8 8	1 +7 8	2 +6 8	3 +5 8	4 +4 8	5 +3 8	6 +2 8	7 +1 8	8 +0 8

+ 9									
0 +9 9	1 +8 9	2 +7 9	3 +6 9	4 +5 9	5 +4 9	6 +3 9	7 +2 9	8 +1 9	9 +0 9

648

By 5's to 100 Missing Numbers #11

120

Count by 5's

5	10	15	20	25
30	35	40	45	50
55	60	65	70	75
80	85	90	95	100

Count by 5's

5	10	15	20	25
30	35	40	45	50
55	60	65	70	75
80	85	90	95	100

649

Hour, Half Hour Clocks #6

120

4:30	1:00	7:00	8:30
10:00	3:30	3:00	5:30
9:30	8:00	12:30	2:30
9:00	12:00	7:30	5:00

650

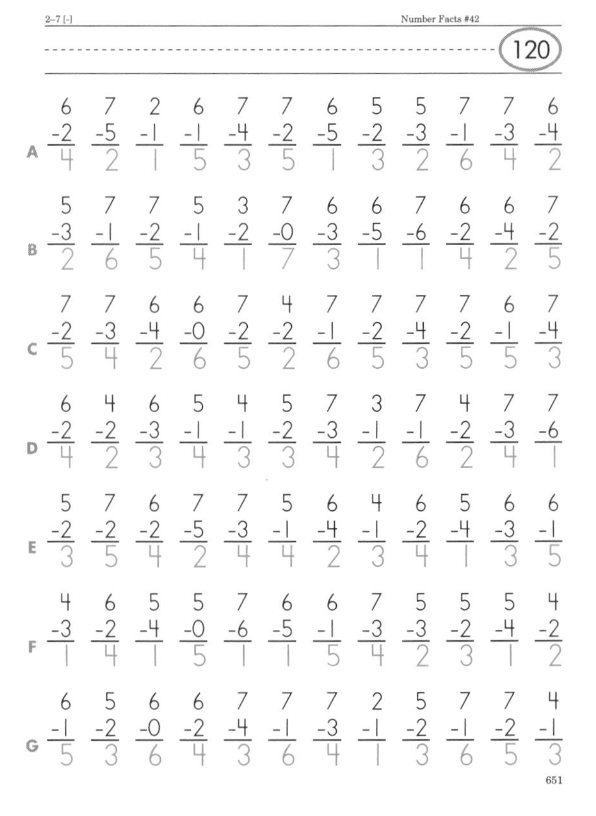

2–7 [-] Number Facts #42

120

A	6 -2 4	7 -5 2	2 -1 1	6 -1 5	7 -4 3	7 -2 5	6 -5 1	5 -2 3	5 -3 2	7 -1 6	7 -3 4	6 -4 2
B	5 -3 2	7 -1 6	7 -2 5	5 -1 4	3 -2 1	7 -0 7	6 -3 3	6 -5 1	7 -6 1	6 -2 4	6 -4 2	7 -2 5
C	7 -2 5	7 -3 4	6 -4 2	6 -0 6	7 -2 5	4 -2 2	7 -1 6	7 -2 5	7 -4 3	7 -2 5	6 -1 5	7 -4 3
D	6 -2 4	4 -2 2	6 -3 3	5 -1 4	4 -1 3	5 -2 3	7 -3 4	3 -1 2	7 -1 6	4 -2 2	7 -3 4	7 -6 1
E	5 -2 3	7 -2 5	6 -2 4	7 -5 2	7 -3 4	5 -1 4	6 -4 2	4 -1 3	6 -2 4	5 -4 1	6 -3 3	6 -1 5
F	4 -3 1	6 -2 4	5 -4 1	5 -0 5	7 -6 1	6 -5 1	6 -1 5	7 -3 4	5 -3 2	5 -2 3	5 -4 1	4 -2 2
G	6 -1 5	5 -2 3	6 -0 6	6 -2 4	7 -4 3	7 -1 6	7 -3 4	2 -1 1	5 -2 3	7 -1 6	7 -2 5	4 -1 3

651

8, 9 [+] Number Facts #43

120

A	5 +4 9	7 +2 9	3 +5 8	7 +2 9	4 +5 9	7 +1 8	3 +5 8	4 +5 9	5 +4 9	2 +6 8	1 +8 9	7 +2 9
B	2 +7 9	3 +6 9	2 +6 8	7 +1 8	6 +3 9	0 +8 8	4 +5 9	6 +3 9	6 +2 8	9 +0 9	2 +7 9	5 +3 8
C	1 +8 9	6 +3 9	2 +6 8	1 +8 9	2 +6 8	1 +8 9	6 +2 8	3 +5 8	2 +7 9	5 +3 8	3 +5 8	5 +4 9
D	3 +5 8	2 +6 8	5 +3 8	3 +6 9	3 +5 8	5 +4 9	7 +2 9	5 +4 9	3 +5 8	6 +3 9	3 +6 9	6 +2 8
E	0 +9 9	3 +6 9	4 +5 9	7 +2 9	2 +7 9	1 +7 8	3 +6 9	5 +3 8	2 +6 8	2 +7 9	3 +6 9	3 +5 8
F	4 +4 8	2 +7 9	8 +0 8	5 +4 9	6 +2 8	5 +3 8	7 +2 9	3 +6 9	4 +4 8	8 +1 9	4 +5 9	2 +7 9
G	6 +2 8	8 +1 9	5 +4 9	5 +3 8	5 +4 9	6 +2 8	4 +4 8	2 +7 9	4 +5 9	3 +6 9	6 +3 9	2 +6 8

652

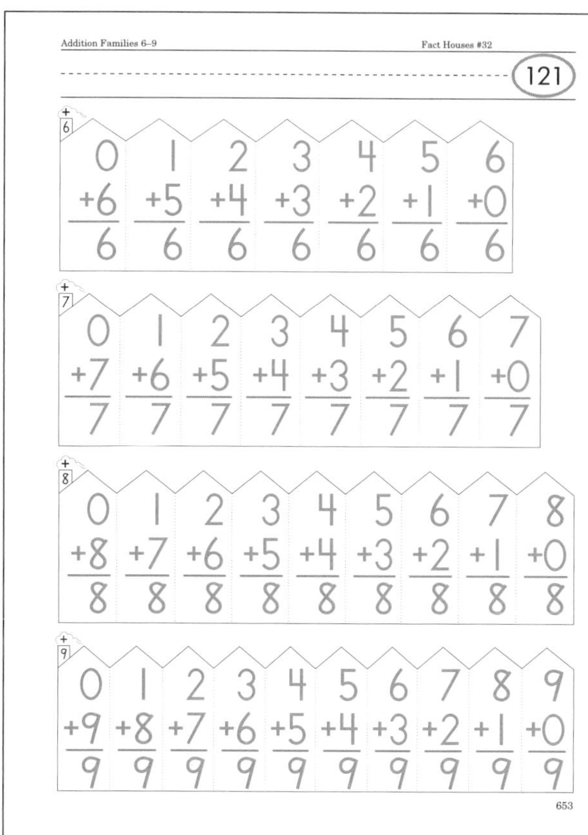

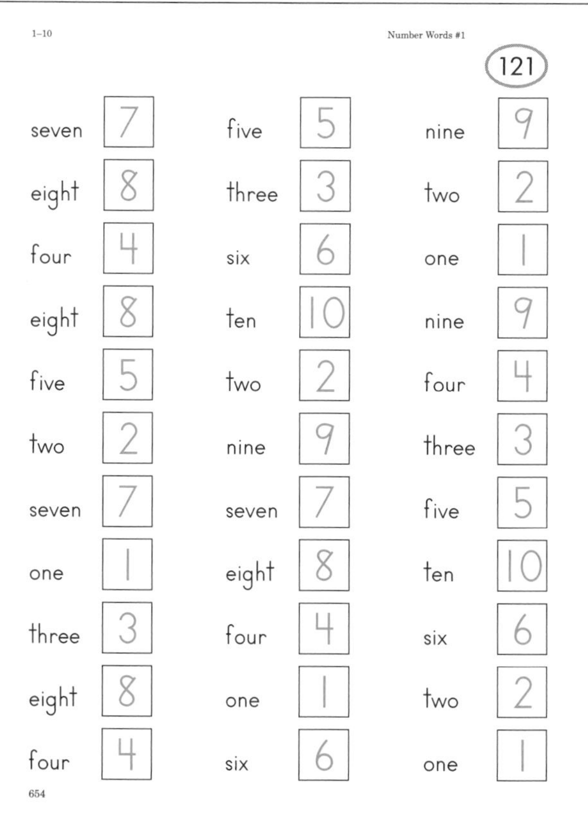

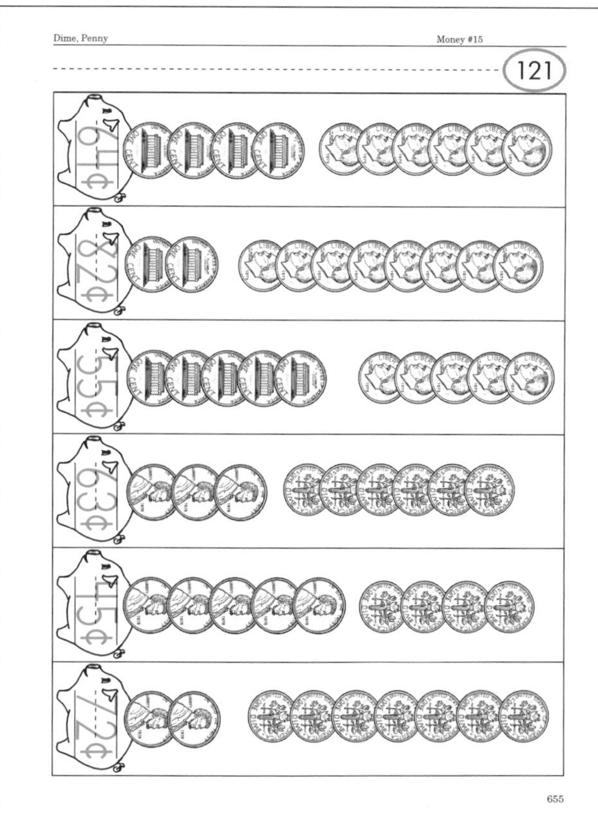

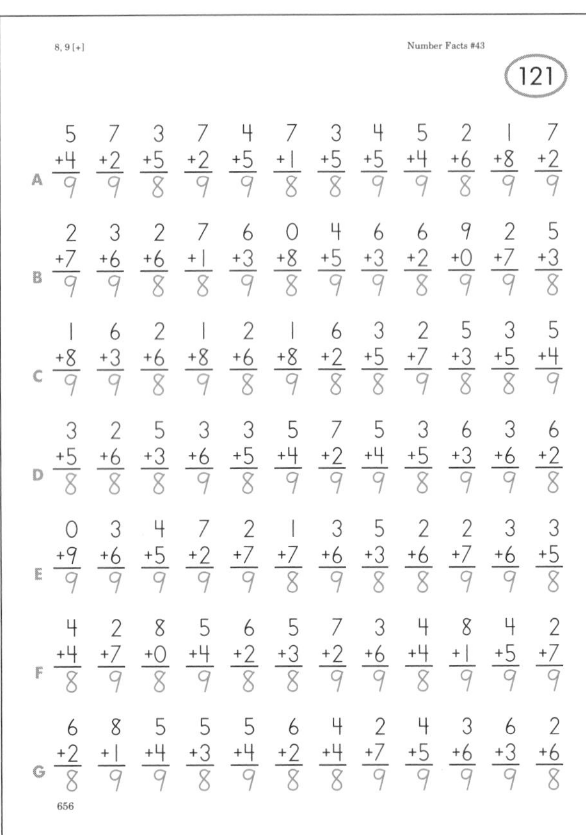

8, 9 [+] Number Facts #43

121

A	5+4=9	7+2=9	3+5=8	7+2=9	4+5=9	7+1=8	3+5=8	4+5=9	5+4=9	2+6=8	1+8=9	7+2=9
B	2+7=9	3+6=9	2+6=8	7+1=8	6+3=9	0+8=8	4+5=9	6+3=9	6+2=8	9+0=9	2+7=9	5+3=8
C	1+8=9	6+3=9	2+6=8	1+8=9	2+6=8	1+8=9	6+2=8	3+5=8	2+7=9	5+3=8	3+5=8	5+4=9
D	3+5=8	2+6=8	5+3=8	3+6=9	3+5=8	5+4=9	7+2=9	5+4=9	3+5=8	6+3=9	3+6=9	6+2=8
E	0+9=9	3+6=9	4+5=9	7+2=9	2+7=9	1+7=8	3+6=9	5+3=8	2+6=8	2+7=9	3+6=9	3+5=8
F	4+4=8	2+7=9	8+0=8	5+4=9	6+2=8	5+3=8	7+2=9	3+6=9	4+4=8	8+1=9	4+5=9	2+7=9
G	6+2=8	8+1=9	5+4=9	5+3=8	5+4=9	6+2=8	4+4=8	2+7=9	4+5=9	3+6=9	6+3=9	2+6=8

656

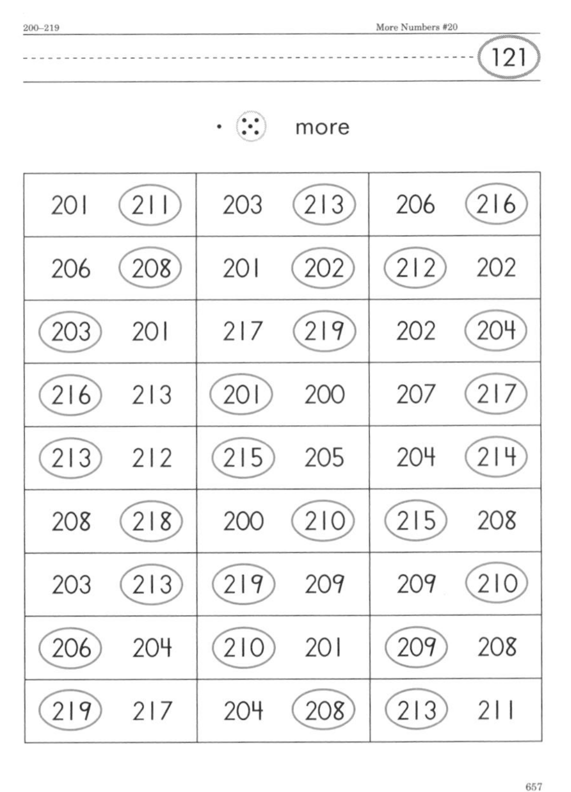

200–219 More Numbers #20

121

• more

201	**211**	203	**213**	206	**216**
206	**208**	201	**202**	**212**	202
203	201	217	**219**	202	**204**
216	213	**201**	200	207	**217**
213	212	**215**	205	204	**214**
208	**218**	200	**210**	**215**	208
203	**213**	**219**	209	209	**210**
206	204	**210**	201	**209**	208
219	217	204	**208**	**213**	211

657

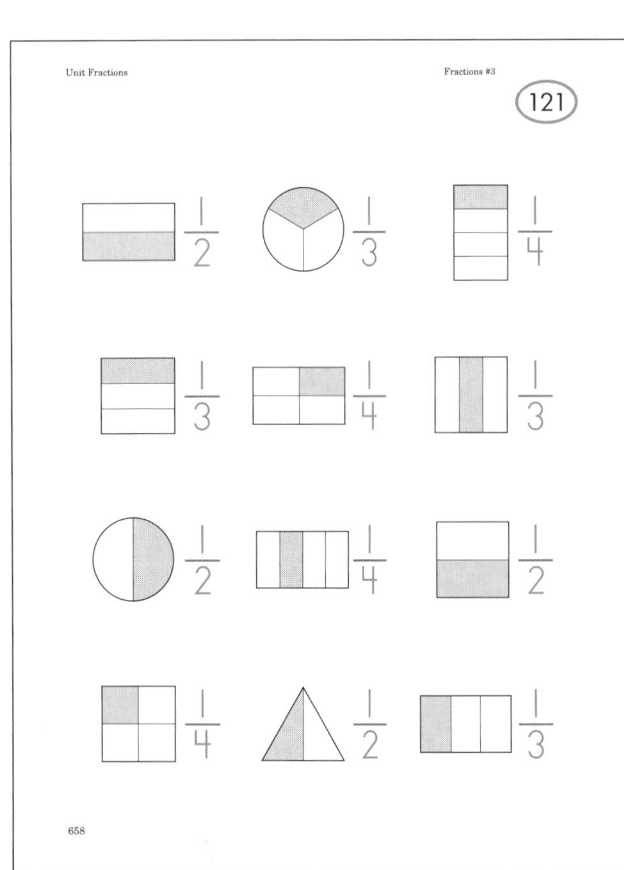

Unit Fractions Fractions #3

121

1/2 1/3 1/4

1/3 1/4 1/3

1/2 1/4 1/2

1/4 1/2 1/3

658

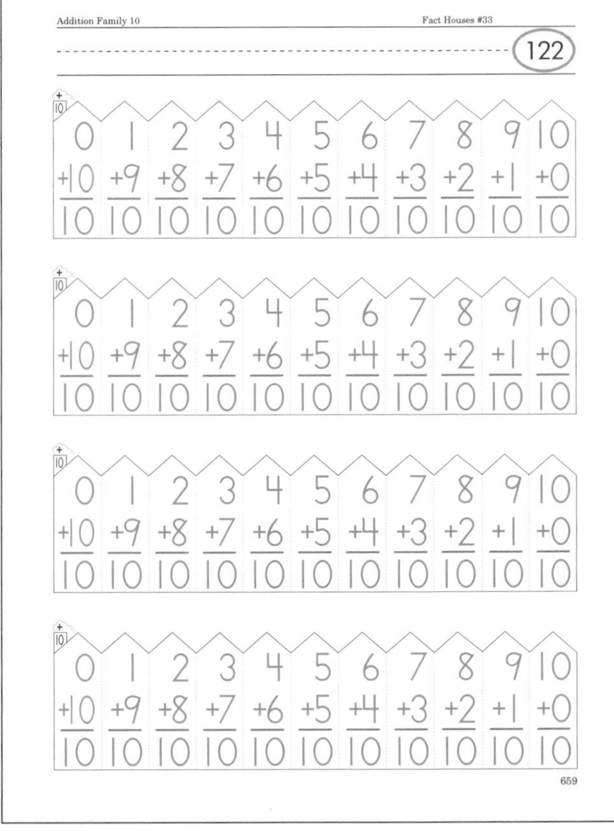

Addition Family 10 Fact Houses #33

122

0+10=10 1+9=10 2+8=10 3+7=10 4+6=10 5+5=10 6+4=10 7+3=10 8+2=10 9+1=10 10+0=10

0+10=10 1+9=10 2+8=10 3+7=10 4+6=10 5+5=10 6+4=10 7+3=10 8+2=10 9+1=10 10+0=10

0+10=10 1+9=10 2+8=10 3+7=10 4+6=10 5+5=10 6+4=10 7+3=10 8+2=10 9+1=10 10+0=10

0+10=10 1+9=10 2+8=10 3+7=10 4+6=10 5+5=10 6+4=10 7+3=10 8+2=10 9+1=10 10+0=10

659

200–219 Less Numbers #20

122

less ⊙ ∵

206	216	201	**200**	213	**211**
204	208	216	**213**	215	**208**
219	**217**	**203**	213	219	**209**
209	210	206	**204**	210	**201**
209	**208**	**200**	210	**208**	218
204	214	215	**205**	213	**212**
207	217	**203**	213	**201**	211
206	208	**201**	202	212	**202**
203	**201**	**217**	219	**202**	204

660

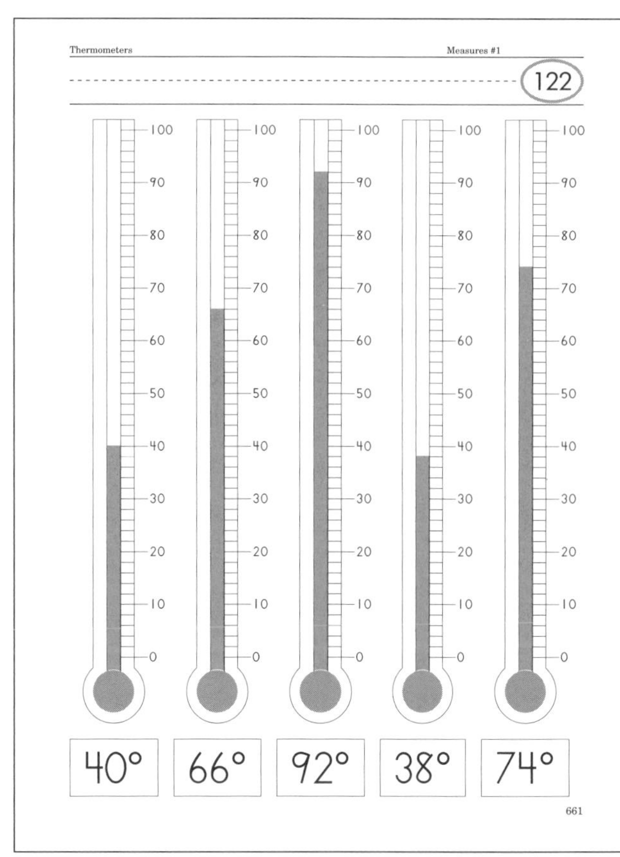

3–9 [+] 4–7 [-] Number Facts #44

122

A	6 + 2 = 8	3 + 2 = 5	7 - 2 = 5	6 + 3 = 9
B	7 - 2 = 5	1 + 8 = 9	7 - 3 = 4	5 - 2 = 3
C	7 - 4 = 3	2 + 1 = 3	2 + 4 = 6	5 - 4 = 1
D	5 + 4 = 9	3 + 4 = 7	2 + 6 = 8	6 - 2 = 4
E	6 + 3 = 9	6 - 2 = 4	3 + 2 = 5	3 + 3 = 6
F	2 + 5 = 7	2 + 2 = 4	7 + 2 = 9	5 + 3 = 8
G	7 - 3 = 4	7 - 1 = 6	7 - 4 = 3	6 - 1 = 5
H	4 + 2 = 6	4 + 4 = 8	7 - 6 = 1	3 + 4 = 7
I	6 - 1 = 5	7 - 2 = 5	4 + 3 = 7	2 + 6 = 8
J	3 + 5 = 8	4 + 5 = 9	7 - 0 = 7	5 + 4 = 9
K	4 + 2 = 6	6 - 3 = 3	3 + 5 = 8	7 - 4 = 3
L	2 + 5 = 7	7 - 6 = 1	5 - 3 = 2	5 - 2 = 3
M	5 + 3 = 8	7 - 4 = 3	6 - 1 = 5	4 + 4 = 8
N	7 - 5 = 2	6 - 5 = 1	3 + 6 = 9	5 - 3 = 2
O	2 + 7 = 9	4 + 3 = 7	6 - 3 = 3	2 + 3 = 5
P	5 - 2 = 3	6 + 2 = 8	5 + 2 = 7	7 - 5 = 2
Q	4 - 3 = 1	7 - 5 = 2	6 - 3 = 3	6 - 4 = 2

662

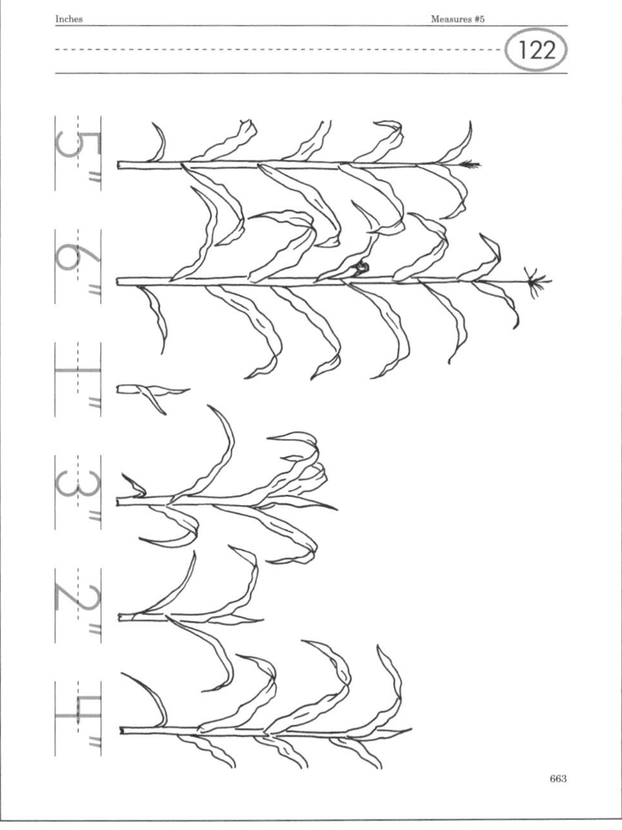

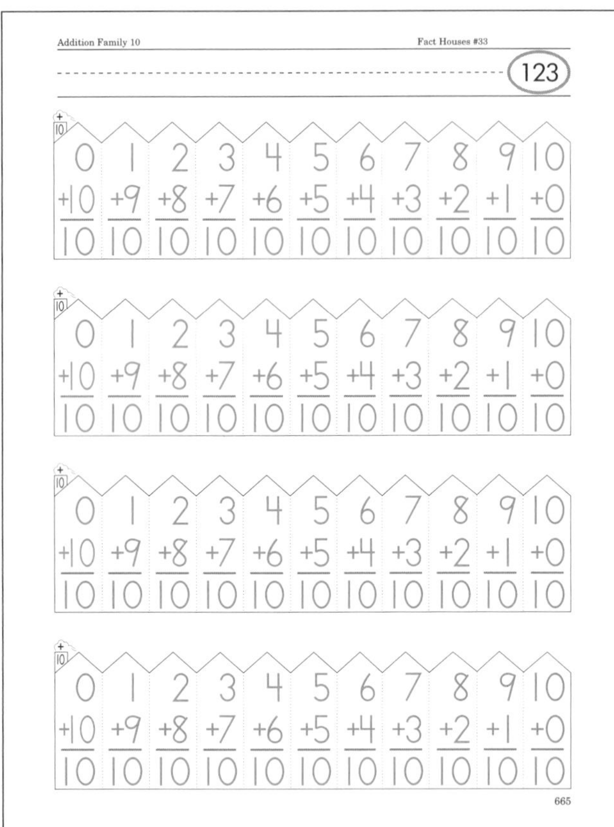

Addition Family 10 — Fact Houses #33 — 123

0	1	2	3	4	5	6	7	8	9	10
+10	+9	+8	+7	+6	+5	+4	+3	+2	+1	+0
10	10	10	10	10	10	10	10	10	10	10

0	1	2	3	4	5	6	7	8	9	10
+10	+9	+8	+7	+6	+5	+4	+3	+2	+1	+0
10	10	10	10	10	10	10	10	10	10	10

0	1	2	3	4	5	6	7	8	9	10
+10	+9	+8	+7	+6	+5	+4	+3	+2	+1	+0
10	10	10	10	10	10	10	10	10	10	10

0	1	2	3	4	5	6	7	8	9	10
+10	+9	+8	+7	+6	+5	+4	+3	+2	+1	+0
10	10	10	10	10	10	10	10	10	10	10

665

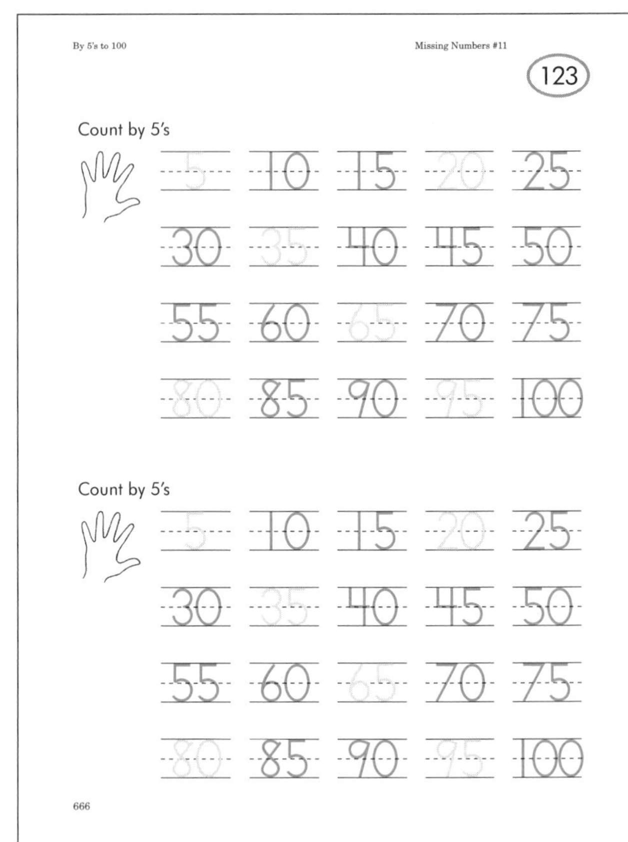

By 5's to 100 — Missing Numbers #11 — 123

Count by 5's

5	10	15	20	25
30	35	40	45	50
55	60	65	70	75
80	85	90	95	100

Count by 5's

5	10	15	20	25
30	35	40	45	50
55	60	65	70	75
80	85	90	95	100

666

Hour, Half Hour — Clocks #7 — 123

6:30	3:00	7:00	10:30
8:00	12:00	11:30	5:00
1:30	3:30	1:00	5:30
10:00	8:30	12:30	7:30

667

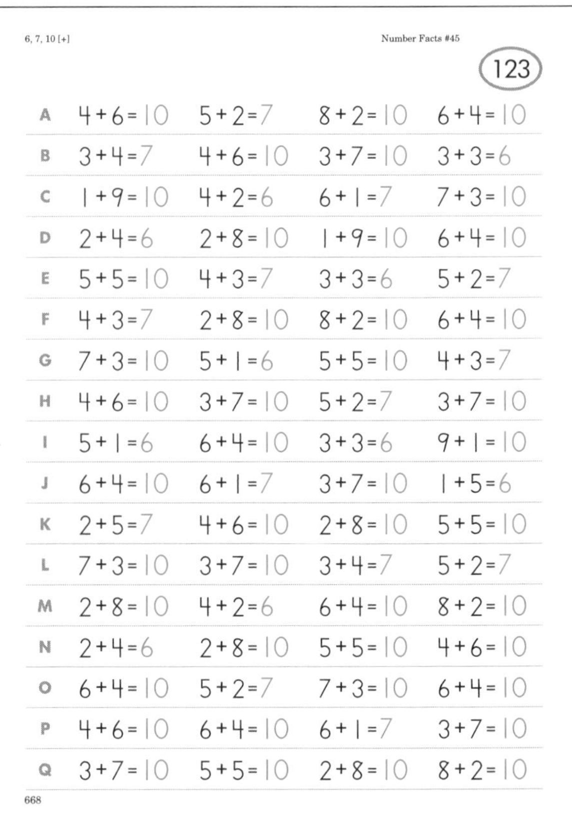

6, 7, 10 [+] — Number Facts #45 — 123

A	4+6=10	5+2=7	8+2=10	6+4=10
B	3+4=7	4+6=10	3+7=10	3+3=6
C	1+9=10	4+2=6	6+1=7	7+3=10
D	2+4=6	2+8=10	1+9=10	6+4=10
E	5+5=10	4+3=7	3+3=6	5+2=7
F	4+3=7	2+8=10	8+2=10	6+4=10
G	7+3=10	5+1=6	5+5=10	4+3=7
H	4+6=10	3+7=10	5+2=7	3+7=10
I	5+1=6	6+4=10	3+3=6	9+1=10
J	6+4=10	6+1=7	3+7=10	1+5=6
K	2+5=7	4+6=10	2+8=10	5+5=10
L	7+3=10	3+7=10	3+4=7	5+2=7
M	2+8=10	4+2=6	6+4=10	8+2=10
N	2+4=6	2+8=10	5+5=10	4+6=10
O	6+4=10	5+2=7	7+3=10	6+4=10
P	4+6=10	6+4=10	6+1=7	3+7=10
Q	3+7=10	5+5=10	2+8=10	8+2=10

668

2–7 [-] Number Facts #42

123

A	6 -2 4	7 -5 2	2 -1 1	6 -1 5	7 -4 3	7 -2 5	6 -5 1	5 -2 3	5 -3 2	7 -1 6	7 -3 4	6 -4 2
B	5 -3 2	7 -1 6	7 -2 5	5 -1 4	3 -2 1	7 -0 7	6 -3 3	6 -5 1	7 -6 1	6 -2 4	6 -4 2	7 -2 5
C	7 -2 5	7 -3 4	6 -4 2	6 -0 6	7 -2 5	4 -2 2	7 -1 6	7 -2 5	7 -4 3	7 -2 5	6 -1 5	7 -4 3
D	6 -2 4	4 -2 2	6 -3 3	5 -1 4	4 -1 3	5 -2 3	7 -3 4	3 -1 2	7 -1 6	4 -2 2	7 -3 4	7 -6 1
E	5 -2 3	7 -2 5	6 -2 4	7 -5 2	7 -3 4	5 -1 4	6 -4 2	4 -1 3	6 -2 4	5 -4 1	6 -3 3	6 -1 5
F	4 -3 1	6 -2 4	5 -4 1	5 -0 5	7 -6 1	6 -5 1	6 -1 5	7 -3 4	5 -3 2	5 -2 3	5 -4 1	4 -2 2
G	6 -1 5	5 -2 3	6 -0 6	6 -2 4	7 -4 3	7 -1 6	7 -3 4	2 -1 1	5 -2 3	7 -1 6	7 -2 5	4 -1 3

669

Place Value Form E

124

hundreds	tens	ones		hundreds	tens	ones
	7	8		2	1	8
1	2	5		1	3	3
		3			9	1
	4	9		2	0	5
		6				9
1	6	7		1	4	7
1	0	1		2	0	0
	2	2		1	8	4
2	1	4			6	2
1	5	0		2	0	9

671

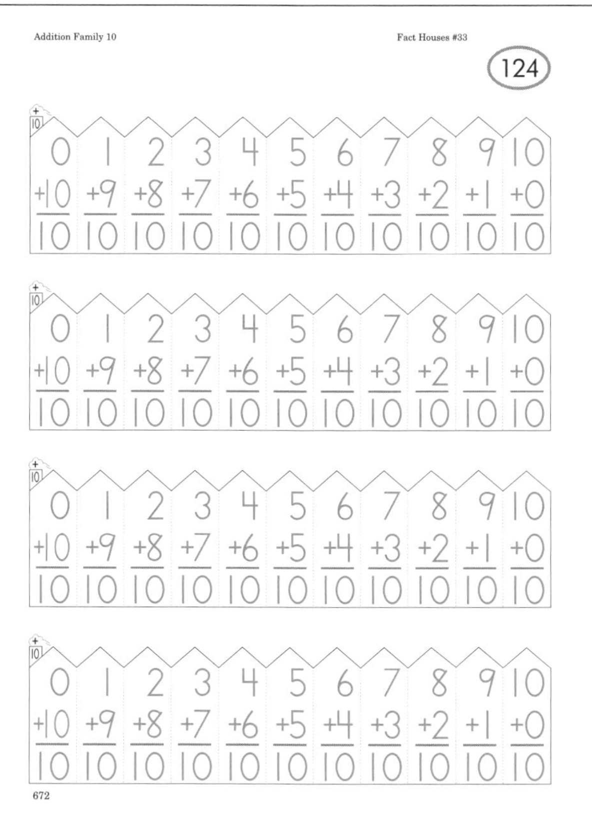

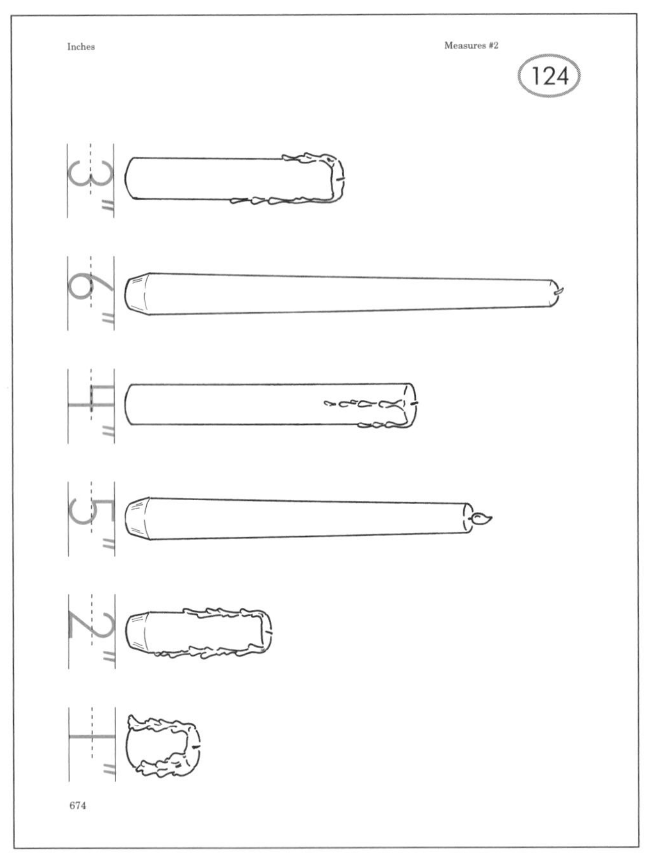

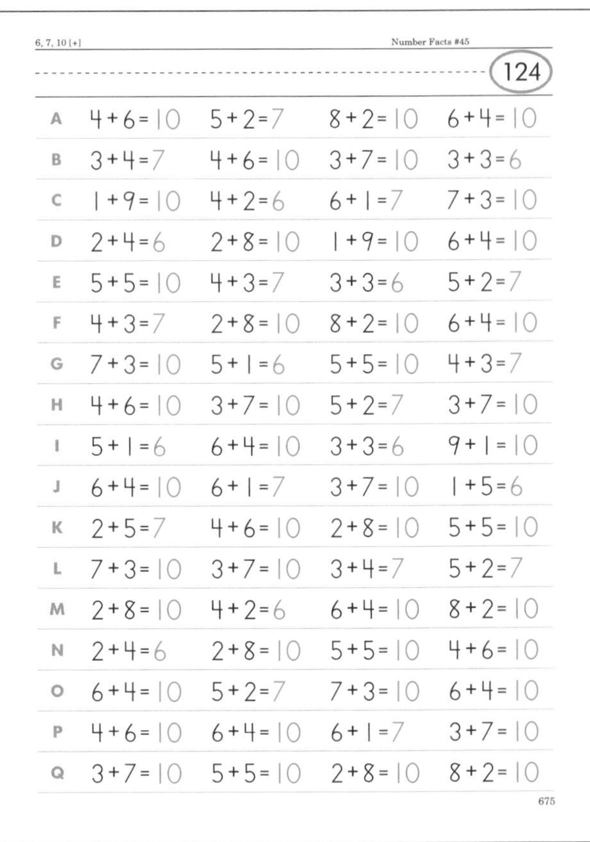
6, 7, 10 [+]
Number Facts #45
124

A	4+6=10	5+2=7	8+2=10	6+4=10
B	3+4=7	4+6=10	3+7=10	3+3=6
C	1+9=10	4+2=6	6+1=7	7+3=10
D	2+4=6	2+8=10	1+9=10	6+4=10
E	5+5=10	4+3=7	3+3=6	5+2=7
F	4+3=7	2+8=10	8+2=10	6+4=10
G	7+3=10	5+1=6	5+5=10	4+3=7
H	4+6=10	3+7=10	5+2=7	3+7=10
I	5+1=6	6+4=10	3+3=6	9+1=10
J	6+4=10	6+1=7	3+7=10	1+5=6
K	2+5=7	4+6=10	2+8=10	5+5=10
L	7+3=10	3+7=10	3+4=7	5+2=7
M	2+8=10	4+2=6	6+4=10	8+2=10
N	2+4=6	2+8=10	5+5=10	4+6=10
O	6+4=10	5+2=7	7+3=10	6+4=10
P	4+6=10	6+4=10	6+1=7	3+7=10
Q	3+7=10	5+5=10	2+8=10	8+2=10

675

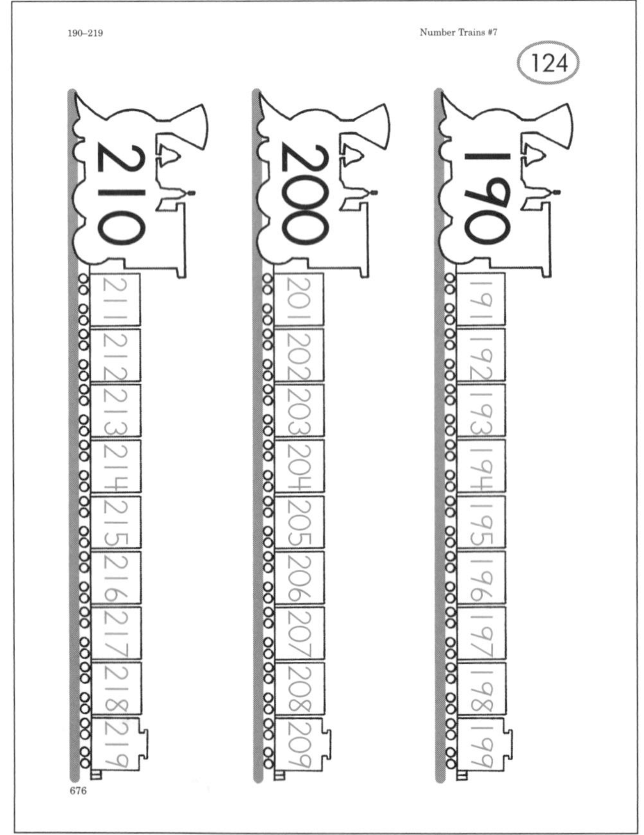

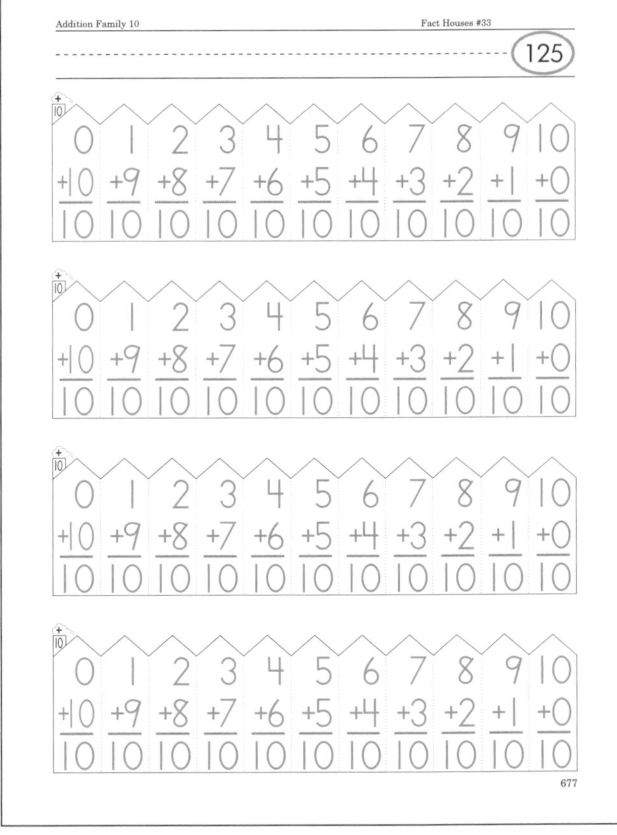

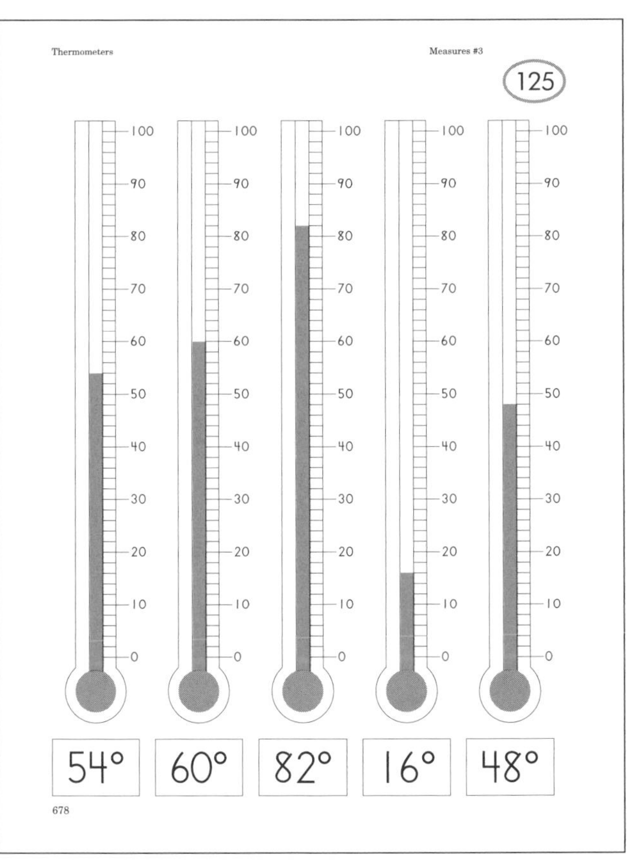

3–9 [+] 4–7 [-]

Number Facts #44

125

A	6 + 2 = 8	3 + 2 = 5	7 - 2 = 5	6 + 3 = 9
B	7 - 2 = 5	1 + 8 = 9	7 - 3 = 4	5 - 2 = 3
C	7 - 4 = 3	2 + 1 = 3	2 + 4 = 6	5 - 4 = 1
D	5 + 4 = 9	3 + 4 = 7	2 + 6 = 8	6 - 2 = 4
E	6 + 3 = 9	6 - 2 = 4	3 + 2 = 5	3 + 3 = 6
F	2 + 5 = 7	2 + 2 = 4	7 + 2 = 9	5 + 3 = 8
G	7 - 3 = 4	7 - 1 = 6	7 - 4 = 3	6 - 1 = 5
H	4 + 2 = 6	4 + 4 = 8	7 - 6 = 1	3 + 4 = 7
I	6 - 1 = 5	7 - 2 = 5	4 + 3 = 7	2 + 6 = 8
J	3 + 5 = 8	4 + 5 = 9	7 - 0 = 7	5 + 4 = 9
K	4 + 2 = 6	6 - 3 = 3	3 + 5 = 8	7 - 4 = 3
L	2 + 5 = 7	7 - 6 = 1	5 - 3 = 2	5 - 2 = 3
M	5 + 3 = 8	7 - 4 = 3	6 - 1 = 5	4 + 4 = 8
N	7 - 5 = 2	6 - 5 = 1	3 + 6 = 9	5 - 3 = 2
O	2 + 7 = 9	4 + 3 = 7	6 - 3 = 3	2 + 3 = 5
P	5 - 2 = 3	6 + 2 = 8	5 + 2 = 7	7 - 5 = 2
Q	4 - 3 = 1	7 - 5 = 2	6 - 3 = 3	6 - 4 = 2

679

6, 7, 10 [+]

Number Facts #45

125

A	4 + 6 = 10	5 + 2 = 7	8 + 2 = 10	6 + 4 = 10
B	3 + 4 = 7	4 + 6 = 10	3 + 7 = 10	3 + 3 = 6
C	1 + 9 = 10	4 + 2 = 6	6 + 1 = 7	7 + 3 = 10
D	2 + 4 = 6	2 + 8 = 10	1 + 9 = 10	6 + 4 = 10
E	5 + 5 = 10	4 + 3 = 7	3 + 3 = 6	5 + 2 = 7
F	4 + 3 = 7	2 + 8 = 10	8 + 2 = 10	6 + 4 = 10
G	7 + 3 = 10	5 + 1 = 6	5 + 5 = 10	4 + 3 = 7
H	4 + 6 = 10	3 + 7 = 10	5 + 2 = 7	3 + 7 = 10
I	5 + 1 = 6	6 + 4 = 10	3 + 3 = 6	9 + 1 = 10
J	6 + 4 = 10	6 + 1 = 7	3 + 7 = 10	1 + 5 = 6
K	2 + 5 = 7	4 + 6 = 10	2 + 8 = 10	5 + 5 = 10
L	7 + 3 = 10	3 + 7 = 10	3 + 4 = 7	5 + 2 = 7
M	2 + 8 = 10	4 + 2 = 6	6 + 4 = 10	8 + 2 = 10
N	2 + 4 = 6	2 + 8 = 10	5 + 5 = 10	4 + 6 = 10
O	6 + 4 = 10	5 + 2 = 7	7 + 3 = 10	6 + 4 = 10
P	4 + 6 = 10	6 + 4 = 10	6 + 1 = 7	3 + 7 = 10
Q	3 + 7 = 10	5 + 5 = 10	2 + 8 = 10	8 + 2 = 10

680

221–240

Writing Practice #28

125

221	221	231	231
222	222	232	232
223	223	233	233
224	224	234	234
225	225	235	235
226	226	236	236
227	227	237	237
228	228	238	238
229	229	239	239
230	230	240	240

681

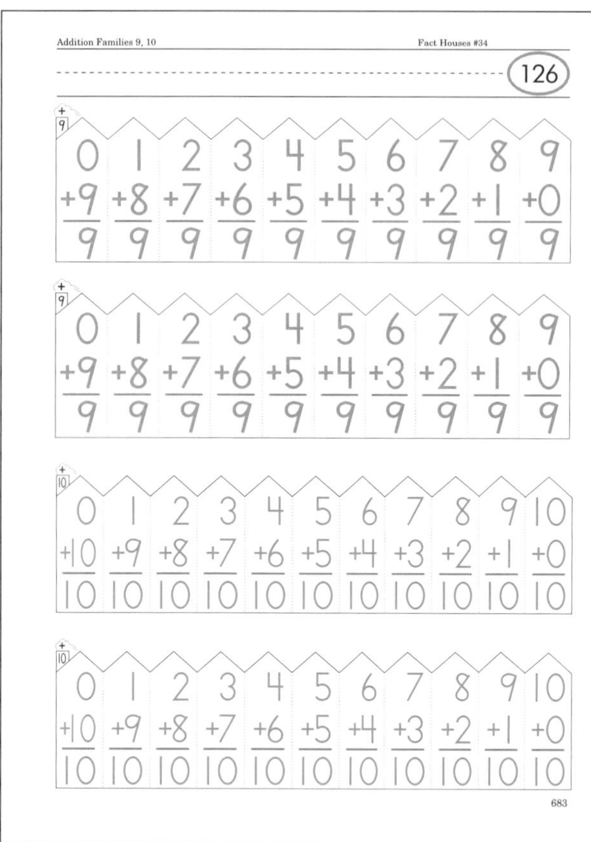

Addition Families 9, 10 — Fact Houses #34 — 126

9									
0	1	2	3	4	5	6	7	8	9
+9	+8	+7	+6	+5	+4	+3	+2	+1	+0
9	9	9	9	9	9	9	9	9	9

9									
0	1	2	3	4	5	6	7	8	9
+9	+8	+7	+6	+5	+4	+3	+2	+1	+0
9	9	9	9	9	9	9	9	9	9

10										
0	1	2	3	4	5	6	7	8	9	10
+10	+9	+8	+7	+6	+5	+4	+3	+2	+1	+0
10	10	10	10	10	10	10	10	10	10	10

10										
0	1	2	3	4	5	6	7	8	9	10
+10	+9	+8	+7	+6	+5	+4	+3	+2	+1	+0
10	10	10	10	10	10	10	10	10	10	10

683

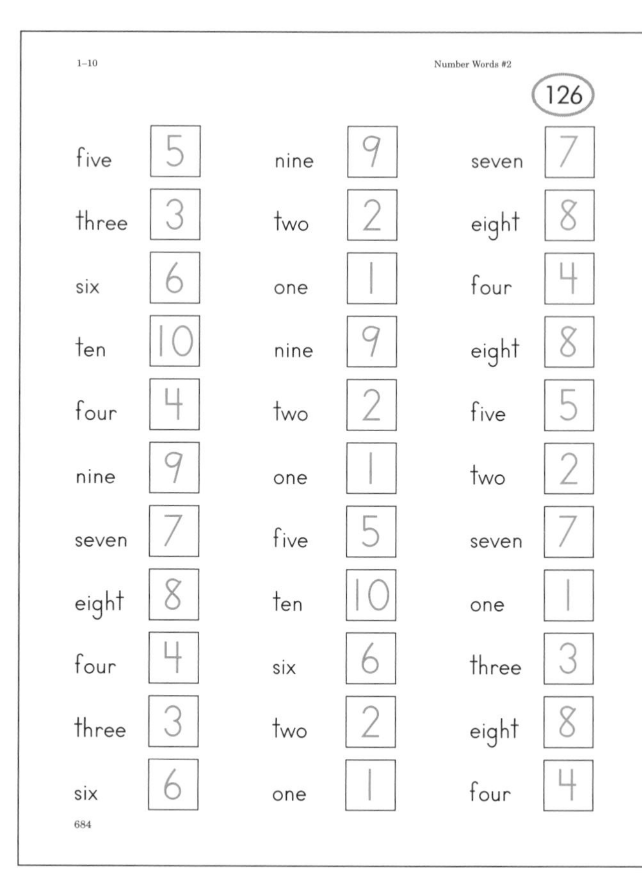

1–10 — Number Words #2 — 126

five	5	nine	9	seven	7
three	3	two	2	eight	8
six	6	one	1	four	4
ten	10	nine	9	eight	8
four	4	two	2	five	5
nine	9	one	1	two	2
seven	7	five	5	seven	7
eight	8	ten	10	one	1
four	4	six	6	three	3
three	3	two	2	eight	8
six	6	one	1	four	4

684

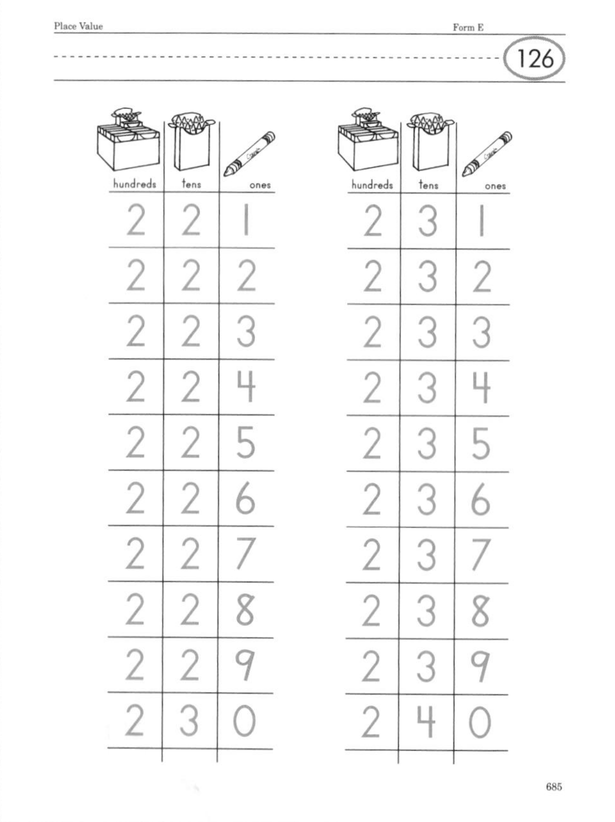

Place Value — Form E — 126

hundreds	tens	ones
2	2	1
2	2	2
2	2	3
2	2	4
2	2	5
2	2	6
2	2	7
2	2	8
2	2	9
2	3	0

hundreds	tens	ones
2	3	1
2	3	2
2	3	3
2	3	4
2	3	5
2	3	6
2	3	7
2	3	8
2	3	9
2	4	0

685

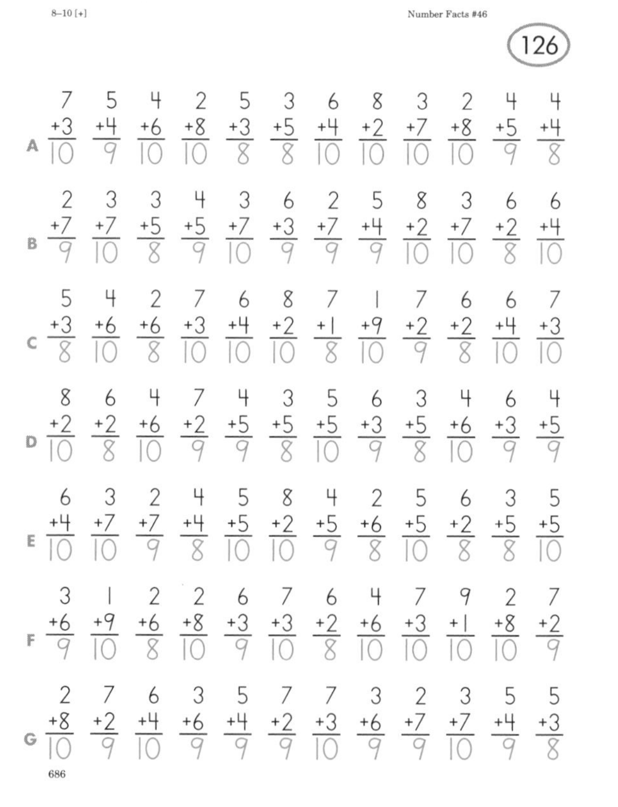

8–10 [+] — Number Facts #46 — 126

A	7 +3 10	5 +4 9	4 +6 10	2 +8 10	5 +3 8	3 +5 8	6 +4 10	8 +2 10	3 +7 10	2 +8 10	4 +5 9	4 +4 8
B	2 +7 9	3 +7 10	3 +5 8	4 +5 9	3 +7 10	6 +3 9	2 +7 9	5 +4 9	8 +2 10	3 +7 10	6 +2 8	6 +4 10
C	5 +3 8	4 +6 10	2 +6 8	7 +3 10	6 +4 10	8 +2 10	7 +1 8	1 +9 10	7 +2 9	6 +2 8	6 +4 10	7 +3 10
D	8 +2 10	6 +2 8	4 +6 10	7 +2 9	4 +5 9	3 +5 8	5 +5 10	6 +3 9	3 +5 8	4 +6 10	6 +3 9	4 +5 9
E	6 +4 10	3 +7 10	2 +7 9	4 +4 8	5 +5 10	8 +2 10	4 +5 9	2 +6 8	5 +5 10	6 +2 8	3 +5 8	5 +5 10
F	3 +6 9	1 +9 10	2 +6 8	2 +8 10	6 +3 9	7 +3 10	6 +2 8	4 +6 10	7 +3 10	9 +1 10	2 +8 10	7 +2 9
G	2 +8 10	7 +2 9	6 +4 10	3 +6 9	5 +4 9	7 +2 9	7 +3 10	3 +6 9	2 +7 9	3 +7 10	5 +4 9	5 +3 8

686

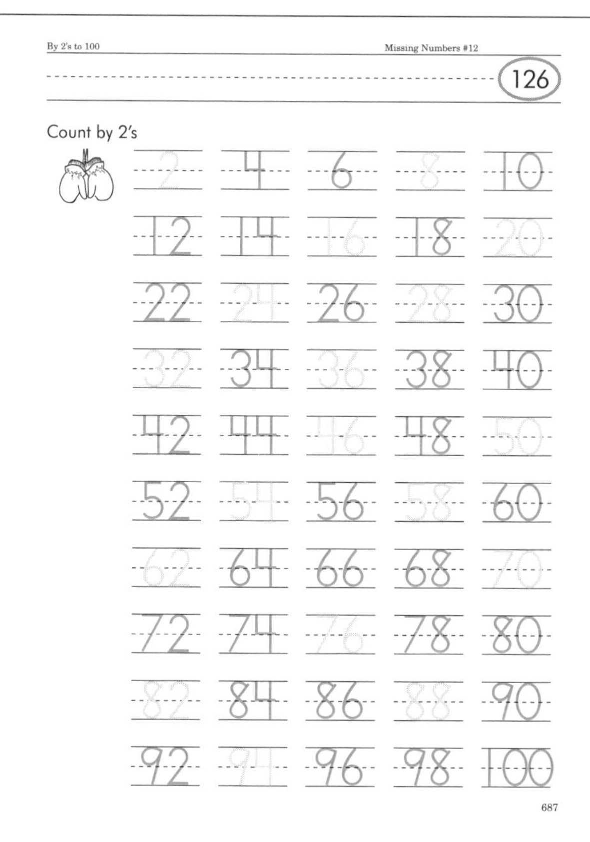

By 2's to 100 Missing Numbers #12

126

Count by 2's

2	4	6	8	10
12	14	16	18	20
22	24	26	28	30
32	34	36	38	40
42	44	46	48	50
52	54	56	58	60
62	64	66	68	70
72	74	76	78	80
82	84	86	88	90
92	94	96	98	100

687

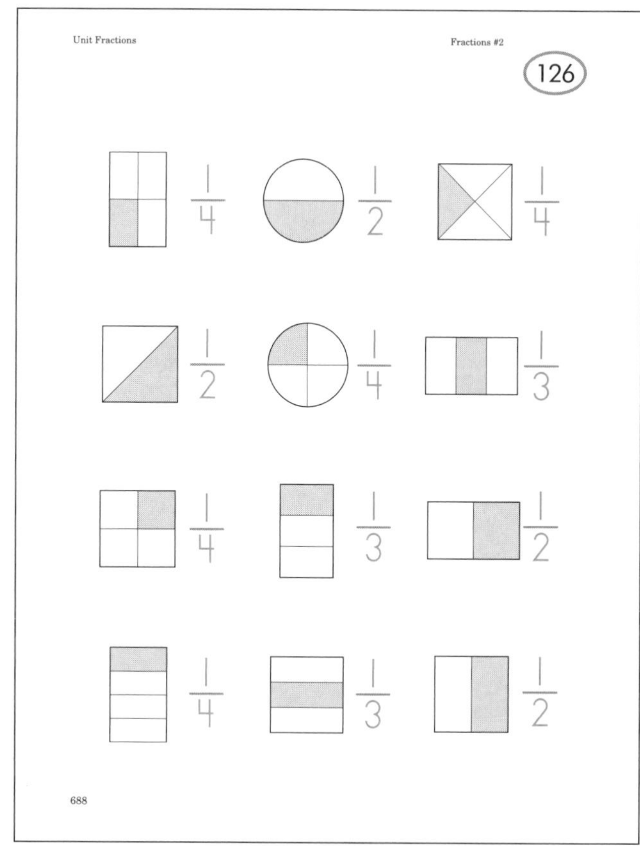

Unit Fractions Fractions #2

126

$\frac{1}{4}$	$\frac{1}{2}$	$\frac{1}{4}$
$\frac{1}{2}$	$\frac{1}{4}$	$\frac{1}{3}$
$\frac{1}{4}$	$\frac{1}{3}$	$\frac{1}{2}$
$\frac{1}{4}$	$\frac{1}{3}$	$\frac{1}{2}$

688

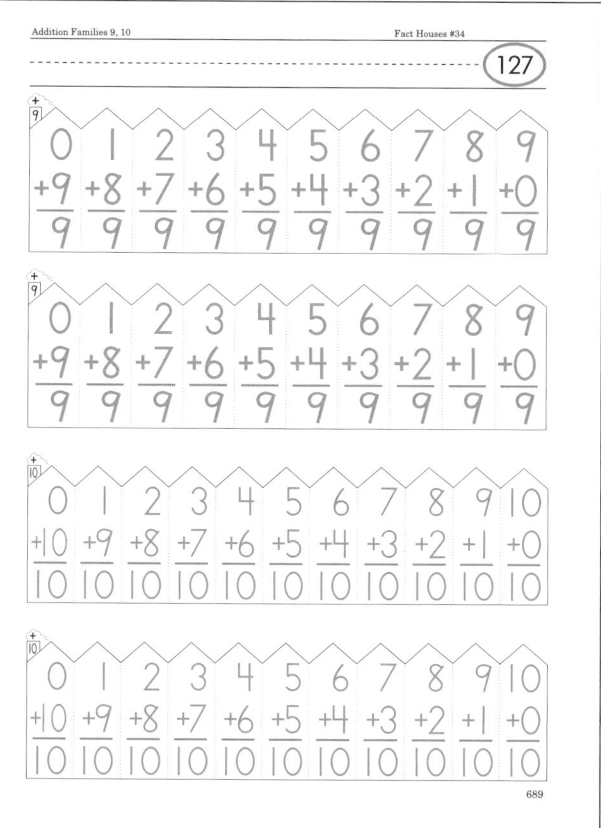

Addition Families 9, 10 Fact Houses #34

127

+9

0	1	2	3	4	5	6	7	8	9
+9	+8	+7	+6	+5	+4	+3	+2	+1	+0
9	9	9	9	9	9	9	9	9	9

+9

0	1	2	3	4	5	6	7	8	9
+9	+8	+7	+6	+5	+4	+3	+2	+1	+0
9	9	9	9	9	9	9	9	9	9

+10

0	1	2	3	4	5	6	7	8	9	10
+10	+9	+8	+7	+6	+5	+4	+3	+2	+1	+0
10	10	10	10	10	10	10	10	10	10	10

+10

0	1	2	3	4	5	6	7	8	9	10
+10	+9	+8	+7	+6	+5	+4	+3	+2	+1	+0
10	10	10	10	10	10	10	10	10	10	10

689

220–239 Before and After #14

127

226	227	228	229	230	231
231	232	233	225	226	227
228	229	230	233	234	235
229	230	231	220	221	222
222	223	224	234	235	236
236	237	238	227	228	229
232	233	234	224	225	226
230	231	232	235	236	237
221	222	223	223	224	225

690

5–10 [+] 3–7 [-] Number Facts #47

127

A	2+7=9	3+6=9	6+2=8	2+8=10
B	7-3=4	5-2=3	6-2=4	4+4=8
C	6-2=4	7-2=5	5+5=10	3+4=7
D	5-2=3	5+5=10	2+7=9	7+3=10
E	3+7=10	7-3=4	6-3=3	6+3=9
F	2+6=8	6-1=5	3-2=1	7-4=3
G	7+3=10	7-2=5	5+1=6	8+2=10
H	1+8=9	3+7=10	3+2=5	5+3=8
I	7-4=3	5-1=4	5+5=10	5-3=2
J	3+2=5	8+2=10	3+6=9	7-3=4
K	2+8=10	3+5=8	7-4=3	6-2=4
L	4+5=9	4+2=6	6+4=10	6+2=8
M	6-3=3	7-2=5	3+5=8	5+2=7
N	4+6=10	6+4=10	7-3=4	2+3=5
O	1+7=8	7+2=9	5+4=9	2+8=10
P	5-1=4	4-1=3	6-3=3	4+5=9
Q	6+4=10	7+3=10	8+2=10	7-4=3

691

8–10 [+] Number Facts #46

127

	7	5	4	2	5	3	6	8	3	2	4	4
	+3	+4	+6	+8	+3	+5	+4	+2	+7	+8	+5	+4
A	10	9	10	10	8	8	10	10	10	10	9	8
	2	3	3	4	3	6	2	5	8	3	6	6
	+7	+7	+5	+5	+7	+3	+7	+4	+2	+7	+2	+4
B	9	10	8	9	10	9	9	9	10	10	8	10
	5	4	2	7	6	8	7	1	7	6	6	7
	+3	+6	+6	+3	+4	+2	+1	+9	+2	+2	+4	+3
C	8	10	8	10	10	10	8	10	9	8	10	10
	8	6	4	7	4	3	5	6	3	4	6	4
	+2	+2	+6	+2	+5	+5	+5	+3	+5	+6	+3	+5
D	10	8	10	9	9	8	10	9	8	10	9	9
	6	3	2	4	5	8	4	2	5	6	3	5
	+4	+7	+7	+4	+5	+2	+5	+6	+5	+2	+5	+5
E	10	10	9	8	10	10	9	8	10	8	8	10
	3	1	2	2	6	7	6	4	7	9	2	7
	+6	+9	+6	+8	+3	+3	+2	+6	+3	+1	+8	+2
F	9	10	8	10	9	10	8	10	10	10	10	9
	2	7	6	3	5	7	7	3	2	3	5	5
	+8	+2	+4	+6	+4	+2	+3	+6	+7	+7	+4	+3
G	10	9	10	9	9	9	10	9	9	10	9	8

692

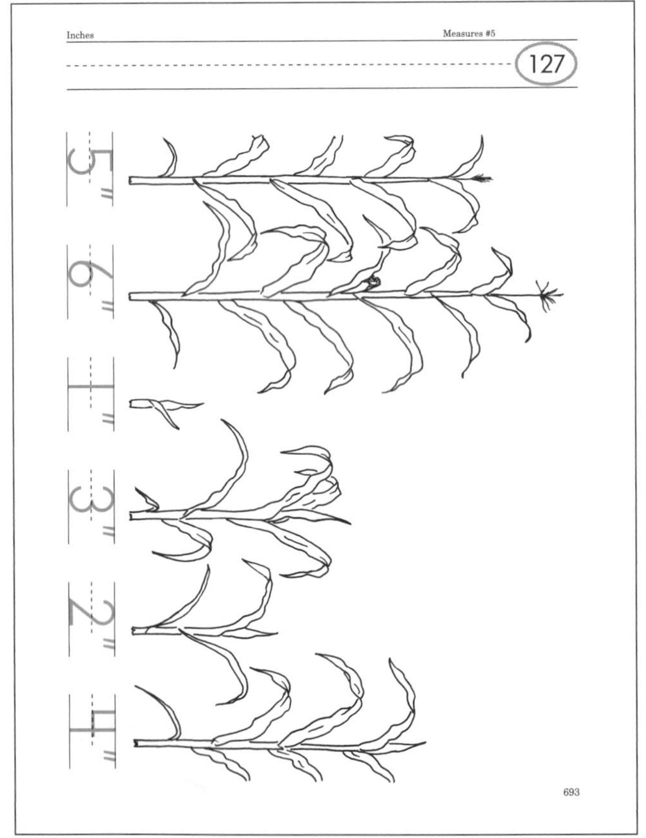

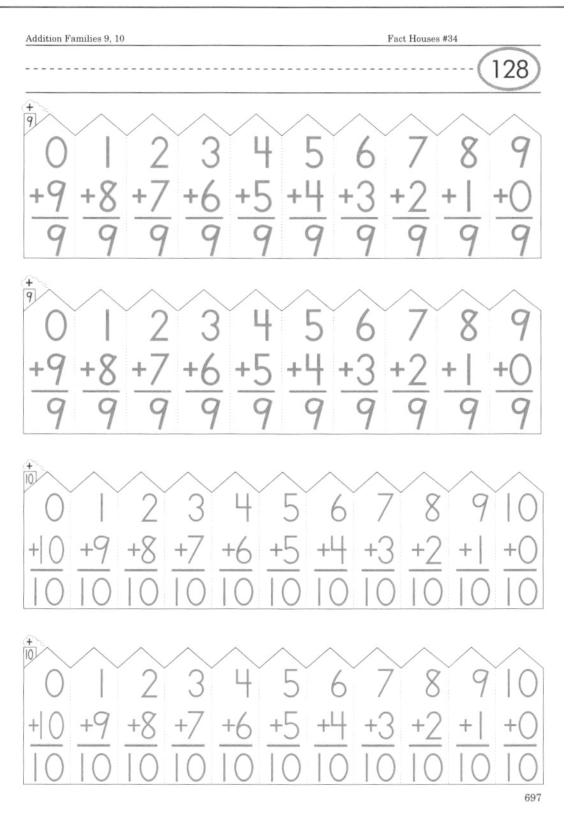

Addition Families 9, 10 — Fact Houses #34

128

+ 9									
0 +9 = 9	1 +8 = 9	2 +7 = 9	3 +6 = 9	4 +5 = 9	5 +4 = 9	6 +3 = 9	7 +2 = 9	8 +1 = 9	9 +0 = 9
0 +9 = 9	1 +8 = 9	2 +7 = 9	3 +6 = 9	4 +5 = 9	5 +4 = 9	6 +3 = 9	7 +2 = 9	8 +1 = 9	9 +0 = 9

+ 10										
0 +10 = 10	1 +9 = 10	2 +8 = 10	3 +7 = 10	4 +6 = 10	5 +5 = 10	6 +4 = 10	7 +3 = 10	8 +2 = 10	9 +1 = 10	10 +0 = 10
0 +10 = 10	1 +9 = 10	2 +8 = 10	3 +7 = 10	4 +6 = 10	5 +5 = 10	6 +4 = 10	7 +3 = 10	8 +2 = 10	9 +1 = 10	10 +0 = 10

697

Hour, Half Hour — Clocks #7

128

6:30	3:00	7:00	10:30
8:00	12:00	11:30	5:00
1:30	3:30	1:00	5:30
10:00	8:30	12:30	7:30

698

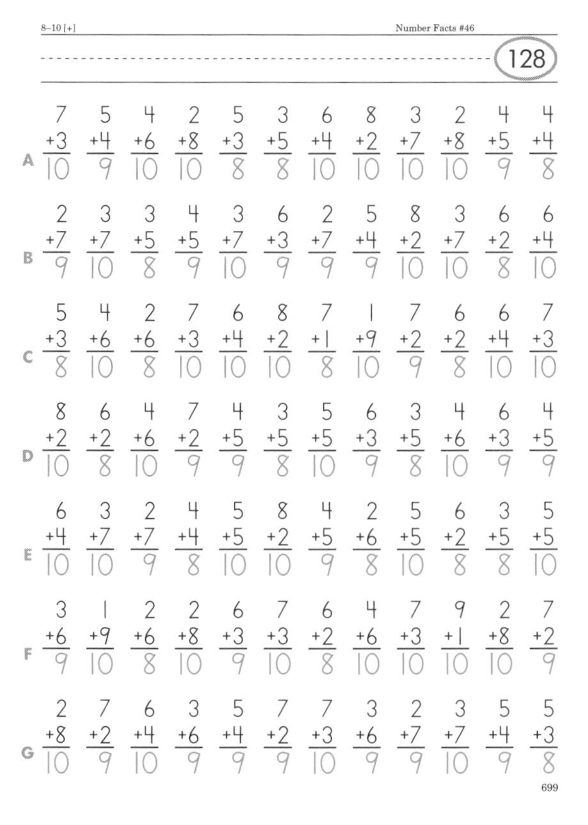

8–10 [+] — Number Facts #46

128

A	7 +3 = 10	5 +4 = 9	4 +6 = 10	2 +8 = 10	5 +3 = 8	3 +5 = 8	6 +4 = 10	8 +2 = 10	3 +7 = 10	2 +8 = 10	4 +5 = 9	4 +4 = 8
B	2 +7 = 9	3 +7 = 10	3 +5 = 8	4 +5 = 9	3 +7 = 10	6 +3 = 9	2 +7 = 9	5 +4 = 9	8 +2 = 10	3 +7 = 10	6 +2 = 8	6 +4 = 10
C	5 +3 = 8	4 +6 = 10	2 +6 = 8	7 +3 = 10	6 +4 = 10	8 +2 = 10	7 +1 = 8	1 +9 = 10	7 +2 = 9	6 +2 = 8	6 +4 = 10	7 +3 = 10
D	8 +2 = 10	6 +2 = 8	4 +6 = 10	7 +2 = 9	4 +5 = 9	3 +5 = 8	5 +5 = 10	6 +3 = 9	3 +5 = 8	4 +6 = 10	6 +3 = 9	4 +5 = 9
E	6 +4 = 10	3 +7 = 10	2 +7 = 9	4 +4 = 8	5 +5 = 10	8 +2 = 10	4 +5 = 9	2 +6 = 8	5 +5 = 10	6 +2 = 8	3 +5 = 8	5 +5 = 10
F	3 +6 = 9	1 +9 = 10	2 +6 = 8	2 +8 = 10	6 +3 = 9	7 +3 = 10	6 +2 = 8	4 +6 = 10	7 +3 = 10	9 +1 = 10	2 +8 = 10	7 +2 = 9
G	2 +8 = 10	7 +2 = 9	6 +4 = 10	3 +6 = 9	5 +4 = 9	7 +2 = 9	7 +3 = 10	3 +6 = 9	2 +7 = 9	3 +7 = 10	5 +4 = 9	5 +3 = 8

699

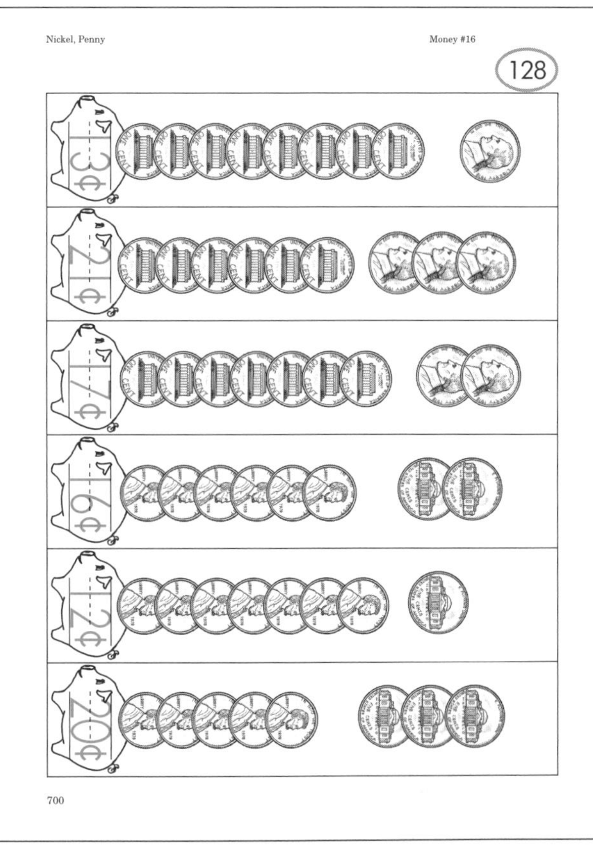

Nickel, Penny — Money #16

128

13¢

21¢

17¢

16¢

12¢

20¢

700

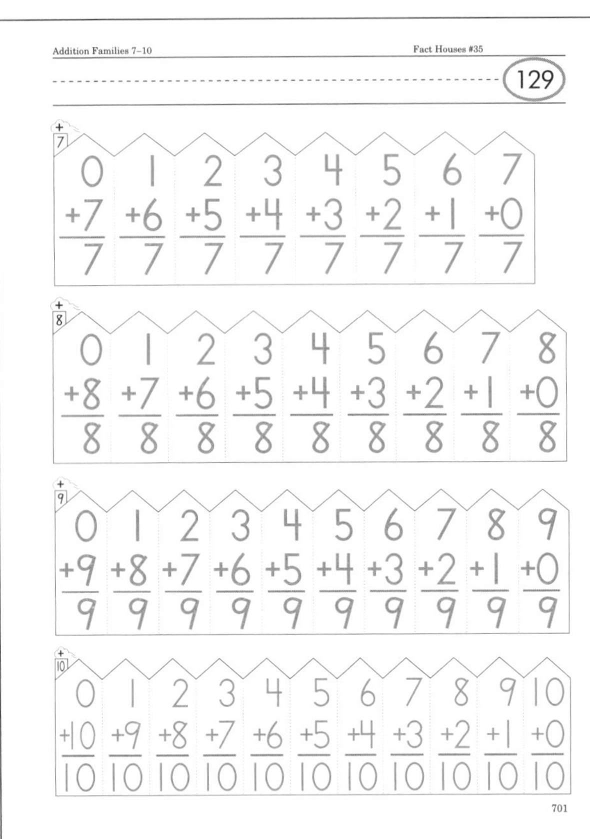

Addition Families 7–10 Fact Houses #35 129

+ 7										
0 +7 = 7	1 +6 = 7	2 +5 = 7	3 +4 = 7	4 +3 = 7	5 +2 = 7	6 +1 = 7	7 +0 = 7			

+ 8										
0 +8 = 8	1 +7 = 8	2 +6 = 8	3 +5 = 8	4 +4 = 8	5 +3 = 8	6 +2 = 8	7 +1 = 8	8 +0 = 8		

+ 9										
0 +9 = 9	1 +8 = 9	2 +7 = 9	3 +6 = 9	4 +5 = 9	5 +4 = 9	6 +3 = 9	7 +2 = 9	8 +1 = 9	9 +0 = 9	

+ 10										
0 +10 = 10	1 +9 = 10	2 +8 = 10	3 +7 = 10	4 +6 = 10	5 +5 = 10	6 +4 = 10	7 +3 = 10	8 +2 = 10	9 +1 = 10	10 +0 = 10

701

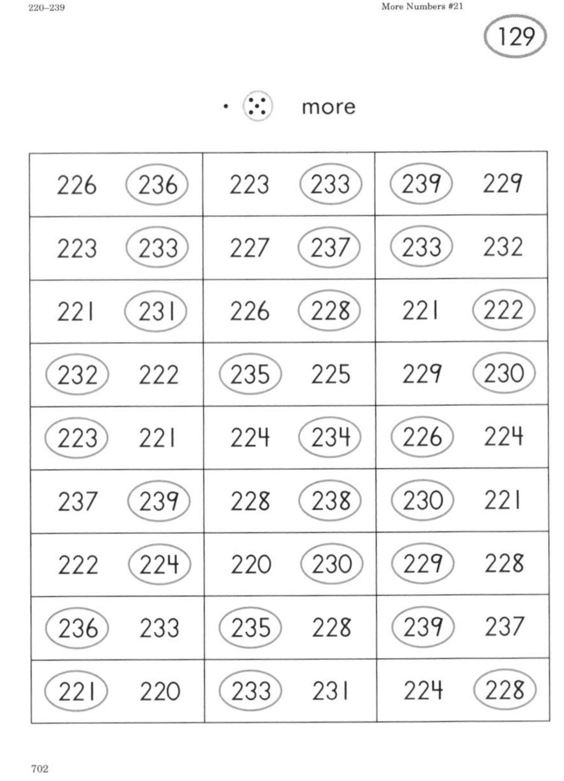

220–239 More Numbers #21 129

• 5 more

226	**236**	223	**233**	**239**	229
223	**233**	227	**237**	**233**	232
221	**231**	226	**228**	221	**222**
232	222	**235**	225	229	**230**
223	221	224	**234**	**226**	224
237	**239**	228	**238**	**230**	221
222	**224**	220	**230**	**229**	228
236	233	**235**	228	**239**	237
221	220	**233**	231	224	**228**

702

Story Problems #1 129

Mother had 6 lemons. She cut 2 lemons to mix drink. How many lemons were left?	6 − 2 = 4	lemons
Jim put 3 little cakes in a box. Joan put 7 cakes in the box. How many cakes is that in all?	3 + 7 = 10	cakes
Joan had 7 cups of drink. She gave 5 cups to the men. How many cups were left?	7 − 5 = 2	cups
The men made 5 big bales. They will make 3 more bales. How many bales is that in all?	5 + 3 = 8	bales

703

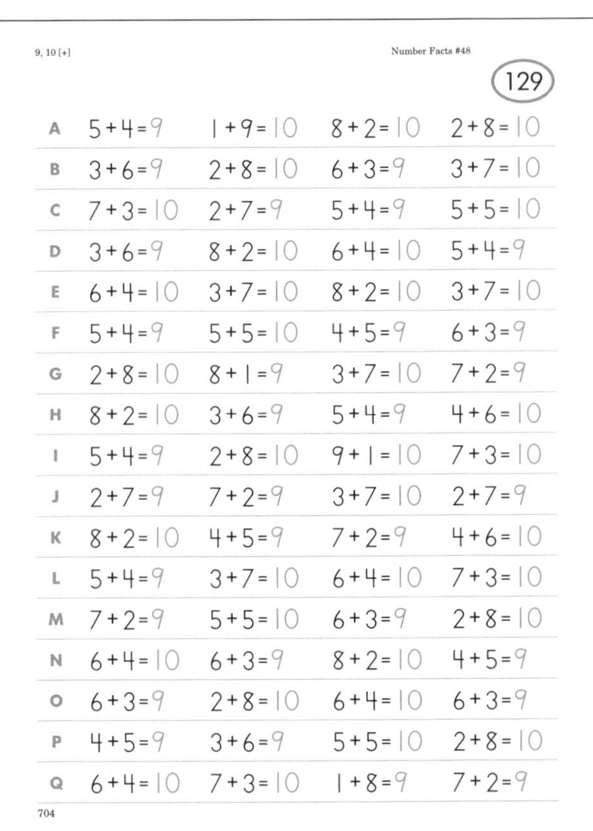

9, 10 [+] Number Facts #48 129

A	5+4=9	1+9=10	8+2=10	2+8=10
B	3+6=9	2+8=10	6+3=9	3+7=10
C	7+3=10	2+7=9	5+4=9	5+5=10
D	3+6=9	8+2=10	6+4=10	5+4=9
E	6+4=10	3+7=10	8+2=10	3+7=10
F	5+4=9	5+5=10	4+5=9	6+3=9
G	2+8=10	8+1=9	3+7=10	7+2=9
H	8+2=10	3+6=9	5+4=9	4+6=10
I	5+4=9	2+8=10	9+1=10	7+3=10
J	2+7=9	7+2=9	3+7=10	2+7=9
K	8+2=10	4+5=9	7+2=9	4+6=10
L	5+4=9	3+7=10	6+4=10	7+3=10
M	7+2=9	5+5=10	6+3=9	2+8=10
N	6+4=10	6+3=9	8+2=10	4+5=9
O	6+3=9	2+8=10	6+4=10	6+3=9
P	4+5=9	3+6=9	5+5=10	2+8=10
Q	6+4=10	7+3=10	1+8=9	7+2=9

704

5–10 [+] 3–7 [-] — Number Facts #47 — 129

A	2+7=9	3+6=9	6+2=8	2+8=10
B	7-3=4	5-2=3	6-2=4	4+4=8
C	6-2=4	7-2=5	5+5=10	3+4=7
D	5-2=3	5+5=10	2+7=9	7+3=10
E	3+7=10	7-3=4	6-3=3	6+3=9
F	2+6=8	6-1=5	3-2=1	7-4=3
G	7+3=10	7-2=5	5+1=6	8+2=10
H	1+8=9	3+7=10	3+2=5	5+3=8
I	7-4=3	5-1=4	5+5=10	5-3=2
J	3+2=5	8+2=10	3+6=9	7-3=4
K	2+8=10	3+5=8	7-4=3	6-2=4
L	4+5=9	4+2=6	6+4=10	6+2=8
M	6-3=3	7-2=5	3+5=8	5+2=7
N	4+6=10	6+4=10	7-3=4	2+3=5
O	1+7=8	7+2=9	5+4=9	2+8=10
P	5-1=4	4-1=3	6-3=3	4+5=9
Q	6+4=10	7+3=10	8+2=10	7-4=3

705

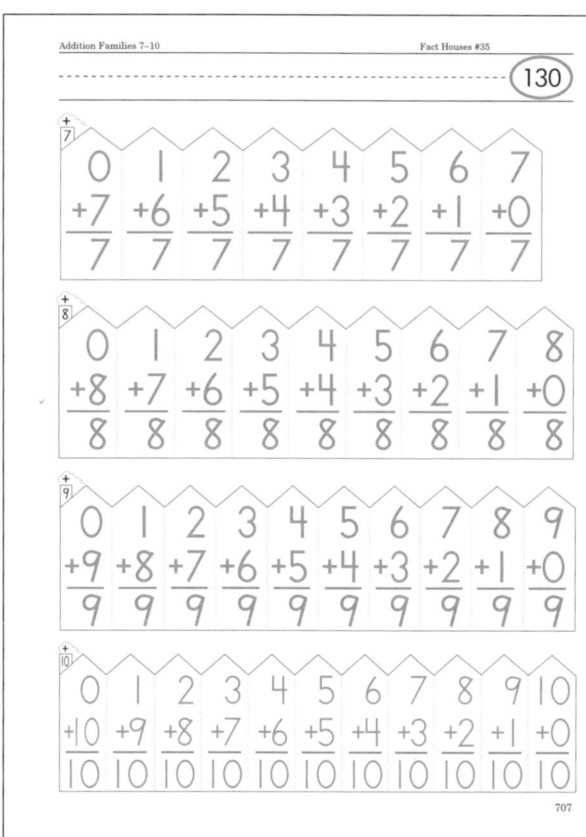
Addition Families 7–10 — Fact Houses #35 — 130

+7

0	1	2	3	4	5	6	7
+7	+6	+5	+4	+3	+2	+1	+0
7	7	7	7	7	7	7	7

+8

0	1	2	3	4	5	6	7	8
+8	+7	+6	+5	+4	+3	+2	+1	+0
8	8	8	8	8	8	8	8	8

+9

0	1	2	3	4	5	6	7	8	9
+9	+8	+7	+6	+5	+4	+3	+2	+1	+0
9	9	9	9	9	9	9	9	9	9

+10

0	1	2	3	4	5	6	7	8	9	10
+10	+9	+8	+7	+6	+5	+4	+3	+2	+1	+0
10	10	10	10	10	10	10	10	10	10	10

707

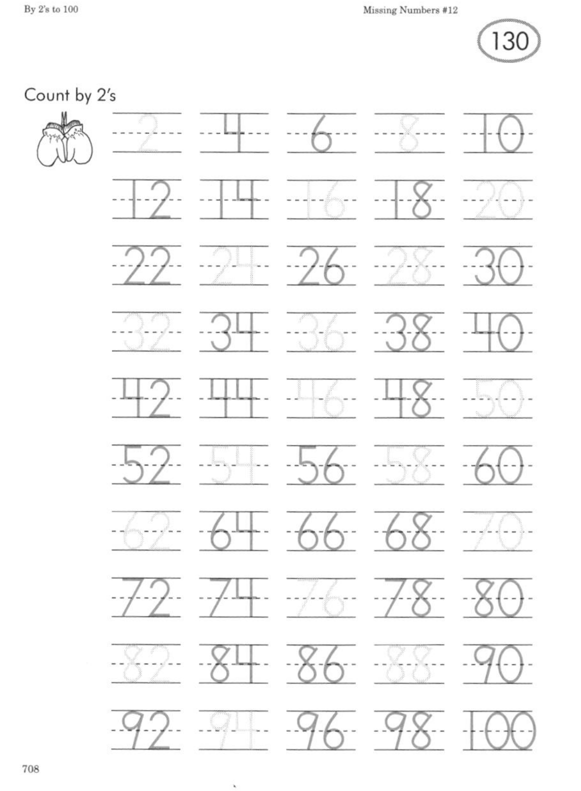
By 2's to 100 — Missing Numbers #12 — 130

Count by 2's

2	4	6	8	10
12	14	16	18	20
22	24	26	28	30
32	34	36	38	40
42	44	46	48	50
52	54	56	58	60
62	64	66	68	70
72	74	76	78	80
82	84	86	88	90
92	94	96	98	100

708

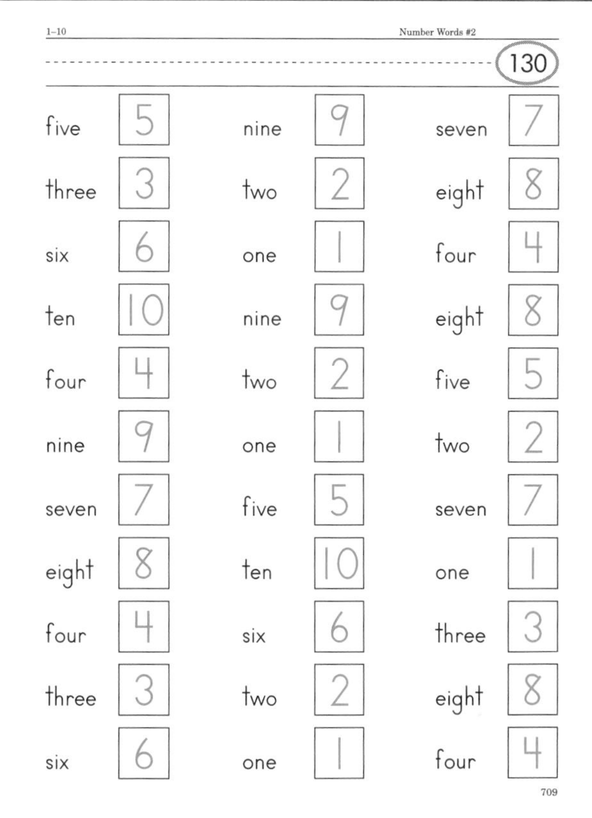
1–10 — Number Words #2 — 130

five	5	nine	9	seven	7
three	3	two	2	eight	8
six	6	one	1	four	4
ten	10	nine	9	eight	8
four	4	two	2	five	5
nine	9	one	1	two	2
seven	7	five	5	seven	7
eight	8	ten	10	one	1
four	4	six	6	three	3
three	3	two	2	eight	8
six	6	one	1	four	4

709

9, 10 [+] Number Facts #48

130

A	5+4=9	1+9=10	8+2=10	2+8=10
B	3+6=9	2+8=10	6+3=9	3+7=10
C	7+3=10	2+7=9	5+4=9	5+5=10
D	3+6=9	8+2=10	6+4=10	5+4=9
E	6+4=10	3+7=10	8+2=10	3+7=10
F	5+4=9	5+5=10	4+5=9	6+3=9
G	2+8=10	8+1=9	3+7=10	7+2=9
H	8+2=10	3+6=9	5+4=9	4+6=10
I	5+4=9	2+8=10	9+1=10	7+3=10
J	2+7=9	7+2=9	3+7=10	2+7=9
K	8+2=10	4+5=9	7+2=9	4+6=10
L	5+4=9	3+7=10	6+4=10	7+3=10
M	7+2=9	5+5=10	6+3=9	2+8=10
N	6+4=10	6+3=9	8+2=10	4+5=9
O	6+3=9	2+8=10	6+4=10	6+3=9
P	4+5=9	3+6=9	5+5=10	2+8=10
Q	6+4=10	7+3=10	1+8=9	7+2=9

710

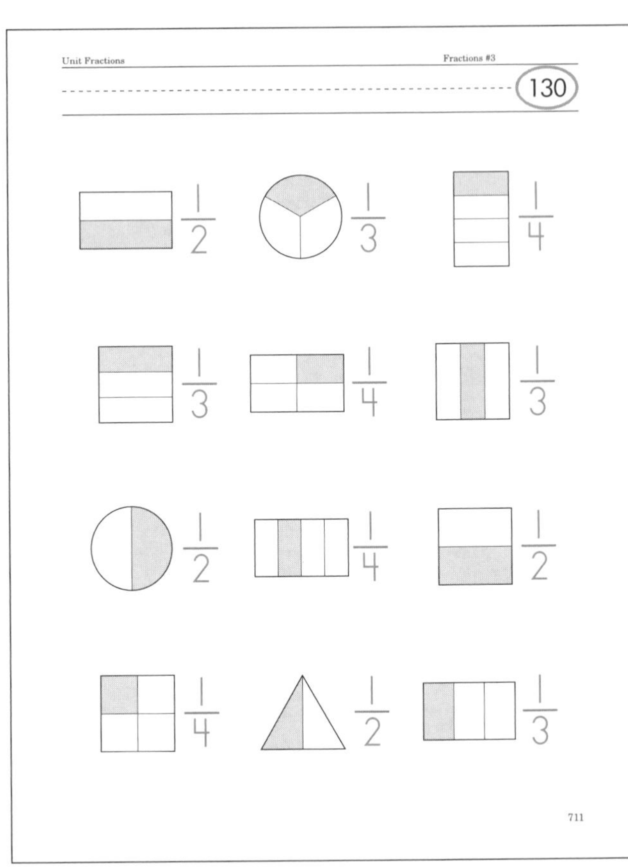
Unit Fractions Fractions #3

130

$\frac{1}{2}$ $\frac{1}{3}$ $\frac{1}{4}$

$\frac{1}{3}$ $\frac{1}{4}$ $\frac{1}{3}$

$\frac{1}{2}$ $\frac{1}{4}$ $\frac{1}{2}$

$\frac{1}{4}$ $\frac{1}{2}$ $\frac{1}{3}$

711

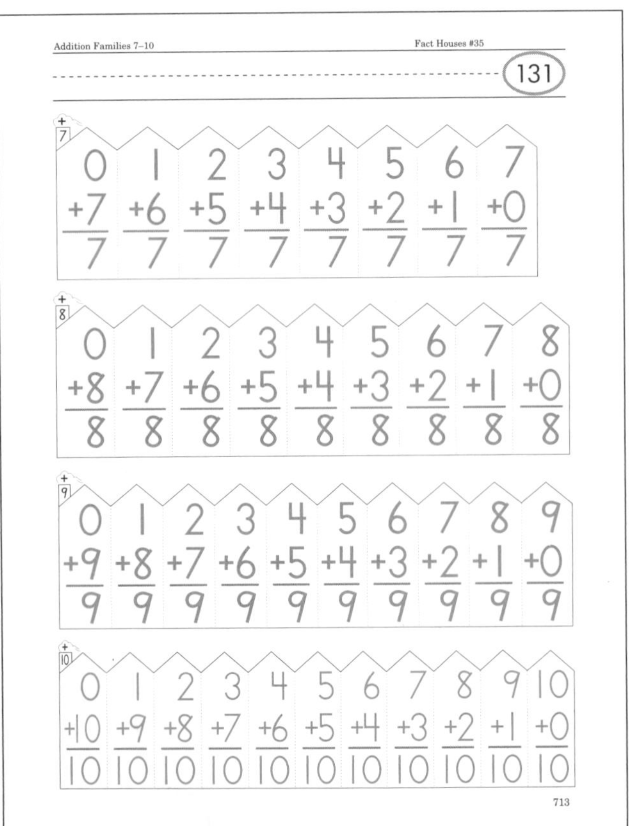
Addition Families 7–10 Fact Houses #35

131

+7

0	1	2	3	4	5	6	7
+7	+6	+5	+4	+3	+2	+1	+0
7	7	7	7	7	7	7	7

+8

0	1	2	3	4	5	6	7	8
+8	+7	+6	+5	+4	+3	+2	+1	+0
8	8	8	8	8	8	8	8	8

+9

0	1	2	3	4	5	6	7	8	9
+9	+8	+7	+6	+5	+4	+3	+2	+1	+0
9	9	9	9	9	9	9	9	9	9

+10

0	1	2	3	4	5	6	7	8	9	10
+10	+9	+8	+7	+6	+5	+4	+3	+2	+1	+0
10	10	10	10	10	10	10	10	10	10	10

713

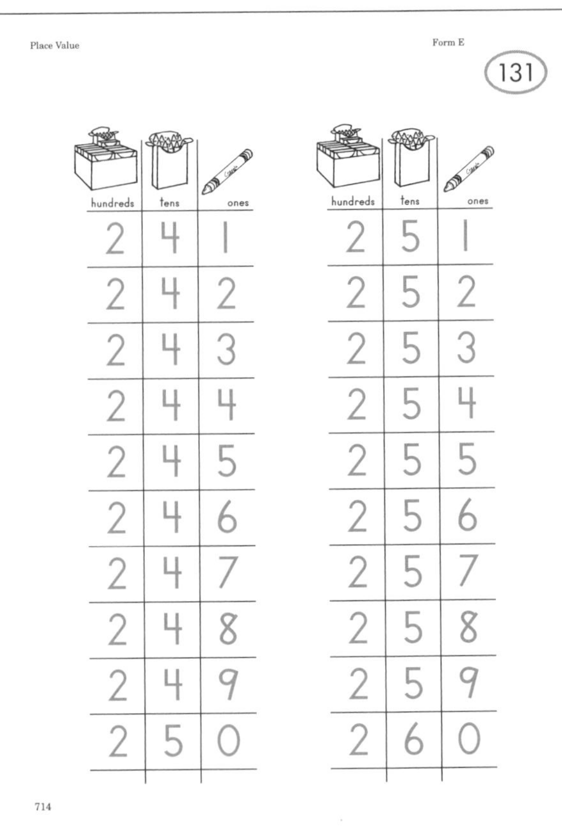
Place Value Form E

131

hundreds	tens	ones
2	4	1
2	4	2
2	4	3
2	4	4
2	4	5
2	4	6
2	4	7
2	4	8
2	4	9
2	5	0

hundreds	tens	ones
2	5	1
2	5	2
2	5	3
2	5	4
2	5	5
2	5	6
2	5	7
2	5	8
2	5	9
2	6	0

714

9, 10 [+] Number Facts #48

131

A	5+4=9	1+9=10	8+2=10	2+8=10
B	3+6=9	2+8=10	6+3=9	3+7=10
C	7+3=10	2+7=9	5+4=9	5+5=10
D	3+6=9	8+2=10	6+4=10	5+4=9
E	6+4=10	3+7=10	8+2=10	3+7=10
F	5+4=9	5+5=10	4+5=9	6+3=9
G	2+8=10	8+1=9	3+7=10	7+2=9
H	8+2=10	3+6=9	5+4=9	4+6=10
I	5+4=9	2+8=10	9+1=10	7+3=10
J	2+7=9	7+2=9	3+7=10	2+7=9
K	8+2=10	4+5=9	7+2=9	4+6=10
L	5+4=9	3+7=10	6+4=10	7+3=10
M	7+2=9	5+5=10	6+3=9	2+8=10
N	6+4=10	6+3=9	8+2=10	4+5=9
O	6+3=9	2+8=10	6+4=10	6+3=9
P	4+5=9	3+6=9	5+5=10	2+8=10
Q	6+4=10	7+3=10	1+8=9	7+2=9

715

220–239 Less Numbers #21

131

less

221	231	**223**	233	**226**	236
226	228	**227**	237	**223**	233
221	222	233	**232**	239	**229**
232	**222**	235	**225**	**229**	230
223	**221**	**224**	234	226	**224**
237	239	**228**	238	230	**221**
222	224	**220**	230	229	**228**
236	**233**	235	**228**	239	**237**
221	**220**	233	**231**	**224**	228

716

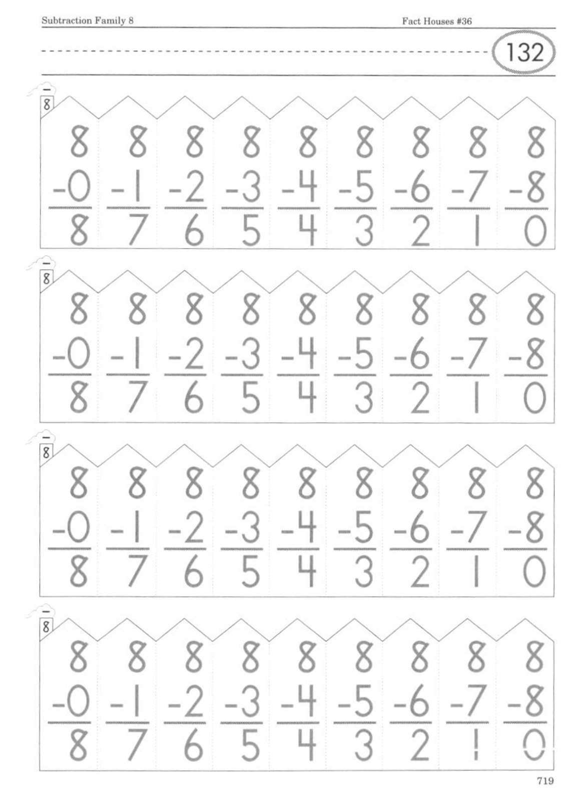

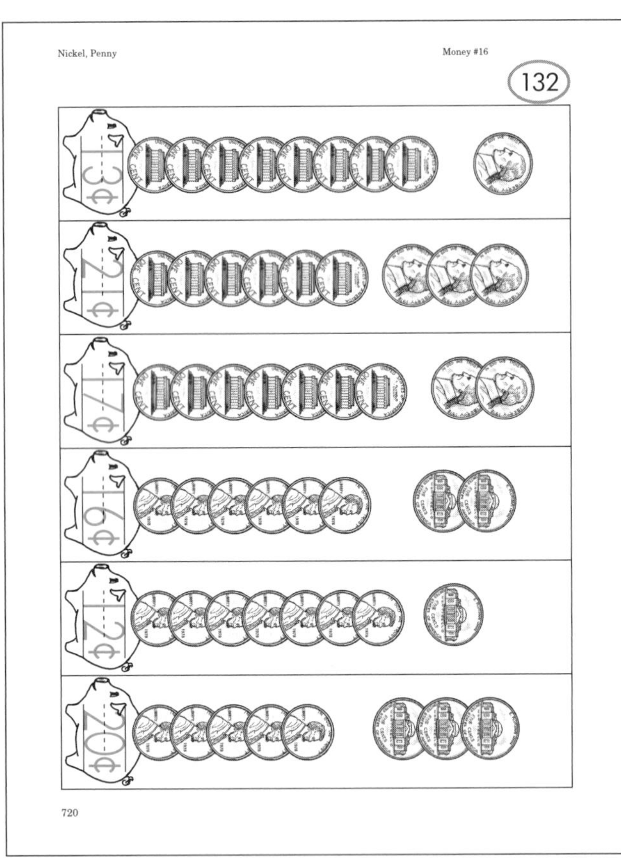
Nickel, Penny | Money #16

132

13¢

21¢

17¢

16¢

12¢

20¢

720

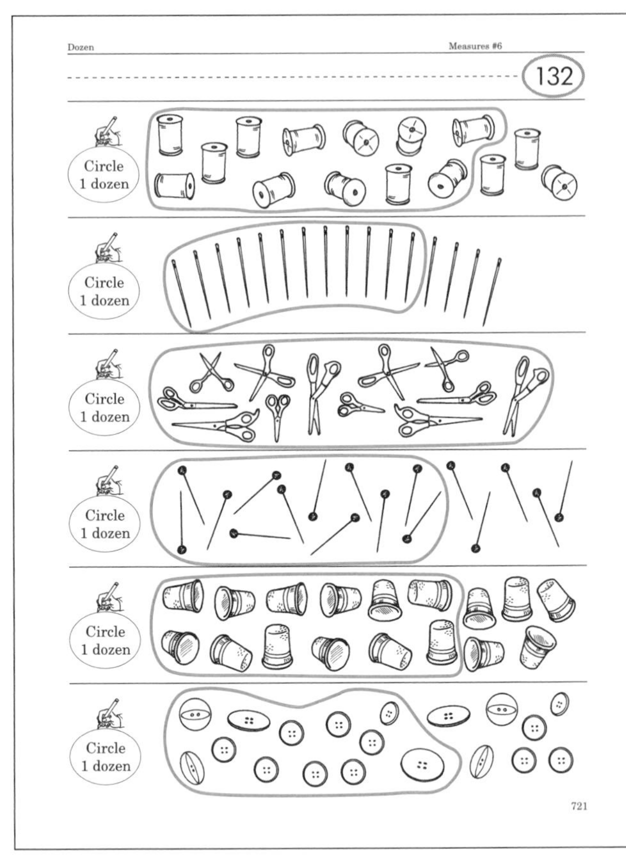
Dozen | Measures #6

132

Circle 1 dozen

Circle 1 dozen

Circle 1 dozen

Circle 1 dozen

Circle 1 dozen

Circle 1 dozen

721

9, 10 [+] | Number Facts #48

132

A	5+4=9	1+9=10	8+2=10	2+8=10
B	3+6=9	2+8=10	6+3=9	3+7=10
C	7+3=10	2+7=9	5+4=9	5+5=10
D	3+6=9	8+2=10	6+4=10	5+4=9
E	6+4=10	3+7=10	8+2=10	3+7=10
F	5+4=9	5+5=10	4+5=9	6+3=9
G	2+8=10	8+1=9	3+7=10	7+2=9
H	8+2=10	3+6=9	5+4=9	4+6=10
I	5+4=9	2+8=10	9+1=10	7+3=10
J	2+7=9	7+2=9	3+7=10	2+7=9
K	8+2=10	4+5=9	7+2=9	4+6=10
L	5+4=9	3+7=10	6+4=10	7+3=10
M	7+2=9	5+5=10	6+3=9	2+8=10
N	6+4=10	6+3=9	8+2=10	4+5=9
O	6+3=9	2+8=10	6+4=10	6+3=9
P	4+5=9	3+6=9	5+5=10	2+8=10
Q	6+4=10	7+3=10	1+8=9	7+2=9

722

Number Grid | Form F

132

51	52	53	54	55	56	57	58	59	60
61	62	63	64	65	66	67	68	69	70
71	72	73	74	75	76	77	78	79	80
81	82	83	84	85	86	87	88	89	90
91	92	93	94	95	96	97	98	99	100
101	102	103	104	105	106	107	108	109	110
111	112	113	114	115	116	117	118	119	120
121	122	123	124	125	126	127	128	129	130
131	132	133	134	135	136	137	138	139	140
141	142	143	144	145	146	147	148	149	150

723

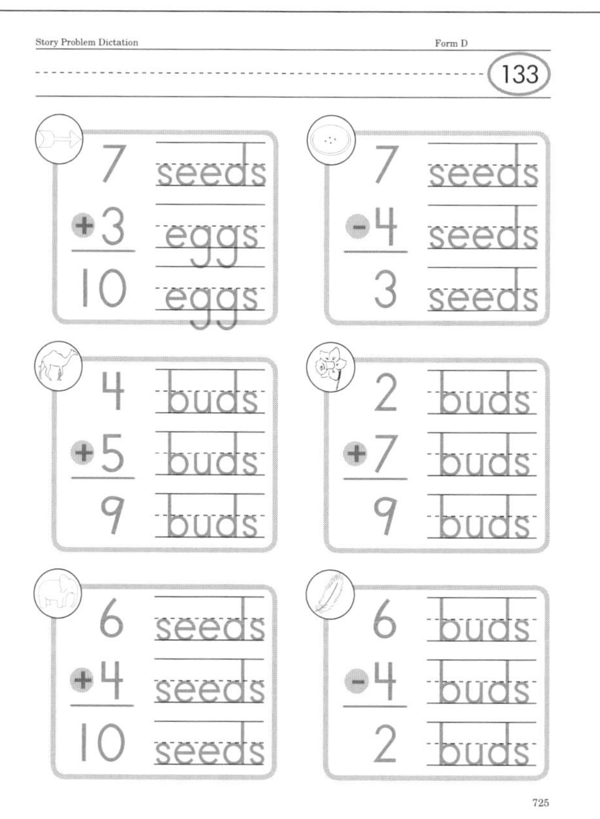
Story Problem Dictation Form D

133

7	seeds	7	seeds
+3	eggs	−4	seeds
10	eggs	3	seeds
4	buds	2	buds
+5	buds	+7	buds
9	buds	9	buds
6	seeds	6	buds
+4	seeds	−4	buds
10	seeds	2	buds

725

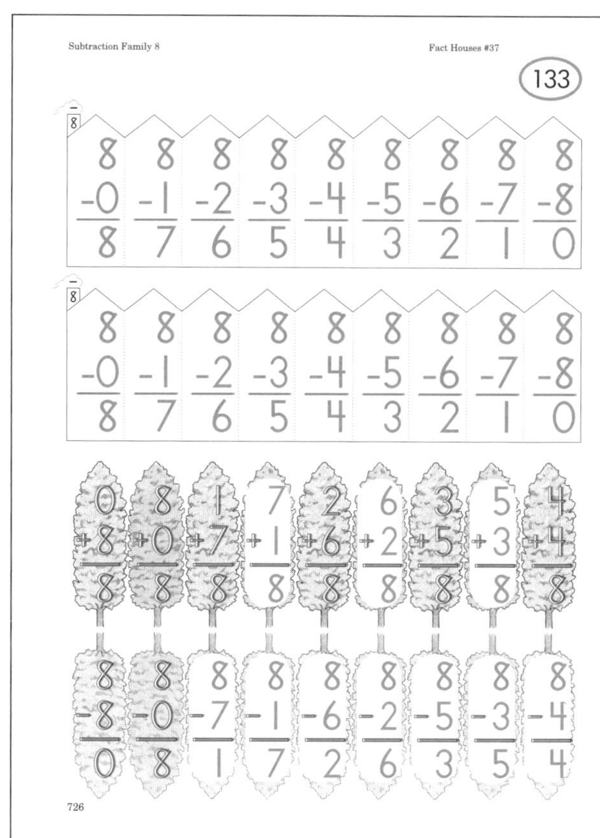
Subtraction Family 8 Fact Houses #37

133

8	8	8	8	8	8	8	8	8
−0	−1	−2	−3	−4	−5	−6	−7	−8
8	7	6	5	4	3	2	1	0

8	8	8	8	8	8	8	8	8
−0	−1	−2	−3	−4	−5	−6	−7	−8
8	7	6	5	4	3	2	1	0

0	8	1	7	2	6	3	5	4
+8	+0	+7	+1	+6	+2	+5	+3	+4
8	8	8	8	8	8	8	8	8

8	8	8	8	8	8	8	8	8
−8	−0	−7	−1	−6	−2	−5	−3	−4
0	8	1	7	2	6	3	5	4

726

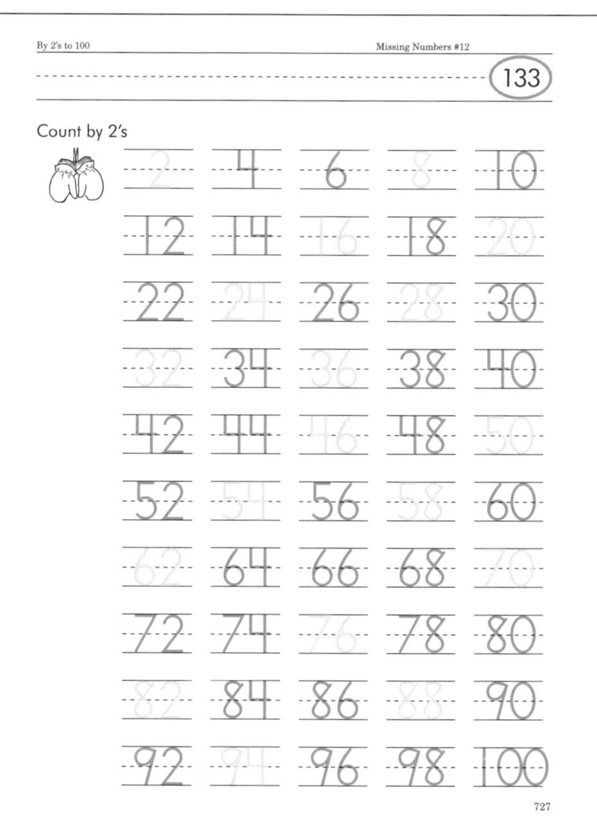
By 2's to 100 Missing Numbers #12

133

Count by 2's

2	4	6	8	10
12	14	16	18	20
22	24	26	28	30
32	34	36	38	40
42	44	46	48	50
52	54	56	58	60
62	64	66	68	70
72	74	76	78	80
82	84	86	88	90
92	94	96	98	100

727

Hour, Half Hour Clocks #7

133

6:30	3:00	7:00	10:30
8:00	12:00	11:30	5:00
1:30	3:30	1:00	5:30
10:00	8:30	12:30	7:30

728

8 [-] — Number Facts #49 — 133

A	8-0=8	8-5=3	8-3=5	8-1=7	8-2=6	8-5=3	8-4=4	8-1=7	8-2=6	8-1=7	8-4=4	8-7=1
B	8-3=5	8-2=6	8-5=3	8-3=5	8-4=4	8-1=7	8-8=0	8-4=4	8-3=5	8-4=4	8-5=3	8-2=6
C	8-6=2	8-4=4	8-8=0	8-4=4	8-2=6	8-3=5	8-6=2	8-2=6	8-1=7	8-3=5	8-2=6	8-1=7
D	8-3=5	8-4=4	8-8=0	8-1=7	8-5=3	8-6=2	8-4=4	8-3=5	8-1=7	8-5=3	8-3=5	8-4=4
E	8-4=4	8-2=6	8-3=5	8-1=7	8-6=2	8-1=7	8-2=6	8-5=3	8-3=5	8-1=7	8-4=4	8-7=1
F	8-2=6	8-3=5	8-5=3	8-3=5	8-4=4	8-2=6	8-3=5	8-1=7	8-6=2	8-4=4	8-1=7	8-5=3
G	8-3=5	8-1=7	8-6=2	8-4=4	8-3=5	8-4=4	8-5=3	8-1=7	8-3=5	8-2=6	8-5=3	8-6=2

729

5–10 [+] 3–7 [-] — Number Facts #47 — 133

A	2+7=9	3+6=9	6+2=8	2+8=10
B	7-3=4	5-2=3	6-2=4	4+4=8
C	6-2=4	7-2=5	5+5=10	3+4=7
D	5-2=3	5+5=10	2+7=9	7+3=10
E	3+7=10	7-3=4	6-3=3	6+3=9
F	2+6=8	6-1=5	3-2=1	7-4=3
G	7+3=10	7-2=5	5+1=6	8+2=10
H	1+8=9	3+7=10	3+2=5	5+3=8
I	7-4=3	5-1=4	5+5=10	5-3=2
J	3+2=5	8+2=10	3+6=9	7-3=4
K	2+8=10	3+5=8	7-4=3	6-2=4
L	4+5=9	4+2=6	6+4=10	6+2=8
M	6-3=3	7-2=5	3+5=8	5+2=7
N	4+6=10	6+4=10	7-3=4	2+3=5
O	1+7=8	7+2=9	5+4=9	2+8=10
P	5-1=4	4-1=3	6-3=3	4+5=9
Q	6+4=10	7+3=10	8+2=10	7-4=3

730

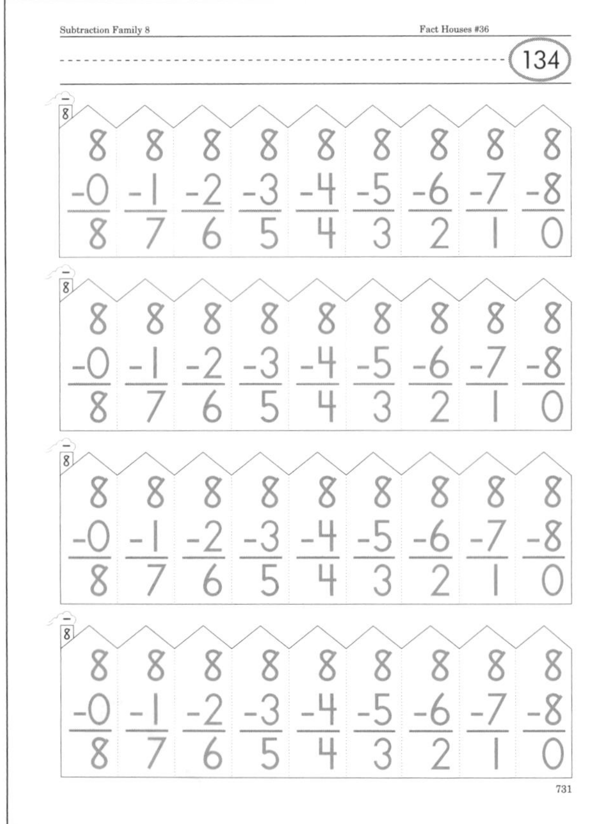

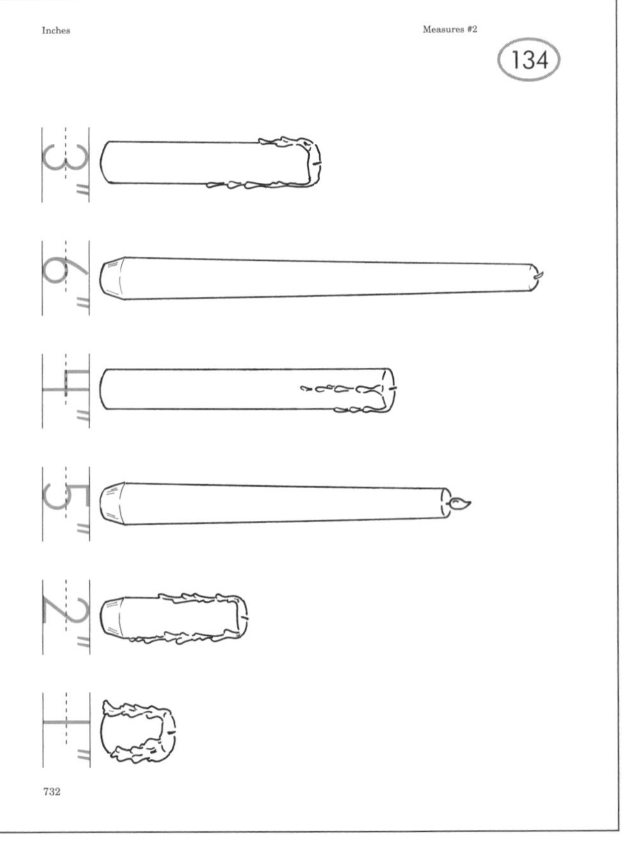

8 [-] Number Facts #49

134

A	8 −0 = 8	8 −5 = 3	8 −3 = 5	8 −1 = 7	8 −2 = 6	8 −5 = 3	8 −4 = 4	8 −1 = 7	8 −2 = 6	8 −1 = 7	8 −4 = 4	8 −7 = 1
B	8 −3 = 5	8 −2 = 6	8 −5 = 3	8 −3 = 5	8 −4 = 4	8 −1 = 7	8 −8 = 0	8 −4 = 4	8 −3 = 5	8 −4 = 4	8 −5 = 3	8 −2 = 6
C	8 −6 = 2	8 −4 = 4	8 −8 = 0	8 −4 = 4	8 −2 = 6	8 −3 = 5	8 −6 = 2	8 −2 = 6	8 −1 = 7	8 −3 = 5	8 −2 = 6	8 −1 = 7
D	8 −3 = 5	8 −4 = 4	8 −8 = 0	8 −1 = 7	8 −5 = 3	8 −6 = 2	8 −4 = 4	8 −3 = 5	8 −1 = 7	8 −5 = 3	8 −3 = 5	8 −4 = 4
E	8 −4 = 4	8 −2 = 6	8 −3 = 5	8 −1 = 7	8 −6 = 2	8 −1 = 7	8 −2 = 6	8 −5 = 3	8 −3 = 5	8 −1 = 7	8 −4 = 4	8 −7 = 1
F	8 −2 = 6	8 −3 = 5	8 −5 = 3	8 −3 = 5	8 −4 = 4	8 −2 = 6	8 −3 = 5	8 −1 = 7	8 −6 = 2	8 −4 = 4	8 −1 = 7	8 −5 = 3
G	8 −3 = 5	8 −1 = 7	8 −6 = 2	8 −4 = 4	8 −3 = 5	8 −4 = 4	8 −5 = 3	8 −1 = 7	8 −3 = 5	8 −2 = 6	8 −5 = 3	8 −6 = 2

733

241–260 Writing Practice #29

134

241	241	251	251
242	242	252	252
243	243	253	253
244	244	254	254
245	245	255	255
246	246	256	256
247	247	257	257
248	248	258	258
249	249	259	259
250	250	260	260

734

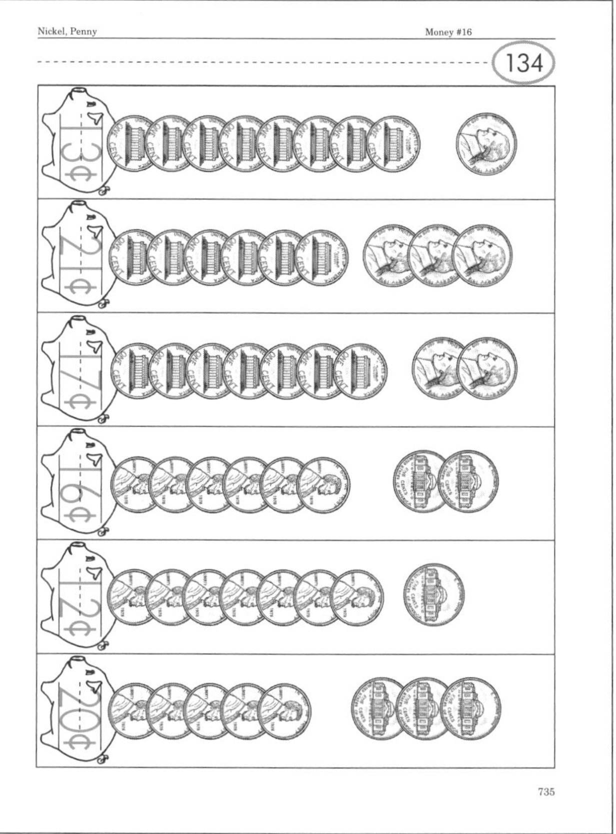

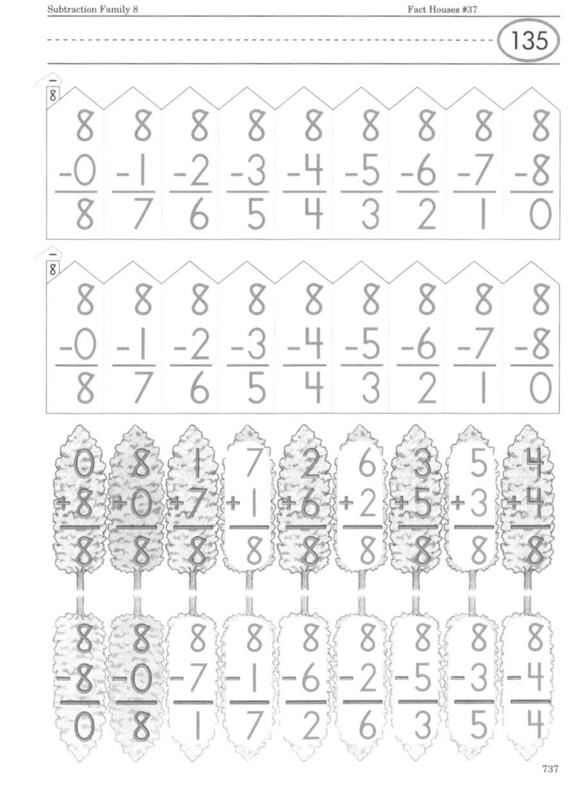

1–10 Number Words #2

135

five	5	nine	9	seven	7
three	3	two	2	eight	8
six	6	one	1	four	4
ten	10	nine	9	eight	8
four	4	two	2	five	5
nine	9	one	1	two	2
seven	7	five	5	seven	7
eight	8	ten	10	one	1
four	4	six	6	three	3
three	3	two	2	eight	8
six	6	one	1	four	4

739

4, 5, 6, 8 [-] Number Facts #50

135

A	6 - 1 = 5	8 - 4 = 4	6 - 1 = 5	6 - 3 = 3
B	8 - 5 = 3	5 - 3 = 2	5 - 4 = 1	8 - 3 = 5
C	6 - 2 = 4	6 - 0 = 6	8 - 2 = 6	6 - 5 = 1
D	8 - 6 = 2	5 - 1 = 4	8 - 4 = 4	5 - 4 = 1
E	5 - 2 = 3	8 - 6 = 2	4 - 3 = 1	8 - 1 = 7
F	8 - 3 = 5	6 - 1 = 5	8 - 2 = 6	5 - 1 = 4
G	8 - 7 = 1	8 - 5 = 3	6 - 2 = 4	5 - 3 = 2
H	8 - 2 = 6	8 - 3 = 5	8 - 6 = 2	8 - 5 = 3
I	8 - 5 = 3	6 - 3 = 3	6 - 1 = 5	4 - 1 = 3
J	4 - 3 = 1	8 - 7 = 1	5 - 2 = 3	8 - 4 = 4
K	6 - 4 = 2	8 - 4 = 4	8 - 1 = 7	5 - 3 = 2
L	8 - 4 = 4	8 - 6 = 2	6 - 2 = 4	8 - 3 = 5
M	8 - 6 = 2	8 - 3 = 5	8 - 2 = 6	8 - 6 = 2
N	6 - 1 = 5	8 - 5 = 3	6 - 1 = 5	8 - 3 = 5
O	6 - 4 = 2	6 - 2 = 4	8 - 5 = 3	6 - 1 = 5
P	5 - 0 = 5	4 - 2 = 2	5 - 1 = 4	8 - 7 = 1
Q	6 - 3 = 3	8 - 5 = 3	5 - 3 = 2	8 - 6 = 2

740

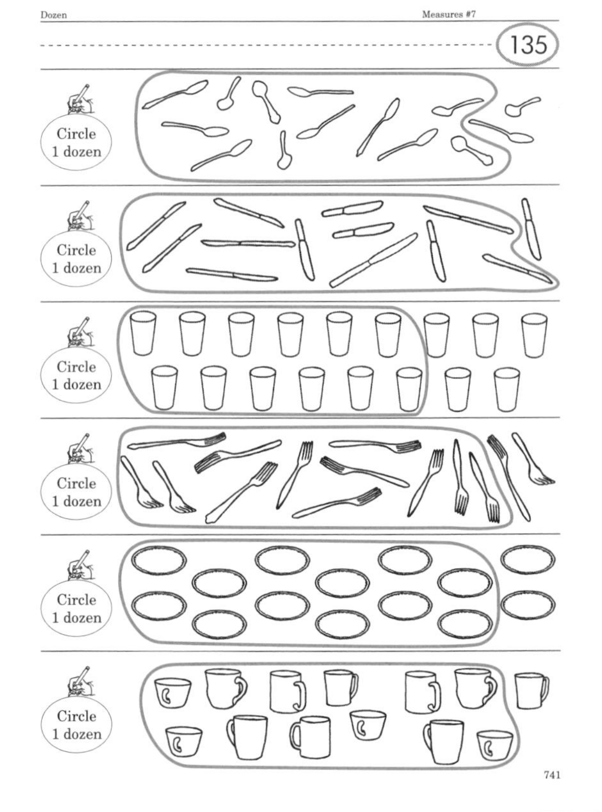

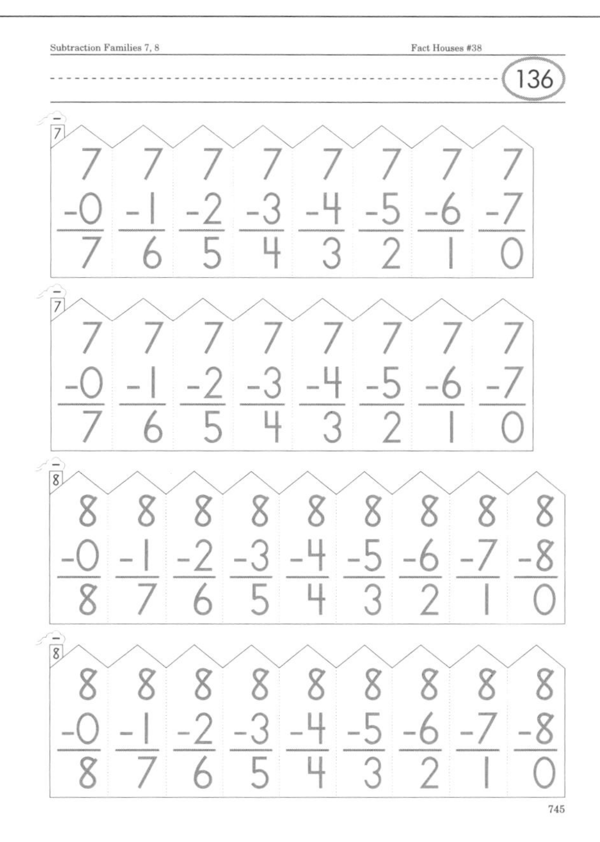

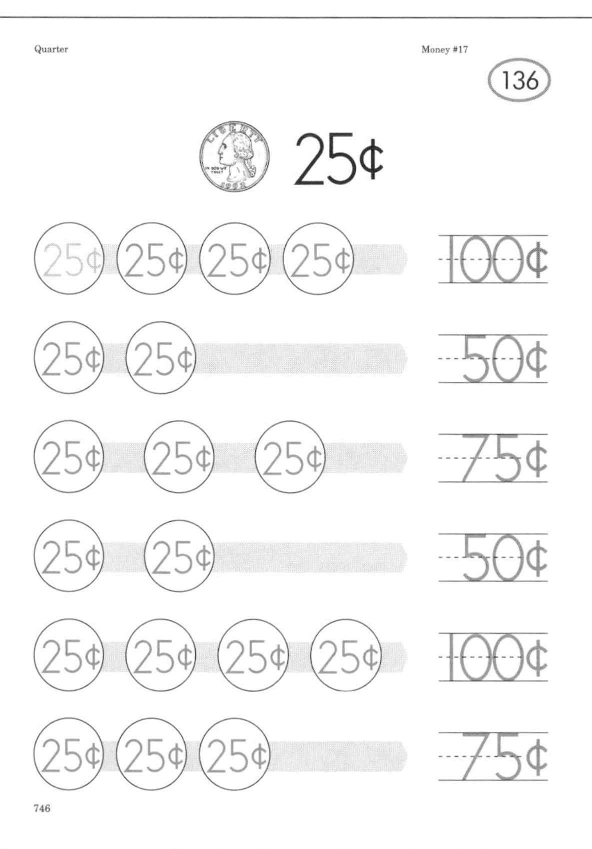

4, 5, 6, 8 [-] Number Facts #50

136

A	6 - 1 = 5	8 - 4 = 4	6 - 1 = 5	6 - 3 = 3
B	8 - 5 = 3	5 - 3 = 2	5 - 4 = 1	8 - 3 = 5
C	6 - 2 = 4	6 - 0 = 6	8 - 2 = 6	6 - 5 = 1
D	8 - 6 = 2	5 - 1 = 4	8 - 4 = 4	5 - 4 = 1
E	5 - 2 = 3	8 - 6 = 2	4 - 3 = 1	8 - 1 = 7
F	8 - 3 = 5	6 - 1 = 5	8 - 2 = 6	5 - 1 = 4
G	8 - 7 = 1	8 - 5 = 3	6 - 2 = 4	5 - 3 = 2
H	8 - 2 = 6	8 - 3 = 5	8 - 6 = 2	8 - 5 = 3
I	8 - 5 = 3	6 - 3 = 3	6 - 1 = 5	4 - 1 = 3
J	4 - 3 = 1	8 - 7 = 1	5 - 2 = 3	8 - 4 = 4
K	6 - 4 = 2	8 - 4 = 4	8 - 1 = 7	5 - 3 = 2
L	8 - 4 = 4	8 - 6 = 2	6 - 2 = 4	8 - 3 = 5
M	8 - 6 = 2	8 - 3 = 5	8 - 2 = 6	8 - 6 = 2
N	6 - 1 = 5	8 - 5 = 3	6 - 1 = 5	8 - 3 = 5
O	6 - 4 = 2	6 - 2 = 4	8 - 5 = 3	6 - 1 = 5
P	5 - 0 = 5	4 - 2 = 2	5 - 1 = 4	8 - 7 = 1
Q	6 - 3 = 3	8 - 5 = 3	5 - 3 = 2	8 - 6 = 2

747

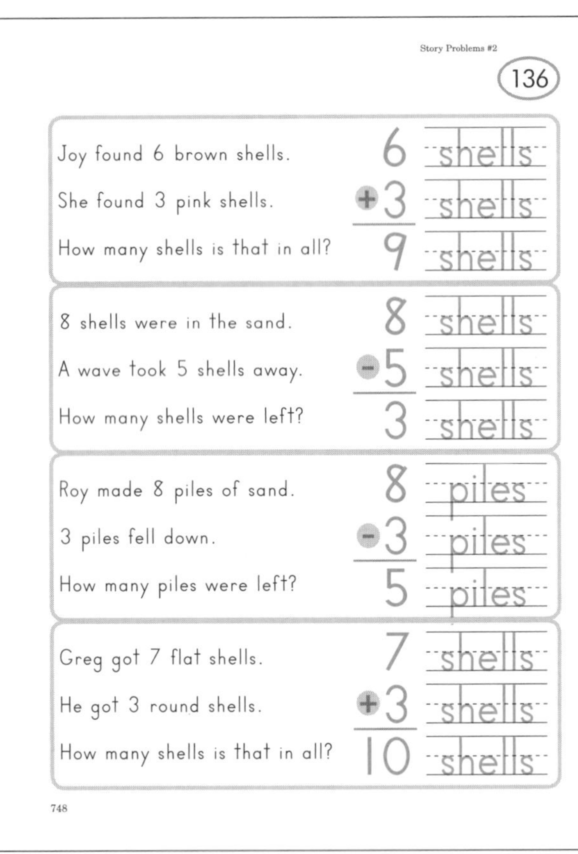

Story Problems #2

136

Joy found 6 brown shells. She found 3 pink shells. How many shells is that in all?
6 shells + 3 shells = 9 shells

8 shells were in the sand. A wave took 5 shells away. How many shells were left?
8 shells − 5 shells = 3 shells

Roy made 8 piles of sand. 3 piles fell down. How many piles were left?
8 piles − 3 piles = 5 piles

Greg got 7 flat shells. He got 3 round shells. How many shells is that in all?
7 shells + 3 shells = 10 shells

748

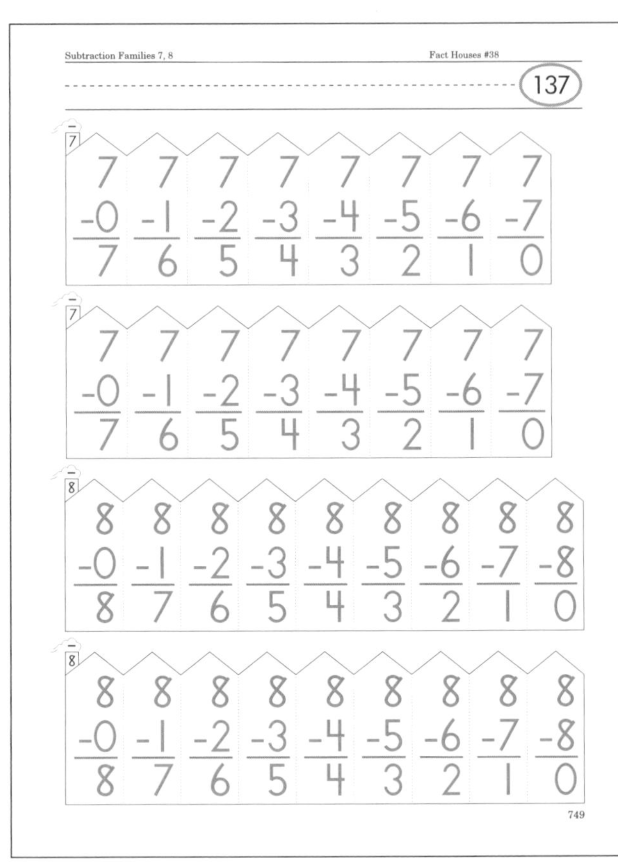

Subtraction Families 7, 8

Fact Houses #38

137

7	7	7	7	7	7	7	7
-0	-1	-2	-3	-4	-5	-6	-7
7	6	5	4	3	2	1	0

7	7	7	7	7	7	7	7
-0	-1	-2	-3	-4	-5	-6	-7
7	6	5	4	3	2	1	0

8	8	8	8	8	8	8	8	8
-0	-1	-2	-3	-4	-5	-6	-7	-8
8	7	6	5	4	3	2	1	0

8	8	8	8	8	8	8	8	8
-0	-1	-2	-3	-4	-5	-6	-7	-8
8	7	6	5	4	3	2	1	0

749

Number Grid

Form F

137

61	62	63	64	65	66	67	68	69	70
71	72	73	74	75	76	77	78	79	80
81	82	83	84	85	86	87	88	89	90
91	92	93	94	95	96	97	98	99	100
101	102	103	104	105	106	107	108	109	110
111	112	113	114	115	116	117	118	119	120
121	122	123	124	125	126	127	128	129	130
131	132	133	134	135	136	137	138	139	140
141	142	143	144	145	146	147	148	149	150
151	152	153	154	155	156	157	158	159	160

750

4, 5, 6, 8 [-]

Number Facts #50

137

A	6 - 1 = 5	8 - 4 = 4	6 - 1 = 5	6 - 3 = 3
B	8 - 5 = 3	5 - 3 = 2	5 - 4 = 1	8 - 3 = 5
C	6 - 2 = 4	6 - 0 = 6	8 - 2 = 6	6 - 5 = 1
D	8 - 6 = 2	5 - 1 = 4	8 - 4 = 4	5 - 4 = 1
E	5 - 2 = 3	8 - 6 = 2	4 - 3 = 1	8 - 1 = 7
F	8 - 3 = 5	6 - 1 = 5	8 - 2 = 6	5 - 1 = 4
G	8 - 7 = 1	8 - 5 = 3	6 - 2 = 4	5 - 3 = 2
H	8 - 2 = 6	8 - 3 = 5	8 - 6 = 2	8 - 5 = 3
I	8 - 5 = 3	6 - 3 = 3	6 - 1 = 5	4 - 1 = 3
J	4 - 3 = 1	8 - 7 = 1	5 - 2 = 3	8 - 4 = 4
K	6 - 4 = 2	8 - 4 = 4	8 - 1 = 7	5 - 3 = 2
L	8 - 4 = 4	8 - 6 = 2	6 - 2 = 4	8 - 3 = 5
M	8 - 6 = 2	8 - 3 = 5	8 - 2 = 6	8 - 6 = 2
N	6 - 1 = 5	8 - 5 = 3	6 - 1 = 5	8 - 3 = 5
O	6 - 4 = 2	6 - 2 = 4	8 - 5 = 3	6 - 1 = 5
P	5 - 0 = 5	4 - 2 = 2	5 - 1 = 4	8 - 7 = 1
Q	6 - 3 = 3	8 - 5 = 3	5 - 3 = 2	8 - 6 = 2

751

240–259 Before and After #15

137

240	241	242	246	247	248
243	244	245	251	252	253
249	250	251	254	255	256
252	253	254	242	243	244
248	249	250	253	254	255
255	256	257	245	246	247
250	251	252	241	242	243
244	245	246	247	248	249
257	258	259	256	257	258

752

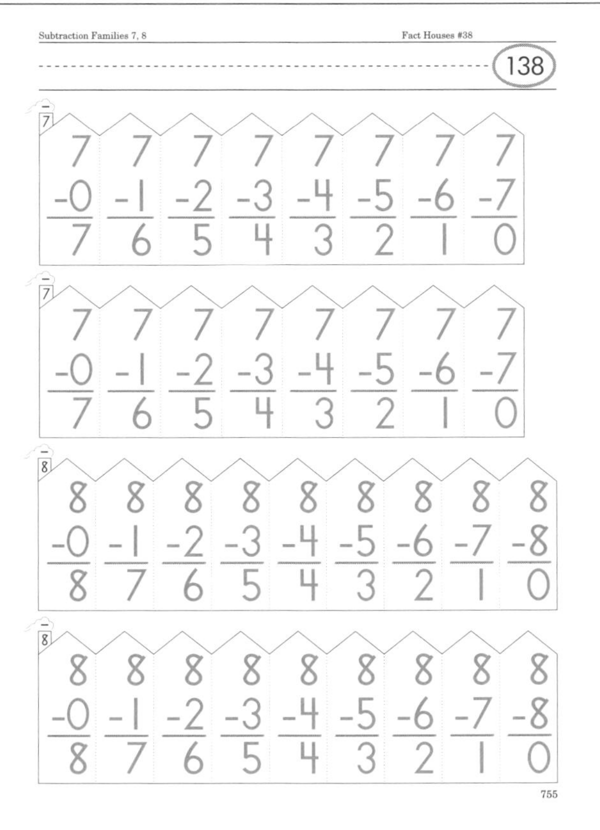
Subtraction Families 7, 8 Fact Houses #38

138

7	7	7	7	7	7	7	7
-0	-1	-2	-3	-4	-5	-6	-7
7	6	5	4	3	2	1	0

7	7	7	7	7	7	7	7
-0	-1	-2	-3	-4	-5	-6	-7
7	6	5	4	3	2	1	0

8	8	8	8	8	8	8	8	8
-0	-1	-2	-3	-4	-5	-6	-7	-8
8	7	6	5	4	3	2	1	0

8	8	8	8	8	8	8	8	8
-0	-1	-2	-3	-4	-5	-6	-7	-8
8	7	6	5	4	3	2	1	0

755

By 10's, by 5's Missing Numbers #13

138

Count by 10's

10 20 30 40 50
60 70 80 90 100

Count by 10's

10 20 30 40 50
60 70 80 90 100

Count by 5's

5 10 15 20 25
30 35 40 45 50
55 60 65 70 75
80 85 90 95 100

756

7, 8 [-]

Number Facts #51

138

A	8 -2 6	7 -5 2	8 -4 4	7 -3 4	8 -6 2	8 -5 3	7 -2 5	7 -5 2	7 -6 1	7 -5 2	7 -1 6	8 -3 5
B	8 -6 2	8 -3 5	8 -2 6	8 -6 2	7 -3 4	8 -7 1	7 -3 4	8 -6 2	8 -4 4	8 -5 3	8 -1 7	8 -0 8
C	7 -3 4	8 -3 5	7 -2 5	8 -4 4	8 -5 3	7 -2 5	8 -1 7	7 -1 6	8 -3 5	7 -6 1	8 -7 1	8 -2 6
D	7 -6 1	8 -5 3	8 -7 1	8 -2 6	8 -5 3	8 -4 4	7 -2 5	7 -3 4	8 -2 6	8 -1 7	8 -6 2	7 -4 3
E	7 -3 4	7 -6 1	8 -3 5	7 -1 6	7 -5 2	8 -7 1	8 -2 6	7 -4 3	8 -6 2	7 -3 4	8 -4 4	7 -5 2
F	8 -3 5	7 -4 3	8 -4 4	7 -2 5	8 -5 3	8 -3 5	7 -1 6	8 -6 2	7 -4 3	7 -0 7	8 -1 7	7 -3 4
G	7 -4 3	8 -5 3	7 -5 2	7 -4 3	7 -5 2	8 -5 3	8 -3 5	8 -4 4	8 -6 2	8 -3 5	8 -7 1	8 -3 5

758

7–10 [+]

Number Facts #52

138

A	5+4=9	6+4=10	3+4=7	2+8=10
B	6+2=8	5+3=8	5+5=10	3+5=8
C	5+4=9	6+2=8	5+2=7	4+5=9
D	3+7=10	8+2=10	3+6=9	7+3=10
E	4+3=7	2+5=7	5+3=8	6+2=8
F	6+2=8	4+6=10	7+2=9	3+4=7
G	3+6=9	2+7=9	7+3=10	6+3=9
H	5+3=8	2+5=7	3+6=9	3+4=7
I	3+6=9	7+3=10	2+7=9	3+7=10
J	4+6=10	3+6=9	8+2=10	6+4=10
K	5+3=8	6+2=8	5+4=9	4+3=7
L	5+2=7	7+3=10	6+4=10	3+7=10
M	6+4=10	3+7=10	2+5=7	4+5=9
N	5+4=9	3+5=8	6+3=9	7+2=9
O	2+7=9	7+3=10	3+6=9	4+5=9
P	6+2=8	2+6=8	5+2=7	2+7=9
Q	8+2=10	4+6=10	3+5=8	4+5=9

759

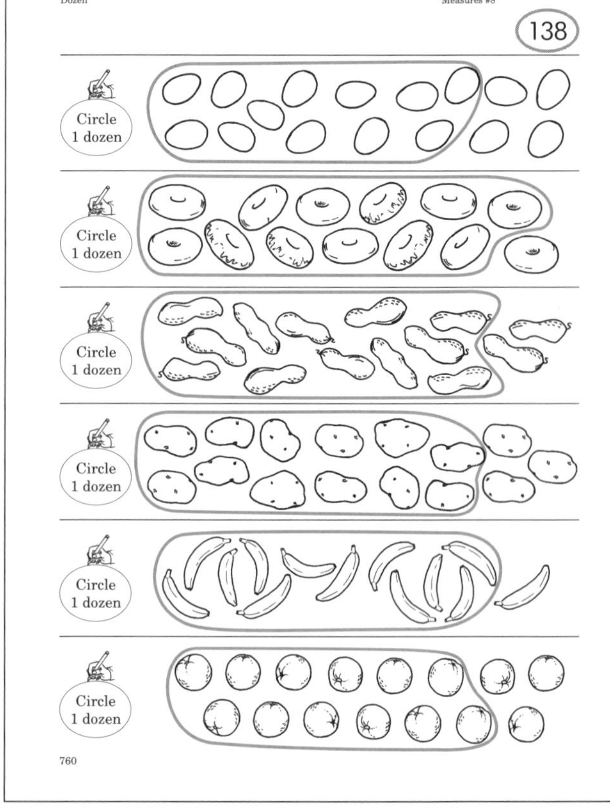

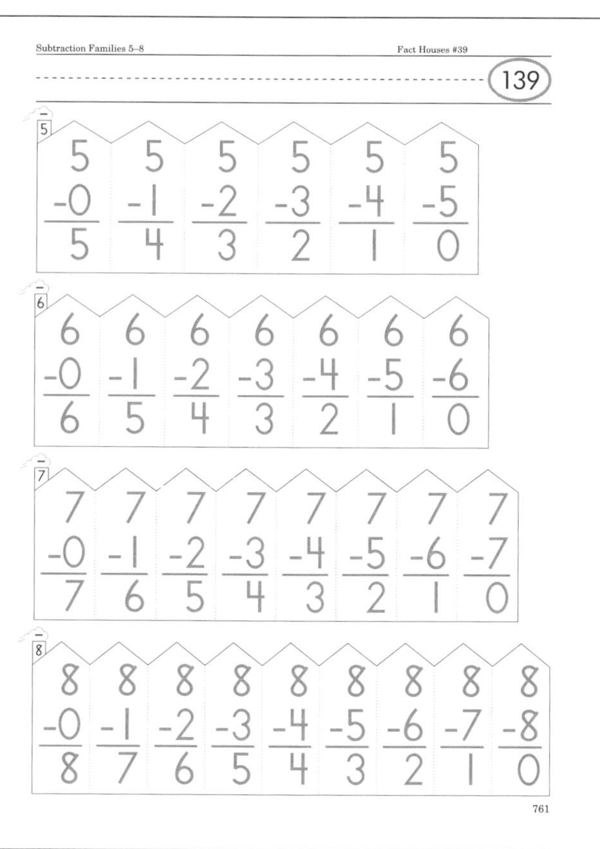

Subtraction Families 5–8 Fact Houses #39

139

5	5	5	5	5	5
5 -0 5	5 -1 4	5 -2 3	5 -3 2	5 -4 1	5 -5 0

6	6	6	6	6	6	6
6 -0 6	6 -1 5	6 -2 4	6 -3 3	6 -4 2	6 -5 1	6 -6 0

7	7	7	7	7	7	7	7
7 -0 7	7 -1 6	7 -2 5	7 -3 4	7 -4 3	7 -5 2	7 -6 1	7 -7 0

8	8	8	8	8	8	8	8	8
8 -0 8	8 -1 7	8 -2 6	8 -3 5	8 -4 4	8 -5 3	8 -6 2	8 -7 1	8 -8 0

761

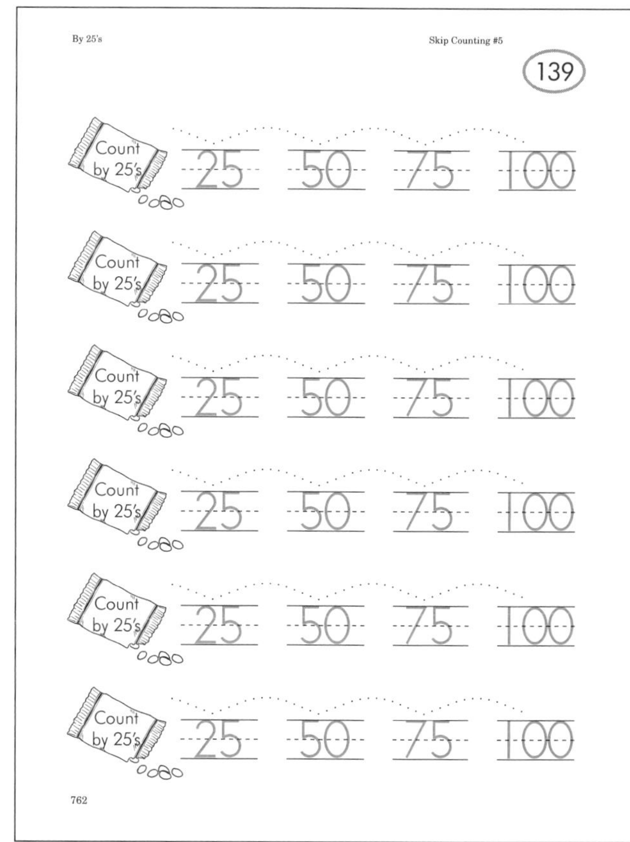

By 25's Skip Counting #5

139

Count by 25's 25 50 75 100

Count by 25's 25 50 75 100

Count by 25's 25 50 75 100

Count by 25's 25 50 75 100

Count by 25's 25 50 75 100

Count by 25's 25 50 75 100

762

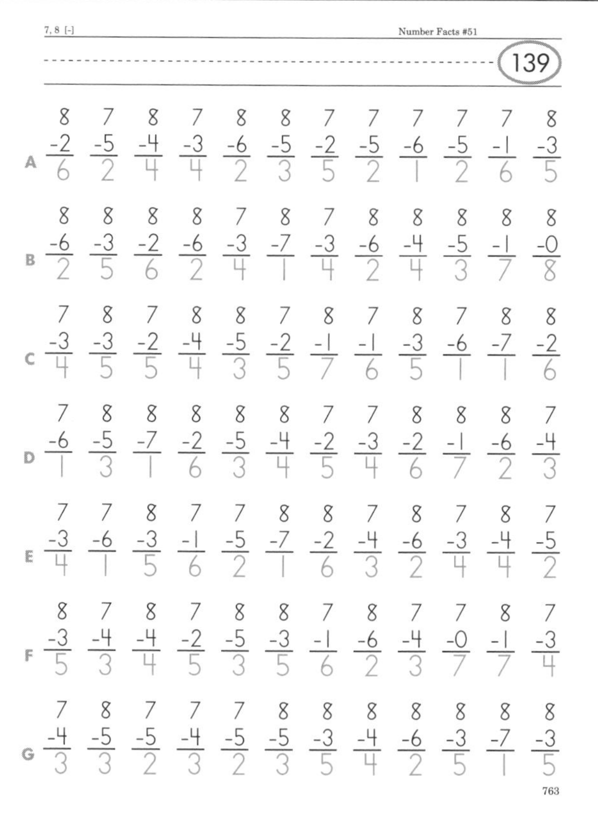

7, 8 [-] Number Facts #51

139

A	8 -2 6	7 -5 2	8 -4 4	7 -3 4	8 -6 2	8 -5 3	7 -2 5	7 -5 2	7 -6 1	7 -5 2	7 -1 6	8 -3 5
B	8 -6 2	8 -3 5	8 -2 6	8 -6 2	7 -3 4	8 -7 1	7 -3 4	8 -6 2	8 -4 4	8 -5 3	8 -1 7	8 -0 8
C	7 -3 4	8 -3 5	7 -2 5	8 -4 4	8 -5 3	7 -2 5	8 -1 7	7 -1 6	8 -3 5	7 -6 1	8 -7 1	8 -2 6
D	7 -6 1	8 -5 3	8 -7 1	8 -2 6	8 -5 3	8 -4 4	7 -2 5	7 -3 4	8 -2 6	8 -1 7	8 -6 2	7 -4 3
E	7 -3 4	7 -6 1	8 -3 5	7 -1 6	7 -5 2	8 -7 1	8 -2 6	7 -4 3	8 -6 2	7 -3 4	8 -4 4	7 -5 2
F	8 -3 5	7 -4 3	8 -4 4	7 -2 5	8 -5 3	8 -3 5	7 -1 6	8 -6 2	7 -4 3	7 -0 7	8 -1 7	7 -3 4
G	7 -4 3	8 -5 3	7 -5 2	7 -4 3	7 -5 2	8 -5 3	8 -3 5	8 -4 4	8 -6 2	8 -3 5	8 -7 1	8 -3 5

763

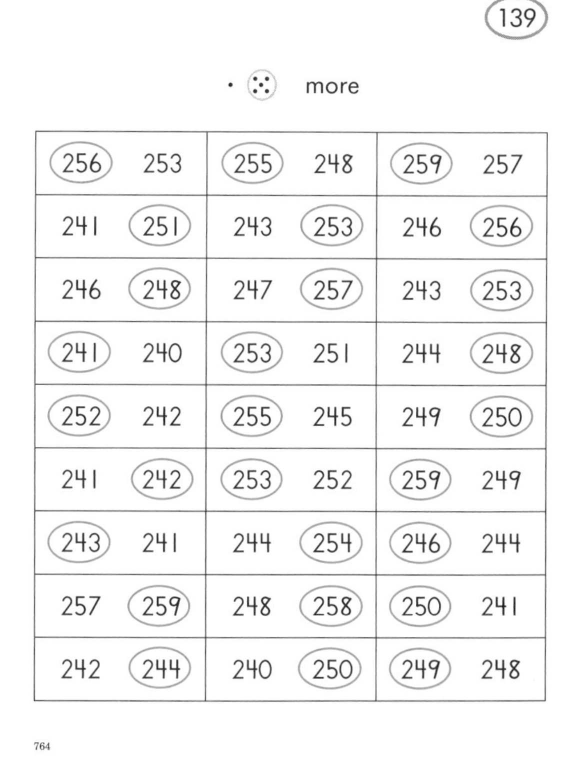

240–259 More Numbers #22

139

• more

256	253	**255**	248	**259**	257
241	**251**	243	**253**	246	**256**
246	**248**	247	**257**	243	**253**
241	240	**253**	251	244	**248**
252	242	**255**	245	249	**250**
241	**242**	**253**	252	**259**	249
243	241	244	**254**	**246**	244
257	**259**	248	**258**	**250**	241
242	**244**	240	**250**	**249**	248

764

Quarter — Money #18

139

25¢	25¢

765

Number Dictation — Form B

140

	1	2	3
apple	8:30	12:30	3:30
nest	7:30	11:30	1:30
igloo	4:00	6:30	9:30
octopus	2:30	11:30	5:30
umbrella	8:00	10:30	4:30

767

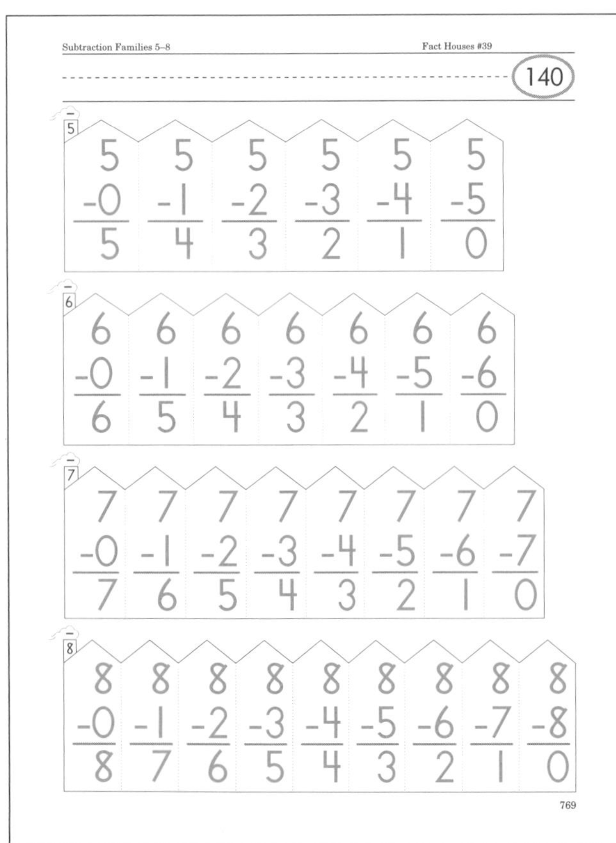

Subtraction Families 5–8 — Fact Houses #39

140

5: 5 − 0 = 5, 5 − 1 = 4, 5 − 2 = 3, 5 − 3 = 2, 5 − 4 = 1, 5 − 5 = 0

6: 6 − 0 = 6, 6 − 1 = 5, 6 − 2 = 4, 6 − 3 = 3, 6 − 4 = 2, 6 − 5 = 1, 6 − 6 = 0

7: 7 − 0 = 7, 7 − 1 = 6, 7 − 2 = 5, 7 − 3 = 4, 7 − 4 = 3, 7 − 5 = 2, 7 − 6 = 1, 7 − 7 = 0

8: 8 − 0 = 8, 8 − 1 = 7, 8 − 2 = 6, 8 − 3 = 5, 8 − 4 = 4, 8 − 5 = 3, 8 − 6 = 2, 8 − 7 = 1, 8 − 8 = 0

769

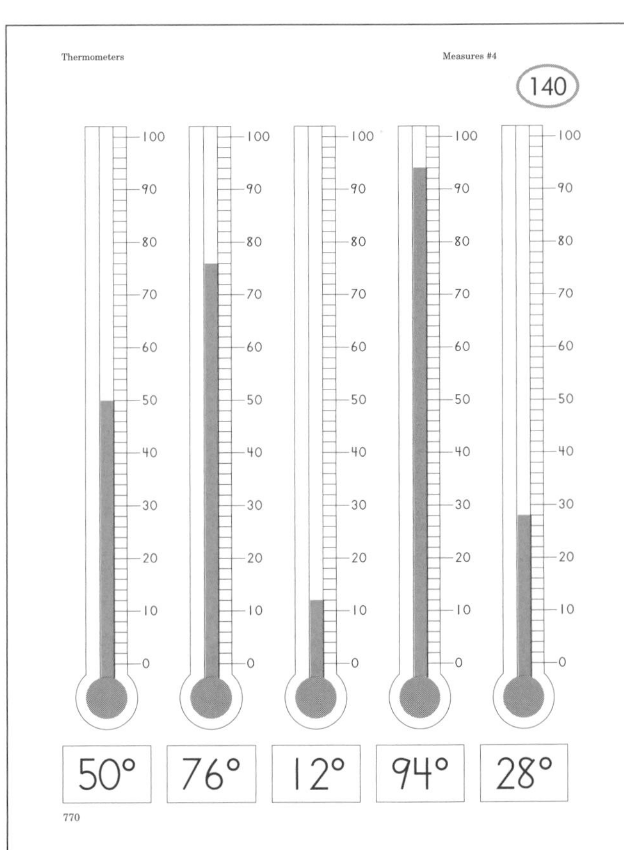

Thermometers — Measures #4

140

50°	76°	12°	94°	28°

770

7, 8 [-] Number Facts #51

140

A	8 -2 6	7 -5 2	8 -4 4	7 -3 4	8 -6 2	8 -5 3	7 -2 5	7 -5 2	7 -6 1	7 -5 2	7 -1 6	8 -3 5
B	8 -6 2	8 -3 5	8 -2 6	8 -6 2	7 -3 4	8 -7 1	7 -3 4	8 -6 2	8 -4 4	8 -5 3	8 -1 7	8 -0 8
C	7 -3 4	8 -3 5	7 -2 5	8 -4 4	8 -5 3	7 -2 5	8 -1 7	7 -1 6	8 -3 5	7 -6 1	8 -7 1	8 -2 6
D	7 -6 1	8 -5 3	8 -7 1	8 -2 6	8 -5 3	8 -4 4	7 -2 5	7 -3 4	8 -2 6	8 -1 7	8 -6 2	7 -4 3
E	7 -3 4	7 -6 1	8 -3 5	7 -1 6	7 -5 2	8 -7 1	8 -2 6	7 -4 3	8 -6 2	7 -3 4	8 -4 4	7 -5 2
F	8 -3 5	7 -4 3	8 -4 4	7 -2 5	8 -5 3	8 -3 5	7 -1 6	8 -6 2	7 -4 3	7 -0 7	8 -1 7	7 -3 4
G	7 -4 3	8 -5 3	7 -5 2	7 -4 3	7 -5 2	8 -5 3	8 -3 5	8 -4 4	8 -6 2	8 -3 5	8 -7 1	8 -3 5

771

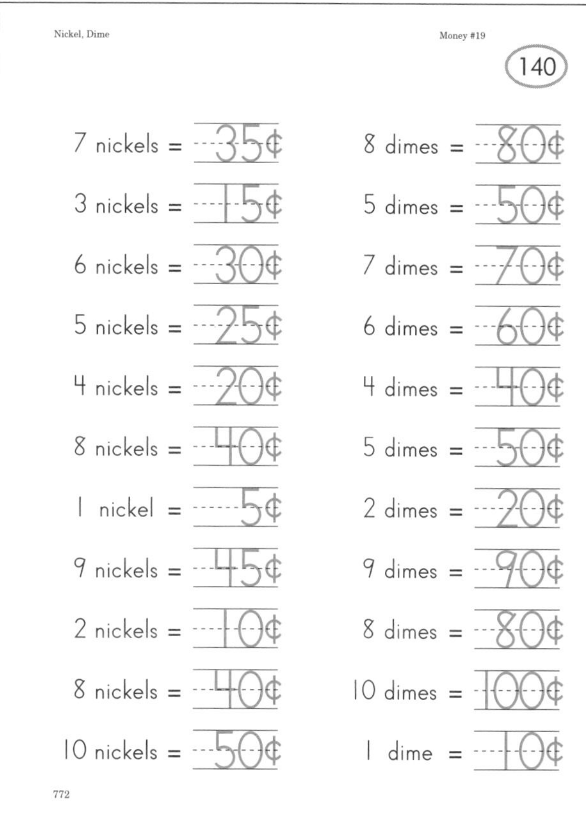

Nickel, Dime Money #19

140

7 nickels =	35¢	8 dimes =	80¢
3 nickels =	15¢	5 dimes =	50¢
6 nickels =	30¢	7 dimes =	70¢
5 nickels =	25¢	6 dimes =	60¢
4 nickels =	20¢	4 dimes =	40¢
8 nickels =	40¢	5 dimes =	50¢
1 nickel =	5¢	2 dimes =	20¢
9 nickels =	45¢	9 dimes =	90¢
2 nickels =	10¢	8 dimes =	80¢
8 nickels =	40¢	10 dimes =	100¢
10 nickels =	50¢	1 dime =	10¢

772

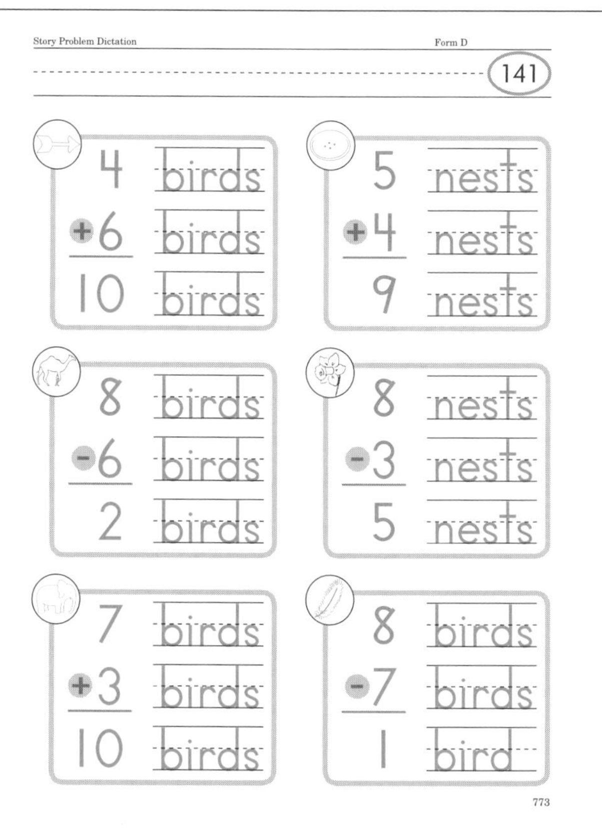

Story Problem Dictation Form D

141

4 birds +6 birds 10 birds	5 nests +4 nests 9 nests
8 birds -6 birds 2 birds	8 nests -3 nests 5 nests
7 birds +3 birds 10 birds	8 birds -7 birds 1 bird

773

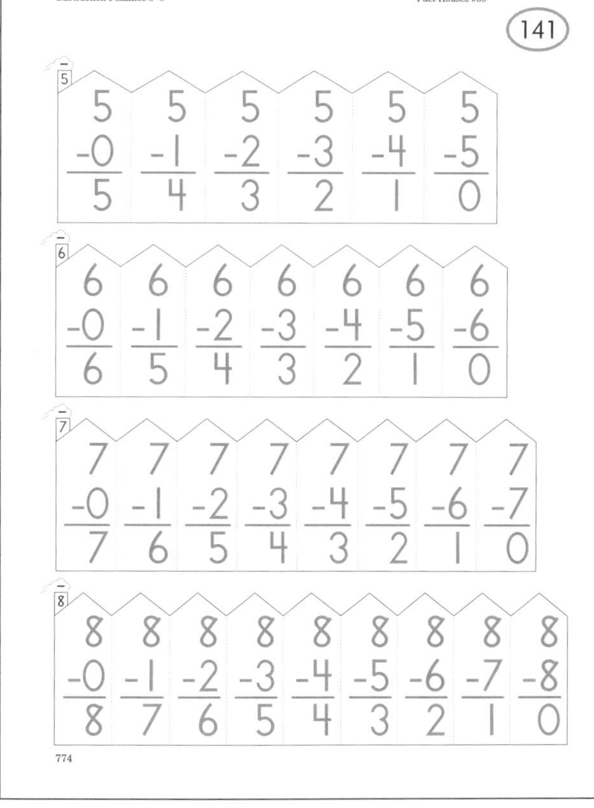

Subtraction Families 5–8 Fact Houses #39

141

5: 5-0=5, 5-1=4, 5-2=3, 5-3=2, 5-4=1, 5-5=0

6: 6-0=6, 6-1=5, 6-2=4, 6-3=3, 6-4=2, 6-5=1, 6-6=0

7: 7-0=7, 7-1=6, 7-2=5, 7-3=4, 7-4=3, 7-5=2, 7-6=1, 7-7=0

8: 8-0=8, 8-1=7, 8-2=6, 8-3=5, 8-4=4, 8-5=3, 8-6=2, 8-7=1, 8-8=0

774

Number Grid Form F 141

71	72	73	74	75	76	77	78	79	80
81	82	83	84	85	86	87	88	89	90
91	92	93	94	95	96	97	98	99	100
101	102	103	104	105	106	107	108	109	110
111	112	113	114	115	116	117	118	119	120
121	122	123	124	125	126	127	128	129	130
131	132	133	134	135	136	137	138	139	140
141	142	143	144	145	146	147	148	149	150
151	152	153	154	155	156	157	158	159	160
161	162	163	164	165	166	167	168	169	170

775

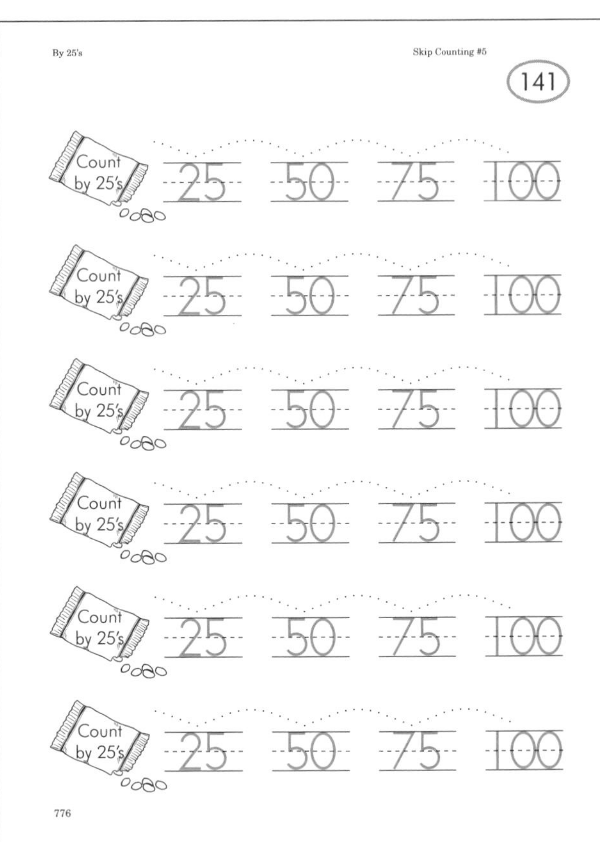
By 25's Skip Counting #5 141

Count by 25's	25	50	75	100
Count by 25's	25	50	75	100
Count by 25's	25	50	75	100
Count by 25's	25	50	75	100
Count by 25's	25	50	75	100
Count by 25's	25	50	75	100

776

7, 8 [-] Number Facts #51 141

A	8-2=6	7-5=2	8-4=4	7-3=4	8-6=2	8-5=3	7-2=5	7-5=2	7-6=1	7-5=2	7-1=6	8-3=5
B	8-6=2	8-3=5	8-2=6	8-6=2	7-3=4	8-7=1	7-3=4	8-6=2	8-4=4	8-5=3	8-1=7	8-0=8
C	7-3=4	8-3=5	7-2=5	8-4=4	8-5=3	7-2=5	8-1=7	7-1=6	8-3=5	7-6=1	8-7=1	8-2=6
D	7-6=1	8-5=3	8-7=1	8-2=6	8-5=3	8-4=4	7-2=5	7-3=4	8-2=6	8-1=7	8-6=2	7-4=3
E	7-3=4	7-6=1	8-3=5	7-1=6	7-5=2	8-7=1	8-2=6	7-4=3	8-6=2	7-3=4	8-4=4	7-5=2
F	8-3=5	7-4=3	8-4=4	7-2=5	8-5=3	8-3=5	7-1=6	8-6=2	7-4=3	7-0=7	8-1=7	7-3=4
G	7-4=3	8-5=3	7-5=2	7-4=3	7-5=2	8-5=3	8-3=5	8-4=4	8-6=2	8-3=5	8-7=1	8-3=5

777

Hour, Half Hour Clocks #8 141

7:00	6:30	2:00	5:30
2:30	11:00	9:00	8:30
3:00	1:30	12:00	11:30
6:00	4:00	3:30	7:30

778

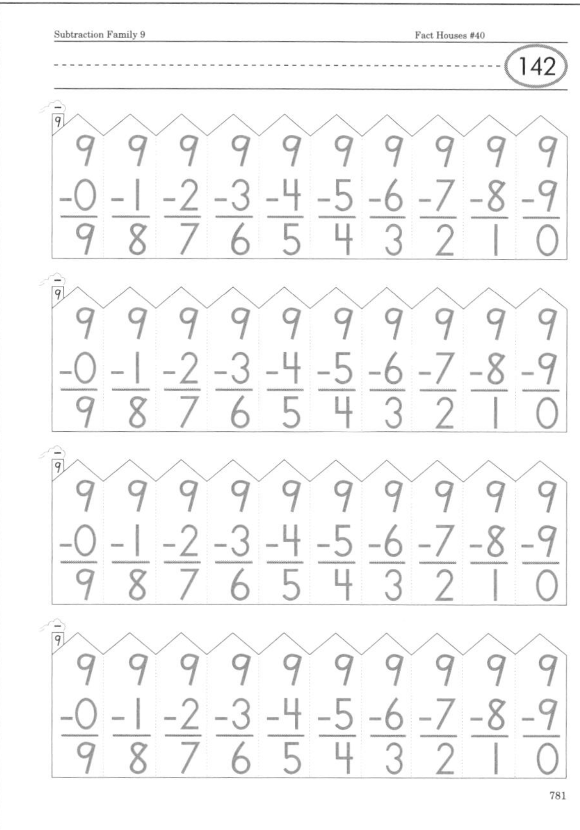

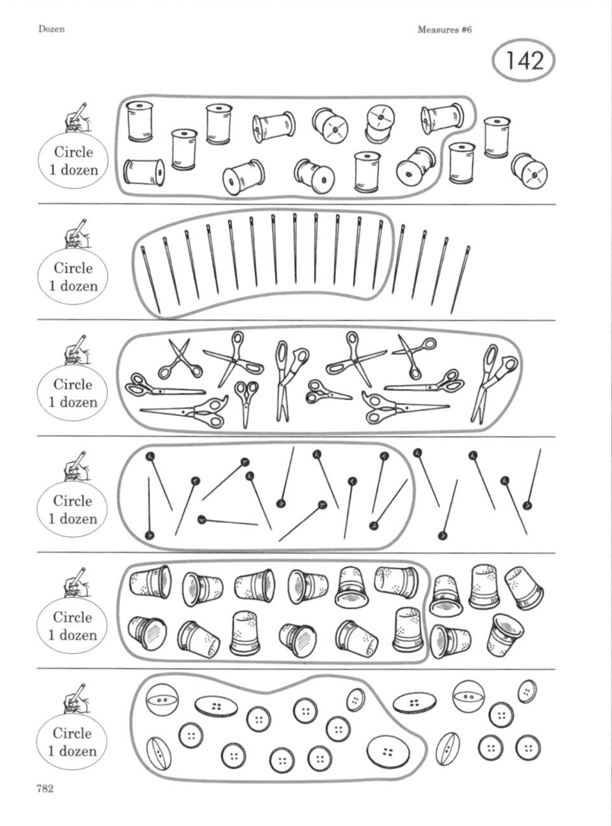

7–10 [+] Number Facts #52

142

A	5+4=9	6+4=10	3+4=7	2+8=10
B	6+2=8	5+3=8	5+5=10	3+5=8
C	5+4=9	6+2=8	5+2=7	4+5=9
D	3+7=10	8+2=10	3+6=9	7+3=10
E	4+3=7	2+5=7	5+3=8	6+2=8
F	6+2=8	4+6=10	7+2=9	3+4=7
G	3+6=9	2+7=9	7+3=10	6+3=9
H	5+3=8	2+5=7	3+6=9	3+4=7
I	3+6=9	7+3=10	2+7=9	3+7=10
J	4+6=10	3+6=9	8+2=10	6+4=10
K	5+3=8	6+2=8	5+4=9	4+3=7
L	5+2=7	7+3=10	6+4=10	3+7=10
M	6+4=10	3+7=10	2+5=7	4+5=9
N	5+4=9	3+5=8	6+3=9	7+2=9
O	2+7=9	7+3=10	3+6=9	4+5=9
P	6+2=8	2+6=8	5+2=7	2+7=9
Q	8+2=10	4+6=10	3+5=8	4+5=9

783

240–259 Less Numbers #22

142

less ⊙ ∴

246	248	**241**	242	252	**242**
243	**241**	**257**	259	**242**	244
256	**253**	241	**240**	**241**	251
243	253	**246**	256	**247**	257
259	**249**	253	**252**	**243**	253
255	**245**	**249**	250	**244**	254
246	**244**	**248**	258	250	**241**
240	250	249	**248**	255	**248**
259	**257**	253	**251**	**244**	248

784

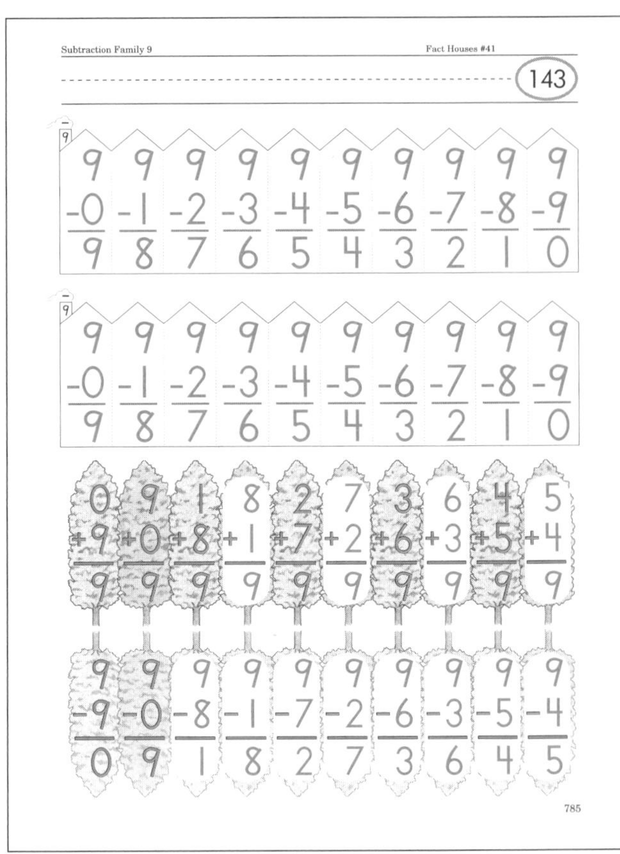
Subtraction Family 9 Fact Houses #41

143

9	9	9	9	9	9	9	9	9	9
-0	-1	-2	-3	-4	-5	-6	-7	-8	-9
9	8	7	6	5	4	3	2	1	0

9	9	9	9	9	9	9	9	9	9
-0	-1	-2	-3	-4	-5	-6	-7	-8	-9
9	8	7	6	5	4	3	2	1	0

0	9	1	8	2	7	3	6	4	5
+9	+0	+8	+1	+7	+2	+6	+3	+5	+4
9	9	9	9	9	9	9	9	9	9

9	9	9	9	9	9	9	9	9	9
-9	-0	-8	-1	-7	-2	-6	-3	-5	-4
0	9	1	8	2	7	3	6	4	5

785

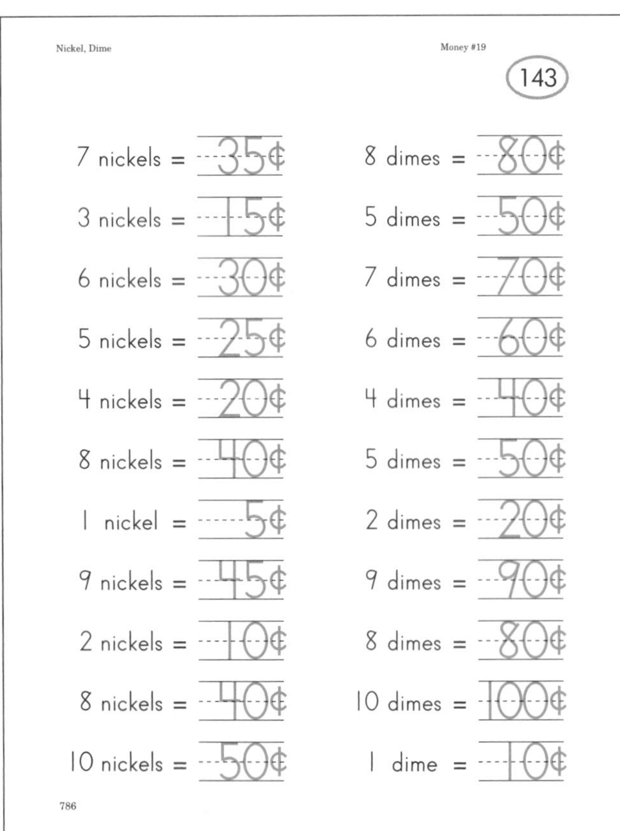
Nickel, Dime Money #19

143

7 nickels = 35¢	8 dimes = 80¢
3 nickels = 15¢	5 dimes = 50¢
6 nickels = 30¢	7 dimes = 70¢
5 nickels = 25¢	6 dimes = 60¢
4 nickels = 20¢	4 dimes = 40¢
8 nickels = 40¢	5 dimes = 50¢
1 nickel = 5¢	2 dimes = 20¢
9 nickels = 45¢	9 dimes = 90¢
2 nickels = 10¢	8 dimes = 80¢
8 nickels = 40¢	10 dimes = 100¢
10 nickels = 50¢	1 dime = 10¢

786

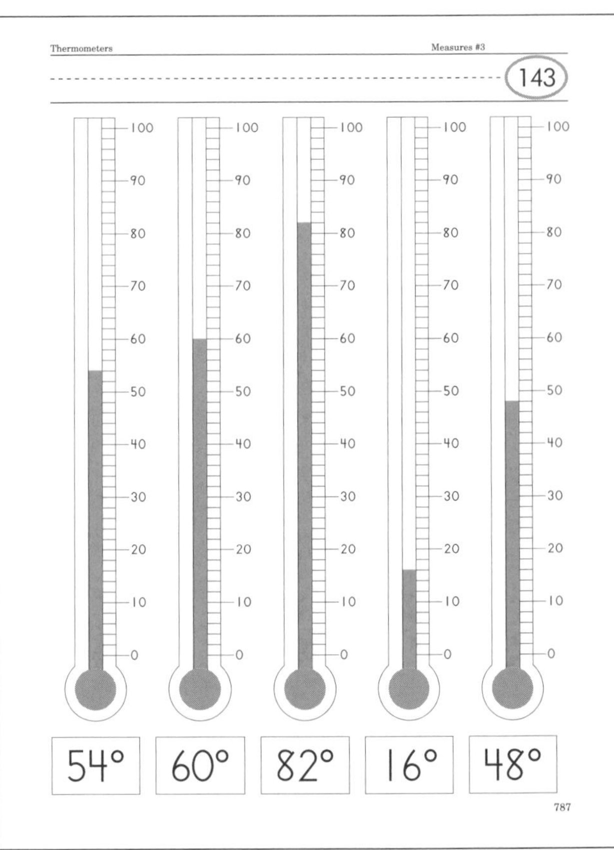
Thermometers Measures #3

143

54° 60° 82° 16° 48°

787

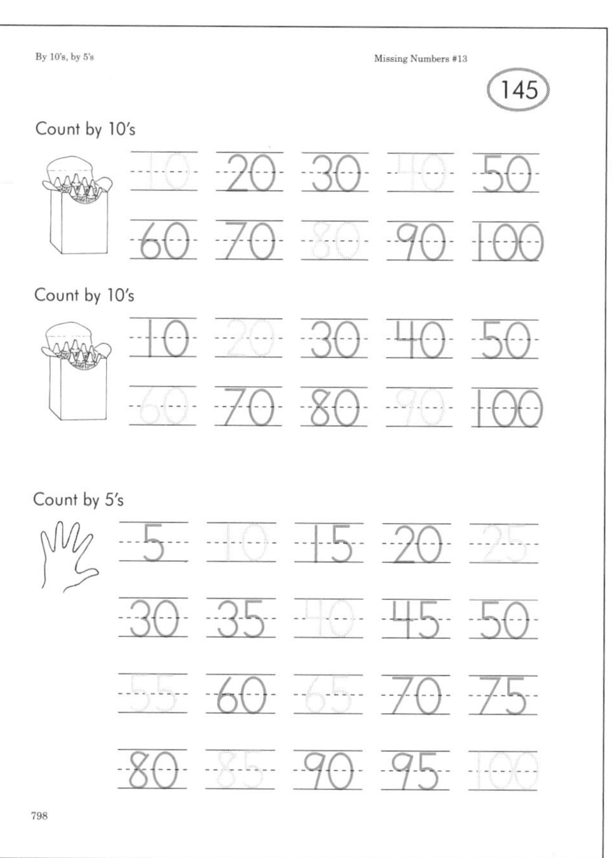

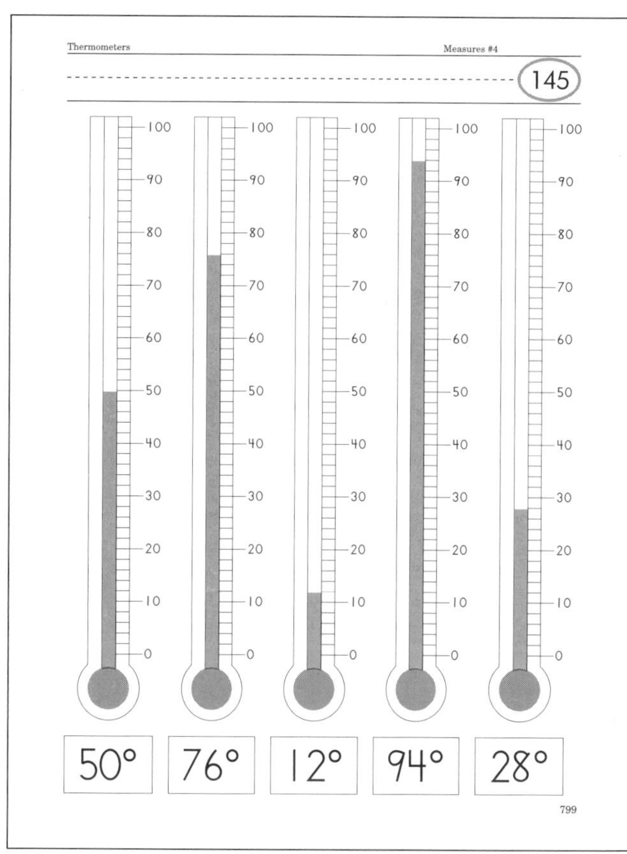

5, 6, 7, 9 [-]

Number Facts #54

145

A	9 -1 8	7 -1 6	9 -3 6	9 -2 7	9 -4 5	9 -7 2	9 -2 7	9 -3 6	9 -4 5	9 -2 7	7 -2 5	7 -1 6
B	9 -4 5	9 -7 2	7 -4 3	6 -2 4	9 -6 3	7 -3 4	9 -4 5	6 -3 3	9 -8 1	7 -4 3	9 -5 4	9 -7 2
C	9 -3 6	9 -2 7	9 -6 3	7 -1 6	5 -3 2	7 -1 6	9 -3 6	7 -2 5	9 -2 7	9 -4 5	9 -3 6	9 -4 5
D	7 -2 5	9 -7 2	5 -1 4	9 -4 5	9 -5 4	7 -3 4	9 -6 3	7 -6 1	9 -4 5	9 -7 2	9 -6 3	9 -8 1
E	7 -4 3	7 -1 6	9 -5 4	9 -7 2	7 -4 3	9 -3 6	9 -4 5	9 -2 7	9 -6 3	9 -3 6	9 -2 7	9 -7 2
F	6 -1 5	7 -5 2	7 -2 5	9 -7 2	9 -5 4	9 -6 3	9 -8 1	7 -1 6	6 -4 2	5 -4 1	6 -1 5	7 -4 3
G	9 -3 6	9 -2 7	7 -4 3	9 -5 4	7 -2 5	9 -4 5	7 -3 4	7 -4 3	7 -6 1	7 -0 7	9 -7 2	6 -2 4

800

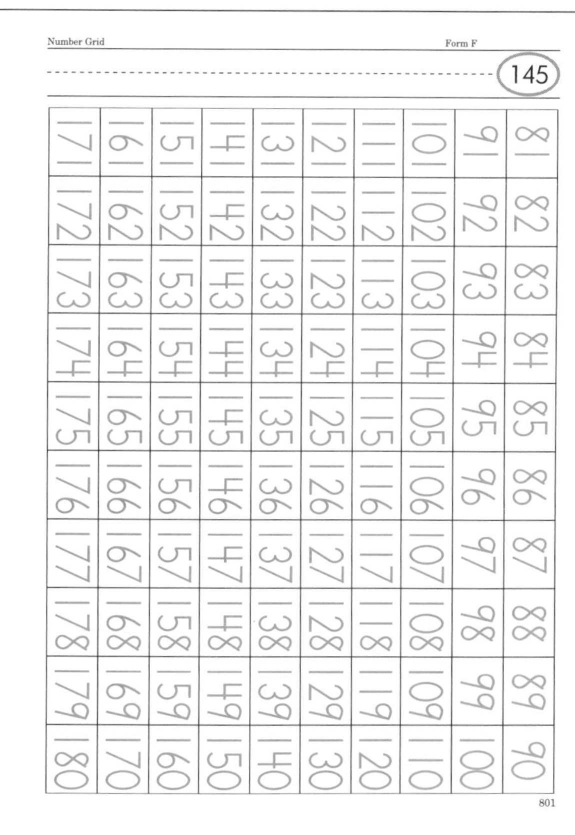

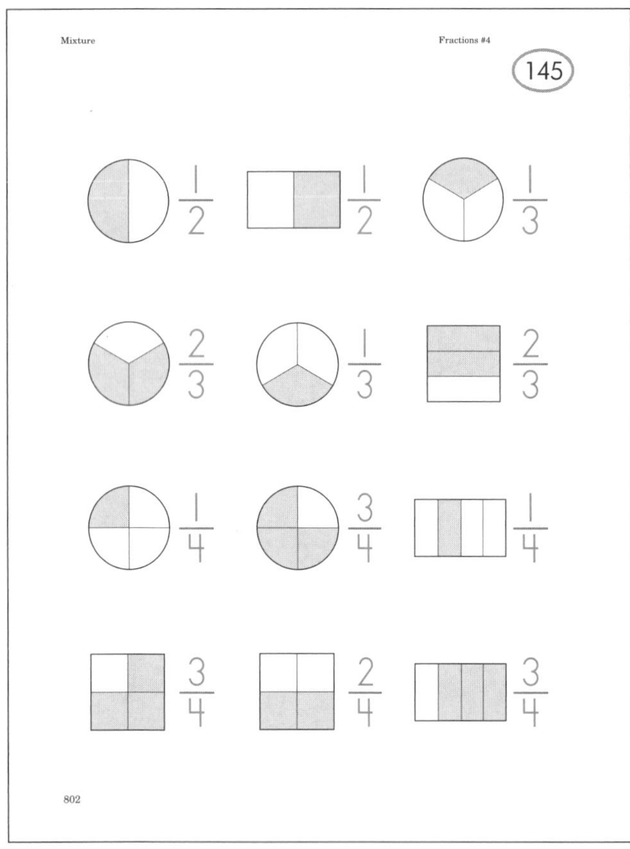
Mixture
Fractions #4
145
1/2
1/2
1/3
2/3
1/3
2/3
1/4
3/4
1/4
3/4
2/4
3/4
802

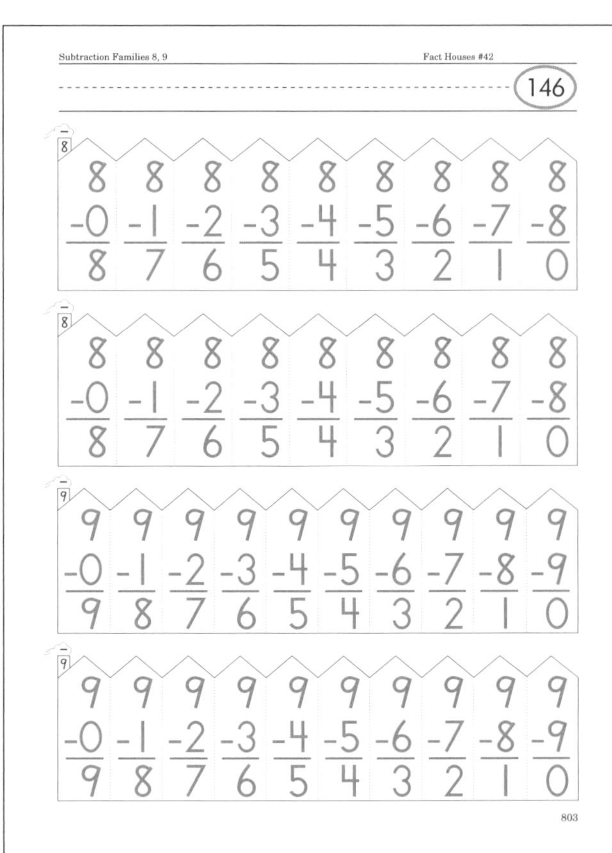
Subtraction Families 8, 9
Fact Houses #42
146
803

5, 6, 7, 9 [-]
Number Facts #54
146
804

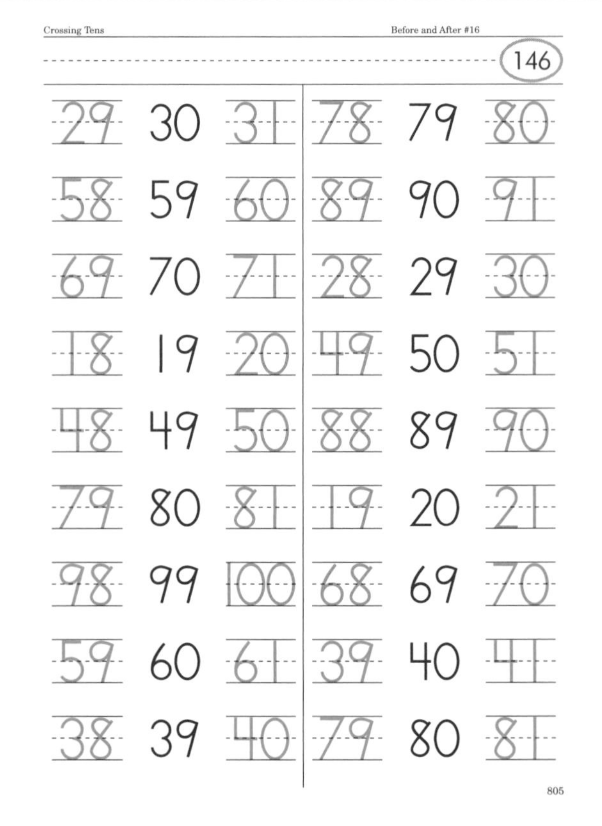
Crossing Tens
Before and After #16
146
805

Place Value #3

146

126 has 1 hundreds	201 has 0 tens
171 has 1 ones	169 has 1 hundreds
216 has 1 tens	220 has 0 ones
183 has 1 hundreds	98 has 9 tens
59 has 9 ones	154 has 1 hundreds
165 has 6 tens	182 has 2 ones
232 has 2 hundreds	97 has 9 tens
204 has 4 ones	175 has 1 hundreds
48 has 4 tens	142 has 2 ones
231 has 2 hundreds	213 has 1 tens
147 has 7 ones	130 has 1 hundreds

806

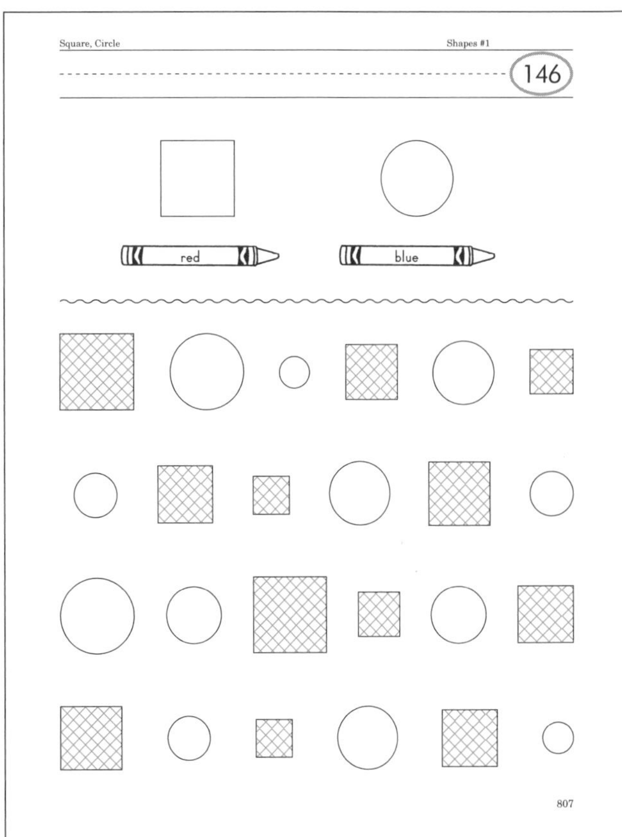

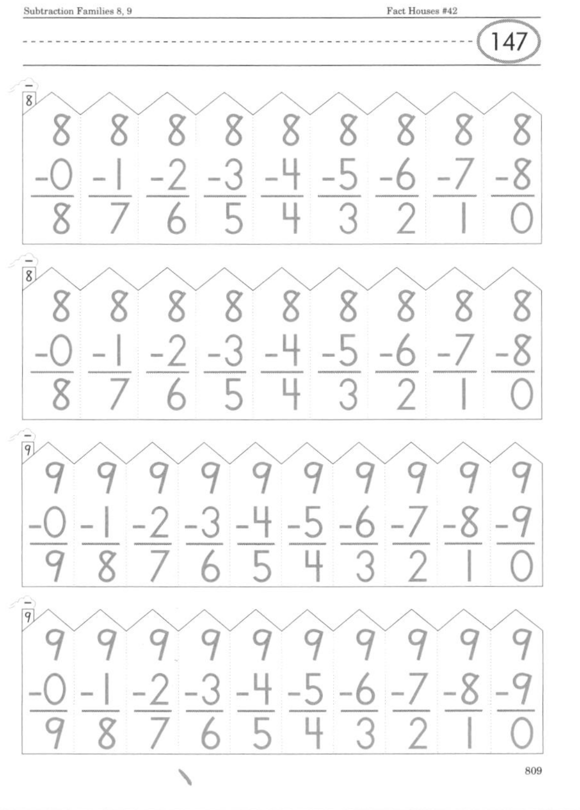

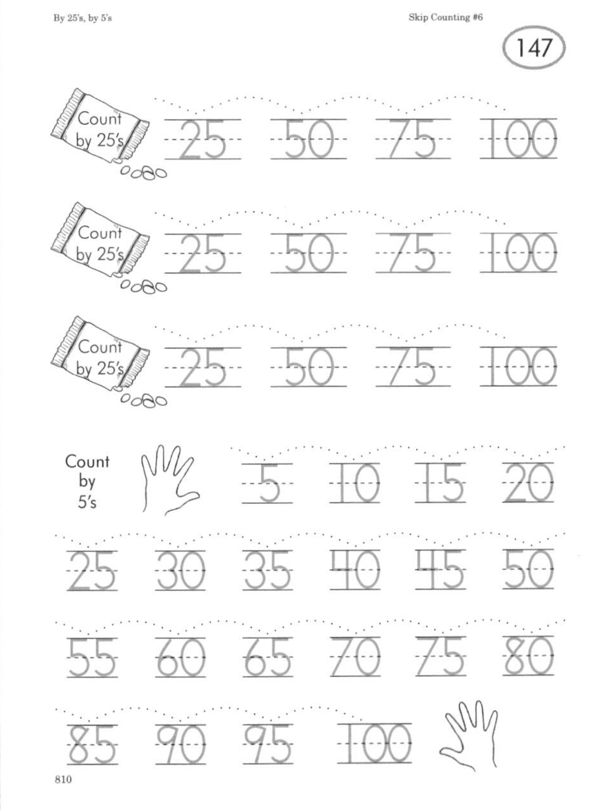

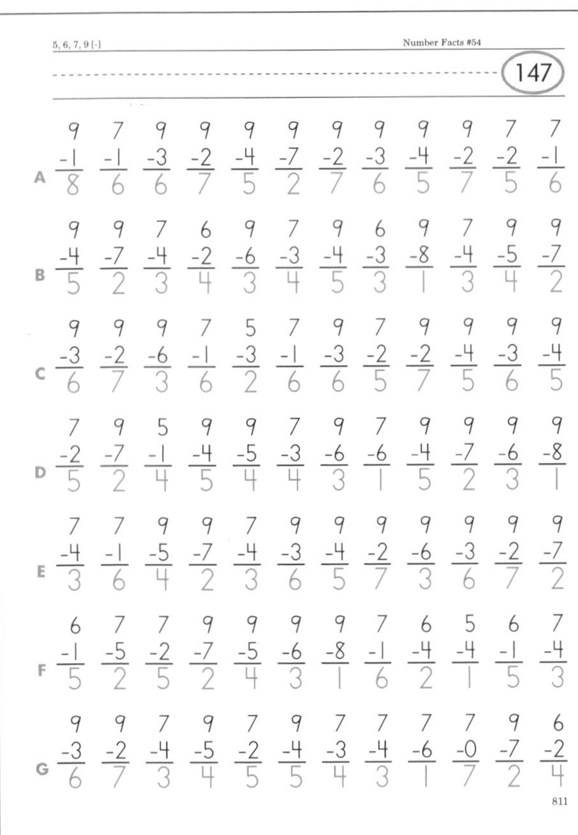

5, 6, 7, 9 [-] Number Facts #54

147

A	9 -1 8	7 -1 6	9 -3 6	9 -2 7	9 -4 5	9 -7 2	9 -2 7	9 -3 6	9 -4 5	9 -2 7	7 -2 5	7 -1 6
B	9 -4 5	9 -7 2	7 -4 3	6 -2 4	9 -6 3	7 -3 4	9 -4 5	6 -3 3	9 -8 1	7 -4 3	9 -5 4	9 -7 2
C	9 -3 6	9 -2 7	9 -6 3	7 -1 6	5 -3 2	7 -1 6	9 -3 6	7 -2 5	9 -2 7	9 -4 5	9 -3 6	9 -4 5
D	7 -2 5	9 -7 2	5 -1 4	9 -4 5	9 -5 4	7 -3 4	9 -6 3	7 -6 1	9 -4 5	9 -7 2	9 -6 3	9 -8 1
E	7 -4 3	7 -1 6	9 -5 4	9 -7 2	7 -4 3	9 -3 6	9 -4 5	9 -2 7	9 -6 3	9 -3 6	9 -2 7	9 -7 2
F	6 -1 5	7 -5 2	7 -2 5	9 -7 2	9 -5 4	9 -6 3	9 -8 1	7 -1 6	6 -4 2	5 -4 1	6 -1 5	7 -4 3
G	9 -3 6	9 -2 7	7 -4 3	9 -5 4	7 -2 5	9 -4 5	7 -3 4	7 -4 3	7 -6 1	7 -0 7	9 -7 2	6 -2 4

811

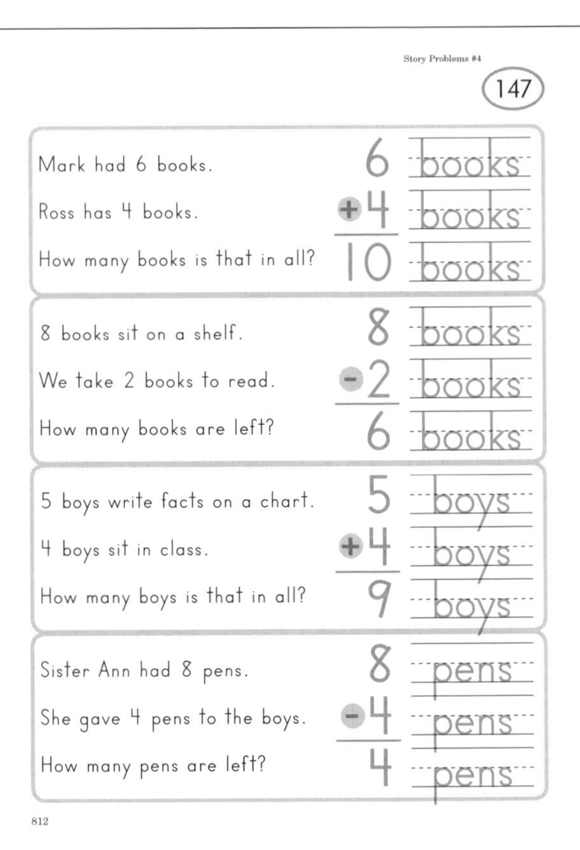

Story Problems #4

147

Mark had 6 books. 6 books
Ross has 4 books. +4 books
How many books is that in all? 10 books

8 books sit on a shelf. 8 books
We take 2 books to read. -2 books
How many books are left? 6 books

5 boys write facts on a chart. 5 boys
4 boys sit in class. +4 boys
How many boys is that in all? 9 boys

Sister Ann had 8 pens. 8 pens
She gave 4 pens to the boys. -4 pens
How many pens are left? 4 pens

812

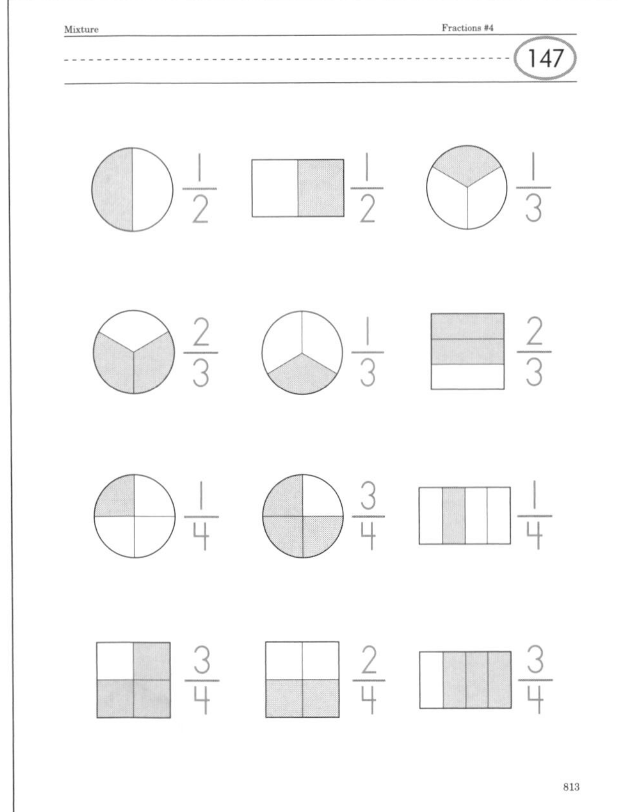

Mixture Fractions #4

147

1/2 1/2 1/3

2/3 1/3 2/3

1/4 3/4 1/4

3/4 2/4 3/4

813

Flash Card Drill Form C

148

1 2 3 4 5

1 2 3 4 5

1 2 3 4 5

1 2 3 4 5

1 2 3 4 5

Individual answers
(See page 365
for instructions.)

815

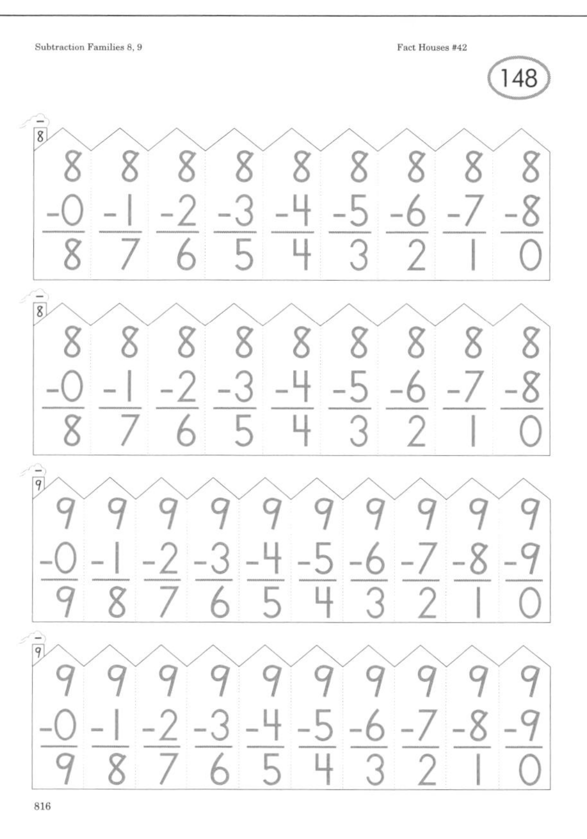

Subtraction Families 8, 9 — Fact Houses #42 — 148

8	8	8	8	8	8	8	8	8
-0	-1	-2	-3	-4	-5	-6	-7	-8
8	7	6	5	4	3	2	1	0

8	8	8	8	8	8	8	8	8
-0	-1	-2	-3	-4	-5	-6	-7	-8
8	7	6	5	4	3	2	1	0

9	9	9	9	9	9	9	9	9	9
-0	-1	-2	-3	-4	-5	-6	-7	-8	-9
9	8	7	6	5	4	3	2	1	0

9	9	9	9	9	9	9	9	9	9
-0	-1	-2	-3	-4	-5	-6	-7	-8	-9
9	8	7	6	5	4	3	2	1	0

816

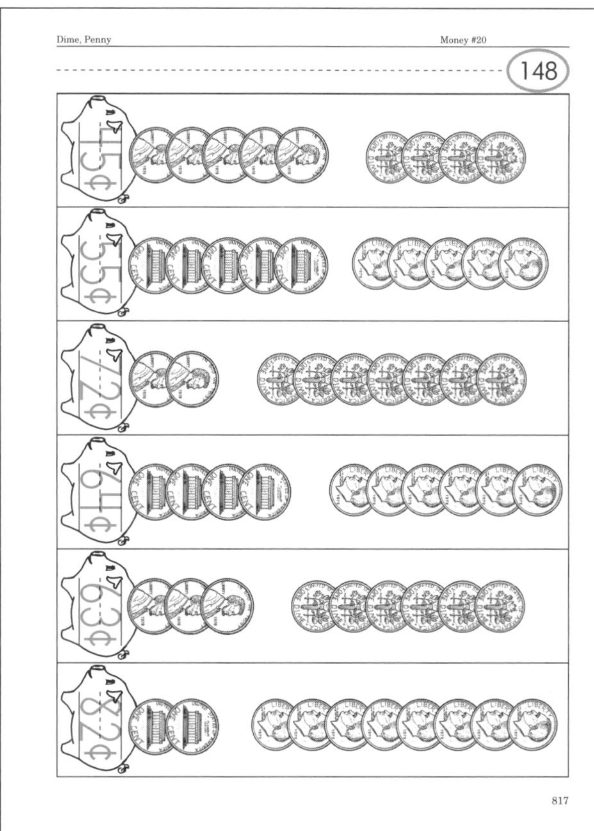

Dime, Penny — Money #20 — 148

45¢

55¢

72¢

64¢

63¢

82¢

817

Crossing Tens — Before and After #16 — 148

29	30	31	78	79	80
58	59	60	89	90	91
69	70	71	28	29	30
18	19	20	49	50	51
48	49	50	88	89	90
79	80	81	19	20	21
98	99	100	68	69	70
59	60	61	39	40	41
38	39	40	79	80	81

818

8, 9 [-] — Number Facts #55 — 148

A	9 - 3 = 6	8 - 5 = 3	8 - 7 = 1	8 - 3 = 5
B	8 - 3 = 5	9 - 7 = 2	9 - 4 = 5	8 - 6 = 2
C	9 - 7 = 2	9 - 5 = 4	9 - 6 = 3	9 - 3 = 6
D	8 - 5 = 3	8 - 4 = 4	9 - 2 = 7	9 - 5 = 4
E	9 - 4 = 5	8 - 6 = 2	9 - 3 = 6	9 - 7 = 2
F	9 - 2 = 7	8 - 5 = 3	9 - 7 = 2	9 - 6 = 3
G	9 - 5 = 4	9 - 3 = 6	9 - 6 = 3	9 - 3 = 6
H	8 - 3 = 5	8 - 2 = 6	8 - 4 = 4	8 - 5 = 3
I	9 - 8 = 1	9 - 2 = 7	9 - 4 = 5	8 - 3 = 5
J	9 - 3 = 6	9 - 4 = 5	8 - 1 = 7	8 - 2 = 6
K	9 - 7 = 2	8 - 6 = 2	8 - 3 = 5	9 - 5 = 4
L	9 - 5 = 4	9 - 6 = 3	9 - 5 = 4	9 - 2 = 7
M	8 - 2 = 6	8 - 3 = 5	8 - 6 = 2	9 - 5 = 4
N	8 - 5 = 3	9 - 3 = 6	9 - 6 = 3	9 - 7 = 2
O	9 - 2 = 7	9 - 8 = 1	9 - 3 = 6	9 - 6 = 3
P	8 - 4 = 4	8 - 3 = 5	9 - 4 = 5	8 - 3 = 5
Q	8 - 6 = 2	8 - 2 = 6	9 - 8 = 1	9 - 3 = 6

819

8–10 [+] 7–9 [-] Number Facts #56

148

A	7-5=2	5+4=9	2+8=10	4+4=8
B	7-2=5	8-3=5	7-1=6	6+4=10
C	8-2=6	3+7=10	5+4=9	3+5=8
D	6+2=8	8-3=5	5+5=10	9-3=6
E	9-2=7	2+7=9	9-6=3	7-5=2
F	2+7=9	6+4=10	3+5=8	9-4=5
G	7-3=4	9-3=6	8-1=7	3+6=9
H	4+6=10	9-1=8	9-4=5	9-2=7
I	7-2=5	9-2=7	3+7=10	8-3=5
J	6+3=9	8-5=3	9-1=8	3+6=9
K	3+7=10	9-5=4	7-1=6	2+8=10
L	9-3=6	6+2=8	9-7=2	5+4=9
M	8-6=2	9-3=6	8-3=5	9-5=4
N	9-4=5	8-6=2	7+2=9	6+4=10
O	9-6=3	9-4=5	7-3=4	9-3=6
P	8-4=4	3+6=9	3+7=10	3+5=8
Q	6+2=8	8-4=4	8-2=6	8-1=7

820

Subtraction Families 6–9 Fact Houses #43

149

6: 6-0=6, 6-1=5, 6-2=4, 6-3=3, 6-4=2, 6-5=1, 6-6=0

7: 7-0=7, 7-1=6, 7-2=5, 7-3=4, 7-4=3, 7-5=2, 7-6=1, 7-7=0

8: 8-0=8, 8-1=7, 8-2=6, 8-3=5, 8-4=4, 8-5=3, 8-6=2, 8-7=1, 8-8=0

9: 9-0=9, 9-1=8, 9-2=7, 9-3=6, 9-4=5, 9-5=4, 9-6=3, 9-7=2, 9-8=1, 9-9=0

821

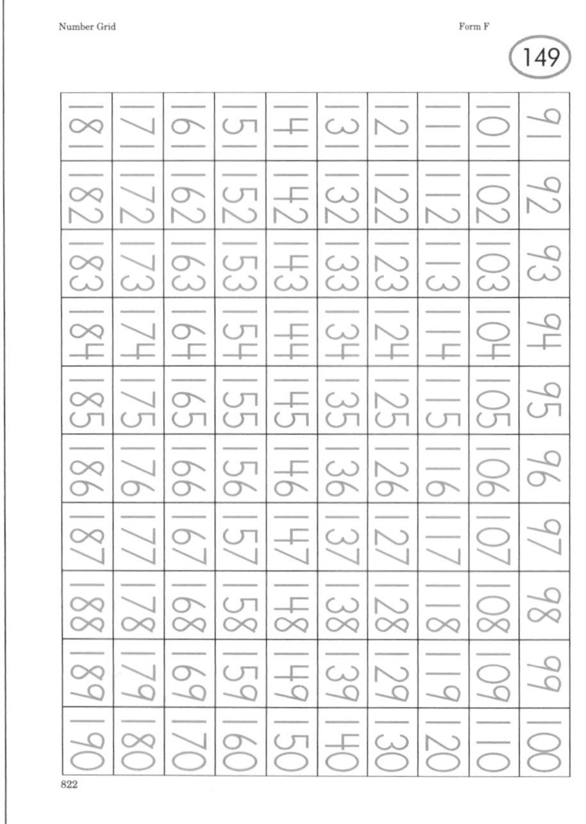
Number Grid Form F

149

91	92	93	94	95	96	97	98	99	100
101	102	103	104	105	106	107	108	109	110
111	112	113	114	115	116	117	118	119	120
121	122	123	124	125	126	127	128	129	130
131	132	133	134	135	136	137	138	139	140
141	142	143	144	145	146	147	148	149	150
151	152	153	154	155	156	157	158	159	160
161	162	163	164	165	166	167	168	169	170
171	172	173	174	175	176	177	178	179	180
181	182	183	184	185	186	187	188	189	190

822

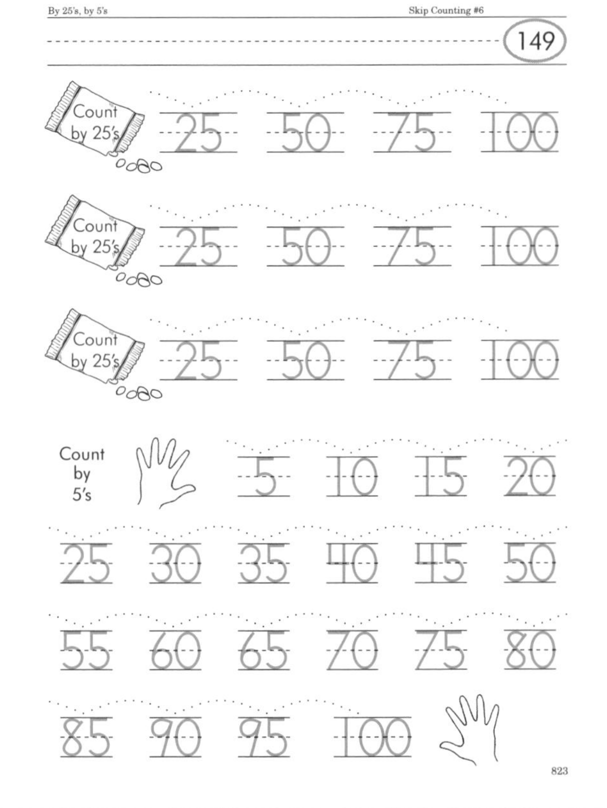
By 25's, by 5's Skip Counting #6

149

Count by 25's 25 50 75 100

Count by 25's 25 50 75 100

Count by 25's 25 50 75 100

Count by 5's 5 10 15 20

25 30 35 40 45 50

55 60 65 70 75 80

85 90 95 100

823

8, 9 [-] Number Facts #55

149

A	9 - 3 = 6	8 - 5 = 3	8 - 7 = 1	8 - 3 = 5
B	8 - 3 = 5	9 - 7 = 2	9 - 4 = 5	8 - 6 = 2
C	9 - 7 = 2	9 - 5 = 4	9 - 6 = 3	9 - 3 = 6
D	8 - 5 = 3	8 - 4 = 4	9 - 2 = 7	9 - 5 = 4
E	9 - 4 = 5	8 - 6 = 2	9 - 3 = 6	9 - 7 = 2
F	9 - 2 = 7	8 - 5 = 3	9 - 7 = 2	9 - 6 = 3
G	9 - 5 = 4	9 - 3 = 6	9 - 6 = 3	9 - 3 = 6
H	8 - 3 = 5	8 - 2 = 6	8 - 4 = 4	8 - 5 = 3
I	9 - 8 = 1	9 - 2 = 7	9 - 4 = 5	8 - 3 = 5
J	9 - 3 = 6	9 - 4 = 5	8 - 1 = 7	8 - 2 = 6
K	9 - 7 = 2	8 - 6 = 2	8 - 3 = 5	9 - 5 = 4
L	9 - 5 = 4	9 - 6 = 3	9 - 5 = 4	9 - 2 = 7
M	8 - 2 = 6	8 - 3 = 5	8 - 6 = 2	9 - 5 = 4
N	8 - 5 = 3	9 - 3 = 6	9 - 6 = 3	9 - 7 = 2
O	9 - 2 = 7	9 - 8 = 1	9 - 3 = 6	9 - 6 = 3
P	8 - 4 = 4	8 - 3 = 5	9 - 4 = 5	8 - 3 = 5
Q	8 - 6 = 2	8 - 2 = 6	9 - 8 = 1	9 - 3 = 6

824

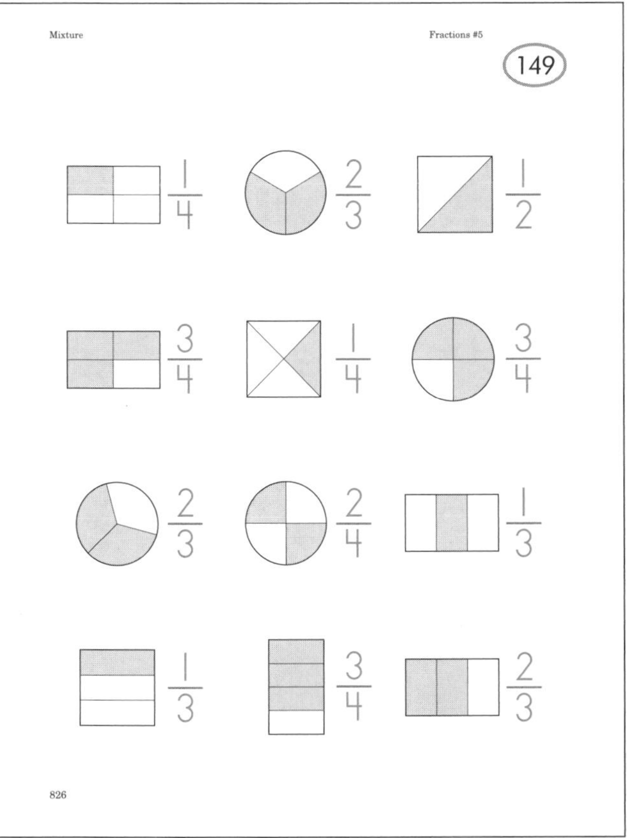

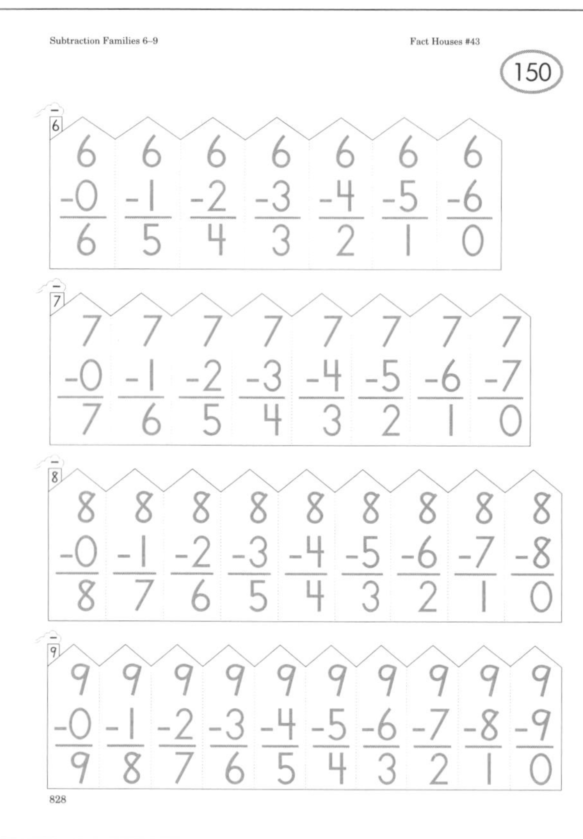

Subtraction Families 6–9 | Fact Houses #43

150

6	6	6	6	6	6	6
-0	-1	-2	-3	-4	-5	-6
6	5	4	3	2	1	0

7	7	7	7	7	7	7	7
-0	-1	-2	-3	-4	-5	-6	-7
7	6	5	4	3	2	1	0

8	8	8	8	8	8	8	8	8
-0	-1	-2	-3	-4	-5	-6	-7	-8
8	7	6	5	4	3	2	1	0

9	9	9	9	9	9	9	9	9	9
-0	-1	-2	-3	-4	-5	-6	-7	-8	-9
9	8	7	6	5	4	3	2	1	0

828

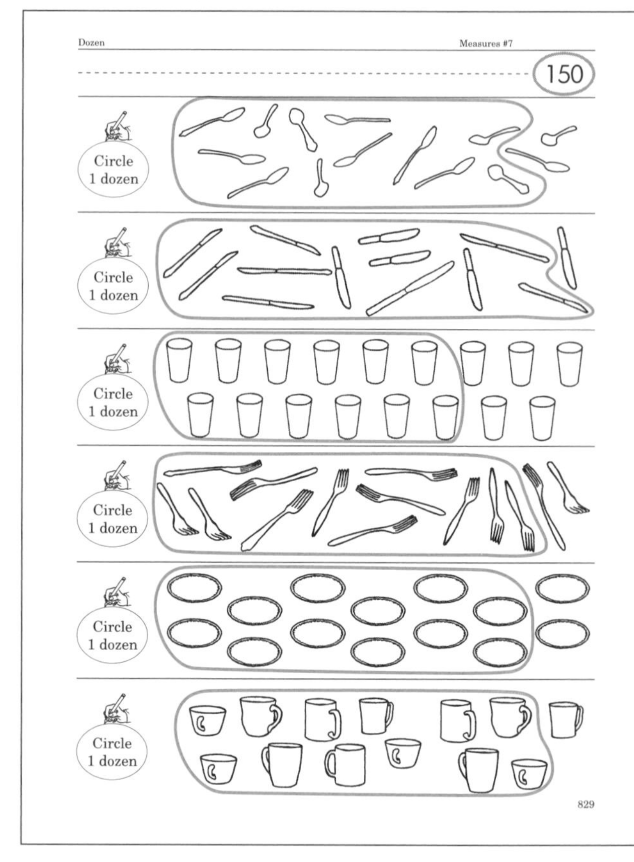

Dozen | Measures #7

150

Circle 1 dozen

Circle 1 dozen

Circle 1 dozen

Circle 1 dozen

Circle 1 dozen

Circle 1 dozen

829

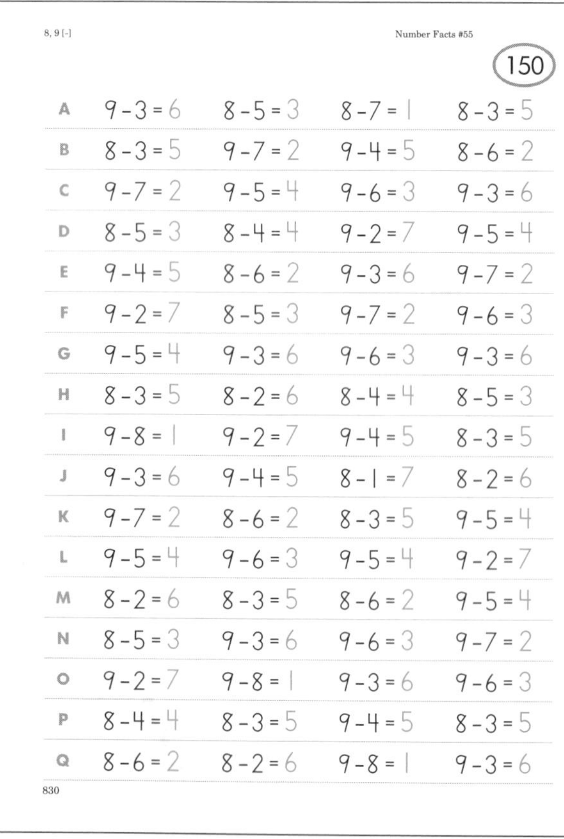

8, 9 [-] | Number Facts #55

150

A	9 - 3 = 6	8 - 5 = 3	8 - 7 = 1	8 - 3 = 5
B	8 - 3 = 5	9 - 7 = 2	9 - 4 = 5	8 - 6 = 2
C	9 - 7 = 2	9 - 5 = 4	9 - 6 = 3	9 - 3 = 6
D	8 - 5 = 3	8 - 4 = 4	9 - 2 = 7	9 - 5 = 4
E	9 - 4 = 5	8 - 6 = 2	9 - 3 = 6	9 - 7 = 2
F	9 - 2 = 7	8 - 5 = 3	9 - 7 = 2	9 - 6 = 3
G	9 - 5 = 4	9 - 3 = 6	9 - 6 = 3	9 - 3 = 6
H	8 - 3 = 5	8 - 2 = 6	8 - 4 = 4	8 - 5 = 3
I	9 - 8 = 1	9 - 2 = 7	9 - 4 = 5	8 - 3 = 5
J	9 - 3 = 6	9 - 4 = 5	8 - 1 = 7	8 - 2 = 6
K	9 - 7 = 2	8 - 6 = 2	8 - 3 = 5	9 - 5 = 4
L	9 - 5 = 4	9 - 6 = 3	9 - 5 = 4	9 - 2 = 7
M	8 - 2 = 6	8 - 3 = 5	8 - 6 = 2	9 - 5 = 4
N	8 - 5 = 3	9 - 3 = 6	9 - 6 = 3	9 - 7 = 2
O	9 - 2 = 7	9 - 8 = 1	9 - 3 = 6	9 - 6 = 3
P	8 - 4 = 4	8 - 3 = 5	9 - 4 = 5	8 - 3 = 5
Q	8 - 6 = 2	8 - 2 = 6	9 - 8 = 1	9 - 3 = 6

830

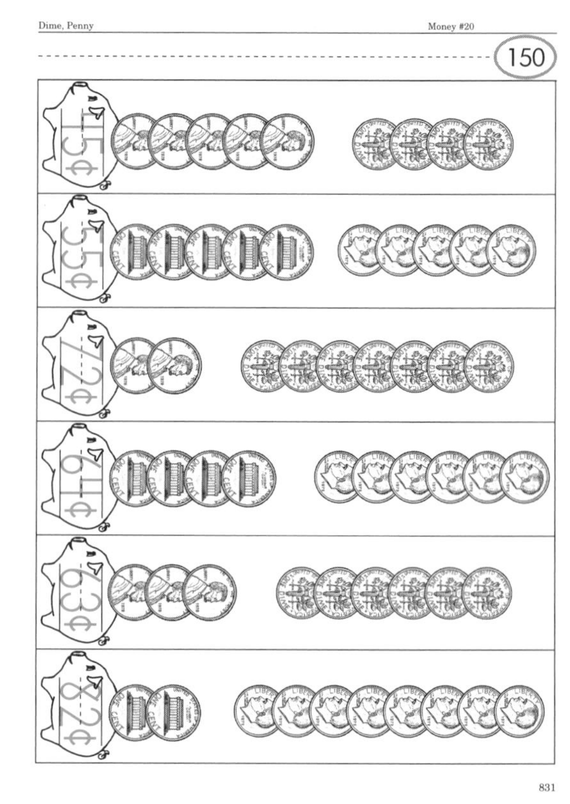

Dime, Penny | Money #20

150

831

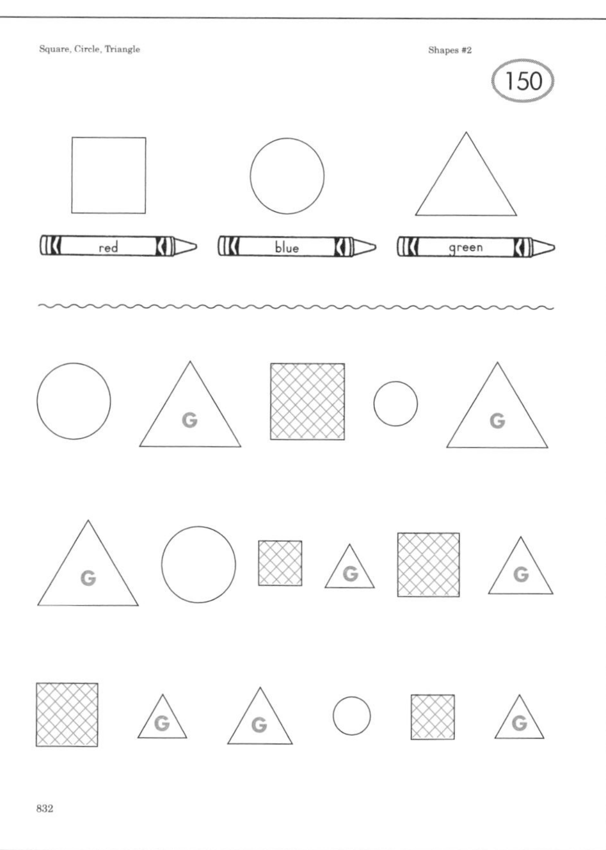
Square, Circle, Triangle — Shapes #2 — 150

832

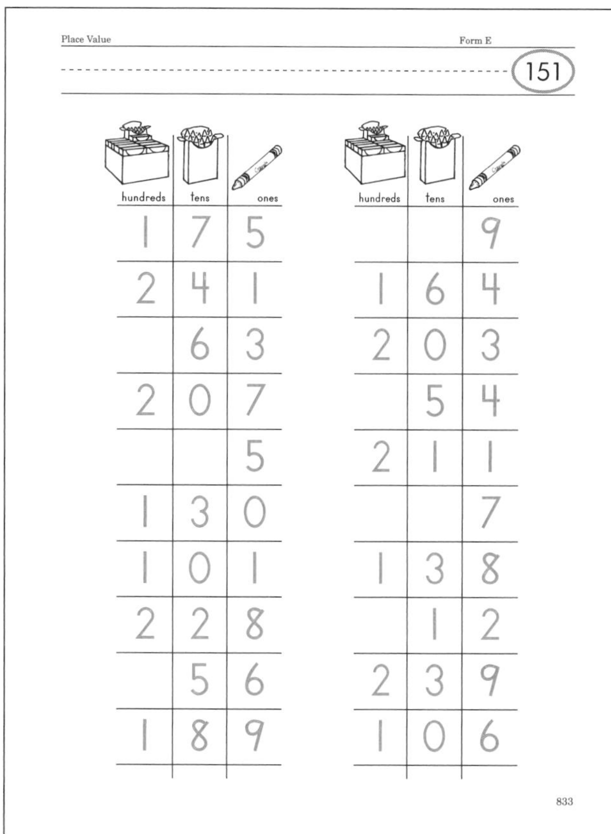
Place Value — Form E — 151

hundreds	tens	ones
1	7	5
2	4	1
	6	3
2	0	7
		5
1	3	0
1	0	1
2	2	8
	5	6
1	8	9

hundreds	tens	ones
		9
1	6	4
2	0	3
	5	4
2	1	1
		7
1	3	8
	1	2
2	3	9
1	0	6

833

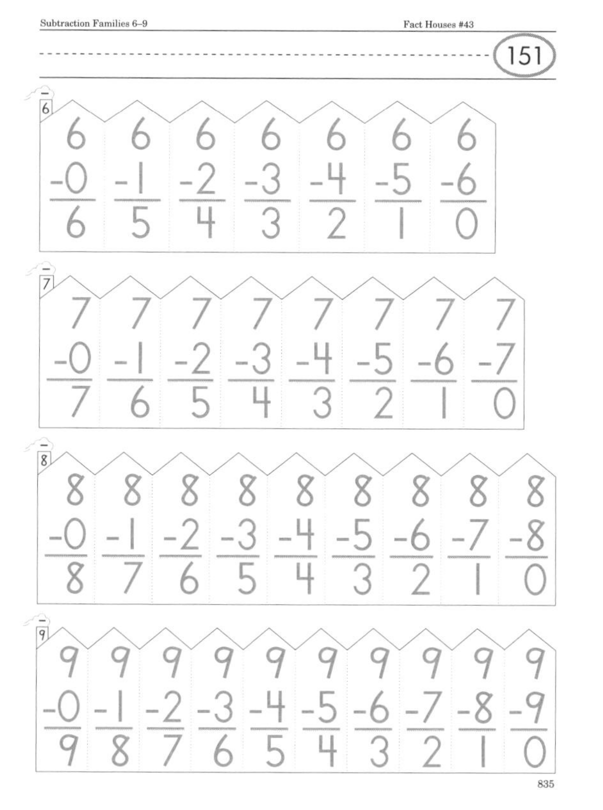
Subtraction Families 6–9 — Fact Houses #43 — 151

6: 6 − 0 = 6, 6 − 1 = 5, 6 − 2 = 4, 6 − 3 = 3, 6 − 4 = 2, 6 − 5 = 1, 6 − 6 = 0

7: 7 − 0 = 7, 7 − 1 = 6, 7 − 2 = 5, 7 − 3 = 4, 7 − 4 = 3, 7 − 5 = 2, 7 − 6 = 1, 7 − 7 = 0

8: 8 − 0 = 8, 8 − 1 = 7, 8 − 2 = 6, 8 − 3 = 5, 8 − 4 = 4, 8 − 5 = 3, 8 − 6 = 2, 8 − 7 = 1, 8 − 8 = 0

9: 9 − 0 = 9, 9 − 1 = 8, 9 − 2 = 7, 9 − 3 = 6, 9 − 4 = 5, 9 − 5 = 4, 9 − 6 = 3, 9 − 7 = 2, 9 − 8 = 1, 9 − 9 = 0

835

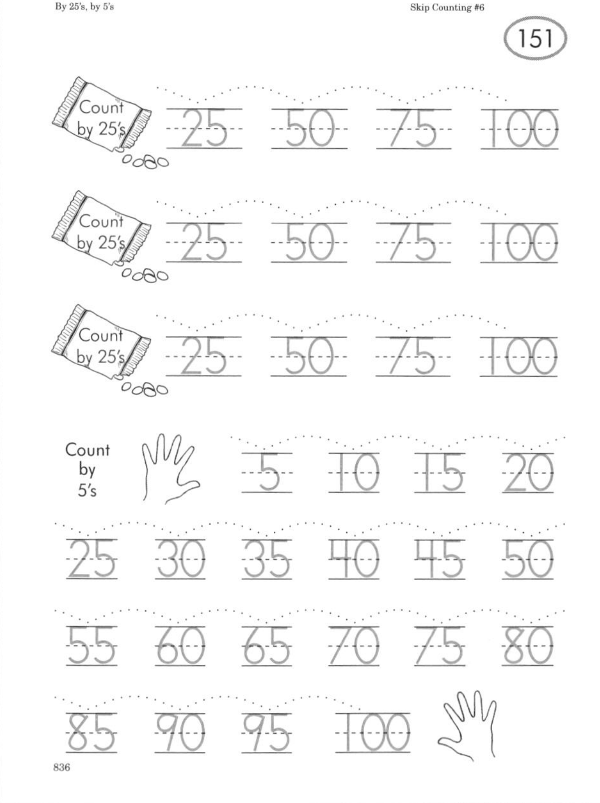
By 25's, by 5's — Skip Counting #6 — 151

Count by 25's: 25 50 75 100

Count by 25's: 25 50 75 100

Count by 25's: 25 50 75 100

Count by 5's: 5 10 15 20

25 30 35 40 45 50

55 60 65 70 75 80

85 90 95 100

836

8, 9 [-] — Number Facts #55 — 151

A	9 - 3 = 6	8 - 5 = 3	8 - 7 = 1	8 - 3 = 5
B	8 - 3 = 5	9 - 7 = 2	9 - 4 = 5	8 - 6 = 2
C	9 - 7 = 2	9 - 5 = 4	9 - 6 = 3	9 - 3 = 6
D	8 - 5 = 3	8 - 4 = 4	9 - 2 = 7	9 - 5 = 4
E	9 - 4 = 5	8 - 6 = 2	9 - 3 = 6	9 - 7 = 2
F	9 - 2 = 7	8 - 5 = 3	9 - 7 = 2	9 - 6 = 3
G	9 - 5 = 4	9 - 3 = 6	9 - 6 = 3	9 - 3 = 6
H	8 - 3 = 5	8 - 2 = 6	8 - 4 = 4	8 - 5 = 3
I	9 - 8 = 1	9 - 2 = 7	9 - 4 = 5	8 - 3 = 5
J	9 - 3 = 6	9 - 4 = 5	8 - 1 = 7	8 - 2 = 6
K	9 - 7 = 2	8 - 6 = 2	8 - 3 = 5	9 - 5 = 4
L	9 - 5 = 4	9 - 6 = 3	9 - 5 = 4	9 - 2 = 7
M	8 - 2 = 6	8 - 3 = 5	8 - 6 = 2	9 - 5 = 4
N	8 - 5 = 3	9 - 3 = 6	9 - 6 = 3	9 - 7 = 2
O	9 - 2 = 7	9 - 8 = 1	9 - 3 = 6	9 - 6 = 3
P	8 - 4 = 4	8 - 3 = 5	9 - 4 = 5	8 - 3 = 5
Q	8 - 6 = 2	8 - 2 = 6	9 - 8 = 1	9 - 3 = 6

837

Crossing Tens — Before and After #17 — 151

129	130	131	188	189	190
198	199	200	119	120	121
159	160	161	168	169	170
158	159	160	189	190	191
148	149	150	128	129	130
169	170	171	149	150	151
118	119	120	178	179	180
179	180	181	139	140	141
138	139	140	179	180	181

838

Subtraction Family 10 — Fact Houses #44 — 152

10	10	10	10	10	10	10	10	10	10	10
-0	-1	-2	-3	-4	-5	-6	-7	-8	-9	-10
10	9	8	7	6	5	4	3	2	1	0

10	10	10	10	10	10	10	10	10	10	10
-0	-1	-2	-3	-4	-5	-6	-7	-8	-9	-10
10	9	8	7	6	5	4	3	2	1	0

10	10	10	10	10	10	10	10	10	10	10
-0	-1	-2	-3	-4	-5	-6	-7	-8	-9	-10
10	9	8	7	6	5	4	3	2	1	0

10	10	10	10	10	10	10	10	10	10	10
-0	-1	-2	-3	-4	-5	-6	-7	-8	-9	-10
10	9	8	7	6	5	4	3	2	1	0

839

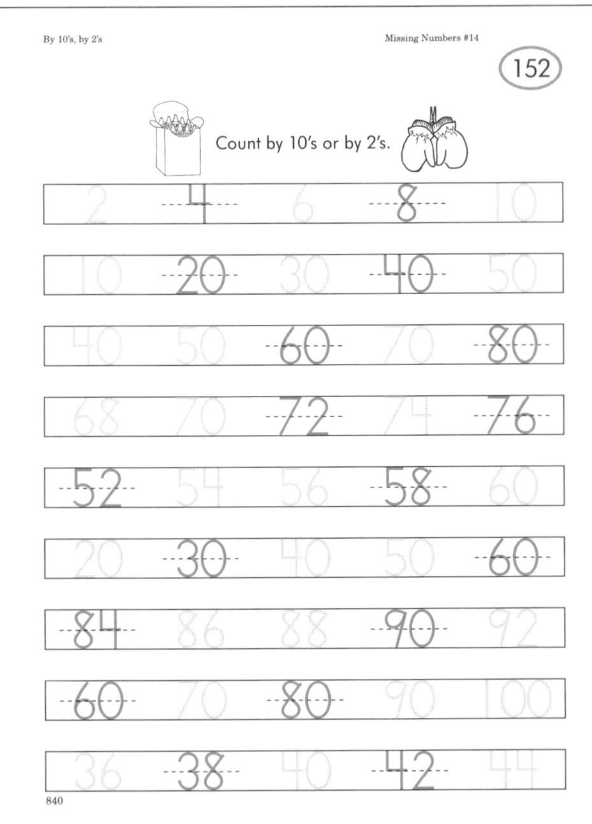
By 10's, by 2's — Missing Numbers #14 — 152

Count by 10's or by 2's.

2	4	6	8	10
10	20	30	40	50
40	50	60	70	80
68	70	72	74	76
52	54	56	58	60
20	30	40	50	60
84	86	88	90	92
60	70	80	90	100
36	38	40	42	44

840

8–10 [+] 7–9 [–] Number Facts #56

152

A	7-5=2	5+4=9	2+8=10	4+4=8
B	7-2=5	8-3=5	7-1=6	6+4=10
C	8-2=6	3+7=10	5+4=9	3+5=8
D	6+2=8	8-3=5	5+5=10	9-3=6
E	9-2=7	2+7=9	9-6=3	7-5=2
F	2+7=9	6+4=10	3+5=8	9-4=5
G	7-3=4	9-3=6	8-1=7	3+6=9
H	4+6=10	9-1=8	9-4=5	9-2=7
I	7-2=5	9-2=7	3+7=10	8-3=5
J	6+3=9	8-5=3	9-1=8	3+6=9
K	3+7=10	9-5=4	7-1=6	2+8=10
L	9-3=6	6+2=8	9-7=2	5+4=9
M	8-6=2	9-3=6	8-3=5	9-5=4
N	9-4=5	8-6=2	7+2=9	6+4=10
O	9-6=3	9-4=5	7-3=4	9-3=6
P	8-4=4	3+6=9	3+7=10	3+5=8
Q	6+2=8	8-4=4	8-2=6	8-1=7

841

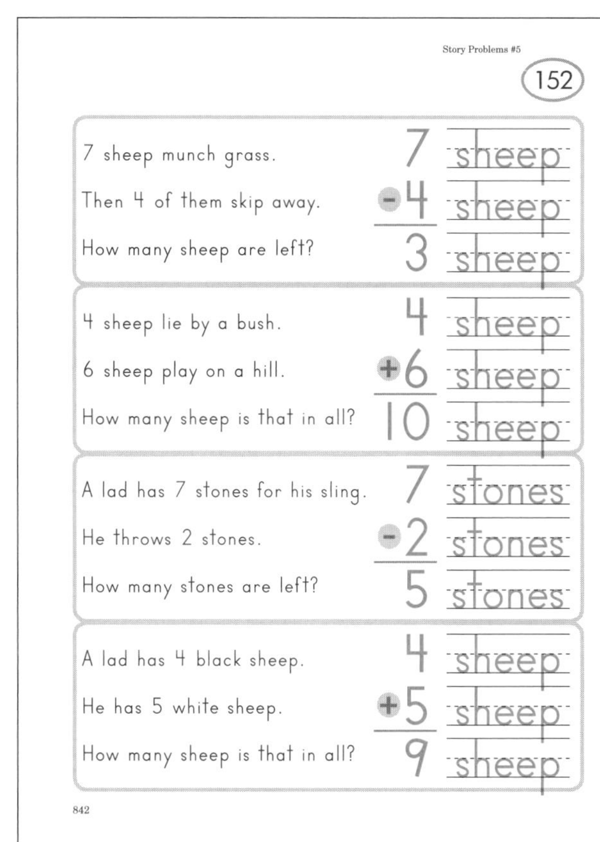
Story Problems #5

152

7 sheep munch grass. Then 4 of them skip away. How many sheep are left? 7 sheep − 4 sheep = 3 sheep

4 sheep lie by a bush. 6 sheep play on a hill. How many sheep is that in all? 4 sheep + 6 sheep = 10 sheep

A lad has 7 stones for his sling. He throws 2 stones. How many stones are left? 7 stones − 2 stones = 5 stones

A lad has 4 black sheep. He has 5 white sheep. How many sheep is that in all? 4 sheep + 5 sheep = 9 sheep

842

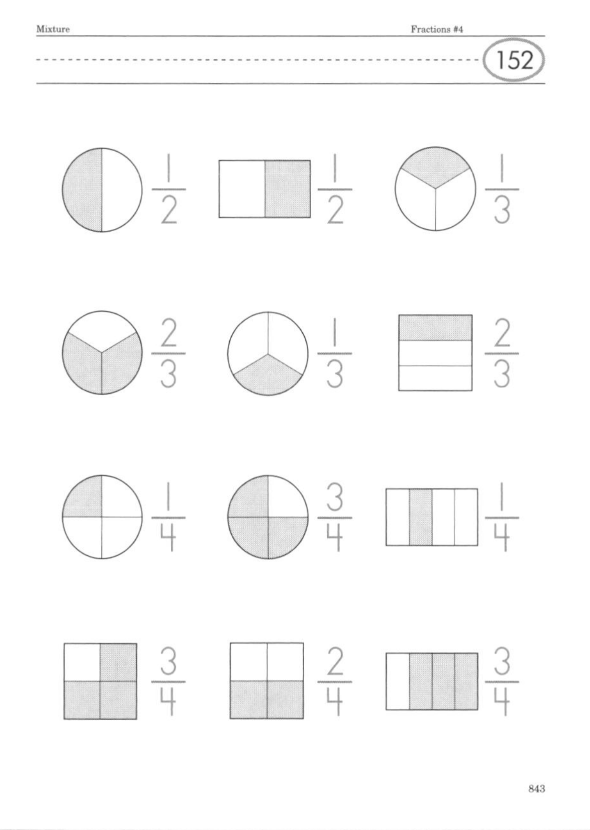
Mixture Fractions #4

152

843

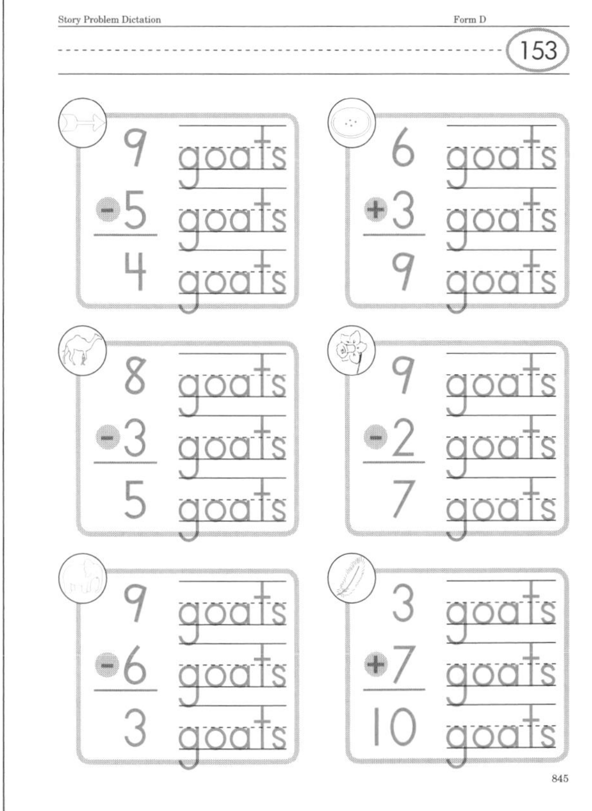
Story Problem Dictation Form D

153

9 goats − 5 goats = 4 goats

6 goats + 3 goats = 9 goats

8 goats − 3 goats = 5 goats

9 goats − 2 goats = 7 goats

9 goats − 6 goats = 3 goats

3 goats + 7 goats = 10 goats

845

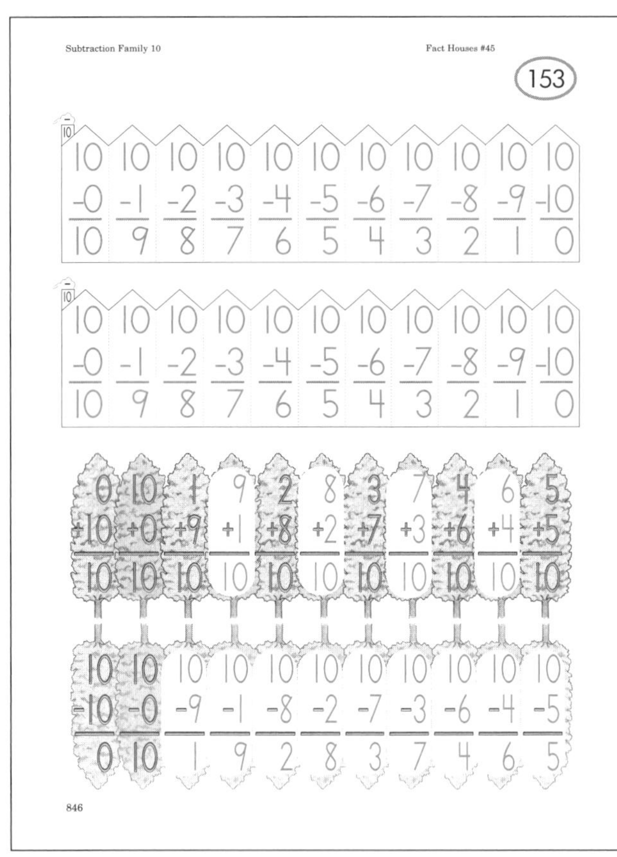
Subtraction Family 10 — Fact Houses #45 — 153

10	10	10	10	10	10	10	10	10	10	10
-0	-1	-2	-3	-4	-5	-6	-7	-8	-9	-10
10	9	8	7	6	5	4	3	2	1	0

10	10	10	10	10	10	10	10	10	10	10
-0	-1	-2	-3	-4	-5	-6	-7	-8	-9	-10
10	9	8	7	6	5	4	3	2	1	0

0	10	1	9	2	8	3	7	4	6	5
+10	+0	+9	+1	+8	+2	+7	+3	+6	+4	+5
10	10	10	10	10	10	10	10	10	10	10

10	10	10	10	10	10	10	10	10	10	10
-10	-0	-9	-1	-8	-2	-7	-3	-6	-4	-5
0	10	1	9	2	8	3	7	4	6	5

846

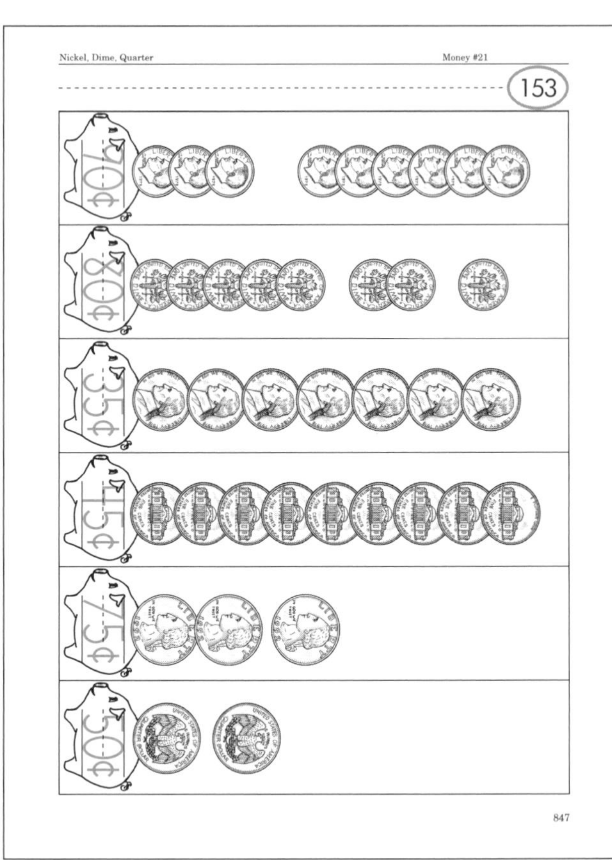
Nickel, Dime, Quarter — Money #21 — 153

20¢
80¢
35¢
45¢
75¢
50¢

847

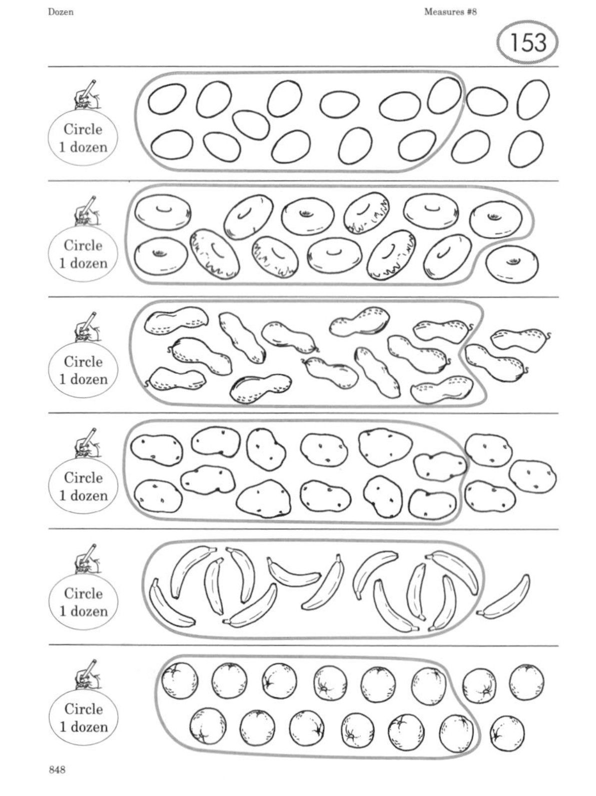
Dozen — Measures #8 — 153

Circle 1 dozen
Circle 1 dozen
Circle 1 dozen
Circle 1 dozen
Circle 1 dozen
Circle 1 dozen

848

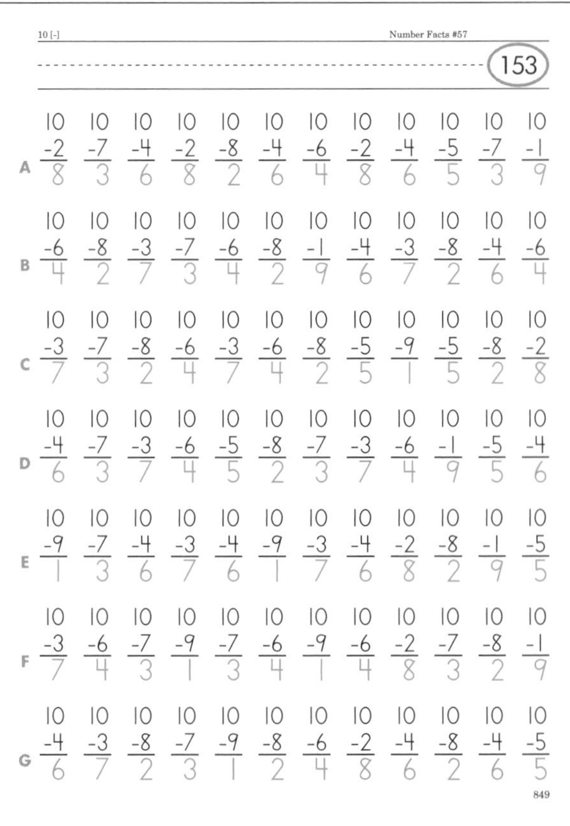
10 [-] — Number Facts #57 — 153

A	10 -2 = 8	10 -7 = 3	10 -4 = 6	10 -2 = 8	10 -8 = 2	10 -4 = 6	10 -6 = 4	10 -2 = 8	10 -4 = 6	10 -5 = 5	10 -7 = 3	10 -1 = 9
B	10 -6 = 4	10 -8 = 2	10 -3 = 7	10 -7 = 3	10 -6 = 4	10 -8 = 2	10 -1 = 9	10 -4 = 6	10 -3 = 7	10 -8 = 2	10 -4 = 6	10 -6 = 4
C	10 -3 = 7	10 -7 = 3	10 -8 = 2	10 -6 = 4	10 -3 = 7	10 -6 = 4	10 -8 = 2	10 -5 = 5	10 -9 = 1	10 -5 = 5	10 -8 = 2	10 -2 = 8
D	10 -4 = 6	10 -7 = 3	10 -3 = 7	10 -6 = 4	10 -5 = 5	10 -8 = 2	10 -7 = 3	10 -3 = 7	10 -6 = 4	10 -1 = 9	10 -5 = 5	10 -4 = 6
E	10 -9 = 1	10 -7 = 3	10 -4 = 6	10 -3 = 7	10 -4 = 6	10 -9 = 1	10 -3 = 7	10 -4 = 6	10 -2 = 8	10 -8 = 2	10 -1 = 9	10 -5 = 5
F	10 -3 = 7	10 -6 = 4	10 -7 = 3	10 -9 = 1	10 -7 = 3	10 -6 = 4	10 -9 = 1	10 -6 = 4	10 -2 = 8	10 -7 = 3	10 -8 = 2	10 -1 = 9
G	10 -4 = 6	10 -3 = 7	10 -8 = 2	10 -7 = 3	10 -9 = 1	10 -8 = 2	10 -6 = 4	10 -2 = 8	10 -4 = 6	10 -8 = 2	10 -4 = 6	10 -5 = 5

849

Number Grid — Form F — 153

101	102	103	104	105	106	107	108	109	110
111	112	113	114	115	116	117	118	119	120
121	122	123	124	125	126	127	128	129	130
131	132	133	134	135	136	137	138	139	140
141	142	143	144	145	146	147	148	149	150
151	152	153	154	155	156	157	158	159	160
161	162	163	164	165	166	167	168	169	170
171	172	173	174	175	176	177	178	179	180
181	182	183	184	185	186	187	188	189	190
191	192	193	194	195	196	197	198	199	200

850

Subtraction Family 10 — Fact Houses #44 — 154

10	10	10	10	10	10	10	10	10	10	10
-0	-1	-2	-3	-4	-5	-6	-7	-8	-9	-10
10	9	8	7	6	5	4	3	2	1	0

10	10	10	10	10	10	10	10	10	10	10
-0	-1	-2	-3	-4	-5	-6	-7	-8	-9	-10
10	9	8	7	6	5	4	3	2	1	0

10	10	10	10	10	10	10	10	10	10	10
-0	-1	-2	-3	-4	-5	-6	-7	-8	-9	-10
10	9	8	7	6	5	4	3	2	1	0

10	10	10	10	10	10	10	10	10	10	10
-0	-1	-2	-3	-4	-5	-6	-7	-8	-9	-10
10	9	8	7	6	5	4	3	2	1	0

851

Crossing Tens — Before and After #17 — 154

129	130	131	188	189	190
198	199	200	119	120	121
159	160	161	168	169	170
158	159	160	189	190	191
148	149	150	128	129	130
169	170	171	149	150	151
118	119	120	178	179	180
179	180	181	139	140	141
138	139	140	179	180	181

852

8–10 [+] 7–9 [-] — Number Facts #56 — 154

A	7-5=2	5+4=9	2+8=10	4+4=8
B	7-2=5	8-3=5	7-1=6	6+4=10
C	8-2=6	3+7=10	5+4=9	3+5=8
D	6+2=8	8-3=5	5+5=10	9-3=6
E	9-2=7	2+7=9	9-6=3	7-5=2
F	2+7=9	6+4=10	3+5=8	9-4=5
G	7-3=4	9-3=6	8-1=7	3+6=9
H	4+6=10	9-1=8	9-4=5	9-2=7
I	7-2=5	9-2=7	3+7=10	8-3=5
J	6+3=9	8-5=3	9-1=8	3+6=9
K	3+7=10	9-5=4	7-1=6	2+8=10
L	9-3=6	6+2=8	9-7=2	5+4=9
M	8-6=2	9-3=6	8-3=5	9-5=4
N	9-4=5	8-6=2	7+2=9	6+4=10
O	9-6=3	9-4=5	7-3=4	9-3=6
P	8-4=4	3+6=9	3+7=10	3+5=8
Q	6+2=8	8-4=4	8-2=6	8-1=7

853

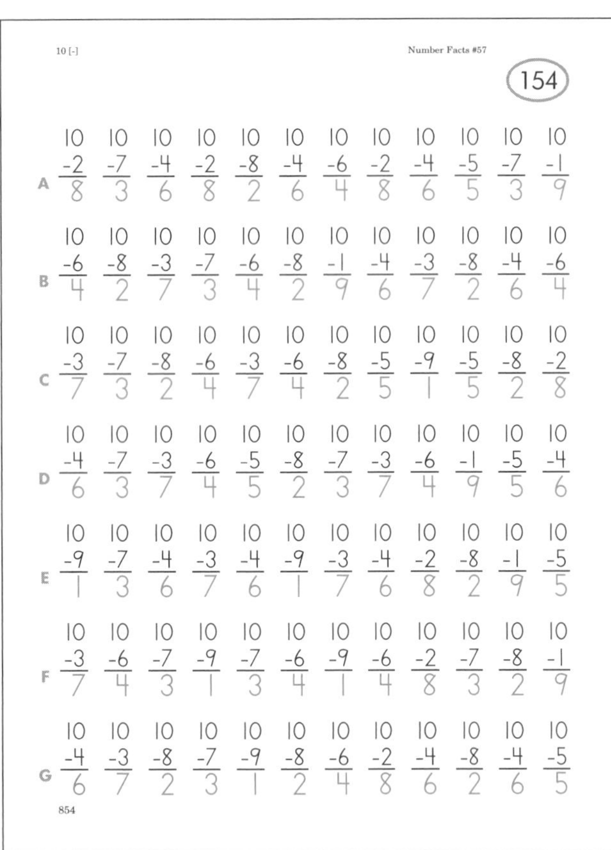
10 [-] Number Facts #57

154

A	10 -2 8	10 -7 3	10 -4 6	10 -2 8	10 -8 2	10 -4 6	10 -6 4	10 -2 8	10 -4 6	10 -5 5	10 -7 3	10 -1 9
B	10 -6 4	10 -8 2	10 -3 7	10 -7 3	10 -6 4	10 -8 2	10 -1 9	10 -4 6	10 -3 7	10 -8 2	10 -4 6	10 -6 4
C	10 -3 7	10 -7 3	10 -8 2	10 -6 4	10 -3 7	10 -6 4	10 -8 2	10 -5 5	10 -9 1	10 -5 5	10 -8 2	10 -2 8
D	10 -4 6	10 -7 3	10 -3 7	10 -6 4	10 -5 5	10 -8 2	10 -7 3	10 -3 7	10 -6 4	10 -1 9	10 -5 5	10 -4 6
E	10 -9 1	10 -7 3	10 -4 6	10 -3 7	10 -4 6	10 -9 1	10 -3 7	10 -4 6	10 -2 8	10 -8 2	10 -1 9	10 -5 5
F	10 -3 7	10 -6 4	10 -7 3	10 -9 1	10 -7 3	10 -6 4	10 -9 1	10 -6 4	10 -2 8	10 -7 3	10 -8 2	10 -1 9
G	10 -4 6	10 -3 7	10 -8 2	10 -7 3	10 -9 1	10 -8 2	10 -6 4	10 -2 8	10 -4 6	10 -8 2	10 -4 6	10 -5 5

854

Hour, Half Hour Clocks #8

154

7:00	6:30	2:00	5:30
2:30	11:00	9:00	8:30
3:00	1:30	12:00	11:30
6:00	4:00	3:30	7:30

855

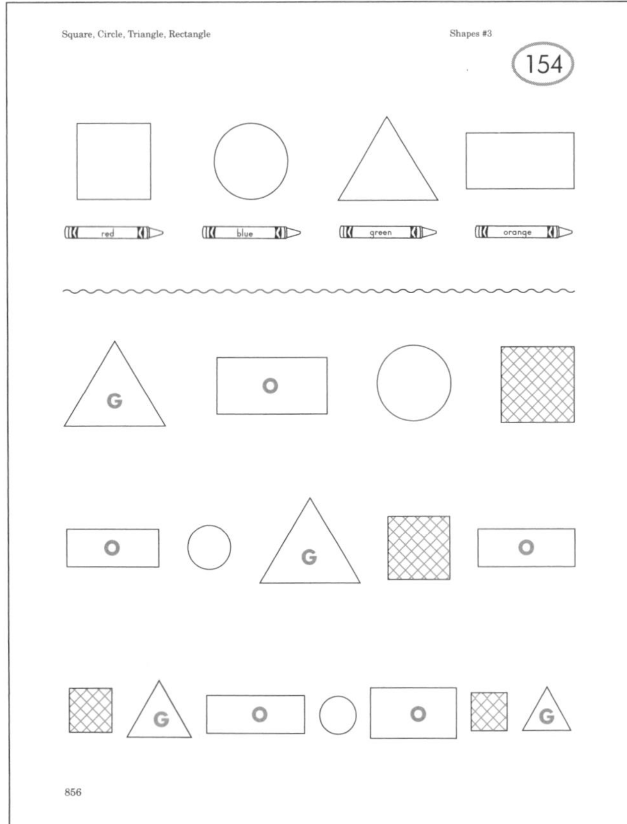
Square, Circle, Triangle, Rectangle Shapes #3

154

red blue green orange

G O O G O O G O

856

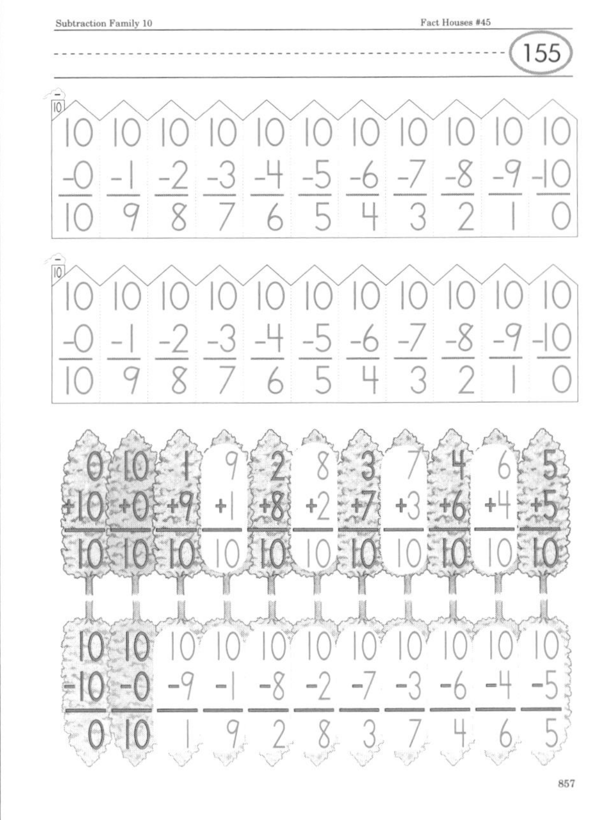
Subtraction Family 10 Fact Houses #45

155

10 -0 10	10 -1 9	10 -2 8	10 -3 7	10 -4 6	10 -5 5	10 -6 4	10 -7 3	10 -8 2	10 -9 1	10 -10 0
10 -0 10	10 -1 9	10 -2 8	10 -3 7	10 -4 6	10 -5 5	10 -6 4	10 -7 3	10 -8 2	10 -9 1	10 -10 0
0 +10 10	10 +0 10	1 +9 10	9 +1 10	2 +8 10	8 +2 10	3 +7 10	7 +3 10	4 +6 10	6 +4 10	5 +5 10
10 -10 0	10 -0 10	10 -9 1	10 -1 9	10 -8 2	10 -2 8	10 -7 3	10 -3 7	10 -6 4	10 -4 6	10 -5 5

857

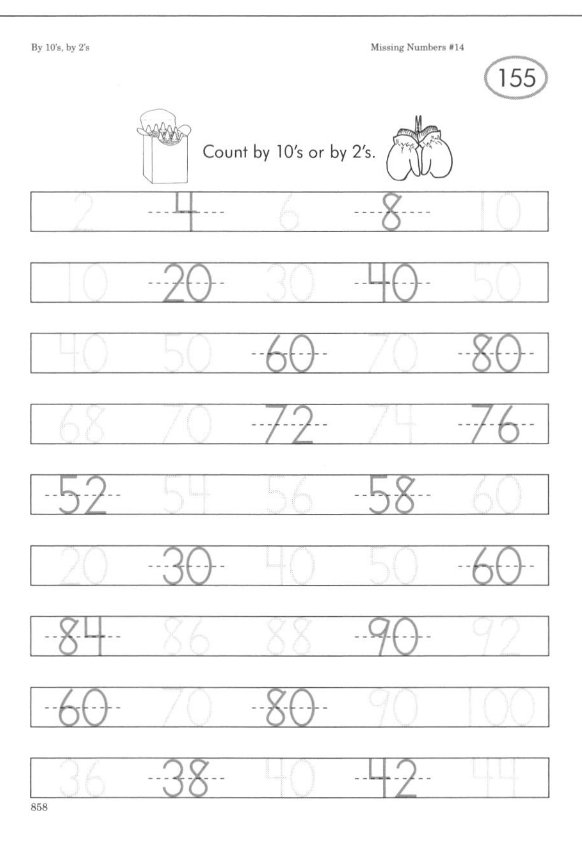

6-8, 10 [-] Number Facts #58

155

A	8 - 6 = 2	10 - 4 = 6	7 - 4 = 3	10 - 2 = 8
B	6 - 2 = 4	10 - 2 = 8	10 - 5 = 5	8 - 5 = 3
C	10 - 3 = 7	7 - 4 = 3	8 - 5 = 3	10 - 6 = 4
D	7 - 4 = 3	10 - 6 = 4	6 - 1 = 5	8 - 7 = 1
E	10 - 5 = 5	10 - 8 = 2	10 - 3 = 7	7 - 2 = 5
F	8 - 1 = 7	8 - 4 = 4	10 - 4 = 6	10 - 7 = 3
G	8 - 2 = 6	6 - 3 = 3	7 - 5 = 2	10 - 3 = 7
H	10 - 8 = 2	8 - 3 = 5	7 - 3 = 4	10 - 7 = 3
I	8 - 5 = 3	8 - 0 = 8	10 - 2 = 8	8 - 3 = 5
J	10 - 5 = 5	8 - 5 = 3	10 - 7 = 3	10 - 2 = 8
K	10 - 9 = 1	10 - 6 = 4	7 - 3 = 4	10 - 7 = 3
L	8 - 3 = 5	6 - 5 = 1	7 - 6 = 1	8 - 4 = 4
M	10 - 4 = 6	7 - 2 = 5	10 - 5 = 5	8 - 6 = 2
N	10 - 3 = 7	10 - 4 = 6	8 - 2 = 6	10 - 3 = 7
O	6 - 3 = 3	8 - 1 = 7	10 - 6 = 4	7 - 1 = 6
P	10 - 8 = 2	10 - 4 = 6	10 - 7 = 3	7 - 5 = 2
Q	8 - 4 = 4	7 - 3 = 4	7 - 2 = 5	10 - 9 = 1

859

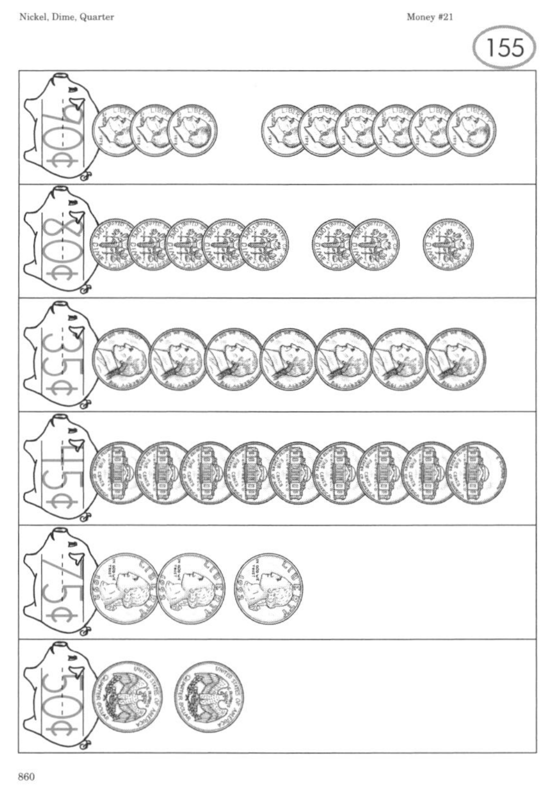

Place Value #4

155

136 has 1 hundreds	213 has 2 hundreds
241 has 1 ones	158 has 1 hundreds
94 has 9 tens	62 has 2 ones
73 has 3 ones	205 has 0 tens
182 has 8 tens	224 has 2 hundreds
45 has 4 tens	192 has 9 tens
231 has 2 hundreds	206 has 6 ones
117 has 7 ones	181 has 1 hundreds
220 has 2 hundreds	238 has 8 ones
179 has 9 ones	49 has 4 tens
57 has 5 tens	160 has 1 hundreds

861

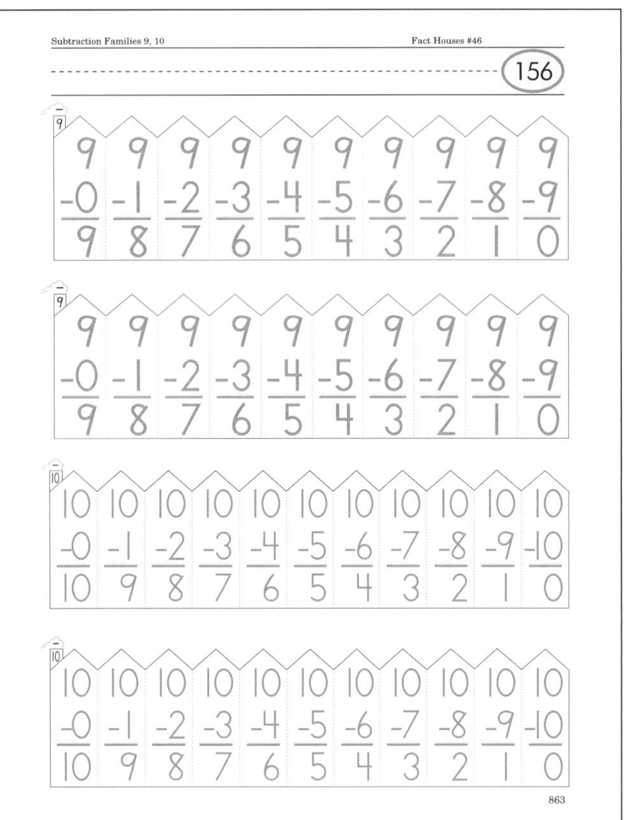
Subtraction Families 9, 10 Fact Houses #46

156

9	9	9	9	9	9	9	9	9	9	
-0	-1	-2	-3	-4	-5	-6	-7	-8	-9	
9	8	7	6	5	4	3	2	1	0	
9	9	9	9	9	9	9	9	9	9	
-0	-1	-2	-3	-4	-5	-6	-7	-8	-9	
9	8	7	6	5	4	3	2	1	0	
10	10	10	10	10	10	10	10	10	10	10
-0	-1	-2	-3	-4	-5	-6	-7	-8	-9	-10
10	9	8	7	6	5	4	3	2	1	0
10	10	10	10	10	10	10	10	10	10	10
-0	-1	-2	-3	-4	-5	-6	-7	-8	-9	-10
10	9	8	7	6	5	4	3	2	1	0

863

Hour, Half Hour Clocks #9

156

1:30 10:00 8:00 4:30

12:30 12:00 10:30 5:00

11:30 3:30 7:00 5:30

4:00 9:00 8:30 6:00

864

8–10 [+] Number Facts #59

156

A	2+8=10	3+6=9	1+7=8	1+9=10
B	3+7=10	7+3=10	5+5=10	3+6=9
C	6+2=8	3+7=10	6+3=9	5+5=10
D	8+1=9	6+3=9	6+4=10	4+4=8
E	2+6=8	8+2=10	2+8=10	3+7=10
F	7+2=9	4+5=9	1+8=9	2+7=9
G	6+4=10	3+5=8	4+6=10	6+4=10
H	3+6=9	6+4=10	6+3=9	2+8=10
I	5+5=10	3+7=10	7+3=10	4+5=9
J	5+4=9	2+7=9	5+3=8	4+4=8
K	3+7=10	8+2=10	6+4=10	3+6=9
L	5+5=10	3+6=9	5+4=9	7+3=10
M	7+3=10	4+5=9	7+2=9	4+5=9
N	2+7=9	4+6=10	5+3=8	6+2=8
O	6+4=10	2+8=10	4+5=9	6+3=9
P	3+5=8	2+7=9	7+3=10	8+2=10
Q	1+9=10	2+8=10	5+4=9	2+7=9

865

6–8, 10 [-] Number Facts #58

156

A	8-6=2	10-4=6	7-4=3	10-2=8
B	6-2=4	10-2=8	10-5=5	8-5=3
C	10-3=7	7-4=3	8-5=3	10-6=4
D	7-4=3	10-6=4	6-1=5	8-7=1
E	10-5=5	10-8=2	10-3=7	7-2=5
F	8-1=7	8-4=4	10-4=6	10-7=3
G	8-2=6	6-3=3	7-5=2	10-3=7
H	10-8=2	8-3=5	7-3=4	10-7=3
I	8-5=3	8-0=8	10-2=8	8-3=5
J	10-5=5	8-5=3	10-7=3	10-2=8
K	10-9=1	10-6=4	7-3=4	10-7=3
L	8-3=5	6-5=1	7-6=1	8-4=4
M	10-4=6	7-2=5	10-5=5	8-6=2
N	10-3=7	10-4=6	8-2=6	10-3=7
O	6-3=3	8-1=7	10-6=4	7-1=6
P	10-8=2	10-4=6	10-7=3	7-5=2
Q	8-4=4	7-3=4	7-2=5	10-9=1

866

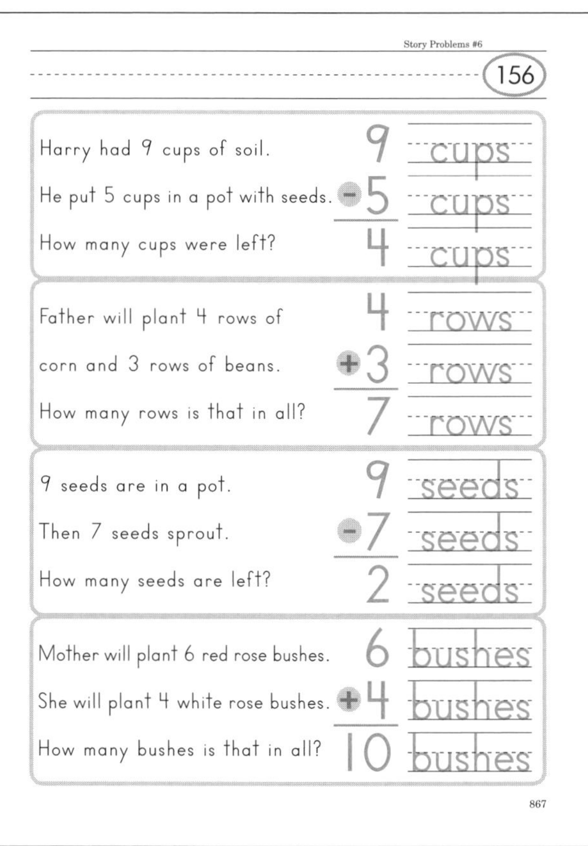

Story Problems #6

156

Harry had 9 cups of soil.	9	cups
He put 5 cups in a pot with seeds.	− 5	cups
How many cups were left?	4	cups

Father will plant 4 rows of	4	rows
corn and 3 rows of beans.	+ 3	rows
How many rows is that in all?	7	rows

9 seeds are in a pot.	9	seeds
Then 7 seeds sprout.	− 7	seeds
How many seeds are left?	2	seeds

Mother will plant 6 red rose bushes.	6	bushes
She will plant 4 white rose bushes.	+ 4	bushes
How many bushes is that in all?	10	bushes

867

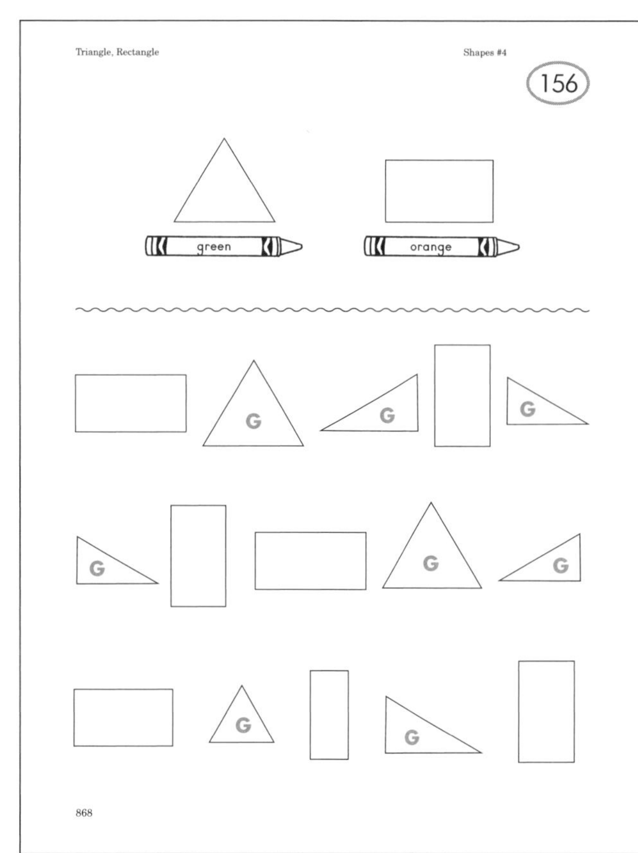

Triangle, Rectangle

Shapes #4

156

868

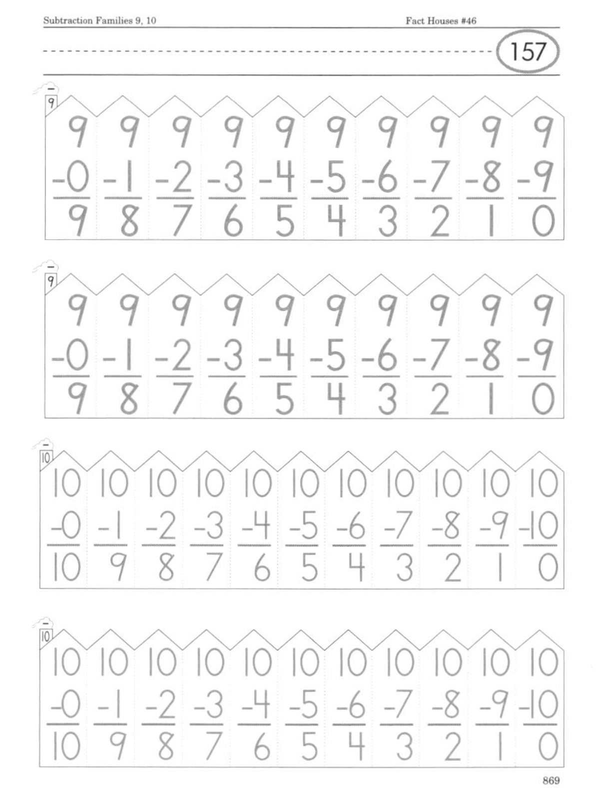

Subtraction Families 9, 10

Fact Houses #46

157

9	9	9	9	9	9	9	9	9	9
-0	-1	-2	-3	-4	-5	-6	-7	-8	-9
9	8	7	6	5	4	3	2	1	0

9	9	9	9	9	9	9	9	9	9
-0	-1	-2	-3	-4	-5	-6	-7	-8	-9
9	8	7	6	5	4	3	2	1	0

10	10	10	10	10	10	10	10	10	10	10
-0	-1	-2	-3	-4	-5	-6	-7	-8	-9	-10
10	9	8	7	6	5	4	3	2	1	0

10	10	10	10	10	10	10	10	10	10	10
-0	-1	-2	-3	-4	-5	-6	-7	-8	-9	-10
10	9	8	7	6	5	4	3	2	1	0

869

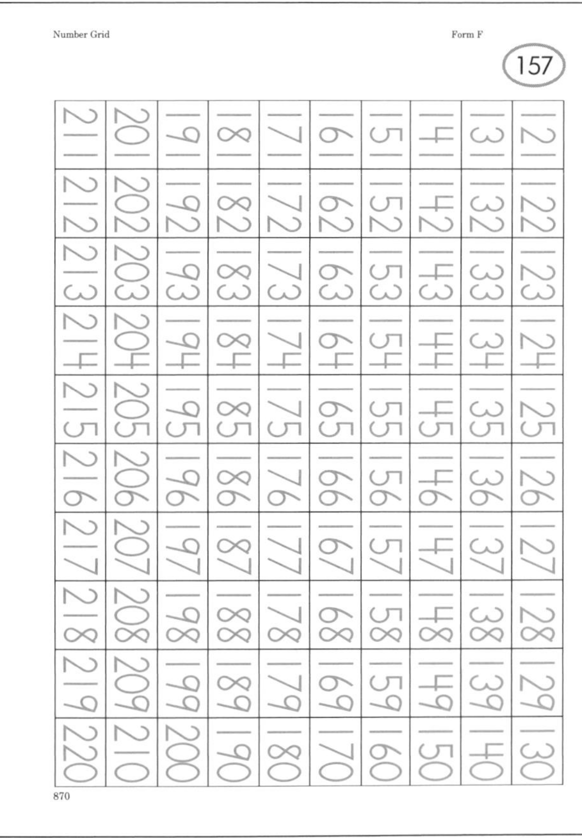

Number Grid

Form F

157

121	122	123	124	125	126	127	128	129	130
131	132	133	134	135	136	137	138	139	140
141	142	143	144	145	146	147	148	149	150
151	152	153	154	155	156	157	158	159	160
161	162	163	164	165	166	167	168	169	170
171	172	173	174	175	176	177	178	179	180
181	182	183	184	185	186	187	188	189	190
191	192	193	194	195	196	197	198	199	200
201	202	203	204	205	206	207	208	209	210
211	212	213	214	215	216	217	218	219	220

870

6–8, 10 [-] Number Facts #58

157

A	8 - 6 = 2	10 - 4 = 6	7 - 4 = 3	10 - 2 = 8
B	6 - 2 = 4	10 - 2 = 8	10 - 5 = 5	8 - 5 = 3
C	10 - 3 = 7	7 - 4 = 3	8 - 5 = 3	10 - 6 = 4
D	7 - 4 = 3	10 - 6 = 4	6 - 1 = 5	8 - 7 = 1
E	10 - 5 = 5	10 - 8 = 2	10 - 3 = 7	7 - 2 = 5
F	8 - 1 = 7	8 - 4 = 4	10 - 4 = 6	10 - 7 = 3
G	8 - 2 = 6	6 - 3 = 3	7 - 5 = 2	10 - 3 = 7
H	10 - 8 = 2	8 - 3 = 5	7 - 3 = 4	10 - 7 = 3
I	8 - 5 = 3	8 - 0 = 8	10 - 2 = 8	8 - 3 = 5
J	10 - 5 = 5	8 - 5 = 3	10 - 7 = 3	10 - 2 = 8
K	10 - 9 = 1	10 - 6 = 4	7 - 3 = 4	10 - 7 = 3
L	8 - 3 = 5	6 - 5 = 1	7 - 6 = 1	8 - 4 = 4
M	10 - 4 = 6	7 - 2 = 5	10 - 5 = 5	8 - 6 = 2
N	10 - 3 = 7	10 - 4 = 6	8 - 2 = 6	10 - 3 = 7
O	6 - 3 = 3	8 - 1 = 7	10 - 6 = 4	7 - 1 = 6
P	10 - 8 = 2	10 - 4 = 6	10 - 7 = 3	7 - 5 = 2
Q	8 - 4 = 4	7 - 3 = 4	7 - 2 = 5	10 - 9 = 1

871

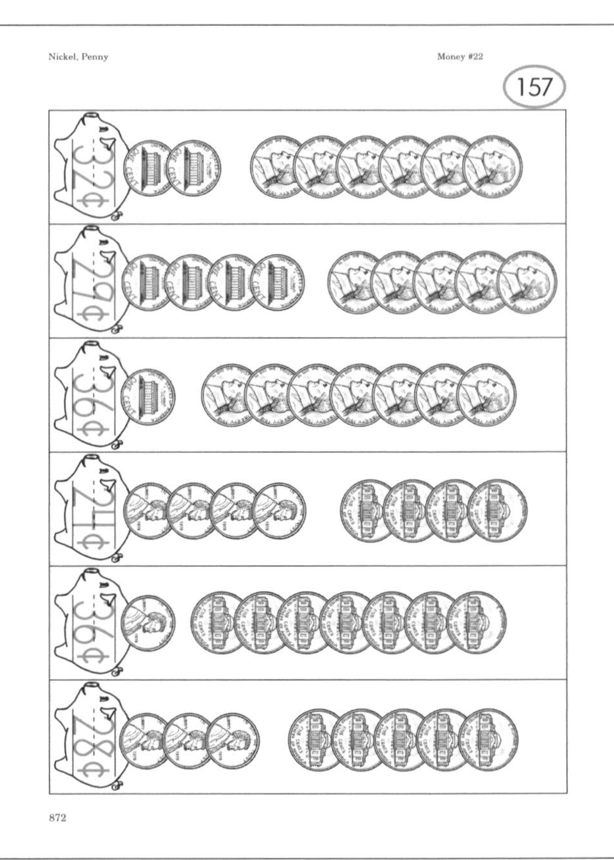
Nickel, Penny Money #22

157

32¢

29¢

36¢

21¢

36¢

28¢

872

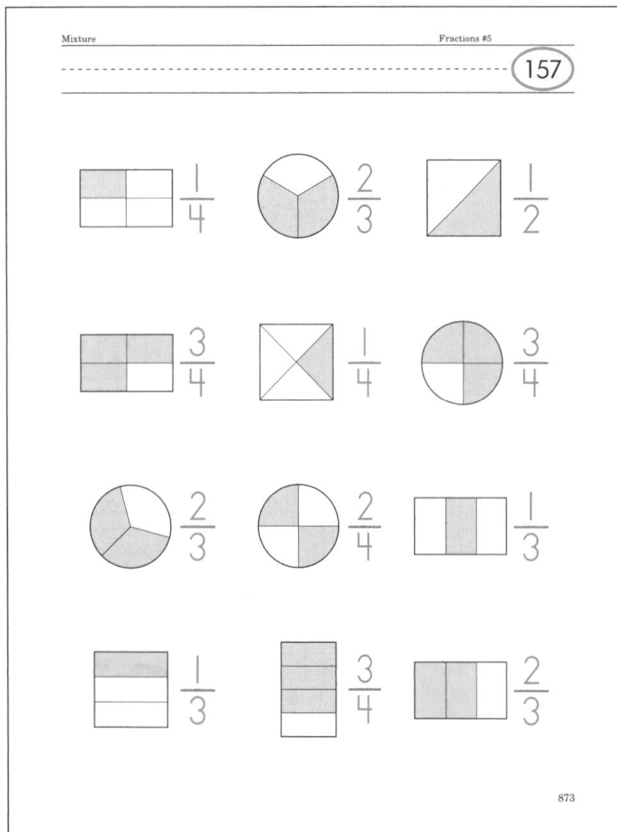
Mixture Fractions #5

157

1/4 2/3 1/2

3/4 1/4 3/4

2/3 2/4 1/3

1/3 3/4 2/3

873

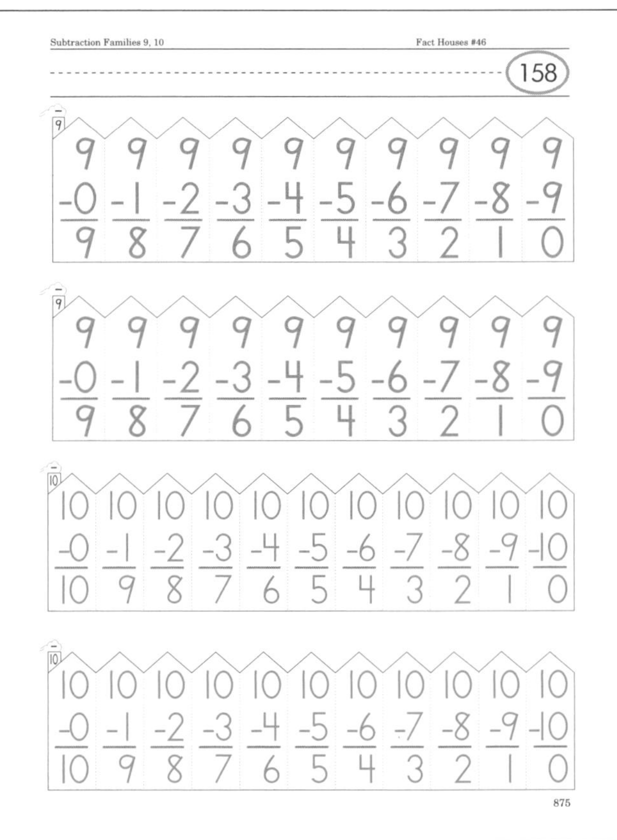
Subtraction Families 9, 10 Fact Houses #46

158

9 - 0 = 9, 9 - 1 = 8, 9 - 2 = 7, 9 - 3 = 6, 9 - 4 = 5, 9 - 5 = 4, 9 - 6 = 3, 9 - 7 = 2, 9 - 8 = 1, 9 - 9 = 0

9 - 0 = 9, 9 - 1 = 8, 9 - 2 = 7, 9 - 3 = 6, 9 - 4 = 5, 9 - 5 = 4, 9 - 6 = 3, 9 - 7 = 2, 9 - 8 = 1, 9 - 9 = 0

10 - 0 = 10, 10 - 1 = 9, 10 - 2 = 8, 10 - 3 = 7, 10 - 4 = 6, 10 - 5 = 5, 10 - 6 = 4, 10 - 7 = 3, 10 - 8 = 2, 10 - 9 = 1, 10 - 10 = 0

10 - 0 = 10, 10 - 1 = 9, 10 - 2 = 8, 10 - 3 = 7, 10 - 4 = 6, 10 - 5 = 5, 10 - 6 = 4, 10 - 7 = 3, 10 - 8 = 2, 10 - 9 = 1, 10 - 10 = 0

875

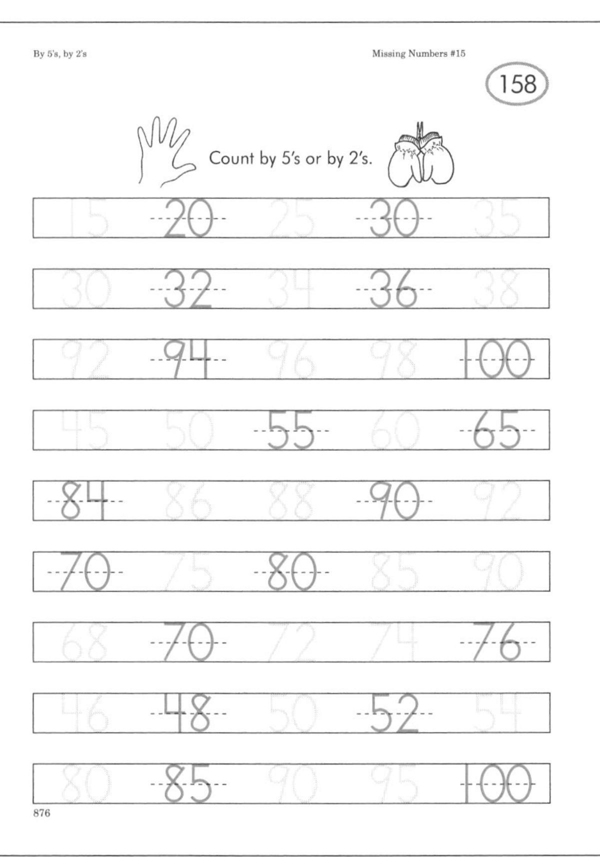

9, 10 [-] Number Facts #60

158

A	10 -9 = 1	10 -2 = 8	9 -6 = 3	9 -5 = 4	10 -8 = 2	10 -4 = 6	10 -5 = 5	9 -2 = 7	9 -6 = 3	9 -5 = 4	10 -1 = 9	10 -6 = 4
B	9 -4 = 5	10 -3 = 7	10 -6 = 4	10 -2 = 8	9 -5 = 4	9 -7 = 2	10 -8 = 2	9 -4 = 5	10 -4 = 6	10 -6 = 4	9 -5 = 4	10 -7 = 3
C	10 -2 = 8	10 -4 = 6	10 -3 = 7	9 -3 = 6	9 -6 = 3	10 -6 = 4	10 -8 = 2	9 -2 = 7	10 -3 = 7	10 -7 = 3	9 -6 = 3	9 -3 = 6
D	10 -6 = 4	9 -7 = 2	10 -4 = 6	9 -7 = 2	10 -5 = 5	9 -6 = 3	10 -7 = 3	10 -5 = 5	9 -6 = 3	9 -3 = 6	10 -4 = 6	9 -4 = 5
E	10 -2 = 8	10 -8 = 2	10 -3 = 7	10 -6 = 4	10 -7 = 3	9 -1 = 8	9 -3 = 6	10 -8 = 2	10 -2 = 8	10 -3 = 7	9 -2 = 7	10 -8 = 2
F	9 -4 = 5	10 -5 = 5	10 -7 = 3	10 -3 = 7	10 -2 = 8	10 -6 = 4	9 -5 = 4	10 -2 = 8	10 -4 = 6	9 -4 = 5	10 -5 = 5	9 -5 = 4
G	10 -6 = 4	9 -1 = 8	9 -2 = 7	10 -4 = 6	10 -3 = 7	9 -2 = 7	10 -1 = 9	10 -7 = 3	10 -8 = 2	9 -7 = 2	10 -4 = 6	10 -3 = 7

877

8–10 [+] Number Facts #59

158

A	2+8=10	3+6=9	1+7=8	1+9=10
B	3+7=10	7+3=10	5+5=10	3+6=9
C	6+2=8	3+7=10	6+3=9	5+5=10
D	8+1=9	6+3=9	6+4=10	4+4=8
E	2+6=8	8+2=10	2+8=10	3+7=10
F	7+2=9	4+5=9	1+8=9	2+7=9
G	6+4=10	3+5=8	4+6=10	6+4=10
H	3+6=9	6+4=10	6+3=9	2+8=10
I	5+5=10	3+7=10	7+3=10	4+5=9
J	5+4=9	2+7=9	5+3=8	4+4=8
K	3+7=10	8+2=10	6+4=10	3+6=9
L	5+5=10	3+6=9	5+4=9	7+3=10
M	7+3=10	4+5=9	7+2=9	4+5=9
N	2+7=9	4+6=10	5+3=8	6+2=8
O	6+4=10	2+8=10	4+5=9	6+3=9
P	3+5=8	2+7=9	7+3=10	8+2=10
Q	1+9=10	2+8=10	5+4=9	2+7=9

878

Place Value #5

158

232 has 2 hundreds	241 has 4 tens
138 has 8 ones	127 has 1 hundreds
214 has 1 tens	143 has 3 ones
150 has 1 hundreds	209 has 0 tens
96 has 6 ones	65 has 6 tens
172 has 7 tens	181 has 1 hundreds
73 has 3 ones	84 has 4 ones
197 has 1 hundreds	168 has 1 hundreds
51 has 5 tens	102 has 2 ones
215 has 2 hundreds	246 has 2 hundreds
139 has 9 ones	120 has 2 tens

879

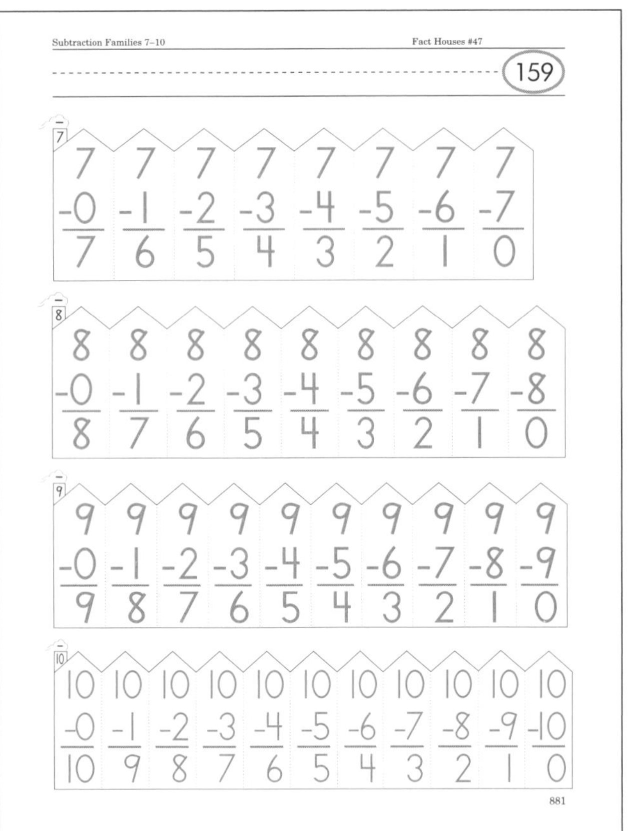
Subtraction Families 7–10 Fact Houses #47

159

7	7	7	7	7	7	7	7
-0	-1	-2	-3	-4	-5	-6	-7
7	6	5	4	3	2	1	0

8	8	8	8	8	8	8	8	8
-0	-1	-2	-3	-4	-5	-6	-7	-8
8	7	6	5	4	3	2	1	0

9	9	9	9	9	9	9	9	9	9
-0	-1	-2	-3	-4	-5	-6	-7	-8	-9
9	8	7	6	5	4	3	2	1	0

10	10	10	10	10	10	10	10	10	10	10
-0	-1	-2	-3	-4	-5	-6	-7	-8	-9	-10
10	9	8	7	6	5	4	3	2	1	0

881

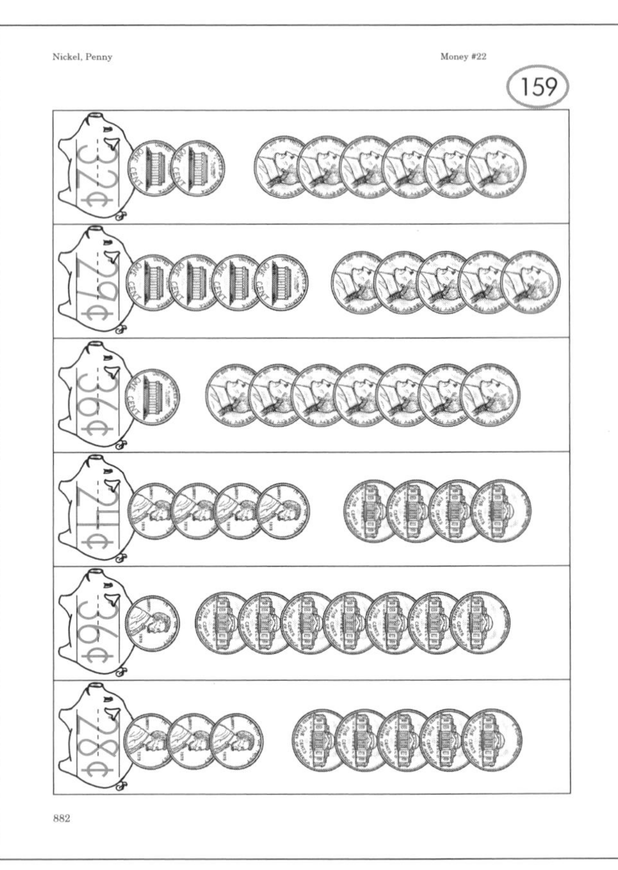

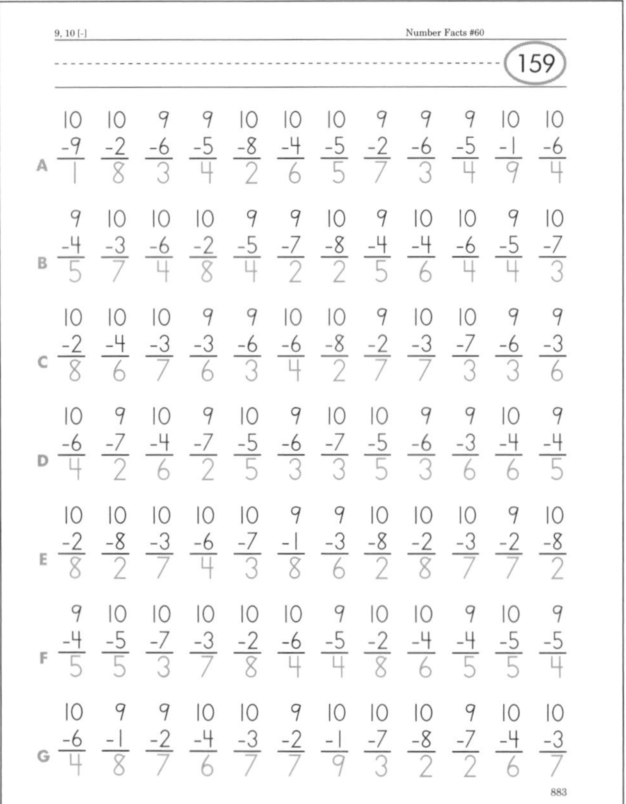
9, 10 [-] Number Facts #60

159

A	10 -9 = 1	10 -2 = 8	9 -6 = 3	9 -5 = 4	10 -8 = 2	10 -4 = 6	10 -5 = 5	9 -2 = 7	9 -6 = 3	9 -5 = 4	10 -1 = 9	10 -6 = 4
B	9 -4 = 5	10 -3 = 7	10 -6 = 4	10 -2 = 8	9 -5 = 4	9 -7 = 2	10 -8 = 2	9 -4 = 5	10 -4 = 6	10 -6 = 4	9 -5 = 4	10 -7 = 3
C	10 -2 = 8	10 -4 = 6	10 -3 = 7	9 -3 = 6	9 -6 = 3	10 -6 = 4	10 -8 = 2	9 -2 = 7	10 -3 = 7	10 -7 = 3	9 -6 = 3	9 -3 = 6
D	10 -6 = 4	9 -7 = 2	10 -4 = 6	9 -7 = 2	10 -5 = 5	9 -6 = 3	10 -7 = 3	10 -5 = 5	9 -6 = 3	9 -3 = 6	10 -4 = 6	9 -4 = 5
E	10 -2 = 8	10 -8 = 2	10 -3 = 7	10 -6 = 4	10 -7 = 3	9 -1 = 8	9 -3 = 6	10 -8 = 2	10 -2 = 8	10 -3 = 7	9 -2 = 7	10 -8 = 2
F	9 -4 = 5	10 -5 = 5	10 -7 = 3	10 -3 = 7	10 -2 = 8	10 -6 = 4	9 -5 = 4	10 -2 = 8	10 -4 = 6	9 -4 = 5	10 -5 = 5	9 -5 = 4
G	10 -6 = 4	9 -1 = 8	9 -2 = 7	10 -4 = 6	10 -3 = 7	9 -2 = 7	10 -1 = 9	10 -7 = 3	10 -8 = 2	9 -7 = 2	10 -4 = 6	10 -3 = 7

883

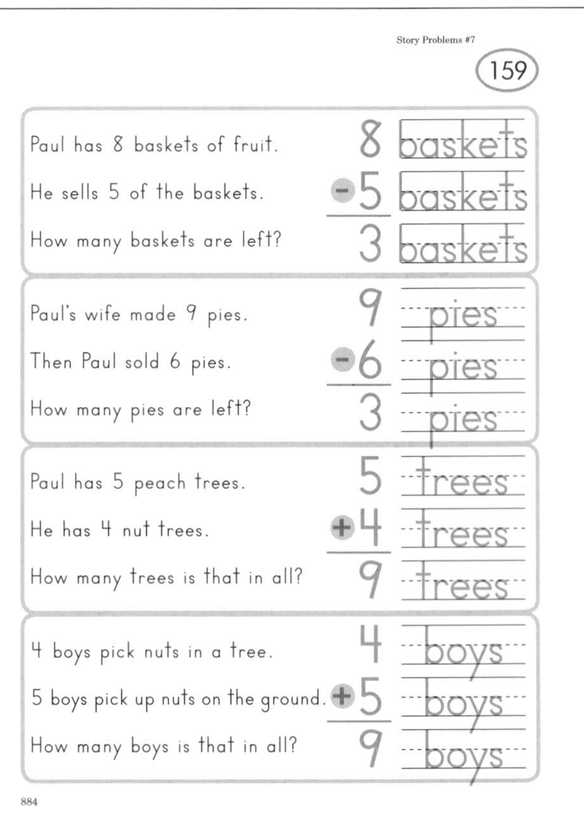
Story Problems #7

159

Paul has 8 baskets of fruit. 8 baskets
He sells 5 of the baskets. - 5 baskets
How many baskets are left? 3 baskets

Paul's wife made 9 pies. 9 pies
Then Paul sold 6 pies. - 6 pies
How many pies are left? 3 pies

Paul has 5 peach trees. 5 trees
He has 4 nut trees. + 4 trees
How many trees is that in all? 9 trees

4 boys pick nuts in a tree. 4 boys
5 boys pick up nuts on the ground. + 5 boys
How many boys is that in all? 9 boys

884

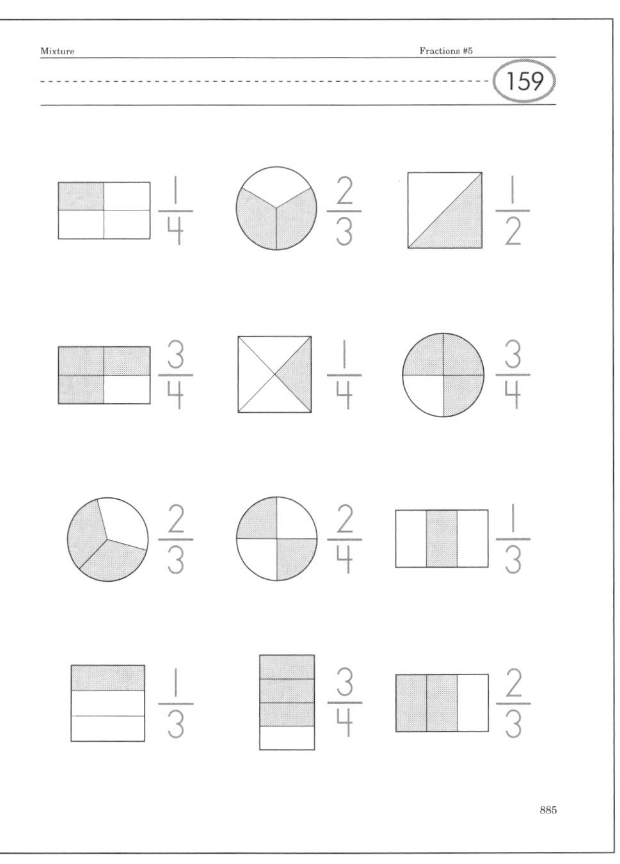
Mixture
Fractions #5
159
1/4
2/3
1/2
3/4
1/4
3/4
2/3
2/4
1/3
1/3
3/4
2/3
885

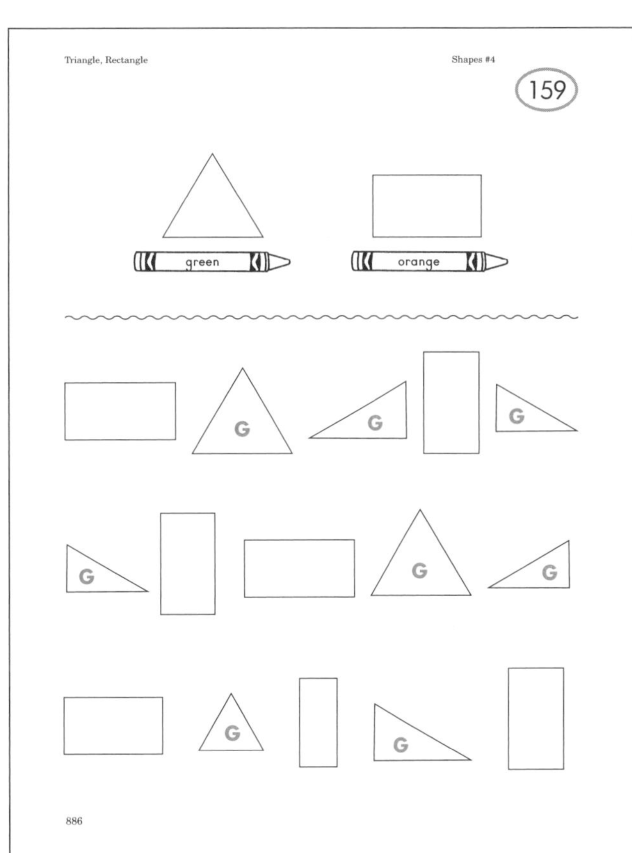
Triangle, Rectangle
Shapes #4
159
green
orange
G
886

Flash Card Drill
Form C
160
Individual answers
(See page 365
for instructions.)
887

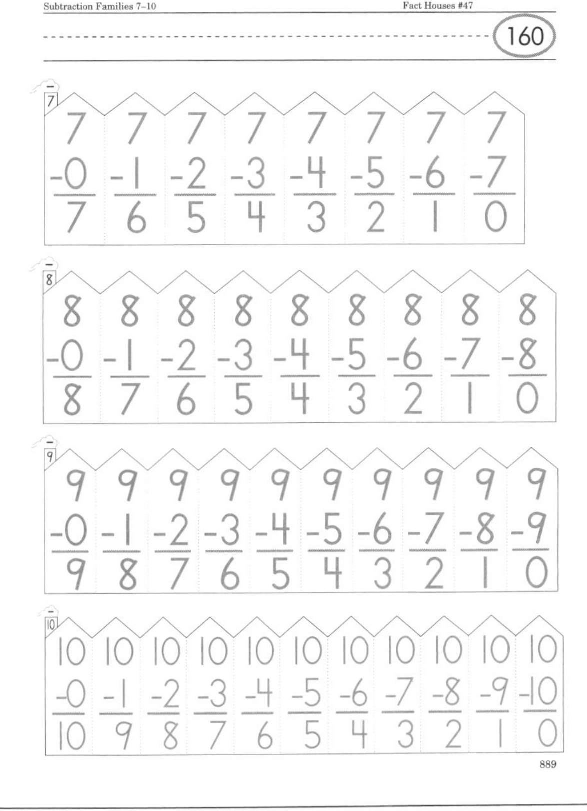
Subtraction Families 7–10
Fact Houses #47
160
7 -0 7; 7 -1 6; 7 -2 5; 7 -3 4; 7 -4 3; 7 -5 2; 7 -6 1; 7 -7 0
8 -0 8; 8 -1 7; 8 -2 6; 8 -3 5; 8 -4 4; 8 -5 3; 8 -6 2; 8 -7 1; 8 -8 0
9 -0 9; 9 -1 8; 9 -2 7; 9 -3 6; 9 -4 5; 9 -5 4; 9 -6 3; 9 -7 2; 9 -8 1; 9 -9 0
10 -0 10; 10 -1 9; 10 -2 8; 10 -3 7; 10 -4 6; 10 -5 5; 10 -6 4; 10 -7 3; 10 -8 2; 10 -9 1; 10 -10 0
889

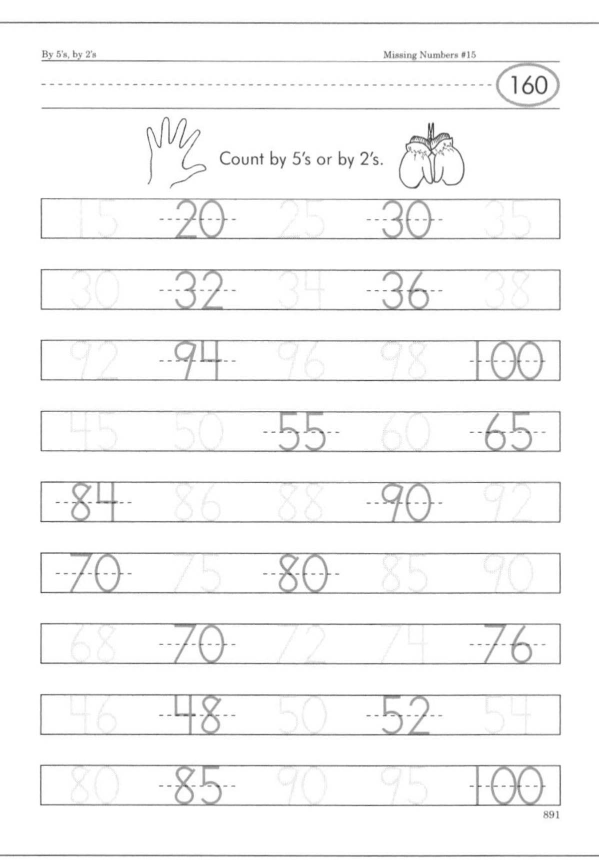

9, 10 [-]

Number Facts #60

160

A	10 -9 1	10 -2 8	9 -6 3	9 -5 4	10 -8 2	10 -4 6	10 -5 5	9 -2 7	9 -6 3	9 -5 4	10 -1 9	10 -6 4
B	9 -4 5	10 -3 7	10 -6 4	10 -2 8	9 -5 4	9 -7 2	10 -8 2	9 -4 5	10 -4 6	10 -6 4	9 -5 4	10 -7 3
C	10 -2 8	10 -4 6	10 -3 7	9 -3 6	9 -6 3	10 -6 4	10 -8 2	9 -2 7	10 -3 7	10 -7 3	9 -6 3	9 -3 6
D	10 -6 4	9 -7 2	10 -4 6	9 -7 2	10 -5 5	9 -6 3	10 -7 3	10 -5 5	9 -6 3	9 -3 6	10 -4 6	9 -4 5
E	10 -2 8	10 -8 2	10 -3 7	10 -6 4	10 -7 3	9 -1 8	9 -3 6	10 -8 2	10 -2 8	10 -3 7	9 -2 7	10 -8 2
F	9 -4 5	10 -5 5	10 -7 3	10 -3 7	10 -2 8	10 -6 4	9 -5 4	10 -2 8	10 -4 6	9 -4 5	10 -5 5	9 -5 4
G	10 -6 4	9 -1 8	9 -2 7	10 -4 6	10 -3 7	9 -2 7	10 -1 9	10 -7 3	10 -8 2	9 -7 2	10 -4 6	10 -3 7

892

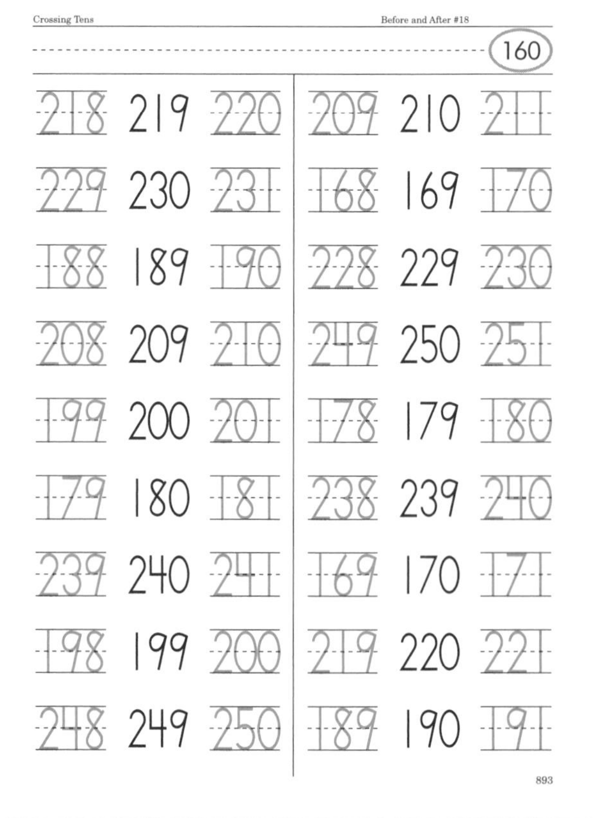

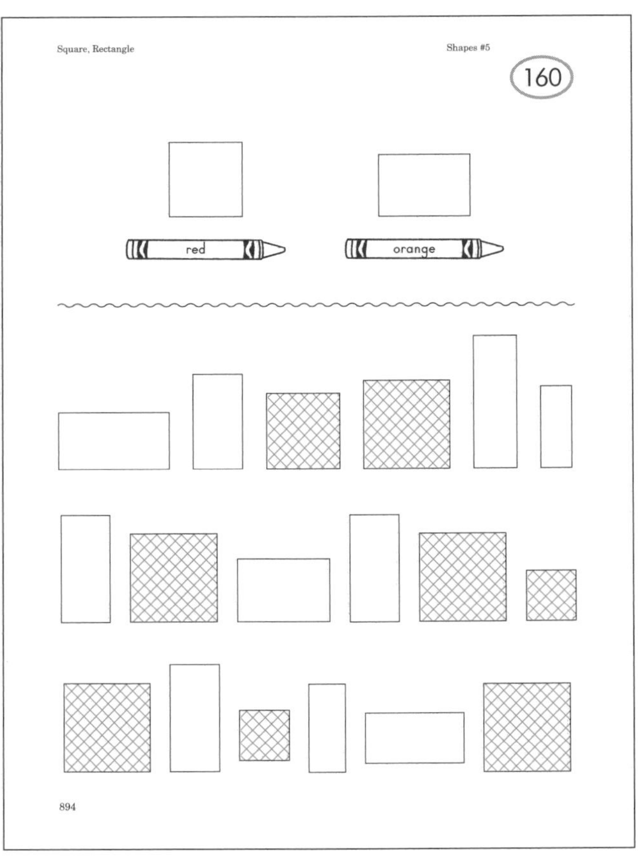
Square, Rectangle
Shapes #5
160
red
orange
894

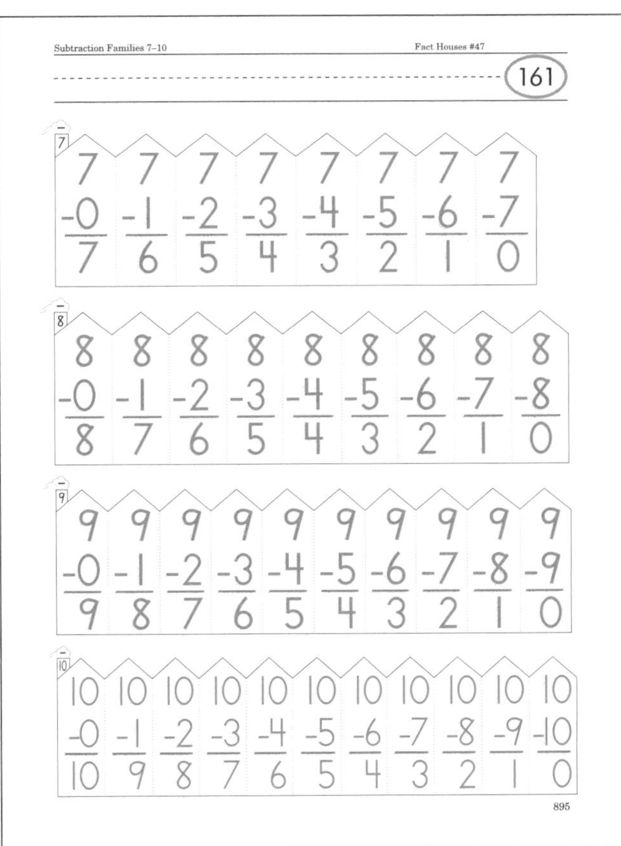
Subtraction Families 7–10
Fact Houses #47
161
895

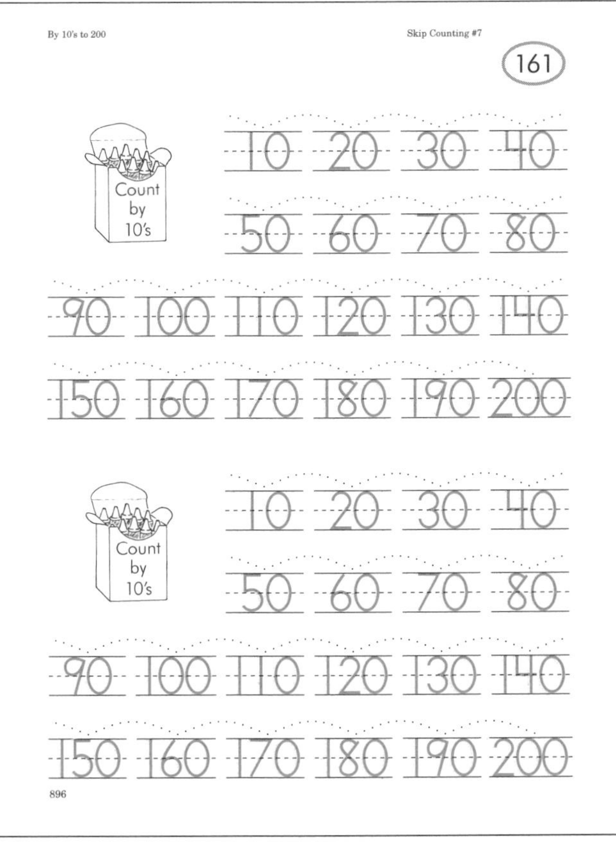
By 10's to 200
Skip Counting #7
161
Count by 10's
10 20 30 40
50 60 70 80
90 100 110 120 130 140
150 160 170 180 190 200
Count by 10's
10 20 30 40
50 60 70 80
90 100 110 120 130 140
150 160 170 180 190 200
896

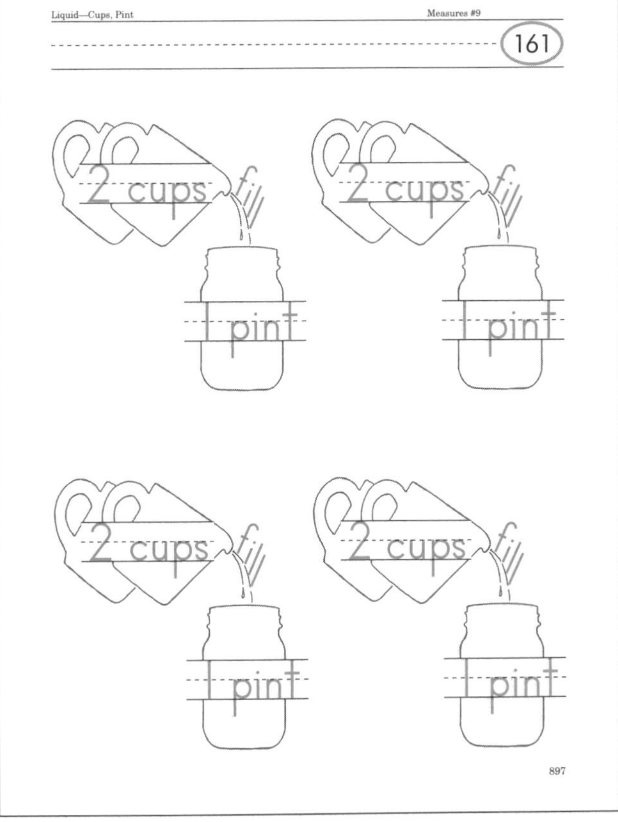
Liquid—Cups, Pint
Measures #9
161
2 cups
fill
1 pint
2 cups
fill
1 pint
2 cups
fill
1 pint
2 cups
fill
1 pint
897

8–10 [+] Number Facts #59

161

A	2+8=10	3+6=9	1+7=8	1+9=10
B	3+7=10	7+3=10	5+5=10	3+6=9
C	6+2=8	3+7=10	6+3=9	5+5=10
D	8+1=9	6+3=9	6+4=10	4+4=8
E	2+6=8	8+2=10	2+8=10	3+7=10
F	7+2=9	4+5=9	1+8=9	2+7=9
G	6+4=10	3+5=8	4+6=10	6+4=10
H	3+6=9	6+4=10	6+3=9	2+8=10
I	5+5=10	3+7=10	7+3=10	4+5=9
J	5+4=9	2+7=9	5+3=8	4+4=8
K	3+7=10	8+2=10	6+4=10	3+6=9
L	5+5=10	3+6=9	5+4=9	7+3=10
M	7+3=10	4+5=9	7+2=9	4+5=9
N	2+7=9	4+6=10	5+3=8	6+2=8
O	6+4=10	2+8=10	4+5=9	6+3=9
P	3+5=8	2+7=9	7+3=10	8+2=10
Q	1+9=10	2+8=10	5+4=9	2+7=9

898

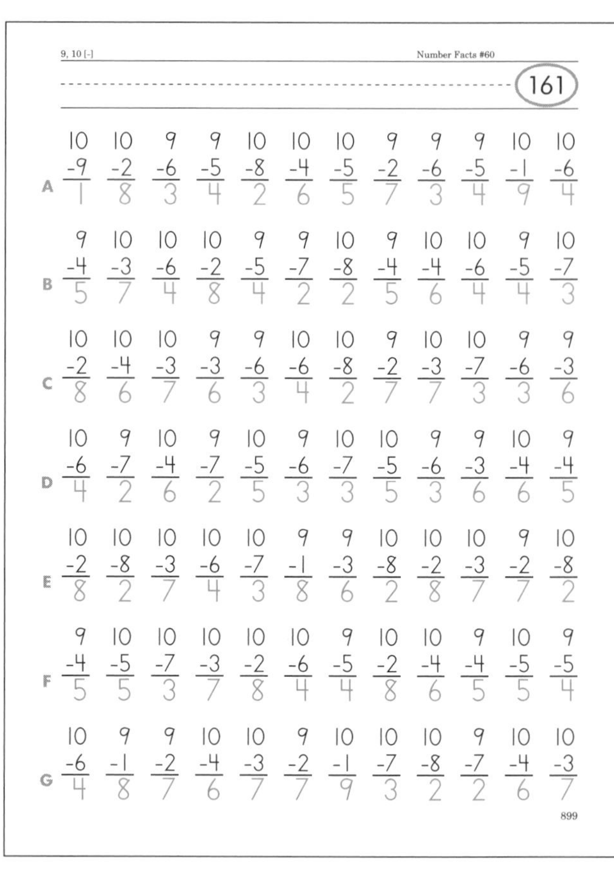
9, 10 [-] Number Facts #60

161

A	10 -9 1	10 -2 8	9 -6 3	9 -5 4	10 -8 2	10 -4 6	10 -5 5	9 -2 7	9 -6 3	9 -5 4	10 -1 9	10 -6 4
B	9 -4 5	10 -3 7	10 -6 4	10 -2 8	9 -5 4	9 -7 2	10 -8 2	9 -4 5	10 -4 6	10 -6 4	9 -5 4	10 -7 3
C	10 -2 8	10 -4 6	10 -3 7	9 -3 6	9 -6 3	10 -6 4	10 -8 2	9 -2 7	10 -3 7	10 -7 3	9 -6 3	9 -3 6
D	10 -6 4	9 -7 2	10 -4 6	9 -7 2	10 -5 5	9 -6 3	10 -7 3	10 -5 5	9 -6 3	9 -3 6	10 -4 6	9 -4 5
E	10 -2 8	10 -8 2	10 -3 7	10 -6 4	10 -7 3	9 -1 8	9 -3 6	10 -8 2	10 -2 8	10 -3 7	9 -2 7	10 -8 2
F	9 -4 5	10 -5 5	10 -7 3	10 -3 7	10 -2 8	10 -6 4	9 -5 4	10 -2 8	10 -4 6	9 -4 5	10 -5 5	9 -5 4
G	10 -6 4	9 -1 8	9 -2 7	10 -4 6	10 -3 7	9 -2 7	10 -1 9	10 -7 3	10 -8 2	9 -7 2	10 -4 6	10 -3 7

899

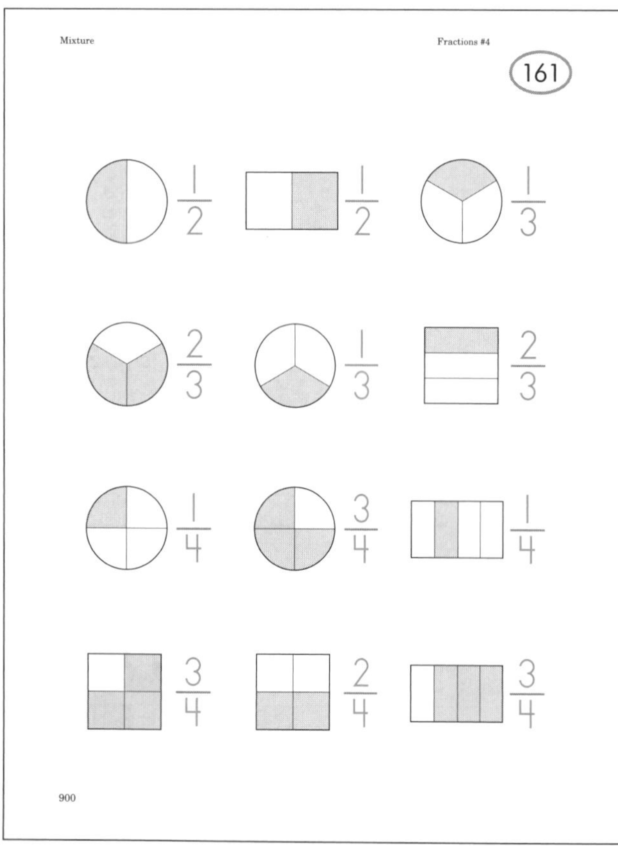
Mixture Fractions #4

161

900

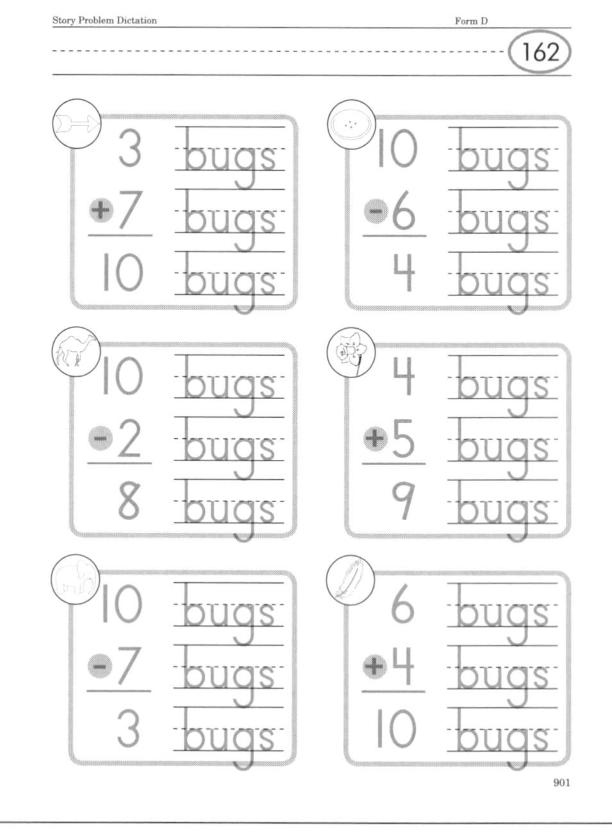
Story Problem Dictation Form D

162

901

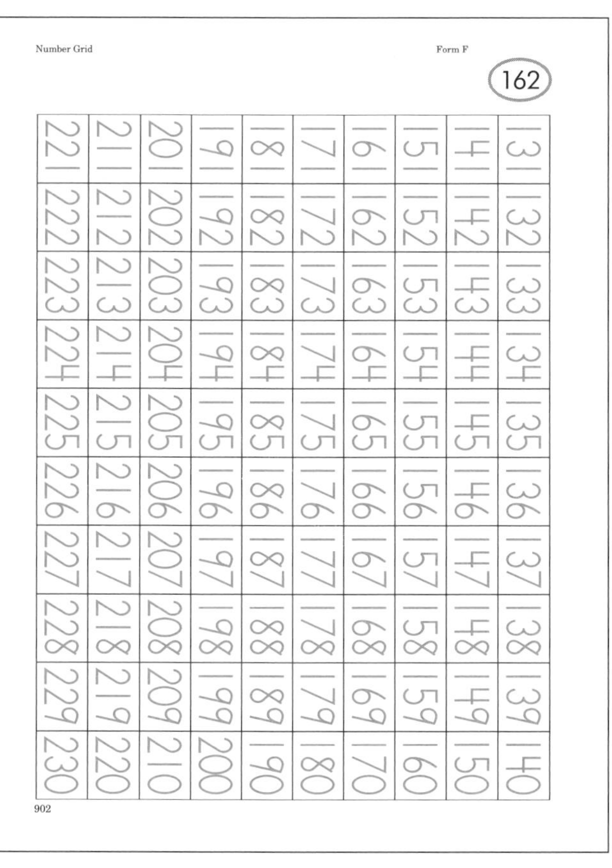
Number Grid Form F

162

131	132	133	134	135	136	137	138	139	140
141	142	143	144	145	146	147	148	149	150
151	152	153	154	155	156	157	158	159	160
161	162	163	164	165	166	167	168	169	170
171	172	173	174	175	176	177	178	179	180
181	182	183	184	185	186	187	188	189	190
191	192	193	194	195	196	197	198	199	200
201	202	203	204	205	206	207	208	209	210
211	212	213	214	215	216	217	218	219	220
221	222	223	224	225	226	227	228	229	230

902

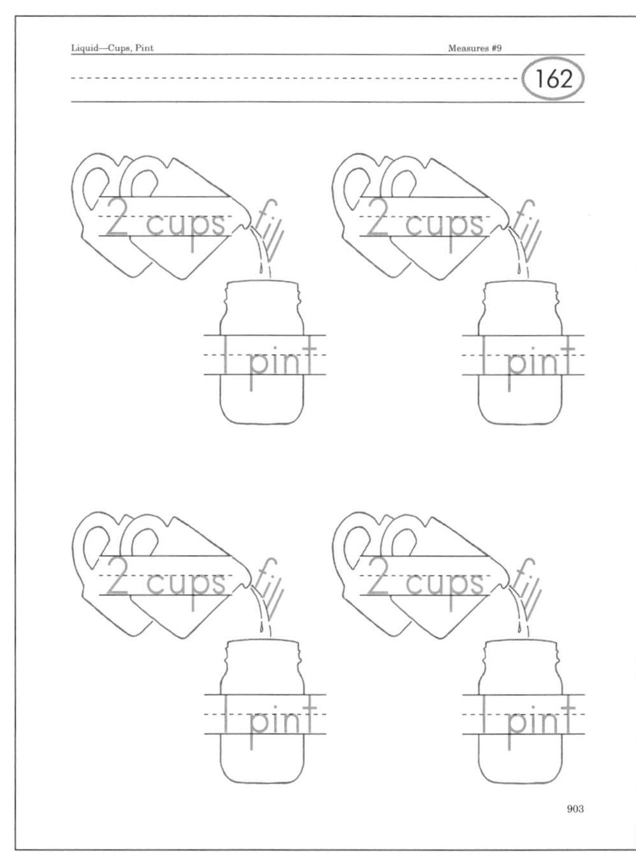
Liquid—Cups, Pint Measures #9

162

903

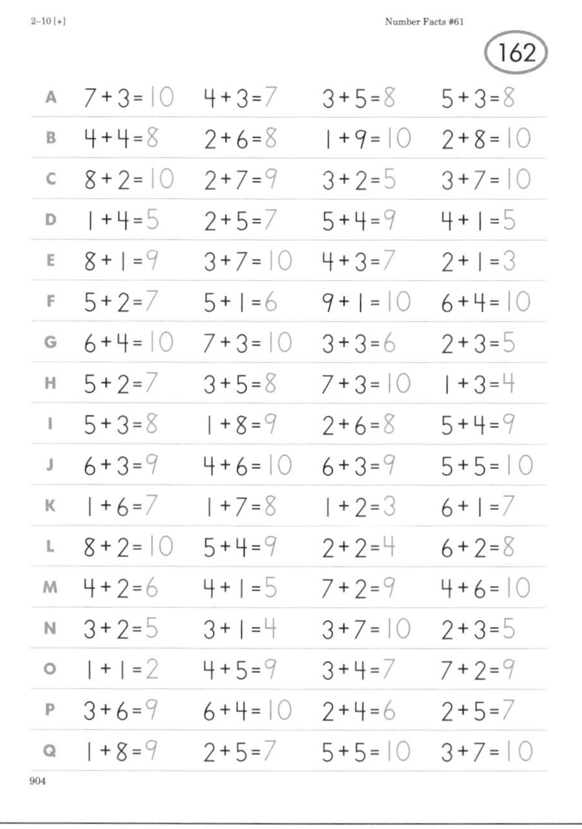
2–10 [+] Number Facts #61

162

A	7 + 3 = 10	4 + 3 = 7	3 + 5 = 8	5 + 3 = 8
B	4 + 4 = 8	2 + 6 = 8	1 + 9 = 10	2 + 8 = 10
C	8 + 2 = 10	2 + 7 = 9	3 + 2 = 5	3 + 7 = 10
D	1 + 4 = 5	2 + 5 = 7	5 + 4 = 9	4 + 1 = 5
E	8 + 1 = 9	3 + 7 = 10	4 + 3 = 7	2 + 1 = 3
F	5 + 2 = 7	5 + 1 = 6	9 + 1 = 10	6 + 4 = 10
G	6 + 4 = 10	7 + 3 = 10	3 + 3 = 6	2 + 3 = 5
H	5 + 2 = 7	3 + 5 = 8	7 + 3 = 10	1 + 3 = 4
I	5 + 3 = 8	1 + 8 = 9	2 + 6 = 8	5 + 4 = 9
J	6 + 3 = 9	4 + 6 = 10	6 + 3 = 9	5 + 5 = 10
K	1 + 6 = 7	1 + 7 = 8	1 + 2 = 3	6 + 1 = 7
L	8 + 2 = 10	5 + 4 = 9	2 + 2 = 4	6 + 2 = 8
M	4 + 2 = 6	4 + 1 = 5	7 + 2 = 9	4 + 6 = 10
N	3 + 2 = 5	3 + 1 = 4	3 + 7 = 10	2 + 3 = 5
O	1 + 1 = 2	4 + 5 = 9	3 + 4 = 7	7 + 2 = 9
P	3 + 6 = 9	6 + 4 = 10	2 + 4 = 6	2 + 5 = 7
Q	1 + 8 = 9	2 + 5 = 7	5 + 5 = 10	3 + 7 = 10

904

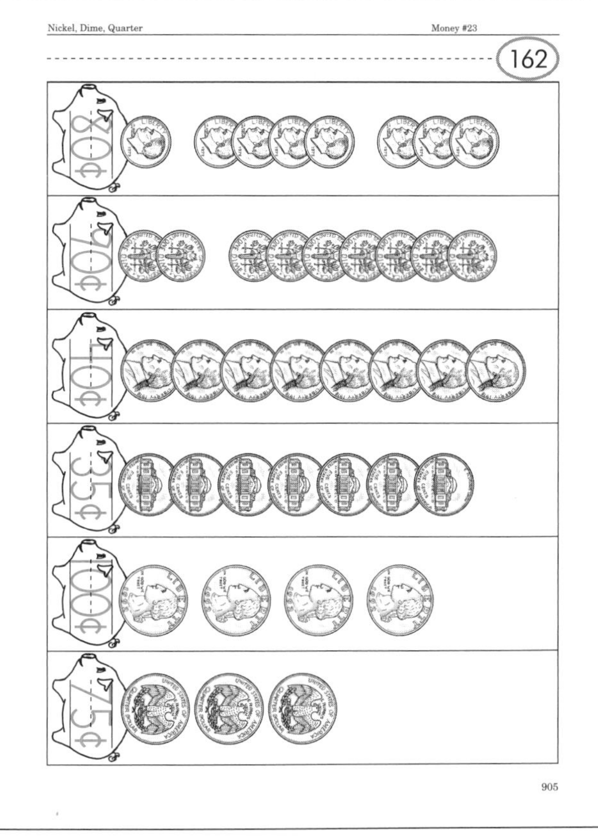
Nickel, Dime, Quarter Money #23

162

905

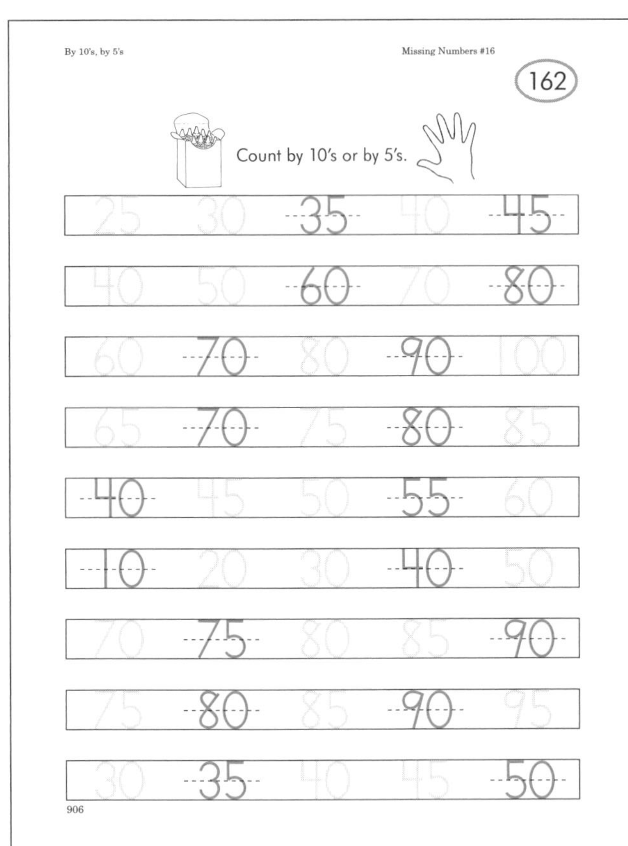
By 10's, by 5's — Missing Numbers #16 — 162

Count by 10's or by 5's.

25	30	35	40	45
40	50	60	70	80
60	70	80	90	100
65	70	75	80	85
40	45	50	55	60
10	20	30	40	50
70	75	80	85	90
75	80	85	90	95
30	35	40	45	50

906

By 10's to 200 — Skip Counting #7 — 163

Count by 10's

10 20 30 40
50 60 70 80
90 100 110 120 130 140
150 160 170 180 190 200

Count by 10's

10 20 30 40
50 60 70 80
90 100 110 120 130 140
150 160 170 180 190 200

907

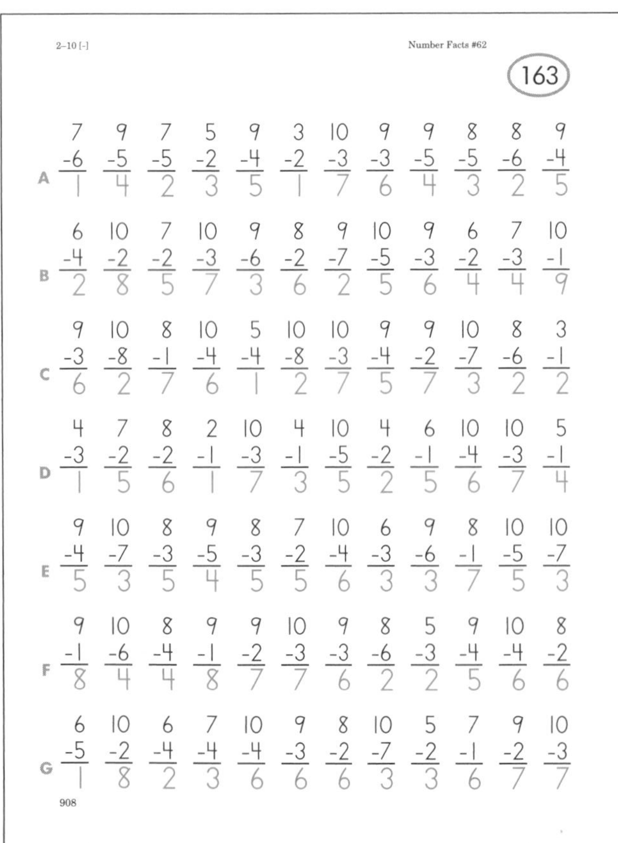
2–10 [-] — Number Facts #62 — 163

A	7-6=1	9-5=4	7-5=2	5-2=3	9-4=5	3-2=1	10-3=7	9-3=6	9-5=4	8-5=3	8-6=2	9-4=5
B	6-4=2	10-2=8	7-2=5	10-3=7	9-6=3	8-2=6	9-7=2	10-5=5	9-3=6	6-2=4	7-3=4	10-1=9
C	9-3=6	10-8=2	8-1=7	10-4=6	5-4=1	10-8=2	10-3=7	9-4=5	9-2=7	10-7=3	8-6=2	3-1=2
D	4-3=1	7-2=5	8-2=6	2-1=1	10-3=7	4-1=3	10-5=5	4-2=2	6-1=5	10-4=6	10-3=7	5-1=4
E	9-4=5	10-7=3	8-3=5	9-5=4	8-3=5	7-2=5	10-4=6	6-3=3	9-6=3	8-1=7	10-5=5	10-7=3
F	9-1=8	10-6=4	8-4=4	9-1=8	9-2=7	10-3=7	9-3=6	8-6=2	5-3=2	9-4=5	10-4=6	8-2=6
G	6-5=1	10-2=8	6-4=2	7-4=3	10-4=6	9-3=6	8-2=6	10-7=3	5-2=3	7-1=6	9-2=7	10-3=7

908

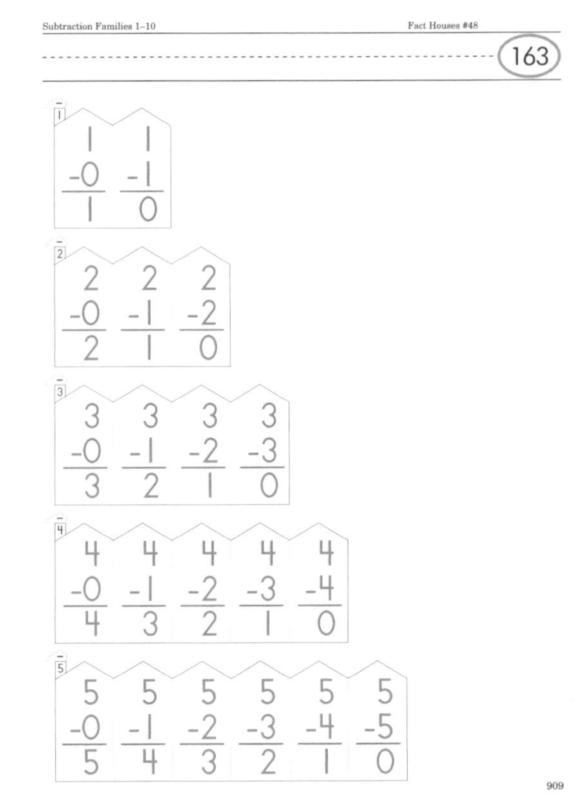
Subtraction Families 1–10 — Fact Houses #48 — 163

1: 1-0=1, 1-1=0
2: 2-0=2, 2-1=1, 2-2=0
3: 3-0=3, 3-1=2, 3-2=1, 3-3=0
4: 4-0=4, 4-1=3, 4-2=2, 4-3=1, 4-4=0
5: 5-0=5, 5-1=4, 5-2=3, 5-3=2, 5-4=1, 5-5=0

909

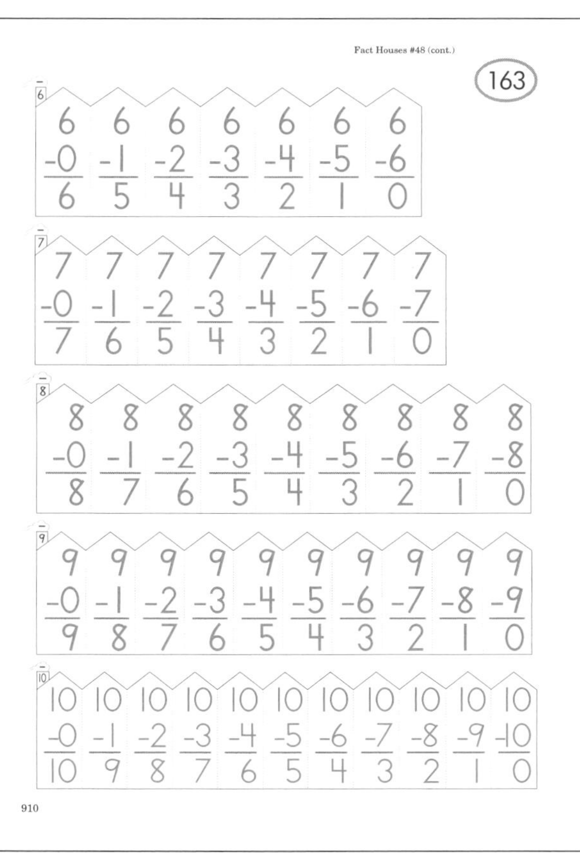

Fact Houses #48 (cont.)

163

6	6	6	6	6	6	6
-0	-1	-2	-3	-4	-5	-6
6	5	4	3	2	1	0

7	7	7	7	7	7	7	7
-0	-1	-2	-3	-4	-5	-6	-7
7	6	5	4	3	2	1	0

8	8	8	8	8	8	8	8	8
-0	-1	-2	-3	-4	-5	-6	-7	-8
8	7	6	5	4	3	2	1	0

9	9	9	9	9	9	9	9	9	9
-0	-1	-2	-3	-4	-5	-6	-7	-8	-9
9	8	7	6	5	4	3	2	1	0

10	10	10	10	10	10	10	10	10	10	10
-0	-1	-2	-3	-4	-5	-6	-7	-8	-9	-10
10	9	8	7	6	5	4	3	2	1	0

910

Place Value #3

163

126 has 1 hundreds	201 has 0 tens
171 has 1 ones	169 has 1 hundreds
216 has 1 tens	220 has 0 ones
183 has 1 hundreds	98 has 9 tens
59 has 9 ones	154 has 1 hundreds
165 has 6 tens	182 has 2 ones
232 has 2 hundreds	97 has 9 tens
204 has 4 ones	175 has 1 hundreds
48 has 4 tens	142 has 2 ones
231 has 2 hundreds	213 has 1 tens
147 has 7 ones	130 has 1 hundreds

911

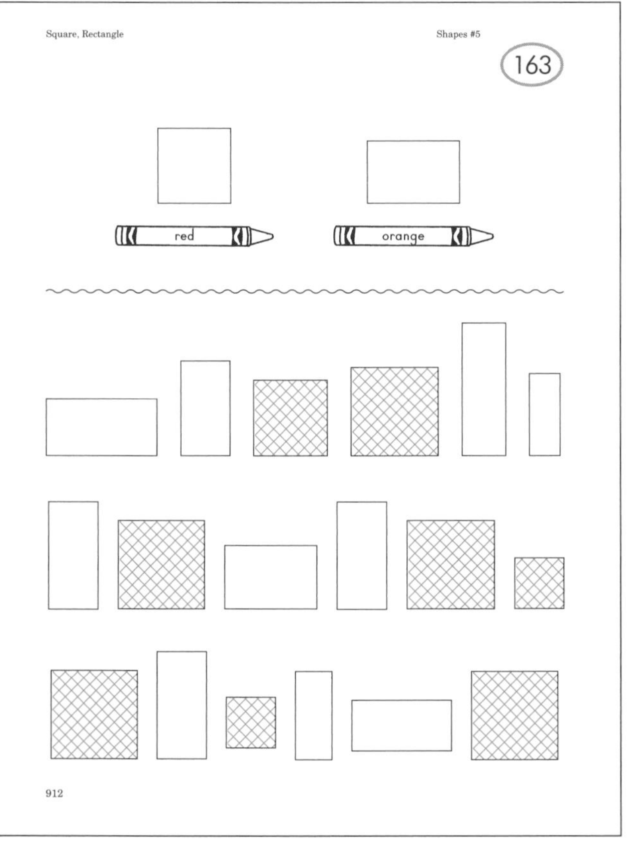

Square, Rectangle

Shapes #5

163

912

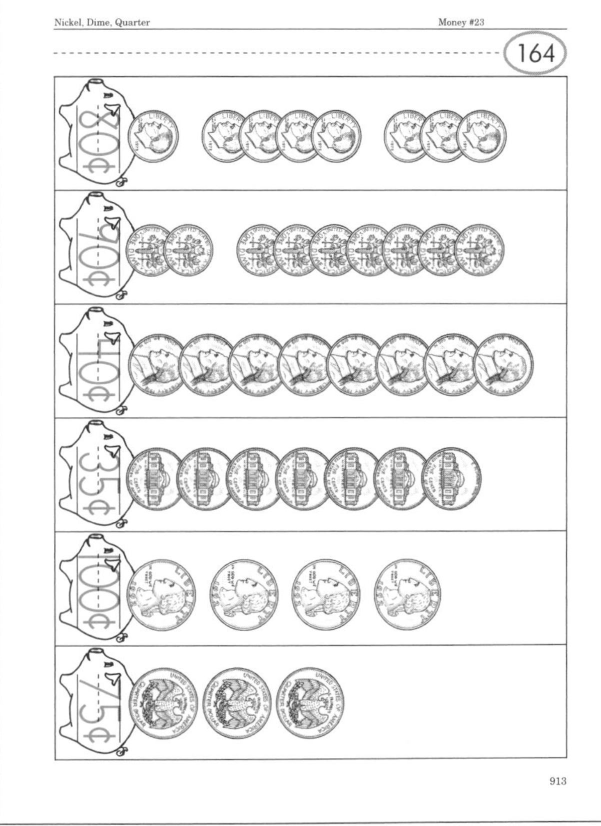

Nickel, Dime, Quarter

Money #23

164

913

Liquid—Cup, Pint, Quart

Measures #10

164

914

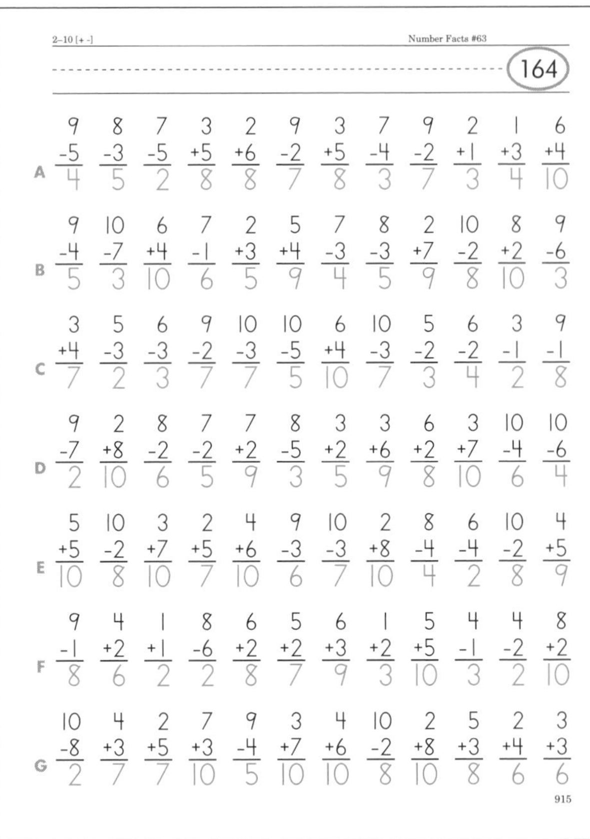
2–10 [+ -]

Number Facts #63

164

A	9 -5 4	8 -3 5	7 -5 2	3 +5 8	2 +6 8	9 -2 7	3 +5 8	7 -4 3	9 -2 7	2 +1 3	1 +3 4	6 +4 10
B	9 -4 5	10 -7 3	6 +4 10	7 -1 6	2 +3 5	5 +4 9	7 -3 4	8 -3 5	2 +7 9	10 -2 8	8 +2 10	9 -6 3
C	3 +4 7	5 -3 2	6 -3 3	9 -2 7	10 -3 7	10 -5 5	6 +4 10	10 -3 7	5 -2 3	6 -2 4	3 -1 2	9 -1 8
D	9 -7 2	2 +8 10	8 -2 6	7 -2 5	7 +2 9	8 -5 3	3 +2 5	3 +6 9	6 +2 8	3 +7 10	10 -4 6	10 -6 4
E	5 +5 10	10 -2 8	3 +7 10	2 +5 7	4 +6 10	9 -3 6	10 -3 7	2 +8 10	8 -4 4	6 -4 2	10 -2 8	4 +5 9
F	9 -1 8	4 +2 6	1 +1 2	8 -6 2	6 +2 8	5 +2 7	6 +3 9	1 +2 3	5 +5 10	4 -1 3	4 -2 2	8 +2 10
G	10 -8 2	4 +3 7	2 +5 7	7 +3 10	9 -4 5	3 +7 10	4 +6 10	10 -2 8	2 +8 10	5 +3 8	2 +4 6	3 +3 6

915

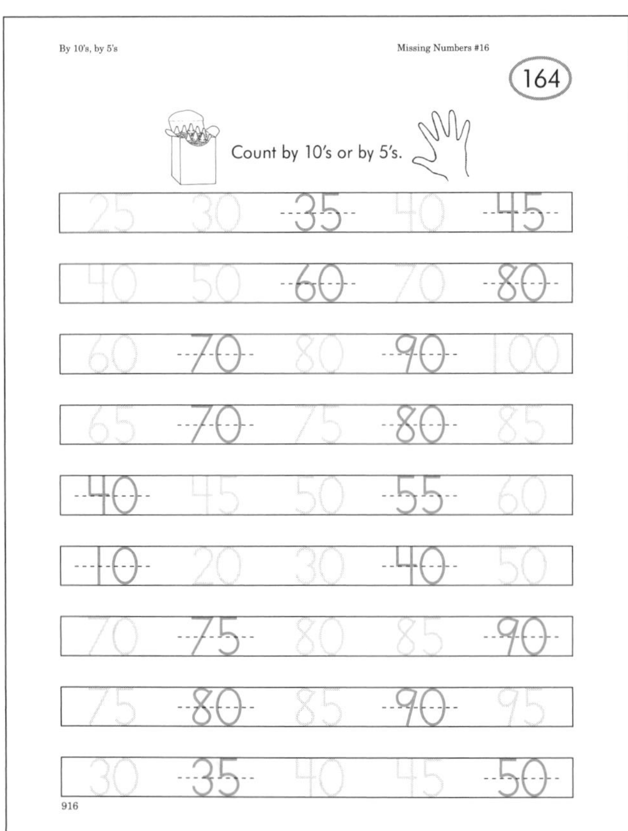
By 10's, by 5's

Missing Numbers #16

164

Count by 10's or by 5's.

25 30 35 40 45

40 50 60 70 80

60 70 80 90 100

65 70 75 80 85

40 45 50 55 60

10 20 30 40 50

70 75 80 85 90

75 80 85 90 95

30 35 40 45 50

916

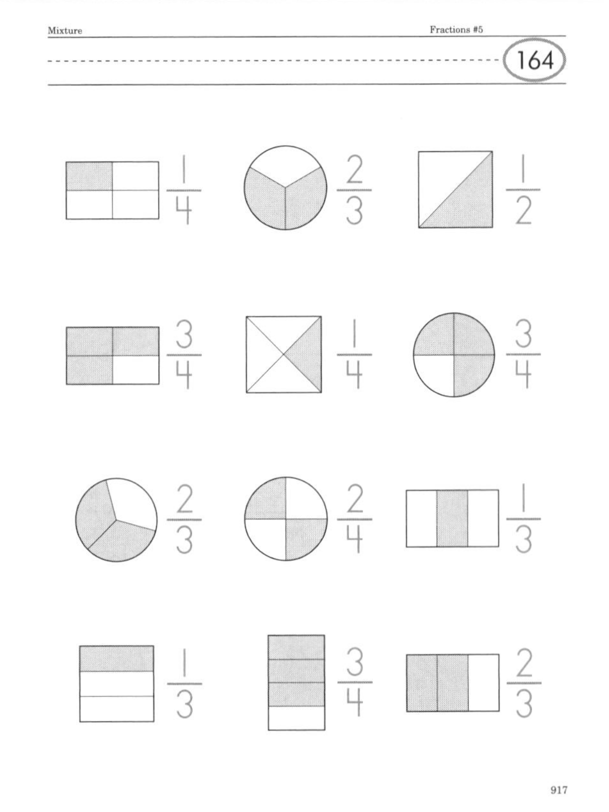
Mixture

Fractions #5

164

$\frac{1}{4}$ $\frac{2}{3}$ $\frac{1}{2}$

$\frac{3}{4}$ $\frac{1}{4}$ $\frac{3}{4}$

$\frac{2}{3}$ $\frac{2}{4}$ $\frac{1}{3}$

$\frac{1}{3}$ $\frac{3}{4}$ $\frac{2}{3}$

917

Flash Card Drill
Form C
165
Individual answers
(See page 365
for instructions.)
919

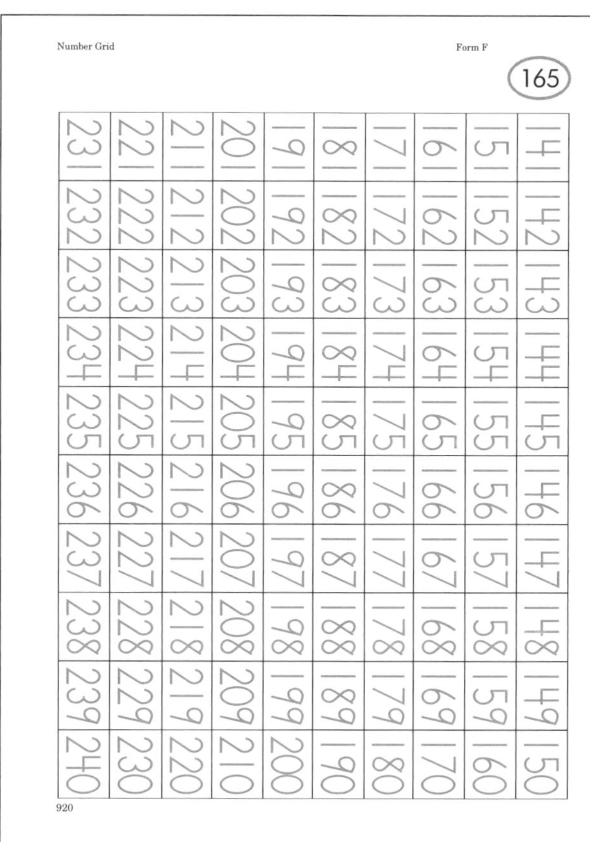
Number Grid
Form F
165
920

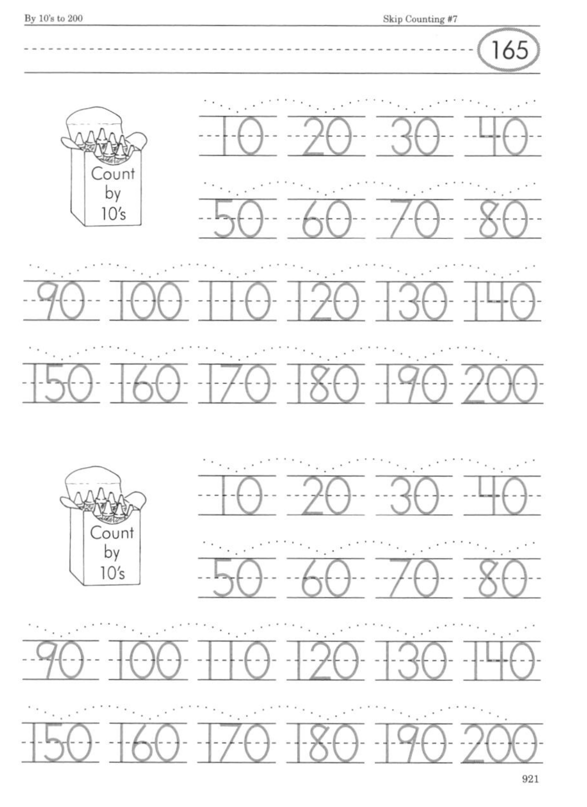
By 10's to 200
Skip Counting #7
165
Count by 10's
10 20 30 40
50 60 70 80
90 100 110 120 130 140
150 160 170 180 190 200
921

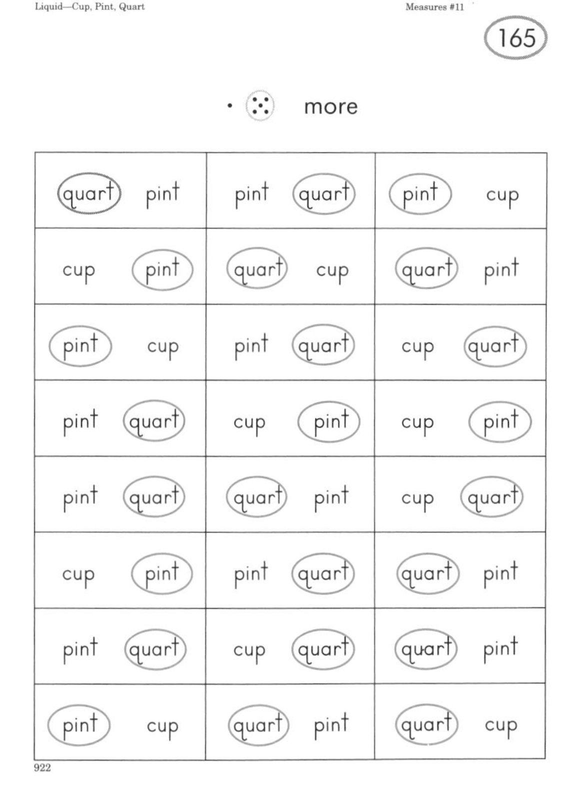
Liquid—Cup, Pint, Quart
Measures #11
165
more
922

5–10 [+ -] Number Facts #64

165

A	9-2=7	6-4=2	9-4=5	3+6=9
B	8-7=1	10-4=6	8-6=2	7+3=10
C	7-6=1	6-3=3	3+3=6	6+4=10
D	5+4=9	9-2=7	7-3=4	2+5=7
E	3+6=9	3+7=10	10-9=1	10-2=8
F	8-5=3	8-2=6	4+5=9	8-3=5
G	4+5=9	9-3=6	5+5=10	7-5=2
H	2+3=5	10-4=6	9-2=7	2+4=6
I	4+3=7	9-5=4	6+2=8	10-6=4
J	4+6=10	6-5=1	7-2=5	4+3=7
K	4+2=6	2+7=9	10-8=2	6+4=10
L	5+3=8	9-6=3	9-7=2	9-3=6
M	10-5=5	2+6=8	8-4=4	7+2=9
N	8+2=10	3+7=10	10-7=3	6+4=10
O	3+4=7	2+8=10	5+2=7	6-2=4
P	5+3=8	10-3=7	3+7=10	9-8=1
Q	3+2=5	3+5=8	5-3=2	6+3=9

923

2–10 [+] Number Facts #61

165

A	7+3=10	4+3=7	3+5=8	5+3=8
B	4+4=8	2+6=8	1+9=10	2+8=10
C	8+2=10	2+7=9	3+2=5	3+7=10
D	1+4=5	2+5=7	5+4=9	4+1=5
E	8+1=9	3+7=10	4+3=7	2+1=3
F	5+2=7	5+1=6	9+1=10	6+4=10
G	6+4=10	7+3=10	3+3=6	2+3=5
H	5+2=7	3+5=8	7+3=10	1+3=4
I	5+3=8	1+8=9	2+6=8	5+4=9
J	6+3=9	4+6=10	6+3=9	5+5=10
K	1+6=7	1+7=8	1+2=3	6+1=7
L	8+2=10	5+4=9	2+2=4	6+2=8
M	4+2=6	4+1=5	7+2=9	4+6=10
N	3+2=5	3+1=4	3+7=10	2+3=5
O	1+1=2	4+5=9	3+4=7	7+2=9
P	3+6=9	6+4=10	2+4=6	2+5=7
Q	1+8=9	2+5=7	5+5=10	3+7=10

924

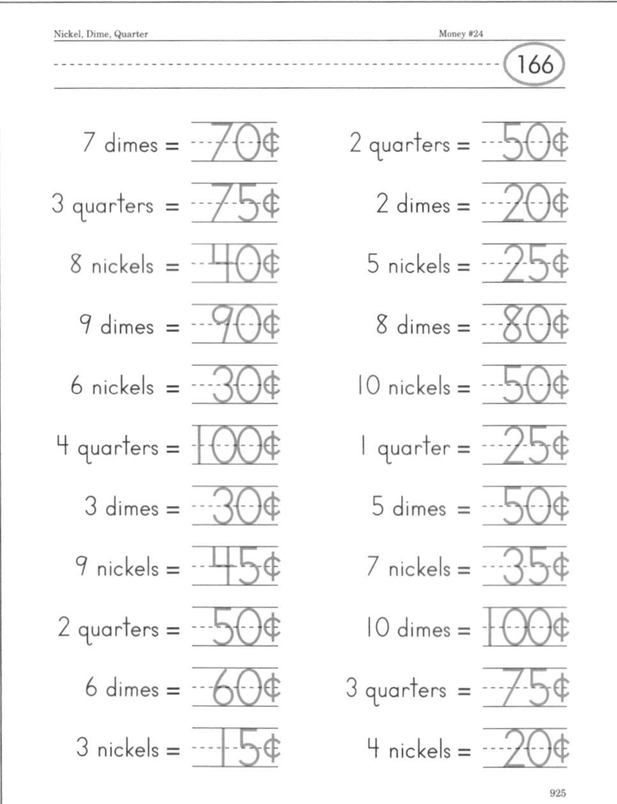
Nickel, Dime, Quarter Money #24

166

7 dimes = 70¢
3 quarters = 75¢
8 nickels = 40¢
9 dimes = 90¢
6 nickels = 30¢
4 quarters = 100¢
3 dimes = 30¢
9 nickels = 45¢
2 quarters = 50¢
6 dimes = 60¢
3 nickels = 15¢

2 quarters = 50¢
2 dimes = 20¢
5 nickels = 25¢
8 dimes = 80¢
10 nickels = 50¢
1 quarter = 25¢
5 dimes = 50¢
7 nickels = 35¢
10 dimes = 100¢
3 quarters = 75¢
4 nickels = 20¢

925

2–10 [-] Number Facts #62

166

A	7 -6 1	9 -5 4	7 -5 2	5 -2 3	9 -4 5	3 -2 1	10 -3 7	9 -3 6	9 -5 4	8 -5 3	8 -6 2	9 -4 5
B	6 -4 2	10 -2 8	7 -2 5	10 -3 7	9 -6 3	8 -2 6	9 -7 2	10 -5 5	9 -3 6	6 -2 4	7 -3 4	10 -1 9
C	9 -3 6	10 -8 2	8 -1 7	10 -4 6	5 -4 1	10 -8 2	10 -3 7	9 -4 5	9 -2 7	10 -7 3	8 -6 2	3 -1 2
D	4 -3 1	7 -2 5	8 -2 6	2 -1 1	10 -3 7	4 -1 3	10 -5 5	4 -2 2	6 -1 5	10 -4 6	10 -3 7	5 -1 4
E	9 -4 5	10 -7 3	8 -3 5	9 -5 4	8 -3 5	7 -2 5	10 -4 6	6 -3 3	9 -6 3	8 -1 7	10 -5 5	10 -7 3
F	9 -1 8	10 -6 4	8 -4 4	9 -1 8	9 -2 7	10 -3 7	9 -3 6	8 -6 2	5 -3 2	9 -4 5	10 -4 6	8 -2 6
G	6 -5 1	10 -2 8	6 -4 2	7 -4 3	10 -4 6	9 -3 6	8 -2 6	10 -7 3	5 -2 3	7 -1 6	9 -2 7	10 -3 7

927

5–10 [+ -] Number Facts #64

166

A	9-2=7	6-4=2	9-4=5	3+6=9
B	8-7=1	10-4=6	8-6=2	7+3=10
C	7-6=1	6-3=3	3+3=6	6+4=10
D	5+4=9	9-2=7	7-3=4	2+5=7
E	3+6=9	3+7=10	10-9=1	10-2=8
F	8-5=3	8-2=6	4+5=9	8-3=5
G	4+5=9	9-3=6	5+5=10	7-5=2
H	2+3=5	10-4=6	9-2=7	2+4=6
I	4+3=7	9-5=4	6+2=8	10-6=4
J	4+6=10	6-5=1	7-2=5	4+3=7
K	4+2=6	2+7=9	10-8=2	6+4=10
L	5+3=8	9-6=3	9-7=2	9-3=6
M	10-5=5	2+6=8	8-4=4	7+2=9
N	8+2=10	3+7=10	10-7=3	6+4=10
O	3+4=7	2+8=10	5+2=7	6-2=4
P	5+3=8	10-3=7	3+7=10	9-8=1
Q	3+2=5	3+5=8	5-3=2	6+3=9

928

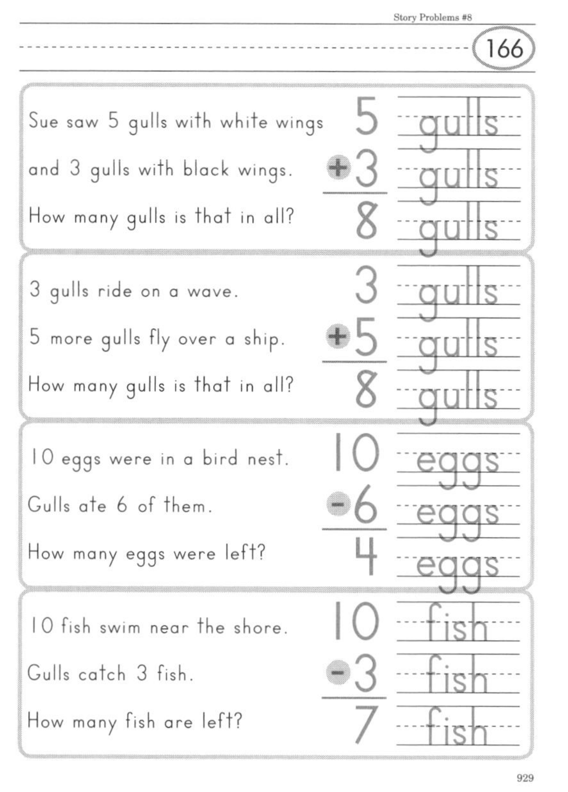

Story Problems #8

166

Sue saw 5 gulls with white wings and 3 gulls with black wings. How many gulls is that in all? 5 gulls + 3 gulls = 8 gulls

3 gulls ride on a wave. 5 more gulls fly over a ship. How many gulls is that in all? 3 gulls + 5 gulls = 8 gulls

10 eggs were in a bird nest. Gulls ate 6 of them. How many eggs were left? 10 eggs − 6 eggs = 4 eggs

10 fish swim near the shore. Gulls catch 3 fish. How many fish are left? 10 fish − 3 fish = 7 fish

929

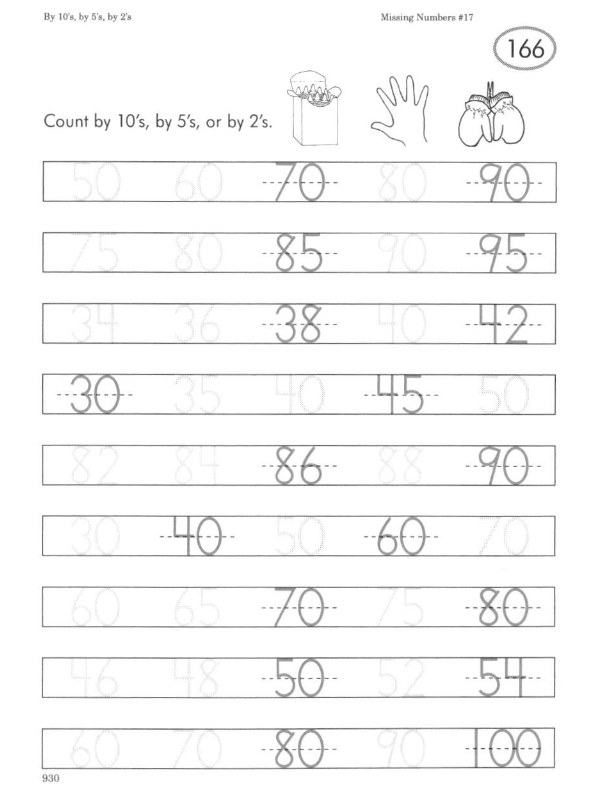

By 10's, by 5's, by 2's Missing Numbers #17

166

Count by 10's, by 5's, or by 2's.

50 60 70 80 90

75 80 85 90 95

34 36 38 40 42

30 35 40 45 50

82 84 86 88 90

30 40 50 60 70

60 65 70 75 80

46 48 50 52 54

60 70 80 90 100

930

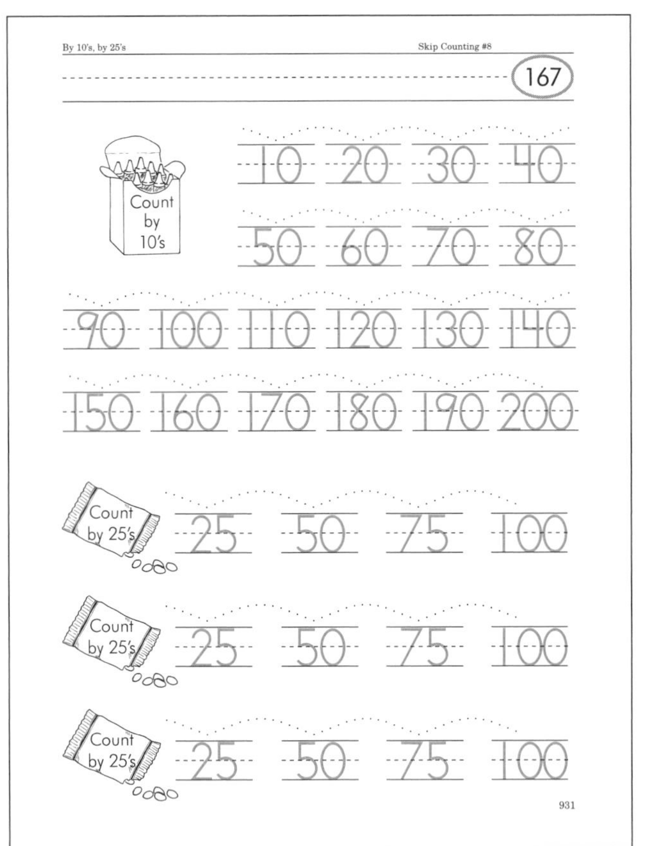

By 10's, by 25's — Skip Counting #8 — 167

Count by 10's

10 20 30 40

50 60 70 80

90 100 110 120 130 140

150 160 170 180 190 200

Count by 25's

25 50 75 100

Count by 25's

25 50 75 100

Count by 25's

25 50 75 100

931

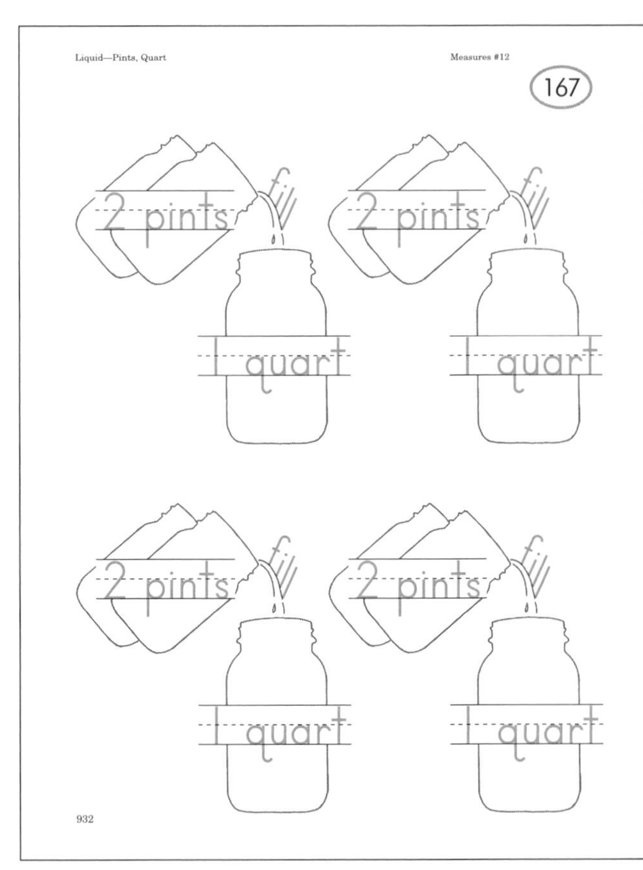

Liquid—Pints, Quart — Measures #12 — 167

2 pints — fill — 1 quart

2 pints — fill — 1 quart

2 pints — fill — 1 quart

2 pints — fill — 1 quart

932

Hour, Half Hour — Clocks #9 — 167

1:30 10:00 8:00 4:30

12:30 12:00 10:30 5:00

11:30 3:30 7:00 5:30

4:00 9:00 8:30 6:00

933

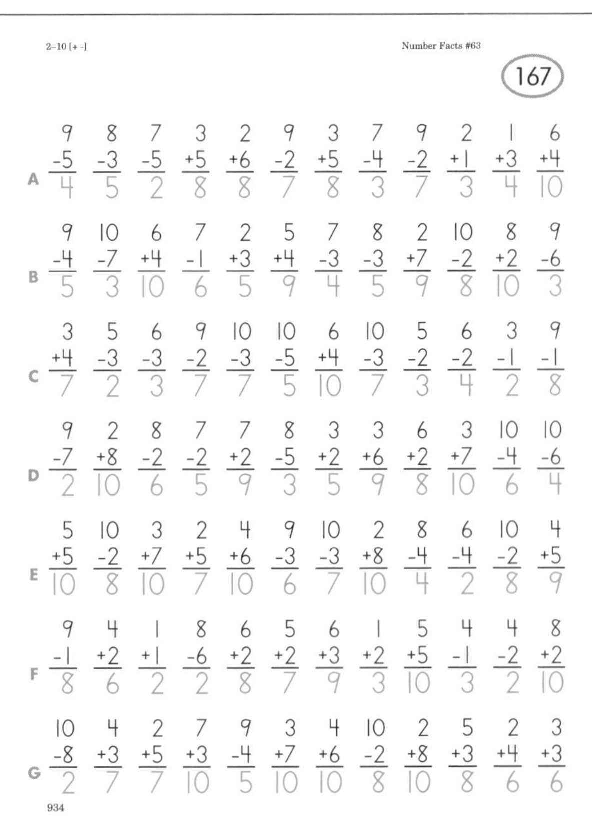

2–10 [+ -] — Number Facts #63 — 167

A	9 -5 4	8 -3 5	7 -5 2	3 +5 8	2 +6 8	9 -2 7	3 +5 8	7 -4 3	9 -2 7	2 +1 3	1 +3 4	6 +4 10
B	9 -4 5	10 -7 3	6 +4 10	7 -1 6	2 +3 5	5 +4 9	7 -3 4	8 -3 5	2 +7 9	10 -2 8	8 +2 10	9 -6 3
C	3 +4 7	5 -3 2	6 -3 3	9 -2 7	10 -3 7	10 -5 5	6 +4 10	10 -3 7	5 -2 3	6 -2 4	3 -1 2	9 -1 8
D	9 -7 2	2 +8 10	8 -2 6	7 -2 5	7 +2 9	8 -5 3	3 +2 5	3 +6 9	6 +2 8	3 +7 10	10 -4 6	10 -6 4
E	5 +5 10	10 -2 8	3 +7 10	2 +5 7	4 +6 10	9 -3 6	10 -3 7	2 +8 10	8 -4 4	6 -4 2	10 -2 8	4 +5 9
F	9 -1 8	4 +2 6	1 +1 2	8 -6 2	6 +2 8	5 +2 7	6 +3 9	1 +2 3	5 +5 10	4 -1 3	4 -2 2	8 +2 10
G	10 -8 2	4 +3 7	2 +5 7	7 +3 10	9 -4 5	3 +7 10	4 +6 10	10 -2 8	2 +8 10	5 +3 8	2 +4 6	3 +3 6

934

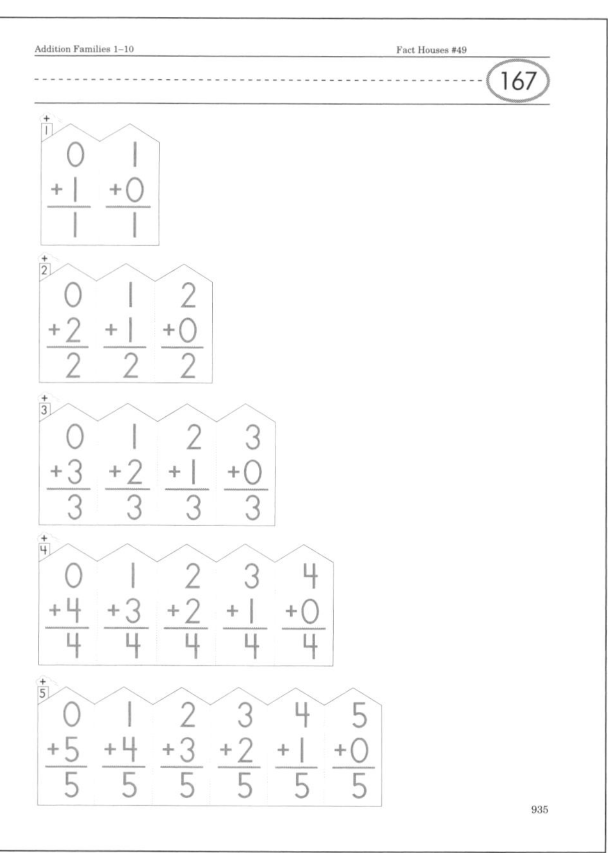

Addition Families 1–10 Fact Houses #49

167

+ 1		
0	1	
+1	+0	
1	1	

+ 2		
0	1	2
+2	+1	+0
2	2	2

+ 3			
0	1	2	3
+3	+2	+1	+0
3	3	3	3

+ 4				
0	1	2	3	4
+4	+3	+2	+1	+0
4	4	4	4	4

+ 5					
0	1	2	3	4	5
+5	+4	+3	+2	+1	+0
5	5	5	5	5	5

935

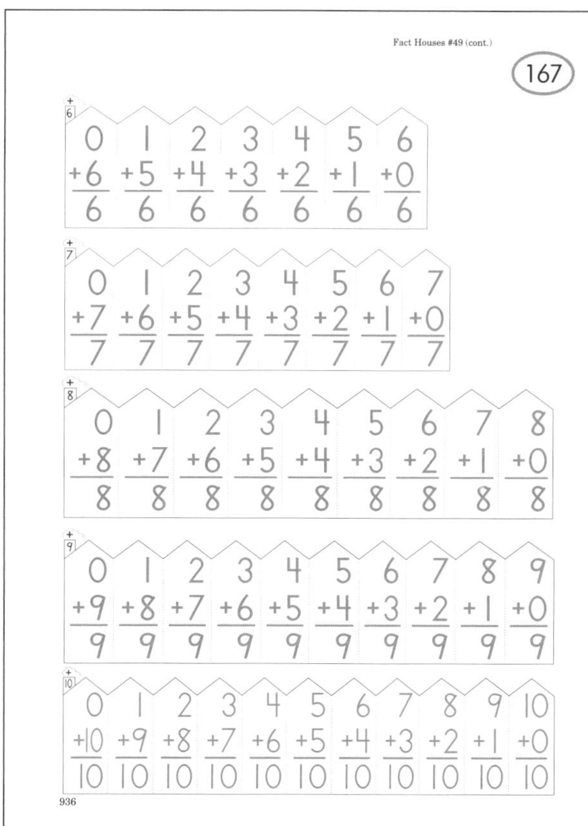

Fact Houses #49 (cont.)

167

+ 6						
0	1	2	3	4	5	6
+6	+5	+4	+3	+2	+1	+0
6	6	6	6	6	6	6

+ 7							
0	1	2	3	4	5	6	7
+7	+6	+5	+4	+3	+2	+1	+0
7	7	7	7	7	7	7	7

+ 8								
0	1	2	3	4	5	6	7	8
+8	+7	+6	+5	+4	+3	+2	+1	+0
8	8	8	8	8	8	8	8	8

+ 9									
0	1	2	3	4	5	6	7	8	9
+9	+8	+7	+6	+5	+4	+3	+2	+1	+0
9	9	9	9	9	9	9	9	9	9

+ 10										
0	1	2	3	4	5	6	7	8	9	10
+10	+9	+8	+7	+6	+5	+4	+3	+2	+1	+0
10	10	10	10	10	10	10	10	10	10	10

936

Flash Card Drill Form C

168

1 2 3 4 5

1 2 3 4 5

1 2 3 4 5

1 2 3 4 5

1 2 3 4 5

Individual answers
(See page 365 for instructions.)

937

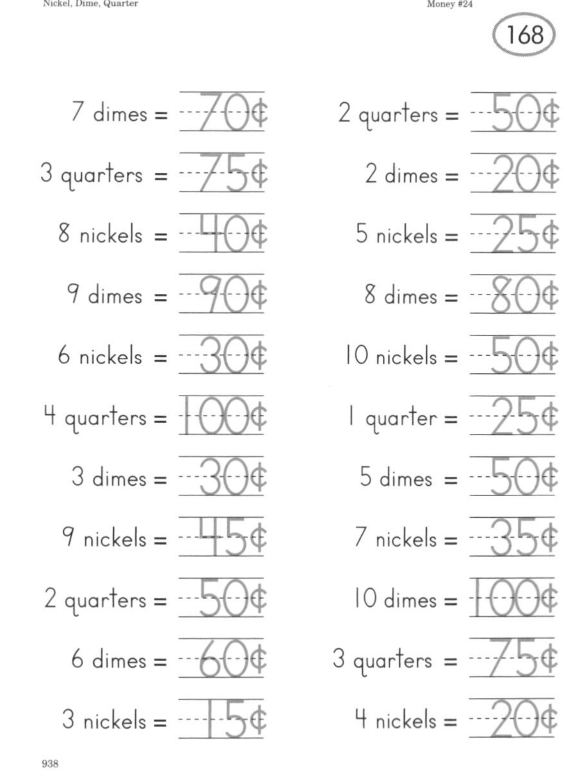

Nickel, Dime, Quarter Money #24

168

7 dimes = 70¢	2 quarters = 50¢
3 quarters = 75¢	2 dimes = 20¢
8 nickels = 40¢	5 nickels = 25¢
9 dimes = 90¢	8 dimes = 80¢
6 nickels = 30¢	10 nickels = 50¢
4 quarters = 100¢	1 quarter = 25¢
3 dimes = 30¢	5 dimes = 50¢
9 nickels = 45¢	7 nickels = 35¢
2 quarters = 50¢	10 dimes = 100¢
6 dimes = 60¢	3 quarters = 75¢
3 nickels = 15¢	4 nickels = 20¢

938

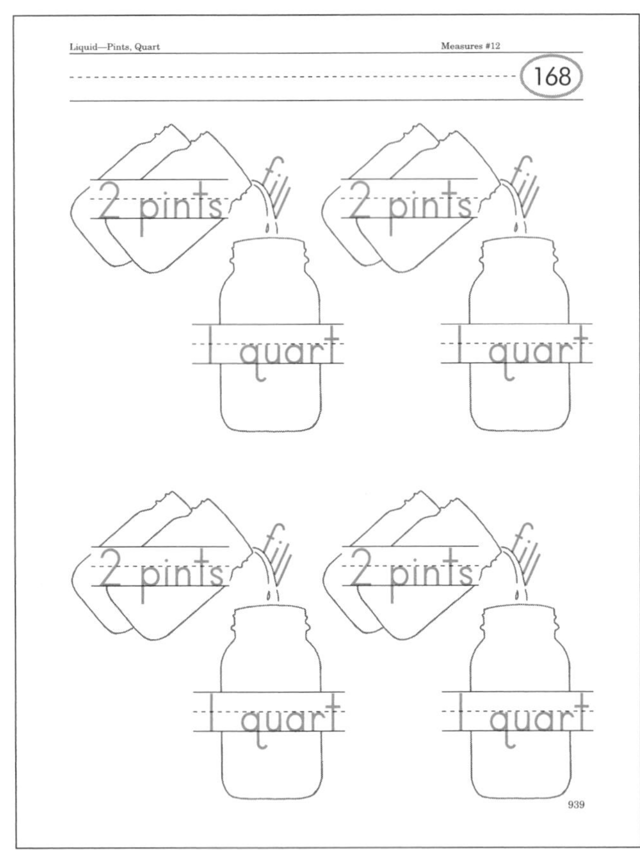

2–10 [+] Number Facts #61

168

A	7+3=10	4+3=7	3+5=8	5+3=8
B	4+4=8	2+6=8	1+9=10	2+8=10
C	8+2=10	2+7=9	3+2=5	3+7=10
D	1+4=5	2+5=7	5+4=9	4+1=5
E	8+1=9	3+7=10	4+3=7	2+1=3
F	5+2=7	5+1=6	9+1=10	6+4=10
G	6+4=10	7+3=10	3+3=6	2+3=5
H	5+2=7	3+5=8	7+3=10	1+3=4
I	5+3=8	1+8=9	2+6=8	5+4=9
J	6+3=9	4+6=10	6+3=9	5+5=10
K	1+6=7	1+7=8	1+2=3	6+1=7
L	8+2=10	5+4=9	2+2=4	6+2=8
M	4+2=6	4+1=5	7+2=9	4+6=10
N	3+2=5	3+1=4	3+7=10	2+3=5
O	1+1=2	4+5=9	3+4=7	7+2=9
P	3+6=9	6+4=10	2+4=6	2+5=7
Q	1+8=9	2+5=7	5+5=10	3+7=10

940

5–10 [+ -] Number Facts #64

168

A	9-2=7	6-4=2	9-4=5	3+6=9
B	8-7=1	10-4=6	8-6=2	7+3=10
C	7-6=1	6-3=3	3+3=6	6+4=10
D	5+4=9	9-2=7	7-3=4	2+5=7
E	3+6=9	3+7=10	10-9=1	10-2=8
F	8-5=3	8-2=6	4+5=9	8-3=5
G	4+5=9	9-3=6	5+5=10	7-5=2
H	2+3=5	10-4=6	9-2=7	2+4=6
I	4+3=7	9-5=4	6+2=8	10-6=4
J	4+6=10	6-5=1	7-2=5	4+3=7
K	4+2=6	2+7=9	10-8=2	6+4=10
L	5+3=8	9-6=3	9-7=2	9-3=6
M	10-5=5	2+6=8	8-4=4	7+2=9
N	8+2=10	3+7=10	10-7=3	6+4=10
O	3+4=7	2+8=10	5+2=7	6-2=4
P	5+3=8	10-3=7	3+7=10	9-8=1
Q	3+2=5	3+5=8	5-3=2	6+3=9

941

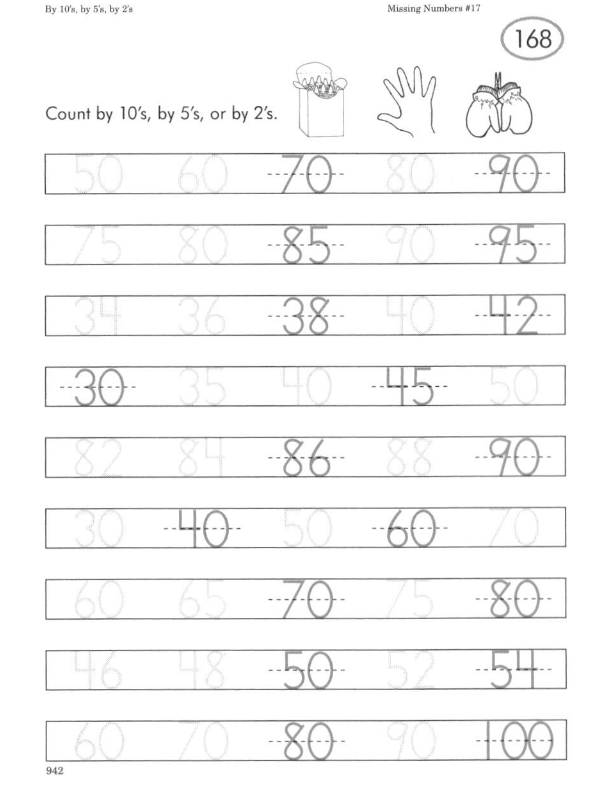

By 10's, by 5's, by 2's Missing Numbers #17

168

Count by 10's, by 5's, or by 2's.

50	60	70	80	90
75	80	85	90	95
34	36	38	40	42
30	35	40	45	50
82	84	86	88	90
30	40	50	60	70
60	65	70	75	80
46	48	50	52	54
60	70	80	90	100

942

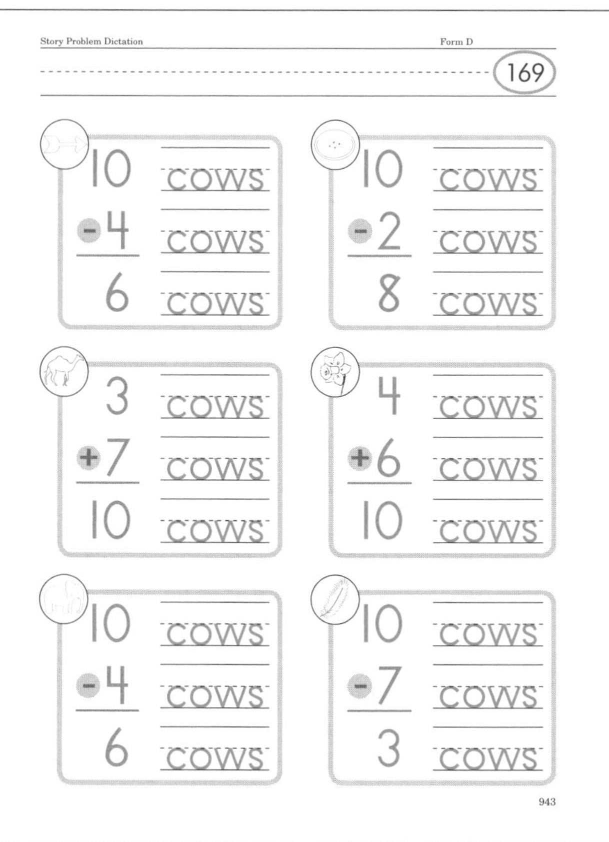

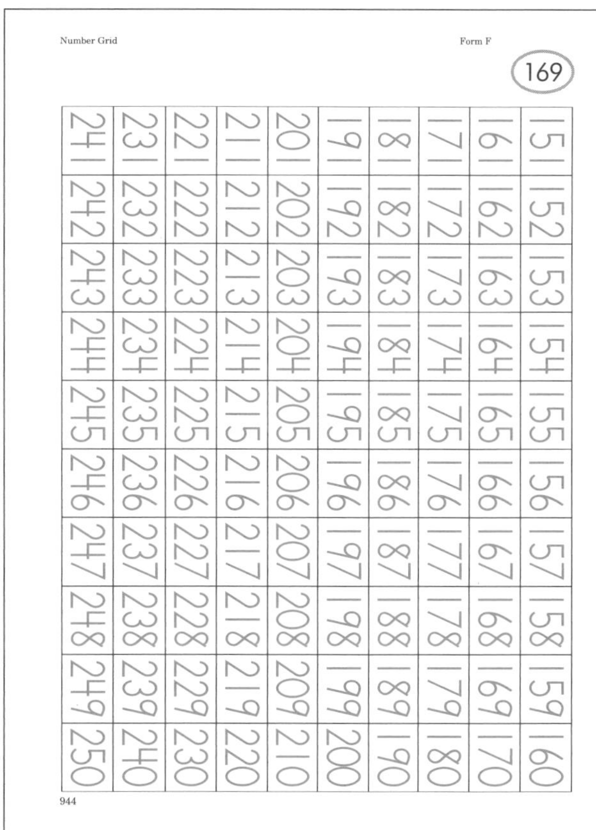
Number Grid

Form F

169

151	152	153	154	155	156	157	158	159	160
161	162	163	164	165	166	167	168	169	170
171	172	173	174	175	176	177	178	179	180
181	182	183	184	185	186	187	188	189	190
191	192	193	194	195	196	197	198	199	200
201	202	203	204	205	206	207	208	209	210
211	212	213	214	215	216	217	218	219	220
221	222	223	224	225	226	227	228	229	230
231	232	233	234	235	236	237	238	239	240
241	242	243	244	245	246	247	248	249	250

944

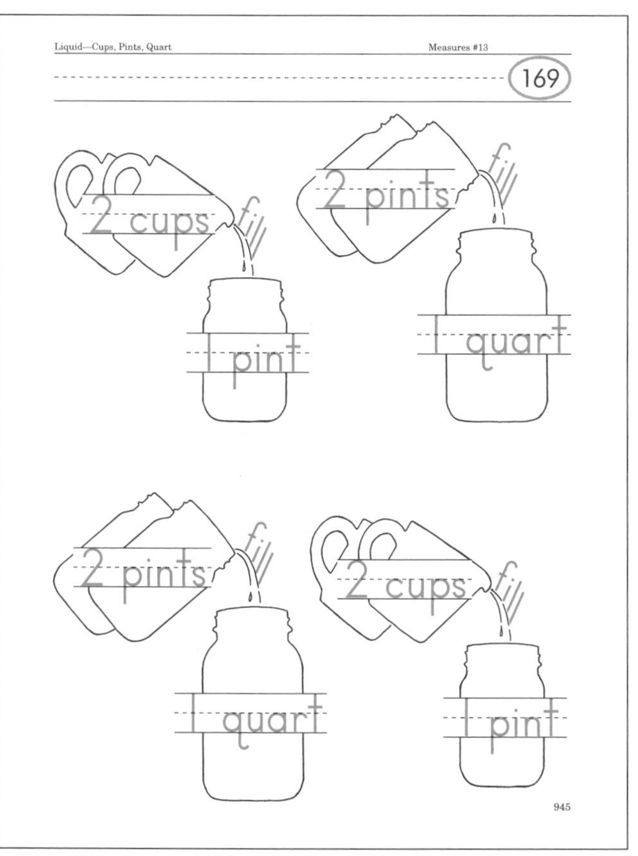

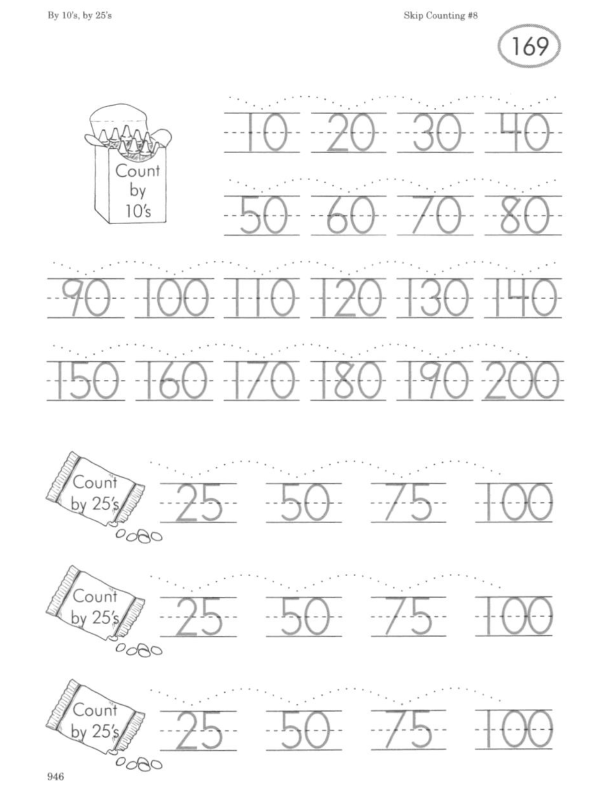

2–10 [-]   Number Facts #62

169

A	7 -6 1	9 -5 4	7 -5 2	5 -2 3	9 -4 5	3 -2 1	10 -3 7	9 -3 6	9 -5 4	8 -5 3	8 -6 2	9 -4 5
B	6 -4 2	10 -2 8	7 -2 5	10 -3 7	9 -6 3	8 -2 6	9 -7 2	10 -5 5	9 -3 6	6 -2 4	7 -3 4	10 -1 9
C	9 -3 6	10 -8 2	8 -1 7	10 -4 6	5 -4 1	10 -8 2	10 -3 7	9 -4 5	9 -2 7	10 -7 3	8 -6 2	3 -1 2
D	4 -3 1	7 -2 5	8 -2 6	2 -1 1	10 -3 7	4 -1 3	10 -5 5	4 -2 2	6 -1 5	10 -4 6	10 -3 7	5 -1 4
E	9 -4 5	10 -7 3	8 -3 5	9 -5 4	8 -3 5	7 -2 5	10 -4 6	6 -3 3	9 -6 3	8 -1 7	10 -5 5	10 -7 3
F	9 -1 8	10 -6 4	8 -4 4	9 -1 8	9 -2 7	10 -3 7	9 -3 6	8 -6 2	5 -3 2	9 -4 5	10 -4 6	8 -2 6
G	6 -5 1	10 -2 8	6 -4 2	7 -4 3	10 -4 6	9 -3 6	8 -2 6	10 -7 3	5 -2 3	7 -1 6	9 -2 7	10 -3 7

947

5–10 [+ -]   Number Facts #64

169

A	9-2=7	6-4=2	9-4=5	3+6=9
B	8-7=1	10-4=6	8-6=2	7+3=10
C	7-6=1	6-3=3	3+3=6	6+4=10
D	5+4=9	9-2=7	7-3=4	2+5=7
E	3+6=9	3+7=10	10-9=1	10-2=8
F	8-5=3	8-2=6	4+5=9	8-3=5
G	4+5=9	9-3=6	5+5=10	7-5=2
H	2+3=5	10-4=6	9-2=7	2+4=6
I	4+3=7	9-5=4	6+2=8	10-6=4
J	4+6=10	6-5=1	7-2=5	4+3=7
K	4+2=6	2+7=9	10-8=2	6+4=10
L	5+3=8	9-6=3	9-7=2	9-3=6
M	10-5=5	2+6=8	8-4=4	7+2=9
N	8+2=10	3+7=10	10-7=3	6+4=10
O	3+4=7	2+8=10	5+2=7	6-2=4
P	5+3=8	10-3=7	3+7=10	9-8=1
Q	3+2=5	3+5=8	5-3=2	6+3=9

948

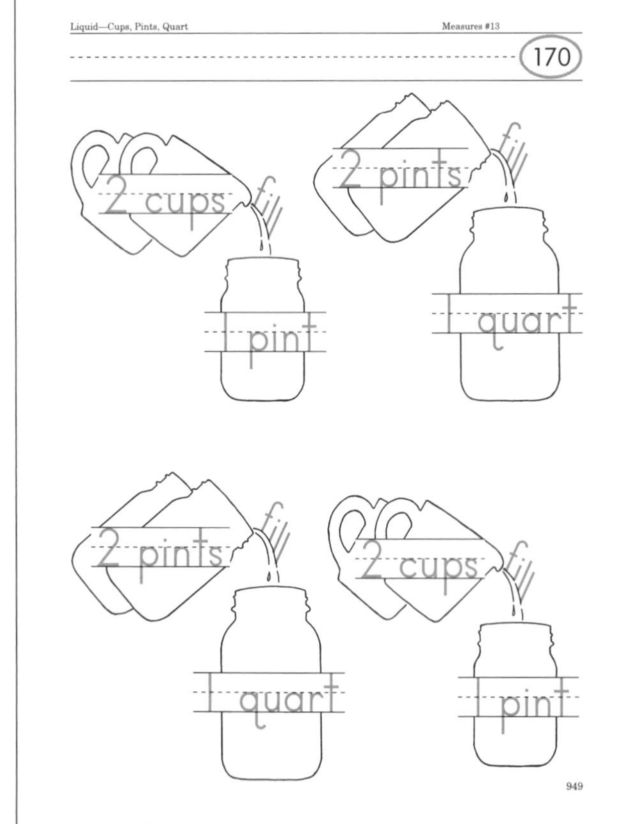

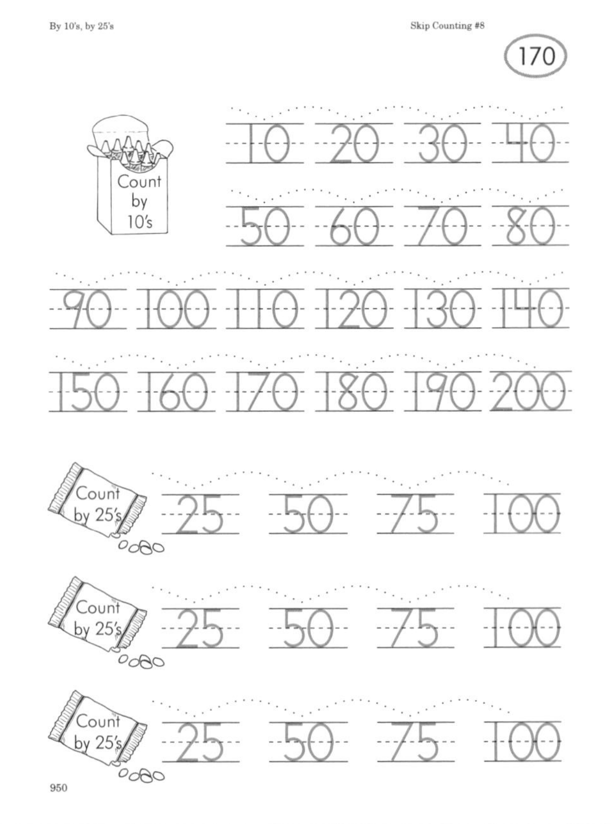

Hour, Half Hour — Clocks #10 — 170

1:30	4:00	8:30	12:30
6:00	5:30	9:00	4:30
3:00	6:30	2:00	7:30
2:30	11:00	9:30	1:00

951

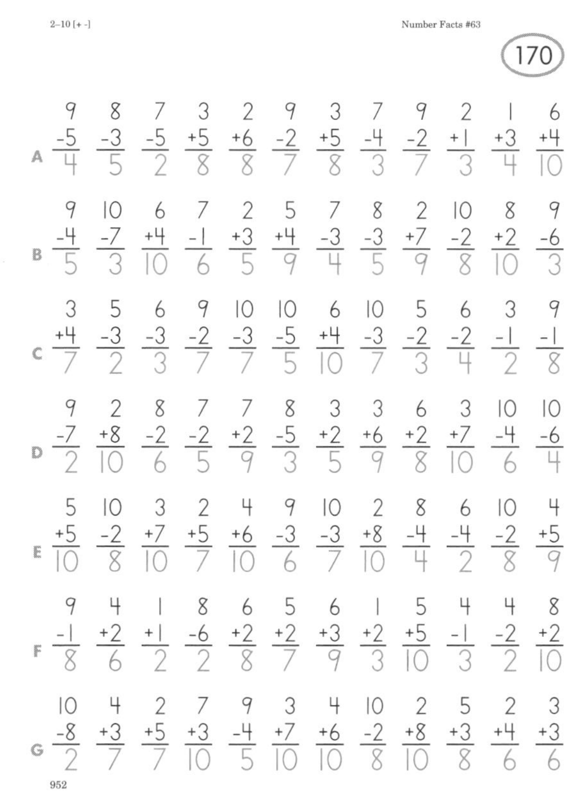

2–10 [+ -] — Number Facts #63 — 170

A	9 -5 4	8 -3 5	7 -5 2	3 +5 8	2 +6 8	9 -2 7	3 +5 8	7 -4 3	9 -2 7	2 +1 3	1 +3 4	6 +4 10
B	9 -4 5	10 -7 3	6 +4 10	7 -1 6	2 +3 5	5 +4 9	7 -3 4	8 -3 5	2 +7 9	10 -2 8	8 +2 10	9 -6 3
C	3 +4 7	5 -3 2	6 -3 3	9 -2 7	10 -3 7	10 -5 5	6 +4 10	10 -3 7	5 -2 3	6 -2 4	3 -1 2	9 -1 8
D	9 -7 2	2 +8 10	8 -2 6	7 -2 5	7 +2 9	8 -5 3	3 +2 5	3 +6 9	6 +2 8	3 +7 10	10 -4 6	10 -6 4
E	5 +5 10	10 -2 8	3 +7 10	2 +5 7	4 +6 10	9 -3 6	10 -3 7	2 +8 10	8 -4 4	6 -4 2	10 -2 8	4 +5 9
F	9 -1 8	4 +2 6	1 +1 2	8 -6 2	6 +2 8	5 +2 7	6 +3 9	1 +2 3	5 +5 10	4 -1 3	4 -2 2	8 +2 10
G	10 -8 2	4 +3 7	2 +5 7	7 +3 10	9 -4 5	3 +7 10	4 +6 10	10 -2 8	2 +8 10	5 +3 8	2 +4 6	3 +3 6

952

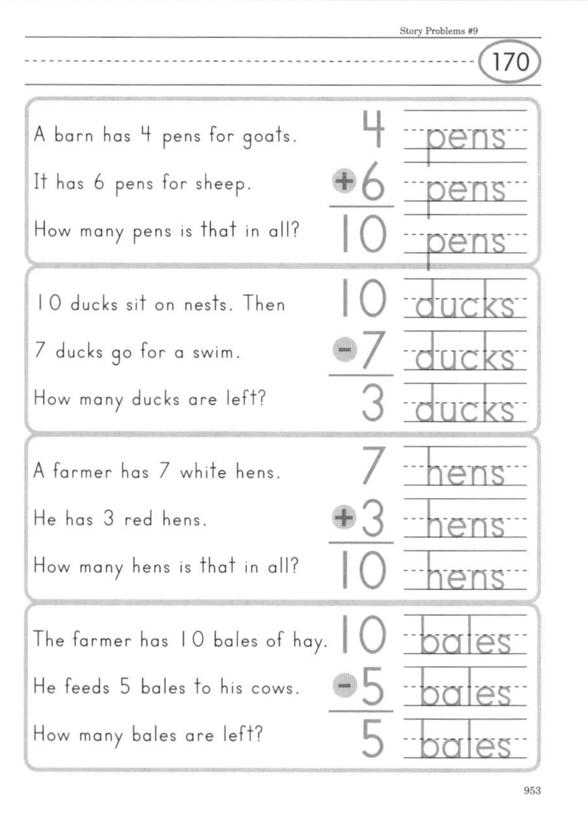

Story Problems #9 — 170

A barn has 4 pens for goats. — 4 pens
It has 6 pens for sheep. — +6 pens
How many pens is that in all? — 10 pens

10 ducks sit on nests. Then — 10 ducks
7 ducks go for a swim. — -7 ducks
How many ducks are left? — 3 ducks

A farmer has 7 white hens. — 7 hens
He has 3 red hens. — +3 hens
How many hens is that in all? — 10 hens

The farmer has 10 bales of hay. — 10 bales
He feeds 5 bales to his cows. — -5 bales
How many bales are left? — 5 bales

953

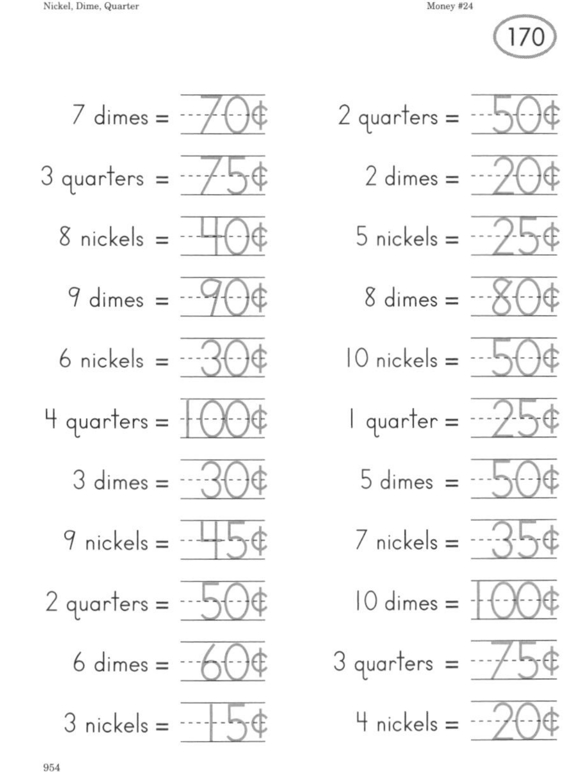

Nickel, Dime, Quarter — Money #24 — 170

7 dimes = 70¢	2 quarters = 50¢
3 quarters = 75¢	2 dimes = 20¢
8 nickels = 40¢	5 nickels = 25¢
9 dimes = 90¢	8 dimes = 80¢
6 nickels = 30¢	10 nickels = 50¢
4 quarters = 100¢	1 quarter = 25¢
3 dimes = 30¢	5 dimes = 50¢
9 nickels = 45¢	7 nickels = 35¢
2 quarters = 50¢	10 dimes = 100¢
6 dimes = 60¢	3 quarters = 75¢
3 nickels = 15¢	4 nickels = 20¢

954

Patterns

Student's Desk Number Line

Copy the two sections and tape them together, overlapping the two 10's. Secure the line to the desk with clear, self-adhesive covering, one inch longer and wider than the paper.

Thermometer

next page →

Copy the number scale and lines. Tape the sections together overlapping the two 50s, and glue the scale to a large stiff cardboard. Cut a slit below the zero mark and another above the 100 mark. Thread 40 inches of smooth white ribbon through the slits so that it passes beside the scale markings on the front. The lower half of the ribbon may be colored with a red marker or glued or sewed to the back of a red ribbon.

Slide the ribbon through the slots to adjust the "mercury" level.

0 1 2 3 4 5 6 7 8 9 10

10 11 12 13 14 15 16 17 18 19 20

50

40

30

20

10

100

90

80

70

60

50

Number Line Markers for Skip Counting

Cut ten triangles from purple construction paper, using the large triangle pattern. When you are at Lesson 57, mount them above the 10's on your classroom number line.

Cut ten triangles from pink construction paper, using the small triangle pattern. When you are at Lesson 66, mount them above your number line at 5, 15, 25, and so on.

Cut four rings from green construction paper, using the circle pattern. When you are at Lesson 132, mount them on the number line so that they circle 25, 50, 75, and 100.

Place-value Chart

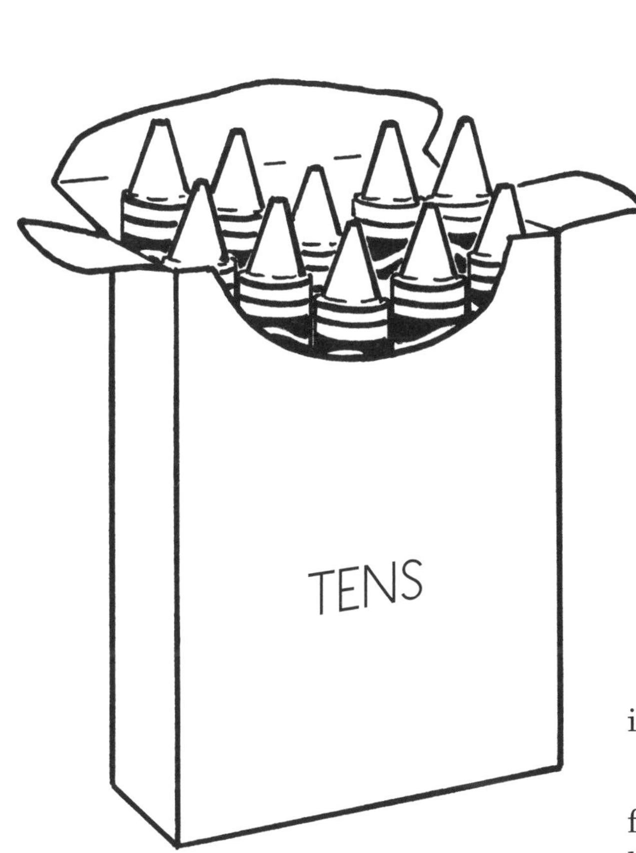

Use these patterns to make the chart illustrated below.

Prepare three cards for each digit from 0 through 9. Place paper clips to hold one digit in each column.

hundreds	tens	ones

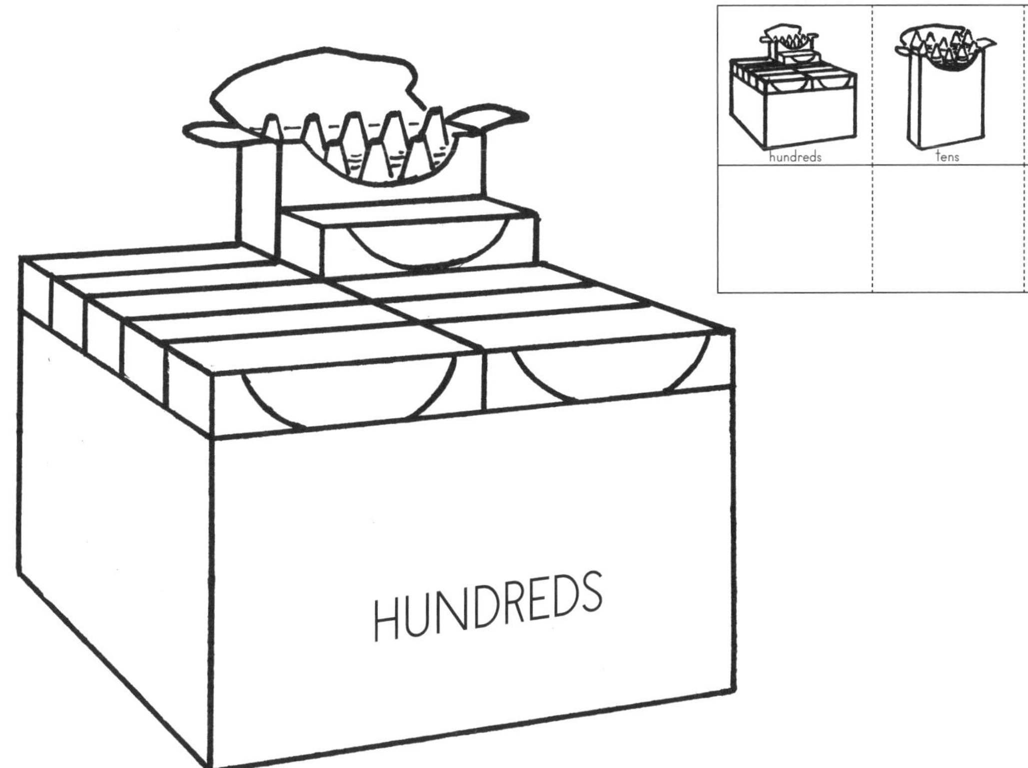

Footprint Poster

Enlarge the diagram with grid drawing lines spaced one inch apart to make a 14- by 18-inch poster like the one pictured below.

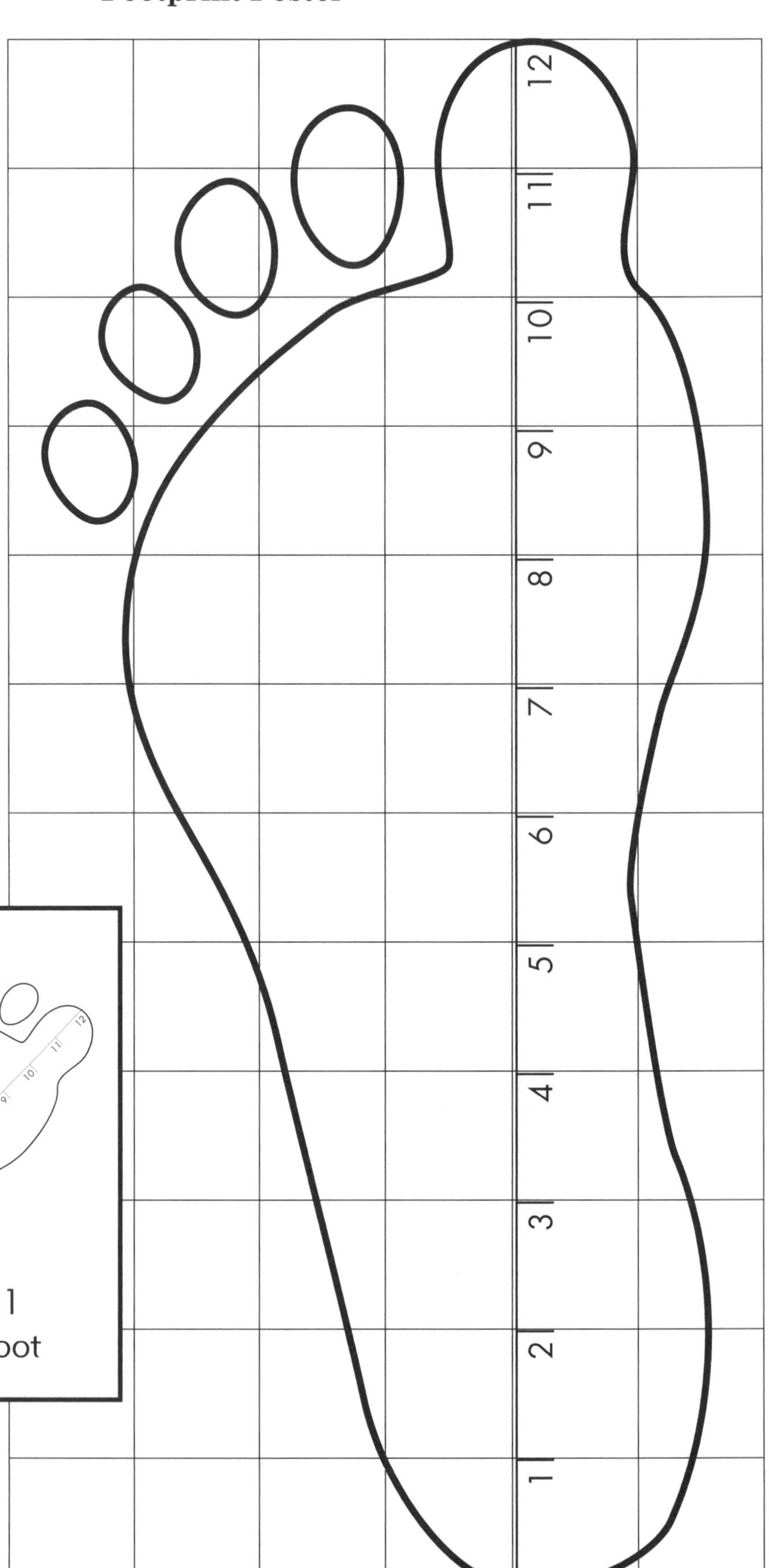

12 inches make 1 foot

Shape Posters

Make these posters large enough to be easily seen by the whole class. Use a red marker for the letters in the square, blue for the circle, green for the triangle, and orange for the rectangle.

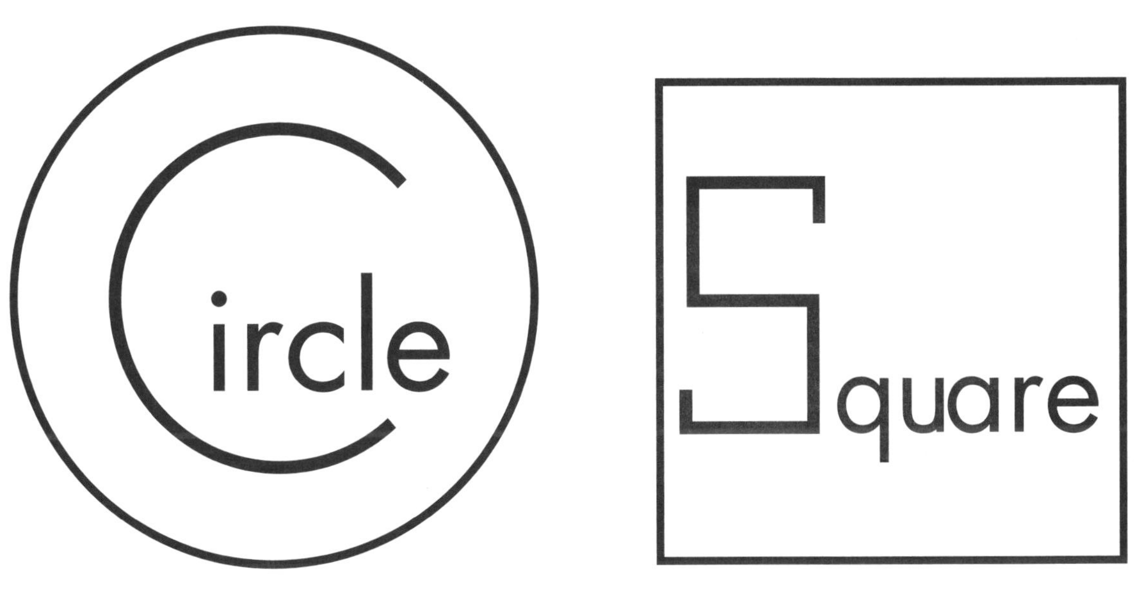

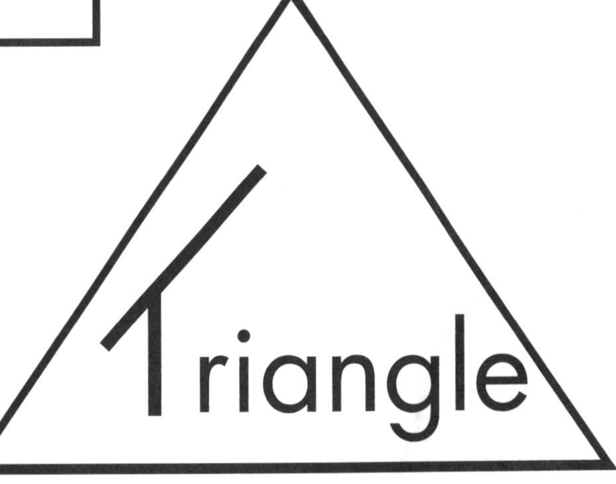

Measures

You may reproduce these patterns for a tracing guide when you need a cup, pint, or quart on the chalkboard.

Fact Trees

You may reproduce this pattern for a tracing guide when you put fact trees on the chalkboard.

Individual Flash Cards

The following pages may be used to reproduce small flash cards for the children to study individually. Copy or paste each page onto stiff paper, and then cut apart. On the back of each card, write the complete fact with the answer.

0 + 1	1 + 0	0 + 2
1 + 1	2 + 0	0 + 3
1 + 2	2 + 1	3 + 0

$\begin{array}{r} 0 \\ +\ 4 \\ \hline \end{array}$	$\begin{array}{r} 1 \\ +\ 3 \\ \hline \end{array}$	$\begin{array}{r} 2 \\ +\ 2 \\ \hline \end{array}$
$\begin{array}{r} 3 \\ +\ 1 \\ \hline \end{array}$	$\begin{array}{r} 4 \\ +\ 0 \\ \hline \end{array}$	$\begin{array}{r} 0 \\ +\ 5 \\ \hline \end{array}$
$\begin{array}{r} 1 \\ +\ 4 \\ \hline \end{array}$	$\begin{array}{r} 2 \\ +\ 3 \\ \hline \end{array}$	$\begin{array}{r} 3 \\ +\ 2 \\ \hline \end{array}$

4 + 1	5 + 0	0 + 6
1 + 5	2 + 4	3 + 3
4 + 2	5 + 1	6 + 0

$\begin{array}{r} 0 \\ +\ 7 \\ \hline \end{array}$	$\begin{array}{r} 1 \\ +\ 6 \\ \hline \end{array}$	$\begin{array}{r} 2 \\ +\ 5 \\ \hline \end{array}$
$\begin{array}{r} 3 \\ +\ 4 \\ \hline \end{array}$	$\begin{array}{r} 4 \\ +\ 3 \\ \hline \end{array}$	$\begin{array}{r} 5 \\ +\ 2 \\ \hline \end{array}$
$\begin{array}{r} 6 \\ +\ 1 \\ \hline \end{array}$	$\begin{array}{r} 7 \\ +\ 0 \\ \hline \end{array}$	$\begin{array}{r} 0 \\ +\ 8 \\ \hline \end{array}$

1 + 7	2 + 6	3 + 5
4 + 4	5 + 3	6 + 2
7 + 1	8 + 0	0 + 9

1 + 8	2 + 7	3 + 6
4 + 5	5 + 4	6 + 3
7 + 2	8 + 1	9 + 0

$\begin{array}{r} 4 \\ -\ 0 \\ \hline \end{array}$	$\begin{array}{r} 4 \\ -\ 1 \\ \hline \end{array}$	$\begin{array}{r} 4 \\ -\ 2 \\ \hline \end{array}$
$\begin{array}{r} 4 \\ -\ 3 \\ \hline \end{array}$	$\begin{array}{r} 4 \\ -\ 4 \\ \hline \end{array}$	$\begin{array}{r} 5 \\ -\ 0 \\ \hline \end{array}$
$\begin{array}{r} 5 \\ -\ 1 \\ \hline \end{array}$	$\begin{array}{r} 5 \\ -\ 2 \\ \hline \end{array}$	$\begin{array}{r} 5 \\ -\ 3 \\ \hline \end{array}$

$\begin{array}{r} 5 \\ -\ 4 \\ \hline \end{array}$	$\begin{array}{r} 5 \\ -\ 5 \\ \hline \end{array}$	$\begin{array}{r} 6 \\ -\ 0 \\ \hline \end{array}$
$\begin{array}{r} 6 \\ -\ 1 \\ \hline \end{array}$	$\begin{array}{r} 6 \\ -\ 2 \\ \hline \end{array}$	$\begin{array}{r} 6 \\ -\ 3 \\ \hline \end{array}$
$\begin{array}{r} 6 \\ -\ 4 \\ \hline \end{array}$	$\begin{array}{r} 6 \\ -\ 5 \\ \hline \end{array}$	$\begin{array}{r} 6 \\ -\ 6 \\ \hline \end{array}$

$\begin{array}{r} 7 \\ -0 \\ \hline \end{array}$	$\begin{array}{r} 7 \\ -1 \\ \hline \end{array}$	$\begin{array}{r} 7 \\ -2 \\ \hline \end{array}$
$\begin{array}{r} 7 \\ -3 \\ \hline \end{array}$	$\begin{array}{r} 7 \\ -4 \\ \hline \end{array}$	$\begin{array}{r} 7 \\ -5 \\ \hline \end{array}$
$\begin{array}{r} 7 \\ -6 \\ \hline \end{array}$	$\begin{array}{r} 7 \\ -7 \\ \hline \end{array}$	$\begin{array}{r} 8 \\ -0 \\ \hline \end{array}$

8 − 1	8 − 2	8 − 3
8 − 4	8 − 5	8 − 6
8 − 7	8 − 8	9 − 0

9 − 1	9 − 2	9 − 3
9 − 4	9 − 5	9 − 6
9 − 7	9 − 8	9 − 9

10 − 1	10 − 2	10 − 3
10 − 4	10 − 5	10 − 6
10 − 7	10 − 8	10 − 9

Index

This index gives lesson numbers where the concepts are first introduced or further developed. **T-** indicates lessons that have the concept in a teaching session (*Follow-up* or *Class Time*). **W-** indicates the appearance in workbook lessons.